APP INST

Go to the App store

Search for: "Iceland Road Guide"

Download the App

After download open the App

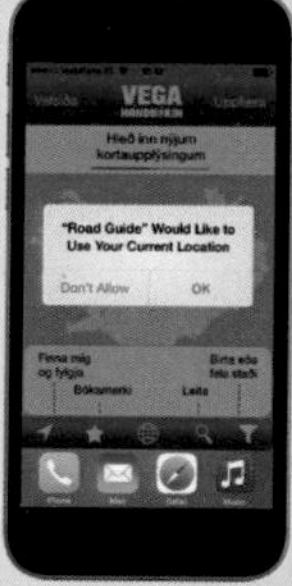
Allow the App to use your location

Choose upgrade

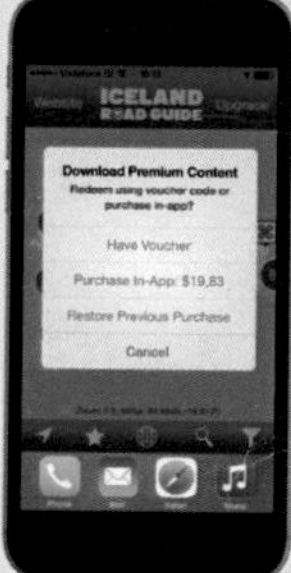
Choose the method "have voucher"

Enter the code

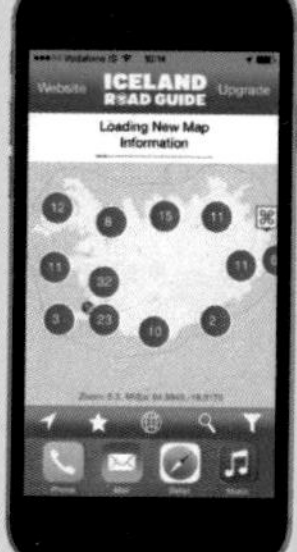
Enjoy!

VOUCHER **bd2049**

Works for 2 phones or pads

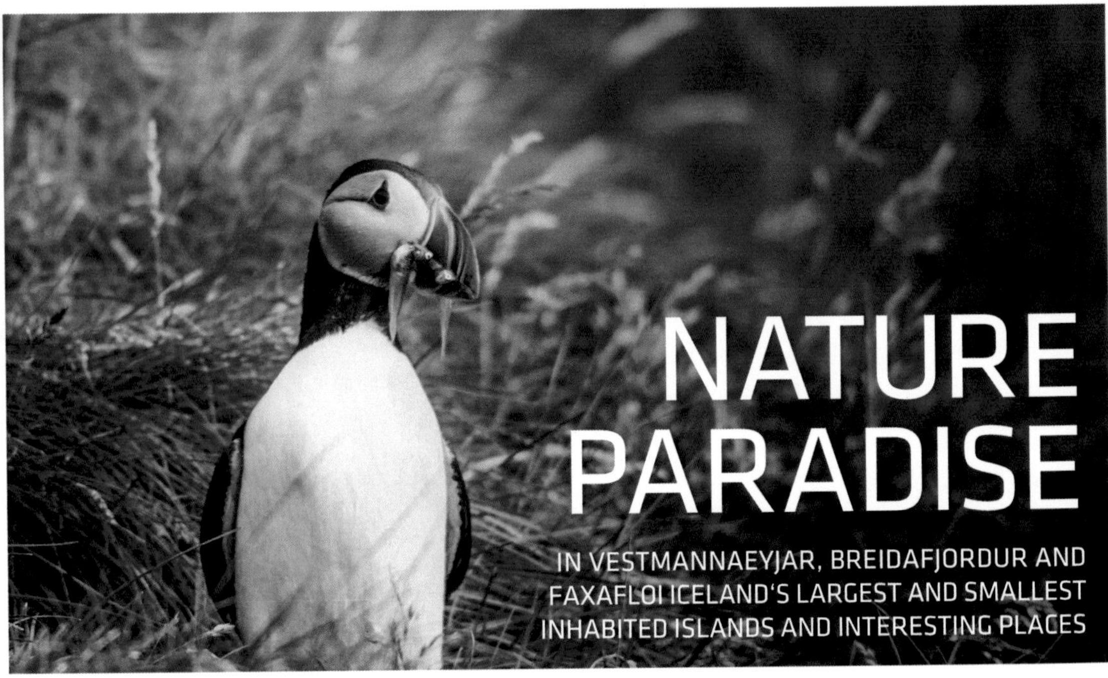
NATURE
PARADISE
IN VESTMANNAEYJAR, BREIDAFJORDUR AND
FAXAFLOI ICELAND'S LARGEST AND SMALLEST
INHABITED ISLANDS AND INTERESTING PLACES

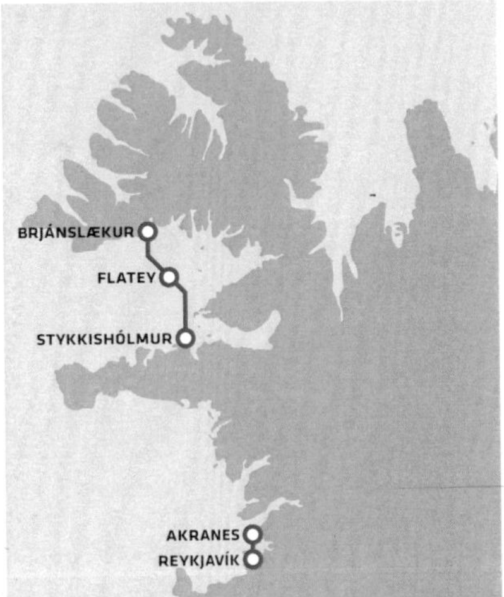
BRJÁNSLÆKUR
FLATEY
STYKKISHÓLMUR
AKRANES
REYKJAVÍK
LANDEYJAHÖFN
VESTMANNAEYJAR

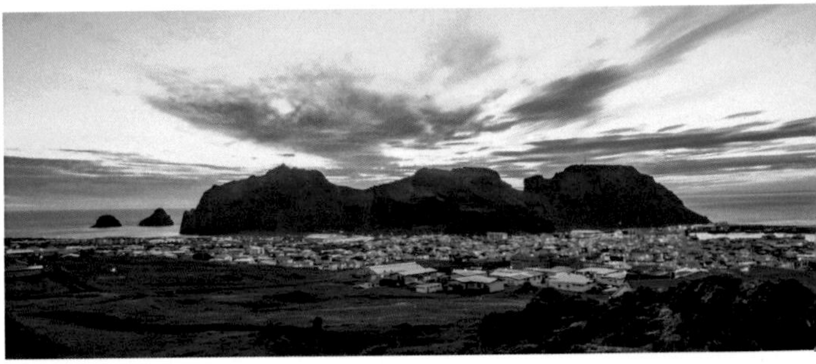

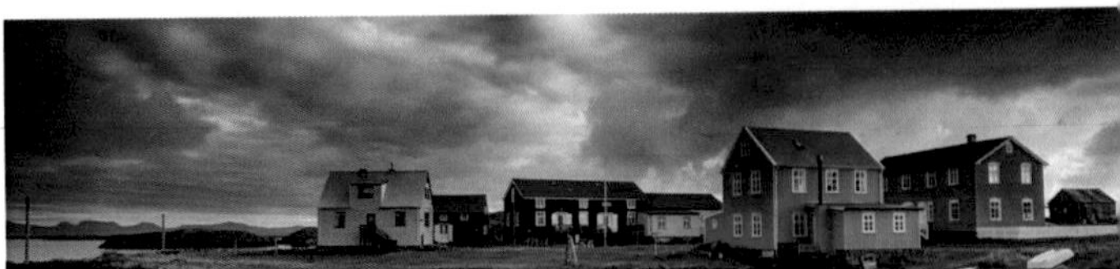

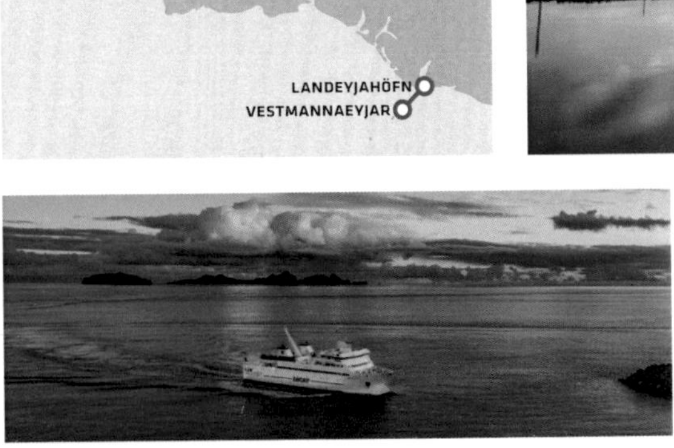

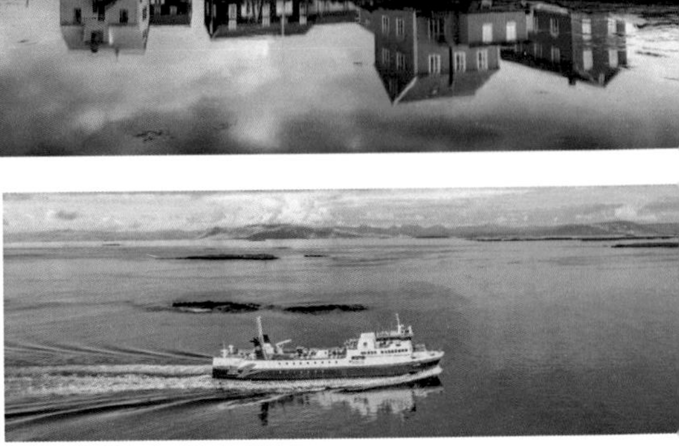

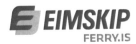

Original text:
Steindór Steindórsson frá Hlöðum

Editor:
Hálfdan Örlygsson
Þórdís Guðrún Arthursdóttir

Supervision of maps and the Atlas:
Þórdís Guðrún Arthursdóttir

Advertisements:
Elsa M. Ágústsdóttir
Óttar Sveinsson

VEGAHANDBÓKIN EHF.

TABLE OF

Important reading

CONTENT

Iceland Road Guide – 15th edition.
– Former title: *The Visitor´s Key to Iceland*
– Former title: *Iceland Road Atlas*

This book was published under the title Iceland Road Guide 1975, 1978, 1981 and 1988.
Revised 1996, 1999, 2001 and 2003 under the title The Visitor´s Key to Iceland.
Revised 2005, 2007 and 2009 under the title Iceland Road Atlas.
Revised 2011, 2013, 2015 and 2017 under the title Iceland Road Guide.

All plans in this book are based on maps prepared by the Icelandic Geodetic Survey and the original maps produced by Geodætisk Institut in Copenhagen. This book is published by special agreement with Icelandic Geodetic Survey.

Original design: Jakob Hálfdanarson, engineer.

Map drawing: Narfi Þorsteinsson directed the original drawing of the maps which form the basis of the maps in this edition and have been converted into machine-readable form. Sigurgeir Skúlason was in charge of the text on the maps.
Ólafur Valsson produced the maps.

English version: Einar Guðjohnsen and Pétur Kidson Karlsson (based on the original Icelandic editions 1973 and 1974) with additional material 1988 by Leo Munro and Helgi Magnússon.
Revision of the 1996 edition (based on additional material by Örlygur Hálfdanarson): Wincie Jóhannsdóttir.
Revision of the 1999, 2001, 2003, 2005, 2007, 2009, 2011, 2013 and 2015 edition Örlygur Hálfdanarson/ Eva Hálfdanardóttir

Layout: Marcel Kircheis
Printing and bound by: Prentmiðlun ehf., Poland

ISBN 978-9935-9254-7-3

HOW TO USE THIS BOOK

Please spend a few minutes reading these pages before you start using and enjoying the Iceland Road Guide.

Information is arranged according to the Public Roads Administration's regional numbering system, which is also used on road signs throughout the country. Roads are listed in numerical order. **The Ring Road, Highway 1,** is covered in **pages 51-151.** It is followed by roads in Regions 2 to 9, and finally by the mountain roads, which are prefixed by a letter F. Almost all roads have both numbers and names.

There are eight regions. The regional boundaries are shown on the map on page 5.

All roads in each region are identified on the regional maps, next to these is a list of the roads (both their names and numbers) with their corresponding page(s) in the guide.

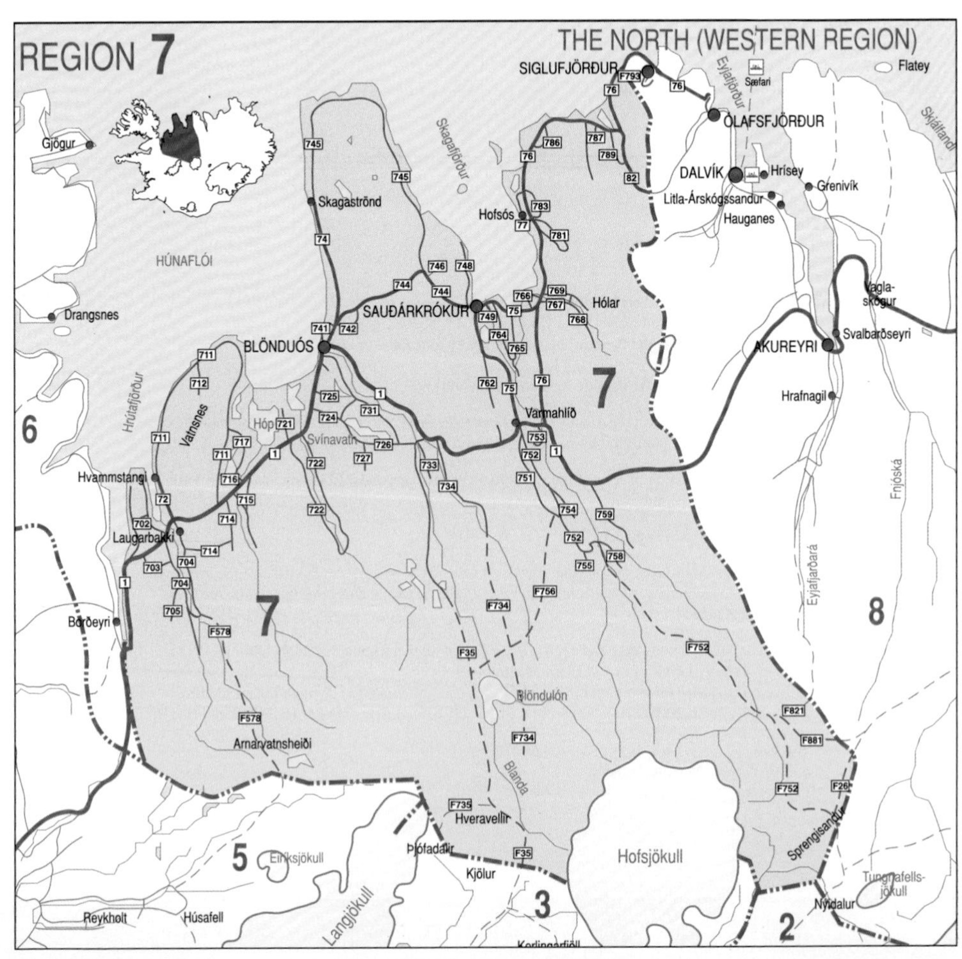

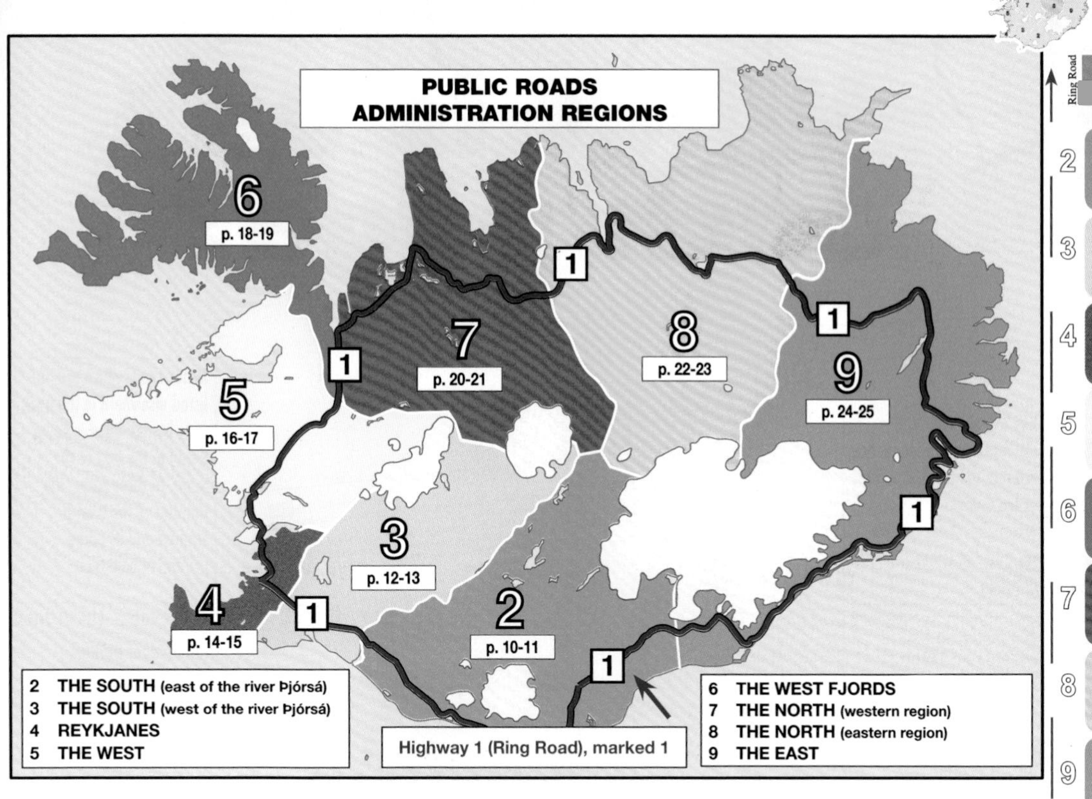

Iceland is divided into eight regions, numbered from 2 to 9.
There is no region 1.

This map shows the regions, and also Highway 1 (the Ring Road), which passes through all regions. The numbers of all roads in each area (with the exception of Highway 1) begin with the relevant regional number. For example, all roads in Region 2 have numbers beginning with 2. The roads within each region are listed in numerical, rather than alphabetical, order. For example, the first road in Region 3, Skeiða- og Hrunamannavegur, is no. 30, and the last, Arnarbælisvegur, is no. 375.

Use the colour bars on the side to find each new section easily.

Use the region color chart for quick region reference.

If you are taking the Ring Road from Reykjavík to the west and the north, start at page 51.
If you are travelling east from Reykjavík, begin instead at page 151 and follow the pages in reverse order until you get to Reykjavík via Hvalfjörður and Kjalarnes.

What is on each page?

Key locations and the distances between them are listed at the top and bottom of the map. This makes it easy to use for travel in either direction.

The numer in the triangle (1-24) is a refernece to an Atlas (p. 562-587) so you can orient yourself within a bigger region.

Every region has its own colour code.

The road-map includes symbols which indicate various services available in the area.

Advertisements detail various services available in the area.

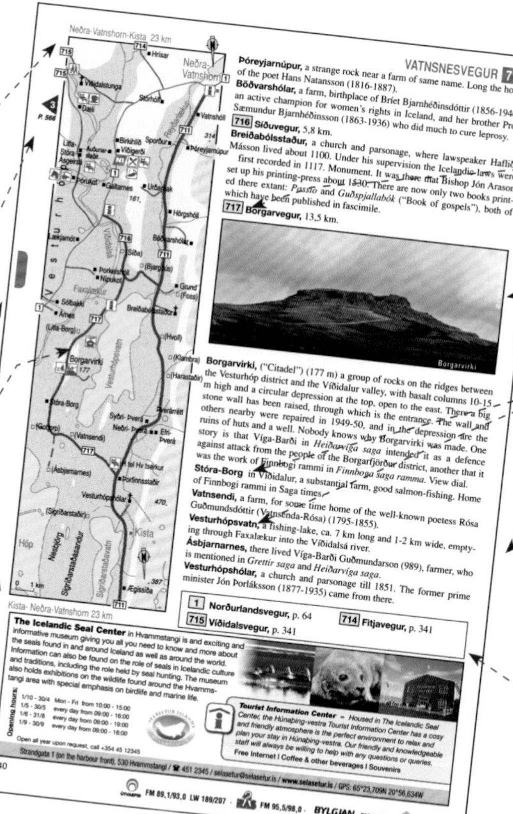

Neðra-Vatnshorn-Kista 23 km

VATNSNESVEGUR 711

Þóreyjarnúpur, a strange rock near a farm of same name. Long the home of the poet Hans Natansson (1816-1887).
Böðvarshólar, a farm, birthplace of Bríet Bjarnhéðinsdóttir (1856-1940), an active champion for women's rights in Iceland, and her brother Prof. Sæmundur Bjarnhéðinsson (1863-1936) who did much to cure leprosy.
716 **Síðuvegur,** 5,8 km.
Breiðabólsstaður, a church and parsonage, where lawspeaker Hafliði Másson lived about 1100. Under his supervision the Icelandic laws were first recorded in 1117. Monument. It was there that Bishop Jón Arason set up his printing-press about 1530. There are now only two books printed there extant: *Passio* and *Guðspjallabók* ("Book of gospels"), both of which have been published in fascimile.
717 **Borgarvegur,** 13,5 km.

Borgarvirki

Borgarvirki, ("Citadel") (177 m) a group of rocks on the ridges between the Vesturhóp district and the Víðidalur valley, with basalt columns 10-15 m high and a circular depression at the top, open to the east. There a big stone wall has been raised, through which is the entrance. The wall and others nearby were repaired in 1949-50, and in the depression are the ruins of huts and a well. Nobody knows why Borgarvirki was made. One story is that Víga-Barði in *Heiðarvíga saga* intended it as a defence against attack from the people of the Borgarfjörður district, another that it was the work of Finnbogi rammi in *Finnboga saga ramma*. View dial.
Stóra-Borg in Víðidalur, a substantial farm, good salmon-fishing. Home of Finnbogi rammi in Saga times.
Vatnsendi, a farm, for some time home of the well-known poetess Rósa Guðmundsdóttir (Vatnsenda-Rósa) (1795-1855).
Vesturhópsvatn, a fishing-lake, ca. 7 km long and 1-2 km wide, emptying through Faxalækur into the Víðidalsá river.
Ásbjarnarnes, there lived Víga-Barði Guðmundarson (989), farmer, who is mentioned in *Grettir saga* and *Heiðarvíga saga*.
Vesturhópshólar, a church and parsonage till 1851. The former prime minister Jón Þorláksson (1877-1935) came from there.

1 **Norðurlandsvegur,** p. 64
715 **Víðidalsvegur,** p. 341
714 **Fitjavegur,** p. 341

Kista- Neðra-Vatnshorn 23 km

The Icelandic Seal Center in Hvammstangi is and exciting and informative museum giving you all you need to know and more about the seals found in and around Iceland as well as around the world. Information can also be found on the role of seals in Icelandic culture and traditions, including the role held by seal hunting. The museum also holds exhibitions on the wildlife found around the Hvammstangi area with special emphasis on birdlife and marine life.

Opening hours:
1/10 - 30/4 Mon - Fri from 10:00 - 15:00
1/5 - 30/5 every day from 09:00 - 16:00
1/6 - 31/8 every day from 09:00 - 19:00
1/9 - 30/9 every day from 09:00 - 16:00

Open all year upon request, call +354 45 12345

Tourist Information Center – Housed in The Icelandic Seal Center, the Húnaþing-vestra Tourist Information Center has a cosy and friendly atmosphere is the perfect environment to relax and plan your stay in Húnaþing-vestra. Our friendly and knowledgeable staff will always be willing to help with any questions or queries. Free Internet I Coffee & other beverages I Souvenirs

Strandgata 1 (on the harbour front), 530 Hvammstangi / ☎ 451 2345 / selasetur@selasetur.is / www.selasetur.is / GPS: 65°23,709N 20°56,634W

340

FM 89,1/93,0 LW 189/207 . FM 95,5/98,0 . BYLGJAN FM 98,9 . FM 94,3

Minor roads which are not listed elsewhere in the book may be described in some detail in the text of the page. In these cases, the number of the road is framed and its name printed in bold type.

Hundreds of pictures and photographs bring to life the information accompanying the maps.

Words in bold type are listed in the index at the back of the book.

Each map is accompanied by interesting information on the history and natural features of the area.

The relevant page number(s) for information on other roads is listed at the bottom of the text.

Frequencies for the National Radio, Bylgjan and FM957 are listed at the bottom of each page.

This edition includes a detailed 24-page Atlas, on pages **p. 562-587**.
On a scale of **1:500,000**, you can get a clear **overview** of all of the Icelandic regions and refer quickly back and forth to place descriptions by page number. For instance, if you are reading **p. 340** as you travel towards Hvammstangi, you can orient yourself within a bigger region by noting the arrow referring you to Map 3 (P. 566) in the Atlas, on **p. 566**.

READ THIS
SO YOU DON'T GET LOST!

One of the advantages of this Guide is that it is equally easy to use when **travelling in either direction** on any road.

The road descriptions begin with Highway 1 (the Ring Road), starting from Reykjavík and continuing clockwise round the country through the West, North, East and South Regions and reaching Reykjavík again by Suðurlandsvegur.

It may seem odd to have to read the map and the corresponding information upwards and not from the top down as you are probably used to doing. There is a natural reason for this, which you will soon understand and get used to immediately.

Of course, it is also possible to follow Highway 1 in an **anti-clockwise** direction from Reykjavík. To do this, begin your journey at **Rauðavatn** on page 151 and follow each page from top to bottom, and in reverse order (i.e. going from **page 151 to 150** and so on until you returned to Reykjavík via Hvalfjörður and Kjalarnes).

There are street maps of all main towns and villages in the country, with symbols showing services offered by advertisers in this Guide.

If you are taking the Ring Road from Reykjavík to the west and the north, start at page 51.
If you are travelling east from Reykjavík, begin instead at page 151 and follow the pages in reverse order until you get to Reykjavík via Hvalfjörður and Kjalarnes.

KEY TO MAP SYMBOLS

Hospital / Clinic	Licensed premises	Sea angling	ATM	Lighthouse
Police station	Guesthouse	Whale watching	Post office	School
Chemist	Sleeping bag accommodation	Snowcat trips	Grocery store	Community centre
Emergency phone	Youth hostel	Ski slopes	Bakery	Radio
Fire extinguiser	Summerhouse rental	Shooting arena	Roadhouse	N1 station
Clinic	Summerhouse colony	Cross-country skiing area	Museum	Olís station
Information	Tourist hut	Ski slopes	Live music	Skeljungur station
Information centre	Campsite	Golf course	Library	ÓB gas station
Public toilets	Waste tank dischange	Jet ski rental	Aquarium	Orkan gas station
Town centre	Caravan park	Bicycle rental	Bird view	Orkan X station
Place of interest	Hot tub	Boat rental	Rubbish container	Bónus Groceries
Walking routes	Swimming pool	River rafting	Handcrafts	Landsbanki Bank
Picnic spot	Gymnasium	Water skiing	Ice-cream shop	Open Forest
View dial	Sports area	Glacier tours	Book store	Golf course
Spas & natural hot pools	Seal view	Bus tours	Coffee house	National Museum of Iceland
Garbage containers	Playgroud	Jeep tours	Car ferry	
Petrol station	Farmyard animal zoo	Shark fishing	Boat trips	1 61 702 F622 Road numbers
Auto mechanic	Tourist cowshed	Open all year	Airport	
Tyre service	Horse rental	Greenhouse	Airport	Paved road
4W bike rental	Stable area	Church	Tunnel	Gravel road
Car rental	Race track	Graveyard	Factory	Primary highland gravel road
Restaurant	Fishing permits	Bank	Hydroelectric station	Highland gravel road

Above and below each map are the names of the distance points, and normally the distance between them. Some place names are also printed in red on the maps themselves. On p. 62, for example, the distance points are Grænumýrartunga - Reykjaskóli and Reykjaskóli - Grænumýrartunga. Grænumýrartunga is printed in red, but in parentheses. The parentheses, together with the open square □ which is also printed in red, show that the farm is abandoned. If farming had been discontinued but the buildings were still maintained, then the square would be filled in: ■ At the top of the page, Reykjaskóli is printed in red, and also with a filled square, since the school is in operation. On p. 168, the distance points are Hvolsvöllur - Hlíðarendi; the name Hvolsvöllur is printed in red at the bottom of the map, with the symbol for a built-up area also in red. At the top of the map, Hlíðarendi is printed in red, but instead of the farm symbol there is the symbol for a church, in red. If the farm Hlíðarendi were abandoned, then the name would be in parentheses, but not around the symbol for the church, since it is in use.

	Symbol	Meaning
	■	Farm
(Farm name)	■	Farm and distance point
	■	Farm; uninhabited, but buildings maintained
(Farm name)	■	Farm, uninhabited, distance point
	□	Abandoned farm
	□	Abandoned farm, distance point
	✝	Church
	✝	Church and distance point
		Built-up area

The Meaning of Icelandic Place Names

Most Icelandic place names, both of towns, villages, and natural features in the landscape, mean something. This can help the reader to identify and understand them. For instance, words containing the compounds *hver, laug,* and *reyk(ja)* indicate the proximity of hot springs. It should be noted that words or compounds in declension sometimes appear rather different from the nominative.

The last part of a place name is usually the name of the geographical feature, e.g. Þing*vellir* (*vellir* is the plural of völlur = plain), Þjórs*á* (*á* = river), Akra*fjall* (*fjall* = mountain), Sel*foss* (*foss* = falls).

The following list is intended primarily as an aid to map-reading.

alda = hilly ridge (plural: *öldur*)
á = river
ás = small hill, ridge
bær = farm, township
bakki = river bank
bjarg = cliff, rock
borg = city; crag
botn = bottom, head of valley or fiord
brekka = slope
brú = bridge
bunga = rounded peak
dalur = valley
djúp = long inlet; deep
drag = watercourse (plural: *drög*)
drangur = isolated column of rock
dyngja = dome
eiði = isthmus
ey = island (plural: *eyjar*)
eyri = sandspit, delta
fell = mountain; hill
fjall = mountain (plural: *fjöll*)
fjörður = fiord; broad inlet; valley (plural: *firðir*)
fljót = large river
foss = waterfall
gígur = crater
gil = gorge, ravine
gjá = chasm, fissure
grunn = shoal, shallow
háls = ridge, isthmus
hamar = crag
heiði = heath, moor
hlíð = mountain side
hnjúkur/*hnúkur* = peak
höfði = promontory
höfn = harbour
hóll = rounded hill (plural: *hólar*)
hólmur = islet
holt = stony hill
hraun = lava-field, lava
hryggur = ridge
hver = hot spring
hvoll = hill
jökull = glacier
jökulsá = glacial river
kirkja = church
klettur = rock, cliff
kot = small farm
kvísl = river; branch of river
lækur = brook
laug = warm spring
lón = lagoon
melur = gravel; barren plain
múli = headland, spur
mynni = mouth
mýri = swamp
nes = headland, ness
núpur = spur, peak
oddi = point, tongue of land
öræfi = desert
ós = estuary
reykur = smoke, steam
rif = reef
sandur = sand(s)
skagi = peninsula
skarð = mountain pass
sker = skerry
skógur = wood, shrubland
slétta = plain
staður = place; parsonage (plural: *staðir*)
stapi = bluff , crag
súlur = (mountain) peaks
tangi = narrow peninsula
tindur = summit
tjörn = small lake; pond
tunga = tongue (of land)
vað = ford (plural: *vöð*)
varða = cairn (plural: *vörður*)
vatn = lake; water (plural: *vötn*)
vegur = road; track
ver = grassy spot
vík = inlet; small bay
vogur = inlet; creek
völlur = plain (plural: *vellir*)

Conversion table

Temperature

0°C = 32°F
10°C = 50°F
20°C = 68°F
-5°C = 23°F
-10°C = 14°F

To convert Centigrade into Fahrenheit: Multiply by 9, divide by 5, and add 32.
To convert Fahrenheit into Centigrade: Subtract 32, multiply by 5, and divide by 9.

Length

1 metre = 1.094 yards
1 yard = 0.914 metre
1 kilometre = 0.6214 mile
1 mile = 1.609 kilometres

Area

1 square metre = 1.196 square yards
1 square yard = 0.836 square metre
1 square kilometre = 0.386 square mile
1 square mile = 2.59 square kilometres

Volume

1 litre = 1.76 pints (2.1 US pints)
1 pint = 0.568 litre
1 litre = 0.22 gallon (0.263 US gallons)
10 litres = 2.2 gallons (2.63 Us gallons)
1 gallon = 4.546 litres

Weight

1 kilogram = 2.205 pounds
1 pound (lb) = 0.454 kilogram
1 tonne (metric ton) = 1 kilogram = 0.984 long ton
1 ton = 1016.04 kilograms

© RG
Fingrafoss

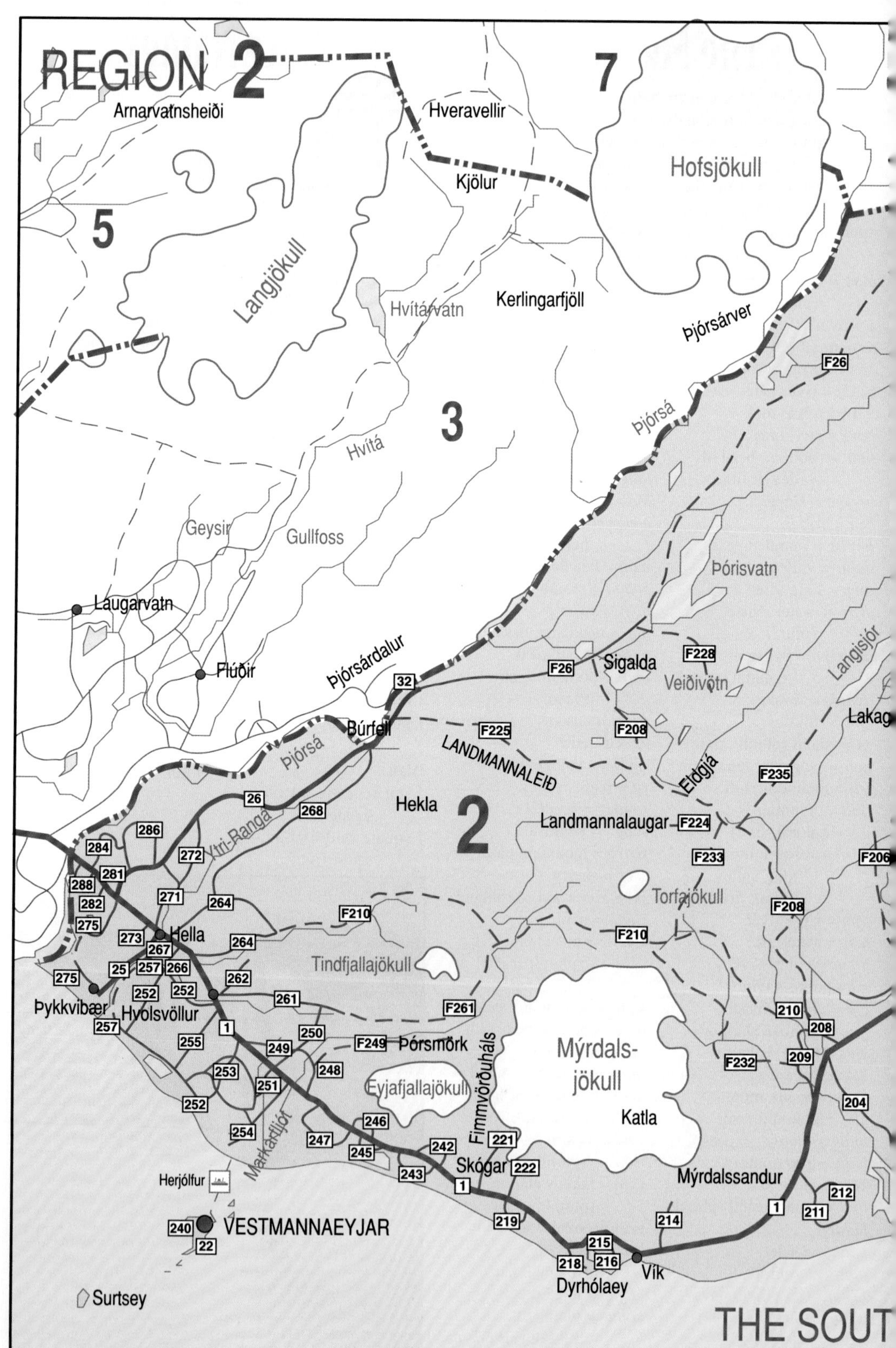
REGION 2
Arnarvatnsheiði
Hveravellir
Kjölur
7
Hofsjökull
5
Langjökull
Hvítárvatn
Kerlingarfjöll
Þjórsárver
F26
3
Þjórsá
Hvítá
Geysir
Gullfoss
Þórisvatn
Laugarvatn
Flúðir
Þjórsárdalur
32
F26
Sigalda
F228
Veiðivötn
Langisjór
Búrfell
F225
F208
LANDMANNALEIÐ
Eldgjá
F235
Þjórsá
26
268
Hekla
2
Landmannalaugar
F224
F233
F206
Ytri-Rangá
286
284
272
281
288
271
264
282
275
Torfajökull
F208
F210
273
Hella
267
264
F210
Tindfjallajökull
275
25
257
266
262
252
252
261
F261
Þykkvibær
Hvolsvöllur
257
1
250
255
249
F249
Þórsmörk
Mýrdals-
jökull
210
208
253
248
251
Eyjafjallajökull
Fimmvörðuháls
F232
209
252
Markarfljót
204
254
246
247
245
242
221
Katla
Herjólfur
243
Skógar
222
Mýrdalssandur
1
212
240
VESTMANNAEYJAR
22
219
214
1
211
215
218
216
Vík
Dyrhólaey
Surtsey

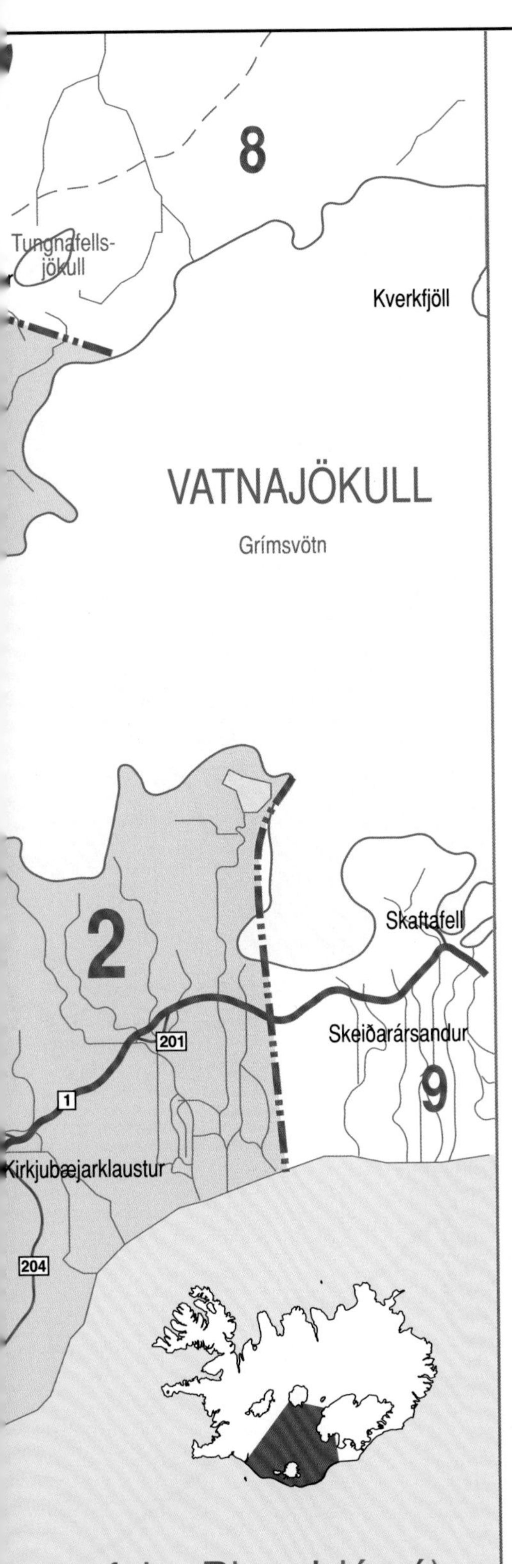
8
Tungnafells-
jökull
Kverkfjöll
VATNAJÖKULL
Grímsvötn
2
Skaftafell
Skeiðarársandur
9
201
1
Kirkjubæjarklaustur
204
east of the River Þjórsá)

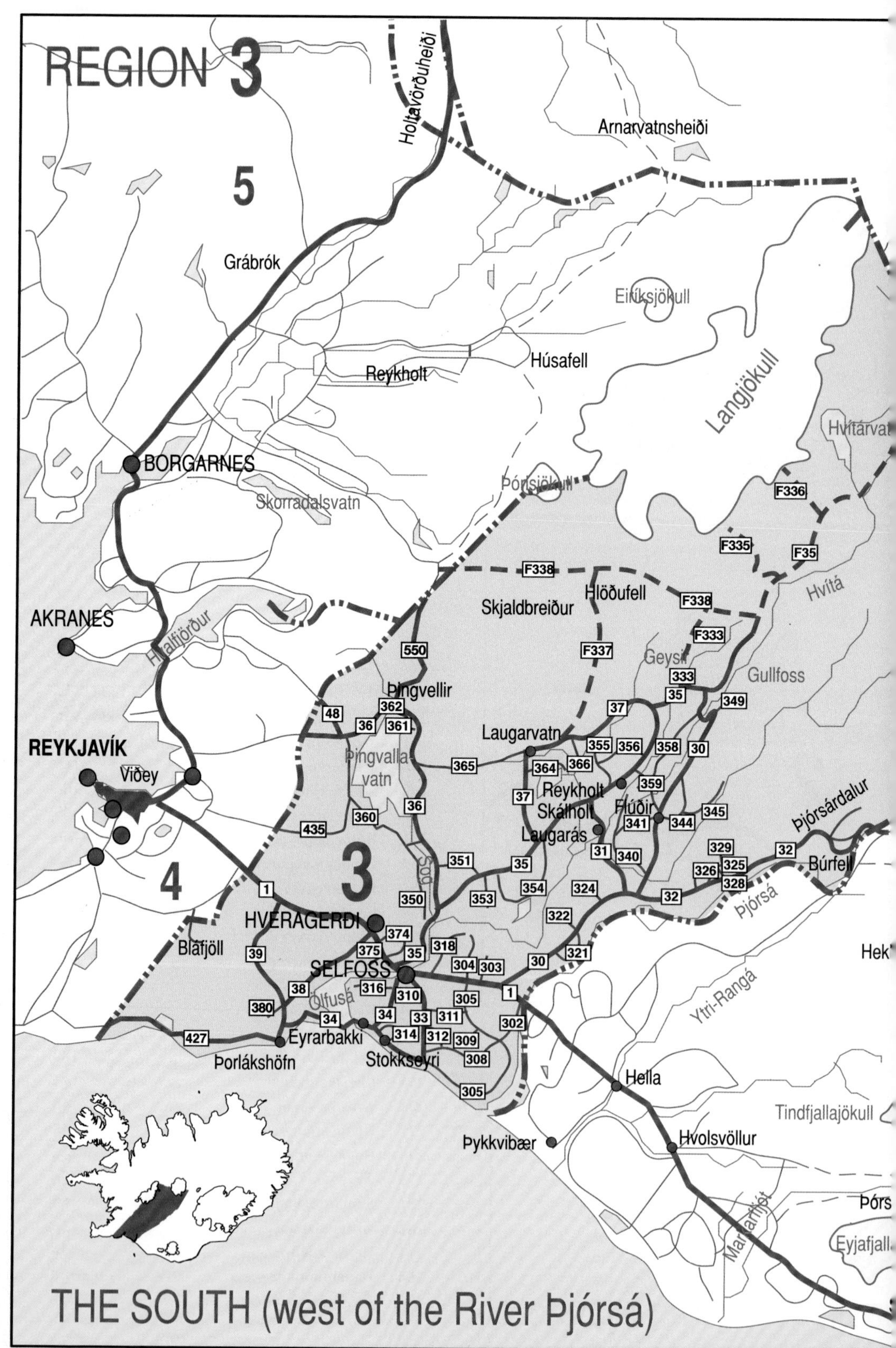
REGION 3
5
Holtavörðuheiði
Arnarvatnsheiði
Grábrók
Eiríksjökull
Húsafell
Reykholt
Langjökull
Hvítárvatn
BORGARNES
Skorradalsvatn
Þórisjökull
F336
F335
F35
F338
Hlöðufell
Skjaldbreiður
Hvítá
AKRANES
Hvalfjörður
550
F337
F333
Geysir
333
Gullfoss
35
Þingvellir
362
48
36
361
37
349
Laugarvatn
355
356
358
30
REYKJAVÍK
Þingvallavatn
365
364
366
Viðey
359
37
Reykholt
Skálholt
Flúðir
36
360
341
344
345
435
Laugarás
Þjórsárdalur
329
31
340
32
3
351
35
325
Búrfell
326
328
Sog
4
1
350
353
354
324
32
Þjórsá
HVERAGERÐI
322
374
Bláfjöll
39
375
35
318
321
Hek
SELFOSS
304
303
30
38
316
Ölfusá
310
1
305
380
34
34
33
311
302
Ytri-Rangá
427
Eyrarbakki
314
312
309
Þorlákshöfn
Stokkseyri
308
Hella
305
Tindfjallajökull
Þykkvibær
Hvolsvöllur
Þórs
Markarfljót
Eyjafjall
THE SOUTH (west of the River Þjórsá)

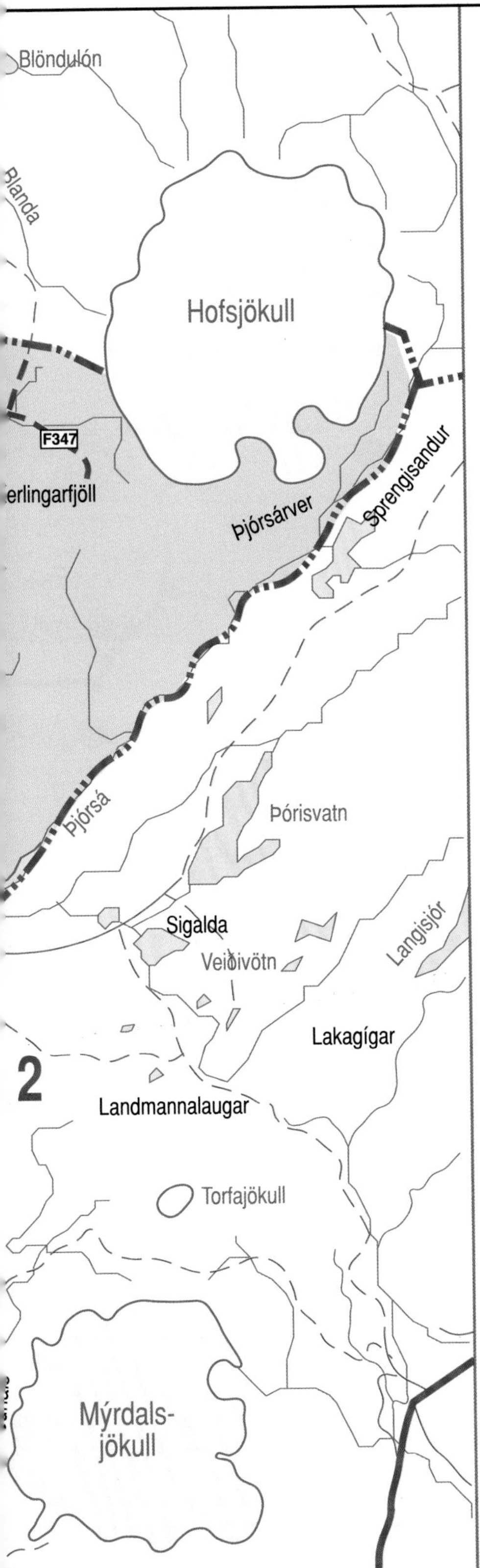

Blöndulón
Blanda
Hofsjökull
F347
erlingarfjöll
Þjórsárver
Sprengisandur
Þjórsá
Þórisvatn
Sigalda
Veiðivötn
Langisjór
Lakagígar
2
Landmannalaugar
Torfajökull
Mýrdals-
jökull

REGION 4
FAXAFLÓI
BORGARNES
Borgarfjörður
5
Akrafjall
AKRANES
47
460
Hvalfjörður
1
Esja
458
Grundarhverfi
Kollafjörður
REYKJAVÍK
SELTJARNARNES
Viðey
MOS
1
Bessastaðir
Álftanes
KÓPAVOGUR
40
41
415
GARÐABÆR
HAFNARFJÖRÐUR
Straumsvík
Garðskagi
45
Garður
45
SANDGERÐI
429
423
45
41
KEFLAVÍK
Keflavík Airport
420
41
Vogar
46
421
NJARÐVÍK
417
42
407
44
Hafnir
Kleifar-
vatn
Bláfjöll
425
43
4
428
Blue Lagoon
426
427
Reykjanes
425
427
427
Þor
GRINDAVÍK
REYKJANES

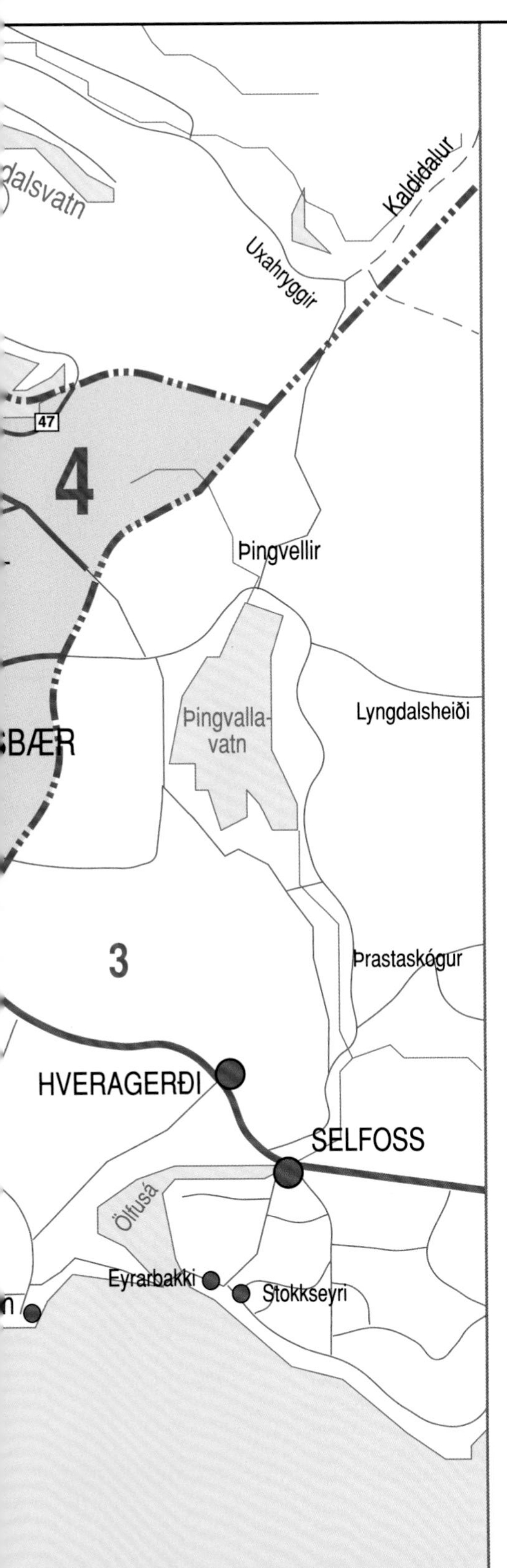
dalsvatn
Kaldidalur
Uxahryggir
47
4
Þingvellir
Þingvalla-
vatn
Lyngdalsheiði
BÆR
3
Þrastaskógur
HVERAGERÐI
SELFOSS
Ölfusá
Eyrarbakki
Stokkseyri

Road no. Page

REGION 5

THE WEST

Brjánslækur
Vatnsfjörður
Skálmarfjörður
Flatey
Baldur
BREIÐAFJÖRÐUR
STYKKISHÓLMUR
Hellissandur
Rif
ÓLAFSVÍK
Grundarfjörður
Fróðárheiði
Snæfellsnes
Vatnaheiði
Snæfellsjökull
Vegamót
Búðir
Arnarstapi
FAXAFLÓI
5

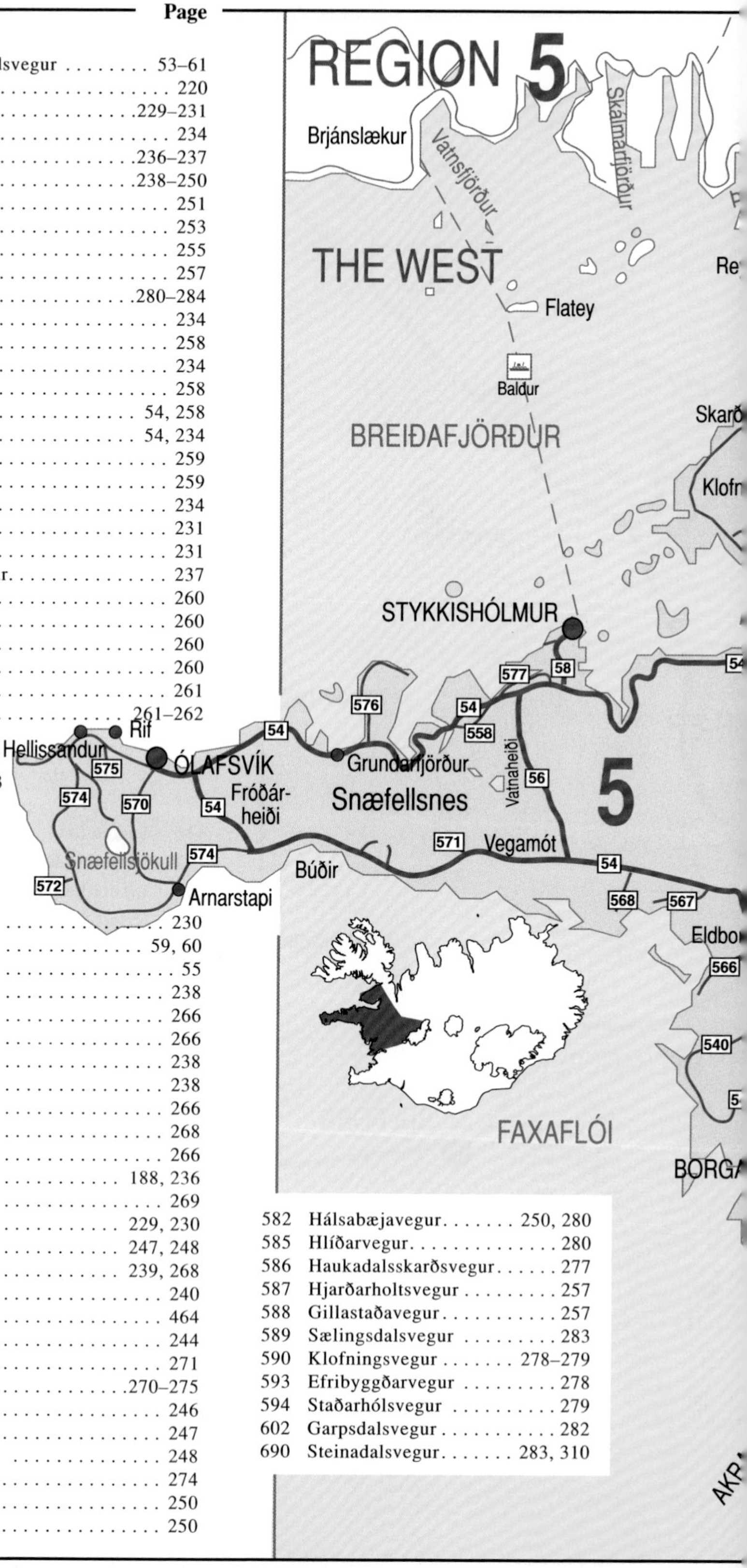

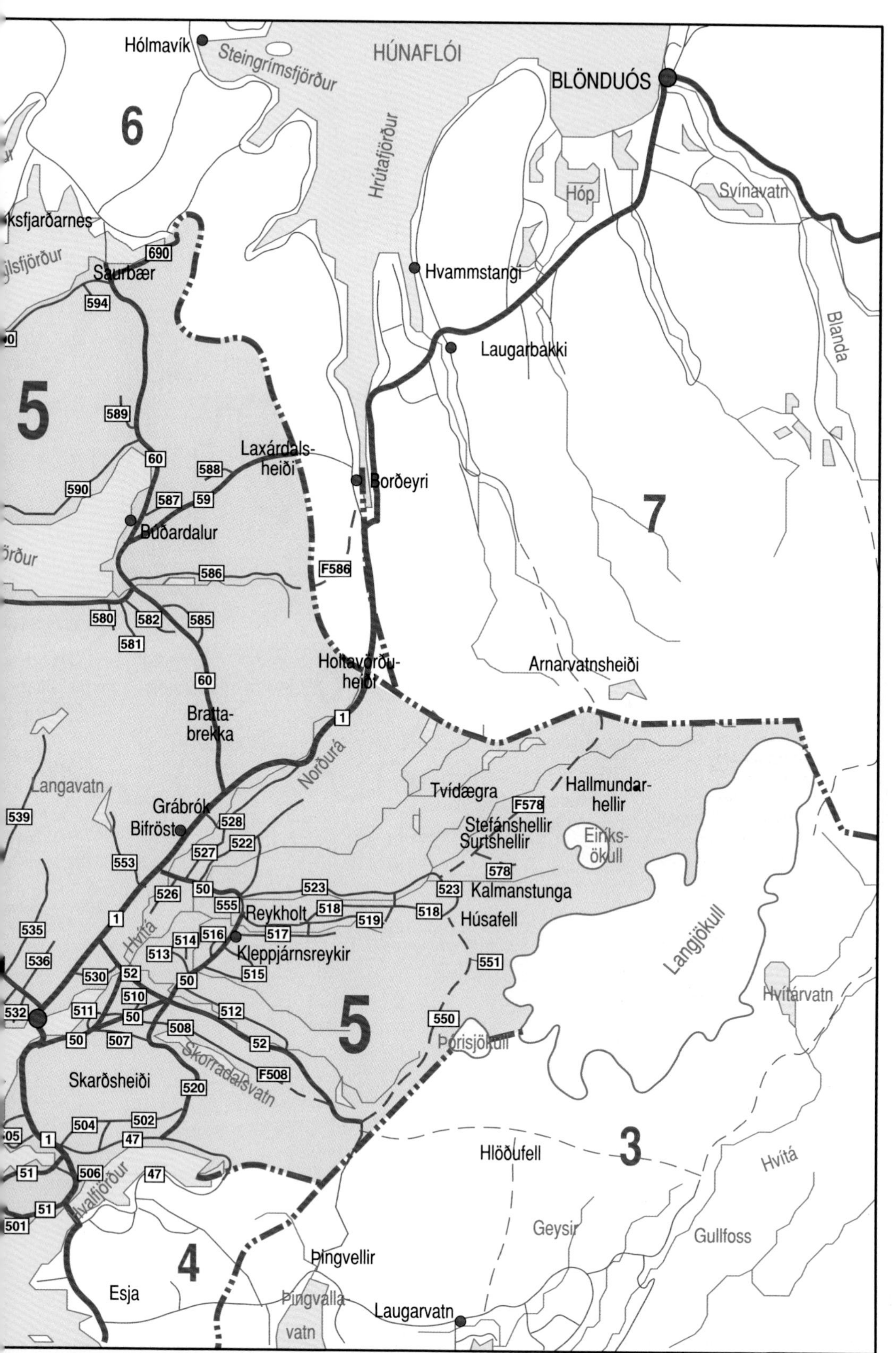
Hólmavík
Steingrímsfjörður
HÚNAFLÓI
BLÖNDUÓS
6
Hrútafjörður
Hóp
Svínavatn
ksfjarðarnes
690
Saurbær
594
Hvammstangi
Blanda
Laugarbakki
5
589
Laxárdals-
heiði
60
588
590
Borðeyri
587
59
7
Búðardalur
F586
586
580
582
585
581
Holtavörðu-
heiði
Arnarvatnsheiði
60
Bratta-
brekka
1
Norðurá
Langavatn
Tvídægra
Hallmundar-
hellir
F578
Grábrók
539
Bifröst
528
Stefánshellir
Surtshellir
Eiríks-
jökull
527
522
553
578
523
Kalmanstunga
526
50
523
555
Reykholt
518
518
Húsafell
1
519
535
Hvítá
517
Langjökull
514
516
513
Kleppjárnsreykir
536
551
530
52
515
50
510
Hvítárvatn
532
511
50
512
5
550
50
507
508
Þórisjökull
52
Skorradalsvatn
Skarðsheiði
F508
520
502
504
05
1
47
3
Hlöðufell
51
506
47
Hvalfjörður
Hvítá
51
Geysir
501
Gullfoss
4
Þingvellir
Esja
Þingvalla-
vatn
Laugarvatn

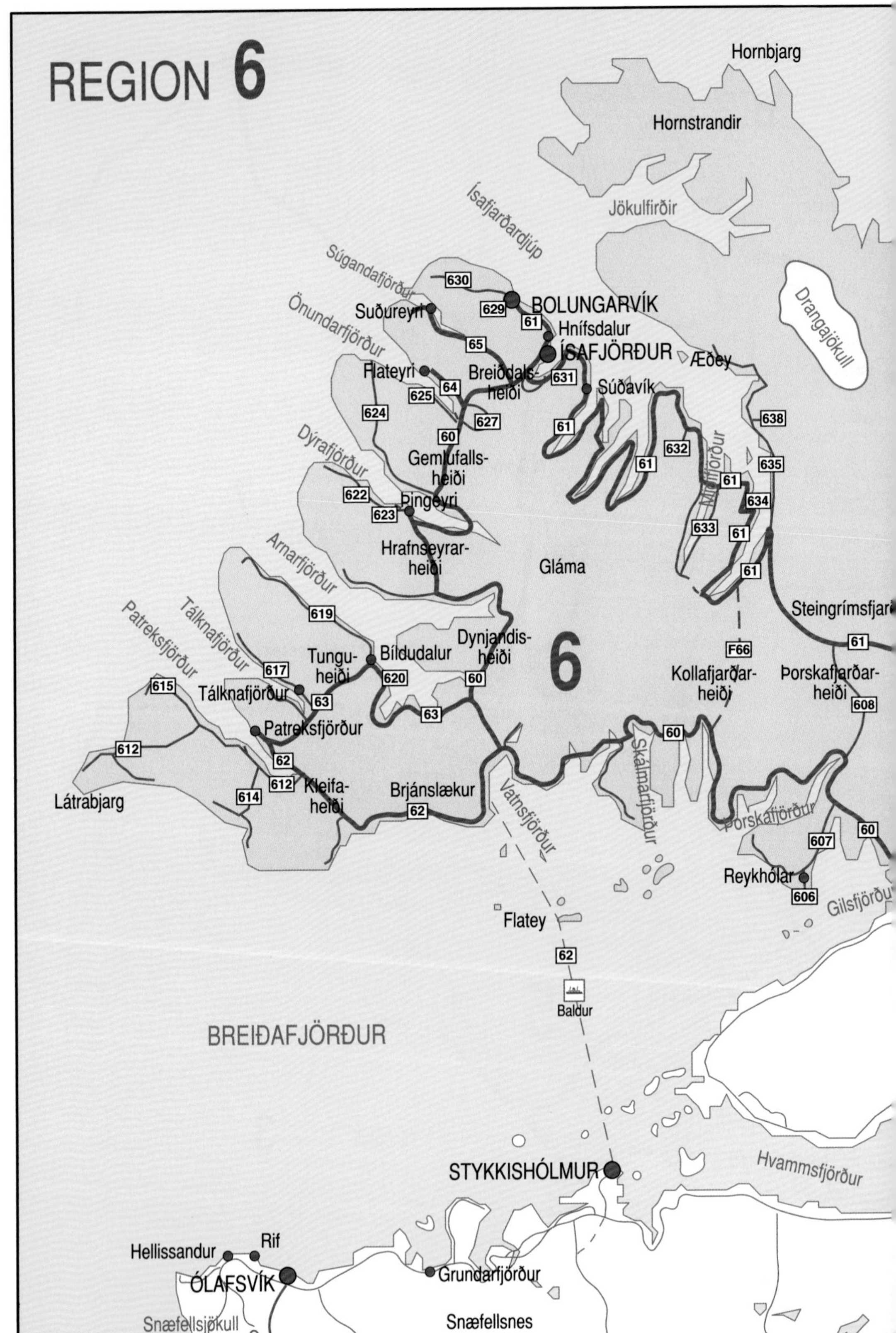
REGION 6
Hornbjarg
Hornstrandir
Jökulfirðir
Ísafjarðardjúp
Drangajökull
Súgandafjörður
Önundarfjörður
Suðureyri
BOLUNGARVÍK
Hnífsdalur
ÍSAFJÖRÐUR
Æðey
Flateyri
Breiðdals-
heiði
Súðavík
Dýrafjörður
Gemlufalls-
heiði
Þingeyri
Hrafnseyrar-
heiði
Gláma
Arnarfjörður
Patreksfjörður
Tálknafjörður
Tungu-
heiði
Bíldudalur
Dynjandis-
heiði
6
Steingrímsfjar
Kollafjarðar-
heiði
Þorskafjarðar-
heiði
Tálknafjörður
Patreksfjörður
Látrabjarg
Kleifa-
heiði
Brjánslækur
Vatnsfjörður
Skálmarfjörður
Þorskafjörður
Reykhólar
Gilsfjörður
Flatey
Baldur
BREIÐAFJÖRÐUR
STYKKISHÓLMUR
Hvammsfjörður
Hellissandur
Rif
ÓLAFSVÍK
Grundarfjörður
Snæfellsjökull
Snæfellsnes
630
629
61
65
631
625
64
624
627
60
61
632
638
635
61
634
622
623
633
61
61
619
F66
61
617
620
60
615
63
63
608
612
60
62
612
614
62
607
60
606
62

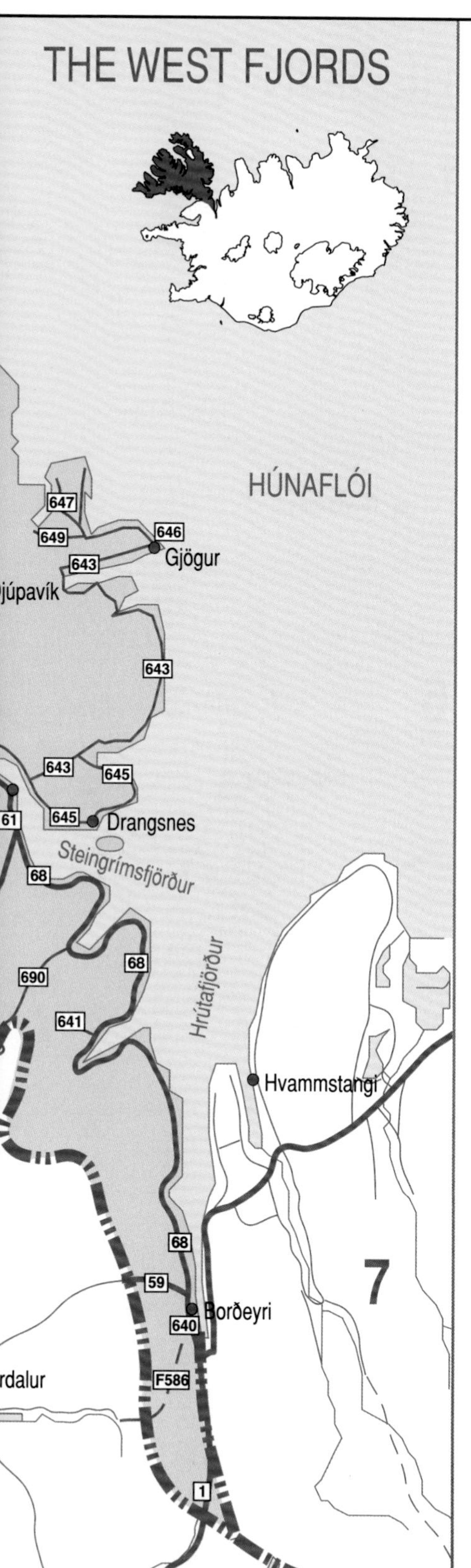

Road no.		Page
1	Ring Road/Norðurlandsvegur	59–60
59	Laxárdalsvegur	257
60	Vestfjarðavegur	280–292
61	Djúpvegur	292–301
62	Barðastrandarvegur	303–304
63	Bíldudalsvegur	305
64	Flateyrarvegur	290
65	Súgandafjarðarvegur	308
67	Hólmavíkurvegur	311
68	Innstrandavegur	309-311
602	Garpsdalsvegur	282
606	Karlseyjarvegur	312
607	Reykhólasveitarvegur	312
608	Þorskafjarðarvegur	313
611	Siglunesvegur	304
612	Örlygshafnarvegur	315
614	Rauðasandsvegur	315
615	Kollsvíkurvegur	315
617	Tálknafjarðarvegur	305
619	Ketildalavegur	317
622	Svalvogavegur	289
623	Flugvallarvegur Dýrafjörður	289
624	Ingjaldssandsvegur	290
625	Valþjófsdalsvegur	290
627	Önundarfjarðarvegur	290
628	Hjarðardalsvegur	290
629	Syðradalsvegur	293
630	Skálavíkurvegur	293
631	Flugvallarvegur Ísafjörður	292, 297
632	Laugardalsvegur	299
633	Mjóafjarðarvegur	299
634	Reykjanesvegur	299
635	Snæfjallastrandarvegur	318
638	Laugalandsvegur	318
640	Borðeyrarvegur	62, 309
641	Krossárdalsvegur	310
643	Strandavegur	319–321
645	Drangsnesvegur	319
646	Flugvallarvegur Gjögri	321
647	Munaðarnesvegur	321
649	Ófeigsfjarðarvegur	321
690	Steinadalsvegur	283, 310

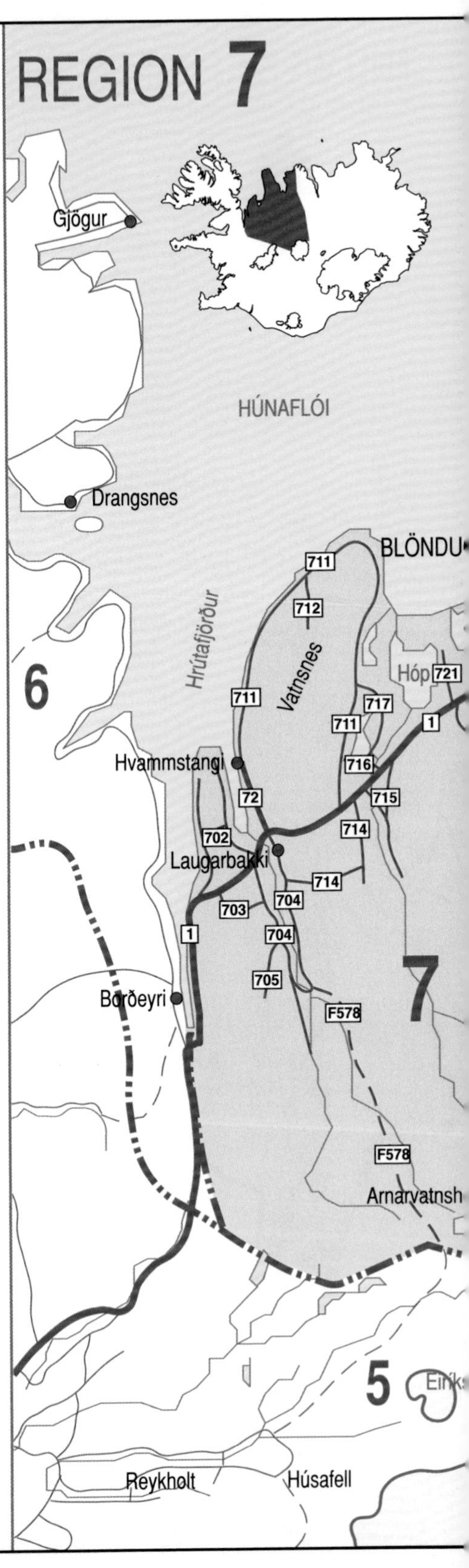

REGION 7
Gjögur
HÚNAFLÓI
Drangsnes
BLÖNDU
Hrútafjörður
Vatnsnes
Hóp
6
711
712
721
717
1
716
715
714
72
702
703
704
705
Hvammstangi
Laugarbakki
Borðeyri
F578
7
Arnarvatnsh
5
Reykholt
Húsafell

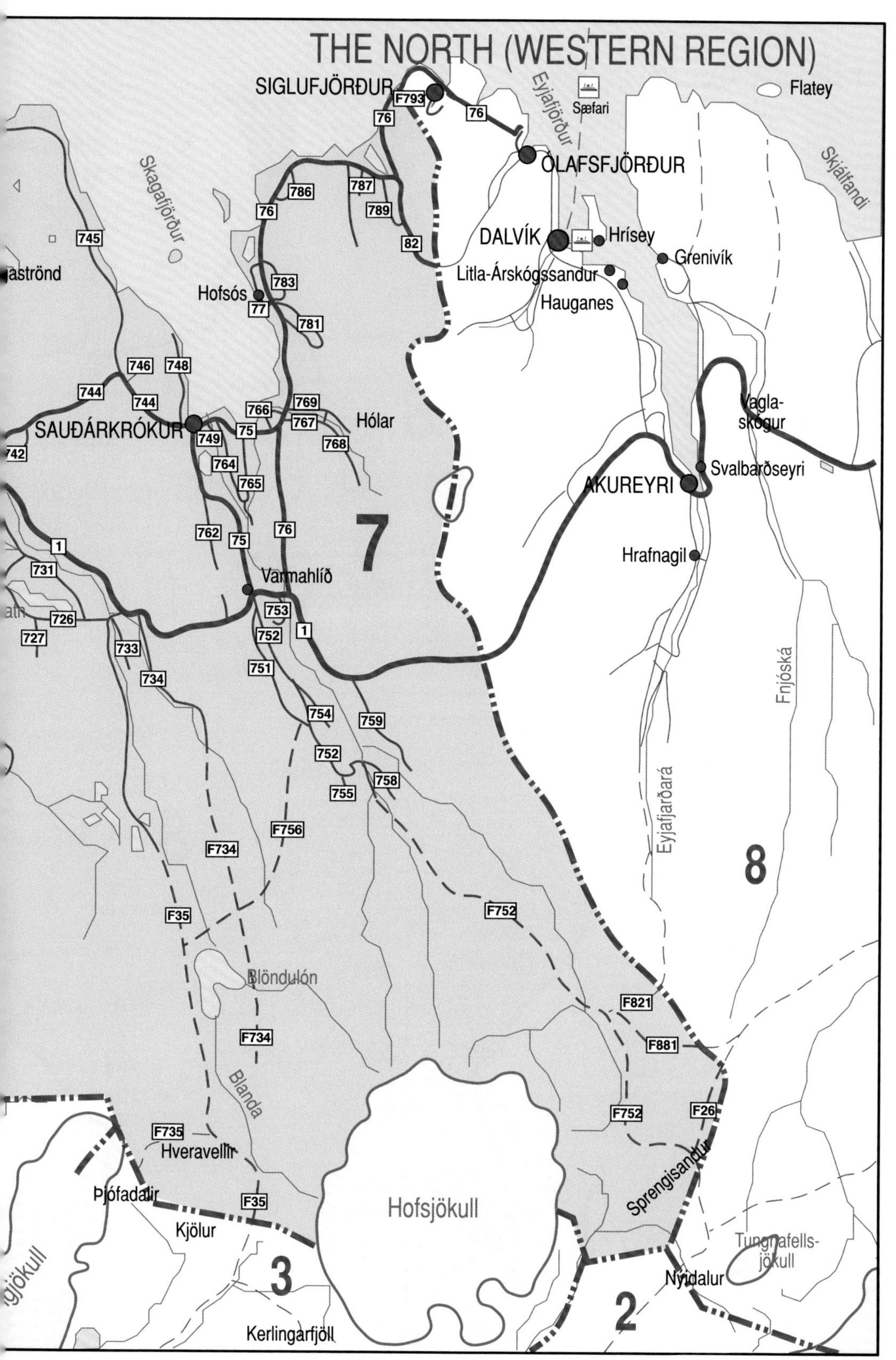
THE NORTH (WESTERN REGION)
SIGLUFJÖRÐUR
ÓLAFSFJÖRÐUR
DALVÍK
Hrísey
Grenivík
Litla-Árskógssandur
Hauganes
Sæfari
Flatey
Eyjafjörður
Skjálfandi
Skagafjörður
Hofsós
SAUÐÁRKRÓKUR
Hólar
Varmahlíð
AKUREYRI
Svalbarðseyri
Vagla-
skógur
Hrafnagil
Fnjóská
Eyjafjarðará
Blöndulón
Blanda
Hveravellir
Þjófadalir
Kjölur
Kerlingarfjöll
Hofsjökull
Sprengisandur
Nýidalur
Tungnafells-
jökull
7
8
3
2
F793
76
786
787
789
82
745
783
77
781
746
748
744
766
769
767
75
768
749
764
765
762
1
731
726
727
753
752
751
733
734
754
759
758
755
F756
F734
F35
F752
F821
F881
F26
F735

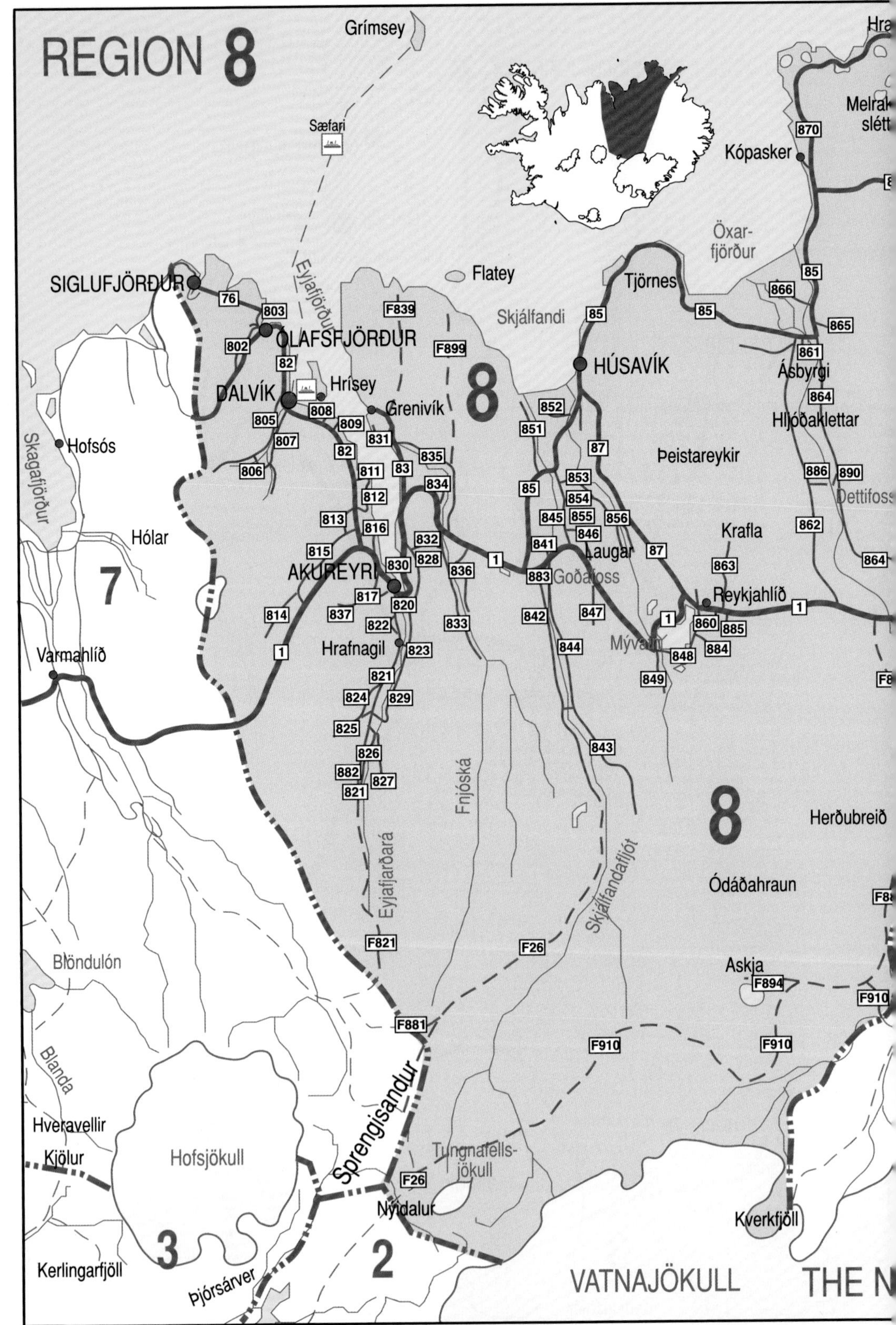
REGION 8
Grímsey
Sæfari
Flatey
Skjálfandi
SIGLUFJÖRÐUR
ÓLAFSFJÖRÐUR
DALVÍK
Hrísey
Grenivík
Eyjafjörður
HÚSAVÍK
Tjörnes
Kópasker
Öxar-
fjörður
Ásbyrgi
Hljóðaklettar
Þeistareykir
Krafla
Reykjahlíð
Laugar
Goðafoss
Mývatn
Hofsós
Skagafjörður
Hólar
AKUREYRI
Hrafnagil
Varmahlíð
Fnjóská
Eyjafjarðará
Skjálfandafljót
Herðubreið
Ódáðahraun
Askja
Blöndulón
Blanda
Hveravellir
Kjölur
Hofsjökull
Sprengisandur
Tungnafells-
jökull
Nýidalur
Kverkfjöll
Kerlingarfjöll
Þjórsárver
VATNAJÖKULL

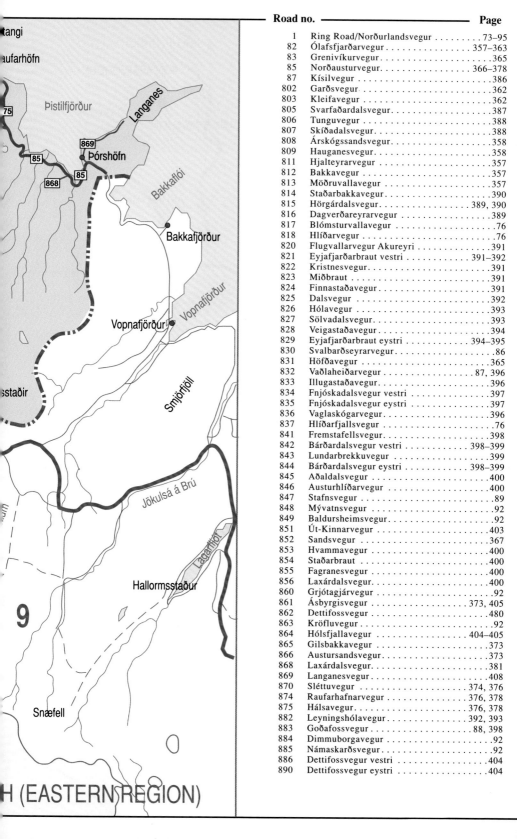

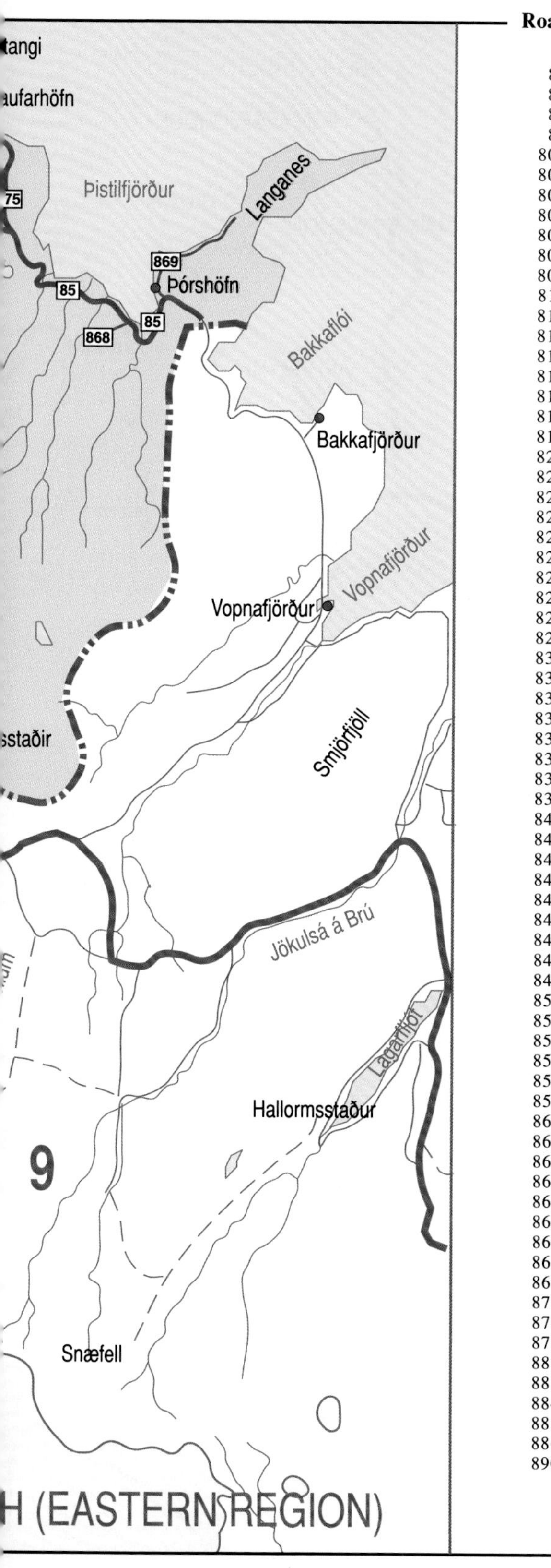
Þistilfjörður
Langanes
75
869
Þórshöfn
85
868
85
Bakkaflói
Bakkafjörður
Vopnafjörður
Vopnafjörður
Smjörfjöll
Jökulsá á Brú
Lagarfljót
Hallormsstaður
9
Snæfell

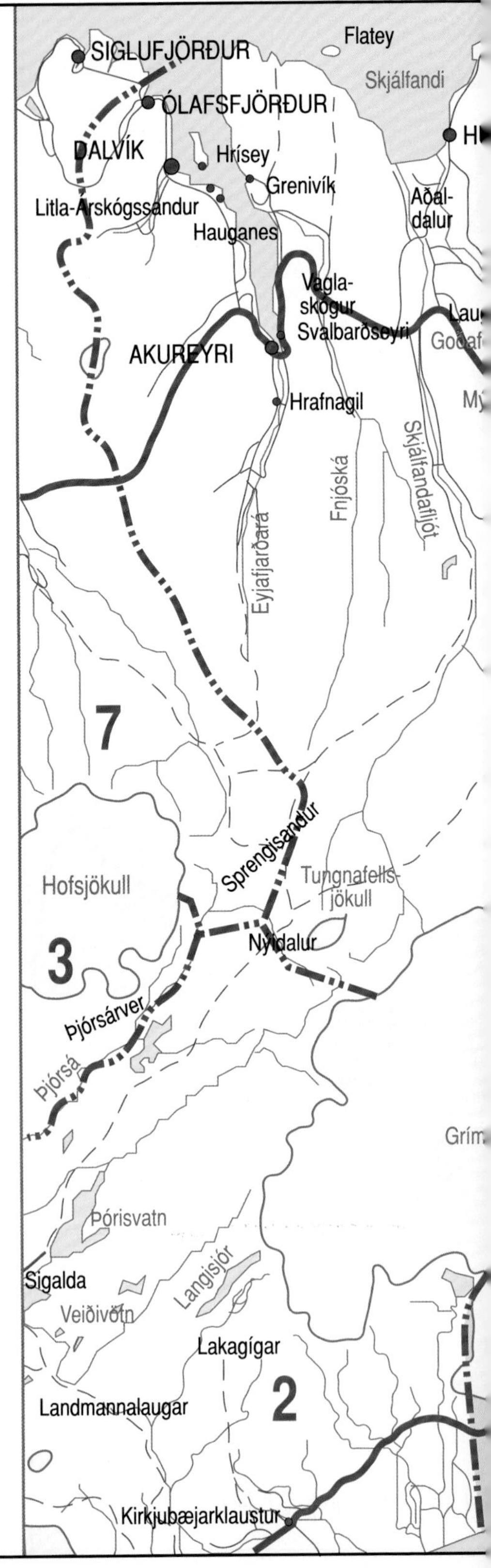

SIGLUFJÖRÐUR
Flatey
Skjálfandi
ÓLAFSFJÖRÐUR
DALVÍK
Hrísey
Grenivík
Litla-Árskógssandur
Hauganes
Aðal-
dalur
Vagla-
skógur
Svalbarðseyri
AKUREYRI
Hrafnagil
Fnjóská
Skjálfandafljót
Eyjafjarðará
7
Sprengisandur
Hofsjökull
Tungnafells-
jökull
Nýidalur
3
Þjórsárver
Þjórsá
Þórisvatn
Sigalda
Langisjór
Veiðivötn
Lakagígar
Landmannalaugar
2
Kirkjubæjarklaustur

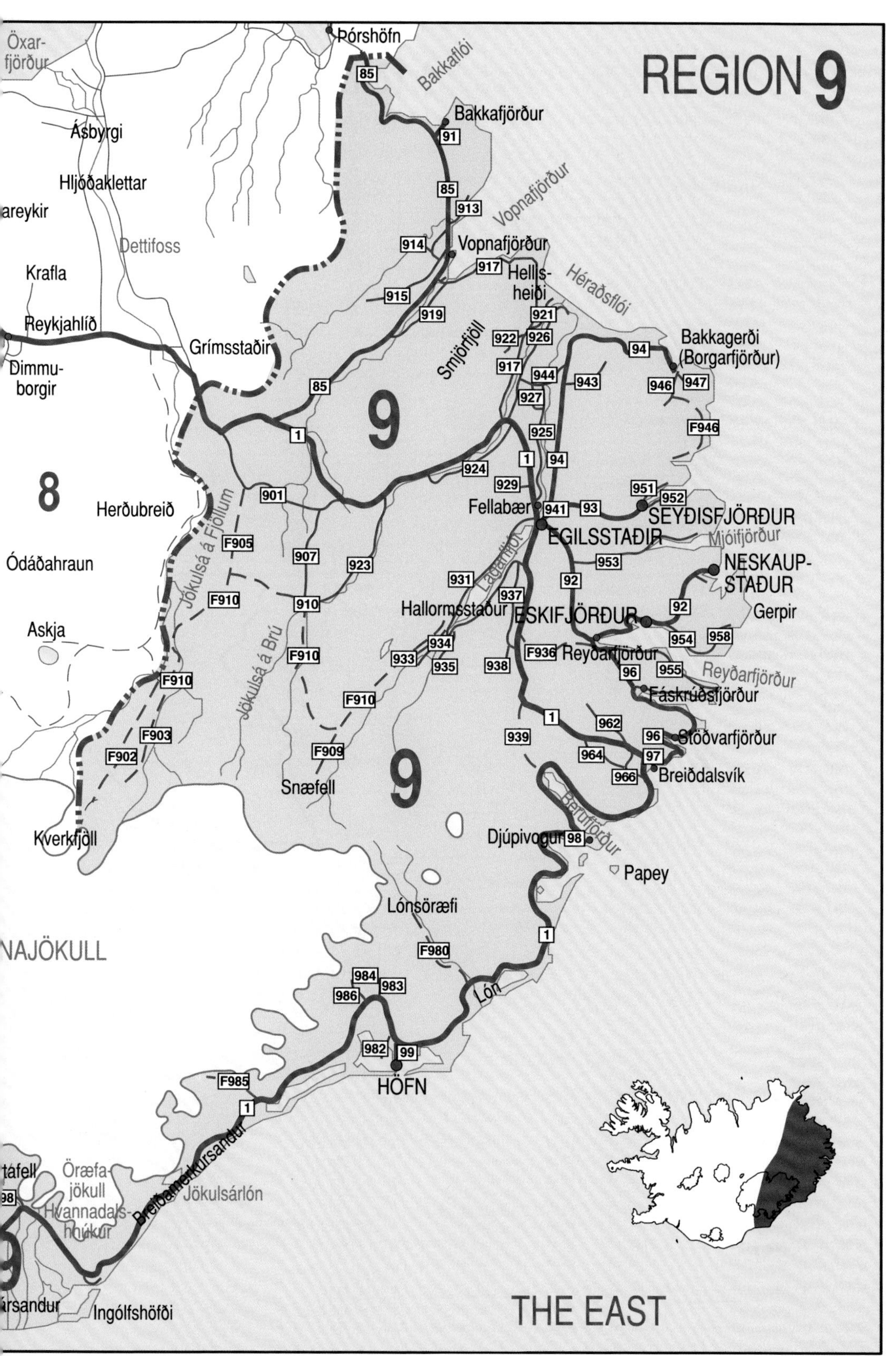
REGION 9
THE EAST
Þórshöfn
Bakkaflói
Bakkafjörður
Vopnafjörður
Vopnafjörður
Héraðsflói
Hellisheiði
Smjörfjöll
Bakkagerði (Borgarfjörður)
Fellabær
SEYÐISFJÖRÐUR
EGILSSTAÐIR
Mjóifjörður
NESKAUPSTAÐUR
Gerpir
Hallormsstaður
ESKIFJÖRÐUR
Reyðarfjörður
Reyðarfjörður
Fáskrúðsfjörður
Stöðvarfjörður
Breiðdalsvík
Berufjörður
Djúpivogur
Papey
Snæfell
Lónsöræfi
Lón
HÖFN
Breiðamerkursandur
Jökulsárlón
Öræfajökull
Hvannadalshnúkur
Ingólfshöfði
Öxarfjörður
Ásbyrgi
Hljóðaklettar
Dettifoss
Krafla
Reykjahlíð
Dimmuborgir
Grímsstaðir
Herðubreið
Ódáðahraun
Askja
Kverkfjöll
Jökulsá á Fjöllum
Jökulsá á Brú
Lagarfljót
8
9
9
9
NAJÖKULL
85
91
85
913
914
917
915
919
921
922
926
917
944
927
925
94
943
946
947
F946
1
94
924
929
951
952
941
93
953
92
92
937
931
901
907
923
F905
F910
910
F910
934
933
935
938
F936
954
958
96
955
F910
F910
F903
F902
F909
1
962
939
96
964
97
966
98
1
F980
984
983
986
982
99
F985
1

Mountain Roads

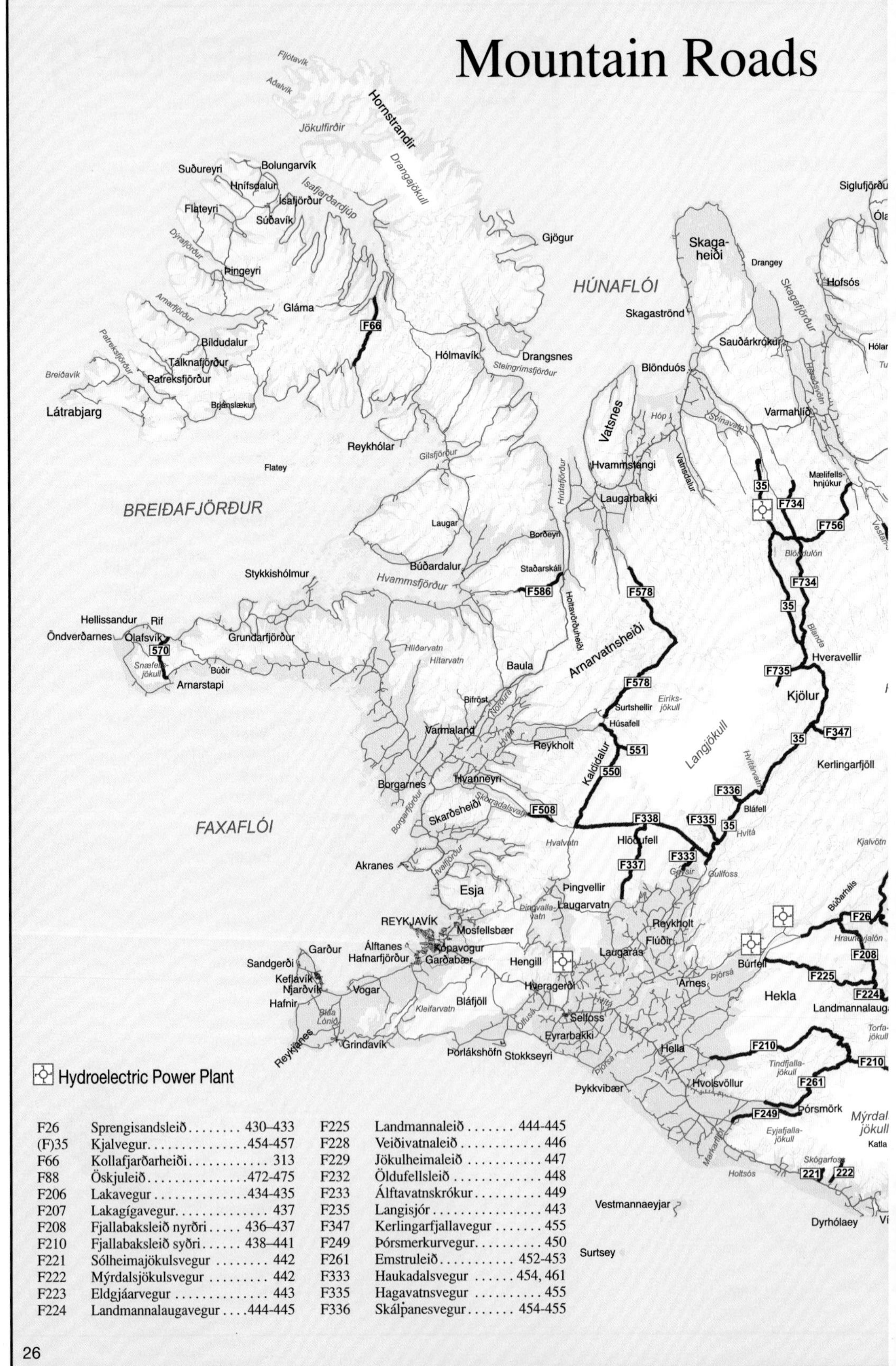

F26	Sprengisandsleið........ 430–433	F225	Landmannaleið 444-445
(F)35	Kjalvegur...............454-457	F228	Veiðivatnaleið 446
F66	Kollafjarðarheiði............ 313	F229	Jökulheimaleið 447
F88	Öskjuleið...............472-475	F232	Öldufellsleið 448
F206	Lakavegur 434-435	F233	Álftavatnskrókur.......... 449
F207	Lakagígavegur.............. 437	F235	Langisjór 443
F208	Fjallabaksleið nyrðri..... 436–437	F347	Kerlingarfjallavegur 455
F210	Fjallabaksleið syðri...... 438–441	F249	Þórsmerkurvegur.......... 450
F221	Sólheimajökulsvegur 442	F261	Emstruleið........... 452-453
F222	Mýrdalsjökulsvegur 442	F333	Haukadalsvegur 454, 461
F223	Eldgjáarvegur 443	F335	Hagavatnsvegur 455
F224	Landmannalaugavegur 444-445	F336	Skálpanesvegur....... 454-455

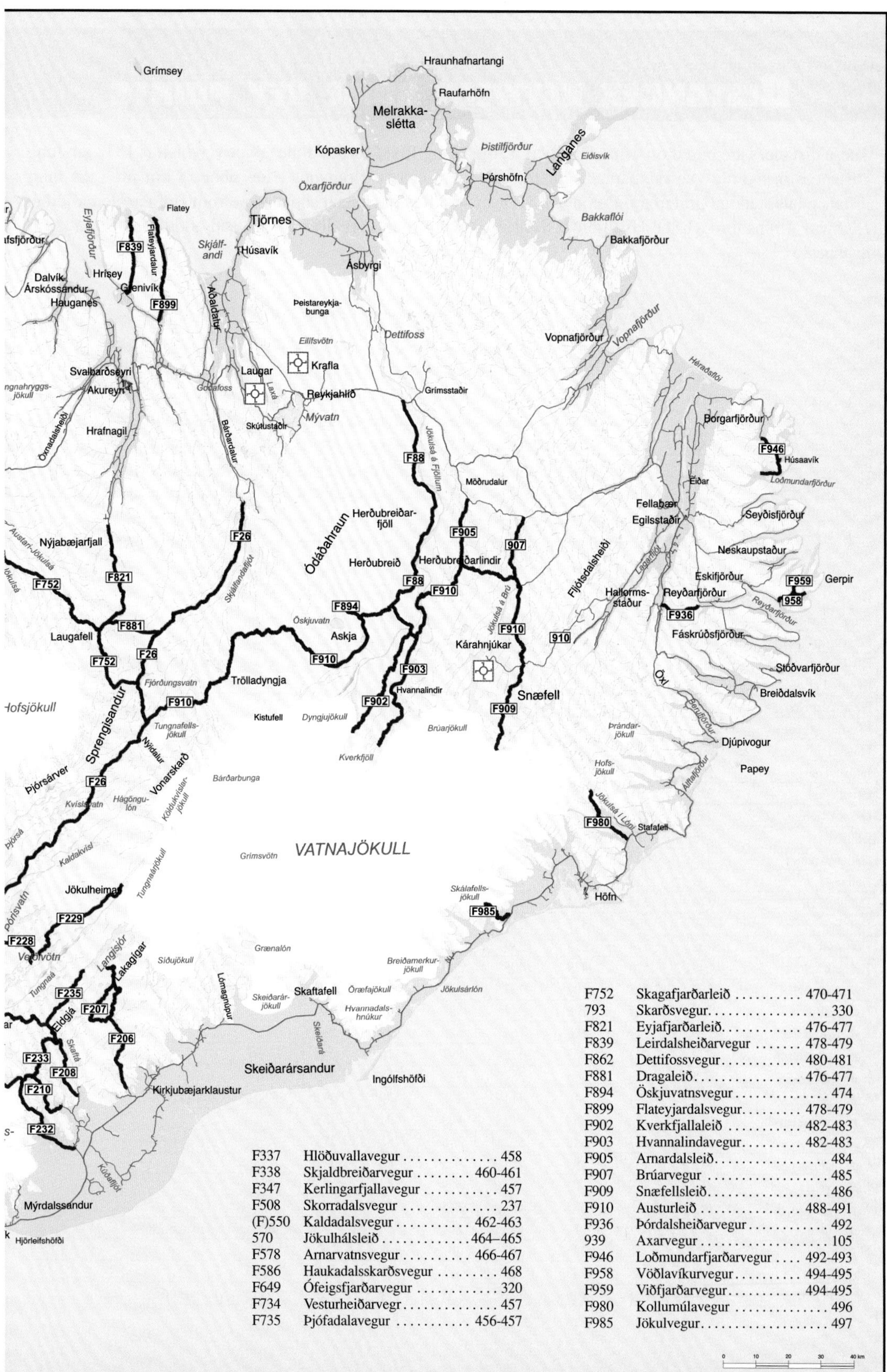
Grímsey
Hraunhafnartangi
Raufarhöfn
Melrakka-
slétta
Kópasker
Þistilfjörður
Langanes
Eiðisvík
Þórshöfn
Öxarfjörður
Bakkaflói
Bakkafjörður
Flatey
Tjörnes
Eyjafjörður
Skjálf-
andi
Húsavík
Ásbyrgi
F839
Flateyjardalur
Dalvík
Hrísey
Árskógssandur
Grenivík
Hauganes
F899
Aðaldalur
Þeistareykja-
bunga
Dettifoss
Eilífsvötn
Vopnafjörður
Krafla
Svalbarðseyri
Laugar
Akureyri
Goðafoss
Laxá
Reykjahlíð
Grímsstaðir
Héraðsflói
Mývatn
Skútustaðir
Hrafnagil
Bárðardalur
Öxnadalsheiði
Borgarfjörður
F946
Húsavík
F88
Jökulsá á Fjöllum
Möðrudalur
Eiðar
Loðmundarfjörður
Fellabær
Egilsstaðir
Seyðisfjörður
Herðubreiðar-
fjöll
F26
Nýjabæjarfjall
Ódáðahraun
F905
907
Neskaupstaður
Fljótsdalsheiði
F821
Herðubreið
Herðubreiðarlindir
Eskifjörður
F959
Gerpir
F752
F88
F910
Hallorms-
staður
Reyðarfjörður
958
F894
Jökulsá á Brú
F936
F881
Öskjuvatn
Askja
F910
910
Fáskrúðsfjörður
Laugafell
Kárahnjúkar
F752
F26
F910
F903
Stöðvarfjörður
Fjórðungsvatn
Trölladyngja
Hvannalindir
Öxi
Breiðdalsvík
F910
F902
Snæfell
Hofsjökull
F909
Kistufell
Dyngjujökull
Tungnafells-
jökull
Brúarjökull
Þrándar-
jökull
Berufjörður
Djúpivogur
Sprengisandur
Nýidalur
Kverkfjöll
Vonarskarð
Hofs-
jökull
Papey
Þjórsárver
F26
Bárðarbunga
Hágöngu-
lón
Köldukvíslar-
jökull
Kvíslavatn
Álftafjörður
Jökulsá í Lóni
F980
Stafafell
Þjórsá
VATNAJÖKULL
Kaldakvísl
Grímsvötn
Tungnaárjökull
Skálafells-
jökull
Jökulheimar
Höfn
F985
Þórisvatn
F229
F228
Veiðivötn
Grænalón
Langisjór
Lakagígar
Síðujökull
Breiðamerkur-
jökull
Tungnaá
F235
Lómagnúpur
Skeiðarár-
jökull
Skaftafell
Öræfajökull
Jökulsárlón
F207
Eldgjá
Hvannadals-
hnúkur
Skaftá
F206
Skeiðará
F233
F208
Skeiðarársandur
Ingólfshöfði
F210
Kirkjubæjarklaustur
F232
Kúðafljót
Mýrdalssandur
Hjörleifshöfði
0 10 20 30 40 km

Distances between some key points

These distances are based on using Highway 1, the "Ring Road" around the country, which is 1332 km long. Distances in red are via Skeiðarársandur (on the south coast). Highway 1 lies about 8 km from the long-distance bus station (Umferðarmiðstöðin, BSÍ) in central Reykjavík and about 4 km from Höfn in Hornafjörður. Highway 1 runs through the Hvalfjörður Tunnel. Driving round Hvalfjörður instead adds another 42 km to distances.

	Vík	Selfoss	Rvík	Borgarnes	Ísafjörður	Akureyri	Egilsstaðir	Höfn	Notes
Akranes	219	90	49	38	419	352	616	491	
Akureyri	558	429	388	314	558	1332	264	510	
Bakkafjörður	671	692	652	578	822	263	162	408	
Bíldudalur	589	460	420	346	205	539	802	861	via road no 60
Bjarkalundur	385	256	215	141	232	334	598	657	via road no 59
Blönduós	414	285	244	170	414	144	408	654	
Bolungarvík	638	509	468	394	13	571	835	909	
Borgarfjörður eystri	580	709	723	649	893	335	71	317	
Borgarnes	244	115	74	1332	381	314	578	515	
Breiðdalsvík	428	557	614	660	904	346	82	165	
Búðardalur	323	194	153	80	302	272	536	595	via road no 59
Dalvík	582	453	412	338	582	44	307	553	
Djúpivogur	367	496	552	611	967	409	146	103	
Egilsstaðir	509	638	652	578	822	264	1332	246	
Eskifjörður	506	636	692	627	871	313	49	243	via road no 96
Eyrarbakki	142	13	59	118	499	432	651	414	via road no 34
Fagurhólsmýri	161	290	347	406	787	612	348	111	
Fáskrúðsfjörður	474	603	660	628	872	313	50	211	via road no 96
Flateyri	609	480	439	366	22	558	822	881	
Flókalundur	501	372	331	257	116	4580	714	773	via road no 59
Grindavík	213	84	50	119	500	433	697	485	via road no 41
Grundarfjörður	347	218	177	103	408	374	637	619	via road no 59
Gullfoss	176	71	115	156	537	471	679	441	from Vík via road no 30
Hallormsstaður	513	642	678	604	848	290	26	250	
Hella	93	36	93	151	553	466	602	365	
Hellissandur	374	245	204	130	442	409	672	645	via road no 59
Hofsós	497	368	327	253	497	132	396	642	via road no 76
Hólmavík	403	274	233	159	224	336	600	675	
Húsavík	649	520	479	405	649	91	219	465	via road no 87
Hvammstangi	367	238	197	123	367	203	466	639	
Hveravellir	266	162	206	247	527	204	468	532	
Hvolsvöllur	80	49	106	164	545	479	589	352	
Höfn í Hornafirði	272	401	457	516	897	510	246	1340	
Ísafjörður	625	496	455	381	1949	558	822	897	
Keflavík	223	94	46	114	496	429	692	495	via road no 41
Kirkjubæjarklaustur	73	202	258	317	698	631	438	201	
Kópasker	746	617	576	502	746	188	218	464	via road no 864
Landmannalaugar	121	138	195	254	635	568	535	298	
Laugarvatn	167	39	77	118	499	432	673	435	
Mýri / Bárðardal	645	516	475	401	645	87	252	498	
Neskaupstaður	529	658	715	650	894	336	72	266	via road no 96
Norðurfjörður / Westfjords	505	376	335	261	307	438	702	777	
Ólafsfjörður	573	443	403	329	573	61	325	571	
Ólafsvík	364	235	195	121	433	399	663	636	via road no 59

	Vík	Selfoss	Rvík	Borgarnes	Ísafjörður	Akureyri	Egilsstaðir	Höfn	Notes
Patreksfjörður	562	433	392	319	178	511	775	834	via road no 60
Raufarhöfn	772	651	610	536	780	222	263	509	
Reyðarfjörður	491	620	676	611	855	297	33	227	via road no 96
Reykholt / Borgarfjörður	278	149	108	39	385	318	581	549	
Reykjahlíð / Mývatn	657	528	487	413	657	99	165	411	
Reykjavík	186	57	1347	74	455	388	652	458	
Sandgerði	232	103	54	123	504	437	701	504	via road no 41
Sauðárkrókur	460	331	291	217	461	120	384	630	
Selfoss	129	1332	57	115	497	430	638	401	
Seyðisfjörður	537	666	679	606	849	291	28	273	
Siglufjörður	556	427	386	312	556	77	341	587	via road no 76
Skaftafell	140	269	326	385	766	637	373	136	
Skagaströnd	436	307	266	193	436	163	427	673	
Skógar (by Eyjafjöll)	33	98	154	213	594	527	542	305	
Stykkishólmur	342	213	172	98	388	354	618	614	via road no 59
Stöðvarfjörður	446	575	632	651	895	337	73	183	
Suðureyri / Súgandafjörður	624	495	454	380	23	575	838	896	
Tálknafjörður	577	448	407	333	192	526	790	849	via Bíldudalur and road no 62
Varmahlíð	464	335	294	220	464	94	358	604	
Vegamót / Snæfellsnes	309	180	139	65	390	356	620	580	
Vík / Mýrdal	1332	129	186	244	626	559	509	272	
Vopnafjörður	641	662	621	547	791	233	131	377	
Þingeyri	570	441	400	326	49	519	783	842	
Þingvellir / Service Centre	174	45	50	90	472	405	669	446	
Þorlákshöfn	157	28	51	110	491	425	666	429	via road no 39 and 34
Þórshöfn	707	679	638	564	808	250	197	443	

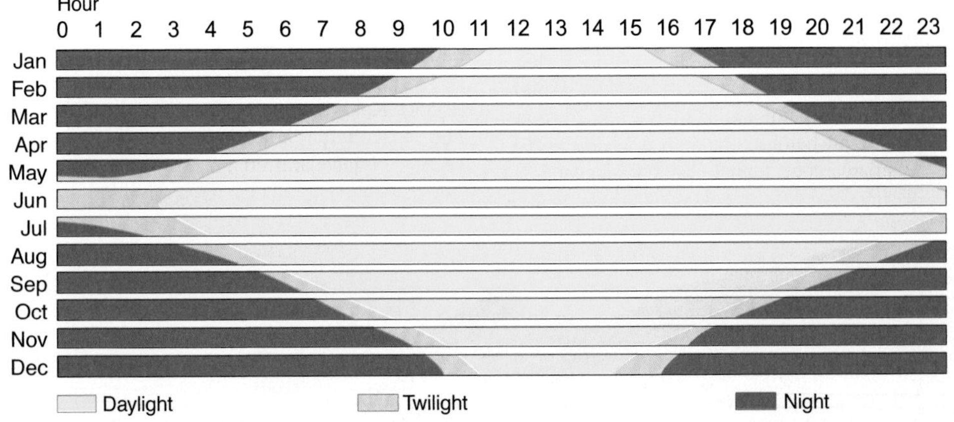

MOUNTAIN ROADS

Road Number	Place	Height in meters
1	Reynisfjall	119
1	Hellisheiði	374
1	Holtavörðuheiði	407
1	Vatnsskarð	420
1	Öxnadalsheiði	540
1	Víkurskarð	325
1	Fljótsheiði	247
1	Mývatnsheiði	335
1	Námaskarð	410
1	Vegaskarð	500
1	Langidalur	600
1	Breiðdalsheiði	470
1	Almannaskarð	153
26	Sigalda	500
32	Skeljafell	300
36	Mosfellsheiði	260
39	Þrengsli	288
365	Gjábakkahraun	300
42	Vatnsskarð	180
48	Kjósarskarð	260
50	Ferstikluháls	170
50	Geldingadragi	217
52	Uxahryggir	410
54	Fróðárheiði	361
55	Heydalur	165
59	Laxárdalsheiði	200
60	Brattabrekka	402
60	Svínadalur	220
60	Hjallaháls	335
60	Ódrjúgsháls	160
60	Klettsháls	332
60	Helluskarð	468
60	Dynjandisheiði	500
60	Hrafnseyrarheiði	552
60	Gemlufallsheiði	270
60	Vestfjarðargöng, tunnel - Breiðdalsleggur	199

Road Number	Place	Height in meters
61	Steingrímsfjarðarheiði.	439
62	Kleifaheiði	404
63	Miklidalur	369
63	Hálfdán	500
65	Vestfjarðargöng, tunnel - Súgandafjarðarleggur	177
68	Stikuháls	165
68	Ennisháls	290
690	Steinadalsheiði	330
605	Tröllatunguheiði	420
608	Þorskafjarðarheiði	490
612	Hafnarfjall	330
615	Hænuvíkurháls	320
624	Sandsheiði	530
643	Bjarnarfjarðarháls	180
643	Veiðileysuháls	220
744	Þverárfjall	322
82	Lágheiði	409
85	Brekknaheiði	160
85	Sandvíkurheiði	275
92	Fagridalur	350
92	Oddsskarð (tunnel)	632
93	Fjarðarheiði	620
94	Vatnsskarð	431
901	Möðrudalsleið	660
917	Hellisheiði eystri	655
939	Öxi	532
953	Mjóafjarðarheiði	578
F26	By Jökuldalur	820
F208	By Grænafjall	700
F208	Frostastaðaháls	625
F35	Kjalvegur - Bláfellsháls	600
F35	Kjalvegur - Fjórðungsalda	672
(F)550	Kaldidalur	720
F66	Kollafjarðarheiði	460
F821	Nýjabæjarafrétt	940

Facts about Iceland

Country	km²	
Iceland	102775	
Terra Firma	23805	
Glaciers	11922	
Lakes	2757	
Wastelands	64538	
Ring Road	1332	km
All roads	12955	km
Coastline	4970	km
Population	338349	1)

Largest islands	km²
Flatey	2,8
Grímsey	5,3
Heimaey	13,4
Hjörsey (Faxaflói)	5,5
Hrísey	8,0
Málmey	2,4
Papey	2

Highest mountains	m
Bárðarbunga	2000
Eiríksjökull	1675
Eyjafjallajökull	1666
Hekla	1491
Herðubreið	1682
Hofsjökull	1765
Kerling	1538
Kverkfjöll	1920
Snæfell	1833
Tungnafellsjökull	1540
Þorvaldsfell (Askja)	1510
Öræfajökull	2110

Highest Falls	m
Foss,Morsárjökull	228
Glymur	190
Goðafoss	12
Gullfoss	32
Háifoss	122
Hengifoss	128
Hjálparfoss,Fossá	13
Reykjarfoss,Svartá,Skagafjörður	13
Seljalandsfoss	65
Skógafoss	62
Dettifoss	44
Hrauneyjafoss	29

Largest Glaciers	km²
Drangajökull	160
Hofsjökull	925
Langjökull	953
Mýrdalsjökull	596
Vatnajökull	8300

Largest Lakes	km²
Hvítárvatn	30
Lögurinn	53
Mývatn	37
Þingvallavatn	82
Þórisvatn	83-88

Deepest Lakes	m
Hvalvatn	160
Jökulsárlón	248
Þingvallavatn	114
Þórisvatn	113
Öskjuvatn	217

Longest Rivers	km
Hvítá/Ölfusá	185
Jökulsá á Dal	150
Jökulsá á Fjöllum	206
Lagarfljót	140
Skjálfandafljót	178
Þjórsá	230

Longest Bridges	m
Skeiðará	880
Borgarfjörður	520
Súla	420
Ölfusarós	360
Gígjukvísl	336
Kúðafljót	302
Lagarfljót	301
Hornafjarðarfljót	254
Markarfljót	250
Jökulsá í Lóni	247

1) Source: Statistics Iceland, 1 January 2017

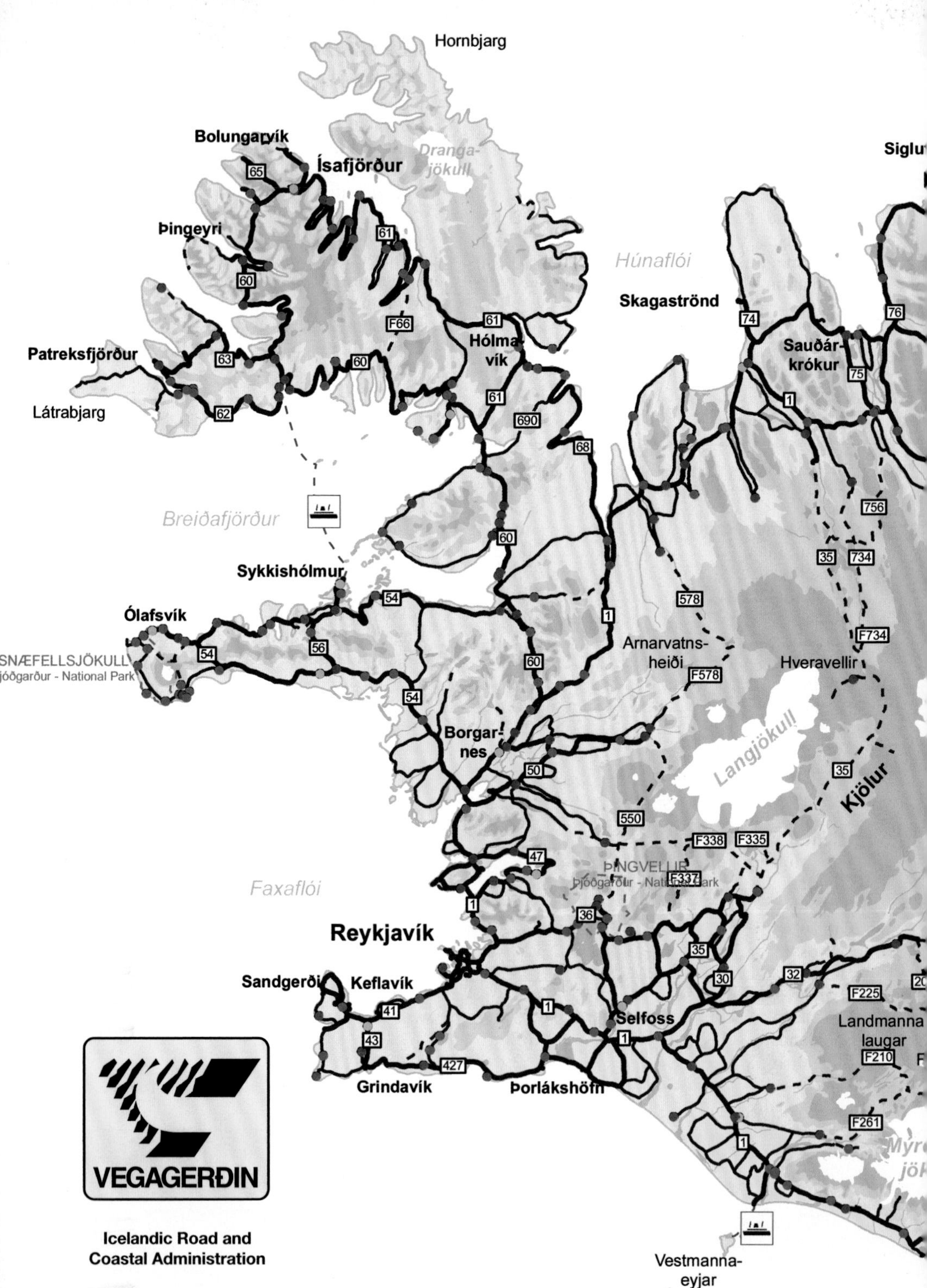

VEGAGERÐIN

Icelandic Road and
Coastal Administration

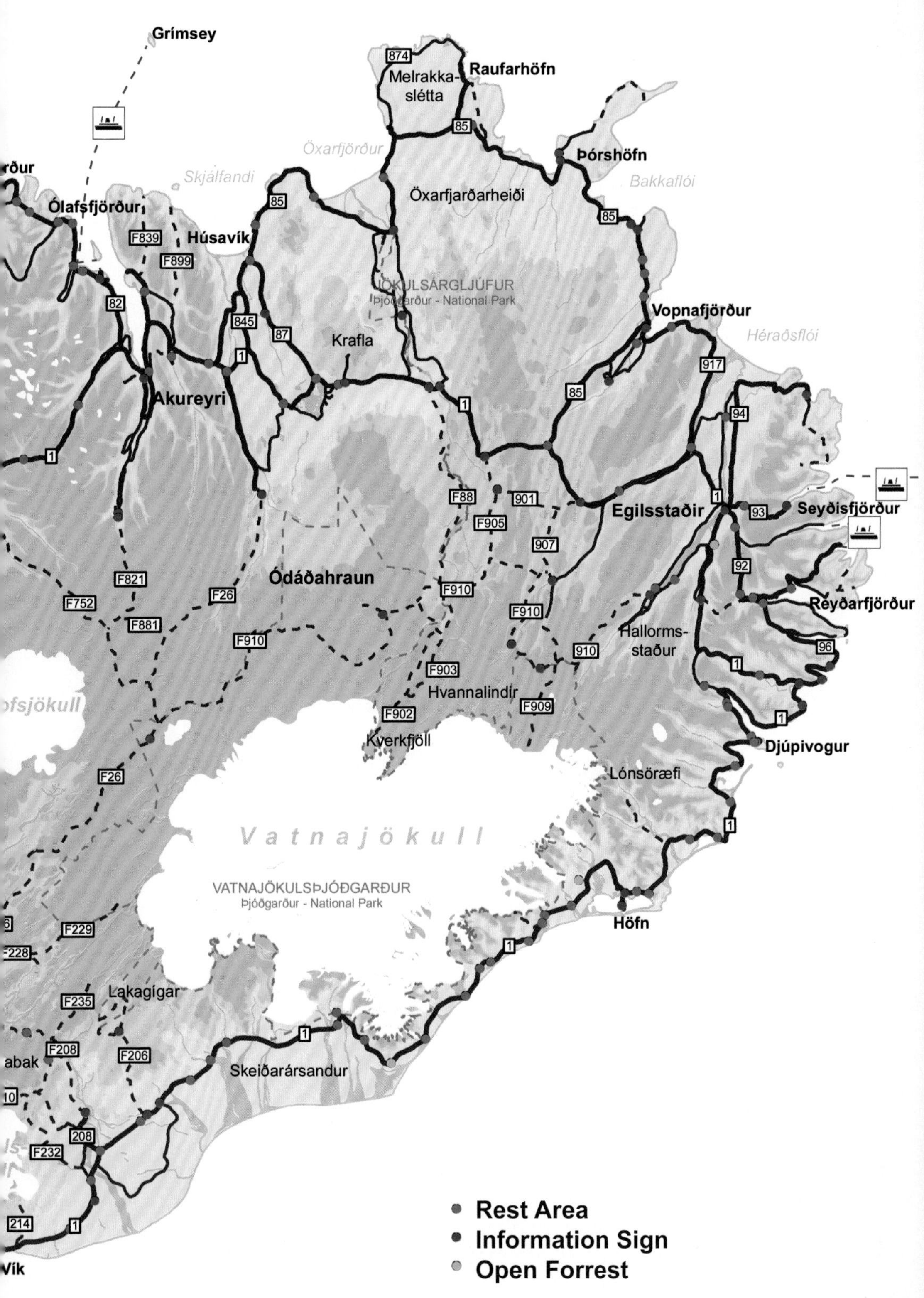
Grímsey
Raufarhöfn
Melrakka-
slétta
Öxarfjörður
Skjálfandi
Þórshöfn
Bakkaflói
Ólafsfjörður
Húsavík
Öxarfjarðarheiði
JÖKULSÁRGLJÚFUR
Þjóðgarður - National Park
Vopnafjörður
Héraðsflói
Krafla
Akureyri
Egilsstaðir
Seyðisfjörður
Ódáðahraun
Reyðarfjörður
Hallorms-
staður
Hvannalindir
Kverkfjöll
Djúpivogur
Lónsöræfi
Vatnajökull
VATNAJÖKULSÞJÓÐGARÐUR
Þjóðgarður - National Park
Höfn
Lakagígar
Skeiðarársandur
Vík
Rest Area
Information Sign
Open Forrest

ITA Huts in

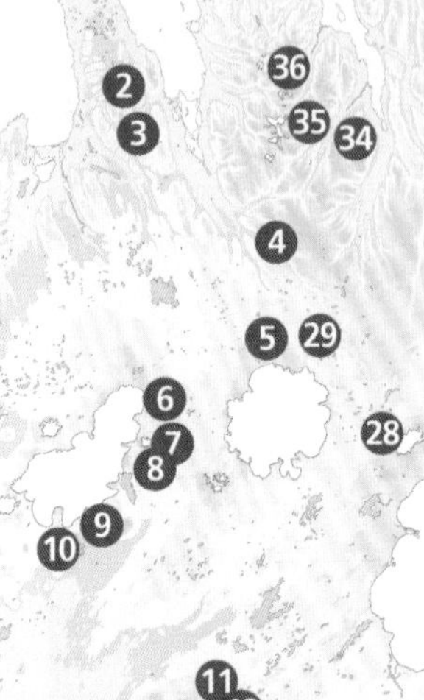

Iceland Tourin
Association
www.fi.is

1 
Norðurfjörður Valgeirsstaðir (p. 591)
Sleeps: 20
Service:
GPS Co-ordinates: 66°03.080 21°33.970

2 
Trölli í Tröllabotnum (p. 579)
Sleeps: 16
Service:
GPS Co-ordinates: 65°42.603 19°53.163

3 
Þúfnavellir í Víðidal (p. 579)
Sleeps: 12
Service:
GPS Co-ordinates: 65°38.330 19°49.480

4 
Hildarsel í Austurdal (p. 597)
Sleeps: 36
Service:
GPS Co-ordinates: 65°15.330 18°43.910

5 
Ingólfsskáli í Lambahrauni (p. 597)
Sleeps: 28
Service:
GPS Co-ordinates: 65°00.470 18°53.790

6 
Þjófadalir (p. 596)
Sleeps: 12
Service:
GPS Co-ordinates: 64°48.900 19°42.510

7 
Þverbrekknamúli (p. 596)
Sleeps: 20
Service:
GPS Co-ordinates: 64°43.100 19°36.860

8 
Hvítárnes (p. 596)
Sleeps: 30
Service:
GPS Co-ordinates: 64°37.007 19°45.394

9 
Hagavatn (p. 596)
Sleeps: 12
Service:
GPS Co-ordinates: 64°27.760 20°14.700

10 
Hlöðuvellir (p. 577)
Sleeps: 15
Service:
GPS Co-ordinates: 64°23.911 20°33.387

11 
Landmannalaugar (p. 589)
Sleeps: 78
Service:
GPS Co-ordinates: 63°59.600 19°03.660

12 
Hrafntinnusker Höskuldsskáli
Sleeps: 52 (p. 589)
Service:
GPS Co-ordinates: 63°56.014 19°10.109

Iceland (highland)

13 

Álftavatn (p. 589)
Sleeps: 70
Service:
GPS Co-ordinates: 63°51.470 19°13.640

14 

Hvanngil (p. 589)
Sleeps: 60
Service:
GPS Co-ordinates: 63°50.026 19°12.507

15 **Emstrur** (p. 589)
Sleeps: 60
Service:
GPS Co-ordinates: 63°45.980 19°22.450

16 **Þórsmörk** Skagfjörðsskáli (p. 599)
Sleeps: 75
Service:
GPS Co-ordinates: 63°40.960 19°30.890

17 **Leirás** í Múladal (p. 585)
Sleeps: 6
Service:
GPS Co-ordinates: 64°39.053 14°57.772

18 **Múlaskáli** á Lónsöræfum (p. 599)
Sleeps: 25
Service:
GPS Co-ordinates: 64°33.199 15°09.077

19 **Kollumúlavatn** (p. 599) (p. 599)
Sleeps: 22
Service:
GPS Co-ordinates: 64°36.680 15°08.750

20 

Geldingafell (p. 585)
Sleeps: 16
Service:
GPS Co-ordinates: 64°41.690 15°21.690

21 **Snæfell** (p. 584)
Sleeps: 62
Service:
GPS Co-ordinates: 64°48.250 15°38.600

22 

Karlsstaðir í Vöðlavík (p. 584)
Sleeps: 33
Service:
GPS Co-ordinates: 65°01.803 13°40.354

23 **Húsavík** (p. 598, 588)
Sleeps: 33
Service:
GPS Co-ordinates: 65°23.716 13°44.160

24 

Breiðavík (p. 598)
Sleeps: 33
Service:
GPS Co-ordinates: 65°27.830 13°40.286

25 **Herðubreiðarlindir** Þorsteinsskáli (p. 598)
Sleeps: 30
Service:
GPS Co-ordinates: 65°11.560 16°13.390

26 **Bræðrafell** í Ódáðahrauni (p. 597)
Sleeps: 12
Service:
GPS Co-ordinates: 65°11.310 16°32.290

27 

Sigurðarskáli í Kverkfjöllum (p. 597)
Sleeps: 82
Service:
GPS Co-ordinates: 64°44.850 16°37.890

28 

Nýidalur (p. 598)
Sleeps: 90
Service:
GPS Co-ordinates: 64°44.130 18°04.350

29 **Laugafell** (p. 598)
Sleeps: 35
Service:
GPS Co-ordinates: 65°01.630 18°19.950

30 

Dyngjufell í Dyngjufjalladal (p. 598)
Sleeps: 16
Service:
GPS Co-ordinates: 65°07.480 16°55.280

31 

Dreki í Dyngjufjöllum (p. 581)
Sleeps: 60
Service:
GPS Co-ordinates: 65°02.520 16°35.720

32 

Botni í Suðurárbotnum (p. 582)
Sleeps: 16
Service:
GPS Co-ordinates: 65°16.180 17°04.100

33 **Heilagsdalur** (p. 582)
Sleeps: 18
Service:
GPS Co-ordinates: 65°27.334 16°47.514

34 

Lambi á Glerárdal (p. 582)
Sleeps: 6
Service:
GPS Co-ordinates: 65°34.880 18°17.770

35 

Baugasel í Barkárdal (p. 589)
Sleeps: 10
Service:
GPS Co-ordinates: 65°39.400 18°36.700

36 

Á Tungnahrygg
Sleeps: 10
Service:
GPS Co-ordinates: 65°41.340 18°50.820

ÚTIVIST HUTS

Skælingar

Útivist's mountain hut at Stóragil in Skælingar was rebuilt by members in 1996-1997. An old hut for the annual sheep round-up that the local farmers had stopped using was previously located on the site. The surrounding countryside is magnificent, with large lava formations reminiscent of a landscaped park. There is a short hike to Hólaskjól from the hut, and ideal day tours include hikes to Uxatindar or Gjátindur. A rough vehicle track extends from the road leading to Gjátindur, to the hut. The hut is heated with a small oil stove and has mattresses and gas for cooking, but no tableware. Water is fetched from a brook nearby. The hut is not insulated and is therefore not suitable for winter stays. It can accommodate 16 people.
GPS coordinate is N 63°58.849′ W 18°31.319′

Álftavötn

A good jeep track leads most of the way to the house, although the last 2-300 m must be traversed on foot. Consequently the area is very quiet and peaceful, as well as extremely beautiful. A popular riding trail passes in front of the hut and a fence has been erected to the north so that riders can rest their horses. There is much vegetation near the hut and excellent camping facilities with running water and a water toilet. Lodging is available indoors for up to 24 people. Numerous hikes may be taken in the vicinity, including a day hike to Strútslaug or Gjátindur.
Hólaskjól is a short walk away.
GPS coordinate: N 63° 53.890′ W 18°41.467′

Dalakofinn

The location of Dalakofinn hut is excellent for all kinds of tours in the Fjallabak area and other mountain huts are within reach for ongoing hikers. It's ideal for access to nearby natural wonders, i.e. the colourful geothermal areas and rhyolite mountains. The location is also great for for snow scooter og cross country skiers during winter. The hut is easily accessible from farm Keldur without any river fording.
GPS coordinate: N 63° 57.048′ W 19°21.584′

Básar in Goðaland

The huts can accommodate 80-90 people and are occupied by wardens from early May until October. In summer there is running water and water toilets near the huts and on many of the campsites. The huts are heated with oil stoves and the electrical station Básabína uses water from a nearby brook to generate electricity for lighting. Útivist has published a hiking map with descriptions of paths around Þórsmörk and Goðaland. It is safe to say that the heart of Útivist beats at Básar.
GPS coordinate: N 63°40.559′ W 19°29.014′

Fimmvörðuskáli

Fimmvörðuhálsskáli hut is located on the highest part of the hill, just west of the marked path between Skógar and Þórsmörk. The hut is heated with an oil stove and provides the most necessary cooking utensils and tableware. Special arrangements have been made regarding toilets, as it is not possible to insert a septic tank on the site; hence travellers are asked to follow set rules. It should be pointed out that running water in the area cannot be counted on and in late summer it is difficult to find snow for melting. The hut can accommodate 20 people.
GPS coordinate: N 63°37.320′ W 19°27.093′

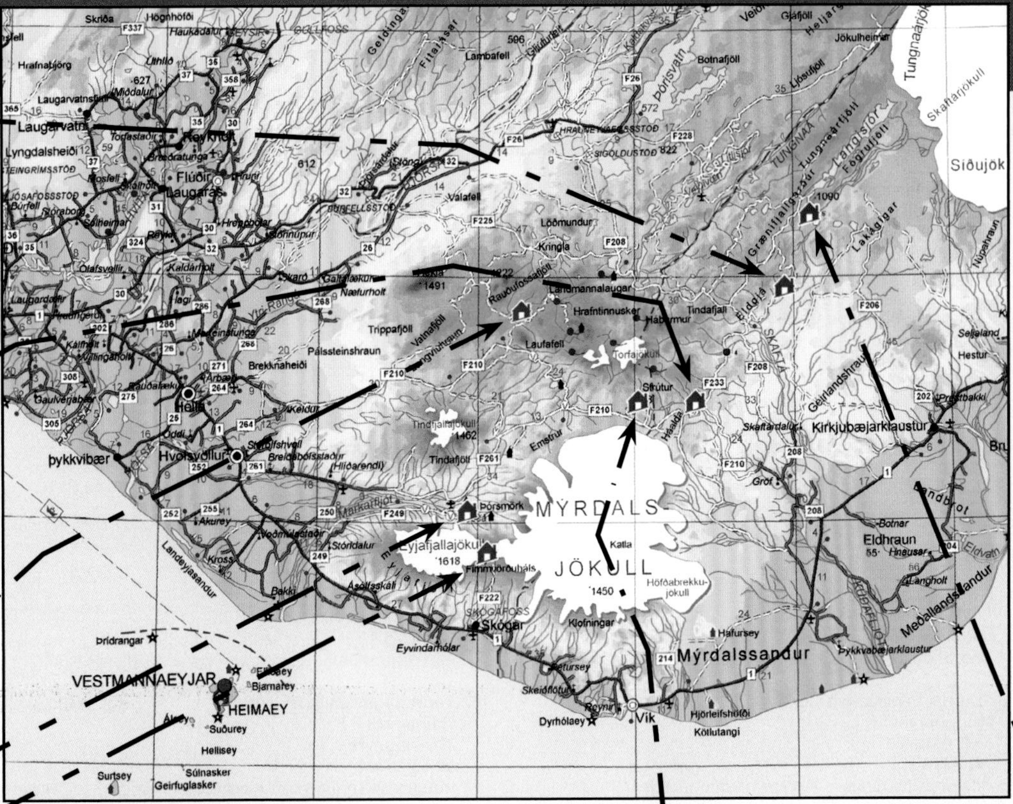

Strútur on Mælifellssandur

The hut was built in autumn 2002 and is fully-equipped, with oil heating, cooking facilities and a water toilet. Vehicles access the hut from Mælifellssandur via a jeep track that leads north from Syðri-Fjallabaksleið to the western part of Mælifell. Day hikes to fantastic locations may be taken from the hut, including Rauðibotn, Hólmsárlón, Strútslaug and Torfajökull. The hut is an ideal rest stop for hikers from Álftavötn en route to Hvanngil or Emstrur. The hut sleeps 26.

GPS coordinate: N 63°50.330′ W 18°58.477′

Sveinstindur

The hut at Mt. Sveinstindur is to the south-east of the mountain. Vehicle access is via tracks leading to Langisjór lake, and a marked trail used by hydrographers is followed to the east until the hut is reached. In early summer the trail may have patches of wet sand. A hiking path has been marked out from the tracks leading to Langisjór to the hut, and a marked path also extends to the top of the mountain from the southwest. The hut is heated with a small oil stove and gas for cooking is provided, along with necessary utensils. Drinking water is piped into the hut in summer.
The hut sleeps 20.

GPS coordinate: N 64°05.176′ W 18°24.946′

Information Centres in Iceland

1. Tourist Information Centre Reykjavík (p. 510)
Aðalstræti 2
101 Reykjavík
☎ 590-1550
info@visitreykjavik.is

2. Tourist Information Centre (p. 207)
Strandgata 6
220 Hafnarfjörður
☎ 585-5500
info@hafnarfjordur.is • www.hafnarfjordur.is

3. Tourist Information Centre (p. 209)
Flugstöð Leifs Eiríkssonar
235 Reykjanesbær
☎ 570-7790
airoport@ita.is • www.visitreykjanes.is

4. Tourist Information Centre (p. 221)
Kjósastofa / Ásgarður, Kjós
276 Mosfellsbær
☎ 857 0100
kjosarstofa@kjos.is • www.westiceland.is

5. Tourist Information Centre (p. 232)
Kirkjubraut 54
300 Akranes
☎ 433-1065
info@visitakranes.is • www.visitakranes.is

6. Tourist Information Centre (p. 56)
Hyrnutorg, Borgarbraut 58-60
310 Borgarnes
☎ 437-2214
info@ westiceland.is • www.westiceland.is

7. Tourist Information Centre (p. 261)
Snorrastofa
320 Reykholt
☎ 433-8000
gestastofa@snorrastofa.is • www.snorrastofa.is

8. Tourist Information Centre (p. 254)
Aðalgata 29
340 Stykkishólmur
☎ 433-8120
travelinfo@stykkisholmur.is • www.westiceland.is

9. Tourist Information Centre (p. 248)
Grundargata 35
350 Grundarfjörður
☎ 438-1881
info@sagan.is • www.westiceland.is

10. Tourist Information Centre (p. 276)
Kirkjutún 2
355 Snæfellsbær
☎ 433-9930
info@snb.is • www.westiceland.is

11. Visitors Centre - Snæfellsjökull National Park
Hellnar (p. 276)
360 Hellissandur
☎ 436-6888
snaefellsjokull@ust.is • www.ust.is/snaefellsjokull.is

12. Tourist Information Centre (p. 282)
Leifsbúð
370 Búðardalur
☎ 434-1441
info@dalir.is • www.dalir.is

13. Tourist Information Centre (p. 285)
Maríutröð
380 Reykhólahreppur
☎ 894-1011
info@reykholar.is • www.westiceland.is

14. Tourist Information Centre (p. 294)
Aðalstræti 7
400 Ísafjörður
☎ 450-8060
info@vestfirdir.is • www.westfjords.is

15. Tourist Information Centre (p. 293)
Vitastígur 1
415 Bolungarvík
☎ 450-7010
touristinfo@bolungarvik.is • www.westfjords.is

16. Tourist Information Centre (p. 288)
Hafnarstræti 5
470 Þingeyri
☎ 456-8304
thingeyri@thingeyri.is • www.westfjords.is

17. Tourist Information Centre (p. 311)
Höfðagata 8 - 10
510 Hólmavík
☎ 451-3111
info@holmavik.is • www.westfjords.is

18. Tourist Information Centre (p. 338)
Strandgata 1
530 Hvammstangi
☎ 451-2345
selasetur@selasetur.is • www.selasetur.is

19. Tourist Information Centre (p. 70)
Varmahlíð
560 Varmahlíð
☎ 455-6161
info@skagafjordur.is • www.visitskagafjordur.is

20. Tourist Information Centre (p. 331)
Gránugata 24
580 Siglufjörður
☎ 464-9120
info@fjallabyggd.is • www.northiceland.is

21. Tourist Information Centre (p. 81)
Hof Menningarhús, Strandgata 12
600 Akureyri
☎ 450-1050
info@visitakureyri.is • www.northiceland.is

22. Tourist Information Centre (p. 371)
Húsavíkurstofa, Hafnarstétt 1
640 Húsavík
☎ 464-4340
info@visithusavik.is • www.visithusavik.is

23. Tourist Information Centre (p. 91)
Mývatnsstofa, Hraunvegur 8
660 Mývatn
☎ 464-4390
info@visitmyvatn.is • www.visitmyvatn.is

24. Visitors Centre - Jökulsárgljúfur National Park
Gljúfrastofa, Ásbyrgi (p. 405)
671 Kópasker
☎ 470-7100
asbyrgi@vjp.is • www.vjp.is

25. Tourist Information Centre (p. 380)
Langanesvegur 18b
680 Þórshöfn
☎ 468-1515
sund@langanesbyggd.is • www.northiceland.is

26. Tourist Information Centre (p. 102)
Miðvangur 1-3
700 Egilsstaðir
☎ 471-2320
east@east.is • www.east.is

27. Visitors Centre - Jökulsárgljúfur National Park
Snæfellsstofa, Skriðuklaustur (p. 428)
701 Egilsstaðir
☎ 470-0840
snaefellsstofa@vjp.is • www.vjp.is

28. Tourist Information Centre (p. 415)
Ferjuleira 1
710 Seyðisfjörður
☎ 472-1551
ferdamenning@sfk.is • ww.visitseydisfjordur.com

29. Tourist Information Centre (p. 109)
Langabúð
765 Djúpavogur
☎ 478-8228
ugnius@djupivogur.is • www.east.is

30. Visitors Centre - Skaftafell National Park
Skaftafellsstofa (p. 121)
785 Öræfi
☎ 470-8300
skaftafell@vjp.is • www.vjp.is

31. Tourist Information Centre (p. 144)
Austurvegur 4
800 Selfoss
☎ 480-1990
tourinfo@arborg.is • www.south.is

32. Tourist Information Centre (p. 175)
Þjórsárstofa, Árnesi
801 Selfoss
☎ 486-6115
thjorsarstofa@skeidgnup.is • www.south.is

33. Tourist Information Centre (p. 146)
Sunnumörk 2-4
810 Hveragerði
☎ 483-4601
tourinfo@hveragerdi.is • www.south.is

34. Tourist Information Centre (p. 140)
Austurvegur 8
860 Hvolsvöllur
☎ 487-8043
tourinfo@hvolsvollur.is • www.south.is

35. Tourist Information Centre (p. 132)
Víkurbraut 28
870 Vík
☎ 487-1395
info@vik.is • www.visitvik.is

36. Visitors Centre - Vatnajökull National Park
Skaftárstofa, Klausturvegur 10 (p. 124)
880 Kirkjubæjarklaustur
☎ 487-4620
info@klaustur.is • www.south.is

37. Tourist Information Centre (p. 154)
Safnahúsið við Ráðhúströð
900 Vestmannaeyjar
☎ 481-3555
tourinfo@vestmannaeyjar.is • www.south.is

See more map p. 42-43

Information Centres in Iceland

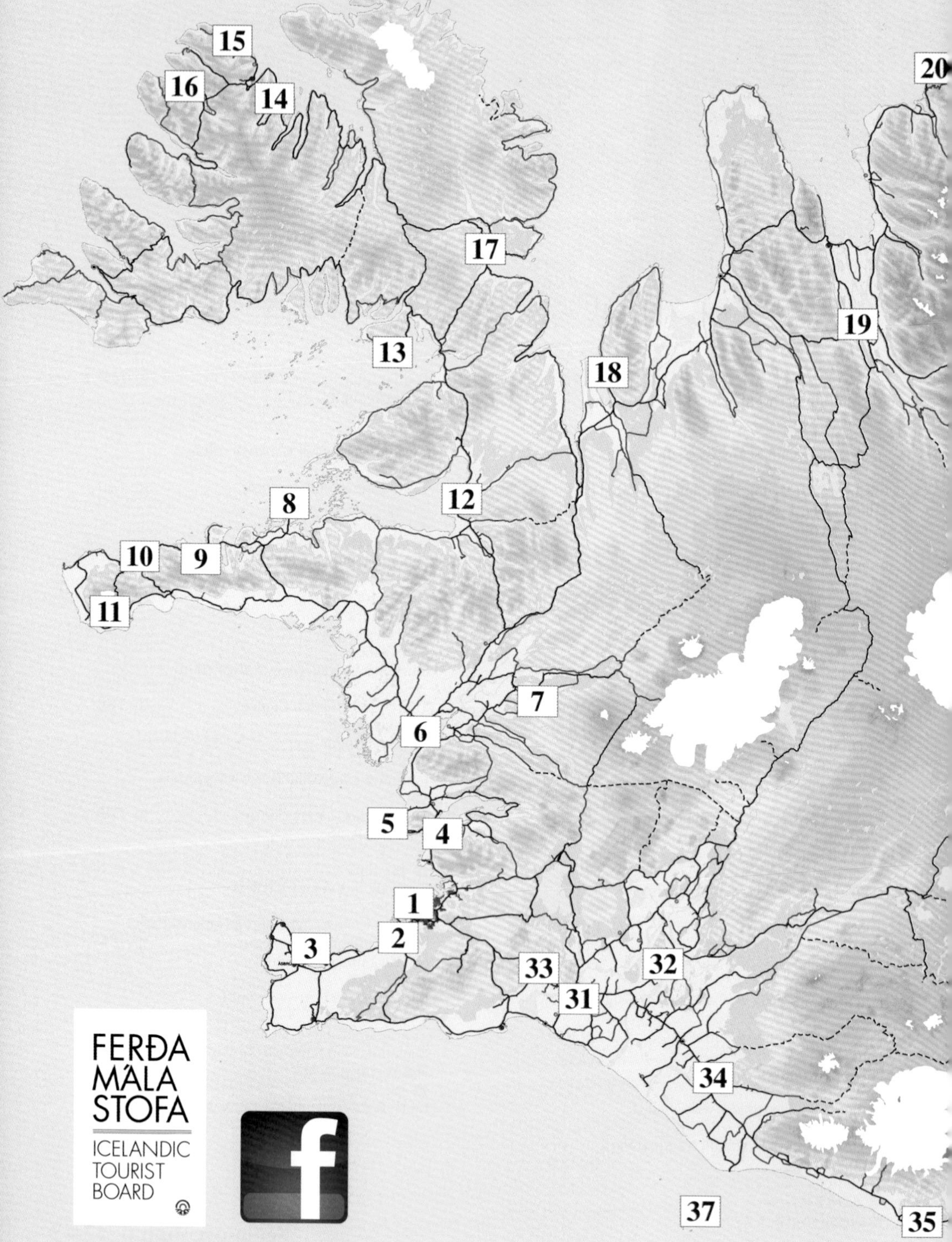

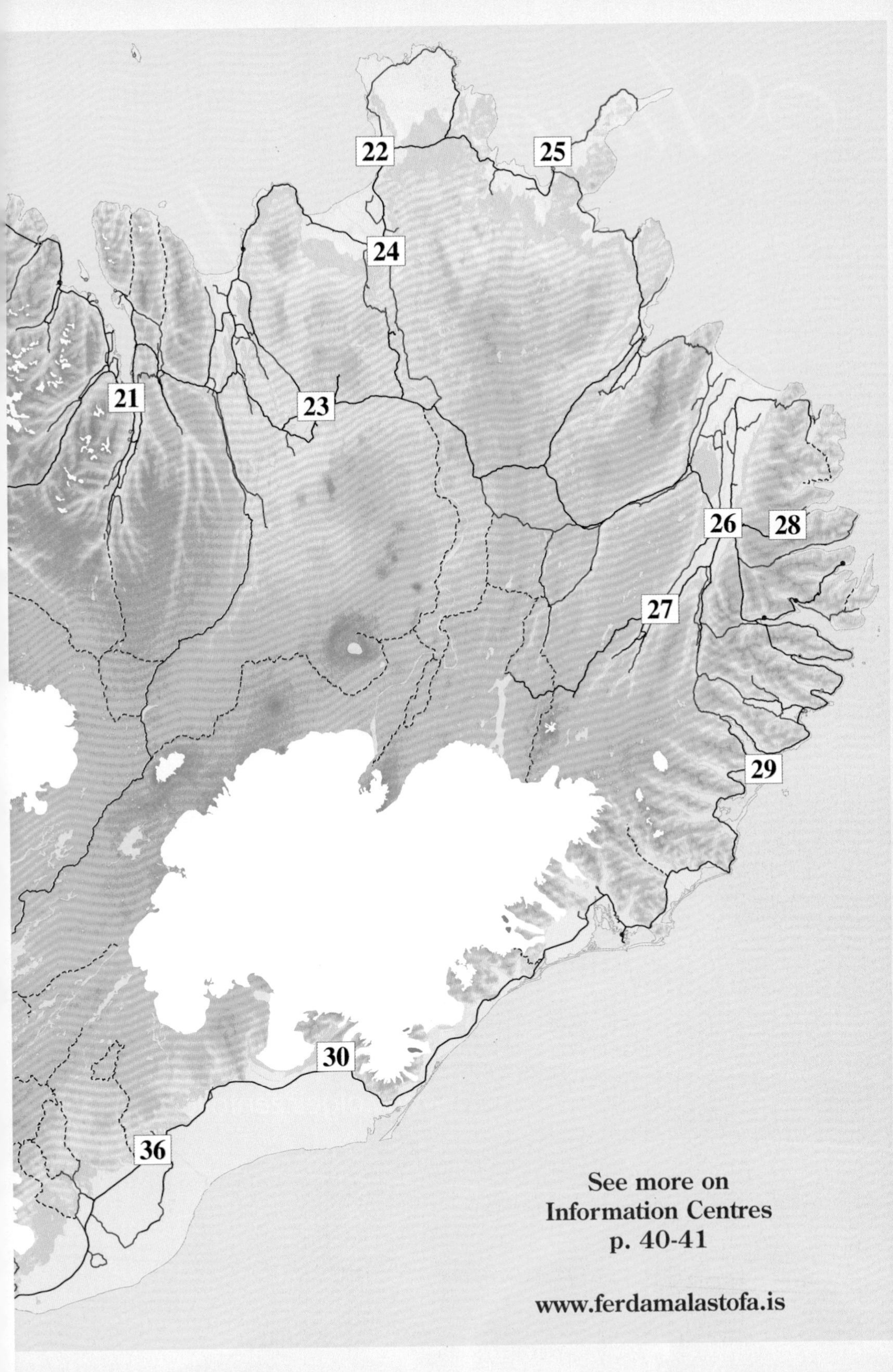
22
25
24
21
23
26
28
27
29
30
36
See more on
Information Centres
p. 40-41
www.ferdamalastofa.is

Aurora
Borealis

As the effects of solar wind are greatest in the belts around the magnetic poles, the aurora (Northern and Southern Lights) are most visible at those locations. In Iceland we are lucky enough to be within the North Polar belt during the nights, in normal conditions. Changes in solar winds cause the belt to grow or shrink, so the Lights are seen at varying latitudes. An example of this kind of variation can be seen when solar flares send massive emissions of material into space. When the material reaches the earth, the northern and southern belts can stretch a long way towards the equator, and there are examples of aurora having been seen at the equator itself."

The Aurora Borealis or Northern Lights can be seen in all parts of Iceland from September through to March – as long as the "Aurora Belt" is over Iceland, the skies are clear and it is dark. Just as for stargazing, it is best to get away from the light pollution of urban areas in order to enjoy the Aurora Borealis in all their glory. Ideally, choose a sheltered place as your observation point, as clear winter nights in Iceland tend to be cold, especially if a wind is blowing.

The best time to observe the Aurora is between about 9 pm and 2 am, although they can, of course, often be seen both earlier and later. In Iceland the Midnight Sun means that the Northern Lights cannot be seen in summer, although they are still there.

Source - www.visindavefur.is

If you would like to catch the Northern Lights no matter what the season, you can visit the Aurora Reykjavík Northern Lights Center, home of the Icelandic Northern Lights. It features a continuously running HD panoramic film of these amazing auroral displays in Iceland. There you can read up on the auroras through stories and legends from around the world, learn something about the science behind this amazing phenomenon and gaze at spectacular Northern Lights photography from top Icelandic photographers.

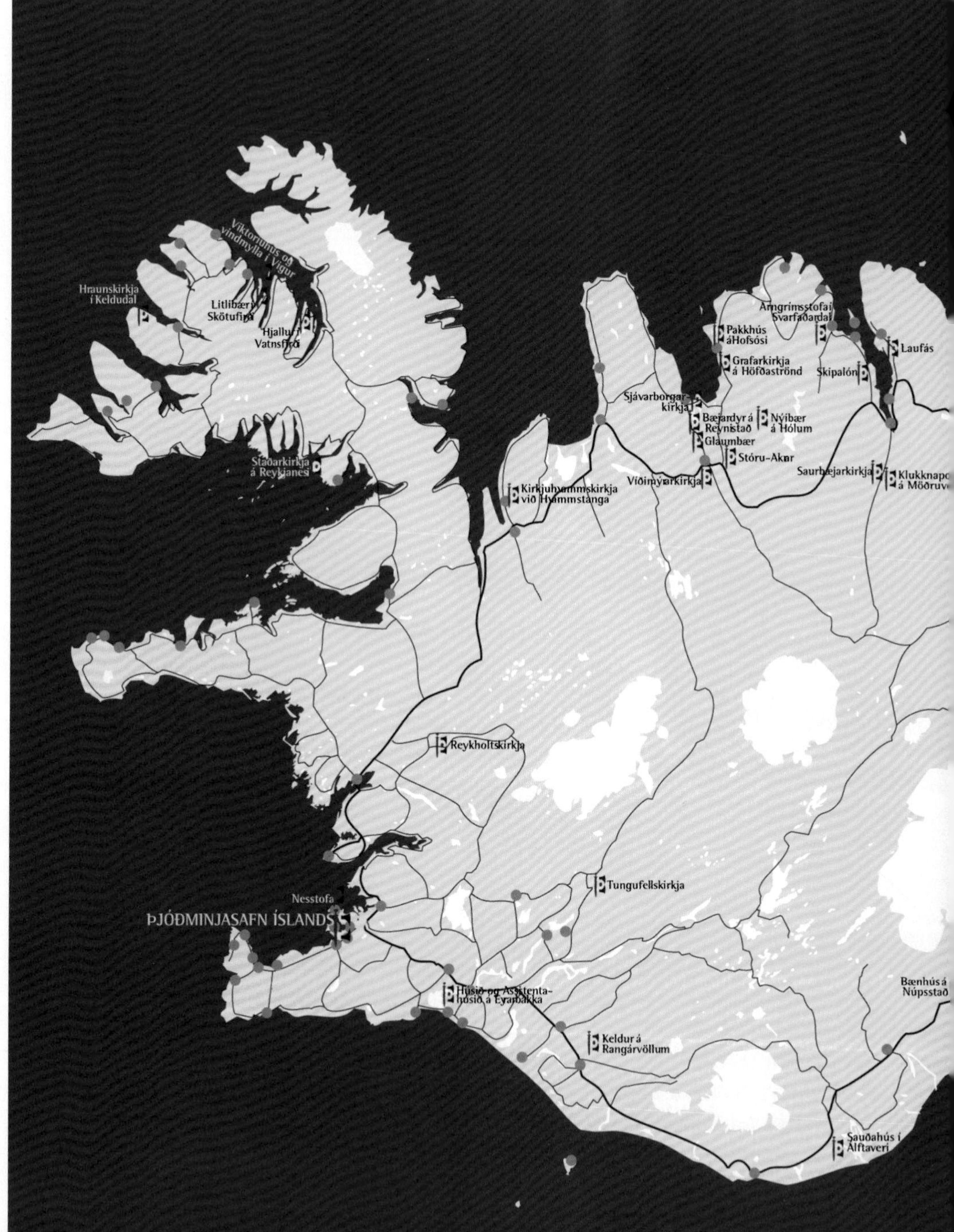

NATIONAL MUSEUM OF

National Museum Historic Buildings Collection
Towns and Villages
Roads

ICELAND

HISTORIC BUILDING COLLECTION OF THE NATIONAL MUSEUM

ÞJÓÐMINJASAFN ÍSLANDS
National Museum of Iceland

Truly a treasure to find

-The Fine Art of Knifemaking

Master craftsman Palli Kristjánsson and his co-creator Soffía Sigurðardóttir are hard at work bringing an ancient Viking tradition into the present, where they create an array of handsome knives for collectors, chefs, and all those who appreciate the workmanship that goes into a finely crafted tool.

Icelandic Artisans at work

Damascus steel as well as stainless steel from Denmark, Germany and Sweden are choice materials favored by Palli and Soffia. Many of the blades are Viking Age replicas decorated with finely etched designs. Traditional Icelandic materials are used to create beautifully carved handles - birch, rowan, horse's hooves, reindeer antlers, goat and sheep horn and even fossilized wood.

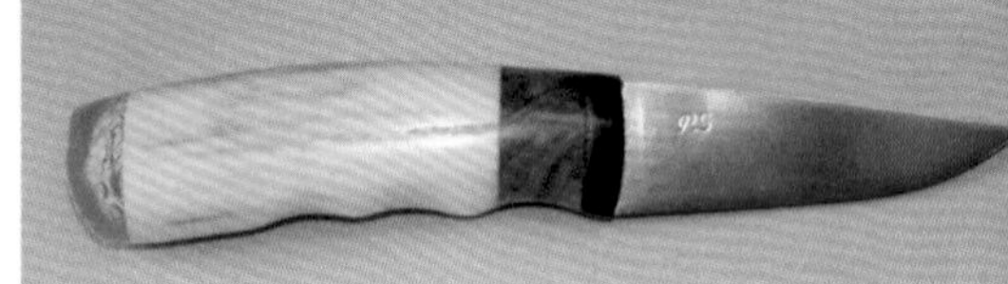

Custom made for a lifetime

Chefs, cooking schools and cooking enthusiasts tend to love to show off these one of a kind handmade kitchen tools that have become something of a sought after souvenir from Iceland. If you have your own design ideas you can special order on-line.

Walk-ins are welcome at their workshop at Álafossvegur 29 in Mosfellsbær. Opening hours are 9 - 6, Monday through Friday, from 9 - 4 on Saturdays or if you are in the neighborhood outside of those hours, you are always welcome to pop in for a chat.

Tel. +354 899 6903
Álafossvegur 29 / 270 Mosfellsbær

palli@knifemaker.is / www.knifemaker.is
soffia@knifemaker.is / www.kitchenknives.is

Your trip starts here

If you are taking the Ring Road from Reykjavík to the west and the north, start at page 51. If you are travelling east from Reykjavík, begin instead at page 151 and follow the pages in reverse order until you get to Reykjavík via Hvalfjörður and Kjalarnes.

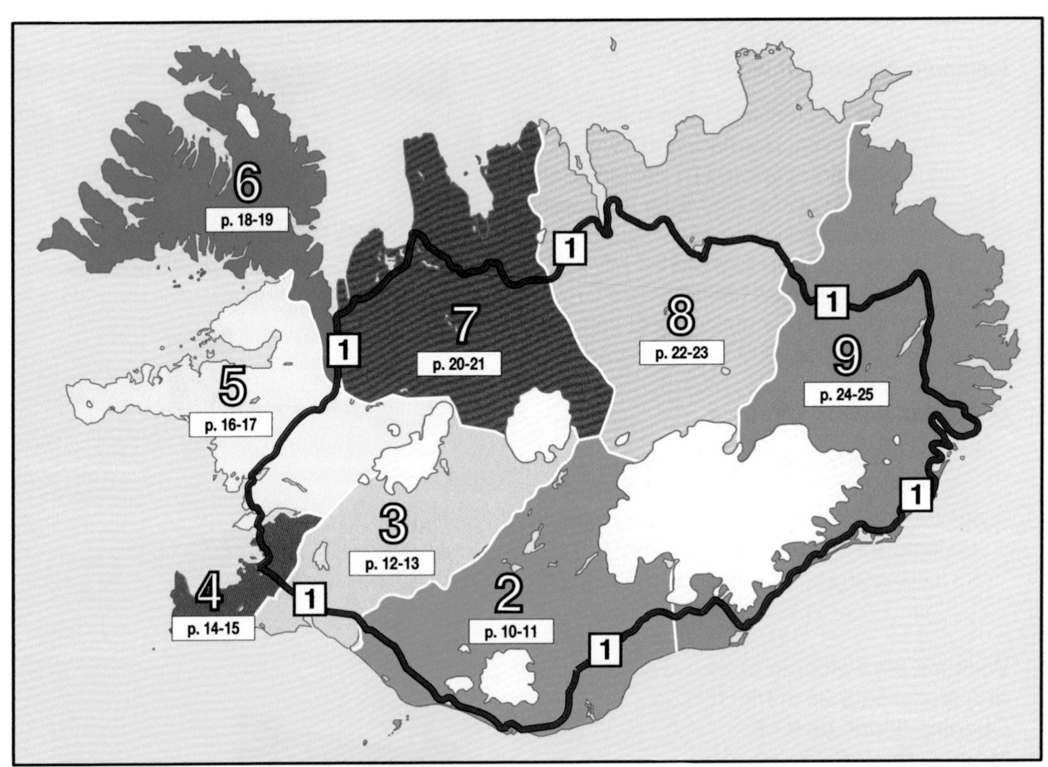

Iceland is divided into eight regions, numbered from 2 to 9.

There is no Region 1.

This map shows the regions, and also Highway 1 (the Ring Road), which passes through all regions. The numbers of all roads in each area (with the exception of Highway 1) begin with the relevant regional number. For example, all roads in Region 2 have numbers beginning with 2. The roads within each region are listed in numerical, rather than alphabetical, order. For example, the first road in Region 3, Skeiða- og Hrunamannavegur, is no. 30, and the last, Arnarbælisvegur, is no. 375.

See more detailed information on how to use this book on p. 4-7

1 VESTURLANDSVEGUR

Esja, (914 m) For many citizens of Reykjavík this mountain is virtually a part of the city, and indeed it often protects it from the full fury of the north-east winds in winter. Good viewing points are **Kerhólakambur** (850 m), **Kistufell** (830 m) and **Þverfell** (guest book). There are many routes up the mountain, the most popular being from Mógilsá and Esjuberg.

Mógilsá, a mixed forest in the Alps-like surroundings of Mt. Esja, one of Reykjavík's most popular areas for outdoor recreation. The Mógilsá Research Station's clonal archives, a wide variety of paths and a path network leading from the research station. An excellent variation on the traditional Mt. Esja hike – sort of like a 'mini' Mt. Esja hike!

Mosfellskirkja, a church in Mosfellsdalur. In front of the church is a monument of Ólafía Jóhannsdóttir often called „Mother Teresa of the North". She was born in Mosfell in 1863 and was a womens rights activist.

Álafoss, a village by Varmá, built around a woollen mill of the same name which was founded in 1896. The mill buildings are now artists' studios. There you will also find the workshop of Páll Kristjánsson and Soffía Sigurðardóttir. They are amazing creators of handmade knives, using traditional Viking method, making every knife and sheath unique. There is a possibility to attend a knife making course and/or visit their workshop.

Reykjalundur, a sanatorium and workshop, built 1945, originally for TB patients. Now a general rehabilitation centre.

Mosfellsbær, (pop. 9,783) a town and surrounding community with the usual services. Some light industry.

Lágafell, once a farm and often the residence of priests. There is a church built in 1889, it is a wooden church with a concrete foundation. Extensions and renovations have been made to the original building.

Úlfarsfell, (295 m) a mountain and a farm of the same name. The cliffs on west the mountain are now called **Hamrahlíð**, formerly **Lágafellshamrar**. On the east side of Úlfasfell is Skyggnir a satellite communication base for phone, television and air control.

Korpúlfsstaðir, a farm built after 1922 by Thor Jensen (1863-1947). He took over a cottage farm and made it one of the largest and richest farms in the country. The large farm building which, among other things, housed 300 cows, still stands. The Thors family are descended from him; among them Ólafur Thors (1892-1964) a prominent politician and former prime minister, and the author Thor Vilhjálmsson (1925-2011). On pastures where cattle once grazed, Reykjavik Golf Club now has a fine 27-hole golf course that will challenge even the most seasoned golfer.

Keldnaholt, a group of research laboratories for farming, building and industry.

Gufunes, a farm. Since 1935 the site of a telecommunication centre, both for domestic and foreign communication. The sculpture garden of Hallsteinn Sigurðsson is on a slope above the plant.

Grafarholt, one of Reykjavík´s suburbian districts. Reykjavik Golf Club also has an 18-hole golf course in Grafarhólt. Established in 1934, RGK is the country´s oldest golf club. The Grafarholt golf course opened in 1963. Near the road is a large split rock, thought to be inhabited by the "hidden people". The rock has been moved twice. The first time it was moved it split in two. One piece weighs 15 tons and the other 35.

Esjuberg-Ártúnshöfði 18 km

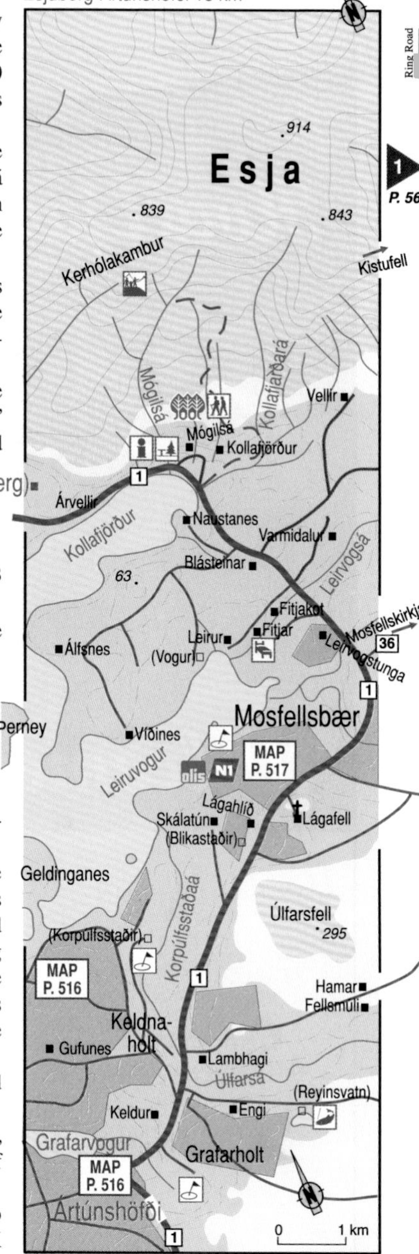

Ártúnshöfði-Esjuberg 18 km

1 P. 564

36 **Þingvallavegur,** p. 187

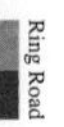

HVALFJARÐAR SVEIT

Hvalfjarðarsveit

- countryside beauty on crossroads

Welcome

1 VESTURLANDSVEGUR

Hlésey, a small farm and a place of Viking culture. It is the private home of Jóhanna Harðardóttir an artist and a heathen priestess of Ásatrú, the religion of the settlers of Iceland. As a skilled Rune reader she uses the wisdom of the god Óðin to channel a path from past to future. There are no set opening hours, but if you are interested in a rune reading or in Jóhanna's artwork, you can make an advance appointment.

Kúludalsá, a farm and a river of the same name. The river runs just east of the farm.

Hvalfjörður Tunnel (Whale Fjord). Built in 1996–1998, the tunnel is 5650 m. This first underwater tunnel in Iceland shortened the journey north and west from Reykjavík by 47 km. It is the only road for which payment is collected of vehicle owners.

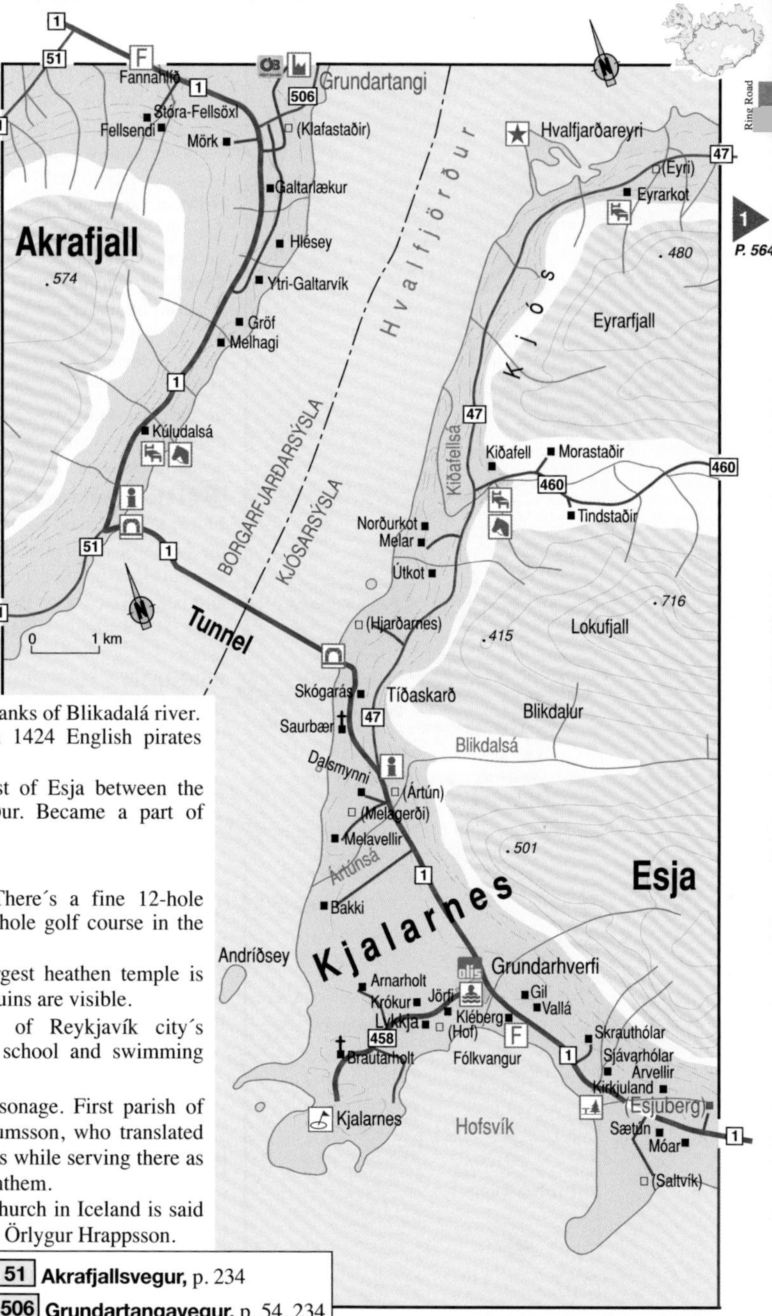

Ártún, an abandoned farm on the banks of Blikadalá river.

Saurbær, a farm and church. In 1424 English pirates raided the farm.

Kjalarnes, the district to the west of Esja between the fjords Kollafjörður and Hvalfjörður. Became a part of Reykjavík in 1998.

458 Brautarholtsvegur, 2 km.

Brautarholt, church and farm. There´s a fine 12-hole golf course. This was the first 12-hole golf course in the country.

Hof, a farm where the second largest heathen temple is supposed to have been, though no ruins are visible.

Grundarhverfi, (pop. 562) one of Reykjavík city´s suburbs. It boasts an elementary school and swimming pool.

Móar, a farm and formerly a parsonage. First parish of the poet and priest Matthías Jochumsson, who translated *Hamlet* and other Shakespeare plays while serving there as well as writing Iceland's national anthem.

Esjuberg, a farm where the first church in Iceland is said to have been built by the Hebridean Örlygur Hrappsson.

47 Hvalfjarðarvegur, p. 220
51 Akrafjallsvegur, p. 234
460 Eyrarfjallsvegur, p. 224
506 Grundartangavegur, p. 54, 234

1 P. 564

Esjuberg-Grundartangi 16 km

Höfn-Grundartangi 17 km

Belgsholt, a windmill was installed in 2011. It was the first windmill in Iceland, producing upto 30kW, providing the farm most of the electricity it needs. The windmill was damaged in a severe storm in 2012. It was later rebuilt and is again in use.

Höfn, a farm and in earlier times the seat of chieftains. In the 17th century the home of Steinunn Finnsdóttir, the first known Icelandic poetess.

Ölver, (602 m) in the birch woods below this mountain there is a community centre and summer cottages.

Melar, a farm and, until 1855, a church but the site is now much eroded by the sea. Served by Helgi Sigurðsson 1815 (1808-88), who was the major force in the establishment of the National Museum and the first Icelander to study photography, which he did in Copenhagen alongside his academic studies 1842-45.

505 Melasveitarvegur, 11,68 km.

Leirá, ("Clay river") a farm and church, from earliest times the home of influential men. Chief Justice Magnús Stephensen put up a printing press at a nearby farm, **Leirárgarðar**, and later moved it to Beitistaðir. Good salmon fishing in the river. Hot springs, swimming pool, school and community centre.

Beitistaðir, a farm where there was a printing press which was brought there from Leirárgarðar in 1814 and was moved in 1819 to Viðey, then the only printing-house in the country.

Galtarholtslækur, a small stream flowing into Eiðisvatn. This is where the executioner drowned, in the novel *Íslandsklukkan* by Nobel prize-winning author Halldór Laxness.

Grundartangi, (on Rd. 506), ferrosilicon plant built 1977 – 1980 belongin to Icelandic Alloys Ltd. At the beginning 180 people were working in the plant. New aluminium plant commenced production 1998. Now there are 12 companies operating in the area with over 1000 employees, most of them living in the capital area.

Katanes, abandoned farm by the sea. During the last century a monster was said to have come from the sea and found a hiding-place in the small lake Katanestjörn. Extensive preparations were made to kill the monster but the story turned out to be a hoax.

506 Grundartangavegur, 2,46 km.

47 Hvalfjarðarvegur, p. 220
51 Akrafjallsvegur, p. 234
502 Svínadalsvegur, p. 258
504 Leirársveitarvegur, p. 258

Grundartangi-Höfn 17 km

1 VESTURLANDSVEGUR

530 Ferjubakkavegur, 5 km.

Brennistaðir, a community centre, Valfell.

Einkunnir, a 265 ha park, protected for recreational use and the preservation of the typical landscape of the area since 2006. The main characteristics for this area are rocky islands or bluffs that rise from the vast flat wetlands. Diverse fauna. A 5km hiking path extends from Einkunnir to the parsonage at Borg.

Borg á Mýrum, church and parsonage. Originally settled by Skallagrímur Kveldúlfsson father of the poet Egill Skallagrímsson of *Egils saga*. Many of his relatives and descendants lived there, including Snorri Sturluson for a time. Tradition has it that Kjartan Ólafsson, one of the main characters of *Laxdæla saga*, is buried there.

Borgarnes, (pop. 1,946) a small town on Borgarfjörður. One of the very few costal towns in Iceland not dependent on fishing. Engaged mainly in commerce, service and industry. The first building know to have been built in Borgarnes was built by a Scot in 1858 for salmon-canning. Rivers and lakes in the area are rich of salmons and trout's. The settler Skallagrímur Kveldúlfsson is buried in Borgarnes, his burial mound now being the central feature in a beautiful public garden, Skallagrímsgarður. Landnámssetið, the Icelandic Settlement Centre, is situated in the picturesque township of Borgarnes. The Borgarfjordur area is the setting for Egils Saga, one of the most graphic of the settlement sagas, and this historical context combined with the charming natural beauty of the site make it an ideal location for the Centre. Over a thousand years ago, Viking adventurers discovered a large untouched island in the north Atlantic and claimed the land for their own. A rapid period of settlement ensued and thus the Icelandic nation was born. The prime objective of the Icelandic Settlement Centre at Borgarnes is to dramatically recreate the fascinating sagas surrounding the birth of this island nation.

Brákarsund, ("Brák's channel") between the town and the island Brákarey ("Brák's island"), both named for Brák, a slave of Skallagrímur's. Fleeing her master's anger, she tried to swim out to the island but he threw a boulder which hit her between the shoulders and killed her. A memorial in her remembrance behind the Settlment Center.

Borgarfjarðarbrú, second longest bridge in Iceland at 520 m, opened to traffic in 1980.

Seleyri, a spit of land. Through there lies a water pipe to Borgarnes from Hafnarfjall. A good spot for fishing sea trout and sea char.

Hafnarfjall, (844 m) a basalt mountain, barren and with big screes on the slopes. Some light-coloured granophyre crags in the screes, called **Flyðrur**.

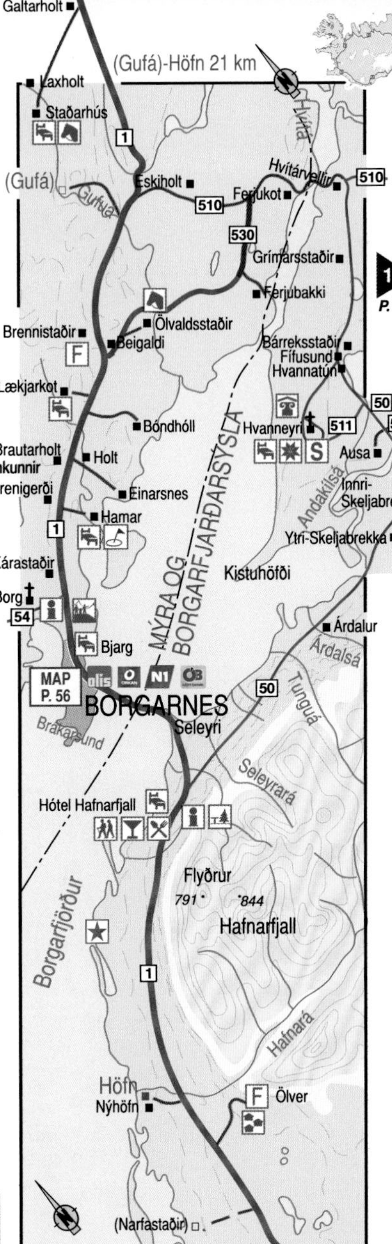

50 Borgarfjarðarbraut, p. 231	**54 Snæfellsnesvegur,** p. 238
505 Melasveitarvegur, p. 54, 258	**507 Mófellsstaðavegur,** p. 259
508 Skorradalsvegur, p. 259	**510 Hvítárvallavegur,** p. 231
511 Hvanneyrarvegur, p. 231	

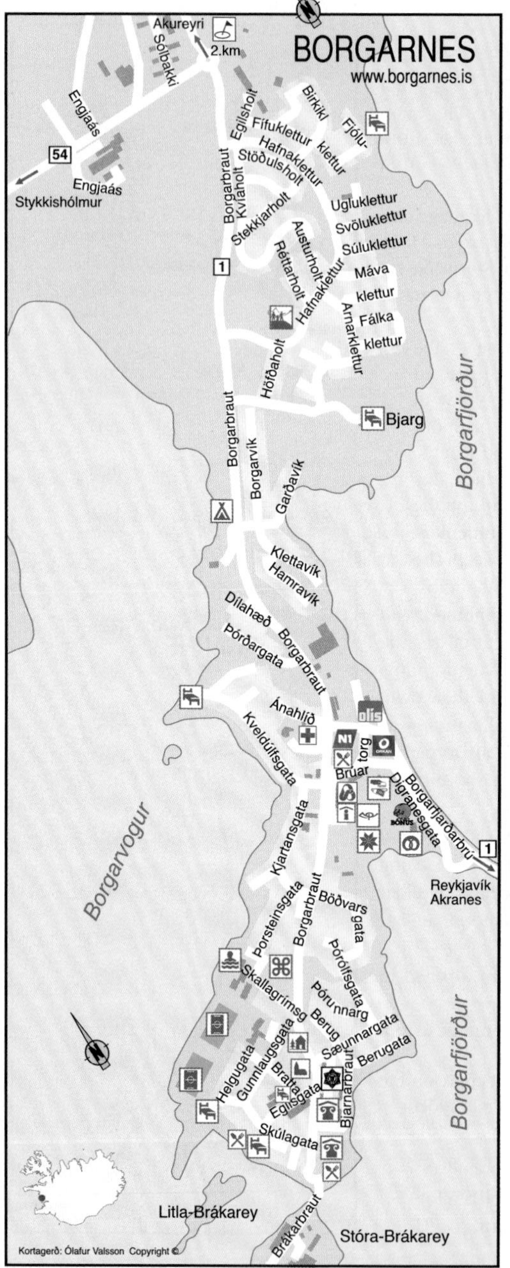
BORGARNES
www.borgarnes.is
Akureyri
2.km
Sólbakki
Engjaás
54
Stykkishólmur
Egilsholt
Birkikl
Fjólu-
Fífuklettur
Hafnaklettur
Stöðulsholt
klettur
Borgarbraut
Kvíaholt
Stekkjarholt
Uglukiettur
Svölukiettur
Súlukiettur
Máva
klettur
Fálka
klettur
Austurholt
Réttarholt
Hafnaklettur
Arnarklettur
1
Höfðaholt
Bjarg
Borgarfjörður
Borgarvík
Garðavík
Klettavík
Hamravík
Dílahæð
Þórðargata
Ánahlíð
Kveldúlfsgata
torg
Brúar
Digranesgata
Borgarfjarðarbrú
Kjartansgata
Reykjavík
Akranes
Borgarvogur
Böðvarsgata
Þorsteinsgata
Þórólfsgata
Skallagrímsg
Þórunnarg
Berug
Sæunnargata
Berugata
Helgugata
Gunnlaugsgata
Brattag
Egilsgata
Bjarnarbraut
Skúlagata
Litla-Brákarey
Brákarbraut
Stóra-Brákarey
Kortagerð: Ólafur Valsson Copyright ©

Borgarnes
Bed & Breakfast
Skúlagata 21 - 310 Borgarnes
Tel: 434-1566, 842-5866
www.borgarnesbb.is
Situated in a quiet
residental area by the sea.
Borgarnes Swimming Pool
Tel.: 433-7100 / sundlaug@borgarbyggd.is
Out and indoor pool / Wading pool
3 water slides / Hot tubs / Bubbling Water Area
Gym / Sauna / Natural Steambath
OPEN: WEEKDAYS 6⁰⁰-22⁰⁰ / WEEKENDS 9⁰⁰-18⁰⁰
Geirabakarí
Bakery
Coffee House
Digranesgata 6
310 Borgarnes
☎ 437-1920
Open daily

netto
Grocery store

EGILS SAGA EXHIBITION
SETTLEMENT EXHIBITION
EGILS SAGA EXHIBITION
SETTLEMENT EXHIBITION
TWO SAGA EXHIBITIONS WITH AUDIO GUIDE IN 15 LANGUAGES
Welcome to
The Settlement Center in Borgarnes
Open All Year: 10:00 – 21:00
Tel. 437 1600
www.settlementcenter.is
landnam@landnam.is
DELICIOUS DISHES AT A STUNNING RESTAURANT

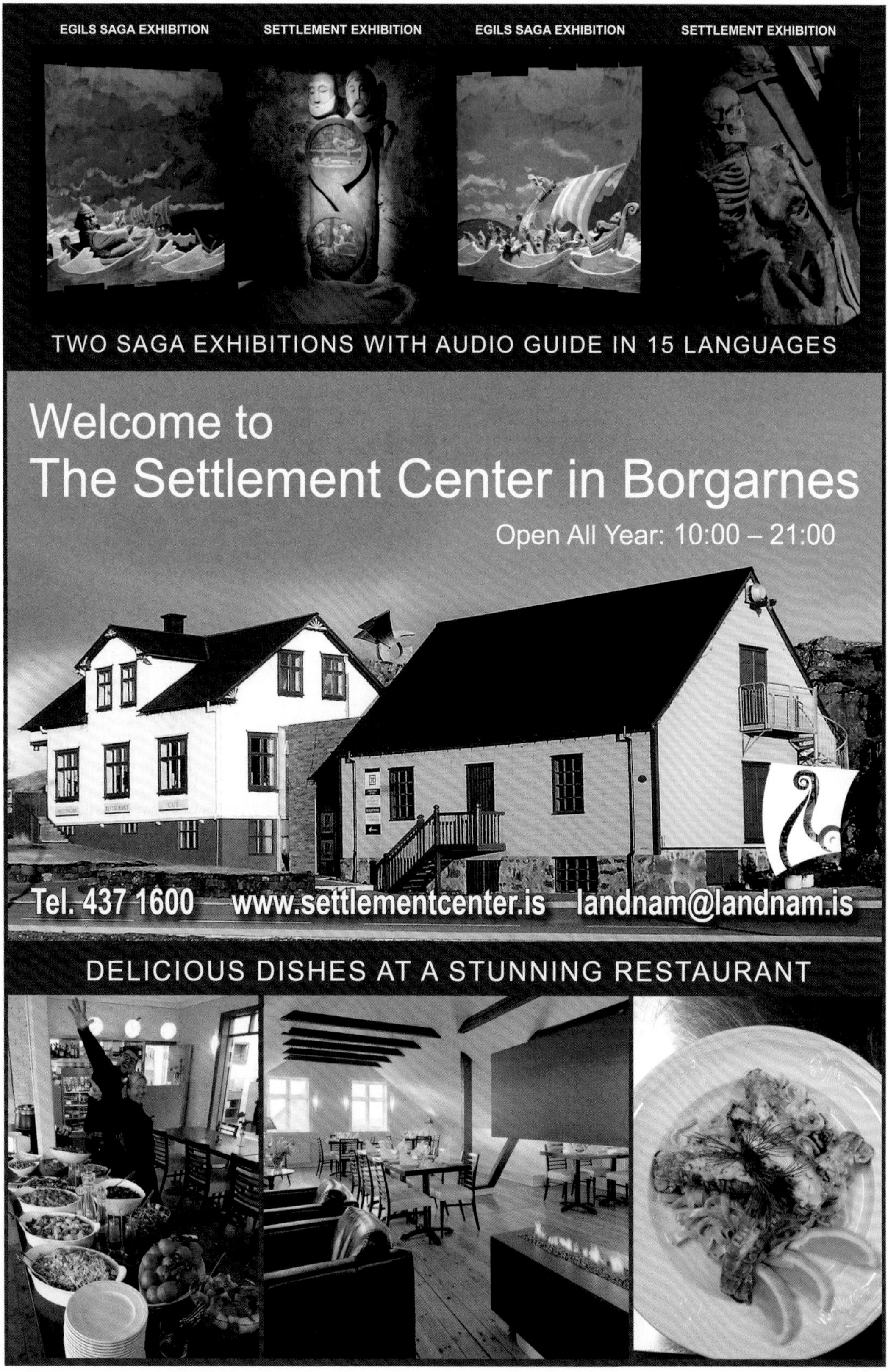

(Laxfoss)-(Gufá) 18 km
(Laxfoss) 1 Laxfoss 527 Höll Hjarðarholt
Norðurá 522
229
(Litlaskarð)
Einifell
1 P. 564
(Stóra-Gröf)
527 Varmaland
(Stóru-Skógar)
Stafholtsveggir
Munaðarnes 527 522
Hlöðutún
Gljúfurá 1 Arnarholt 50
Borgir 50
Baulan 526
Tómasarhagi
553 Hofstaðir
Sólheimatunga
Svignaskarð
Daníelslundur Stafholt
Tún Stórafjall 76
Gljúfurá Bjargarsteinn
Skarðslækur Ystatunga Svarfhóll
Litlagröf Melkot
Flóðatangi
1
Norðurá
Galtarholt
Laxholt
Staðarhús
Faxaborg
Hvítárvellir 510
Eskiholt Ferjukot
(Gufá) 510
Gufá 530 Hvítá
0 1 km
1
(Gufá)-(Laxfoss) 18 km

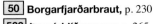

Paradísarlaut

Laxfoss, waterfall in the river Norðurá and a farm of the same name. Good salmon-fishing below the falls. Plant fossils found nearby.

Munaðarnes, a farm on whose land a great many summer houses have been built for the Union of state and municipal employees.

Varmaland, (on Rd. 527) a school centre built near a large hot spring. Greenhouses and swimming pool. There is a walking path through the woods to a cliff called Hnjúkurinn.

Gljúfurá, a branch of Langá and tributary of Norðurá it flows through an impressive long, straight canyon.

Svignaskarð, a substantial farm since early times, where many men of consequences have lived. Snorri Sturluson owned it for some time. The view from the view-dial on the crags, **Kastali**, just north of the farm is extremely good on clear days, with the glaciers Eiríksjökull, Geitlandsjökull, Þórisjökull and Ok to the east, Skarðsheiði and Hafnarfjall to the south and Baula to the north.

Ferjukot, a farm by the bridge on Hvítá with good salmon-fishing. At Ferjukot is a salmon and history museum. Groups are only facilitated by appointment. Once sport tournaments were held on the banks of the river Hvítá and later hourse tournaments by a place now known as **Faxaborg**.

Hvítá, ("White river") the biggest river in western Iceland, dividing the counties Borgarfjarðarsýsla and Mýrasýsla. Like other rivers of the same name, it is a glacial river, coming from the western foot of Eiríksjökull. Along with its tributary Norðurá, however, which is 117 km long and has its source at the north-eastern end of Langjökull. In 1648 a Dutchman built a salmon-fishing lodge by the mouth of the river.

50 **Borgarfjarðarbraut,** p. 230
522 **Þverárhlíðarvegur,** p. 265
527 **Varmalandsvegur,** p. 230
553 **Langavatnsvegur,** p. 269
510 **Hvítárvallavegur,** p. 231
526 **Stafholtsvegur,** p. 230
530 **Ferjubakkavegur,** p. 55

The Glanni waterfalls in Norðurá river

Grábrók

Dalsmynni, ("Mouth of the valley") has been a farm site since the original settlement. The settler was Rauða-Björn ("Iron-oxide-Björn"), who was the first to work iron from the moors.

Hraunsnefsöxl, a mountain ridge, half of which is said to have split off and fallen down into the valley shortly before the original settlement, leaving a 100 m high cliff face on the mountain and another 100 m of gravel and rock scree below it. At **Hraunsnef** is a guesthouse and a restaurant. There you can get a map with information about where the local fairies, hidden people, gnomes, dwarves and trolls live.

528 Norðurárdalsvegur, 16 km.

Bifröst, (pop. 182) a business college first operated by the co-operative movement in Iceland. Now a university.

Hreðavatn, a lake and farm of the same name. There is trout-fishing in the lake and several small islands covered with the rich vegetation which is a feature of the immediate area. Lignite, mined at one time, is found a little above the farm, also plant fossils from the warm interval of the Tertiary period. Some distance west of the lake there is a lone pyramid-shaped peak, **Vikrafell** (539 m). By the lake is a forrest **Jafnaskarðsskógur**.

Hreðavatnsskáli, probably Icelands oldest restaurant by the road. First built in 1933 but moved in 1946 to its current location.

Glanni, waterfall in the river Norðurá. The river bank has interesting lave formation and a magical landscape. Well worth a visit. Close to the waterfall is a fine 9-hole golf course, Glannavöllur. Near Bifröst a road leads down to a car park next to the club house and close to the waterfall.

Grábrókarhraun, a rough lava-field about 3,000 years old, covered with moss and birch bushes. The lava came from three craters, **Grábrók**, which is the largest, **Grábrókarfell**, and a small crater that has been more or less dug up and used as gravel for the road. There is an excellent view from the top of Grábrók.

Jafnaskarðsskógur, an expansive forest with delightful walking paths and routes shown on a walking map published by the Stafholtstungur Youth Association.

60 Vestfjarðavegur, p. 280

522 Þverárhlíðarvegur, p. 265

527 Varmalandsvegur, p. 230

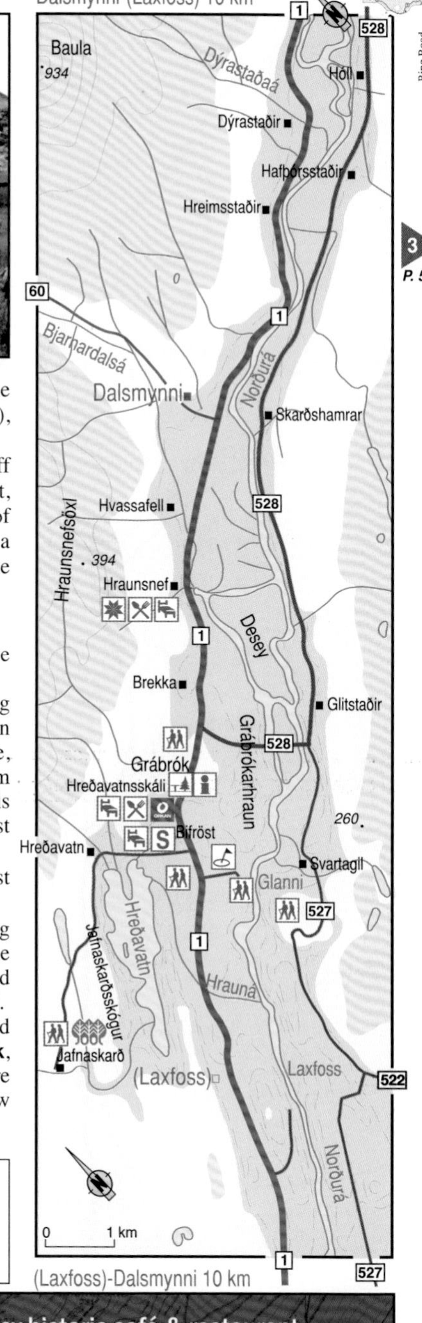

3 P. 566

Ring Road
3
P. 566

(Fornihvammur)-Dalsmynni 20 km

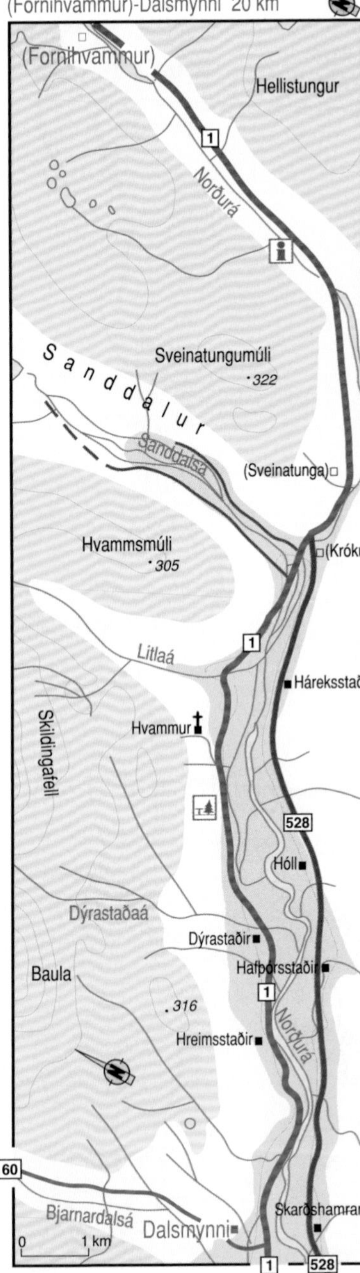

Dalsmynni-(Fornihvammur) 20 km

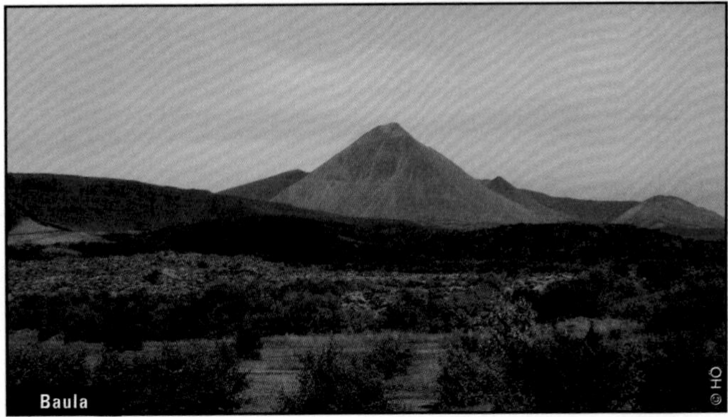
Baula

© HO

Fornihvammur, once important as the first farm on descending south into the Norðurá valley after the difficult crossing over the Holtavörðuheiði moor. A shelter was built there in 1840 and a farm in 1853. Now abandoned.

Sveinatunga, once a farm. There is the oldest concrete building in Iceland, built 1895.

528 Norðurárdalsvegur, 16 km.

Háreksstaðir, a farm on the southern side opposite Hvammur. The farm of the settler Örn the Old, who laid claim to the valley from Sveinatunga down to Arnarbæli or Bæli. Bæli is a rigde that goes across the valley to **Klettstía**, now the river **Norðurá** has carved its way through there.

Hvammur, church. The first mention of a church at Hvammur is in 1200 AD. Today´s church dates from 1880. It was extensively renovated in 1970.

Baula, (934 m) a rhyolite mountain, most likely a lava bulge from the ice age. The mountain is cone-shaped and steep, with screes and boulders on all sides. There are no particular obstacles for climbers but care should be taken because of falling rocks. On the top there is a small rock shelter and the view from there is excellent in all directions. In a rock shelter is a guest book, there is also a cairn. To the west and north of Baula is **Litla-Baula** ("Little-Baula") and **Skildingafell**. All of these mountains were formed over 3 million years ago. The river **Dýrastaðaá** runs from a lovely little valley, **Sátudalur**, through a deep canyon with many waterfalls, to join **Norðurá** between the farms **Hóll** and **Hafþórsstaðir**.

60 Vestfjarðavegur, p. 280
525 Grjóthálsvegur, p. 265
528 Norðurárdalsvegur, p. 59

Grænumýrartunga, an abandoned farm at the northern descent off the moor Holtavörðuheiði. Once a resting place and inn.

Miklagil, a river whose source is along the Tröllakirkja mountain; flows north from Holtavörðuheiði. Formerly an obstacle to travellers.

Konungsvarða, ("The king's cairn") a cemented cairn built at the northern end of Grunnavatnshæð ("Shallow lake hill") in 1936 to commemorate the trip of King Christian X, of Denmark and Iceland, and his queen Alexandrine across Holtavörðuheiði moor that year. The king's initials are carved on the cairn.

Konungsvarða.

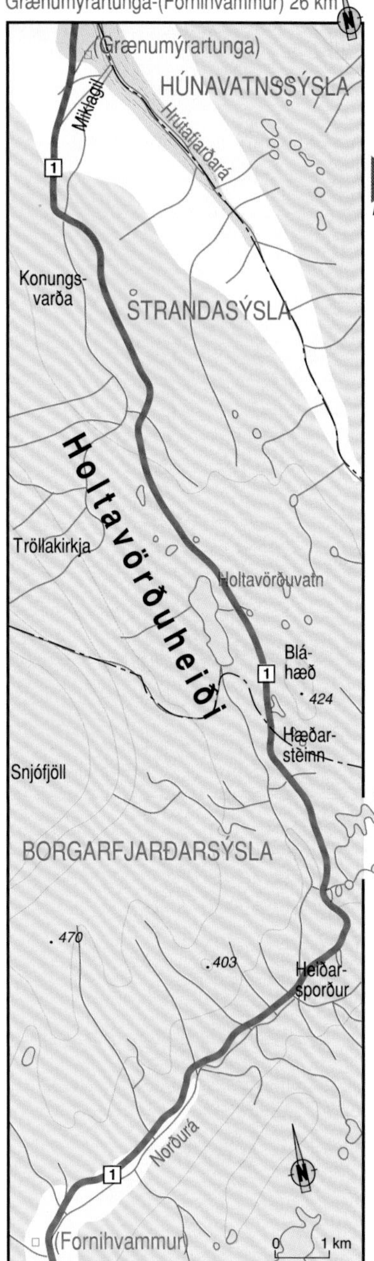

Ring Road
3
P. 566

Holtavörðuvatn, a fair-sized lake in a hollow west of the road. Trout-fishing. Swans and diving birds often seen there in summertime.

Hæðarsteinn, a big rock at the southern end of the high ridge; boundary between the counties Mýrasýsla and Strandasýsla.

Haukadalsskarð, north of Tröllakirkja and Klambrafells and south of Geldingafell was once a much travelled route between the North and the West. It was used if the weather was bad at Holtavörðuheiði.

Tröllakirkja, ("Giants' church") (1,001 m) a mountain to the north of Snjófjöll. The highest mountain in this area, with a good deal of permanent snow and ice.

Snjófjöll, ("Snow mountains") (808 m) a wide mountain ridge to the southwest of Holtavörðuheiði.

Holtavörðuheiði, moors with extensive and rather flat hills and mountains between Norðurárdalur and Hrútafjörður, quite marshy and with many lakes, maximum altitude about 400 m. The road across Holtavörðuheiði has long been the main route between the north and south of Iceland. Once considered to be haunted. Good view towards Eiríksjökull and Langjökull.

Never drive off roads

Reykjaskóli-Grænumýrartunga 21 km

Hrútey, Eyjanes, Sæberg, Reykjaskóli (Reykjatangi), Reykir, Hrútafjarðarháls, Akurbrekka, Þóroddsstaðir, Borðeyrarbær, 287, Laugarholt, Borðeyri, (Lyngholt), (Gilsstaðir), 172, Brautarholt, Oddsstaðir, Valdasteinsstaðir, Hvalshöfði, HRÚTAFJÖRÐUR, STRANDASÝSLA, HÚNAVATNSSÝSLA, Brandagil, Markhöfði, Fjarðarhorn, Smáragil, Staður, Staðarskáli, Staðarflöt, Fagrabrekka, Bálkastaðir, Hrútatungurétt, Hrútatunga, Melar, Sika, Brú, (Foss), Ormsá, Óspaksstaðir, Hrútafjarðará, Hrútatunga, (Grænumýrartunga), 0, 1 km

702, 1, 68, 59, 640, 68, 1, 705, F586, 1

3 P. 566

Grænumýrartunga-Reykjaskóli 21 km

Reykjatangi, the small peninsula which one can see tidemarks showing changes in the sea-level through the ages.
Þóroddsstaðir, a farm since the original settlement. According to *Grettis saga* Þorbjörn öxnamegin was killed there by Grettir Ásmundarson the strong, as the name Spjótsmýri ("Spear-marsh"), still reminds us.
Gilsstaðir, a farm on the shore, formerly a point for the ferry to Borðeyri.
Borðeyri, a village and a trading place since 1846.

640 Borðeyrarvegur, 0,64 km.

Brandagil, a farm from where a jeep-track goes over to Hnúkur in Miðfjörður. The track can be difficult. By the lakes on the ridge are large collonies og the Great Northern Loon.
Staður, a farm, church and former parsonage. It was long a dispatch centre for overland postmen and a resting place for all travellers, as the **Staðarskáli** roadhouse. Memorial to overland postmen by the roadside.
Melar, a substantial farm for many centuries, see p. 309.
Brú, once a telephone exchange and post office built in 1950, when the service was moved from Borðeyri.
Hrútafjarðará, a long river with many tributaries, originating in the lakes of the Holtavörðuheiði and Tvídægra moors. Forms the boundary between the counties Vestur-Húnavatnssýsla to the east and Strandasýsla and Mýrasýsla to the west and south. A well-known salmon river.

59 Laxárdalsvegur, p. 257	**68 Innstrandavegur,** p. 309
702 Heggstaðanesvegur, p. 334	**F586 Haukadalsskarðsvegur,** p. 468

1 NORÐURLANDSVEGUR

Stóri-Ós, a farm, in Saga times the home of Þórður hreða, a well-known warrior and craftsman.

Reykir, a farm above Laugarbakki. In Saga times the home of Miðfjarðar-Skeggi, famed for taking the sword Sköfnungur from the burial mound of Hrólfur kraki.

Laugarbakki, (pop. 47) a village south of the bridge across Miðfjarðará. It was previously called Langafit, and horse fights were held there, as told in the Saga of Grettir the strong. The first house was built there in 1933. Community centre Ásbyrgi, sport centre, campsite, grocery store, handcraft market, organic greenhouse, Skrúðvangur, and a hotel. At Grettisból is a farmers market in the summer time. Laugarbakki is a geothermal site, which sustains this village and also that of Hvammstangi.

Melstaður, a farm since Saga times, a church and parsonage. The home of the poet Kormákur and later Oddur Ófeigsson of *Bandamanna saga*. After the country had been Christianized in the year 1000, it became still more important and was considered the second-richest parish in the north, the present church indeed containing a number of interesting old objects. From 1598 to 1648 Arngrímur Jónsson lærði ("the learned"), lived there and wrote many of his books about Icelandic history and culture. His books, giving accurate information about the country and its people, were written in Latin and were of international interest at the time. Among them are: *Crymogæa, Anatome Blefkeniana, Brevis Commentarius de Islandiae, Specimen Islandiae historicum* and *Gronlandia*.

Tannastaðir, a farm and the birthplace of Björn Gunnlaugsson (1788-1876) mathematician, surveyor and the first person to make an exact map of Iceland.

Hrútafjarðarháls, the long range of hills between Hrútafjörður and Miðfjörður, wet and marshy. Where it continues to the north it is called **Heggsstaðanes** or **Bálkastaðanes**. There is Europes biggest Great Northern Loon colony. More info Brandagil p. 62.

Reykjaskóli, a centre for school field trips, formerly a boarding school, heated by water from the Reykjahver hot spring. Interesting museum of shark fishing. On the shoreline next to Reykjaskóli is a natural hot pool to bathe in.

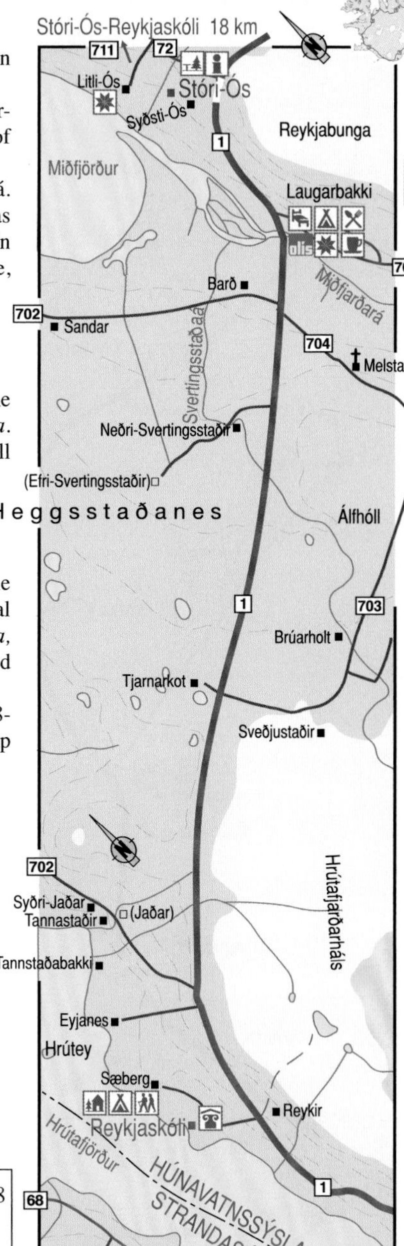

Ring Road
3 P. 566

68 Innstrandavegur, p. 309	**72 Hvammstangavegur,** p. 338
702 Heggstaðanesvegur, p. 334	**703 Hálsbæjarvegur,** p. 334
704 Miðfjarðarvegur, p. 335	**711 Vatnsnesvegur,** p. 338

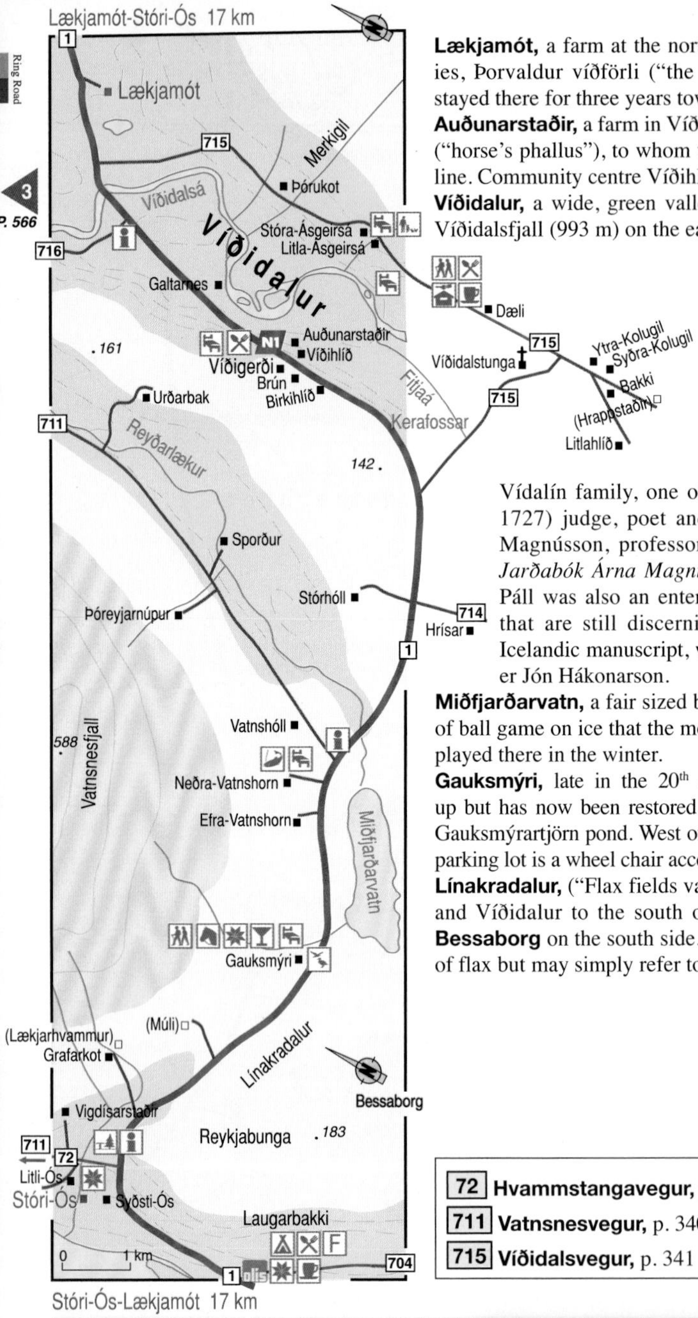

Lækjamót-Stóri-Ós 17 km

3 P. 566

Lækjamót, a farm at the northern end of Víðidalur. The first missionaries, Þorvaldur víðförli ("the widely travelled") and Bishop Friðrekur, stayed there for three years towards the end of the 11th century.

Auðunarstaðir, a farm in Víðidalur named after the settler Auðun skökull ("horse's phallus"), to whom the British royal family can trace its family line. Community centre Víðihlíð nearby.

Víðidalur, a wide, green valley, with low hills on the western side and Víðidalsfjall (993 m) on the eastern side. The 65 km long Víðidalsá flows through the valley, a good salmon river, coming from north-western Stórisandur.

Kerafossar in the river Fitjaá is a good place for fishing.

Víðidalstunga, a substantial farm since early times and a church, built on the tongue of land between the rivers **Fitjaá** and **Víðidalsá**. From the 15th century until about 1900 it was the seat of the Vídalín family, one of whom was Páll Jónsson Vídalín (1667–1727) judge, poet and schoolmaster. Also, together with Árni Magnússon, professor and manuscript collector, the author of *Jarðabók Árna Magnússonar og Páls Vídalín* (a farm register). Páll was also an enterprising farmer who cultivated large fields that are still discernible. *Flateyjarbók*, the largest extant old Icelandic manuscript, was written there at the request of the farmer Jón Hákonarson.

Miðfjarðarvatn, a fair sized but shallow lake. *Grettis saga* tells of a kind of ball game on ice that the men from Miðfjörður, Vatnsnes and Víðidalur played there in the winter.

Gauksmýri, late in the 20th century a march land of 10 ha was dried up but has now been restored. It can be seen from the road and is called Gauksmýrartjörn pond. West of the lake is a bird watching house. From the parking lot is a wheel chair accecible path to the bird watching house.

Línakradalur, ("Flax fields valley") a shallow valley between Miðfjörður and Víðidalur to the south of Vatnsnesfjall, with **Reykjarbunga** and **Bessaborg** on the south side. The name seems to indicate the cultivation of flax but may simply refer to cotton grass.

72 **Hvammstangavegur,** p. 338
704 **Miðfjarðarvegur,** p. 335
711 **Vatnsnesvegur,** p. 340
714 **Fitjavegur,** p. 341
715 **Víðidalsvegur,** p. 341
716 **Síðuvegur,** p. 340

Stóri-Ós-Lækjamót 17 km

1 NORÐURLANDSVEGUR

Hnausar, a farm built on the debris of a landslide that fell from Vatnsdalsfjall in 1545, called Skíðastaðaskriða. The slide destroyed the farm Skíðastaðir and killed 14 people. The lake **Hnausatjörn** was formed by the slide.

Hnausakvísl, the river between the lakes Flóðið and Húnavatn. Calm and deep, it is a good fishing river.

Sveinsstaðir, a substantial farm by Vatnsdalshólar where, in 1522, there was a battle between the Catholic bishop Jón Arason and Teitur Þorleifsson.

Vatnsdalshólar, a cluster of small hills at the mouth of Vatnsdalur, supposedly uncountable, the debris of a tremendous landslide from Vatnsdalsfjall. About 4 km² in area. Other geographical features in Iceland considered to be uncountable are the islands of Breiðafjörður and the lakes on Arnarvatnsheiði moor.

Þrístapar, a group of three small hills on the north side of the road, the site of the last execution in Iceland, January 12th 1830, when Natan Ketilsson' murderers, Agnes and Friðrik, were beheaded. The popular novel Burial Rites by the Australian author, Hanna Kent, deals with this dramatic event. As a teenager Kent was an exchange student in northern Iceland. See p. 339.

Þing, the district between the rivers Gljúfurá and Giljá, flat and fertile.

Hóp, the fifth largest lake in Iceland, 29-44 km² depending on the tide which affects the water level. Fed by Víðidalsá and Gljúfurá, it empties out through Bjargaós.

Gljúfurá, a river in a narrow canyon dividing the counties Austur- and Vestur-Húnavatnssýsla.

Ásmundarnúpur, (665 m) the northern tip of Víðidalsfjall, a steep peak with loose screes.

Dalsá, a river flowing from Melrakkadalur.

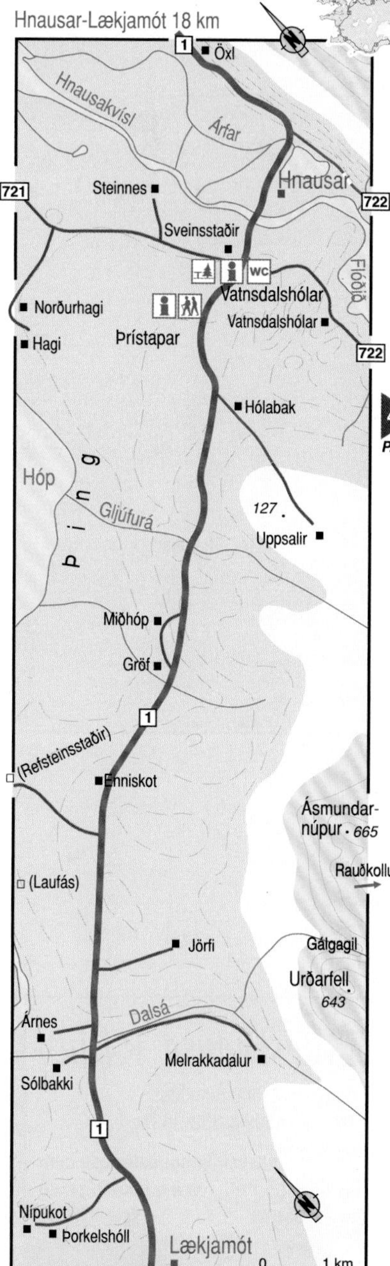

Ring Road

4
P. 567

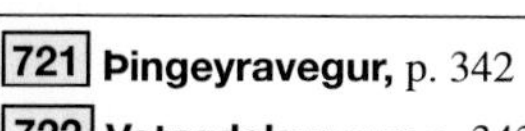

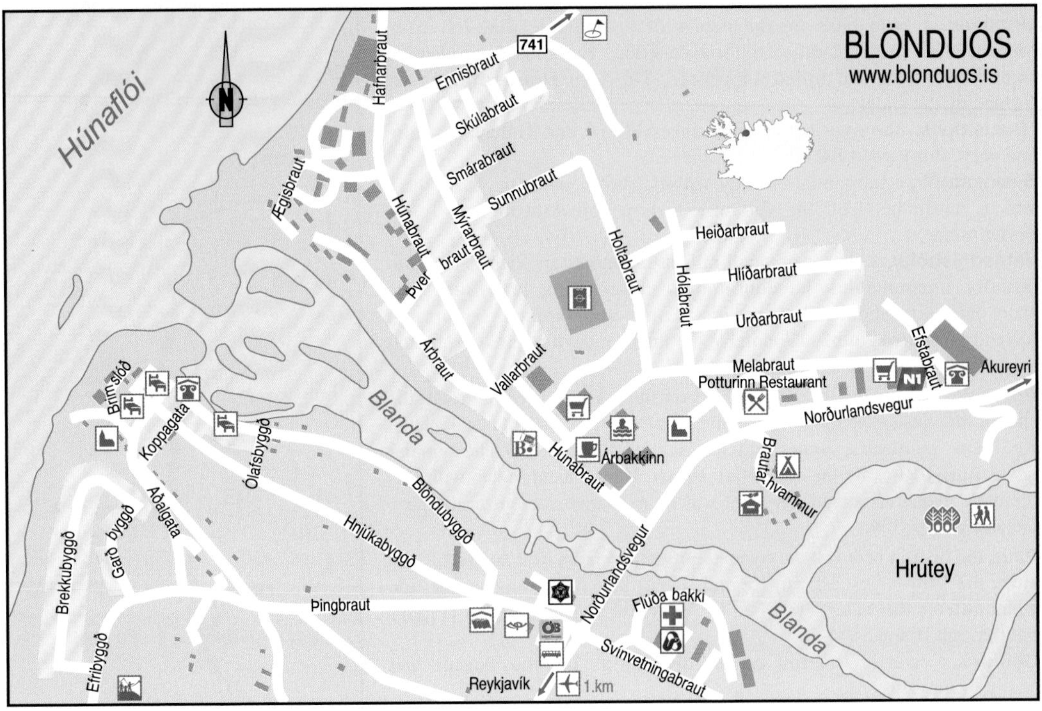

BLÖNDUÓS
www.blonduos.is

Húnaflói
741
Hafnarbraut
Ennisbraut
Skúlabraut
Smárabraut
Sunnubraut
Ægisbraut
Húnabraut
Mýrarbraut
Þverbraut
Holtabraut
Heiðarbraut
Hlíðarbraut
Urðarbraut
Hólabraut
Árbraut
Vallarbraut
Melabraut
Potturinn Restaurant
Efstabraut
Akureyri
N1
Norðurlandsvegur
Brim slóð
Koppagata
Blanda
Ólafsbyggð
Árbakkinn
Húnabraut
Brautarhvammur
Hrútey
Aðalgata
Garð byggð
Brekkubyggð
Blöndubyggð
Hnjúkabyggð
Norðurlandsvegur
Flúða bakki
Blanda
Þingbraut
Svínvetningabraut
Efribyggð
Reykjavík
1.km

1 NORÐURLANDSVEGUR

Blönduós, (pop. 795) a town at the mouth of the river Blanda, built on both sides of the river. A harbour and trading post since 1875. Industry connected with agriculture, trading and transport services. Hospital, hotel, guesthouse, campsite, swimming pool, restaurant, café, the Textile Museum and the Atlantic Salmon Museum. Vatnsdæla Saga is an action-packed family chronicle from the 13th century. A 46m long tapestry depicting the Saga´s storyline is now being handsewn and visitors can add their personal touch to its creation. Information can be had at the Textile Museum. Forestry research on **Hrútey**, an island in the river just east of town which is also a public park. Good salmon-fishing. See town map.

725 Miðásavegur, 3,47 km.

Hjaltabakki, a farm, church and parsonage until 1895.

Laxá á Ásum, one of the best salmon river in Iceland, in which is the waterfall Mánafoss, flowing from Laxárvatn to Húnavatn. Harnessed for electricity in 1933.

Torfalækur, a farm with fertile grasslands.

Stígandahróf, the place on the Búðartangi peninsula on **Húnavatn**, between the church at Þingeyrar and the farm **Akur**, where the settler Ingimundur the Old beached his ships after sailing from Norway. He named the lake Húnavatn ("Cup Lake") after finding a mama bear with two cups there.

Ásar, the district between the rivers Gilljá and Blanda. Its ancient name was Kolkumýrar.

Stóra-Giljá, a farm where Þorvaldur Koðránsson víðförli ("widely travelled") lived. He was a Christian missionary in Iceland who travelled around with the bishop Friðrekur, from Sachen. Þorvaldur later founded a monastery in Constantinople (Mikligarður, in Icelandic) and died there. There is a memorial to these missionaries at the nearby stone **Gullsteinn,** ("Golden stone") which was revered by the heathens. When Friðrekur chanted to exorcise it, the stone split.

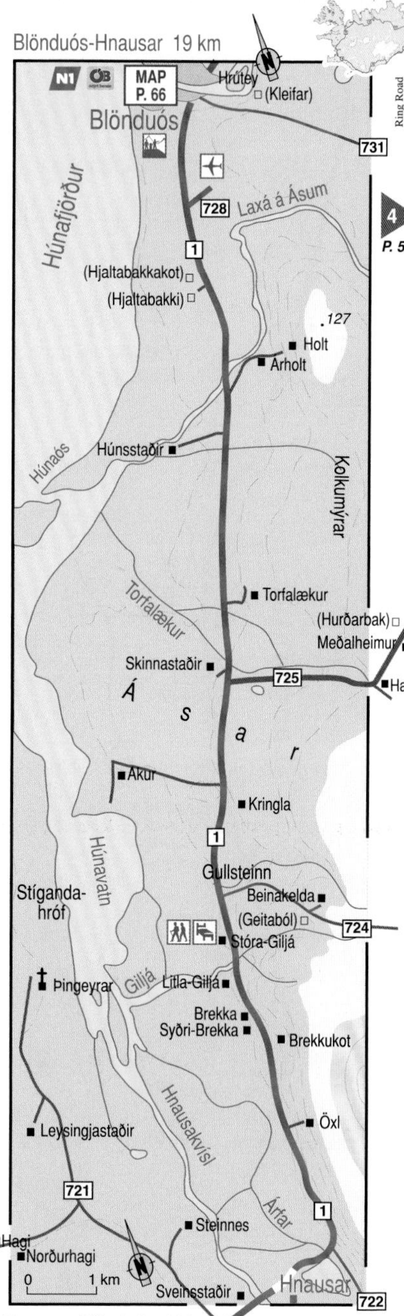

4 P. 567

Auðólfsstaðir-Blönduós 23 km

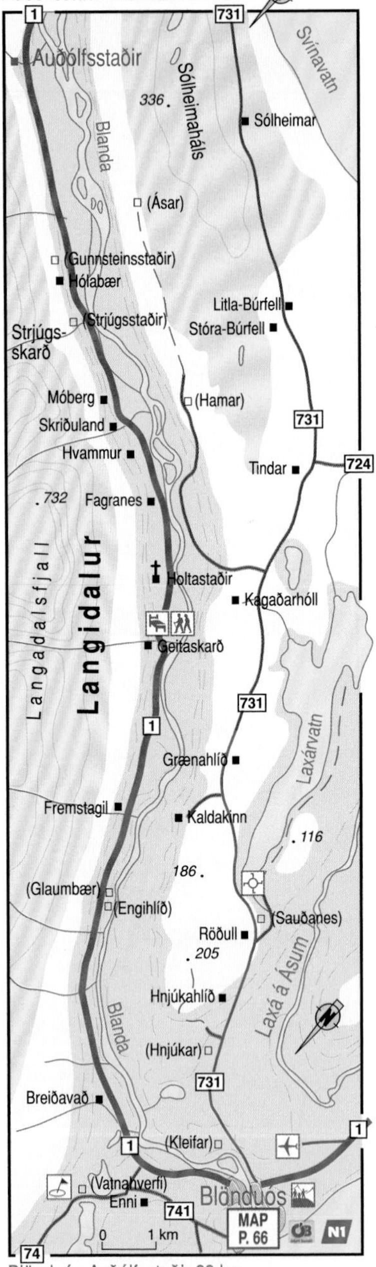

1 731 Auðólfsstaðir Sólheimaháls Svínavatn 336. Sólheimar Blanda (Ásar) (Gunnsteinsstaðir) Hólabær Litla-Búrfell Strjúgs-skarð (Strjúgsstaðir) Stóra-Búrfell Móberg Skriðuland (Hamar) 731 Hvammur Tindar 724 .732 Fagranes Langadalsfjall Langidalur Holtastaðir Kagaðarhóll Geitaskarð 731 1 Grænahlíð Laxárvatn Fremstagil Kaldakinn .116 186. (Glaumbær) (Engihlíð) (Sauðanes) Röðull .205 Hjúkahlíð Laxá á Ásum Blanda (Hnjúkar) 731 Breiðavað 1 1 (Kleifar) (Vatnahverfi) Enni 741 Blönduós MAP P. 66 0 1 km 74

Blönduós-Auðólfsstaðir 23 km

Langidalur, ("Long valley") the district along the east side of Blanda from Breiðavað to the junction of Svartá and Blanda, green and fertile with many big farms. To the east of it is the 25 km long mountain **Langadalsfjall**, 700-800 m high, steep with many peaks and three deep passes over to Laxárdalur in the east. There have been many big landslides on this mountain, such as those from Illveðurshnjúkur ("Foul weather peak") north of Geitaskarð pass and from Móbergsfjall ("Tuff mountain"), which left bare a vertical rockface called Móbergsstofur or Stofur.

Auðólfsstaðir, a farm since the time of the settlement. A jeep-track from there across Auðólfsstaðaskarð pass to Laxárdalur.

Strjúgur, there lived one of Icelands greatest poets in the 16th century, Þórður Magnússon.

Hvammur, from there are the brothers Guðmundur (1903–1989) and Jóhann Frímann poet (1906–1990).

Holtastaðir, a substantial farm and a church. Formerly a ferry point.

Geitaskarð, a substantial farm of historical note, built below a pass of the same name. Farmers there have often been district judges and outstanding men of the district. The home of Kolfinna, the sweetheart of the poet Hallfreður vandræðaskáld of Saga times.

Blanda, glacial river about 125 km long, with a large hydroelectric plant, flowing from the western sides of Hofsjökull. Two bridges, one by Blönduós and the other by Langamýri in Blöndudalur. The magnificent canyon Blöndugil is south of the head of Blöndudalur. Good fishing.

74 **Skagastrandarvegur,** p. 322 | 724 **Reykjabraut,** p. 344

731 **Svínvetningabraut,** p. 346 | 741 **Neðribyggðarvegur,** p. 322

© Olgeir Andresson
The church at Bólstaðahlíð

Stóra-Vatnsskarð, a farm at the eastern end of the Vatnsskarð pass.
Vatnshlíð, the easternmost farm in Húnavatnssýsla. Good fishing in the nearby lake, Vatnshlíðarvatn, which along with Krókagil canyon between the mountains Vatnshlíðarhnjúkur and Grísafell acts as a boundary between the counties Skagafjarðarsýsla and Húnavatnssýsla.
Vatnsskarð, (ca. 440 m) a mountain pass between the districts of Húnaflói and Skagafjörður. Good views in the western part from Saxhöfði, on the south side of the road and Víðivörðuháls, on the north side. From Botnastaðabrún farthest west in the pass there is also a fine view over the Svartárdalur valley below.
Þverárdalur, a pass, actually a valley open at both ends, connecting Svartárdalur and Laxárdalur. The river Hlíðará flows along this short valley originating in the Hólsvötn lakes way up in the mountains to the northeast.
Húnaver, a community centre to the south of the river Hlíðará.
Bólstaðarhlíð, a church and substantial farm for centuries. For 300 years, 1528-1825, the home of successive generations of the same family, which produced numerous children, many of whom have been famous or influential people in their time. Descendants are still known as the Bólstaðarhlíð family.
Æsustaðaskriður, steep screes by Æsustaðir.
Æsustaðir, the southernmost farm in Langidalur, at one time a parsonage.

731 Svínvetningabraut, p. 346 **734 Svartárdalsvegur,** p. 347

Stóra-Vatnsskarð-Auðólfsstaðir 20 km

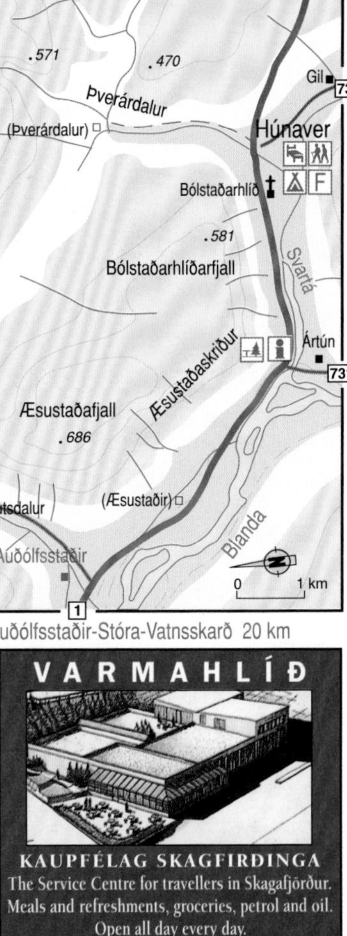

Auðólfsstaðir-Stóra-Vatnsskarð 20 km

Ring Road
4
P. 567

Grundarstokkur-Stóra-Vatnsskarð 15 km

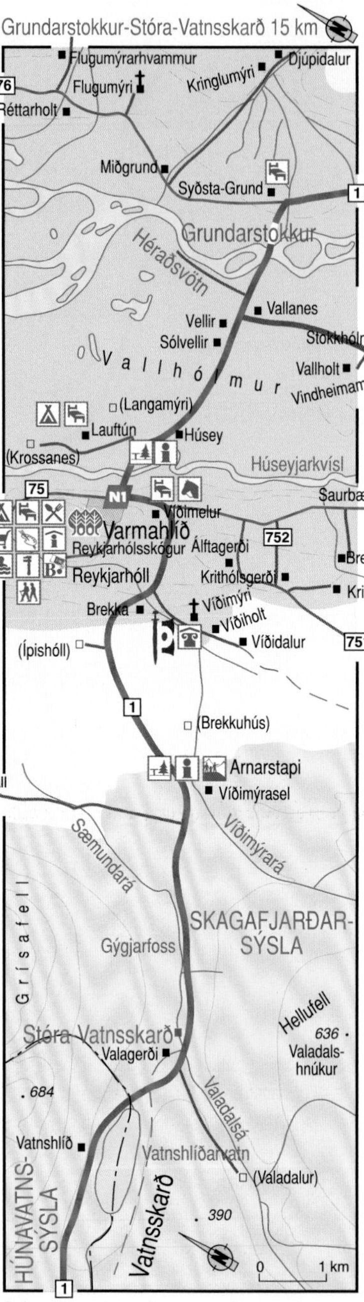

5 P. 568

4 P. 567

Stóra-Vatnsskarð-Grundarstokkur 15 km

Grundarstokkur, the bridged part of the many-armed river Héraðsvötn. It was bridged in 1937. A new bridge by Vellir took over in 1981, it is 188m long.

Vellir, a farm in Hólmur. The birthplace of the historian Gísli Konráðsson (1787–1877).

753 Vindheimavegur, 6,88 km to road 752.

Vallhólmur, (or Hólmur) the flat area between the rivers Héraðsvötn and Húseyjarkvísl.

Langamýri, a farm and a holiday home run by the state church. Birthplace of the grammarian Konráð Gíslason (1808-91). He was one of a group of writers and poets who led the national awakening to the importance of maintaining the Icelandic language and gaining sovereignty.

Húseyjarkvísl, a clear river formed by many smaller rivers originating on distant Eyvindarstaðaheiði moor.

Varmahlíð, (pop. 128) a community that has been built up at the crossroads during recent years. Geothermal heat, swimming pool sport cenre, hotel, information centre, grocery store and a gas station. A very good view from the hill **Reykjarhóll** (111 m) a short distance above Varmahlíð in Reykjarhólsskógur.

Reykjarhólsskógur, a forest rich in diversity, linked to a larger outdoor recreation area in Varmahlíð.

Víðimýri, a farm and church. A place of historical importance for centuries, and frequently the home of outstanding leaders, among them Kolbeinn ungi Arnórsson and Kolbeinn Tumason. The church was built 1834 and is one of the most precious gems of Icelandic architecture. In the keeping of the National Museum since 1936. The church is open for guests in the summer.

Brekka, from there came the poet Andrés Björnsson (1883–1916).

Brekkuhús, formerly sheep-cots belonging to the nearby farm Brekka. The poet Bólu-Hjálmar (1796-1875) died there.

Arnarstapi, ("Eagle crag") a hill at the eastern end of Vatnsskarð and a very good viewpoint. A memorial to the poet Stephan G. Stephansson (1853-1927) has been erected on the hill. Stephan lived for a while in nearby **Víðimýrarsel** and later emigrated to Canada; he is now often called Klettafjallaskáldið or "The poet of the Rocky Mountains".

Valadalsá, a river flowing from the valley Valadalur. It becomes the river **Sæmundará**, in which is the waterfall **Gýgjarfoss**.

75 Sauðárkróksbraut, p. 323	**76 Siglufjarðarvegur,** p. 327
751 Efribyggðarvegur, p. 353	**752 Skagafjarðarvegur,** p. 353

1 NORÐURLANDSVEGUR

Miklibær, a farm, church and parsonage, often mentioned in the Sagas and the stage for various dramas through the ages. In 1786, for instance, Rev. Oddur Gíslason (1740-1786) disappeared when travelling from one farm to another and was never seen again. The female ghost Solveig was blamed. She had been a maid in his household, fallen in love with him, been rejected, gone mad and finally cut her own throat, after which she haunted Oddur wherever he went, especially in the dark. Solveig's remains were found in the churchyard wall in 1937 and given a Christian burial at Glaumbær. The grave of the poet Bólu-Hjálmar is at Miklibær, marked with a stone monument.

Stóru-Akrar and **Minni-Akrar,** two farms. Remnants of a farmhouse built in the mid 18th century for Skúli Magnússon, later Treasurer, known as the Father of Reykjavík. The living room, entrance building and corridors are of a late type of stave construction. In the keeping of the National Museum since 1954. The poet Bólu-Hjálmar lived at Minni-Akrar for 27 years. Formerly a ferry point. Community centre Héðinsminni.

Haugsnes, an abandoned farm on the south banks of the river Djúpá. In 1246 this was the site of the battle Haugsnesbardagi, where Þórður kakali and Brandur Kolbeinsson fought, with the loss of Brandur and 105 of his men, the greatest loss of life in any battle ever fought in Iceland.

Djúpidalur, a substantial farm for centuries, in a valley of the same name. Owned by the same family since 1733. The river, Djúpadalsá, coming from the valley used to be a bad obstacle until the bridge was built.

Glóðafeykir, (990 m) an impressive mountain, steep and rocky, above Flugumýri. The story goes that Helga Sigurðardóttir, mistress of the catholic bishop Jón Arason, hid out on this mountain while Danish warships were in the north in 1551, the summer after Jón was beheaded in the struggles of the Reformation.

Flugumýri, a farm and a church, an important place since early times. For a while the home of Earl Gissur Þorvaldsson, the only Icelander to have been titled "Earl". In 1253 the farm was burned down (Flugumýrarbrenna, "The burning of Flugumýri"), when his opponents tried to take his life. Formerly the official meeting-place for the priests of the diocese of Hólar. Above the farm is **Virkishóll** ("Fort Hill"), a name probably given to the hill in the time of Earl Gissur. At Flugumýri is a horse breeding farm from where the well know stead Ófeigur 882 is from.

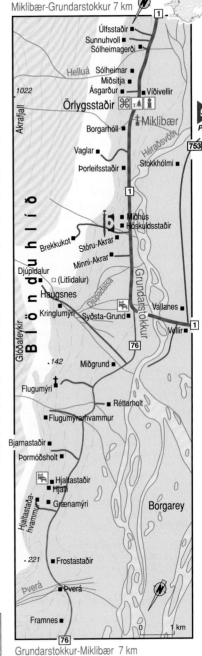

Miklibær-Grundarstokkur 7 km

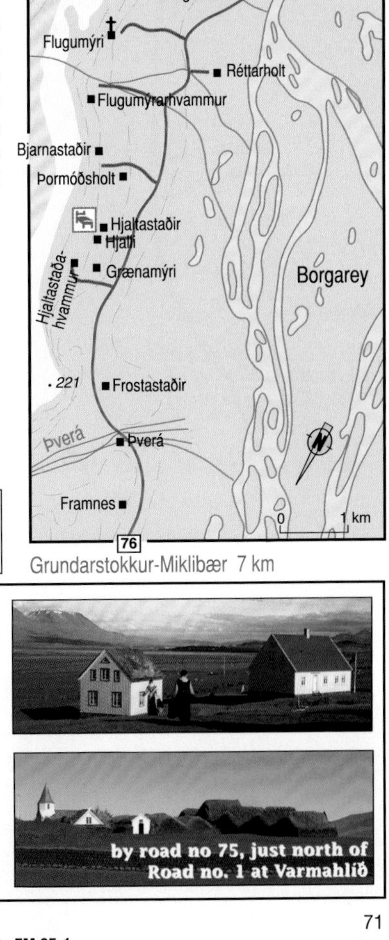

Grundarstokkur-Miklibær 7 km

5 P. 568

76 Siglufjarðarvegur, p. 329

753 Vindheimavegur, p. 70

Silfrastaðir-Miklibær 10 km

Tyrfingsstaða-bunga
Stekkjarflatir
Keldudand
(Tyrfingsstaðir)
Egilsá
Kjálki
759
Egilsá
Norðurá
1
5 p. 568
Flatatunga
.712
759
Skeljungssteinn
Silfrastaðafjall
Silfrastaðir
Sólheimafjall
Héraðsvötn
208.
(Bóla)
Bólugil
Litli-Dalur
Laugardalur
Uppsalir
Héraðsdalur
Kúskerpi
1
Úlfsstaðir
754
Sunnuhvoll
Sólheimagerði
Sólheimar
Héraðsvötn
Miðsitja
Miðsitjuskarð
Ásgarður
Örlygsstaðir
Víðivellir
.202
Borgarhóll
Miklibær
Vaglar
0 1 km
1

Miklibær-Silfrastaðir 10 km

Silfrastaðir, a church and a substantial farm. The turf-roofed church which was formerly at Silfrastaðir is now located in Reykjavík (local history) Museum. The present church at Silfrastaðir is a curiously constructed octagonal timber building dating from about 1900. Below the road, not far from the farm, there is a big stone, **Skeljungssteinn**. According to folktales the ghost Skeljungur was tied to it, two holes through the stone being the proof of this.

Bóla, a farm where the poet Hjálmar Jónsson (1796-1875), lived for some time and from which he got his name, Bólu-Hjálmar. A memorial to him has been erected by the road. The farm is named for the slave-woman, possibly a giantess, Bóla from Silfrastaðir, who escaped and hid in the rocky canyon Bólugil above the farm, from where she made forays to steal farmers' crops and cattle until she was finally killed by Skeljungur, the shepherd (and later ghost, see above) at Silfrastaðir. The canyon is very rugged with many waterfalls, some of which can be seen from the road.

Örlygsstaðir, an important historical site with some ruins a short distance above the home-field of Víðivellir. This was the scene of one of the most fateful battles of old, Örlygsstaðabardagi, in 1238, when Sturla Sighvatsson was killed together with his father and brothers and about 60 others. Memorial to the battle.

Víðivellir, an old manor farm, often a parsonage, the seat of district judges and other magistrates. The home of the Rev. Pétur Pétusson (1754-1842) who was the first person to grow potatoes in Skagafjörður. Birthplace of Gottskálk, father of the famous sculptor Bertel Thorvaldsen who was half Danish and lived in Denmark.

754 **Héraðsdalsvegur,** p. 353 759 **Kjálkavegur,** p. 354

Stóru-Akrar p. 71 ©ÞMS

The Ferryman at Héraðsvötn ©ÞGA

Egilsá.

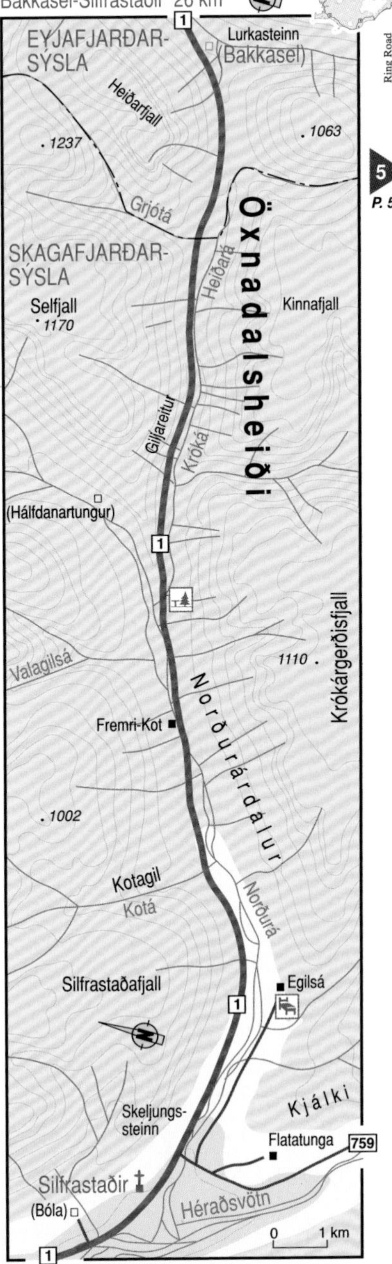

5
P. 568

Grjótá, a small river on Öxnadalsheiði, dividing the counties Eyjafjarðarsýsla and Skagafjarðarsýsla.

Öxnadalsheiði, the moor and valley connecting Norðurárdalur and Öxnadalur. The highest point of the road is about 540 m.

Hörgárdalsheiði, a moor and valley connecting Norðurárdalur and Hörgárdalur. There is an old mountain trail over Hörgárdalsheiði.

Hálfdanartungur, an abandoned farm in Norðurárdalur, said to be haunted.

Valagilsá, a small river that emerges from a narrow and deep canyon, not far from Fremri-Kot. In 1954, when there were landslides and rivers were in spate, the river broke down the bridge.

Fremri-Kot, a farm in Norðurárdalur and now the only farm on the north side of the river. Ytri-Kot, abandoned after a big landslide in 1954, is believed to be the Þorbrandsstaðir mentioned in *Landnámabók* ("The Book of Settlements"), a farm where food was free for all travellers.

Norðurárdalur, a narrow mountain valley east of Silfrastaðir. Trout-fishing in the river.

Kotagil, one of the most magnificent canyons by the road between Reykjavík and Akureyri.

Egilsá, the only farm on the south side of the river.

Kjálki, the district on the east side of Héraðsvötn, from the River Norðurá to Merkigil in Austurdalur.

Flatatunga, a farm in the Kjálki district. Some very old wood carvings preserved there considered to be a detail from *The Last Judgement* carved in the 11th century in Byzantine style. Now in the National Museum.

759 **Kjálkavegur,** p. 354

Ring Road
5
P. 568

Steinsstaðir-Bakkasel 18 km

Bakkasel-Steinsstaðir 18 km

Hraundrangi

Öxnadalur, a deep and narrow valley about 35 km long with high mountains on both sides. Around the middle of the valley are numerous mounds, the debris from old landslides.

Bakki, a farm and a church on the west side of the river. Around 1200 the home of Guðmundur dýri, well-known for both his quarrels and his great enterprise. The church, built in 1843, is the oldest in the Eyjafjörður ditrict.

Steinsstaðir, a farm where the 19th century poet and naturalist Jónas Hallgrímsson lived as a young man. Trees have been planted there in his memory. View dial. The waterfall **Gljúfrabúi** ("Canyon dweller") in the gully nearby.

Þverá, a farm and a river of the same name. From there leads an old riding trail over Kambsskarð to Skjóldalur.

Hraundrangi, (1,075 m) a pinnacle on the rocky mountain ridge between Öxnadalur and Hörgárdalur. According to legend a treasure chest was hidden there waiting for the first climber to fetch it. Hraundrangi was first climbed in 1956 by a party of three, an American and two Icelanders, but none of them appeared to be richer after the ascent. The flat area on top of it turned out to be less than 0.5 m^2.

Hraun, a farm in the hills on the west side of the river, birthplace of Jónas Hallgrímsson (1807-45), naturalist and one of the most important Romantic poets in Iceland. **Hraunsvatn**, a good trout-fishing lake 50-60 m deep, is in the valley behind the hills. Hallgrímur, father of Jónas, drowned in it.

Þverbrekka, abandoned farm on the west side of the river, once the home of Víga-Glúmur of Saga times. **Þverbrekkuhnjúkur** (1,142 m), one of the highest and most rugged mountains in the vicinity is above the farm. There is a guest book in a cairn at the top of the peak. Above some small hills on the side of the mountain is a small lake **Þverbrekkuvatn**.

Lurkasteinn, a rock not far from Bakkasel, where Þórður hreða killed Sörli sterki in Saga times. It is said that travellers who are passing the rock for the first time should through a stone in its direction and say a prayer before heading on the Öxnadalsheiði moor.

Bakkasel, formerly a farm and an inn, now abandoned.

1 NORÐURLANDSVEGUR

Laugaland, a farm which is mentioned in the Sagas. Geothermal heat. Swimming pool.
Vaglir, self-sowing birch and willows have spread after being protected. Also a planted forest of larch, pine and spruce. National Forest.
Vindheimaöxl, an impressive rocky ridge above the farm Vindheimar ("Home of the wind"). A small glacier, **Vindheimajökull,** south of there, its highest points **Strýta** (1,451 m) and **Kista** (1,447 m). The rivers Húsá and Fossá flow from the glacier, the two separate valleys derive their names from the rivers. Good mountaineering country.
Ytri-Bægisá, a farm, church and parsonage until 1941. Among the clergymen who served there were Jón Þorláksson (1744-1819) and Arnljótur Ólafsson (1823-1904). Jón was an outstanding poet and the translator of many works, among them *Paradise Lost* by Milton and *Messias* by Klopstock.
Hörgárdalur, a valley about 50 km long on the west side of Eyjafjörður, high mountains with small glaciers on both sides. Good fishing in the river Hörgá, which usually has some glacial water in it.
Bægisá, a river joining Öxnadalsá between the farms Ytri-and Syðri-Bægisá. Bægisá flows from the glacier **Bægisárjökull** at the end of Bægisárdalur, a valley surrounded by majestic mountains: **Landafjall,** a narrow ridge between the valleys Bægisárdalur and Öxnadalur on the west, and on the east, the mountain **Tröllafjall** ("Giants' mountain") (1,471 m), which also dominates Glerárdalur above Akureyri on the east side. This is magnificent mountaineering country.
Miðhálsstaðir, an abandoned farm, now used for experiments in forestry by the Forestry Association of Eyjafjörður.

814 **Staðarbakkavegur,** p. 390 815 **Hörgárdalsvegur,** p. 390

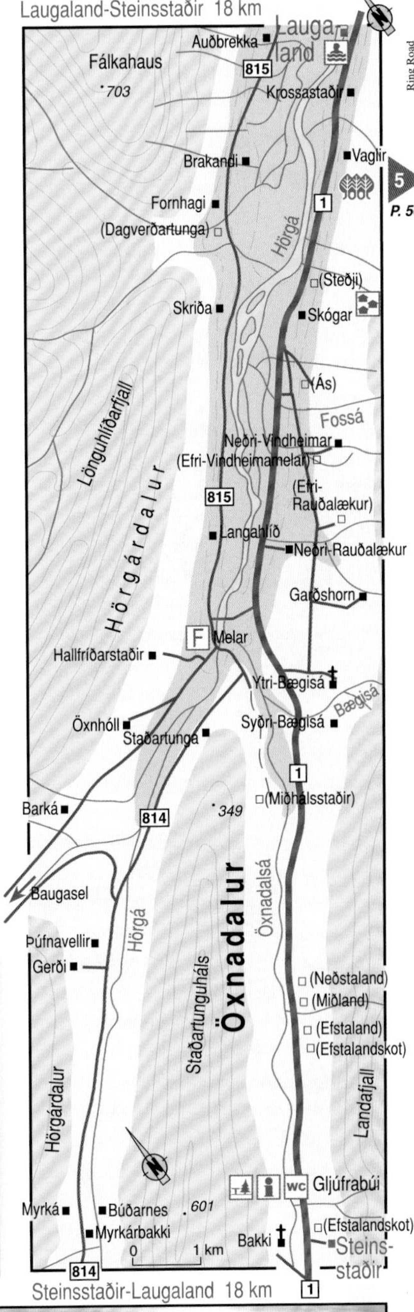

Akureyri-Laugaland 13 km

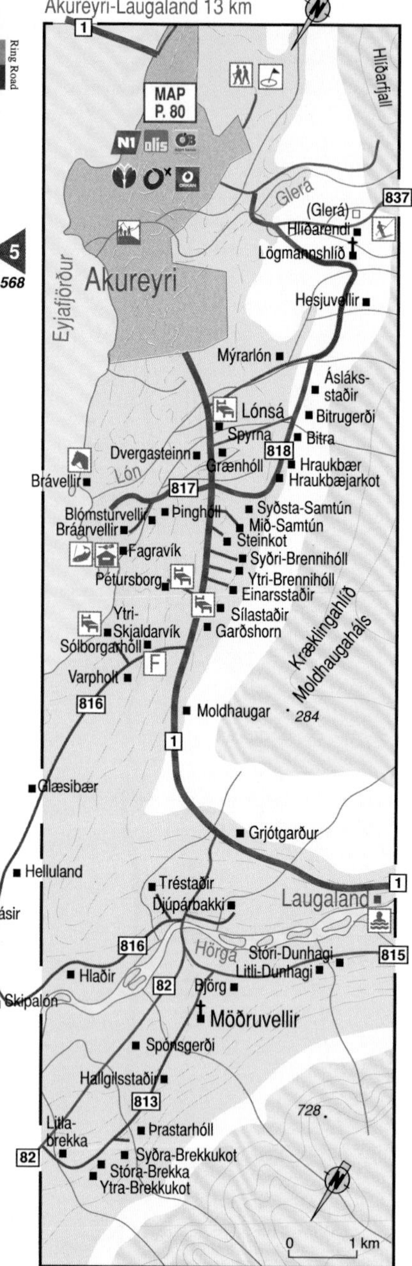

Laugaland-Akureyri 13 km

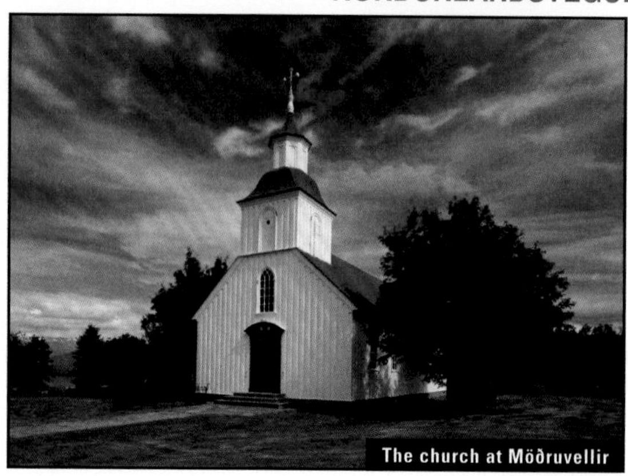
The church at Möðruvellir

Glerárdalur, a long uninhabited valley above Lögmannshlíð, surrounded by the highest mountains in the north of Iceland, the highest being **Kerling** (1,538 m), **Tröllafjall** and **Vindheimajökull** from 1,100 to 1,400 m high. Magnificent outdoor area both in summer and winter. The Akureyri Ski Resort is on the lower slopes of the mountain **Hlíðarfjall**. Fossils have been found in the valley. The river Glerá emerges from the valley and flows through the northern outskirts of Akureyri.

837 Hlíðarfjallsvegur, 7,5 km. Leads to Hlíðarfjall Ski Resort which is open November - April. Good view of the town Akureyri.

Lögmannshlíð, a farm and a church with an interesting 17th century altar-piece.

817 Blómsturvallavegur, 1,65 km. **818 Hlíðarvegur,** 2,5 km.

Sólborgarhóll, a community centre, Hlíðarbær.

Kræklingahlíð, a mountain side from Hörgárósar to Glerá. On top of it lies **Hlíðarfjall** and **Stórihnjúkur**, 912 m.

Moldhaugnaháls, ("Heaps-of-earth ridge") a low mountain ridge between Hörgárdalur and Kræklingahlíð. Coming from the west, the view opens towards Akureyri. A war memorial was erected there by British soldiers in 1942 to commemorate their stay in Iceland.

Möðruvellir, a substantial farm of great historical importance for many centuries. Church and parsonage. See p. 357.

82 Ólafsfjarðarvegur, p. 357
813 Möðruvallavegur, p. 357
815 Hörgárdalsvegur, p. 389
816 Dagverðareyrarv., p. 389

www.visitakureyri.is

Hof Cultural and Conference Center | 600 Akureyri | ☎450 1050 | info@visitakureyri.is

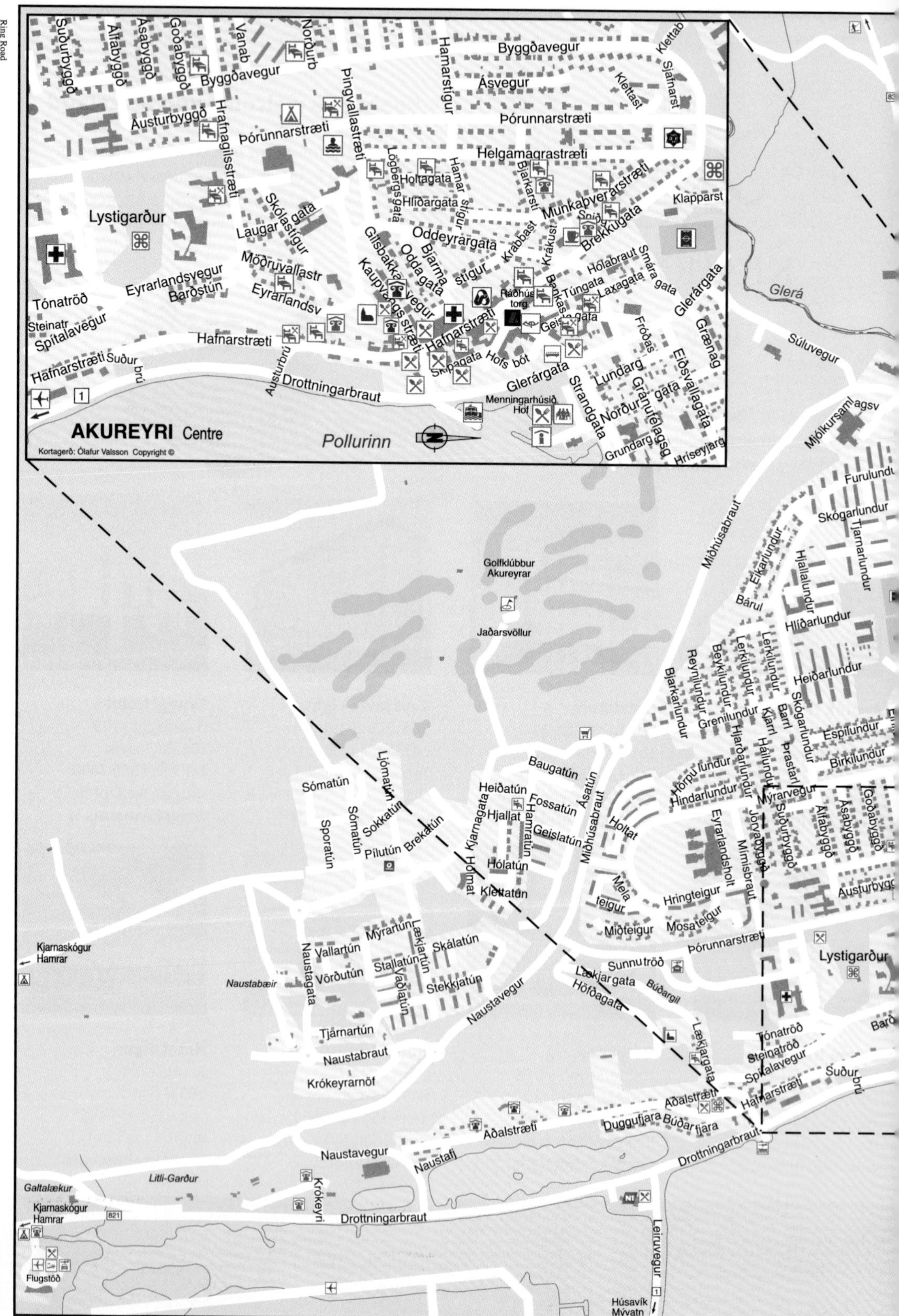
AKUREYRI Centre
Kortagerð: Ólafur Valsson Copyright ©
Pollurinn
Suðurbyggð
Álfabyggð
Ásabyggð
Goðabyggð
Vanab
Norðurb
Byggðavegur
Austurbyggð
Hrafnagilsstræti
Þórunnarstræti
Þingvallastræti
Hamarstígur
Ásvegur
Klettab
Sjafnarst
Klettast
Helgamagrastræti
Lögbergsgata
Holtagata
Hlíðargata
Hamarstígur
Bjarkarstígur
Munkaþverárstræti
Klapparst
Lystigarður
Skólastígur
Laugargata
Oddeyrargata
Brekkugata
Möðruvallastr
Eyrarlandsvegur
Barðstún
Eyrarlandsv
Tónatröð
Steinatr
Spítalavegur
Hafnarstræti
Suður brú
Austurbrú
Drottningarbraut
Gilsbakkavegur
Kaupvangsstræti
Oddagata
Bjarmastígur
Krabbast
Krákust
Hólabraut
Smáragata
Ráðhústorg
Túngata
Laxagata
Glerárgata
Grænag
Fróðas
Skipagata
Hofsbót
Menningarhúsið Hof
Strandgata
Lundarg
Eiðsvallagata
Gránufélagsg
Norðurg
Grundarg
Hríseyjarg
Glerá
Súluvegur
Mjólkursamlagsv
Miðhúsabraut
Furulundur
Skógarlundur
Tjarnarlundur
Hjallalundur
Eikarlundur
Bárul
Hlíðarlundur
Heiðarlundur
Golfklúbbur Akureyrar
Jaðarsvöllur
Reynilundur
Beykilundur
Lerkilundur
Bjarkarlundur
Grenilundur
Kjarri
Barrl
Skógarlundur
Espilundur
Birkilundur
Hjarðarlundur
Hálundur
Þrastarl
Hörpulundur
Hindarlundur
Mýrarvegur
Suðurbyggð
Álfabyggð
Ásabyggð
Goðabyggð
Jörvabyggð
Eyrarlandsholt
Mímisbraut
Austurbyggð
Baugatún
Ásatún
Heiðatún
Fossatún
Hjallat
Hamratún
Geislatún
Miðhúsabraut
Holtat
Sómatún
Ljómatún
Sokkatún
Sporatún
Pílutún
Brekatún
Kjarnagata
Hólatún
Hólmat
Klettatún
Melateigur
Hringteigur
Miðteigur
Mosateigur
Þórunnarstræti
Lystigarður
Sunnutröð
Lækjargata
Höfðagata
Búðargil
Mýrartún
Vallartún
Lækjartún
Skálatún
Stallatún
Vörðutún
Vaðlatún
Stekkjatún
Naustagata
Naustabæir
Naustavegur
Tjarnartún
Naustabraut
Krókeyrarnöf
Kjarnaskógur Hamrar
Tónatröð
Steinatröð
Spítalavegur
Hafnarstræti
Suður brú
Aðalstræti
Duggufjara
Búðarfjara
Drottningarbraut
Naustafj
Naustavegur
Litli-Garður
Galtalækur
Krókeyri
821
Leiruvegur
Flugstöð
Húsavík Mývatn
1

AKUREYRI
www.akureyri.is
Kortagerð: Ólafur Valsson Copyright ©
Reykjavík
Eyjafjörður
Pollurinn
Glerá
600
603
Borgarsíða
Bakkasíða
Bæjarsíða
Búðarsíða
Bogasíða
Móðusíða
Vestursíða
Brekkusíða
Bröttusíða
Síðubraut
Móasíða
Rimasíða
Múlasíða
Miðsíða
Reykjasíða
Austursíða
Þverasíða
Frostagata
Melasíða
Flögusíða
Fagrasíða
Flatasíða
Hörgárbraut
Bugðusíða
Lindasíða
Fjölnisgata
Draupnisgata
Hlíðarbraut
Baldursnes
Njarðarnes
Goðanes
Freyjunes
Fannagil
Fálkagil
Fornagil
Urðargil
Víkurgil
Fossagil
Skottugil
Merkigil
Valagil
Vesturgil
Vörðugil
Skriðugil
Skessugil
Vættagil
Skútagil
Skuggagil
Snægil
Huldugil
Kiðagil
Drekagil
Tröllagil
Dvergagil
Réttarhv
Borgarbraut
Núpasíða
Kjalarsíða
Keilusíða
Stapasíða
Ekrusíða
Tungusíða
Teigarsíða
Arnarsíða
Bakkahlíð
Sunnuhlíð
Brattah
Fosshlíð
Mánahlíð
Barmah
Steinahlíð
Smárahlíð
Skarðshlíð
Seljahlíð
Litlahlíð
Sólborg Háskólinn á Akureyri
Norðurslóð
Hvammsh
Borgarh
Drangsh
Höfðahlíð
Hraunholt
Hlíðarbraut
Dalsbraut
Háhlíð
Harðarangur
Áshlíð
Langahlíð
Einholt
Krossanesbraut
Langholt
Þverholt
Stafholt
Miðholt
Bárufell
Sæberg
Undirhlíð
Stórholt
Lynghol
Skálag
Kambagerði
Kolgerði
Klettagerði
Kleifargerði
Grundargerði
Kristagerði
Hraungerði
Stóragerði
Hólsgerði
Háagerði
Dalsgerði
Hamragerði
Akurgerði
Stekkjargerði
Kotárgerði
Klettaborg
Mýrarvegur
Kambsmýri
Engimýri
Kringlumýri
Grænamýri
Rauðamýri
Víðimýri
Langamýri
Hrafnabj
Norðurbyggð
Þingvallastræti
Byggðavegur
Ásvegur
Klettast
Sjafnarst
Hamarstígur
Þórunnarstræti
Helgamagrastræti
Lögbergsg
Holtagata
Bjarkarst
Munkaþverárstræti
Klapparst
Hlíðargata
Oddeyrargata
Krabbast
Brekkugata
Krákust
Hólabraut
Smárag
Bjarmast
Tungata
Laxag
Geislag
Ráðhústorg
Hafnarst
Hofsbót
Skipagata
Glerárgata
Lundarg
Fróðasu
Drottningarbraut
Austurbrú
Strandgata
Norðurgata
Eiðsvallagata
Gránufélagsgata
Grundarg
Hríseyjarg
Hjalteyrargata
Kaldbaksgata
Laufásgata
Grímseyjarg
Sjávargata
Oddeyrarbryggja
Glerárgata
Hvannavellir
Tryggvabraut
Þórsstígur
Furuvellir
Árstígur
Víðivellir
Reynivellir
Eyrarvegur
Grænagata
Fjólugata
Norðurgata
Ránargata
Ægisgata
Grenivellir
Skipatangi
Naustatangi
Norður tangi
Vesturbakki
Austurbakki
Fiskitangi
Silfurtangi
Krossanesbraut
Óseyri
Ósvör
Sandgerðisbót

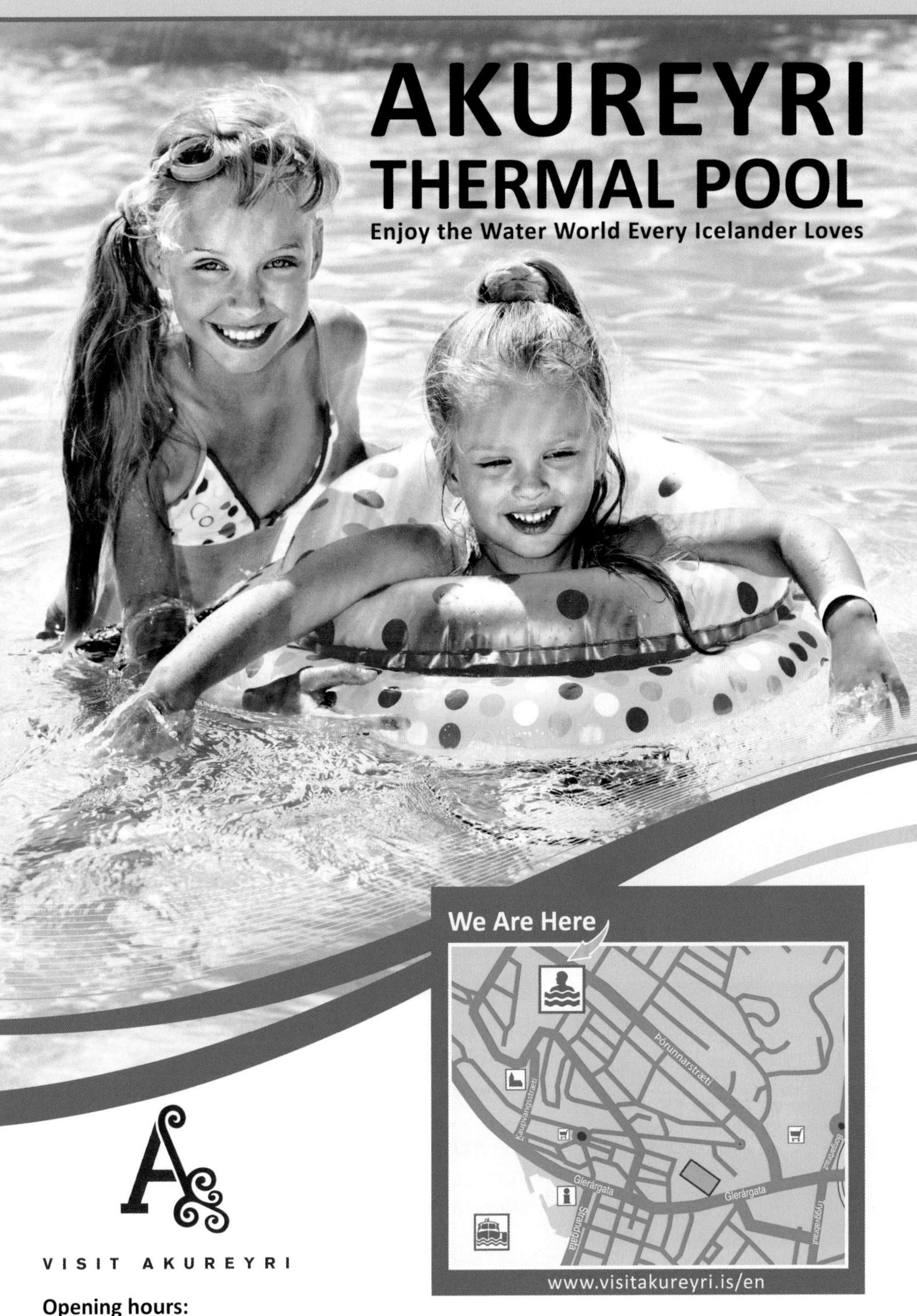
AKUREYRI
THERMAL POOL
Enjoy the Water World Every Icelander Loves
We Are Here
Þórunnarstræti
Kaupvangsstræti
Glerárgata
Glerárgata
Strandgata
Borgarbraut
Tryggvabraut
www.visitakureyri.is/en
VISIT AKUREYRI

The writer's homes

Memorial Musems at Nonnahús, Davíðshús and Sigurhæðir.
Dedicated to the writers who use to live there,
Nonni, Matthías Jochumssons and Davíð Stefánsson.

Nonnahús

Aðalstræti 54, 600 Akureyri
☎ 462-3555 & 462-4162
nonni@nonni.is • **www.nonni.is**

The museum is open every day from 10:00 - 17:00, from June 1st till September 1st. Other times by arrangement.

Davíðshús

Bjarkarstígur 6, 600 Akureyri
☎ 462-4162 • minjasafnid@minjasafnid.is
www.minjasafnid.is

The museum is open every day from 13:00 - 17:00, from June 1st till August 31st. Other times by arrangement.

Sigurhæðir

Eyrarlandsvegur 3, 600 Akureyri
☎ 462-6649 & 462-4162
minjasafnid@minjasafnid.is • **www.minjasafnid.is**

The museum is open every day from 13:00 - 17:00, from June 1st till August 31st. Other times by arrangement.

Ask for a Day or an Annual pass for all the Museums. They are available at the Museums, Tourist Info in Hof and Saga Travel Info office.

1 NORÐURLANDSVEGUR

Vaðlaskógur, woodland on the east shore of Pollurinn.

Hallland, the southernmost farm along Svalbarðsströnd. The poet Hjálmar Jónsson (Bólu-Hjálmar) was born there in 1796, when his mother sought shelter for one night.

Akureyri, (pop. 18,342) is the second largest urban area, after the capital area of Reykjavík, and the centre of trade and services in northern Iceland. It is also a town of culture and education, often called a school town as it boasts many educational estabishments, including a university. Fishing and fish processing centres also make their mark on the town. The original "Akureyri" is a small gravel bank below Búðargil formed from the deposits of a creek flowing through the gulley. The market town's first settlement was built there, and the town's oldest house, Laxdalshús at Hafnarstræti 11, can still be found at this location. The house was built in 1795. There are records of trade in Akureyri going as far back as 1602. In 1787 the town gained municipal rights, and it obtained its municipal charter in 1862, since then it has had its own town council. Akureyri is heated with geothermal water coming from Laugaland and Hjalteyri in Eyjafjörður. There is contiguous open area around Akureyri where the biosphere and landscape are extremely diverse, and vegetation in many places is especially lush. In the urban area there are also interesting natural features, and on the hills of Akureyri there are many intriguing plants. Within the Akureyri town limits there are many interesting recreation areas and hiking paths. The Akureyri Botanical Garden is known far and wide for its beautiful walking paths and luxuriant flora. One of Akureyri's gems, it was founded in 1912, and it contains nearly every plant found in Iceland ca. 450 and nearly 7,000 foreign plants. The town has many museums, e.g. notable museums like Akureyri Museum, Aviation Museum, Industrial Museum, Motorcycle Museum, Art Museum, Nonni Museum, Memorial Museums Sigurhæð and Davíðshús commemoration the life's of two of Iceland's most loved poets. There are also galleries and exhibitions who offers insight in the diversity of the culture and the nation as a whole. Visitors can choose between varied accommodation and excellent range of restaurants, some of which specialise in local food. Akureyri also boasts one of Iceland's most popular swimming facilities, 18-hole golf course, the best skiing area in the country and free city bus. The town is a good base for many of Iceland's most beautiful natural wonders as waterfalls, volcanic areas and canyons. Selection of exciting activities as river rafting, hiking, fishing, whale watching and horse riding as well as tours to local villages and national parks, northern light tours and visits to the small island in the fjord. Akureyri and the surrounding area offers a number of annual events as well as many occasional concerts, exhibitions, theatre ect. For more details visit the event calender at **www.visitakureyri.is/en**.

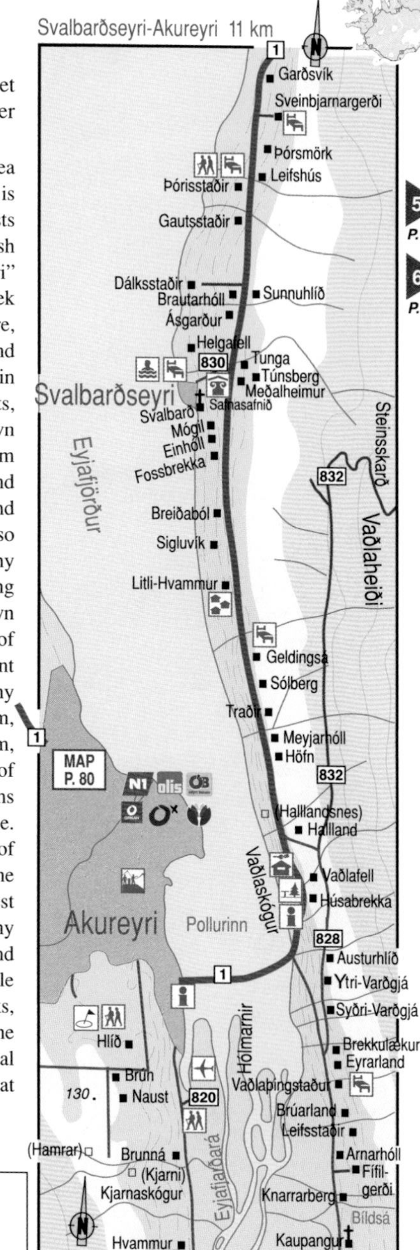

5 P. 568
6 P. 569

820 Flugvallarvegur, p. 391	**821 Eyjafj. braut vestri,** p. 391
828 Veigastaðavegur, p. 394	**829 Eyjafj. braut eystri,** p. 394
830 Svalbarðseyrarvegur, p. 86	**832 Vaðlaheiðarvegur,** p. 86, 396

Ring Road
5 P. 568
6 P. 569

Víkurskarð-Svalbarðseyri 10 km

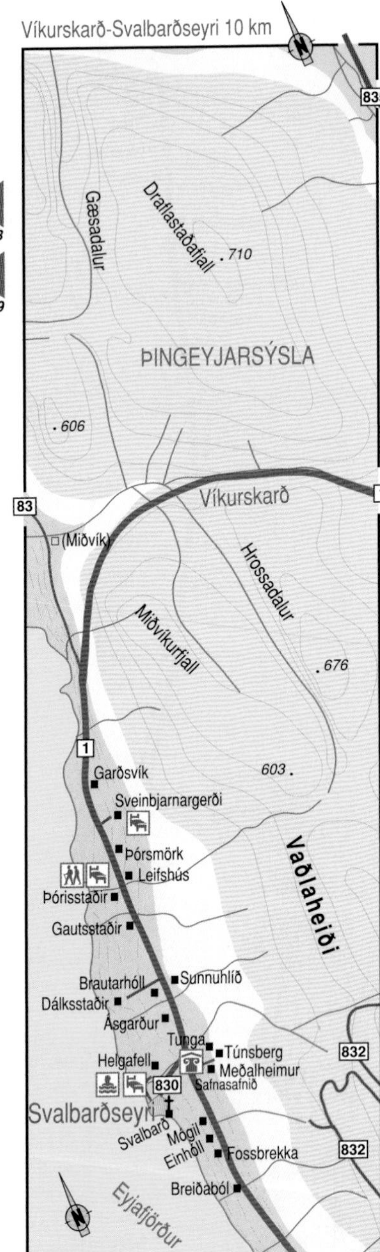

Svalbarðseyri-Víkurskarð 10 km

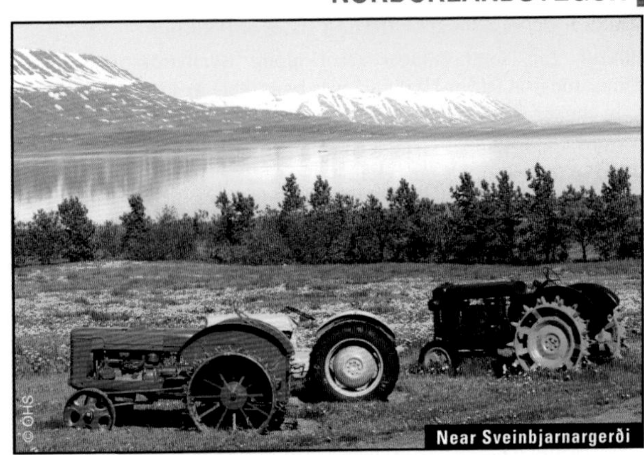

Near Sveinbjarnargerði

Víkurskarð, (325 m) a fairly wide pass in the mountain range between the Svalbarðsströnd coast and Fnjóskadalur.

Svalbarðsströnd, a coast and mountainside east of Eyjafjörður, below Vaðlaheiði, between the farms Varðgjá and Miðvík at Víkurskarð. The northernmost part of it is commonly called Kjálki. Very little lowland though there are some broad terraces in the mountainside, providing a good deal of space for cultivation in the southern parts. Grassy areas along the coast, many farms.

Vaðlaheiði, (600-700 m) the mountain range on the east side of Eyjafjörður between the passes Víkurskarð to the north and Bíldsárskarð to the south. Mostly quite grassy. The view from Vaðlaheiði across the fjord towards Akureyri with its backdrop of majestic mountains is renowned. A tunnel beneath Vaðlaheiði heath is under construction. The project has run into a series of setbacks, including huge amounts of hot water flooding the tunnel.

Svalbarðseyri, (pop. 326) a village. A former trading place and a herring-salting station. At Svalbarðseyri you will find a meat processing plant, a base for contractors, public service, a guesthouses, an elementary school, a swimming pool and sports facilities. There is a beautiful forest grove at the turn-off to Svalbarðseyri as well as Safnasafnið, an interesting folk art gallery, housed in the old local assembly building, displaying folk art and special collections like embroidery, models, souvenirs, books, dolls, toys and tools. The museum is open during the summer. The beach by the village provides an excellent location for bird watching in two picturesque ponds.

Svalbarð, church and ancient manor farm. Geothermal heat.

832 Vaðlaheiðarvegur, the old road over Vaðlaheiði, to Fnjóskadalur.

830 Svalbarðseyrarvegur, 1 km.

83 Grenivíkurvegur, p. 365 **835 Fnjóskadalsvegur eystri,** p. 397

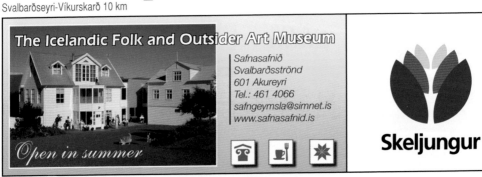

The old bridge at Fnjóská

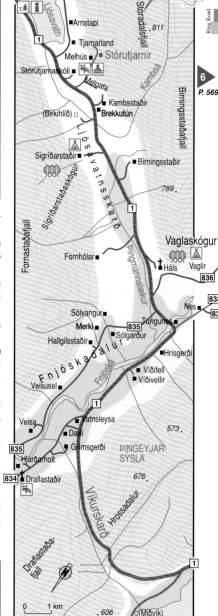

Stórutjarnir, ("Big ponds") a farm in the eastern section of Ljósavatnsskarð. Geothermal heat, swimming pool, school and a summer hotel.

Ljósavatnsskarð, ("Lake of lights pass") a wide valley open at both ends, connecting Fnjóskadalur and Bárðardalur. Widespread birch bushes on the mountain slopes.

Sigríðarstaðaskógur, on the land of **Sigríðarstaðir** with extensive birchwoods, which are now protected by the Forestry Service. National forest.

Háls, farm, church and parsonage. Above the farm is the mountain **Hálshnjúkur** (682 m).

Vaglaskógur, one of two major birchwood forests in Iceland, about 300 hectares or 750 acres, highest trees 12-13 m. Centre of the Forestry Service. Summer outings and gatherings are held there. Campsites. Marked walking routes. National forest.

Fnjóskárbrú, the old concrete arch bridge on the river Fnjóská built 1908, at that time the longest bridge of its type in Scandinavia. Now a footbridge. A new arch bridge was opened in the year 2000. It is the longest bridge of its kind in Iceland. The new bridge near Nes was opened in 1969.

Fnjóskadalur, a long and narrow valley with steep scree mountains on the east side. Long gravel ridges along the slopes, old tidemarks from the ice age, when there was a lake in the valley. Many farms have been abandoned during the last years and the three valleys that continue to the south, **Bleiksmýrardalur**, **Hjaltadalur** and **Timburvalladalur**, now have no functioning farms. The river Fnjóská is a good fishing river.

Stórutjarnir - Víkurskarð 19 km

Arnstapi
Tjarnarland
Melhús
Stórutjarnir
Stórutjarnaskóli
Ljósavatn
Stóradalsfjall
811
Melgata
Kambsá
Kambsstaðir
Brekkutún
(Birkihlíð)
Ljósavatnsskarð
Birningsstaðafjall
Sigríðarstaðir
Birningsstaðir
Sigríðarstaðaskógur
789
Fornastaðafjall
Fornhólar
Þingmannalækur
Vaglaskógur
Háls
Vaglir
836
833
Nes
832
Sólvangur
Merki
835
Tungunes
Sólgarður
Hallgilsstaðir
Hrísgerði
Fnjóskadalur
Fnjóská
Víðifell
Víðivellir
Veisusel
1
Veisa
Vatnsleysa
Dæli
573
835
Grímsgerði
ÞINGEYJARSÝSLA
Hjarðarholt
834
Draflastaðir
676
Víkurskarð
Hrossadalur
Draflastaðafjall
1
0 1 km
606
83
(Miðvík)

Víkurskarð - Stórutjarnir 19 km

6 P. 569

Einarsstaðir-Stóru-Tjarnir 19 km

6 P. 569

Fljótsheiði, (280 m) an extensive and long but low mountain range, green and wet in places with many small lakes. There used to be many farms in this area, now all abandoned.

Fosshóll, a farm since 1930 and a trading place. Fosshóll is a small commerce community at Goðafoss waterfall. There one can find a shop, a gas station, a restaurant, a handcrafts market as well as accommodations. This is a nice spot to stop while travelling on the highway, observe Goðafoss in the Skjálfandi River and enjoy the scenery at Ljósavatnsskarð Passage where there are several historical sites, such as Ljósavatn Lake and Þorgeirskirkja, but this church is named after Þorgeir goði, who was the one who decided that Icelanders should switch from being heathens and become Christians. In the Skjálfandi River, a little to the north of Fosshóll, one can visit Þingey which this county and district are named after. There is an effort being made to refine the availability of information about the remarkable historical heritage which the region has to offer and there is an instructor at Þorgeirskirkja to welcome tourists and offer them information about the district.

883 **Goðafossvegur,** 0,34 km.

Goðafoss, ("Falls of the gods") among the finest in the country, not very high but cut into two horseshoe-shaped falls, Not far above the falls the river Skjálfandafljót divides in two, forming the island **Hrútey**. According to the Sagas Þorgeir of Ljósavatn threw his statues of the gods into the falls when Iceland converted to Christianity in the year 1000, hence the name. The lavafield by the falls, Bárðardalshraun, came from Trölladyngja north of Vatnajökull more than 7,000 years ago and reached as far as 100 km from the crater.

Hrifla, a farm on the banks of Skjálfandafljót. The birthplace of Jónas Jónsson (1885-1968), one of the most influential politicians of the 20th century, and a great social innovator. He founded the Progressive Party.

Djúpá, a river, runs from Ljósavatn in Skjálfandafljót.

Ljósavatn, ("Lake of lights") a deep lake, 3.28 km^2, good fishing. Farm of the same name. In the year 1000 the home of the lawspeaker and chieftain Þorgeir, who threw his idols into Goðafoss after having converted to Christianity. A new church, **Þorgeirskirkja**, was consecrated there in summer 2000, marking the 1000th anniversary of the conversion of Iceland.

Arnstapi, a farm, birthplace of Guðmundur Finnbogason (1873-1944), state librarian and renowned author.

85 **Norðausturvegur,** p. 366
841 **Fremstafellsvegur,** p. 398
842 **Bárðardalsvegur vestri,** p. 398
844 **Bárðardalsvegur eystri,** p. 398
845 **Aðaldalsvegur,** p. 400
846 **Austurhlíðarvegur,** s. 400

Stóru-Tjarnir-Einarsstaðir 19 km

Goðafoss

1 NORÐURLANDSVEGUR

Arnarvatn, a farm and a lake of the same name. Fishing permits for the **Arnarvatnsá** river can be got there.
Helluvað, one of the first farms in the Mývatn district when approaching from the west. Long the home of the poet Jón Hinriksson (1829-1921).
Hofsstaðir, a farm by Laxá and belonging to the Mývatn district. Ruins found there in 1908 believed to be a farm from the 10th or the 11th century.
Laxá, one of the best known and most popular fishing rivers in Iceland. Considered the fairest of rivers with its many grassy or wooded islands, deep pools and swift currents. Comes from Lake Mývatn and runs through Laxárdalur and Aðaldalur. Hydroelectric plant at Brúar.
Laxárdalur, a shallow but fairly narrow valley, 26 km long from Brúar to Helluvað. Laxá runs along it on a lava bed. Luxuriant vegetation.
Másvatn, a lake with good fishing above Reykjadalur, its outlet, **Máslækur,** runs into the river Reykjadalsá.
Narfastaðir, in 1995 a church bell believed to date from before 1200 was dug up there. It is made of copper and is 14,5 cm high, with the same diameter. There are very few bells of this age existing.
Kárhóll, an Aurora Observatory research centre. This is a joint project directed by Icelandic and Chinese scientists. The aim is to further advance knowledge on the phenomenon of the Aurora Borealis.

847 Stafnsvegur, 5,68 km.
Laugar, (pop. 106) a small school and commerce community in the eastern part of the Þingeyjar region. A public school was built there in 1924 which is still running. The schools dorms are used as a hotel in summer. Geothermal heat. Heating distribution. The first indoor swimming pool in the country was built there in 1925. A new outdoor swimming pool with large hot tub was built in 2005. At Laugar one can find among other things a repair shop, a gasoline station, a market, a restaurant, a savings bank and a post office. A fish drying factory is also found there which specializes in drying fish heads and other produce that are exported to Nigeria. Beautiful and peaceful surroundings.
Breiðamýri, a farm and community centre beside which is a grove of trees planted before 1920.
Einarsstaðir, a substantial farm and a church by the crossroads of Norðurlandsvegur (Road no. 1) and Aðaldalsvegur (Road no. 845). The birthplace of the Rev. Bergur Guðsteinsson, a 12th century translator of the story of Archbishop Thomas of Canterbury. Long the home of Einar Jónsson (1915-87), a well known medium and healer.

845 Aðaldalsvegur, p. 400
846 Austurhlíðarvegur, p. 400
848 Mývatnsvegur, p. 92

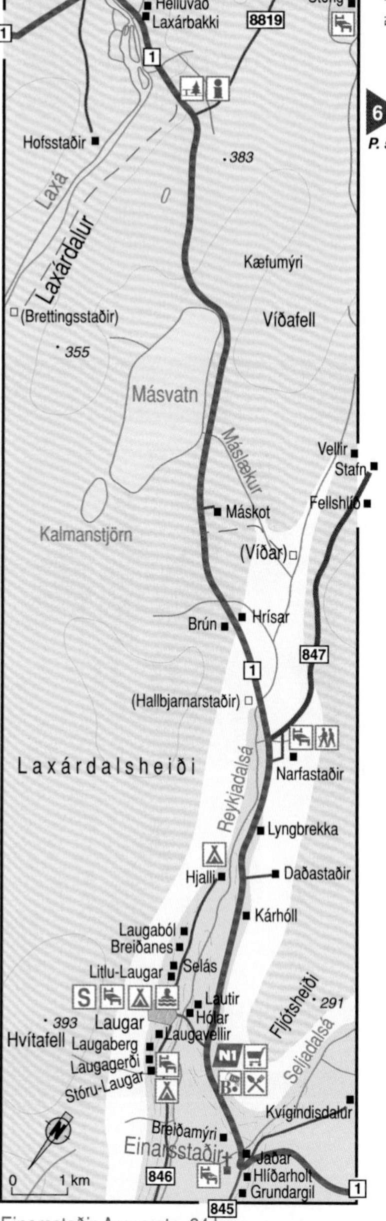

Ring Road
6 P. 569

Mývatn, ("Midge lake") among the largest lakes in Iceland, 36.5 km², altitude 277 m, with a very indented shoreline, almost cut into two halves by a long peninsula and islands. Rather shallow, the average depth being 2.5 m, 4.5 m at its deepest, with lots of diatomite (kieselguhr) in the lake bed. Many islands, islets and pseudo craters, rich plant life in the lake and around it. A greater variety of birds, especially ducks, than anywhere else in Iceland, or even a large part of the world. The lake abounds in trout and there is very good trout fishing. Lots of midges and hence the name. The surrounding area is extremely beautiful with many interesting lava fields, geothermal heat in caves and canyons and steep mountains in the background. **Reykjahlíð,** (pop. 166 in the town, 425 in the district) the "capital" of the Mývatn district, on the land of a farm claiming about 6,000 km² of land, more than any other farm in Iceland, its land reaching from the Gæsafjöll mountains and Dettifoss falls all the way to the Vatnajökull glacier. A church and formerly a parsonage. Not far from the home field of Reykjahlíð is the rift Stóragjá which has warm water in it and was a popular place for bathing, it is not suited for bathing now. One of the longest series of eruptions in the history of Iceland, Mývatnseldar ("The Lake Mývatn fires") took place near there in 1724-29. There were eruptions of lava in many places, the greatest quantity of lava coming from a crater-row associated with the mountain **Leirhnjúkur**. Lava surrounded the old church in 1729, a new church being built beyond the lava field. From 1975-84 there was a series of tremors and eruptions originating in the old volcano Kröfluaskja to the north of the lake, but no lava to speak of reached the Mývatn area.

Vindbelgur, a basalt mountain (529m) rising majestically in the landscape. A track from Vagnbrekka farm leads up the mountain. It takes about an hour to ascend the steep mountainside. A fine view from the top is your reward.

Ytri-Neslönd, there is a fine natural history museum, Sigurgeir´s Bird Museum, showcasing all of Iceland´s indigenous birds, with the exception of the Red Phalarope. The view from the museum over Mývatn is breathtaking.

Slútnes, a small island well-known for rich plant life and numerous birds. Slútnes is in the area of Grímstaðir.

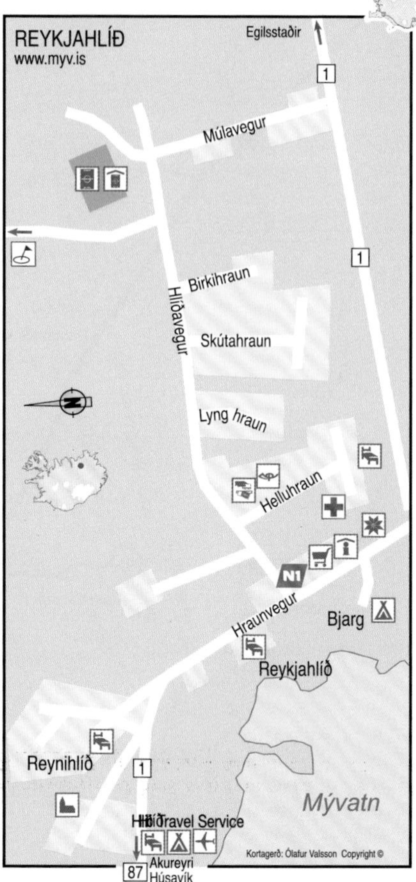

The entire Mývatn area along with the river Laxá and its banks all the way to the sea, is protected by law.

6
P. 569

87 **Kísilvegur,** p. 386

848 **Mývatnsvegur,** 20 km.

Grænavatn, ("Green lake") a farm by lake of the same name, out of which flows Grænilækur into Mývatn. The same family in the direct male line has lived at there since 1818. Large turf farmhouse from about 1913, of a late type. In the keeping of the National Museum since 2000.

Skútustaðir, church, parsonage, the Skjólbrekka community centre. Numerous craters, **Skútustaðagígar** and pseudocraters in the area which are a protected natural feature. Marked walking routes.

Heilagsdalur, shallow dale below Bláfjall. Grass, bushes and pretty streams. Lavafield to the east. It is likely that this was formerly a resting-place for travellers riding down from Ódáðahraun. Some traces of old tracks and cairns visible.

Bláfjall, (1,222 m) an old volcano.

Ódáðahraun, the largest lava-field in Iceland, extending between the glaciers Mývatnsjökull and Vatnajökull between the rivers Jökulsá and Skjálfandafljót, covering 4440 km^2. The plateau covers 800 m at its highest point and has many mountains, the highest being **Herðubreið** (1,682 m) and **Dyngjufjöll** (1,510 m).

849 **Baldursheimsvegur,** 8 km.

Baldursheimur, a farm where in 1860 an interesting pagan grave was found. This discovery was an important incentive to the founding of the National Museum.

Litlaströnd, home of the poet Jón Stefánsson (Þorgils gjallandi) (1851–1915).

Gautlönd, a farm since the original settlement. Since 1818 the same family has lived there, many of its members having been prominent politicians and local leaders.

Vogar, a farm from which came Benedikt Jónsson Gröndal, writer and Chief Justice (1762–1825).

Hverfjall, (312 m) a roundish crater about 140 m deep and 1,300 m diameter. Said to be one of the largest such craters in the world.

Dimmuborgir, ("Dark crags") a magnificent lava landscape with strange formations, columns, caves, arches, etc. It seems this was formed from a lava-lake, out of which molten lave flowed, causing much upheaval. One of the strangest spots is **Kirkjan** ("The Church"), an enormous arch. Some rich vegetation, including birch-bushes, now protected. It is easy to get lost if the marked paths are not followed. Dimmuborgir is under threat of silting up with windblown sand from the highlands, in the past parts have been totally submerged. To counteract this a conservation program was initiated and ownership handed over to the Soil Conservation Service in 1942.

Lúdentsborgir, a row of craters east of Mývatn. They are a continuation of Þrengslaborgir, having erupted at the same time. Named for the explosion crater Lúdent to the southwest, which has a diameter of 600–800 m and depth of 60–70 m. The crater rims rise about 100 m above the surrounding terrain. In 1968 Lúdentsborgir was the training area for Neil Armstrong and other astronauts before the moon landing.

Þrengslaborgir, a very impressive row of craters, north of the mountain Bláfjall, from which lava, known as Laxárhraun, flowed over the centre of the Mývatn district continued down Laxárdalur valley and north along Aðaldalur, covering a total area of 170 km^2. Believed to be 2,000 years old and Mývatn in its present form of a similar age.

Höfði, a public park on Hafurshöfði point opposite Kálfaströnd, given to the people of Mývatn by the desendents of Héðinn Valdimarsson (1892–1948), a leader of the Icelandic labour movement. Beautiful trees and garden. Magnificent views.

Kálfaströnd, a farm on a peninsula of the same name which provides some of the prettiest and most varied scenery on the Lake Mývatn shore. Many rock islands in the lake. Marked walking routes.

863 **Kröfluv.,** 7,5 km. **885** **Námaskarðsv.,** 1,3 km.

860 **Grjótagjárv.,** 4 km. **884** **Dimmuborgav.,** 1,3 km.

Stóragjá, a rift near Reykjahlíð. Used to be a popular bathing place but is not suited for bathing now.

Grjótagjá, a rift with hot water south of Jarðbaðshólar. Formerly a popular bathing place, but in the disturbances 1975-84 the water became too hot for bathing. **The water is now over 50°C (122°F) and bathing is strictly forbidden.**

Jarðbaðshólar, crater hills south of the road. Steam vents there have long been used for steam baths, which are considered beneficial for rheumatism. Southeast from Jarðbaðshólar, about 1km from the main road in Bjarnarflag are the Nature Baths at Mývatn. The lagoons are man-made structures with bottoms containing sand and gravel. The nature of the water is in some aspects very unique. It contains a large amount of minerals, alkaline and is therefore very suitable for bathing. Because of the mineral content, undesirable bacteria and vegetation do not thrive in the lagoon which makes the use of chlorine or other disinfectant unnecessary.

Bjarnarflag, the area west of Námafjall. The water from the drill hole at Bjarnarflag is piped into bathing lagoons at Mývatns Nature Baths.

Krafla, (818 m) a tuff mountain north of Námafjall. Considerable geothermal heat on the west side of Krafla with fumaroles and mud-springs (solfataras). At the northwest side is **Víti,** ("Hell") an explosion crater, 300 m in diameter with green water in the bottom. **Leirhnjúkur** ("Clay peak"), is west of Krafla and on the southeast side is **Hrafntinnuhryggur** ("Raven flint). Construction of a geothermally powered electric plant started in 1974. Its first stage has been completed and provides 30 MW. From 1975-84 there was a series of tremors and eruptions in the area, 9 eruptions altogether along a 7,5 km long fissure. These originated in the old volcano Kröfluaskja.

Námafjall, the mountain south of Námaskarð, with geothermal heat all over the east side of the mountain, which looks light yellow from a distance. Sulphur was mined there for centuries from the Hlíðarnámur mines and exported. **Great care must be taken and all warnings observed as there have been many accidents.**

Námaskarð, a narrow pass between the mountains Námafjall and Dalfjall.

7 P. 570

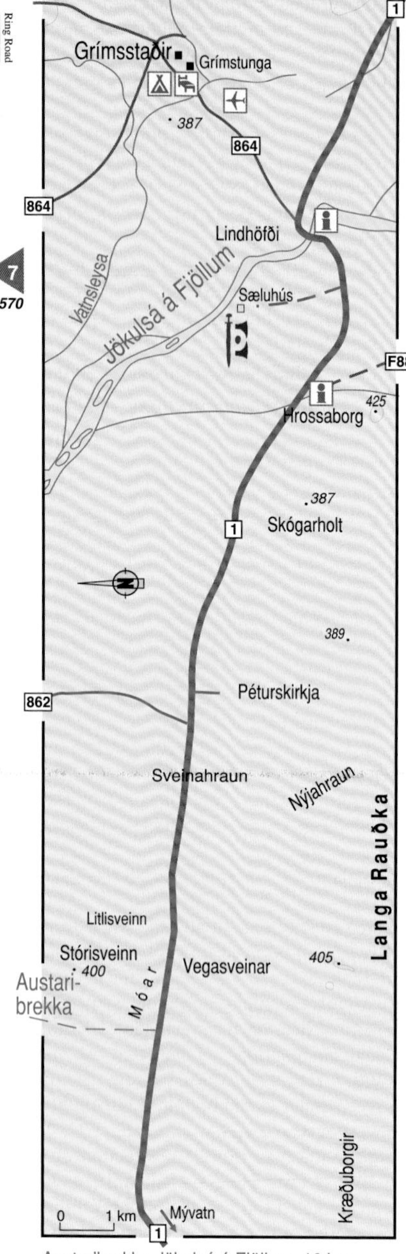

Austaribrekka-Jökulsá á Fjöllum 16 km

The Sæluhús shelter by the Jökulsá river.

Grímsstaðir á Fjöllum, ("Grímsstaðir in the mountains") a farm at a crossroads in the district Fjöll ("Mountains"), or Hólsfjöll, long an important resting place for travellers in this area. Before the bridge was built over Jökulsá there was a ferry point on the river, supervised from Grímsstaðir.

Jökulsá á Fjöllum, a large glacial river, the largest in the north of Iceland, coming from the Vatnajökull glacier and Kverkfjöll mountains. A big tributary, Kreppa, joins Jökulsá by Herðubreiðarlindir. Many falls in the river, the greatest being Dettifoss.

Sæluhús, a shelter built in 1881 near the ferry point on Jökulsá. This building was in many ways better than such shelters used to be, made of stones cemented together and having three floors: the basement for the horses and the upper ones for accommodation for travellers. However, the place soon got the reputation of being haunted and there are some ghost stories and folktales connected with the shelter. In the keeping of the National Museum since 1988.

Hrossaborg, an old crater, elliptical, about 500 m long. From there a jeep-track leads to Herðubreiðarlindir (about 60 km) and Askja (about 100 km).

Péturskirkja, ("Pétur's church") a shelter for sheep herders, built by the farmer Pétur Jónsson in 1925. Gunnar Gunnarsson´s novel *Aðventa* (The Good Shepherd) takes place in this area, telling the story of Benedikt Sigurjónsson (Fjalla-Bensi, or "Mountain-Benny") searching for sheep in late December. He spent Christmas Eve in the old shelter beside Péturskirkja.

Nýjahraun, a lava-field that came from the 30 km long Sveinagjá rift in 1875. The road crosses the northern tip of this lava-field.

Sveinar, craters on the Sveinagjá rift, both north and south of the road. In direct line and south of Sveinar are **Rauðuborgir**.

Skógarmannafjöll, ("Outlaw mountains") (400 m) two parallel tuff mountains.

Búrfell, (953 m) an impressive table mountain.

Kræðuborgir, a crater row several km long, the highest craters being 50-60 m. A considerable lavafield has its origins in these craters.

Austaribrekka, the east side of a wide but shallow subsided valley. Jeep-tracks from there to Dettifoss, Hólmatungur, Hljóðaklettar and Kelduhverfi.

862 **Dettifossvegur,** p. 403 864 **Hólsfjallavegur,** p. 404 - 405
F88 **Öskjuleið**, p. 472

In the Vegaskarð area.

Vegaskarð, a pass between the mountains **Vegahnjúkur** (783 m) to the south and **Sauðahnjúkur** (641 m) to the north.

Víðidalur, a valley and once one of the country´s most remote farmsteads, it was abandoned in 2000.

Biskupsháls, ("Bishops' ridge") a tuff mountain ridge between Grímsstaðir and Víðidalur, the boundary between the counties Suður-Þingeyjarsýsla and Norður-Múlasýsla. In earlier days it is said the bishops of Hólar in the north and Skálholt in the south were to meet there when visiting and travelling through their districts. According to folktales the bishops did not quite agree on the limits of their districts and therefore decided to erect a cairn on Biskupsháls to mark the agreed eastern border. Then each of them was to ride all the way round his bishopric and they would set the western boundary where they met again. They both set off, the bishop of Skálholt riding as fast as he could and the bishop of Hólar taking it easy and enjoying himself en route. They met in Hrútafjörður (V-Hún), the bishop of Skálholt obviously having travelled much farther and the western boundary was set there. In the light of this story, the two cairns on Biskupsháls, which are called **Biskupavörður** ("The bishops' cairns"), might have been built about the year 1200 or even earlier.

Hólsfjöll, a small and isolated district east of Jökulsá á Fjöllum, 300-400 m above sea level and the highest inhabited district in Iceland. Sandy in places and subject to erosion, yet having good grasslands and pastures for sheep. The smoked lamb (hangikjöt) from Hólsfjöll is renowned. Low tuff mountains on the east side, the highest points being **Grímsstaðakerling** (859 m) and **Hólskerling** (801 m). Formerly there were eight farms in the district but now there are only two left, **Grímsstaðir** and **Grímstunga**. A church at Víðirhóll and formerly a parsonage.

864 **Hólsfjallavegur,** p. 404

Vegaskarð-Jökulsá á Fjöllum 16 km

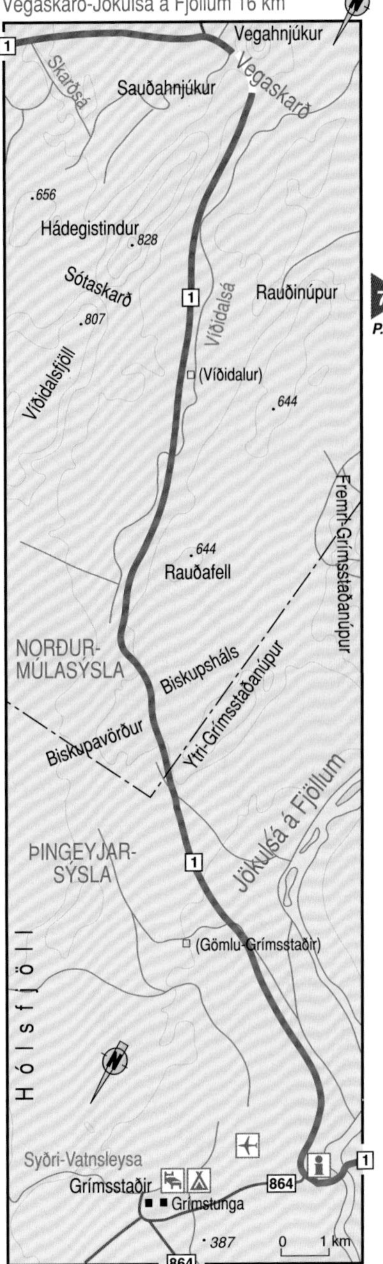

Jökulsá á Fjöllum-Vegaskarð 16 km

7 P. 570

7
P. 570

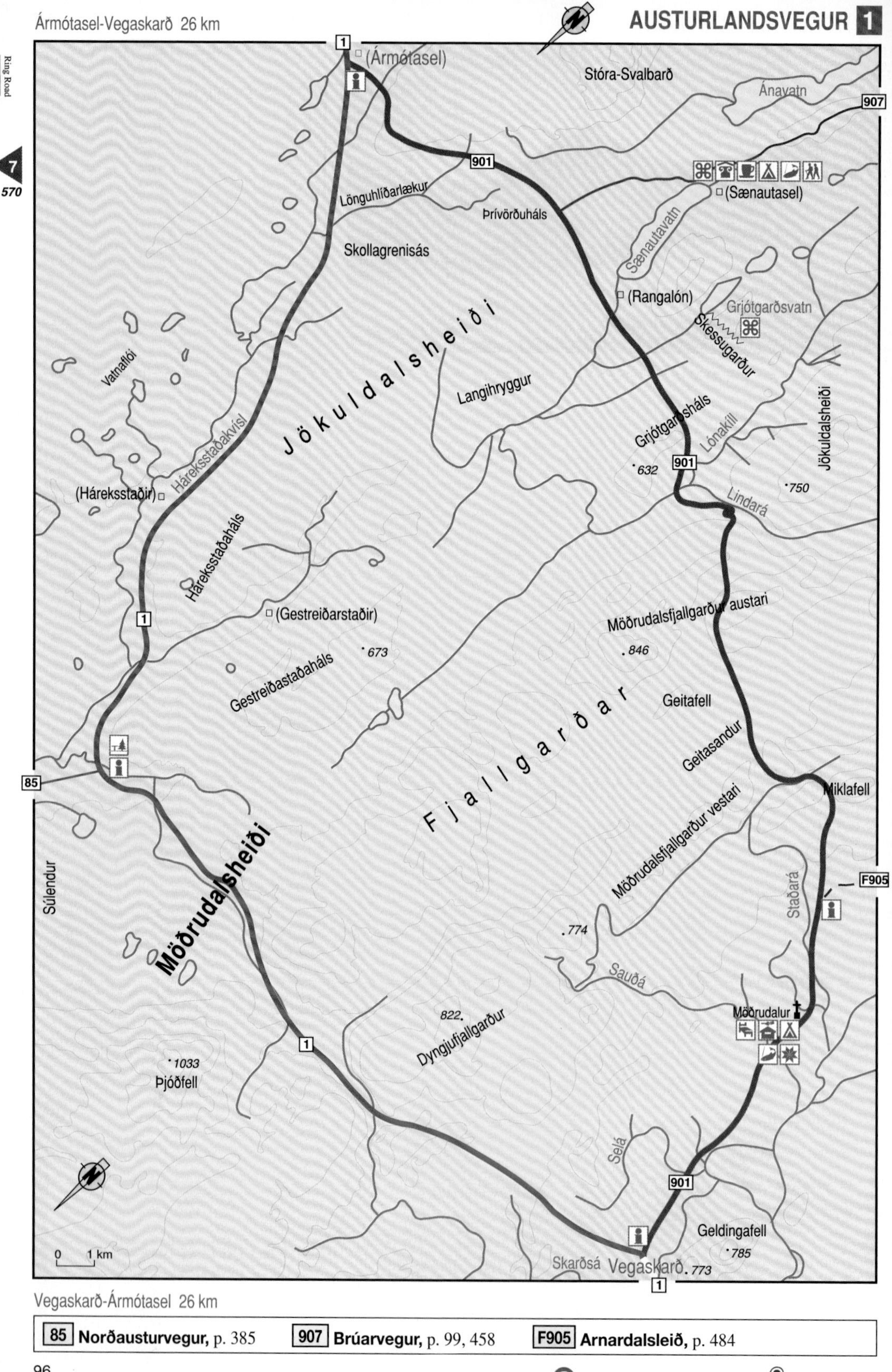

Vegaskarð-Ármótasel 26 km

85 **Norðausturvegur,** p. 385	907 **Brúarvegur,** p. 99, 458	F905 **Arnardalsleið,** p. 484

The church at Möðrudalur

Möðrudalur

Hárekssta̧ðir, an abandoned farm on Jökuldalsheiði which was first built in 1841 by Jón Sölvason (1803-1864). Prior to that time the place was the site of medieval farm ruins. Hárekssta̧ðir was the first farm built in this area in the 20th century and among the most succsessfull ones before it was abandoned in 1925. Several tales exist about the people who lived in the area long ago. There is a sheep pen used by the people of Vopnafjörður to sort out their sheep.

Gestreiðarstaðir, an abandoned farm on Jökuldalsheiði. The name may indicate that this farm dates back to the middle ages, as do names of places in the area that are in one way or the other connected with the name of the farm.

Jökuldalsheiði, a vast moor covered with low hills and mountains southwest of Vopnafjörður and along the Jökuldalur valley, with higher mountains on both sides. Mostly grassy and wet with many lakes, good fishing in all of them. About 100 years ago there were many farms in this region but during the great eruption of Askja in 1875 large quantities of ashes and pumice fell there so that most of the inhabitants moved away, a number of them emigrating to North America. The last inhabitants left the area in 1946.

Þjóðfell, a tuff mountain, easily accessible from the highway at 1033 meters. Splendid view.

901 **Möðrudalsvegur,** 40 km.

Rangalón, a farm in the middle of Jökuldalsheiði moor, by the northern end of **Sænautavatn**, which has good trout-fishing.

Skessugarður, ("Giantess' rampart") an ancient end morrain lying at right angles across the Grjótgarðsháls ridge, just to the west of the mountain Sænautafell about 2 km south of the road. One of the most magnificent natural formations in Iceland, forming a 5 m high wall made of gigantic boulders of porphorytic basalt.

Möðrudalsfjallgarður, (750-950m) western and eastern, two mountain ranges of tuff, with steep sides, barren. Between them lies a flat plain, **Geitasandur** ("Goat sands"). Very good view from the western ridge across Möðrudalur and towards Vatnajökull and Ódáðahraun with the majestic Herðubreið, often called the queen of the northern mountains, in the middle.

Möðrudalur, a farm on Efra-Fjall (469 m) situated at a higher altitude than any other farm in Iceland; also one of the most isolated. Möðrudalur has extensive lands considered very well suited for sheep-farming and has thus been a substantial farm for centuries. Formerly a parsonage. The present church was built by the farmer Jón Stefánsson, who painted the altar-piece himself. From Möðrudalur there is a very good view of the surrounding mountains, especially the majestic **Herðubreið**, 1682 m in heigth, is one of the most beautiful mountains in Iceland and from there one can also see Dyrafjöll mountains, part of Vatnajökull glacier and **Kverkfjöll** on its northern fringe. An indication of the isolated character of the farm is the tale of a traveller who stayed there overnight in 1814. According to him, the farmer had six grown-up children who had never been to another farm even though the oldest of them was married and a parent of three children. Now a travel service is run at Mörðudalur as well a goat- and sheep farm.

1 AUSTURLANDSVEGUR

Skjöldólfsstaðir, a substantial farm since the original settlement. Guesthouse, campsite, restaurant, gas station and a swimming pool.

Jökulsá á Brú or **Jökulsá á Dal**, a glacial river, at 150 km the longest river in eastern Iceland. Considered the muddiest of Icelandic rivers, it carried about 112 tons of clay and sand to the ocean daily. The river is reduced in volume, both water and deposits, when the generators of the Kárahnjúkar Hydroelectric Power Station started to revolve. The deposits will remain behind the gigantic dam in the river's canyons and the mainstay of the water will be diverted to river Lagarfljót.There are five bridges over the river.

Dimmugljúfur.

Dimmugljúfur, a narrow canyon, more than 160 m deep, situated below the Kárahnjúkar Hydropower Plant, the largest hydroelectric power plant in Iceland.

Jökuldalur, a long valley going up from Fljótsdalshérað, mostly with low mountains on both sides. Narrow, especially far inland where there is little or no flat land, though the slopes are grassy and provide good grazing. Scattered population.

Gilsá, a swift river that comes down the valley almost parallel to the road and joins Jökulsá. The bridge was built in 1972.

Ánavatn, a good fishing lake about 7 km long. There were two farms by the lake, **Veturhús** on the north and Heiðarsel on the south, the latter being the last farm to be abandoned in the region of Jökuldalsheiði in the year 1941.

Sænautasel, a farm (occupied 1843–1943) at the southern end of the lake Sænautavatn ("Sea-monster lake"). It achieved notoriety through the Halldór Laxness' account *A Midwinter Night on Jökuldalsheiði Moor*. It was renovated in 1992-3 and is considered well worth a visit. Land reclamation and revegetation.

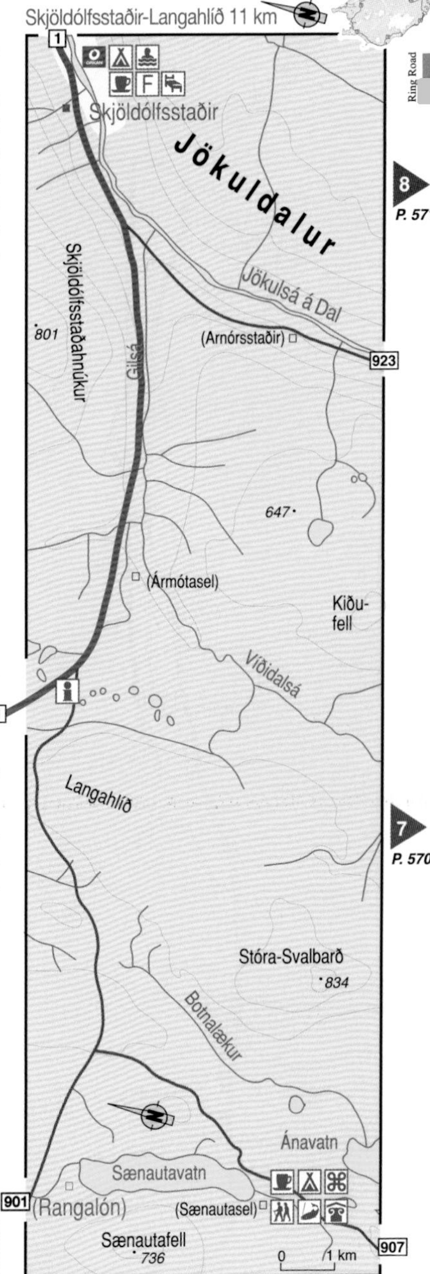

Langahlíð-Skjöldólfsstaðir 11 km

901 **Möðrudalsvegur,** p. 96
907 **Brúarvegur,** p. 485
923 **Jökuldalsvegur,** p. 424

Ring Road

8
P. 571

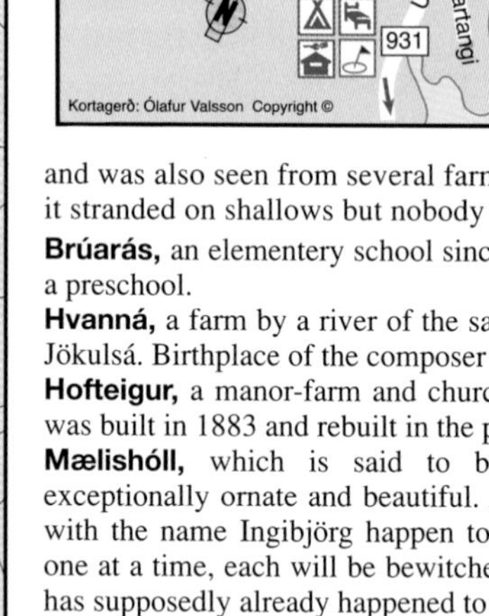

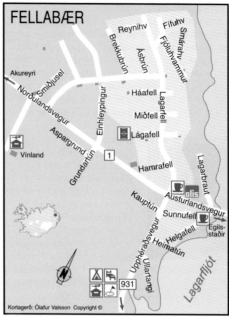

Jökulsárbrú, the present bridge was built in 1994, about 1 km south of that built in 1931. The river runs through a fairly deep, narrow (17-18 m) gorge at this point. The new bridge is the highest in Iceland, 40 m above the river. The first bridge, sponsored by German merchants, was built before 1564. According to the folktales of Jón Árnason, a monster, said to have been somewhat bigger than a horse, was seen in the river above the bridge and was also seen from several farms swimming upstream. At one place it stranded on shallows but nobody dared to go and take a closer look.

Brúarás, an elementery school since 1979. Now also a music school and a preschool.

Hvanná, a farm by a river of the same name, built close to the big river, Jökulsá. Birthplace of the composer Jón Jónsson from Hvanná (1910-63).

Hofteigur, a manor-farm and church, parsonage until 1925. The church was built in 1883 and rebuilt in the period 1970-72

Mælishóll, which is said to be the home of "hidden people", exceptionally ornate and beautiful. According to legend, if three women with the name Ingibjörg happen to own the farm **Hnefilsdalur** nearby, one at a time, each will be bewitched and disappear into Mælishóll. This has supposedly already happened to two such Ingibjörgs.

Goðanes, a promontory by Jökulsá downstream from the river Teigará. A temple of Thor was built there in Saga times and some ruins can still be seen on the promontory. A spring which comes up not far from the ruins is reddish because of iron compounds. The name of the spring is Blótkelda ("The spring of sacrifices") or Blóðkelda ("The spring of blood"), it being believed that the colour and taste of the water derived from the blood of sacrificial animals (or even people).

924 Jökuldalsvegur eystri, 23 km.

917 Hlíðarvegur, p. 422 **925 Hróarstunguvegur,** p. 425

1 AUSTURLANDSVEGUR

Eyvindará, a river and farm of the same name.

Egilsstaðabær (Egilsstaðir), located in the heart of East-Iceland in the broad valley of Fljótsdalshérað. Dense population can be found in Hallormsstaður but the largest rural district is Egilsstaðir/Fellabær, the only full scale town in Fljótsdalshérað. Together they form the core of the valley with the population of about 3,493 inhabitants. This core is the communication- and service center of East Iceland. The main occupations include light industry, various services, supermarkets and stores, tourism, and agriculture, while handcraft shops of the area are widely known. A diverse educational service is available in the area in musical schools, nursery schools, elementary- and high schools and college. Egilsstaðir supports an attractive swimming pool and a nine hole golf course. Regular sightseeing excursions are available, as well as hiking tours on marked trails. A local drama club and many choires are example of the fertile cultural life in Egilsstaðir. The Museum Center reflect the history of the area. A first class hotel, summertime lodging, farm accommodation, and coffee and guest houses make the traveller's stay comfortable. An important attraction is the glacially hollowed Lake Lögurinn, which empties into the wide bay Héraðsflói through Lagarfljót River. Through the area flows the Lagarfljót lake which is home to Iceland's most renowned water monster, Lagarfljótsormur (The Lagarfljóts wyrm), considered to be the sister of the Loch Ness monster. Whether hunting for reindeer, geese or ptarmigan, the chances are high. Trout fishing is widely possible, and salmon fishing is available in several rivers in the neighbourhood. The transportation connections are optimal and scheduled passenger traffic is available during the high season of tourism in summer. A domestic airport and substitute airport for international flight is located in Egilsstaðir with only one hour's flight from Reykjavík and a mere two hours flight from Europe. More info www.visitegilsstadir.is

Egilsstaðir, a substantial farm. A centre of communications after the bridge was built on Lagarfljót. Hotel and grain farming. Wild aspen grows in the woods of Egilsstaðir.

941 Flugvallarvegur, 0,55 km. **929 Hafrafellsvegur,** 7,3 km.

Selskógur, a small forest on the outskirts of Egilsstaðir. Hiking trails through the forest.

Lagarfljótsbrú, (301 m) this was for years the longest bridge in Iceland.

Fellabær, (pop. 404) a village across the bridge from Egilsstaðir. Main activities trading, service and industry.

Hafrafell, (216 m) a rocky mountain by the road. **Grímstorfa** ("Grímur´s turf"), a wooded ledge on its eastern side very difficult to reach whether from above or below, was for a while the hiding place of Grímur Droplaugarson, according to the Sagas.

Hróarstunga, the district north of Rangá between the big rivers Jökulsá and Lagarfljót, the southernmost part being Lágheiði moor, across which the road goes. Long and low hills with wet ground, fens and marshes in between, many lakes.

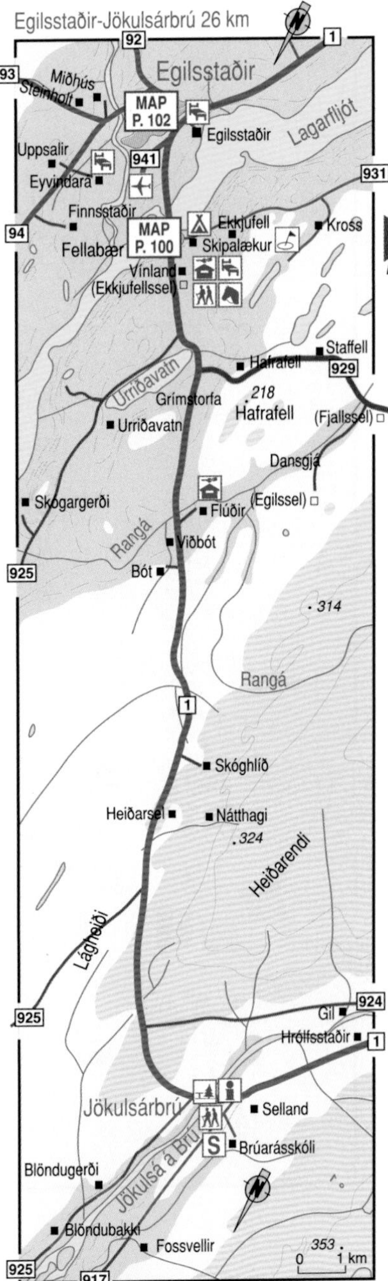

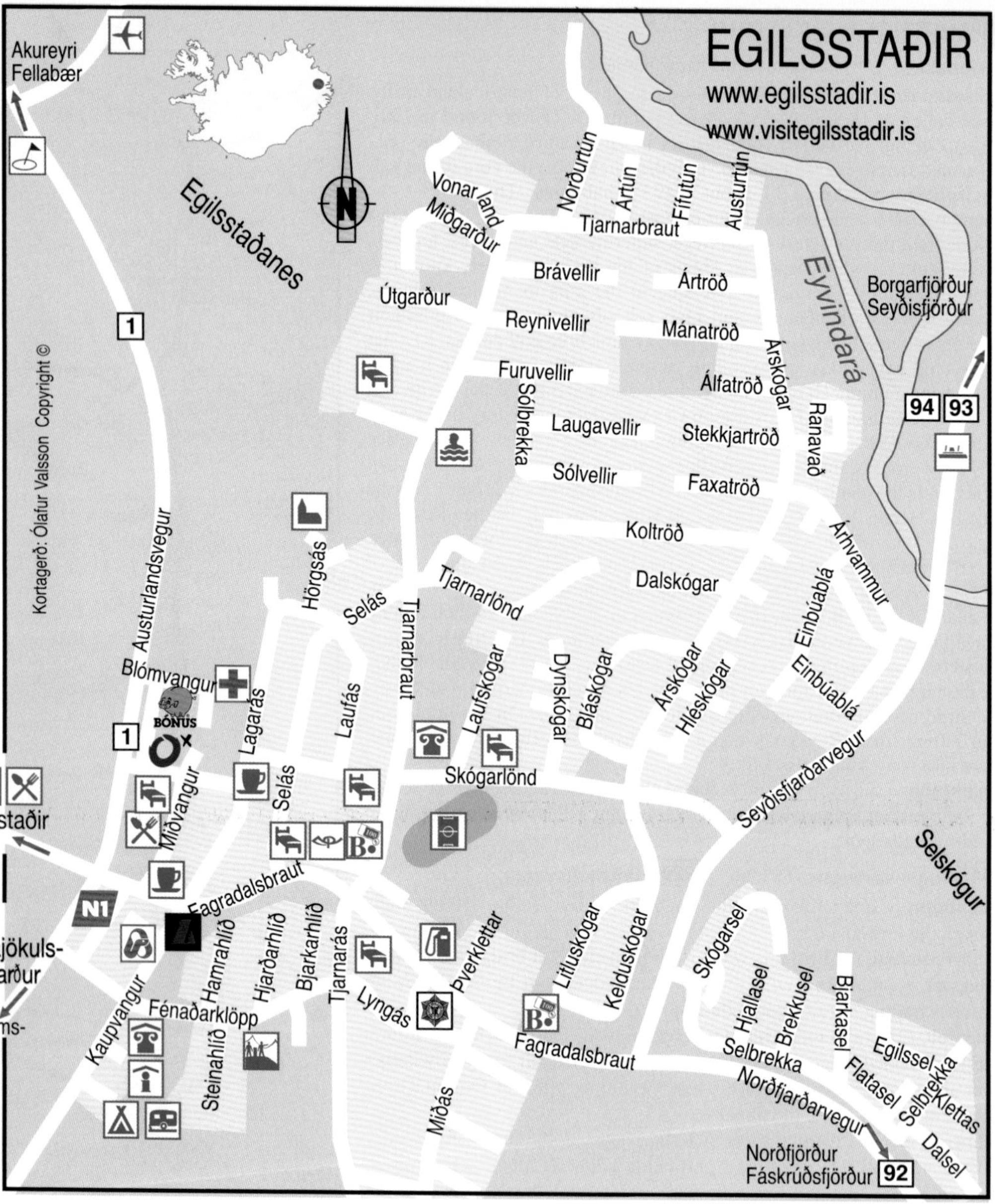

EGILSSTAÐIR

www.egilsstadir.is
www.visitegilsstadir.is

Kortagerð: Ólafur Valsson Copyright ©

Akureyri
Fellabær
Egilsstaðanes
1
Austurlandsvegur
Blómvangur
BÓNUS
Miðvangur
Egilsstaðir
N1
Vatnajökuls-
þjóðgarður
Höfn
Hallorms-
staður
Kaupvangur
Fénaðarklöpp
Steinahlíð
Hamrahlíð
Hjarðarhlíð
Bjarkarhlíð
Tjarnarás
Fagradalsbraut
Lagarás
Selás
Laufás
Hörgsás
Tjarnarbraut
Tjarnarlönd
Laufskógar
Skógarlönd
Lyngás
Miðás
Þverklettar
Útgarður
Vonarland
Miðgarður
Norðurtún
Ártún
Fífutún
Austurtún
Tjarnarbraut
Brávellir
Reynivellir
Furuvellir
Sólbrekka
Laugavellir
Sólvellir
Ártröð
Mánatröð
Álfatröð
Stekkjartröð
Faxatröð
Koltröð
Dalskógar
Árskógar
Ranavað
Eyvindará
Borgarfjörður
Seyðisfjörður
94
93
Árhvammur
Einbúablá
Dynskógar
Bláskógar
Árskógar
Hléskógar
Seyðisfjarðarvegur
Selskógur
Litluskógar
Kelduskógar
Skógarsel
Hjallasel
Brekkusel
Bjarkasel
Selbrekka
Egilssel
Flatasel
Selbrekka
Klettas
Dalsel
Norðfjarðarvegur
Fagradalsbraut
Norðfjörður
Fáskrúðsfjörður
92

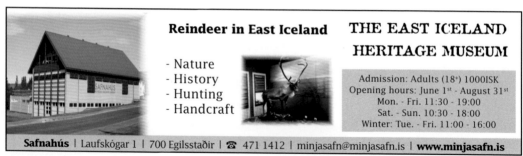

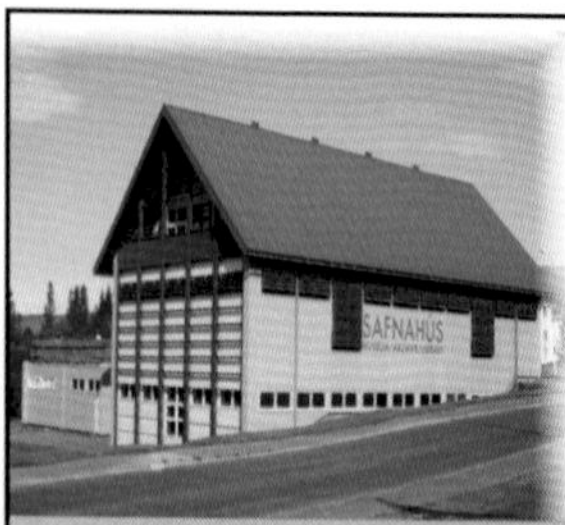

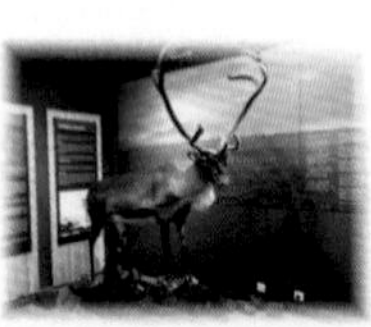

Ring Road
9 P. 572

Litla-Sandfell-Egilsstaðir 21 km

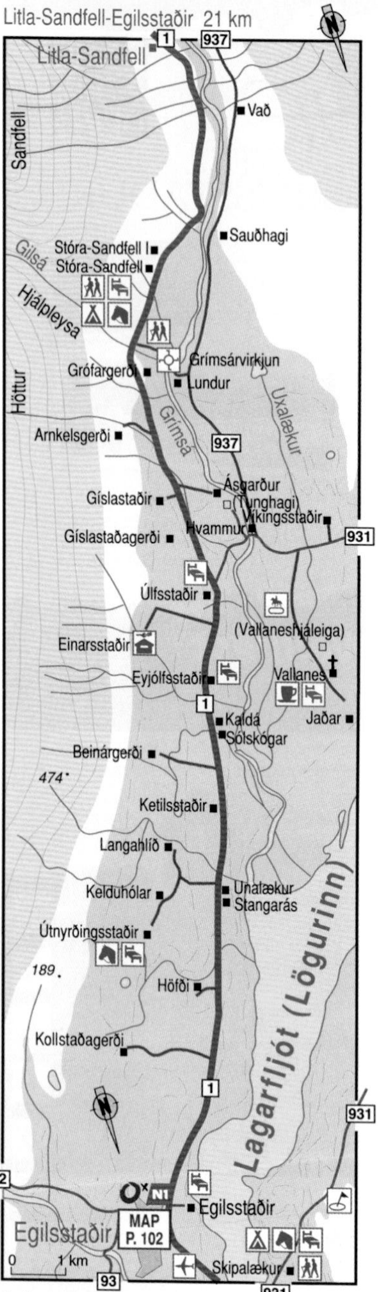

Grímsárvirkjun, a hydro-electric power plant built in 1958.

Hjálpleysa, ("Lack of help") a pass or a side valley often used by hiking travellers to and from Reyðarfjörður. There is **Valtýshellir** cave.

Höttur, (1,106 m) a rhyolite mountain by Hjálpleysa.

Vallanes, a farm and church. See more p. 427.

Grímsá, a river formed by the two rivers Geitdalsá coming from lakes in the highlands east of Hornbrynja through Norðurdalur, and Múlaá coming from the Ódáðavötn lakes. Until it reaches the lake Skriðuvatn in Suðurdalur Múlaá is called Öxará.

Eyjólfsstaðir, formerly a substantial farm, has extensive birchwood forests that are now protected and in the care of the district's Forestry Association. There are some hiking trails in the forrest and two waterfalls, one which can be accessed from behind.

Einarsstaðir, a summerhouse colony.

Ketilsstaðir, a farm, formerly the seat of district judges, also formerly a church and a free church. Now a horse farm. New farms are being built nearby. One of several noted judges from Ketilsstaðir was Pétur Þorsteinsson (1720-95). He was among those who imported reindeer and he had a number of books written and printed, especially religious works, hymns etc. His son was Sigurður Pétursson (1759-1827), a poet and playwright whose plays were the first to be printed in Iceland (1844 and later).

Útnyrðingsstaðir, a farm, birthplace of Þorsteinn M. Jónsson (1885-1977), member of parliament, headmaster and publisher, owner of one of the largest private collections of Icelandic books, now in the Árni Magnússon Institute. Now a horse farm.

Höfði, now a forest farm owned by Iceland Forest Service.

92 **Norðfjarðarvegur,** p. 409
93 **Seyðisfjarðarvegur,** p. 414
931 **Upphéraðsvegur,** p. 426
937 **Skriðdalsvegur,** p. 105

Egilsstaðir-Litla-Sandfell 21 km

1 AUSTURLANDSVEGUR

Breiðdalsheiði, (470 m) a mountain road across the moor between Skriðdalur and Breiðdalur, steep at the Breiðdalur end. A small lake, Heiðarvatn, not far from the road, where trout has been introduced and seems to thrive well. Between the road and the lake is Tjarnarflöt, where legend has it the men of Vopnafjörður and Breiðdalur fought in the old days. Reindeer may be seen along the road on Breiðdalsheiði.

Ódáðavötn, two lakes above the Skriðdalur valley. Formerly a frequented route between Fljótsdalur and Djúpivogur. In 1964 dams were built by the lakes in order to maintain an even flow of water for the Grímsárvirkjun hydroelectric plant.

939 Axarvegur, 18,6 km between Skriðdalur og Berufjörður, highest point 532 m. Rather steep in Berufjörður, many beautiful waterfalls. The road is open for all cars in the summer time.

Skriðdalur, a long valley between Hérað and Breiðdalsheiði, wide at its mouth and dividing into two valleys, Norðurdalur and Suðurdalur. The eastern mountains are mostly of multi-coloured rhyolite.

Haugahólar, a group of hills, most likely the debris from an old landslide. The farm **Haugar** by the hills and the 3 km long lake **Skriðuvatn** nearby.

Arnhólsstaðir, a farm by the river Jóka which runs out of the valley Þórudalur. There is a jeep track along the east bank of Jóka to Reyðarfjörður. Formerly the main horse track from the Upphérað district.

Múlakollur (Þingmúli), 508 m, a tuff mountain, splitting Skriðdalur in to two valleys. Some fosiles have been found there.

Þingmúli, ("Meeting mountain") a farm, church and parsonage until 1890, formerly an official meeting place and hence the name of the two counties, Suður-Múlasýsla og Norður-Múlasýsla. Some ruins from earlier times are still to be seen. Place-names indicate that there was a heathen temple there. A mountain (508 m) of the same name between the valleys. Some fossils found there.

938 Múlavegur syðri, 6 km.

937 Skriðdalsvegur, 19 km.

Þórisá, a river in the land of the farm Eyrarteigur. In 1995 a heathen tomb was found there, thought to be from the time of settlement. It was lined with horse skins, unusual in this country, richly furnished with weapons and other objects, containing among other things a fragment of a silver coin thought to be from the time of Athelstan, King of England 925–940. It also contained the skeletons of a man, a horse and a dog. This is one of the most remarkable archeological finds in Iceland.

Skúmhöttur, (1,229 m) a rhyolite mountain between Skriðdalur and the head of Reyðarfjörður, one of the highest mountains in this region.

Heiðarvatn-Litla-Sandfell 23 km

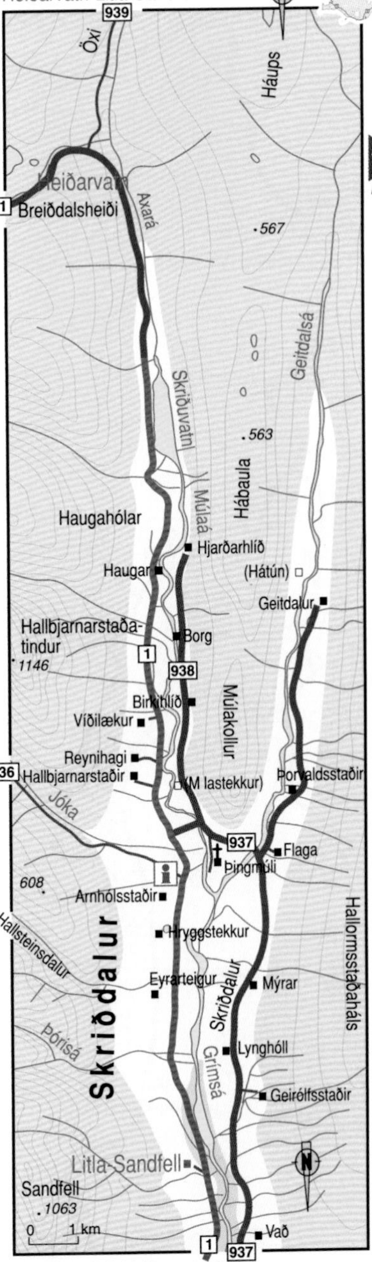

10 P. 573

11 P. 574

Litla-Sandfell-Heiðarvatn 23 km

936 Þórdalsheiðarvegur, p. 492

Streitishvarf-Heiðarvatn 44 km

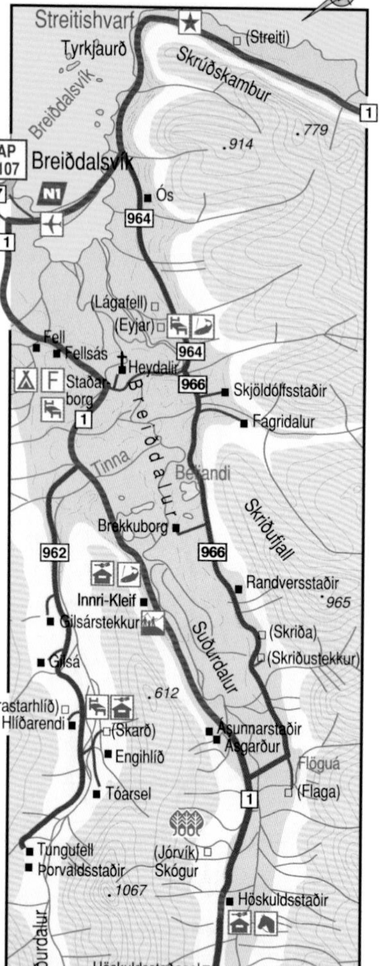

MAP P. 107

10 P. 573

Skrúðskambur, a rock-wall by the road, where a giant was supposed to have lived. His two brothers lived on the islands Papey and Skrúður.

Streitishvarf, the peninsula on the south side of the Breiðdalsvík bay. Streiti has great natural hiking trails and view points out to the islands. A lighthouse has been there since 1922.

Tyrkjaurð, ("Turks' scree") above Streitishvarf, where legend has it that a farmer killed 18 Algerian pirates when he found them asleep.

Breiðdalseyjar, several islands in the south of Breiðdalsvík. The islands are home to seals, eider ducks, and many other seabirds.

Breiðdalsvík, ("Broad valley bay") a short, wide bay with a wide beach of black sand across the end of the bay. A town of the same name (pop. 130). The small town lies at the entrance to the valley between the headlands of Kambanes and Streitishvarf. The first house was built in 1883 by the Gránufélagið association. The community developed slowly at first, but grew rapidly when major harbour improvements were made in the mid 20th century. Nothing is known for sure about the settlement until about 1880 when the Gránufélagið built a warehouse. Yet full-time settlement did not begin until 1896, when the Brynesverslun store in Seyðisfjörður built a branch store at the top of Selnes at the eastern corner of Selnesbót. In the spring of 1906 the store burned down and the same year a new store was built to the west of the inlet. That building still exists today, making it the oldest building in Breiðdalsvík. The old co-op has been rebuilt as a geology centre, which is fitting as Breiðdalur is East Iceland's volcanic region, as indicated by the colours of the mountains.

964 Breiðdalsvegur, 9 km. **966 Suðurbyggðarvegur,** 14 km.

Heydalir, often called Eydalir, a farm, church and parsonage, formerly considered one of the richest parishes in Iceland. Among the best known clergymen of Heydalir was the poet Einar Sigurðsson (1538-1626) who wrote one of the most popular of all Icelandic Christmas hymns. Above the road is **Staðarborg** the first community centre in Breiðdalur. Beautiful walking trails connect Heydalir and Staðarborg.

Flöguá, a river which runs down from Flögutindur and Smátindur peaks, in cliff steps ending in a 60 m fall through a hole in the cliff making an eye or an arch around the tip of a waterfall **Flögufoss**.

Tinna, a river running through Tinnudalur from the peaks Njáll and Bera. The peaks are named after a giant couple that lived in the mountains and were eventually turned into stone. A wonderful walking trail leads up the valley alongside the river.

Breiðdalur, the biggest of the valleys cutting into the eastern mountains, wide towards the sea but dividing into two valleys, Norðurdalur and Suðurdalur, further inland. The highway goes through the latter. The valley is surrounded by mountains 1,100-1,200m high and extremely colourful because of rhyolite which came from the Breiðdalseldstöð volcano in the tertiary period. Big gravel beds in the middle of the valley are gravel plains, seashores from when the ocean reached further inland. These are quite common in the eastern fjords and their height above the present sea level varies markedly. At the farm Þorgrímsstaðir at the head of the valley there is a small electrical power station for home use, harnessing a stream where the water falls 255m.

962 Norðurdalsvegur í Breiðdal, 12 km.

Breiðdalsá, one of the most beautiful salmon fishing rivers in Iceland.

Beljandi, ("The roarer") a waterfall in Breiðdalsá, one of most beautiful waterfalls in Breiðdalur. It is accessible by jeep or in walking distance from the road (966).

Jórvík, a perfect place for a picnic, hiking and nature exploring. Walking path from Jórvík to Norðurdalur. The land was given to the National Forest Association for cultivation, 600 ha of forest. A small ravine runs up the slope towards the mountain. The forest contains traditional Icelandic tree types such as natural aspen and birch combined with cultivated areas and remains of forest cultivation experience of the first half of the 19th century. National Forest.

Heiðarvatn-Streitishvarf 44 km

96 Suðurfjarðavegur, p. 421
97 Breiðdalsvíkurvegur, p. 421

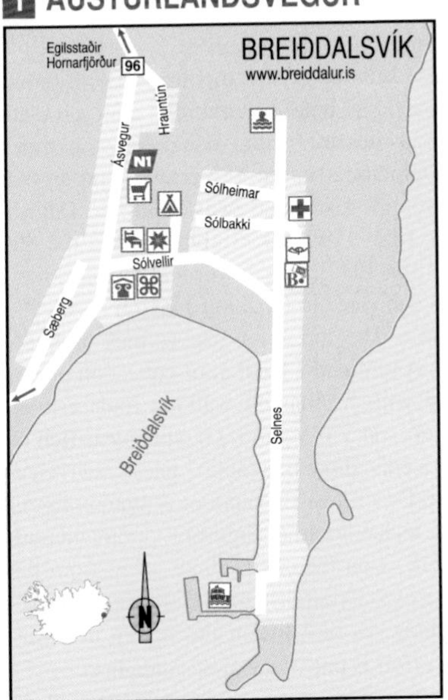

Berufjörður, a long, fairly wide fjord with many islets and reefs, and high and beautiful mountains on both sides, the highest being Búlandstindur to the south. Many interesting peaks and pinnacles, particularly around the head of the fjord. Very little flat land, especially on the south side. Rhyolite is common in the mountains and ignimbrite is found on the Berufjarðarströnd shore.

Berufjörður, a farm, church and parsonage until 1906. The birthplace of Professor Eiríkur Magnússon (1833-1913), librarian in Cambridge. There is a museum Nönnusafn. From Berufjörður an old trail, now improved for jeeps, goes across Öxi to Skriðdalur. When the Algerian pirates attacked the Westman Islands in 1627 they also attacked many places on the eastern fjords, among others Berufjörður where they burned the farm, killed many of the animals and took whatever valuables they could get their hands on.

Kistufell, (1,111 m) the highest mountain in this area, rising gradually up from Öxi but with steep rocky faces on the other sides.

939 Axarvegur, see p.105.

Berufjarðarskarð, (700 m) a mountain pass and trail between the head of Berufjörður and Breiðdalur, formerly frequently travelled, steep at both ends. Marked walking routes through the pass and also through Jórvíkurskarð, Reindalsheið and Streitishvarf. A map of interesting walking routes in the Eastern Fjords are available in most places in region.

Skáli, a farm of the original settlement. The home of the ghost Skála-Brandur, well-known from the folk tales of Sigfús Sigfússon.

Gautavík, a farm and trading post until the 17th century, at that time one of the main harbours in eastern Iceland. The landing place of the missionary Þangbrandur when he came to convert Iceland in the 11th century. Old ruins still to be seen. A protected site.

Bláþjörg, blue green cliff on the shore, a short distance from the farm Fagrihvammur, formed in a massive volcanic eruption.

Berunes, a church and a substantial farm, often the seat of district judges. Local place names indicate official gatherings. There is a lighthouse on Gíslatangi point, as many islets and skerries in the fjord make navigation quite dangerous.

Karlsstaðir, there´s a café, guesthouse and performance centre under the trademark Havarí. Havarí produces vegetarian sausages and chips from home-grown turnips.

Berufjörður-Streitishvarf 34 km

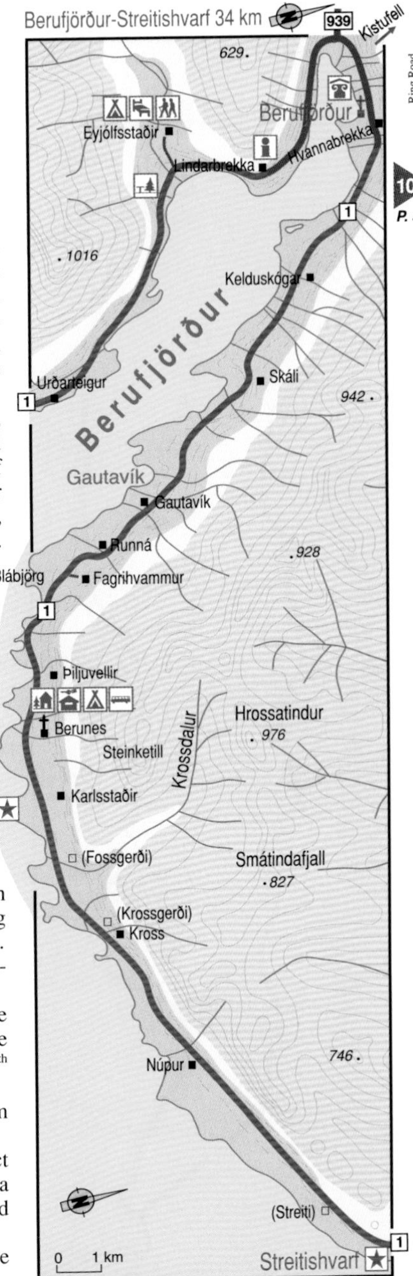

Streitishvarf-Berufjörður 34 km

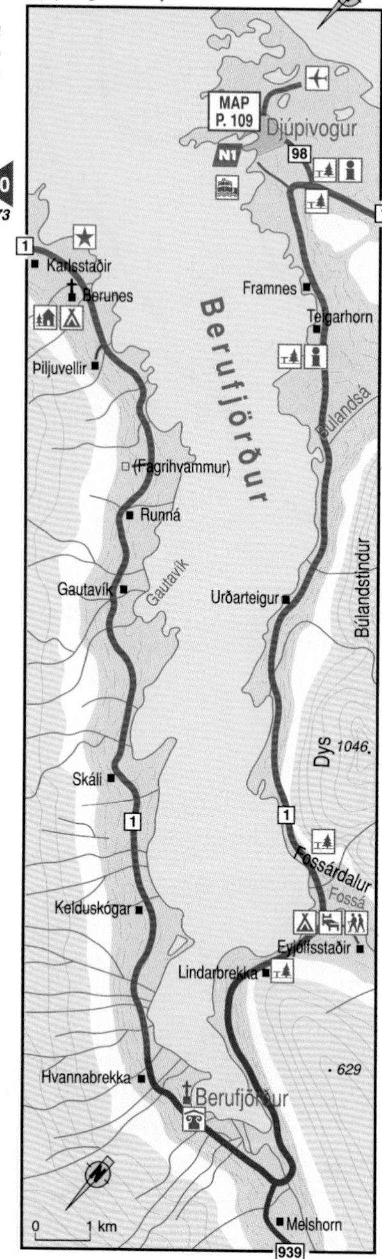

98 Djúpavogsvegur, 2,5 km.

Djúpivogur, (pop. 349) a village situated at the mouth of Berufjörður fjord, on the south coast. There is a hotel, swimming pool and an elementary school The primary industries are fishing, fish processing, trade and services. Trading began in Djúpivogur in the 17th century and an old store, Langabúð, can still be found. Langabúð was built by Danish merchants and is believed to date from 1790. An exhibition about the life and work of Ríkarður Jónsson, (1888-1977), tree carver and sculptor, may be found there, as well as a room dedicated to Eysteinn Jónsson (1906-93) and his wife Sólveig Eyjólfsdóttir. The top floor has various artefacts relating to the history of the area. A bird and a hand craft collection is in a house next to Langabúð. A map with 52 marked walking trails can be bought in Langabúð, Hótel Framtíð and Við Voginn. Djúpivogur is rich of local handcraft. In the local souvenir shop Bakkabúð, guests can view variety of souvenirs from the area. Don't miss the outdoor sculpture, Eggin í Gleðivík, by the world famous Icelandic artist Sigurður Guðmundsson, consisting of 34 eggs. The artwork is on the coast, about 1 km from the centre of the village, in a convenient walking distance. Djúpivogur and its environs are ideal for bird watching, as bird life in the region is highly diverse. The Djúpavogur forestry effort is one of the area's delights.

Teigarhorn, a farm about 5 km from Djúpivogur. Timber house built in 1880-82. A photographic studio was operated there around 1900. In the keeping of the National Museum since 1992. Zeolites found there are said to be the most beautiful and varied anywhere in the world. A protected natural feature.

Búlandstindur, (1,068 m) one of the highest and most majestic mountains in the east of Iceland. In continuation west of Búlandstindur is **Goðaborg** ("Crag of the gods"), where it is said the idols of the heathen gods were carried up and thrown off the cliffs when Iceland converted to Christianity in the year 1000.

Urðarteigur, a farm.

Fossárdalur, a valley. Fossá waterfall falls from a high cliff by Fossárvík. The river runs from **Líkárvatn** ("Lake of the dead"). It is said that it got its name when two men died when they went fishing there.

939 Axarvegur, 20 km across Öxi between Berufjörður and Skriðdalur. See p. 105.

Beruhóll, a small hill below the farm of Berufjörður, said to be the burial mound of Bera who lived there with her husband Sóti. The story goes that once when Bera and Sóti were returning with a group of people from a visit to Breiðdalur they ran into bad weather on the mountain and lost their way. All of them died at **Mannabeinahjalli** exept Sóti who walked over a cliff on the mountain in Sótabotn where he was buried. And Bera who kept going, letting her horse and dog find the way, but didn´t notice where she was until the horse went galloping into the stable so she was knocked out of the saddle and broke her neck.

Teigarhorn

10 P. 573

Djúpivogur

Bragðavellir, a farm. In 1952 two ancient Roman coins were found there, which might indicate that Roman seafarers visited Iceland long before the settlement.
Hamar, once the site of a prayer house. A "sibyl's grave" mound in the home field.
Hamarsá, among the longest and biggest rivers of the eastern mountains, getting some glacial colour from the glacier Þrándarjökull.
Hamarsdalur, a long valley with birch bushes. The glacier **Þrándarjökull** (1,248 m) near the head of the valley.
Vígðilækur, a spring 2–3 km north of Hamar. Consecrated by Bishop Guðmundur the Good around the year 1200.
Djáknadys, ("Deacon's cairn") a heap of rocks by the road on the north side of Hamarsfjörður, between the farms Strýta and Hamar. According to folktales the priest of Háls and deacon of Hamar quarrelled there and killed each other. All travellers passing there for the first time were to throw three stones in the heap in order to prevent mishaps during the trip. The cairn is a protected site.
Valtýskambur, a cliff east of Rauðuskriður. The cliff got its name when a menn called Valtýr saved his live after he had committed a crime. He save himself by standing on his head on the cliff during a mess at Háls, after that he went free.
Háls, an abandoned farm, formerly a church and parsonage until 1816.
Strýta, a farm where two famous artists were born: the sculptor Ríkarður Jónsson (1888-1977) and his brother, the painter Finnur Jónsson (1892-1993). A rock in the home field is believed to be a church of the "hidden people".
Papey, a large island opposite Búland and Hamarsfjörður, surrounded by islets. Formerly a substantial farm but now deserted. The name indicates that Irish monks lived there before the settlement. A popular tourist attraction, church and lighthouse. Daily boat trips during summer.

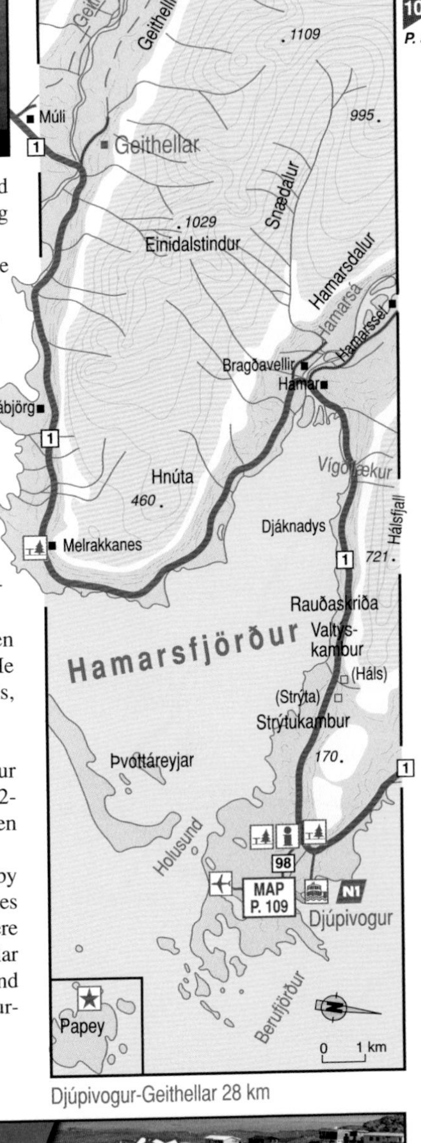

Djúpivogur-Geithellar 28 km

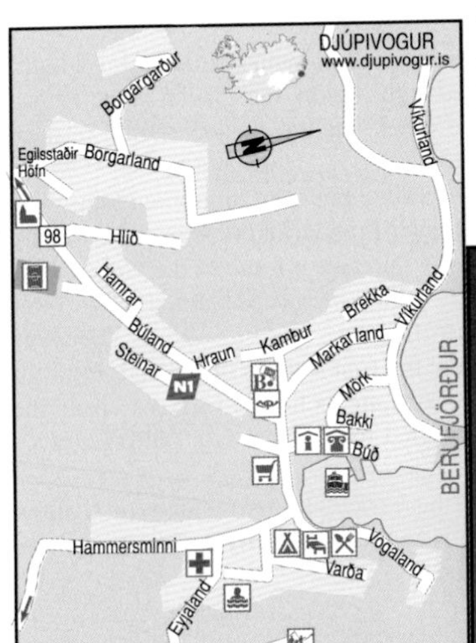

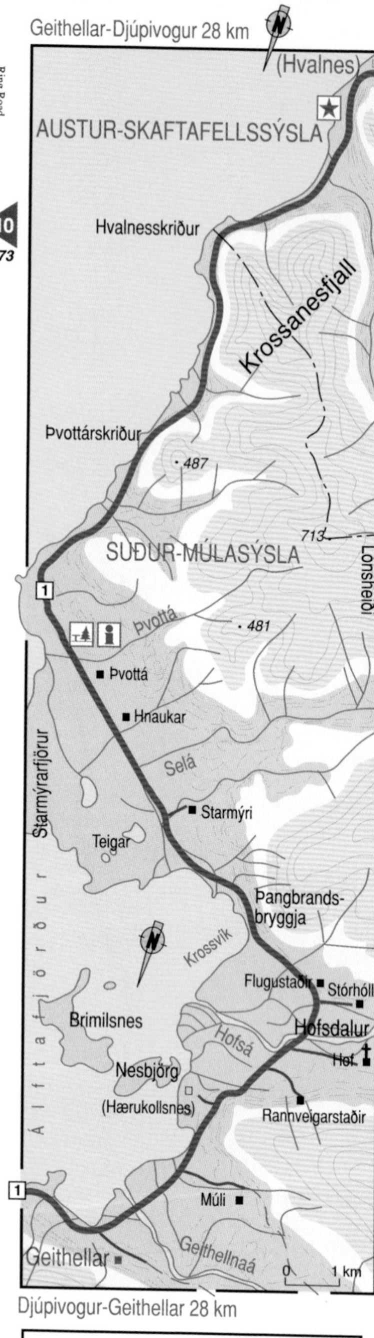

10
P. 573

Hvalnesskriður and **Þvottárskriður** lie between **Lón** and **Álftafjörður**. The road was moved there from **Lónsheiði**.

Lónsheiði, (389 m) the mountain track and road between Álftafjörður and Lón, 18 km long. A rock, Sýslusteinn, marks the boundary of the counties Suður-Múlasýsla and Austur-Skaftafellssýsla. This road is no longer in use.

Þvottá, ("Ablution River") a farm and the home of Síðu-Hallur in Saga times after he moved from Hof. The 10th century Norwegian priest and missionary Þangbrandur stayed there one winter, converted Síðu-Hallur and his folk to Christianity and baptized them in the river, hence its name. Many place-names connected with him, such as Þangbrandsbrunnur, a well still in use, and Þangbrandstóft, protected ruins. A monument in the memory of Síðu-Hallur was unveiled in 1999; it is located close to the highway. A church until 1754 and a parsonage a little longer. The birthplace of Jón Bjarnason (1845-1914), a clergyman and leader among those Icelanders who emigrated to Canada.

Starmýri, ("Sedge marsh") a farm north of Lónsheiði, a chapel in early times. The name is said to be from Stari the settler, but more likely it is derived from an extensive sedge-grown meadow.

Þangbrandsbryggja, a cliff 50 m above the road, 2–3km from Starmýri. Named after the priest Þangbrandur a missonary who came to Iceland in the year 997.

Hof, a farm and a place of settlement, for a while the home of Síðu-Hallur, a chieftain of the 10th century. His son, Þiðrandur was killed in the field at Hof, now called **Þiðrandalág**. A church and parsonage until 1905. Birthplace of the brothers Eysteinn Jónsson (1906-93), member of parliament, minister of state and chairman of the Progressive Party, and the Rev. Jakob Jónsson (1904-89), well-known cleric and author.

The farm Hof in 1902. Goðaborg on the left.

Hofsdalur, a valley off southern Álftafjörður, with a side-valley Flugustaðadalur, mostly uninhabited. Through it runs the glacial river Hofsá, which comes from **Hofsjökull** and other smaller glaciers. Birch bushes, especially in Tunga between the valleys.

Geithellnadalur, a long and narrow valley between high mountains. The river Geithellnaá comes from the glacier Þrándarjökull. It once had many farms, now mostly deserted. Formerly the easiest route to the valley **Víðidalur**, to the west of Hofsjökull, while it was inhabited. The river Geithellnaá has many waterfalls and gorges.

Geithellar, long a manor farm where the first settlers of Iceland, Ingólfur Arnarson and Hjörleifur Hróðmarsson, are believed to have spent the winter when they visited Iceland the first time. There is a "sibyl's grave" mound in the home field.

Álftafjörður, the southernmost of the eastern fjords, actually a shallow and wide lagoon closed by a sand reef called **Starmýrarfjörur**, with an outlet through **Melrakkanesós**.

Stafafell in 1902.

Stafafell, a manor farm, church and a parsonage until 1920. An old pulpit and altar piece are preserved in the church. A jeep track to the colourful Lónsöræfi goes south of Jökulsá, fording Skyndidalsá, and over Kjarrdalsheiði moor to **Illikambur**. From there on a selection of hiking tours can be made, for example to Sauðhamarstindur (1,319 m) and to the eastern section of Vatnajökull, or across Jökulsá by a footbridge and across Kollumúli to the valley Víðidalur, populated in the 19th century, or to the impressive **Tröllakrókar** with wind-eroded needles and pinnacles. This whole area, known as **Lónsöræfi** ("The lón (lagoon) wilderness"), is particularly attractive and varied walking country, giving fairly easy access to the eastern peaks of the Vatnajökull glacier, e.g. Grendill. Hiking tours of various lengths are organized from Stafafell.

Jökulgilstindur, (1313 m) the highest mountain in the area. A considerable glacier on the north side of the mountain with an outlet through the Jökulgil canyon to the valley Flugustaðadalur in the district of Álftafjörður. Very interesting country for mountain lovers.

Bær, a farm near the sea, in settlement times the home of Úlfljótur, the first lawspeaker, to whom a monument was set up 1985. View dial.

Svínhólar, a farm near the road to the south of Lónsheiði. Metal ores (e.g. copper) have been found there.

Lón, the easternmost district of Austur-Skaftafellssýsla, a wide area between the two capes, Eystrahorn and Vesturhorn. Two long sand-reefs enclose the two lagoons Lón, whose outlet is Bæjarós, and Papafjörður, with its outlet through Papós. Majestic mountains all around the district, which is rather barren and thinly populated.

Hvalnes, the easternmost farm, now abandoned, in the district of Lón, impressively situated under the rock-walls of **Eystra-Horn**, also called Hvalneshorn. These mountains are batholites mostly made of gabbro and granophyre, and very interesting from the geological point of view. Hvalneskrókur formerly a point place for fishermen. Lighthouse. Turf houses were built there for the film *Paradísarheimt* based on a novel by Halldór Laxness.

F980 **Kollumúlavegur,** p. 496

Stafafell-Hvalnes 17 km

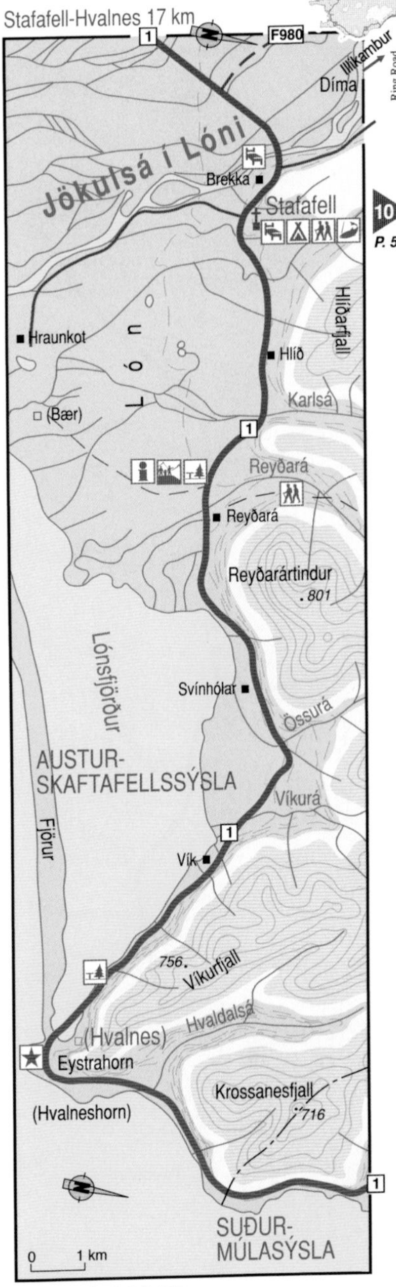

Hvalnes-Stafafell 17 km

Ring Road
12 P. 575
10 P. 573

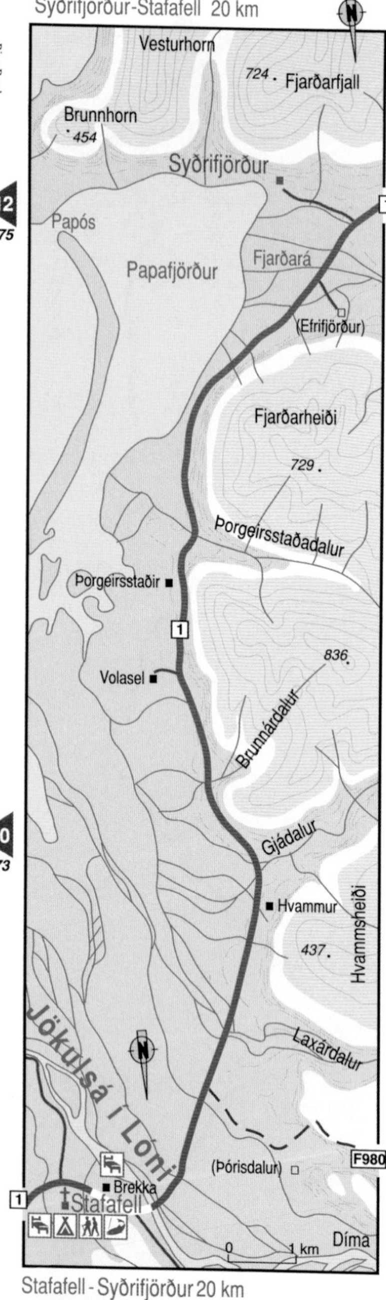

Vesturhorn, (454 m) the mountain jutting out between Lón and Hornafjörður, a bat ho lite made of gabbro, with high cliffs and steep screes. Brunnhorn (683 m) a separate peak near Papós to the east of Vesturhorn.

Papós, the outlet from Papafjörður in the land of Syðri-Fjörður. Formerly a fishing station and a trading place 1860-97. There was a boarding school there from 1898 to 1899. South of the ruins of this village are older ruins, Papatættur, said to be the remains of the buildings of Irish hermits from before the settlement.

Syðrifjörður, the sunrise can´t be seen there from September 29th till early march.

Endalausidalur, ("Endless valley") a narrow, uninhabited valley between Laxárdalur and Efri-Fjörður, open at both ends with rivers flowing in both directions. Within this valley are two others **Loklausidalur** and **Slaufrudalur**. There is a big batholite (10 km^2) made of gabbro at Slaufrudalur. There is Bleikitindur, 615m.

Jökulsá í Lóni, a big river coming from the eastern side of Vatnajökull. A major tributary is Skyndidalsá, coming from the glacier Lambatungujökull. Formerly difficult to ford, now bridged by one of the longer bridges of Iceland (247m). **Díma,** a cliff skerry in the river bed a little above the road, is a protected natural feature.

Þórisdalur, a farm in the district of Lón. Once the home of Þórður Þorkelsson Vídalín (1661-1742) a rector at Skálholt, clergyman, doctor, natuarlist etc. He wrote an important work on the nature of glaciers which was published in 1754 in German in the *Hamburgisches Magazin*, translated into Icelandic and published in 1965. The story goes that Þórður was so cunning that he could force ghosts to return to those who sent them, and so skilled that from Þórisdalur he could detect a ghost coming up through Almannaskarð on its way to Stafafell. He took his horse, arrived at Stafafell ahead of the ghost and turned it back. Yet Þórður was so good and kind that he would not even hurt a fly with his magic. From Þórisdalur the jeep-track goes across the river Skyndidalsá and up over Kjarrdalsheiði moor to Illikambur, this route being preferable to that starting from Stafafell because of Jökulsá.

An old sheep fold in Þórisdalur in the Lón district.

F980 **Kollumúlavegur,** p. 496

Hornafjörður, a big lagoon with an outlet through Hornafjarðarós. Very deep, the current is so strong that it was a big hindrance to navigation until the advent of the motorboat. The current also carries sand and mud, building up deposits on navigation routes, so a great deal of work is necessary to ensure that vessels can come in and out at all times.

99 Hafnarvegur, 5,36 km.

Höfn, (pop. 1,633) a town situated on the coast of Hornafjörður fjord, belonged to the municipality of Nesjahreppur until the town became its own municipality with some 300 inhabitants in 1946. It was granted town status on December 31st 1988. The municipality merged with Nesjahreppur and Mýrahreppur in 1994, and four years later all the district municipalities merged into a single Municipality of Hornafjörður. Höfn is situated by the mouth of Hornafjörður fjord and major structures have been erected to safeguard the passing of ships. The primary industries are fishing, tourism, trade and manufacturing. The town has a district commissioner's office, a health care centre, the site of the Hornafjörður Cultural Centre, a university centre, a new ventures centre and the Austur-Skaftafellssýsla Upper Secondary School, a swimming pool and a nature reserve at Ósland. Vatnajökull National Park's visitor centre in Höfn is located in the building Gamlabúð next to the harbour area. It houses an exhibition about the region's geology, glaciers and culture. There is also a tourist information desk by the harbour. The majority of migrating birds to Iceland first reach land in the Hornafjörður region; hence a bird research centre has been set up at Höfn. Trade was moved from Papós to Höfn in 1897. At the Höfn harbour there is a memorial to the arrival of first settler Ingólfur Arnarson to Iceland, a gift from Norwegian seafarers in 1997.

Mígandi, a small beautifull waterfall. It is possible to walk on a ledge behind it.

Nes, the easternmost district of the Hornafjörður area, reaching from Hornafjörður and the river Hornafjarðarfljót on the west side to Skarðsfjörður on the east. Quite fertile and good farming country, being mostly flat land with small hills and wet areas in between. The coastline is particularly interesting with its innumerable inlets, small peninsulas and islets.

Skarðsfjörður, a wide and shallow lagoon reaching in to Almannaskarð.

Horn, formerly a church, point place for fishermen and seal hunters. A former NATO radar station on the nearby **Stokksnes** peninsula.

Almannaskarð, (153 m) a narrow mountain pass between Hornafjörður and Lón. Steep scree mountains on both sides, **Skarðstindur** (488 m) on the north, **Hádegistindur** ("Midday peak") (724 m) and **Klifatindur** (890 m) on the south. There is a fine view to the west from Almannaskarð. A 1300 m long tunnel lies under Almannaskarð.

12 P. 575

Syðrifjörður- 99 Hafnarvegur 16 km

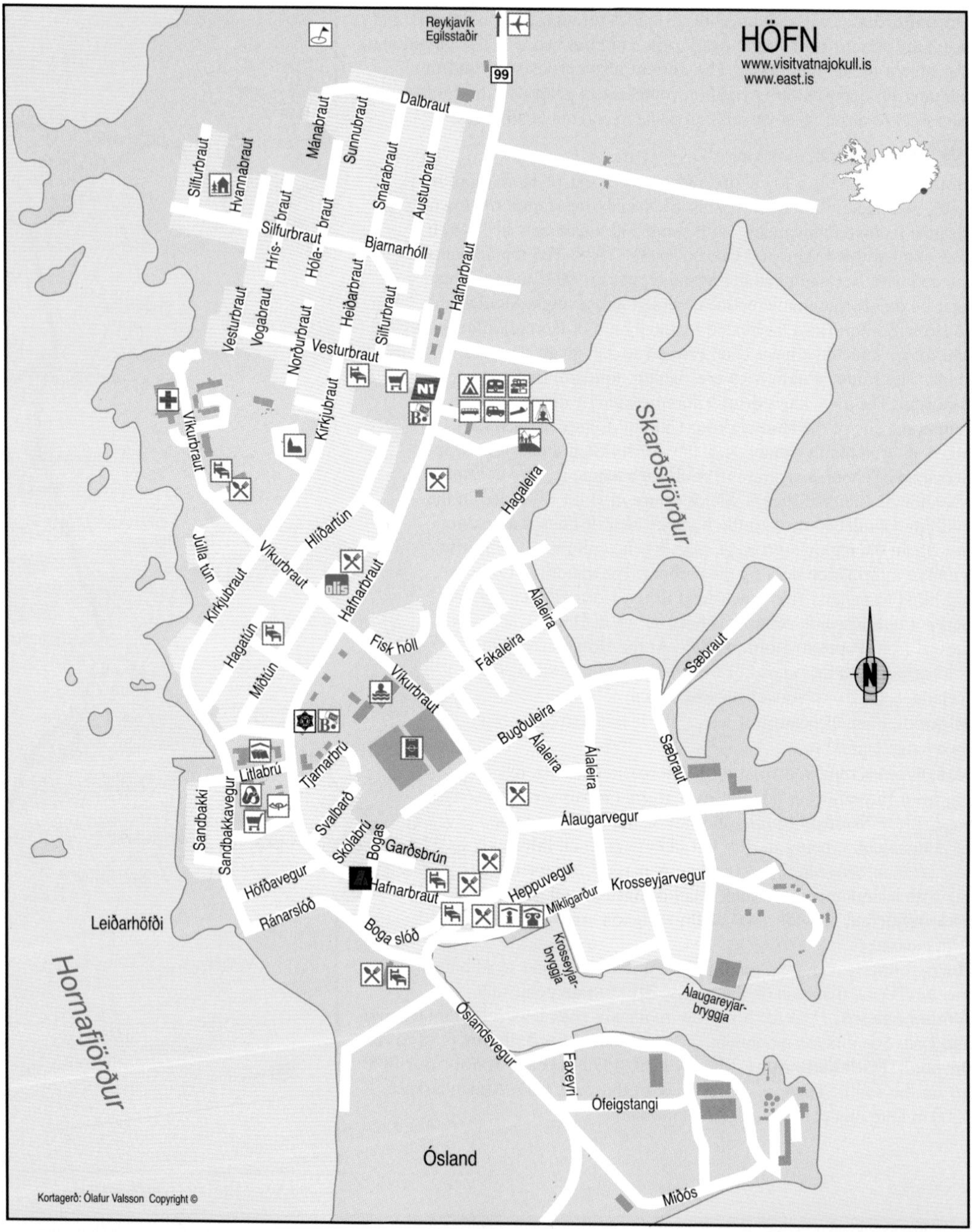

HÖFN

www.visitvatnajokull.is
www.east.is

Reykjavík
Egilsstaðir
99

Dalbraut
Mánabraut
Sunnubraut
Silfurbraut
Hvannabraut
Smárabraut
Austurbraut
Hrís-braut
Hóla-braut
Silfurbraut
Bjarnarhóll
Hafnarbraut
Vesturbraut
Vogabraut
Norðurbraut
Heiðarbraut
Silfurbraut
Vesturbraut
Kirkjubraut
Víkurbraut
Skarðsfjörður
Hagaleira
Hlíðartún
Júlla tún
Víkurbraut
Kirkjubraut
Hafnarbraut
Álaleira
Hagatún
Fisk hóll
Fákaleira
Sæbraut
Miðtún
Víkurbraut
Bugðuleira
Álaleira
Álaleira
Sæbraut
Litlabrú
Tjarnarbrú
Sandbakki
Sandbakkavegur
Svalbarð
Álaugarvegur
Skólabrú
Bogas
Garðsbrún
Höfðavegur
Hafnarbraut
Heppuvegur
Krosseyjarvegur
Mikligarður
Leiðarhöfði
Ránarslóð
Boga slóð
Krosseyjar-bryggja
Álaugareyjar-bryggja
Hornafjörður
Óslandsvegur
Faxeyri
Ófeigstangi
Ósland
Miðós

Kortagerð: Ólafur Valsson Copyright ©

Golf

WELCOME TO HORNAFJÖRÐUR

Glacier hiking

Ring Road
12 P. 575

Hornafjarðarfljót- 99 Hafnarvegur 16 km

Skógey, revegetation and soil conservation area.

983 Miðfellsvegur, 1,1 km. **984 Hoffellsvegur,** 3,5 km.

Hoffell, a farm since the time of the settlement, beautifully situated amidst mountains, glaciers, rivers and gravel beds. **Goðaborg** ("Crag of the gods") (1,425 m), the highest point on the mountain range reaching into the glacier, was once believed to be a house built by gods or spirits even though it looked like a rock. A shepherd is said to have strayed there when looking for sheep and found a big, grey, ferocious-looking bull standing in a huge open doorway. It seemed to the shepherd that he was wading through leaves, but he did not pay any attention to this until he came down to Setbergsheiði moor where his shoe came off and he found that the leaves that fell out of it were in fact gold coins. It is said that Judge Jón Helgason of Hoffell fetched gold from **Goðaborg** every year. Jasper, opal, marble and other stones are also found.

Ketillaugarfjall, (668 m) a colourful batholite mountain. According to legend, a woman named Ketillaug disappeared into the mountain carrying a kettle full of gold. Walking route up the mountain, beautiful view.

Þveit, the largest lake in Austur-Skaftafellssýsla, thought to be haunted.

Bjarnanes, a manor farm since ancient times and a historical place, church and parsonage. In the 15th century this was the home of Teitur Gunnlaugsson the rich, a lawman responsible for the execution of the aggressive and unpopular bishop Jón Gerreksson, by having him drowned in Brúará in Árnessýsla. In the 16th century there were great disputes about the ownership of Bjarnanes, which finally was placed under the bishopric of Skálholt.

Nesjahverfi, (pop. 91) a community, built up around the community centre Mánagarður.

Laxá, a river flowing from Laxárdalur, which turns into **Endalausidalur**, reaching east into the Lón district. By the farm **Hólmur** at the top of Laxárdalur, in 1996, an old grave was discovered and excavations carried out near the ruins of a farm from the Viking age. This has given rise to theories that the site also contains the ruins of a heathen temple; however, scholars differ in their opinions regarding this. Should the theory prove correct this would be the first time that a place of sacrifice from the Viking age is found in Iceland and indeed in the entire Nordic Region.

982 Airport Road, 0,68 km.

Árnanes, airport for Hornafjörður.

Hólar, a substantial farm, birthplace of the painter Jón Þorleifsson (1891–1961).

Dilksnes, a site of a small archaelogical find.

99 **Hafnarvegur,** p. 113

99 Hafnarvegur-Hornafjarðarfljót 16 km

1 AUSTURLANDSVEGUR

Skálafell, the easternmost farm in the district of Suðursveit. Birthplace of Jón Eiríksson (1728-87), councillor to the King of Denmark and one of the most influential advocates of Iceland in Denmark, hence the memorial to him by the roadside. Nearby the river **Kolgríma** comes rushing out of its narrow canyon.

Skinneyjarhöfði, a skerry or low cape on the coast, the only elevated land on a long stretch. Formerly a point place for fishermen, but always difficult. Skinney used to be among the bigger farms of the Mýrar district but was abandoned because of floods.

Brunnhóll, a church, consecrated in 1899. Before there were churches at Holt and Einholt.

Mýrar, the district between the rivers Hornafjarðarfljót and Kolgríma, flat, wet, with many low rock-hills and extensive gravelbeds. The coast is characterised by long, wide sandbars with mudflats and lagoons. Vatnajökull dominates the background with many glaciertongues in between high and majestic mountains. Glacial rivers, counting from the east: Hólmsá, Heinabergsvötn and Kolgríma, spread all over, continually changing their courses. The streams of Heinabergsvötn, for instance, were bridged in 1947 but the following year they changed their course and started running into Kolgríma, so the bridge has stood on dry land ever since. The glacier-tongues **Fláajökull** and Heinabergsjökull stretch far down into the district. It is possible to drive to Fláajökull along Hólmsá. **Heinabergsjökull** divides into two arms around the mountain Hafrafell, north of which there is another mountain, **Snjófjall**, with a peculiar glacier hollow on the south side. The valley Vatnsdalur ("Water (or lake) valley") on the western side of Heinabergsjökull often collects large quantities of water dammed up by the glacier, **Heinabergsvötn**. Once in a while this water forces its way out under the glacier, causing big floods in the rivers. The low mountain **Jökulfell** (150 m) in front of Fláajökull was hidden by ice at the beginning of the century, but began to come into view around 1920.

986 Rauðabergsvegur, 4,1 km.

Haukafell, 2,5 km west of the farm Rauðaberg.

Hornafjarðarfljót, a big glacial river flowing mostly from **Hoffellsjökull** and emptying into Hornafjörður. Very wide but shallow, dividing into two main rivers: Austurfljót and Suðurfljót ("East and south rivers"). The bridge (225 m) built in 1961 was the second longest in the country until 1973.

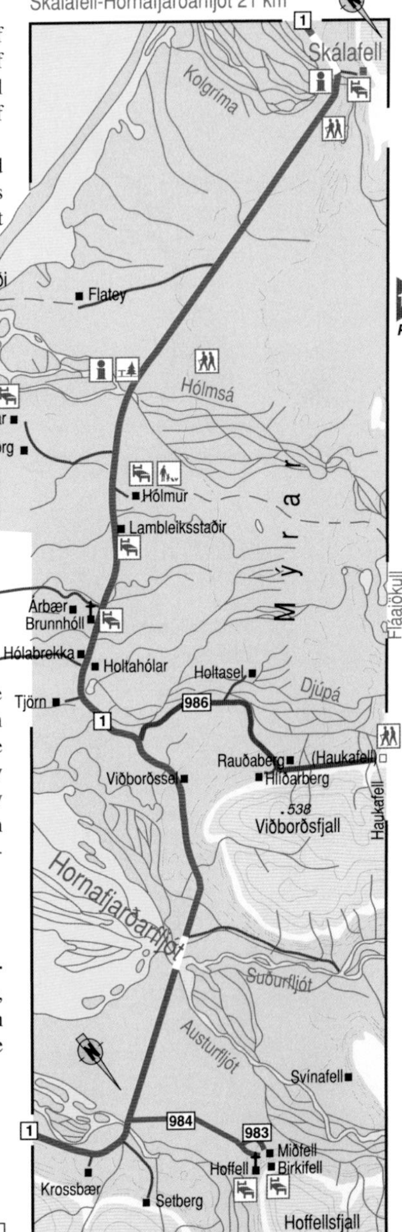

12 P. 575

983 Miðfellsvegur, p. 116 **984 Hoffellsvegur,** p. 116

12 P. 575

1
Fellsá
Reynivellir
Breiðabólsstaður
Gerði
Hali
Steinafjall
790
Steinasandur
Steinavötn
Suðursveit
1
Kálfafell
Hrollaugsstaðir
Kálfafellsstaður
Jaðar
850
Brunnavellir
(Brunnar)
Vagnstaðir
Staðardalur
Borgarhöfn
Lækjarhús
Borgarhafnarfjall
Hestgerði
(Hreggsgerði)
Hestgerðishnúta
(Hreggsgerðishnúta)
881
Hestgerðislón
Miðvatn
Fremstavatn
Sunnuhlíð
Uppsalir
F985
Smyrlabjörg
Smyrlabjargaárvirkjun
595
Skálafellshnúta
Skálafell
Kolgríma
0 1 km
1

Skálafell-Breiðabólsstaður 26 km

Breiðabólsstaður, a group of farms below the mountain Breiðabólsstaðarfjall, originally settled by Hrollaugur, son of Earl Rögnvaldur of the Möre district in Norway. One of the farms is **Hali**, birthplace of the author Þórbergur Þórðarson (1889-1974), there is a monument in his and his brothers honour. There is a walking path leading from the monument with 13 signs that have quotes from his books. The walk takes about an hour if all the signs are visited. There is also a museum at Hali dedicated to Þórbergur, **Þórbergssetur**. Guided tours are available.

Steinafjall, (789 m) an impressive rock-wall rising up from the flatlands.

Steinasandur, mud flats, once the bed of the various streams of the river Steinavötn which were formerly more extensive.

Kálfafellsstaður, a group of farms, a church and parsonage, community centre. It is said that an old route used to go up from Kálfafellsstaður, through the valley Staðardalur and north across the Vatnajökull glacier. The birthplace of the writer Torfhildur Þ. Hólm (1845-1918), the first woman novelist in Iceland. Below the home field is a "sibyl's grave" mound and they say that any person that attends to it will have good luck.

Suðursveit, the district between the river Kolgríma and the Breiðamerkursandur sands. The bottom of **Kálfafellsdalur** is very steep with a glacier-tongue, **Brókarjökull** ("Breeches glacier"), dividing around the rock Brók, and hence the name. The area provides some of the most majestic mountaineering country in Iceland.

F985 **Jökulvegur,** to the glacier Vatnajökul, 16 km. From there are pick-ups for jeep and skidoo tours on Skálafellsjökull glacier.

Smyrlabjörg, a farm which harnessed a nearby waterfall 1969, to provide 1,200 kW. Since then the falls have disappeared, except in torrential rain.

F985 **Jökulvegur,** p. 497

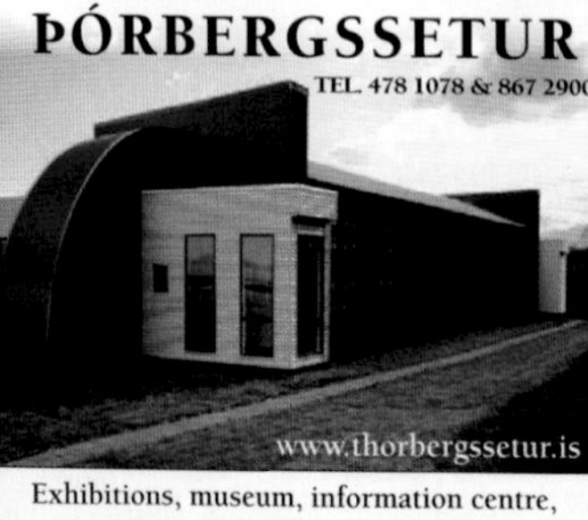

1 AUSTURLANDSVEGUR

Breiðamerkurfjall, (774 m) mountain on the western edge of Breiðamerkurjökull. In about 1700 the glaciers on both sides united in front of the mountain, and it remained a glacier island until 1946. Since then the glaciers have retreated.
Fjallsárlón, a lagoon carved out by a crawling glacier. The lagoon has grown considerably in size since 2000, due to the glacier retreating more rapidly. Boat tours on the lagoon are available.
Breiðamerkursandur, extensive sand area created by glaciers and glacial rivers. The principal breeding grounds of the Great Skua in Iceland. There used to be several farms in the western section of the sands, but they were destroyed by advancing glaciers in the 17th century. One of the farms was Breiðá, home of Kári Sölmundarson of *Njáls saga*.
Jökulsá á Breiðamerkursandi, the biggest river on the sands, though very short, only about 1,500 m. Comes from a 248 m deep lake, or lagoon, **Jökulsárlón**, the deepest lake in Iceland, at the foot of the glacier. There are usually icebergs floating on the lake. The river, which used to seriously hinder travel, was bridged 1966-67, but the bridge is now in danger due to the encroachment of the sea. Boat trips are available.
Breiðamerkurjökull, a wide glacier-tongue coming down to the Breiðamerkursandur sands, flat and relatively free of crevasses. It almost reached the sea in 1891-92, but has retreated considerably since then. Long moraine lines descend from Mávabyggðir and Esjufjöll, two extensive glacier islands or nunataks.

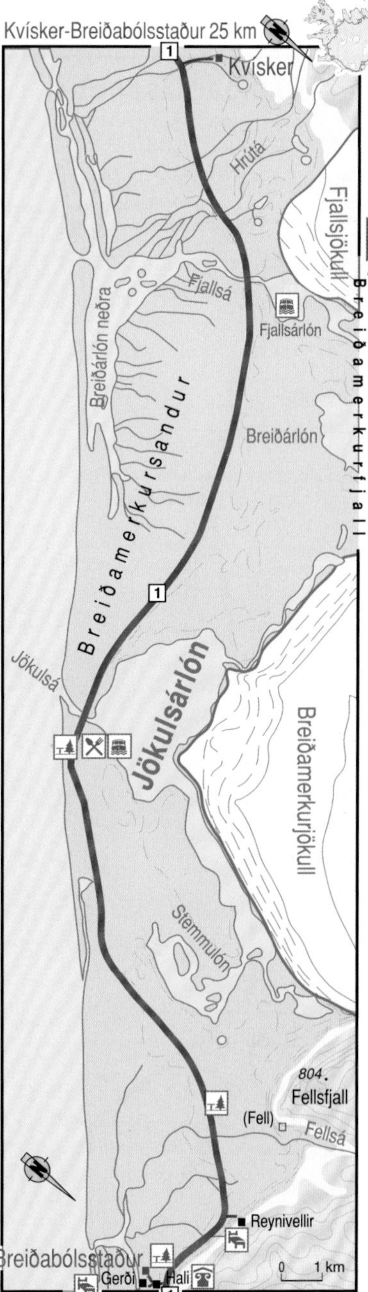

Hof-Kvísker 25 km

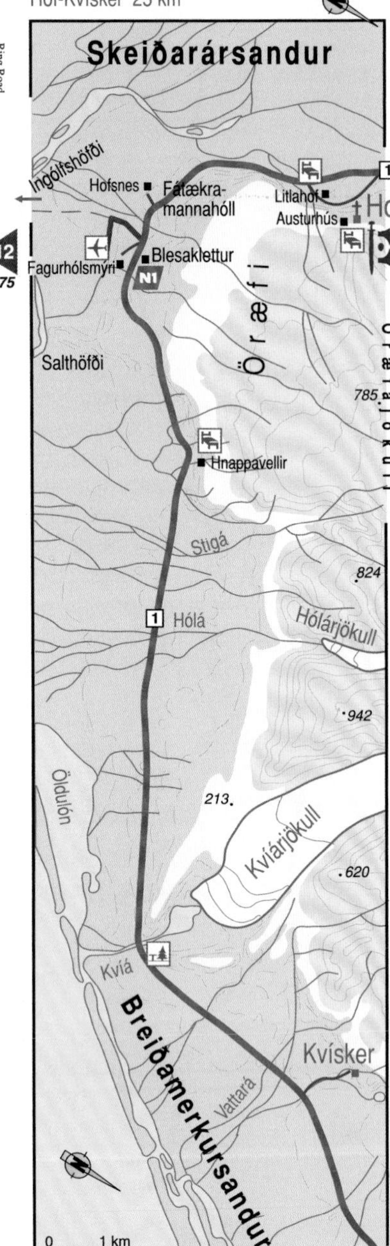

Kvísker-Hof 25 km

12 P. 575

The church at Hof

Hof, a group of farms and a church of turf, built in 1883. The youngest turf church in the country. In the keeping of the National Museum since 1951. Ruins of the nearby farm **Gröf**, which was buried in ashes and pumice in the eruption of 1362, have been excavated.

Ingólfshöfði, a cape on the coast 9-10 km south of Fagurhólsmýri, 76 m high, 1,200 m long and 750 m wide, birdcliffs and a lighthouse. Formerly a point-place for fishermen, though always difficult and dangerous. Named after the first settler, Ingólfur Arnarson, who spent his first winter there in 874, commemorated by a monument raised there in 1974.

Fagurhólsmýri, a farm and weather station. The farm is built on formerly coastal cliffs, beautiful view.

Hnappavellir, a group of farms where the old building style of the Öræfi district has lasted longer than in other places. This is one of the most popular climbing area in the country, many routes.

Öræfi, the westernmost district of Austur-Skaftafellssýsla between the sands Skeiðarársandur and Breiðamerkursandur, a semi-circle around the base of Öræfajökull. For long one of the most isolated districts of Iceland with no harbours on the coast, Vatnajökull to the north and dangerous rivers to east and west. Until 1962 mice, rats and cats were unknown in the district. Magnificent views and great variety in landscape and nature. Only seven farms or groups of farms along the 43 km road between the farms Skaftafell and Kvísker.

Öræfajökull, a great glacier-covered stratovolcano connected to the Vatnajökull massif. The volcano has erupted twice in historical times, 1362 and 1727. Its highest point, **Hvannadalshnjúkur** (2,110 m), is also the highest point in Iceland. Many farms were destroyed in these eruptions, the earlier one being more destructive. Older names were Hnappafell mountain and Hnappafellsjökull glacier. Glacier Guides at Skaftafell offer guided trips to Hvannadalshnjúkur peak with all technical equipment that is needed (crampons, harness, ice axe and ropes). The trip takes 10-15 hours going over challenging terrain.

1 AUSTURLANDSVEGUR

Skaftafell, the westernmost estate in Öræfi built high on the southern slopes of Skaftafellsheiði moor because of the destructive forces of Skeiðará. Extensive birchwoods, rich vegetation (*Saxifraga cotyledon, Campanula rotundifolia* etc. etc.), gullies, canyons, waterfalls, glaciers and valleys. Extensive and varied view from the view-dial at Sjónarsker. In 1967 the land of Skaftafell was purchased by the state and made into a National Park because of the great variety of natural beauty. Skaftafellsstofa is an information and education centre where visitors can find answers to their questions about the Skaftafell area, along with information about hiking trails, accommodation and nearby recreational options. Skaftafellstofa has an exhibition room where the story of fire and ice is told; the way in which volcanoes and glaciers have struggled to form the surrounding region and the effects of eruptions and glacial outburst floods on daily lives of people. Park Wardens operate in the Park, assisted by Park Rangers during the summer months. Visitors are encouraged to seek information and advice from Park staff. Hiking trips led by rangers give visitors the opportunity to get to know the magnificent Skaftafell area and find out about the history and natural phenomena of the area, in the company of a well-informed guide. The hikes follow a variety of routes, and everyone should be able to find a suitable outing. Also on offer are short trips walking on glacier, 2 and a half hour and 5 hours, that explore the peculiar landscape on the glacier tongues. The Guides educate on the nature of glaciers, as well as the geological history and human settlement in the region. More sporty orientated are Climbing tours and the ascension of Iceland's highest peak Hvannadalshnjúkur 2110 m. Glacier equipment is provided for all tours.

See information on Vatnajökull National Park on p. 122.

Sel, a small turf farmhouse of the southern type built in 1912. The baðstofa (communal living space) is built over the cowshed for warmth. Nearby barns are of ancient type of construction. In the keeping of the National Museum since 1972.

998 Skaftafellsvegur, 1,86 km.

Svínafell, a manor farm since early days and once one of the most important farms in the eastern region of Iceland. The home of Flosi Þórðarson well known from *Njáls saga* and of his family, known as Svínfellingar, who played an important role in the events of the 12th and 13th century. Beautiful surroundings, good weather, birch bushes and the longest tongue of the glacier Svínafellsjökull almost in the home field.

Falljökull, a glacier tongue, steep and fissured, descending like a waterfall from the mountain.

Sandfell, an abandoned farm, a church until 1914 and a parsonage until 1931, one of the oldest farms in the Öræfi district. The easiest and most-travelled route to Öræfajökull and Hvannadalshnjúkur starts from Sandfell. The traveller goes first up Sandfellsheiði moor where it is possible to ascend to about 1,300 m before stepping onto the glacier, where there are 400-500 m of rather steep glacier, usually with many big crevasses, to be covered before reaching the 4 km wide plateau to the north of the mountain Rótarfjallshnjúkur (1,848 m). This has to be crossed to get to the 2,110 m high Hvannadalshnjúkur, rising about 200 m from the north-west edge of the plateau. This final peak is usually icy and greatly fissured. The whole climb is quite strenuous and takes 15-20 hours. Standard glacier-climbing techniques should be applied. Ice-axes, crampons and lines are essential, and inexperienced people must have guides.

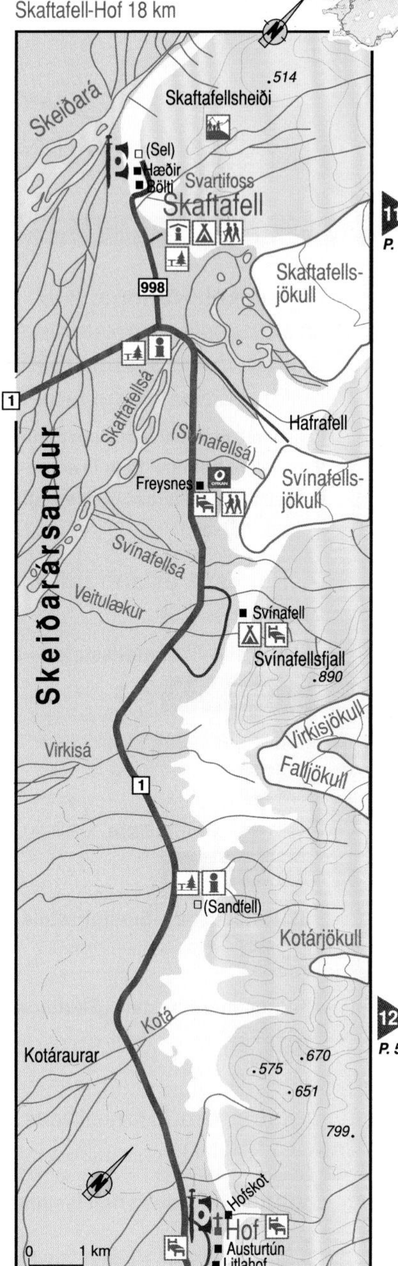

Vatnajökull National Park, established in 2008, covers all of Vatnajökull glacier and extensive surrounding areas. These include the former national parks at Skaftafell and Jökulsárgljúfur. Today's national park covers about 14% of Iceland, making it one of the largest protected areas in Europe.

In general, national parks are protected areas considered unique for their nature or cultural heritage. Vatnajökull National Park is above all unique through the great variety of landscape features created by the combined forces of rivers, glacial ice, and volcanic and geothermal activity.

Visitor centres and information offices:

Skaftafell - Skaftafellsstofa

Höfn – Gamlabúð

Ásbyrgi – Gljúfrastofa

Skriðuklaustur – Snæfellsstofa

Kirkjubæjarklaustur – Skaftárstofa

Other information offices cooperating with the park:

Guesthouse Hoffell (southeast Iceland)

Guesthouse Hólmur (southeast Iceland)

Guesthouse Skálafell (southeast Iceland)

All of the aforementioned visitor centres and information offices are located in lowland areas and are accessible by normal vehicles troughout the year. Opening hours do vary; for details please visit the park's website: *www.vjp.is*

The highland areas

A large part of the park is located in higland areas. Highland ranger stations serve as information offices, with rangers providing information and educational services. Please note that under normal circumstances ranger stations are accessible and operate in the summer only.

Highland ranger stations:

Askja, Kverkfjöll, Hvannalindir, Snæfell, Lónsöræfi, Laki, Eldgjá, Langisjór, Nýidalur.

Most of the roads in highland areas require 4x4 vehicles. The roads become impassable in winter and remain closed until June or sometimes July. Travellers are encouraged to seek information about road conditions prior to their travels. Detailed road maps are available in visitor centres, information centres and from park rangers.

Please note that off-road driving is illegal in Iceland and punishable by law.

WELCOME TO VATNAJÖKULL NATIONAL PARK!

Morsárdalur og Svínafellsjökull – South

Laki - West

Dettifoss – North

Snæfellsstofa Visitor Centre – East

Skaftafell Visitor Centre – South

Photos: ©Guðmundur Ögmundsson

Further information about Vatnajökull National Park, event schedule, campsites, hiking routes, recreation and activities are available on www.vjp.is, in visitor centres, information offices and from park rangers.

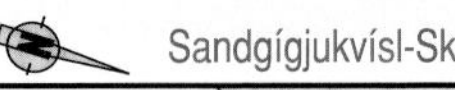

Ring Road

11 P. 574

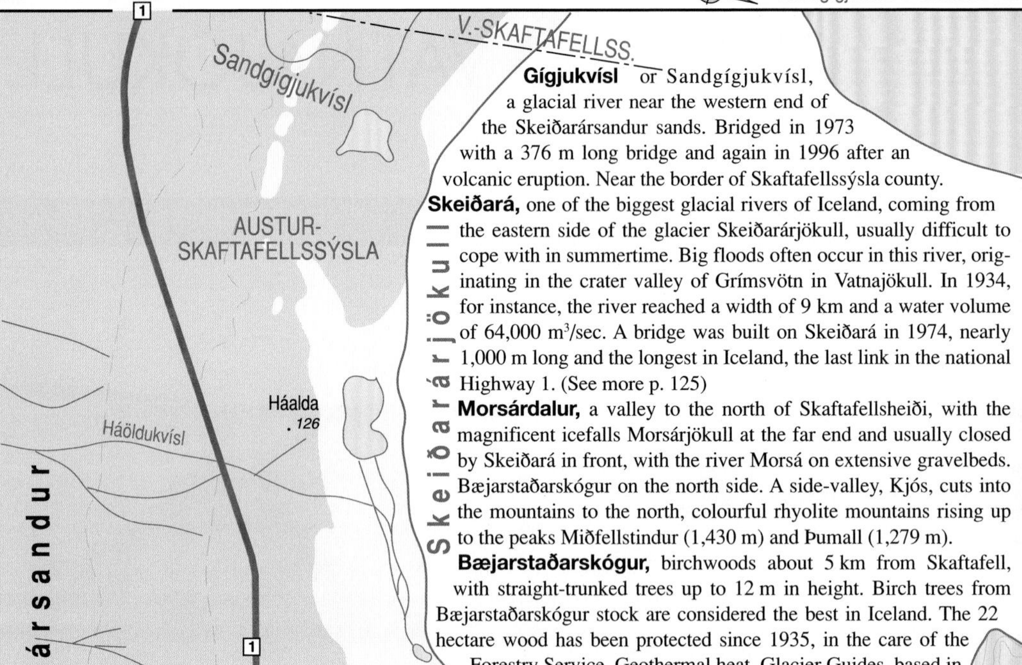

Gígjukvísl or Sandgígjukvísl, a glacial river near the western end of the Skeiðarársandur sands. Bridged in 1973 with a 376 m long bridge and again in 1996 after an volcanic eruption. Near the border of Skaftafellssýsla county.

Skeiðará, one of the biggest glacial rivers of Iceland, coming from the eastern side of the glacier Skeiðarárjökull, usually difficult to cope with in summertime. Big floods often occur in this river, originating in the crater valley of Grímsvötn in Vatnajökull. In 1934, for instance, the river reached a width of 9 km and a water volume of 64,000 m[3]/sec. A bridge was built on Skeiðará in 1974, nearly 1,000 m long and the longest in Iceland, the last link in the national Highway 1. (See more p. 125)

Morsárdalur, a valley to the north of Skaftafellsheiði, with the magnificent icefalls Morsárjökull at the far end and usually closed by Skeiðará in front, with the river Morsá on extensive gravelbeds. Bæjarstaðarskógur on the north side. A side-valley, Kjós, cuts into the mountains to the north, colourful rhyolite mountains rising up to the peaks Miðfellstindur (1,430 m) and Þumall (1,279 m).

Bæjarstaðarskógur, birchwoods about 5 km from Skaftafell, with straight-trunked trees up to 12 m in height. Birch trees from Bæjarstaðarskógur stock are considered the best in Iceland. The 22 hectare wood has been protected since 1935, in the care of the Forestry Service. Geothermal heat. Glacier Guides, based in Skaftafell, offer guided tours in the woods.

998 Skaftafellsvegur, 1,86 km.

Skaftafell-Sandgígjukvísl 24 km

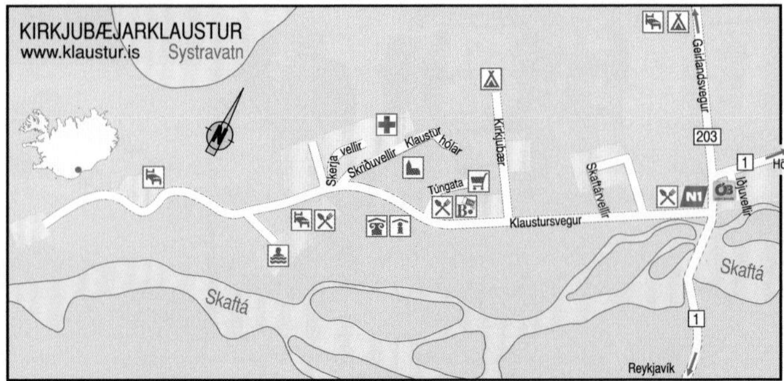

Kálfafell, farm, church. Parsonage until 1880. Served by the Rev. Páll Pálsson (1836-90), the first Icelander to teach the deaf. He first started teaching in 1867, publishing two textbooks for the deaf the same year, *Bible Stories* and *Luther's Theology*. It was almost 130 years before a new textbook for the deaf was published in 1995.

Djúpá, ("Deep river") a sizeable glacial river. A short walk along the eastern bank north of the bridge over the main road takes one to where the waterfall Gufufoss ("Steam falls") tumbles over the edge of a deep and impressive canyon. Canyon and waterfall are spectacular.

Núpsstaður, the first farm west of Skeiðarársandur. A restored chapel from around 1850 and farmhouses from around 1900 in the care of the National Museum. It was extremely difficult to make one's way across the sands before the rivers were bridged, horseback being the only feasible mode of travel. The most skilled and experienced travellers in the area were known, respectfully, as "water men" and the best horses as "water horses". Núpsstaðir was the home of the last such water man, the well-known Hannes Jónsson (1880-1968) who carried the post between Síða and Hornafjörður.

Lómagnúpur, (668 m) a headland which once rose from the sea, now rising from the sands. One of Iceland's highest perpendicular inland cliffs. In July 1789 a large part of the south-western side of the cliff collapsed and evidence of this may be seen in the rock to this day. An avalanche fell on the east side of Lómagnúpur, west of Hellisflái and to the east of Stóragil, in June 1998. This avalanche was on a much smaller scale then the one in 1789.

Núpsvötn, a wide and many-streamed glacial river on the western side of Skeiðarársandur, joined by the river **Súla** some distance upstream. This river often rises considerably, causing big floods when the lake **Grænalón** by the edge of Skeiðarárjökull forces its way out under the glacier. The whole valley between Lómagnúpur and Skeiðarársandur is very interesting for the tourist but difficult to reach because of the rivers. The rivers Núpsá and Hvítá join in two falls into a beautiful canyon and from then on they are called Núpsvötn. It is possible to make one's way along the eastern side of the canyon with the help of an iron chain which has been bolted to the rock. A fine day's hike from the valley across **Eystrafjall** to **Núpsstaðarskógar** and Eggjar to Grænalón or to the impressive Súlutindar by the western edge of Skeiðarárjökull.

Skeiðarársandur, a vast sand desert about 20 by 30 km between the districts Fljótshverfi in the west and Öræfi in the east. It is said that there were once many farms in this area, but these were destroyed by tremendous floods from Grímsvötn in Vatnajökull breaking their way under the glacier. The largest of these Skeiðarárhlaup, as the floods are called, have been compared with the Amazon river. In 1974 bridges were built across the rivers Núpsvötn, Sandgígjukvísl and Skeiðará thus completing the main highway round Iceland. Considerable volcanic activity in Vatnajökull glacier in 1996 destroyed one bridge and damaged another. Much quagmire remains and travellers are warned that great care should be taken and no attempt made to drive off the main road in this area.

Kálfafell-Sandgígjukvísl 19 km

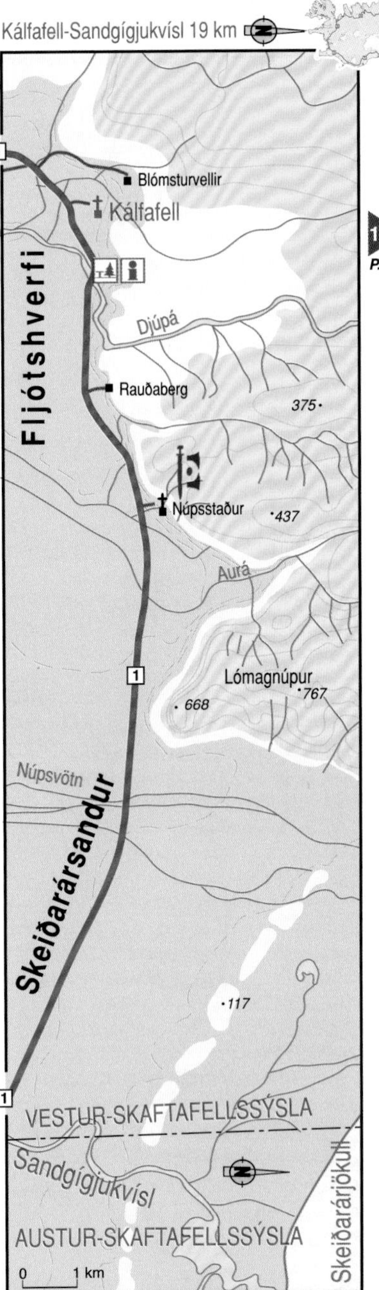

Sandgígjukvísl-Kálfafell 19 km

11 P. 574

At Núpsstaður

Lómagnúpur seen from the east

11 P. 574

1
251
Múlakot
Hörgsdalur
Hörgsland
.188
Hörgslandskot
Fossálar
Brunnasandur
Síða
.294
399.
.329
Foss
Þórutjörn
.373
Dverghamrar
Hraunból
Sléttaból
Orustuhóll
90.
.267
Eyjalón
Þverá
1
Brunahraun
Eldvatn
Dalshöfði
Seljaland
Hruni
Slétta
Teygingalækur
Hverfisfljót
Fljótshverfi
Brunná
Hótel Núpar
Núpar
Hvoll
201
Brúará
Maríubakki
Djúpá
(Blómstur-
vellir)
Kálfafell
Laxá
0 1 km
1
Kálfafell-Hörgsland 20 km

Múlakot, a schoolhouse built 1909. One of many such houses, now rare, built after the new school laws were enacted in 1907. Renovated and protected.

Hörgsdalur, a farm and a former parsonage.

Hörgsland, a farm. Often a parsonage. One clergyman, Magnús Pétursson, who lived there in the 17th century, was a poet and said to be skilled in black magic, one of his feats being to divert a fleet of Turkish pirate ships away from the shores of the country. He was also skilled at slaying ghosts. A hospital in the 17th and 18th century.

Brunasandur, a green area along the edge of Brunahraun, which started to grow after the eruption of 1783-44. The first farm was built there in 1822.

Foss, a farm taking its name from an unusual waterfall coming off the cliffs on the mountainside.

Þverá, a jeeptrack leeds from Þverá to road F206 Lakavegur through an amazing world of waterfalls, lavaformations and caves.

Dverghamrar, ("Dwarf crags") rocks with hexagonal columns by the roadside. Such columns are often found where lava has flowed into water and been abruptly cooled.

Brunahraun, the eastern part of the Skaftáreldahraun lava of 1783-4, coming from the Lakagígar craters and following the river Hverfisfljót. An interesting walk to the old **Hverfisfljótsgljúfur** canyon.

Orustuhóll, ("Battle hill") a tuff cliff-sided hill (90 m) south of the highway. A grand view from the top.

Eldvatn, ("Fire water") (on Brunasandur), a clear river flowing from under the lava-field and eventually into Hvalsíki.

Hverfisfljót, a glacial river coming from the southwest part of Vatnajökull, Síðujökull. Divides the districts Fljótshverfi to the east and Síða to the west and flows into Hvalsíki.

Fljótshverfi, the district between the rivers **Hverfisfljót** and Núpsvötn, the easternmost district of Vestur-Skaftafellssýsla.

Núpar, a farm formerly called Gnúpar, where the settler Gnúpa-Bárður settled after having moved from Bárðardalur in the north across the interior through Vonarskarð and down to Fljótshverfi. The Sagas say that Bárður had each of his animals carry its own food across the desert. Behind the farm is the mountain Núpafjall. There you can find the cave **Gapi**.

201 Vallavegur, 3,59 km.

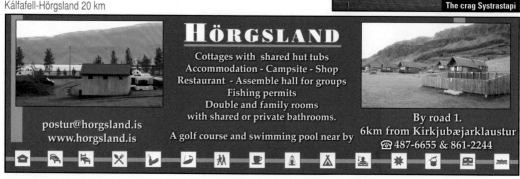

The crag Systrastapi

1 SUÐURLANDSVEGUR

Skaftá, a glacial river and one of the big rivers of Iceland. Comes from the glacier Skaftárjökull in Vatnajökull, divides the districts Skaftártunga and Síða, then turns eastward along Síða and thence southward along Landbrot.

Hólmur, a farm. The home of Bjarni Runólfsson (1891-1938), a self-taught electrical engineer, who built many power-stations throughout Iceland. This was the side of a carpentery school from 1945 to 1963.

Síða, the district from Skaftá to Þverá. Lies on the south side of some low mountains.

205 Klausturvegur, 1,35 km. **202 Prestbakkavegur,** 4,6 km.

Kirkjubæjarklaustur, ("The church farm convent") (pop. 140) for long one of the biggest farms of the county Skaftafellssýsla. Now a village with the community centre Kirkjuhvoll, a Vatnajökull National Park information centre, a weather station, elementary school, sport centre and a swimming pool. Christian Irishmen are supposed to have lived there before the Norse settlement, and after Ketill the foolish settled there no heathen people were allowed to live at this spot. A convent was situated there from 1186 until the Reformation in the 15th century. Many place-names remind us of the convent, such as **Systrastapi** ("The sisters' crag"), **Systrafoss** ("The sisters' falls"), **Systravatn** ("The sisters' lake") and **Sönghóll** ("Hill of chanting") to the south of the river Skaftá, where the monks of Þykkvibær on their way to visit the nuns of Kirkjubæjarklaustur would start their chanting as Kirkjubæjarklaustur came into sight. West of Systrastapi is **Eldmessutangi** ("Fire sermon point") where, in the eruption of 1783, the advancing lava miraculously stopped before it reached the church where Rev. Jón Steingrímsson was delivering his famous "eldmessa" ("Fire sermon"). It was common belief that it was due to his prayers that the lava-stream stopped. National Forest.

Kirkjugólf, ("Church floor") curious basaltic rock formation just east of Kirkjubæjarklaustur. Resembles the tiled floor of an ancient cathedral.

Stjórn, a clear river running across the Stjórnarsandur sands where the land has been effectively recultivated. On a sunny day the water, which runs down over dark rocks, can warm up enough for bathing.

Prestbakki, a farm. Church built in 1859.

Keldunúpur,a farm and a mountain of the same name. There is a cave **Gunnarshellir**, named after Gunnar Keldugnúpsfífl. In the year 1948 people found a big cross carved in to the wall of the cave.

203 Geirlandsvegur, 2,66 km.

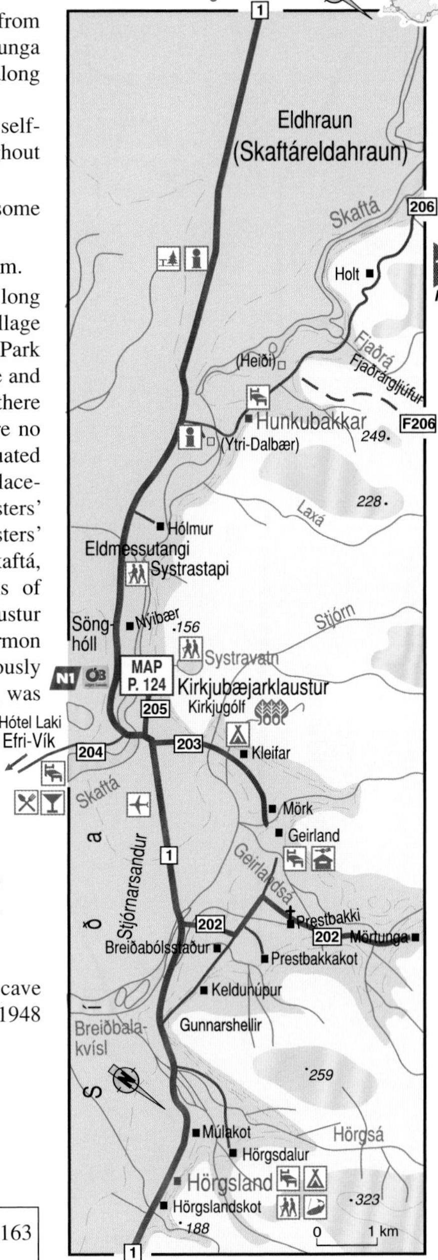

204 Meðallandsvegur, p. 162
206 Holtsvegur, p. 128, 163
F206 Lakavegur, p. 434

Ásar-Hunkubakkar 18 km

Eldvatn, ("Fire water") an outlet from the river Skaftá, which together with Tungufljót and Hólmsá forms Kúðafljót.

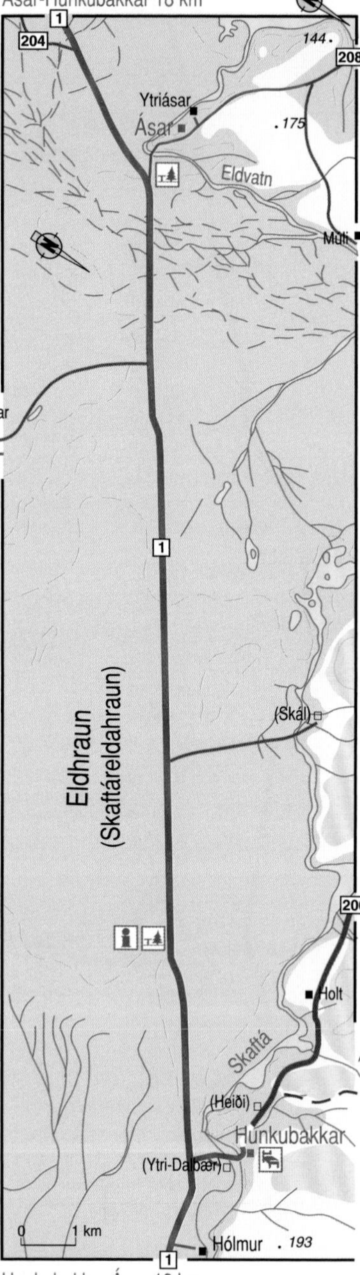

Eldhraun, ("Fire lava") or **Skaftáreldahraun** a lava-flow, from a row of craters, Lakagígar, along a 25 km long fissure named after the mountain Laki. The lavaflow from this eruption of 1783-84 was 565 km², considered one the largest in the world from one eruption in historical times. The eruption is usually called Skaftáreldar ("The Skaftá river fires") or Síðueldur. More than 20 farms had to be abandoned, and the eruptions were followed by "Móðuharðindin", a period of famine and disease named for the ash mist from the eruption. More than 9,000 people died, approx. 20% of the Icelandic nation. This was one of the heaviest blows to the population of Iceland since the settlement in 874. Much has been written by Icelandic and foreign scientists about the craters of Laki and the eruption.

Skál, a farm and church abandoned in 1783 due to the Skaftáreldar eruptions. An old route eastwards through the lava along the the river is marked with cairns.

Holt, a farm destroyed by the Skaftáreldar eruptions, after which it was moved. Birthplace of the author Jón Björnsson (1907-94). There is an extensive and beautiful view from the **Holtsborg** crag, on which grows burnet rose (*Rosa pimpinellifolia*). To the west of Holt is **Holtsdalur**, a pleasant valley to walk through.

Fjaðrá, a minor river running through a magnificent rocky canyon, falling into Skaftá between the farms Holt and Heiði.

Heiði, abandoned farm. The jeep-track to Laki starts beyond Heiði, passes the abandoned farm **Heiðarsel** and goes past the abandoned farm **Eintúnaháls** ("One-field ridge"). In the canyon is a odd looking waterfall often named **Slæðufoss**. The river Stjórn must be forded, as must Geirlandsá just by the waterfall Fagrifoss ("Beautiful falls"). The track then leads east and north over the barren Mörtungusker, fords the river Hellisá, then just east of Blágil, crosses the mountain Galti and then leads to Laki along the Varmárdalur valley north of Galti. Most years this track is fairly good after the beginning of July for any 4-wheel drive vehicles, though the fords can be a hindrance. The craters of Laki are extremely interesting.

206 Holtsvegur, 1,1 km to Hunkubakkar, but 4,7 km to Holt.

Hunkubakkar, a farm. There starts a jeep track (42 km) to Laki, see Road F206. Birthplace of State architect Guðjón Samúelsson (1887-1950) who designed a number of the well-known buildings in Reykjavík such as Hallgrímskirkja church, The National Theatre, The main University building and the Landspítali hospital.

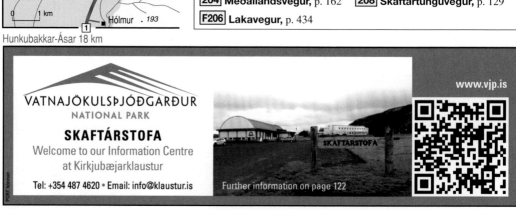

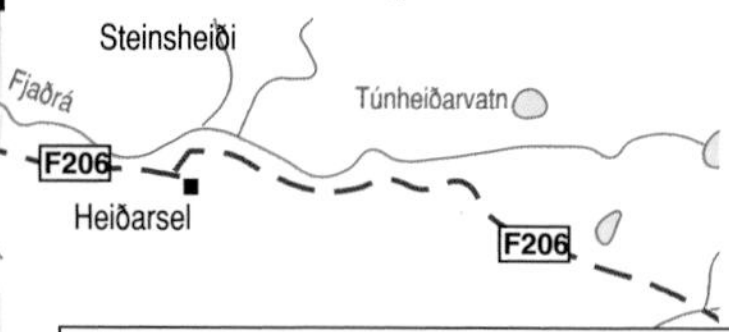

204 Meðallandsvegur, p. 162 **208 Skaftártunguvegur,** p. 129

F206 Lakavegur, p. 434

Hunkubakkar-Ásar 18 km

14 P. 577

11 P. 574

1 SUÐURLANDSVEGUR

Laufskálavarða, a low gravel ridge with many small cairns. Every traveller who passed for the first time was supposed to build a cairn for good luck. An information board is located by the cairns.

Kúðafljót, a big glacial river formed by the rivers **Eldvatn**, Tungufljót, Hólmsá and Skálm. About 4 km wide and difficult to ford before it was bridged, because of quicksands. Seals and trout in the river mouth. The Irish settler Vilbaldi had a boat named Kúði, from which the river gets its name. It is thought the boat may have been an Irish coracle.

Hólmsá, a glacial river drawing its water from the north and east of the Mýrdalsjökull glacier, and often getting a good share of the floods when the volcano Katla erupts. Many outlets from the north of Mýrdalsjökull combine to form the river Brennivínskvísl ("The schnaps branch"), which joins Hólmsá after this has emerged from Rauðibotn, the southern end of the Eldgjá canyon, in many falls and rapids.

Skaftártunga, a settlement between the river Hólmsá and the river Skaftá.

Hrífunes or Hrísnes, the southernmost farm in the Skaftártunga area, where an extensive wood has been largely destroyed by sandstorms.

209 Hrífunesvegur, 12,4 km.

Ásar, a farm and parsonage. For a time the home of Hróar Tungugoði Unason (920).

Flaga, a farm and formerly a popular resting place for travellers.

Tungufljót, a clear river that comes from the mountains Svartahnúksfjöll and Bláfjall.

208 Skaftártunguvegur, 15 km. **210 Ljótarstaðavegur,** 6 km.

Gröf, a farm and church. The church was built in 1896 and totally rebuilt in 1932. It can seat 100 worshippers. Surrounding the cemetery is a fine turf wall that is much admired for its skillful construction.

204 Meðallandsvegur, p. 162 **211 Álftaversvegur,** p. 130
F208 Fjallabaksleið nyrðri, p. 436

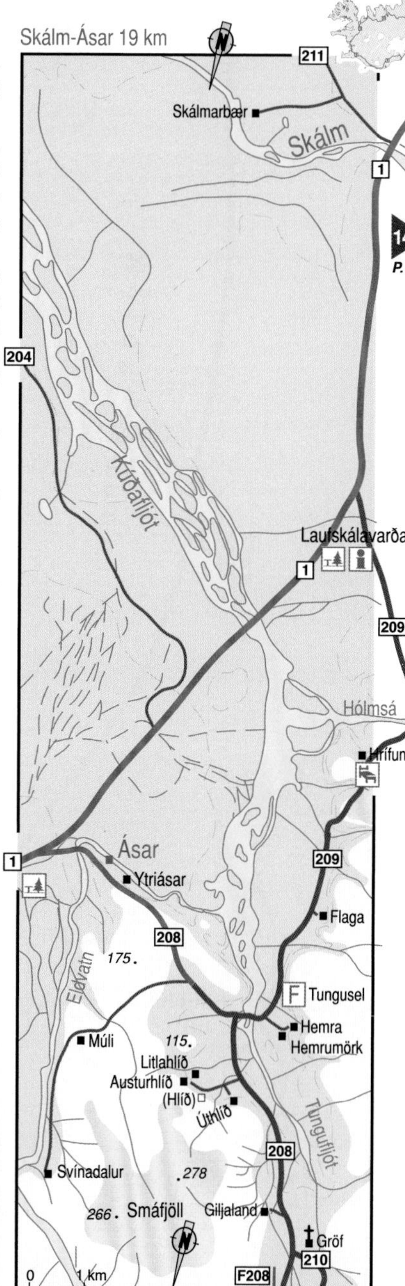

Ring Road

14 P. 577

Blautakvísl-Skálm 16 km

Skálm-Blautakvísl 16 km

Hjörleifshöfði

Hafursey, (582 m) a rugged tuff mountain with gorges, gullies and peculiar rock formations. A nesting place for fulmars.

Mýrdalssandur, a 700 km² desert southeast of Mýrdalsjökull, created by floods from Katla and changing glacial rivers. Landgræðsla ríkisins, the Soil Conservation Service of Iceland has revegetated areas along the road to minimize the effect of drifting sand on road traffic.

Mýrdalsjökull, (1,480 m) the fourth largest glacier in Iceland, about 701 km². Many glacier tongues protrude from the main glacier towards Mýrdalssandur, such as **Kötlujökull**, Öldufellsjökull, Sandfellsjökull and Höfðabrekkujökull. Under Mýrdalsjökull above Höfðabrekkujökull is the volcano **Katla** , which has erupted 16 times in the past 1,100 years, about once every 70 years or so. The interval between eruptions varies from 40 to 80 years. The first recorded eruption was in 894 and the last one in 1918. The eruptions usually start quite abruptly, sending torrents of melted glacier down across Mýrdalssandur, so huge they sweep away everything in their path. Many farms have been destroyed and many lives lost in some of these floods.

211 Álftaversvegur, 8 km. **212 Hryggjavegur,** 8,5 km.

Álftaver, a small district between Mýrdalssandur and Kúðafljót. Some hills and pseudo-craters on the north side have provided considerable protection from many of the floods from Katla. The craters are a protected natural feature. A view dial is located on Álftaver Road, near the crossroads at the Ring Road, a board with information about Þykkvabæjarklaustur nearby.

Þykkvabæjarklaustur, farm, church and a monastery from 1168 until the Reformation in the 17th century. Its first abbot was Þorlákur Þórhallsson the Holy, the only Icelander to have been canonized by the Roman Catholic church, which was confirmed by the Pope in 1984. The 23rd of December is Þorláksmessa, his saints day. Plaque commemorating the monastery can be seen where the altar once was. In the sands above the farm a very big medieval farmstead which was buried in a flood from **Katla** has been dug up. About 6 km distance south of Þykkvabæjarklaustur on an almost impassable path are two sheephouses of turf from about 1900. One of them has lymegrass between rafters and turf roofing and a unique type of timber frame. In the keeping of the National Museum since 1974.

1 SUÐURLANDSVEGUR

Reynisfjall, (324 m) a steep mountain, with a discontinued loran-station on top. Big rockfalls have occurred. A nesting-place for fulmars and puffins.

Reynisdrangar, 66 m high rocks and needles in the sea.

Vík, a village with 326 inhabitants, an official trading post since 1887. Vík attracts a great number of tourists year-round, who come to experience its famed natural beauty. A large arctic tern nesting colony is located east of Vík, while Mt. Reynisfjall, to the west, is home to a vast number of bird species, including puffin, fulmar, auk and kittiwake. A great diversity of flowers and grasses may be found on the eastern side of Mt. Reynisfjall, the most extensive in one place in all of Iceland. The entire area is perfect for nature lovers and many lovely hiking paths exist in Vík and its surrounding regions. Brydebúð, the origins of which date from 1831, contains an information centre, a café, and exhibitions about living conditions, nature, climate and ship strandings on the southern coast. There is a memorial to German seafarers in Vík, and a storehouse opposite Brydebúð contains the Skaftfellingur, a 60-ton vessel built in 1916-1917, which sailed with people and goods to "harbours" on the harbourless coast of Vestur-Skaftafellssýsla for some 20 years, beginning in 1918. Various services are available in Vík, including a hotel, guesthouse, hostel and campground. There is also a field for sports, 9 hole golf course, a swimming pool, bank, health care centre, preschool, elementary school and a music school. Vík was the home of Sveinn Pálsson, MD (1762-1840), the first Icelandic natural historian.

214 Kerlingardalsvegur, 2,4 km.

Kerlingardalur, a valley and farm of the same name. The river Kerlingardalsá flows past the mouth of the valley. A road runs up along Kerlingardalur, over Höfðabrekkuheiðar heaths to the bridge at Selfjall. A lovely route, with unique rock formations in Lambaskörð and a magnificent view from Léreftshöfði.

Þakgil, ("Roof Canyon") draws its name from the good shelter it gives. Now there is a campsite and some cabins, open during the summer. Beautiful walking routes. The road to Þakgil is 14 km and is passable for all cars.

Höfðabrekka, a farm and formerly a church. The farm was once situated at the foot of the mountain, but was moved higher up after the Katla eruption of 1660 and then down again in 1964. Some centuries ago Jóka was the lady of the house. It was said that she got so angry at one of the farmhands for making her daughter pregnant that after her death she haunted him and the farm for years. This notorious ghost was known as Höfðabrekku-Jóka.

Hjörleifshöfði, (221 m) a headland named after Hjörleifur, the foster-brother of Ingólfur Arnarson, the first settler in Iceland. According to *Landnámabók* ("The Book of Settlements") Hjörleifur stayed there for a while and was killed there. There is a large fulmar colony in the cliffs and there was a farm there until 1937. Formerly on the coast but now several km inland. There is a trail leading to the headland, but it is only passible for cars with 4x4.

Kötlutangi, the southernmost pointv of Iceland. Formed by floods from Mýrdalsjökull. In the Katla eruption of 1918 the land increased for 2 km to the south, but the sea has since worn much of the increase away.

215 Reynishverfisvegur, 4km.

216 Þórisholtsvegur, 1 km.

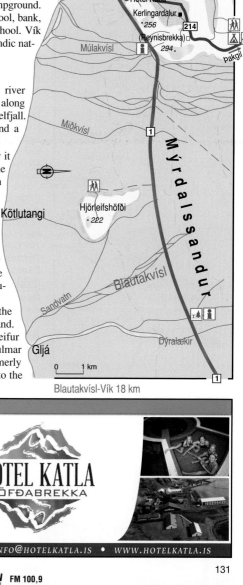

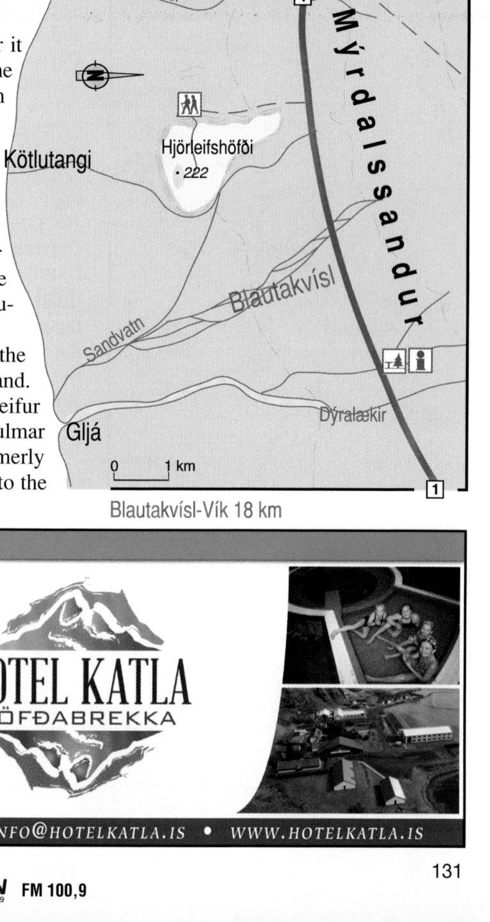

Ytri-Sólheimar-Vík 22 km

14 P. 577

VÍK

www.vik.is
info@vik.is

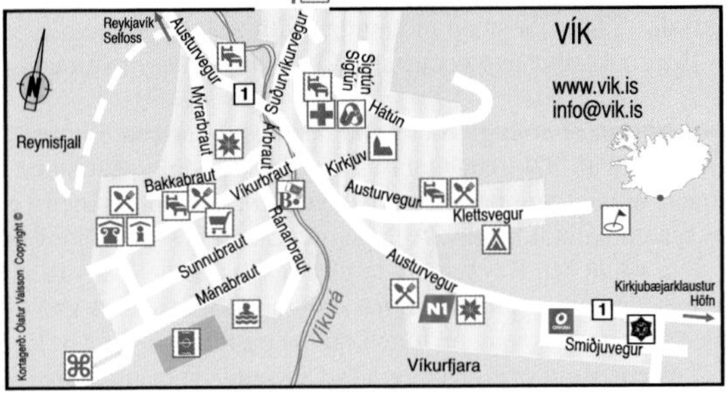

Sólheimar, westernmost farms in Mýrdalur. The home of the settler Loðmundur the Old. **Sólheimajökull**, a glacier tongue coming from the southwest of the glacier Mýrdalsjökull, is named for the farm. The spectacular surroundings of the glacier are marked by rugged and majestic rock formations thoroughly shaped by the glacier. This is an easy walk on crampons up onto the ice field where a wonderland of ice sculptures, ridges and deep crevasses await your discovery. Guieds offer guided tours on the glacier and at the beginning of the tour an experienced glacier guide will teach you how to use basic ice equipment, crampons and ice axe required for your trip into this magical frozen world.

Mýrdalur, the district between the deserts Sólheimasandur and Mýrdalssandur. Immensely varied landscape: green pastures and fields with valleys, gullies and canyons, and the glacier Mýrdalsjökull in the background.

218 Dyrhólavegur, 6 km. **219 Péturseyjarvegur,** 4 km.

Pétursey, (275 m) a solitary mountain.

Skeiðflöt, a church. In a hill on the south side of the farm is a five-pointed star.

Dyrhólahverfi, a cluster of farms, which includes Dyrhólar, home of *Njáls saga*'s Kári Sölmundarson.

Loftsalir, a farm. The cave Loftsalahellir, which was used for official gatherings up to the turn of the century is in the mountain Geitafjall.

Dyrhólaey, ("Doorway hill island") a cape or headland 110-120 m high, with perpendicular cliffs on the southern and western sides and a narrow rock rim with an arch-shaped opening through it protruding into the sea. Boats and even small planes can pass through the arch, hence the name Dyrhólaey, or Portland as it has been called. **Dyrhólahöfn** west of Dyrhólaey used to be a point place for fishermen. Cliffs and pillars off the coast, one of them, Háidrangur (56 m), climbed by Hjalti Jónsson in 1893. Dyrhólaey is a nature sanctuary.

Dyrhólaós, a lagoon.

Skammidalur, a farm where interesting fossils have been found.

215 Reynishverfisvegur, 4 km. **216 Þórisholtsvegur,** 1 km.

Reynir, a church untill 1987.

Garðar, the southernmost farm in Iceland. Some interesting caves and hexagonal pillar rocks near by at the sea end of the mountain Reynisfjall.

Reynisfjara, a beach with beautiful basalt columns and now a café. Be very careful on the beach as powerful rogue waves regularly come much further in.

221 Sólheimajökulsvegur, p. 442 **222 Mýrdalsjökulsvegur,** p. 442

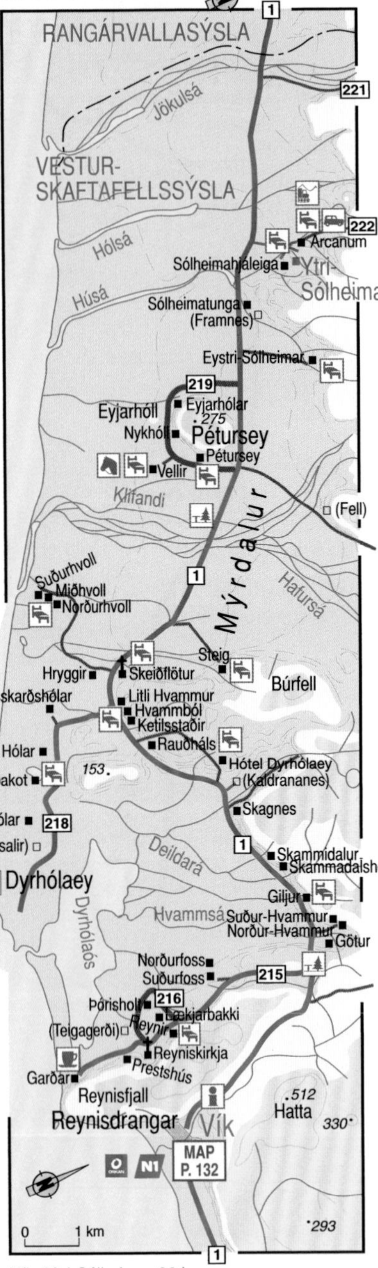

Vík -Ytri-Sólheimar 22 km

Drangshlíð - Ytri-Sólheimar 13 km

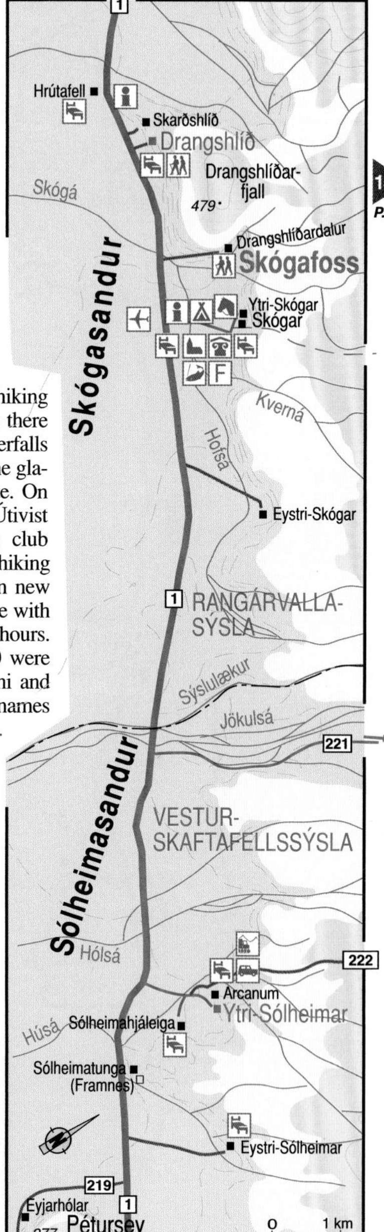

Ytri-Sólheimar-Drangshlíð 13 km

14 P. 577

Skógar, formerly the site of a regional secondary school and a major farm. There was also a church here until the year 1890. Skógar is the location of the Skógar Museum, the largest Folk Museum outside the Reykjavík area. It preserves among other things old tools, implements, a church and farm houses fully furnished, showing the living conditions of the gone past. The chief attraction of the Skógar Museum, and no doubt its most historically valuable asset, is the eight-oar fishing boat Pétursey, Icelands best-kown boat of its kind. The legendary ring from Thrasi's treasure chest, once hidden behind the Skógafoss waterfall, is also on display. The latest addition to the Skógar Museum is the Museum of Transport which explores the history of transport, communications and technology in Iceland.

Skógafoss, (60 m) a waterfall in the river **Skógá,** one of the highest in Iceland. There are many other waterfalls further up in the river. Legend has it that the settler Þrasi hid his chest of gold behind Skógafoss.

Fimmvörðuháls, ("Five cairn ridge") (1,000 m) a ridge between the glaciers Eyjafjallajökull and Mýrdalsjökull, itself formerly covered by glacier. From Skógar one can take a jeep track to Fimmvörðuháls from where there is a good hiking track to Goðaland and Þórsmörk. However, it is even more interesting to get there along the marked hiking path up beside the river Skógá with its many waterfalls which can not be seen from the jeep track. There is a good hike to the peak of the glacier Eyjafjallajökull from Fimmvörðuháls, though this is not the shortest route. On Fimmvörðuháls there are two huts, a new one belonging to the touring club Útivist and an older one just south of Fimmvörðuháls belonging to the touring club Ferðafélag Íslands (FÍ). In the spring of 2010 a volcanic eruption started on the hiking path in Goðaland. It lasted approximately 2 weeks and now one can walk on new mountains and see how alive the Icelandic nature is. An exciting new experience with or without a local guide. Estimated hiking time from Skógar to Þórsmörk 7–10 hours. The two craters that were formed in the eruption in Fimmvörðuháls in 2010 were named Magni og Móði and the new lava field was named Goðahraun. Magni and Móði were the sons of Thor, the Thunder God. Many places in this area cary names linked to the Norwegian mythology. See more info on Fimmvörðuháls on p. 164.

Skógasandur, a large part this sandy area has been revegetated with lupine and extensive grassfields have been developed on the sand.

Jökulsá á Sólheimasandi, a short but swift glacial river coming from the glacier Sólheimajökull. Also known as **Fúlilækur** ("Foul river") on account of the strong sulphur smell. This river used to be a serious obstacle to travel. A bridge was built over it in 1921 and another in 1967.

Sólheimasandur, a sand desert east of Jökulsá, the eastern continuation Skógasandur on the other side of the river.

219 **Péturseyjarvegur,** p. 132
221 **Sólaheimajökulsvegur,** p. 442
222 **Mýrdalsjökulsvegur,** p. 442

13
P. 576

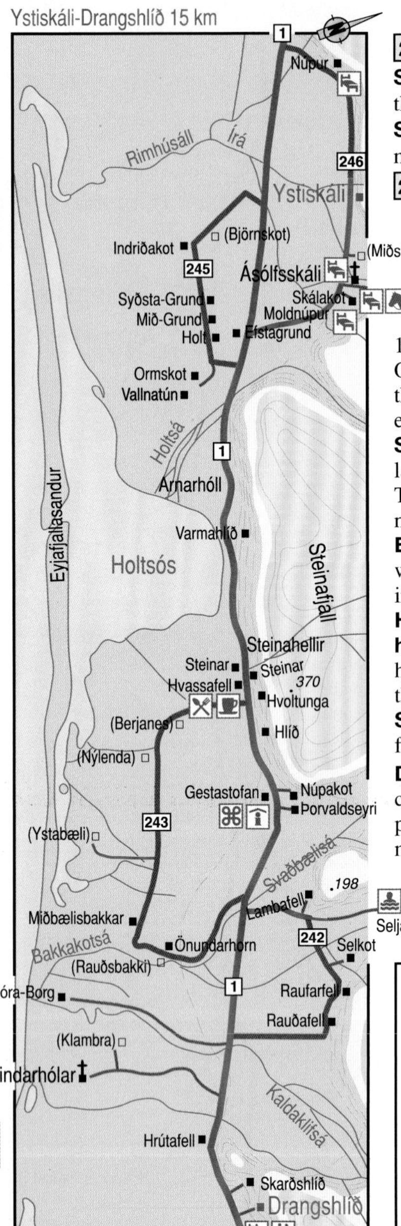

14
P. 577

246 Skálavegur, 5,4 km. **245 Hverfisvegur,** 3,6 km.

Steinahellir, a cave used for official gatherings until the second half of the 19th century.

Steinar, ("Rocks") a farm previously with a church. Has been moved many times because of rockfalls.

242 Raufarfellsvegur, 4,4 km. **243 Leirnavegur,** 6,4 km.

Þorvaldseyri, a farm, the leader in grain cultivation ever since this was reintroduced in Iceland, which includes a special Icelandic grain.

Þorvalseyri Visitor Centre, an information centre dedicated to the dramatic eruption in Eyjafjallajökull volcano in 2011.

Seljavellir, there a swimming pool was built in the mountain side in 1923 by the Youth movement, making use of natural hot water on the spot. One of the shortest climbing routes to the glacier Eyjafjallajökull starts in the vicinity. This route is quite steep and some crevasses may be expected en route.

Stóra-Borg, a farm to the east of Bakkakotsá, quite well-known in Iceland because of the semi-historical novel, *Anna of Stóra-Borg*, by Jón Trausti. Digs in an ancient cemetery and farmhouses have revealed a number of important remains.

Eyvindarhólar, a farm and a church. Parsonage until 1904. The church was dedicated to the Blessed Virgin. The present church was consecreted in 1961.

Hrútafell, a farm. In a rock just east of the farm there is the cave **Rútshellir**, probably the first man-made dwelling in Iceland. Recent research has revealed that there was a forge there of an ancient type, so Rútshellir is the site of remains of great importance.

Skarðshlíð, a farm. Interesting caves shaped by ocean waves in the homefield.

Drangshlíð, takes its name from a unique cliff in the middle of a field called **Drangurinn**. Ledgend says that Grettir Ásmundsson "*the strong*" pushed this cliff from the mountain Hrútafell leaving a scar in the mountain. Under this cliff are caves which have been used through the ages. A protected natural feature.

1 SUÐURLANDSVEGUR

Eyjafjöll, the district between the rivers Álar and Jökulsá on Sólheimasandur. Most of the district is flat land, wet and sandy, between the ocean and steep mountain slopes which, though rocky, are often very grassy. Numerous streams and falls coming off the 300-400 m high mountainside, cut in many places by valleys through which fall glacial rivers from the glacier Eyjafjallajökull which towers in the background.

Eyjafjallajökull, (1,666 m) a volcano covered by about 100 km^2 of glacier. Three eruptions in historical times, in 1612, 1821-22 and 2010. It is comparatively easy to climb this glacier and there is a choice of routes. One of the easiest and safest is from Langanes on the road to Þórsmörk, by Grýtutindur and Sker. See more info p. 164.

Stóri-Dalur, a farm and a church, often mentioned in *Njáls saga*. In Saga times the home of Runólfur Úlfsson, one of the chief opponents of Christianity when it was made legal in the year 1000.The present church was built in 1969. Though unusual in style it´s charming and beautiful.

Kattarnef, ("Cat's nose"), a rocky point protruding towards Markarfljót, previously an obstacle to travellers when the river was high.

Hamragarðar, an abandoned farm. Many streams and waterfalls nearby, among them one of the most unusual small waterfalls in the country, **Gljúfrabúi** ("Canyon dweller"), half hidden in a gorge. A great variety of flora on the slopes by the falls.

Seljalandsfoss, one of the higher waterfalls in Iceland, though it has little water. A path at the bottom of the cliff makes it possible to walk behind the fall. The waterfall and its surroundings are floodlit at night.

Seljaland, a farm where many small caves are to be found, one of them **Kverkarhellir**, previously used for official gatherings. Above the farm is the cave **Seljalandshellir**, sometimes called **Papahellir**, where there are many ancient remains and cross marks in the tuff walls, near the highway.

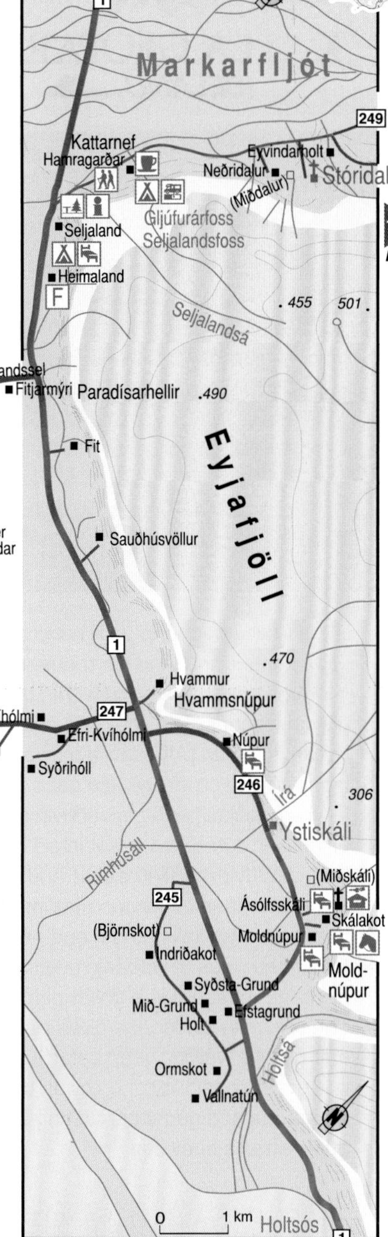

247 Sandhólmavegur, 10,6 km.

Paradísarhellir, ("Paradise cave") a cave up in the cliff-wall west of the farm **Fit**, an easy climb. According to folktales the outlaw Hjalti Magnússon, lover of Anna of Stóra-Borg, had his hideout there in the 16th century. A path leads to it from sheep pens above the main road.

Heimaland, a community centre. **Drífandi**, a high waterfall but with very little water, falls of the cliffs behind the house. If the wind is strong it blows the waterfall back up on the cliff.

Ystiskáli, a farm where the doctor Sveinn Pálsson (1772-1840) lived and wrote a work on the flora of the district. He was the first person to make important discoveries about the movements of glaciers.

Ásólfsskáli, a farm and church. The original settler was Ásólfur the Christian, driven from his home by heathens. The story goes that wherever he came to stay, barren rivers would suddenly teem with fish.

Holtsós, a sea lagoon, which the river Holtsá runs into.

245 Hverfisvegur, 3,6 km. **246 Skálavegur,** 5,4 km.

WHAT IS A GEOPARK?

The Global Geopark Network was established in response to an increasing need for comprehensive protection, development and management of many of the world´s most significant natural sites of geological, archaeological and esthetic value. Global Geoparks Networks, endorsed by UNESCO, now include 112 sites in 32 countries, ensuring high quality geo destinations with geological sites of national and international importance.

Katla Geopark is Iceland's first and only Global Geopark, with an area of 9542 km^2, and a population of 2700 inhabitants. The Geopark was named after one of its majestic volcanoes which lies gently heaving under the glacier Mýrdalsjökull. A top priority of the park is protection of the natural environment, to promote local sustainable development, introduce local culture and place a strong emphasis on nature tourism.

Katla Geopark opens up a natural wonderland to the visitor. The forces of magma and meltwater have shaped the land for thousands of years. Three of the nation's most volcanically active systems are to be found within the Geopark: Eyjafjallajökull, Katla and Grímsvötn, all lying beneath glacial icecaps. The region is characterised by eruptive craters and fissures (Laki and Eldgjá), rootless cones (Álftaversgígar and Landbrotshólar) and lava fields (Skaftárhraun from Laki) with fragile moss coverage. Ice caps topping the highest volcanoes result in outlet glaciers (Sólheimajökull) and glacial rivers (Markarfljót, Kúðafljót, Skaftá) and moraines. Large floods or glacier outbursts associated with subglacial eruptions, have formed outwash plains in the lowlands (Markarfljótsaurar and Mýrdalssandur). Black sandy beaches with beautiful columnar basalt rock formations (Reynisfjara) and cliffs with nesting puffins (Dyrhólaey), beautiful waterfalls (-foss) and numerous remnants of habitation (Kúabót, Vík, Hjöreifshöfði) telling the tales of volcanic events of the past affecting the inhabitants of the area. Skogar heritage museum is a great place to experience nostalgic history and turf buildings.
The versatile landscape gives rise to various activities and adventures, for example ice climbing and glacier walking, jeep safaris, hiking, caving, horse-riding, sightseeing, fishing and birding. There is a great possibility of enjoying the areas local culture and heritage by visiting its interesting museums and geosites, tasting locally produced foods and relaxing in one of the areas swimming pools after a busy day.

THE HILLS ARE ALIVE WITH THE SOUND OF FIRE AND ICE

It can be safely said that Katla Geopark is one of the most dynamic, diverse and geologically exciting regions of the world, ranging from landforms created millions of years ago to freshly minted lava that came with the eruption of Eyjafjallajökull in 2010. There is practically nowhere else on earth where fire and ice collide so dramatically, where the ebb and flow of the landscape is in such constant motion and all of this happening, as it were, in our own backyard. With over 150 volcanic eruptions recorded here since record keeping began in the 9th century, it is the most volcanically active area of Iceland.

Please take advantage of local guides for great adventures and in particular for safety reasons if venturing onto glaciers. Beware of strong currents and unpredictable waves on the south coast beaches and please follow footpaths and refrain from walking on fragile growth formations such as the extensive moss covering the Skaftárhraun lava field.

ATTRACTION

Geology & Culture

1 Alviðruhamrar
2 Drangurinn í Drangshlíð
3 Dyrhólaey
5 Eyjarhóll, Pétursey
6 Hjörleifshöfði
9 Hverfisfljót við Eldvatnstanga
10 Katla, Mýrdalsjökull, Mýrdalssandur
11 Kirkjugólf
16 Nauthúsagil
17 Skaftáreldahraun
19 Skógafoss
20 Steinahellir
22 Systrastapi, Klausturheiði, Systravatn
25 Efra-Hvolshellar
31 Paradísarhellir
33 Þríhyrningur

Mainly Geology

34 Álftaversgígar
38 Dverghamrar
39 Dýralækjasker
41 Eldgjárhraun
43 Eyjafjallajökull, Gígjökull, Steinsholtsjökull
44 Fagrifoss
45 Fimmvörðuháls, Magni & Móði
46 Fjaðrárgljúfur
49 Hólmsárfoss
58 Merkjárfoss (Gluggafoss)
59 Reynisfjall, Reynisdrangar, Reynisfjara
61 Seljalandsfoss, Gljúfrabúi
62 Skaftá
64 Sólheimajökull, Sólheimaheiði

Mainly Geology

74 Kirkjubæjarklaustur
75 Kúabót
80 Vík (older part of the village)
81 Þykkvabæjarklaustur

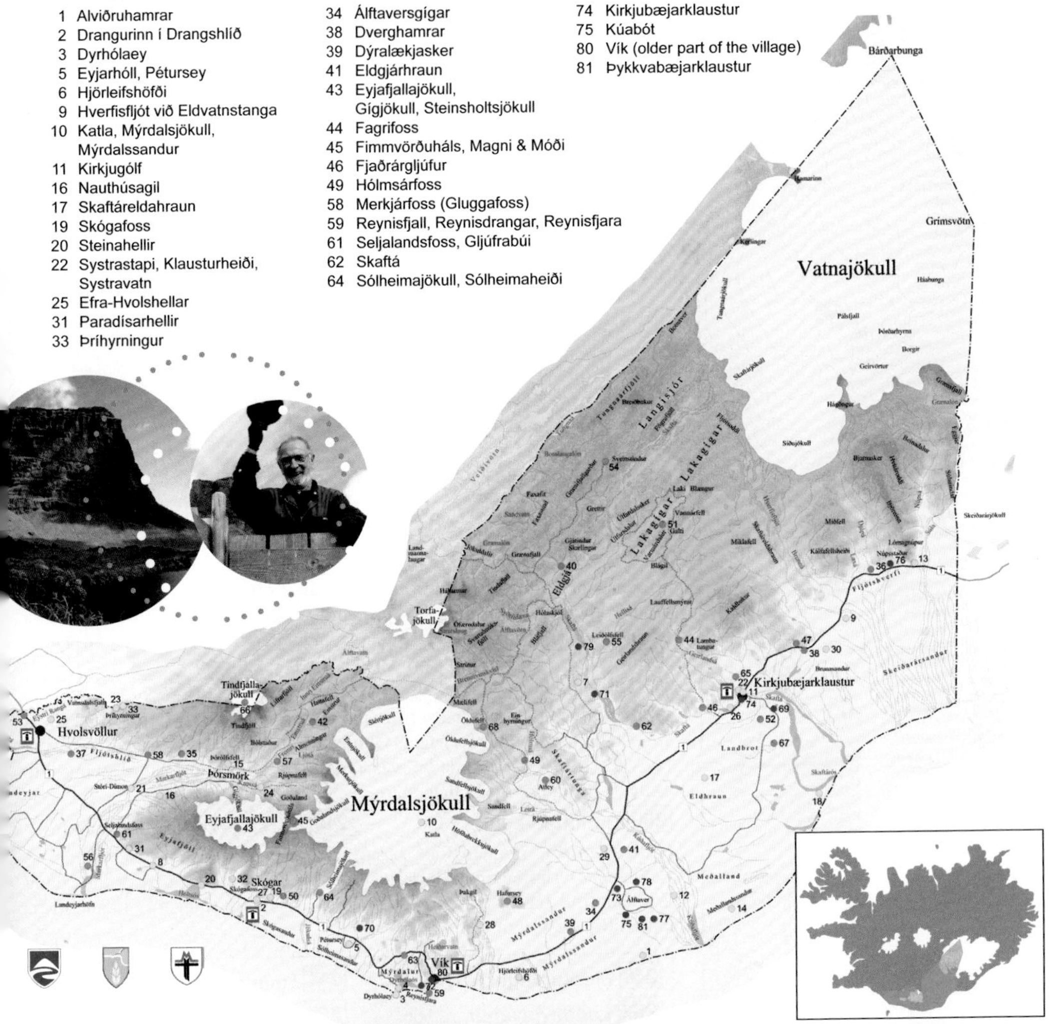

For more information and maps of geosites and hikingtrails within Katla Gopark visit our information centers located in the main populaton centres Hvolsvöllur, Vík and Kirkjubæjarklaustur and at www.katlageopark.is.

THE BEDROCK OF BIODIVERSITY STARTS WITH GEODIVERSITY

Geodiversity refers to the soil, rocks, minerals, landforms and various processes such as earthquakes, volcanoes that have shaped these elements over time. Mountains, caves, beaches, deserts, rivers, oceans and even the weather are all elements of geo-diversity. Geological diversity is in fact the foundation of life, giving support to the ecosystems as well as providing places to live, resources for industry, soils from which we grow our food, areas for recreation, places of healing, places of worship, learning and inspiration. We look to Katla geopark´s magnificent geo diversity for inspiration, for peace, for healing, and as a way to refresh our souls, without which the world would be a dreary place to live indeed.

Hvolsvöllur-Markarfljót 23 km

13 P. 576

Ring Road

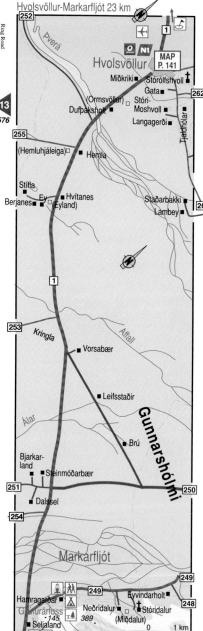

Hvolsvöllur, (pop. 929) the main village in Rangárþing eystra district, a municipality formed in 2002 through the merging of six municipalities between the rivers Eystri-Rangá and Jökulsá á Sólheimasandi. Centre of trade and travel, built up since 1930. Lava Iceland Volcano and Earthquake Centre offers a spectacular interactive experience on volcanicity and seismology, the powerful forces that shape this land. The Sögusetrið historical centre is the site of two museums, one depicting Njáls Saga and the other – the Kaupfélagasafn – focusing on the history of trade in South Iceland. There Njáls Saga is also being sewed in *refill*, which is a special form of viking tapestry (**www.njalurefill.is**) Primary industries are trade, tourism, service and manufacturing, eg. a processing plant of the major butcher and meat-packing company Sláturfélag Suðurlands, founded in 1907 making it the oldest firm of its kind in Iceland. In summer there is a market with local products.

© Mats Wibe Lund

Hvolsvöllur

Þverá, a clear river into which all the streams from Fljótshlíð flow. Previously this river got a good share of glacial water from Markarfljót, which would turn Þverá into a menace that often broke down the fertile land of the district. A series of protective rock barriers was built in order to keep Markarfljót in its own course and since then grasslands are being recultivated.

Vorsabær, a farm where Höskuldur Hvítanesgoði of *Njáls saga* lived.

Gunnarshólmi, grasslands near the rivers Álar and Markarfljót. *Njáls saga* tells us that this is where Gunnar from Hlíðarendi turned and went back to Hlíðarendi, where he was eventually killed, instead of going into exile as he had been sentenced to.

250 Dímonarvegur, 12 km. **249 Þórsmerkurvegur,** 16,4 km.

Stóra-Dímon, remnants of basalt islands of the same rock type as Pétursey, Dyrhóley and Hjörleifshöfði. On the northern part of the island are beautiful basalt column formations. In *Njáls saga* this mountain is called Rauðuskriður.

248 Merkurvegur, p. 166	**251 Hólmabæjarvegur,** p. 166
252 Landeyjavegur, p. 166	**254 Landeyjahafnarvegur,** p. 166
255 Akureyjavegur, p. 166	**261 Fljótshlíðarvegur,** p. 168
262 Vallarvegur, p. 168	**F249 Þórsmerkurvegur,** p. 450

Markarfljót-Hvolsvöllur 23 km

1 SUÐURLANDSVEGUR

267 Selalækjarvegur, 2,5 km.

Selalækur, there lived congressman Gunnar Sigurðsson (1888–1962).

Rangárvellir, the district between the two rivers Ytri-Rangá and Eystri-Rangá. The upper parts covered by lava fields and sands, the middle flat and sandy and the lowest part wet.

266 Oddavegur, 4,3 km.

Oddi.

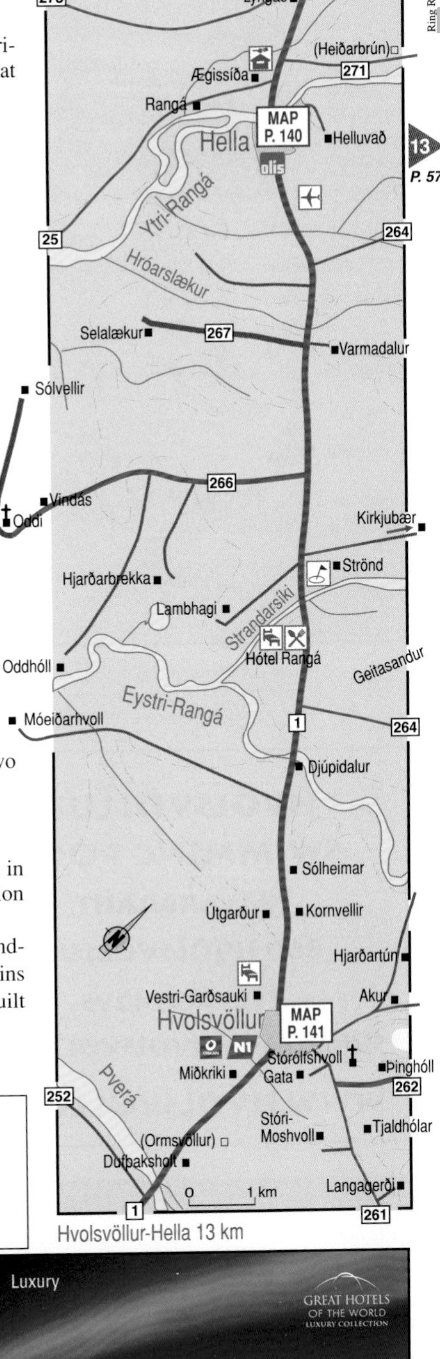

Oddi, a farm, church and parsonage. A major historic site. It first became famous around the middle of the 12th Century, when a church was built there, and thus is one of the oldest church sites in Iceland. In the year 1078, Sæmundur the Learned became priest of Oddi. He had studied for the clergy in France (at the Sorbonne). Sæmundur established a school at Oddi, which is believed to have stood for two centuries.A view dial at **Gammabrekka**.

Oddhóll, there lives one of Icelands best riders Sigurbjörn Bárðarson.

Strönd, once an elementery school, now a golf course.

Geitasandur, a sandy plain. The area has been used for experiments in soil reclamation, re-vegetation and forestry by the Soil Conservation Service of Iceland.

Eystri-Rangá, a river that comes from Rangárbotnar north of Tindfjallajökull. Mostly clear, though there is a small glacial tributary. It joins Þverá and later Ytri-Rangá to form the river Hólsá. First bridge built 1914, the second bridge 1969. Good salmon river.

Djúpidalur, once a slaughter house.

25 Þykkvabæjarvegur, p. 156
261 Fljótshlíðarvegur, p. 168-169
264 Rangárvallavegur, p. 170
273 Bugavegur, p. 156
252 Landeyjavegur, p. 166
262 Vallarvegur, p. 168
271 Árbæjarvegur, p. 158

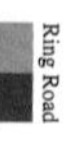

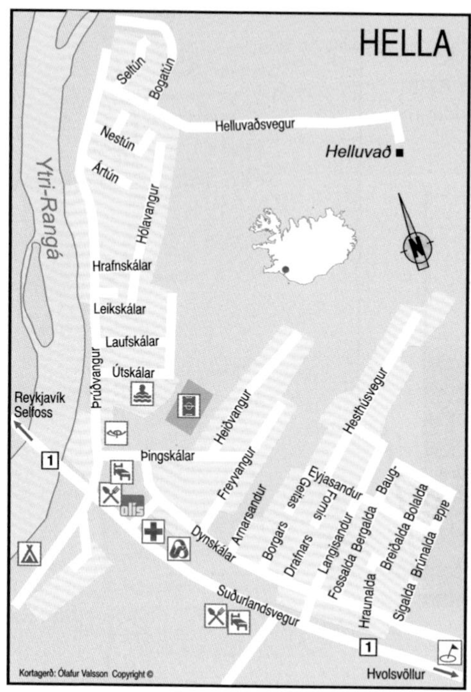

HELLA
Seltún
Bogatún
Helluvaðsvegur
Helluvað
Nestún
Ártún
Hólavangur
Ytri-Rangá
Hrafnskálar
Leikskálar
Laufskálar
Útskálar
Þrúðvangur
Reykjavík
Selfoss
1
Þingskálar
Heiðvangur
Freyvangur
Hesthúsvegur
Arnarsandur
Dynskálar
Borgars
Drafnars
Eyjasandur
Langisandur
Fossalda
Bergalda
Baug-
Breiðalda
Bolalda
Hraunalda
Sigalda
Brúnalda
Suðurlandsvegur
1
Hvolsvöllur
Kortagerð: Ólafur Valsson Copyright ©

© Markaðsstofa Suðurlands

Hella
© Markaðsstofa Suðurlands

Hella, p. 142.

© Markaðsstofa Suðurlands

© Markaðsstofa Suðurlands

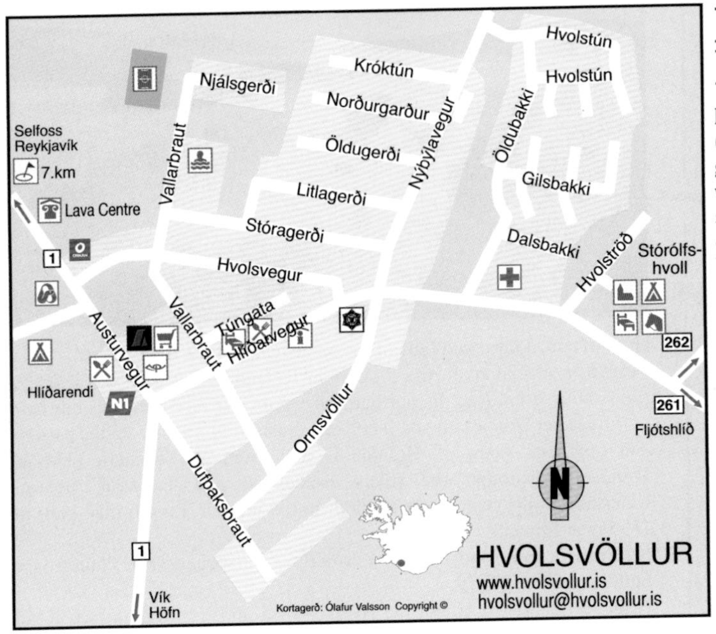

Hvolsvöllur, p. 138.

Eastern Rangárþing

Eastern Rangárþing, (pop. 1752) is a new name given to a municipality which was formed in 2002 when small municipalities merged into one. This new municipality lies between two great rivers, the Eystri-Rangá to the west and the Jökulsá á Sólheimasandi to the east. Many beautiful nature sites are located in this area, for example, Þórsmörk, the Tindfjöll mountains, the Eyjafjallajökull glacier, black beaches and the waterfalls Skógafoss and Seljalandsfoss. Various kinds of recreation are available, such as visits to museums, swimming pools, a sport centre, a community centre, horse rentals, golf courses, galleries, fishing sites, guided hiking and adventure tours etc. The local government of East Rangárþing is at Hvolsvöllur.

Ring Road

13 P. 576

Þjórsá-Hella 19 km

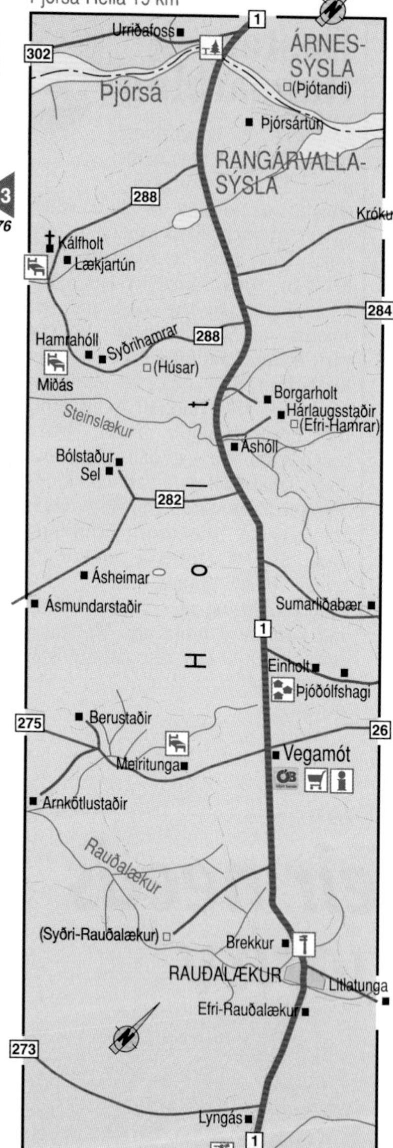

Hella-Þjórsá 19 km

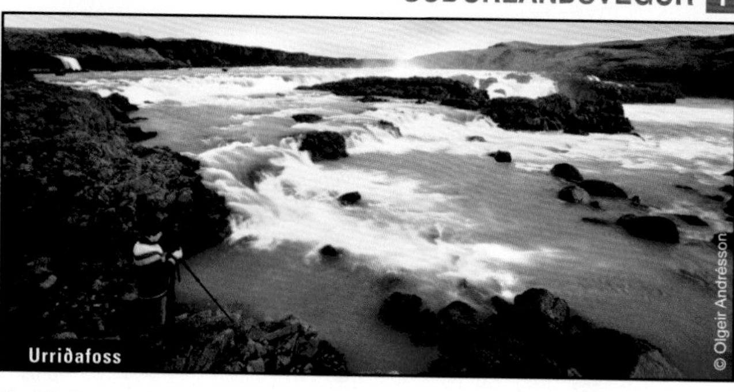
Urriðafoss

© Olgeir Andrésson

Urriðafoss, a farm and falls of the same name in the river Þjórsá.
Þjórsá, a glacial river, the longest in Iceland, about 230 km, average flow about 400m³/sec. Its northernmost source is on Sprengisandur east of the glacier Hofsjökull and it collects most of its water from the eastern and southern sides of Hofsjökull and from the western side of Vatnajökull through the rivers Kaldakvísl and Tungnaá. Several waterfalls in the river, most of them in the interior. First bridge built in 1895 near Þjótandi.
Kálfholt, a farm and church. Formerly a parsonage. The church was built between 1978-79.
Holt, the district between the rivers Þjórsá and Ytri-Rangá (see Road 26).
Efri-Rauðalækur and **Syðri-Rauðalækur,** farms taking their names from a reddish-coloured stream. A small settlement by the main road just west of Hella.
Ægissíða, a farm with 11 man-made caves in the home-field (see Road 25).
Ytri-Rangá, (Rangá West) a spring fed river coming from the lavafields off Rangárbotnar beneath Mt. Hekla. Icelands best salmon fishing river in 2006. First bridge built in 1912 and a new bridge in 1960.
Hella, is the district´s most populated area and its economic hub, with 816 inhabitants. Hella´s industry is based primarily on serving the needs associated with agricultural production in the surrounding area and on services to inhabitants and tourists. Hella boasts a grocery store, bakery, hotel, guesthouse, summer houses, campsite, restaurants, shops, pharmacy, pool, primary school, riding area, rescue team, garage, tyre centre and petrol station as well as various other businesses and public services.

25 **Þykkvabæjarvegur,** p. 156
271 **Árbæjarvegur,** p. 158
275 **Ásvegur,** p. 156
284 **Heiðarvegur,** p. 158
302 **Urriðafossvegur,** p. 178
26 **Landvegur,** p. 158
273 **Bugavegur,** p. 156
282 **Ásmundarstaðavegur,** p. 156
288 **Kálfholtsvegur,** p. 156

1 SUÐURLANDSVEGUR

Ölfusá-Hvítá, one of the biggest rivers in Iceland, 185 km long. It has many tributaries, the last and greatest being the river Sog, and it is after the clear Sog has joined the glacial Hvítá ("White river") that the river is named Ölfusá.

Selfoss, (pop. 7191) is a part of the Municipality of Árborg. A town situated by the bridge of the river Ölfusá. In 1891 a bridge, which used to be the biggest construction in Iceland, was built across Ölfusá, after which the town began to grow. A new bridge was built in 1945. Selfoss is the largest town in South Iceland and the main service centre of trade and industry. The Tourist Information Centre is located at Austurvegur 4, there you will find souvenirs, travel books and maps, internet and a booking service. Various accommodation options can be found in the town for example a hotel, a few guesthouses and a campsite. Many interesting restaurants and cafés are situated in Selfoss. At Svarfhóll, on the outskirt of Selfoss, there is an attractive 9 hole golf course on the bank of the Ölfusá river. Furthermore the town has an outdoor and an indoor swimming pool with steam bath and hot tubs, galleries and a bus terminal. Like all good service centres Selfoss has a a hospital, great variety of shops, two comprehensive schools and a college. There you will also find The Bobby Fisher Center, a museum dedicated to the master of the Royal Game, chess. The largest dairy company in Iceland is in Selfoss. The National Circular Highway no. 1 leads through the town. North of Selfoss is Hellisskógur forrest with nice walking paths by the Ölfusá river and a view over the golf course. The distance from the capital is 57 km.

Laugardælir, the site of a church. Bobby Fisher (1948-2008) the Grand Chessmaster is buried there. Selfoss gets its hot water supply from nearby Þorleifskot.

304 Oddgeirshólavegur, 13 km.

Stóra-Ármót, a research sheep and dairy farm.

Oddgeirshólar, a substantial farm and formerly the site of a church, beautifully situated near the river Hvítá.

303 Ölvisholtsvegur, 4,2 km.

Flói, the agricultural area between the rivers Ölfusá-Hvítá and Þjórsá, reaching inland to the Merkurhraun lavafield. Flat country with the occasional hill, the Þjórsárhraun lava field being the "bedrock" under the soil. In 1927 a remarkable irrigation project was undertaken, using the river Hvítá and constructing the Flóaáveita system of 300 km of ditches and 450 km of dykes to irrigate an area of 12 thousand hectares.

Þingborg, a former school and community centre. Today there´s a souvenir store offering handmade woolen goods and a gallery. The main ditch of the irrigation system Flóaáveita is just west of Þingborg.

Brúnastaðir, a farm near Hvítá, where the irrigation water of Flóaáveita is taken from Hvítá at the rate of 19 m³/sec.

30 Skeiða- og Hrunamannavegur, p. 172
33 Gaulverjabæjarvegur, p. 178
35 Biskupstungnabraut, p. 180
305 Villingaholtsvegur, p. 178
34 Eyrarbakkavegur, p. 178
302 Urriðafossvegur, p. 178
310 Votmúlavegur, p. 178

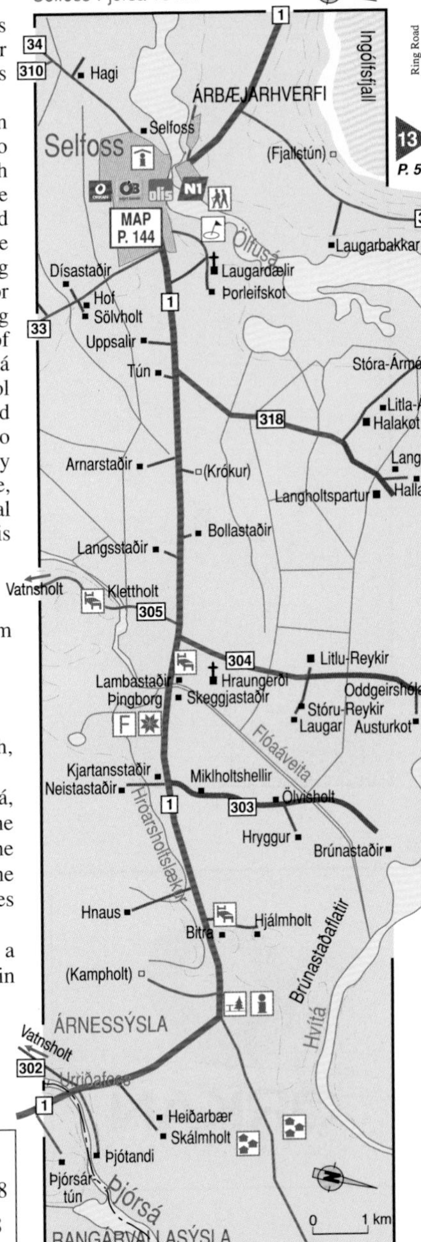

Ring Road
13 P. 576

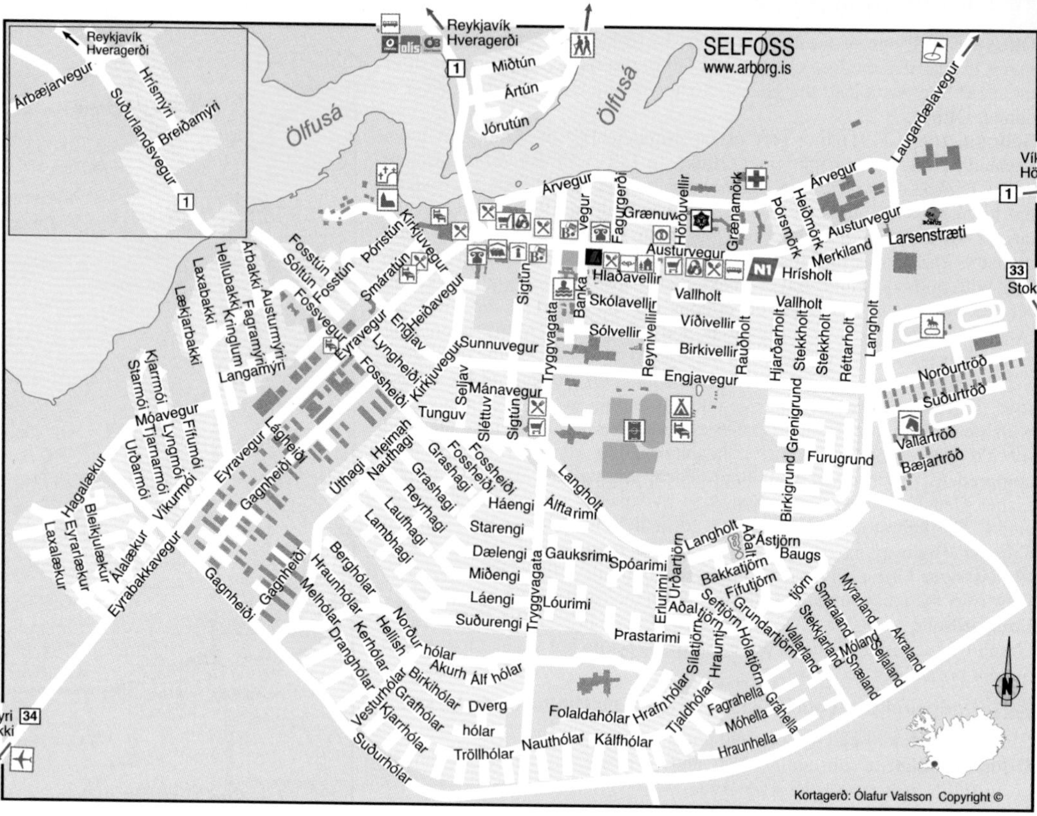

SELFOSS
www.arborg.is

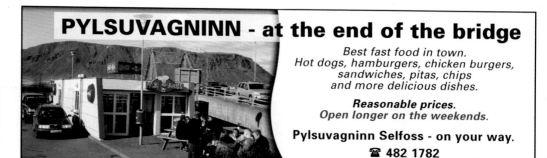

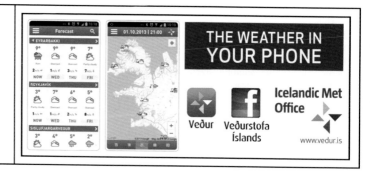

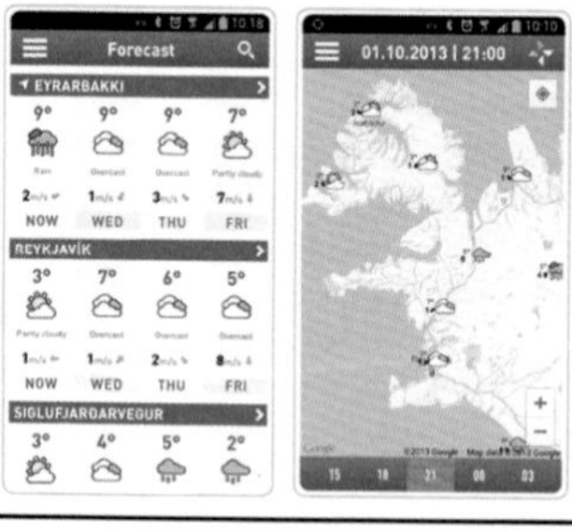

Reykjavík
Hveragerði

Vík
Höfn

Stokkseyri 34
Eyrarbakki

Ölfusá

Miðtún
Ártún
Jórutún
Árvegur
Austurvegur
Larsenstræti
Eyravegur
Kirkjuvegur
Tryggvagata
Engjavegur
Sunnuvegur
Mánavegur
Langholt
Fossheiði
Gagnheiði
Eyrabakkavegur
Laugardælavegur
Norðurtröð
Suðurtröð
Vallartröð
Bæjartröð
Furugrund
Folaldahólar
Nauthólar
Kálfhólar
Tröllhólar

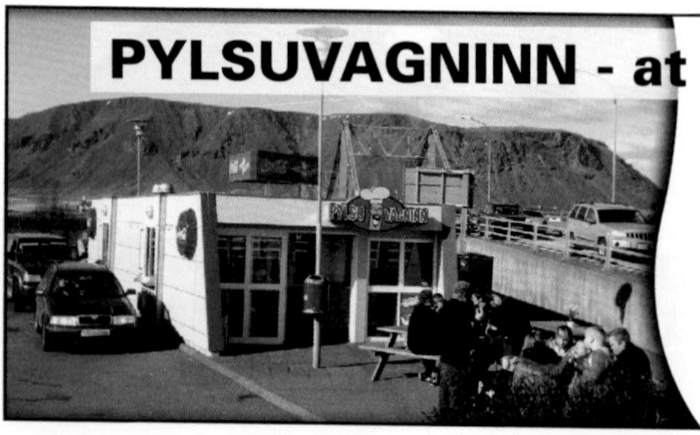

Kortagerð: Ólafur Valsson Copyright ©

Welcome to the Swimming Pools in Árborg

Free of charge for children under 18 years old

Selfoss Swimming Pool

Open all year

Monday to Friday: 06:30 – 21:30

Saturaday – Sunday: 09:00 – 19:00

Stokkseyri Swimming Pool

Opening hours 18. August – 31. May:

Monday to Friday: 16:30 – 20:30

Saturaday: 10:00 – 15:00

Sunday: Closed

Opening hours 1. June – 17. Aug. :

Monday to Friday: 13:00 – 21:00

Saturaday: 10:00 – 17:00

Sunday: 10:00 – 17:00

Prices

Adult (18-66 years old)

One ticket	600 kr.
10 tickets	3.500 kr.
30 tickets	7.500 kr.
Open ticket for one year	26.500 kr.

Admission is free of charge for people older then 67 years upon presenting an ID card. Admission is free of charge for disabled people upon presenting a Disabled Person Card.

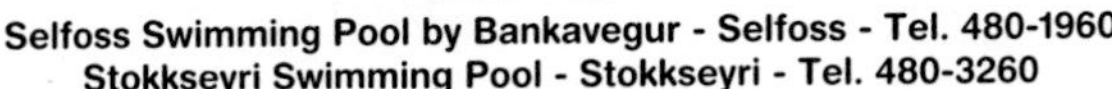

Selfoss Swimming Pool by Bankavegur - Selfoss - Tel. 480-1960
Stokkseyri Swimming Pool - Stokkseyri - Tel. 480-3260

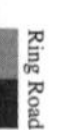

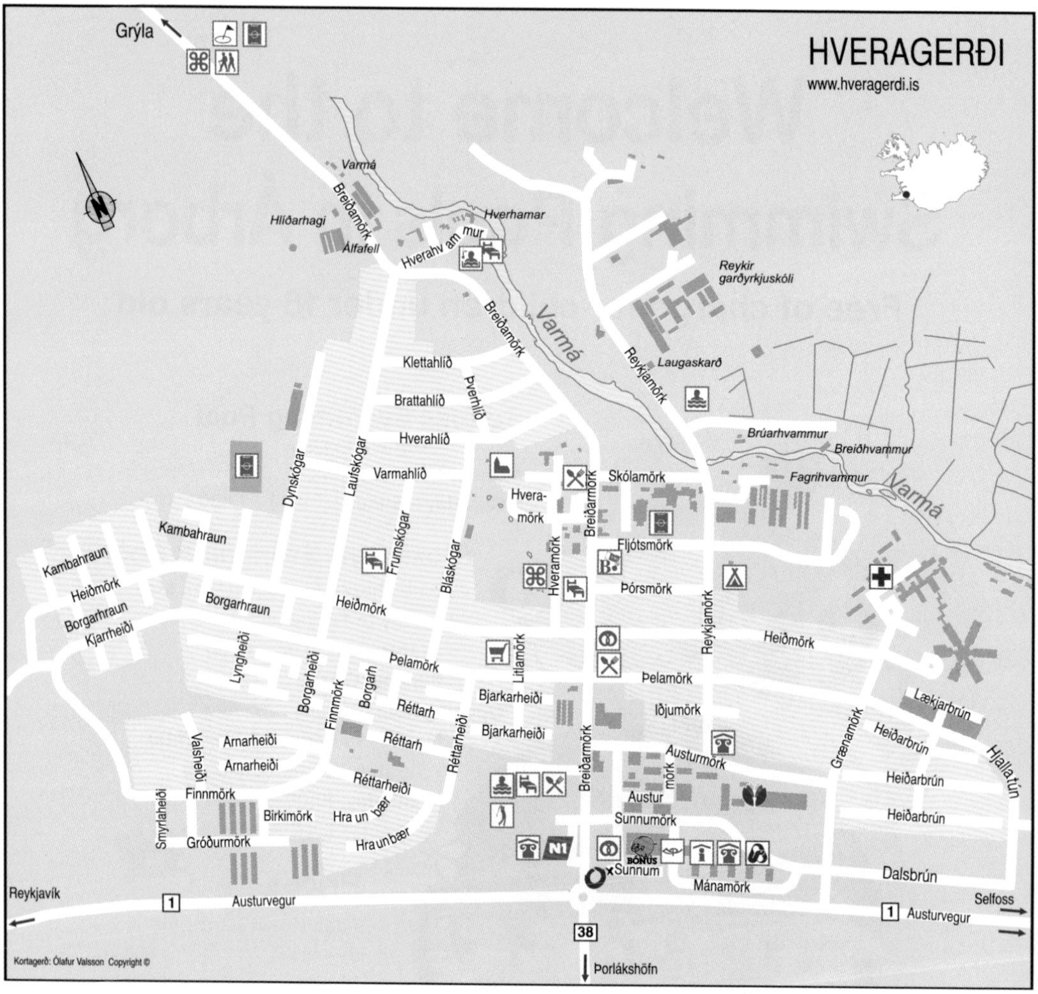

HVERAGERÐI
www.hveragerdi.is
Grýla
Varmá
Breiðamörk
Hlíðarhagi
Álfafell
Hverhamar
Hverahvammur
Reykir garðyrkjuskóli
Varmá
Breiðamörk
Reykjamörk
Laugaskarð
Klettahlíð
Brattahlíð
Þverhlíð
Hverahlíð
Varmahlíð
Brúarhvammur
Breiðhvammur
Fagrihvammur
Varmá
Skólamörk
Hvera-
mörk
Breiðamörk
Fljótsmörk
Dynskógar
Laufskógar
Frumskógar
Bláskógar
Kambahraun
Kambahraun
Heiðmörk
Borgarhraun
Kjarrheiði
Borgarhraun
Heiðmörk
Hveramörk
Þórsmörk
Reykjamörk
Heiðmörk
Lyngheiði
Borgarheiði
Finnmörk
Borgarh
Þelamörk
Litlamörk
Réttarh
Bjarkarheiði
Bjarkarheiði
Þelamörk
Iðjumörk
Lækjarbrún
Valsheiði
Arnarheiði
Arnarheiði
Réttarh
Réttarheiði
Réttarheiði
Breiðamörk
Austurmörk
Austur
mörk
Grænamörk
Heiðarbrún
Heiðarbrún
Heiðarbrún
Hjallatún
Smyrlaheiði
Finnmörk
Birkimörk
Hraunbær
Hraunbær
Gróðurmörk
Sunnumörk
N1
BÓNUS
Sunnum
Mánamörk
Dalsbrún
Reykjavík
1
Austurvegur
38
1
Austurvegur
Selfoss
Þorlákshöfn
Kortagerð: Ólafur Valsson Copyright ©

TRIP GUIDE
ICELAND
DAY TOURS
&ACTIVITIES
Best price guarantee
www.tripguide.is

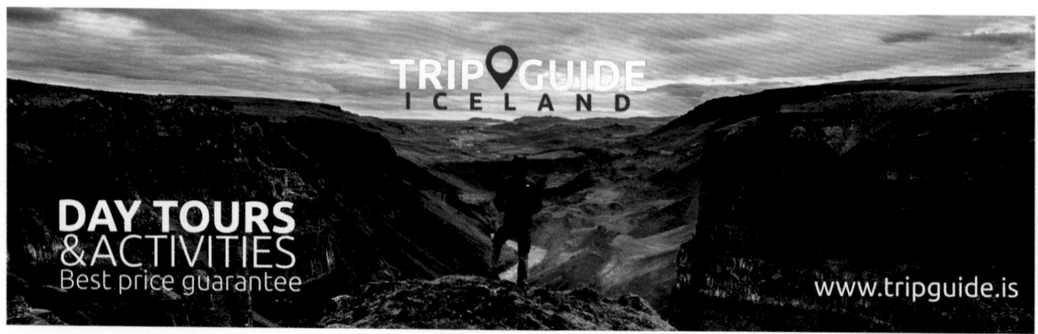

Hellisheiði-Selfoss 22 km

Ring Road

Skálafell .574
Hellisheiði
Hengladalsá
2 P. 565
313·
Kambar
Gufu-dalur
Reykjakot
38
Núpar
Hveragerði
MAP P. 146
Reykir
(Vötn)
Þúfa
Saurbær
Kröggólfsstaðir
(Öxnalækur)
Varmá
Ölfus-borgir
Vellir
Rauðilækur
Kross
Gljúfurárholt
Klettagljúfur
Sogn
Ásnes
374
Gljúfur
(Arnarbæli)
Kvistir
Gljúfurholtsá
Nátthagi
Egilsstaðir (Auðsholts-hjáleiga)
Auðsholt
Grænhóll
Kotströnd
375
Bakkár-holt
Sandhóll
Bakkárholtsá
Hvammur
Ingólfshvoll
Efstaland
Rauðilækur
Akurgerði
Hjarðarból
Lambhagi
Hjallartunga
Kvíarhóll
Nautaflatir
Kirkjuferjuhjáleiga
374
Kirkjuferja
Bræðraból
Hvoll
Ingólfsfjall
1
Kögunarhóll
Silfurberg
Kjarr
Ölfusá
Þórustaðir
Sængurkonu-steinn
(Fjallstún)
Árbæjarhverfi
35
34
1
Hagi
Selfoss
Geirakot
Björk
Eyði-Sandvík
Ölfusá
Selfoss
Þorleifskot
Jórvík
Fossmúli
MAP P. 144
Laugardælir
Byggðarhorn
Votmúli
Lækjamót
Austurkot
0 1 km
310
33

Selfoss-Hellisheiði 22 km

Hellisheiði, a plateau to the south of Hengill. Covered with many lavafields old and new. The most recent, from the year 1000, the same year Iceland converted to Christianity, is called Kristnitökuhraun ("Conversion lava").

Skálafell, (574 m) mountain providing one of the best views in southern Iceland, an easy climb.

Kambar, the eastern slope of Hellisheiði. The road lies along the path of lava that flowed down the slope. From Kambabrún ("Kambar's edge") there is a fine view across the southern lowlands, all the way to the glacier Eyjafjallajökull, the Westman Islands and Surtsey.

Hveragerði, (pop. 2,510) a small town that has been built up since 1930. Main activities are tourism, health care, greenhouses and trading. One of the biggest assets of the town is the Geothermal park in the centre of the town. Such a natural wonder in the middle of a residential area is extremely rare in the world. The farm Ljósbrá houses one of Iceland´s largest private stone collections. There are interesting hiking trails within the town. The Poets´Trail winds its way through historical parts of the town visiting three streets that made up the "artists´ quarters" between the years 1940-1965. These are Bláskógar(Blue woods), the street of painters; Frumskógar (Jungles), the street of poets, formerly known as Skáldagata, and Laufskógar (Leaf Woods), the street of the musicians. The Geothermal Trail visits the principal geothermal areas in and around town. Hveragerði is the home of the Horticultural College of Iceland. The regions art gallery is located in Hveragerði with its changing exhibitions. A vegetarian rehabilitation and Health Clinic in located here with e.g. clay baths, inand outdoor swimming pools and various treatments. The Hveragerði surroundings are a paradise for outdoors people. There are good hiking trails within the town that link up with a network of trails on the land belonging to the Agricultural University of Iceland at the foot of Reykjafjall Mountain and in Ölfusborgir. After an earthquake struck southern Iceland on May 29th, 2008 a new hot springs area appeared directly above the town. The area demonstrates how the forces of nature shape the land, as the hot springs are quite diverse and constantly changing. The earthquake measured 6.3 on the Richter scale. South Iceland Tourist Information Centre located in Hveragerði, has an earthquake simulator, a lite up earthquake rift under the floor and various information about the earthquake.

Reykir, once the home of Gissur jarl ("Earl") Þorvaldsson (1208-1268).

Ölfusborgir, summer houses.

Klettagljúfur, settlement.

Kotströnd, church site. The cemetery is walled off with an exquisitely constructed wall of lava rock.

Grænhóll, a horse breeding farm.

374 Hvammsvegur, 7,6 km. **375 Arnarbælisvegur,** 4,3 km.

Arnarbæli, an old manor farm, church until 1909 and a parsonage until 1940, now a group of farms. The farm was badly hit by the earthquakes of 1706 and 1896. The area around the farm is called **Arnarbælisforir**.

Ingólfsfjall, (551 m) a tuff mountain named after Ingólfur Arnarson, the first settler in Iceland. Legend has it that Ingólfur is buried in Inghóll, a small hill on the mountain. South of the mountain are some gray coloured rocks called **Silfurberg** ("Silver rocks").

Kögunarhóll, a single cone under the mountain Ingólfsfjall. The white crosses by Kögunarhóll are to commemorate those who have died in car accidents on the road between Reykjavík and Selfoss.

Fjallstún, a deserted farm. The settler Ingólfur Arnarsson wintered there in his third year in Iceland. (See Road 35.)

33 **Gaulverjabæjarvegur,** p. 178
34 **Eyrarbakkavegur,** p. 178
35 **Biskupstungnabraut,** p. 180
38 **Þorlákshafnarvegur,** p. 192
310 **Votmúlavegur,** p. 178

1 SUÐURLANDSVEGUR

Vífilsfell, (655 m) a steep tuff mountain named after Vífill, a freed slave of Ingólfur Arnarson's.
Jósepsdalur, a narrow valley east and south of Vífilsfell. Once a troll lived there according to old folk tales.
Svínahraun, a 5,000 year old lava-flow between Sandskeið and Kolviðarhóll. Lava from eruptions around the year 1000 lies on top of it, as can be seen quite clearly on approaching from the west.
Hellisheiði Power Plant, there is a Geothermal Energy Exhibition on how geothermal energy is harnessed. Experienced guides are provide informative presentations backed by multimedia shows about sustainable green energy as a global energy source. Geothermal resources can be found worldwide. Some refreshments are available at Kaffi Kolviðarhóll.
Bolavellir, ("Bull meadows") grasslands to the north of Svínahraun (see **Hengill**, below).
Kolviðarhóll, formerly a popular resting place for travellers across Hellisheiði, first with a primitive shelter and later an inn. Still later Kolviðarhóll became a popular ski lodge, but it is now deserted. From the road bend by Kolviðarhóll a rock formation resembling a well-known Icelandic poet, Matthías Jochumsson the author of the national anthem, can be seen in the mountainside to the south.
Hveradalir, a valley in the southern slopes of the mountain Reykjafell, where considerable geothermal heat is to be found.
Hengill, a tuff mountain or a mountain range, with widespread geothermal heat some of which has been harnessed. Good hiking in summertime and skiing in wintertime, especially in **Innstidalur**, the westernmost valley of Hengladalir. Highest point 803 m, **Skeggi**, a rocky point on the northwest side, overlooking a small valley, **Marardalur**, a fairly large, grassy plain closed in by cliffs and screes on all sides, with a narrow canyon leading out of it to the west. The valley is easily closed off, and bulls were often kept there. They often managed to escape, however, and roamed the moors, e.g. the **Bolavellir** meadows (see above). The bulls were fierce and a danger to travellers, other dangers including ghosts, as place names such as Draugahlíð ("Ghosts' hillside") and Draugatjörn ("Ghosts' pond") indicate.
Kristnitökuhraun, ("Conversion lava") a lava-field on Hellisheiði that came from a 6.5 km long fissure east of the mountain Reykjafell. According to the Sagas, the eruption started in the year 1000 while Icelanders were discussing at the Althing at Þingvellir whether to convert from paganism to Christianity. Hence the name.
Hellukofinn ("flat-stone hut"), on the Hellisheiði uplands, was built in 1830 by re-stacking rocks taken from a centuries-old cairn that had stood on the same bedrock. Measuring 1.85 m on each side and 2 m high, the hut can shelter 4-5 persons in a blizzard.

39 **Þrengslavegur,** p. 194 417 **Bláfjallavegur,** p. 225

Fóelluvötn-Hellisheiði 16 km

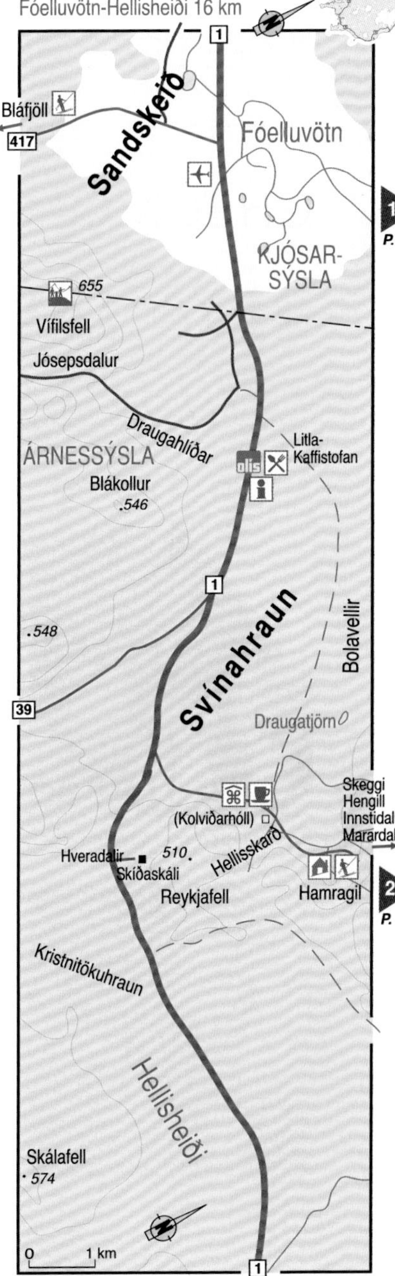

Hellisheiði-Fóelluvötn 16 km

1 P. 564
2 P. 565

1 SUÐURLANDSVEGUR

Rauðavatn, a small lake on the eastern outskirts of Reykjavík. East of the lake is a grove where mountain pines were planted in the beginnig of last century.

Rauðhólar, a group of red hills, pseudocraters. Great quantities of pumice have been taken from them and used to build roads and the runways of Reykjavík Airport. The pseudocraters have thus been to a great extent spoiled but are now protected.

Elliðavatn, the largest lake in the vicinity of Reykjavík. Also a farm of the same name, where in the 18th century a Swedish-German baron, by the name of Hastfer, started a sheep-breeding station. On the Þinganes point and surrounding area by the lake remains have been found which confirm that the Kjalarnesþing meetings were held there of old, for a period at least. It might even have been there that they prepared to establish the Althing at Þingvellir in the year 930. Archeological digs there have brought to light important relics from as far back as the settlement.

Heiðmörk, a recreation and forestry area belonging to Reykjavík and the neighbouring communities, a nature reserve since 1948. Millions of trees have been planted there. Good walking routes and a view-dial. Arctic Adventures offers moutain bike tours in Heiðmörk.

Gunnarshólmi, a farm. South of the road is **Silungapollur,** a former preschool.

Tröllabörnin, ("The giants' children") a group of small pseudocraters by the road. Portected since 1983.

Gvendarbrunnar, named after Guðmundur bishop Arason (1160–1237) From there the people of Reykjavík get its drinking water.

Lækjarbotnar, formerly a farm and a popular resting-place for travellers.

Bláfjöll, a mountain range south of Vífilsfell, a skiing and outdoor-sports area a few km from the main road. Good skiing area, both Alpine and cross-country in Bláfjöll and Heiðin há, especially in late winter and springtime. Skilifts, lodge etc. The lava-fields west of Bláfjöll can be very dangerous, however, because of cracks, subsidence and open-roofed caves where the fall down to the rough floor may be as much as 10 m.

Lyklafell, a small mountain on the north side of the road in Fóellu vötn. There 3 counties meet Árnessýsla, Gullbringusýsla and Kjósarsýsla.

Sandskeið, a fairly large sandy plateau, the bed of an old lake, now partly cultivated. Airstrip and headquarters of the Icelandic Gliding Association. On a low, rocky hill to the west of Sandskeið are the remains of an old mountain hut. The road used to lie over Sandskeið, south of the airstrip. It has now been moved north across the **Fóelluvötn** area, where considerable lakes are formed in the spring melts. They empty down over the Fossvellir plains into the river Hólmsá. In Fossvallaklif pass there is a stone marked 1887 showing when the first road for vehicles was laid.

41	**Reykjanesbraut,** p. 204	413	**Breiðholtsbraut,** p. 202
417	**Bláfjallavegur,** p. 225	435	**Nesjavallaleið,** p. 187

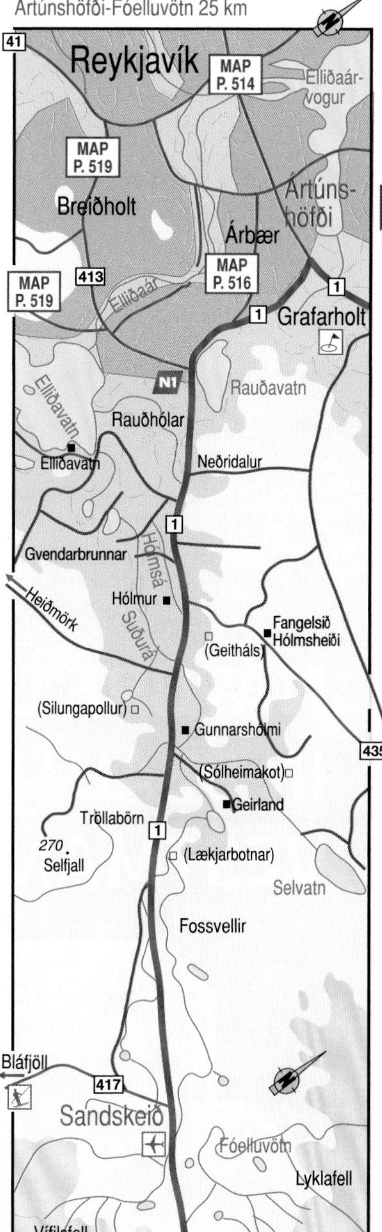

Ring Road
1
P. 564

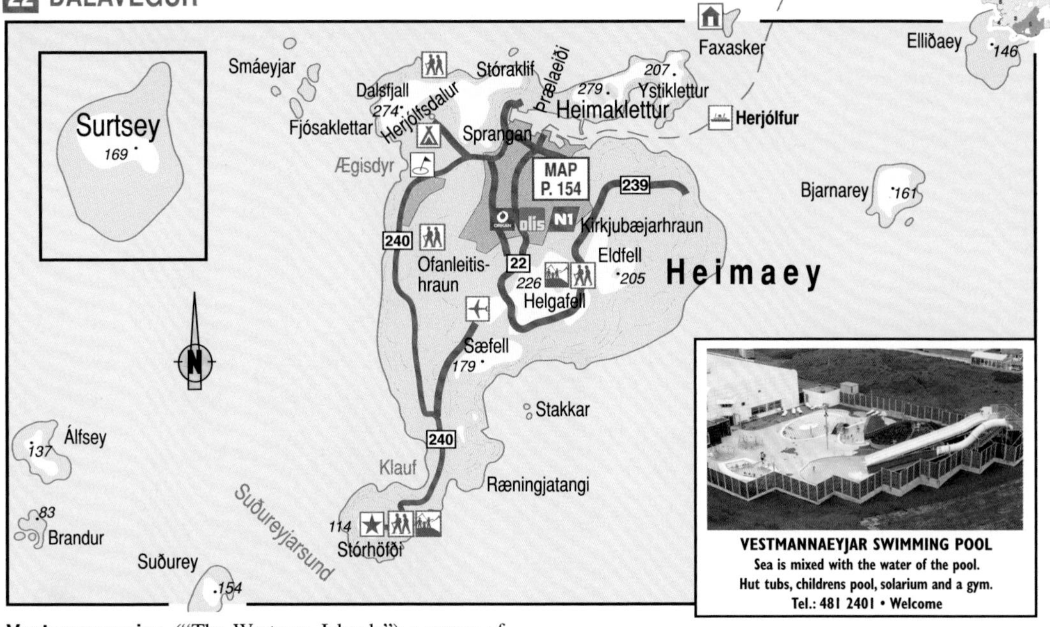

Vestmannaeyjar, ("The Westman Islands") a group of 15-18 steep and rocky islands, with green mountain sides and ridges. All the islands come from submarine eruptions, the oldest from about 10,000 years ago and others from 5,000 years ago when the mountain Helgafell erupted and the Ofanleitishraun lava field was formed. In 1963 there was a submarine eruption which went on for almost 5 years and eventually formed the island Surtsey. Then, in 1973, there was an eruption on the only inhabited island of the group, Heimaey. No lives were lost, though almost 400 of the 1,200 houses of the town were buried under lava from the new volcano **Eldfell** ("Fire mountain"). Before the town was evacuated in the 1973 eruption the population was 5,300, now it's 4,292. **Eldheimar/Pompei of the North,** a new museum around the evacuation of houses that have been covered with ash since the volcanic eruption 1973. The islands of Vestmannaeyjar are famous for the millions of birds in puffin and other sea bird colonies there. The hunting of puffins is widely practiced throughout the islands and each year thousands of fulmar and guillemot eggs are collected from the cliffs by locals who lower each other on long ropes to get at them. Since 1900 Heimaey has been one of the most important fishing towns in Iceland. A very good aquarium is located there, an historical museum and a library. A replica of a 11th century wooden church has been build in the Islands as a gift from Norway on a occation of the 1000th anniversary of the adoption of Christianity in the year 2000 to commemorate the arrival of Hjalti Skeggjason and Gissur the White in Iceland in 1000 AD, whose mission was to convert Icelanders to the new faith. The church was to be built in the place where the two first landed on their way to Þingvellir. A special Vestmannaeyjar activity is Sprangan at Skiphellar ("Ship caves") where children and teenagers practice lowering each other and swinging along the cliffs on ropes. Informtion Centre in the Museum building by City Hall. Ferry connections between Vestmannaeyjar and Bakki.

239 Eldfellsvegur. **240 Stórhöfðavegur,** 7 km.

Ræningjatangi, ("Pirate point") near Stórhöfði. In 1627 sea rovers from Algeria landed there and killed scores of people. A number escaped by hiding in caves and the lava fields, but about 240 people were taken to Algeria and sold there as slaves. A few were rescued about ten years later. One of the most famous of these was Guðríður Símonardóttir, known as Tyrkja-Gudda ("Turk-Guðríður"), who later married the priest and poet Hallgrímur Pétursson, author of the *Passíusálmar* ("Passion Hymns").

Stórhöfði, a good spot to watch the puffin colonies.

Helgafell, (226 m) the elder of the volcanos on Heimaey. View dial.

Herjólfsdalur, an open valley in the outskirts of town where, since 1874, the people of Vestmannaeyar have celebrated their annual festival (known as their "national" holiday) over the 3-day weekend in the beginning of August.

Fjósaklettar, in Herjólfsdalur is the site where man-made caves were discovered in 1999. It is speculated that these caves were once used to house cattle.

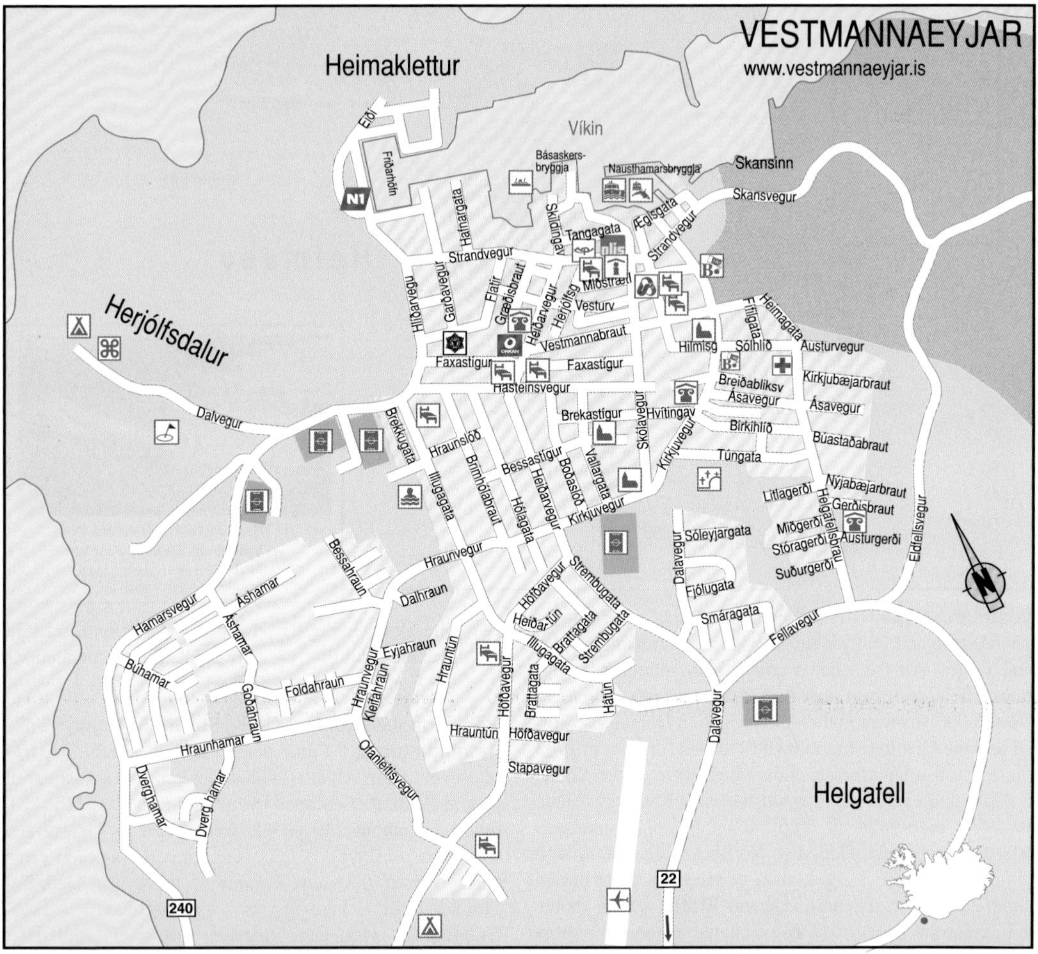

VESTMANNAEYJAR

www.vestmannaeyjar.is

Heimaklettur
Víkin
Básaskers-bryggja
Nausthamarsbryggja
Skansinn
Skansvegur
Friðarhöfn
Eiði
Hafnargata
Skildingav
Tangagata
Ægisgata
Strandvegur
Herjólfsdalur
Hlíðarvegur
Garðavegur
Flatir
Græðisbraut
Heiðarvegur
Herjólfsg
Miðstræti
Vesturv
Vestmannabraut
Faxastígur
Hásteinsvegur
Dalvegur
Brekkugata
Hraunslóð
Illugagata
Brimhólabraut
Bessastígur
Heiðarvegur
Boðaslóð
Vallargata
Hólagata
Brekastígur
Skólavegur
Hvítingav
Kirkjuvegur
Hilmisg
Sólhlíð
Fífilgata
Heimagata
Austurvegur
Breiðabliksv
Ásavegur
Kirkjubæjarbraut
Birkihlíð
Búastaðabraut
Túngata
Litlagerði
Nýjabæjarbraut
Gerðisbraut
Helgafellsbraut
Miðgerði
Stóragerði
Austurgerði
Suðurgerði
Eldfellsvegur
Sóleyjargata
Dalavegur
Fjólugata
Smáragata
Fellavegur
Hraunvegur
Bessahraun
Dalhraun
Áshamar
Hamarsvegur
Búhamar
Goðahraun
Foldahraun
Hraunvegur
Kleifahraun
Eyjahraun
Hrauntún
Höfðavegur
Heiðartún
Illugagata
Brattagata
Strembugata
Hátún
Hraunhamar
Dverghamar
Ofanleitisvegur
Stapavegur
Dalavegur
Helgafell
240
22

Welcome to Vestmannaeyjar

Fly from Reykjavík Airport – 20 min.

Ferry from Landeyjahöfn – 30 min.

Vestmannaeyjar tourist information
Tel. +354 ***488-2555***
www.vestmannaeyjar.is
tourinfo@vestmannaeyjar.is

SLIPPURINN

EATERY

Slippurinn (The Ship Yard) is a family run eatery located in a former machine workshop by the harbor of Westman Islands.

One of the most acclaimed restaurant on the south coast, Slippurinn is famous for its use of locally grown ingredients, serving the freshest catch from the sea around the island and outstanding meat dishes.
The bar makes its own cocktails using seasonal herbs and offers a great selection of Icelandic beers.

TEL. +354 481 1515

STRANDVEGUR 76 - 900 VESTMANNAEYJAR
WWW.SLIPPURINN.COM • INFO@SLIPPURINN.COM

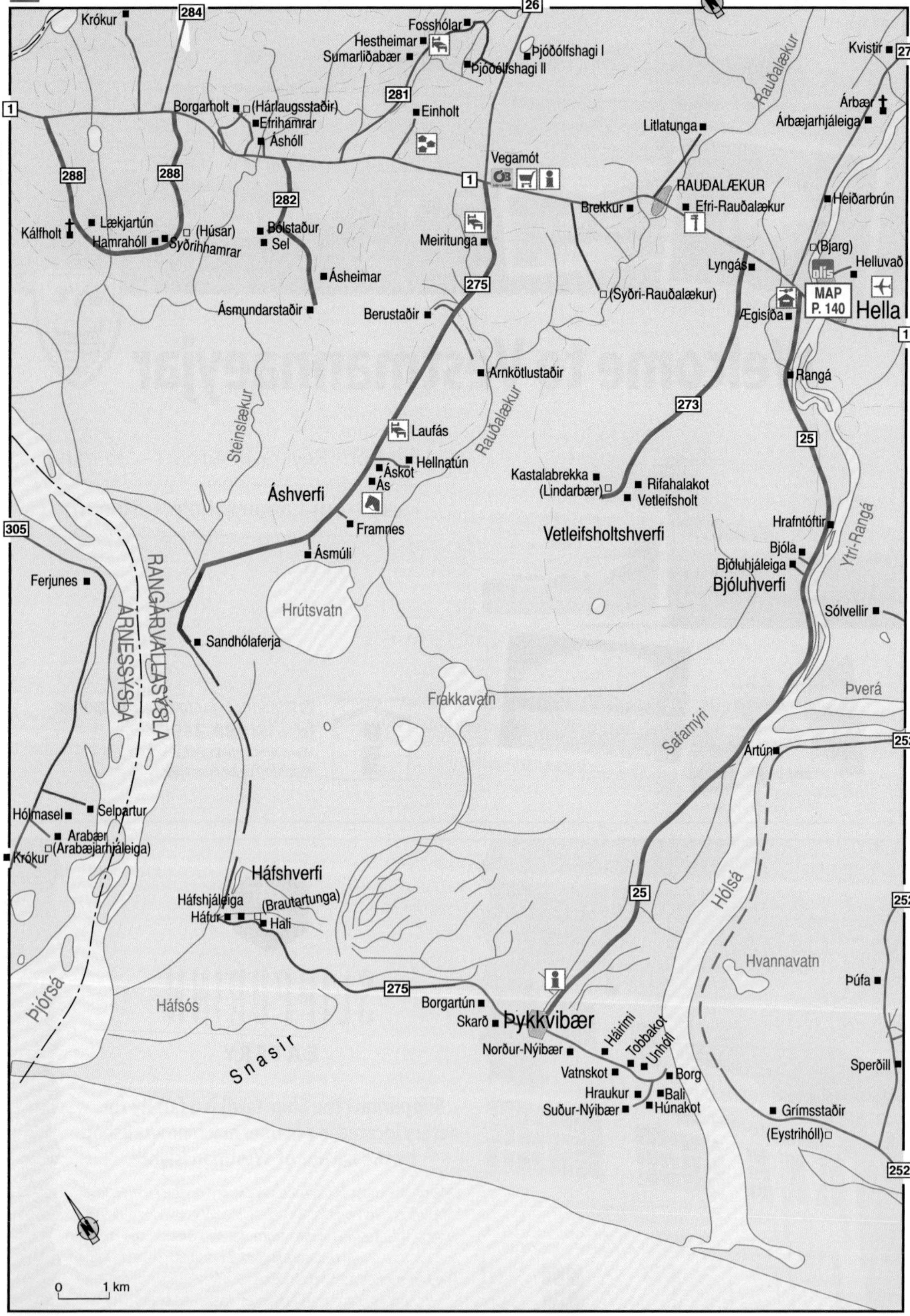

Krókur
284
26
Fosshólar
Hestheimar
Sumarliðabær
Þjóðólfshagi I
Þjóðólfshagi II
Kvistir
271
1
Borgarholt
(Hárlaugsstaðir)
Efrihamrar
Áshóll
281
Einholt
Rauðalækur
Litlatunga
Árbær
Árbæjarhjáleiga
13
P. 576
288
288
Vegamót
1
RAUÐALÆKUR
Brekkur
Efri-Rauðalækur
Heiðarbrún
282
Kálfholt
Lækjartún
Hamrahóll
(Húsar)
Syðrihamrar
Bólstaður
Sel
Meiritunga
(Bjarg)
Helluvað
Lyngás
Ásheimar
275
(Syðri-Rauðalækur)
Ásmundarstaðir
Berustaðir
Ægisíða
MAP P. 140
Hella
1
Arnkötlustaðir
Rangá
273
Steinslækur
Rauðalækur
Laufás
25
Hellnatún
Áskot
Ás
Kastalabrekka
(Lindarbær)
Rifahalakot
Vetleifsholt
Áshverfi
Framnes
Vetleifsholtshverfi
Hrafntóftir
Ytri-Rangá
305
Ásmúli
Bjóla
Bjóluhjáleiga
Bjóluhverfi
Ferjunes
RANGÁRVALLASÝSLA
ÁRNESSÝSLA
Hrútsvatn
Sólvellir
Sandhólaferja
Þverá
Frakkavatn
Safamýri
Ártún
252
Hólmasel
Selpartur
Arabær
(Arabæjarhjáleiga)
Krókur
Háfshverfi
Hólsá
25
252
Háfshjáleiga
Háfur
(Brautartunga)
Hali
Hvannavatn
Þúfa
Þjórsá
Háfsós
275
Borgartún
Skarð
Þykkvibær
Háirimi
Tobbakot
Unhóll
Norður-Nýibær
Vatnskot
Borg
Sperðill
Snasir
Hraukur
Bali
Suður-Nýibær
Húnakot
Grímsstaðir
(Eystrihóll)
252
0 1 km

Ásahreppur-Þykkvibær

1	Suðurlandsvegur, p. 142	26	Landvegur, p. 128	252	Landeyjavegur, p. 166
271	Árbæjarvegur, p. 158	284	Heiðarvegur, p. 158	305	Villingaholtsvegur, p. 178

25 Þykkvabæjarvegur, 16 km.

Ægissíða, a farm on the western banks of the Rangá river. There are 11 man-made caves in the home-field, one of them large and used for storing hay up until 1980. Some of the caves have peculiar carvings on the walls, believed by some to have been made by Irish hermits before the settlement in the 9th century. There was a ford on the Rangá near Ægissíða, and this used to be a much-travelled route.

Ytri-Rangá, a clear river originating on the sands between Hekla and Þjórsá. Good fishing.

Bjóluhverfi, a group of farms near Rangá, one of them being **Hrafntóftir**, dwelling-place of the settler Ketill hængur during his first winter in Iceland, and the birthplace of his son Hrafn Hængsson, who was the first law-speaker after the enactment of the laws of Úlfljótur.

Safamýri, formerly extensive marshes, extremely grassy. Has now mostly been drained after dykes were built along the rivers on the east side.

Þykkvibær, a district to the south of Safamýri, formerly surrounded by rivers with the ocean on the south side, probably the oldest country-village in Iceland. A church at **Hábær**. Formerly the rivers threatened this district but dykes have changed this. One of the main potato-growing districts in Iceland. Potato processing plant.

273 Bugavegur, 5,4 km.

Vetleifsholt, a farm and the settling place of Ráðormur. A small hill, Kollhóll, below the farm, said to be a home of the "hidden people" and not to be spoiled in any way, otherwise bad luck will follow.

Syðri-Rauðalækur, an abandoned farm where two caves were made in 1896-97 and 1916, possibly the most recent man-made caves in Iceland.

275 Ásvegur, 12 km.

Ás, a substantial farm, the main one of a group of farms known together as **Áshverfi**. The birthplace of Gísli Bjarnason (1678-1707), who died at sea from smallpox, the disease then being brought to Iceland with his belongings. It became the worst epidemic since the Plague, killing 12,000 in the diocese of Skálholt and 6,000 in the north.

Hrútsvatn, ("Ram's lake") southwest of Ás, the biggest lake in the district of Holt, 2,4 km^2. A monster resembling a brown ram is said to live in the lake, hence the name.

Sandhólaferja, a farm by Þjórsá, one of the principal ferry points east of the river until the bridge was built. In early Saga times some historical killings took place at Sandhólaferja when Sigmundur and Steinn came from Eyrarbakki and both of them wanted to be first across the river.

Háfshverfi, a group of farms, and a church until 1914 when it was moved to **Hábær** in Þykkvibær. The land there is so flat that the two lakes, Hrútsvatn and **Frakkavatn**, are only 5 m above sea level. It is easiest to get to Háfshverfi via Þykkvibær. Háfur was the settling place of Þorkell bjálfi.

Þjórsárós, the Þjórsá estuary, becoming 3-4 km wide below Sandhólaferja. Half-closed on the sea side by a long sandreef forming a lake or lagoon. Seals are common there. In the Sagas it said that ships often landed in Þjórsárós.

281 Sumarliðabæjarvegur, 5,6 km.

282 Ásmundarstaðavegur, 3,2 km.

288 Kálfholtsvegur, a 7 km long circle.

Kálfholt, a farm and a church, formerly a parsonage.

© Markaðsstofa Suðurlands

26 LANDVEGUR

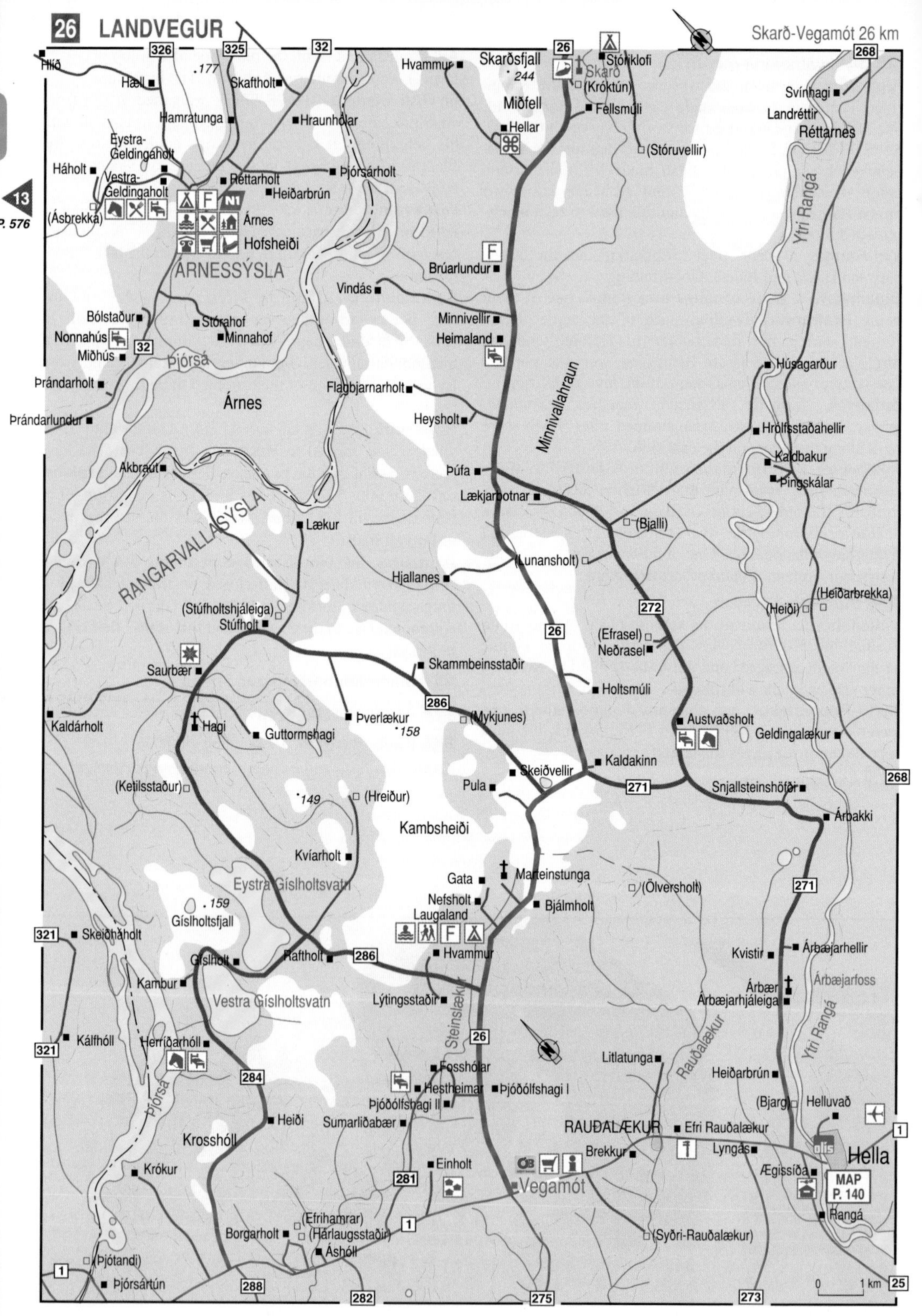

13 P. 576

Skarð, a farm and church, long a manor farm. Much of its land, like that of many farms in the Landsveit district, was destroyed by sand erosion. The farmhouse was formerly at the foot of the **Skarðsfjall** mountain, where there are now several-meter-high sand dunes. Good view from the mountain.

Fellsmúli, a farm and parsonage since 1912.

Hvammur, a farm, long the home of Eyjólfur Guðmundsson (1857-1940), a leader in his district and in the fight against the sand erosion that threatened the grasslands of the upper Landsveit district.

Hellar, ("Caves") a farm where some man-made caves are used as hay-barns. The Bishop of Iceland celebrated Mass in the cave in 2000 to mark the 1000th anniversary of the conversion of Iceland.

Brúarlundur, the community centre of the Landsveit district, built near the now deserted church-farm of **Stóruvellir**, formerly a parsonage and manor farm.

Flagbjarnarholt, a farm. Not far from there is Þinghóll ("Meeting hill") where some ruins, excavated in 1883, indicate that official gatherings were held there, though this is not mentioned in old records.

Árnes, ("River peninsula") an island in the Þjórsá river, at one time the official meeting place for Árnessýsla, and hence the name of the county. Some ruins can still be seen, and place names like Þinghóll (see above). There are more ruins on the west side of the river. It is believed that the river was formerly all to the east of Árnes, and later broke through on the west side where the main channel is now. Two waterfalls in the river by Árnes, Búðafoss in the west channel and Hestafoss in the east channel.

272 Bjallavegur, 8,65 km.

Land or **Landsveit,** the district north of Holt between Þjórsá and Rangá. Most of the land is old, dry lava-fields covered with soil and vegetation. Much has been done to stop the sand erosion and recultivate the lava-fields.

Marteinstunga, a farm and church.

Laugaland, a school and community centre. Geothermal heat. This heat has been harnessed to provide central heating to much of the district. A swimming pool and a campsite.

Þjóðólfshagi, a farm with a man-made cave.

Holt, the district between the rivers Þjórsá and Rangá, mostly rolling hills with marshes in between. The soil is very thick and the district green and grassy.

271 Árbæjarvegur, 12,5 km.

Lækjarbotnar, a farm where once lived Gissur, whom the giantesses were going to catch. From the mountain Búrfell he heard a voice say, "Sister, lend me a pot", and from the mountain Bjólfell came the answer, "What do you want it for?" From Búrfell, "Cook a man in it." From Bjólfell, "Who is he?" and from Búrfell, "Gissur from Botnar, Gissur from Lækjarbotnar". He escaped (see **Tröllkonuhlaup**).

Landréttir, sheep-folds by Rangá.

Hrólfsstaðahellir, a farm, birthplace of the poet Guðmundur Guðmundsson (1874-1919). In a hill in the home field are some man-made caves, among them **Hrútshellir**("Ram´s cave"), named for a ghost ram that has often been seen there.

Snjallsteinshöfði, a farm, in Saga times the home of Steinn hinn snjalli ("the clever"), a relative of Gunnar from Hlíðarendi of *Njáls saga*. Formerly a church. Some ancient runic writings on the cliff east of the farm.

Árbær, a farm and church by Ytri-Rangá.

286 Hagabraut, a 20 km long circle.

Skeiðvellir, a horse breeding farm.

Akbrautarholt, a small hill near the farm Akbraut, where ruins of an old church and a graveyard are to be found, interesting columnar rocks.

Hagi, a farm and church. In the church there is a carved font by the artist Ríkarður Jónsson given to the church on its 100th birthday.

Kaldárholt, a farm by the river Þjórsá west of Hagi. Geothermal heat.

284 Heiðarvegur, 11 km.

Gíslholt, a farm between two lakes both named after the farm. The mountain Gíslholtsfjall (159 m) north of the farm is the highest point in the district of Holt. A small lake on top of the mountain.

Herríðarhóll, a traditional farm with horse breeding, sheep and milking cows, situated between river Þjórsá and lake Gíslholt.

281 Sumarliðabæjarvegur, 5,6 km.

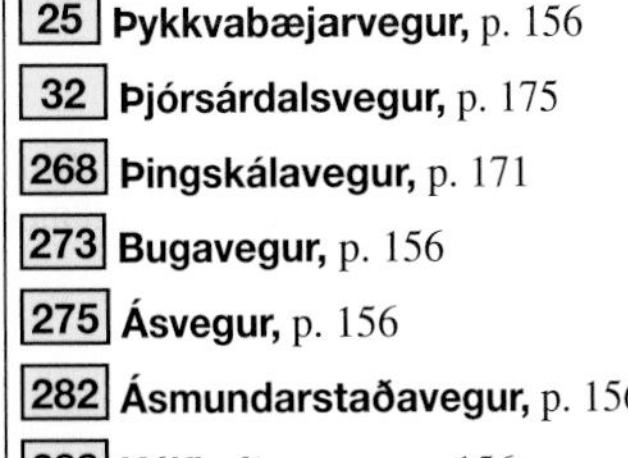

1 Suðurlandsvegur, p. 142
25 Þykkvabæjarvegur, p. 156
32 Þjórsárdalsvegur, p. 175
268 Þingskálavegur, p. 171
273 Bugavegur, p. 156
275 Ásvegur, p. 156
282 Ásmundarstaðavegur, p. 156
288 Kálfholtsvegur, p. 156

321 Skeiðháholtsvegur, p. 172
325 Gnúpverjavegur, p. 175
326 Hælsvegur, p. 175

13 P. 576

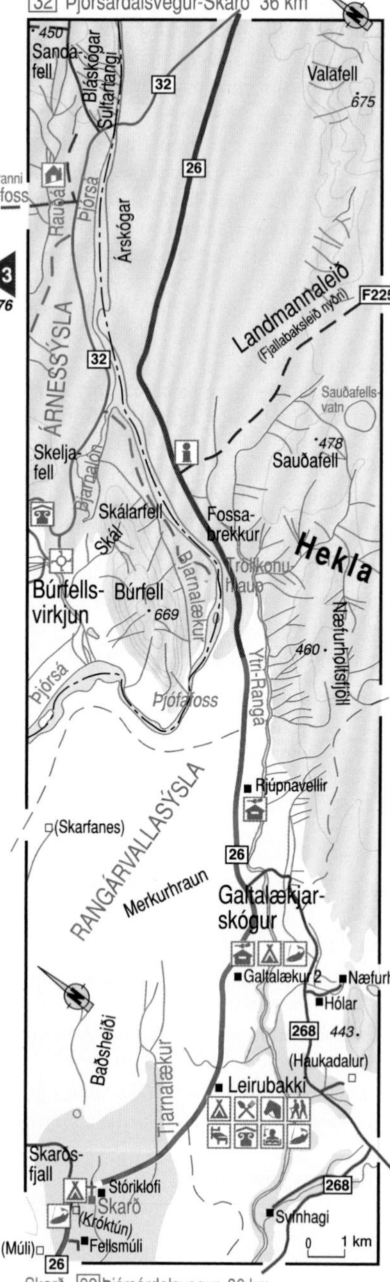

Þjófafoss.

Fossabrekkur, ("Waterfall slopes") an interesting place by the river Rangá, an oasis in the pumice desert, falls and rich vegetation (angelica etc.).

Tröllkonuhlaup, ("Giantess' leap") a waterfall in Þjórsá. Giantesses believed to live in Búrfell and Bjólfell used the rocks in the river as stepping stones when they tried to catch Gissur of Lækjarbotnar.

Hekla, (1,491 m) the most famous volcano in Iceland, a ridge more than 4 km long. There have been at least 18 eruptions in recorded history, the first in 1104 and the latest in 2000, when scientists were able to predict the eruption half an hour in advance using the alarm system of the Icelandic Meteorological Office. In the eruption of 1947 the peak rose 50 m. The easiest climbing route is along the northern ridge. The first known ascent was made by the explorers Eggert Ólafsson and Bjarni Pálsson in June 20th 1750.

Þjófafoss, a waterfall in the Þjórsá river south of Búrfell; a 5 km long jeep-track leads there, very difficult to drive. Legend says that thieves were thrown into the waterfall, hence the name.

Þjórsárhraun, a great lava-field that came about 8,000 years ago from cracks near the Veiðivötn lakes and flowed along Þjórsárdalur, Landsveit, Skeið and Flói to reach the sea between the rivers Ölfusá and Þjórsá, a distance of 130 km and covering some 800 km^2. One of the largest known lava-flows anywhere on Earth.

Skarfanes, a deserted farm now belonging to the Forestry Service. Extensive birchwoods protected since 1941. Can be reached via jeep-tracks from Þjófafoss and Skarð.

Galtalækur, the northernmost farm in the Landsveit district. The old mountain tracks Fjallabaksvegur nyrðri and Sprengisandsvegur start there. Formerly a popular stopping place for those who climbed Hekla.

Baðsheiði, ("Bath moor") the area north of Skarð, geothermal heat, where there was once a steam-bath.

Leirubakki, there is the Hekla Museum.

Stóri-Klofi, a farm and formerly a church. Best known from judge Torfi Jónsson of the 15th century. The Klofi farmhouse went under sand dunes and was rebuilt across from Skarð.

32 **Þjórsárdalsvegur,** p. 176 | 268 **Þingskálavegur,** p. 171
F225 **Landmannaleið,** p. 444

26 LANDVEGUR

Þórisvatn, the second largest lake in Iceland, 70 km², 109 m deep. This lake is regulated and may rise by as much as 5 meters, reaching 80 km². Its upper end is cut in two by the mountain Útigönguhöfði, forming two bays. The shores are mostly steep and desolate. Formerly the outlet was **Þórisós**, but there is now a regulated outlet down to the power station of Sigalda.

Sigalda, (543 m) low mountain ridges on both sides of Tungnaá. The Sigalda power station was opened in 1977, power 150,000 kW.

Þóristungur, the triangle between the rivers Kaldakvísl and Tungnaá north of Hrauneyjafoss.

Hrauneyjafoss, a 29 m high waterfall in the river Tungnaá where a new 210,000 kW power station was built in 1981.

Búðarháls, a long ridge, 600-700 m above sea level, between the rivers Þjórsá and Kaldakvísl, mostly desolate and bare. Jeep-traffic was once frequent along this ridge.

Tungnaá, a glacial river coming from the west side of Vatnajökull. Formerly a serious obstacle for travellers, which could only be crossed by ferry at **Hald** and **Bjallavað** and forded at **Hófsvað**. Two power stations have been built on Tungnaá at Sigalda and Hrauneyjafoss.

Sultartangi, a former isthums at the crossing of the rivers Tungnaá and Þjórsá. A 6 km wide dam has been constructed there and given the name Sultartangastífla. Sultartangastífla was built there to provide a reservoir for the Búrfellsvirkjun Power Statation. A tunnel goes out of the reservoir to the south-west through Sandfell to the Sultartangi Power Plant (120 MW), inaugurated in October 1999. The tunnel is 12 m high and 3,4 km long.

Árskógar, desolate and sandy lava fields on the east of Þjórsá up to Tungnaá. Landgræðsla ríkisins, the Soil Conservation Service of Iceland, has revegetated extensive land areas in this region.

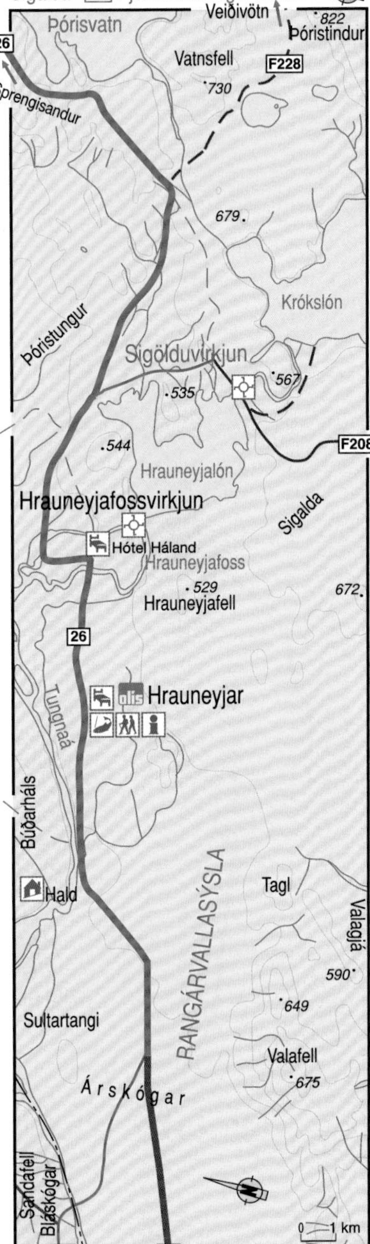

14 P. 577

32 **Þjórsárdalsvegur,** p. 176	F208 **Fjallabaksleið,** p. 436
F26 **Sprengisandsleið,** p. 430	F228 **Veiðivatnaleið,** p. 446

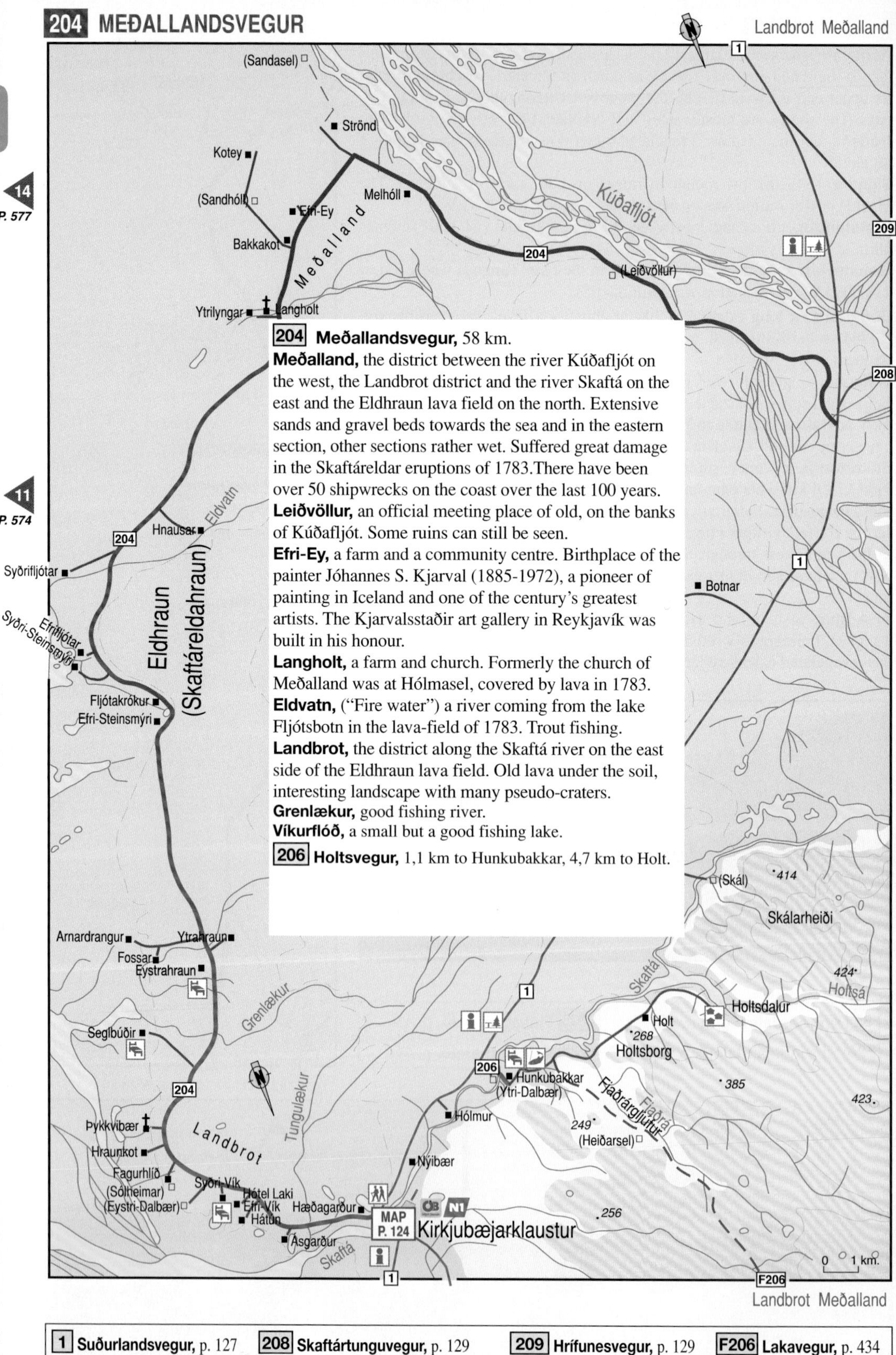

204 Meðallandsvegur, 58 km.

Meðalland, the district between the river Kúðafljót on the west, the Landbrot district and the river Skaftá on the east and the Eldhraun lava field on the north. Extensive sands and gravel beds towards the sea and in the eastern section, other sections rather wet. Suffered great damage in the Skaftáreldar eruptions of 1783.There have been over 50 shipwrecks on the coast over the last 100 years.

Leiðvöllur, an official meeting place of old, on the banks of Kúðafljót. Some ruins can still be seen.

Efri-Ey, a farm and a community centre. Birthplace of the painter Jóhannes S. Kjarval (1885-1972), a pioneer of painting in Iceland and one of the century's greatest artists. The Kjarvalsstaðir art gallery in Reykjavík was built in his honour.

Langholt, a farm and church. Formerly the church of Meðalland was at Hólmasel, covered by lava in 1783.

Eldvatn, ("Fire water") a river coming from the lake Fljótsbotn in the lava-field of 1783. Trout fishing.

Landbrot, the district along the Skaftá river on the east side of the Eldhraun lava field. Old lava under the soil, interesting landscape with many pseudo-craters.

Grenlækur, good fishing river.

Víkurflóð, a small but a good fishing lake.

206 Holtsvegur, 1,1 km to Hunkubakkar, 4,7 km to Holt.

1 Suðurlandsvegur, p. 127 **208 Skaftártunguvegur,** p. 129 **209 Hrífunesvegur,** p. 129 **F206 Lakavegur,** p. 434

Vatnajökull National Park
Europe's Greatest Outdoor Playground!

Formerly a national park in itself, **Skaftafell** lies at the foot of the massive icecap that gives **Vatnajökull National** Park its name. The Vatnajökull massif is not only the biggest glacier in the world outside of the polar regions, but together with its surrounding mountain ranges has officially become Europe's largest national park. A vast land where boundless glacial tongues stretch to the horizon in all directions, flanked by jagged peaks and lush greenery, where iceberg-packed lagoons feed raging rivers, there are few places on Earth that can compare in sheer scale or awe-inspiring beauty. For this reason, as well as its proximity to endless hiking, climbing, and adventure options, Skaftafell has become the hub of glacier and mountain operations in Iceland, and you can find Glacier Guides in the heart of it all!

For those with a passion for nature at its purest or a thirst for outdoor adventure, Skaftafell promises to be the ultimate destination! With a range of activities from mild to wild, Glacier Guides has developed a menu of outdoor activities that caters to everyone.

Our **easy glacier walks** follow the path of least resistance through glacier and mountain landscapes, while our longer hikes take a more adventurous approach into the world of deep blue crevasses and towering ice falls. For those craving a serious challenge, consider a guided multi-day summit trip to Iceland's highest peak, **Hvannadalshnúkur**, at 2110m, or put your nerves and skills to the wall for some vertical **ice climbing**!

If glaciers are an interest but not quite the same obsession they are to us, get into something totally different like **mountain biking** or **rock climbing**, or jump on a **combo tour** for a change of scenery after an introduction to the ice! Check out puffins and other sea birds at the **Ingólfshöfði Cape**, or relax on the decks of a cruise boat as it meanders through a maze of curious seals and towering icebergs on the famous **Jökulsárlón** glacial lagoon!

Whatever your passion, you'll find plenty of it in Vatnajökull National Park!

www.adventures.is

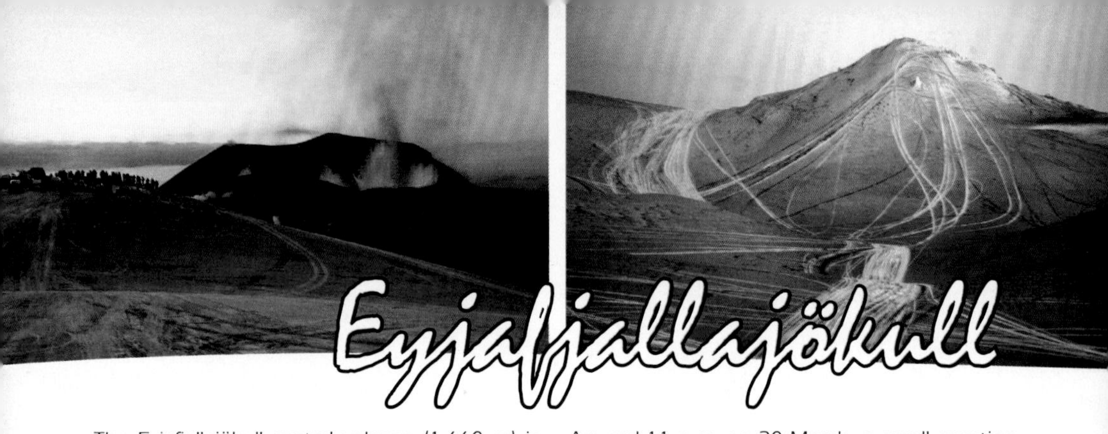

Eyjafjallajökull

The Eyjafjallajökull central volcano (1,660 m) is less than a million years old and therefore still considered as young. No high-temperature area appears on the surface, probably because the volcano's magma chamber is small and lies at great depth. The jökull part of the name means glacier; this one is 80 km2 in size and the seventh largest in Iceland. Its ice generally fills the 2.5-km2 caldera on top of the volcano, from where the outlet glacier Gígjökull flows downwards to the lowlands. During most of the volcano's existence, it has been covered by either

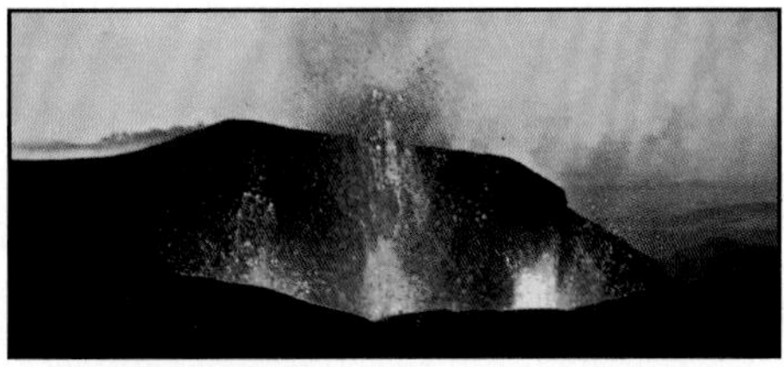

this glacial ice or that of Ice Age glaciations, so that uncounted eruptions under ice have largely produced hyaloclastite material and gradually piled it up to form the mountain.

One recorded eruption occurred in 1612, while another started on the evening of 19 December 1821 and lasted, including short periods of inactivity, until January 1823.

The Fimmvörðuháls volcanic eruption

In 1994, scientists noticed magma flowing under Eyjafjallajökull central volcano, with accompanying earthquakes. A similar event occurred in 2000. In the following years, measurements indicated that fissures around the glacier peak were beginning to enlarge, with clear signs of increasing geothermal heat below. In mid-2009, a magma influx began once more, accompanied by earthquakes. In the first three months of 2010, the seismic activity inside the volcano was nearly constant. Everyone wondered whether the magma would ever reach the surface, since the source of these earthquakes generally lay at a depth of about 10 km.

Around 11 p.m. on 20 March, a small eruption finally began in the northern part of Fimmvörðuháls pass. The lava from this eruption flowed north, towards Þórsmörk, but there was never much seismic activity and the eruption ended on 12 April.

The Eyjafjallajökull volcanic eruption

About 11 p.m. on 13 April, an earthquake measuring 2.5 occurred, located approximately 6 km beneath Eyjafjallajökull. About 7 a.m. the next morning, apparently after volcanic activity had been melting ice at the summit for several hours, the volume of water emerging from under Gígjökull outlet glacier started increasing fast. Two major jökulhlaups, or glacial floods, gushed down from their source in the caldera on 14 April, although little damage was caused by these, while additional, minor jökulhlaups flowed from the caldera over the next few days. As long as the rising lava still contacted water in the caldera, steam explosions resulted that threw the lava up in bits, creating an ash cloud and seriously affecting Europe's air traffic. However, just over a week after the eruption began, the lava no longer encountered water and began running north under the Gígjökull ice, thereby producing much less ash. By Day 10 of the eruption, the amount of fresh lava had stabilised and was much less than at the beginning.

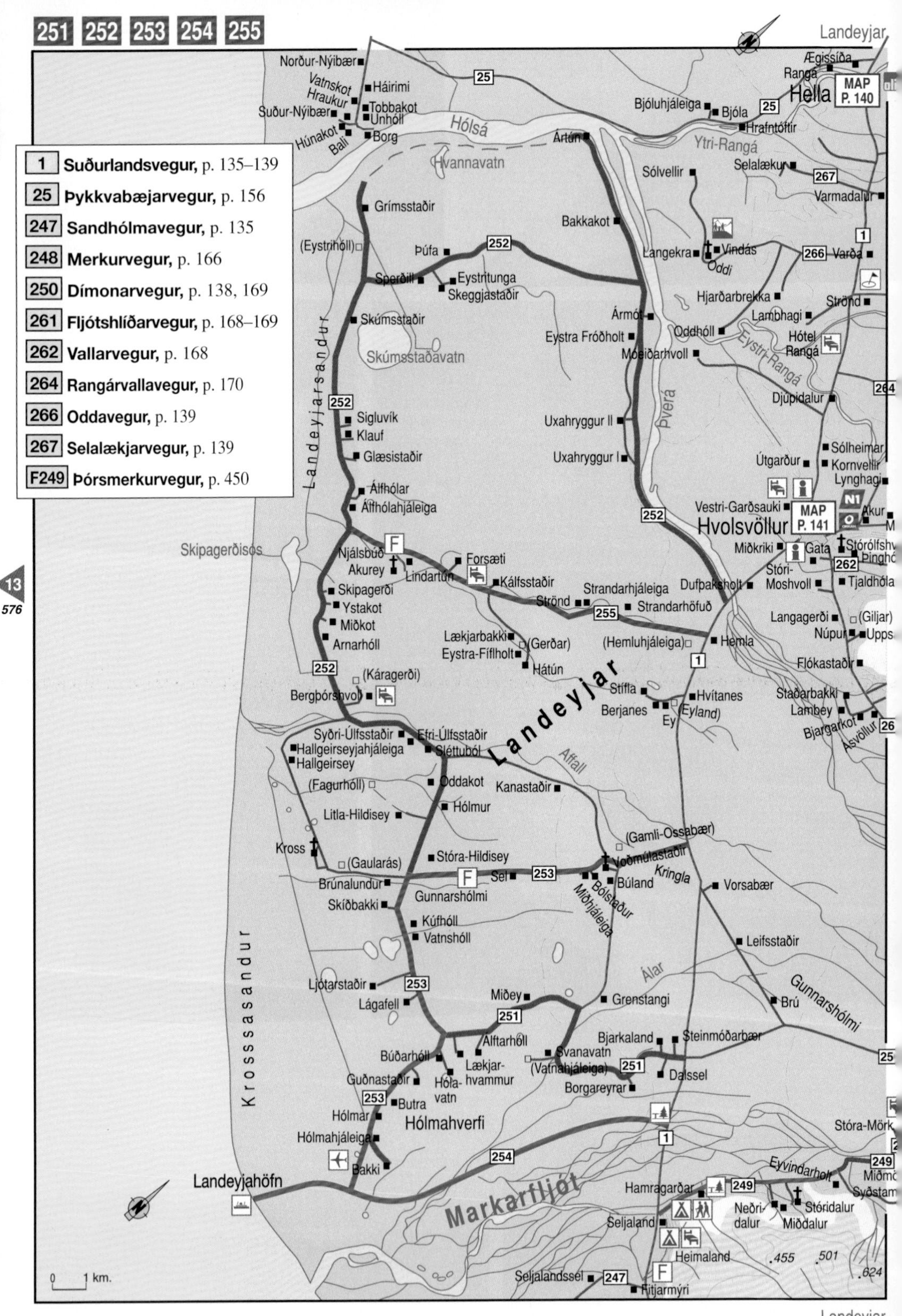
1 Suðurlandsvegur, p. 135–139
25 Þykkvabæjarvegur, p. 156
247 Sandhólmavegur, p. 135
248 Merkurvegur, p. 166
250 Dímonarvegur, p. 138, 169
261 Fljótshlíðarvegur, p. 168–169
262 Vallarvegur, p. 168
264 Rangárvallavegur, p. 170
266 Oddavegur, p. 139
267 Selalækjarvegur, p. 139
F249 Þórsmerkurvegur, p. 450
Norður-Nýibær
Vatnskot
Hraukur
Suður-Nýibær
Húnakot
Bali
Háirimi
Tobbakot
Unhóll
Borg
Hólsá
Hvannavatn
Ártún
Ægissíða
Rangá
Hella
MAP P. 140
Bjóluhjáleiga
Bjóla
Hrafntóftir
Ytri-Rangá
Sólvellir
Selalækur
Varmadalur
Grímsstaðir
Bakkakot
(Eystrihóll)
Þúfa
Langekra
Vindás
Oddi
Varða
Sperðill
Eystritunga
Skeggjastaðir
Hjarðarbrekka
Strönd
Skúmsstaðir
Ármót
Lambhagi
Eystra Fróðholt
Oddhóll
Hótel Rangá
Skúmsstaðavatn
Móeiðarhvoll
Eystri-Rangá
Landeyjarsandur
Djúpidalur
Sigluvík
Klauf
Uxahryggur II
Þverá
Glæsistaðir
Uxahryggur I
Útgarður
Sólheimar
Kornvellir
Lynghagi
Álfhólar
Álfhólahjáleiga
Vestri-Garðsauki
Hvolsvöllur
MAP P. 141
Akur
Skipagerðisós
Njálsbúð
Akurey
Lindartún
Forsæti
Kálfsstaðir
Miðkriki
Gata
Stórólfshvoll
Stóri-Moshvoll
Tjaldhólar
Skipagerði
Ystakot
Miðkot
Arnarhóll
Strönd
Strandarhjáleiga
Dufþaksholt
Strandarhöfuð
Langagerði
(Giljar)
Núpur
Lækjarbakki
Eystra-Fíflholt
(Gerðar)
(Hemluhjáleiga)
Hemla
Flókastaðir
(Káragerði)
Hátún
Landeyjar
Stífla
Bergþórshvoll
Berjanes
Hvítanes
Ey
(Eyland)
Staðarbakki
Lambey
Bjargarkot
Ásvöllur
Syðri-Úlfsstaðir
Efri-Úlfsstaðir
Hallgeirseyjahjáleiga
Hallgeirsey
Sléttuból
Affall
(Fagurhóll)
Oddakot
Kanastaðir
Litla-Hildisey
Hólmur
Kross
(Gamli-Ossabær)
Voðmúlastaðir
(Gaularás)
Stóra-Hildisey
Sel
Kringla
Brúnalundur
Búland
Bólstaður
Miðhjáleiga
Vorsabær
Skíðbakki
Gunnarshólmi
Kúfhóll
Vatnshóll
Leifsstaðir
Krossasandur
Ljótarstaðir
Álar
Gunnarshólmi
Lágafell
Miðey
Grenstangi
Brú
Álftarhóll
Bjarkaland
Steinmóðarbær
Búðarhóll
Lækjarhvammur
Svanavatn
(Vatnahjáleiga)
Dalssel
Guðnastaðir
Hólavatn
Borgareyrar
Butra
Hólmar
Hólmahverfi
Hólmahjáleiga
Stóra-Mörk
Bakki
Landeyjahöfn
Markarfljót
Eyvindarholt
Miðmörk
Syðstamörk
Hamragarðar
Neðri-dalur
Stóridalur
Miðdalur
Seljaland
Heimaland
Seljalandssel
Fitjarmýri
0 1 km.

13
P. 576

© Markaðsstofa Suðurlands

Stóra Dímon

Landeyjar, ("Land islands") the district bordered by the rivers Þverá to the north and Hólsá and Álar to the west and east. Mostly flat country, wet and sandy towards the sea. Divided by the river **Affall** into Austur- and Vestur-Landeyjar.

252 **Landeyjavegur,** 55 km.

251 **Hólmabæjavegur,** 10,5 km.

Bergþórshvoll, a farm on the western banks of Affall, a parsonage. This was the home of Njáll Þorgeirsson of *Njáls saga*. Many place-names remind us of the Saga, such as Flosalág, Káragerði (a farm), Káragróf, Línakrar etc. *Njáls saga* tells of the burning of Bergþórshvoll in 1011, and archeological studies verify that the house did indeed burn in the early 11th century.

Hallgeirsey, a farm by the mouth of the river Affall. For a while a cooperative store was located there, and goods were landed from the sea.

Kross, a farm and church, and a parsonage until 1920.

Voðmúlastaðir, a farm and church.

Gamli-Ossabær, ruins 1 km from Voðmúlastaðir and 3 km from Vorsabær, believed to have been the farm of Höskuldur Hvítanesgoði of *Njáls saga*.

255 **Akureyjavegur,** 11 km.

Akurey, farm, church, community centre.

Njálsbúð, community centre.

253 **Bakkavegur**.

254 **Landeyjahafnarvegur,** 11 km.

Gunnarshólmi, community centre.

Hólmar, or Hólmahverfi, a group of farms. From there a jeep-track goes down to the coast.

Krosssandur, this is the nearest point to Vestmannaeyjar, which are about 10 km away.

Bakki, an airport for Vestmannaeyjar (Westman Islands). Electricity, telephone and water are led from there to Vestmannaeyjar.

Markarfljót, a glacial river with its main source on the Mýrdalsjökull glacier and another on the Eyjafjallajökull glacier, but its longest branch comes from Reykjadalir west of the Torfajökull glacier. It carries a good deal of stones and gravel. It has often overflowed its banks in the lowlands causing great damage to farming country, but recently-built dykes have given good protection. The Markarfljót is 100 km long with a total drainage area of ca. 1,070 km^2 and an average flow of 85 m^3 per sec. The 242 m bridge over Markarfljót was opened in 1934. A new bridge to the west of the farm Seljaland was opened in 1992, and a bridge was built at Emstrur (see Road F210) in 1978. The river was formerly widely believed to harbour monsters, and there is a modern account of people who claim to have seen a strange creature 12-15 m long in it. According to folk-tales the monster originated from a large skate, or ray-fish, thrown into the river by a local farmer after it had been hung up to dry. The farmer hoped to protect the people of the Fljótshlíð district from glacial floods, especially those in Markarfljót. The skate came to life and turned into a monster. It is said that when fording Markarfljót or Þverá on horseback there is a danger of "skidding on the skate".

249 **Þórsmerkurvegur,** from Road 1 by Seljalandsmúli east of Markarfljót to Road F29 Merkurvegur.

248 **Merkurvegur,** 3,46 km to Stóra-Mörk.

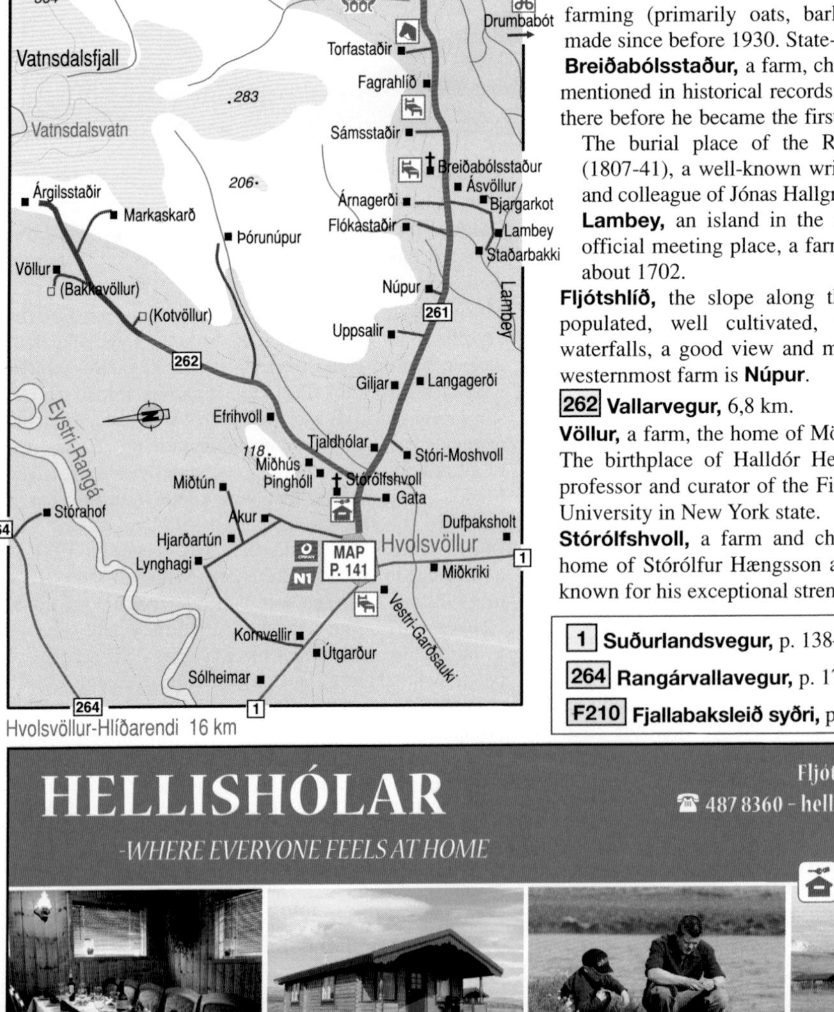

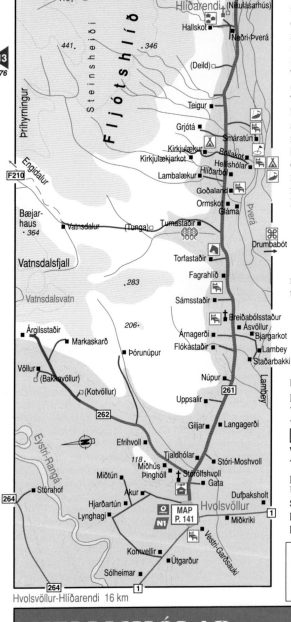

13 P. 576

Grjótá, a farm, the home of Þráinn Sigfússon of *Njáls saga*.

Kirkjulækur and Kirkjulækjarkot, farms on the west of the Grjótá river, usually called Kirkjulækjartorfan. A centre for Pentecostals. A small cave by the stream northwest of the farm was used for official gatherings until 1894.

Kvoslækur, a school by the river Kvoslækjará.

Vatnsdalsvatn, a lake on the mountain Vatnsdalsfjall (279 m). A monster is said to live in the lake.

Tumastaðir, a farm, since 1935 a forestry centre belonging to the Forestry Service. Good access to paths and trails. The 'Republic Grove' and tree collection with numerous species. National Forest.

Drumbabót, a desert-like area with battered 1200 year old tree stumps. Research have shown that the whole forest was most likely wiped-out in one glacial outburst flood from the Mýrdalsjökull glacier. The road to Drumbabót is only accessible by jeep as rivers need to be crossed. Please exercise care!

Sámsstaðir, a farm where experiments in grain-farming (primarily oats, barley and rye) have been made since before 1930. State-operated.

Breiðabólsstaður, a farm, church and parsonage, often mentioned in historical records. Jón Ögmundsson served there before he became the first catholic bishop at Hólar.

The burial place of the Rev. Tómas Sæmundsson (1807-41), a well-known writer and nationalist, friend and colleague of Jónas Hallgrímsson.

Lambey, an island in the river Þverá, formerly an official meeting place, a farm and church, abandoned about 1702.

Fljótshlíð, the slope along the river Þverá. Densely populated, well cultivated, with many rivers and waterfalls, a good view and many beautiful spots. The westernmost farm is **Núpur**.

262 Vallarvegur, 6,8 km.

Völlur, a farm, the home of Mörður gígja of *Njáls saga*. The birthplace of Halldór Hermannsson (1878-1958), professor and curator of the Fiske Collection at Cornell University in New York state.

Stórólfshvoll, a farm and church. In Saga times the home of Stórólfur Hængsson and his son Ormur, well-known for his exceptional strength.

1 **Suðurlandsvegur,** p. 138–139
264 **Rangárvallavegur,** p. 170
F210 **Fjallabaksleið syðri,** p. 438

Þórólfsfell, (574 m) a tuff mountain, named after the settler Þórólfur Askssonur, he was the great grandfather of Njáll in Njáls saga. In *Njáls saga* it says that Njáll had a farm in Þórólfsfell, yet no remains are now to be seen. On the southwest side is an interesting cave, **Mögugilshellir**, now spoiled by the river.

Fljótsdalur, a farm and a Youth Hostel. Emstruleið ("The Emstra route"), a difficult summer road, often hardly passable because of unbridged rivers, leads from there to Fjallabaksleið syðri ("The southern behind-the-mountains route") at Hvanngil.

Bleiksárgljúfur, a deep and narrow canyon, in places so narrow that it seems feasible to jump across but is in fact much too dangerous to attempt, and several deaths have occurred there. The first acted movie scenes to be taken in Iceland were taken there in 1923, for the film *Hadda Padda* by Guðmundur Kamban.

250 Dímonarvegur, 12,1 km .

Múlakot, a farm formerly widely known in Iceland for beautiful tree gardens. A fine view from the farm. One of the locality´s oldest guesthouses and former home of the artist Ólafur Túbal (1897-1964). Many of Iceland´s leading artists stayed here and painted local landscape compositions. The Iceland Forest Service's first tree planting station, from 1935. The tallest trees in Iceland, were found in Múlakot in 2005, some 24 m high, – black cottonwood that grew out of sucker shoots in 1963. National Forest.

Merkjá, a river falling off the cliffs in a beautiful waterfall, Merkjárfoss or Gluggafoss ("Window falls"). Þórðarfoss waterfall just west of there.

Hlíðarendakot, a farm where the poet Þorsteinn Erlingsson (1858-1914) was brought up. Near the farm is his memorial, a bust by the sculptor Nína Sæmundsson (1892-1965). Memorial to her at Hlíðarendi church. The waterfall **Drífandi** in the background.

Nikulásarhús, an abandoned farm were Jónína Sæmundsdóttir was born (1892–1965) better know as Nína Sæmundsson sculptor. She studied in in Copenhagen and Rome but lived in Hollywood for the longest time and was well know for her art.

Hlíðarendi, a farm and church, long a manor farm, one of the most famous in Iceland. It was the home of Gunnar Hámundarson of *Njáls saga*. Also the birthplace of Bishop Þorlákur helgi (St. Thorlak), and the childhood home of the poet Bjarni Thorarensen (1786-1841). In the 17th century it was the home of Gísli Magnússon (1621-96), who experimented with gardening and grain-farming, and imported and planted Caraway (Carum carvi) which now grows wild in many parts of Iceland.

Þverá, now a clear river formed by the numerous streams of Fljótshlíð and flowing along the whole length of Fljótshlíð. Formerly a large part of the glacial river Markarfljót joined Þverá, and in those days it was a menace, breaking down large areas of good farming land. Eventually embankments were built along Markarfljót, the furthest inland being at the mountain Þórólfsfell. Vegetation is increasing on the former floodlands.

1 **Suðurlandsvegur,** p. 138 F261 **Emstruleið,** p. 452

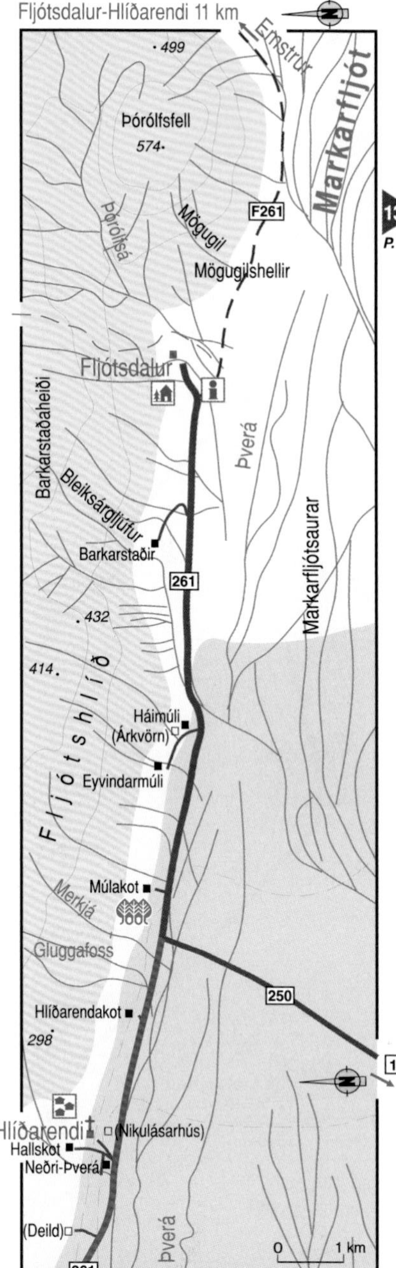

13
P. 576

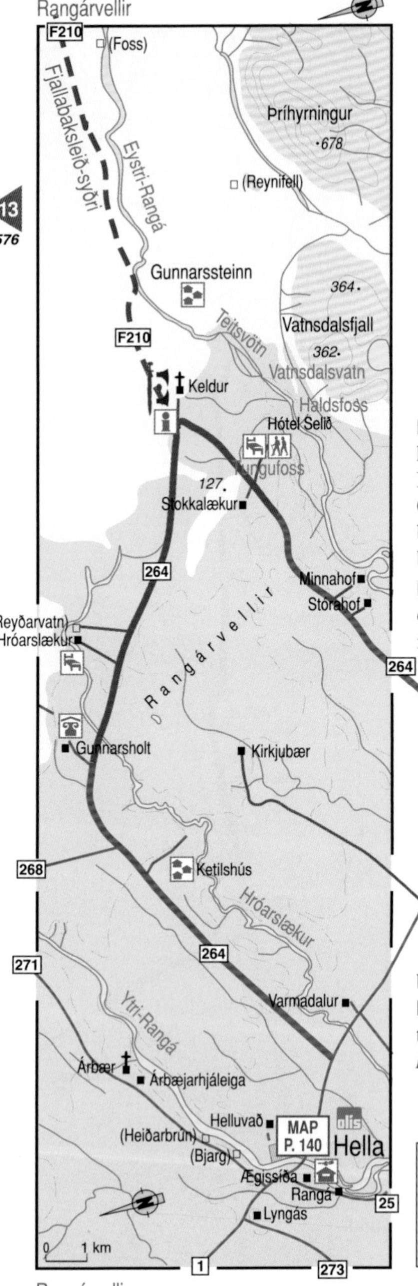

Keldur.

Þríhyrningur, (678 m) a tuff mountain, dominating the surroundings. The hiding place of Flosi of *Njáls saga* and his men after they set fire to Bergþórshvoll, burning Njáll inside.

Gunnarssteinn, where Gunnar of Hlíðarendi of *Njáls saga* and his brothers fought some 30 men after being ambushed at **Knafahólar**. Some bones etc. have been found to verify this.

Keldur, a manor farm since Saga times, mentioned in *Njáls saga* as one of the main farms of the family of Oddi. Over 20 houses are preserved, including the primary living quarters and the accommodation for livestock. The farmhouses are of ancient type of turf houses. The hall, probably dating from the 16th century, is of so called stave construction with Romanesque-style ornament. The date 1641 is carved on a ledge in the hall, but it is likely that the hall is much older. Beneath the hall is a tunnel believed to date from the 11th -13th century, probably for escape in times of conflict. In the keeping of the National Museum since 1947.

Stóra-Hof, a farm since the original settlement. The settler was Ketill hængur, a man of noble family who had many outstanding descendants. After him it was the home of Valgarður hinn grái (the grey) and his son Mörður, frequently mentioned in *Njáls saga*, the latter being one of the main opponents of his relative, Gunnar of Hlíðarendi.

Kirkjubær, long a substantial farm, in the middle of the Rangárvellir area, the only farm in a great area of grass between the sands. Often mentioned in *Njáls saga*, being the home of Otkell Skarfson. Now a horse-breeding farm.

1 **Suðurlandsvegur,** p. 139
25 **Þykkvabæjarvegur,** p. 156
268 **Þingskálavegur,** p. 171
271 **Árbæjarvegur,** p. 158
273 **Bugavegur,** p. 156
F210 **Fjallabaksvegur syðri,** p. 438

268 ÞINGSKÁLAVEGUR

Hekla, (1,491 m) the most famous volcano in Iceland and one of the best-known volcanoes in the world and has been active for thousands of years. The mountain is a long ridge with a 4 km long crack along the top. There have been 20 eruptions in recorded history, the first in 1104 and the latest in February 2000, when scientists were able to predict the eruption half an hour in advanse using the alarm system of the Icelandic Meteorological Office. Folk tales tell us the souls of the damned were once believed to pass through the crater of Hekla on their way to Hell. First ascent of Hekla was made June 20th 1750 by the explorers Eggert Ólafsson and Bjarni Pálsson. It is easiest to climb the mountain from the northwest side or following the north ridge. The climb takes about 8 hours.

Næfurholt, a farm closest to Hekla. The farm has been moved many times because of volcanic eruptions and other natural disasters.

Hraunteigur, birch-woods along the river Rangá across from Galtalækur. A bridge over Rangá not far upstream from there, only 2,6 m wide.

Bjólfell, (443 m) a mountain to the southwest of Hekla. The farms Næfurholt, Hólar and Haukadalur on the north and west of the mountain. Once believed to be the home of a giantess, the sister of the giantess at Búrfell (see road 26).

Selsund, a farm to the south of Hekla, where the first ascent of Hekla in 1750 was begun. In the earthquakes of 1912 a crack opened nearby and one side of the crack subsided all of four metres.

Bolholt, a farm. The area is being cultivated and many trees have been planted there through the years.

Víkingslækur, an anabandoned farm because of sand erosion, once a manor farm.

Þingskálar, an ancient official meeting-place with some protected ruins.

Gunnarsholt, formerly a substantial farm and a church, abandoned in 1925. A monument in memory of the church built there around 1200 and abandoned in 1837 when it was engulfed by sand. Now a growing settlement. It houses the headquarters of the Soil Conservation Service of Iceland which runs a big seed processing station. A team of scientists and executives and are working to improve and restore land quality throughout the country. A new Visitor Centre Telling the Story of Restoring the Land is now open. Learn about the unique story of Iceland´s environmental history: A 1000 years of devastation by nature and human activity and 100 years of restoring of the land.

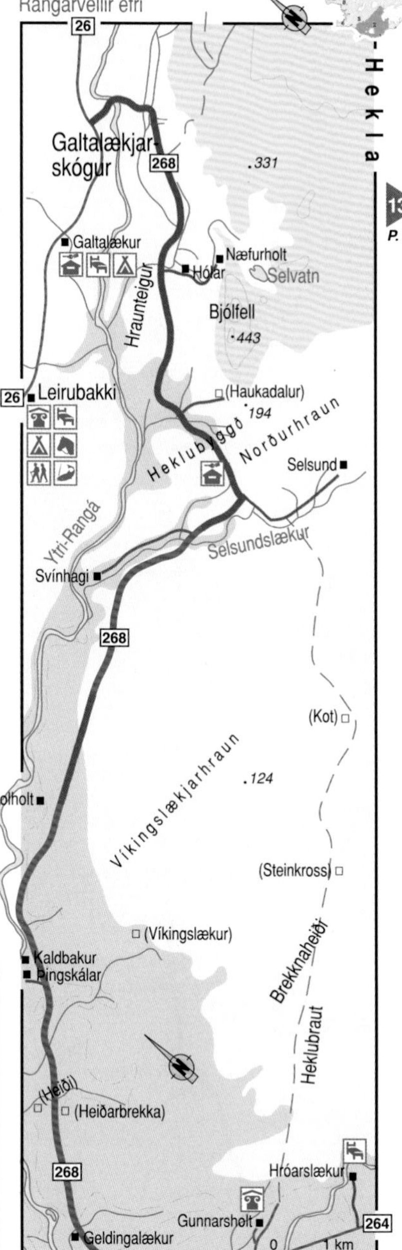

26 **Landvegur,** p. 160 264 **Rangárvallavegur,** p. 170

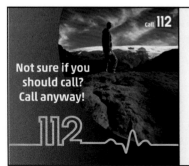

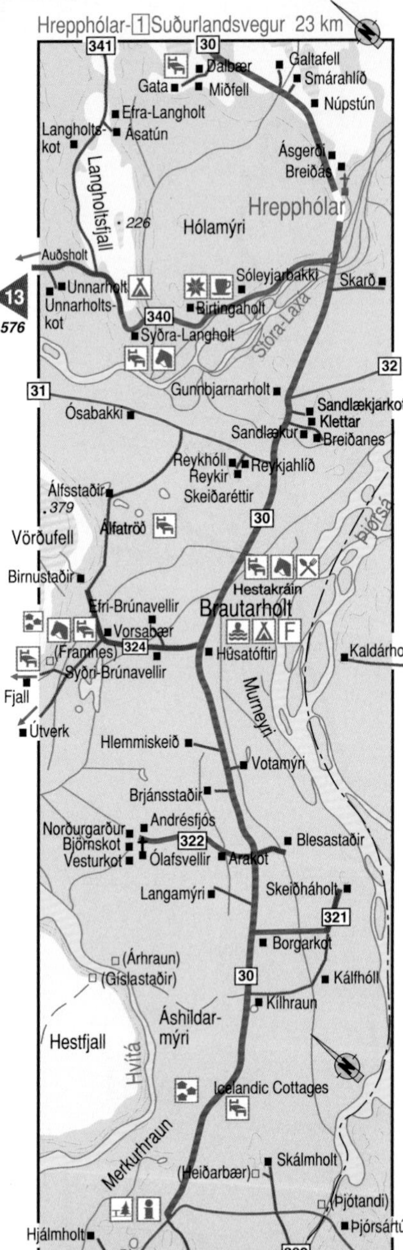

340 Auðsholtsvegur, 11 km.

324 Vorsabæjarvegur, 7,8 km.

Birtingaholt, a farm, long the home of Ágúst Helgason (1862-1948), outstanding among farmers. His three brothers, all ministers, were Guðmundur (1853-1922) of Reykholt, Kjartan (1865-1931) of Hruni and Magnús (1857-1940), the first rector of the teachers' school in Reykjavík. Now there is a pottery workshop and a café called Bragginn.

Álfaskeið, a small valley on the south side of the mountain Langholtsfjall.

Laxárholt, by the bridge across Laxá, ancient place of official meetings.

Stóra-Laxá, a clear river that starts on the south of Kerlingarfjöll and flows through impressive canyons in the interior. Good salmon river. A jeep track goes along the canyon.

Hreppar, the northernmost districts of Árnessýsla, between Hvítá and Þjórsá, Ytrihreppur or Hrunamannahreppur to the west and Eystrihreppur or Gnúpverjahreppur to the east. Uneven land with many ridges and mountains but green and grassy, good farming country.

Húsatóftir, there is Hestakráin, restaurant and guesthouse.

Brautarholt, (pop. 57) a school, swimming pool, campsite and a community centre. Geothermal heat.

322 Ólafsvallavegur, 3 km.

321 Skeiðháholtsvegur, 6 km.

Ólafsvellir, a farm, church and parsonage until 1925.

Áshildarmýri, a hollow in the old **Merkurhraun** lava-field. A memorial has been erected there to commemorate the Áshildarmýri agreement (Áshildarmýrarsamþykkt) of 1496 when the people gathered to protest against bad government and demand improvements.

Skeið, the district between the rivers Hvítá and Þjórsá, from Flói to Stóra-Laxá and Sandlækjarós. Flat and wet in many places, lava under the soil. The irrigation system, Skeiðaáveita, is from 1924.

1 Suðurlandsvegur, p. 143	**31 Skálholtsvegur,** p. 174
32 Þjórsárdalsvegur, p. 175	**302 Urriðafossvegur,** p. 178
341 Langholtsvegur, p. 173	

Brúarhlöð, narrows and rapids of the river Hvítá. Interesting rock formations. Birch bushes on the banks. Arctic Rafting offer tours down Hvítá river with a relay at Brúrarhlöð. There rafters are invited to jump of the cliffs into the river.

349 Tungufellsvegur, 2,7 km.

Tungufell, a farm and church. Towerless wooden church built in 1856. In the keeping of the National Museum since 1987. The farm furthest from the sea in southern Iceland, 58 km from the head of Hvalfjörður. From Tungufell a jeep-track continues northward to Svínárnes and the Kerlingarfjöll mountains. A walking route to Gullfoss, starts 5,5 km from Tungufell.

Hlíð, formerly a farm. Birthplace of the famous outlaw Eyvindur Jónsson (1714-1782), known as Fjalla-Eyvindur ("Eyvindur of the mountains").

344 Hrunavegur, 7,7 km.

345 Kaldbaksvegur, 8,38 km.

Reykjadalur, a farm. A church and a parsonage until 1819.

Hruni, a farm, church and a parsonage. The birthplace of Earl Gissur Þorvaldsson (1208-1268). A well-known folktale, the Dance in Hruni, is connected with this place. The church once stood on a cliff above the present farm, and people would dance, drink and play cards in the church on Christmas night. One Christmas the Devil appeared and dragged the church building and all the people down into the underworld. The present church at Hruni was built in 1865 and can seat 200 people.

Hvítárholt, a farm near the river Hvítá where Saga age ruins have been excavated, showing the oldest building style of Iceland. A Roman copper coin dating from 275-276 AD was found there.

341 Langholtsvegur, 7,7 km.

Flúðir, (pop. 430) a village in the geothermal area of Hellisholt. Greenhouses, community centre, swimming pool, hotel, restaurant, grocery and liquor store. Good walking routes in the area. See more on p. 198.

Hellisholt, a farm south of Flúðir where in 1899, Dr. Helgi Pjeturss discovered moraines which yielded important information about the Ice Age in Iceland.

Galtafell, a farm and the birthplace of the sculptor Einar Jónsson (1873– 1954), whose works can be seen in a special gallery in Reykjavík, the Einar Jónsson Museum, close to Hallgrímskirkja. One can see the influence of the surrounding landscape in some of his works.

Hrepphólar, a farm and a place of settlement, a church and parsonage until 1880. One of the clergymen was Jón Egilsson (1548-1636), who began a new age of historical writings in Iceland when he wrote *Biskupsannálar* ("The annals of the bishops").

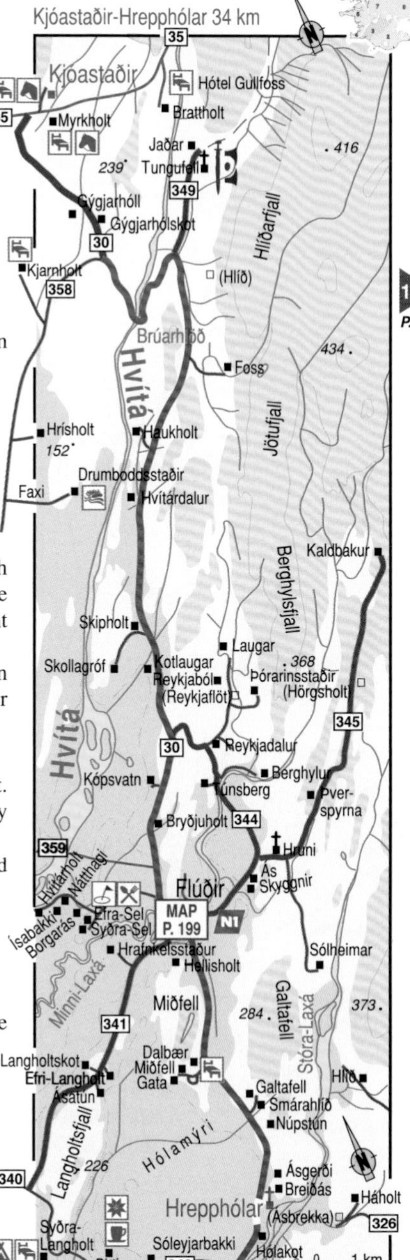

35 Biskupstungnabraut, p. 183
326 Hælsvegur, p. 175
340 Auðsholtsvegur, p. 172
341 Langholtsvegur, p. 173
358 Einholtsvegur, p. 183
359 Bræðratunguvegur, p. 198

Spóastaðir-Reykir 15 km

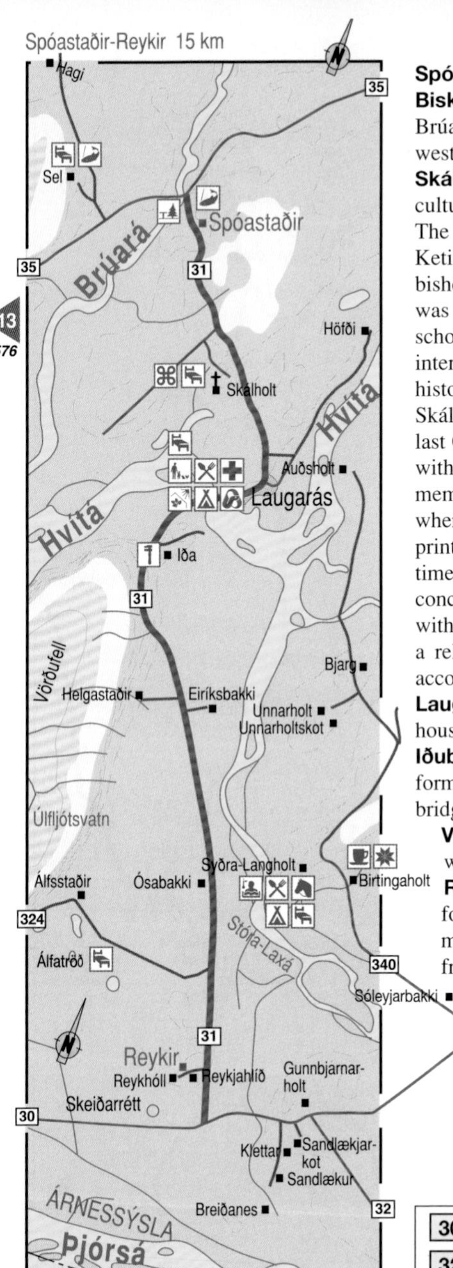

Reykir-Spóastaðir 15 km

Spóastaðir, a farm near the bridge on Brúará, formerly a ferry point.

Biskupstungur, ("Bishop's tongues") a tongue of land between the rivers Brúará and Hvítá, divided into two tongues by the Tungufljót river. The western sections are wet in places, the eastern and northern sections drier.

Skálholt, one of the most historic places in Iceland, presently a place of culture and spirituality, with its church and cultural centre. Also a farm. The first settler at Skálholt was Teitur Ketilbjarnarson grandfather of the first bishop, Ísleifur Gissurarson. Skálholt was the seat of bishops 1056-1796, a school after the Reformation and intermittently in Catholic times. Many historical events are connected with Skálholt, such as the execution of the last Catholic bishop, Jón Arason, along with two of his sons in 1550. A memorial has been erected on the spot where Jón Arason was beheaded. A printing press was operated there for a time. The present cathedral was concecrated in 1963 and is decorated with important works by Icelandic artists. A crypt of former bishops and a related museum is there. A visitor centre in summer, restaurant and accommodation. Concerts five weekends in June-July.

The cathedral at Skálholt

Laugarás, (pop. 97) a village by Hvítá, medical centre, many greenhouses and Slakki, a small petting zoo popular with families.

Iðubrú, a suspension bridge over the river Hvítá built in 1957. There was formerly a busy ferry-point there. The farm **Iða** on the south side of the bridge.

Vörðufell, (391 m) a mountain with the lake **Úlfljótsvatn** on top which has its outlet through the gorge Úlfsgil.

Reykir, a group of farms, geothermal heat. Near Reykir are the sheepfolds **Skeiðaréttir**, among the largest in Iceland and noted for merry-making at round-up times. They were built in 1881 with lave blocks from the area and renovated in 1981. Landgræðsla ríkisins, the Soil Conservation Service of Iceland, has revegetated extensive land areas in this region. The first soil conservation area in Iceland was established at Reykir when in 1908 an area was fenced off to provide protection from grazing.

30 **Skeiða- og Hrunamannavegur,** p. 172
32 **Þjórsárdalsvegur,** p. 175
35 **Biskupstungnabraut,** p. 182
324 **Vorsabæjarvegur,** p. 172
340 **Auðsholtsvegur,** p. 172

32 ÞJÓRSÁRDALSVEGUR

Gaukshöfði, a rocky bluff by the river Þjórsá near the mouth of the Þjórsárdalur valley. In the 19th century old bones and a spearhead were found, believed to have belonged to Gaukur Trandilsson, who was killed there. His home was at Stöng in Þjórsárdalur. Excellent viewing point, especially towards Hekla.

Hagi, a substantial farm under the mountain, Hagafjall. Nearby is Hagaey, a large island in the Þjórsá river

329 Mástunguvegur, 8 km.

Skáldabúðir, a farm by Mástunguvegur. From there a jeep-track leads inland on the east side of the river Stóra-Laxá, to Sultarfit and on to Fossárdrög. Upstream from the abandoned farm, Grímsstaðir, Stóra-Laxá goes through long and majestic canyons.

328 Stóra-Núpsvegur, 2,4 km.

Stóri-Núpur, a farm and a church. The home of Hjalti Skeggjason, a chieftain well-known for his part in the conversion of Iceland to Christianity in year 1000. Birthplace of contemporary painter Jóhann Briem (1907–91) and long the home of his grandfather, minister and hymn-writer Valdimar Briem (1848–1930).

Skaftholtréttir sheep-folds, by Skaftholt. Considered to be the oldest in Iceland, from the 12th century. They were built from lava blocks from Þjórsárdalshraun lavafields.

Þjórsárholt, a farm where hot steam coming from rifts was formerly used for baths.

325 Gnúpverjavegur, 10,4 km.

326 Hælsvegur, 3,3 km.

Ásar, a farm.

Steinsholt, a farm and formerly a church and parsonage, or until 1789, when they were moved to Stóri-Núpur.

Árnes, campsite, pool and visitor centre. Þjórsárstofa offers interesting insights on the locality´s nature, people and history.

Þrándarholt, a farm with the rocky mountain **Þrándur** above. According to the Sagas, Þórður Andrésson, the last member of the Oddi clan, was killed there by Gissur Þorvaldsson. Nearby is **Árnes** ("River point") which used to be a place of official meetings. It is now an island in the Þjórsá river but was formerly connected to the west bank. On the west side is a the waterfall **Búðafoss**, on the east side is the waterfall Hestafoss.

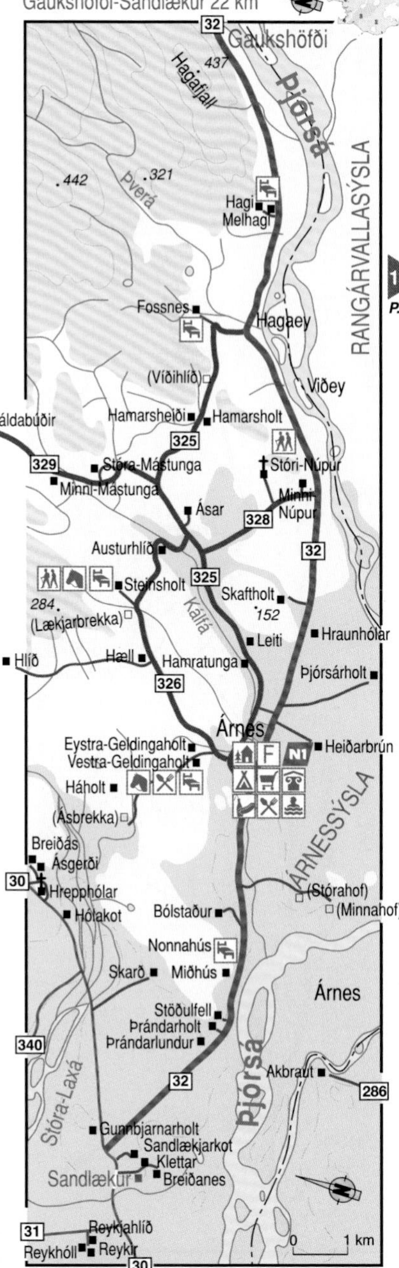

30 **Skeiða- og Hrunamannavegur,** p. 172
31 **Skálholtsvegur,** p. 174
286 **Hagabraut,** p. 158
340 **Auðsholtsvegur,** p. 172

26 Landvegur-Gaukshöfði 32 km

13
P. 576

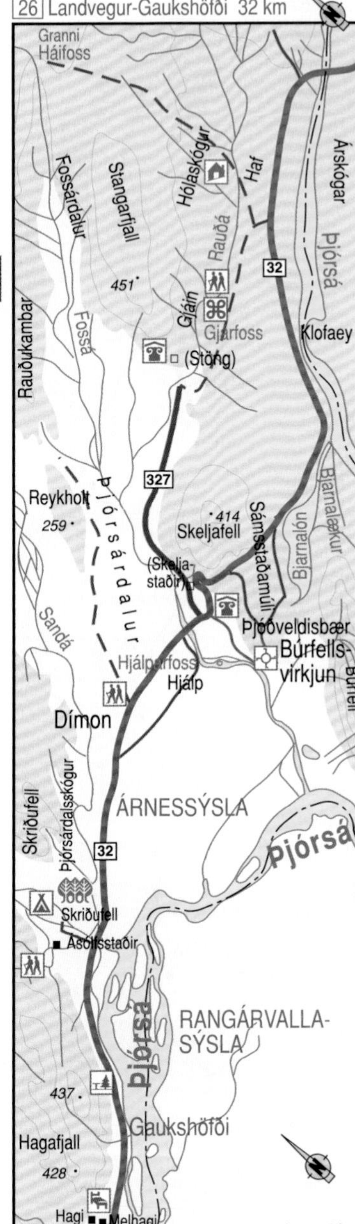

Gaukshöfði- 26 Landvegur 32 km

Gjáin

Þjórsá, a glacial river, the longest river in Iceland, 230 km, with an average flow of 360 m^3/sec. Gathers most of its water from the glaciers Vatnajökull and Hofsjökull, but its northernmost origin is on the Sprengisandur sands. Several waterfalls, especially in the interior. In 1973 a 185 m bridge was built north of Búrfell.

Háifoss, ("High falls") a 122 m high waterfall, the 4th highest in Iceland, in the river Fossá in the **Fossárdalur** valley. Another waterfall, Granni, nearby. About 2 hours' walk from Stöng, but it is easier to reach by a road called Línuvegur ("Lines road"), the access road for repair and maintenance of electricity lines.

Rauðukambar, ("Red crests") multi-coloured rhyolite mountain, geothermal heat.

Gjáin, a gorge with beautiful rock formations and waterfalls like **Gjárfoss** in the river Rauðá ("Red river").

Hólaskógur, a piece of land just inside the boundaries of Þjórsárdalur. An emergency hut was built there in 1970, and in 1998 a guest lodge was constructed.

327 Stangarvegur, 11 km.

Stöng, protected ruins of a farm, excavated in 1939, believed to have been buried under pumice and ashes from the Hekla eruption of 1104.

Skeljastaðir, the ruins of the church farm that served Þjórsárdalur of old. A great many skeletons have been excavated from the churchyard, giving much information about the people.

Þjóðveldisbær, ("Farm of the republic") a farm building below the spur **Sámsstaðamúli,** constructed in the medieval style in commemoration of the 1,100 years of settlement in Iceland in 1974. A small stave church, enclosed with turf, has been built next to the farmhouse replica. The design is conjectural, based on ruins of a church found in excavations at Stöng.

26 Landvegur, p. 160

Búrfellsvirkjun, a power-station, 270 MW, built in 1969 on the river Þjórsá. A big dam was built to the northeast of **Búrfell** and the water diverted through tunnels to the generators under Sámsstaðamúli.

Hjálparfoss, ("The help falls") a beautiful waterfall in the river Fossá opposite the power-station.

Dímon, remarkable strata has been found there.

Þjórsárdalur, the easternmost valley of Árnessýsla. There is only one farm in this valley now, Ásólfsstaðir, but ruins of 20 farms have been found. It is believed that the valley was deserted after heavy pumice rain from the eruption of Hekla in 1104. The valley of Þjórsárdalur has been partly revegetated by Landgræðsla ríkisins, the Soil Conservation Service of Iceland, **Þjórsárdalsskógur**. Extensive birchwoods in many places. Two rivers, Sandá and Fossá flow through the valley, and the Þjórsá river closes it to the south. National Forest.

Quality and hospitality

Árnes / Borg / Brautarholt / Flúðir
Laugarás / Laugarvatn / Reykholt / Sólheimar

www.south.is

www.sveitir.is

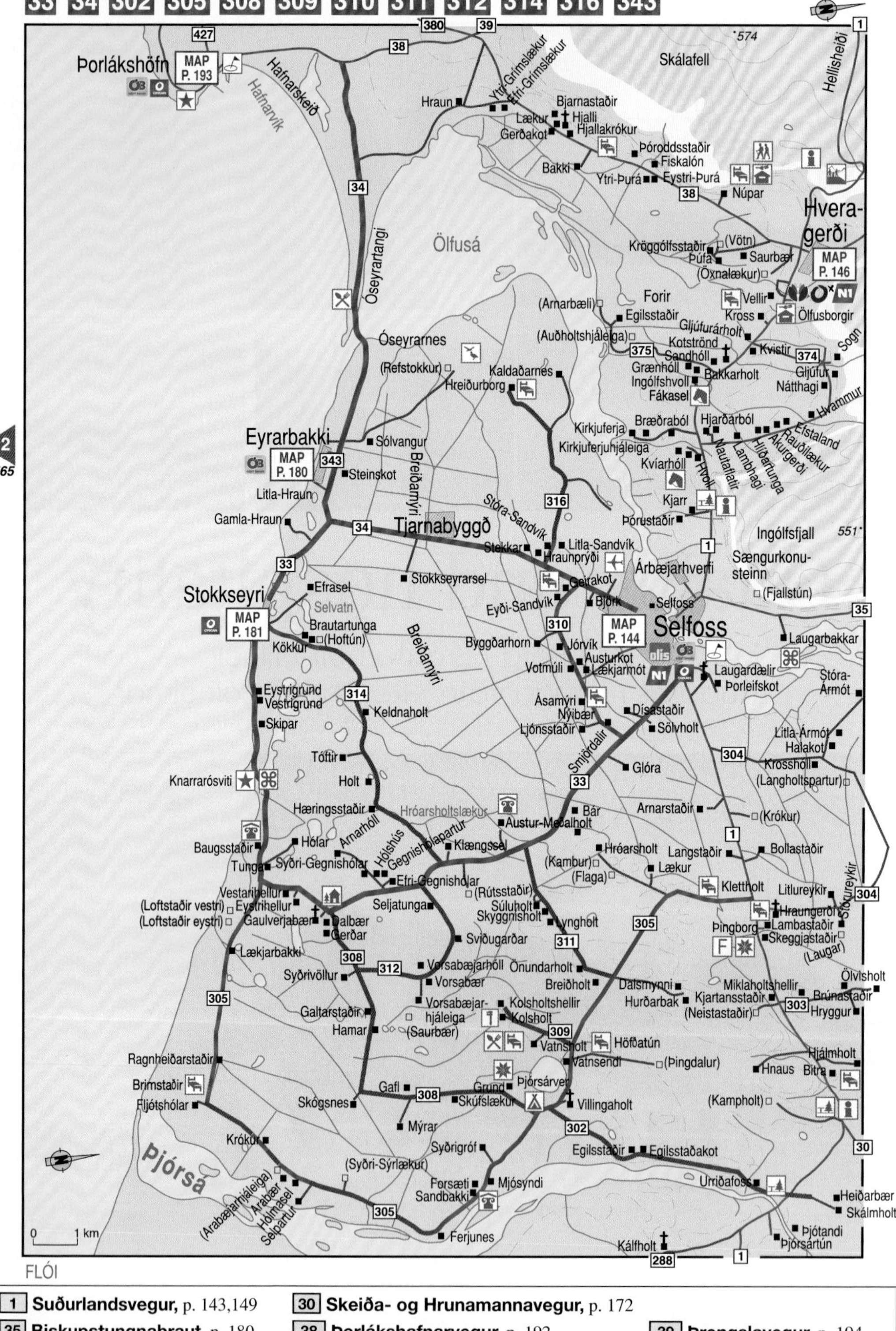

1 **Suðurlandsvegur,** p. 143,149
30 **Skeiða- og Hrunamannavegur,** p. 172
35 **Biskupstungnabraut,** p. 180
38 **Þorlákshafnarvegur,** p. 192
39 **Þrengslavegur,** p. 194
288 **Kálfholtsvegur,** p. 156
303 **Ölvisholtsvegur,** p. 143
304 **Oddgeirshólav.,** p. 143
374 **Hvammsvegur,** p. 148
375 **Arnarbælisvegur,** p. 148
380 **Hlíðarendavegur,** p. 192
427 **Suðurstrandarvegur,** p. 227

34 **Eyrarbakkavegur,** 24 km.

316 **Kaldaðarnesvegur,** 6 km. **343** **Álfsstétt,** 2 km.

Flói, the district between the rivers Ölfusá and Þjórsá up to the old lava field Merkurhraun.

Ölfusá, one of the biggest rivers in Iceland. With its source river, Hvítá, which comes from the Hvítárvatn lake near the Langjökull glacier, it is 185 km long.

Eyrarbakki, (pop. 517) is a part of the Municipality of Árborg. The village was once the largest commercial community and the main harbour on the South Coast of Iceland. A large number of houses from the period 1890-1920 are preserved in Eyrarbakki, which gives it a unique position among towns in South-Iceland. Iceland's oldest school for children, founded in 1852, is in Eyrarbakki. To complete this historical atmosphere, there are two museums to visit; the Eyrarbakki Maritime Museum and the Árnessýsla Folk Museum, located at **Húsið** „The House" in Eyrarbakki, built in 1765 and one of the oldest surviving buildings in Iceland. Húsið and Assistentahúsið, two connected buildings: the House is a type of log building, brought in kit form to Iceland and erected in 1765 for the local merchant. The Assistants' House is a timber-frame structure, added in 1881. In the keeping of the National Museum since 1992. Modern services, for example a gas station, a camping place, guesthouse, Women's Library and a restaurant, are also in Eyrarbakki. To the west of the village is Óseyrarnes, an old ferry point on the Ölfusá river, where once stood the farm Refstokkur, home of Bjarni Herjólfsson, one of Iceland's first permanent settlers and a great seafarer. On his way to Greenland he got lost in a fog, sailed in a different direction and discovered a land to the west, which he didn't explore. This led to Leifur Eiríksson expedition to Vineland (North America). The seashore at Eyrarbakki is popular for hiking and bird watching. The Flói Bird Reserve lies northwest of Eyrarbakki. The reserve covers an area of about 5 sq km (1.93 sq miles). The land is low, only about 2 m above sea level. It is an important nesting area, especially for wetland birds, and listed by the Bird Life International Association.

Litla-Hraun, a state penitentiary.

Kaldaðarnes, a substantial farm and often the home of local leaders, formerly a church. During Catholic times there was a holy cross at Kaldaðarnes and people made long pilgrimages to see it. Immediately after the Reformation in 1550 the cross was taken to the Bishop´s house at Skálholt, where it was chopped up and burned on the orders of the Bishop, who died shortly thereafter. His death was commonly accounted God's revenge. There was a leprosy hospital in Kaldaðarnes in the 18th century. During World War II the British forces had big camps there and built an airfield for warplanes. A monument honouring the presence of the RAF in Kaldaðarnes was unveiled at Selfoss Airport in 1999 in the presence of British pilots who were stationed in Kaldaðarnes during the war.

Stóra-Sandvík and **Litla-Sandvík,** one of the biggest farms in the Flói district.

33 **Gaulverjabæjarvegur,** 27 km.

310 **Votmúlavegur,** 5 km. **311** **Önundarholtsvegur,** 5 km.

Rútsstaðir, a cluster of farms now deserted. The birthplace of the painter Ásgrímur Jónsson (1876-1958). An art gallery in Reykjavík is devoted to his works.

314 **Holtsvegur,** 10 km. **308** **Hamarsvegur,** 11 km.

312 **Vorsabæjarvegur í Flóa,** 5,3 km.

Stokkseyri, (pop. 524) is a part of the Municipality of Árborg. The village is located on the Þjórsárhraun lava field, which extends offshore outside Stokkseyri and Eyrarbakki to form skerries up to 400 – 700 m from the coast. The lava is the largest lava field on earth since the end of the last ice-age. The seashore at Stokkseyri is known for its beauty – skerries, breaking waves and bird life, and thus popular for hiking. The village has a rich art and cultural life. Paintings- and glass galleries, Ghost Centre and a Museum of Icelandic Wonders along with artist's workshop and gallerys which are all situated in the Cultural centre, an old fish processing factory that has found a new role due to changes in the fishing industry. In Stokkseyri there is also a Hunting Museum with a large collection of mounted animals and firearms. Culture is not the only thing the town has to offer. It also has a seafood restaurant, an outdoor swimming pool, kayak sailing tours and a campsite. Þuríðarbúð is a bunkhouse that shows the conditions fishermen had to live with in the past. It is named after Þuríður Einarsdóttir (1777-1863), famous as a woman foreman, or captain, on one of the large rowing boats used for fishing at the time. Further east from Stokkseyri is the Baugsstaðir creamery and Knarrarósviti lighthouse, whose design is an interesting blend of functionalism and art nouveau (jugenstil) schools in architecture.

Baugsstaðir, one of Iceland's oldest dairies, preserved largely unchanged as a museum.

Loftsstaðir, by the farm is a cone like hill with a grand view.

305 **Villingaholtsvegur,** 30 km.

Hróarsholt, an old manor farm, stands beneath a cliff ridge, Hróarsholtsklettar. A monument was erected there in 1999 in honour of Freystein Gunnarsson (1892–1976), principal who was born at **Voli,** a farm not far away, now deserted.

Villingaholt, a church and parsonage till 1856. An elementery school and community centre, Þjórsárver. A campsite.

Fljótshólar, a farm with a spectacular view of the mountains and its surroundings.

302 **Urriðafossvegur,** 8 km. A view deck by Urriðafoss waterfall.

309 **Kolsholtsvegur,** 2,1 km.

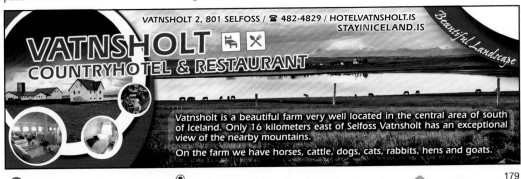

Minni-Borg- 1 Suðurlandsvegur 20 km

2 P. 565

Borg, a farm, community centre, swimming pool and a campsite. Not far from there are some old craters, **Borgarhólar**.

Stóra-Borg, a farm and church, moved from Klausturhólar in 1932.

351 Búrfellsvegur, 9,3 km, see Road 36.

Klausturhólar, a farm from the original settlement, a church and parsonage till 1887.

Seyðishólar, a group of craters from which much of the lava of Grímsnes has come. Much gravel and pumice, which is red there, has been taken from the hills for building so they have been spoiled. Good view from the hills.

Kerið, a 55 m deep explosion crater about 3,000 years old, in **Tjarnarhólar**, a group of crater-hills. A must for sightseers. The story goes that when the water level rises in Kerið, it falls to an equal extent in the small lake on the mountain Búrfell in the Grímsnes district, and vice versa. A protected natural feature.

Snæfoksstaðir, formerly a farm and church, and a parsonage until 1801.

Öndverðarnes, a farm from the original settlement, formerly a church. Ruins of this and the graveyard can still be seen.

Þrastaskógur, woodlands along the river Sog.

Alviðra, a farm. The last farmer who lived there, Magnús Jóhannesson, donated the farms Alviðra and Öndverðarnes II to Árnessýsla county and the Icelandic Enviroment Association in 1973.

Grímsnes, the district marked by the rivers Sog on the south and Hvítá-Brúará on the east. The southern parts mostly flat and covered by old lava-fields with extensive birch-bushes. The upper parts wet in places, with an interesting mountain region furthest inland. A very popular area for summer houses.

Fjallstún, a place name below the mountain Ingólfsfjall, where legend has it that the first settler Ingólfur Arnarson had one of his first winter quarters in Iceland. Protected ruins. There have been many rock slides in the mountain above the site. One of the rocks is **Sængurkonusteinn,** ("Childbed stone") and it is said a pregnant travelling woman who was turned away at the farm gave birth to her child there. The farm was buried in a landslide the same night.

1 Suðurlandsvegur-Minni-Borg 20 km

1 **Suðurlandsvegur,** p. 143
304 **Oddgeirshólavegur,** p. 143
351 **Búrfellsvegur,** p. 189
354 **Sólheimavegur,** p. 196
36 **Þingvallavegur,** p. 189
350 **Grafningsv. neðri,** p. 189
353 **Kiðjabergsvegur,** p. 196

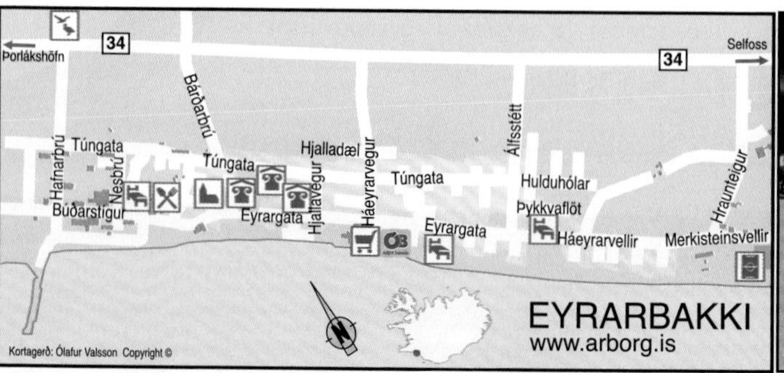

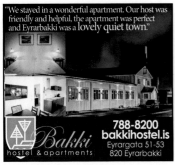

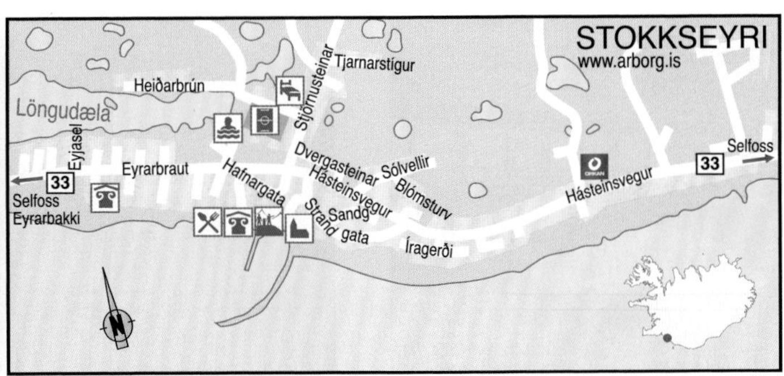
STOKKSEYRI
www.arborg.is
Tjarnarstígur
Heiðarbrún
Löngudæla
Stjörnusteinar
Eyjasel
Eyrarbraut
Hafnargata
Dvergasteinar
Sólvellir
Hásteinsvegur
Blómsturv
Sandg
Strand gata
Íragerði
Hásteinsvegur
33
Selfoss
Eyrarbakki
33
Selfoss

Vatnsleysa-Minniborg 27 km

Bergsstaðir, an abandoned farm where a hollowed rock was at one time used for keeping whey in. It is enchanted, so that if water gets in, it does not mix with the whey nor does the whey ever freeze. If, however, the farm people neglect to keep whey in it, they will have bad luck. This has happened three times within living memory. The first time the farmer at Bergsstaðir lost 150 sheep, the second time 40 sheep and finally, in 1960, all his cows (see Road 35, Haukadalur).

Vatnsleysa, ("Lack of water") a farm. The waterfall **Faxi** in Tungufljót nearby, also called **Vatnsleysufoss**.

Reykholt, (pop. 236) a village in a geothermal area with many greenhouses. A gas station, bank, community centre, swimming pool, guesthouse, campsite and restaurants.

Friðheimar, offers tours of its tomato-growing greenhouse. Its restaurant has delicious meals made from tomatoes. The Centre also has a horse show featuring the Icelandic Horse.

Biskupstungur, the district between the rivers Brúará on the west and Hvítá on the east divided by the river Tungufljót (see Road 31).

Torfastaðir, a church and parsonage. The church was consecrated in 1893 in the presence of 335 people, double the number of parishoners at the time.

Mosfell, a farm, church and parsonage, built below a mountain (254 m) of the same name. The settling place of Ketilbjörn the old, the forefather of the Haukdælir, a powerful and influential family for many centuries.

Svínavatn, ("Pig lake") a farm by a lake of the same name. Road 37 to Laugarvatn nearby.

31 **Skálholtsvegur,** p. 174
37 **Laugarvatnsvegur,** p. 190
354 **Sólheimavegur,** p. 196
355 **Reykjavegur,** p. 190
356 **Tjarnarvegur,** p. 190
358 **Einholtsvegur,** p. 183
359 **Bræðratunguvegur,** p. 198

Minniborg-Vatnsleysa 27 km

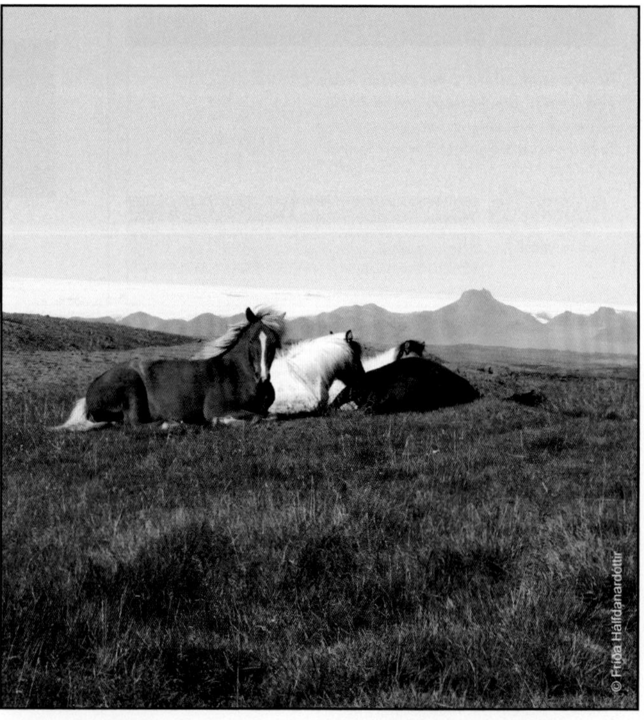
© Fríða Hálfdanardóttir

35 BISKUPSTUNGNABRAUT

Gullfoss, ("Golden falls") in the river Hvítá, one of the most beautiful waterfalls in Iceland and a favourite with tourists. It falls 32 m in two cascades. The canyon below the falls is 2,500 m long and 70 m deep, a magnificent sight. Gullfoss is state property. A tourist store is located near the falls. See also **Brattholt.**

Pjaxi, a dell in the canyon not far below Gullfoss. Birch-bushes and rich vegetation. The name is probably derived from the Latin word *pax*, meaning peace.

Brattholt, a farm to which part of **Gullfoss** used to belong. Well-known because of the struggle of the farmer Tómas Tómasson (1845-1926) and his daughter Sigríður Tómasdóttir (1871-1957) to prevent Gullfoss being sold to foreign buyers. A statue of Sigríður by Gullfoss commemorates her victory.

Haukadalur, see special map on next page.

Geysir, see next page.

Bjarnarfell, (727 m) a mountain west of Geysir, good viewing point.

Faxi, a wide waterfall, kind of a smaller version of Gullfoss. Campsite.

358 Einholtsvegur, 7,5 km.

334 Gullfossvegur, 0,72 km.

Drumbosstaðir, there is Arctic Raftings base camp for river rafting in south Iceland.

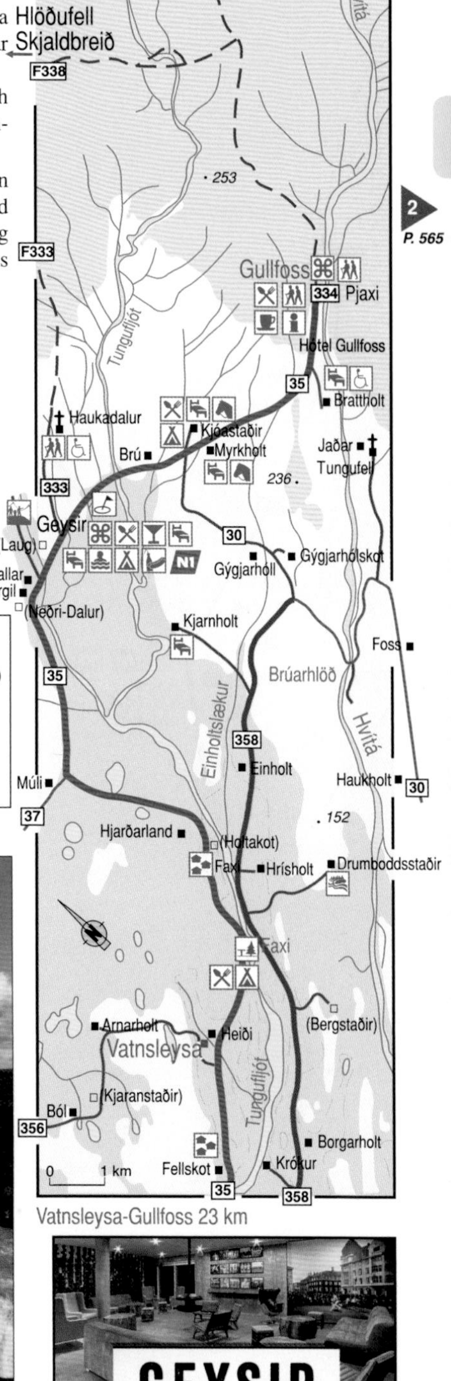

Gullfoss

Geysir

2 P. 565

Haukadalur, a church and formerly a substantial farm and historically important home of local leaders. Now a local headquarters of the Forestry Service and the State Soil Conservation Service. The land of Haukadalur had been badly damaged by erosion when in 1938 a Dane, Kristian Kirk, bought the farm to give it to the Forestry Service to be protected and re-forested. Much has been done since then and a memorial to Kirk has been erected there. National Forest, **Haukadalsskógur**. In Saga times the family of Haukadalur, Haukdælir as they were called, was one of the most important and powerful families in the country. Teitur Ísleifsson founded a school in Haukadalur in the 10th century and many learned men got their education there, the best-known being Ari Þorgilsson (1067-1148), who wrote the oldest extant book in Iceland, *Íslendingabók* (The Book of Icelanders). According to folktales the giant Bergþór of Bláfell is buried near the church of Haukadalur. The iron ring on the church door is said to be from Bergþór's walking-stick and the iron spike from the stick, 1.4 m long, is said to be kept there and was recorded as one of the belongings of the church in the 15th century. The whey stone at **Bergsstaðir** (see p. 182) was supposedly made by Bergþór, also. There is much geothermal heat in the land of Haukadalur. From Haukadalur there is a reasonably good road over the heath as far as road F338 which is a mountain track.

Haukadalsheiði, a land reclamation area.

Laugarfell, a small mountain by Geysir. View dial.

Geysir, one of the most famous spouting hot springs of the world, its name the source of the English word "geyser". It is believed that Geysir started spouting in the 13th century. However, at the beginning of last century it stopped altogether, possibly because it was half choked by visitors throwing rocks and turf into the spring in order to activate it. In 1935 it was re-awakened by lowering the water level and at its best spouted to a height of 60 m. The nearby **Strokkur** spouts with great frequency and Geysir itself spouts once in a while. Hotel, campsite, restaurant and store.

Konungssteinar, ("The king's stones") three stones on the slope west of the hot spring area. Their name derives from the fact that three Danish kings on official visits to Iceland, Christian IX in 1874, Frederick VIII in 1907 and Christian X in 1922, used them as seats while waiting for Geysir to spout.

333 Haukadalsvegur, 2,11 km.

Geysir

Hvítá

Geysir

Kárastaðir, the first farm in the Þingvallasveit district when approaching from Mosfellsheiði moor.

Vinaskógur, ("Friends' wood") a grove of trees on the land of Kárastaðir. Trees planted there are all associated with the President of Iceland and are the gifts of foreign friends. It is customary for foreign heads of state who visit Iceland to plant a tree there. Vinaskógur was started on the 60th birthday of President Vigdís Finnbogadóttir when the foreign embassies in Iceland, under the leadership of the German Ambassador, together gave Iceland a birch grove in honour of the President.

Skálafell, (754 m) a mountain with a telecommunications station on top, for both telephone and television. Very good skiing country, with ski-lifts and cabins.

Mosfellsheiði, an extensive moorland area between the Mosfellssveit district and the lake Þingvallavatn. A shield-volcano from a warm period of the ice age, covered by basalt lava, some of which also reached the Reykjavík area. The highest point, **Borgarhólar** (410 m), remnants of the crater.

434 **Skálafellsvegur,** 4 km.

Móskarðshnúkar, rhyolite mountains between Skálafell and Esja, several cone-shaped, light-coloured peaks, the highest 807 m.

Skeggjastaðir, an abandoned farm in the Mosfellssveit district. An interesting waterfall, **Tröllafoss** ("Giants' falls"), not far from there in the river Leirvogsá.

Gljúfrasteinn, was the home and workplace of Halldór Laxness (winner of the Nobel Prize for Literature in 1955) and his family for more than half a century. The house is now a museum, where the author´s home is preserved just as it was when he lived and worked there.

Laxnes, a farm where Halldór Laxness was brought up.

Reykjahlíð, a community in the Mosfellsdalur valley with many greenhouses. Geothermal water is piped from there to Reykjavík, a distance of 20 km.

Mosfell, a farm, church and a parsonage, on the slopes of a mountain of the same name. In Saga times Egill Skallagrímsson of *Egils saga* spent his last days at Mosfell and the story goes that he buried two chests of silver coins in the area.

Hrísbrú, a farm by Mosfell. A church was already there when Iceland became Christian in the year 1000 but was moved to Mosfell in the years 1130-60. Some excavation have been done there.

Mosfellsdalur, a wide, green valley between the mountains Mosfell and Helgafell. Much geothermal heat.

Grímmannsfell, (454 m) a small mountain on the north side of the road.

Hengill, (803 m) a mountain to the south of the road, its highest point being **Skeggi** at the northwestern edge. From there, and elsewhere along the mountains edge, there are spectacular views, particularly over the Faxaflói bay and Lake Þingvallavatn. Hengill is a central volcano and acid rocks are found in Sleggja on the southwestern side. There are volcanic rifts to the north and south of Hengill, the most recent eruptions having been about 2,000 years ago. On the western slopes is **Marardalur,** a fairly large, grassy plain closed in by cliffs and screes on all sides, with a narrow canyon leading out of it to the west. The valley is easily closed off, and bulls were often kept there, signs of walls can still be found. Bulls used to be pastured on many moors, from Bolavellir by Kolviðarhóll up to Hofmannaflöt on Bláskógaheiði moor. The bulls became quite fierce and there are many stories of travellers' encounters with them. The enormous loss of cattle in the Móðuharðindi period 1783-85 put an end to the highland pasturing of bulls. Reindeer frequented the area near Marardalur up until 1925. They were the last reindeer on the Reykjanes peninsula.

Dyrafjöll, an interesting tuff mountain range where a recreation area has been organised, with marked footpaths. Forestation has started.

Nesjavellir, a geothermal power station, owned by the Reykjavík Heating Service (Orkuveita Reykjavíkur). There is a great deal of geothermal heat under the northern and northeastern slopes of the mountain Hengill. Beautiful walking routes.

435 **Nesjavallaleið,** 27 km. A beautiful route, many marked walking routes on the way.

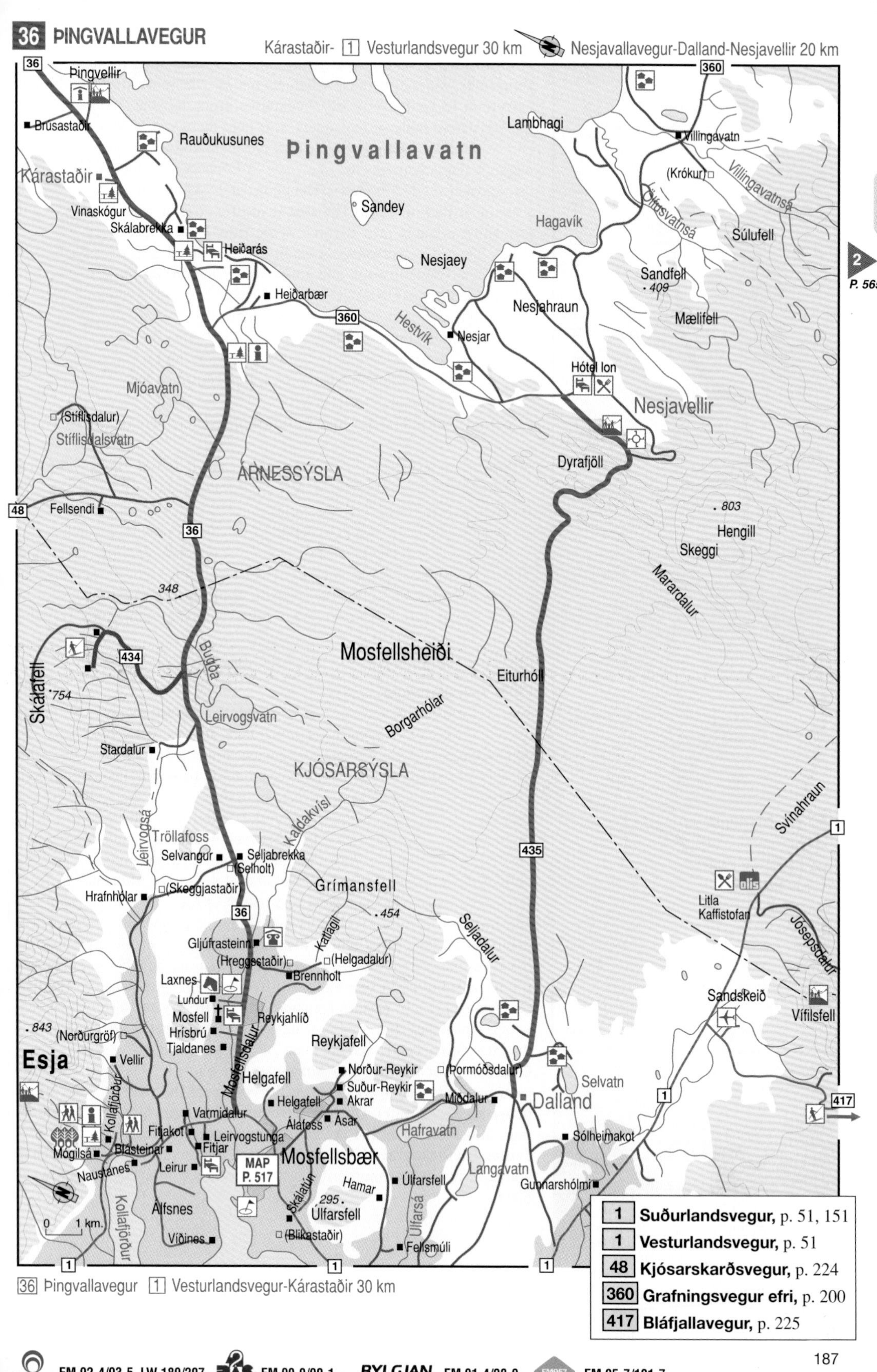

1	**Suðurlandsvegur,** p. 51, 151
1	**Vesturlandsvegur,** p. 51
48	**Kjósarskarðsvegur,** p. 224
360	**Grafningsvegur efri,** p. 200
417	**Bláfjallavegur,** p. 225

Sog-Kárastaðir 26 km

36
Úlfljótsvatn
Steingrímsstöð
Kaldárhöfði
Dráttarhlíð
172
Sog
Þingvallavatn
Miðfellshraun
Miðfell
Miðfell
323
365
Mjóanes
36
Arnarfell
238
(Arnarfell)
(Gjábakki)
Hrafnagjá
Vatnsvík
Þingvallavatn
361
(Vatnskot)
Rauðukusunes
36
(Skógarkot)
Hakið
363
36
Þingvellir
362
Kárastaðir
Almannagjá
Oxarárfoss
Þjónustumiðstöð
Brúsastaðir
550
Öxará
(Svartagil)
0 1 km

Kárastaðir-Sog 26 km

2 P. 565

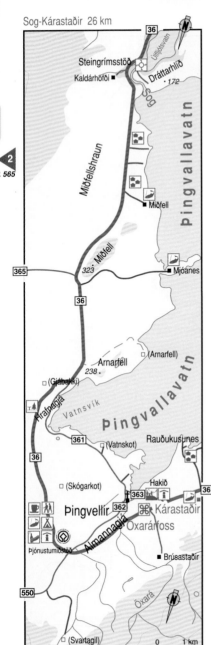

Hrafnabjörg, (765 m) a rocky tuff mountain dominating the area.

Þingvellir National Park ("Parliament plains") the most important historical site in Iceland. For nearly 9 centuries, from the year 930 the Althing, the legislative body of Icelanders, was held there annually near the north end of the lake. Some marked ruins are there and in the canyon Almannagjá. A flagpole marks the likely site of Lögberg ("Law cliff") where the law-speaker recited the laws. The plains and surrounding area were made a National Park in 1928. The area is mostly covered with birch and willow and has many lava fissures, some filled with icy cold, crystal-clear water. There is a parsonage, church and a national graveyard where the poets Einar Benediktsson and Jónas Hallgrímsson are buried. Þingvellir were added to the UNESCO World Heritage List in the summer of 2004. At Hakið, a viewspot where tourists may walk down into Almannagjá fault, a Visitor Centre has been built for the Þingvellir National Park. In this centre, tourists are introduced to the history and nature of Þingvellir with the aid of multimedia techniques. Þingvellir is a very popular camping place in summer. Tourist centre.

Flosagjá, **Nikulásárgjá** and **Peningagjá** waterfilled rifts, east of the church.

Silfra, a rift that leads to Þingvallavatn lake. It is one of the best dive sites in the world with exceptionally clear waters.

Þingvallavatn, at 82 km^2, the largest lake in Iceland. Its surface is 103 m above sea level, its average depth 34,1 m, but it reaches a depth of 114 m, i.e. 11 m below sea level. Fed largely by underwater springs the water is always extremely cold, the only river feeding it being Öxará, and the river Sog being its outlet. Two islands, **Sandey** and **Nesjaey**, both old craters. Many summer houses around the lake. Angling permits available in the information centre.

361 Vallavegur, 9 km. **362 Efrivallavegur,** 1,5 km.

363 Valhallarvegur, 0,5 km.

Þjónustumiðstöð, a service and information centre visitors can get all general information about the National Park, its nature and history.

Almannagjá, ("Public ravine")in ancient times many of those attending the Alþing camped on the level grassy bottom of the ravine. Almannagjá is the largest and most famous tectonic fissure in the Þingvellir National Park. Its western edge is higher than the eastern one which is considerably lower. The entire piece of land between Almannagjá and Hrafnagjá is a graben (fault trough). View-dial on the edge of Almannagjá.

Hakið, the interpretive centre at Hakið is at the top of Almannagjá. There visitors can discover the history and nature of the area with the help of a multimedia program. The history and nature of Þingvellir is described in detail on large screens where diverse and interesting photographs and drawings may be viewed. At the exhibition visitors can choose either narration or subtitles in one of four different languages (Danish, English, German or French) besides Icelandic and control by use of touch-screens which topics they view and in what order. Lavatories can also be found in the interpretive centre and are open 24/7 all year round.

Öxará, a river flowing into Almannagjá in a lovely waterfall. The story goes that our forefathers changed the course of the river in order to get better access to water. **Drekkingarhylur** ("The drowning pool"), a deep pool in the river near the bridge in Almannagjá, formerly a place of execution. Up to the early 18th century women found guilty of crimes such as adultery, incest and murdering infants were tied in sacks and drowned there.

Þingvellir

365 Lyngdalsheiðarvegur, p. 201 **550 Kaldadalsvegur,** p. 236

Álftavatn, a shallow lake through which flows the river Sog. The Sog is so wide and slow-moving below the lake that a rise in the level of Ölfusá River, beyond Sog, can cause it to back up and raise the level of the lake. Extensive birchwoods near the lake make it a popular area for summer houses.

351 Búrfellsvegur, 9,3 km to road 35.

Búrfell, (536 m) a mountain with a farm and church of the same name at its foot. A lake on top of the mountain. It is said that the water level rises and falls there in relation to its fall and rise in the explosion crater Kerið, and vice versa.

350 Grafningsvegur neðri, 12,2 km.

Ljósifoss, a waterfall in the river Sog by Efri-Brú. Two power stations in the Sog are associated with it, Ljósifoss, harnessed in 1935-37 and 1934-44, total power 15 MW and Írafoss-Kistufoss, harnessed in 1950-53, power 48 MW.

Efri-Brú, birthplace of the poet Tómas Guðmundsson (1901-83).

Kaldárhöfði, a farm by the river Sog, between the lakes Þingvallavatn and **Úlfljótsvatn**. In an islet in Úlfljótsvatn called Torfnes a heathen grave from the 10th century was found in 1946. A man and a child had been buried there in a boat, together with weapons and other objects.

Dráttarhlíð, the hill to the south of Lake Þingvallavatn by the river Sog. In 1956-59 a tunnel was dug through there and the power station **Steingrímsstöð,** a power station built on the lower side with a drop of 22 m, power 26,4 MW.

Sog, the largest clear river in Iceland, the outlet from Þingvallavatn and running into the river Hvítá, now running through the Steingrímsstöð power station. Total length 19 km with a volume of 114 m³/sec. A very good salmon-river.

35 Biskupstungnabraut, p. 180 **360 Grafningsvegur efri,** p. 200

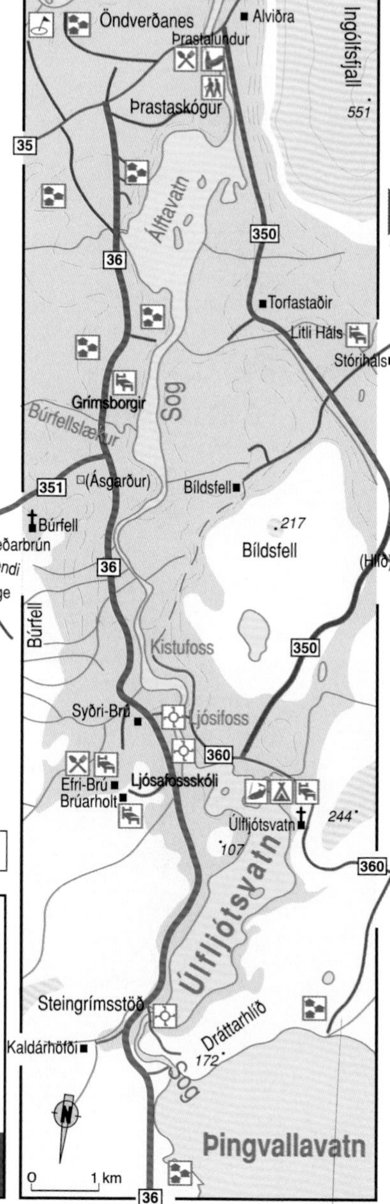

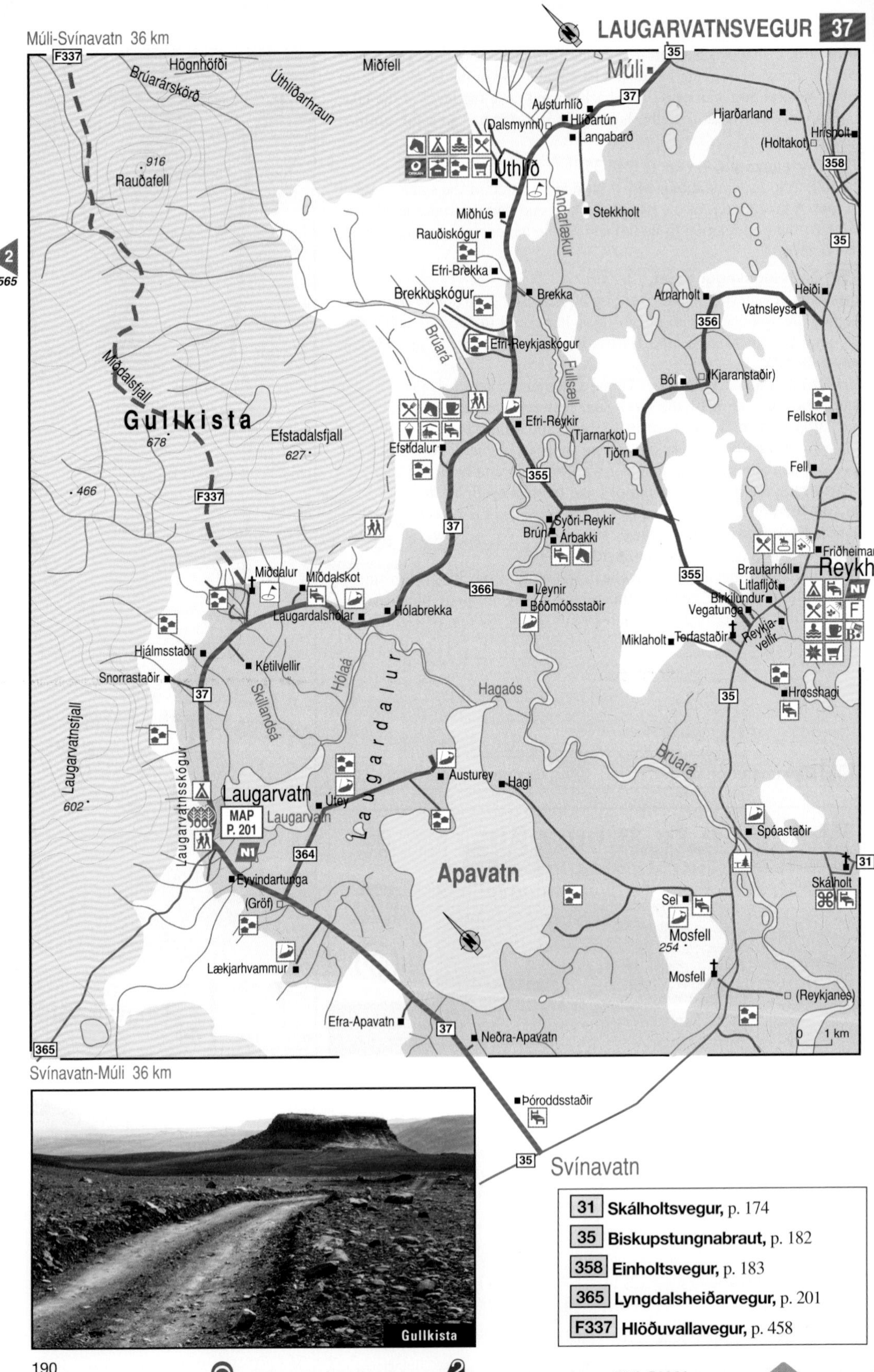

31 Skálholtsvegur, p. 174
35 Biskupstungnabraut, p. 182
358 Einholtsvegur, p. 183
365 Lyngdalsheiðarvegur, p. 201
F337 Hlöðuvallavegur, p. 458

Úthlíð, a farm since the original settlement, a church. Extensive lavafield, Úthlíðarhraun, widely grown with birch bushes. Some ruins of the heathen temple of Geir goði can be seen in the homefield, e.g. a sacrificial blood bowl, also what is believed to be his burial mound.

Brekkuskógur, an area covered with birch bushes, belongs to the farm Brekka. In recent years a great many summer houses have been built there, e.g. by the Association of Academics.

Efri-Reykir, a farm by Brúará. It provides hot water for 19 farms and 500 summer houses in the area.

355 Reykjavegur, 8 km. **356 Tjarnarvegur,** 9 km.

Brúará, a clear river originating on the **Rótarsandur** sands and falling through impressive canyons, **Brúarárskörð**, between the mountains Rauðafell and Högnhöfði. The most impressive canyons of Árnessýsla, 3-4 km long, dug by Brúará through layers of loose sediments of agglomerate. On the flat land Brúará flows into a long, narrow rift in the middle of the river bed. There is a footbridge there, but there was once a natural bridge, which it is said the cook at the bishopric of Skálholt had destroyed in 1602, when the country was suffering hard times. He wanted to stop travellers from getting to Skálholt and begging for food, but was himself drowned in the river a short while later.

Efstidalur, the innermost farm in the Laugardalur valley. Now there is a guesthouse, restaurant and a café.

Álfhóll ("Fairies' hill") is behind the farm, a fine viewing point towards the mountains behind and the districts below. Extensive birch bushes in the neighbourhood.

366 Böðmóðsstaðavegur, 2,4 km.

Böðmóðsstaðir, geothermal heat, green houses.

Laugardalur, a valley or depression under the slopes of the mountains **Laugarvatnsfjall** and Efstadalsfjall, with two large lakes, Laugarvatn and Apavatn.

Gullkista, ("Chest of gold") an interesting little box-shaped peak on the mountain Miðdalsfjall (678 m).

Miðdalur, a farm, church and a 9 hole golf course.

Laugarvatn, (pop. 177) a village that has grown around a number of schools: a junior college, an intermediate school and an elementary school. This is a geothermal area, and it is said that when Christianity was legalized in the year 1000, the chieftains from the north refused to be baptised in the cold waters of Þingvellir, and were brought to Laugarvatn to be baptised in the warm spring, **Vígðalaug** ("Consecrated spring"). The bodies of the last Catholic bishop, Jón Arason, and his sons were washed there after they had been beheaded at Skálholt in 1550, and were later taken to Hólar in Skagafjörður for burial. Three children were baptised in Vígðalaug at the celebrations in 2000 commemorating the conversion of Iceland. A natural steambath, Fontana, with sandy beaches by the lake. At Laugarvatn you will also find a gas station, grocery store, restaurants, hotels, a swimming pool, beach volleyball court and a gallery. A popular camping area in summer. Beautiful walking routes in the area.

Laugarvatn, a lake, 2,14 km^2, with geothermal heat on the banks and the bottom, mostly shallow and rich in plant-life.

Laugarvatnsskógur, expansive forest, combination of birch and planted species. Declared protected in early 20th century. National Forest.

364 Eyjavegur, 4,9 km.

Apavatn, ("Ape lake") a lake of 14 km^2, good trout-fishing. Two farms, Efra-Apavatn and Neðra-Apavatn, south of the lake. In the 11th century the home of the poet Sighvatur Þórðarson.

Þorlákshöfn-Hveragerði 20 km

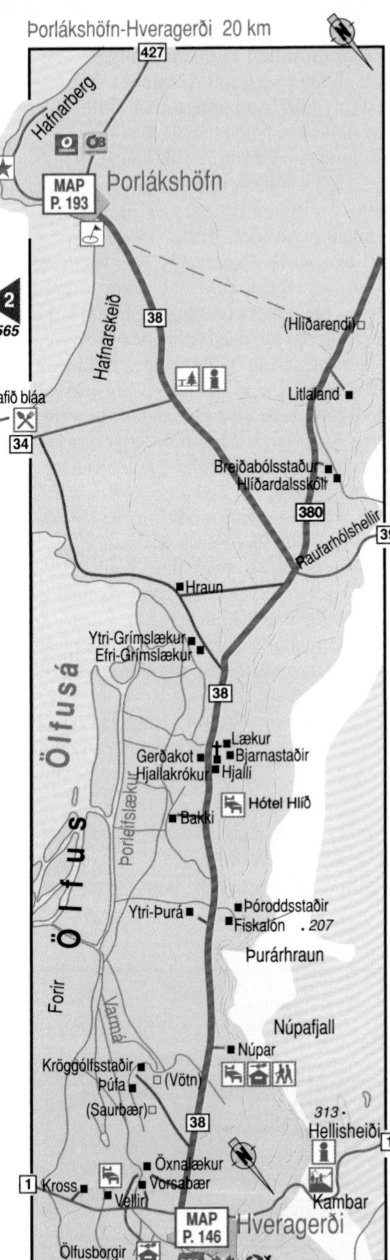

Hveragerði-Þorlákshöfn 20 km

Þorlákshöfn, (pop. 1,572) a young but rapidly growing village, named after Iceland's only saint, St. Þorlákur, Bishop of Skálholt (1133-1193). Just outside of the town is a challenging 18 hole golf course and in town is a large sports hall with excellent outdoor and indoor swimming pools, a spa and a gym. For those who want to get to know the history of this old fishing village there is a path, guided with signs, through some of the town's sites of interest. The town library and folk museum is situated in the town hall, where there is an exhibition of stuffed fish and sea animals and a small gallery. Services offered to visitors are expanding and improving every year and now include a campsite and an art gallery. During the days when fishermen rowed out to sea, a fleet of 20-30 boats was common, and the population swelled to three or four hundred during the fishing season. The modern town grew up around the successful Meitill hf. fisheries company in the middle of the last century. The population increased again in the 1970s after an eruption on the island of Heimaey. Þorlákshöfn is one of many icelandic communities that owes its present existance to soil conservation work. The area was threatened by drift sand and sandstorms, and an 7500 ha area around Þorlákshöfn was fenced off in 1935. Initiating extensive soil conservation and restoration work that is still ongoing today. Þorlákshöfn is also a great place for surfing both for beginners and more advanced surfers. Arctic Surfers offer tours in the area.

380 Hlíðarendavegur, 5,4 km.

Hafið Bláa, a restaurant located at the coast with a great view over the sand coast and the Atlantic Ocean.

Ölfus, a municipality, the most westerly district in Árnessýsla. It covers a total area of 750 km^2 and has a population of over 2,000 people. The most important industries are fishing, fish processing, retail services, agriculture and light industries.

Vindheimar, a farm where Adventist have built and earlier run a intermediate school, **Hlíðardalsskóli**.

Hraun, a farm where judge Lénharður was killed in 1502.

Hjalli, a substantial farm and church. In Saga times the home of lawspeaker Skafti Þóroddsson. Bishop Ögmundur Pálsson, the last Catholic bishop at Skálholt, was captured there by Danish soldiers in 1541.

Þurá, ("Dry river") a farm where part of the lava flow of Kristnitökuhraun ("Conversion lava") came down from Hellisheiði moor in the year 1000, now called **Þurárhraun**.

1 Suðurlandsvegur, p. 149	**34 Eyrarbakkavegur,** p. 178
39 Þrengslavegur, p. 194	**427 Suðurstrandarvegur,** p. 227

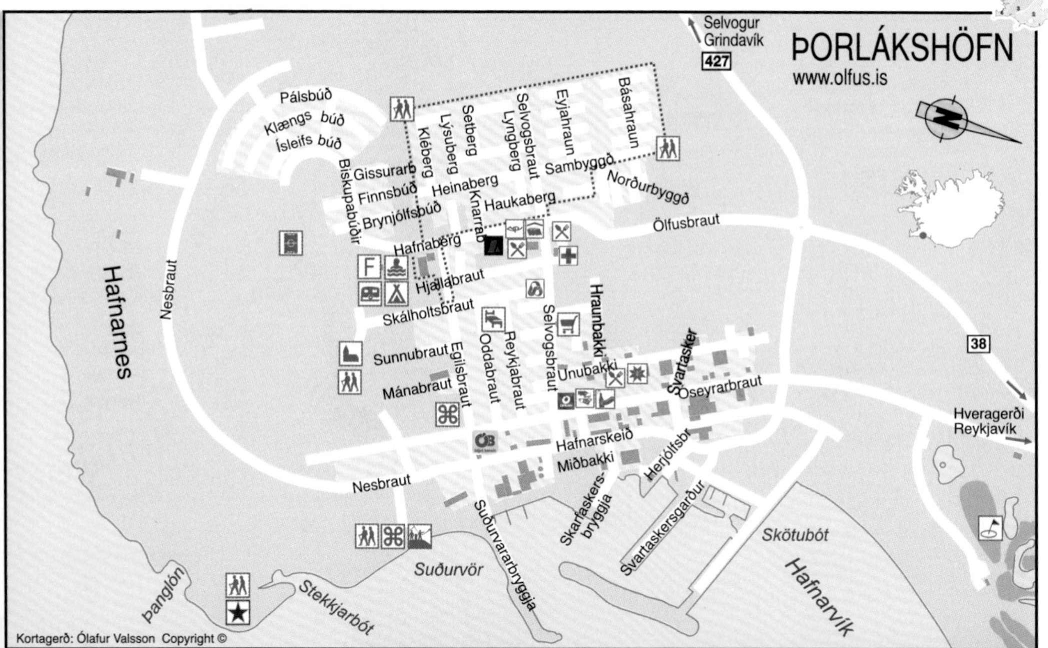
ÞORLÁKSHÖFN
www.olfus.is
Selvogur
Grindavík
427
38
Hveragerði
Reykjavík
Hafnarnes
Nesbraut
Pálsbúð
Klængs búð
Ísleifs búð
Biskupabúðir
Gissurarb
Finnsbúð
Brynjólfsbúð
Klébreg
Lýsuberg
Setberg
Lyngberg
Selvogsbraut
Eyjahraun
Básahraun
Sambyggð
Norðurbyggð
Heinaberg
Knarrab
Haukaberg
Ölfusbraut
Hafnaberg
Hjallabraut
Skálholtsbraut
Sunnubraut
Egilsbraut
Mánabraut
Oddabraut
Reykjabraut
Selvogsbraut
Hraunbakki
Unubakki
Svartasker
Óseyrarbraut
Hafnarskeið
Miðbakki
Herjólfsbr
Nesbraut
Suðurvararbryggja
Skarfaskers-bryggja
Svartaskersgarður
Skötubót
Hafnarvík
Suðurvör
Stekkjarbót
Þanglón
Kortagerð: Ólafur Valsson Copyright ©

39 ÞRENGSLAVEGUR

1 Suðurlandsvegur-38 Þorlákshafnarvegur 14 km

Rauðuhnúkar
417
KJÓSARSÝSLA
417
Drottning
407
1 P. 564
655
Vífilsfell
Jósepsdalur
Ólafsskarð
586
Draugahlíðar
Blákollur
546
1
Litla-Kaffistofan
Svínahraun
(Kolviðarhóll)
Hellisheiðarvirkjun
Bruni
Stóra-Reykjafell
510
Hveradalir
Hellisheiði
Bláfjöll
Leiti
546
Lambafell
Þrengsli
39
Stórimeitill
521
ÁRNESSÝSLA
Lambafellshraun
Stóra-Sandfell
Litlimeitill
Heiðin há
Votaberg
Litla-Sandfell
Eldborgarhraun
509
Geitafell
Hrossagjá
39
Krossfjöll
Hjallafjall
Þúfnavellir
Raufarhólshellir
Búrfell
Hlíðardalsskóli
Breiðabólsstaður
Litlaland
(Hlíðarendi)
38
Efri-Grímslækur
Ytri-Grímslækur
Hraun
Selvogsheiði
Þorlákshöfn
38
0 1 km

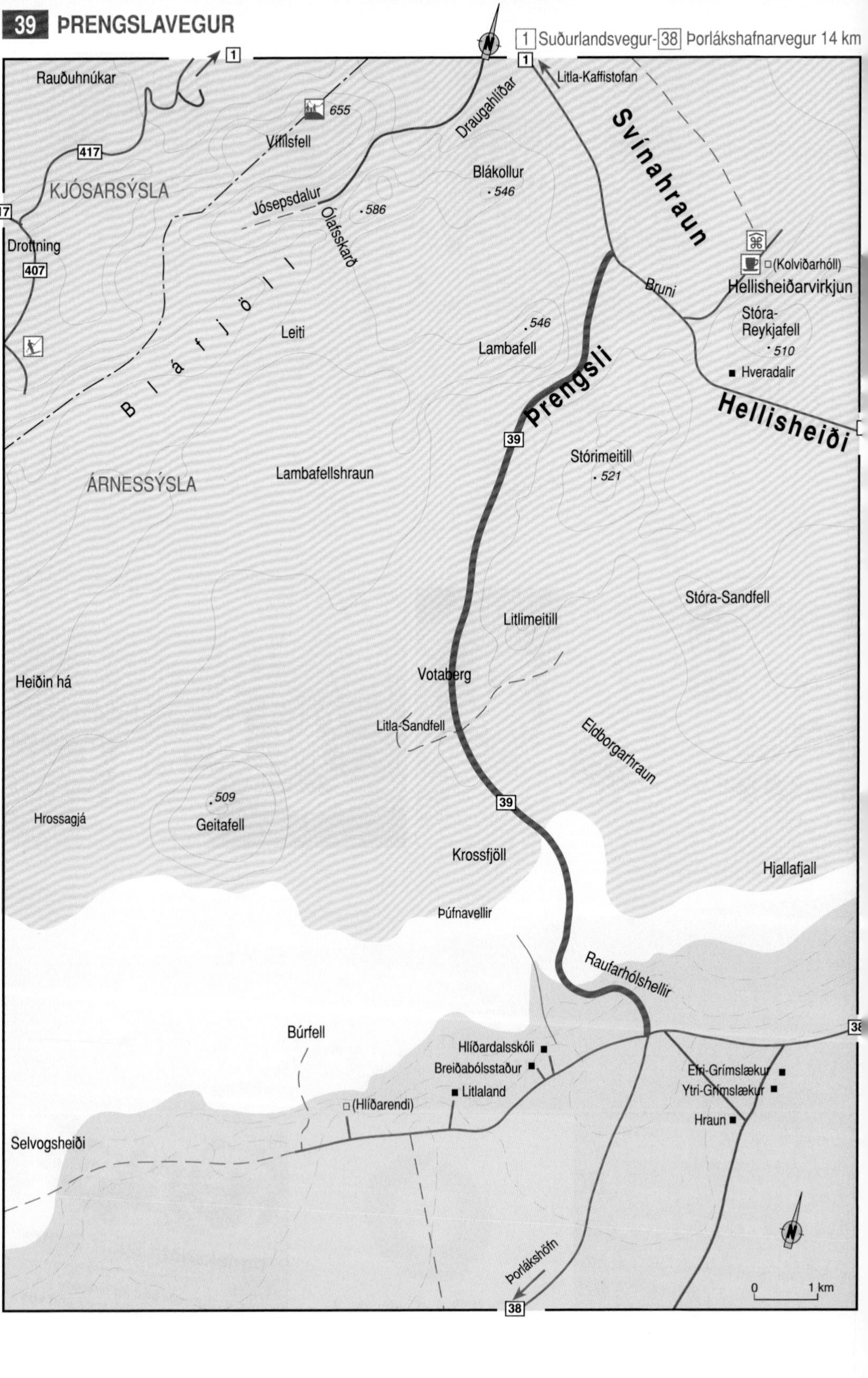

417 **Bláfjallavegur,** 4,3km from Bláfjallavegur Road by Rauðuhnúkar to the skiing area.

Leiti, craters by the eastern slopes of the Bláfjöll mountains, not far south of Ólafsskarð pass. About 5,000 years ago great masses of lava came from there and spread across an extensive area. The Lambahraun lava field on the moors east of Bláfjöll, over Hraunsheiði to the sea by Þorlákshöfn, the Svínahraun and Elliðaárhraun lava fields as well as Rauðhólar and the cave Raufarhólshellir are all part of this lava field. Highway 1 crosses part of it, from the river Elliðaár to the Draugahlíðar slopes. The Þrengslavegur road goes across this lava south of Þrengsli. Two younger lava flows, Svínahraunsbrunar, from the middle of the 14th century, coming from two small craters called Eldborg east of Leiti.

Raufarhólshellir, about 1 km long cave, one of the largest caves in Iceland. Difficult to traverse due to piles of loose rocks that have fallen from the roof. Beautiful in the bottom. Good lights are essential. The road passes over the cave.

Stalagmites and stalactites in the caves are a protected natural feature!

1 **Suðurlandsvegur,** p. 148, 151 **38** **Þorlákshafnarvegur,** p. 192 **417** **Bláfjallavegur,** p. 225

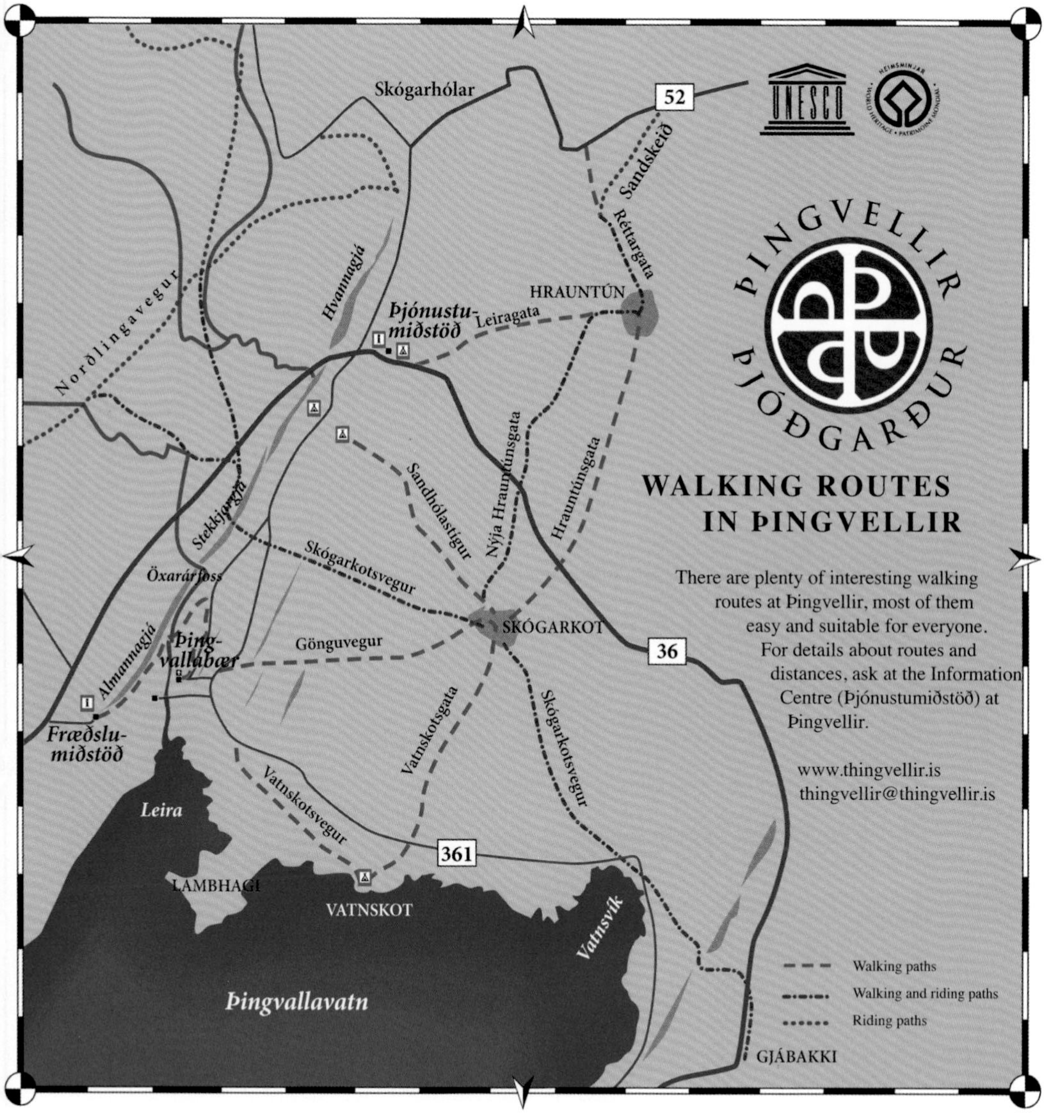
Skógarhólar
52
UNESCO
ÞINGVELLIR ÞJÓÐGARÐUR
Sandskeið
Réttargata
HRAUNTÚN
Hvannagjá
Þjónustu-miðstöð
Leiragata
Norðlingavegur
Nýja Hrauntúnsgata
Hrauntúnsgata
Sandhólastígur
Stekkjargjá
Skógarkotsvegur
Öxarárfoss
SKÓGARKOT
36
Gönguvegur
Almannagjá
Þing-vallabær
Fræðslu-miðstöð
Vatnskotsgata
Skógarkotsvegur
Vatnskotsvegur
Leira
361
LAMBHAGI
VATNSKOT
Vatnsvík
Þingvallavatn
GJÁBAKKI
Walking paths
Walking and riding paths
Riding paths
WALKING ROUTES IN ÞINGVELLIR
There are plenty of interesting walking routes at Þingvellir, most of them easy and suitable for everyone. For details about routes and distances, ask at the Information Centre (Þjónustumiðstöð) at Þingvellir.
www.thingvellir.is
thingvellir@thingvellir.is

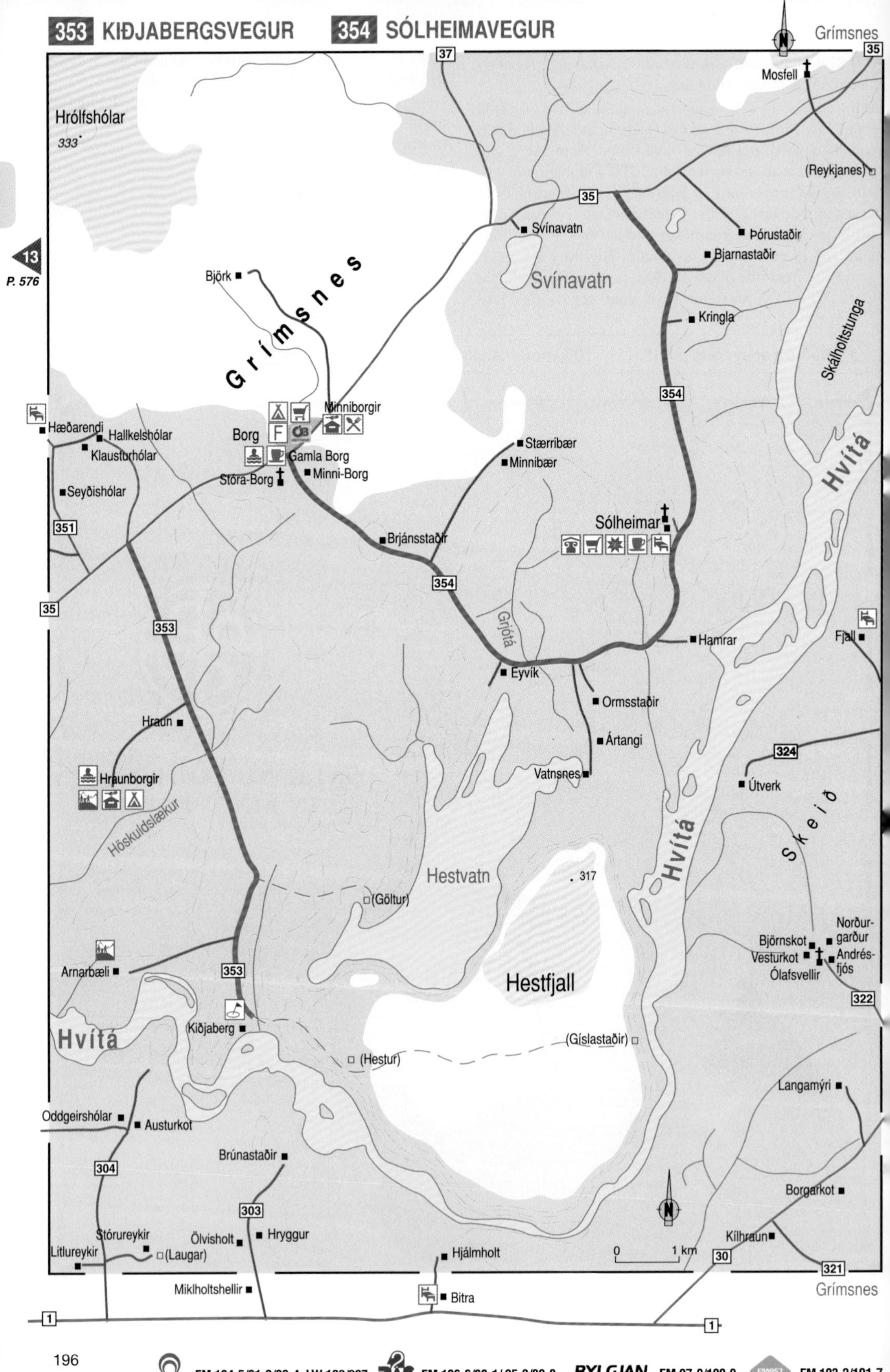
Grímsnes
37
35
Mosfell
Hrólfshólar
333
(Reykjanes)
13
P. 576
35
Svínavatn
Þórustaðir
Bjarnastaðir
Svínavatn
Björk
Grímsnes
Kringla
Skálholtstunga
354
Minniborgir
Hæðarendi
Hallkelshólar
Borg
F
Klausturhólar
Gamla Borg
Stærribær
Minnibær
Hvítá
Stóra-Borg
Minni-Borg
Seyðishólar
Sólheimar
351
Brjánsstaðir
354
35
Grjótá
353
Hamrar
Fjall
Eyvík
Ormsstaðir
Hraun
Ártangi
324
Vatnsnes
Útverk
Hraunborgir
Höskuldslækur
Hvítá
Skeið
Hestvatn
317
(Göltur)
Norður-
garður
Björnskot
Vesturkot
Andrés-
fjós
Ólafsvellir
Arnarbæli
353
Hestfjall
322
Hvítá
Kiðjaberg
(Gíslastaðir)
(Hestur)
Langamýri
Oddgeirshólar
Austurkot
Brúnastaðir
304
Borgarkot
303
Stórureykir
Ölvisholt
Hryggur
Kílhraun
Litlureykir
(Laugar)
Hjálmholt
0
1 km
30
321
Miklholtshellir
Bitra
Grímsnes
1
1

At Stóragil above the campsite at Laugarvatn.

Grímsnes, the district marked by the rivers Sog on the south and Hvítá-Brúará on the east. Named after the settler Grímur who settled there. The southern parts mostly flat and covered by old lava-fields with extensive birch-bushes. The upper parts wet in places, with an interesting mountain region furthest inland. A very popular area for summer houses.

Klausturhólar, a farm and a place of settlement, a church and a parsonage until 1887. A leprosy hospital was operated there for a while.

Mosfell, a farm, church and parsonage, built below a mountain (254 m) of the same name. The settling place of Ketilbjörn the old, the forefather of the Haukdælir, a powerful and influential family for many centuries.

Svínavatn, ("Pig lake") a farm by a lake of the same name. Road 37 to Laugarvatn nearby.

Hestvatn, a lake of 6 km^2, 60 m deep, the bottom thus being 12 m below sea level. Good trout-fishing. Sometimes Hvítá flows into the lake.

Hestfjall, ("Horse mountain") (317 m) a mountain by Hvítá, believed to be part of an old shield-volcano made of tuff with a cap of basalt. Old seashore lines found 120 m up in the mountainsides. Highest point called Hesteyru ("Horse ears"), probably part of the crater rim. Very good view from Hestfjall, which is a gentle climb. In the year 2000 two big earthquakes shook South Iceland, one who originated in Hestfjall.

354 Sólheimavegur, 15 km.

Sólheimar, a world renowned sustainable community known for its artistic and ecological atmosphere where about 90 people live and work together. It was founded in 1930 by Sesselja Hreindís Sigmundsdóttir (1902-1974). It is a small village set out in the countryside, characterized by vegetation, open common spaces and buildings that nicely co-exist with the landscape. Sólheimar is blessed with enough space for residential and common housing and there are ideal conditions for outdoor activities in the village, which play a big part in the residents' health and wellbeing. The Sólheimar community focuses on the growth and development of man and nature. The social emphasis is that different individuals are offered variable opportunities to work, live, and socialize.

353 Kiðjabergsvegur, 8 km.

Kiðjaberg, a farm from the time of the settlement, interesting surroundings. **Today there´s an 18-hole golf course in beautiful natural surroundings.**

Hvítá, ("White river") comes out of the lake Hvítárvatn. Once it reaches the low land it flows to the southwest, between the Biskupstungur and Hrunamannahreppur districts. Lower down it runs between the districts Grímsnes and Skeið, then bends south of the mountain Hestfjall to flow west above the Flói district until the river Sog joins it below the mountain Ingólfsfjall. From this confluence to the river mouth it is called Ölfusá, which has more water in it than any other Icelandic river, with a flow of 371 cubic meters/minute at Selfoss and a drainage basin of 6,100 km^2. Hvítá, Ölfusá and a number of their tributaries all offer good salmon fishing.

1 Suðurlandsvegur, p. 143
30 Skeiða- og Hrunamannavegur, p. 172
35 Biskupstungnabraut, p. 182
37 Laugarvatnsvegur, p. 190
303 Ölvisholtsvegur, p. 143
304 Oddgeirshólavegur, p. 143
321 Skeiðháholtsvegur, p. 172
322 Ólafsvallavegur, p. 172
324 Vorsabæjarvegur, p. 172
351 Búrfellsvegur, p. 180, 189

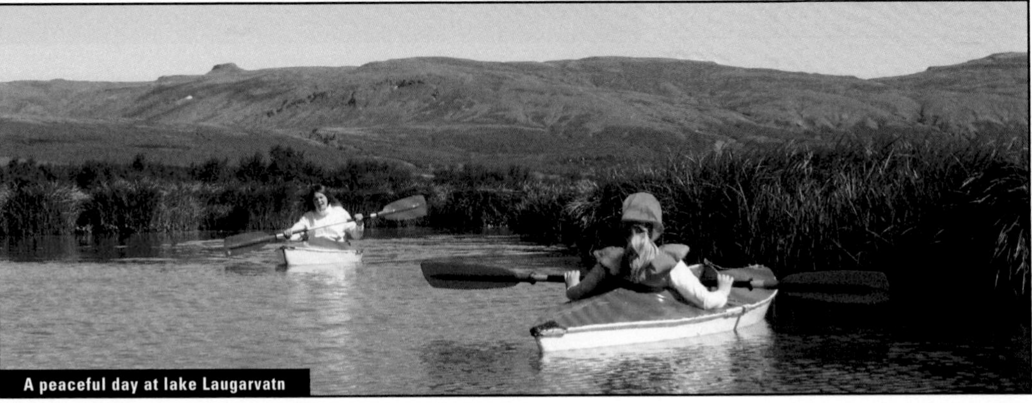

A peaceful day at lake Laugarvatn

13
P. 576

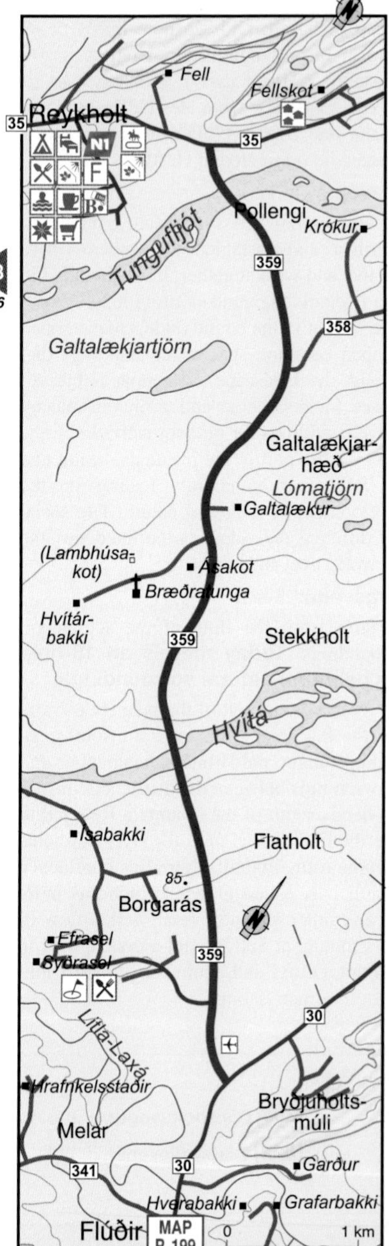

Tungufljót, formerly a glacial river coming from the lake **Sandvatn** and joining Hvítá. There used to be large mud-flats around Sandvatn and in dry periods these caused much sand erosion down in the farming country. To prevent this the water level of Sandvatn was raised in 1994 by closing the two outlets, Sandá and Ásbrandsá and creating a new outlet in the Sandá river flowing east into Hvítá. Ásbrandsá is now a clear river and along with small streams from Haukadalsheiði moor forms Tungufljót, which has become good for salmon-raising after the salmon-ladder was made in the Faxi (or Tungufoss) waterfall.

Bræðratunga, a farm and church, often the home of chieftains and outstanding men, such as Ásgrímur Elliðagrímson in *Njáls saga,* Earl Gissur Þorvaldsson, and the lawyers Gísli Hákonarson (1583-1631) and later Magnús Sigurðsson (1651-1707) known for his cases against Professor Árni Magnússon of Copenhagen, cf. *Íslandsklukkan* by Halldór Laxness.

Hvítá, ("White river") comes out of the lake Hvítárvatn. See p. 197.

Flúðir, (pop. 430) a village in the geothermal area of Hellisholt. Greenhouses, community centre, swimming pool, hotel, restaurant, grocery and liquor store. Good walking routes. The Secret Lagoon at Hverahólmi, the geothermal area near Flúðir, was made in 1891 and is the oldest swimming pool in Iceland. Through the ages it has been a tradition to take a bath in the warm water from the hot springs in the area. In the year 1909 the first swimming lessons took place in the pool and every year after that until 1947, when the new pool in Flúðir was opened. The Secret Lagoon then fell into oblivion, but has now been reopened after renovation. Around the Secret Lagoon you can find several hot spots. At Efra-Seli, close to Flúðir, is an 18-hole golf course.

30 **Skeiða- og Hrunamannavegur,** p. 173
35 **Biskupstungnabraut,** p. 182
341 **Langholtsvegur,** p. 173
358 **Einholtsvegur,** p. 183

Flúðir

Beach volleyball at Flúðir

Funny boat competition

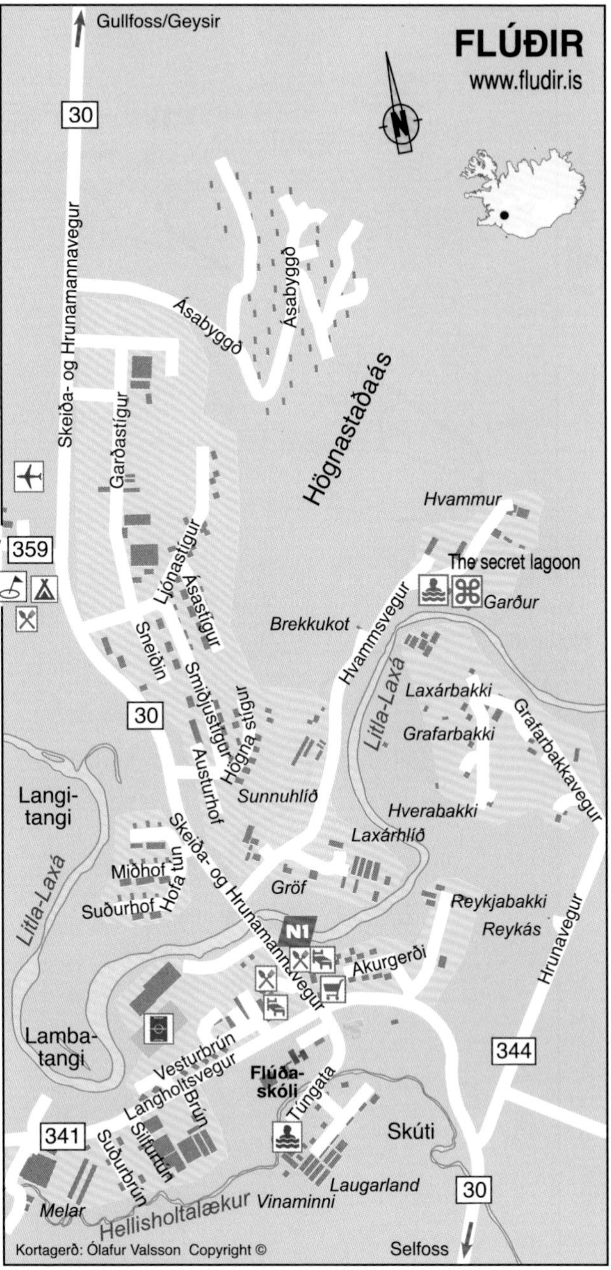

FLÚÐIR

www.fludir.is

Gullfoss/Geysir
30
Skeiða- og Hrunamannavegur
Ásabyggð
Ásabyggð
Högnastaðaás
Garðastígur
Ljónastígur
Ásastígur
359
Sneiðin
Smiðjustígur
Högna stígur
30
Austurhof
Hvammur
The secret lagoon
Garður
Brekkukot
Hvammsvegur
Litla-Laxá
Laxárbakki
Grafarbakki
Grafarbakkavegur
Sunnuhlíð
Hverabakki
Langi-tangi
Laxárhlíð
Miðhof
Hofa tún
Skeiða- og Hrunamannavegur
Gröf
Litla-Laxá
Suðurhof
Reykjabakki
Reykás
Hrunavegur
N1
Akurgerði
Lamba-tangi
Vesturbrún
Langholtsvegur
Flúða-skóli
Túngata
Brún
344
341
Silfurtún
Suðurbrún
Skúti
Laugarland
30
Melar
Hellisholtalækur
Vinaminni
Kortagerð: Ólafur Valsson Copyright ©
Selfoss

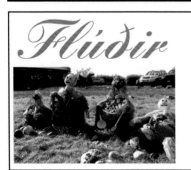

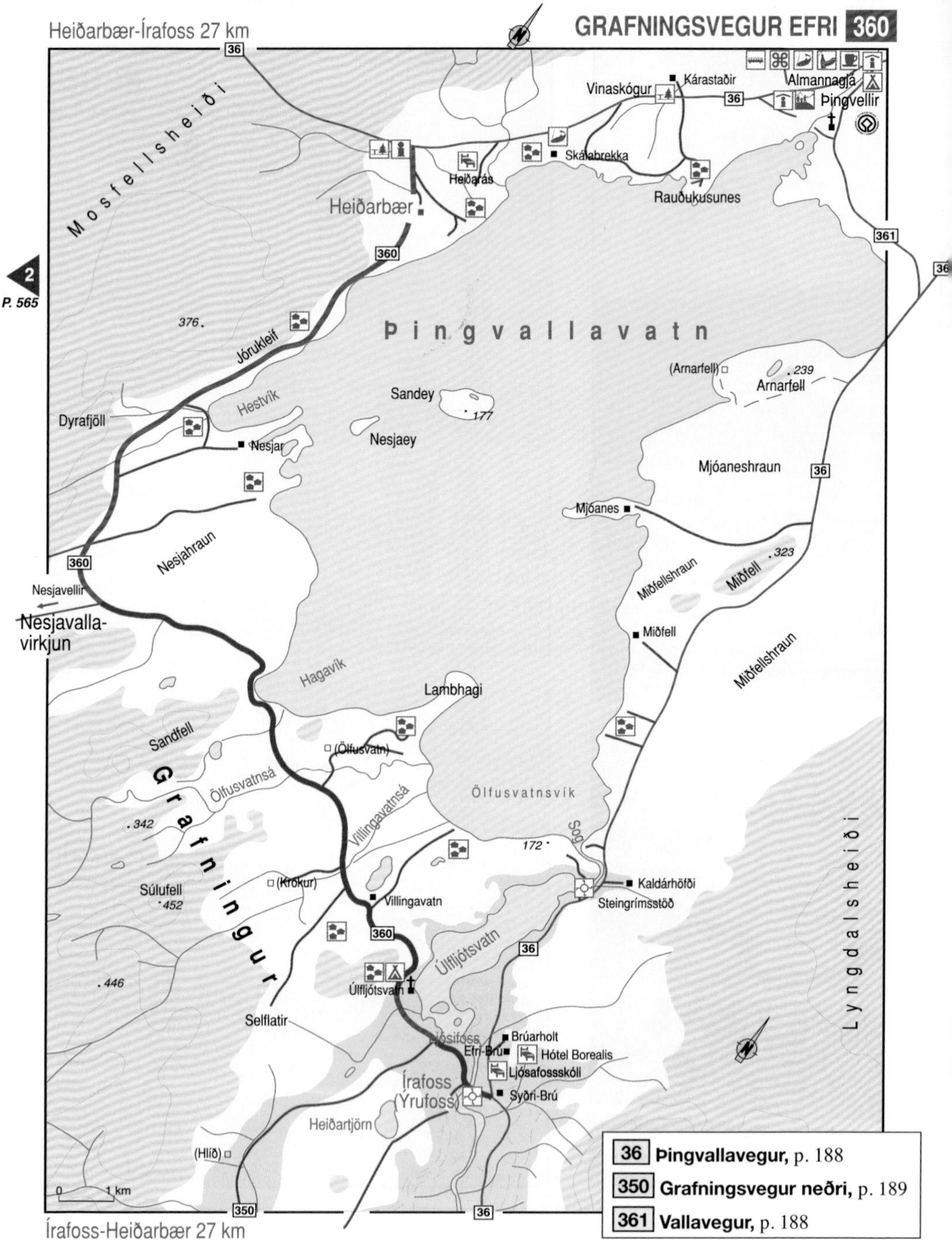

2 P. 565

Írafoss-Heiðarbær 27 km

36 Þingvallavegur, p. 188
350 Grafningsvegur neðri, p. 189
361 Vallavegur, p. 188

Jórukleif, a rocky wall above the **Hestvík** inlet.
Nesjavellir, much geothermal heat, harnessed for Reykjavík (see Road 36).
Dyrafjöll, (442 m) an interesting tuff mountain range where a recreation area has been organised, with marked footpaths. Forestation has been started.
Hagavík, a deserted farm where Dr. Helgi Tómasson (1896– 1958) planted more trees than any other individual in Iceland. A large lavafield, Hagavíkurhraun, to the north of the mountain Hengill.

Grafningur, the district to the west of Lake Þingvallavatn and the river Sog, with Mosfellsheiði and Dyrafjöll and several low mountain ridges, Grafningsfjöll, to the west, with the mountain Hengill beyond them. Many valleys, often wooded, between the mountains and ridges.
Úlfljótsvatn, the Scout Movement has a campsite open to the public. It´s intended for families and offers a variety of activities for kids. The church was built in 1914 on the site where once stood an ancient church.

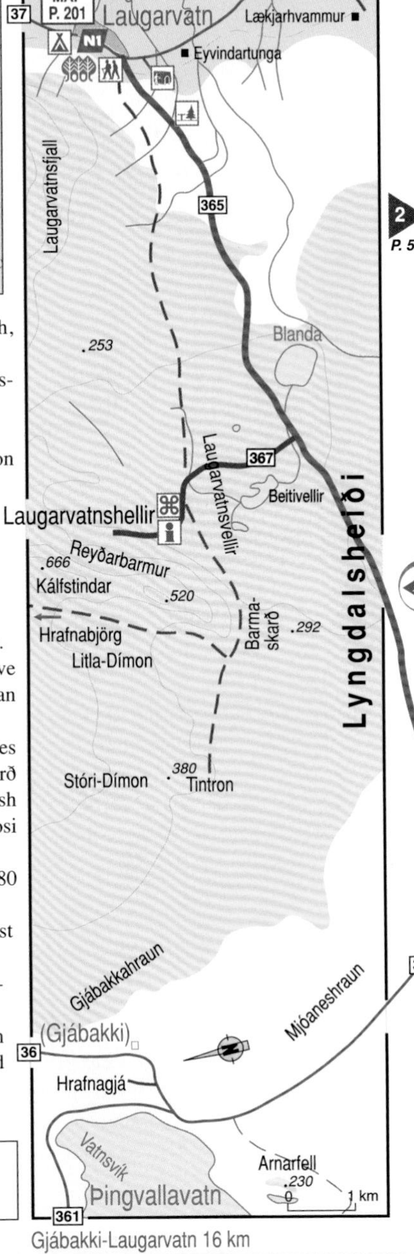

2 P. 565

Laugarvatn Hostel / ☎ 899-5409

Lyngdalsheiði, an old, flat shield-volcano. The road passes to the north, across the Gjábakkahraun lava field.

Kálfstindar, (826 m) a row of tuff peaks to the north of the Laugarvatnsvellir plains.

367 Laugarvatnshellavegur, 3,45 km.

Laugarvatnsvellir, dry flatlands to the east of Reyðarbarmur. Two caves on the west side of the flats were often used to house sheep but were the home of people during the first decades of this century. A young couple lived there in 1910-11 and had an "inn" in a tent near by. It was again inhabited in 1918 by a single man who lived there for a year and a married couple who stayed until 1922. During that time they had a daughter and the husband helped his wife to delivered the baby himself. Afterwards he had to travel far, through deep snow that closed all paths, to fetch the midwife. Everything went well and the daughter is the only living Icelander to have been born and lived in a cave. South of Laugarvatnsvellir are **Beitivellir**, an old resting place.

Vopnalág, ("Weapons hollow") and **Kárahella,** ("Kári's slab") place names to the east of Reyðarbarmur where the road comes down from Barmaskarð pass. It is said that Kári Sölmundarson in *Njáls saga* waited there to ambush Flosi and his men when they came from Alþingi in the spring of 1012. Flosi realised they were there and turned north.

Stóra-Dímon and **Litla-Dímon,** two small tuff mountains, 347 m and 380 m high respectively.

Tintron, an old steam vent in the lava, very deep and dark at the bottom, just south of Stóra-Dímon; a side track leads to there.

Hrafnagjá, a long lava rift marking the eastern edge of the plain of Þingvellir.

Gjábakkahellir, a 364 m long lava tube cave that was formed during an eruption 9000 years ago. First found in the year 1907 during road construction.

36 Þingvallavegur, p. 188
37 Laugarvatnsvegur, p. 190
361 Vallavegur, p. 188

P. 564

Nesstofa

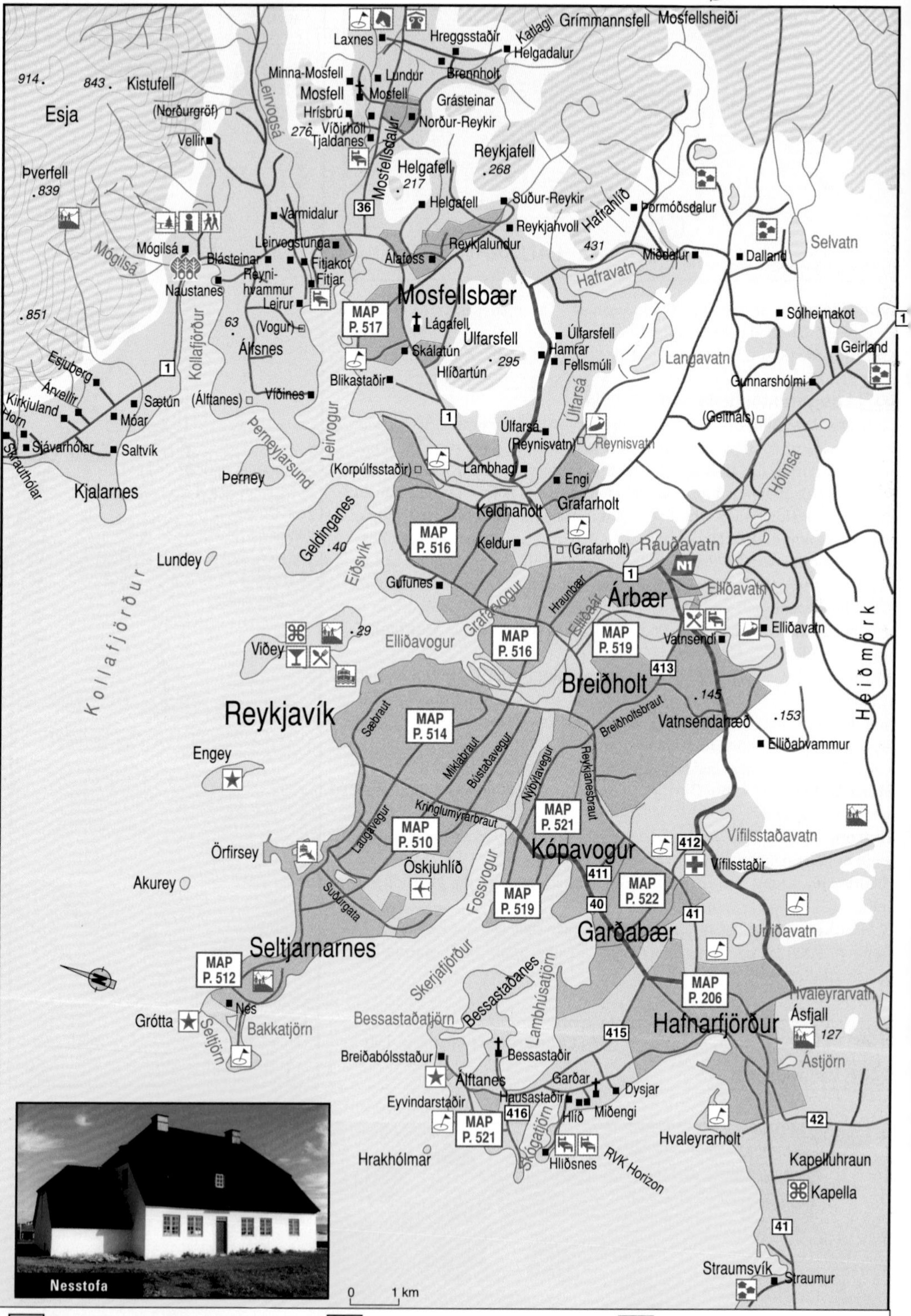

1 **Vesturlandsvegur,** p. 51	**1** **Suðurlandvegur,** p. 151	**36** **Þingvallavegur,** p. 187
41 **Reykjanesbraut,** p. 204	**42** **Krýsuvíkurvegur,** p. 213	**411** **Arnarnesvegur,** p. 204
412 **Vífilsstaðavegur,** p. 204	**415** **Álftanesvegur,** p. 204	**416** **Bessastaðavegur,** p. 204

Suður-Reykir, a geothermal area providing Reykjavík with hot water for heating.

Miðdalur, the home of the painter, sculptor and graphic artist Guðmundur Einarsson (1895-1963).

Seltjarnarnes, (pop. 4,450) a town on a peninsula west of Reykjavík which gained municipal rights in 1974. On the hill Valhúsahæð the falcon farm of the King of Denmark was once located, exporting some 200-300 bird per annum, each of them worth four horses. The first view-dial to be put up in Iceland is on Valhúsahæð. **Nesstofa,** a stone built house from 1761-63, at the request of the Danish government, for the newly appointed Director of Public Health, Bjarni Pálsson. The house was designed by Jacob Fortling, mason to the Danish court. It was built close to the old farmhouse. The stone in the house is Icelandic dolerite and was carved by a Danish stonemason. The stones were cemented with chalk imported from Denmark. In the house was a flat and an office for the Director, and also a pharmacy which was the first in the country. In the keeping of the National Museum since 1979 and now houses a Medical Museum. The birthplace of Sveinbjörn Sveinbjörnsson (1847-1926), composer of the Icelandic national anthem. The northernmost part of Seltjarnarnes peninsula, including the lighthouse, is a nature reserve and public park. The island **Grótta**, with its lighthouse, can be reached dry-footed at low tide, but care must be taken as the tide can rise quite swiftly and cover the causeway in less than the time it takes to walk across it. Swimming pool and a 9 hole golf course. (See town map under Reykjavík.)

Hafnarfjörður, its name simply means 'harbour fjord' and refers to the excellent natural harbour, which has Iceland's longest history of continuous port trade - since the 1300s. Hafnarfjörður is Iceland's third-largest town, with 28,703 residents. And yet that number is open to debate, since legend has it that some of Iceland's elves and hidden people live in Hafnarfjörður's lava cliffs and rocks, in peaceful coexistence with the town's human residents. In fact, it is possible to tour the elf lands, and those with second sight may even be lucky enough to spot one or two! Naturally the town also offers plenty of more conventional outdoor activities, from golf and swimming to horse riding and scenic walking routes. Museums and galleries turn the spotlight on history, music and visual arts. And every summer hordes of Norsemen invade the town for the annual Viking Festival, held in June. So relax and enjoy your favourite activity. The staff of the Tourist Information Centre is always ready to welcome you and is happy to provide any advice or information you may need during your stay. Hafnarfjörður nestles comfortably among the lava, and the splendour of the great outdoors is everywhere. One need go no further than the beautiful Hellisgerði park, founded in 1922, which has been ingeniously landscaped amongst the lava. Birdwatchers are sure to enjoy the Ástjörn nature reserve, and for walkers there are many lovely routes in and around the town. For those who wish to venture a little further afield, many places of outstanding natural beauty may be found within an easy distance of Hafnarfjörður, although a car is required for visitors planning their own itinerary. Inland from Mt. Ásfjall is a lovely area with lava and mountain scenery containing various walking routes. Enjoy the peaceful surroundings of Hvaleyrarvatn lake, or climb Mt. Helgafell (338m) for stunning panoramic views. Hafnarfjörður is famous for having one of Iceland's largest settlements of elves, dwarves and other mystical beings, which (translating from the Icelandic) are collectively called 'Hidden Folk.' Centuries-old folklore has it that whole clans of such beings reside in the rocks that make up part of the town's centre. We do not doubt this at all.

1
P. 564

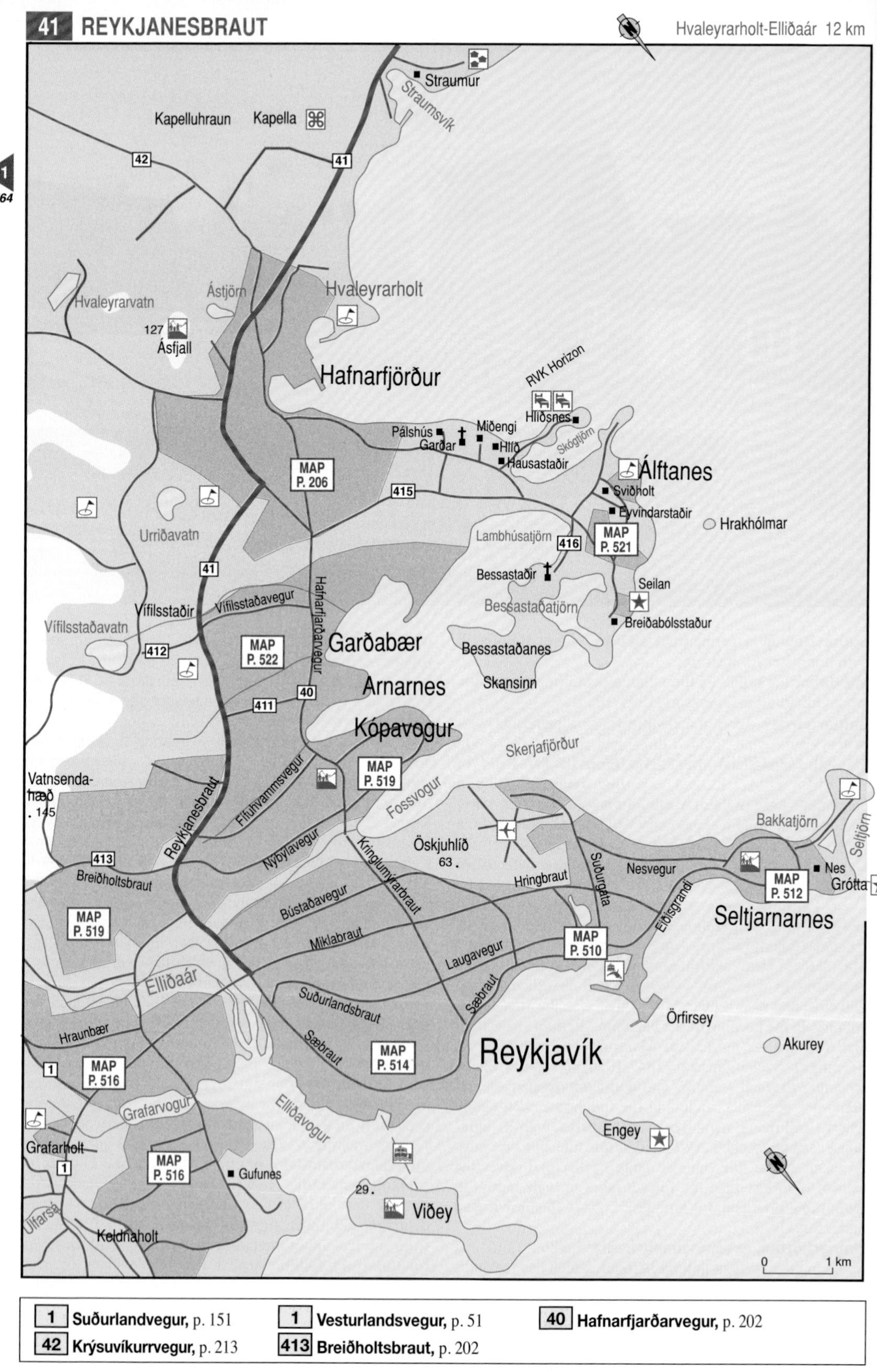

1 **Suðurlandvegur,** p. 151	1 **Vesturlandsvegur,** p. 51	40 **Hafnarfjarðarvegur,** p. 202
42 **Krýsuvíkurrvegur,** p. 213	413 **Breiðholtsbraut,** p. 202	

Hafnarfjörður, see p. 203.

Garðabær, (pop. 15,230) a town between Kópavogur and Hafnarfjörður, gained municipal rights in 1976. The municipalities of Garðabær and **Álftanes** merged together into one municipality in 2013. Within the town's boundaries there is a variety of natural features, extraordinary lava formations, caves etc., as well as ancient remains, now protected. Farming used to be the main occupation in Garðabær along with some fishing from the Álftanes peninsula, not far away from the fishing banks. Today it's a urban area in the capital region with industry and service. An elementary school was founded at Hausastaðir in Garðabær in 1791, marking the inception of public education in Iceland. The peninsula Álftanes has a magnificent pastoral setting by the sea. It is home to the ancient farmstead of Bessastaðir, the official presidential residence. On Arnarnes, near the junction of the roads Arnarnesvegur and Hegranesvegur, there is a concrete column, a restoration of one built by the German geophysicist Alfred Wegener in 1930 to test his theory of continental drift, which he originally advanced in the years 1908-12. See more p. 522.

Kópavogur, (pop. 35,246) a town between Reykjavík and Hafnarfjörður, the second largest town in Iceland. The first inhabitants of today's Kópavogur settled there in 1936. In 1945 the population was 521, in 1955, when Kópavogur gained municipal rights, it was 3,783. Kópavogur is an old site of the official meeting Kópavogsþing, one of four such assemblies in Gullbringusýsla. A fateful event in the history of Kópavogsþing was when the Icelanders were forced to acknowledge Fredrik III, King of Denmark, as absolute monarch in 1662. A monument commemorating these events was erected at the actual site of Kópavogsþing in 1962. At the same place there are also traces of old ruins, believed to be the former assembly house. A view-dial on the hill Víghóll.

Reykjavík, see p. 500.

415 **Álftanesvegur,** 5,25 km.

416 **Bessastaðavegur,** 0,82 km.

Eyvindarstaðir, a farm on the Álftanes peninsula. Residence of Sveinbjörn Egilsson (1791-1852), rector of Lærði skólinn (see below) in Reykjavík and author of *Lexicon Poëticum*, a dictionary of poetic language. The childhood home of his son, the poet and naturalist Benedikt Gröndal (1826-1907).

Bessastaðir, an ancient manor farm, official residence of the President of Iceland. First mention of Bessastaðir is in *Íslendinga saga* (The Saga of the Icelanders) by Sturla Þórðarson; the place then belonged to Snorri Sturluson. Later it became the first royal estate in Iceland, being in the possession of the King of Norway. From 1805 Bessastaðir was the site of the highest educational institution in Iceland, Lærði skólinn ("The learned school"), for 40 years. The eminent poet Grímur Thomsen (1820-96) was born at Bessastaðir and lived there from 1867. Upon his death, Bessastaðir became a private estate and remained so until 1941, since when it has been the official residence of the President of the Republic: Sveinn Björnsson (1881-1952) lived there from 1941 to 1952, first as governor then (from 1944) as president, Ásgeir Ásgeirsson (1894–1972) from 1952 to 1968, Kristján Eldjárn (1916-82) from 1968 to 1980, Vigdís Finnbogadóttir (b. 1930) from 1980 to 1996, Ólafur Ragnar Grímsson (b. 1943) from 1996 to 2016 and Guðni Th. Jóhannesson (b. 1968) from 2016. The main building is among the oldest houses in Iceland, built in 1761–66. It has since been added to and renovated. Further renovations were made in 1987 in Bessastaðastofa, revealing some relics of major importance under the floorboards. The church at Bessastaðir was built 1777–1823. Ruins of a fort from the 17th century at Skansinn.

412 **Vífilsstaðavegur,** 3 km.

411 **Arnarnesvegur,** 2 km.

Vífilsstaðir, the home of Vífill, freed slave of the first settler, Ingólfur Arnarson, and the one who found Ingólfur's pillars when they drifted ashore at Reykjavík. Vífilsstaðir was formerly a TB sanatorium and a hospital for respiratory diseases.

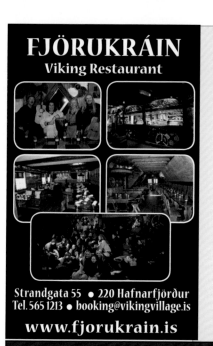

HAFNARFJÖRÐUR

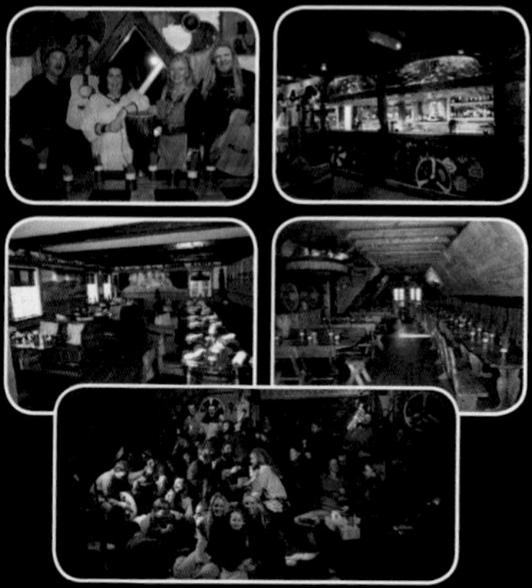

www.hafnarfjordur.is

Hvaleyrarhöfði
Hvaleyri
Hvaleyrarlón
Golfklúbburinn Keilir
Hvaleyrarholt
Hvaleyrarhraun
Hellnahraun
Vellir
Reykjanesbraut
Óseyrarbraut
Hvaleyrarbakki

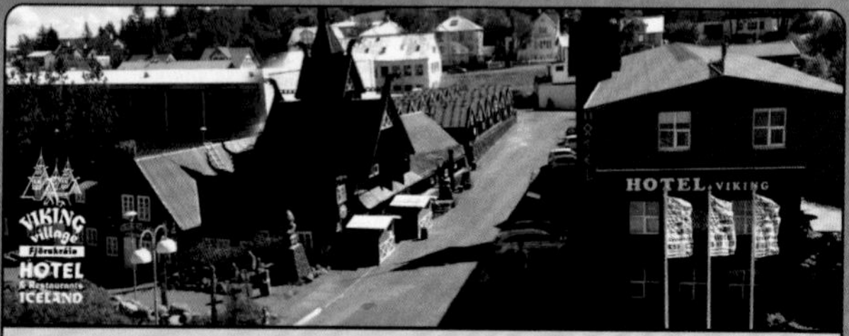

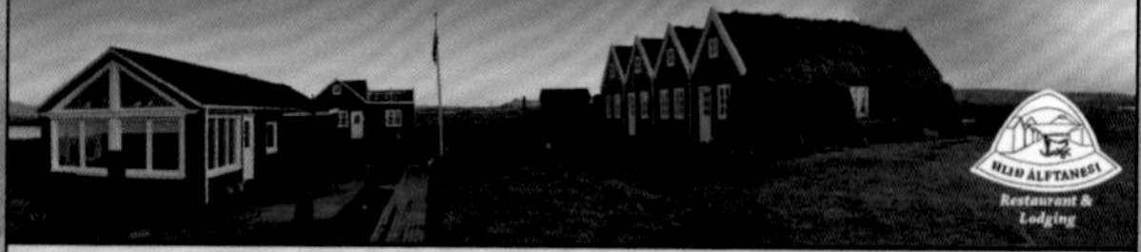

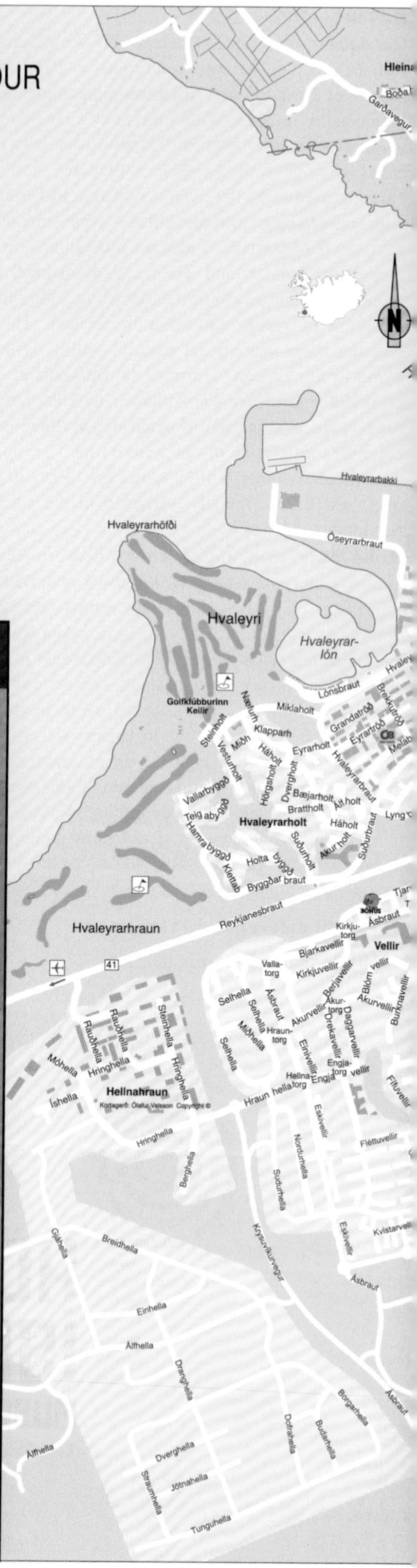

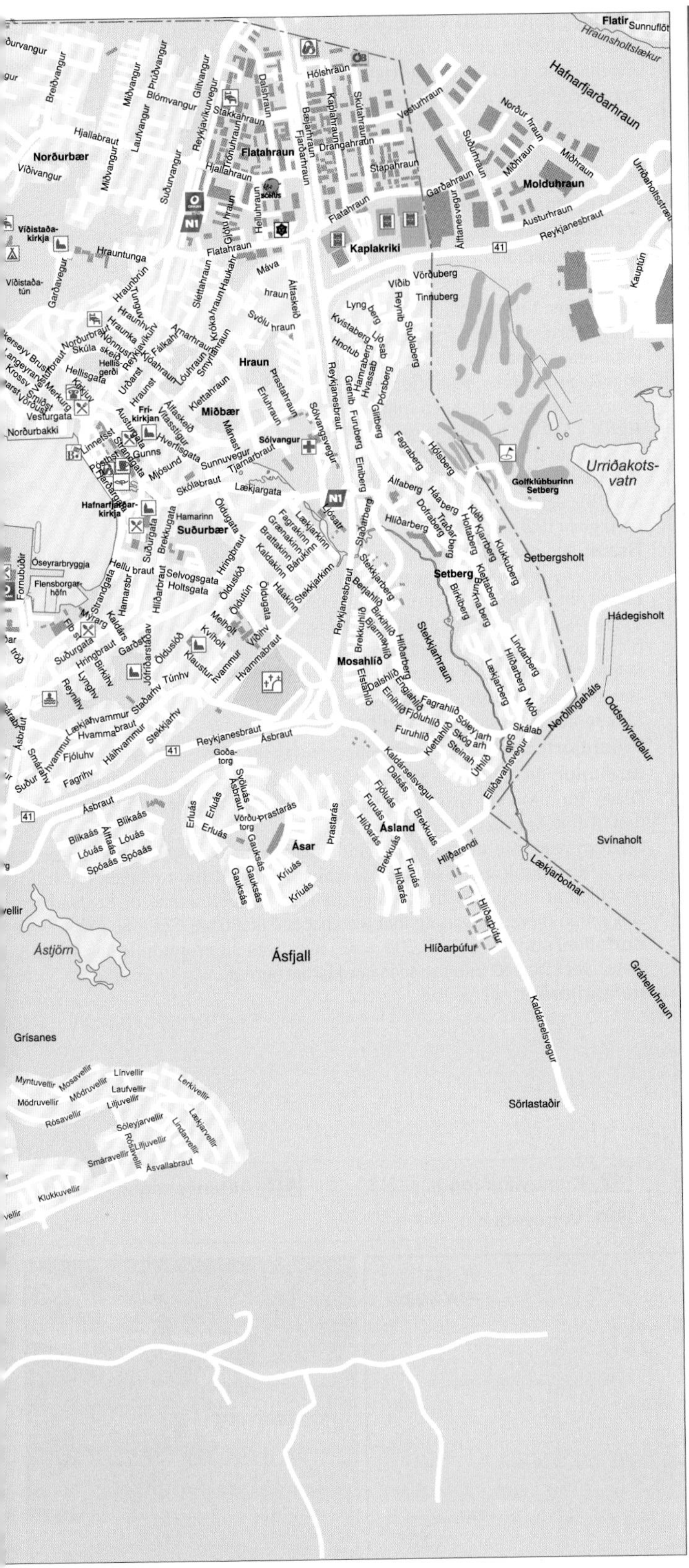

HAFNARFJÖRÐUR
Free admission in the museums
BYGGÐASAFN HAFNARFJARÐAR

Vogar-Hvaleyrarholt 20 km

1 P. 564

Vogar, (pop. 1,134) a village at the extreme south of Vatnsleysuströnd, with a harbour and lighthouse, fishing and fish processing, industrial mechanics, pork and poultry farming. Preschool, elementary school, sports centre, swimming pool, community centre, campsite and motel. By the elementary school there is a memorial to Jón Daníelsson the strong (1771-1855), made of a stone weighing 450 kg, which Jón is said to have picked up and carried.

420 Vatnsleysustrandarvegur, 11,3 km.

Vatnsleysuströnd, a community along the coast southwest of Straumsvík to Vogastapi sea cliffs, the farms being close to sea. Little grass except around the farms, otherwise mostly lava all the way to the Reykjanes mountains. Fish hatcheries.

Kálfatjörn, a church and parsonage until 1907. The church is one of largest country churches in Iceland. Surrounding the church is the beautiful 9-hole golf course, Kálfatjörn. 2-3 km to **Staðarborg**, a several hundred year old stone-built sheep fold.

Keilir, (379 m) a cone-shaped tuff mountain with fine views. It is usually possible to drive to Höskuldarvellir just east of Keilir.

Kúagerði, west of the Afstapahraun lava field, which probably flowed after the settlement of Iceland. Was the site of one of the few fresh-water springs in this area.

Hraun, the name for the area west and south of Straumsvík. The bay was formed between Lambhagatjarnir to the east and Hraun to the west. In Hraun there are many ruins and remains of old farms and outhouses. There is evidence of fishing being conducted from the shore, of fishermen´s lodgings, storage rooms, walls and areas for processing fish. Scattered in the lava plains there are many freshwater ponds that come and go with the tide. Some of these ponds are home to dwarf trout that life on the freshwater-seawater boundary.

Brunntjörn, the biggest freshwater pond in the area.

Straumur, the farmer of Kikjuból in Garðskagi was executed there by the Danes for allowing Kristján skrifara to be killed, but he allow the execution of Jón Arason bishop in Skálholt 1550.

Straumsvík, site of an aluminium smelting plant, with a good harbour. Located in the Kapella lava field, which is named for a chapel, the ruins of which are opposite the factory. In 1950 a small statue of St. Barbara was found there, indicating that the chapel dated from Catholic times.

Búrfellshraun, lava ca. 7,000 years old, from an eruption in the Búrfell crater, that flowed into the sea near Hafnarfjörður.

Hafnarfjörður, see p. 203.

Hvaleyrarholt-Vogar 20 km

42 Krýsuvíkurvegur, p. 213
415 Álftanesvegur, p. 204
421 Vogavegur, p. 209

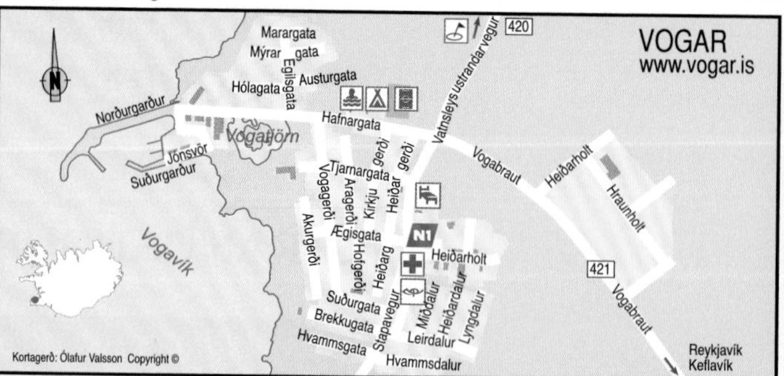

41 REYKJANESBRAUT

Sandgerði-Vogar 21 km

1 P. 564

Hvalsnes, ("Whale point") a church, formerly also a farm. The present church building built of hewn stone in 1887. Hallgrímur Pétursson (1614-74), the author of the *Passion Hymns*, served there before moving to Saurbær in Hvalfjörður. The church Hallgrímskirkja in Reykjavík is named after him.

Keflavík Airport, international airport on Miðnesheiði moor, built by Americans during and after the Second World War, later handed over to Icelanders. Outside the terminal building are the sculptures *Þotuhreiður* ("Jet Nest") by Magnús Tómasson and *Regnboginn* ("Rainbow") by Rúrí.

Reykjanesbær, (pop. 16,235) was at one time a fishing town, but this is not the case any longer. There is now more emphasis on industry, services connected to the airport and the commercial harbor at Helguvík, and harnessing energy and natural resources on the Reykjanes peninsula. The municipality of Reykjanesbær was created in 1994 when the inhabitants of the three towns Keflavík, Njarðvík and Hafnir voted to merge them into one. The downtown area has undergone a number of improvements. The Duus complex and Fischer's house form the old commercial centre of the town, while the docks in front of them were previously the heart of Keflavík. The marina at Gróf is particularly attractive. In a little cave at the marina one can find Giganta, a full sized ogress, resting in a rocking chair. She is a well known children's book character by author Herdís Egilsdóttir. At the marina you can also see Baldur KE 97 or "the Golden Nugget" (1961), which was the first Icelandic boat to use stern tow. In Reykjanesbær you'll find churches, a hospital, a health clinic, a college, a sports training center, Vatnaveröld water park, the Viking ship Icelander and Viking exhibition in Vikingworld, the Icelandic Museum of Rock n' Roll, and the Duushús Cultural Centre, which houses the Reykjanes Art Museum, the Grímur Karlsson Boat Museum, exhibitions from the Reykjanesbær Heritage Museum plus Reykjanes Geopark Visitor Center and a tourist info. At Ásbrú, the former NATO base on Reykjanes peninsula, you'll find Keilir – Atlantic Centre for Excellence, the Eldey centre for new business ventures, and the Research Centre for Energy Sciences. Hiking maps are available from the information office.

421 Vogavegur, 2,24 km. **423 Miðnesheiðarvegur,** 1,66 km.

424 Keflavíkurvegur, 2,5 km. **429 Sandgerðisvegur,** 6,4 km.

Stekkjarkot, by Fitjar. The home of non-farming fishermen from about 1850. It has now been rebuilt as a folk museum and is also used for gatherings of various kinds.

Vogastapi, or Stapi, an 80 m high sheer sea cliff, below which there used to be good fishing grounds. Said to be haunted. On the way from Vogastapi to the airport are a series of large stone figures sculpted by Áki Gränz. These represent trolls transformed to stone when caught by the rays of the rising sun. View-dial at Grímshóll.

43 Grindavíkurvegur, p. 216
44 Hafnavegur, p. 219
45 Garðskagavegur, p. 219
420 Vatnsleysustrvegur, p. 208

Vogar-Sandgerði 21 km

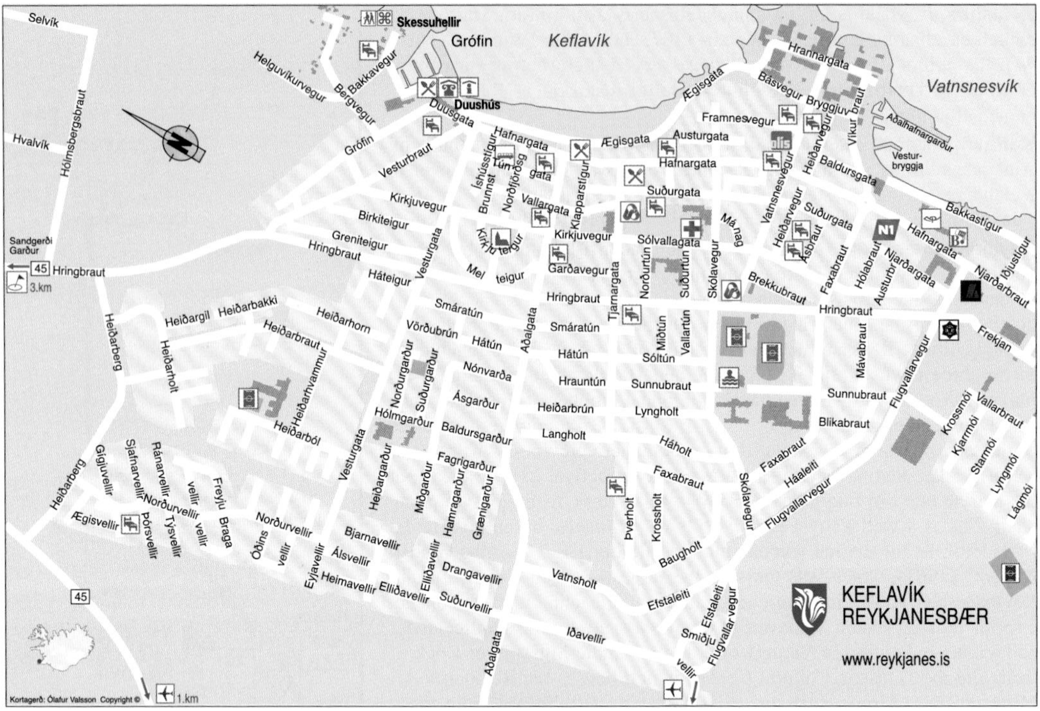

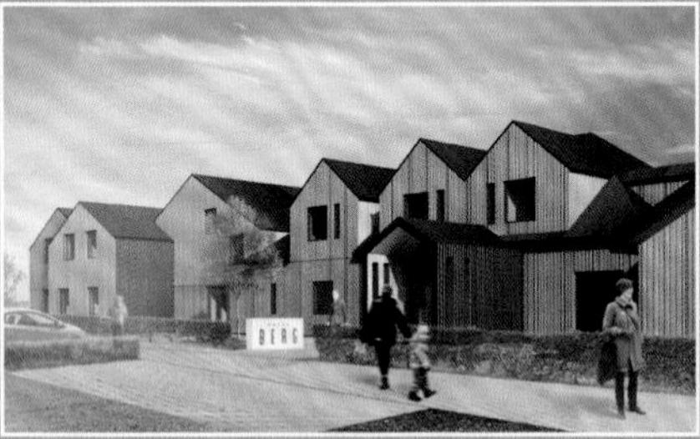

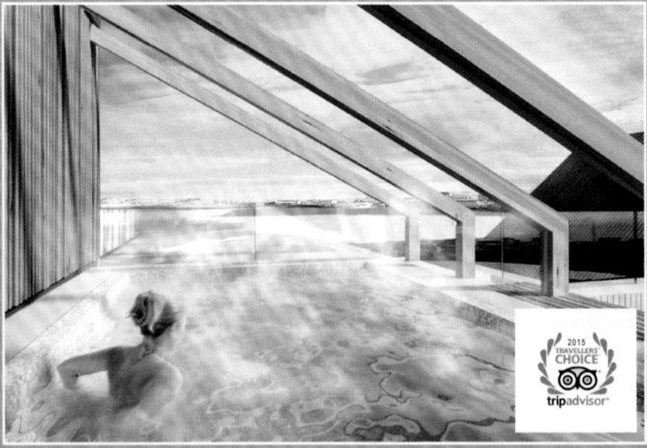

Keflavík
Vatnsnesvík
Skessuhellir
Grófin
Duushús
Selvík
Hvalvík
Hólmsbergsbraut
Helguvíkurvegur
Bakkavegur
Bergvegur
Duusgata
Vesturbraut
Hafnargata
Tún
Túngata
Ægisgata
Austurgata
Framnesvegur
Hrannargata
Básvegur
Bryggjuvegur
Vikurbraut
Aðalhafnargarður
Vesturbryggja
Baldursgata
Suðurgata
Kirkjuvegur
Birkiteigur
Greniteigur
Hringbraut
Háteigur
Vesturgata
Vallargata
Klapparstígur
Sólvallagata
Garðavegur
Melteigur
Smáratún
Vörðubrún
Hátún
Nónvarða
Ásgarður
Hólmgarður
Baldursgarður
Fagrigarður
Heiðargil
Heiðarbakki
Heiðarhorn
Heiðarbraut
Heiðarberg
Heiðarholt
Heiðarhvammur
Heiðarból
Gígjuvellir
Sjafnarvellir
Ránarvellir
Norðurvellir
Týsvellir
Þórsvellir
Freyjuvellir
Bragavellir
Ægisvellir
Óðinsvellir
Eyjavellir
Bjarnavellir
Álsvellir
Heimavellir
Elliðavellir
Drangavellir
Suðurvellir
Vatnsholt
Iðavellir
Aðalgata
Hraunstún
Heiðarbrún
Langholt
Lyngholt
Sunnubraut
Sóltún
Miðtún
Vallartún
Hátún
Háholt
Faxabraut
Krossholt
Þverholt
Baugholt
Efstaleiti
Smiðjuvellir
Flugvallarvegur
Skólavegur
Brekkubraut
Hólabraut
Austurbraut
Njarðargata
Njarðarbraut
Iðjustígur
Bakkastígur
Frekjan
Mávabraut
Blikabraut
Háaleiti
Vallarbraut
Krossmói
Kjarrmói
Starmói
Lyngmói
Lágmói
Hringbraut 3.km
45
1.km
KEFLAVÍK
REYKJANESBÆR
www.reykjanes.is
Kortagerð: Ólafur Valsson Copyright ©

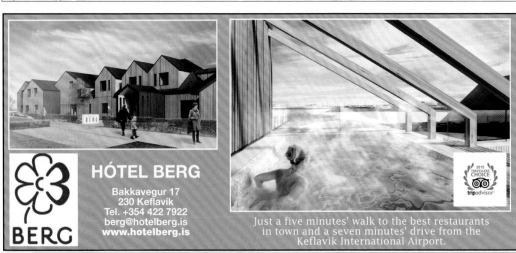

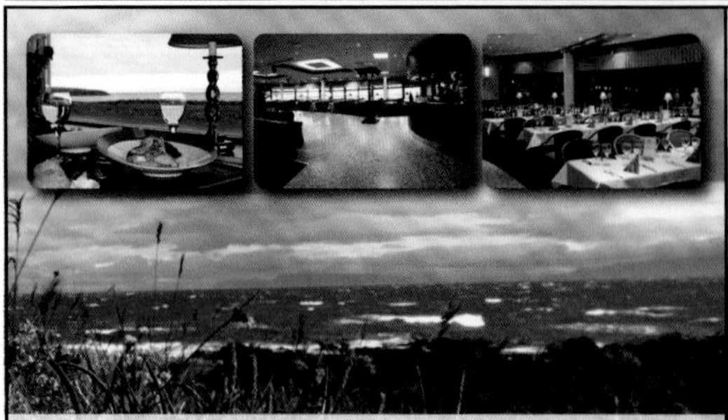

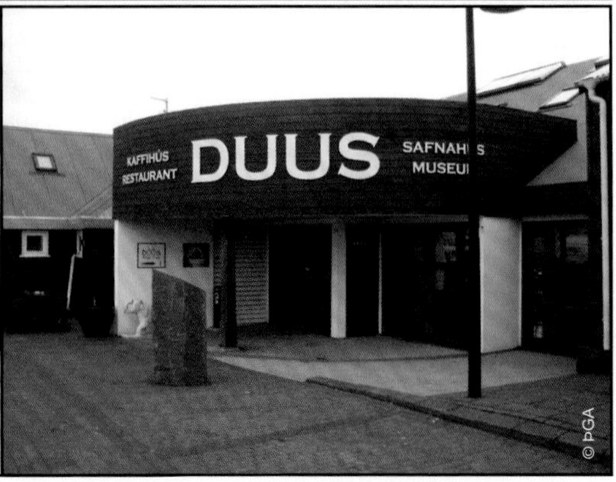

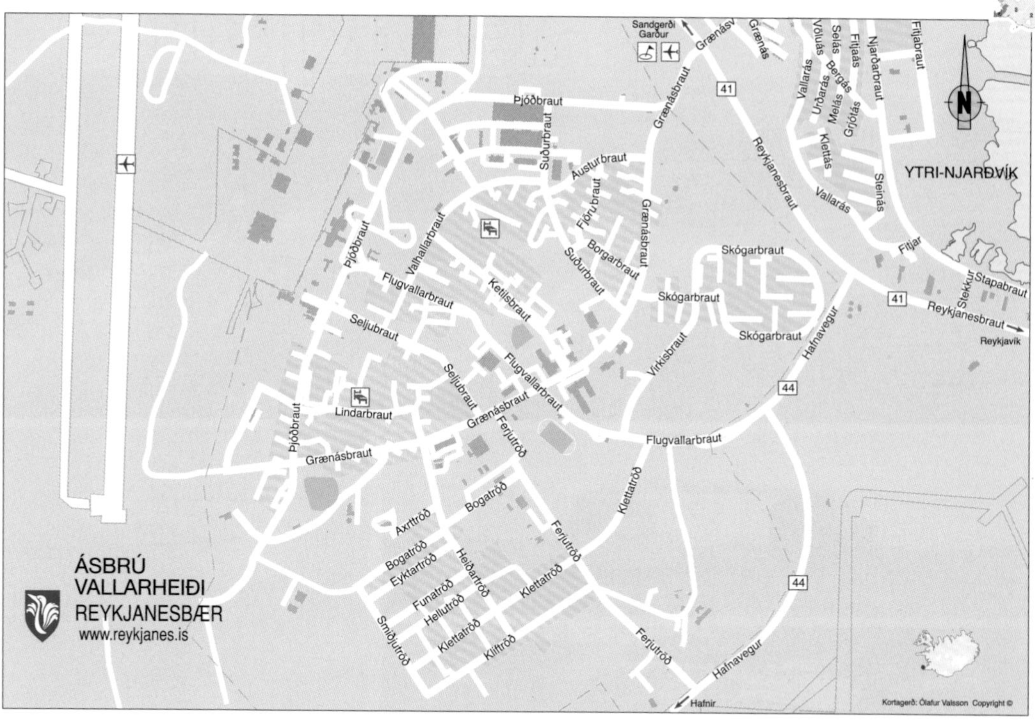
ÁSBRÚ
VALLARHEIÐI
REYKJANESBÆR
www.reykjanes.is
YTRI-NJARÐVÍK
Sandgerði
Garður
Reykjavík
Hafnir
Þjóðbraut
Suðurbraut
Austurbraut
Grænásbraut
Grænásv
Grænás
Reykjanesbraut
Valhallarbraut
Fjörubraut
Borgarbraut
Flugvallarbraut
Ketilsbraut
Seljubraut
Skógarbraut
Virkisbraut
Hafnavegur
Lindarbraut
Ferjutröð
Klettatröð
Bogatröð
Axrtröð
Eyktartröð
Heiðartröð
Funatröð
Hellutröð
Kliftröð
Smiðjutröð
Vallarás
Urðarás
Völuás
Selás
Bergás
Melás
Fitjaás
Grjótás
Njarðarbraut
Fitjabraut
Klettás
Steinás
Fitjar
Stekkur
Stapabraut
41
44
Kortagerð: Ólafur Valsson Copyright ©

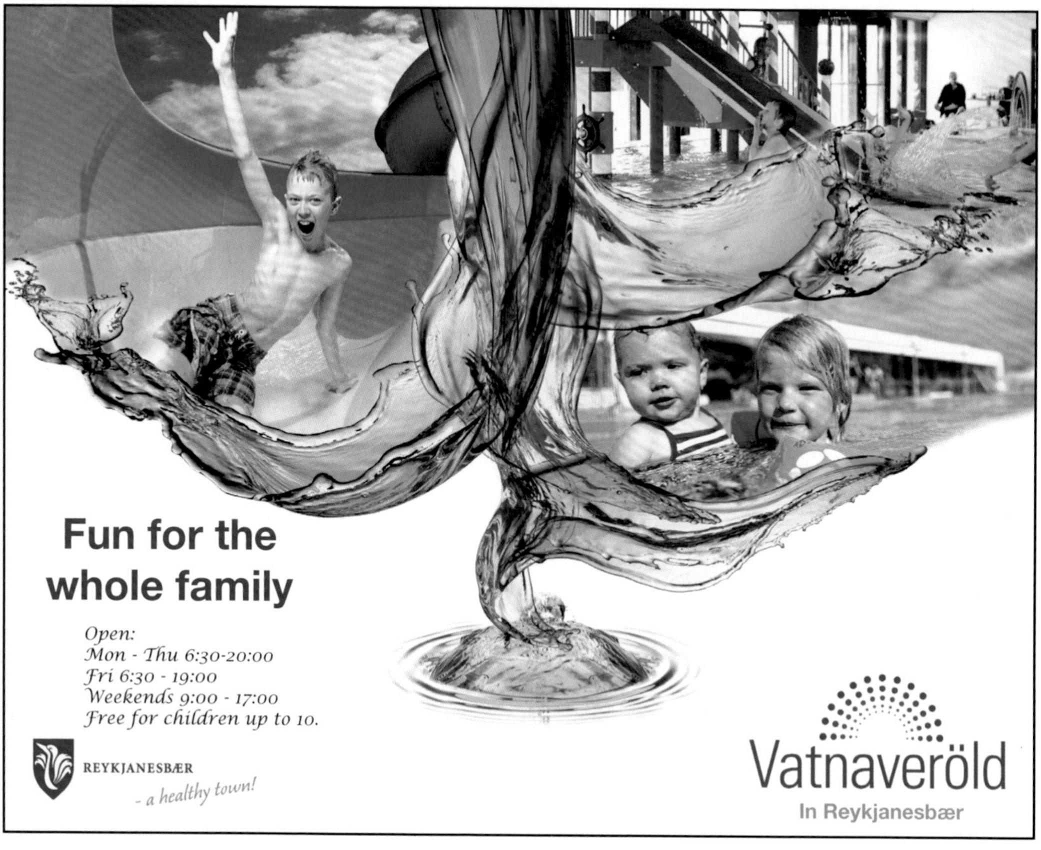
Fun for the whole family
Open:
Mon - Thu 6:30-20:00
Fri 6:30 - 19:00
Weekends 9:00 - 17:00
Free for children up to 10.
REYKJANESBÆR
- a healthy town!
Vatnaveröld
In Reykjanesbær

Reykjanes

42 KRÝSUVÍKURVEGUR

Fjallið eina, ("The lone mountain") a single tuff mountain (223 m) with surprisingly panoramic views from the top.

428 Vigdísarvallavegur, 21 km.

Sveifluháls, a tuff ridge with a maximum height of 395 m. Descends in steep cliffs to the lake Kleifarvatn. The old route from Krýsuvík to Hafnarfjörður and Reykjavík went over Sveifluháls along the path Ketilstígur. At the south end of the ridge is a single mountain **Mælifell**, 228 m.

Kleifarvatn, nearly 10 km^2 and up to 97 m deep, the third largest lake in southern Iceland. The water level rises and falls at intervals according to precipitation. Formerly a dead lake, but some trout have been imported and are prospering. At the crag Innri-Stapi on the shore there is a bronze plaque commemorating the guide Stefán Stefánsson, whose ashes were scattered in the lake, as he requested.

Djúpavatn, ("Deep Lake") a small lake west of the Sveifluháls ridge. A side-track goes to it from the Krýsuvík road west of the Vatnsskarð pass and south along Sveifluháls. Trout have been imported into this and other nearby lakes.

Austurengjahver, a big steam hot spring south of the Kleifarvatn lake, east of road. It grew very much larger after an earthquake in 1924.

Seltún, a geothermal area in Krýsuvík. **Paths have been laid so as to offer better access to the hot springs. Walk only on marked paths.**

Krýsuvík, ancient manor farm and church now abandoned along with other nearby farms. Much geothermal heat, with drill-holes for possible exploitation. The church was lost in a fire in the year 2010. A special school for young people, a treatment community for the upbringing and education of drug addicts. The land belongs to Hafnarfjörður. To the south, on the coast, are the Krýsuvíkur bird cliffs. The only place possible to climb the cliff is at **Ræningjastígur**.

Grænavatn, ("Green Lake") a lake in an explosion crater, 44 m deep. Another old crater also with water, Gestsstaðavatn, on the other side of the road.

Hafnarfjörður-Krýsuvík 23 km

Krýsuvík-Hafnarfjörður 23 km

41 Reykjanesbraut, p. 208
417 Bláfjallavegur, p. 225
427 Suðurstrandarvegur, p. 228

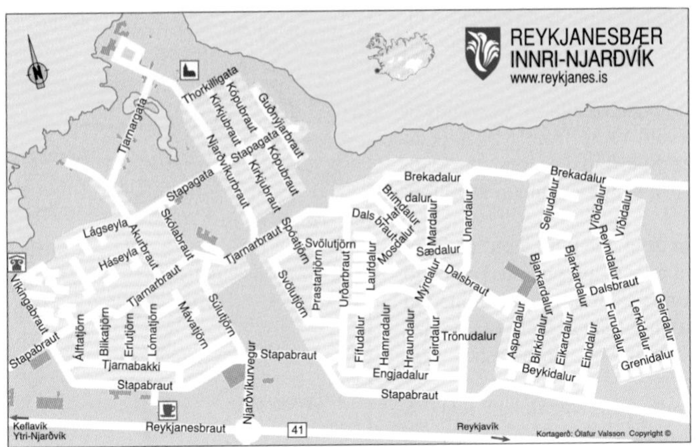

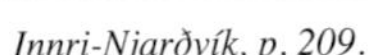
Innri-Njarðvík, p. 209.

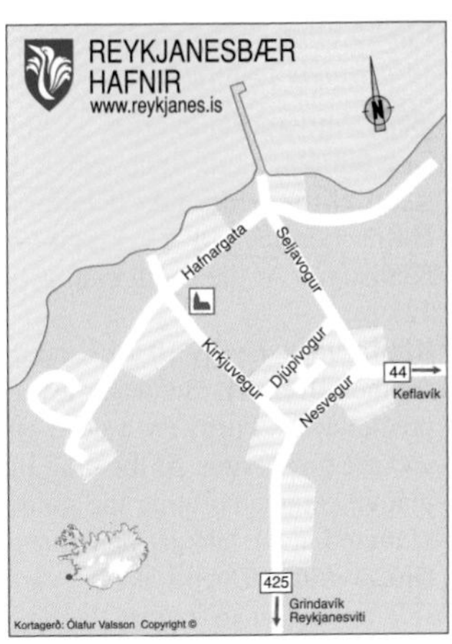

Hafnir, p. 219.

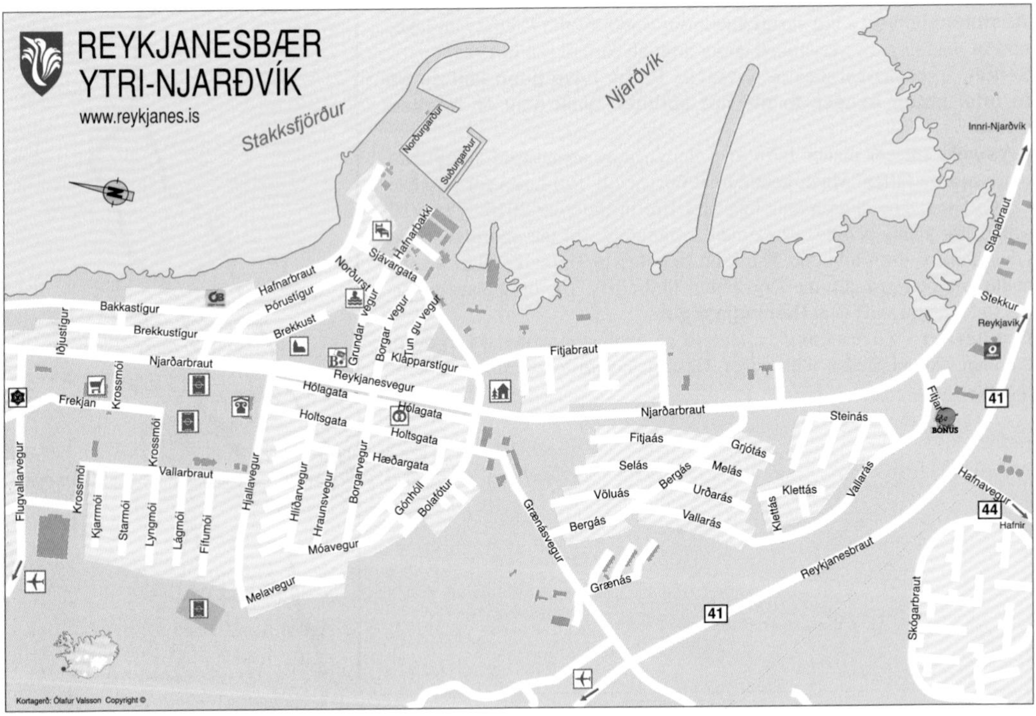

REYKJANESBÆR
YTRI-NJARÐVÍK
www.reykjanes.is

Stakksfjörður
Njarðvík
Innri-Njarðvík
Reykjavík
Hafnir
Njarðarbraut
Reykjanesvegur
Reykjanesbraut
Fitjabraut
Grænásvegur
Stapabraut
Flugvallarvegur
Kortagerð: Ólafur Valsson Copyright ©

Ytri-Njarðvík, p. 209.

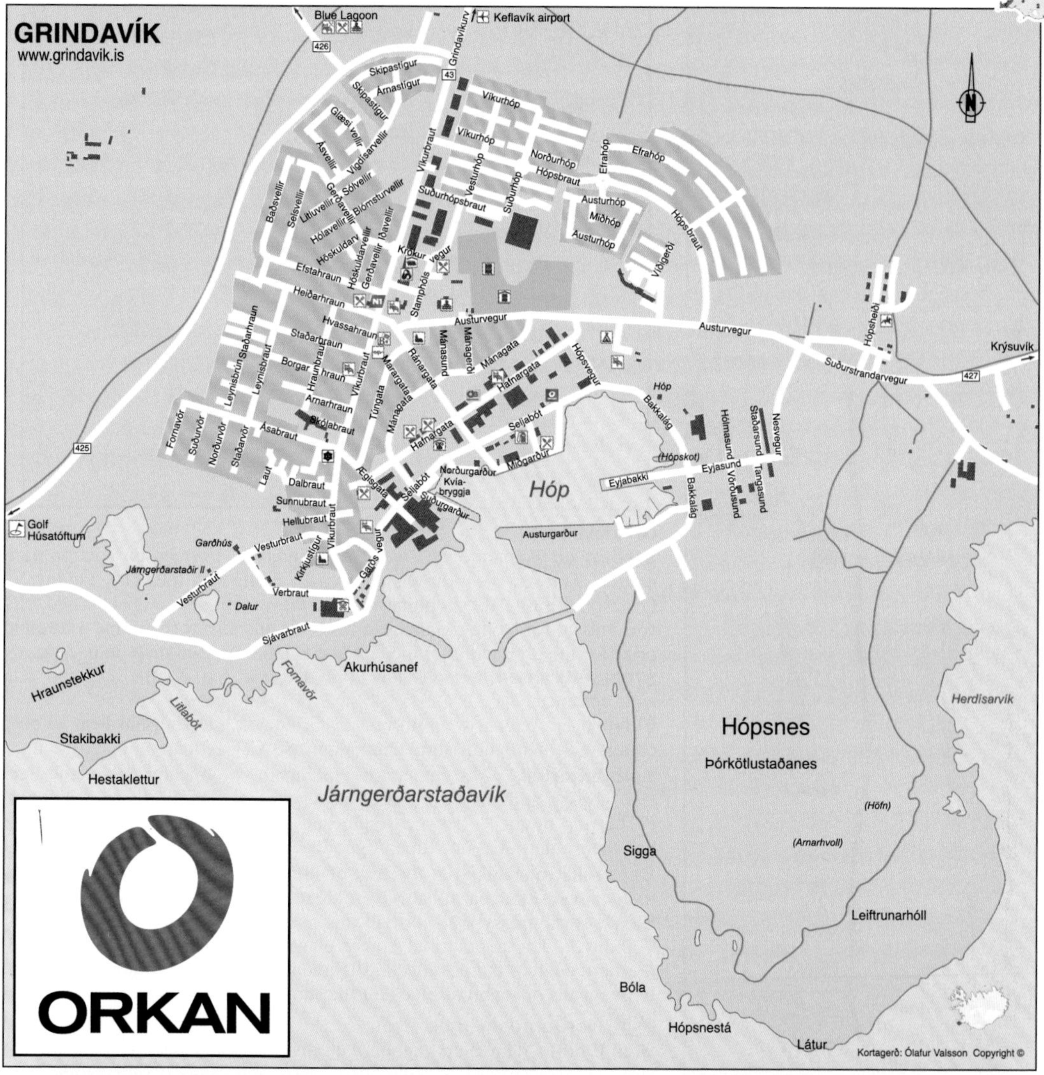

GRINDAVÍK
www.grindavik.is
Blue Lagoon
Keflavík airport
Krýsuvík
Víkurhóp
Norðurhóp
Efrahóp
Hópsbraut
Suðurhópsbraut
Austurhóp
Miðhóp
Víðigerði
Austurvegur
Suðurstrandarvegur
Hópsheiði
Hóp
Bakkalág
(Hópskot)
Eyjabakki
Eyjasund
Hólmasund
Staðarsund
Nesvegur
Vörðusund
Tangasund
Austurgarður
Norðurgarður
Kvíabryggja
Seljabót
Suðurgarður
Miðgarður
Hafnargata
Mánagata
Ránargata
Mánasund
Mánagerði
Víkurbraut
Túngata
Marargata
Hvassahraun
Staðarhraun
Borgarhraun
Hraunbraut
Arnarhraun
Skólabraut
Ásabraut
Heiðarhraun
Efstahraun
Stamphólsvegur
Grindavíkurvegur
Skipastígur
Árnastígur
Gæsi vellir
Ásvellir
Vígdísarvellir
Sólvellir
Litluvellir
Gerðavellir
Blómsturvellir
Hólavellir
Höskuldarvellir
Baðsvellir
Selsvellir
Leynisbrún
Leynisbraut
Fornavör
Suðurvör
Norðurvör
Staðarvör
Laut
Dalbraut
Sunnubraut
Hellubraut
Vesturbraut
Kirkjustígur
Garðsvegur
Verbraut
Sjávarbraut
Garðhús
Járngerðarstaðir II
Dalur
Golf
Húsatóftum
Akurhúsanef
Hraunstekkur
Fornavör
Litlabót
Stakibakki
Hestaklettur
Járngerðarstaðavík
Hópsnes
Þórkötlustaðanes
(Höfn)
(Arnarhvoll)
Sigga
Leiftrunarhóll
Bóla
Hópsnestá
Látur
Herdísarvík
Hóp
ORKAN
Kortagerð: Ólafur Valsson Copyright ©

SALTHÚSIÐ RESTAURANT
Stamphólsvegur 2, 240 Grindavík
Tel. 426 9700 & 699 2665
salthusid@salthusid.is
www.salthusid.is
...dedicated to Icelandic delicacies...

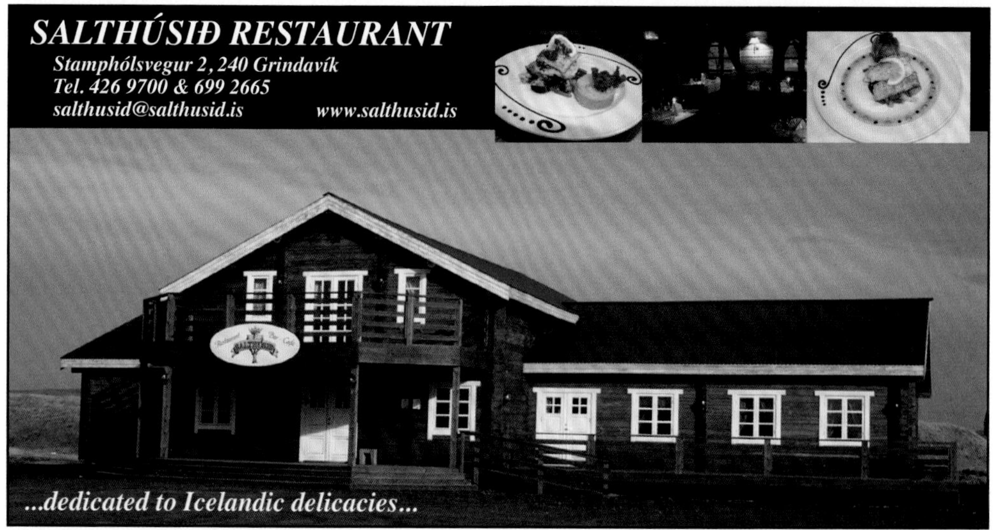

Grindavík-Vogastapi 14 km

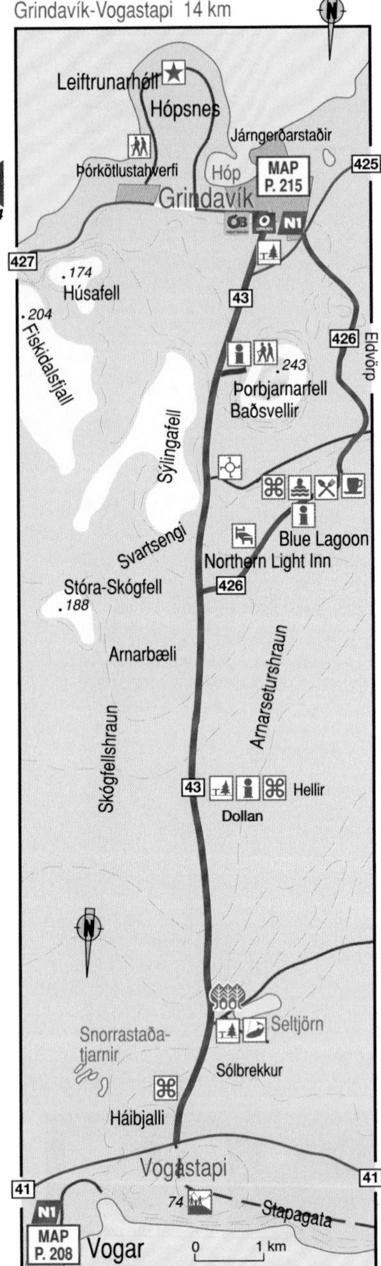

Vogastapi-Grindavík 14 km

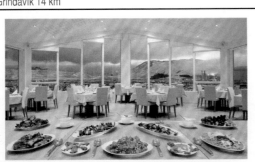

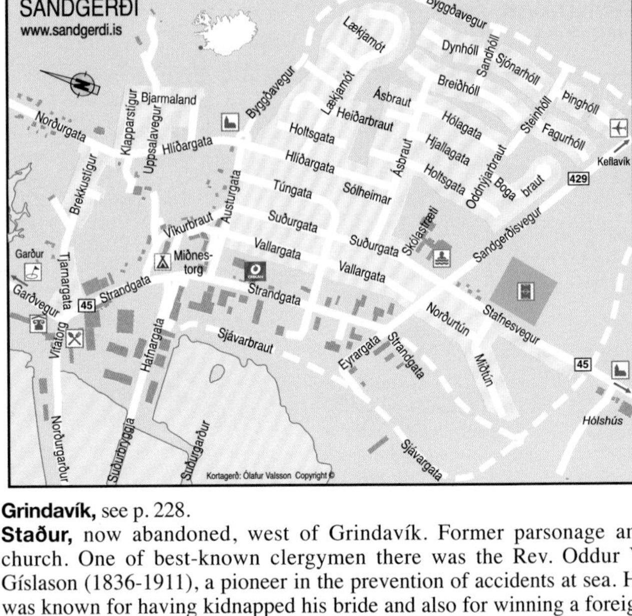

Grindavík, see p. 228.

Staður, now abandoned, west of Grindavík. Former parsonage and church. One of best-known clergymen there was the Rev. Oddur V. Gíslason (1836-1911), a pioneer in the prevention of accidents at sea. He was known for having kidnapped his bride and also for winning a foreign prize for the production of medicinal cod liver oil, (see map on p. 226).

Arnarseturshæð, a good view point and rest stop. By the rest stop is a cave entrance.

Eldvörp, a crater row northwest of Grindavík. Geothermal heat in one crater, with steam emission, temperature 80°C, (see map on p. 226).

Þorbjarnarfell, (243 m) a tuff mountain, a volcano from the Ice Age, grassy and easy to climb, fine views. In a ravine there, **Þjófagjá** ("Thieves' ravine"), between eight and fifteen thieves are said to have had their hide-out at one time. A good walking route.

Baðsvellir, marshland at the foot of Þorbjarnarfell mountain. The name might suggest that earth baths were there once.

Svartsengi, grassy area north of the mountain Sýlingafell to the north of Grindavík. The geothermal power plant at Svartsengi is located at the northern edge of the postglacial Illahraun lava field. It produced electricity by means of steam turbines for the surrounding districts.

426 Norðurljósavegur, 7 km.

Bláa lónið, ("The Blue Lagoon") an internationally popular recreational and therapeutic pool of deliciously warm and mineral rich geothermal water carved out of the Svartsengi lava field. The tectonically supercharged brine flows from Svartsengi power plant, and its beautiful blue color comes from light refracting micro-organisms that thrive in this unusual ecosystem.

Seltjörn and **Sólbrekkur**, outdoor recreation areas near the town of Reykjanesbær. Trout has been released into Seltjörn and fishing licences are sold. Sólbrekkur has an outdoor barbecue and play equipment for children. One of the planned outdoor recreation areas at Vogar is at **Háibjalli** and **Snorrastaðatjarnir**. All the ponds are in grabens and the woods are sheltered beneath tall fault walls.

41 Reykjanesbraut, p. 209

425 Nesvegur, p. 226

427 Suðurstrandavegur, p. 228

Reykjanes

Vitinn
SEAFOOD RESTAURANT
Vitinn restaurant is located, just minutes from Keflavik airport, in the town of Sandgerði and is therefore an excellent place to visit on the way to or from the airport. This beautiful restaurant, brings the freshest seafood straight to your plate.
Vitinn specialty is the Rock Crab, a delicacy found only in this part of Iceland and on the US East coast. This is one of the few if not the only restaurant in Europe that offers this treat fresh from the sea. Special live holding tanks in the back garden of the restaurant guarantee the crabs so you can be sure of the very best dining experience.
The menu and the presentation of each course show off Icelandic cuisine at its best. Besides seafood, there is also a delicious offering of Icelandic specialties such as lamb steak. However, it is not restricted to classic Icelandic foods alone but provides a truly international variety.
Vitatorg 7, 245 Sandgerð
Tel. +354 423 775
info@vitinn.i
www.vitinn.i

44 Hafnavegur, 8,7 km. **45 Garðskagavegur,** 24 km.

Hafnir, (pop. 112) a community with big farms and much sea fishing. Church at Kirkjuvogur. From the nearby mountain Stapafell a great deal of material has been taken for use on construction work at Keflavík Airport. Nearby is one of the anchors of the ship *Jamestown* which drifted ashore, unmanned, at Ósabotnar by Hafnir in 1870, the other one is in Sandgerði.

Básendar, or Bátsendar, former trading place and fishing centre just south of the Stafnes lighthouse. A record high tide on January 9th 1799 destroyed most buildings althought all the people but one managed to escape.

Stafnes, formerly an ancient manor farm with many smaller farms around it. Lighthouse. This coast has proved very dangerous for ships.

Hvalnes, a church built out of stone in 1887. One of Iceland's most cherished poets, Hallgrímur Pétursson, served there as a priest from 1644-1651. Inside the church is a tombstone made made by him for his daughter which he lost at an young age.

429 Sandgerðisvegur, 6,38 km.

Sandgerðisbær, (pop. 1,673) a town with a busy harbour, much fishing and fish processing. There you can find a good campsite and a sport centre with a swimming pool. The Suðurnes Science and Learning Centre is an environmental travel and learning centre based on the local Icelandic reality. It relates to the sea, the shore, the fish, the birds and the fresh-water ecology in the immediate environment. There you can find high quality research facilities and accommodation for researchers. There are two exhibitions in the Center: a natural history museum and the magnificent exhibition Attraction of the Poles on the work, life and death of the French medical doctor and polar scientist Jean-Baptiste Charcot. His research ship named *Pourquoi-Pas?*, perished off the coast of Iceland in 1936.

Garðskagi, the outermost point of the Miðnes peninsula, the north-pointing "toe" of the Reykjanes peninsula. Quite densely populated. Old and new lighthouses, birdwatching station. In the old lighthouse, built in 1897, there is a map of the Garðskagi reef showing where ships have stranded, and other information about the coast. In earlier times there was more cultivation of land in this area than in most other parts of Iceland. Whales can be seen swimming in the sea at Garðskagi.

Útskálar, a church and parsonage.

Garður, (pop. 1,511) a village focusing on fish processing and service. The art project Fresh Breeze at Garður is an Art Festival which puts its mark on the village with all the art work. There is also a Folk museum with various interesting artifacts from the story of Garður and machine collection by Garðskagaviti lighthouse with restaurant Flösin is on the second floor. At Garður there is also a good campsite, walking routes, swimming pool and hot tubs.

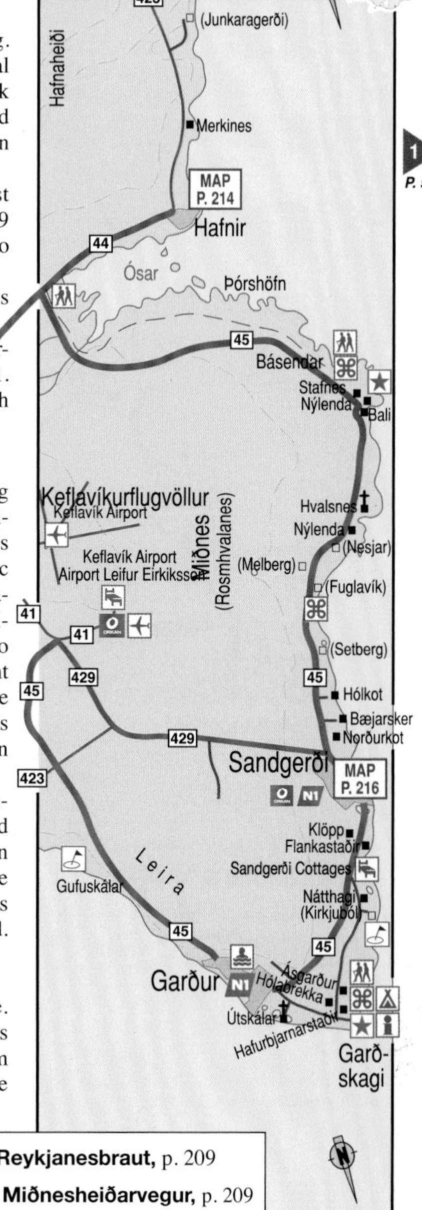

1 P. 564

41 Reykjanesbraut, p. 209

423 Miðnesheiðarvegur, p. 209

425 Nesvegur, p. 226

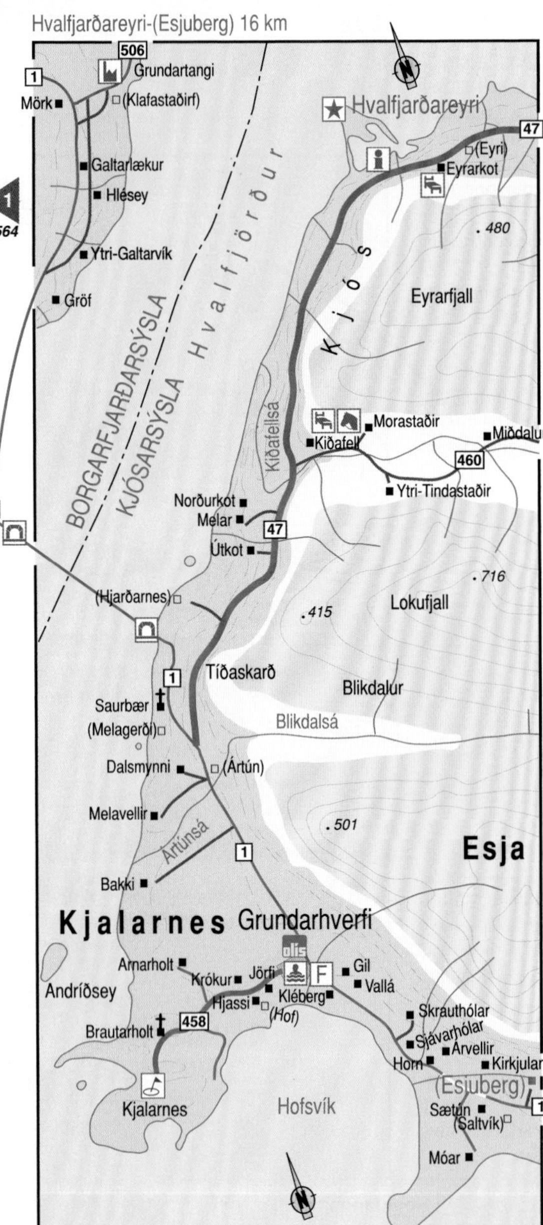

(Esjuberg) - Hvalfjarðareyri 16 km

Hvalfjarðareyri, once a ferry point to Kalastaðakot. Many beautiful stones can be found there.

Tíðaskarð, a small pass above the farm Saurbær.

Hvalfjarðargöng, a tunnel see p. 53.

Saurbær, a farm and church. In 1424 English pirates raided the farm.

458 Brautarholtsvegur, 2,5 km.

Andríðsey, an island. It is said that a farmer from the time of settlement was buried there.

Brautarholt, church and a manor farm.

Hof, a farm where the second largest heathen temple is supposed to have been, though no ruins are visible.

Kjalarnes, the district to the west of Esja between the fjords Kollafjörður and Hvalfjörður. Became a part of Reykjavík in 1998.

Grundarhverfi, a community of 562 inhabitants. **Fólkvangur,** a community centre in Grundarhverfi.

Esjuberg, a farm where the first church in Iceland is said to have been built by the Hebridean Örlygur Hrappsson.

Saltvík, training area for the police.

Móar, a farm and formerly a parsonage. First parish of the poet and priest Matthías Jochumsson, who translated *Hamlet* and other Shakespeare plays while serving there as well as writing Iceland's national anthem.

1 **Vesturlandsvegur,** p. 53
460 **Eyrarfjallsvegur,** p. 224
506 **Grundartangavegur,** p. 54, 234

47 HVALFJARÐARVEGUR

Hvalfjörður, ("Whale fjord") the longest fjord in the southwest of Iceland, about 30 km long and up to 84 m deep. Formerly a good harbour, and during the Second World War a big naval base run by the Allied Forces, where convoys often used to gather. In 1402 the plague was brought to Hvalfjörður and from there it spread around the island. Fishing often used to be good and great quantities of herring have been caught there.
Botnssúlur, (1,089 m) a group of high mountains with five peaks rising at the head of the fjord, the remnant of an old volcano. A fine viewing point.
Hlaðhamar, cliffs on the shore, once a loading place for ships.
Múlafjall, (391 m) a steep mountain with many cliff-faces between Botnsdalur and Brynjudalur.
Brynjudalur, the valley to the south of Múlafjall. Falls in the river near the road were spectacular until salmon-ladders were blasted in the cliff to by-pass them.
Hvítanes, an abandoned farm where the British Navy had its headquarters during the war. Some ruins remain.
Karlinn í Skeiðhóli, ("The old man of Skeiðhóll") also known as **Staupasteinn** ("Dram rock"), **Prestasteinn** ("Priests' rock") or **Steðji**. A goblet-like rock by the old road. Formerly a popular resting place for travellers. A protected natural feature.
Hvammur or **Hvammsvík,** beautiful area and many walking routes. Some forestry at **Hvammsmörk.**
Reynivallaháls, (415 m) a long mountain ridge between Hvalfjörður and Kjós, with steep slopes and cliffs on the seaward side.
Neðri-Háls, an organic dairy farm in the Kjós district.
Maríuhöfn, ("Mary's harbour") in Laxárvogur inlet. Iceland's major centre of commerce in the 14th century.
Laxá, a well-known salmon river.
Bugða, a short river flowing from Meðalfellsvatn into Laxá. Good fishing.
Kjós, the district from Kiðafellsá to the head of Hvalfjörður, most of it being a wide valley between the mountains Eyrarfjall and Reynivallaháls with a single mountain, Meðalfell, in the centre. A well-cultivated area with trout and salmon rivers.

48 **Kjósarskarðsvegur,** p. 224 — **460** **Eyrarfjallsvegur,** p. 224
461 **Meðalfellsvegur,** p. 224

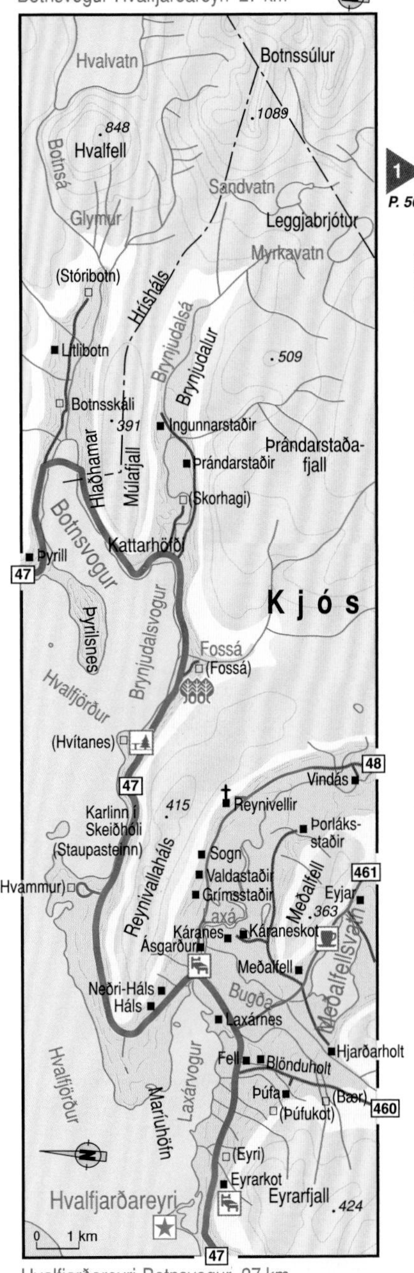

1 P. 564

Glymur

Melahverfi-Botnsvogur 27 km

1 P. 564

Melahverfi, a small village. The first houses were built in the area in 1980 soon after the ferrosilicon factory at Grundartangi started in 1979 by some employees. Even today most inhabitants of Melahverfi work in the Grundartangi area.

Saurbær, a farm, church and parsonage. Hallgrímur Pétursson (1614-74), the author of the *Passíusálmar* ("Passion Hymns"), served there 1651-69 and is buried there. Many local features bear his name, such as Hallgrímslind ("Hallgrímur's fountain") and Hallgrímssteinn ("Hallgrímur's rock"), against which he is said to have sat when composing the *Passíusálmar.* Like Hallgrímskirkja in Reykjavík this church was built in his memory. It is decorated with stained glass windows by the artist Gerður Helgadóttir.

Ferstikla, a roadhouse and a small whale museum.

Miðsandur, formerly a farm which began to grow into a village after the U.S. Navy made its headquarters there during the last war. Many oil tanks. A nearby whaling station.

Geirshólmur, a small steep-sided island where, according to the Sagas, a large band of outlaws hid out under the leadership of Hörður Grímkelsson.

Þyrill, (388 m) a basalt mountain with cliffs on three sides. Some rare kinds of zeolites are found there. Above the farm of the same name there is a steep gully through the cliffs called **Helguskarð** ("Helga's pass") where the Sagas say Helga, daughter of a Norwegian Earl and mistress of the outlaw Hörður Grímkelsson, made her escape along with her two young sons. She climbed up there after swimming with them from Geirshólmur after her lover had been hunted down and killed along with his band of outlaws.

Botnsá, a river in which is the waterfall **Glymur** ("Clamour"), the highest falls in Iceland at 200 m. The river divides the counties Kjósarsýsla and Borgarfjarðarsýsla.

Botnsdalur, a short valley with widespread birch bushes two abandoned farms **Stóribotn** and **Litlibotn**. An old track called Leggjabrjótur ("Leg-breaker") leads from there across to Þingvellir.

Hvalfell, (848 m) tuff mountain. On the east side of Hvalfell is the lake **Hvalvatn** ("Whale lake"), 160 m deep and the second deepest lake in Iceland. There are folktales about a man who betrayed a woman of the "hidden people" by refusing to have their child christened. He was changed into a terrible whale that killed many fishermen, including two brothers whose father was a priest and a "poet of power". He placed poetry spells on the whale forcing it to swim into Hvalfjörður, along the river at its head, up the waterfall Glymur - which brought roars of protest from the whale, and into the lake. It is said that whale bones have been found in the lake.

1 **Vesturlandsvegur,** p. 54
51 **Akrafjallsvegur,** p. 234
502 **Svínadalsvegur,** p. 258
504 **Leirársveitarvegur,** p. 258
520 **Dragavegur,** p. 264

Botnsá

Botnsvogur-Melahverfi 27 km

1
P. 564

Kjósarskarð, a pass between the districts of Kjós and Þingvallasveit. 22 km between Vesturlandsvegur (Highway 1) and Þingvallavegur (Road 36).

Írafell, a farm near the top end of the Kjós district, for which was named Írafells-Móri, a famous ghost of olden times said to be still in evidence now and again, though he was most active at the nearby farm, Möðruvellir in Kjós.

Vindáshlíð, a church site below the mountain Sandfell. YMCA summer camp.

Reynivellir, a church and parsonage.

461 Meðalfellsvegur, 10,7 km.

Meðalfell, ("Middle mountain") a farm since the settlement and a manor farm of old at the foot of a mountain of same name. Summer houses. Fishing in Meðalfell lake.

460 Eyrarfjallsvegur, 11 km.

Kiðafell, a farm since it was originally settled by Svartkell hinn katneski, who later moved to Eyri.

© ÓHS

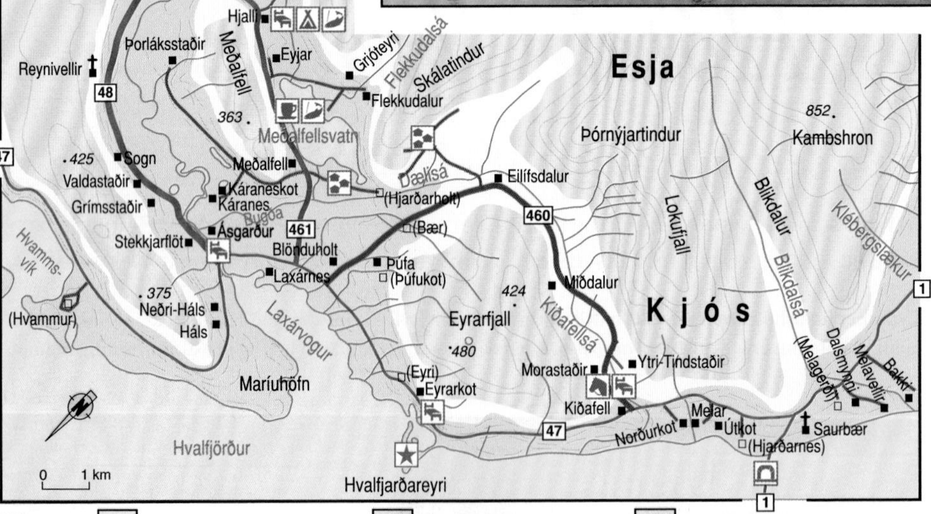

1 **Vesturlandsvegur,** p. 53 36 **Þingvallavegur,** p. 187 47 **Hvalfjarðarvegur,** p. 221

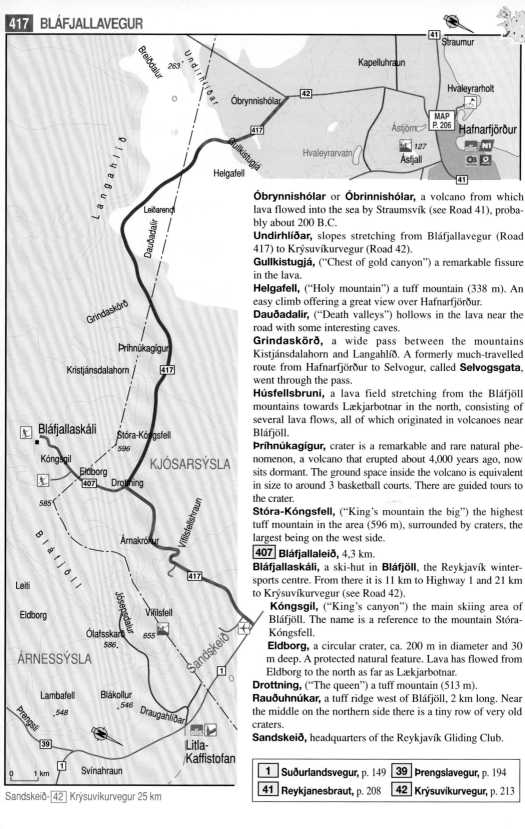

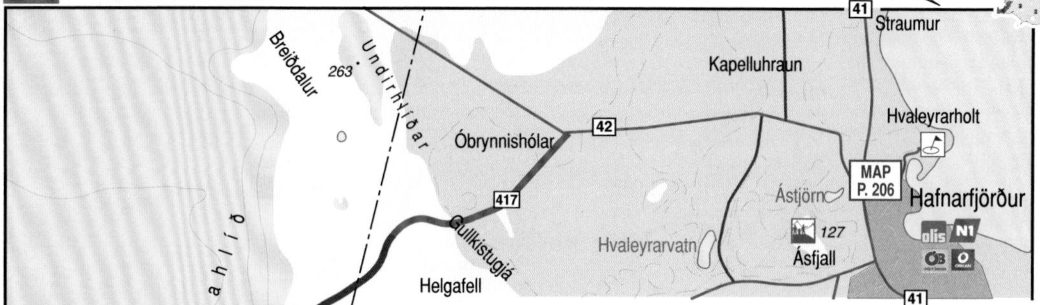

MAP P. 206

1 P. 564

Óbrynnishólar or **Óbrinnishólar,** a volcano from which lava flowed into the sea by Straumsvík (see Road 41), probably about 200 B.C.

Undirhlíðar, slopes stretching from Bláfjallavegur (Road 417) to Krýsuvíkurvegur (Road 42).

Gullkistugjá, ("Chest of gold canyon") a remarkable fissure in the lava.

Helgafell, ("Holy mountain") a tuff mountain (338 m). An easy climb offering a great view over Hafnarfjörður.

Dauðadalir, ("Death valleys") hollows in the lava near the road with some interesting caves.

Grindaskörð, a wide pass between the mountains Kistjánsdalahorn and Langahlíð. A formerly much-travelled route from Hafnarfjörður to Selvogur, called **Selvogsgata,** went through the pass.

Húsfellsbruni, a lava field stretching from the Bláfjöll mountains towards Lækjarbotnar in the north, consisting of several lava flows, all of which originated in volcanoes near Bláfjöll.

Þríhnúkagígur, crater is a remarkable and rare natural phenomenon, a volcano that erupted about 4,000 years ago, now sits dormant. The ground space inside the volcano is equivalent in size to around 3 basketball courts. There are guided tours to the crater.

Stóra-Kóngsfell, ("King's mountain the big") the highest tuff mountain in the area (596 m), surrounded by craters, the largest being on the west side.

407 Bláfjallaleið, 4,3 km.

Bláfjallaskáli, a ski-hut in **Bláfjöll**, the Reykjavík winter-sports centre. From there it is 11 km to Highway 1 and 21 km to Krýsuvíkurvegur (see Road 42).

Kóngsgil, ("King's canyon") the main skiing area of Bláfjöll. The name is a reference to the mountain Stóra-Kóngsfell.

Eldborg, a circular crater, ca. 200 m in diameter and 30 m deep. A protected natural feature. Lava has flowed from Eldborg to the north as far as Lækjarbotnar.

Drottning, ("The queen") a tuff mountain (513 m).

Rauðuhnúkar, a tuff ridge west of Bláfjöll, 2 km long. Near the middle on the northern side there is a tiny row of very old craters.

Sandskeið, headquarters of the Reykjavík Gliding Club.

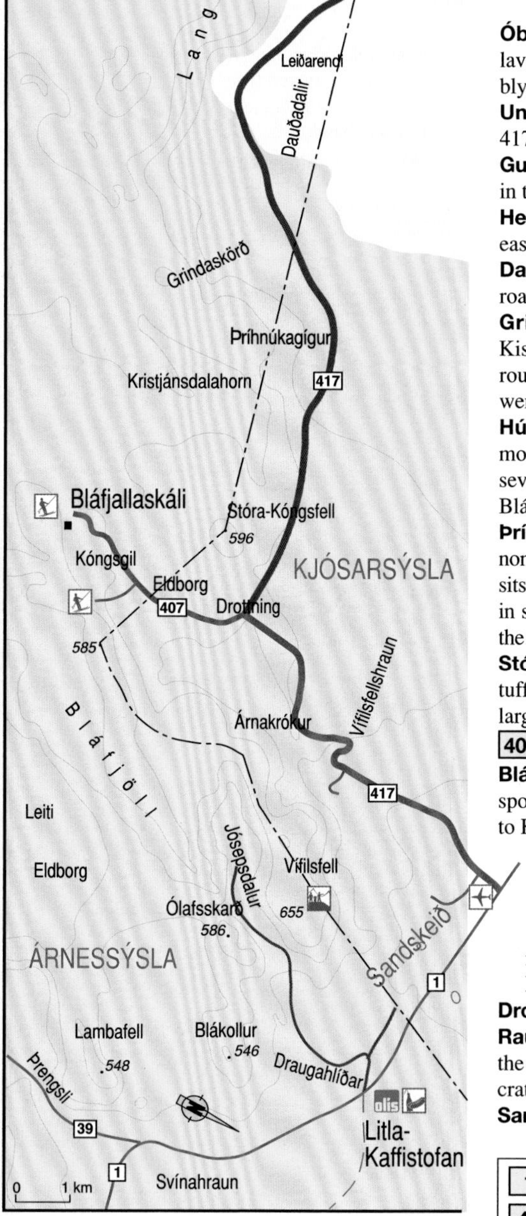

Sandskeið-42 Krýsuvíkurvegur 25 km

1 Suðurlandsvegur, p. 149	**39 Þrengslavegur,** p. 194
41 Reykjanesbraut, p. 208	**42 Krýsuvíkurvegur,** p. 213

1 P. 564

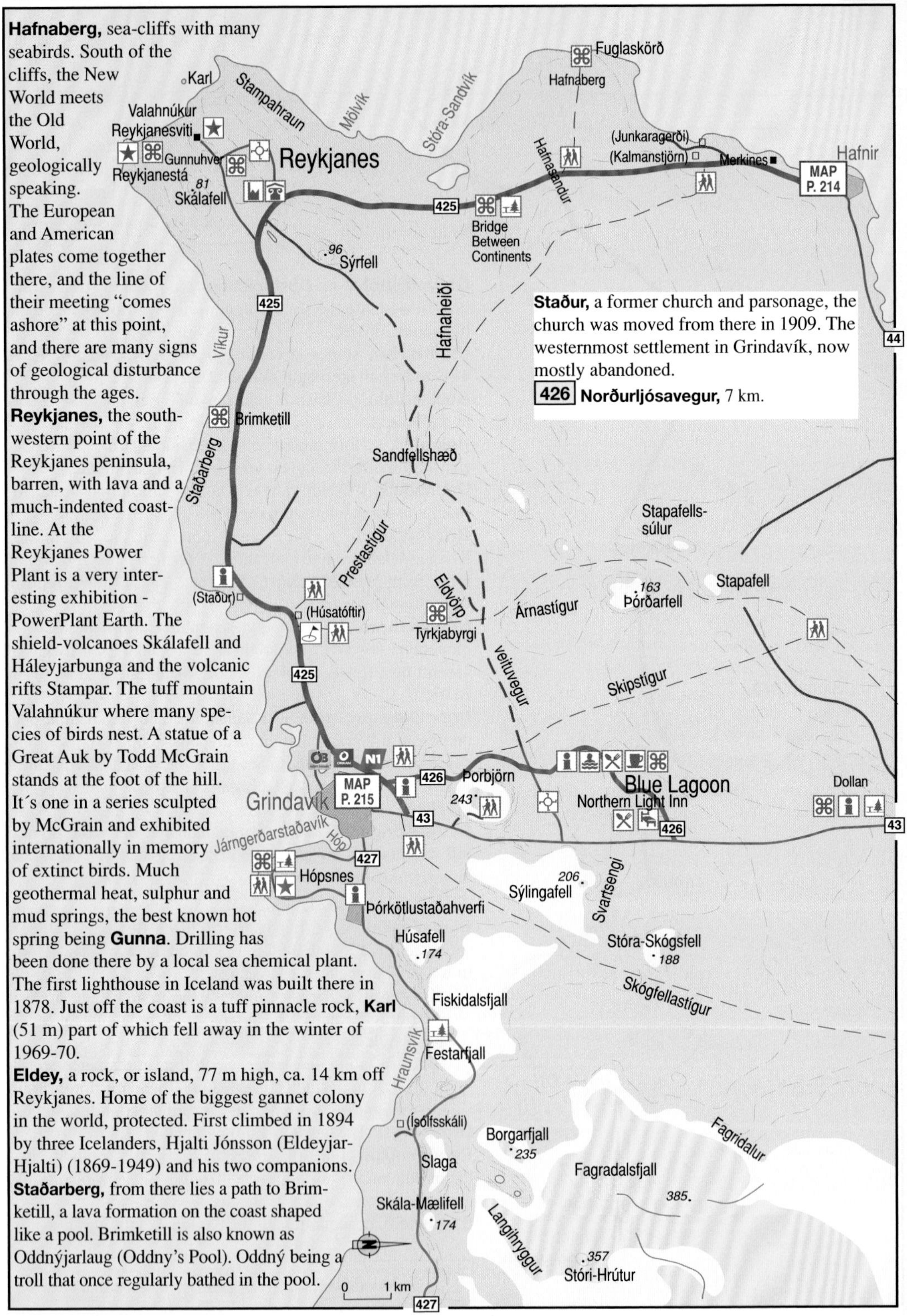

Hafnaberg, sea-cliffs with many seabirds. South of the cliffs, the New World meets the Old World, geologically speaking. The European and American plates come together there, and the line of their meeting "comes ashore" at this point, and there are many signs of geological disturbance through the ages.

Reykjanes, the south-western point of the Reykjanes peninsula, barren, with lava and a much-indented coast-line. At the Reykjanes Power Plant is a very interesting exhibition - PowerPlant Earth. The shield-volcanoes Skálafell and Háleyjarbunga and the volcanic rifts Stampar. The tuff mountain Valahnúkur where many species of birds nest. A statue of a Great Auk by Todd McGrain stands at the foot of the hill. It´s one in a series sculpted by McGrain and exhibited internationally in memory of extinct birds. Much geothermal heat, sulphur and mud springs, the best known hot spring being **Gunna**. Drilling has been done there by a local sea chemical plant. The first lighthouse in Iceland was built there in 1878. Just off the coast is a tuff pinnacle rock, **Karl** (51 m) part of which fell away in the winter of 1969-70.

Eldey, a rock, or island, 77 m high, ca. 14 km off Reykjanes. Home of the biggest gannet colony in the world, protected. First climbed in 1894 by three Icelanders, Hjalti Jónsson (Eldeyjar-Hjalti) (1869-1949) and his two companions.

Staðarberg, from there lies a path to Brimketill, a lava formation on the coast shaped like a pool. Brimketill is also known as Oddnýjarlaug (Oddny's Pool). Oddný being a troll that once regularly bathed in the pool.

Staður, a former church and parsonage, the church was moved from there in 1909. The westernmost settlement in Grindavík, now mostly abandoned.

426 Norðurljósavegur, 7 km.

Karl
Valahnúkur
Reykjanesviti
Gunnuhver
Reykjanestá
81
Skálafell
Stampahraun
Mölvík
Stóra-Sandvík
Reykjanes
Fuglaskörð
Hafnaberg
Hafnasandur
(Junkaragerði)
(Kalmanstjörn)
Merkines
Hafnir
MAP P. 214
425
Bridge Between Continents
96
Sýrfell
425
Hafnaheiði
44
Víkur
Brimketill
Staðarberg
Sandfellshæð
Stapafells-súlur
Prestastígur
Eldvörp
163
Þórðarfell
Stapafell
(Staður)
(Húsatóftir)
Árnastígur
Tyrkjabyrgi
425
Skipstígur
Eldvörp-veituvegur
Grindavík
MAP P. 215
426
Þorbjörn
243
Blue Lagoon
Northern Light Inn
Dollan
43
43
426
Járngerðarstaðavík
Hóp
427
Hópsnes
Þórkötlustaðahverfi
206
Sýlingafell
Svartsengi
Húsafell
174
Stóra-Skógsfell
188
Skógfellastígur
Fiskidalsfjall
Festarfjall
Hraunsvík
(Ísólfsskáli)
Borgarfjall
235
Fagridalur
Slaga
Fagradalsfjall
385
Skála-Mælifell
174
Langihryggur
357
Stóri-Hrútur
0 1 km
427

43 **Grindavíkurvegur,** p. 216 | 44 **Hafnavegur,** p. 219 | 427 **Suðurstrandarvegur,** p. 228

427 SUÐURSTRANDAVEGUR

Stóra-Eldborg and **Litla-Eldborg,** two nicely shaped craters off the highway to the south of the mountain **Geitahlíð**. There is also a large crater on Geitahlíð. Eldborg is a protected natural feature.

Herdísarvík, formerly a substantial farm with much seafishing. The craggy mountain Herdísarvíkurfjall, from which much lava has flowed, above the farm. The poet Einar Benediktsson (1864-1940) lived there in later life, and died there. He is buried in the national graveyard at Þingvellir. Herdísarvík is now owned by the University of Iceland.

Brennisteinsfjöll, ("Sulphur mountains") a mountain ridge in the Reykjanes range, whence much lava has flowed all the way into the sea at Herdísarvík. It poured down from high ground, forming rocky cascades. Formerly this lava was thought to have flowed before the settlement of Iceland, but riding-trails have since been found that continue under the lava, so some of it must be younger than that. In the late 19th century the Scot W.G. Spence Paterson, for a time teacher at the Möðruvellir school and later British consul at Hafnarfjörður, started sulphur-mining east of the mountains but this never paid. The popular route between Hafnarfjörður and Selvogur once went via **Grindaskörð** and east of the mountains.

Hlíðarvatn, a good fishing lake.

Vogsósar, near Hlíðarvatn in Selvogur. Formerly a parsonage. Best known for the clergyman-sorcerer Eiríkur Magnússon (1638-1715).

Strandarkirkja, ("Coast church") a church in Selvogur, now far from farms and the only remains of the once flourishing community Strönd ("Coast"), at one time the home of some of the richest and most powerful men in Iceland. It is popularly believed that this church has a special power to aid success or good luck. Many gifts are therefore donated to it in connection with people's hopes and fears. It is one of the richest churches in the country.

Selvogur, the westernmost settlement in Árnessýsla. Formerly a thriving fishing centre, now much eroded by sand.

Kvenngönguhólar, ("Women walk hills") at Kaldraðanes, p. 179, there was a holy cross there which people came from all over to see and touch. When the women at Selvogur couldn´t go to the cross the walked to Kvenngönguhólar to look over to Kaldraðanes, hence the name.

38 **Þorlákshafnarvegur,** p. 192 | 42 **Krýsuvíkurvegur,** p. 213

Krýsuvík-Hlíðardalsskóli 42 km

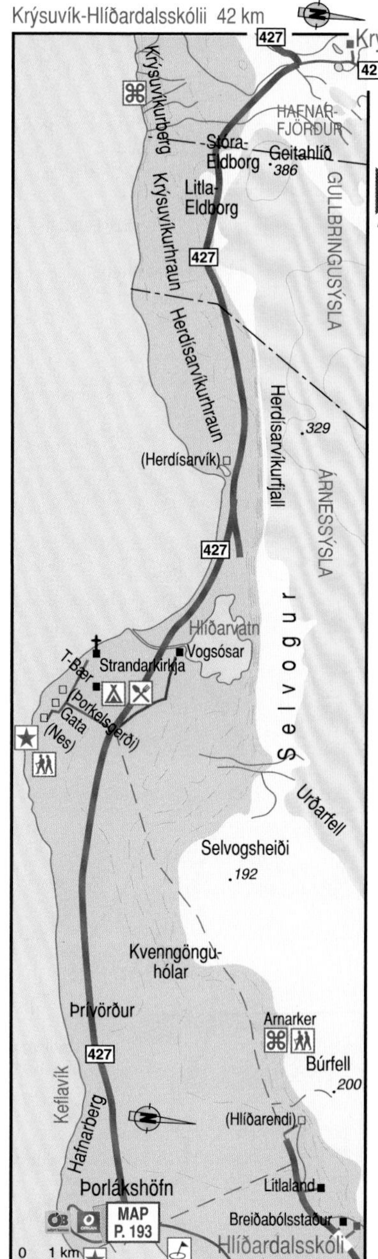

Hlíðardalsskóli-Krýsuvík 42 km

1 P. 564

Strandarkirkja

1
P. 564

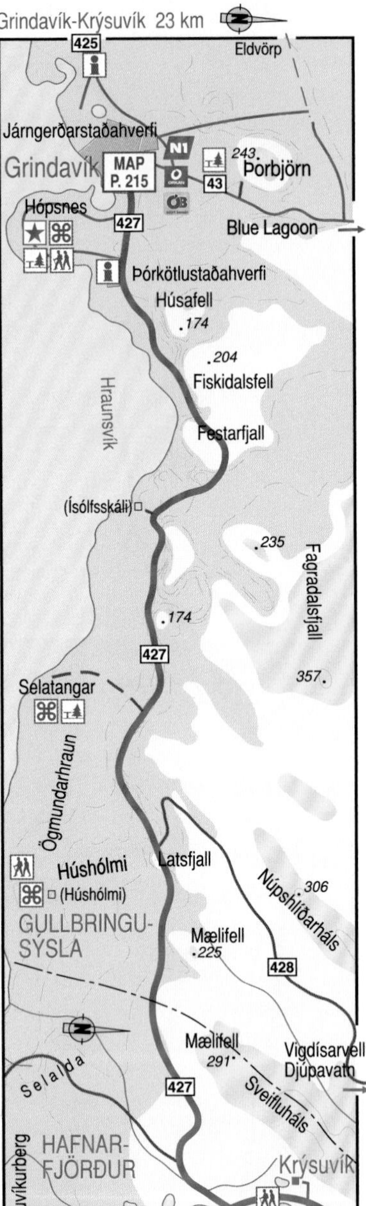

Krýsuvík-Grindavík 23 km

Grindavík, (pop. 3,214) a fishing village that became a market town in 1974. The town consists of three main areas: **Þórkötlustaðahverfi**, **Járngerðarstaðahverfi**, now the main part of town; and **Staðarhverfi** to the far west, which today is mostly deserted. Information signs in each area document its history. Entering the harbour remains a challenge for sailors, despite extensive improvements there. Nonetheless, this harbour has been used for fishing for centuries, and contributed greatly to the wealth of the bishop at Skálholt. The peninsula of Reykjanes was so important for fishing and trade that the English and Germans fought there over the most sheltered places for boats. This struggle climaxed on June 11th 1532, when the Germans allied with some natives and killed about 20 Englishmen. This event marked a turning point in Iceland's commercial history, ending an era of English dominance. Main industries: fishing and fish processing. The Saltfish Museum celebrates the history of salted cod in Iceland. The town has a church, compulsory school, community centre and swimming pool. There is a monument to drowned sailors by Ragnar Kjartansson, while glass art by Einar Lárusson depicts the historical raid here by Muslim pirates. A local thistle, Cirsium arvense, is otherwise rare in Iceland; it is said that it first appeared when the blood of the Muslim pirates mixed with that of the Christians. The French trawler Cap Fragnet stranded by Þórkötlustaðahverfi in 1931. For the first time in history, a line thrower was used in order to reach the crew and rescue 38 people.

Festarfjall, (190 m) the remains of an old volcano, taking its name from **Festi**, a basalt column that goes through the mountain.

Fagradalsfjall, there Frank M. Andrew, commander of US troops in Europe, along with 13 others was killed when his airplain crashed into the mountain in May 1943.

Selatangar, protected remains of an old fishing-station on the coast south of the Núpshlíðarháls ridge. The ghost Tanga-Tómas, or Tumi, was said to haunt the place.

Ögmundarhraun, a lava field believed to have flowed in 1151 from a row of craters between the ridges Núpshlíðarháls and Sveifluháls.

Húshólmi and Óbrennishólmi, situated in the Ögmundarhraun lava field, above Hólmasund strait, in the westernmost section of the Krýsuvíkurbjarg cliffs, just west of Selatangi point. The Húshólmi and Óbrennishólmi sites exhibit ancient ruins, houses and gardens, sometimes called Old Krýsuvík. There are indications that there once was a church on the site as well. The ruins are thought to be from the earliest years of Iceland's settlement. The Ögmundarhraun lava field flooded the area in the 12th century, covering the settlement. Today one can still see the remnants of three houses and a church, as well as large gardens, a stone sheep enclosure and a shepherd's hut. Access to Húsahólmi is good for hikers. It is also possible to drive to the location in off-road vehicles. The hike from Ísólfsskálavegur road begins at the signpost for Húsahólmi, continuing down along the edge of the lava field until the Húshólmastígur hiking path is reached, then continuing about 1.1 km east through the lava field. The entire hike from Ísólfsskálavegur road takes about one hour.

Krýsuvík, ancient manor farm see p. 213.

Grænavatn, ("Green lake") a lake in an explosion crater, 44 m deep. Another old crater also with water, Gestsstaðavatn, on other side of the road.

Sveifluháls, a tuff ridge, maximum height 397 m, which drops in steep cliffs down to the Kleifarvatn lake. At the south end of Sveifluháls is a lone peak, **Mælifell** (225 m).

Krýsuvíkurberg, a cliff by the sea where thousands of sea birds nest. A track leads to the cliff. To the west of Selalda are a row of cliffs known as The Boys. Beneath them is a lovely pasture and old sheep shelter.

42 **Krýsuvíkurvegur,** p. 213
43 **Grindavíkurvegur,** p. 216
425 **Nesvegur,** p. 226
428 **Vigdísarvallavegur,** p. 213

50 BORGARFJARÐARBRAUT

Kljáfoss, a waterfall in the river Hvítá. A bridge. There are records of a bridge there from the Sturlunga age in the 13th century.
Deildartunga, a manor farm, now and in ages past.
555 Deildartunguvegur, 0,6 km.
Deildartunguhver, this hot water spring is protected by conservation laws and is the most powerful hot spring in Iceland, with 200 l/sec. of 100°C hot water, supplying the towns of Borgarnes and Akranes with hot water. The only place in Iceland where a variety of hard fern (*Blechnum spicant* var. *fallax*) is found. Closeby is Krauma, a natural hot spring spa where the water is used in bathing pools and a sauna. It has changing facilities, a restaurant and souvenir shop.
Reykjadalsá, a calm, winding river flowing through the Reykholtsdalur valley.
Kleppjárnsreykir, (pop. 42) a community where there is hot-house cultivation using heat from one of Borgarfjörður's bigger hot springs, 70 l/sec.
Stóri-Kroppur, a farm below Kroppsmúli spur. Airstrip.
Flókadalur, a broad, grassy valley, actually two, down which flow the rivers **Flóka** and **Geirsá**.
Flókadalsá, or Flóka, a river flowing out of Flókadalur.
Varmalækur, the settlement land of Óleifur hjalti. For a time the home of Hallgerður langbrók ("long-breeches") and her husband Glúmur (*Njáls saga*).
Varmalækjarmúli, a steep spur at the end of the Lundarháls ridge.
Blundsvatn, a rather big lake, though shallow, in the Bæjarsveit district.
Bæjarsveit, flatlands between the rivers Grímsá and Flóka. Marshy but grassy with low ridges.
Fossatún, restaurant and accomodation. Beautiful walking routes and views.
Grímsá, a sizeable river flowing down the Lundarreykjadalur valley into Hvítá. Good fishing. Some low waterfalls.
Hestur, a former church and parsonage. Now an experimental sheep breeding station.
Hestfjall, (221 m) a jagged mountain above Hestur.

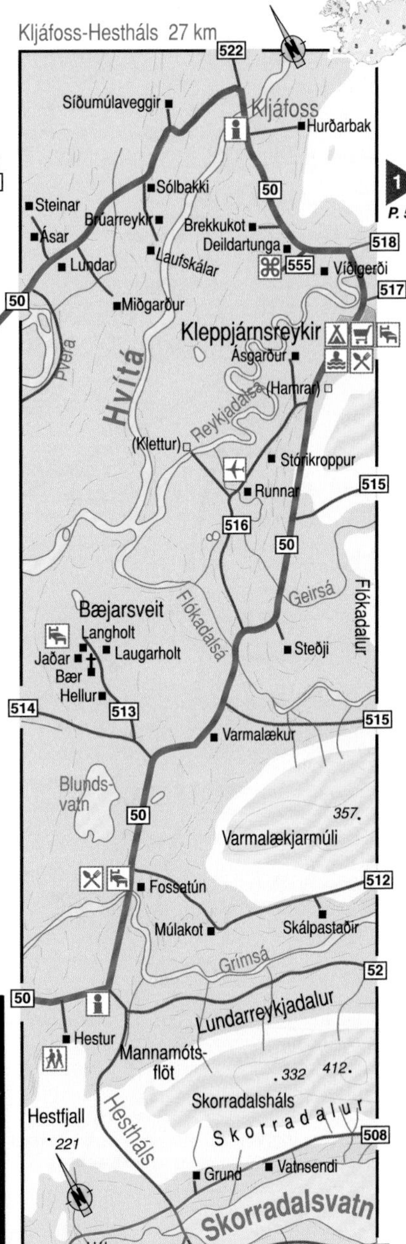

1 Vesturlandsvegur, p. 58
52 Uxahryggjavegur, p. 237
508 Skorradalsvegur, p. 259
513 Bæjarsveitarvegur, p. 260
515 Flókadalsvegur, p. 260
517 Reykdælavegur, p. 261
520 Dragavegur, p. 264
507 Mófellsstaðavegur, p. 259
512 Lundareykjadalsvegur, p. 237
514 Laugarholtsvegur, p. 260
516 Stóra-Kroppsvegur, p. 260
518 Hálsasveitarvegur, p. 261
522 Þverárhlíðarvegur, p. 265

Borgir-Kljáfoss 14 km

P. 564

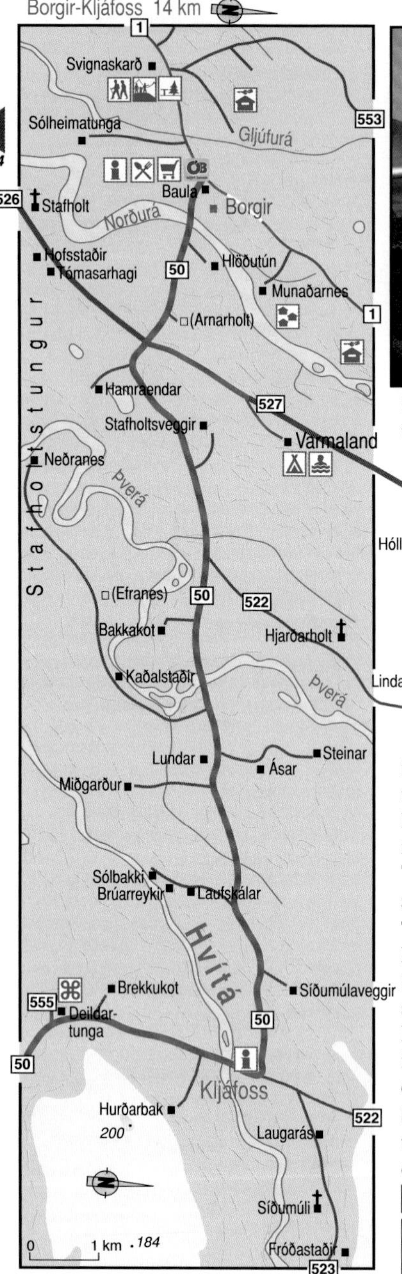

Kljáfoss-Borgir 14 km

By Deildartunguhver

© Andreas G

Norðurá, a river originating up on Holtavörðuheiði moor and flowing through the Norðurárdalur valley and the Stafholtstungur district into the river Hvítá. It is smooth, deep and navigable lower down. Good salmon fishing. In Norðurá are the waterfalls **Laxfoss** and **Glanni**.

Stafholtstungur, three tongues of land between the rivers Gljúfurá, Norðurá, Þverá and Hvítá. Stony ridges, mostly marshy in between, though the westernmost tongue has a lot of birch bushes.

Arnarholt, a farm in the Stafholtstungur district. A nearby grove of coniferous trees was planted around 1910.

526 Stafholtsvegur, 6 km. **527 Varmalandsvegur,** 13,9 km.

Varmaland, a school centre built by the big hot spring at the farm Stafholtsveggir. The Borgarfjörður school of domestic science was there for years, the building now housing a middle school. Extensive hot-house cultivation. Mushroom production was first started in Iceland at the nearby farm, **Laugaland**, whose buildings now belong to the Icelandic Teacher's Training College.

Stafholt, a church and parsonage in the lower Stafholtstungur district. The church was built 1875-77. Lignite is found at Stafholtskastali by the Norðurá river.

Hjarðarholt, a farm and church, long the home of men of influence and a site of official gatherings. For a time it was the residence of the county of Mýrasýsla sheriffs, one of whom died of exposure right by the farmstead in a dreadful winter storm. At a church conference in 1684 a man was condemned and burnt at the stake (1685) for blasphemy.

Þverá, a clear river formed from several rivers and streams coming from the lakes on the Tvídægra moors. Considered to be one of the best salmon-fishing rivers in Iceland.

555 Deildartunguvegur, 0,6 km.

1 Vesturlandvegur, p. 58	**522 Þverárhlíðarvegur,** p. 265
523 Hvítársíðuvegur, p. 265	**553 Langavatnsvegur,** p. 269

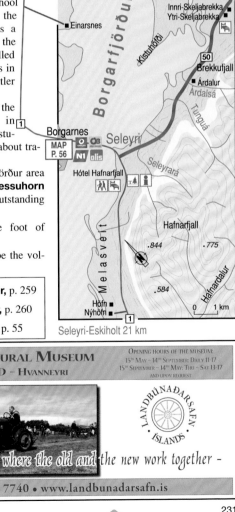

Eskiholt-Seleyri 21 km

Skallagrímsgarður, Borgarnes

Hvítárvellir, a manor farm now and of old, having the best salmon-fishing in Borgarfjörður. Often the home of men of influence. At the beginning of the 20th century the home of the French baron Boilleau, one street in Reykjavík, Barónsstígur, being called after him. In 1859 James Ritchie, a Scotsman, established a cannery at Hvítárvellir and operated it for several years. In the old days markets were held at Hvítárvellir, as ships could be sailed that far upstream.

511 Hvanneyrarvegur, 2,5 km. **510 Hvítárvallavegur,** 10 km.

Hvanneyri, (pop. 272) a substantial farm and a farming school since 1889. The Agricultural Museum of Iceland and the Agricultural University of Iceland from 2005. Ullarselið is a store offering quality woolen goods made locally Some of the best grass-land in Iceland is there, especially in the so-called Hvanneyrarfit. When the college was started many small farms in the surrounding area were taken under Hvanneyri. The first settler at Hvanneyri was Grímur háleyski.

Andakílsárvirkjun, a power station built in 1947 when falls in the river **Andakílsá** were harnessed. Water reservoir in Skorradalsvatn. Hespuhúsið (Wool Dyeing Centre) is an open studio specializing in the dyeing of wool. Here one can learn all about traditional methods of colouring wool.

Skarðsheiði, a high mountain range dominating the Borgarfjörður area on the south side. Highest point **Heiðarhorn,** (1,053 m). **Skessuhorn** ("Giantess' peak") (963 m) is a particularly impressive and outstanding peak when the range is viewed from the north.

Innri-Skeljabrekka and **Ytri-Skeljabrekka,** farms at the foot of Brekkufjall mountain.

Brekkufjall, (409 m) a solid basalt mountain, considered to be the volcanic plug of what was once a volcano.

1 Vesturlandsvegur, p. 55
508 Skorradalsvegur, p. 259
526 Stafholtsvegur, p. 230
507 Mófellsstaðavegur, p. 259
514 Laugarholtsvegur, p. 260
530 Ferjubakkavegur, p. 55

Seleyri-Eskiholt 21 km

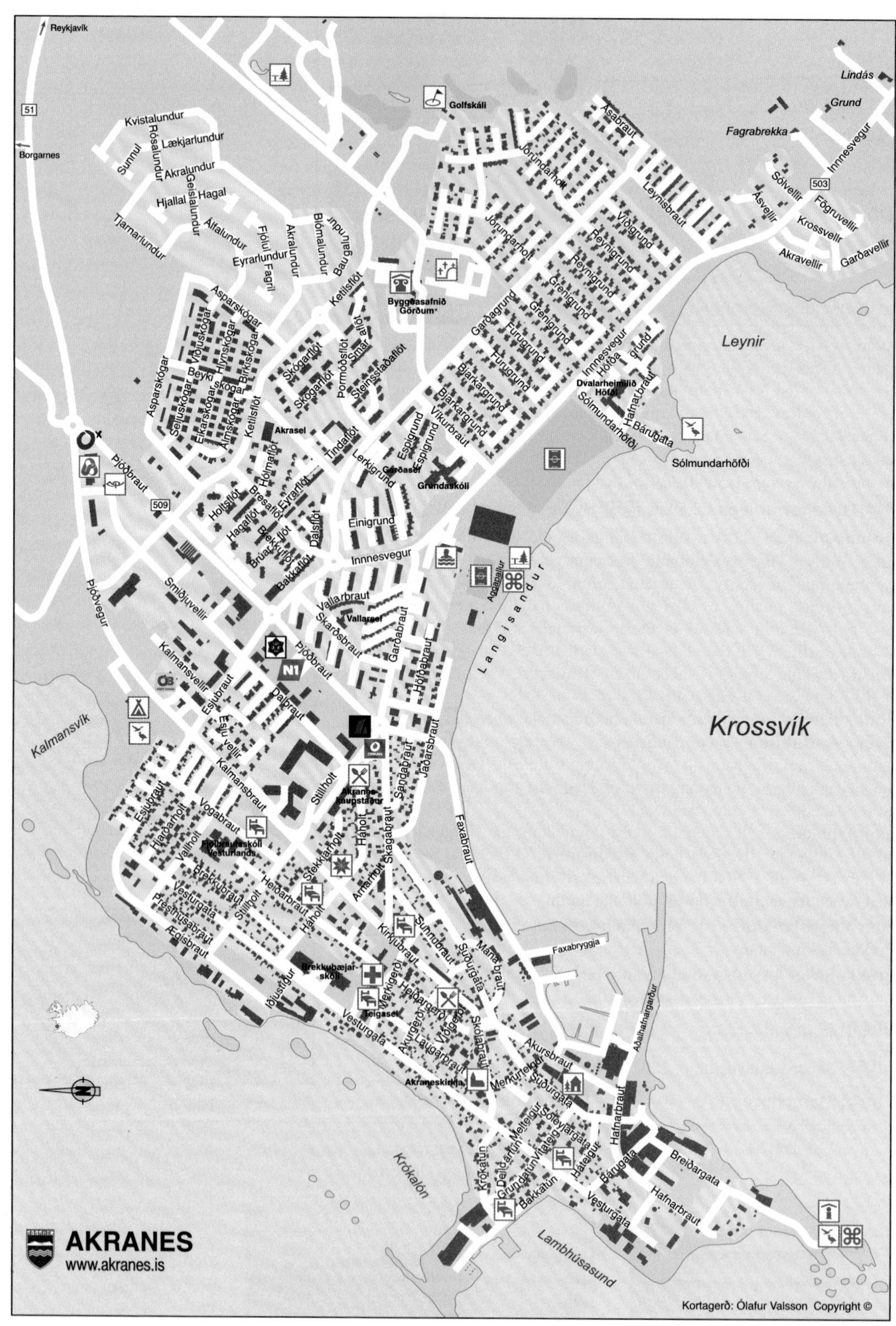

Reykjavík
Borgarnes
51
509
503
Golfskáli
Lindás
Grund
Fagrabrekka
Innnesvegur
Kvistalundur
Rósalundur
Lækjarlundur
Sunnul
Akralundur
Geislalundur
Hjallal
Hagal
Tjarnarlundur
Álfalundur
Eyrarlundur
Fjóluf
Fagril
Akralundur
Blómalundur
Baugalundur
Ketilsflöt
Byggðasafnið Görðum
Jörundarholt
Ásabraut
Leynisbraut
Viðigrund
Reynigrund
Sólvellir
Ásvellir
Fögruvellir
Krossvellir
Akravellir
Garðavellir
Leynir
Asparskógar
Víðiskógar
Hlynskógar
Beyki
Birkiskógar
Seljuskógar
Eikarskógar
Álmskógar
Skógarflöt
Pormóðsflöt
Smáraflöt
Steinsstaðaflöt
Garðagrund
Furugrund
Grenigrund
Bjarkargrund
Höfðagrund
Dvalarheimilið Höfði
Sólmundarhöfði
Hafnarbraut
Bárugata
Akrasel
Tindaflöt
Lerkigrund
Espigrund
Víkurbraut
Garðasel
Grundaskóli
Þjóðbraut
Hólmaflöt
Holtsflöt
Bresaflöt
Eyrarflöt
Hagaflöt
Brekkuflöt
Dalsflöt
Bakkaflöt
Einigrund
Innnesvegur
Smiðjuvellir
Þjóðvegur
Vallarbraut
Vallarsel
Skarðsbraut
Garðabraut
Höfðabraut
Aggapallur
Langisandur
Kalmansvellir
Esjubraut
Dalbraut
N1
Kalmansvík
Krossvík
Kalmansbraut
Stillholt
Akranes kaupstaður
Sandabraut
Jaðarsbraut
Faxabraut
Vogabraut
Hjarðarholt
Vallholt
Fjölbrautaskóli Vesturlands
Stekkjarholt
Háholt
Skagabraut
Brekkubraut
Vesturgata
Presthúsabraut
Ægisbraut
Heiðarbraut
Hánolt
Kirkjubraut
Sunnubraut
Suðurgata
Mánabraut
Faxabryggja
Brekkubæjarskóli
Merkigerði
Heiðargerði
Teigasel
Akurgerði
Laugarbraut
Skólabraut
Akursbraut
Aðalhafnargarður
Akraneskirkja
Merkurteigur
Melteigur
Sóleyjargata
Krókatún
Deildartún
Grundartún
Vitateigur
Háteigur
Bárugata
Breiðargata
Hafnarbraut
Krókalón
Lambhúsasund
AKRANES
www.akranes.is
Kortagerð: Ólafur Valsson Copyright ©

Akranes

Akranes- 1 Vesturlandsvegur 14 km

P. 564

Akranes, (pop. 7,106) a town, gained municipal rights in 1942. The main activities are fishing, fish processing, commerce and industry. Extensive harbour facilities and lighthouses. If you are into photography or just interested in exploring new things in Iceland you need to look at Akranes lighthouses. Down by the harbour you will notice two lighthouses. The bigger one that is currently in use is open to the public so you can go up and enjoy the view from there and there is even a photography exhibition to enjoy in there and an information centre. There you will find a hospital, secondary school, trade school, sports stadium, guesthouses, hostel, hotels, restaurants, grocery stores. As well as being an important fisheries centre, Akranes has repeatedly made its name in sports, both nationally and even internationally. You will find both outdoor and indoor swimming pools, football grounds, a sports stadium, a busy 18-hole golf course, an outdoor shooting range and a popular outdoor recreation area. On Akratorg square is the sculpture *Memorial to sailors*, by Marteinn Guðmundsson and in front of the old people's home, *Grettir's challenge* by Magnús Tómasson. Row boat fishing started there centuries ago and there was some sort of village already in the 17th century.

Garðar, former parsonage, church and manor farm. Now part of Akranes. The Akranes Museum Centre in Garðar comprises the highly interesting Iceland´s Museum of Sports and the Akranes Folk Museum with innumerable items of very great interest. The Centre has been much acclaimed by both Icelanders and foreign visitors. The local folk museum is partly housed in the former parsonage which was built in 1871, of concrete blocks and cement, the first house in Iceland built by this method.

Blautós and **Innsta-Vogsnes,** a nature reserve at the north western rim of the town Akranes. It is rich with bird life, vegetation and interesting geological formations from the last glacial period. Many migration birds stop there on their quest to Canada. One being the brant gees. It is estimated that a quarter of the species stop there and in Grunnafjörður on their route from Ireland. There are also eider duck breeding grounds there. Eider farmers collect eiderdown there as the have for centuries.

Akrafjall, (643 m) a mountain between Hvalfjörður and Grunnafjörður, the nesting place of huge numbers of gulls. An outlawed thief spent the summer on the mountain in 1756. Farmers formed a search party to look for him in the autumn, but he sneaked himself into the search party and helped them search, thus avoiding capture.

503 Innnesvegur, 4,9 km.

Reynir, a farm, the home of farmer Jón Hreggviðsson, made famous by Halldór Laxness in the novel *Íslandsklukkan*.

Innri-Hólmur, a parsonage and substantial farm. For a time home of the Governor Ólafur Stefánsson and his son, Chief Justice Magnús Stephensen, who later moved to Viðey.

509 Akranesvegur, 2,5 km. **501 Innrahólmsvegur,** 3,1 km.

506 Grundartangavegur, 2,5 km.

Grundartangi, a ferrosilicon plant belonging to the Icelandic Alloy Co. The plant started production in 1979, for export only. An aluminium plant commenced production 1998.

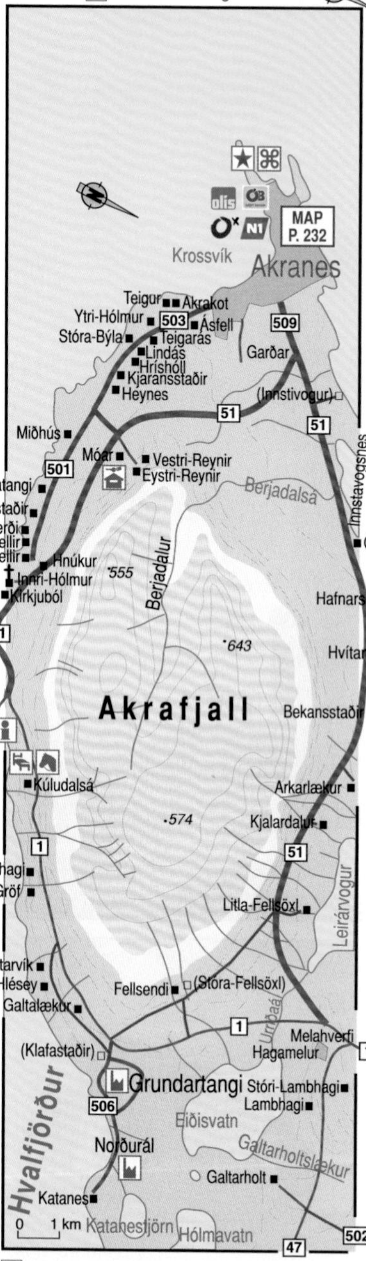

1 Vesturlandsvegur-Akranes 14 km

1 Vesturlandsvegur, p. 53
47 Hvalfjarðarvegur, p. 220
502 Svínadalsvegur, p. 258

Have fun in Akranes this summer

Lots of things to do

A SEASIDE TOWN IN WEST ICELAND

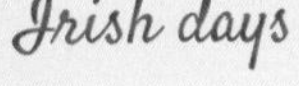

Lively market atmosphere on Saturdays

Spend a day by the sea on Akranes own natural beach Langisandur

Akranes lighthouse open all summer

Sea angling

Blacksmiths and exhibitionsin in the Museum Centre this summer

Spiffy stores
Varied ways to stay
Regular good restaurants

Akrafjall, the natural treasure of Akranes!

Garðalundur
Barbecue
Frisbee-golf and a playground

All kind of activity
Cozy Coffehouses
All in Akranes

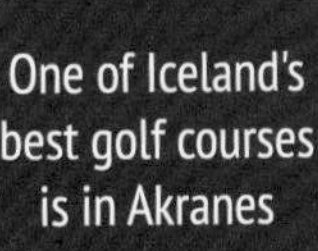

One of Iceland's best golf courses is in Akranes

Come golfing

www.visitakranes.is / www.akranes.is
You find us on Twitter, Facebook and Instagram

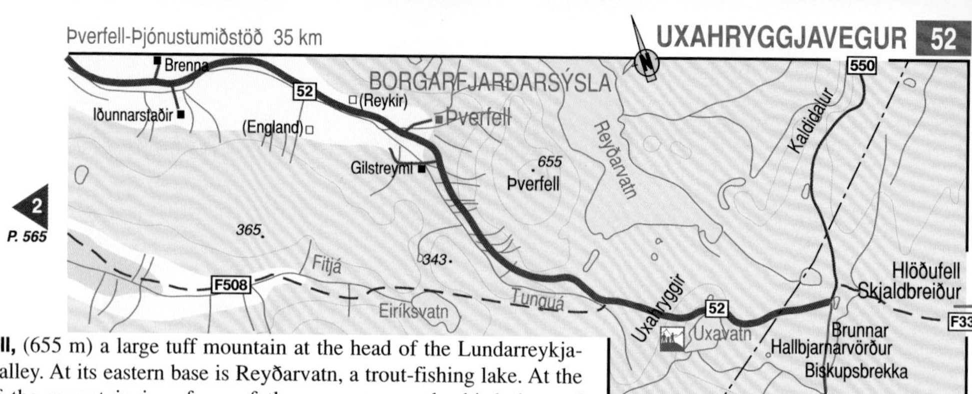

Þverfell, (655 m) a large tuff mountain at the head of the Lundarreykjadalur valley. At its eastern base is Reyðarvatn, a trout-fishing lake. At the foot of the mountain is a farm of the same name, the birthplace of Kristmann Guðmundsson (1901-83), novelist. He lived in Norway for years and wrote a great many novels in Norwegian. His books have been translated into many languages.

Uxahryggjaleið, the route along the stony ridge, Uxahryggir ("Ox ridge"), alongside the Uxavatn lake. View dial.

Kvígindisfell, (786 m) an easy mountain to climb, rewarded with an impressive panoramic view.

Brunnar, an old resting place.

Hallbjarnarvörður, stony mounds with cairns on them, on the Sæluhúshæðir hills. *Landnámabók* ("The Book of Settlements") mentions battles there.

Biskupsbrekka, ("Bishop's slope") a grassy slope beside the road where there is a memorial to Bishop Jón Vídalín, who died there in 1720 on his way to a funeral.

Víðiker, a natural hollow north and west of the Tröllháls ridge. A jeep-track goes west from there to the Hvalvatn lake.

Skjaldbreiður, (1,060 m) an evenly-shaped shield volcano with a large, deep crater, about 300 m in diameter.

Hofmannaflöt, a grassy area east of the mountain Ármannsfell. A track leads from there east through the Goðaskarð pass and north of the Tindaskagi mountains to the mountain Skriða (1,005 m) and to Hlöðuvellir fields. From **Hlöðuvellir** there is also a track south across Rótarsandur sands and the mountain Miðdalsfjall to the Laugardalur valley (see Road 37). It is possible to drive round Hlöðufell. Tourist hut at Hlöðuvellir.

Meyjarsæti, a cone shaped hill by Hofmannaflöt, the passes on both sides are of the brand are Sandkluftir.

Ármannsfell, (768 m) a tuff mountain north of Þingvellir. Below it to the south is **Bolabás,** ("Bulls' stall") where horse races took place.

550 **Kaldadalsvegur,** a road between Þingvellir and Húsafell.

36 **Þingvallavegur,** p. 188 | 361 **Vallarvegur,** p. 188
362 **Efrivallavegur,** p. 188 | 550 **Kaldadalsvegur,** p. 462-463
F508 **Skorradalsv.,** p. 237 | F338 **Skjaldbreiðarvegur,** p. 460-461

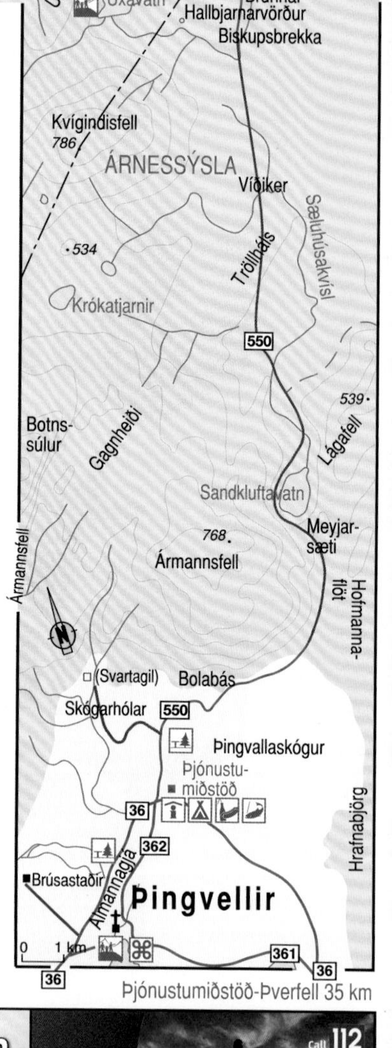

52 UXAHRYGGJAVEGUR

Götuás, there is the junction of Uxahryggjavegur.

Lundarreykjadalur, a valley, ca. 28 km long, rather narrow, between the ridges Skorradalsháls and Lundarháls. It splits at its head to either side of the mountain Tungufell. Grassy but marshy.

Skorradalsháls, a ca. 28 km long ridge from the Kýrmúli spur and in as far as Eiríksvatn. Mostly over 300 m high. Not an old place-name, but sections of it are derived from the names of local farms. For example, Krossöxl ("Cross shoulder") above the farm Kross and Kistufell a little farther on. Above Skarð is Skarðshnöttur with two side-valleys: Skarðsdalur and Tötradalur.

Grímsá, a river flowing from the Reyðarvatn lake down the Lundarreykjadalur valley in numerous falls and rapids. Farthest down river are the waterfalls Hrísbrekknafoss and Jötnabrúarfoss, which is as far as salmon goes. Higher up are the waterfalls Kleppagilsfoss, Selmýrafoss, Kleppafoss, Kerlingafoss, Kálfsgilsfoss and many others.

512 Lundarreykjadalsvegur, 15 km.

Lundur, a church and former parsonage. Site of an ancient heathen temple. In the winter of 1981 a landslide did some damage to the farm.

Gullberastaðir, a farm originally settled by Björn gullberi ("Gold-carrier").

Krosslaug, ("Cross spring") by the road. Men from western Iceland were baptized there in the year 1000, when Iceland converted to Christianity. After that it was a holy place, reputed to have healing powers.

Brautartunga, a farm, community centre, ancient assembly site. Geothermal heat and hothouse cultivation.

England, a farm, hot springs. Formerly a swimming pool. The story goes that a farmer there used to say that Copenhagen wasn´t the only place where there was an England! This was during the time that Iceland was governed from Copenhagen, and Denmark was the foreign country most familiar to Icelanders.

Reykir, a farm and hot spring area. There was a swimming pool by the hot spring where they taught swimming in the mid-19th century.

F508 Skorradalsvegur, 9,3 km. A beautiful route but only accessible by jeeps.

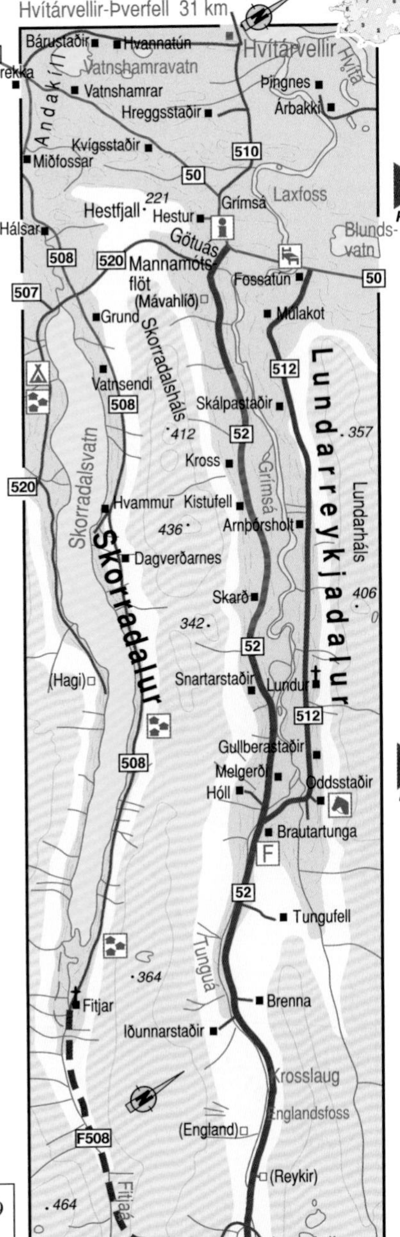

1 P. 564

2 P. 565

50 **Borgarfjarðarbraut,** p. 229

508 **Skorradalsvegur,** p. 259

520 **Dragavegur,** p. 264

507 **Mófellsstaðavegur,** p. 259

510 **Hvítárvallavegur,** p. 231

P. 564

Borgarnes

Álftártunga, farm and church. The church was built with wood in 1795 and part of this structure still remains. It was rebuilt in 1873 and later covered with corrugated iron c. 1900. The church was extensively renovated in 1984-88.

535 Grímsstaðavegur, 12 km.

532 Þursstaðavegur, 4,8 km.

Grímsstaðir, a farm and birth place of Haraldur Níelsson (1863–1928), professor.

Langárfoss, a farm on the northern bank of the Langá river. Waterfalls and rapids in the river. Good salmon-fishing.

Langá, a salmon river, flowing from the Langavatn lake through the Grenjadalur valley. A large salmon-ladder has been installed near the waterfall Sveðjufoss.

Rauðanes, where Skallagrímur had his smithy. He needed a hard, smooth rock to use as an anvil, so he rowed out into the fjord, dived down and found a large boulder, heaved it into the boat and rowed ashore, where he put the boulder outside the door to the smithy. That stone is still in the same place, quite unlike other rocks at Rauðanes, and is thought to need four men to move it.

Borg á Mýrum, **a** church and parsonage. Originally settled by Skallagrímur Kveldúlfsson father of the poet Egill Skallagrímsson of *Egils saga*. Many of his relatives and descendants lived there, including Snorri Sturluson for a time. Tradition has it that Kjartan Ólafsson, one of the main characters of *Laxdæla saga*, is buried there. The sculpture *Sonatorrek* ("Irretrievable Loss of Sons") by Ásmundur Sveinsson (1893-1982), based on the incident in *Egils saga* when Egill Skallagrímsson loses both his sons and eventually composes the long poem, *Sonatorrek*, as a way of dealing with his grief.

536 Stangarholtsvegur, 5,87 km.

1 Vesturlandsvegur, p. 55
533 Álftaneshreppsvegur, p. 266
537 Skíðholtsvegur, p. 266
539 Hítardalsvegur, p. 268

54 SNÆFELLSNESVEGUR

Kolbeinsstaðir, an old manor farm, and the home of many influential men. Church, community centre. The highest peak on the mountain **Kolbeinsstaðafjall**. above the farm is called Tröllakirkja ("Giants' church") (862 m). Another peak is Hrútaborg, with steep crags. A challenging mountain for climbers.

Barnaborgarhraun, a lavafield west of the river Hvítá. The **Barnaborg** crater rises quite high above the lavafield.

Fagraskógarfjall, ("Fair forest mountain") an impressive mountain (644 m) west of the Hítardalur valley. From its western side extends a tuff ridge, **Grettisbæli** ("Grettir's hide-out") where according to the Saga Grettir the strong stayed for a time in a cleft that he roofed over with homespun cloth.

Brúarfoss, ("Bridge falls") a farm on the south bank of the **Hítará** river, by the main road. A waterfall of the same name nearby. There is a bridge over the river there, a fishermen's hut and a summer house. The wrestler and hotellier Jóhannes Jósefsson (1883–1967), called Jóhannes in Borg, who built the Hótel Borg in the centre of Reykjavík, spent many summers there. The story goes that there was once a natural bridge there, a stone arch. A man who had been sentenced to death escaped from his place of execution and ran over the arch, which collapsed into the river as soon as he had reached the other side. This was considered proof of his innocence. There are some unusual pot-holes in the river by Brúarfoss. Grettisstillur, a number of rocks both large and small that lie nearly in single file over the river, can be seen a short distance upstream. According to Grettis Saga, these rocks were put there by the saga strongmen Grettir and Björn Hítadælakappi.

Staðarhraun, a farm, church and once a parsonage. The church contains some old relics, brought there from the church at Hítardalur. A little to the west of Staðarhraun is **Grettisoddi** ("Grettir's point") where Grettir the strong fought alone against great numbers, eventually driving them off after killing 10, mortally wounding 5 and injuring others. He had been on his way to his hide-out on Fagraskógarfjall mountain with stolen cattle.

Melur, birthplace of the Rev. Bjarni Þorsteinsson, composer (1861–1938), famous for collecting Icelandic folk songs and publishing them in the collection *Íslensk Þjóðlög*.

Álftá, ("Swan river") a small clear river, its main source in the Hraundalur valley, running into the Faxaflói bay. Salmon river. Five nearby farms are named for the river.

Urriðaá, ("Sea-trout river") shallow river with its source in Grímsstaðamúli and running into the Langá river.

566 Hítarnesvegur, 7 km.

55 Heydalsvegur, p. 251
535 Grímsstaðavegur, p. 238
537 Skíðholtsvegur, p. 266
540 Hraunhreppsvegur, p. 266
533 Álftaneshreppsvegur, p. 266
536 Stangarholtsvegur, p. 238
539 Hítardalsvegur, p. 268

Kolbeinsstaðir-Álftá 26 km

15 P. 578
1 P. 564

Álftá-Kolbeinsstaðir 26 km

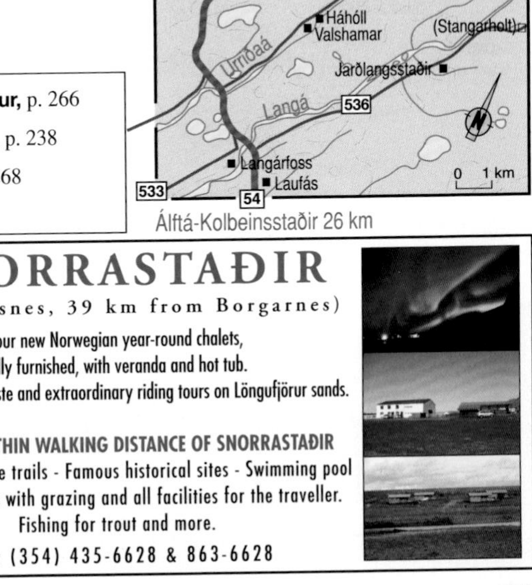

15 P. 578

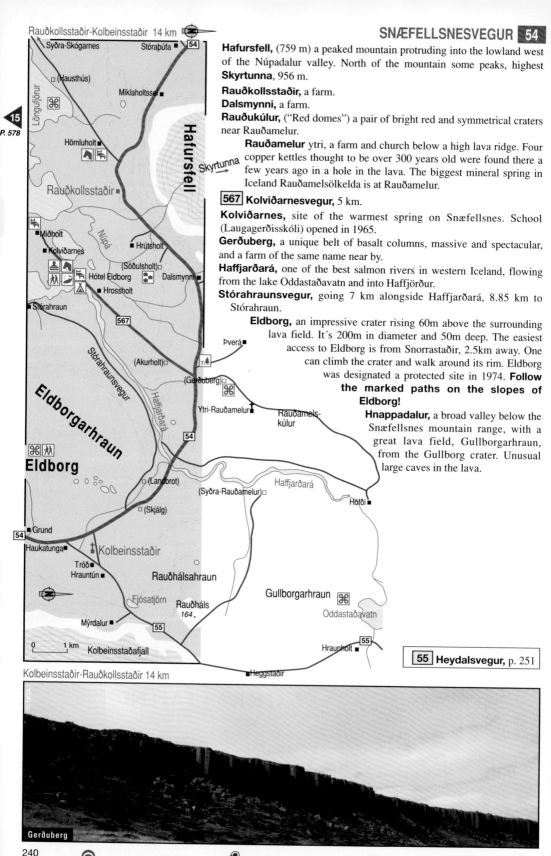

Hafursfell, (759 m) a peaked mountain protruding into the lowland west of the Núpadalur valley. North of the mountain some peaks, highest **Skyrtunna**, 956 m.

Rauðkollsstaðir, a farm.

Dalsmynni, a farm.

Rauðukúlur, ("Red domes") a pair of bright red and symmetrical craters near Rauðamelur.

Rauðamelur ytri, a farm and church below a high lava ridge. Four copper kettles thought to be over 300 years old were found there a few years ago in a hole in the lava. The biggest mineral spring in Iceland Rauðamelsölkelda is at Rauðamelur.

567 Kolviðarnesvegur, 5 km.

Kolviðarnes, site of the warmest spring on Snæfellsnes. School (Laugagerðisskóli) opened in 1965.

Gerðuberg, a unique belt of basalt columns, massive and spectacular, and a farm of the same name near by.

Haffjarðará, one of the best salmon rivers in western Iceland, flowing from the lake Oddastaðavatn and into Haffjörður.

Stórahraunsvegur, going 7 km alongside Haffjarðará, 8.85 km to Stórahraun.

Eldborg, an impressive crater rising 60m above the surrounding lava field. It´s 200m in diameter and 50m deep. The easiest access to Eldborg is from Snorrastaðir, 2.5km away. One can climb the crater and walk around its rim. Eldborg was designated a protected site in 1974. **Follow the marked paths on the slopes of Eldborg!**

Hnappadalur, a broad valley below the Snæfellsnes mountain range, with a great lava field, Gullborgarhraun, from the Gullborg crater. Unusual large caves in the lava.

55 Heydalsvegur, p. 251

Gerðuberg

One of the crater domes at Rauðamelur.

Hofstaðir, a farm just west of the Straumfjarðará river. The poet and naturalist Eggert Ólafsson (1726-68) had meant to live there. He had made improvements to the land, signs of which could still be seen.

Stakkhamar, a farm on the coast. A long reef, Stakkhamarsnes, largely encloses a big lagoon. This is where the Löngufjörur sea sands end, which reach all the way from Hítarnes. Previously a frequently travelled route.

Straumfjarðará, a river flowing from the Baulárvallavatn lake through the valley Dökkólfsdalur. Fishing-river.

Vegamót, ("Crossroads") where the routes to western Snæfellsnes and north across the Vatnaleið pass meet.

Ljósufjöll, the highest mountains on Snæfellsnes, 1,063 m, apart from the glacier, formed of rhyolite. Three pyramid-shaped formations, bare and snowfree on their south side, but with permanent snow on the north.

Fáskrúðarbakki, a church and community centre. The river Fáskrúð nearby.

Miklaholt, a former church and parsonage that was moved to Fáskrúðarbakki. Now a chapel, consecrated in 1946. The oldest existing record of Miklaholt church dates from 1181.

Skógarnes, a farm on the coast. Former trading centre. It was off this coast that the postal steamer *Phönix* stranded in 1881. Strong ebbtide.

Löngufjörur, ("Long beach") sands and mud-flats all along the coast of Hnappadalssýsla from Hítarnes west to Stakkhamar. Light-coloured sand, with low headlands here and there. Shallow and rocky.

56 **Vatnaleið,** p. 253

Hofstaðir-Rauðkollsstaðir 16 km

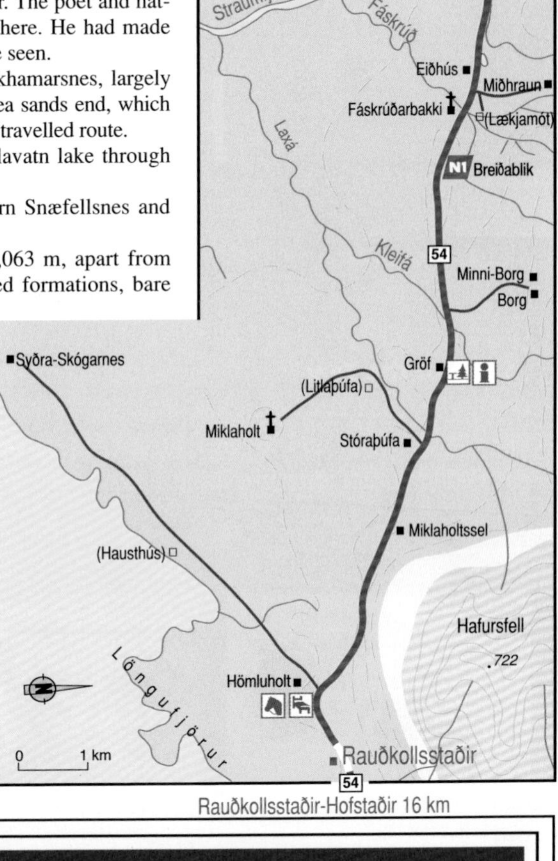

Rauðkollsstaðir-Hofstaðir 16 km

15 P. 578

Bláfeldur-Hofstaðir 27 km

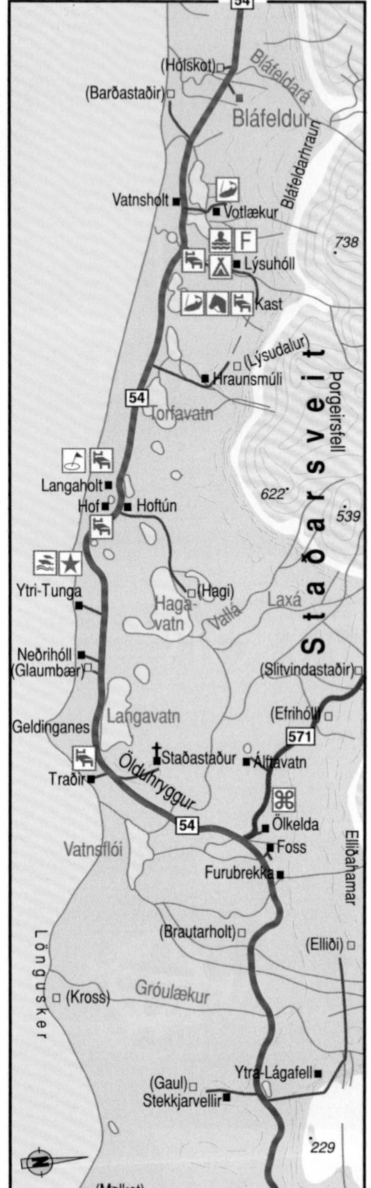

Hofstaðir-Bláfeldur 27 km

Bláfeldur, a farm in Staðarsveit. Now a weather station which is sometimes mentioned in weather news, whereas it can get very windy there.

Bláfeldarskarð, the pass over Bláfeld. An old route to Grundarfjörður.

Bláfeldarhraun, a lava field that flowed from the crater Rauðkúla, on the edge of the mountains.

Lýsuhóll, a farm in the Staðarsveit district. There is a warm mineral spring, one of few in the world. The water is use in the swimming pool and hot tubs at Lýsuhóll. A school and a community centre were built there, in 1969, because of the abundance of hot water. Now there is a travel service run there all year round.

Þorgeirsfell, (622 m) a mountain protruding southwards. Gabbro in this mountain.

Staðarsveit, a flat, grassy and marshy lowland district from the Hofstaðaháls ridge west to the mountain Axlarhyrna. A string of farms between the mountains and the shore. Many lakes above the Ölduhryggur ridge, Langavatn being the nearest one to Staðastaður. Nesting islets and trout-fishing in many of the lakes.

Ölduhryggur, a flat gravel ridge, a former shoreline, extending more or less continuously from the Miklaholt area far to the west. The road runs along this ridge.

Staðarstaður, a parsonage, church - one of the most famous Saga farms on Snæfellsnes. Ari fróði (the Wise), the pioneer of Saga writing, is believed to have lived there. Many well-known clergymen have lived there, four of whom became bishops. A fifth bishop was brought up there. The folktale about Galdra-Loftur, a student at the school at Hólar who dabbled in the black arts, ends at Staðarstaður, where he is dragged into the sea by a shaggy grey paw.

571 Ölkelduvegur, 0,5 km.

Ölkelda, a farm in the Staðarsveit district, taking its name from a mineral spring in the homefield.

Elliðahamar, a sheer, overhanging crag with steep sides. To the north the peaks **Elliðatindar** (864 m) and **Tröllatindar** (930 m). Halfway up the mountain are caves, supposedly connected to a tunnel reaching all the way to Öxarhamar. Iron rungs are said to have been driven into the rock in the old days to provide access to the caves.

Lágfell, a farm. Above the farm, the peak **Lágafellshyrna** (230 m) is the nearest one on the ridge named Hofstaðaháls.

Ólafsvík, (pop. 945) a town forming part of Snæfellsbær Community. Good harbour. Main activities fishing and trading. Hotel, restaurant and pool. Nearby is a fine campsite and a 9-hole golf course. As evidence of early business activity, there is still standing a warehouse dating from 1841, of distinctive architecture. It now houses a part of the Snæfell rural museum and a store. Jónshús, another old house that has been restored, occupies a prominent place in the town. Building materials for the original construction are believed to have been imported in 1892. Near the town is an impressive mountain, Enni.

Fróðá, formerly a church. Nearby is the abandoned farm Forna Fróðá, where the "Fróðá marvels" recounted in the *Eyrbyggja Saga* took place. They involved a long period during which the place was plagued with walking dead, rains of blood etc., the most hair-raising ghost story on record in Iceland.

Fróðárheiði, (361 m) a mountain pass and road across the Snæfellsnes range.

Knörr, there lived Bjarni „ghost buster" Jónsson (1709–1790) a man of magic and sorcery.

Búðahraun, a lava field near Búðir that came from the crater **Búðaklettur** (88 m). There is a cave in Búðaklettur, said to reach all the way to the cave Surtshellir (see Road 518) and be paved with gold. Great variety of plants and ferns, some of which are very rare.

Búðir, an old anchorage, later a trading centre. The 19th century church is unusual, not only in its setting, but also because it was raised by a woman who did not have the support of the church authorities, but special permission from the king in Denmark. This can be seen on a ring on the church door. Fine views. One of the best sand and shingle beaches in Iceland.

Mælifell, (566 m) a rhyolite mountain near Búðir.

Bjarnarfoss, a high but fairly meager waterfall coming off the edge of the plateau. When the wind is from the south, the water is blown back upwards and never reaches the bottom. There are many rare grasses on slopes.

Búðaós, formerly called Hraunhöfn ("Lava harbour"). Boats can enter at high tide but there is a strong ebb. The Hraunhafnará river flows into this inlet.

Kálfárfossar, beautiful waterfalls where Kálfá river splits in two ravines west of the farm Kálfárvellir.

Böðvarsholt, a farm in Staðarsveit at the foot of Böðvarsholtshyrna. The same family has live there over a century. Above the farm are high cliffs called Kambshaus.

574 **Útnesvegur,** p. 270 570 **Jökulhálsleið,** p. 464-465

Fróðá-Bláfeldur 18 km

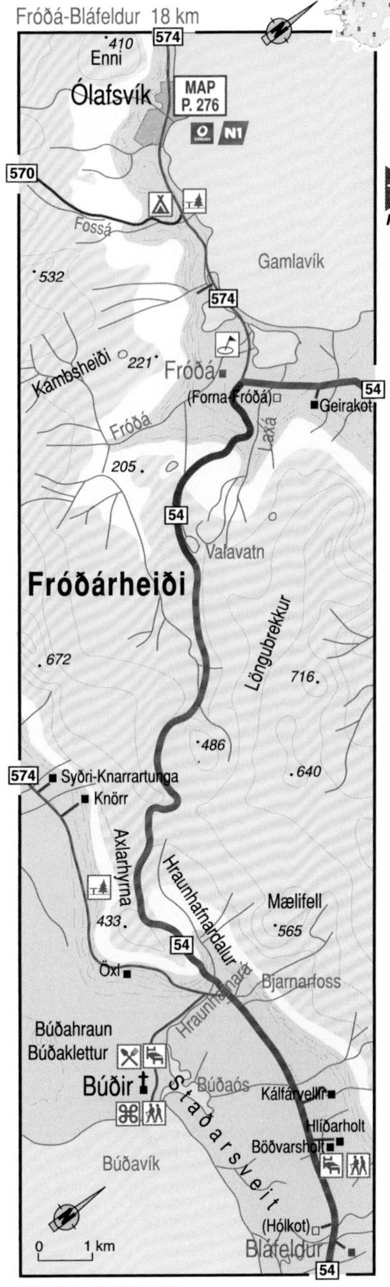

Bláfeldur-Fróðá 18 km

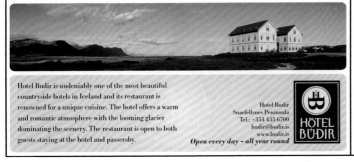

15 P. 578

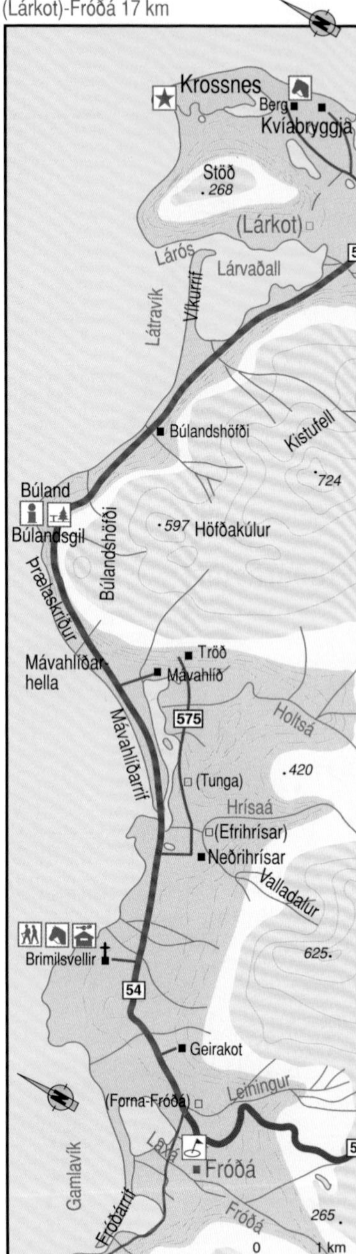

Eyrarsveit, the district reaching across the fjords beyond Búlandshöfði, Grundarfjörður, Kolgrafarfjörður and Hraunsfjörður. Narrow areas of flat land between the sea and high mountains. Impressive scenery.

Kvíabryggja, a prison.

Stöð, (268 m) a single, low, elongated mountain, on the peninsula east of the Lárvaðall lagoon. Formerly called "Coffin" by the Danes.

Lárvaðall, a shallow lagoon off Látravík bay, east of the Búlandshöfði headland.

Búlandshöfði, a headland descending sheer into the sea, with rock belts at its top and base, and scree in between. Formerly a great obstacle to travel because of its steepness, **Þrælaskriða** being the most notorious scree. In Búlandshöfði Dr. Helgi Pjeturss (1872-1949) found interesting strata of sea-shells and remains from the Ice Age 135-180 m above sea-level. This is an important contribution to the knowledge of climatic changes during the Ice Age in Iceland. Similar strata have since been found in other mountains nearby, e.g. Stöð, Kirkjufell, Mýrarhyrna.

Mávahlíð, an old manor below Búlandshöfði. Frequently mentioned in *Eyrbyggja Saga*. Mávahlíð and Brimilsvellir were formerly considered extremely attractive properties. A well-known quatrain on the happiness of marrying Margrét, the daughter of the family at Ingjaldshóll, who was going to inherit them, is evidence of this.

575 Tunguvegur.

Brimilsvellir, formerly a substantial farm and rowing boat fishing-station. Until about 1930 fourteen farmers lived there and the total population was about 100.

Forna-Fróðá, a farm and the site of the Fróðá marvels mentioned in *Eyrbyggja saga*, the most hair-raising ghost story on record in Iceland (see Road 54 Fróðá).

574 **Útnesvegur,** p. 270

Hraunsfjörður-Lárkot 28 km

Hraunsfjörður, a narrow fjord, the first fjord in Iceland to have been bridged - at Mjósund. At the head of the fjord are the abandoned farms **Árnabotn**, Fjarðarhorn and Þórólfsstaðir. There are two fine, high waterfalls there, and an old track over Tröllaháls ridge to Eyrarbotn in Kolgrafarfjörður.

Hraunsfjarðarvatn, a good fishing lake.

Kolgrafarfjörður, now the fjord has been bridged. In Dec. 2012, 30 tons of herring mysteriously died in the fjord close to the bridge. This again happened in Feb. 2013. It´s thought a lack of oxygen in the water, due to how little sea water enters the fjord at its narrow entrance, was the cause.

576 Framsveitarvegur, 10 km.

Hallbjarnareyri, the home of the champion Steinþór á Eyri, mentioned in *Eyrbyggja Saga*. Eyrarfjall is named after this place. Formerly a leprosy hospital.

Melrakkaey, an island in the mouth of Grundarfjörður. Known for its teeming birdlife. Nature reserve.

Setberg, a farm, church and parsonage. A fine view of Grundarfjörður and the Helgrindur mountains. Comparable to the views from Búðir, Mávahlíð or Helgafell.

Grund, a farm at the head of Grundarfjörður. Nearby waterfall, Grundarfoss in the river Grundará.

Helgrindur, (988 m) impressive and majestic mountains south of Grundarfjörður. Permanent snow.

Grundarfjörður, (pop. 825) a township in a fjord of the same name. Has prospered in recent decades: fishing and fish processing. There was formerly a trading-post at the eastern end of the head of the fjord.

Kirkjufell, ("Church mountain") (463 m) an impressive mountain, climbable but difficult and tiring because of rocks. One of the most beautiful mountains on Snæfellsnes. Called "Sugarloaf" by the Danes.

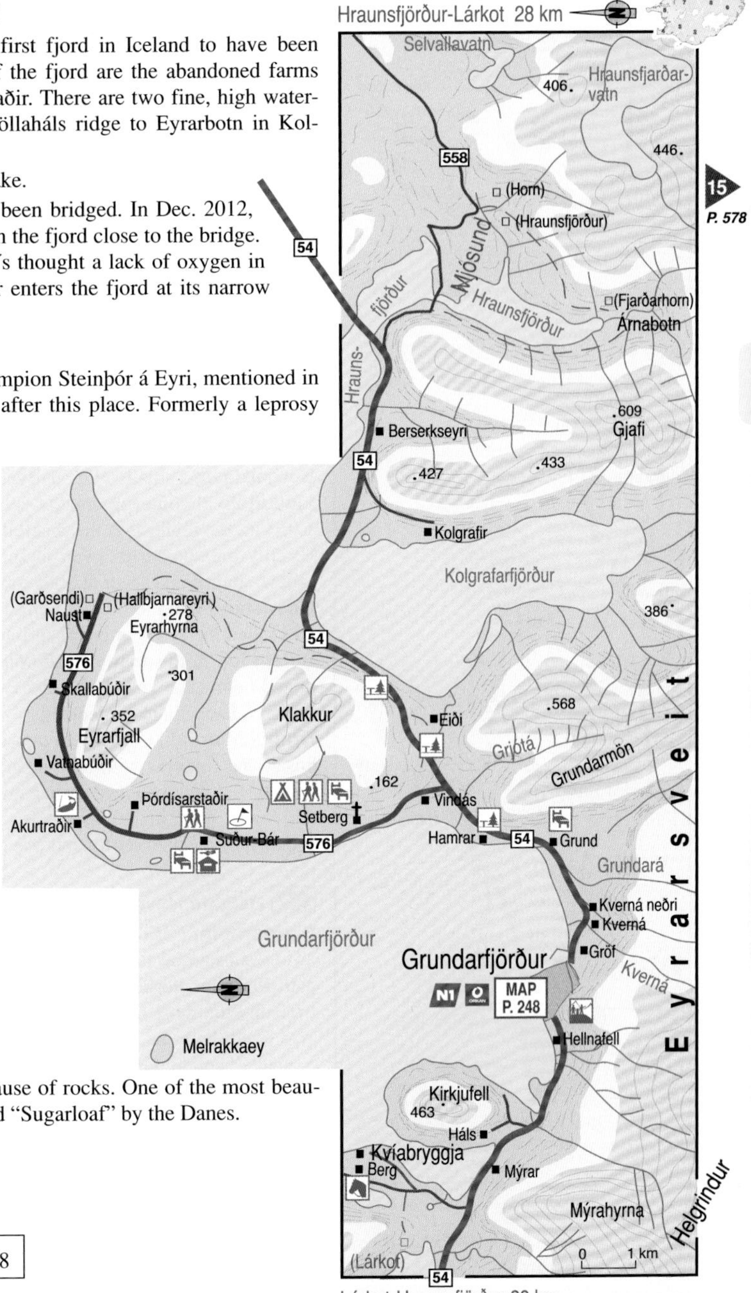

15 P. 578

558 **Berserkjahraunsvegur,** p. 248

Lárkot-Hraunsfjörður 28 km

Narfeyri-Mjósund 33 km

15 P. 578

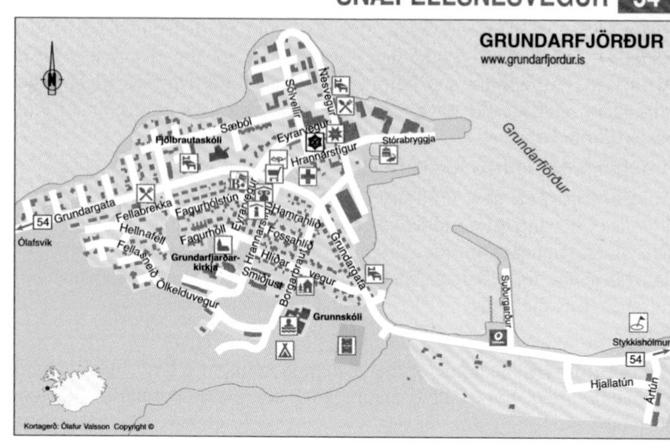

Borgardalur, a small valley halfway between Narfeyri and Kárastaðir.

Ljósufjöll, rhyolite mountains south of Álftafjörður, maximum height 1,063 m, the highest on the Snæfellsnes peninsula, apart from the glacier. Usually big snowdrifts even in summer. To the east is Hestur (864 m), saddle-shaped and sheer at both ends.

Örlygsstaðir, at the head of Álftafjörður. The Sagas tell us Arnkell goði was killed there. The mineral spring Glæsikelda nearby.

Bólstaður, farm site in Álftafjörður, former home of Arnkell goði, abandoned before the year 1000. Excavations made in 1929 uncovered some of the oldest remains in Iceland.

Drápuhlíðarfjall, (527 m) an unusual and colourful mountain containing basalt and rhyolite, with lignite between basalt layers and fossilised tree-trunks. Sulphur pebbles, jasper and other stones. It was long believed there was gold in the mountain, but only very small quantities were found. The most colourful and one of the most beautiful mountains in Iceland.

577 Helgafellssveitarvegur, 11,5 km. **558 Berserkjahraunsvegur.**

Bjarnarhöfn, ("Björn's harbour") the farm of the settler Björn austræni, now a substantial farm with a church and a shark museum. The homeopath Þorleifur Þorleifsson (1801-77) lived there for many years; he was probably the most psychic Icelander ever. Dr. Oddur Hjaltalín (1819-62) also lived there; he was the first person to write a book on the botany of Iceland. The church was built in 1856. It has many old and historically valable artefacs. The alterpiece is believed to have been painted in 1640, there are two cassocks, one of which is more than 500 years old and the other was made in 1762. The church also possesses a chalice from 1286 and a pulpit from 1694. A sign recounting the history of Bjarnarhöfn is located near the higway.

Berserkjahraun, ("Berserkers' lava field") lava from a small row of craters below Kerlingarskarð pass, the largest crater being Rauðakúla. The name is derived from Víga-Styr's berserkers. He got them to cut a path through the lava, then betrayed and killed them. The path is still visible, and beside it the burial mound of the berserkers.

Helgafellssveit, the district between Hraunsfjörður and Álftafjörður. Indented coast with many islands and skerries, inlets and peninsulas.

Mjósund-Narfeyri 33 km

Bjarnarhöfn

56 Vatnaleið, p. 253

58 Stykkishólmsvegur, p. 255

Skógarströnd, the coast along Hvammsfjörður from Álftafjörður to the river Gljúfurá, where Dalasýsla county begins. Some small rivers, fishing in most of them. One valley leading into the mountain range is Heydalur, through which goes Road 55 to the Hnappadalur valley. Birch-bushes.

Breiðabólsstaður, a church and long a parsonage. Sveinn Kristján Bjarnason (1887-1960) was born there, but later moved with his parents to Canada and changed his name to Holger Cahill. In 1932, following an education in art history, he became acting director of the Museum of Modern Art in New York. During the presidency of Franklin D. Roosevelt, Cahill worked closely with him and became one of the most influential people in the American art world.

Drangar, a farm near which Eric the Red killed two men, for which he was outlawed and fled to Greenland.

Brokey, the biggest island in Breiðafjörður, off Skógarströnd, offering many advantages to the farmer. A flour mill was built there and driven by the tides, its remains still visible. One farmer, Jón Pétursson, falcon-hunter (1584-1667), had sailed the seven seas in his youth and was versed in English, German and Danish, rare in a farmer in those days. He encouraged an eider duck colony on Brokey, and was the first to clean eider down. He had 30 children, the last when over 80 years old. Another farmer was the Dane Hans Becker, made governor of North and West Iceland in the early 18th century.

Stóri-Langidalur, a valley east of Eyrarfjall. Pretty and grassy with the salmon-fishing river Langá. Towards its mouth is **Klungurbrekka** slope, named for the wild rose growing there, whose old Icelandic name was Klungur. The parents of Sir William Stephenson (1896-1989) lived at Klungurbrekka before they moved to Canada. William was considerd to be the inspiration for the character of James Bond 007.

Narfeyri, a farm and church north of the Eyrarfjall mountain, the westernmost farm on Skógarströnd. Home of Oddur Sigurðsson (1681-1741), local governor and the farmer Vilhjálmur Ögmundsson (1897-1965), who was famous for his mathematical observations.

Bíldhóll-Narfeyri 23 km

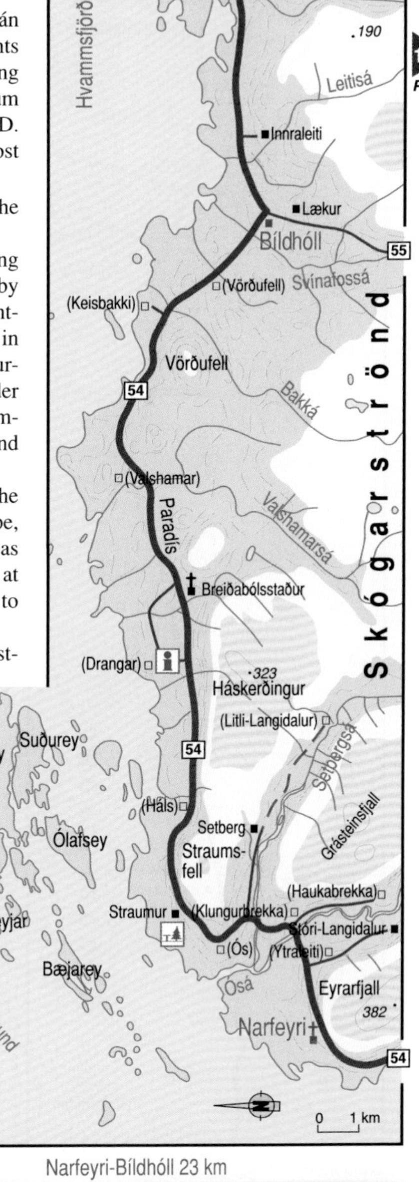

Narfeyri-Bíldhóll 23 km

55 **Heydalsvegur,** p. 251

The church at Bjarnarhöfn

The shark museum at Bjarnarhöfn

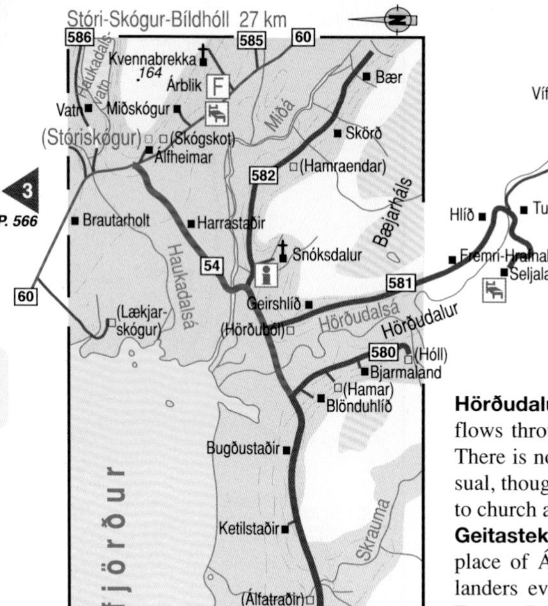

Miðdalir, the lowland area at the "heel" of Hvammsfjörður, along with the valleys through which Road 60 goes and the river Miðá flows.

582 Hálsabæjarvegur, 12,2 km.

Snóksdalur, a church and old manor farm. Home of Daði Guðmundsson who arrested the last Catholic Bishop, Jón Arason, in 1550. Also for a time the home of Magnús Jónsson (1675-1752) who was popular with the ladies and outlawed from the west of Iceland after his fifth conviction for adultery.

581 Hörðudalsvegur eystri, 8 km.

580 Hörðudalsvegur vestri.

Hörðudalur, southernmost valley in Dalasýsla, the river Hörðudalsá flows through it. The valley divides into Vífilsdalur and Laugardalur. There is not and never has been a church in this district, which is unusual, though there used to be small chapels. The local people have to go to church at Snóksdalur.

Geitastekkur, a farm in Hörðudalur, now called **Bjarmaland**. Birthplace of Árni Magnússon (1726-1810) one of the best-travelled Icelanders ever. As a young man he travelled to Denmark, Greenland, France, Russia, Turkey, China and elsewhere, and was a soldier in Russia and Turkey among other places, ending up as a school teacher in Denmark. He wrote a notable book describing his adventures, which is at the same time a remarkable description of his period.

Skrauma, a river to the west of the Hörðudalsá river, flowing through narrow gorges. Legend has it that the son of the giantess Skrauma drowned in the river, at which she laid this curse on it, that 20 men should perish there. In 1806 a father and son from Gautastaðir were the 18th and 19th people to drown in Skrauma.

Gljúfurá, a small river in a narrow ravine. There lie the bounderies of Snæfellsnessýsla county and Dalasýsla county.

Hólmlátur, the innermost farm on Skógarströnd, where Eric the Red spent a winter after his discovery of Greenland.

55 Heydalsvegur, p. 251
60 Vestfjarðavegur, p. 281
582 Hálsabæjarvegur, p. 280
585 Hlíðarvegur, p. 280
586 Haukadalsvegur, p. 277

55 HEYDALSVEGUR

Heydalur, a shallow valley on Rauðamelsheiði moor south of the hill Bílduhóll on the Skógarströnd coast. The road along it joins the Snæfellsnes road near Kolbeinsstaðir. This is the lowest and least snowy road across the Snæfellsnes range.

The lake Hlíðarvatn.

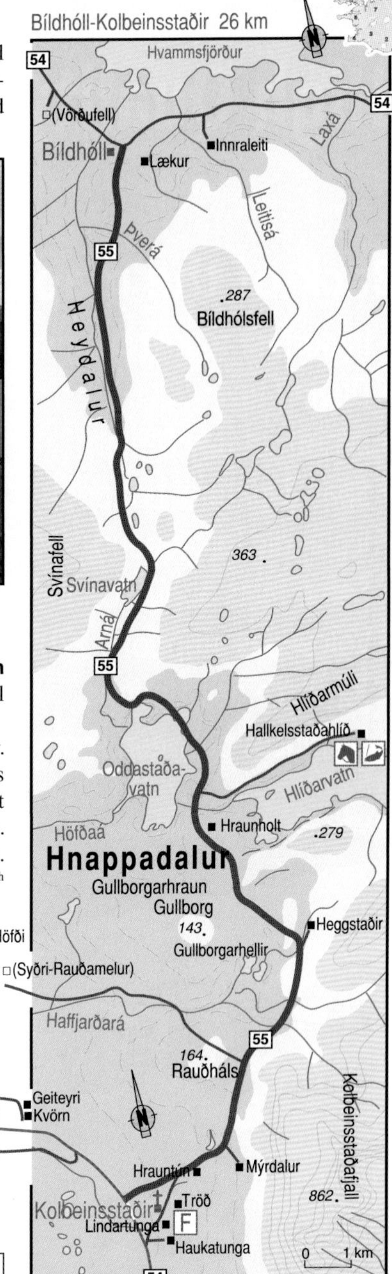

15 P. 578

Hnappadalur, a broad valley, full of lava. Two large lakes, **Hlíðarvatn** and **Oddastaðavatn**, with good trout-fishing. In 1964 a floating hotel shaped like a Viking ship was put on Hlíðarvatn but was not a success.

Gullborgarhraun, a lava field in Hnappadalur from the **Gullborg** crater. There are some large and unusual caves in the lava field. One of these is **Gullborgarhellir**, considered one of the loveliest lava caves in Iceland, not least because of the unusual number of beautiful stalagmites and stalactites. The cave is a protected natural feature and can only be visited with a guide. Some ruins nearby are believed to date from the Sturlunga age in the 13th century, when Aron Hjörleifsson had a hide-out in the lava field. It is said that his main hide-out was in a cave called Aronshellir. In 1979 one more cave was found in this lava field.

Rauðháls, craters in the Rauðhólshraun lava field.

Mýrdalur, a farm at the foot of the mountain Kolbeinsstaðafjall. Behind the farm is Mýrdalsgjá, an unusual ravine.

Lindartunga, a community centre.

Kolbeinsstaðir, an old manor farm, and the home of many influential men. Church, community centre. The highest peak on the mountain **Kolbeinsstaðafjall** above the farm is called **Tröllakirkja** ("Giants' church") (862 m). Another peak is Hrútaborg, with steep crags. A challenging mountain for climbers.

54 Snæfellsnesvegur, p. 238-250

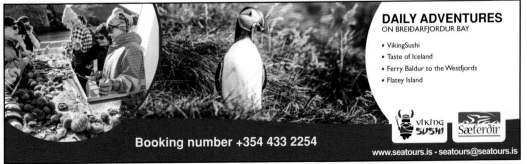

54 Snæfellsvegur-Vegamót 17 km

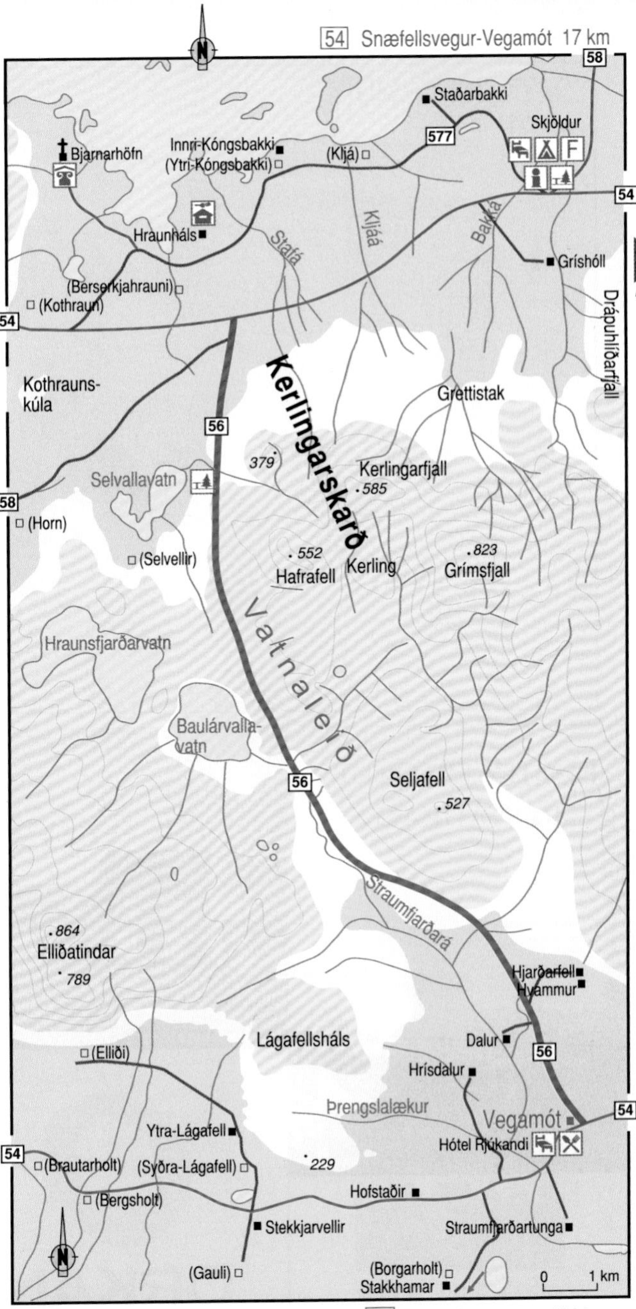

Drápuhlíðarfjall, (527 m) an unusual and colourful mountain containing basalt and rhyolite, with lignite between basalt layers and fossilised tree-trunks. Sulphur pebbles, jasper and other stones. It was long believed there was gold in the mountain, but only very small quantities were found. The most colourful and one of the most beautiful mountains in Iceland.

Grettistak, ("Grettir's challenge") a large tuff boulder that has fallen down from Kerlingafjall. Formerly a resting place for travellers, fine views.

Kerlingarfjall, (585 m) a mountain on the east side of the Kerlingarskarð pass. Vatnaheiði forms a deep depression in the mountain range a short way west of Kerlingarskarð. The present road runs close to Vatnaheiði heath and is called Vatnaleið. There are three angling lakes on the heath: Baulárvallavatn, Hraunsfjarðarvatn and Selvallavatn.

Baulárvallavatn, a good fishing lake notorious for its monsters, as many as 5 having supposedly been seen at once, sunning themselves on the shore and returning to the water at dusk. There was formerly a farm, Baulárvellir, near the lake. One midwinter day in the 19th century the farmer went off, leaving his wife alone with the children. She heard a loud noise as if the farm were being pulled down, and an icy blast filled the room, but she dared not move. The next day several outbuildings were found to have been destroyed, and the huge tracks of an unknown creature could be traced to a hole in the ice on the lake. Just north of there are the lakes Hraunsfjarðarvatn and Selvallavatn.

Kerlingarskarð, ("Old woman pass") a pass (311 m) over the Snæfellsnes mountain range. The pass is named after a rock named **Kerling.** A folktale tells of a giantess of the troll type who was on her way home with her catch after a good nights fishing in the lake when she was caught by the sun and turned to stone. She can still be seen, her line of trout over her shoulder, on a ridge of the mountain Kerlingarfjall opposite the mountain Hafrafell, at the north end of the pass. There is also a fine view from that end of the pass. Burial mounds.

Vegamót, ("Crossroads") where the routes west out onto Snæfellsnes and north across the Vatnaleið pass meet.

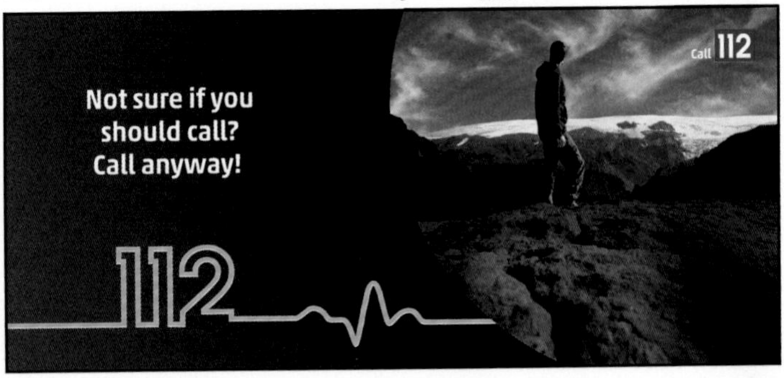

Vegamót – 54 Snæfellsnesvegur 17 km

15 P. 578

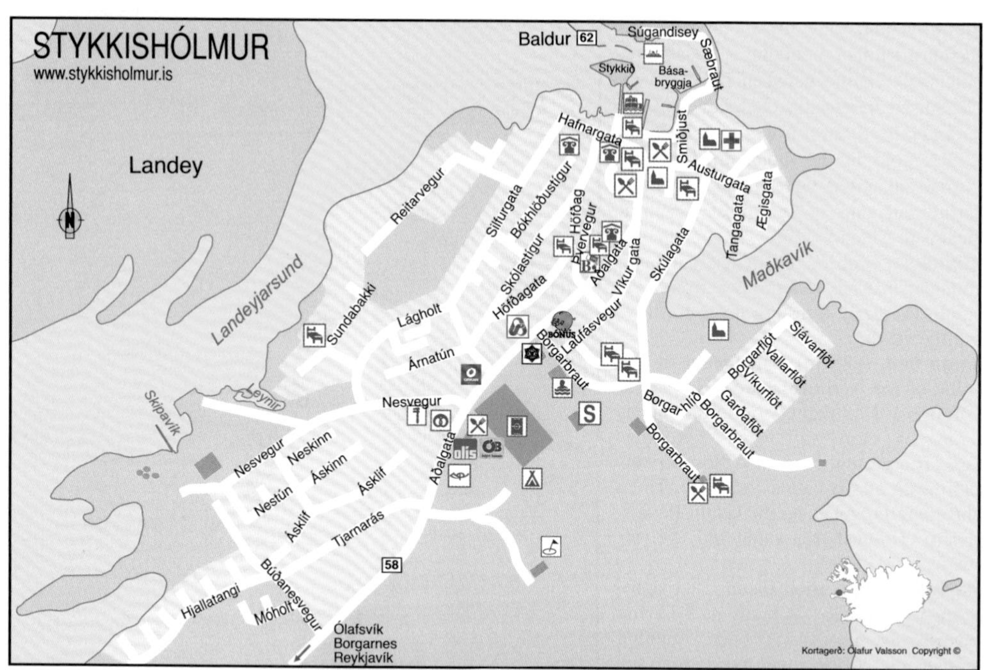

STYKKISHÓLMUR
www.stykkisholmur.is
Landey
Landeyjarsund
Baldur 62
Súgandisey
Stykkið
Bása-bryggja
Sæbraut
Hafnargata
Smiðjust
Austurgata
Tangagata
Ægisgata
Maðkavík
Reitarvegur
Silfurgata
Bókhlöðustígur
Höfðag
Þvervegur
Aðalgata
Skólastígur
Höfðagata
Víkur gata
Skúlagata
Sundabakki
Lágholt
Laufásvegur
Borgarbraut
Árnatún
Nesvegur
Leynir
Skipavík
Neskinn
Áskinn
Ásklif
Nestún
Tjarnarás
Búðanesvegur
Hjallatangi
Móholt
58
Sjávarflöt
Vallarflöt
Borgarflöt
Víkurflöt
Garðaflöt
Borgarhlíð
Ólafsvík
Borgarnes
Reykjavík
Kortagerð: Ólafur Valsson Copyright ©

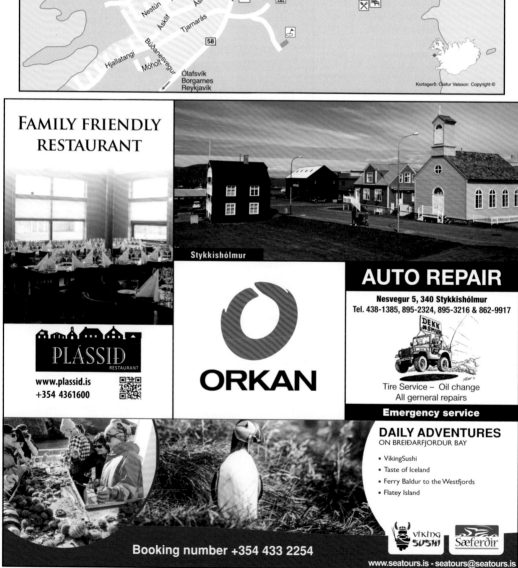

58 STYKKISHÓLMSVEGUR

Stykkishólmur, (pop. 1,164) a town with municipal rights since 1987. It is named after a large skerry in the harbour, which is protected by the rock island Súgandisey. Stykkishólmur has been a centre of fishing, trading and transportation for the Breiðafjörður settlements for centuries. The town is still an ideal destination for those whose who wish to experience diversity of nature, services and life on Breiðafjörður. In summer, daily sightseeing trips go out in the fjord on the Seatours (Sæferðir) boats, while the ferry Baldur connects Snæfellsnes with the West Fjords with daily sailings to Brjánslækur making a stop at Flatey. A great deal of effort has been put into preserving the town's old houses, and old buildings thus have a great influence on the appearance of downtown Stykkishólmur. Norska húsið ("The Norwegian house")built in 1832, was the first two-story-wood frame residence in Iceland. The wood was imported from Norway, hence the name. It was the home of Árni Ó. Thorlacius (1802–1891) and Anna M. Steenback (1807–1894). Árni began regular meteorological observations in Stykkishólmur in 1845 and they have continued uninterrupted to this day, the oldest continuous meteorological observations in Iceland. The Norwegian house has been partially renovated back to its original style. It now serves as the regional museum for the Snæfellsnes area with an open storage on the top floor and rotating exhibitions on the lower level as well as a museum shop. Many craftspeople live in Stykkishólmur, and a crafts market is open in summer. The Danish days festival is held annually on the third weekend of August, when town residents and visitors celebrate with dance, song and various artistic events. In 1879 a church was built in Stykkishólmur. It is one of the old houses that have now been renovated. Now there is also a new at Borg, a striking landmark from land as well as the sea. It is open to tourists. Besides normal church services there are concerts at least fortnightly over the summer. At Stykkishólmur there is the Library of Water, situated at a place with one of the most beautiful views. An American artist Roni Horn created and shaped the Library of Water. It is open daily in summer. There is also the Volcano Museum, a unique exhibition of international art and objects related to volcanic eruptions and their impact. Restaurants, coffee shops, a bakery and a grocery store can be found in Stykkishólmur, as can hotels and other types of accommodation. There is a very good campsite next to a 9 hole golf course and a swimming pool that contains an enjoyable chute for children, as well as hot pots with certificated pure water that comes straight from the borehole. The water is famed for its healing powers, as it is full of minerals and works well for all sorts of skin problems. Besides the football field and athletics track, a tarmac basketball field and playing field can be found on the grounds of the primary school and are open to all. Beautiful walking routes through town and to the beaches and view points.

Hofsstaðir, the farm of Þórólfur Mostraskegg, who originally settled the Þórsnes peninsula. The first known Þing or official meeting place, in Iceland.

Þingvellir, plains on the peninsula south of the Nesvogur inlet. The Þing was moved there from Hofsstaðir and some ruins can still be seen, as well as a sacrificial stone, where people were condemned to be sacrificed. Inside the ring is Þór´s stone, on which the sacrificial victims were broken. Blood stains can still be seen on the stone.

Helgafell, (73 m) this small mountain, though not high, is conspicuous in the plain. It was sacred to people of the Saga age, and they hoped to die on it. The story goes that if you start from the grave of Guðrún Ósvífursdóttir and climb to the Tótt (remains of a chapel) without speaking a single word or looking back on the way, you can have three wishes. However, the wishes must be pure-hearted, told to no one, and made while facing east by the chapel ruins. At the southern foot of Helgafell are a farm of the same name, famous in the Sagas, and a church (former parsonage). The farm was in its time the residence of Snorri goði and later of Guðrún Ósvífursdóttir of *Laxdæla saga*. Her grave can be seen there. From 1184 until the Reformation there was a wealthy monastery nearby. Books and manuscripts from there were burned after the reformation.

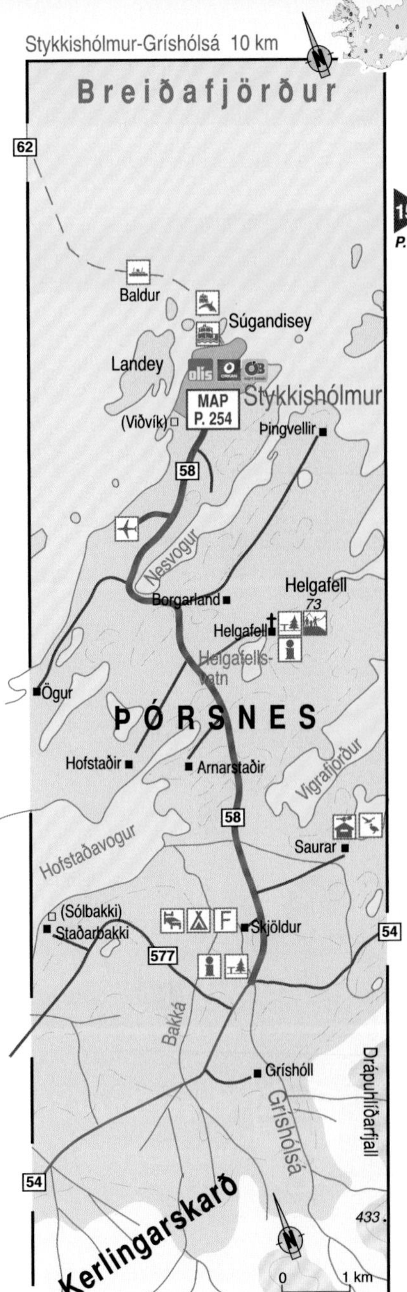

Grísholsá-Stykkishólmur 10 km

15 P. 578

54 **Snæfellsnesvegur,** p. 248
62 **Barðastrandarvegur,** p. 306
577 **Helgafellssveitarvegur,** p. 248

59 LAXÁRDALSVEGUR

Laxárdalur, a long, narrow valley between low grassy ridges, not spectacular though the river Laxá, that flows through it, is a good fishing river. The setting for the *Laxdæla saga* ("Saga of the people of Laxárdalur"). By the old bridge there is a pool called Papi.

Laxárdalsheiði, (200 m), a moor, traversed by Laxárdalsvegur (Road 59) between the villages Búðardalur and Borðeyri. Two Laxá rivers flow down from there, one to Hvammsfjörður, the other to Hrútafjörður. Flattish with many lakes, the biggest being Laxárvatn.

Sólheimar, the innermost farm in Laxárdalur, home of the ghost Sólheima-Móri. The place was so severly haunted at one time that one farmhand after the other died suddenly in the space of a few years. Many horses were killed as well as other livestock. The ghost also enticed people into rivers, pits and gullies.

588 Gillastaðavegur, 1,88 km.

587 Hjarðarholtsvegur, 9 km.

Leiðólfsstaðir, a farm which *Laxdæla saga* tells us was the home of a man and wife who had such magic powers that they could strike people dead. Their son was no less powerful, for when he looked out through a hole in the sack in which he had been trapped, all the grass there withered and has never grown since. Another son was drowned in Hvammsfjörður after which there were no fish in the fjord.

Höskuldsstaðir, home of Höskuldur Dala-Kollsson, father of Ólafur pá ("Peacock"). Ólafur's mother was Irish and of royal blood. Old remains still visible.

Hjarðarholt, a church and manor farm since Saga times. Home of Ólafur pá, birthplace of Kjartan Ólafsson, the main character of *Laxdæla saga*. Former parsonage.

Hrappsstaðir, home of Hrappur who after his death was one of the worst ghosts of the Saga age.

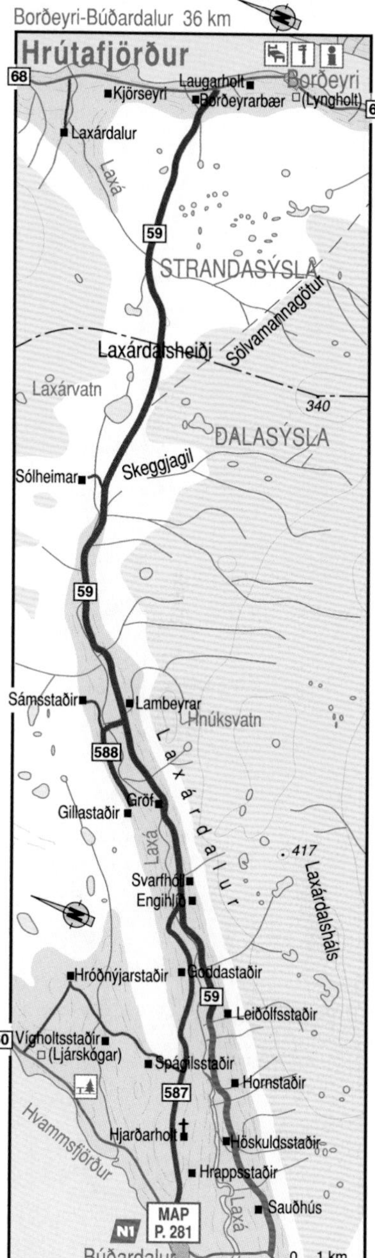

Búðardalur-Borðeyri 36 km

60 Vestfjarðavegur, p. 281 **68 Innstrandavegur,** p. 309

Hjarðarholt 1898

1 P. 564

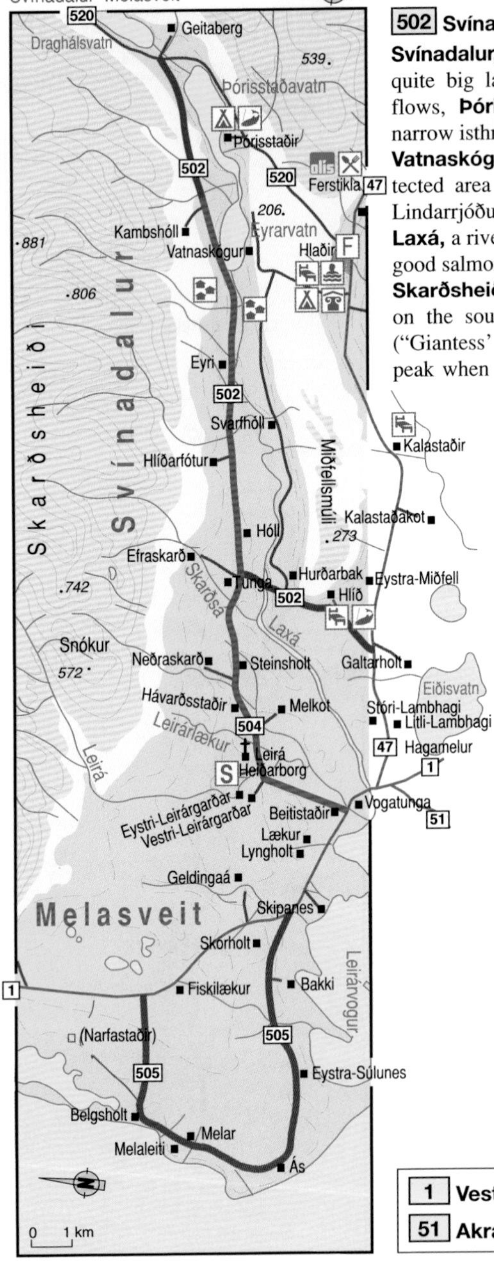

502 Svínadalsvegur, 15 km.

Svínadalur, a valley above Ferstikluháls ridge, in which there are three quite big lakes: **Eyrarvatn** (or Kambhólsvatn), from which the Laxá flows, **Þórisstaðavatn** and **Draghálsvatn**, the road going along a narrow isthmus between the latter two. Trout-fishing in the lakes.

Vatnaskógur, woods alongside the lakes in the valley Svínadalur, a protected area since 1914. The YMCA has a boys' summer camp there, Lindarrjóður.

Laxá, a river flowing from Eyrarvatn and emptying into Leirárvogur. A good salmon river.

Skarðsheiði, a high mountain range dominating the Borgarfjörður area on the south side. Highest point Heiðarhorn, (1,053 m). Skessuhorn ("Giantess' peak") (963 m) is a particularly impressive and outstanding peak when the range is viewed from the north. It is easy to climb from Svínadalur, the best approach being from the outermost valley facing south, or up beside the Skarðsá river.

504 Leirársveitarvegur, 6,7 km.

Beitistaðir, a farm where there was a printing press which was brought there from Leirárgarðar in 1814 and was moved in 1819 to Viðey, then the only printing-house in the country.

Leirá, ("Clay river") a farm and church occupied by men of influence from earliest times. Chief Justice Magnús Stephensen put up a printing press at a nearby farm, Leirárgarðar, and later (1795) moved it to Beitistaðir. Good salmon fishing in the river. Hot springs. A bathing place of old.

505 Melasveitarvegur, 11,7 km.

Melar, a farm and, until 1855, a church but the site is now much eroded by the sea. Served by Helgi Sigurðsson (1815-88), who was the major force in the establishment of the National Museum and the first Icelander to study photography, which he did in Copenhagen alongside his academic studies 1842-45.

1 Vesturlandsvegur, p. 54
47 Hvalfjarðarvegur, p. 222
51 Akrafjallsvegur, p. 234
520 Dragavegur, p. 263

Svínadalur Melasveit

508 Skorradalsvegur, 24 km.

Skorradalur, the southernmost of the Borgarfjörður valleys, 28 km long but narrow. Widespread birch-bushes. In recent years the Forestry Service has done extensive forestation there, developing a quite luxuriant conifer woods. The settler Skorri is buried at Skorrahólar a good way up the valley. Skorradalsskógur is a natural delight with large, old, dense birch trees. Substantial vegetation on the forest floor. Bird life at the river estuary. Fitjaár rivers very diverse. Rare vegetation. Protection of site planned. Difficult to reach by jeep. National Forest.

Skorradalsvatn, a 16 km long lake going right down the valley. Area 14.7 km^2, maximum depth 48 m. The bed of the lake was formed by a glacier, which left a ridge closing the mouth of the valley. The Andakílsá river flows out of the lake, its waters being used in the Andakílsá power station. Trout-fishing.

Klausturskógur (Vatnshornsskógur), a national forrest.

Fitjar, a substantial farm and church, fertile land. Few people live in Skorradal and church services are held 2 to 3 times in summer. Some waterfalls in the Fitjaá river, the biggest being **Hvítserkur**.

Háafell, farm adjacent to Stálpastaðir. Coniferous trees were planted among the low birch bushes there as early as 1938.

Stálpastaðaskógur, popular hiking paths in a forest with numerous slopes. Some 30 tree species from 70 locations around the globe. Labelled tree collection and picnic table. Many of the country's largest Christmas trees originate there. National Forest.

Selsskógur, very pleasant campground among the birch trees. Hiking paths through the forest in many places. Conifer trees are common, as are Norway spruce and Sitka spruce. Located south of Skorradalsvatn, north of Skarðsheiði. National Forest.

Grund, a substantial farm. Bishop Brynjólfur Sveinsson (1605-1675) built a house there which he intended his wife to live in if she would ever become a widow. For long the main farm of the district. Roads from there to Andakíll on both sides of the river Andakílsá, across the Hesthals ridge, down into the valleys Lundarreykjadalur and Skorradalur.

Fossar, there is a power station Andakílsárvirkjun. Built in 1947, power 7,9 MW. Reservoir at lake Skorradalsvatn.

507 Mófellsstaðavegur, 6,7 km.

Efrihreppur, there is a swimming pool called Hreppslaug.

Hestur, formerly a church and parsonage. Now an experimental sheep-breeding station.

Andakíll, a settlement.

50 Borgarfjarðarbraut, p. 237

510 Hvítárvallavegur, p. 231

520 Dragavegur, p. 263

52 Uxahryggjavegur, p. 237

511 Hvanneyrarvegur, p. 231

F508 Skorradalsvegur, p. 237

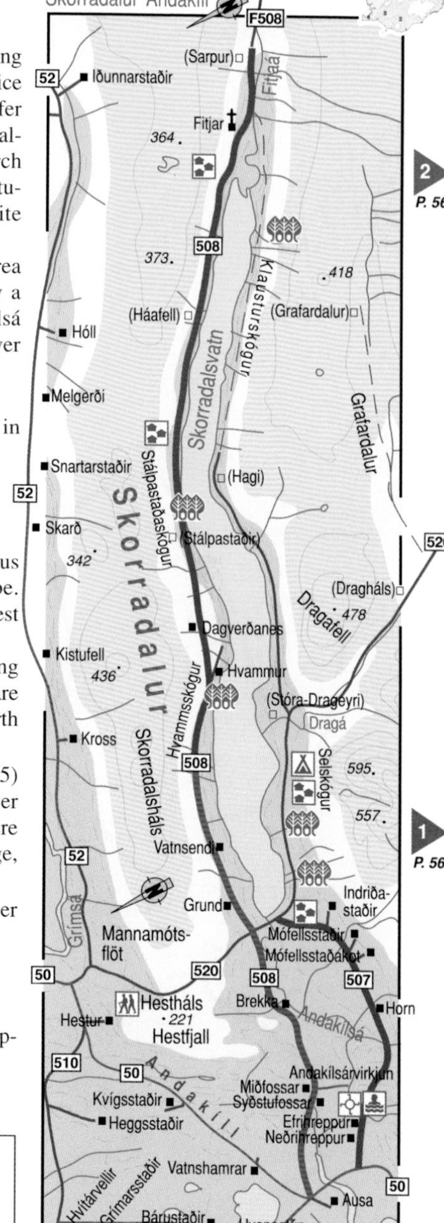

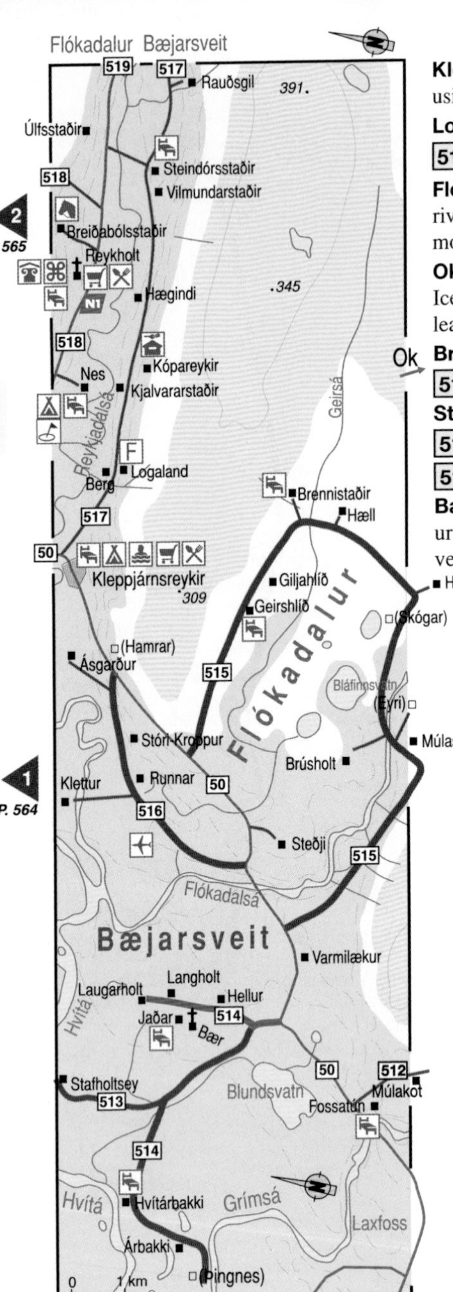

2 P. 565

1 P. 564

Ok

Kleppjárnsreykir, a community where there is hothouse cultivation using heat from one of Borgarfjörður's bigger hot springs, 70 l/sec.

Logaland, a community centre.

515 Flókadalsvegur, 14,6 km.

Flókadalur, a broad, grassy valley, actually two, down which flow the rivers Flókadalsá and Geirsá. In Flókadalsá, which comes from the Ok mountain, there are salmon and trout.

Ok (1,141 m) is made of basalt and was formed by an eruption late in the Ice Age. It has a small glacier on top that has got much smaller recently, leaving the crater bare.

Brennistaðir, a farm and guesthouse.

516 Stóra-Kroppsvegur, 1,5 km.

Stóri-Kroppur, a farm below the Kroppsmúli spur. Airstrip.

514 Hvítárbakkavegur, 4 km.

513 Bæjarsveitarvegur, 2,4 km.

Bær, a church and substantial farm, where Sturla Sighvatsson and Þorleifur Þórðarson fought a bloody battle in 1237. Shortly after Iceland converted to Christianity, or about 1030, the first monastery in Iceland was established at Bær by Bishop Rúðólfur (Rudolph), who is thought to have been a close relative of King Edward of Britain. Rúðólfur ran a school, the first in Iceland as far as is known, and he introduced letters instead of runes. He was later made Abbot of Abington by King Edward. A species of wild onion, exceedingly rare in Iceland, grows in the home field at Bær. They may be a left-over of the monks' kitchen garden.

Bæjarsveit, the flat district between the rivers Grímsá and Flóka. Marshy but grassy with low ridges.

Brún, community centre.

Blundsvatn, a rather big lake, though shallow, in the Bæjarsveit district.

Hvítárbakki, a substantial farm, formerly called Bakkakot. A people's college was founded there in 1905, moved to Reykholt in 1931.

Stafholtsey, an old site of official gatherings, formerly north of the river Hvítá, which has since changed its course.

50 Borgarfjarðarbraut, p. 229, 231
510 Hvítárvallavegur, p. 231
512 Lundarreykjadalsvegur, p. 237
517 Reykdælavegur, p. 261
518 Hálsasveitarvegur, p. 261
519 Reykholtsdalsvegur, p. 261

518 HÁLSASVEITARVEGUR

Stóri-Ás, a church where Miðfjarðar-Skeggi, who took the sword Sköfnungur from the burial mound of Hrólfur kraki in *Hrólfs saga*, is said to be buried.

519 Reykholtsdalsvegur, 13,3 km. **517 Reykdælavegur,** 8,4 km.

Breiðabólstaður, a farm in Reykholtsdalur. Site of a Saga-age tragedy, when Hallbjörn from Kiðjaberg chopped off the head of his wife, Hallgerður, when she refused to move away with him.

Reykholt, a church, parsonage, a medieval institution and a hotel in one of the most famous places in Iceland's history, the home of chieftain/scholar Snorri Sturluson (1179-1241), murdered in his home on 23 September 1241. Snorri, the best-known Icelandic medieval writer was the author of Heimskringla and the Prose Edda, and probably also of the Saga of Egill. Among many famous clergymen to serve Reykholt was Finnur Jónsson (1704–89), later a bishop of Skálholt. Attached to the church is Snorrastofa, a medieval research centre, established to do research and provide information on Snorri and his works, medieval literature and history in general, also the area of Reykholt and Borgarfjörður. A statue of Snorri by Gustav Vigeland presented by Norway was unveiled 1947. Snorralaug ("Snorri's pool"), an outdoor bathing pool with piped warm water and a tunnel leading to it from under the old farmhouse are considered to be among the oldest extant constructions in the country. Much geothermal heat is in the area. The main hot spring, Skrifla, supplies Snorri's pool and the local buildings with hot water. The building of the old district school with its beautiful architecture is both a part of Snorrastofa and the National Library of Iceland. Excavations have been made over the past years by the National museum of Iceland on the old farmhouse site, the passage between the houses and the pool, and on the old churchyard. The old timber-church in Reykholt was built 1886-87 and bears a certain resemblance to Reykjavík Cathredal. In the keeping of the National Museum since 2001.

Skáneyjarbunga, (260 m) the mountain above the farm Skáney, with a fine view.

Skáney, a farm in the Reykholtsdalur valley, the residence in the 16th century of a German doctor, Lazarus Mattheusson, called in to cure syphilis. Wild onions grow there, as at Bær.

Árhver or **Vellir,** a hot spring in the Reykjadalsá river. It spouted regularly at one time, up to 12 m, but now only spouts if soap is thrown into it.

Sturlureykir, a farm in Reykholtsdalur. The first hot spring to be harnessed for domestic heating in Iceland, in 1908.

Reykholtsdalur, a wide, grassy, valley between low ridges. Geothermal heat in many places.

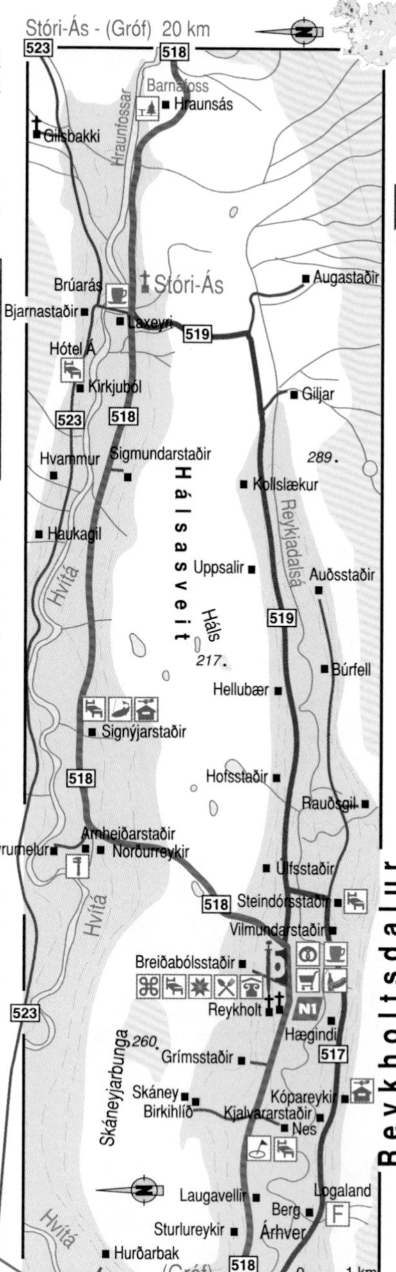

2 P. 565

50 Borgarfjarðarbraut, p. 229 **523 Hvítársíðuvegur,** p. 265

Kalmanstunga-Stóri-Ás 11 km

Eiríksjökull · 938 · Strútur · 660 · Hvítá · Svartá · Surtshellir · F578 · 578 · Kalmanstunga · Kaldidalur · 550 · 523 · Geitá · Fljótstunga · Þorvaldsstaðir · 445 · Tunga · 518 · Norðlingafljót · Kaldá · Hallkelsstaðir · Húsafellsskógur · Húsafell · Kolsstaðir · Gráhraun · 523 · Hvítá · Hringsgil · 518 · Gilsbakki · Hraunsás · Barnafoss · Hraunfossar · Bjarnastaðir · Stóri-Ás · Brúarás · Laxeyri · Augastaðir · 523 · 519 · 0 1 km

2 P. 565

Stóri-Ás-Kalmanstunga 11 km

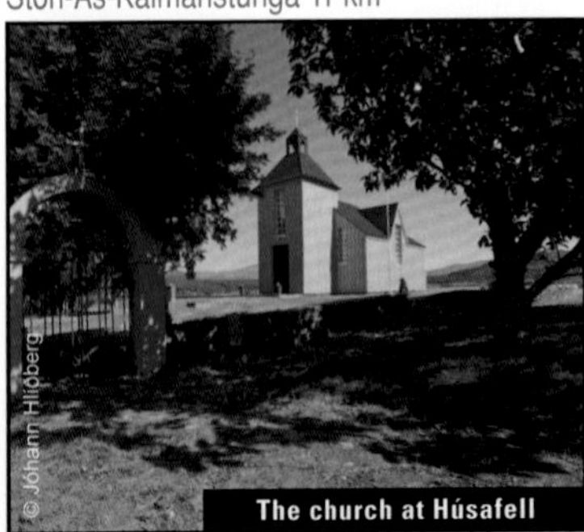
The church at Húsafell

Eiríksjökull, (1,675 m) a tuff mountain with a glacier, one of the most beautiful in Iceland. Road accessible by jeeps to the west side, from where it is an easy 3 hour climb onto the glacier. Excellent view from the top.

Strútur, (938 m) a pyramid-shaped mountain above the farm Kalmanstunga. A very difficult jeep-track to the top.

Húsafell, the innermost farm in the Hálsasveit district. Formerly a parsonage and church. Made famous among other things by Snorri Björnsson (1710-1803), verisfier, poet and strong man, who tried his strength on the boulder **Kvíahella** (180 kg) which still stands at, Kvíar where the sheeps where milked. Birch forest and geothermal heat. An ancient farm has been excavated west of Húsafell. Páll Guðmundsson (b. 1959) a known Icelandic sculptor and artist was born and raised at Húsafell and in fact he still lives there. His artwork can be found all around Húsafell as he sculptures faces on rocks he finds in the nature. Many summerhouses, a hotel, restaurants, 9 hole golf course, swimming pool and beautiful hiking trails.

Barnafoss, ("Children's falls") waterfalls in the river Hvítá. Two children are said to have once fallen off a natural rock bridge over the river and drowned, hence the name. There is now a footbridge over the falls. Interesting ravine.

Hraunfossar, ("Lava falls") along the northern bank of the Hvítá river gorge. Springwater flows from under the lava for about 1 km, cascading in numerous waterfalls between rocks and trees into the river. A beautiful and unusual sight.

Augastaðir, where research into the northern lights has been going on since 1984, financed by the Japanese. This station is similar to those at Mánárbakki and Æðey, but being the headquarters of the research it is larger.

519 **Reykholtsdalsvegur,** p. 261
523 **Hvítársíðuvegur,** p. 265
F550 **Kaldadalsvegur,** p. 462
F578 **Arnarvatnsvegur,** p. 466

The burial cairn Erfingi at Ferstikluháls.

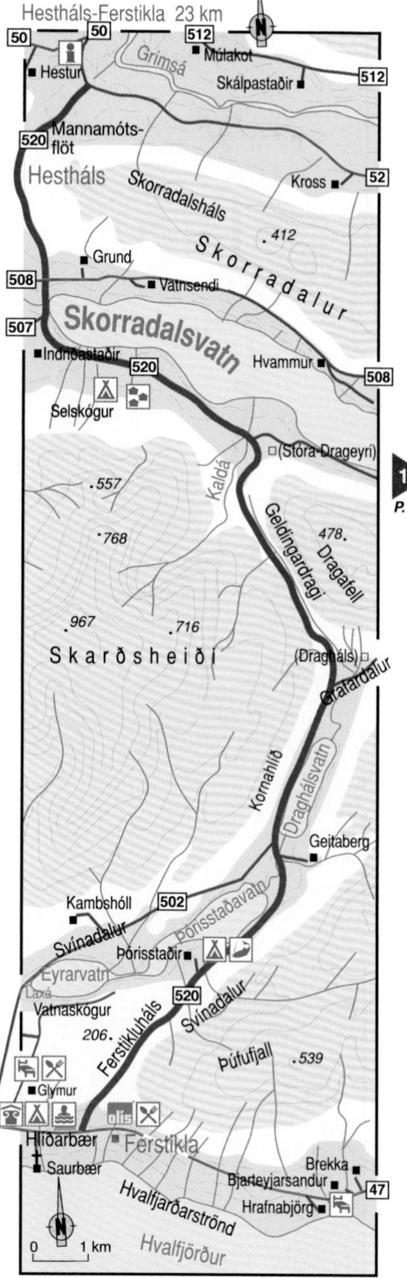

P. 564

Hestháls, low bush-covered ridges between the mountain Hestfjall and the Skorradalsháls ridge. Main route from Grund in Skorradalur. The road is flanked by grasslands where people would hold social gatherings.

Grund, a farm. Bishop Brynjólfur Sveinsson (1605-1675) built a house there which he intended his wife to live in if she was ever widowed.

Skorradalur, the southernmost of the Borgarfjörður valleys, 28 km long but narrow. Widespread birch-bushes. In recent years the Forestry Service has done extensive forestation there, developing a quite luxuriant conifer woods.

Skorradalsvatn, a 16 km long lake going right down the valley. Area 14.3 km^2, maximum depth 60 m. The bed of the lake was formed by a glacier, which left a ridge closing the mouth of the valley. The Andakílsá river flows out of the lake, its waters being used in the Andakílsá power station. Trout-fishing.

Geldingadragi, ("Gelding trail") now usually called Dragi, a pass (243 m) between the valleys Svínadalur and Skorradalur on the main highway, with the mountain **Dragafell** (478 m) to the east. The name is derived from the *Harðar saga og Hólmverja Saga*, in which Hörður and his men stole some geldings which had trouble getting across the pass in deep snow. Geldingadragi forms the eastern boundary of Skarðsheiði.

Drahgháls, the uppermost farm in Svínadalur, a crossroads, with tracks to the Grafardalur valley. Four brothers and sisters, poets and writers, were brought up there, one of them, Sveinbjörn Beinteinsson (1924-93), having been High Priest of the followers of the pagan Nordic religion until his death. There is a statue of Thor at Draghháls, where the pagan ceremonies were performed.

Grafardalur, a farm and once a home of Sveinbjörn Beinteinson (1924–1993) allsherjargoði.

Geitaberg, a farm at the southern end of the lake Geitabergsvatn. Formerly a well-known stopping place for travellers.

Svínadalur, a valley above Ferstikluháls ridge, in which there are three quite big lakes: **Eyrarvatn,** (or Kambhólsvatn) from which the river Laxá flows, **Þórisstaðavatn** and **Draghálsvatn**, the road going along a narrow isthmus between the latter two. Trout-fishing in the lakes.

Ferstikluháls, a ridge between the Svínadalur valley and Hvalfjörður. On its northern edge there is a pile of stones by the road, topped by a cross. This is usually called **Erfingi** ("Heir") and is said to be the burial cairn of a man whose request to be buried there was refused by the authorities. However, when his body was being taken across the ridge, the horses stopped at this point and refused to move another step.

47 **Hvalfjarðarvegur,** p. 222
50 **Borgarfjarðarbraut,** p. 229
52 **Uxahryggjavegur,** p. 237
502 **Svínadalsvegur,** p. 258
507 **Mófellsstaðavegur,** p. 259
508 **Skorradalsvegur,** p. 259
512 **Lundarreykjadalsvegur,** p. 237

Bjarnastaðir-Kalmanstunga 14 km
519 518 523
Kirkjuból Hótel Á
Laxeyri
Stóriás
Bjarnastaðir
Brúarás
Hvítá
Barnafoss
Hraunfossar
Hraunsás
518
Gilsbakki
376
523
Húsafell
(Kolsstaðir)
Gráhraun
Norðlingafljót
518
Hallkelsstaðir
550
445
Tunga
523
Þorvaldsstaðir
Fljótstunga
425
Kalmanstunga
Víðgelmir
438
F578
938
Strútur
Kleppavatn
Surtshellir
Stefánshellir
Fiskivatn
Hallmundarhraun
0 1 km
Hallmundarhellir
Eiríksjökull
Kalmanstunga-Bjarnastaðir 14 km

2 P. 565

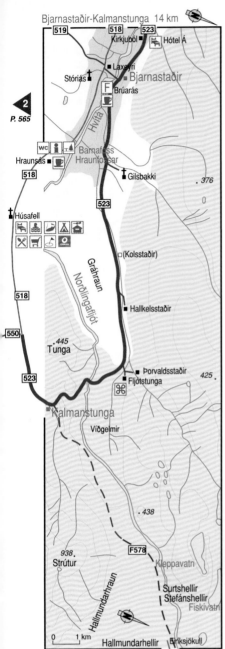

Gilsbakki, a church and manor farm, formerly a parsonage, famous in poems and Sagas. Gunnlaugur Ormstunga ("Serpent-tongue"), a hero of the Sagas, came from there. The farm's land is rich in salmon and trout and formerly it had swan hunting as well. Fine views.

Kalmanstunga, the easternmost and furthest inland farm in the Borgarfjörður district, over 40 km from the sea. It has always been a substantial farm, its land extending over the whole of the Arnarvatnsheiði moor and the Hallmundarhraun lava field. Many trees. It was once on the main horseback route to the north via Kaldidalur, Stórisandur and Arnarvatnsheiði.

Víðgelmir, one of the biggest lava-caves in Iceland, ca. 1 km southeast of Fljótstunga, the uppermost farm in the Hvítársíða district. Many stalagmites and stalacites, some evidence of ancient dwellings there.

Hallmundarhraun, a lava field from craters at the northwestern edge of the Langjökull glacier, reaching north of the Eiríksjökull glacier along the Norðlingafljót river valley to the river Hvítá near Gilsbakki. Parts of it are known as Skógarhraun and Gráhraun. Not difficult to cross in most places. Big caves Kalmanshellir, the biggest known cave in Iceland, Víðgelmir, Surtshellir and Stefánshellir, and other smaller ones.

Surtshellir, in the Hallmundarhraun lava field about 7 km from the farm Kalmanstunga along a road (F578) that is slow but passable for all cars as far as the caves. One of Iceland's longest and best-known caves, it is 1970 m long, or 3500 m along with the cave **Stefánshellir**, which connects up to it. There are many stories connected with Surtshellir, and clear traces of people having lived there.

Arnarvatnsheiði, extensive moors with many fishing-lakes. Accessible by jeep but very difficult in places. The track runs east between the lakes Arnarvatn and Réttarvatn on the Stórisandur sands, whence there are two routes, one to the valleys Víðidalur and Vatnsdalur, the other east to the Kjalvegur (Road F35) north of the mountain Sandkúlufell.

518 **Hálsasveitarvegur,** p. 262 F578 **Arnarvatnsvegur,** p. 466

Hraunfossar

523 Hvítársíðuvegur, 19 km.

Hvítársíða, a farming district along the Hvítá river north of Síðumúlaveggir, Hálsasveit to the south.

Kirkjuból, a farm in the Hvítársíða district, from which come the poets Guðmundur Böðvarsson (1904-1974) and his son Böðvar Guðmundsson (b. 1939).

Síðumúli, a farm and church in the lower part of Hvítársíða.

522 Þverárhlíðarvegur, 20 km.

Þverárhlíð, a farming area above the Stafholtstungur district, separated from the Norðurárdalur valley by the Grjótháls ridge. Broad lowlands with marshes and birch-bushes.

Norðtunga, a church, built in 1953. Nice woods, fenced in and put under the protection of the Forestry Service in 1929.

Norðtunguskógur, a forest planted mostly in straight lines – an example of "Danish-style" planning from the early 20th century. National Forest.

Hjarðarholt, a farm and church. Often the home of sheriffs and wealthy farmers.

Þverá, a clear river formed from several rivers and streams coming from the lakes on the Tvídægra moors. Considered one of the best salmon-fishing rivers in Iceland.

524 Þverárvegur, 2,6 km.

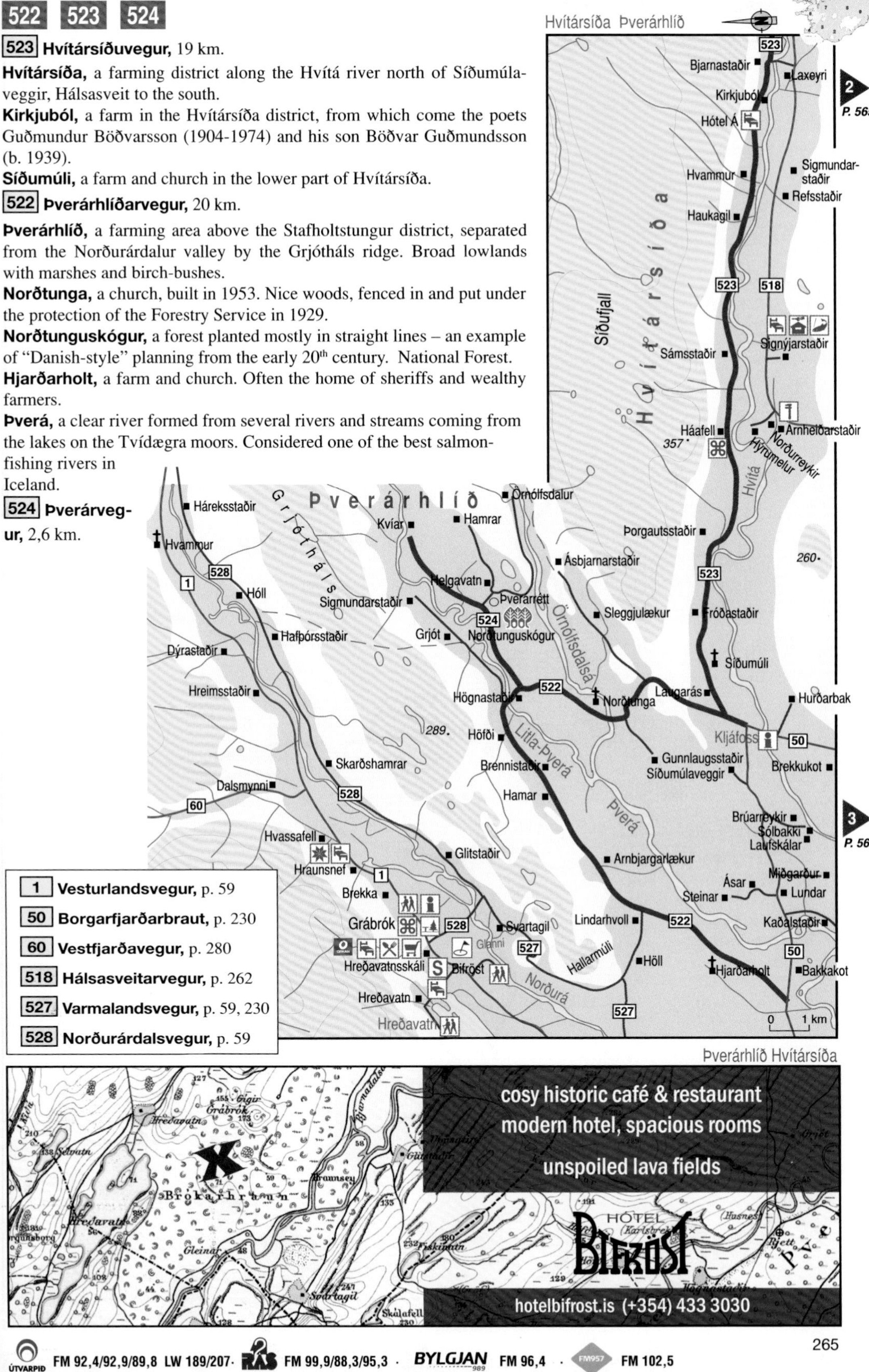

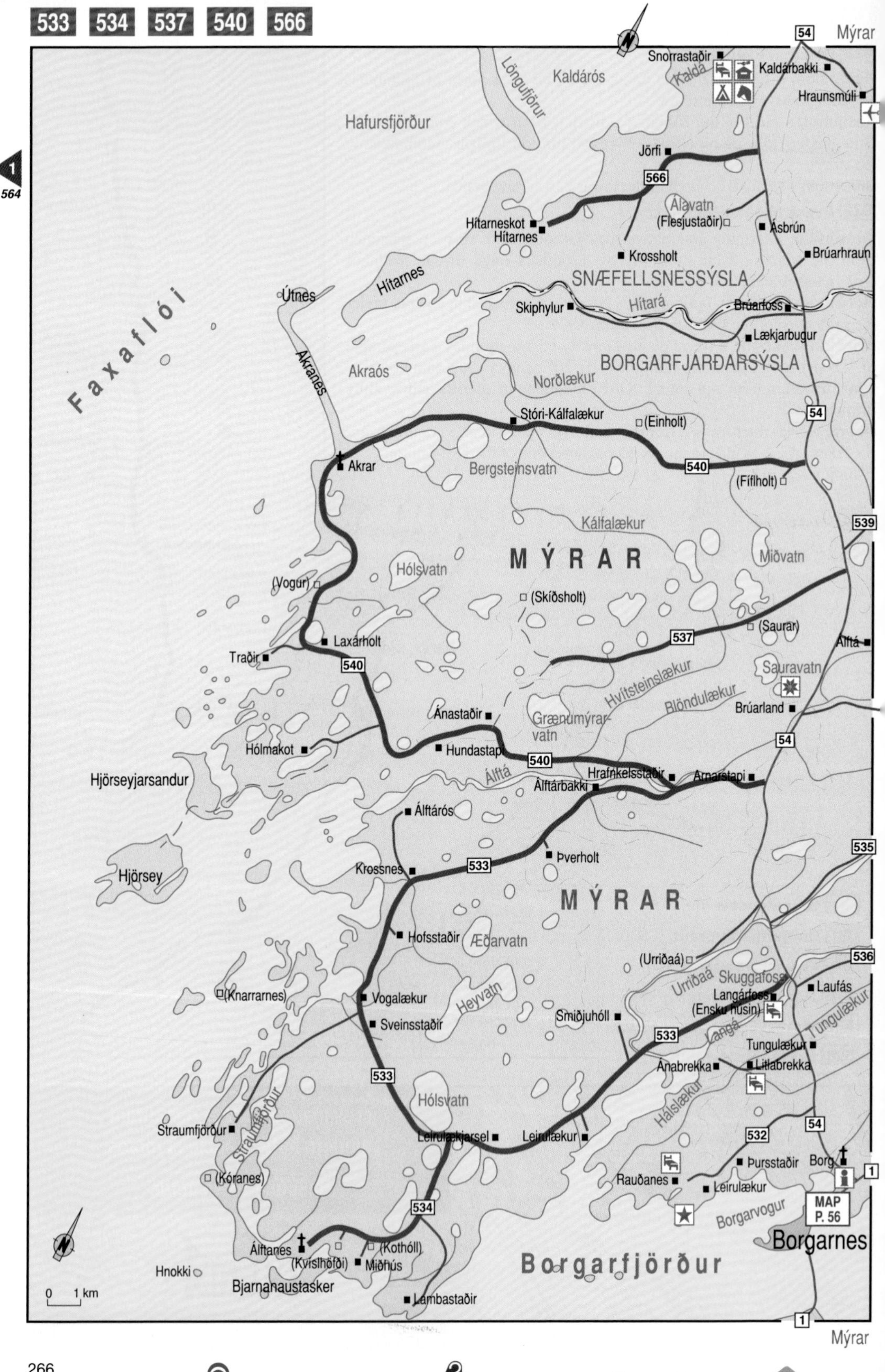
533
534
537
540
566
1
P. 564
Mýrar
54
Snorrastaðir
Kaldá
Kaldárbakki
Hraunsmúli
Kaldárós
Löngufjörur
Hafursfjörður
Jörfi
566
Álavatn
(Flesjustaðir)
Ásbrún
Hítarneskot
Hítarnes
Krossholt
Brúarhraun
Hítarnes
Útnes
SNÆFELLSNESSÝSLA
Skiphylur
Hítará
Brúarfoss
Lækjarbugur
Faxaflói
Akranes
Akraós
BORGARFJARÐARSÝSLA
Norðlækur
Stóri-Kálfalækur
(Einholt)
54
Akrar
Bergsteinsvatn
540
(Fíflholt)
Kálfalækur
539
Hólsvatn
MÝRAR
Miðvatn
(Vogur)
(Skíðsholt)
(Saurar)
537
Laxárholt
Álftá
Traðir
540
Sauravatn
Hvítsteinslækur
Blöndulækur
Ánastaðir
Brúarland
Grænumýrar-
vatn
54
Hólmakot
Hundastapi
540
Hrafnkelsstaðir
Arnarstapi
Hjörseyjarsandur
Álftá
Álftárbakki
Álftárós
Hjörsey
Krossnes
533
Þverholt
535
MÝRAR
Hofsstaðir
Æðarvatn
(Urriðaá)
536
Urriðaá
Skuggafoss
Laufás
(Knarrarnes)
Vogalækur
Heyvatn
Langárfoss
(Ensku húsin)
Smiðjuhóll
Sveinsstaðir
533
Langá
Tungulækur
Tungulækur
Ánabrekka
Litlabrekka
533
Hólsvatn
Hálslækur
Straumfjörður
Straumfjörður
Leirulækjarsel
Leirulækur
54
532
Þursstaðir
Borg
1
(Kóranes)
Rauðanes
Leirulækur
534
MAP
P. 56
Borgarvogur
Borgarnes
Álftanes
(Kothóll)
(Kvíslhöfði)
Miðhús
Hnokki
Borgarfjörður
Bjarnanaustasker
0
1 km
Lambastaðir
1
Mýrar

Snorrastaðir, birthplace of Ólafur Egilsson (1564-1639), pastor, who was taken captive by Algerian pirates when they attacked the Westman Islands. When he later returned to Iceland he wrote a remarkable account of his experiences.

566 **Hítarnesvegur,** 7,15 km.

Jörfi, a farm where Víga-Styr was killed, according to the Sagas. He was an aggressive and violent man, a killer who boasted that he had slain 33 men without making reparation for any of them. Finally he slew the farmer at Jörfi, whose son, a small man and a weakling, killed Víga-Styr, dealing him such a blow that the ax stuck in his brain.

Hítarnes, formerly a parsonage and church. The home of Þórður Kolbeinsson, poet, arch-enemy of Björn Hítdælakappi in *Bjarnar saga Hítdælakappa*. Þórður seduced Björn's wife and eventually killed Björn, but that lost him the woman's love.

Hítará, a good salmon river flowing out of the Hítarvatn lake and into the Akraós estuary. Not far from its mouth is the pool Þangbrandshylur and an old ship anchorage.

Skiphylur, ("Ship's pool") a farm taking its name from a pool in Hítará now called Þangbrandshylur, where it is said the missionary Þangbrandur moored his boat after drifting into the mouth of Hítará when he came to Iceland in 997. Near this pool is the rock **Klukkusteinn** ("Bell rock") which he used as a mooring. A bell-sounding echo is heard when this stone is struck with another stone.

540 **Hraunhreppsvegur,** 33,69 km.

Akrar, a church and old manor farm where Skallagrímur, father of Egill in *Egils saga*, is said to have tilled his fields. West of the farm is a 5 km long peninsula, Akranes, which with Hítarnes separates the **Akraós** estuary from the sea.

Vogur, a farm. There stayed the first doctors for the county of Mýrarsýslu.

Hjörsey, the largest island off this coast. Was a substantial farm, and a church until 1896, with rich land and fishing, but has been much damaged by the sea and sand. This was the home of Oddný, the woman Þórður Kolbeinsson and Björn Hítdælakappi fought over.

Álftá, a fishing river that separates to counties, Álftaneshreppur and Hraunhreppur.

537 **Skíðholtsvegur,** 11,36 km.

533 **Álftaneshreppsvegur,** 31 km.

Knarrarnes, an island with rich farming land, eider ducks and seals. The sea has broken through the isthmus that connected it with the shore.

Straumfjörður, the next farm to the west of Álftanes, named after the inlet by which it stands. Up until the 20th century there was off and on a trading and rowing-boat fishing centre. Very rocky coast with many skerries. The French research ship *Pourquoi pas?* foundered on the Hnokki skerry in 1936, only one of the 39 men on board surviving. Among those drowned was the French scientist Jean-Baptiste Charcot (1867-1936), the leader of the expedition. In the15th century this was the home of Straumfjarðar-Halla, notorious for sorcery, and the local place-names Höllubjarg ("Halla's crag") and Höllubrunnur ("Halla's well") are named for her. An Icelandic movie deals with both the *Pourqui pas?* disaster and Straumfjarðar-Halla.

Kóranes, formerly a general store run by the father of Ásgeir Ásgeirsson (1894-1972), the 2nd president of Iceland, who was born and raised there.

Leirulækur, a farm, the home of Vigfús Jónsson (1648-1728), best known as Leirulækjar-Fúsi. He was a talented poet, famous for his satirical verse, considered to be a "poet of power". Some of his poems have survived to the present day.

Langárfoss, a farm on north bank of the river Langá. Falls and rapids in the river, good salmon-fishing.

Langá, a salmon river flowing from the Langavatn lake through the valley Grenjadalur. There is a big salmon-ladder near the waterfall Sveðjufoss.

534 **Álftanesvegur,** 6,31 km.

Álftanes, a church and substantial farm at the end of the Álftanes peninsula, much eroded by the sea. The manor farm for the district since earliest times. Skallagrímur Kveldúlfsson of *Egils saga* lived there his first years as a farmer. Very rich land. Good view from Virki, a small hill in the home-field.

1 **Vesturlandsvegur,** p. 55
54 **Snæfellsnesvegur,** p. 238
532 **Þursstaðavegur,** p. 238
535 **Grímsstaðavegur,** p. 238
536 **Stangarholtsvegur,** p. 238
539 **Hítardalsvegur,** p. 268

(Hólmur)-Hítardalur 10 km

15 P. 578

Hítardalur-(Hólmur) 10 km

Hítarvatn, a big fishing lake, one of the largest in the lowlands of the county, 8 km^2. In it are several islets where lovely flowering plants grow. Out of the lake runs the river Hítará. East of Hítarvatn is the mountain **Foxufell** (419 m) in which is the cave **Bjarnarhellir**. There are carvings in the cave and a seat has been hewn in the rock.

Hítará, a river flowing out of the Hítarvatn lake and into the Akraós estuary. A good salmon river. The Brúarfoss and Kattarfoss waterfalls are in Hítará, opposite Grettisbæli. A bit above Brúarfoss are the Grettisstillur stepping stones, where large and small stones lie in an almost straight line across the river. Not far from the mouth of Hítará is the pool Þangbrandshylur and an old ship anchorage where it is said the 10th century missionary Þangbrandur moored his ship when he was forced to land again after setting set sail to foreign countries. In a rock by the pool is a mooring-ring, called Klukkusteinn ("Bell rock") because of the reverberations that are set up when it is struck. The pool was formerly called Skiphylur ("Ship's pool"), and a nearby farm bears that name.

Hítardalur, a rather broad valley between the mountains Múlaselsmúli and Fagraskógarfjall. Lava in many places. The valley is closed by a tuff fell, Hólmur (334 m), below which was a farm of the same name, the home of Björn Hítdælakappi ("The hero of Hítardalur"). Björn Arngeirsson Hítdælakappi, a great hero and poet, lived at Hólmur in the early 11th century. There was a feud between him and another poet, Þórður Kolbeinsson of Hítarnes, over the beautiful Oddný eykyndill ("torch of the island") Þorkelsdóttir from Hjörsey, who was engaged to marry Björn but was stolen from him by Þórður. Þórður eventually attacked Björn's home with a force of 24 and killed him. Oddný became ill at the news and in *Bjarnar saga Hítdælakappa* it says that "Þórður would have preferred it if Björn were still alive, were that possible, and he himself might reclaim the love of his wife."

Hítardalur, an old manor farm and a parsonage and church until 1895. Bishop Magnús Einarsson (1098-1148) of Skálholt died there in a fire in 1148 along with 70-80 other people, the greatest loss of life in a fire in Icelandic history. In the home field is **Nafnaklettur** ("Name cliff"), a tuff rock-face where many people have carved their names, including Ebenezer Henderson, the well-known traveller and founder of the Icelandic Bible Society. In the mountain Bæjarfell are two caves, Fjárhellir ("Sheep cave") and Sönghellir ("Song cave"), and in the Drangar cliffs there are clear forms of faces. They are said to be Bárður Snæfellsás and the giantess Hít, who was said to have lived in Hítardalur, which is named for her. An old cornerstone in the Hítardalur church has a carving which the common people considered to be a picture of the giantess Hít, though the clerics said it was an icon. This stone is in the Hítardalur home field, and a cast of it in the National Museum in Reykjavík.

There are 15 km to the Hítardalur farm from Road 54 and 25 km to the lake Hítarvatn.

Nafnaklettur in Hítardalur valley © OH

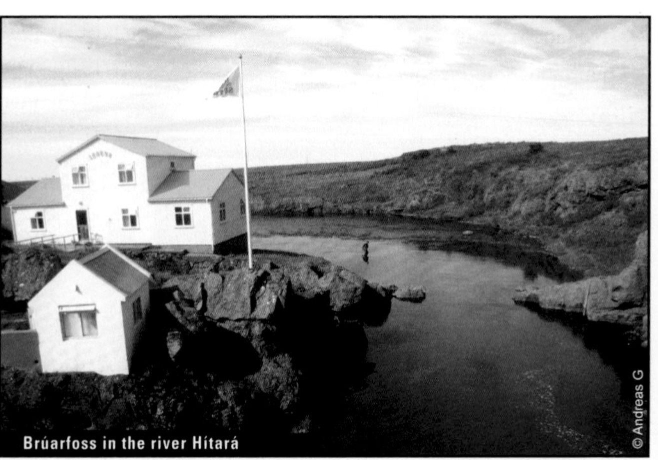
Brúarfoss in the river Hítará © Andreas G

553 LANGAVATNSVEGUR

Langavatnsdalur, the valley north of Langavatn. There were farms there in settlement times, after which it was grazing land for sheep and bulls until the mid-19th century, when the bulls all drowned in the lake. A farm was built there in the early 19th century but the attempt came to tragic end when first, the farmer got lost and died of exposure when he had gone to the nearest farm to fetch fire, and then the daughter was caught stealing a horse, for food, from Hörðudalur (see Roads 57 and 581). There used to be a track up the valley, over Sópandaskarð pass and along the Laugardalur valley to Hörðudalur. It was much-travelled in early times, e.g. in the 13th century, the time of the Sturlungas.

Langavatn, a lake, 5 km long and up to 36 m deep, formed by lava which has dammed the river at the Langá River end. Good fishing. Around the turn of last century the fishing rights belonged to that same French baron C.G. Boilleau that had a salmon canning factory at Hvítárvellir (see Road 53), and for whom the street Barónstígur in Reykjavík is named.

Grísatunga, an abandoned farm above Þinghóll, a crossroads of the major horseback trails of old. One trail went up the Langavatnsdalur valley, the other up along the Gljúfurá river, behind the mountains and down by Hraundalur in the Hraunhreppur district. Before the roads were laid the latter way was often chosen so as to avoid the marshes in the Mýrar district. These bogs and marshes were so notorious that farmers from the upper reaches of the Borgarfjörður lands would make their pack-horse trips to the market town very early in the spring, while the ground was still frozen, travelling as much as two months earlier than most people.

Þinghóll, ("Assembly hill") north and east of the ford in the river Gljúfurá, below the abandoned farm Grísatunga. It is thought that the spring assembly of the Þverárþing west of the river Hvítá was held there for a time, probably from the beginning of the land-quarter assemblies (about 965) until they started having assemblies at Faxið by the river Þverá.

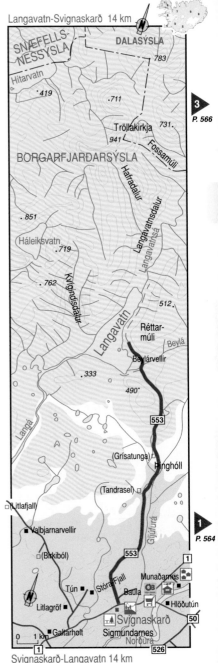

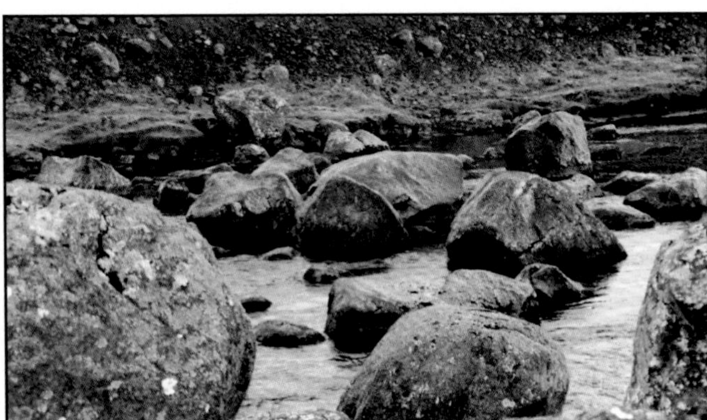

1 **Vesturlandsvegur,** p. 58 50 **Borgarfjarðarbraut,** p. 230

526 **Stafholtsvegur,** p. 230

Langavatn-Svignaskarð 14 km

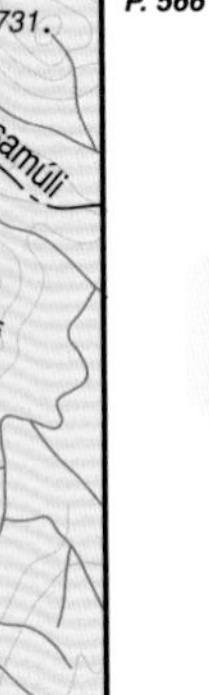

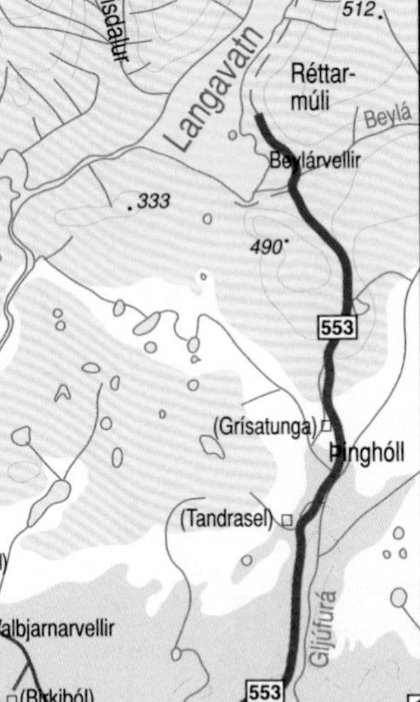

3 P. 566

1 P. 564

Svignaskarð-Langavatn 14 km

The old corner stone in Hítardalur church The portrait of Bárður Snæfellsás and the giantess Hít

15
P. 578

Arnarstapi-Öxl 17 km

Öxl-Arnarstapi 17 km

Stapafell, (526 m) an elongated tuff mountain with much scree, extending south from the lower slopes of the Snæfellsjökull glacier. On top is a rock, **Fellskross**, supposedly the dwelling of the "hidden people" or elves. To the north of Stapafell is the **Sönghellir** ("Singing cave"), known for its echoes. Many names are carved in the rock, including those of Eggert Ólafsson and Bjarni Pálsson who travelled the country in the 18th century.

Klifahraun, a lava-field north and east of Stapafell, ending in the sharp crags **Sölvahamar,** along the top of which the old travel route lay. Through the lava runs the river Sandalækur, north of which the river Grísafossá comes pouring out of the mountain Botnsfjall, to flow into the sea near Sölvahamar.

Sleggjubeina, a small stream towards the west end of the Breiðavík bay, falling down the mountain **Botnafjall** into a deep, narrow, almost circular gorge, **Rauðfeldargjá**, which is near-invisible from the road. It is possible to get quite far up the gorge once the snows have melted, though wellington boots and rainwear are recommended because of spray from the stream. Though the gorge is so narrow, there is sufficient light from above. On the eastern bank of the stream are the overgrown ruins of the farm Grímsstaðir, where the poet Sigurður Breiðfjörð (1798-1846) lived for a time.

Stóri-Kambur, a farm in Breiðavík, often mentioned in *Eyrbyggja saga*, the home of Björn Breiðvíkingakappi, "who was friendlier with the mistress of the house at Fróðá than with her brother, the chieftain at Helgafell", the latter being Snorri goði, who eventually drove Björn away from Iceland. He is thought to have gone west to Vínland (North America) where Icelandic travellers said they had met him.

Breiðavík, the pretty little district between the Búðahraun lava field and the village Arnarstapi, along a bay of the same name. Grassy and sheltered. A long, yellow sand reef, Hraunlandarif, creates the Miðhúsavatn lagoon. Above is the rocky mountain **Knarrarklettar**, where many a traveller has fallen to his death after losing his way on the Fróðárheiði moor.

Öxl, a farm above Búðir below the steep scree mountain **Axlarhyrna** (433 m) where Axlar-Björn ("Björn from Öxl") lived in the 16th century. He was Iceland's most notorious murderer, said to have killed 18 people, mostly travellers to whom he offered hospitality. An information sign about these events are at Axlarhólar, good views. At Öxl is **Ásmundarleiði**, where the settler Ásmundur is said to be buried. Fine view of Faxaflói.

54 **Snæfellsnesvegur,** p. 245 570 **Jökulhálsleið,** p. 464-465

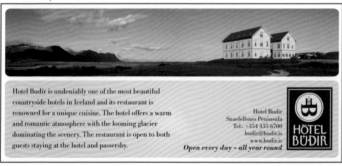

Bárður Snæfellsás

572 Dritvíkurvegur, 2 km.

Malarrif, ("Pebble reef") the southern extremity of this coastline, lighthouse. Large, smooth, black pebbles on the beach. A path to Lóndrangar from there, 30 minutes walk.

Lóndrangar, two pillar rocks by the sea 15 minutes walk from road, the taller one being 75 m. The remains of a volcano, scoria with basalt caverns. The higher one to the east has been climbed. Seabirds nest there.

Svalþúfa, on a ridge east of Lóndrangar, probably the remains of a crater. Below it is the rock Þúfubjarg, where according to a folktale the poet Kolbeinn jöklaskáld ("the glacier poet") had an encounter with the Devil and beat him in a verse-making contest.

Hellnar, a village on a pretty coastline with strange rock formations. The cave **Baðstofa** is there, known for the strange light in it. A church, formerly at **Laugarbrekka**, where the cemetery is. Hellnar is the birthplace of Guðríður Þorbjarnardóttir, the wife of Þorfinnur karlsefni. They attempted to settle in Vínland in the year 1004 and Guðríður gave birth to the first white child to be born in America, Snorri Þorfinnsson. Guðríður was one of the greatest travellers of medieval times, walking all the way to Rome, among other things. She eventually settled down at Glaumbær in Skagafjörður (see Road 75). Most Icelanders are thought to be able to trace their ancestry to her. By Gróuhóll in Hellnar there is a spring that goes by the name of **Lífslind Hellnamanna** ("Spring of life"), but has in recent times been called **Maríulind** ("Spring of Mary") after an image of the Virgin Mary was put up by the spring. It is belived that the spring has healing powers and it is said that it will never dry up. According to legend, Bishop Guðmundur the Good came to this place in 1230 and along with his fellow travellers had a vision of a woman accompanied by three angels. She bade him consecrate the spring, and he did so. Walking route to Arnarstapi. Just below the main road, to the west of Laugarvatn above Þinghamar and the ruins of the farm and church at Laugarbrekka, is a memorial to Guðríður, and a statue of her by Ásmundur Sveinson.

Snæfellsjökull, (1,446 m) an ancient cone volcano, one of finest mountains in Iceland. An impressive sight from as far away as Reykjavík, from where it can be seen in clear weather, seeming to rise from the sea. Many prehistoric eruptions took place in the glacier-covered crater at its peak, and its slopes are covered with lava. The walk to the highest peak of the glacier, Þúfur, takes 5-7 hours and is physically demanding. The glacier dominates the area, the western part of which is covered with lava and known as "under the glacier". In Jules Verne's novel, *A Journey to the Centre of the Earth*, the entrance to the underground way was through the crater of Snæfellsjökull. In the eyes of both "traditional" believers in the supernatural and new agers Snæfellsjökull has more hidden power than any other mountain.

Arnarstapi, a fishing village in very interesting natural surroundings, with weird basalt columns, gorges and caves by the coast, in most of which there are populous sea-bird colonies. The most famous cliff is **Gatklettur** ("Hole cliff"), through which the sea spouts in stormy weather. The path to the caves is reached through the harbour and goes along the top of the cliffs so one sees the caves, and the nesting birds, from above. Walking route to Hellnar.

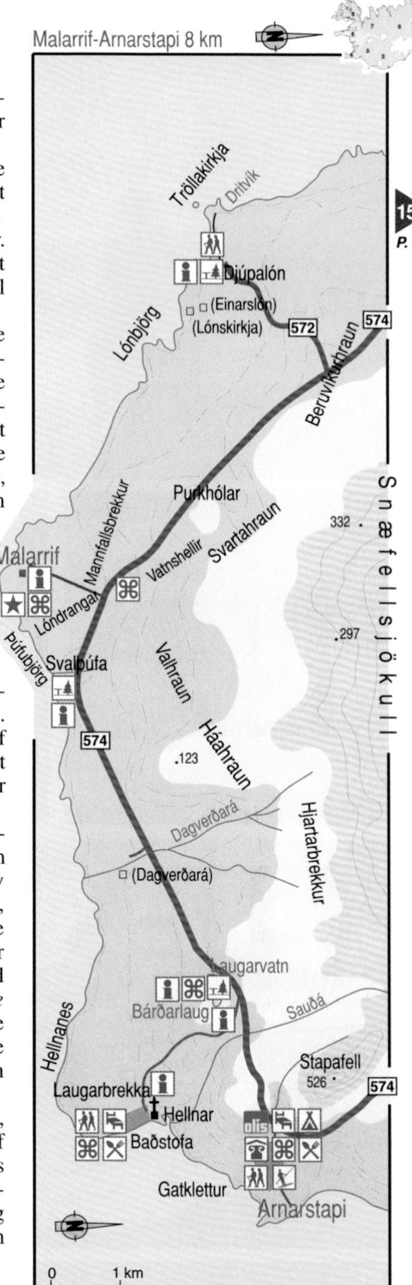

KAFFIHÚS
GAMLA RIF

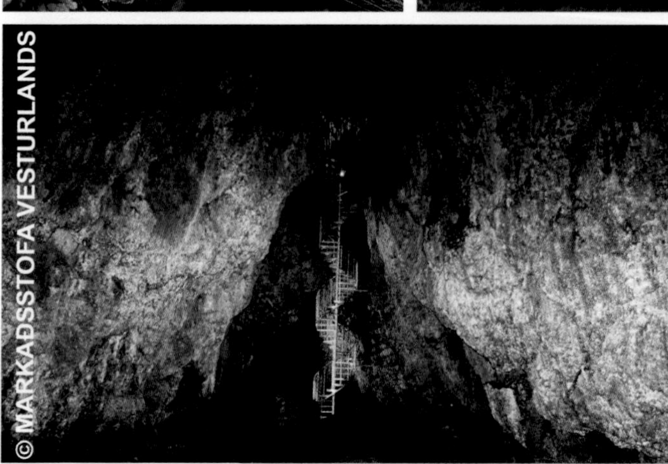

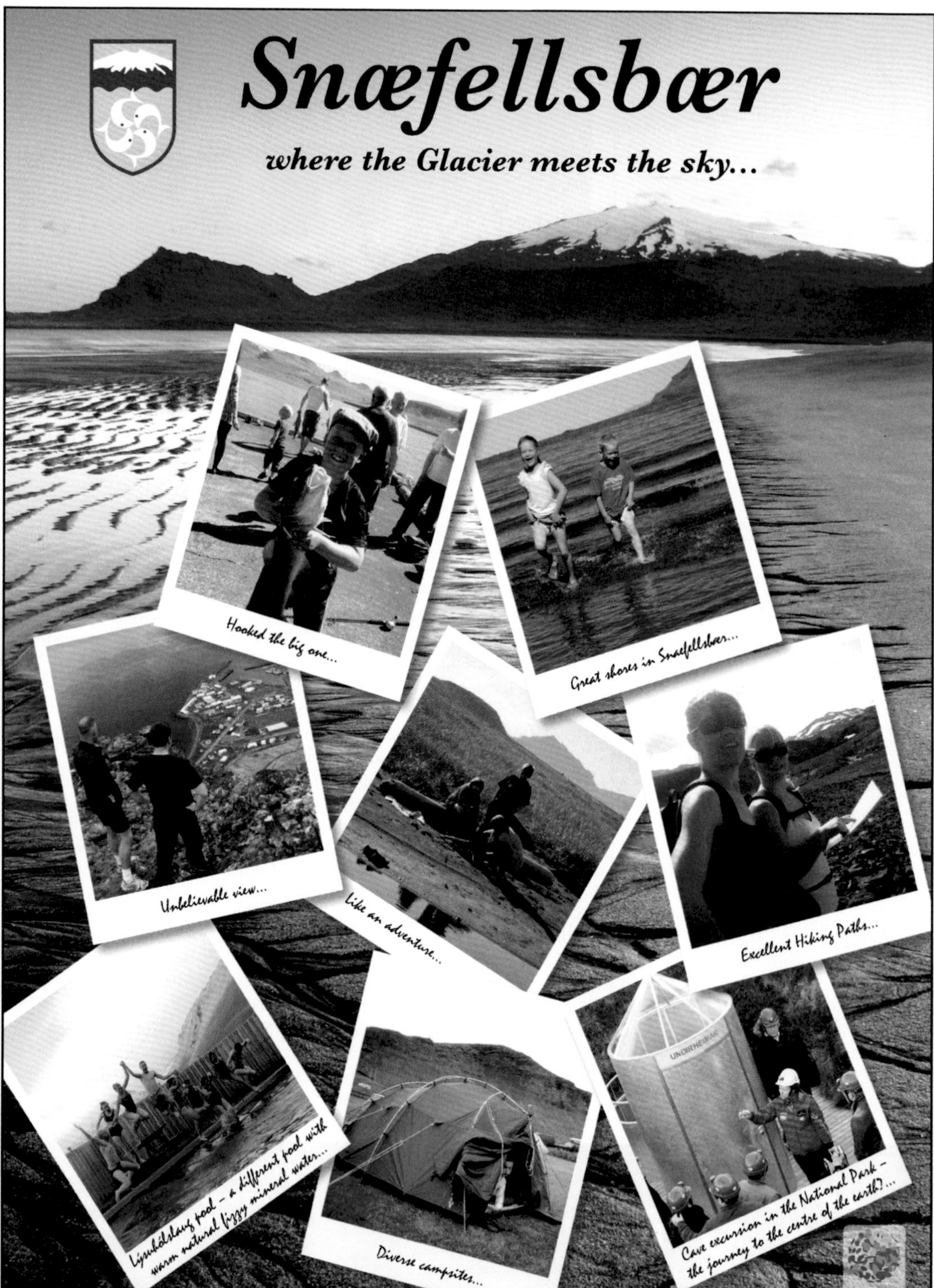

Snæfellsbær
where the Glacier meets the sky...
Hooked the big one...
Great shores in Snæfellsbær...
Unbelievable view...
Like an adventure...
Excellent Hiking Paths...
Lýsuhólslaug pool - a different pool with warm natural fizzy mineral water...
Diverse campsites...
UNDIRHEIMAR
Cave excursion in the National Park - the journey to the centre of the earth?...
EARTHCHECK
Upplýsingamiðstöð Snæfellsbæjar – Tourist information centre – Kirkjutún 2 - Ólafsvík,
Snæfellsbær -) 433 6929 - info@snb.is – www.snb.is - www.facebook.com/snaefellsbaer

Gufuskálar-Malarrif 15 km

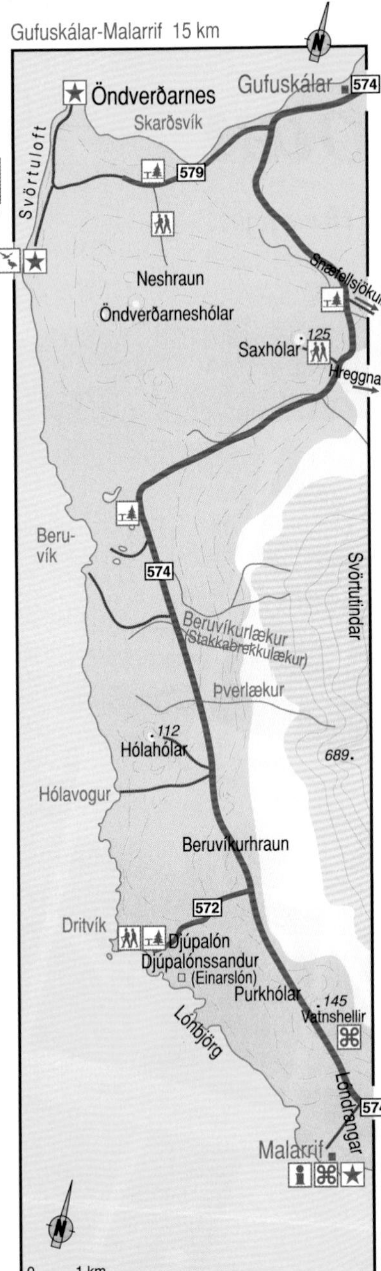

Malarrif-Gufuskálar 15 km

Svörtuloft

579 Öndverðanesvegur, 6,99 km.

Móðulækur, a small stream which legend has it was once a big river but sank into the ground.

Hreggnasi, (469 m) a peak at the end of a tuff ridge sticking north from the glacier. The highest peak on the ridge, **Bárðarkista** ("Bárður's chest") (668 m), is said to be where Bárður Snæfellsás' treasure is hidden.

Saxhóll, 125 m, a crater that erupted 3-4000 years ago. Easy climb and a great view at the top, view dial.

Öndverðarnes, the extreme tip of the Snæfellsnes peninsula. The area between Öndverðarnes and Rif is a great place for bird watching. Formerly a substantial farm with a chapel, now a lighthouse. Deep in the ground is the old well, **Fálki**, with 18 steps leading down to it. South of Öndverðarnes are cliffs known as **Svörtuloft** ("Black skies"), where ships have been wrecked. Nearby is the big Neshraun lava field, with many old craters such as Öndverðarneshólar, Saxhóll etc.

Beruvík, an area where there once were many farms, now abandoned. Some remains of the old fishing-station and settlement.

Hólahólar, old craters, one of which, Berudalur, is like a beautiful, natural amphitheatre, open on one side and with a grassy bottom.

Dritvík, for centuries on of the best and busiest fishing-stations in Iceland, often as many as 60 boats with 300-400 fishermen rowing from there. Rescue hut. To the east is a large rock, Tröllakirkja ("Giants' church"), and in the middle of the inlet another, known as Bárðarskip (Bárður's ship"). At **Djúpalónssandur** between Dritvík and Einarslón are four well-known lifting-stones, on which the fishermen tested their strength. The biggest is known as Fullsterkur ("Fully-strong"), weighs 154 kg and is very difficult to lift. Hálfsterkur ("Half-strong") is 100 kg, Hálfdrættingur ("Weakling"), 54 kg and Amlóði ("Useless"), 23 kg. Men who could not lift Hálfdrættingur were not accepted on the fishing boats. There is a road to Djúpalónssandur.

Einarslón, an abandoned farm, once a church.

Vatnshellir, a 200 m long lava cave on the south slopes of Purkhólahraun lava flow, considered to be 5-8000 years old. A spiral staircase has been put into the cave to enable access but entrance is only allowed on guided tours which are available all year round.

Ólafsvík, (pop. 945) a fishing town below the mountain Enni. A pretty waterfall in the mountainside above it, beyond which is the steep peak Hrói.

Enni, (410 m) a mountain falling sheer to the sea, with cliffs. The travel route used to be along the foot of the cliffs, passable when the tides were right, and dangerous because of falling rocks and surf. The mountain was thought to be haunted.

Svöðufoss, a waterfall in the river Hólmkelsá, visible from the road.

Rif, (pop. 145) a village which was once the most important fishing and trading centre on the Snæfellsnes peninsula. It is again gaining importance with the recent building of a new harbour and the resultant growth in the fishing industry. In 1467 English buccaneers killed the local governor, Björn Þorleifsson, but his widow Ólöf took dreadful revenge. This supposedly included getting the King of Denmark to wage war on England, making her the only Icelander to be responsible for a war between nations. Björnssteinn, the stone where Björn was slain, can still be seen. Near by there is a monument with information about the landing place at Rif which was used by fishermen in medieval times. There is also an airport.

Ingjaldshóll, a church, ancient manor farm and the main setting of *Víglundar saga*. Often the residence of sheriffs and other important officials. The church is believed to be the oldest concrete church in the world, built in 1903. A painting in the church by Áki Gränz shows Christopher Columbus conversing with the local clergyman in 1477 about the voyages of Icelanders to the west (Vinland – now America). Life stories of Columbus indicate that he visited this part of Iceland in the company of English merchants at Rif in order to get information about the earlier Viking voyages to the west. View dial.

Keflavíkurbjarg, a cliff between Hellissandur and Rif. On its west side is **Balalind**, a water source which is claimed to have healing powers. A sign by the road leads to the cliff.

Hellissandur, (pop. 370) Icelands oldest fishing village. A trading and community centre. Hotel, maritime museum and a small park. There is a road leading to Snæfellsjökull, great view.

Gufuskálar, formerly the site of a U.S. loran station with a 420 m high mast, the highest construction in Iceland and at one time (1963) the highest in Europe. It is now to used for long-wave broadcasts of the Icelandic National Radio. Many remains of the old fish-drying installations from the time when there was a great deal of rowing-boat fishing there.

Írskra brunnur, ("Well of the Irishmen") a well from the time of the settlement, in the fields near Gufuskálar, Írskra kirkja ("Church of the Irishmen") ruins on the shore and Írskra búðir ("Irishmen's booth") ruins at the edge of the lava field. At **Gufuskálavör** (vör = landing) one can see grooves worn in the rock over the ages where the rowingboats were pulled ashore. Memorial to Elínborg Þorbjarnardóttir, the last person to make her home there, unveiled in 1987.

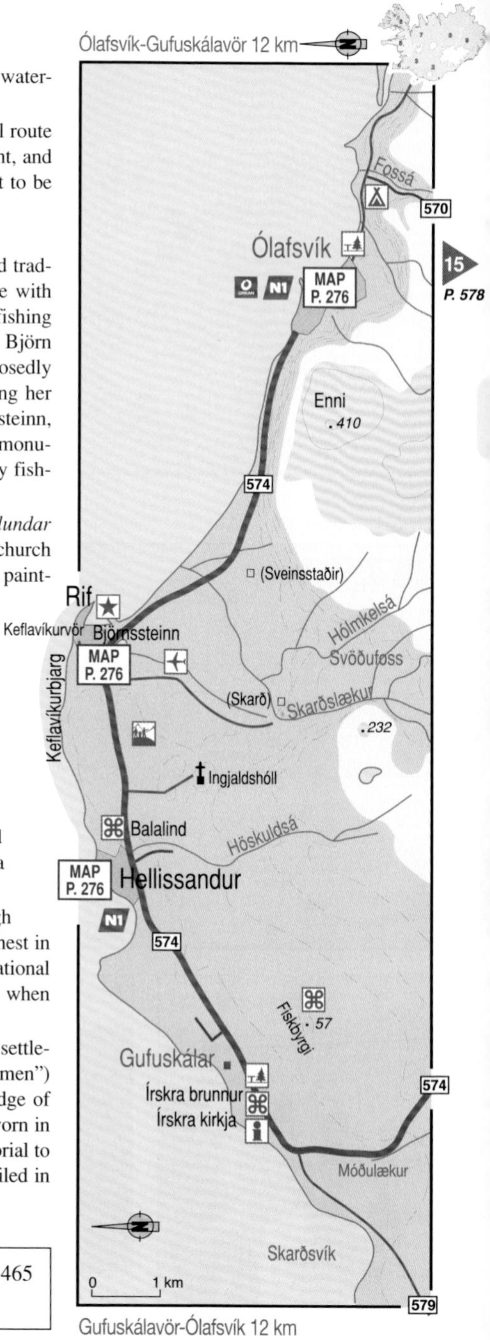

54 Snæfellsnesvegur, p. 245 **570 Jökulhálsleið** p. 465-465
579 Öndverðanesvegur p. 274

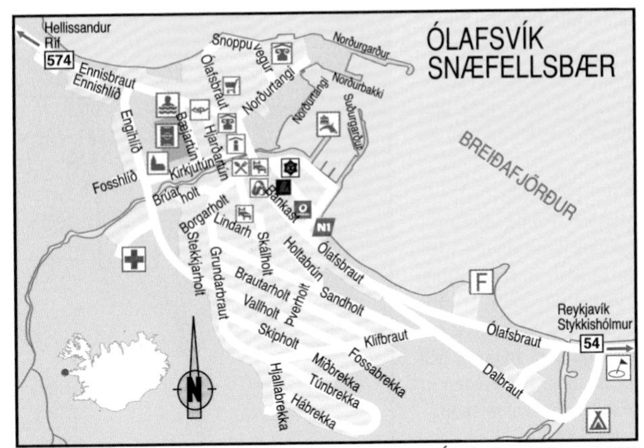

Ólafsvík, p. 245 and 275.

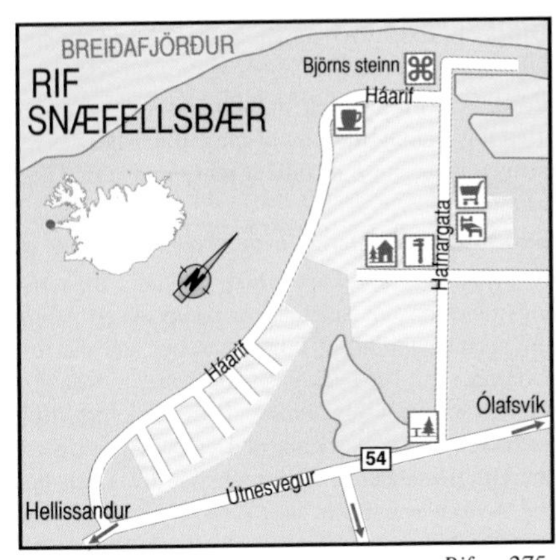

Rif, p. 275.

Hellissandur, p. 275.

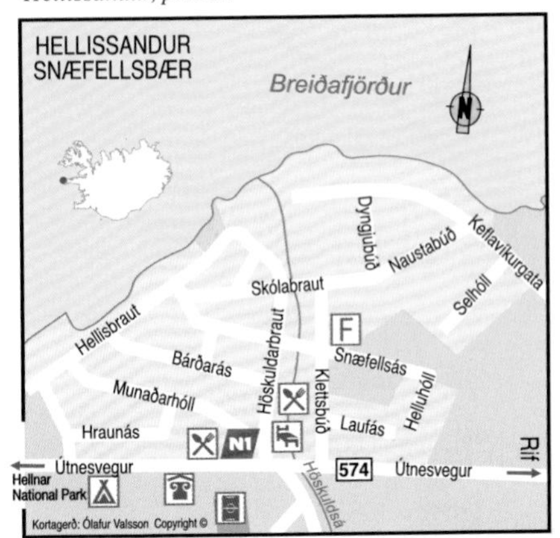

586 HAUKADALSSKARÐSVEGUR

Haukadalsskarð, a pass that was once an important route from the Haukadalur valley over to Hrútafjörður in the north. Little used now but passable for jeeps in summer.

Jörfi, a farm below the peak **Jörfahnúkur** (714 m). Notorious festivities (Jörfagleði) were held there at one time, but the debauchery is said to have been so great that they were abolished early in the 18th century and have never been revived. It is said that 19 illegitimate children were conceived at the last Jörfagleði, which was the last straw for the authorities. A folktale states that one winter a traveller asked for lodging at Jörfi for himself and his horses, but was refused. This enraged the visitor who said the local farmer would lose some of his own horses. At about the same time the following year the farmer's horses became terrified without a reason, rushed up the nearby peak and fell to their deaths on the slippery ice slopes.

Leikskálar, a farm where the same family, in a direct male line, lived from 1760-1915, being named alternately Bergþór and Þorvarður.

Eiríksstaðir, an abandoned farm on the land of Stóra-Vatnshorn, where Eric the Red lived before he went to Greenland. It is believed that his son Leifur the Lucky Eiríksson was born there. Archaeological research has been conducted in the area recently, showing that the timeline described in the sagas can be verified to a considerable extent. The excavations is accessible to the public, and nearby a so-called "theoretical house" has been built. Guides in Viking Age costume describe the life-style of the Viking settlers This is an attempt to show what the farm Eiríksstaðir may have looked like when it was inhabited.

Stóra-Vatnshorn, the same family has lived there since 1658.

Eiríksstaðir in Haukadalur.

Haukadalur, a fairly long, fertile valley going east. At its lower end is **Haukadalsvatn**, a 4 km long fishing-lake, from which flows Haukadalsá, a good salmon river. Formerly well wooded but now hardly any trees.

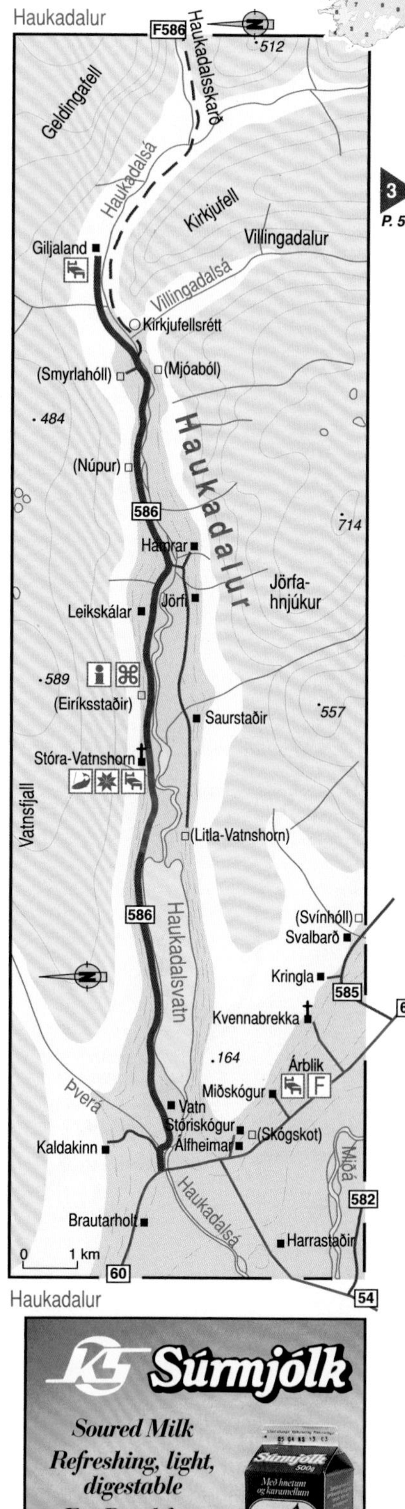

54 **Snæfellsnesvegur,** p. 250
60 **Vestfjarðavegur,** p. 281
582 **Hálsabæjarvegur** p. 280
585 **Hlíðarvegur** p. 280
F586 **Haukadalsskarðsvegur,** p. 468

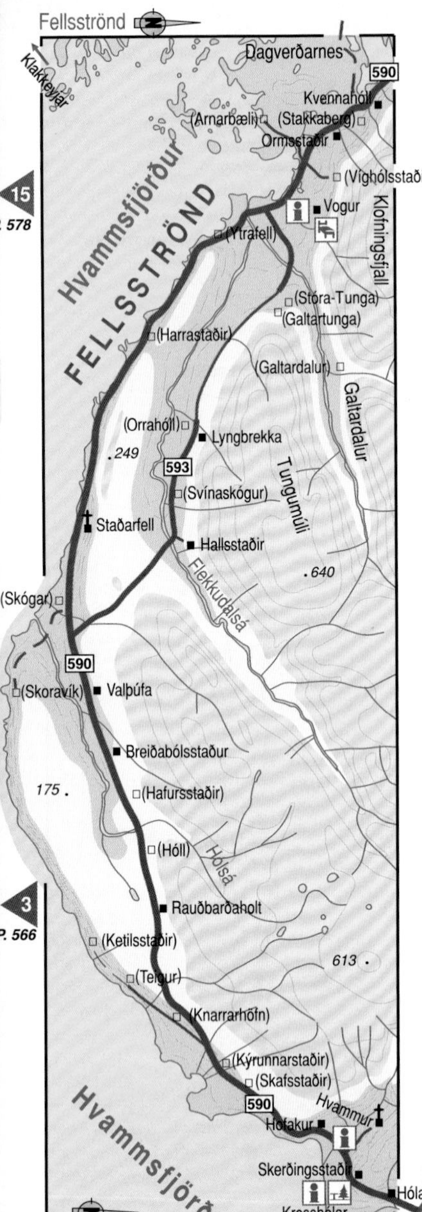

Fellsströnd

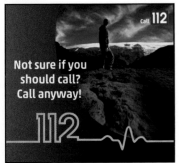

Klakkeyjar, two high, cone-shaped islands. Eric the Red equipped his ship there before setting off to discover Greenland.

Hrappsey, the most famous island in the county of Dalasýsla. Formerly a substantial farm, now abandoned. From 1773-95 there was a printing-press there.

Dagverðarnes, a church on a peninsula of the same name, which is deeply indented with many outlying islands.

Vogur, there is a memorial to Bjarni Jónsson (1863–1926), poet at Vogur.

593 Efribyggðarvegur, 15 km.

Galtardalur, an abandoned farm. Birthplace of the grammarians Dr. Guðbrandur Vigfússon (1827-89), who worked in Copenhagen and Oxford and completed an Icelandic-English Dictionary often associated with Cleasby, and Björn Guðfinnsson (1905-50), an effective and influential grammarian who wrote text-books on his subject.

Staðarfell, a manor farm through the ages, on very good land. Church. Trading place and small harbour. There was a school of domestic science there 1927-76 which is now a rehabilitation centre for alcoholics.

Fellsströnd, the coast along Hvammsfjörður. Just above the shore is a steep, elongated mountain, beyond which is some settled lowland named Efribyggð.

Hvammur, a church and famous Saga-place. The land settled by Auður djúpúðga ("the wise") and long occupied by her descendants. Auður was the daughter of Ketill Suðureyjajarl ("Earl of the Hebrides") and married king Ólafur hvíti of Dublin. After their son Þorsteinn died in battle in Scotland, Auður came to Iceland with her grand-children around the year 890, bringing with her a large number of Scots and Irishmen. Hvammur was also the home of Hvamm-Sturla, forebear of the Sturlunga family, and the birthplace of the writer and law-speaker Snorri Sturluson and his brothers (see Road 518, Reykholt). In the churchyard there is a memorial in honour of Snorri Sturluson, built by the people of Borgarfjörður in 1979 on the 800th anniversary of his birth.

Krosshólar, large crags. *Landnámabók* ("The Book of Settlements") states that Auður djúpúðga had a cross raised there, where she went to pray. The remains of her first farm, Auðartóttir, nearby. A stone cross was erected on the crags in 1965. Auður's descendants considered Krosshólar a holy place.

60 Vestfjarðavegur, p. 282

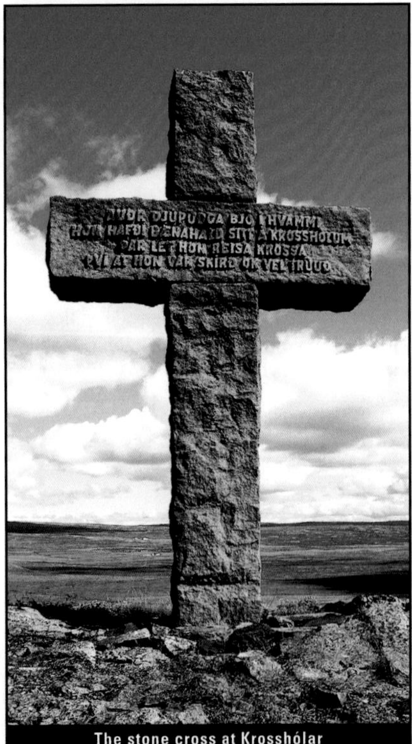
The stone cross at Krosshólar

590 KLOFNINGSVEGUR

Klofningur.

594 Staðarhólsvegur, 3,34 km.

Staðarhóll, formerly a very big manor farm where the Saga writer and district governor Sturla Þórðarson lived.

Salthólmavík, ("Salty islet bay") formerly a trading centre in Saurbær. No harbour but a strong ebbtide. The name indicates salt production at some time.

Tindar, an abandoned farm where lignite was mined, last ca. 1960.

Búðardalur, a farm and former church, occupied by many local leaders. Late in the 18th century Magnús Ketilsson (1732-1803), sheriff and prolific writer, lived there. He experimented with land cultivation.

Skarð, a historic manor farm which has been in the possession of the same family since the 11th century, and probably from the first settlement days. Original settler Geirmundur heljarskinn, the noblest of the original settlers. Skarð was best know when Björn Þorleifsson, sub-governor, and his wife Ólöf Loftsdóttir lived there in the 15th century. In the church is an altarpiece together with other valuable objects believed to have been donated by Ólöf. Two famous vellum manuscripts come from Skarð, both called *Skarðsbók*, the Law-book and the Sagas of Saints. A small harbour nearby where there was once a trading post, also a lignite mine.

Skarðsströnd, the coast between Klofningur and Saurbær. Little lowland but small valleys and many islands.

Klofningsfjall, ("Cloven mountain") (496 m) the outermost mountain in the range. View dial. Great view over the islands in Breiðafjörður fjord.

Klofningur, a belt of rock west of the mountain Klofningsfjall, cleft by a deep chasm through which the highroad goes. Klofningsvegur (Road 590) is 83 km long.

Skarðsströnd
60
Neðri-Brunná
Efri-Brunná
Máskelda
Stórimúli
Efrimúli
Staðarhólskirkja
Purranes
Lambanes
Ásar
Mikligarður
Sauðhóll (Staðarhóll)
594
Kjarlaksvellir
Þverfell
Kverngrjót
Tjaldanes
.550
.441
3
P. 566
590
Seljadalsá
Hafratindur
.923
SKARÐSSTRÖND
Akureyjar
Fagridalur-Innri
Foss
Fagridalur-Ytri
Fagradalsfjall
.813
Nýp
Tindafjall
Búðardalsá
(Tindar)
Búðardalur
(Hvalgrafir)
Klifmýri
.249
(Barmur)
Borgir
.426
Skarð
Krossá
Geirmundarstaðir
(Skarðsstöð)
Mannheimar
15
P. 578
Á
Oddrúnarstaðir
(Kross)
Breiðafjörður
.543
Ballará
Klofningsfjall
Ballará
496
Kvennahóll
(Hnúkur)
Klofningur
0 1 km
Skarðsströnd

60 Vestfjarðavegur, p. 282

For further information:

A unique event occurred in the summer of 1879 when an eagle seized a two-year-old girl named Ragnheiður Eyjólfsdóttir (1877-1959) in the field by the farm Skarð, soared to a great height and flew towards the mountain Krossfjall where it had made a nest. The people of the farm were bringing in the hay when the abduction took place and at first it seemed that little could be done to save the child. One of the locals, Bogi Kristjánsson (1851-1937), was an impulsive and quick-thinking man who was also a good shot. Shooting the eagle crossed his mind but he realised this could only be done as a last result, as he might hit the child by accident and anyway she would plummet to earth if the bird was killed. He therefore grabbed a long pole, mounted a fleet horse and set out in the direction of Krossfjall and the eagle's nest. The girl was big for her age and it soon became obvious that the eagle had taken on more than it could handle, for as it drew near the mountain it tired and lost sufficient altitude for Bogi to hit it in one wing with the pole and force it down. The bird promptly released its burden and flew off. It had grabbed the child's clothes so she had hardly any wounds to speak of; it had also grabbed her hair with its beak. The girl was unconscious when she was rescued. For the first few days after the incident she was gloomy and distracted but she suffered no permanent damage from this unexpected flight.

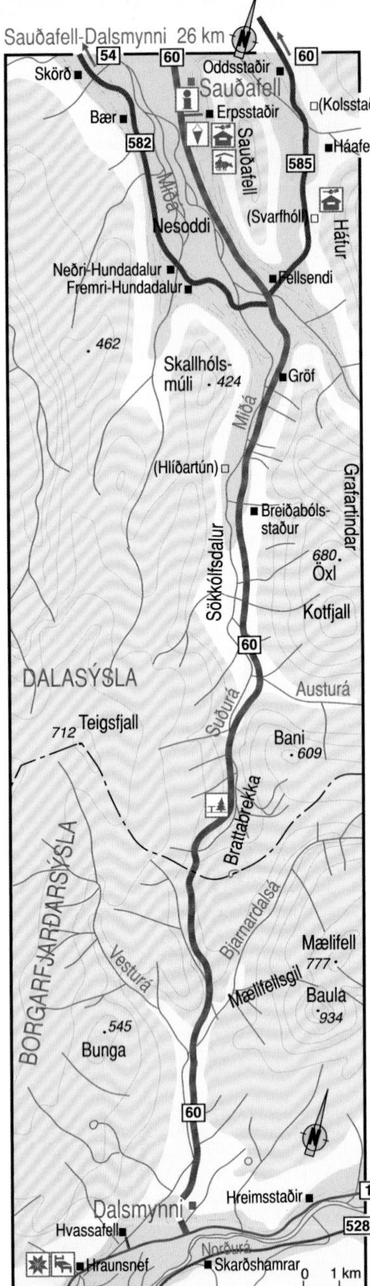

585 **Hlíðarvegur,** 8,6 km.

Sauðafell, a farm at the foot of a mountain of the same name, a manor farm through the ages. The home of Sturla Sighvatsson when the men of Vatnsfjörður attacked it in January 1229, committing gross atrocities against the place and its people, as related in *Sturlunga saga.* Sturla himself escaped as he happened to be away from home that day, and he took revenge by killing the Vatnsfjörður brothers when they were passing Sauðafell three years later. Governor Hrafn Oddsson (1226-1289) lived at Sauðafell. He was made Governor over Iceland, and thus the most powerful man in the country, in 1279. He is best known for his firm opposition to the episcopal powers. It was at Sauðafell that Daði Guðmundsson from Snóksdalur took captive Jón Arason, the last Catholic Bishop, and his sons, later sending them to Skálholt (see Road 31) where they were executed November 7, 1550. Birthplace of Jakob Jóhannesson Smári (1889-1972), well-known poet, grammarian and translator.

Erpsstaðir, a farm, originally settled by Erpur, son of a Scottish earl and an Irish princess. Now a comprehensive tourist services are offered there, while the farm also makes cheeses, ice cream and the Icelandic milk product skyr and sells these directly to the consumer. Visitors can also get information about agriculture and the local community.

Nesoddi, a grassy area by the Miðá river. Ocne a place of gatherings.

Fellsendi, once a substantial farm at the southern end of Sauðafell. Now an old people's home. It ,was built with money bequeathed to the county by the son of a local farmer.

582 **Hálsabæjarvegur,** 12,2 km to road 54, p. 250.

Bær, home of Jón Sigurðsson (ca. 1685-1720), lawwriter and poet.

Hlíðartún, an abandoned farm in Sökkólfsdalur valley.

Breiðabólsstaður, in the valley Sökkólfsdalur, long a substantial farm, the innermost farm north of Brattabrekka.

Bani, ("Death") (609 m) a high rocky mountain, on the slopes of which is a grassy patch called Grettisbæli, where Grettir the strong is said to have dwelt. Bani is said to be so called because 18 people once died on its slopes.

Brattabrekka, ("Steep slope") the road from Highway 1 in the Norðurárdalur valley west to the Dalir district, max. height 402 m. The actual Brattabrekka is the slope down into the Dalir district, where the former post-route lay. The road goes up Bjarnardalur through Miðdalur and down to Suðurárdalur.

Dalsmynni, p. 59.

1 **Vesturlandsvegur,** p. 59

528 **Norðurárdalsvegur,** p. 59

54 **Snæfellsnesvegur,** p. 250

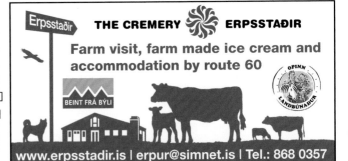

Ásgarður, a substantial farm, formerly also a church. In the land of Ásgarður there is a cone-shaped cliff which is said to be inhabited by elves. Old legend has it that if a group of people walk to the top of the cliff in order of age without looking back, their wishes will be helped along if spoken on top of the cliff.

Fáskrúð, a salmon river, its source on distant Gaflfellsheiði moor.

Ljárskógar, ("The woods of the river Ljá") the largest farm in Dalasýsla county. Birthplace of Jón Jónsson (1914-45), poet and singer, a memorial to him by the road. At now abandoned **Ljárskógasel**, nearby, the poet Jóhannes úr Kötlum (1899-1972) was brought up. In Búðardalur, a monument was erected in memory of Jóhannes in 1999. Many farms in Dalasýsla are named after woods, though there are now few trees. On the land of Ljárskógar, beside the highway, are the so-called **Klofasteinar** ("Cleft stones"), considered by some to be the residence of "hidden people". The stones have twice been moved during roadworks, being replaced in their original position the second time, in 1995. At that time the contractors ran into a number of difficulties, sometimes said to be due to the "hidden people's" being displeased.

Ljá, a small river flowing through the small valley Ljárdalur.

Búðardalur, (pop. 261) a village in Dalabyggð county on the shores of Hvammsfjörður fjord. It has always been easy to reach the village from other regions. Throughout the area, history is evident in numerous place names, not least those of the Laxdæla Saga. Of the 673 inhabitants of Dalabyggð municipality, 261 live in the village, which offers all basic services such as a compulsory school, health centre, a community centre and a dairy which produces the popular Höfðingi, Dala-Yrja and Dala-Brie cheeses. Bogi Sigurðsson (1858-1930), honoured as Father of the Village, opened the first store in Búðardalur in 1899. A former county sheriff, Þorsteinn Þorsteinsson, used to live here; he was one of Iceland's leading book collectors, though his library has now been transferred to Skálholt in South Iceland. Down by the small-craft harbour, Leifsbúð houses a restaurant and exhibit dedicated to the voyages of discovery made by Erik the Red and his son Leif the Lucky.

Saurar, once the home of Saura-Gísli (1820-94), a troublemaker and thorn in the flesh of the authorities.

Kambsnes, ("Comb peninsula") where the *Laxdæla saga* says the settler Auður djúpúðga lost her comb, hence the name.

Kvennabrekka, a parsonage and church. Birthplace of Árni Magnússon, professor and manuscript collector (1663-1730). The Árni Magnússon Institute in Reykjavík is based on his collection and bears his name.

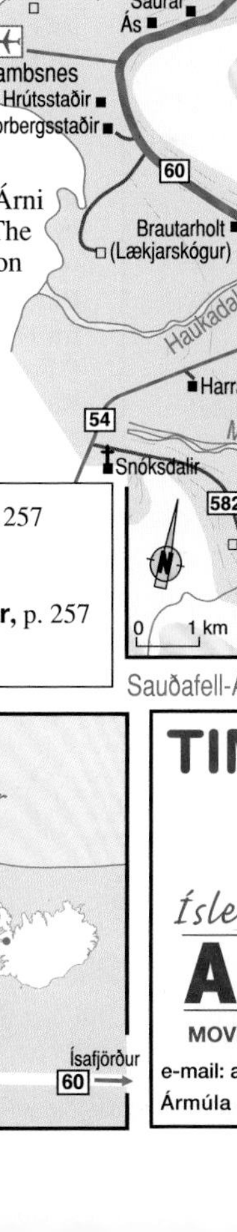

54 **Snæfellsnesvegur,** p. 250	59 **Laxárdalsvegur,** p. 257
582 **Hálsabæjarvegur,** p. 280	585 **Hlíðavegur,** p. 280
586 **Haukadalsskarðsvegur,** p. 277	587 **Hjarðarholtsvegur,** p. 257
590 **Klofningsvegur,** p. 278	

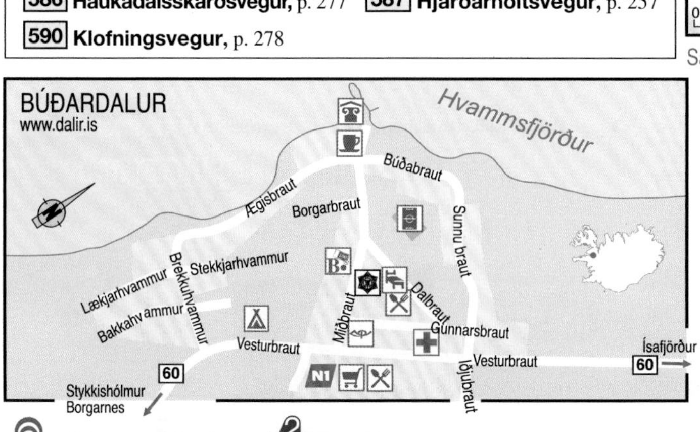

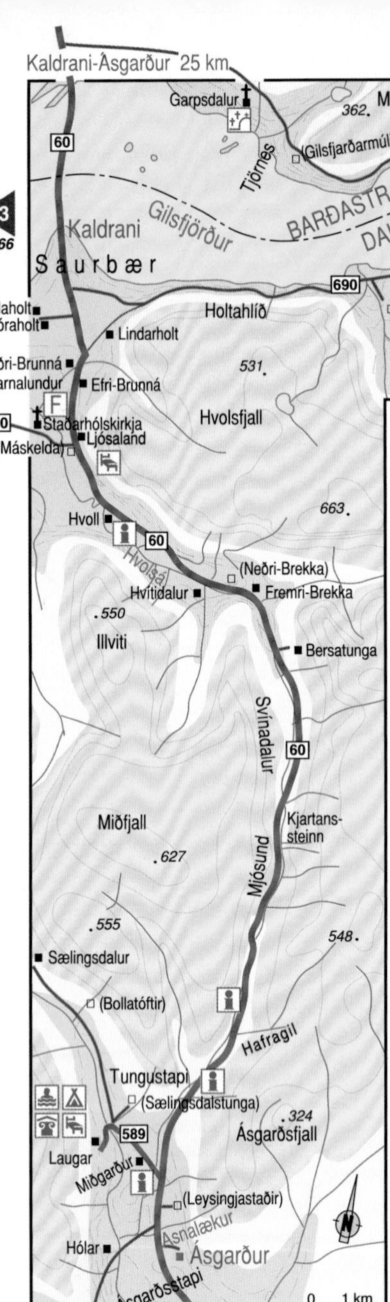

602 **Garpsdalsvegur,** 12,75 km going off Road 60 at the northern end of the bridge across Gilsfjörður, as far as the junction with Road 690 to Steinadalsheiði.

Garpsdalur, a church, a parsonage until 1890. Early in the 19th century a female ghost terrified the local inhabitants. The buildings shook, doors and a boat were broken up and all loose objects were thrown back and forth.

Gilsfjarðarbrekka, the easternmost farm in Barðastrandarsýsla county.

Gilsfjörður, the bridge over this fjord has shortened Road 60 by about 17 km.

Stórholt, a farm having some of the best land in the area. A good beach for gathering edible seaweed, several churches, including Hólar cathedral, had gathering rights.

Kirkjuhvoll, in the centre of the Saurbær district. Church built in 1899, when two parishes (Staðarhóll and Hvoll) were united. Community centre Tjarnarlundur.

Ljósaland, a guesthouse and a restaurant.

Hvoll, a farm. Once a parsonage. The farm has more meadows than any other in the district. A good deal of falling rock from the mountainside.

Illviti, (550 m) a mountain above the farm Hvítidalur.

Saurbær, the northernmost district in the Dalasýsla county, surrounded by high peaks, grassy but marshy. Many small valleys and two bigger ones: Staðarhólsdalur and Hvolsdalur, the road going through the latter.

Bersatunga, the uppermost farm in Hvolsdalur, where he poet Stefán frá Hvítadal ended his days. The name comes from Hólmgöngu-Bersi ("Bersi of the islet-duels") in the Sagas.

Kjartanssteinn, a big stone in the Svínadalur valley, where it is said Kjartan Ólafsson of *Laxdæla saga* was killed.

Hafragil, it was there were Bolli and Guðrún Ósvífursdóttir´s brothers, in *Laxdæla Saga,* waited for Kjartan Ólafsson an then slaid him.

Svínadalur, a deep, narrow valley.

589 **Sælingsdalsvegur,** 2,5 km.

68 **Innstrandavegur,** p. 310 **590** **Klofningsvegur,** p. 279

Laugar, Sælingsdalur © Markaðsstofa Vesturlands

Tungustapi, a big crag below the farm Sælingsdalstunga. It is connected to one of the most beautiful and impressive Icelandic folk tales connected with elves or "hidden people". It was believed that the cathedral and bishopric of the elves was in the crag.

Sælingsdalstunga, an abandoned farm in the valley Sælingsdalur. Snorri goði lived there after moving from Helgafell.

Laugar, a farmstead in the valley Sælingsdalur. Home of Ósvífur, father of Guðrún in *Laxdæla saga*. Geothermal heat and an old spring, Sælingsdalslaug, which was an official meeting place of old. Heritage museum.

Sælingsdalur, a farm in a valley of the same name, with the **Bollatóftir** ruins, where Bolli Þorleifsson of *Laxdæla saga* was slain in revenge for the murder of Kjartan Ólafsson.

690 **Steinadalsvegur,** over **Steinadalsheiði**, a route between Gilsfjörður and Kollafjörður, highest point is 330 m.

Kleifar, the northernmost farm in Dalasýsla county at the head of Gilsfjörður. Above is a high but narrow waterfall, Gullfoss. As the crow flies, it is only 7 km over to Bitrufjörður in Strandasýsla. The river Brekkuá forms the boundary between Dalasýsla and Barðastrandarsýsla counties.

Holtahlíð, a very steep mountainside along Gilsfjörður with no flat land below it, so that the road formerly went along the shore in many places, making travellers dependent on the tides.

Ólafsdalur, a small valley south of Gilsfjörður. A farm of the same name, where Torfi Bjarnason (1838-1915) founded the first agricultural school in Iceland, which he ran 1880-1907, marking a milestone in the history of Icelandic farming. The building still stands. In 1955 a monument was raised to the memory of Torfi and his wife Guðlaug Zakaríasdóttir. www.olafsdalur.is

© Markaðsstofa Vesturlands
Guðrúnarlaug

Laugar, Sælingsdalur

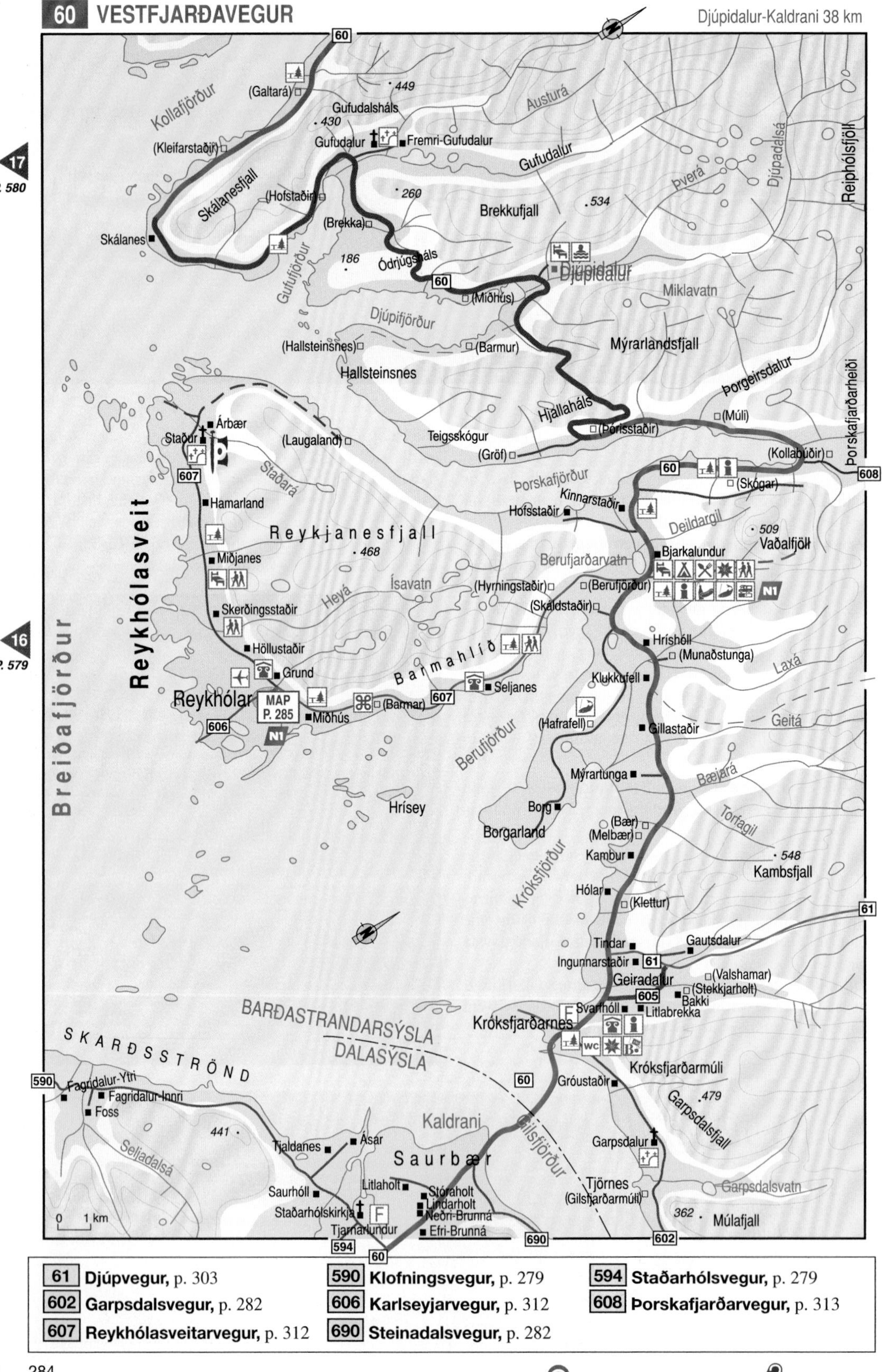

17 P. 580
16 P. 579

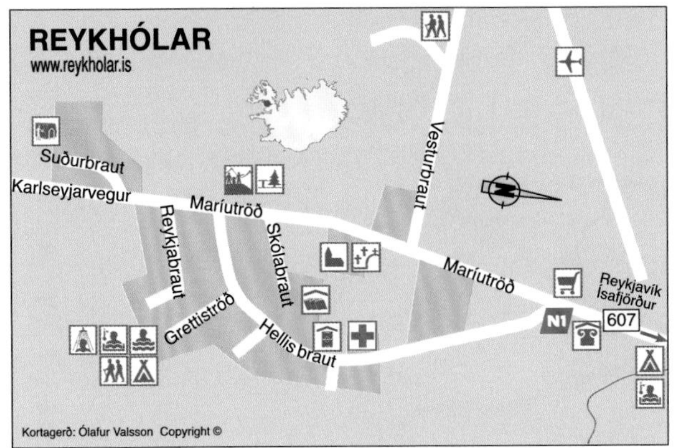

Hallsteinsnes, the land of a settlement farm at the southern end of a peninsula of the same name, on which is the wood **Teigsskógur**, the biggest in the eastern part of the district.
Hjallaháls, a ridge where jasper, zeolites and other unusual stones are to be found.
Kollabúðir, an abandoned farm at the head of Þorskafjörður. By the Músará river was the ancient Þorskafjörður assembly site, where in the latter half of the 19th century the Kollabúðir meetings for freedom and progress were held. See statue at road side. Road 608 goes from there onto Þorskafjarðarheiði moor.
Skógar, ("Woods") a small farm, birthplace of the pastor and poet Matthías Jochumsson (1835-1920), one of the most important poets of the romantic movement in Iceland and writer of the national anthem. A monument in his honour is located on a cliff overlooking the road.

Þorskafjörður, ca. 16 km long, narrow, fjord with strong ebb tides. Little flat land, many flats that can be crossed at low tide.
Vaðalfjöll, two isolated peaks, 6–7 km north of Bjarkalundur, easy to climb. Good view.
Bjarkalundur, a summer hotel, built 1945–47. Jeep track to Vaðalfjöll.
Berufjarðarvatn, south of Bjarkalundur, a lake into which runs the stream Alifiskalækur ("Fed-fish stream"). Trout were introduced into the stream centuries ago, making it the first known fish-breeding station in Iceland.
Berufjörður, a short fjord between the Borgarnes and Reykjanes peninsulas, in which there are many islets with eider duck colonies, Hrísey being the biggest. A farm of the same name at the head of the fjord.
Reykhólasveit, a district, reaching over Króksfjörður, Borgarland, Berufjörður and Reykjanes to Múlaá in Þorskafjörður. The farmhouse at Barmar was rebuilt in 1971–1974, then the only original farmhouse in the Westfjords still standing.
Barmahlíð, the mountainside along the western side of Berufjörður. The poet Jón Thoroddsen (1818–68) wrote a well-known romantic poem about its beauty.
Borgarland, a tiny peninsula with some unusual rock formations.
Gillastaðir, a farm, where the leader Þorvaldur Vatnsfirðingur was burnt to death in 1228.
Bær, an abandoned farm at the head of Króksfjörður.
Tindar, peaks containing rhyolite, normally scarce in the Western fjords.
Geiradalur, a small, grassy valley, marshy and often snowy.
Króksfjarðarnes, a former trading post between Gilsfjörður and Króksfjörður. An old assembly site and now a community centre, Vogaland. Land settled by Þórarinn krókur ("hook") from whom the fjord takes its name.

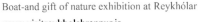

Auðshaugur-Djúpidalur 86 km

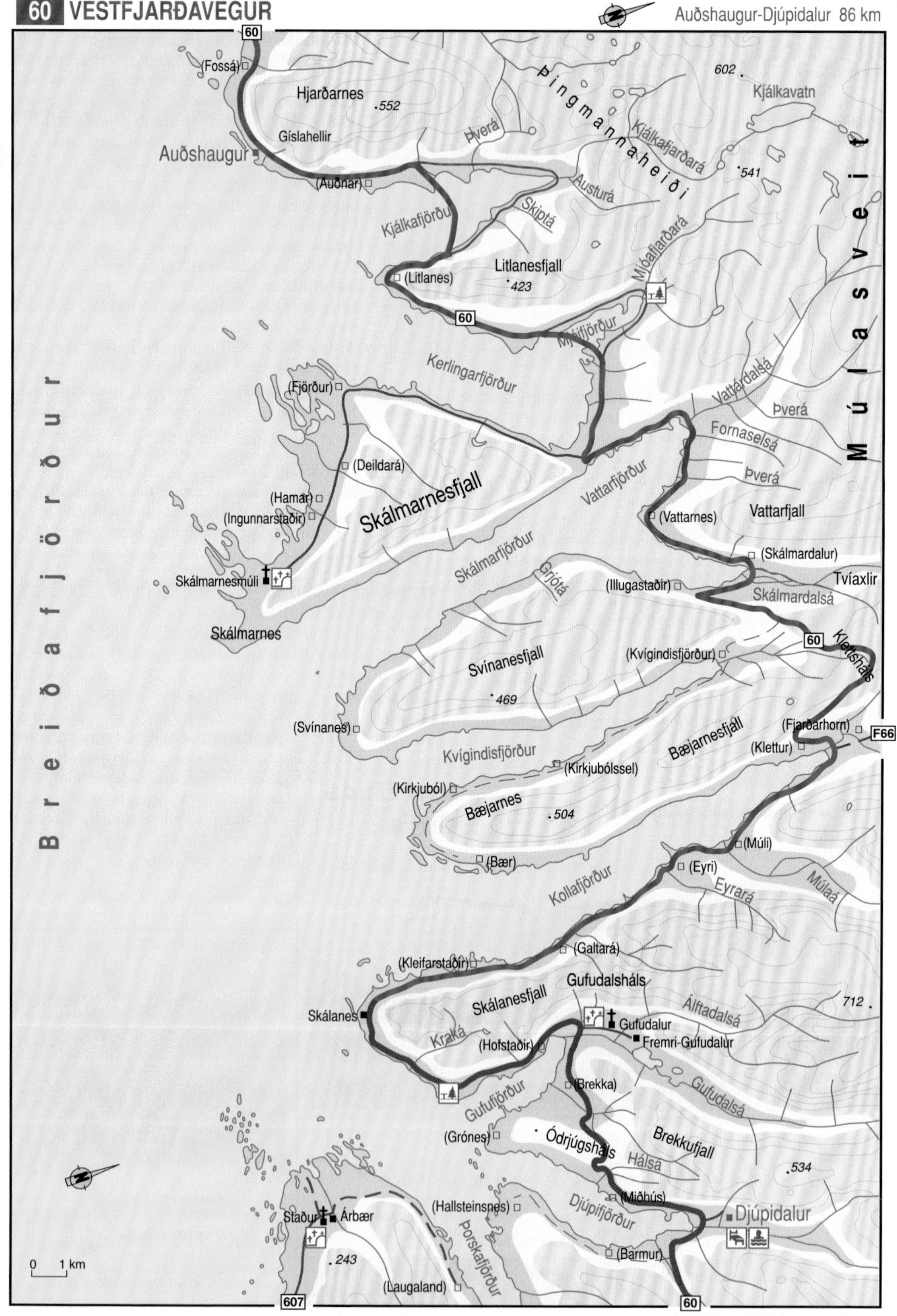

Djúpidalur-Auðshaugur 86 km

F66 **Kollafjarðarheiði,** p. 313 | 607 **Reykhólasveitarvegur,** p. 312

Kjálkafjörður, between the peninsulas Hjarðarnes and Litlanes, ca. 6 km long, rocky and sometimes dangerous for sheep, which can by trapped by high tides, as is the case in most fjords in the area.

Skiptá, a river marking the boundary between the counties Vestur- and Austur-Barðastrandarsýsla.

Litlanes, the peninsula between Kjálkafjörður and Kerlingarfjörður, with the mountain Litlanesfjall (424 m). It is 4–5 km long and 0.5 km wide at its broadest part, very rocky. Now uninhabited.

Kerlingarfjörður, ca. 9 km long, between the Litlanes and Skálmarnes peninsulas, with the inlet Mjóifjörður.

Þingmannaheiði, (400 m) a moor across which there is a mountain road between Vattarfjörður and Vatnsfjörður, ca. 25 km. Stony, bare, often blocked by snow in winter. Its western end goes down the Þingmannadalur valley.

Skálmarnes, mountainous, triangular peninsula between Kerlingarfjörður and Skálmarfjörður, joined by a low isthmus to the southern end of Þingmannaheiði moor. About 300 m high, cliffs on all sides, the only flat land being on the southern side.

Skálmarnesmúli, once the main farm on Skálmarnes, now abandoned, church.

Vattarnes, a point of land and a farm of the same name, now abandoned. Formerly the last stopping place before traversing Þingmannaheiði. Local place-names indicate the site of an ancient assembly.

Skálmarfjörður, ca. 15 km long, between the Skálmarnes and Svínanes peninsulas. Splits at Vattarnes, west of which it is known as Vattarfjörður, where the route onto Þingmannaheiði started. From the valley Skálmardalur there is a route via Skálmardalsheiði moor north to Ísafjarðardjúp.

Svínanes, ("Swine ness") between Skálmarfjörður and Kvígindisfjörður, going steeply down to the sea, but with trees in places. No road. There was a farm of the same name, now abandoned, at the end of the peninsula.

Kvígindisfjörður, a fjord, ca. 15 km long and very narrow. The mountain Svínafellsfjall to the west is very steep, with rocks and scree, but some trees. It is said that the settler Geirmundur heljarskinn kept his pigs on Svínanes, hence the name.

Bæjarnesvegur, the road along the western shore of Kvígindisfjörður to the abandoned farm Bær.

Bæjarnesfjall, (504 m) the mountain forming the Bæjarnes peninsula, very rocky, especially along Klettshlíð.

Múlasveit, the westernmost district in Austur-Barðastrandarsýsla county. Reaching from Bæjarnes, Kvígindisfjörður, Svínanes, Skálmarfjörður, Múlanes, Kerlingarfjörður, Litlanes and Kjálkafjörður.

Klettsháls, a ridge (330 m) between the heads of the valleys in Kollafjörður and Kvígindisfjörður. **The area between Múli in Kollafjörður and Auðshaugur in Kjálkafjörður is totally uninhabited.**

Fjarðarhorn, the innermost farm in Kollafjörður, now deserted. A jeep-track goes from there up to Kollafjarðarheiði moor and down into the valley Laugarbólsdalur in Ísafjörður, 25 km.

Kollafjörður, the westernmost fjord in the Gufudalssveit district, ca. 16 km long, with many fords. Many flats that can be crossed at low tide.

Skálanes, the southernmost farm on the peninsula of the same name. Formerly a trading post and a centre for the islanders of Breiðafjörður, when they brought their sheep to the mainland.

Gufudalur, a church and parsonage until the turn of last century.

Gufufjörður, a small fjord, so shallow that it becomes nothing but mud-flats at low tide. They are, however, impassable because of quicksand.

Djúpifjörður, ("Deep fjord") between the peninsulas Grónes and Hallsteinsnes, short and narrow and - despite its name - shallow, almost drying up at low tide, though there is a channel down the middle.

Djúpidalur, a farm in a valley of the same name, off Djúpifjörður. Birthplace of Björn Jónsson, newspaper editor and Minister of State (1846–1912), father of Sveinn Björnsson (1881–1952), first president of the republic. There are chalk layers in the earth there, and Iceland spar was mined for a time. Geothermal heat.

Dynjandi

© Andreas G

17 P. 580

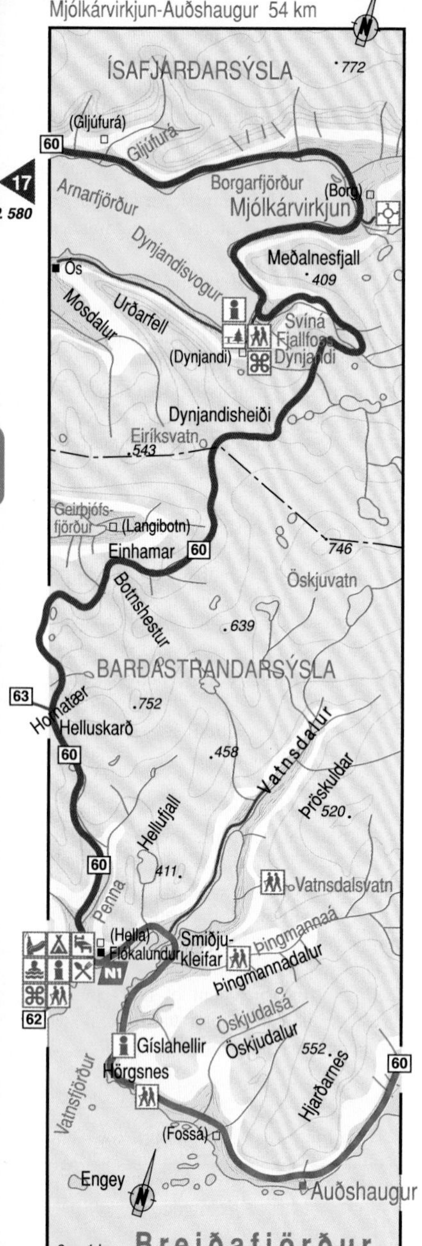

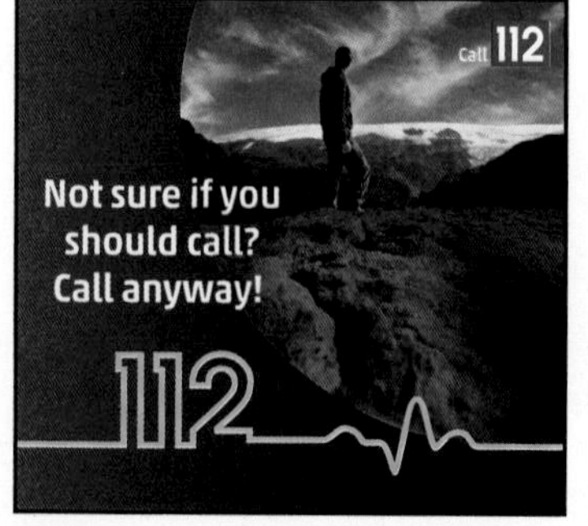

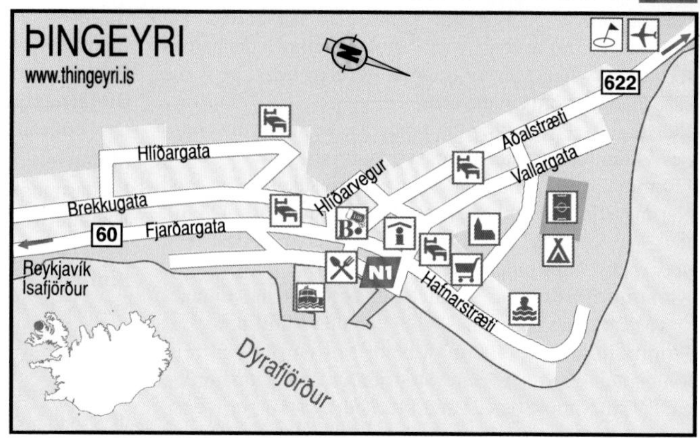

Gljúfurá, an abandoned farm by a river of the same name. Ownership of this farm ensured Jón forseti the right to vote in 1845 (see Road 60, Hrafnseyri).

Mjólkárvirkjun, hydro-electric power station for the Westfjords, built 1958, 8.1 MW.

Dynjandi, an abandoned farm. Above it is the biggest waterfall in the Western fjords and one of finest in Iceland, also named **Dynjandi** ("Resounding"), also known as Fjallfoss, itself 100 m high and very broad. There are five more falls immediately below it: Háifoss, Úðafoss, Göngufoss, Hundafoss and Bæjarfoss. It is possible to walk behind Göngufoss. All six falls can be seen from the shore.

Dynjandisheiði, (500 m) the moor between Geirþjófsfjörður and Dynjandisvogur on Arnarfjörður. The boundary between the counties Barðastrandar- and Vestur-Ísafjarðarsýsla is on these moors.

Langibotn, at the head of Geirþjófsfjörður. Some woods protected by the Forestry Service. The rock **Einhamar**, where Gísli Súrsson of *Gísla saga Súrssonar* was slain, a silhouette of him has been carved into it. His hiding-place is still visible.

Helluskarð, (468 m) the pass where in 1959 the road system for the northern part of the Western fjords was joined to the main Icelandic network. Bíldudalsvegur junction close by.

Hornatær, (700 m and more) several peaks on one of which Hrafna-Flóki is thought to have stood when he named Iceland (see Road 62, Brjánslækur).

Flókalundur, ("Flóki's grove") a wooded area near the crossroads. Some services, summer hotel, summer house area and swimming pool nearby.

Vatnsfjörður, the westernmost fjord of the district, short and broad, with wooded slopes.

Vatnsdalur, a short, well-wooded valley. Vatnsdalsvatn lake, 4 km long, 1.5 km wide, good trout-fishing. The river Vatnsdalsá, only 1 km long, flows out of it.

Smiðjukleifar, ("Smithy rocks") at the mouth of Þingmannadalur, a rocky but wooded slope. The name is derived from an iron ore smithy, said to have belonged to Gestur Oddleifsson the wise of Saga times, but probably more recent.

Hjarðarnes, a mountainous (552 m) peninsula, with wooded slopes, stony and bare higher up. There are three farms on it.

Fossá, there begins the Öskjudalur valley. **Gíslahellir** small cave west of Fossá. It is said that the outlaw Gísli Súrsson dwelled there for a while.

Auðshaugur, there lived Refur and Álfdís, people who helped Gísli Súrsson the outlaw.

62 **Barðastrandarvegur,** p. 303 63 **Bíldudalsvegur,** p. 305

622 **Svalvogavegur,** 30,5 km.

Keldudalur, a short valley. The newly repaired church at Hraun is of older towerless type, built in 1885 and is the only building in Iceland with roof- shingles. The church was deconsecrated in 1971 and has been in the keeping of The National Museum since 1980.

Haukadalur, a short valley. Site of the first fish-freezing plant in the district, later moved to Þingeyri. Grave of French seamen. Site of the main action in *Gísla saga Súrssonar*, one of Iceland´s most famous outlaws. It was off Haukadalur that sheriff Hannes Hafstein was almost drowned in 1899, when British trawlermen he was trying to arrest for fishing in Icelandic waters overturned his boat. Three of his men drowned.

623 **Flugvallarvegur,** 0,04 km.

Sandafell, (367 m) a mountain above the village Þingeyri, named after the ancient manor farm Sandar, often mentioned in records from the time of the Sturlungas in the 13th century. It was long a parsonage, now abandoned, but the cemetery is still there. It is possible to drive up the mountain to a view-dial.

Þingeyri, (pop. 244) a village which is the oldest trading place in the Ísafjarðarsýsla county. Service station, medical centre, store, excellent campsite, and very interesting iron foundry museum. At Þingeyri is a viking based tourism. A Viking ship sails with guests and a Viking Festival is held there every year. A Viking themed area is in the village with tables, benches, barbecue and a stage for shows.

Álftamýri, a church and parsonage until 1880.

Auðkúla, a farm and trading place. In the mountain above it is the biggest rhyolite area in the Western fjords. Also gabbro.

Hrafnseyri, a church and parsonage with a long history. In 1977-78 an archeological dig uncovered the farm site of Án rauðfeldur, the first settler there. His wife was Grélöð Bjartmarsdóttir, and the ruins that were uncovered have been named for her, **Grélutóttir**. The farm was named for Hrafn Sveinbjarnarson, an influential man in the 12th-13th century, probably the first trained doctor in Iceland. It is the birthplace of Jón Sigurðsson (1811-1879), who contributed more than anyone towards Iceland's regaining independence. He was often called Jón forseti ("president") because he was president of the Icelandic Literary Society and long the leader of the house in Parliament. His birthday, the 17th of June, was chosen to be the Icelandic national holiday when the Republic was established in 1944. A chapel was consecrated and a museum about Jón opened in 1981. Jón Sigurðsson's grandfather built a new farmhouse at Hrafnseyri towards the end of the 18th century, almost certainly according to plans drawn up by the Rev. Guðlaugur Sveinsson, dean, of Vatnsfjörður in Ísafjarðardjúp (see Road 61). The farmhouse was one of the first of the gabled farmhouses in Iceland. The buildings, which were collapsing, were torn down, all but one wall which is still standing. The gabled farmhouse has now been re-built in accordance with careful on-site measurements and a model built to the specifications of people who had actually seen the old farmhouse (see Road 61).

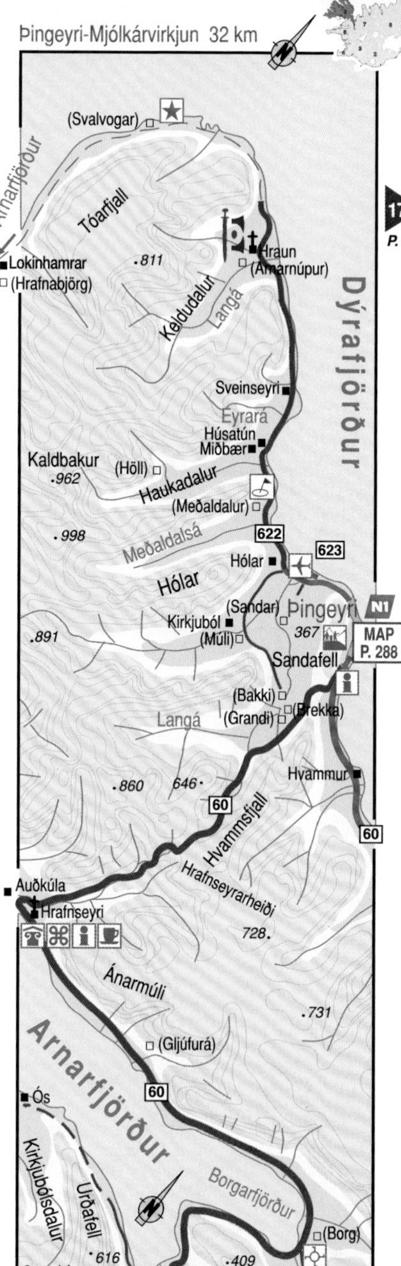

Hrafnseyri

Avalanches

Spend as little time as possible outside and do not go near the avalanche area.

Stay in that part of the house, which is farthest from the hillside. Close windows and doors tightly. Put shutters on windows facing the hillside.

18
P. 581

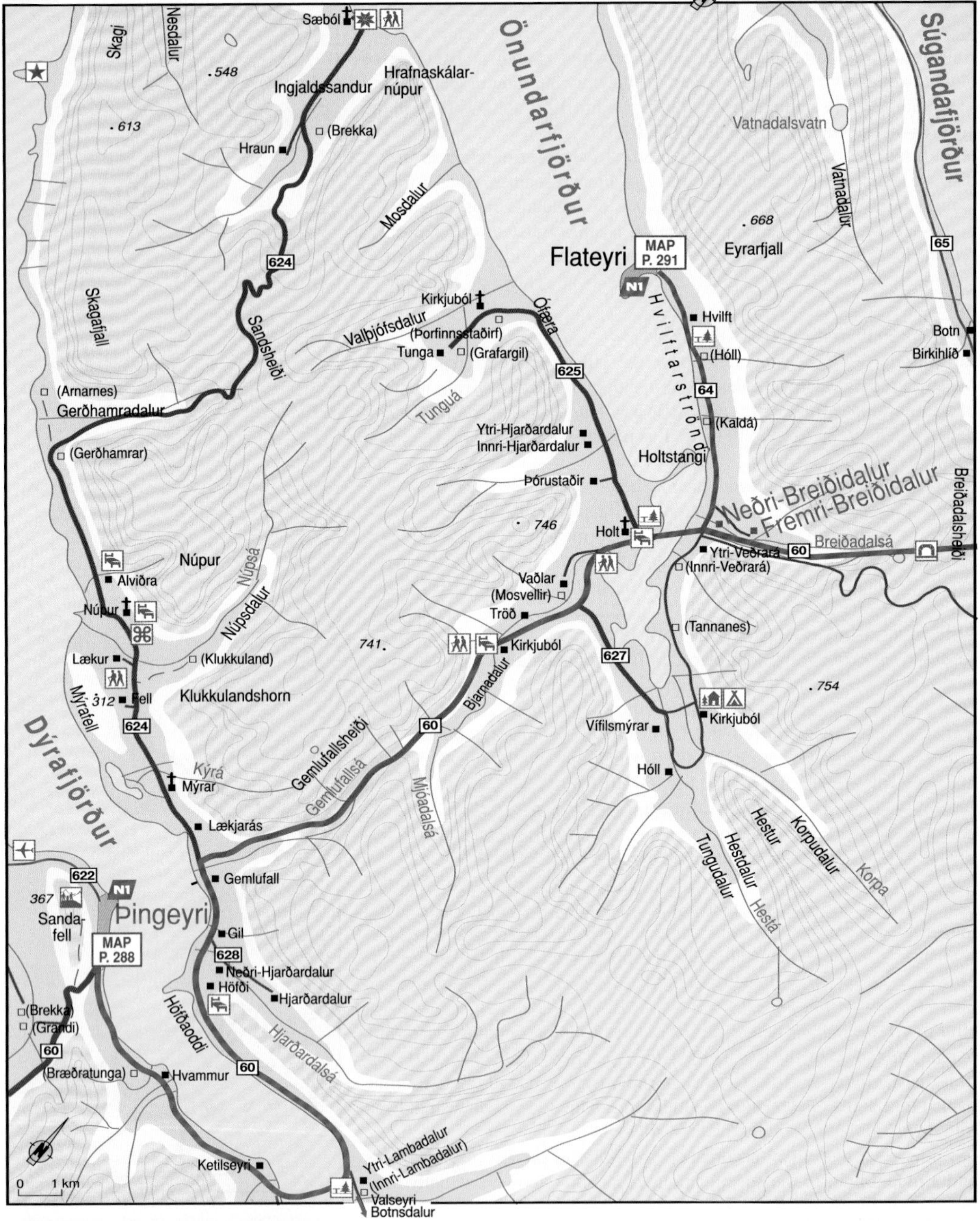

Sæból
Nesdalur
Skagi
.548
Ingjaldssandur
Hrafnaskálar-
núpur
Önundarfjörður
Súgandafjörður
Vatnadalsvatn
Vatnadalur
.613
(Brekka)
Hraun
Mosdalur
.668
Eyrarfjall
624
Flateyri
MAP
P. 291
65
Skagafjall
Kirkjuból
Valþjófsdalur
(Þorfinnsstaðir)
Tunga
(Grafargil)
Ófæra
Hvilftarströnd
Hvilft
(Hóll)
Botn
Birkihlíð
Sandsheiði
625
64
(Arnarnes)
Gerðhamradalur
Tunguá
(Kaldá)
Ytri-Hjarðardalur
Innri-Hjarðardalur
Holtstangi
(Gerðhamrar)
Þórustaðir
Neðri-Breiðidalur
Fremri-Breiðidalur
Breiðadalsheiði
.746
Holt
Breiðadalsá
Ytri-Veðrará
60
(Innri-Veðrará)
Núpur
Núpsá
Alviðra
Vaðlar
(Mosvellir)
Núpur
Núpsdalur
Tröð
(Tannanes)
741.
Kirkjuból
Lækur
(Klukkuland)
627
.754
Mýrafell
.312
Fell
Klukkulandshorn
Kirkjuból
Bjarnadalur
Dýrafjörður
624
Gemlufallsheiði
60
Vífilsmýrar
Kýrá
Mýrar
Gemlufallsá
Mjóadalsá
Hóll
Lækjarás
Hestur
Korpudalur
Hestdalur
Tungudalur
Korpa
622
Gemlufall
367
Sandafell
Þingeyri
Gil
Hestá
MAP
P. 288
628
Neðri-Hjarðardalur
Höfði
Hjarðardalur
(Brekka)
(Grandi)
Höfðaoddi
60
Hjarðardalsá
(Bræðratunga)
Hvammur
60
Ytri-Lambadalur
(Innri-Lambadalur)
Ketilseyri
0 1 km
Valseyri
Botnsdalur

624 **Ingjaldssandsvegur,** 28 km.

Ingjaldssandur, a valley with one farm between the mountains Hrafnaskálanúpur (584 m) to the east and Barði (548 m) to the west. Church at Sæból.

Núpur, a manor farm through the ages, a church and for a while a boarding school founded by Rev. Sigtryggur Guðlaugsson. He and his wife Hjaltlína Guðjónsdóttir also created Skrúður, the oldest botanical garden in Iceland that has been rebuilt.

Ytri-Hús, Rögnvaldur Ólafsson (1874–1917) was born there. He is considered to be the first Icelandic architect although poor healt cut his education short.

Lækur, an eiderdown farm.

Mýrar, a farm and church near the mountain Mýrafell (312 m). An historical place. Birthplace of Þórdís, mother of President Jón Sigurðsson (see Hrafnseyri). Now one of the biggest eider duck breeding grounds in Iceland.

Gemlufall, an old ferry point to Þingeyri.

Gemlufallsheiði, (283 m) a mountain road between Dýrafjörður and Önundarfjörður.

Valseyri, an ancient assembly site, mentioned in *Gísla saga Súrssonar*. Remains of booths.

Botnsdalur, a valley at the head of Dýrafjörður, named for the farm Botn, abandoned in 1925 after damage by an avalanche. It is said there once were seven big farms in this valley. A prominent hill, Dýrahaugur, where some say the settler Dýri is buried. Many trees and a local plantation.

Dýrafjörður, the largest of the fjords in Vestur-Ísafjarðarsýsla county, with the most varied scenery. About 39 km long, mostly narrow. Near the mouth of the fjord are sheer, barren cliffs down to sea, but there is more flat land and grass further in. Two isolated mountains, Mýrafell (312 m) to the north and Sandafell (367 m) to the south, are conspicuous landmarks.

Kirkjuból í Bjarnardal, a farm. A memorial to Hallór Kristjánsson a famer and a poet who used to live there.

64 **Flateyrarvegur,** 3 km.

Flateyri, (pop. 182) a village and authorised trading place, where trading actually started soon after 1790, swimming pool, camping site. Fishing and fish-processing are now the main industries. In 1889 the Norwegian Hans Ellefsen started a whaling station near Flateyri, called Sólbakki, which was burned down in 1901 and then closed. The official reception house of the Icelandic Government, by the lake in Reykjavík, was formerly Ellefsen's residence, presented by him in 1904 to the government minister Hannes Hafstein and moved from Flateyri. There is said to have been a pagan temple on the hill Goðahóll above Flateyri. In the early hours of the 26th of October 1995 an avalanche fell on nineteen houses in Flateyri. Of the 45 people in the houses, 20 died. Before this tragic event the population of Flateyri was 380. A protective wall against avalanches has now been built above the town. The wall has a tower that provides an excellent view.

625 **Valþjófsdalsvegur,** 7 km.

Valþjófsdalur, a valley with several farms. Church at **Kirkjubóli**.

Holt, a church and parsonage, fertile fields, earlier considered one of the wealthiest benefices in Iceland. Birthplace of Bishop Brynjólfur Sveinsson (1605-75). There is a monument to him. Sand-castle building competition have been held there during the first weekend in august.

Önundarfjörður, a fjord between the headlands Barði and Sauðanes, with steep cliffs, opening out towards the mouth, but very narrow at the head, where there is a good deal of flat land. Bridged in 1980.

627 **Önundarfjarðarvegur,** 9 km.

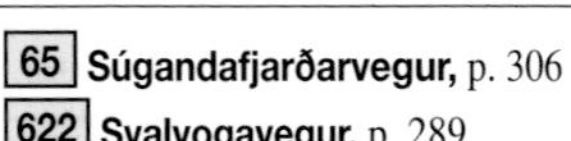

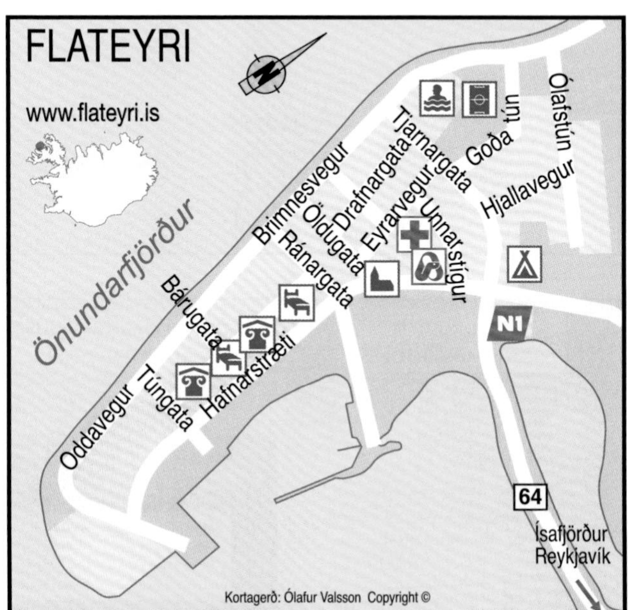

18
P. 581

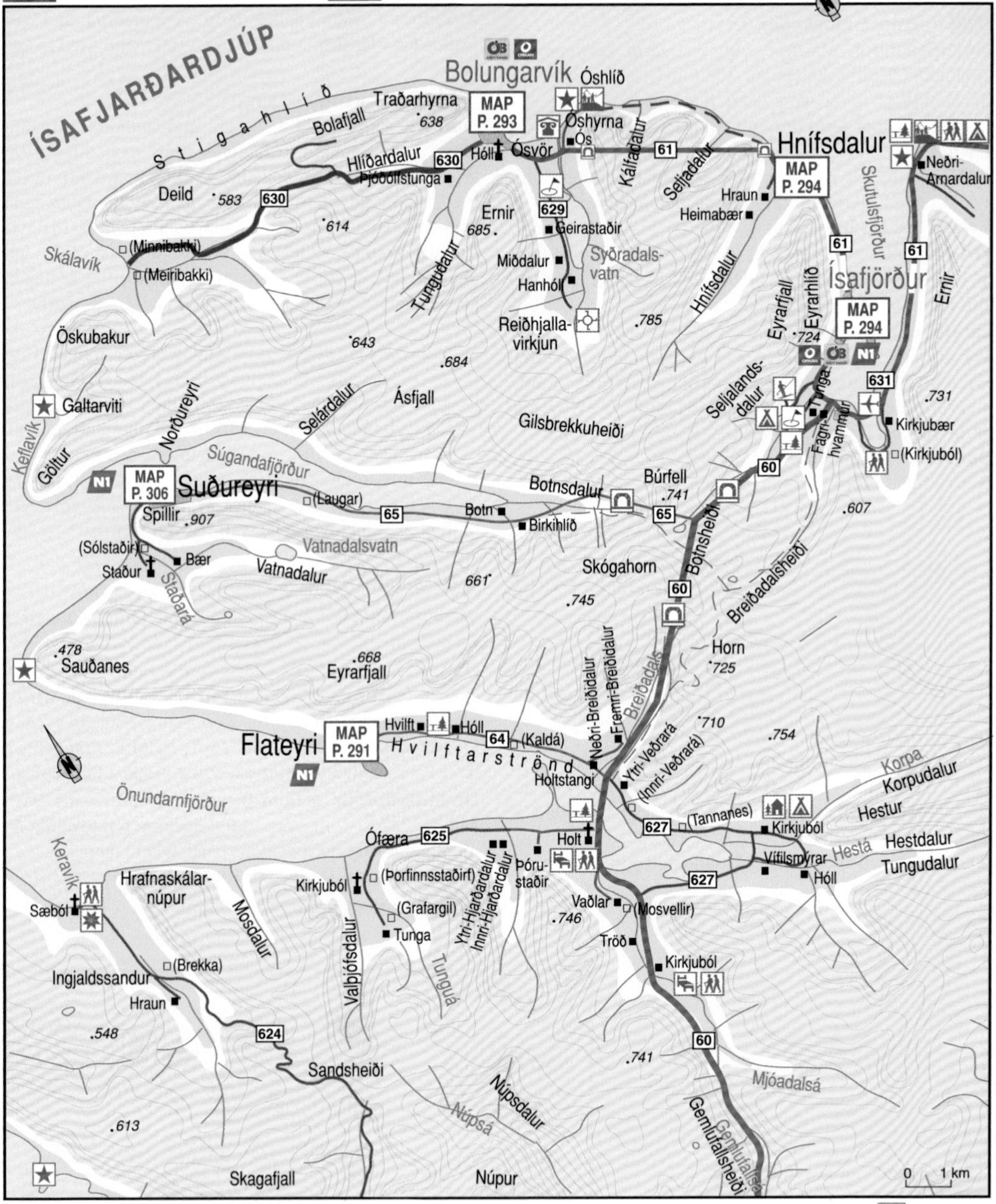

ÍSAFJARÐARDJÚP
Stigahlíð
Bolungarvík
Óshlíð
Traðarhyrna
.638
MAP P. 293
Bolafjall
Óshyrna
Ós
Hóll
Ósvör
61
Kálfadalur
Seljadalur
Hnífsdalur
Neðri-Arnardalur
630
Hlíðardalur
Þjóðólfstunga
Deild
.583
630
.614
629
Ernir
685.
Geirastaðir
Hraun
Heimabær
MAP P. 294
Skutulsfjörður
61
61
Skálavík
(Minnibakki)
(Meiribakki)
Tungudalur
Miðdalur
Hanhóll
Syðradals-vatn
Hnífsdalur
Eyrarfjall
Eyrarhlíð
.724
Ísafjörður
Ernir
MAP P. 294
Öskubakur
.643
Reiðhjalla-virkjun
.785
.684
631
Galtarviti
Norðureyri
Selárdalur
Ásfjall
Gilsbrekkuheiði
Seljalands-dalur
Tunga
Fagri-hvammur
.731
Kirkjubær
(Kirkjuból)
Keflavík
Göltur
Súgandafjörður
MAP P. 306
Suðureyri
Spillir .907
(Laugar)
65
Botn
Birkihlíð
Botnsdalur
Búrfell
.741
65
60
.607
(Sólstaðir)
Staður
Bær
Staðará
Vatnadalsvatn
Vatnadalur
661
Skógahorn
Botnsheiði
60
Breiðadalsheiði
.745
.478
Sauðanes
.668
Eyrarfjall
Neðri-Breiðidalur
Fremri-Breiðidalur
Breiðadalsá
Horn
.725
.710
.754
Hvilft
Hóll
64
(Kaldá)
Flateyri
MAP P. 291
Hvilftarströnd
Holtstangi
Ytri-Veðrará
(Innri-Veðrará)
Korpa
Korpudalur
Önundarfjörður
Hestur
627
(Tannanes)
Kirkjuból
Ófæra
625
Holt
Hestdalur
Keravík
Hrafnaskálar-núpur
Kirkjuból
(Þorfinnsstaðir)
Ytri-Hjarðardalur
Innri-Hjarðardalur
Þóru-staðir
627
Vífilsmýrar
Hestá
Hóll
Tungudalur
Sæból
Mosdalur
(Grafargil)
Tunga
Valþjófsdalur
Vaðlar
(Mosvellir)
.746
Tröð
(Brekka)
Ingjaldssandur
Hraun
Tunguá
Kirkjuból
.548
624
60
Sandsheiði
.741
Mjóadalsá
Núpsdalur
Núpsá
Gemlufallsheiði
Gemlufallsá
.613
Skagafjall
Núpur
0 1 km

61 Djúpvegur

Ísafjarðardjúp, the greatest of the Western fjords. Several smaller fjords open into it.

Ísafjörður, (pop. 2,571) the biggest settlement in the Westfjords, gained municipal status in 28th January 1866. Skutulsfjörður ("Harpoon fjord") is the westernmost south-reaching fjord off Ísafjarðardjúp, surrounded by high, sheer mountains. Near the middle of the fjord, under the mountain Eyrarfjall, a long, flat hook-shaped gravel spit reaches out into the fjord. Inside it is *Pollurinn* ("The puddle"), one of the best natural harbours in Iceland. Between the spit and the mountainside opposite is a narrow channel known as *Sundin*. *Landnámabók* ("The Book of Settlements") tells of two settlers in Skutulsfjörður, Helgi Hrólfsson, who built his farm at Eyri and Þórólfur brækir, who settled in Skálavík. Helgi is said to have found a harpoon washed up on the beach and named the fjord for it. In 1786 a royal decree abolished the trade monopoly in Iceland, and six trading centres were established, Ísafjörður being one. In the spring of 1788 Norwegian merchants came to Ísafjörður, which is what the new trading centre was named, settled just below the parsonage at Eyri and built their stores there. One of these buildings is still there, Aðalstræti 42 in the area known as Hæstikaupstaður ("The highest trading place"). In the oldest part of town, **Neðstikaupstaður**, there are four of the oldest houses in Iceland, one of which houses the maritime museum. They were built in the mid-18th century. In 1816 Ísafjörður lost its trading centre status, but trade continued and there was a lot of growth around mid-century. Ísafjörður again became a legal trading centre by royal decree in 1866. The basis for Ísafjörður's prosperity was the fishing on so-called *þilskip* ("boats with decks") instead of the open rowing boats that were still common at the time. Merchants owned and operated the fishing boats which fished for both cod and shark. From about 1900-1930 there was also a good deal of herring fishing. There was a steady increase in population, reaching 1,085 by 1901. One of the largest companies in Iceland at the time, Ásgeirsverslun, operated in Ísafjörður. The company was by far the biggest producer of the country's most valuable export product, saltfish. In 1996 the town of Ísafjörður was amalgamated with the villages of Suðureyri, Þingeyri and Flateyri to form Ísafjarðarbær (Ísafjörður municipality). The serene beauty of the fjord system is well known by locals but unfamiliar to the outside world. The coast of Snæfjallaströnd really gives you the feeling that you are close to the Arctic Circle with its snow covered hills and the fifth largest glacier in Iceland just around the corner.

Tungudalur, a valley close to the town of Ísafjörður, large areas of birchwood. Many inhabitants of Ísafjörður had summer cottages there but in April 1994 an avalanche destroyed about 40 cottages, sweeping away large tracts of birchwood and costing one man his life. Higher up is the popular skiing area in Seljalandsdalur, along with ski-lodges. Summer camp facilities for scouts and schools. Campsite.

629 Syðradalsvegur, 3 km.

Breiðadalsheiði, (610 m).

Vestfjarðagöng, tunnels built in the 1990's under both Breiðadalsheiði and Botnsheiði moors have completely transformed communications in the area. Two kilometers from the tunnel entrance in Tungudalur valley outside Ísafjörður there is a fork in the road, right under **Botnsheiði**. From the junctions one arm leads to Súgandafjörður (3 km), the other to Önundarfjörður (4 km).

630 Skálavíkurvegur, 11 km.

Skálavík, a small cove, once settled but now abandoned.

Stigahlíð, the mountainside west of Bolungarvík, sheer and rocky with much scree, contains lignite. The mountain itself, Deild, (583 m). Road up to a former radar station from where there are splendid views.

Bolungarvík, (pop. 888) a town and fishing centre on a bay of the same name. Off the inlet are two valleys, Tungudalur and Syðridalur, between which is the mountain Ernir (685 m). Wild but beautiful scenery. Bolungarvík is one of the oldest fishing stations in Iceland, being close to the banks, but landing was often difficult. Now a good harbour and prosperous place, with a fish-processing industry. Good fishing at the end of the pier. In front of the community centre is a memorial to Einar Guðfinnsson (1898-1985) and his wife Elísabet Hjaltadóttir (1900-1981). Einar was a prominent businessman and the driving force behind much of the town´s development. The cairn was built by Jón Sigurpálsson, using stone from Litli-Bær in Skötufjörður, Einar´s birthplace. The bas-relief is by Ríkey Ingimundardóttir.

Hóll, church, formerly a substantial farm and home of local leaders, near Bolungarvík.

Syðradalsvatn, a good fishing lake.

Óshlíð, the mountainside between Hnífsdalur and Bolungarvík, very steep and with much scree. There have often been avalanches and landslides there.

Ósvör, a maritime museum in fisherman's booths that have been rebuilt on old ruins at Óshólar.

Hnífsdalur, (pop. 203) a village in a small valley, enclosed by big mountains. Community centre. A danger area for avalanches, the worst having occurred February 18th 1910, when 20 lives were lost.

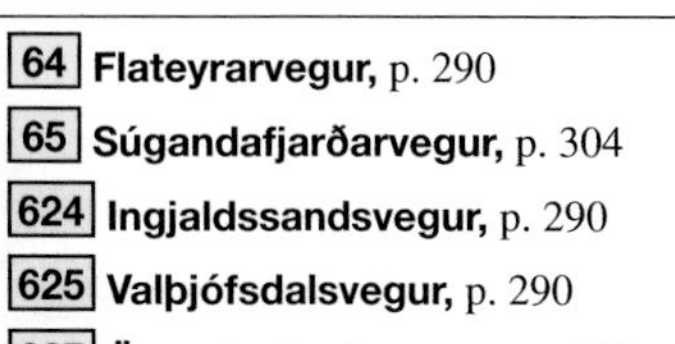

64 Flateyrarvegur, p. 290
65 Súgandafjarðarvegur, p. 304
624 Ingjaldssandsvegur, p. 290
625 Valþjófsdalsvegur, p. 290
627 Önundarfjarðarvegur, p. 290

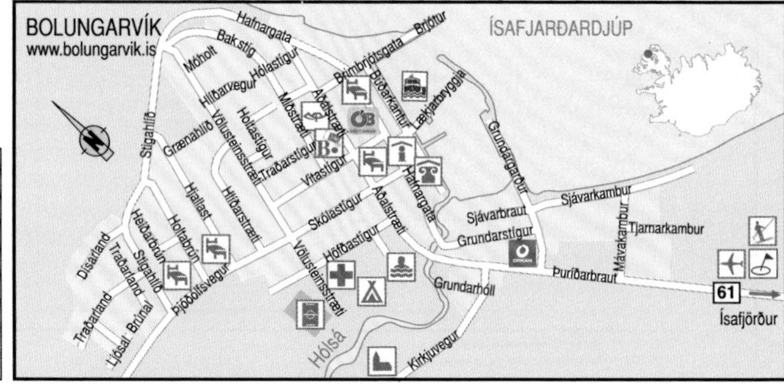

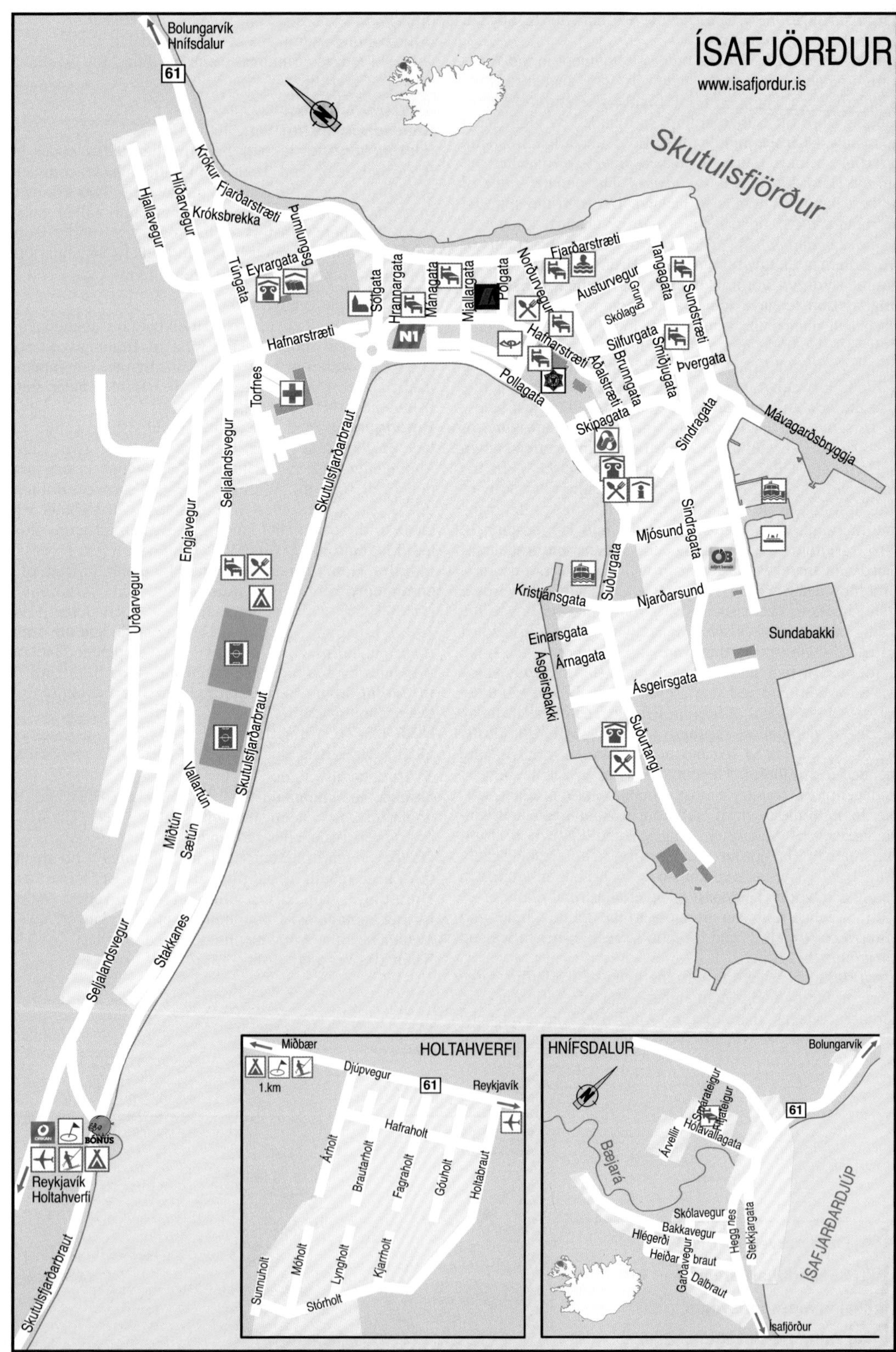
ÍSAFJÖRÐUR
www.isafjordur.is
Skutulsfjörður
Bolungarvík
Hnífsdalur
61
Krókur
Fjarðarstræti
Hlíðarvegur
Hjallavegur
Króksbrekka
Þumlungsg
Eyrargata
Túngata
Hafnarstræti
Sólgata
Hrannargata
Mánagata
Mjallargata
Pólgata
Norðurvegur
Fjarðarstræti
Austurvegur
Tangagata
Sundstræti
Skólagata
Silfurgata
Smiðjugata
Þvergata
Brunngata
Aðalstræti
Pollagata
Skipagata
Sindragata
Mávagarðsbryggja
Torfnes
Seljalandsvegur
Skutulsfjarðarbraut
Engjavegur
Urðarvegur
Mjósund
Sindragata
Suðurgata
Kristjánsgata
Njarðarsund
Sundabakki
Einarsgata
Árnagata
Ásgeirsbakki
Ásgeirsgata
Suðurtangi
Vallartún
Miðtún
Sætún
Stakkanes
Seljalandsvegur
Reykjavík
Holtahverfi
Skutulsfjarðarbraut
HOLTAHVERFI
Miðbær
1.km
Djúpvegur
61
Reykjavík
Hafraholt
Árholt
Brautarholt
Fagraholt
Góuholt
Holtabraut
Sunnuholt
Móholt
Lyngholt
Kjarrholt
Stórholt
HNÍFSDALUR
Bolungarvík
61
Smárateigur
Fitjateigur
Árvellir
Hólavallagata
Bæjará
Skólavegur
Bakkavegur
Hlégerði
Heiðarbraut
Garðavegur
Dalbraut
Hegg nes
Stekkjargata
ÍSAFJARÐARDJÚP
Ísafjörður

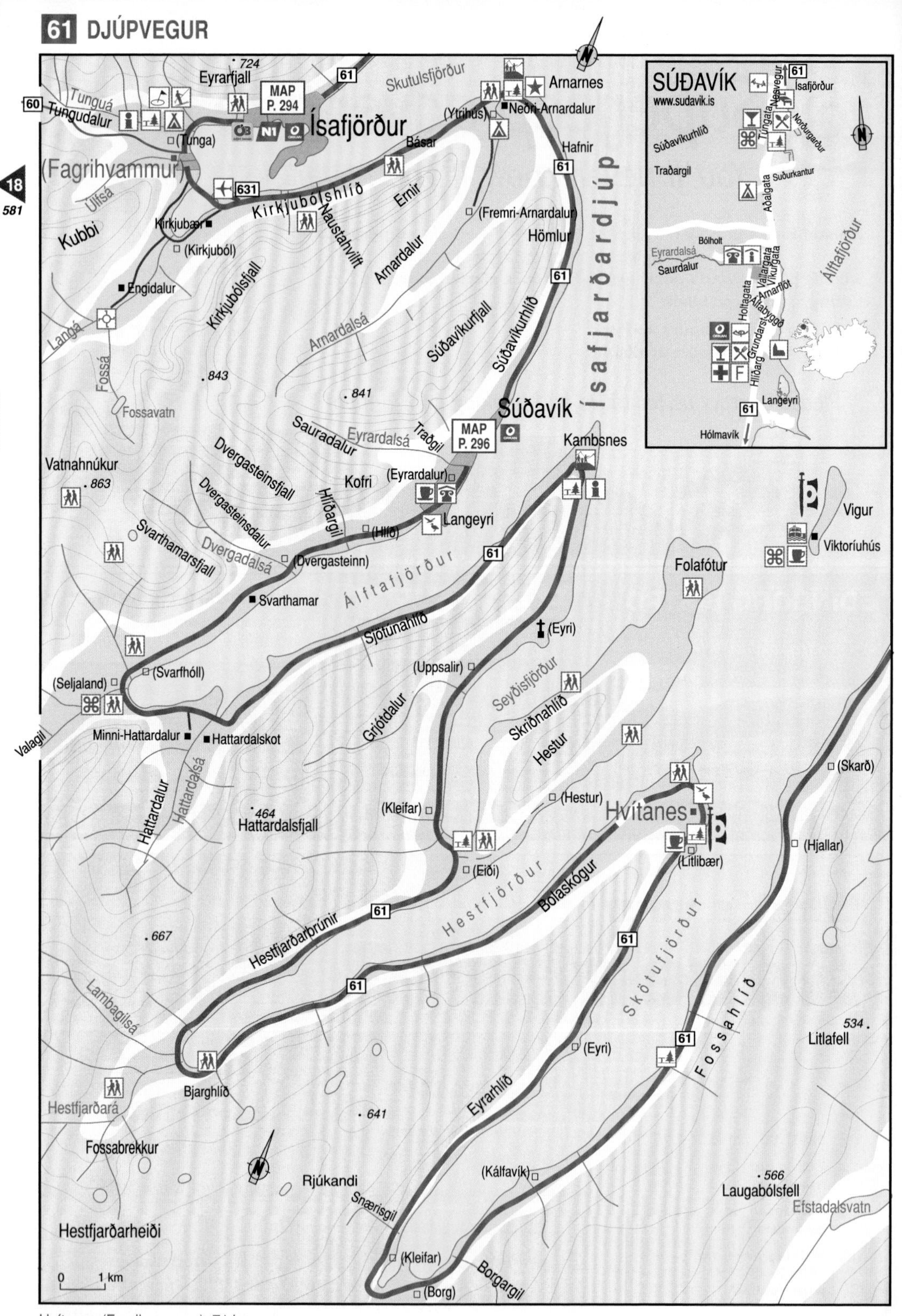

Hvítanes-(Fagrihvammur) 71 km

60 **Vestfjarðarvegur,** p. 292

Skutulsfjörður, the westernmost and shortest fjord off Ísafjarðardjúp. Little flat land, but short valleys at its head.
Tungudalur, see p. 293
Kirkjuból, a farm and formerly a church in Skutulsfjörður where in the 17th century the Rev. Jón Magnússon had a father and son burnt for sorcery.

631 **Airport road.**

Ernir, a narrow mountain ridge with a good viewpoint at Naustahvilft.
Arnardalur, a valley at the end of Arnarnes. The mountain to the west is called Ernir, and that to the east Hömlur. The farm Neðri-Arnardalur was the home of Þorbjörg Kolbrún, whom the poet Þormóður kolbrúnarskáld ("The poet of Kolbrún") praised in verse, as mentioned in *Fóstbræðra saga*. The farm Fremri-Arnardalur was the birthplace of Hannibal Valdimarsson (1903-1991) long a member of parliament, Minister of State and President of ASÍ (The Icelandic Federation of Labour).
Arnarnes, the outermost point of land on Skutulsfjörður. To the east is **Arnarneshamar**, a basalt cape, through which the first road tunnel in Iceland was made in 1948 and remained the only one until the Strákagöng tunnel near Siglufjörður in 1967 (see Road 76). Length c. 35 m. The British trawler *Cæsar* stranded off Arnarnes in April 1971 causing considerable oil pollution which killed many birds.
Súðavíkurhlíð, th slopes from Arnarnes to Súðavík.
Súðavík, (pop. 150) town. Primary industries are fish processing and fishing, with tourism also a growing sector, mostly sea angling. According to the Book of Settlements, Eyvindur kné and his wife Þuríður rymgylta arrived in Iceland at Álftafjörður and Seyðisfjörður in the 10th century, from Agder, Norway. A town began forming in Álftafjörður in the mid-19th century and Súðavík was first mentioned as a village in the 1880 census. In 1883, a group of Norwegians opened a whaling station in Langeyri that was operated for two decades, as well as a whaling station at Dvergasteinseyri. They also set up operations at Hattareyri in Álftafjörður and Uppsalaeyri in Seyðisfjörður. Súðavík was hit by a snow avalanche on January 16th 1995. The avalanche claimed 14 lives, while 12 people were rescued. After the avalanche, a decision was made to construct a new residential area in a secure location near Eyrardalsá river. In April 30th 1995, ground was broken for the new residential area in Súðavík. By older residential area to the new one. A memorial grove to those who were lost was made the avalanche fell. There are numerous marked hiking paths in the Súðavík area, including an old mail route leading from the bottom of Álftafjörður fjord, over to Önundafjörður fjord. There is also a good campsite and a family park Raggagarður, with recreational equipments and a barbecue. The Arctic Fox Centre opened in 2010, a research and exhibition centre, focusing on the arctic fox, the only native terrestrial mammal in Iceland. At the Centre is also a coffee house, a souvenir shop and internet access. The Eyrardalur farm is the oldest house in Súðavík, recently renovated. The farm is a Norwegian timber house and is connected to the whaling history at Langeyri. It is said the Jón Indíafari (1593-1679) lived at Eyrardalur the last years of his life.
Langeyri, a spit of land where Norwegians built a quay and the first whaling station in Iceland in 1883, the famous whaler Svend Foyn being one of the founders. He was a pioneer in Norwegian seal hunting and whale fishing and invented the explosive harpoon which was a revolution in whaling. This station was operated until the early 20th century.
Kofri, (635 m) an unusual mountain above Langeyri. Can be climbed via Hlíðargil canyon.
Dvergasteinn, á Dvergasteinseyri reistu Norðmenn hvalstöð 1896. Síðar var þar síldarsöltun.
Svarthamar, a farm, the home of Jón Ólafsson Indíafari ("who visited India") (1593-1679), one of the most widely travelled Icelanders in the 17th century. A book he wrote about his travels has been translated into many languages.
Valagil, a beautiful ravine with a spectacular and awesome landscape. There is a great variety of lava flow strata that indicate an ancient central volcano under Lambadalsfjall. A marked hiking trail leads from the highway to the ravine.
Hattardalur, a valley with two farms. At Hattareyri there was a herring-salting station for a time.
Eyri, a church and old manor farm, home of Magnús Magnússon (1630-1704), sheriff and writer. The neighbouring farm Tröð, now abandoned, was the birthplace of Magnús Hj. Magnússon (1873-1916), the poet of Þröm, who was the model for Nobel Prize-winning novelist H. Laxness's Ólafur Ljósvíkingur in *Heimsljós*.
Hestur, a peculiar shaped mountain.
Folafótur, ("Colt's foot") the promontory below the mountain Hestur between the sheltered fjords of Seyðisfjörður and Hestfjörður. Formerly a substantial farm of the same name, now abandoned. Was a lively fishing-station earlier. A beautiful place to paddle around in, enjoying the marine wildlife and the coastline from a unique angle.
Hestfjörður, the first shrimp banks to be found off Iceland were discovered off-shore in 1927.

P. 581

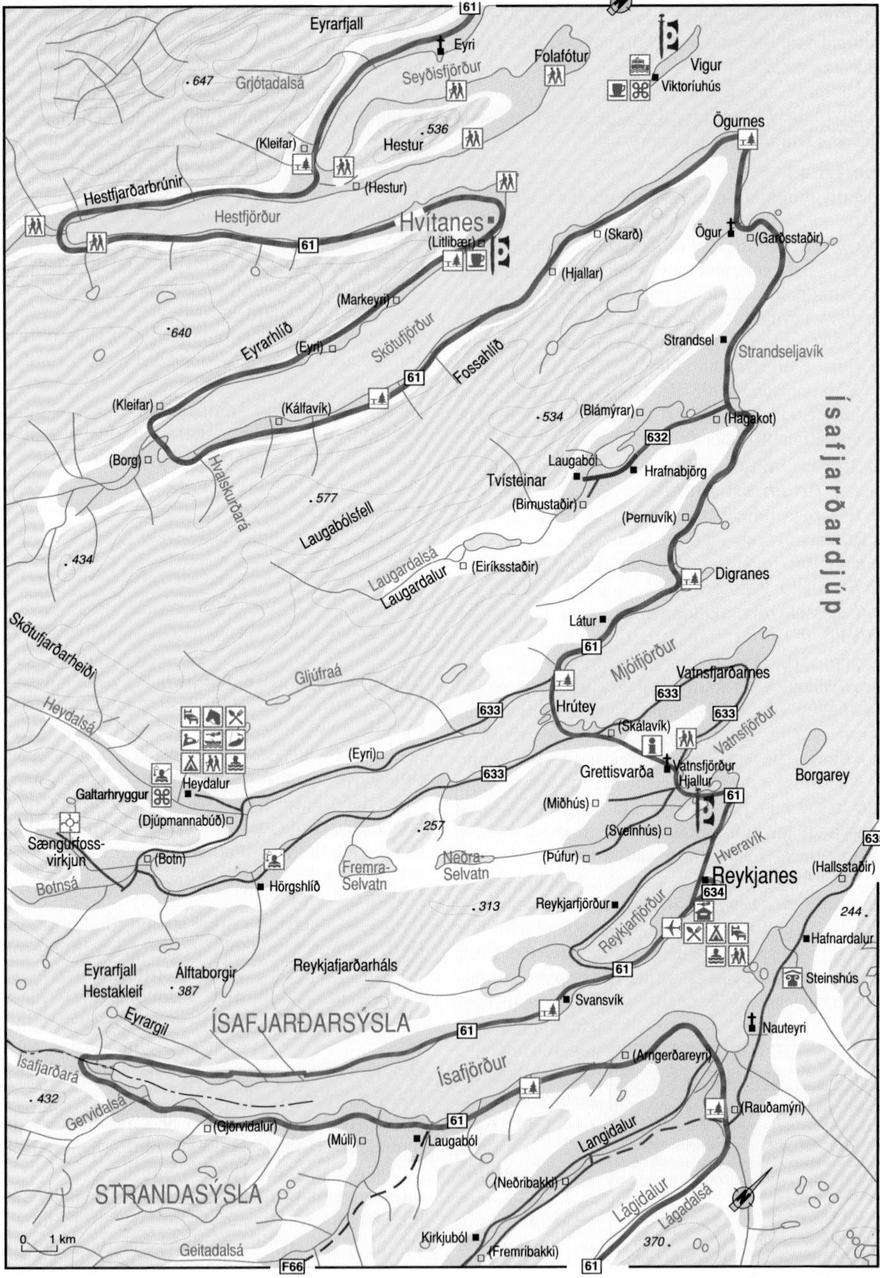

Eyrarfjall
Eyri
.647
Grjótadalsá
Seyðisfjörður
Folafótur
Vigur
Viktoríuhús
Ögurnes
(Kleifar)
.536
Hestur
(Hestur)
Hestfjarðarbrúnir
Hestfjörður
Hvítanes
(Litlibær)
(Skarð)
Ögur
(Garðsstaðir)
(Hjallar)
(Markeyri)
.640
Eyrarhlíð
(Eyri)
Skötufjörður
Fossahlíð
Strandsel
Strandseljavík
(Kleifar)
(Kálfavík)
.534
(Blámýrar)
(Hagakot)
Ísafjarðardjúp
(Borg)
Hvalskurðará
Laugaból
Tvísteinar
Hrafnabjörg
(Birnustaðir)
.577
Laugabólsfell
(Þernuvík)
.434
Laugardalsá
Laugardalur
(Eiríksstaðir)
Digranes
Skötufjarðarheiði
Látur
Mjóifjörður
Gljúfraá
Vatnsfjarðarnes
Heydalsá
Hrútey
(Skálavík)
Vatnsfjörður
(Eyri)
Grettisvarða
Vatnsfjörður
Hjallur
Borgarey
Galtarhryggur
Heydalur
(Miðhús)
(Djúpmannabúð)
.257
(Sveinhús)
Hveravík
Sængurfoss-virkjun
(Botn)
Fremra-Selvatn
Neðra-Selvatn
(Þúfur)
Reykjanes
(Hallsstaðir)
Botnsá
Hörgshlíð
.313
Reykjarfjörður
Reykjarfjörður
244.
Hafnardalur
Eyrarfjall
Hestakleif
Álftaborgir
.387
Reykjafjarðarháls
Steinshús
Svansvík
Eyrargil
ÍSAFJARÐARSÝSLA
Nauteyri
Ísafjarðará
(Arngerðareyri)
Ísafjörður
.432
Gervidalsá
(Rauðamýri)
(Gjörvidalur)
(Múli)
Laugaból
Langidalur
STRANDASÝSLA
(Neðribakki)
Lágidalur
Lágadalsá
0 1 km
Kirkjuból
370.
Geitadalsá
(Fremribakki)
61
61
632
633
634
635
F66

Litlibær, now deserted, was inhabited until 1969. Wooden house from 1895 with outer walls of stone, and turf roof. It originally housed two families. In the keeping of the National Museum since 1999.

Vigur, a lovely island west of the Ögurnes peninsula, 0.59 km^2, rich in eider duck and puffin, formerly a fishing-station. Some relics of old farming methods are preserved on Vigur, including Viktoríuhús and Iceland's only protected windmill, belived to have been built in 1860. In the keeping of the National Museum since 1992. There is also the country's oldest 8-oar rowing boat, which is in fact still in use. Popular tourist place.

Ögur, a substantial farm and church, occupied through the ages by men of influence. Some old relics in the church. About the middle of the 19th century one of the biggest dwelling-houses in rural Iceland was built there and is still standing. The first electric generator on a farm in the Ísafjarðardjúp district was built at Ögur in 1930. Formerly a fishing-station.

Garðsstaðir, an abandoned farm, once the home of poet and sorcerer Þorleifur Þórðarson (1570-1647), best known as Galdra-Leifi ("Leifi the sorcerer") about whom there are many tales. He was for instance said to have got hold of the head of a drowned man, sprinkled it with consecrated wine and bread, and then used it for augery and other magic.

Strandsel, a farm on the shallow bay Strandseljavík. Birthplace of Jón Baldvinsson (1882-1938), member of parliament, one of the pioneers of the trade union movement in Iceland.

632 Laugardalsvegur, 5,1 km.

Laugardalur, a shallow valley.

Heydalur, a 6 km long valley at the end of the fjord **Mjóifjörður**. Geothermal area. Information signs about the varied flora and birdlife in the valley. Walking routes ie to Skötufjörður and Arnarfjörður. At the farm Heydalur is a travel service that is open all year round. They organize all kinds of interesting trips as well as offering good accommodation. The old barn at the farm was converted to an attractive restaurant, emphasising on locally sourced ingredients.

Galtarhryggur, there is a natural pool considered to have healing powers after is was consecrated by Guðmundur góði (1161-1237).

Mjóifjörður, some forest and geothermal heat.

633 Vatnsfjarðarvegur, 42,6 km.

634 Reykjanesvegur, 4,3 km.

Borgarey, an island with many eider duck and puffins

Vatnsfjörður, an ancient manor farm and setting of Sagas, on a fjord of the same name. Church and parsonage. Many clergymen there became wealthy. Among noted farmers was Björn Einarsson Jórsalafari ("who visited Jerusalem") (d.1415) who travelled widely, to Jerusalem among other places. He also went once to Greenland and three times to Rome, travelling like a king with a large retinue. His daughter Kristín was the mother of governor Björn ríki ("the rich") Þorleifsson (1408?-1467) who was killed by Englishmen at Rif (see Skarð). The Rev. Hjalti Þorsteinsson (1665-1754) was the best painter in Iceland in his day. Three Vatnsfjörður pastors in a row wrote annals, the most recent being the Rev. Guðlaugur Sveinsson (1731-1807). In 1791 he published an essay together with sketches which were to cause a revolution in the placing of farmhouses and their appearance, being the first known conception of the Icelandic gabled farmhouse (see Hrafnseyri). Above the farm is the hollow cairn **Grettisvarða**, once thought to have been made by Grettir the strong as a hide-out but more probably a watch tower of some sort, perhaps from the stormy time of the Sturlungas (1220-1262). **Hjallur,** large shack for drying stockfish, with stone walls and turf roof, built around 1880. In the keeping of the National Museum since 1975.

Reykjanes, a narrow peninsula between Ísafjörður and Reykjafjörður. There is a hotel, open all year, in which was once a district school founded in 1934 and renovated around 1960. There is a swimming pool, originally built 1889, green houses and hot springs. From 1774 till the end of the 19th century there was salt-processing by the hot spring. It was operated again in 2008 and is the only place in the world where salt is produced in an environmentally sustainable way. Good walking routes and rich birdlife in the area.

Laugaból, a substantial farm on Ísafjörður, well-wooded. Considered by some to have been the farm of Þorbjörn Þjóðreksson of *Hávarðar saga Ísfirðings*. Long the residence of the poetess Halla Eyjólfsdóttir (1866-1937).

Arngerðareyri, formerly a trading centre, now a landing stage for the Fagranes ferry boat from Ísafjörður.

635 Snæfjallastrandarvegur, p. 318
F66 Kollafjarðarheiði, p. 313

(Lágidalur)-Hólmavík 41 km

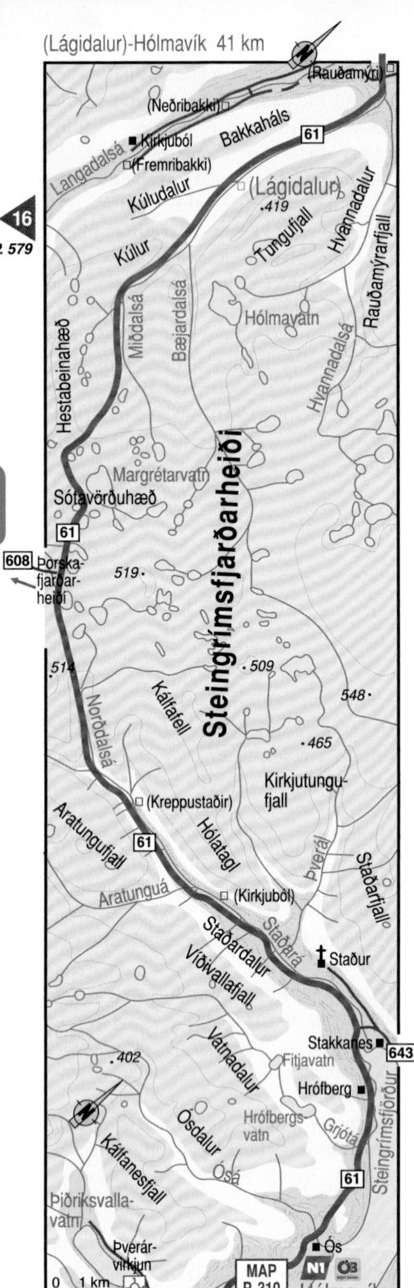

16
P. 579

Steingrímsfjarðarheiði, (440 m) moors with many lakes and brooks. The moors are very flat on top and in the old days many people got lost there in foggy weather.

Þorskafjarðarheiði, (490 m) a moor providing the shortest route between Breiðafjörður and Ísafjarðardjúp and the most-travelled route between Breiðafjörður and Ísafjarðardjúp for centuries. Stony and barren with many small lakes.

Staðará, a river flowing from Steingrímsfjarðarheiði moor down through the valley Staðardalur. Fairly calm and deep at its lower end, a good fishing river.

Staður, a church in the Staðardalur valley, built in 1855, a former parsonage. Staður was considered one of the richest benefices in the entire country. Among the best-known clergymen there was Jón Árnason (1665-1743), Bishop of Skálholt. In the church there is a remarkable pulpit painted with figures of Christ and his disciples, dating back to the year 1731.

68 **Innstrandavegur,** p. 311
608 **Þorskafjarðarvegur,** p. 313
643 **Strandavegur,** p. 319

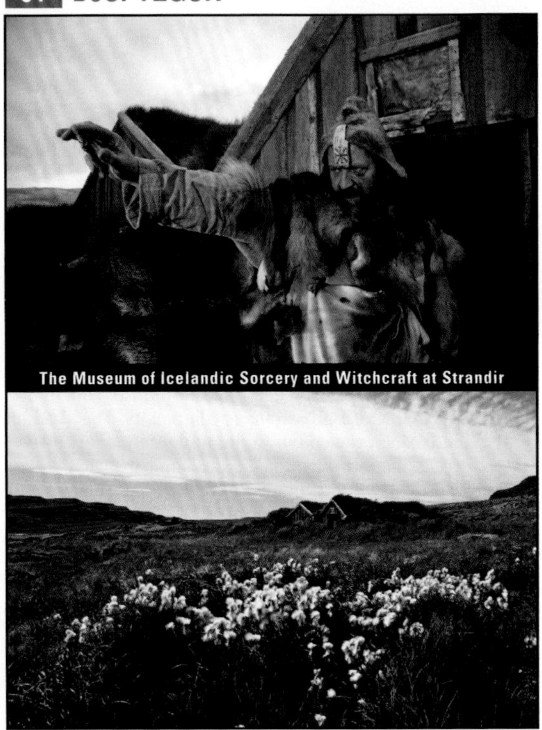

The Museum of Icelandic Sorcery and Witchcraft at Strandir

Skeljavík, there is a memorial to Hermann Jónasson (1896–1976) a member of parliament 1934–67 and prime minister.

Tröllatunga, a church, and a parsonage until 1906. Lignite and plant fossils in places. It used to be said metals and treasure were hidden in the ground, so some Danes obtained official permission to dig, but they found nothing but stones in **Gullhóll** ("Gold hill"). In Tröllatungukirkja church there was an ancient church bell, in the National Museum of Iceland since 1988.

Húsavík, a farm on Steingrímsfjörður. Close by is Húsavíkurkleif where lignite and fossils from the Tertiary period have been found. A stream flows through a gorge there in a small waterfall. Some iron ore is also found there.

Steingrímsfjörður, the biggest fjord in Strandasýsla county, 28 km long and 7 km wide at the mouth. Lowish, rounded mountains descending to the sea in ledges and terraces. Some flat land and many valleys.

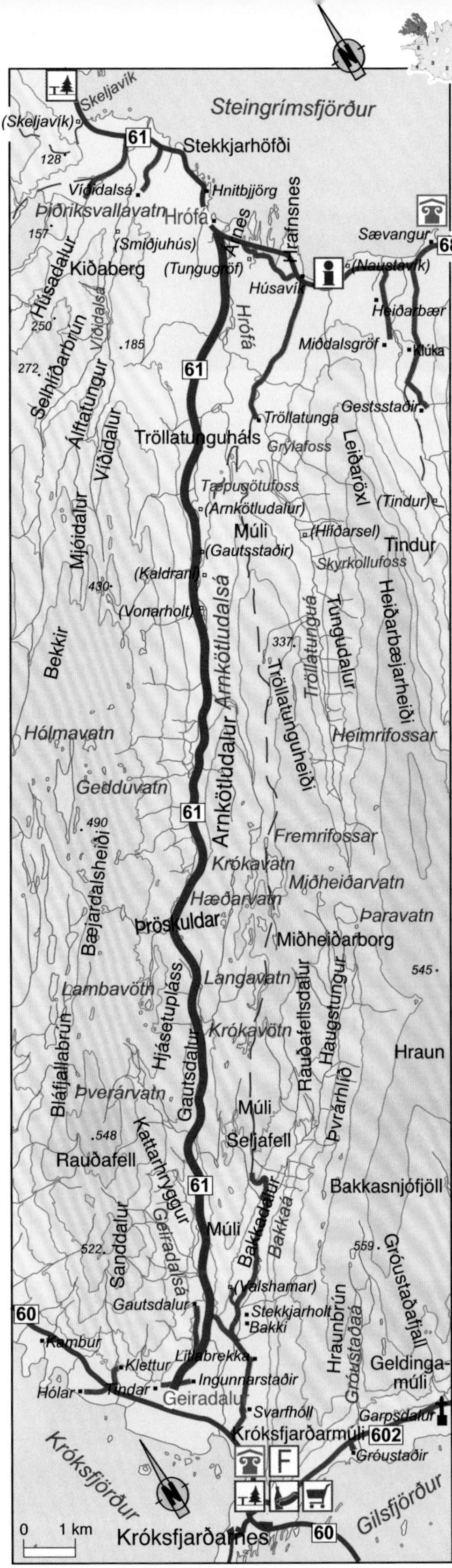

16 P. 579

60 **Vestfjarðavegur,** p. 284
68 **Innstrandavegur,** p. 311
602 **Garpdalsvegur,** p. 282

Flatey

Flatey, an island belonging to a group of about 40 islands who are believed to have been forged under the weight of a great glacier during the last Ice Age. Though Flatey is only about 2km long, 1km wide and rising only 16m m above sea level it is the most notable of all the islands in Breiðafjörður. There is much bird life on the islands where half of all nesting birds in Iceland lay their eggs there. A part of the island is a protected natural site. An Augustinian monastery was erected there in 1172, but was later moved to Helgafell. Klaustursteinn, in the field by Klausturhólar, is thought to mark its site. Flatey has been an official trading place since 1777. The famous manuscript *Flateyjarbók,* written in 1387-1394, takes its name from the island. In the early 19th century Flatey was in the forefront of progress and culture in Iceland. A church was built there in 1926 decorated with a fresco by the contemporary painter Baltasar. The village in Flatey is a good example of a settlement from the turn of the last century. The oldest house on the island was built in 1840 and there are remains of vegetable gardens or indications of their existence. Many of the houses have been restored in their original style. A hotel and a restaurant are open during the summer and a ferry goes to the island from Stykkishólmur and Brjánslækur two times every day during that time.

Hergilsey, an island with geothermal heat, site of some of the events of *Gísla saga Súrssonar*. In the year 1910 an English trawler captain kidnapped the director of the district council in Hergilsey and took him to England, along with the sheriff of Barðastrandasýsla-county. They had, in the line of duty, rowed out to the trawler in an open rowing boat with the intention of arresting the captain for breaking the law by fishing within territorial waters.

Svefneyjar, a group of 52 islands, 2-3 nautical miles off the island of Flatey. There was a substantial manor farm there at one time. Eggert Ólafsson (1726-68) naturalist, poet and cultural leader, one of the most remarkable men in Iceland in the 18th century, was born there. His best known work is the *Ferðabók* which he wrote with Bjarni Pálsson (1719–1779), later the first Surgeon General of Iceland, after their travels and research in Iceland from 1752-57. (*Travels in Iceland* by Eggert Ólafsson and Bjarni Pálsson 1752-1757, first printed by Barnard & Sultzer, Water Lane, Fleet Street, 1805. It contains observations on the manners and customs of the inhabitants, descriptions of lakes, rivers, glaciers, hot-springs and volcanoes, various kinds of earth, stones, fossils and petrifactions, as well as descriptions of animals, insects, fishes, etc.) Eggert and his wife, then newly-wed, were drowned in Breiðafjörður along with all the crew, when they were crossing the fjord on their way to his farm Hofstaðir on the Snæfellsnes peninsula. Eggert is said to have had with him on board the halberd of Gunnar from Hlíðarendi of *Njáls saga* (see Road 54, Hofsstaðir).

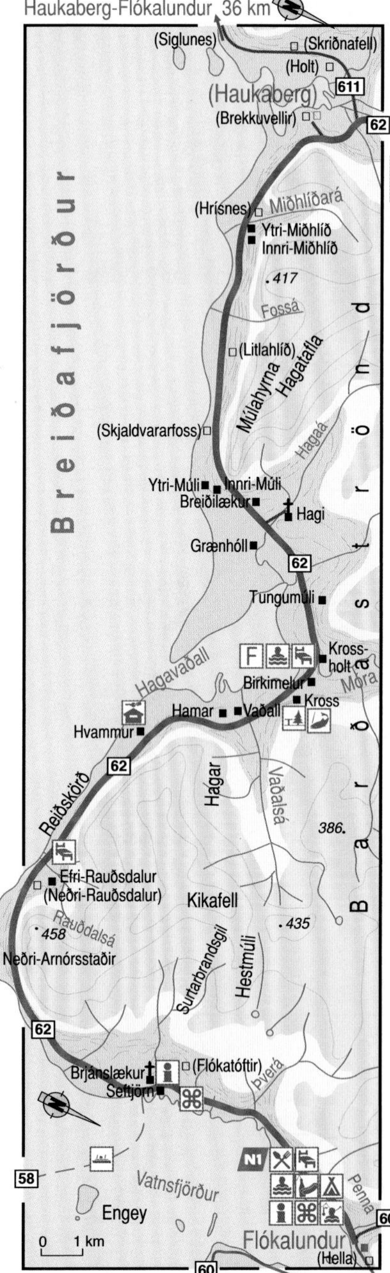

Hagatafla, (603 m) a picturesque mountain west of Hagi.

Hagi, a big manor farm and church. For long the office of a sheriff, the last of whom was the poet Jón Thoroddsen. In Saga times the home of Gestur Oddleifsson the wise. He was one of the wisest men in the land in his time and appears in *Njáls saga* among others. He was thought to have the power of foresight.

Mórudalur, a small valley through which flows the fishing-river Móra. Geothermal heat. A swimming pool, fallen into disuse.

Kross, a community at the mouth of Mórudalur.

Reiðskörð, jagged crags where the criminal Sveinn skotti, the son of the notorious 16th century murderer Björn from Öxl (see Road 574, Öxl), was hanged, after which the place was said to be haunted.

Barðaströnd, the coastline from Vatnsfjörður to the farm Siglunes. Continuous flat land with steep cliffs above and some small valleys, indented by the shallow inlet Hagavaðall, that almost dries up at low tide. Sandy and grassy, with birch-bushes, farms.

Brjánslækur, an ancient manor farm, church, parsonage. Nearby are the **Flókatóttir** remains, said to be ruins of the booth built by Flóki Vilgerðarson or Hrafna Flóki ("Raven-Flóki"), for his first winter's stay in Iceland in the 9th century. He got his nickname because he used ravens to help him find Iceland when he first came there, and is responsible for naming the country Iceland. If they were indeed his booth, these are the oldest ruins of a man-made structure in Iceland. Above the farm is the **Surtarbrandsgil** ravine where there is lignite. It is one of the best places for finding fossils from the Tertiary period, first noticed by the explorers Eggert Ólafsson and Bjarni Pálsson. Car ferry to Stykkishólmur, road 58.

Flókalundur, ("Flóki's grove") a wooded area near the crossroads. Some services, summer hotel, summer house area and swimming pool nearby.

58 Stykkishólmsvegur, p. 255 **60 Vestfjarðavegur,** p. 288
611 Siglunesvegur, p. 304

Patreksfjörður-Haukaberg 25 km

17 P. 580

Haukaberg-Patreksfjörður 25 km

Patreksfjörður, (pop. 687), a village on a fjord of same name, built on the two sandspits Vatneyri and Geirseyri. A very old trading place. The harbour, dug in shallow water on Vatneyri in 1946, is called Patrekshöfn. Main industries fishing and fish-processing. A snow avalanche in 1983 killed 4 people and destroyed many homes. There is a memorial to that event. There is also a memorial honouring British seamen in Icelandic waters and those who died there. This memorial was a joint venture by the citizens of Aberdeen, Hull and Grimsby in the United Kingdom.

Raknadalshlíð, steep, stony cliffs along the fjord east of Patreksfjörður.

Skápadalur, on the shore is Garðar, Icelands oldest steel boat, constructed in Norway 1912. As the boat is very rusty it is not recommended to go on board.

Kleifaheiði, (404 m) a mountain road from the Barðaströnd coast to the head of Patreksfjörður. On the top of the moors, at their western edge, is the *Kleifabúi* cairn in the shape of a man, raised by road workers. It is said the it resembles Hákon J. Kristófersson (1877-1967) a farmer and a congress man from the farm Hagi at Barðaströnd.

Stálfjall, ("Steel mountain") a mountain (650 m) between the Rauðisandur sands and the Barðaströnd coast. Lignite deposits, and during First World War there was some mining there, now discontinued.

611 Siglunesvegur, 7,3 km.

Sjóræningjahúsið

63 Bíldudalsvegur, p. 305

612 Örlygshafnarvegur, p. 314

614 Rauðasandsvegur, p. 314

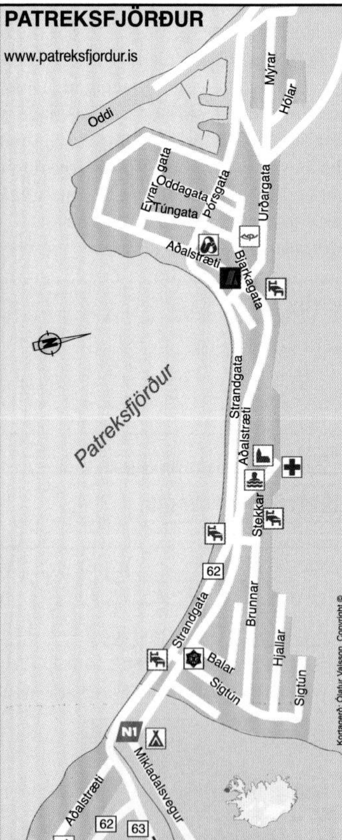

617 Tálknafjarðarvegur, 11,6 km.

Stóri-Laugardalur, a church built in 1907. There is also an old pool that was once used for washing called Djáknalaug.

Litli-Laugardalur, geothermal heat. The hot water is used to heat up a swiming pool and to a hut tub which is open around the clock all year round.

Sveinseyri, farm, community centre and school, swimming pool and forestry.

Tálknafjörður, (pop. 222) The village at Tálknafjörður began forming around 1945 when the Tálknafjörður freezing plant was opened. Until that point there was not much of a community built up, although Bakki was beginning to become a community, as it was home to one of the region's two schools and was used as a base for some fishing outfits. Tálknafjörður is actually one of the younger settlements in the West Fjords, which is no doubt because of the amount of ice that formed at Hópið, making it difficult for timber boats to break though. However, this changed with the dawn of metal boats, and not long after, the new settlement appeared. Fisherman's huts had previously been used out at the end of the fjord as it was shorter to the fishing grounds and the ice didn't obstruct the path. Fishing is still the main industry. The village includes an elementary school, swimming pool, community centre and church, Tálknafjörður Church, consecrated in 2002.

Bíldudalur, (pop. 222) a village in a small inlet of Arnarfjörður. As a well situated for fishing and trading, it was once one of the most important fishing stations in Iceland. Bíldudalur was at its height at the turn of the last century, at the time of Pétur Thorseinsson the father of the present village and a pioneer in fishing and processing, way ahead of his time. Main Occupation today still is fishing but also processing of calcified algae. Main attractions: Bird life and nature. The Sea Monster Museum, gymnasium, hostel, restaurant and a natural hot spring in Reykjarfjörður. The music museum Melodies and memories contains many exhibits related to Icelands's musical history. Monument to drowned seamen. Birthplace of the artist Guðmundur Thorsteinsson (Muggur 1891-1924) the son of Pétur Thorsteinsson.

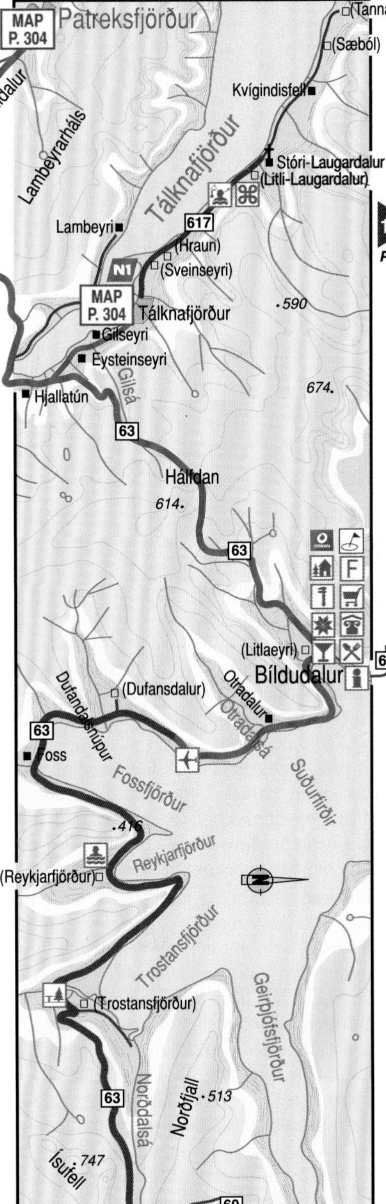

Helluskarð-Patreksfjörður 63 km

60 **Vestfjarðavegur,** p. 288
62 **Barðastrandarvegur,** p. 304
619 **Ketildalavegur,** p. 317

Tálknafjörður swimming pool

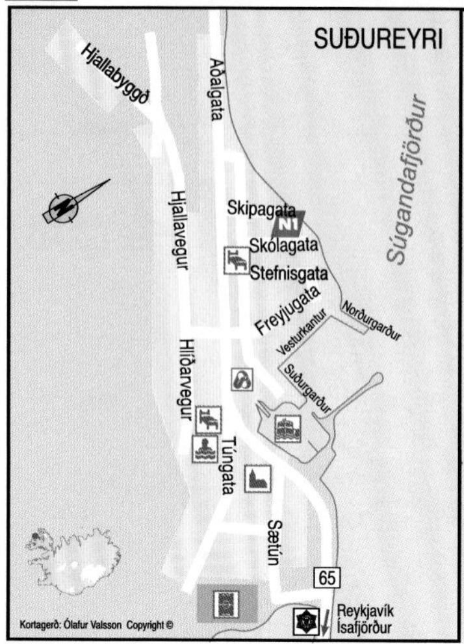

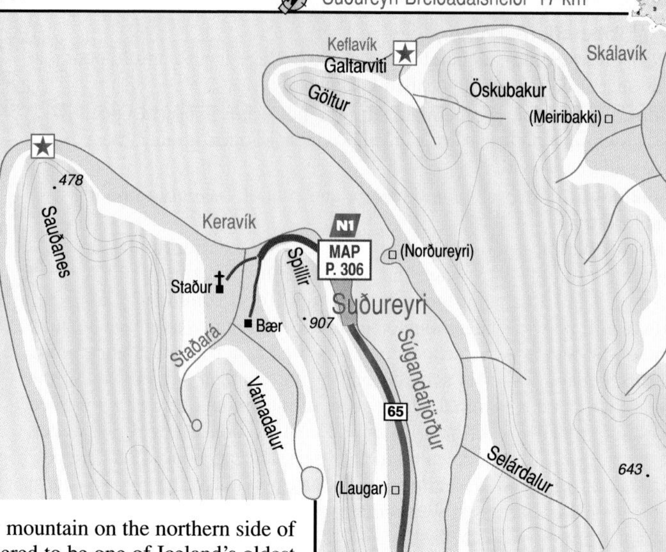

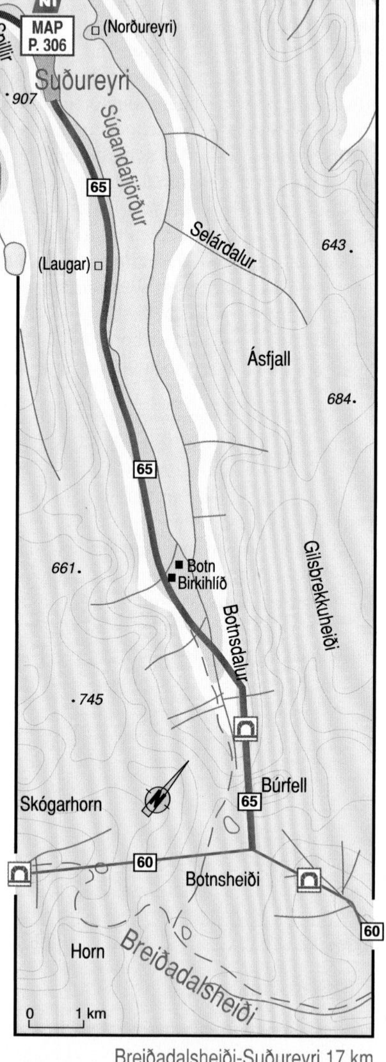

Göltur, (445 m) a distinctive and striking mountain on the northern side of the mouth of Súgandafjörður. It is considered to be one of Iceland's oldest mountains, more then 16 million year old. At Keflavík below Göltur is the Galtarviti lighthouse. Weather station.

Staður, a church not far from the village. Nearby is Sauðanes, where the steamer *Talisman* foundered in 1922.

Suðureyri, (pop. 252) a village which has been an official trading place since just before the turn of last century. Now this small eco-friendly fishing village is a popular destination for guests who like to explore, learn and take part in the local fisherman lifestyle and see how this small village is processing first class fish products for foreign markets. In the evening the small fishing boats sail back home full of fish and the locals meet down by the harbor to hear a good fishing story. The village swimming pool and hot tubs are one of the most popular in the area, being one of the few outside pools in the Westfjords.

Laugar, swimming pool, first built in 1933. Geothermal area. Laugar provides the village of Suðureyri with hot water through a 3 km pipeline.

Botn, a farm at the head of Súgandafjörður, where lignite was sometimes mined, but not since 1940-42. The lignite was used for fuel. Fossils of an american oak have been found there.

Súgandafjörður, a fjord opening out between the mountains Sauðanes and Göltur, ca. 12 km long. Broadish at the mouth, but narrowing near the mountain Spillir to about 1 km. Shallow, steep cliffs, birch-bushes, geothermal heat in places. Danger of avalanches.

Breiðadalsheiði, (610 m) the mountain road between Önundarfjörður and Ísafjörður, one of the highest in Iceland. Formerly frequent avalanche accidents. Motor-road opened in 1936. Tunnels that have been made under the Breiðadalsheiði and Botnsheiði moors are a great improvement to communication in the area.

60 **Vestfjarðavegur,** p. 292

Breiðadalsheiði-Suðureyri 17 km

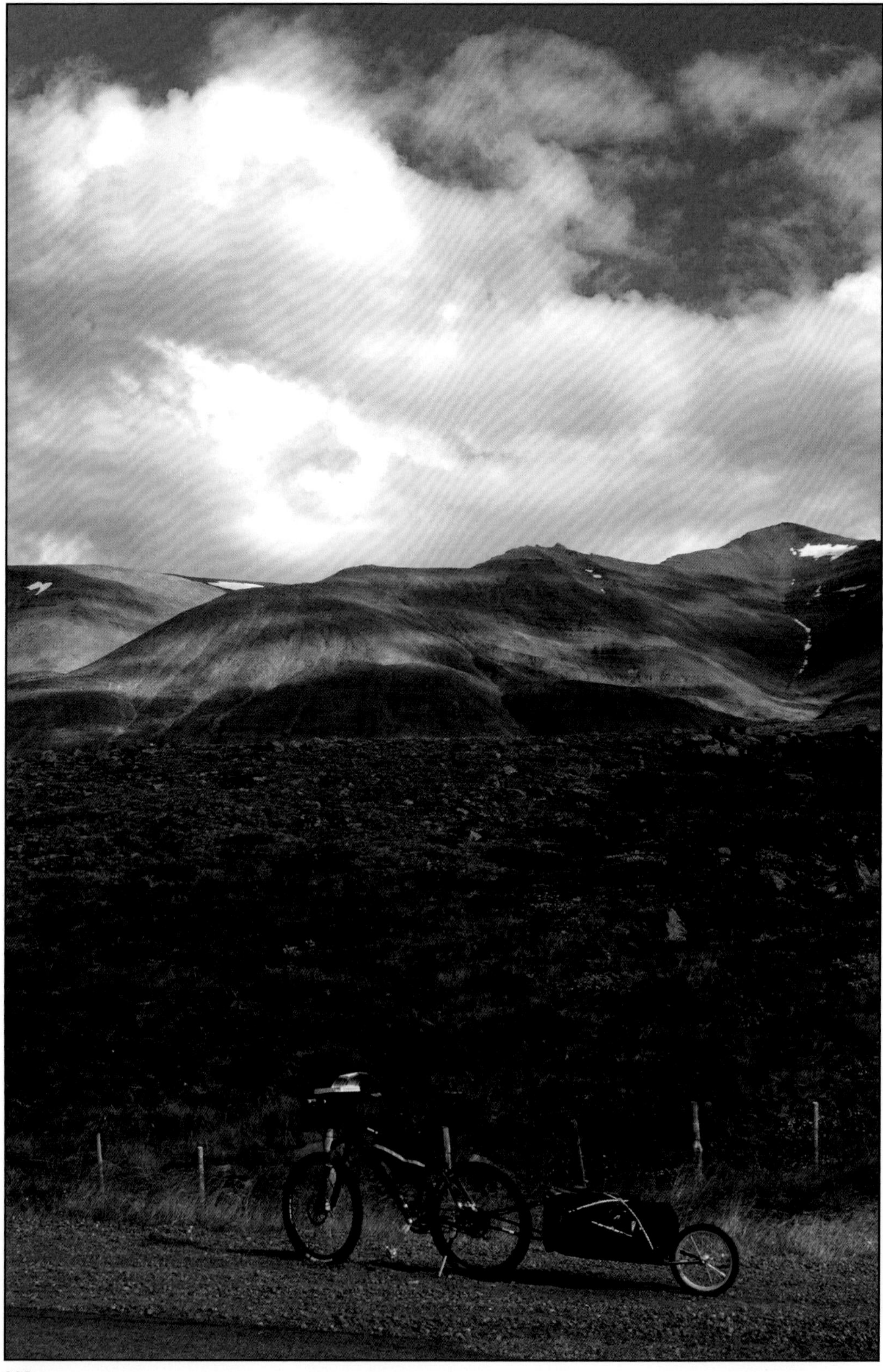

68 INNSTRANDAVEGUR

Prestbakki, a church and parsonage.

Bær, a farm, often the seat of the local sheriff. In the 17th century the sub-governor Þorleifur Kortsson (1615 - 1698) lived there. He was notorious for the number of people he had burnt for witchcraft. His son Hannes was historian to the King, and was sent to Iceland to collect sagas and manuscripts. He was lost at sea in 1682 along with all the manuscripts.

The farm Bær in Hrútafjörður.

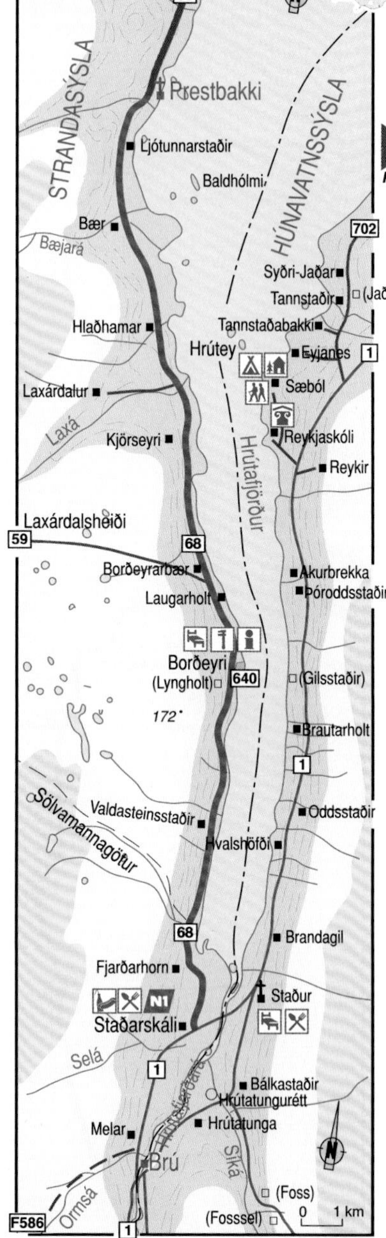

Kjörseyri, a farm, for 40 years the home of the scholar Finnur Jónsson (1842-1924), who wrote about Icelandic national customs and sagas.

Laxárdalsheiði, (200 m), a moor, traversed by Laxárdalsvegur (Road 59) between the villages Búðardalur and Borðeyri. Two Laxá rivers flow down from there, one to Hvammsfjörður, the other to Hrútafjörður. Flattish with many lakes, the biggest being Laxárvatn.

640 Borðeyrarvegur, 0,64 km.

Borðeyri, a trading place, authorised in 1846. For a time the seat of the sheriff's office.

Fjarðarhorn, a farm from where a disused moorland track, **Sölvamannagötur** ("Sea-weed men's road"), goes up onto Laxárdalsheiði moor. The name indicates that men from North Iceland used to go that way to buy the edible sea-weed dulse at Saurbær.

Melar, an old substantial farm and home of local leaders. The same family has lived there since 1530, and all the farmers have been christened Jón, except for one Jósep.

Brú, once a telephone exchange and post office opened about 1950, moved from Borðeyri. Connects North, South and West Iceland.

1 Norðurlandsvegur, p. 62
59 Laxárdalsvegur, p. 257
702 Heggstaðanesvegur, p. 334
F586 Haukadalsskarðsvegur, p. 468

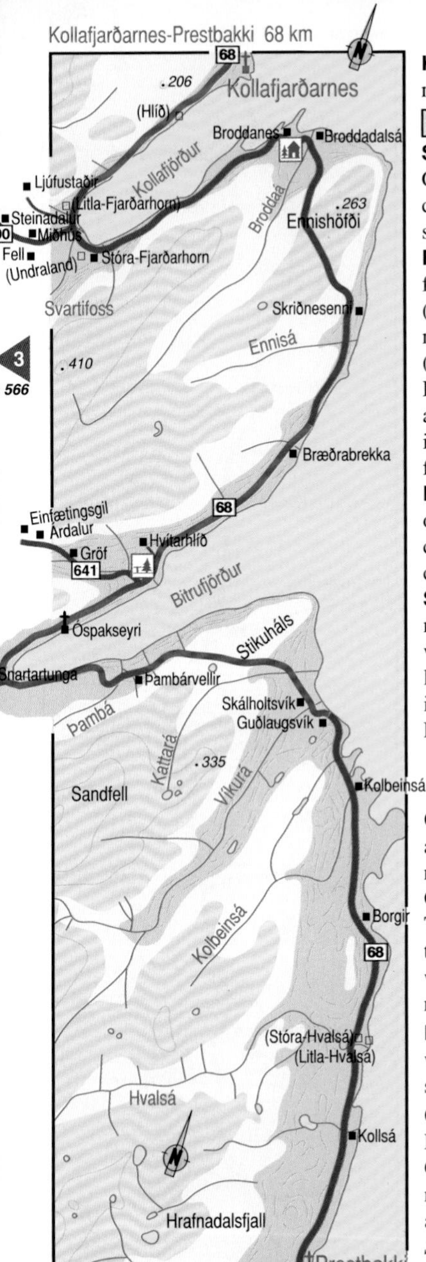

Kollafjörður, a small fjord about 8 km long. Skerries and shoals in the middle known as Skottar, dangerous for boats.

690 Steinadalsvegur, 29 km.

Steinadalsheiði, (330 m) the mountain road between Kollafjörður and Gilsfjörður, 17 km long. The small lake **Heiðarvatn** by the road. Three cairns show the boundary of three counties: Strandasýsla, Austur-Barðastrandarsýsla and Dalasýsla. Available to most cars during the summer.

Fell, an ancient manor farm and church until 1909. Nearby is the waterfall **Svartifoss**, behind which is a cave where the outlaw Fjalla-Eyvindur ("Mountain-Eyvindur") is said to have stayed and which is a good landmark for ships. One of best-known farmers was sheriff Halldór Jakobsson (1736-1810). Among his writings is the history of volcanoes, published in Danish in 1757 and for long a popular reference book abroad. Fell was also the home for a time of the Rev. Oddur Þorsteinsson (ca. 1600), who is said to have been a powerful sorcerer and about whom there are many folk tales.

Broddanes, a farm with many natural advantages, such as seals, eider ducks, driftwood. Some crags in the sea nearby, called Broddar ("Spikes").

Skriðnesenni, the outermost farm on Bitrufjörður, where the same family has lived for 200 years. Nearby is a very steep headland, Ennishöfði.

641 Krossárdalsvegur, 2,84 km.

Óspakseyri, a farm, church and once a trading place named for the robber Óspakur who lived there. The land is that of the settler Þorbjörn bitra, from whom Bitrufjörður takes its name.

Bitrufjörður, a short fjord with little flat land, and small valleys off it.

Guðlaugsvík, a farm. Named after a man, Guðlaugur, who was murdered at Guðlausghöfði according to the *Book of Settlement*.

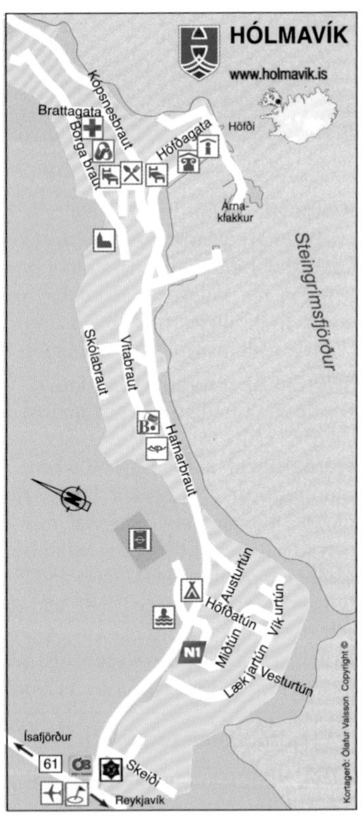

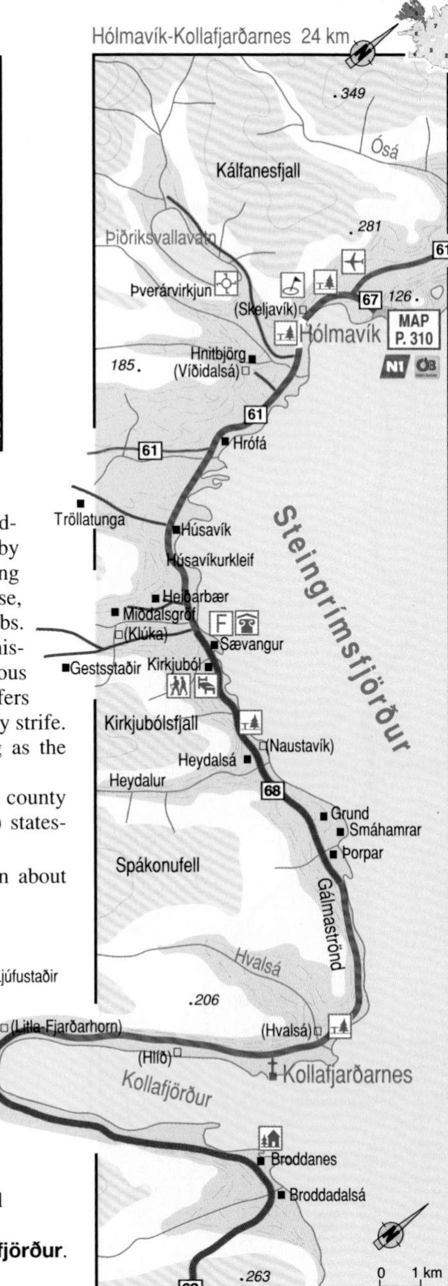

67 Hólmavíkurvegur, 1,63 km.

Hólmavík, (pop. 336) a village in the land of Kálfanes. Before trading started there in 1895, there was trade at Skipatangi in nearby Skeljavík bay. Now the main trading centre for the district. Fishing and fish-processing. At Hólmavík is a library, church, guesthouse, restaurant, coffe house and an outdoor swimming pool with hot tubs. The Museum of Sorcery & Witchcraft in Hólmavík presents the history of witch-hunting in the 17th century Iceland as well as various aspects of magic from younger sources. The museum shop offers souvenirs, books and magical amulets that might assist you in daily strife. The Tourist Information Centre is located in the same building as the museum.

Skeljavík, an abandoned farm where the people of Strandasýsla county erected a monument in 1979 to Hermann Jónasson (1896-1967) statesman and prime minister.

Sævangur, community center. There is an interesting exhibition about the icelandic sheep and sheep farming with special emphasis on the Strandir area. The children can enjoy themselves in their own room, in which are toys and colour books, while the grown-ups can view the exhibition, and the museum also has a small science room where people can taka a look at various things through microscope. One of the main attraction in the Sheep Farming Museum are lambs which the visitors can feed with milk from a bottle. There is also a coffee bar and handicraft- and souvenir store.

Kirkjuból, a farm.

Heydalsá, a farm, site of a secondary school founded in 1896 and operated for 20 years.

Gálmaströnd, the coast to the south of the mouth of **Steingrímsfjörður**. Much driftwood, to which Skálholt cathedral had the rights.

Kollafjarðarnes, a farm and church.

61 Djúpvegur, p. 301
690 Steinadalsvegur, p. 282

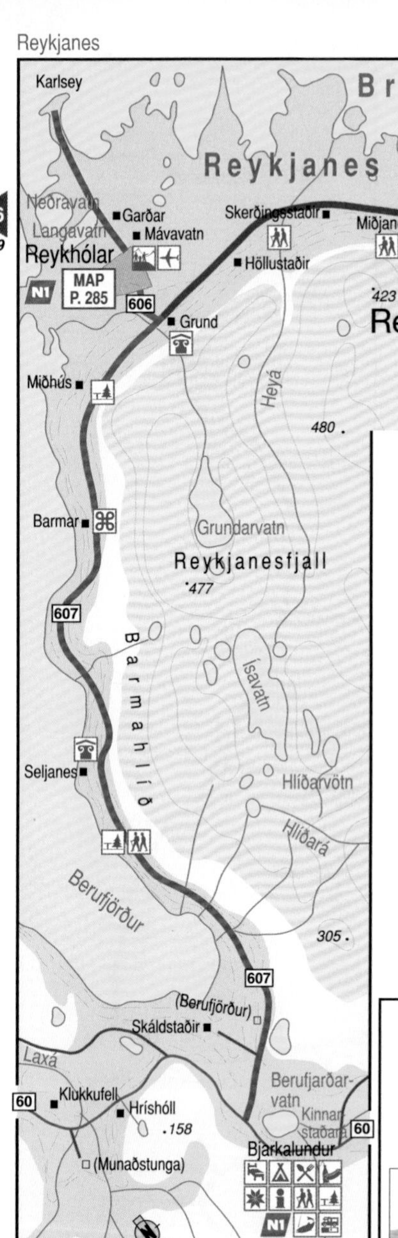

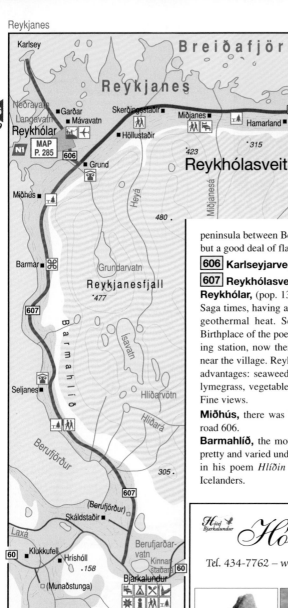

16 P. 579

Staður, formerly a church and parsonage, with fertile land and eider duck colonies. Wooden church built 1864. Ornamented with wood carving, this was one of the first churches in Iceland to be painted, not tarred. In the keeping of the National Museum since 1964.

Reykjanes, the peninsula between Berufjörður and Þorskafjörður. Highland with steep slopes, but a good deal of flat land to the south, with marshes and small lakes.

606 Karlseyjarvegur, 3,6 km.

607 Reykhólasveitarvegur, 21,77 km.

Reykhólar, (pop. 137) one of biggest and richest of manor farms ever since Saga times, having an eventful history. Some 300 skerries and islands. Much geothermal heat. Several powerful and wealthy men have lived there. Birthplace of the poet Jón Thoroddsen (1818–68). Former experimental farming station, now there is a seaweed processing plant and a sea-salt factory near the village. Reykhólar was said to have rights to all the following natural advantages: seaweed, lumpfish, mussels, angelica, eggs, eider down, reeds, lymegrass, vegetables, berries, puffins, carbon, guillemots, ptarmigan, seals. Fine views.

Miðhús, there was born Gestur Pálsson (1852–1891) a poet. Memorial by road 606.

Barmahlíð, the mountainside along the west of Berufjörður, wooded with pretty and varied undergrowth. The poet Jón Thoroddsen describes Barmahlíð in his poem *Hlíðin mín fríða* ("My Bonnie Braes") well-known to most Icelanders.

60 Vestfjarðavegur, p. 284

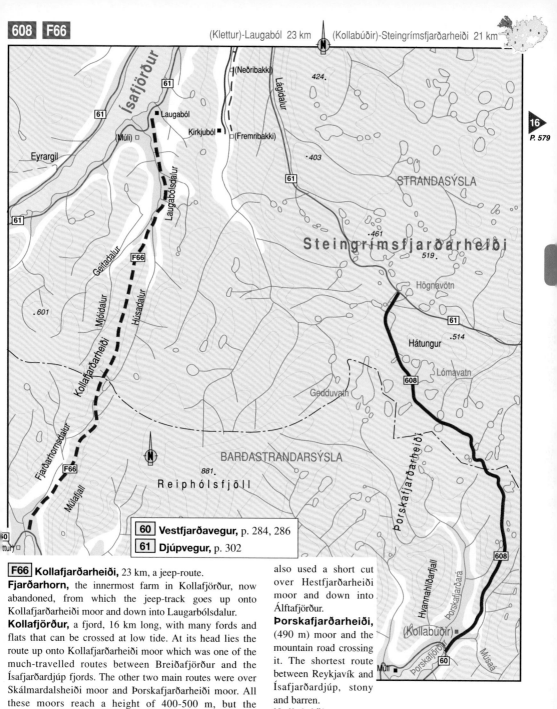

16 P. 579

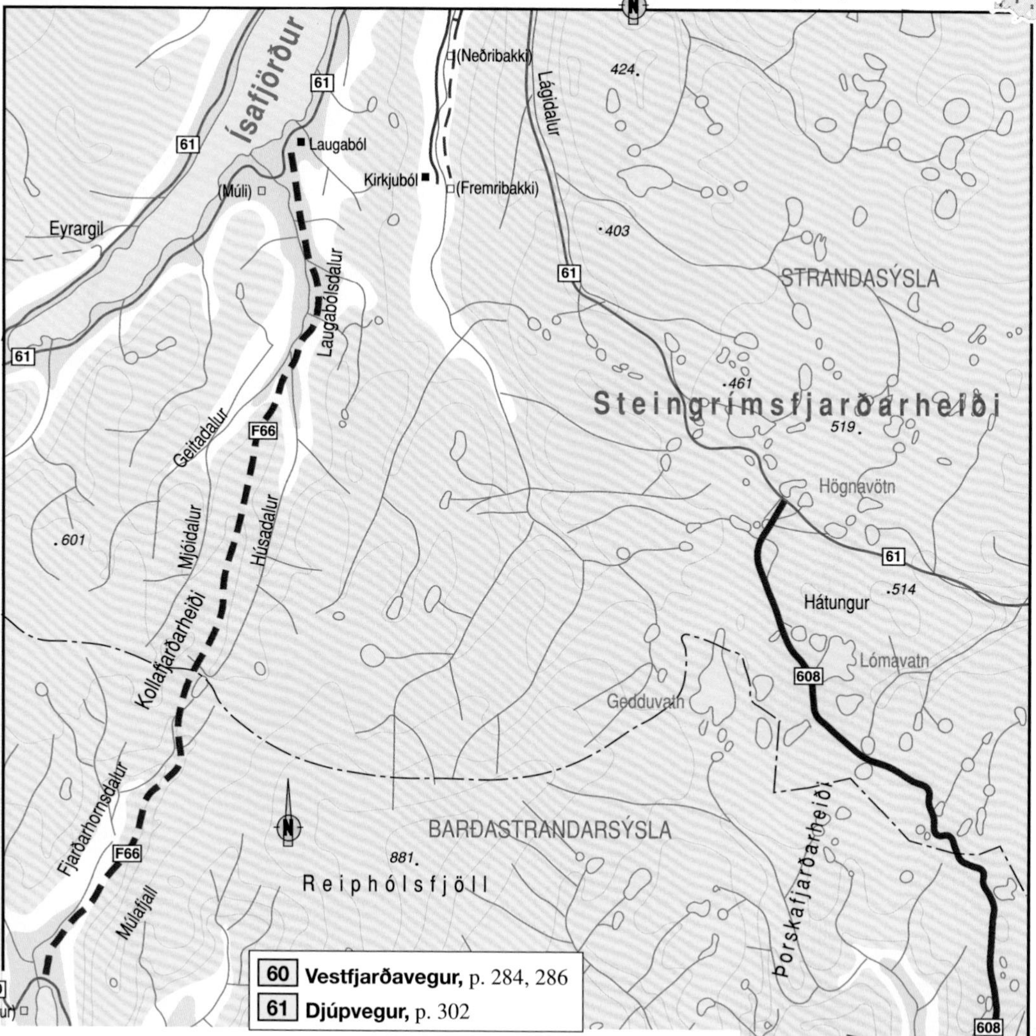

60 **Vestfjarðavegur,** p. 284, 286
61 **Djúpvegur,** p. 302

F66 **Kollafjarðarheiði,** 23 km, a jeep-route.

Fjarðarhorn, the innermost farm in Kollafjörður, now abandoned, from which the jeep-track goes up onto Kollafjarðarheiði moor and down into Laugarbólsdalur.

Kollafjörður, a fjord, 16 km long, with many fords and flats that can be crossed at low tide. At its head lies the route up onto Kollafjarðarheiði moor which was one of the much-travelled routes between Breiðafjörður and the Ísafjarðardjúp fjords. The other two main routes were over Skálmardalsheiði moor and Þorskafjarðarheiði moor. All these moors reach a height of 400-500 m, but the Skálmardalsheiði route offers the shortest distance across the wilderness between farms. It lies up from the head of Skálmarfjörður and comes down via the Gjörvidalur valley at the head of Ísafjörður. The longest route was Þorskafjarðarheiði, going up the valley Kollabúðardalur in Þorskafjörður and coming down Langidalur in Ísafjarðardjúp. The people of Breiðafjörður would travel over these moors to get to Bolungarvík, for winter fishing or to go to Ísafjörður for trade. These routes were in use around 1900 for herding sheep to Ísafjörður. For this they also used a short cut over Hestfjarðarheiði moor and down into Álftafjörður.

Þorskafjarðarheiði, (490 m) moor and the mountain road crossing it. The shortest route between Reykjavík and Ísafjarðardjúp, stony and barren.

Kollabúðir, an abandoned farm at the head of Þorskafjörður; site of the ancient assembly of the Western fjords district, the Þorskafjarðarþing. In late 19th century the scene of the so-called Kollabúðafundir, meetings held in order to further the cause of the political and cultural independence of Iceland. Ruins of the old booths are visible at Kollabúðareyri on the Músará river. Towards the end of the 16th century Kollabúðir was a German trading place.

17
P. 580

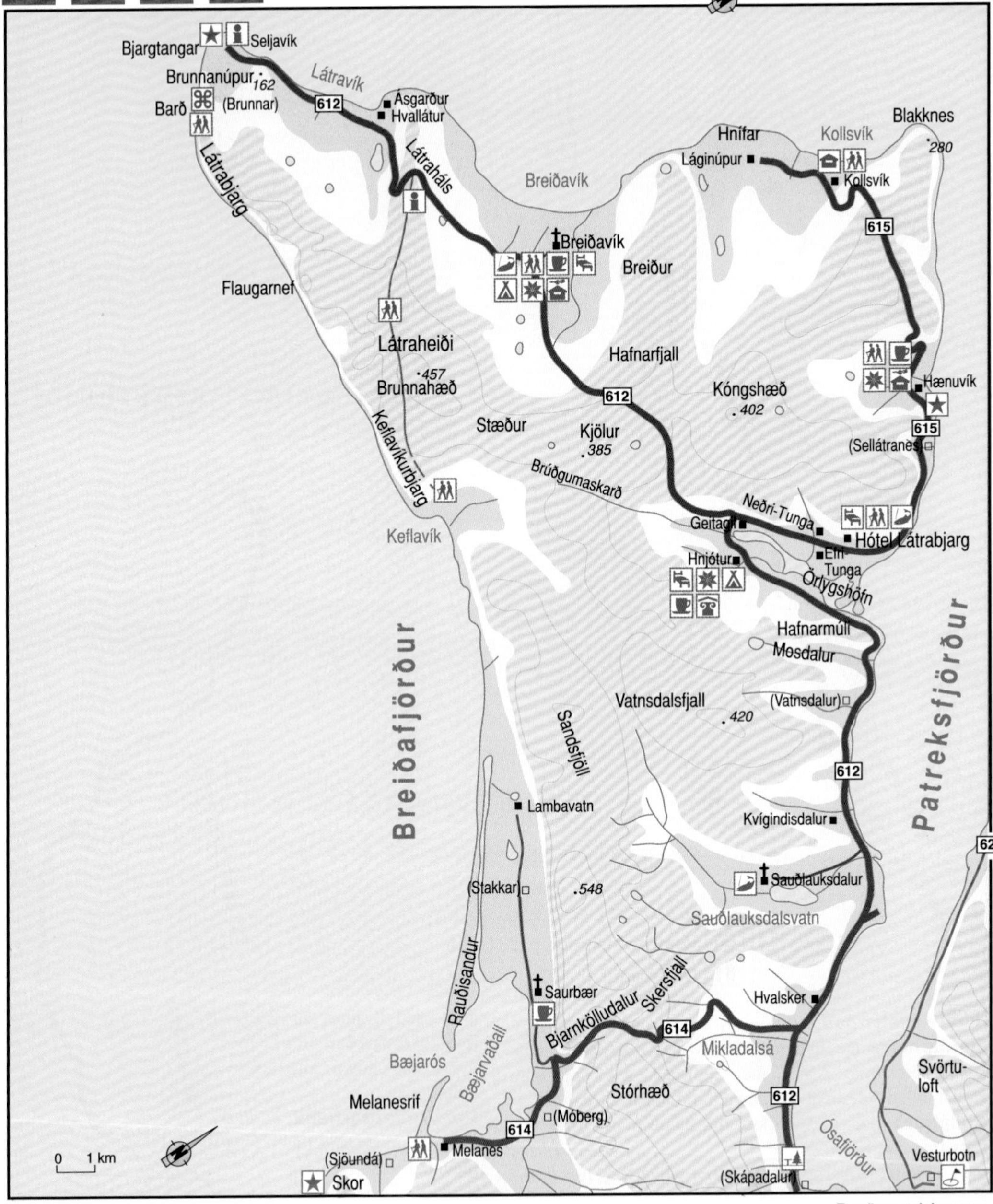

Bjargtangar
Seljavík
Brunnanúpur .162
Barð
(Brunnar)
Látravík
612
Ásgarður
Hvallátur
Látrabjarg
Látraháls
Breiðavík
Hnífar
Láginúpur
Kollsvík
Blakknes
.280
Kollsvík
615
Breiðavík
Breiður
Flaugarnef
Látraheiði
.457
Brunnahæð
Hafnarfjall
Kóngshæð
.402
Hænuvík
612
Stæður
Kjölur
.385
615
(Sellátranes)
Brúðgumaskarð
Keflavíkurbjarg
Neðri-Tunga
Geitagil
Hótel Látrabjarg
Hnjótur
Efri-Tunga
Örlygshöfn
Keflavík
Hafnarmúli
Mosdalur
Breiðafjörður
Patreksfjörður
Vatnsdalsfjall
(Vatnsdalur)
.420
Sandsfjöll
612
Lambavatn
Kvígindisdalur
62
Sauðlauksdalur
(Stakkar)
.548
Sauðlauksdalsvatn
Rauðisandur
Saurbær
Skersfjall
Hvalsker
Bjarnkölludalur
614
Mikladalsá
Bæjarós
Bæjarvaðall
Stórhæð
Svörtuloft
612
Melanesrif
(Móberg)
614
Ósafjörður
0 1 km
(Sjöundá)
Melanes
Vesturbotn
Skor
(Skápadalur)

Rauðasandshreppur

© Gustaf Gústafsson
Rauðisandur

614 Rauðasandsvegur, 9,7 km.

Básar in Seljavík bay**,** between Brunnanúpur and Bjargartangi. There are visible ruins of the walls of the house, the remains of a fence and what was probably a well shelter. It is said that the place used to be a farm, abandoned in the 15th century. If this is true, it was the westernmost place of human habitation in Iceland and consequently the whole of Europe.

Keflavík, an abandoned farm and former fishing station. There are some important remains of a fishing station from long ago. Refuge hut.

Saurbær, often called Bær á Rauðasandi, a church and former home of local leaders, most noted of whom was Eggert Hannesson (1515-83), local governor. English pirates pillaged Bær in his day.

Rauðisandur, ("Red sands") a settled district in an arc between the Skorarhlíðar slopes and the Látrabjarg cliffs, taking its name from the colour of the sand on the coast. A narrow area of flat land, cut across by the Bæjarvaðall lagoon, above which are steep rocky slopes. This is the westernmost township in Iceland and indeed in Europe.

Melanes, the easternmost farm in the Rauðisandur district. Some old soil layers perhaps indicating former grain-growing. Just east of there is the abandoned farm **Sjöundá**, scene of a crime early in the 19th century, on which writer Gunnar Gunnarsson's novel *Svartfugl* is based. Bjarni Bjarnason and Steinunn Sveinsdóttir were found guilty of murdering their spouses, and condemned to death.

Skor, west of the mountain Stálfjall along the Skorarhlíðar slopes lay a rough and dangerous route between the Barðaströnd coast and the Rauðisandur district. Lighthouse built 1953 at Skor. Previously a fishing-station, being one of the few landings in the area. Skor is best known in Icelandic history for being the place from which the magistrate and poet Eggert Ólafsson set out on his fatal voyage in the spring of 1768. His wife and all the boat crew perished with him. Eggert is said to have had with him on board the halberd of Gunnar from Hlíðarendi of *Njáls saga*. Memorial plaque to Eggert at Skor (see Road 62, Svefneyjar).

Skersfjall, a mountain where the road reaches a height of 350 m.

615 Kollsvíkurvegur, 20 km.

Kollsvík, two farms. In the 19th century a whirlwind tore down the buildings, killing the occupants.

Tunga, there was once a community centre and an elementary school. Now a hotel.

612 Örlygshafnarvegur, 46,44 km.

62 Barðastrandarvegur, p. 304

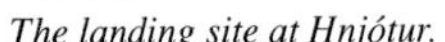

The landing site at Hnjótur.

Memorial at Hnjótur.

Kryppa beneeth Hafnarmúli.

Látrabjarg, a 14 km long cliff, one of the biggest bird-cliffs in Iceland, where eggs have been gathered by absailing. Shipwrecks have occurred there. The highest point (441 m) is at Heiðnakast east of the canyon Saxagjá. It is climbable. In June 2010 a German tourist who was taken pictures from the edge of the cliff fell to his death.

Bjargtangar, the westernmost point of Iceland and also of Europe. The nearest land due south is the Antarctic.

Hvallátur, the westernmost home of Iceland (and thus Europe), just north of Bjargtangar. Formerly a farm and big fishing-station, relics of which are still visible. It was from there that the rescue of the crew of the British trawler *Dhoon* off Látrabjarg in 1947 was organized – one of the boldest rescues off Iceland.

Breiðavík, a church and the westernmost guesthouse in Europe. Good walking routes.

Hnjótur, a farm and a remarkable museum of local objects. This memorial was erected in 1998 in remembrance of rescuers which have saved Icelandic and foreign seamen as well as the memory of those who could not be saved. All this has been the work of dedicated local man, Egill Ólafsson (1925-1999).

Örlygshöfn, a grassy valley by a sea lagoon.

Hafnarmúli, a landing place between Mosdalur and Örlygshöfn. Some ruins are still visable, thought be from the original settlement.

Kryppa, below Hafnarmúli, east of the old landing places. It is said that the people there lived in crofts in this place in former times.

Kvígindisdalur, a weather station.

Sauðlauksdalur, a church and former parsonage in a small valley. Sea and sand erosion. Trout lake. The Rev. Björn Halldórsson (1724-94) was noted for his horticultural activities. He was the first to grow potatoes in Iceland and the first to begin anti-erosion work, building the Ranglátur wall, still visible.

Frá Básum

The landing site at Básar

619 KETILDALAVEGUR

Ketildalir, the district on the southern shore of Arnarfjörður. Some small valleys, partly grassy, trout streams, seafishing, farms. The valleys: Hvestudalur, Hringsdalur, Bakkadalur, Austmannsdalur, Fífustaðadalur and Selárdalur are separated by steep ridges.

Þórishlíðarfjall, there some fossil and lignite have been found.

Samúel Jónsson's house and private church in Selárdalur.

Selárdalur, a church and former parsonage, often mentioned in history. Birthplace of the poet Jón Þorláksson (1744-1899). The most famous pastor there was Páll Björnsson (1621-1706), known as a great scholar but as well; of witchcraft persecution. He was the nephew of Arngrímur the learned and was one of the best educated Icelanders of the 17th century leaving behind many manuscripts. In the winter of 1699 the people of Selárdalur were allegedly targeted by witchcraft. The wife of the Rev. Páll was the principal sufferer and as a result, two men were burned at the stake. Páll was a good speaker and an unusually good linguist e.g. writing verses in Greek. According to a legend, from Páll's time a black sailed schooner was seen off the coast of Selárdalur. People feared that pirates were on board. The pastor went out to the vessel and spoke to the crew in some eastern language and warned them that the district was full of witches. The result was that they exchanged gifts with him and went away. He was an excellent mathematician and studied Oriental mysticism. He was the first Icelander to have built a full decked fishing boat.

Brautarholt, an outlying farm from the Selárdalur parsonage, home of artist Samúel Jónsson (1884-1969). When an altar-piece he wanted to give to Selárdalur church on its centenary was rejected, he built his own church for it. Some of Samúel's statues stand nearby. The altar-piece is now preserved in Listasafn Alþýðu (The Labour Unions' Art Gallery) in Reykjavík.

Bakki, formerly an official trading place, later moved to Bíldudalur. The author Guðmundur Kamban (1888-1945) was brought up there. He was one of the first Icelanders to make motion pictures.

63 Bíldudalsvegur, p. 305

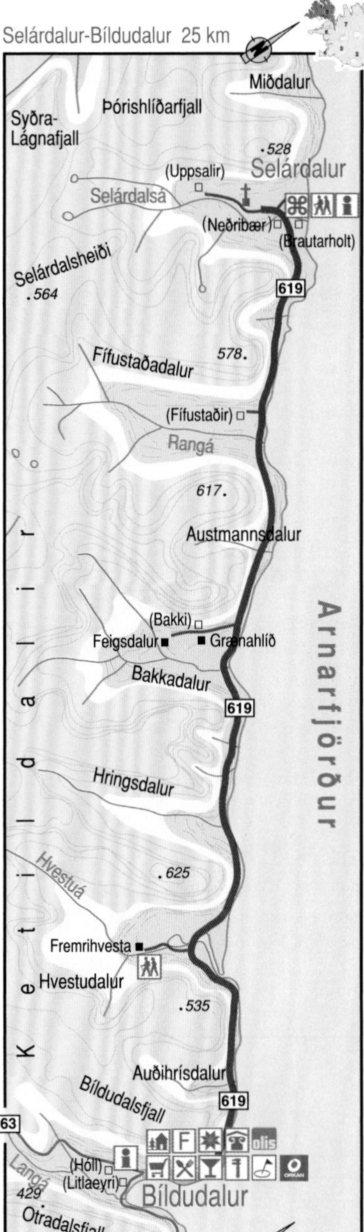

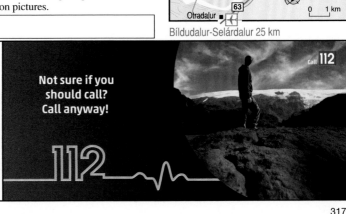

Tyrðilmýri-Hvannadalsá 44 km

18 P. 581

Æðey, the biggest island in Ísafjarðardjúp, 1.26 km², just off the Snæfjallaströnd coast. One of the main breeding grounds of the eider duck in Iceland, fertile, good landing place, pretty scenery. In 1615 some shipwrecked Spanish sailors settled there. After they had been rather aggressive, Ari Magnússon of Ögur attacked them with a force of men, killing them all dishonourably, some on Æðey, others at Sandeyri on Snæfjallaströnd.

Tyrðilmýri, an abandoned farm. The river Mýrará harnessed to generate electricity.

Unaðsdalur, an abandoned farm and church. Guest accommodation and restaurant facilities are open during the summer in the Dalbær community centre.

Bæir, two abandoned farms; Hærribær and Neðribær ("Upper farm and Lower farm"). Made famous by notorious ghosts, whose activities were recorded by the author Þórbergur Þórðarson (1889-1974). Now a TV relay station.

Snæfjallaströnd, ("Snowy mountains coast") the district between the fjord Kaldalón and the mountain Vébjarnarnúpur.

Kaldalón, a fjord ca. 5 km long, largely full of silt. Off it is a broadish valley of the same name. At the head of the valley there are some grassy islets, then moraine brought by a glacier tongue that descends there.

© Gústaf Gústafsson

638 Laugalandsvegur, 3,44 km.

Ármúli, an abandoned farm on the Langadalsströnd coast below a 375 m high mountain of the same name. Formerly a doctor's residence, the last to practice there having been Sigvaldi Kaldalóns, composer (1881-1946), who took his surname from the fjord.

Skjaldfönn, a farm in the **Skjaldfannardalur** valley. From the valley is a beautiful walking route to Hornstrandir.

Laugaland, a farm in the Skjaldfannardalur valley. Birthplace of the poet Steinn Steinarr (1908-58).

Selá, one of the biggest rivers in the Western fjords, coming from the Drangajökull glacier.

Nauteyri, a parsonage.

61 Djúpvegur, p. 298 **634 Reykjanesvegur,** p. 299

Hvannadalsá-Tyrðilmýri 44 km

Klúka, a farm where there is a warm spring, Gvendarlaug, named for Bishop Guðmundur góði ("the good") (1160-1237) and a bathing place for centuries. A hotel and swimming pool. There is also the second part of the Museum of Icelandic Sorcery and Witchcraft, the main exhibition is at Hólmavík, well worth the visit.

Bakki, there is a green house. Also the house Pöntun from Seyðisfjörður, which is Norwegian originally.

645 Drangsnesvegur, 34 km.

Kaldrananes, a farm and church, rich in driftwood, eider duck colonies and seals.

Grímsey, the biggest island in the Strandir district, rather high, used for hay and grazing. Once used for a fox farm. Lighthouse.

Drangsnes, (pop. 76) a village and trading place. Fishing and fish processing. Just beyond the town there is a rock called **Kerling** (Old woman), with distinct human facial features. According to local tales, this is a troll woman who was turned into stone by the sun near the Malarhorn mountain ridge. A signboard at the site, telling the troll woman´s story in Icelandic and two other languages.

© Gústaf Gústafsson

Drangsnes.

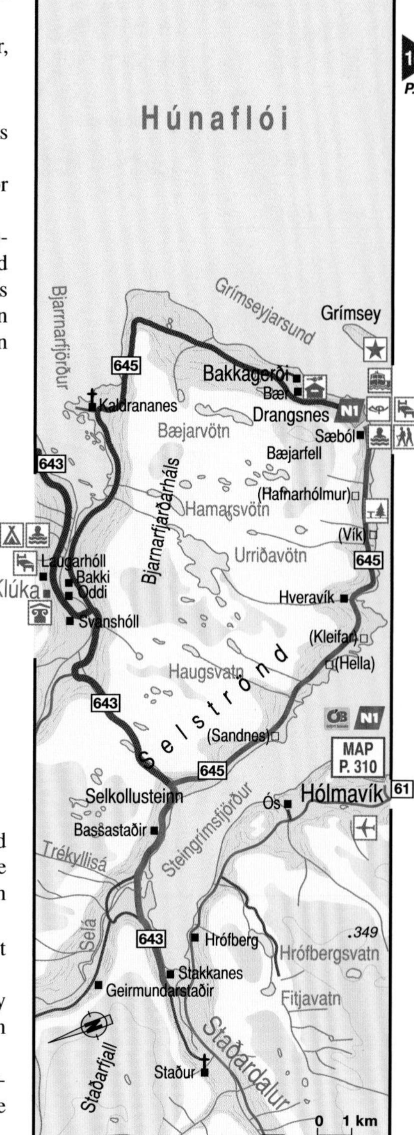

16 P. 579

Bjarnarfjarðarháls, the ridge between Steingrímsfjörður and Bjarnarfjörður, across which the road goes. Many lakes and tarns, the biggest being Urriðavatn, where there is trout-fishing. Geothermal heat in Bjarnarfjörður, used for domestic heating.

Selkollusteinn, a stone by **Bassastaðir**, known from the story about Guðmundur góði ("the good").

Selströnd, ("Seal coast") the northern coast of Steingrímsfjörður. Many isles and skerries, eider duck and seal colonies. Geothermal heat in Hveravík, where there used to be a swimming pool.

Staður, a former parsonage in the valley Staðardalur. Its best known clergyman was Jón Árnason (1665-1743), later bishop of Skálholt. In the church there is a 240 year old pulpit.

Staðardalur, a low, wide, grassy valley at the head of Steingrímsfjörður.

61 Djúpvegur, p. 300

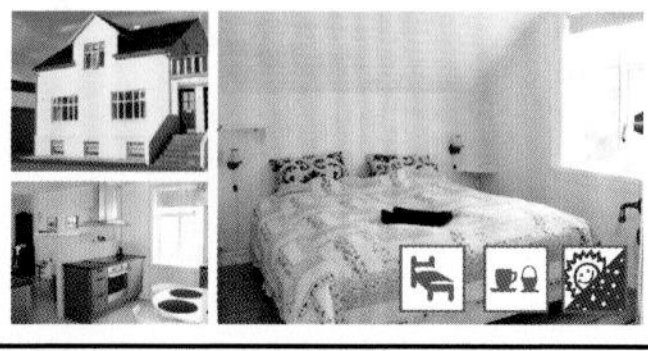

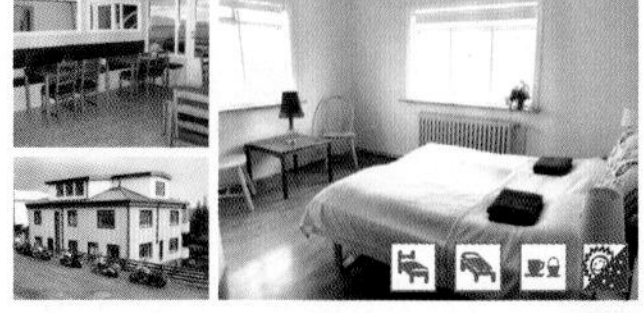

16
P. 579

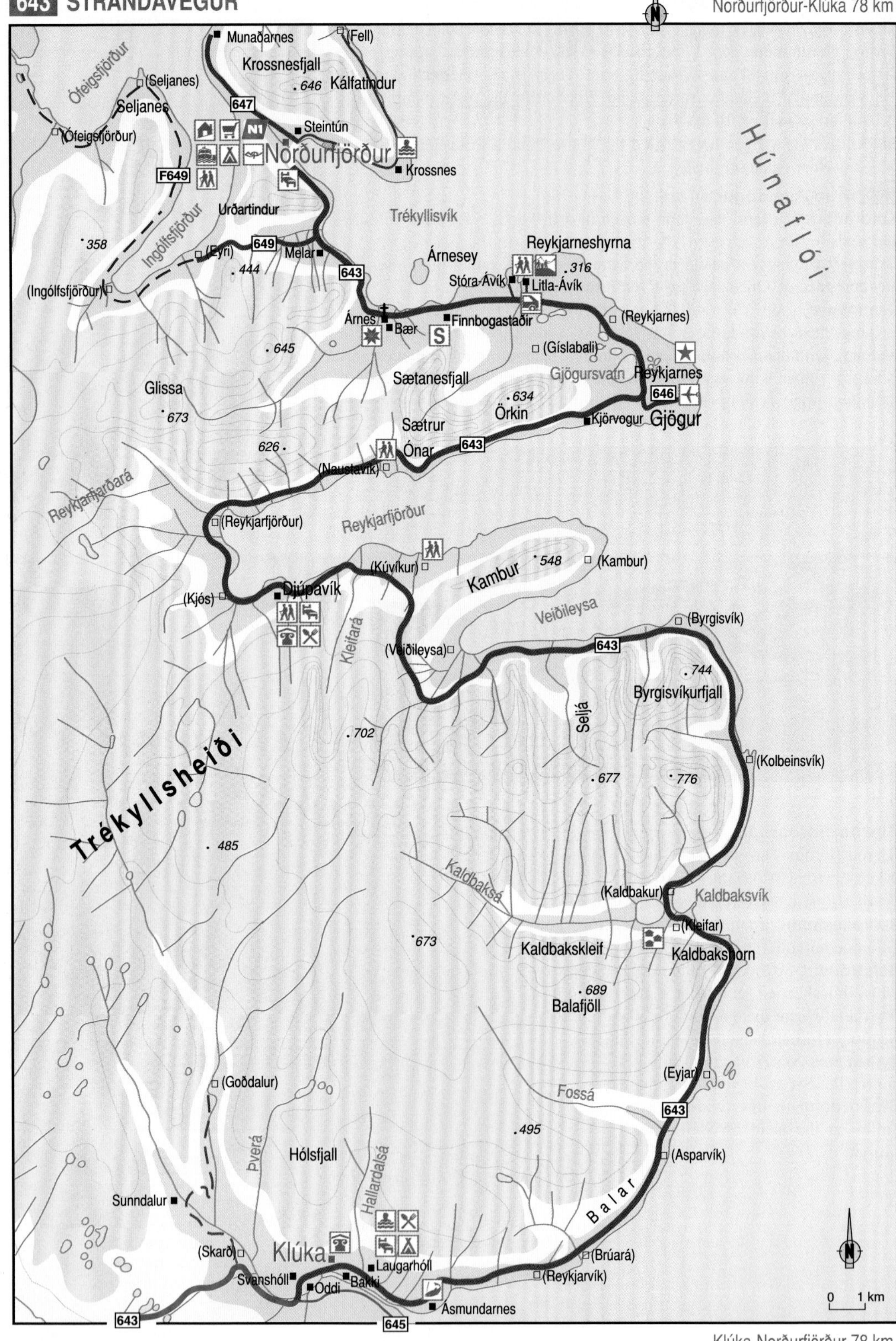

645 **Drangsnesvegur,** p. 319

Ófeigsfjörður, an abandoned farm on a fjord of the same name. Some of the richest land in Strandasýsla because of eider, seals and driftwood. The last shark-fishing from there was in 1915 on the boat *Ófeigur*, which is now preserved in the folk museum at Reykir in Hrútafjörður. Birthplace of the poet, scholar and painter Jón Guðmundsson (1574-1658) who was twice outlawed for sorcery.

Ingólfsfjörður, a long, narrow fjord. In 1942 a herring factory was built at Eyri on the east of the fjord and run for 10 years. The factory building and other installations can still be seen.

647 **Munaðarnesvegur** the distance to Munaðarnes is 4,5 km. Offers a magnificent view of the bays of Ófeigsfjörður, Eyvindarfjörður and the cove of Drangavík and beyond that the magnificent mountain passes of Drangaskörð.

649 **Ófeigsfjarðarvegur** 4 km.

F649 **Ófeigsfjarðarvegur** 15,79 km km from Eyri to Hvalá.

Norðurfjörður, a trading-place on a fjord of the same name, going north from Trékyllisvík bay. **Kálfatindur** (646 m) a mountain at the head of the fjord provides a good viewpoint. A lodge owned by the Icelandic Touring Association, Valgeirsstaðir is located in the bottom of Nordfjordur, just above a sandy beach. A convenience store is in 10 minutes walking distance from the house and a swimming pool is located in **Krossnes**, also close by.

Árnes, a church and former parsonage, vicarage, community center, museum, and a craft house. Down by the shore are some distinctive rocky crags, called **Árnesstapar**.

Finnbogastaðir, a children's boarding school.

Trékyllisvík, a broad bay with a good deal of flat land. One of best farming areas of the northern Strandir district. A biggish island, **Árnesey**, formerly called Trékyllisey, a good breeding-ground for birds. It was off there that Þórður kakali gathered the crew for his journey that led to the Flóabardagi battle in midsummer 1244. Much driftwood. A former shark-fishing centre.

Stóra-Ávík and **Litla-Ávík,** a farm where there is a large stone carried by drift-ice from Greenland. At Stóra-Ávík is Kistuvogur where people were burned for witchcraft. A weather station at Litla-Ávík.

Reykjarnes, the peninsula between Reykjarfjörður and Trékyllisvík bay, low and marshy with many lakes. The striking mountain Reykjarneshyrna (316 m) to the north. A view dial at the foot of the mountain.

646 **Flugvallarvegur,** 1,75 km.

Gjögur, a hamlet with some fishing. Formerly the biggest shark-fishing centre of the district, involving 15-18 open boats with 7-11 men on each. Lighthouse.

Kjörvogur, once a weather station, now it is at Litlu-Ávík.

Sætrafjall, (634 m) a rocky and imposing mountain. Small creeks and skerries below, called **Ónar**, where the Spaniards killed by Ari of Ögur in 1615 had been shipwrecked (see Road 635, Æðey).

Trékyllisheiði, an old moorland riding trail between Steingrímsfjörður and Reykjarfjörður, 300-400 m high.

Kjós, a farm which Símon J. Ágústsson professor (1904–76) came from.

Djúpavík, a village with few inhabitants. Formerly a herring-salting station, and a herring factory was built there in 1934-35, later closed when herring disappeared from the waters north of Iceland. Historical Exhibition in the herring factory.

Kúvíkur, for about 250 years the only trading place in Strandasýsla county. Now abandoned. Home of the poet Jakob Thorarensen (1886-1972), whose grandfather Jakob Thorarensen (1830-1911) ran a store for nearly sixty years.

Reykjarfjörður, a biggish fjord 13-14 km long and 3 km wide at the mouth. Very little flat land.

Veiðileysufjörður, ("Fjord with no fishing") a small fjord enclosed by high, steep mountains.

Byrgisvíkurfjall, (744 m) an imposing rock mountain at Veiðileysufjörður. One of the highest in this area.

Kaldbaksvík, a small bay with two abandoned farms, one being Kaldbakur, the home of the settler Önundur tréfótur ("wooden-leg"), who is said to be buried in the Önundarhaugur mound in the valley Kaldbaksdalur. Summer houses, fishing lake, and geothermal heat at Hveratungur.

Kaldbakshorn, (508 m) a sheer, high mountain ridge. Below it is **Kaldbakskleif** which can be dangerous because of falling rocks, though there have been no known accidents there, perhaps because it was consecrated by bishop Guðmundur góði ("the good") (1160-1237).

Balar, the coast from Bjarnarfjörður to Kaldbaksvík bay. Very little flat land, high and rocky mountains, little grass. The beginning of the northern Strandir district, where mountains are higher, scenery more wild and barren than in the southern Strandir.

Goðdalur, an abandoned farm in a valley of the same name. Destroyed by an avalanche in 1948 in which only the farmer survived.

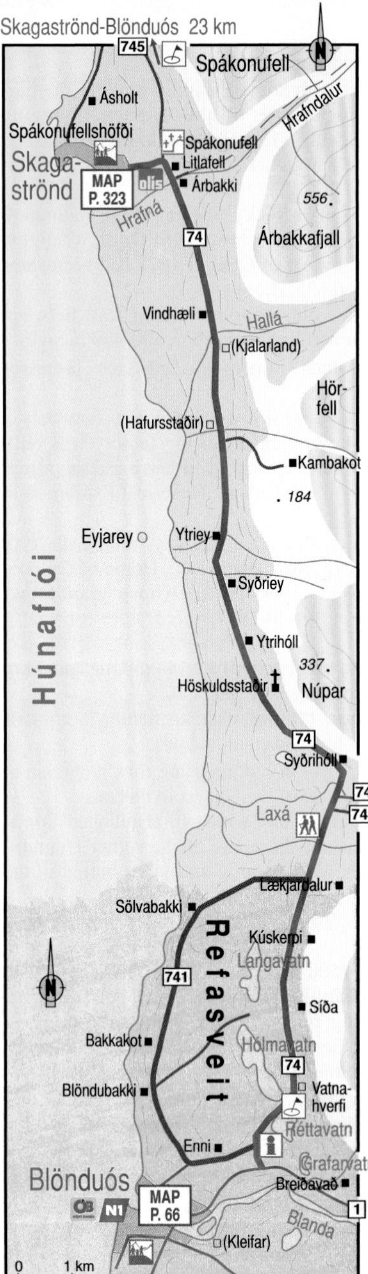

Blönduós-Skagaströnd 23 km

Skagaströnd, (pop. 473) once a trading post run by the Danes with a history dating back into the 16th century and, until the 19th century. It served a huge region stretching west and east. A village started to grow there in the late 19th century, focusing on the fishing industry. Catches by the freezer trawler Arnar are among the highest in Iceland, but numerous smaller boats are also based here and there is a lively fish market. On the other hand, the past few years have seen considerable changes in the business sector. At the biotechnology science hotel BioPol, researchers study marine life in Húnaflói bay, seeking innovative options for utilising ocean resources. A log house restaurant, former Country bar, has got the name Borgin and serves among other dishes of fresh fish from the bay. In a beautiful building down by the sea, Café Bjarmanes opens during the summer months and is popular among travellers. Each year, over a hundred artists spend a residency at Nes, staying there for a month at a time and exercising their creativity in what used to be a fish freezing plant. The Icelandic Directorate of Labour operates a payment office in Skagaströnd for national unemployment benefits. The picturesque campground offers plenty of room for camping vehicles, caravans and tent trailers. The swimming pool is small but enjoyable, and has developed a tradition of offering coffee to people in the hot tub. Built in 1899 and recently restored, Árnes is the village's oldest building and houses a museum depicting domestic conditions and customs early in the 20th century. The headland Spákonufellshöfði is a popular place for walking, with marked trails and information signs about the birds and plants, while on clear spring and summer evenings the midnight sun can be seen setting over the sea to the north. Towering majestically above the village, Spákonufell mountain also offers a number of marked trails. Brochures on the trails at both Spákonufellshöfði and Spákonufell can be obtained at many places in the village. The Museum of Prophecies holds a historical exhibition about a local fortune-teller, cf. Spákonufell. About four kilometres from Skagaströnd, the local golf club's nine-hole course is considered scenic and challenging. The main employment is provided by the fisheries, light industry, trade and services, and there is a compulsory school, church, restaurant, coffee house, community centre, health clinic, sports hall and swimming pool.

Spákonufell, ("Fortune-teller's fell") a former church, once the home of Þórdís spákona ("fortune-teller") mentioned in *Kormáks saga*. Spákonufellsborg (646 m) is the most imposing mountain in this area.

Árbakki, a farm at the mouth of the Hrafndalur valley, birthplace of archeologist and politician Dr. Valtýr Guðmundsson (1860-1928), who taught at the University of Copenhagen.

Ytriey, a farm where there is a monument to the county girls' school that was there from 1883-1900.

Vindhæli, an old manor farm.

Höskuldsstaðir, a church and parsonage. Home of famous pastors, e.g. Magnús Pétursson (1710-84), writer of annals, and Eggert Ó. Briem (1840-93), a great scholar. Birthplace of the brothers Sigurður Stefánsson (1744-98), the last bishop at Hólar, and governor Ólafur Stefánsson (1731-1812) (see Viðey, Rvík). A rune-stone from the early 14th century was found in the churchyard.

Syðri-Hóll, a farm, home of the well-known scholar and writer Magnús Björnsson (1889-1963), to whom there is a memorial by the roadside.

741 Neðribyggðarvegur, 8,4 km.

Refasveit, flat country between the rivers Blanda and Laxá. Two rows of farms, Efribyggð and Neðribyggð ("Upper district and Lower district"), with roads alongside each. Four small lakes in a row: Grafavatn, Réttavatn, Hólmavatn and Langavatn, counting from the south.

1 Norðurlandsvegur, p. 68
731 Svínvetningabraut, p. 345
742 Mýravegur, p. 348
744 Þverárfjallsvegur, p. 348
745 Skagavegur, p. 349

75 SAUÐÁRKRÓKSBRAUT

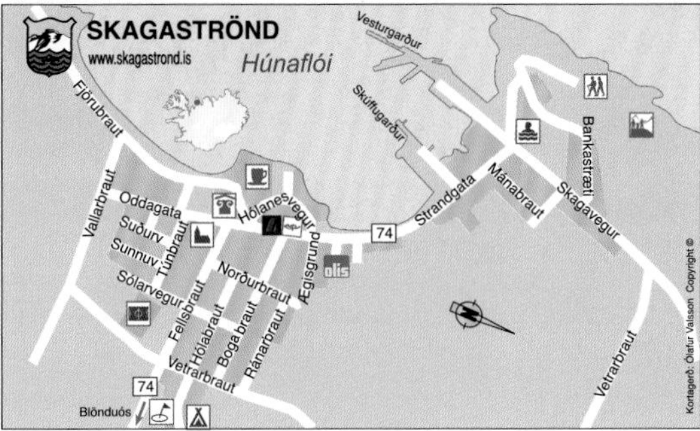

Sauðárkróksbraut
Sauðárkrókur-Varmahlíð 25 km

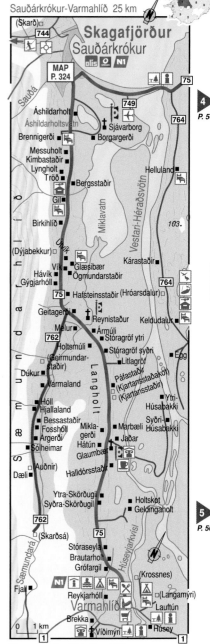

Skagafjörður
Sauðárkrókur
MAP P. 324
75
744
749
764
762
1
(Skarð)
Sauðá
Áshildarholt
Áshildarholtsvatn
Sjávarborg
Borgargerði
Brennigerði
Messuholt
Kimbastaðir
Lyngholt
Tröð
Bergsstaðir
Helluland
Gil
Birkihlíð
Miklavatn
Vestari-Héraðsvötn
(Dýjabekkur)
Úlvík
Vík
Glæsibær
Hávík
Ögmundarstaðir
Kárastaðir
Gýgjarhóll
Hafsteinsstaðir
(Hróarsdalur)
Geitagerði
Reynistaður
Keldudalur
Melur
Ármúli
Stóragröf ytri
Holtsmúli
Stóragröf syðri
(Geirmundar-staðir)
Litlagröf
Egg
Dúkur
Langholt
Páfastaðir
(Kjartansstaðakot)
(Kjartansstaðir)
Varmaland
Ytri-Húsabakki
Sæmundarhlíð
Hóll
Hjallaland
Bessastaðir
Fosshóll
Árgerði
Miklagerði
Marbæli
Syðri-Húsabakki
Jaðar
Sólheimar
Hátún
Glaumbær
(Auðnir)
Dæli
Halldórsstaðir
Ytra-Skörðugil
Syðra-Skörðugil
Holtskot
Geldingaholt
(Skarðsá)
Sæmundará
Stóraseyla
Brautarholt
Grófargil
Húseyjarkvísl
(Krossnes)
Fjall
Reykjarhóll
(Langamýri)
Varmahlíð
Lauftún
Brekka
Víðimýri
Húsey
0 1 km
Varmahlíð-Sauðárkrókur 25 km

4 P. 567

5 P. 568

Sauðárkrókur, (pop. 2,564) a town in Skagafjörður. See p. 326.
Sjávarborg, a tarred wooden church of the older towerless-type was built in 1853. From 1892 its use was secular and in 1975 the building was moved to the northern part of the cliff and turned at the same time. The door now faces south! In the keeping of the National Museum since 1972.
Áshildarholtsvatn, a lake, site of geothermal heat, from where hot water is piped to Sauðárkrókur for domestic heating.
Miklavatn, ("Great lake") 6.18 km^2, a sanctuary with a great variety of bird life.

762 Sæmundarhlíðarvegur, 8 km.

Sæmundarhlíð, the slopes from Vatnsskarð to Reynistaður. Named after the settler Sæmundur suðureyski. Along the slope is a river called Sæmundará but changes its name by Reynistaður, there is called Reynisstaðará and then it changes again and then its is called Staðará.
Reynistaður, a church and manor farm through the ages. Home of Þorfinnur karlsefni and of his descendants to 1259, also of Earl Gissur Þorvaldsson for a while. Convent from 1295 to 1552. The farmhouse porch (**bæjardyrahús**) at Reynistaður, one of the few stave structures dating from the 18th century in Iceland, has been restored. In the keeping of the National Museum since 1999.
Holtsmúli, a famous Icelandic stallion, called Hrafn, 802, was born there in the year 1968.
Glaumbær, a farm, church and parsonage. Home of many men and women of influence. One of Iceland´s few remaining turf farms is there, mainly from the 19th century with some older parts, protected and now the site of the Skagafjörður heritage museum. In the keeping of the National Museum since 1947. Not to be missed. There is a monument by the sculptor Ásmundur Sveinsson in memory of Guðríður Þorbjarnardóttir and her son Snorri Þorfinnsson, the first European born west of the Atlantic. Later in life, Guðríður travelled to Rome, after which she became a nun and hermit in Glaumbær. Guðríður may rightly be considered the greatest Icelandic woman traveller before this century (see Road 574, **Hellnar**). Home of many men of influence. One of Iceland's few remaining turf farms is there, mainly from the 19th century with some older parts, protected and now the site of the Skagafjörður heritage museum. In the keeping of the National Museum since 1947. Not to be missed. **Geldingaholt,** the scene in 1255 of the Battle of Geldingaholt, where Oddur Þórarinsson, one of the bravest men in Iceland in his day, was slain.

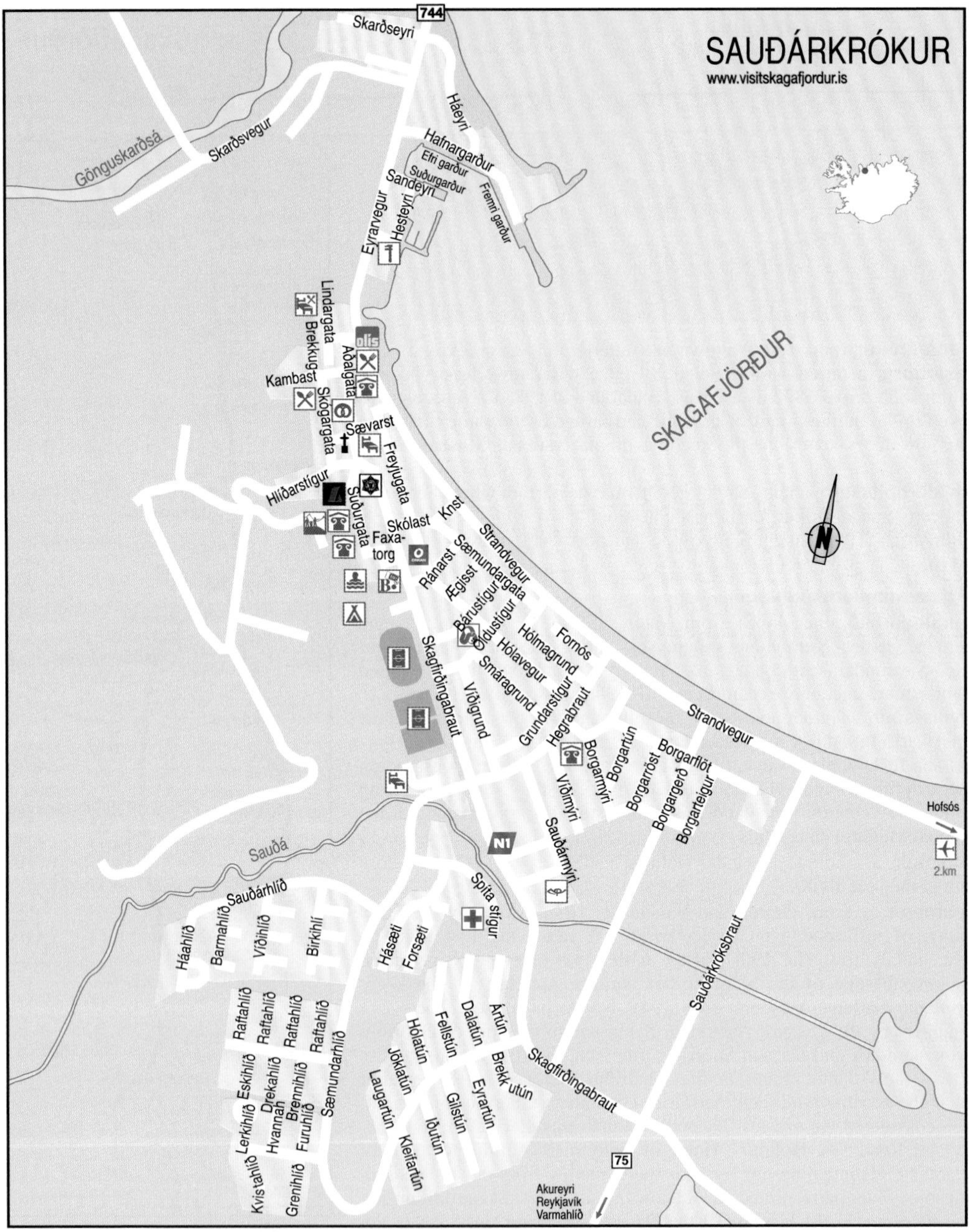

SAUÐÁRKRÓKUR

www.visitskagafjordur.is

SKAGAFJÖRÐUR

744
Skarðseyri
Gönguskarðsá
Skarðsvegur
Háeyri
Hafnargarður
Efri garður
Suðurgarður
Fremri garður
Sandeyri
Hesteyri
Eyrarvegur
Lindargata
Brekkug.
Kambast
Aðalgata
Skógargata
Sævarst
Freyjugata
Hlíðarstígur
Suðurgata
Skólast
Knst
Faxa-torg
Strandvegur
Sæmundargata
Ránarst
Ægisst
Bárustígur
Öldustígur
Hólmagrund
Fornós
Hólavegur
Smáragrund
Skagfirðingabraut
Víðigrund
Grundarstígur
Hegrabraut
Borgartún
Borgarflöt
Borgarröst
Borgargerði
Borgarteigur
Borgarmýri
Víðimýri
Sauðármýri
Hofsós
2.km
Sauðá
Sauðárhlíð
Spítalastígur
Háahlíð
Barmahlíð
Víðihlíð
Birkihlíð
Hásæti
Forsæti
Raftahlíð
Sæmundarhlíð
Eskihlíð
Drekahlíð
Hvannahlíð
Brennihlíð
Lerkihlíð
Furuhlíð
Kvistahlíð
Grenihlíð
Ártún
Dalatún
Fellstún
Hólatún
Jöklatún
Laugatún
Brekkutún
Eyrartún
Gilstún
Iðutún
Kleifartún
Sauðárkróksbraut
75
Akureyri
Reykjavík
Varmahlíð

Aðalgata 15
550 Sauðárkrókur
☎ 453 6454
videosport@simnet.is
www.olafshus.is

Aðalgata 16
550 Sauðárkrókur
☎ 453 6299
videosport@simnet.is
www.kaffikrokur.is

Kaupfélag Skagfirðinga

THE SKAGAFJÖRÐUR CO-OP
Ártorg 1 · 550 Sauðárkrókur · Tel. 455-4500 · Fax 455-4501

Skagfirðingabúð:

The department store in Sauðárkrókur.
One of the biggest of its kind outside Reykjavík.

We look forward to seeing you in Skagfirðingabúð.

Auto Repair

☎ 455 4570
Freyjugata 9
550 Sauðárkrókur

Our campsite and swimming pool are situated in the heart of the town, only a stone´s trow from other services. The Sauðárkrókur Golf Club´s 9-hole golf course, just above the town, is open every day. Visitors are welcome.

Tel. 453 5226

The pool is open:	**Summer opening (June 1st -August 31st)**
Monday - Friday	07:00 - 22:00
Saturday and Sunday	09:00 - 18:00

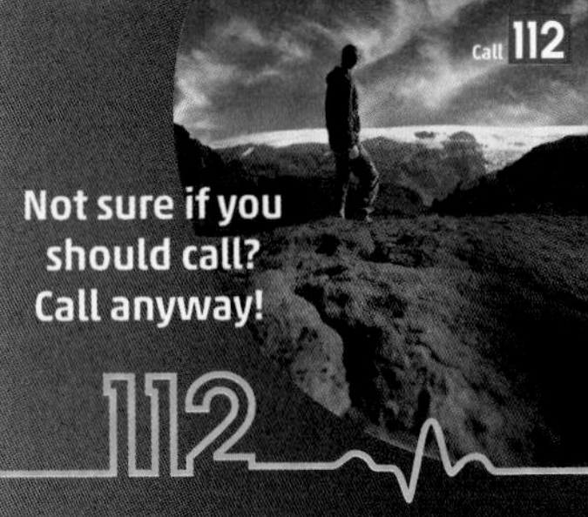

Súrmjólk

Soured Milk
Refreshing, light, digestable
For Breakfast, dessert, or just anytime...

Narfastaðir-Sauðárkrókur 15 km

5 P. 568

4 P. 567

Sauðárkrókur-Narfastaðir 15 km

76 **Siglufjarðarvegur,** p. 327

744 **Þverárfjallsvegur,** p. 348

748 **Reykjastrandarvegur,** p. 352

Hegranes, a strip of land between the estuary branches of the river Héraðsvötn, ca. 15 km long and 5 km wide, with basalt ridges and steep crags but also grassy marshes, lakes and tarns. Sea cliffs at the northern end. An area rich in history and where many excavations are underway.

764 Hegranesvegur, 20,6 km.

749 Flugvallarvegur, 0,49 km.

Garður, a farm on Hegranes. The ancient Hegranesþing assembly was held there and bothy ruins may still be seen.

Geitaberg, (138 m) a beautiful view from Lautinantsvörðu cairn.

Ríp, a church, a parsonage until 1907, where the versifier Hannes Bjarnason (1776–1838) was pastor. Rögnvaldur Pétursson of Winnipeg (1877–1940), long one of the main leaders of Canadian Icelanders, also came from there.

Keldudalur, in 2002 an excavation was started there. An interesting site with a rich history as the rest of Hegranes.

Helluland, aa farm in Hegranes. Home to the painter Sigurður Guðmundsson (1833-74), an influential person in the foundation of The National Museum and its first employee. The farmer Sigurður Ólafsson (1856-1942), known for h is ingenuity, built the first pulley-ferry to cross the Héraðsvötn rivers.

Héraðsvötn, one of the biggest Icelandic rivers, glacial, rising in the Hofsjökull glacier in many branches. It flows in two main streams, Eystri- and Vestari-Jökulsá ("Eastern and Western Jökulsá") north of the highlands and down the valleys of Skagafjörður. After the two streams meet, the river is called Héraðsvötn, but it again divides at its estuary. The bridge over Vesturós, built in 1926, is 113 m long. Before the bridge was built, people would cross the river by ferry; Jón Ósmann (1862-1914) was a ferryman for a long time. A shelter for the ferrymen that used to stand at Furðustrandir at the east end of the bridge, has been rebuilt and a sign board put up nearby. There is a resting place just east of the bridge and a footpath leads down to the shelter. A new bridge a bit to the south of the old bridge, was taken into use in 1994.

Sauðárkrókur, (pop. 2,564) a town at the head of Skagafjörður, authorized trading place since 1857, obtained its municipal charter in 1947. The main occupations are trading, fishing and light industry. Community centre. Secondary school serving the northwest of the country. At the Heritage House are Exhibitions from The Skagafjordur Heritage Museum. The Tannery Visitor Centre at Sauðárkrókur is the only tannery in Europe which makes fishleather. The Visitor Centre provides visitors with an unusual way to experience the tannery and its products: guided tours of the actual tannery, where fish-skin is expertly processed to make high-quality leather. At the Visitor Centre, leather goods made from the tannery's products by outstanding designers and craftspeople are offered for sale. Fishleather from Atlantic Leather has caught the imagination of internationally-known fashion houses and brands such as Prada, Dior and Nike. Airport at Borgarsandur.

A drawing from the church at Hofsstaðir from 1898 by Johannes Klein. This church was replaced by a new church around 1900, which still stands there.

76 SIGLUFJARÐARVEGUR

Kolkuós, at the mouth of the Kolka river. Once an anchorage and trading place.

766 Bakkavegur, 3,6 km.

Brimnes, a farm. In the book of Settlers is said that a great forest was at Brimnes. Now there is no forest but some efforts are being made to change that.

Lækur, an abandoned farm in the Viðvíkursveit district. It was there that the tenor Stefán (Guðmundsson) Íslandi (1907-1994), one of Iceland's best-known singers, sang "publicly" for the first time in the winter of 1924-25.

Hofstaðasel, an ancestral farm that offers unique modern dwellings. Princess Anna stayed there in 2002.

Hofstaðir, a church, where in Catholic times there was a sacred statue of the Virgin Mary. This image was believed to be sacred and attracted many pilgrims, who would promise gifts to secure and answer to their prayers. This image and the cross at Kaldaðarnes were probably the most sacred images in catholic Iceland. It is now in the National Museum of Iceland. However, the church was given a replica which still attracts numerous donations. There are many other artefacts worth seeing in the church at Hofstaðir.

Þverá, a farm, birthplace of Jón Steingrímsson (1728-91), known as the "Fire Pastor" (see Kirkjubæjarklaustur, V-Skaft).

Frostastaðir, a substantial farm, now and through the ages. Home of sheriff Jón Espólín (1769-1836), historiographer and professor at Kongsberg in Norway. Also the birthplace of Þorkell Þorkelsson, chief meterologist (1876-1921).

Hjaltastaðir, the district girls' school was situated there 1878-80.

Flugumýri, a church and manor farm. Home, in the 13th century of the chief Kolbeinn ungi ("the young") and remains of his fort can be seen on a hill to the southeast of the farm. Later Earl Gissur Þorvaldsson lived there for a while. It was during his time there, in 1253, that the Flugumýrarbrenna ("the burning of Flugumýri farm") took place, when his foes attempted to kill him. Twenty five people died in the fire, but Earl Gissur managed to save his life by hiding in a big cask half-full of sour whey (used for storing food), and later took cruel revenge on his enemies. The ecclesiastical conferences of the Hólar bishopric used to be held there. In the churchyard is a tombstone to the historiographer Jón Espólín (1769-1836).

Glóðafeykir, (990 m) an impressive mountain, steep and rocky, above Flugumýri. The story goes that Helga Sigurðardóttir, mistress of the last Catholic bishop Jón Arason, hid out on this mountain while Danish war-ships were in the north in 1551, the summer after Jón was beheaded in the struggles of the Reformation.

1 Norðurlandsvegur, p. 70	**75 Sauðárkróksbraut,** p. 326
767 Hólavegur, p. 355	**769 Ásavegur,** p. 355

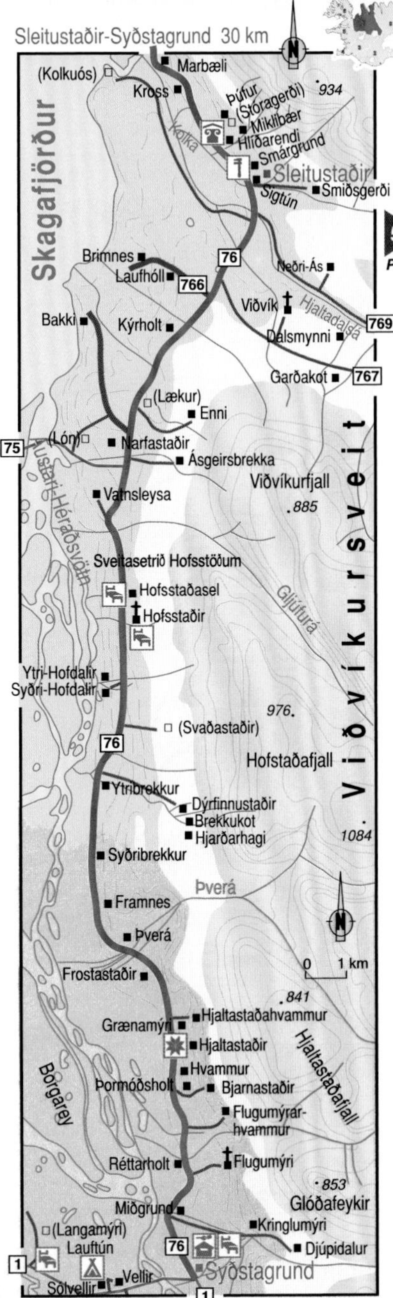

Höfði-Sleitustaðir 22 km

5 P. 568

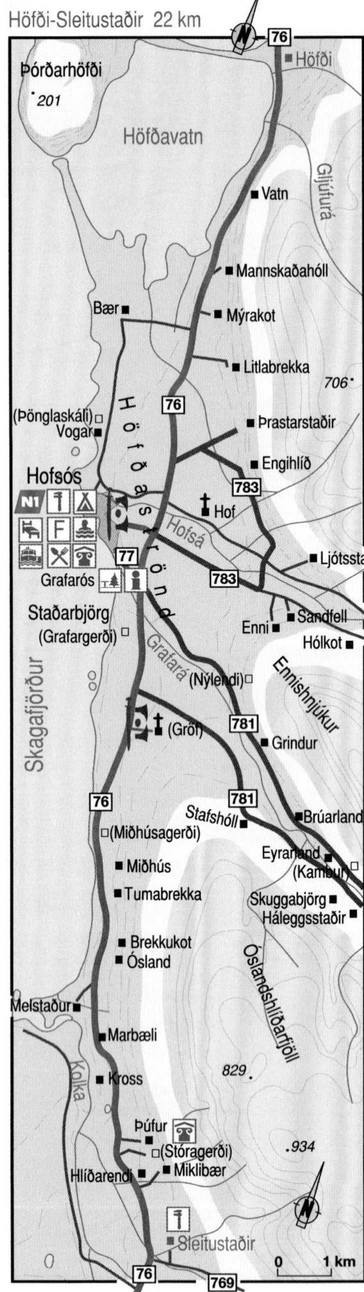

Sleitustaðir-Höfði 22 km

77 Hofsósbraut, 2,3 km.

Bær, a substantial farm and artist residency.

Mannskaðahóll, ("Loss-of-life hill") where Icelanders are said to have fought and defeated English robbers in 1431, killing 80 of them, who were then buried in two mounds near the road. Nearby is Ræningjalág ("Robbers' hollow").

783 Höfðastrandarvegur, 6,76 km. **781 Deildardalsvegur,** 13,4 km.

Hofsós, (pop. 146) one of oldest trading places in Iceland, where there is also one of oldest houses in Iceland (1777), Pakkhúsið (Warehouse), in the keeping of the National Museum since 1954. In another old store, built 1910 is the Icelandic Emigration Centre. It was founded in 1996 and dedicated to commemorate Icelandic emigrants to North America and to promote connections between their descendants and the people of Iceland. The Centre offers four exhibits in three separate buildings, as well as a genealogical information service, library facilities and more. The exhibitions combine text, photographs and tableaux to illustrate the conditions in Iceland that influenced the decision to emigrate, the journey to the 'New World' and the new way of life they encountered. At Hofsós you will also find the only sewing company that specialises in flag making. A recent addition to the community in Hofsós is a new swimming pool donated by two local women. It has been widely recognized for beautiful architecture and design. A local company, Sailing on Skagafjörð, recently started offering scenic boat trips from the Hofsós harbor.

Staðarbjörg, some unusually beautiful columnar basalt on the shore near Hofsós.

Grafará, a river flowing out of the Deildardalur valley. At its mouth was **Grafarós** where there was a trading station from 1835-1915, for a time one of two main trading places in the Skagafjörður district.

Gröf, home of Ragnheiður Jónsdóttir (1646-1715) widow of two bishops, great patron of art. Turf church with wooden frame of stave construction, believed to date originally from the late 17th century. Considered to be the oldest chapel in the country, all timbers were renewed in 1953. In the keeping of the National Museum since 1939.

Höfðaströnd, the farming district between Óslandshlíð and the Höfðahólar landslip.

Stóragerði, there is a transportation museum, privatly run.

Sleitustaðir, a farm since the original settlement, a small community.

769 Ásavegur, p. 355

The Icelandic Emigration Centre

Bakki, an abandoned farm.

Fjall, birthplace of Sölvi Helgason (1820-95) who called himself Sólon Íslandus. He was a well-known wanderer, and once spent time in prison in Copenhagen for passport fraud. Sölvi had artistic talents, was a skilled draughtsman, sketched and painted in water colours. He left many manuscripts with his stories and reflections. Davíð Stefánsson's story *Sólon Íslandus* is based on Sölvi. A memorial to Sölvi at Lónkot.

Fell, a church and once a parsonage, which has been moved to Hofsós. Home of the famous priest-sorcerer Hálfdan Narfason about 1600. (See **Hálfdanarhurð.**) Birthplace of Ólafur Davíðsson (1862-1903), folklore specialist and naturalist.

786 Sléttuhlíðarvegur, 5,2 km.

Sléttuhlíð, the farming area from the Höfðahólar landslip to the river Stafá. Broadish flat land with two hills, Hrolleifshöfði (88 m) by the sea, and the oval-shaped Fell (173 m), at the east end of which is the lake Sléttuhlíðarvatn. The **Hrolleifsdalur** valley goes off there, through it runs the river **Hrolleifsá**, a good fising river.

Málmey, an island with steep cliffs off Sléttuhlíð, 2.4 km^2, max. height 156 m. Grassy and good pasture for sheep. The farm there was abandoned in 1951. According to legend there is a spell on Málmey so that neither mice nor horses will thrive there and no married couple should live on the island for longer than twenty years or the wife will disappear and never be seen again. Folk tales tell of just such occurrences.

Drangey, (200 m) a rocky tuff island, grassy on top, difficult to climb. Birdhunting and egg-collecting. Uninhabited. Famous from *Grettis saga*, as Grettir the strong had a hide-out there, where he and his brother Illugi were slain.

Þórðarhöfði, (202 m) a headland named after the first settler of the area, Þórður. It is a considered an old remain of a volcano from the last Ice Age. A nesting site for seabirds. It can only be reached at low tide. Þórðarhöfði is consider the resident of elves according to folklore.

Lónkot, guesthouse and restaurant. Exhibition of the work of Sölvi Helgason, see **Sléttuhlíð** above.

Höfðavatn, a lagoon at the east end of Þórðarhöfði, 9.27 km^2.

Höfði, the outermost farm on Höfðaströnd, originally settled by Höfða-Þórður. **Höfðahólar**, nearby, formed by a landslip.

Haganesvík-Höfði 21 km

Höfði-Haganesvík 21 km

787 Flókadalsvegur, p. 330

© Sigríður Sigþórsdóttir
Hofsós swimming pool

5
P. 568

Siglufjörður-Haganesvík 24 km

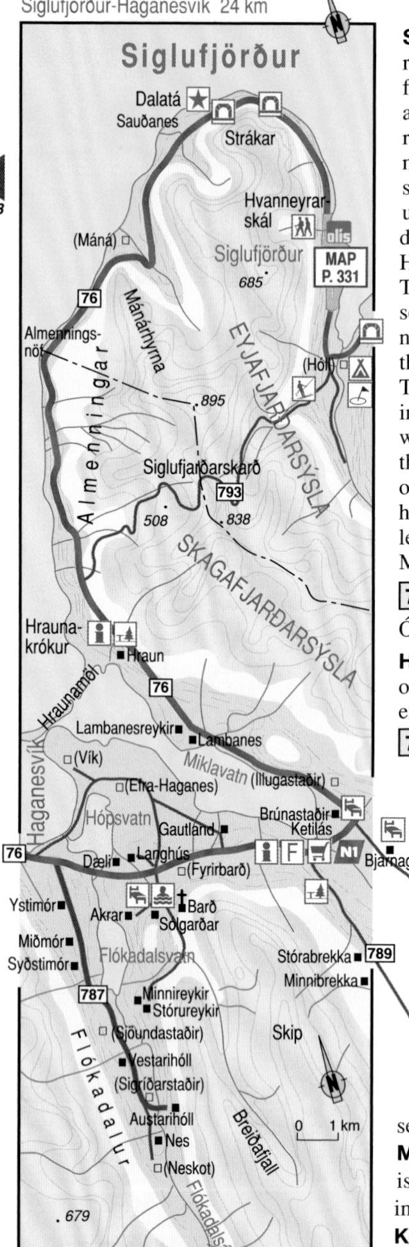

Haganesvík-Siglufjörður 24 km

Siglufjörður, (pop. 1,201) a fishing town on a fjord of same name, surrounded by steep mountains with little flat land. In 1919 an avalanche fell on Engidalur opposite the town, killing 7 people. Siglufjörður was an important herring centre from 1904 to recent times, when the herring disappeared. Good harbour, school, bank, hospital and a herring museum, which was awarded the Micheletti award in 2004. During summer, the atmosphere of the „Herring Era" is recreated on the museum dock and the locals in vintage costumes salt herring and sing and dance to accordion music. The Folk Music Centre is located in Madame House where the Rev. Bjarni Thorsteinsson lived from 1888 to 1898. The centre brings to life the world of Icelandic folk music. Visitors can see people of all ages chanting rímur, singing the tvísöngur, reciting nursery rhymes, and playing folk instruments such as the langspil and the Icelandic fidla. The centre also depicts the life of the Rev. Bjarni Thorsteinsson and how he collected the folk songs. Excellent skiing ground. Beautiful walking routes. A popular destination for birdwatchers. Seven walls have been constructed in the high ground above the town in order to ward off avalanches. Two of them go by the name of Stóri-boli (Big bull), 18 m high, and Litli-boli (Little bull), 14 m high. Together these two walls, completed in 1999, are nearly 1 km in length. There is a beautiful walking route there with an amazing view. Memorial to sailors lost at sea in town.

792 Langeyrarvegur, 2 km. This route leads to the tunnel to Ólafsfjörður, Héðinsfjarðargöng tunnel.

Héðinsfjarðargöng, a tunnel between Siglufjörður and Ólafsfjörður, opened in 2010, making the route between these two fjords much shorter and safer to drive.

793 Skarðsvegur, 13 km.

Siglufjarðarskarð, 630 m, a pass between Siglufjörður and Fljót. Used for sightseeing in the summer, not for those who are afraid of height.

Strákar, (676 m) a mountain dropping sheer into the sea. The tunnel Strákagöng, 800 m long, opened in 1967, goes through it .

Almenningar, the coastline north from the farm Hraun to the mountain Mánárhyrna. Boundary between Skagafjarðarsýsla county and Siglufjörður at Almenningsnöf. Úlfsdalir, two valleys between the Fljót district and Siglufjörður, now abandoned.

Hraun, an old manor farm, the northernmost farm in Skagafjarðarsýsla county. The nearest farm to Siglufjarðarskarð pass.

Hraunakrókur, one of the most important fishing places in the Fljót district of old. Ruins of many fishermen's booths can be seen there.

Miklavatn, a good trout lake, 7.43 km^2, also with sea fish. A narrow isthmus, Hraunamöl, separates it from the sea. There are many interesting remains of fishing in days gone by, well worth seeing.

Ketilás, there are crossroads there that lead to Siglufjörður, Ólafsfjörður and Skagafjörður. Community centre.

787 Flókadalsvegur, 6,4 km.

Flókadalur, a large valley upwards of Vestur-Fljót, lies to the south. It is named after Flóki Villgerðarson (Hrafna-Flóki). Who made the valley his home when he came to Iceland for the second time. Flóki is said to be buried at Stóru-Reykjar at the place named Flókasteinar (Flóki´s rocks).

Barð, a church and parsonage. At Sólgarðar at Barð is a school and a swimming pool.

Haganesvík, once a there was a village there.

Fljót, the northernmost district of Skagafjörður, with two valleys, good, broad, flat land, with the Haganesvík bay. Formerly much cod and shark fishing. Fertile and grassy, with geothermal heat in places, often snowbound in winter.

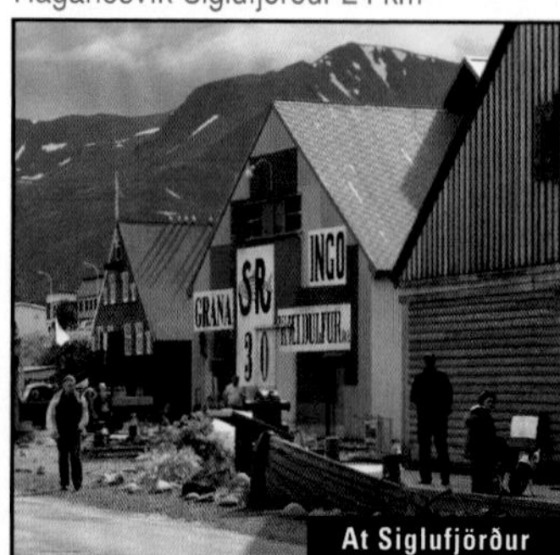

At Siglufjörður

82 Ólafsfjarðarvegur, p. 363 **789 Sléttuvegur,** p. 363

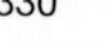

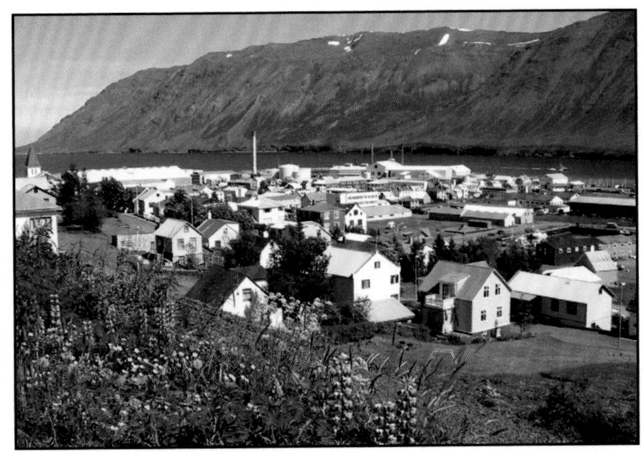

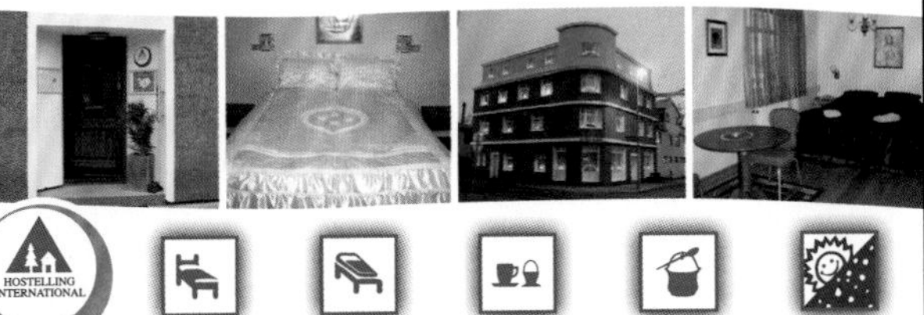

HOSTELLING INTERNATIONAL

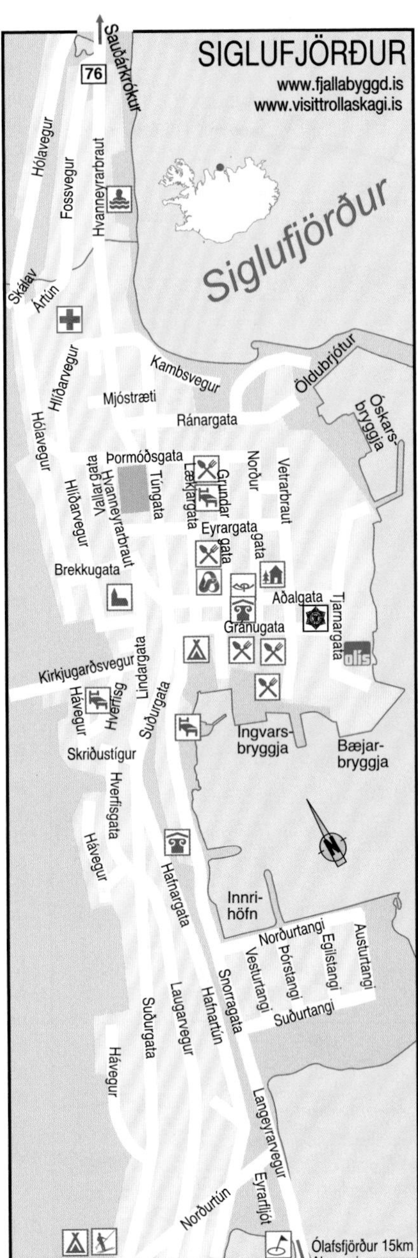

5
P. 568

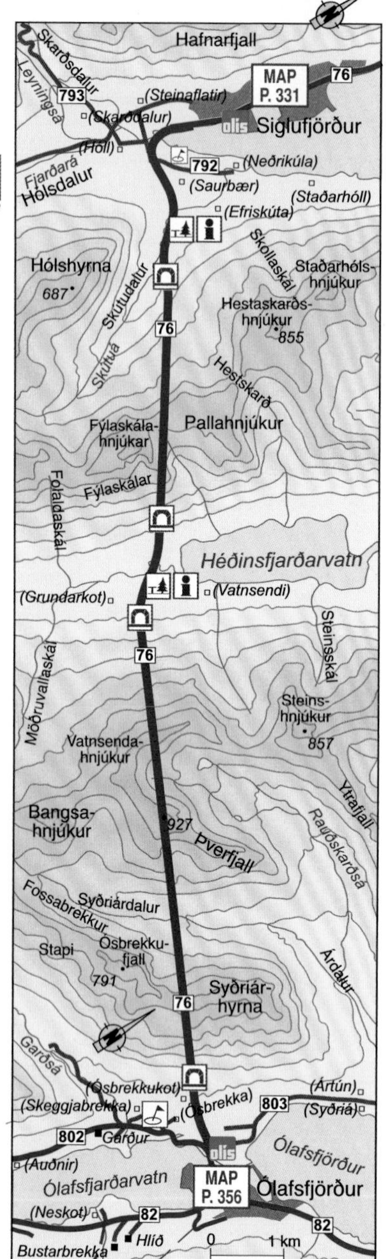

Siglufjörður, see p. 330.

Héðinsfjörður tunnels, lead traffic via a deserted fjord between the settlements to the west and east. The tunnel east from Siglufjörður is 3.9 km long, while the one west from Ólafsfjörður is 7.1 km. These tunnels have created wonderful opportunities for the traveller, making a huge area north of Ring Road No. 1 more accessible, including this area's diverse bird life.

Ólafsfjörður, a valley, 15 km long, grassy but narrow, with fine mountains having jagged peaks at the head of a short (5 km) fjord of the same name. The fjord opens out between high cliffs, **Ólafsfjarðarmúli** to the south and **Hvanndalabjarg** to the north. There is virtually no flat land on the coast. There are various folktales associated with Ólafsfjörður, e.g. about the Rev. Hálfdan Narfason, who rode on the Devil with Farmer Jón from Málmey through Skagafjörður to the Hvanndalir valley in Hvanndalabjarg (see Road 76, Fell and Málmey). In Ódáinsakur ("Field of the undying") in the valley grew a herb that made people immortal.

Ólafsfjarðarvatn, a lake, 2,51 km², at the head of the fjord, empties into the sea. Fishing-lake, sometimes with salt-water fish in it.

Ólafsfjörður, (pop. 796) is one of the two villages in Fjallabyggð municipality. The fjord and high surrounding mountains, together with a lake and estuary, form a magnificent setting. Employment is mostly based on fishing or light industry, but plenty of recreation is also on hand for tourists and outdoor enthusiasts. In the winter, they can choose between slalom and cross-country skiing, and perhaps try skating, fishing through the lake ice or zipping over the landscape on a snow scooter. During summer, the mountains, lake, estuary and black beach are enchanting. A range of hiking routes through valleys and mountains lead to superb panoramas, in the midst of peace and quiet. North of the tunnel going east to Eyjafjörður, the now-abandoned, awe-inspiring road around the Múlinn peninsula climbs to an altitude of 300 m. In fair weather, it provides a terrific view, and the best place to watch the midnight sun in Iceland. Note however that you cannot walk the whole way around the peninsula, since the road has started to collapse down the slope. Ólafsfjörður has Iceland's only ski jump, as well as a splendid natural history museum displaying one of the country's most diverse bird collections, while sports clubs and other local organisations put on numerous events. Many of Iceland's leading blues musicians appear at the Blue North Festival in June, and there is also a classical music festival in August which prides itself on world-class opera singers and musicians during the berry-picking season. Children of all ages from far and wide take part in a football tournament every July. Sailors' Day, a few weeks earlier, has a long tradition here, and emphasises entertainment for the entire family and every visitor. The monument in memory of drowned seamen, which was erected by the church in 1940, was the first of its kind in Iceland.

82 **Ólafsfjarðarvegur,** p. 362
793 **Skarðsvegur,** p. 330
802 **Garðsvegur,** p. 362
803 **Kleifavegur,** p. 362

From Ólafsfjörður

702 Heggstaðanesvegur, 18 km.
Tannastaðir, birthplace of the mathematician Björn Gunnlaugsson (1788-1876), the first person to make an exact map of Iceland.
Sandar, a substantial farm at the head of Miðfjörður.
Álfhóll, ("Hill of the hidden people") by the old road east of Sveðjustaður.
Melstaður, see p. 335.

703 Hálsbæjavegur, 6 km.
Hrútafjarðarháls, a low marshy ridge with gravelly patches between inner Hrútafjörður and the farms of Miðfjörður. Its continuation to the north between the fjords is the peninsula **Heggstaðanes** or **Bálkastaðanes**. The ridge was formerly difficult to cross because of marshes and bogs.

1 **Norðurlandsvegur,** p. 63
68 **Innstrandavegur,** p. 309
704 **Miðfjarðarvegur,** p. 335

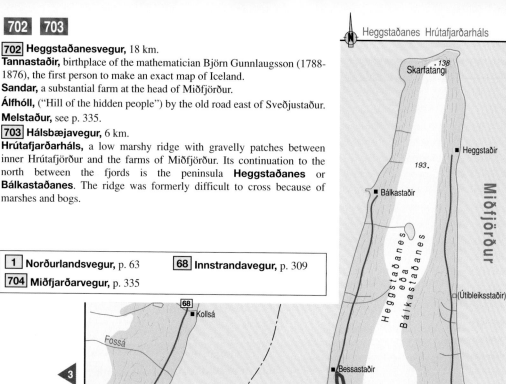

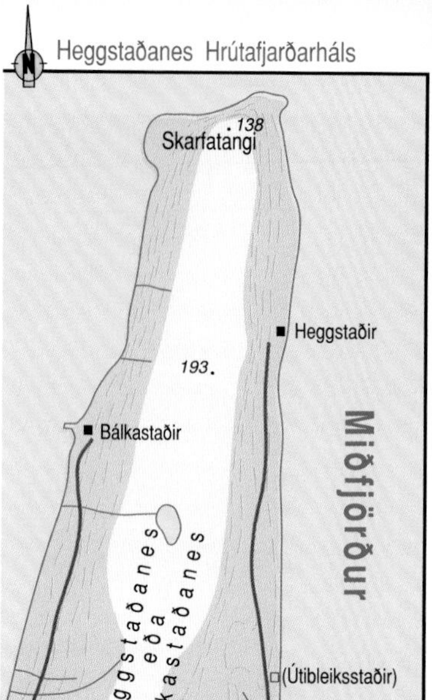

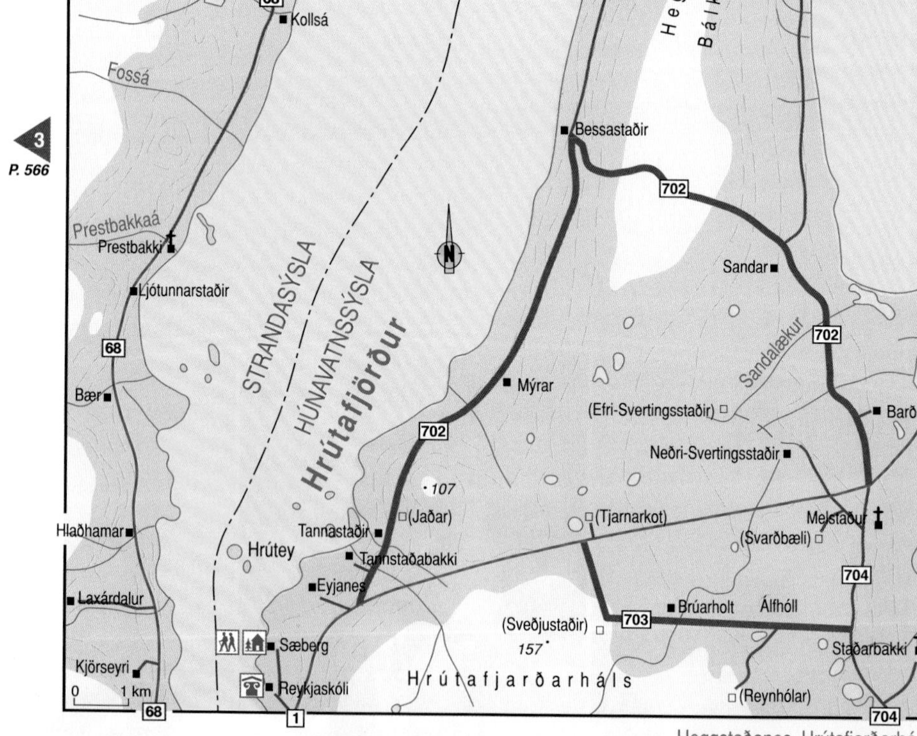

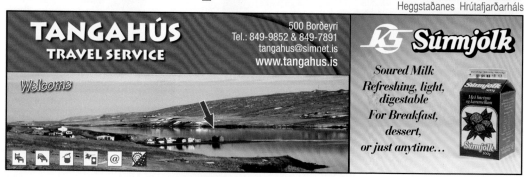

Aðalból, riding trails from there south to Arnarvatnsheiði moor.

Efri-Núpur, a church. The grave of the poetess Vatnsenda-Rósa (1795-1855) is there, with a tombstone erected in 1965 by the women of the district. Route from there south to Arnarvatnsheiði moor.

Torfastaðavatn, a fishing lake. A jeep track leads there from Torafastaðir. A fishing licence can be obtained at Haugur.

Núpsdalstunga, in the Núpsdalur valley, the home, in the 10th century, of Steingerður, mistress of Kormákur the poet.

705 Vesturárdalsvegur, 9 km.

Húkur, from where there is a jeep-track over Hrútafjarðarháls ridge to the farm Brandagil in Hrútafjörður, a very beautiful route in summer.

704 Miðfjarðarvegur, 36 km.

Staðarbakki, a church, the nearest farm to Melstaður. Nowhere in Iceland is there such a short distance between two churches.

Brekkulækur, from there came the writer Friðrik Á. Brekkan (1888–1958).

Bjarg, ("Crag") a farm in Miðfjörður, taking its name from a glacier-eroded rock north of the homefield. Fine panoramas from there. Grettir the strong was brought up at Bjarg, and there is a hummock in the homefield called Grettisþúfa, where his head is said to be buried. Memorial to Grettir's mother, Ásdís.

Melstaður, an old manor farm, parsonage and church. Residence in the 10th century of Kormákur the poet and later of Oddur Ófeigsson, mentioned in the *Bandamanna saga*. It grew in importance after the introduction of Christianity, and was considered the second richest parsonage in northern Iceland. Residence in the 16th century of Björn Jónsson, son of Bishop Jón Arason of Hólar, and later, 1598-1649, of Arngrímur Jónsson the learned, who was a prolific writer. Some interesting old relics in the church.

Reykir, home of Miðfjarðar-Skeggi, who took the sword Sköfnungur from the burial mound of Hrólfur kraki in *Hrólfs saga*.

Laugarbakki, a small village, heated from local hot springs, just south of the Miðfjarðará bridge. Ásbyrgi community centre. See p. 63.

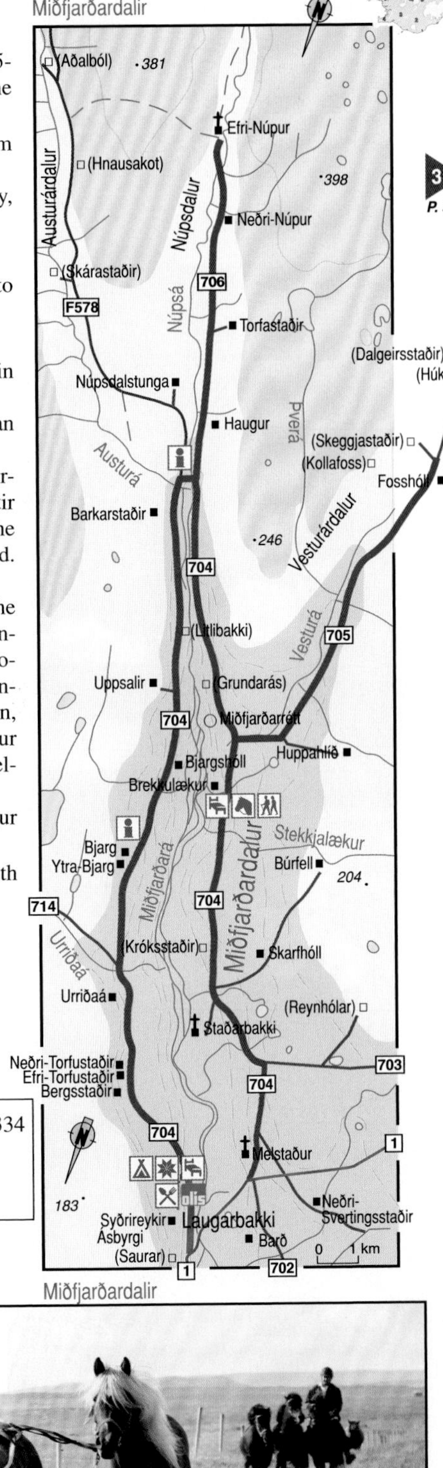

1 Norðurlandsvegur, p. 63
702 Heggstaðanesvegur, p. 334
703 Hálsbæjavegur, p. 334
714 Fitjavegur, p. 341
F578 Arnarvatnsvegur, p. 466-467

Húnaþing-vestra is an exciting destination for travellers who want to experience Icelandic culture, history and nature at its best. Located at the mid-way point between Reykjavík and Akureyri the area is characterised by unspoilt moors and wetlands, majestic mountains, a vivid coastline and rich fishing rivers and lakes.

Hvammstangi on the Vatnsnes peninsula is the capital of the region and from there and its surrounding areas you can find a wide range of excellent services and restaurants along with accommodation at all levels of comfort and value inviting you to experience all the best that the area has to offer.

A great place to start your trip is at the award winning museum run by The Icelandic Seal Center in Hvammstangi. There you will find an extensive educational exhibit detailing the way of life of Icelandic seals and Iceland's best locations for seal watching which are found on the peninsula. The museum building also houses the areas Tourist Information Center where you can learn about everything there is to see and do in Húnaþing-vestra, such as; seal watching boat tours, Iceland´s largest wool factory, horse tours and rental, many unique and interesting museums, quality local handcraft markets, fun and family friendly swimming pool and hot pots, endless nature and wildlife areas and many walking paths to name but a few.

The Vatnsnes peninsula is the undoubted pearl of the region, with Iceland´s largest seal colonies found along its shores and numerous places of interest such as the famous giant rock formation Hvítserkur, Hamarsrétt sheep corral, Illugastaðir with its gruesome history and the unique Borgavirki Viking fort but a selection.

For further information see **www.visithunathing.is** or contact the Tourist Information Center on +354 45 12345 or **info@selasetur.is**

Bergstaðir-Hvammstangi 19 km

3 P. 566

Hamarsrétt, a sheep fold by the ocean.

Skarð, houses and greenhouses heated from springs on the shore. A light housee built in 1947.

Ánastaðir, a farm where in 1882 thirty-two large whales ran aground during an intensely cold spring. This was said to have saved the local people from starvation. Ánastaðastapi is a sharp-pointed rock in the sea.

Káraborg, (476 m) a spectacular crag from which there is a fine view. A riding trail goes past the crag to the Vesturhóp district.

Vatnsnes, the peninsula between Miðfjörður and Húnafjörður, with a high mountain range, **Vatnsnesfjall**, the highest peak being **Þrælsfell** ("Slave mountain") (906 m).

© PMS
The church at Kirkjuhvammur

Hvammstangi, (pop. 564) a village by Miðfjörður fjord: the only trading village in Vestur-Húnavatnssýsla county, legally recognised for commerce in 1895, with trade starting around 1900. Main industries: agriculture, fishing, trade and other services. All of the buildings are heated geothermally, using water piped in from the hot spring at Laugarbakki. While a modern church has now replaced the old one at Kirkjuhvammur, the original church is still standing, cared for by the National Museum, with the only operable watermill in Iceland right by it. Health centre, community centre, museum of commerce, compulsory school and swimming pool. Hvammstangi is also home to the Icelandic Seal Centre, which hosts an exhibition on seals around Iceland, both in the present and the past. In the same building, you can visit art shows over the summer and a tourist information centre. The Seal Centre conducts research on both seals and eco-tourism.

711 Vatnsnesvegur, 77 km.

Kirkjuhvammur, wooden church, of a younger type with a tower, built in 1882. In the keeping of the National Museum since 1976.

72 Hvammstangavegur, 6 km.

1 Norðurlandsvegur, p. 64 **702 Heggstaðanesvegur,** p. 334

Hvammstangi-Bergstaðir 19 km

711 VATNSNESVEGUR

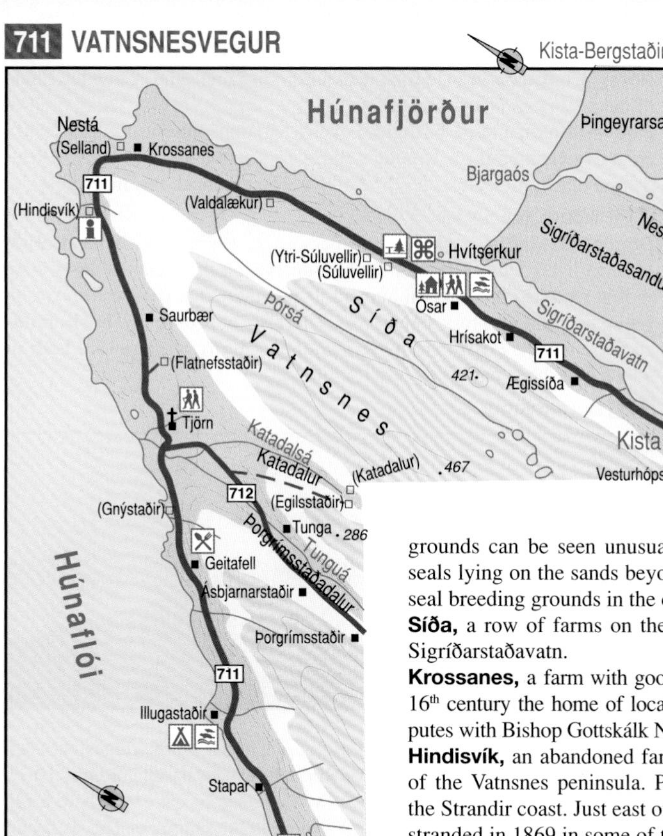

Bjargaós, estuary of Hópið.

Vesturhóp, a good farming district below the Vatnsnesfjall mountain range and south of the lake Sigríðarstaðavatn.

Sigríðarstaðavatn, a fishing lake, 6 km long, narrow and shallow. East of the lake are 50-80 m high cliffs called Nesbjörg.

Hvítserkur, a 15 m high basalt crag rising from the sea near the farm Súluvellir. The action of the surf has eroded it to make it resemble a three-legged monster. On the way to Hvítserkur seal breeding grounds can be seen unusually close to. There are often hundreds of seals lying on the sands beyond the estuary. One of the most accessible seal breeding grounds in the country.

Síða, a row of farms on the east of the Vatnsnes peninsula alongside Sigríðarstaðavatn.

Krossanes, a farm with good land and many natural advantages. In the 16th century the home of local governor Jón Sigmundsson, who had disputes with Bishop Gottskálk Nikulásson in the last years of his life.

Hindisvík, an abandoned farm on an bay of the same name at the end of the Vatnsnes peninsula. Picturesque landscape and a good view of the Strandir coast. Just east of there is Strandvík, where the brig *Valborg* stranded in 1869 in some of the worst weather to have raged in Iceland. Home for a time of the distinguished and talented poet Rev. Sigurður Norland (1885-1971), who also wrote in English, quatrains following Icelandic rules of metre and alliteration, such as:

She is fine as morn in May
Mild, divine and clever
Like a shining summer day
She'll be mine forever

Katadalur, an abandoned farm. Friðrik Sigurðsson lived there with his parents. He was the last man to be executed along with Agnes Magnúsdóttir for the murders at Illugastaðir, January 12th 1830. See p. 65.

Tjörn, a church and parsonage. Ögmundur Sivertsen (1799-1845), naturalist and poet, was pastor there for a time. Roads lead from Tjörn to the valleys Þorgrímsdalur and Katadalur.

712 Þorgrímsstaðavegur, 8 km.

Illugastaðir, an abandoned farm. The farmer, Natan Ketilsson, and his shepherd Pétur Jónsson were murdered there in 1828 (see **Prístapar**, A-Hún). Natan got the farm in 1824 and his family has been there since. From Illugastaðir came captain Hrólfur Jakobsson who drowned in 1910 shortly before his departure to the island Jan Mayen where he and another man had intended to put up a hunting camp, hunt for seal and claim the island for Iceland. It was, however, not until 1921 that Norwegians first settled on Jan Mayen and put up a weather station there.

Svalbarð, a farm. There is a marked seal watching location and a parking lot.

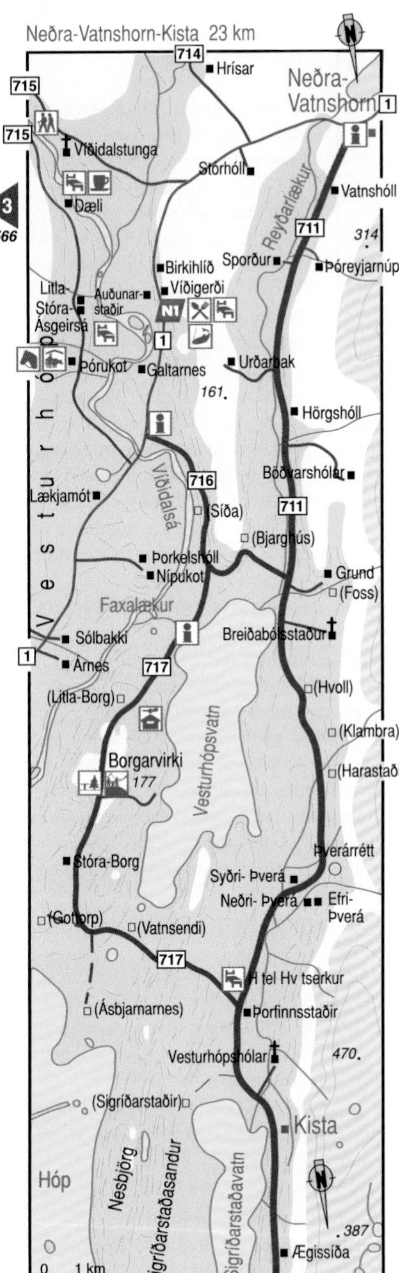

Þóreyjarnúpur, a strange rock near a farm of same name. Long the home of the poet Hans Natansson (1816-1887).

Böðvarshólar, a farm, birthplace of Bríet Bjarnhéðinsdóttir (1856-1940), an active champion for women's rights in Iceland, and her brother Prof. Sæmundur Bjarnhéðinsson (1863-1936) who did much to cure leprosy.

716 Síðuvegur, 5,8 km.

Breiðabólsstaður, a church and parsonage, where lawspeaker Hafliði Másson lived about 1100. Under his supervision the Icelandic laws were first recorded in 1117. Monument. It was there that Bishop Jón Arason set up his printing-press about 1530. There are now only two books printed there extant: *Passio* and *Guðspjallabók* ("Book of gospels"), both of which have been published in fascimile.

717 Borgarvegur, 13,5 km.

Borgarvirki

Borgarvirki, ("Citadel") (177 m) a group of rocks on the ridges between the Vesturhóp district and the Víðidalur valley, with basalt columns 10-15 m high and a circular depression at the top, open to the east. There a big stone wall has been raised, through which is the entrance. The wall and others nearby were repaired in 1949-50, and in the depression are the ruins of huts and a well. Nobody knows why Borgarvirki was made. One story is that Víga-Barði in *Heiðarvíga saga* intended it as a defence against attack from the people of the Borgarfjörður district, another that it was the work of Finnbogi rammi in *Finnboga saga ramma*. View dial.

Stóra-Borg in Víðidalur, a substantial farm, good salmon-fishing. Home of Finnbogi rammi in Saga times.

Vatnsendi, a farm, for some time home of the well-known poetess Rósa Guðmundsdóttir (Vatnsenda-Rósa) (1795-1855).

Vesturhópsvatn, a fishing-lake, ca. 7 km long and 1-2 km wide, emptying through Faxalækur into the Víðidalsá river.

Ásbjarnarnes, there lived Víga-Barði Guðmundarson (989), farmer, who is mentioned in *Grettir saga* and *Heiðarvíga saga*.

Vesturhópshólar, a church and parsonage till 1851. The former prime minister Jón Þorláksson (1877-1935) came from there.

1 Norðurlandsvegur, p. 64 **714 Fitjavegur,** p. 341
715 Víðidalsvegur, p. 341

714 Fitjavegur, 15 km.

Hrappsstaðir, once the outermost farm in Víðidalur, from whence there is a jeep-track south to Arnarvatnsheiði moor, road F578.

Bakkabunga, a hill with rocky edges on the west of the valley Víðidalur, where the remains of plants, including alder, have been found in strata dating from late Tertiary or early Quaternary ages.

Kolugljúfur, a 1 km long and 40–50 m deep ravine. Takes its name from a troll called Kola who dug the ravine and lived theres. Beautiful waterfalls in the ravine.

Víðidalstunga, a church and old manor farm between the rivers Fitjá and **Víðidalsá**. Land belonging to the Vídalín family from 15th century until about 1900. The best-known member of this family was Páll Jónsson Vídalín (1667-1727), magistrate, poet and schoolmaster, author along with Árni Magnússon of the *Jarðabók 1702-12,* an Icelandic Domesday book. The *Flateyjarbók,* the largest extant Icelandic vellum manuscript, was written at Víðidalstunga, on the initiative of the farmer Jón Hákonarson (b. 1350).

Víðidalur, a wide, green valley, with low hills on the western side and **Víðidalsfjall** (993 m) on the eastern side. The river Víðidalsá flows through the valley, a good salmon river, coming from Stórisandur, total length 65 km. Another river connects with Víðidalsá, Fitjá, there you can find a great fishing spot called **Kerafossar**.

Víðihlíð, a community in the Auðunarstaðir lands. Community centre, library, school.

Auðunarstaðir, a farm in Víðidalur named after the settler Auðun skökull ("horse's phallus"), to whom the British royal family can trace its family line. Community centre Víðihlíð nearby.

715 Víðidalsvegur, 13,2 km.

Ásgeirsá, a farm opposite Auðunarstaðir. Home of Hrefna, the wife of Kjartan Ólafsson in *Laxdæla saga.*

Lækjamót, a farm at the northern end of Víðidalur. The first missionaries, Þorvaldur víðförli ("Þorvaldur the widely travelled") and Bishop Friðrekur, stayed there for three years towards the end of the 10th century.

1 Norðurlandsvegur, p. 64	**704 Miðfjarðarvegur,** p. 335
716 Síðuvegur, p. 340	**717 Borgarvegur,** p. 340

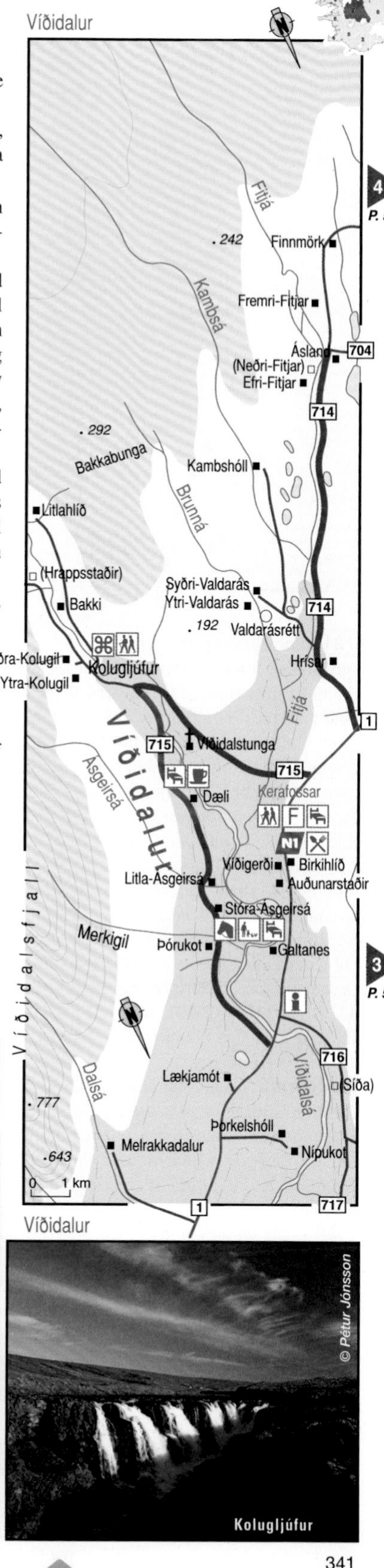

Kolugljúfur

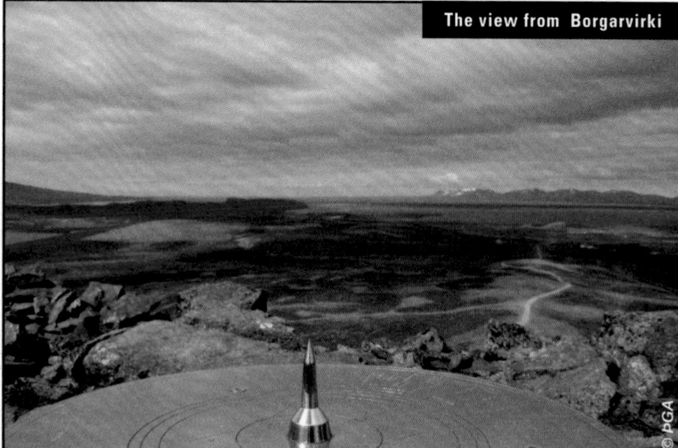

The view from Borgarvirki

4
P. 567

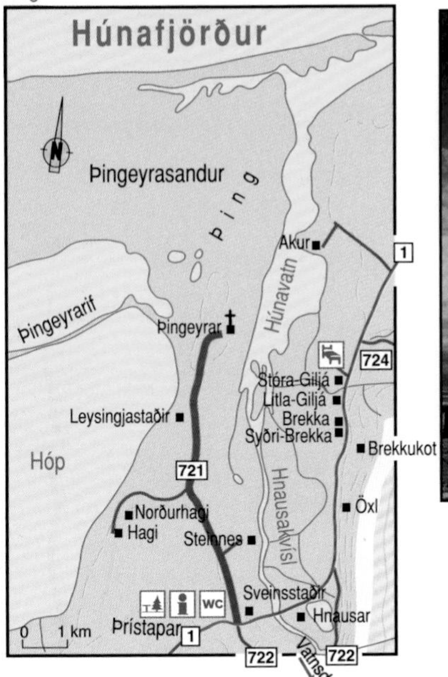

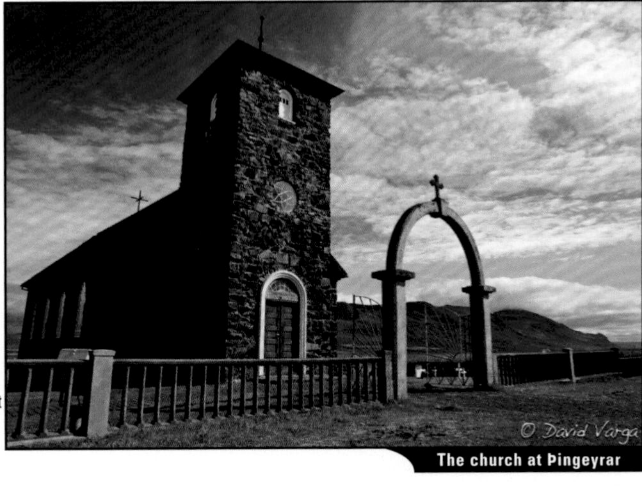

The church at Þingeyrar

721 Þingeyravegur, 6 km.

Þingeyrar, a manor farm of great historical importance, the most important in Húnavatnssýsla county, with more land than most other farms in Iceland, meadows and pastures. Salmon and seal. A stone church built 1864-65 by Ásgeir Einarsson, member of parliament, containing many fine relics. An ancient assembly site, and the site of the first monastery in Iceland, Þingeyraklaustur, established 1133. It was one of the foremost educational centres of that time, the place where more Sagas were written down than anywhere else. Many well-known Icelanders have lived there, e.g Hulda Stefánsdóttir, headmistress and author of a four-volume autobiographical work which is considered among the finest of its kind in Iceland (see **Möðruvellir**, p. 357). Birthplace of Björn M. Ólsen (1850-1919), first rector of the University of Iceland, it is also the birthplace of Jón Eyþórsson (1895-1968) meteorologist.

Þingeyrarif, a sand-bar reaching most of the way across the lake Hóp.

Hóp, the fifth largest lake in Iceland, 29-44 km^2 depending on the tide which affects the water level. Fed by Víðidalsá and Gljúfurá, it empties out through Bjargaós.

Vatnsdalur – Víðidalsfjall

Þing, the plain south and east of Hóp from the river Gljúfurá and east to Húnavatn Lake and the river Giljaá. Grassy and fertile.

Vatnsdalur, a 25 km long valley. On its eastern side is the mountain Vatnsdalsfjall, steep, with rocks and scree, the highest peak being **Jörundarfell** (1,018 m). On the west are low ridges up to Víðidalsfjall with many farms in grassy, fertile country.

Sunnuhlíð, the innermost farm in Vatnsdalur on the eastern side. Opposite it are remains of the farm Þórhallastaðir, where Grettir the strong wrestled with the ghost, Glámur, in *Grettis saga*.

Þórormstunga, the home in mid-19th century of Jón Bjarnason, a self-taught mathematician and astronomer, who worked out almanacs and eclipses and wrote many works on astronomy and natural science.

Marðarnúpur, a farm. Guðmundur Björnsson (1864-1937) Surgeon General and first President of the National Life-Saving Association of Iceland grew up there.

Hof, an old manor farm on the settlement land of Ingimundur gamli ("the old"), who chose it on advice from the gods. His temple is said to have been at **Goðahóll** just above the farm. A memorial to the settler by the road.

Dyngja, 50 m deep, a grassy hollow north of Hof. This spot is considered to be enchanted.

Eyjólfsstaðir, birthplace of Prof. Sigurður Nordal (1886-1974), a distinguished scholar for whom one of the research institutes in the University of Iceland has been named.

Hvammur, a substantial farm. Gedduhryggir, rock layers sloping 40°-50° down into the valley. North of Hvammur is a landslide of boulders, Hvammsurðir. Near the farm the stream Fosslækur tumbles over the Hjalli cliffs in a beautiful high waterfall.

1 **Norðurlandsvegur,** p. 65
722 **Vatnsdalsvegur,** p. 343
724 **Reykjabraut,** p. 344

722 VATNSDALSVEGUR

Forsæludalur, a farm since the original settlement.

Grímstunga, a big sheep farm, church and former parsonage. West of it is a rugged gorge, through which flows the river Álka. The beginning of the old route south via Grímstunguheiði moor to Borgarfjörður, now a jeep-track south to the moors and Stórisandur. The home, in the 10th century of Óttar, father of the poet Hallfreður vandræðaskáld.

Haukagil, a farm taking its name from the Haukagil gorge, which in turn is said to have got its name from two berserkers who were beaten to death and their bodies thrown into it. The poet Hallfreður vandræðaskáld was brought up at Haukagil. A lovely copse of coniferous trees.

Ás, a substantial farm. Birthplace of Halldóra Bjarnadóttir (1873-1981), a pioneer of the Icelandic handicrafts industry. The local meeting place is at Ásbrekka, a new farm nearby. The witch Ljótunn of *Vatnsdæla saga* is said to have lived at Ás.

Undirfell, (also known as Undornfell) a church and former parsonage. Birthplace of the painter Þórarinn B. Þorláksson (1867-1924). A district girls' school had its beginnings there 1879-83.

Kornsá, a farm below which is **Kattarauga** ("Cat's eye"), a large, deep pool with floating islands. A protected natural feature.

Hnjúkur, (111 m) the peak of a hill that almost closes off the valley, below which is farm of the same name. An excellent view of Vatnsdalur from Hnjúkur.

Þórdísarlundur, a grove of trees planted by the Húnvetninga Society in Reykjavík in memory of Þórdís Ingimundardóttir, the first person born in Vatnsdalur.

Vatnsdalshólar, an area of small hills and hillocks at the mouth of Vatnsdalur, the debris of a tremendous landslide from Vatnsdalsfjall, covering about 4 km^2, supposedly uncountable. Other geographical features in Iceland considered to be uncountable are the islands of Breiðafjörður and the lakes on Arnarvatnsheiði moor.

722 Vatnsdalsvegur, 46 km.

Vatnsdalsá, a river having its source in numerous streams on Grímstunga moor and at Stórisandur. Further down it is deep and calm, there called Hnausakvísl (see below), flowing into Húnavatn. A popular salmon river.

Flóðið, a lake near the Vatnsdalshólar hills, created by a landslide in October 1720 that dammed the river. Remains of the landslide can still be seen at the farm Bjarnastaðir east of Flóðið.

Hnausakvísl, the lowest part of the river Vatnsdalsá, between the lakes Flóðið and Húnavatn. Deep and calm, it is an excellent fishing river.

1 **Norðurlandsvegur,** p. 65 | 721 **Þingeyravegur,** p. 342

Vatnsdalur

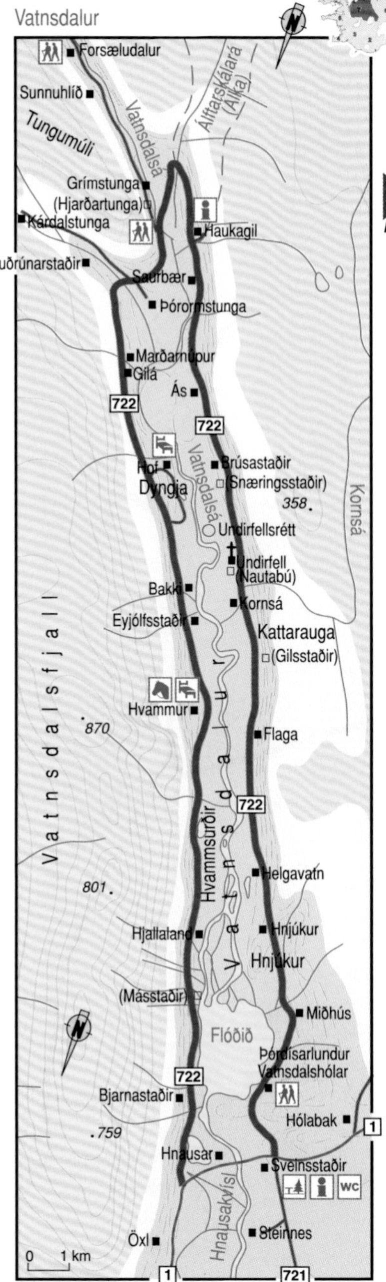

Vatnsdalur

4 P. 567

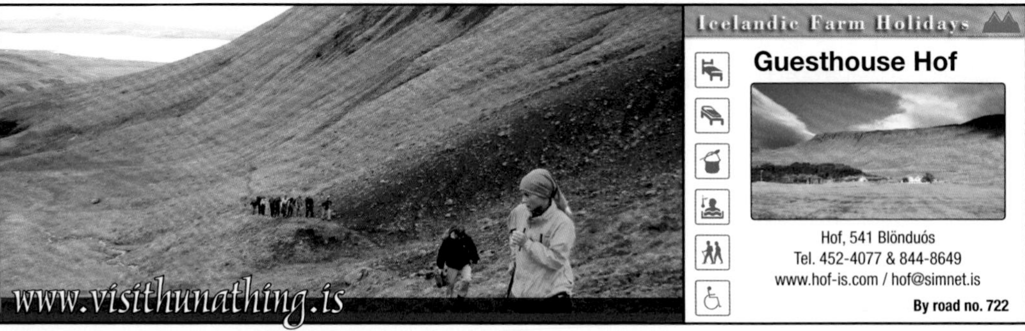

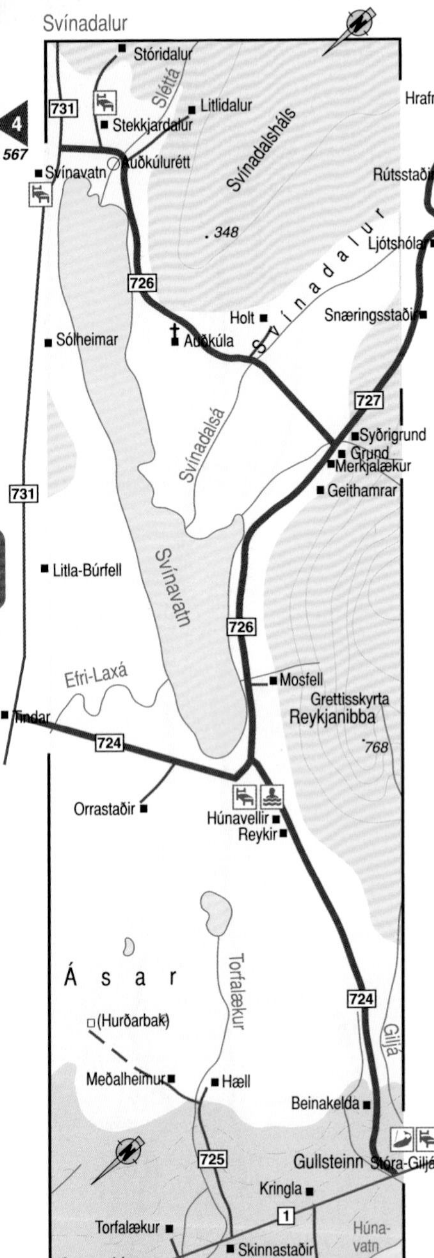

Svínadalur

727 Svínadalsvegur, 8,65 km.

Svínadalur, ("Swine valley") a shallow, broad valley, grassy and fertile, the farms scattered but with good land. *Landnámabók* ("The Book of Settlements") says that the valley got its name from the swine of the settler Ingimundur gamli ("the old"). They vanished one year, but were found the following year, their numbers having increased.

726 Auðkúluvegur, 14,6 km.

Stóridalur, a substantial farm through the ages, 250 m above sea level. The same family has lived there since 1792.

Auðkúla, a church, a parsonage until 1952. A substantial farm, which once owned the whole of Auðkúluheiði moor and Kjölur as far south as the lake Hvítárvatn. The residence of local leaders in the 13th and 14th centuries. The unusual church is octagonal, made of timber.

724 Reykjabraut, 12,8 km.

Reykir, a farm on the Reykjabraut road. Geothermal heat, one of oldest swimming schools in Iceland, swimming teaching having started in 1820. Children's boarding school.

Reykjanibba, (769 m) a mountain above Reykir and Mosfell. On its eastern side are two rhyolite caves called **Grettisskyrta** ("Grettir's shirt") where Grettir is said to have put out his shirt to dry. Long ago the mountain split in two and a large part of it subsided towards the lake, Svínavatn.

Sauðadalur, ("Sheep valley") a valley going south between the mountains Vatnsdalsfjall and Svínadalsfjall. The valley is named for the sheep of the settler Ingimundur gamli ("the old").

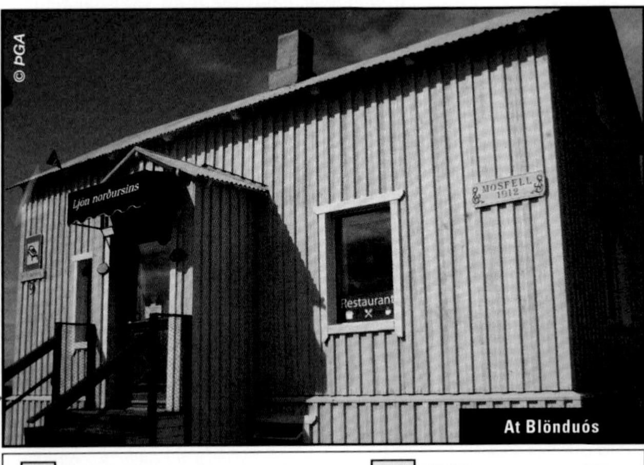

At Blönduós

1 Norðurlandsvegur, p. 67
725 Miðásavegur, p. 67
731 Svínvetningabraut, p. 345

731 SVÍNVETNINGABRAUT

Sólheimaháls, (329 m) long, low ridges east of the Svínavatn lake. West of the ridge are the small lakes Hafratjörn and Lómatjörn, where divers and many kinds of duck can often be seen.

Búrfell, a farm above which are some basalt columns now called Búrfellsfell. Down towards the lake Svínavatn are the "woods" Tindaskógur and Búrfellsskógur, but all that is now left of these is some dwarf birch.

Gunnfríðarstaðir, a farm presented to the local forestry association for tree-planting.

Kagaðarhóll, an imposing farm opposite the southern end of the lake Laxárvatn. There is a fine view from the Hólsberg rock southeast of the farm.

Laxárvatn, a long, narrow trout lake, 2.9 km^2. The level of the lake rose by 1.5 m when the Laxá river was harnessed for hydro-electric power in 1933. Power 480 kW.

Kolkumýrar, *the Book of Settlement* says the a man called Þorbjörn kolka settled there.

Bakásar, the slopes west of the river Blanda, with a few farms.

Mánafoss, waterfall in the river Laxá. In the story of Þorvaldur víðförli ("the widely travelled") it is said that the name comes from Máni the Christian, who caught so many salmon under the falls that he was able to prevent a local famine. Mánafoss is 2.5-3 m high, but rather difficult to reach because of ditches. South of Sauðanes are the Kolkumýrar marshes, grassy pools with low hills in between.

1 **Norðurlandsvegur,** p. 68	74 **Skagastrandarvegur,** p. 322
724 **Reykjabraut,** p. 344	741 **Neðribyggðarvegur,** p. 322

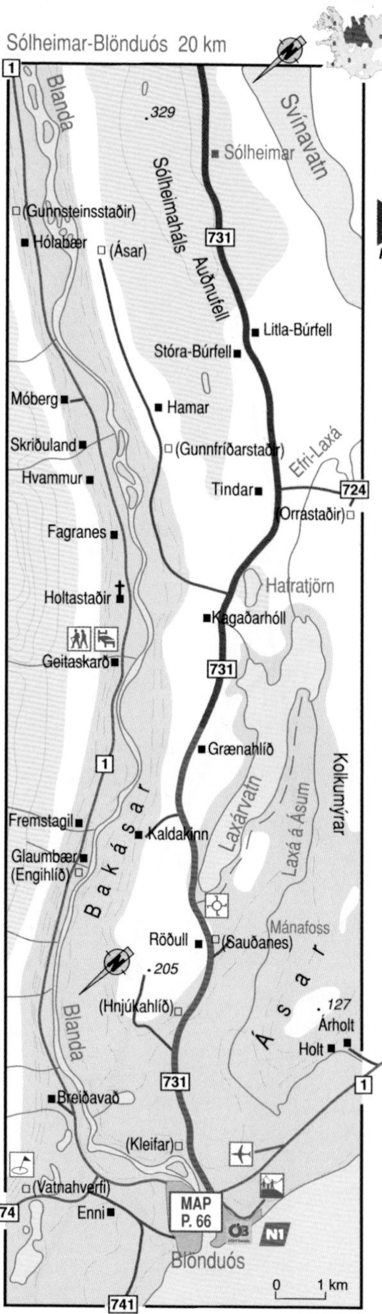

4
P. 567

Ártún-Sólheimar 13 km

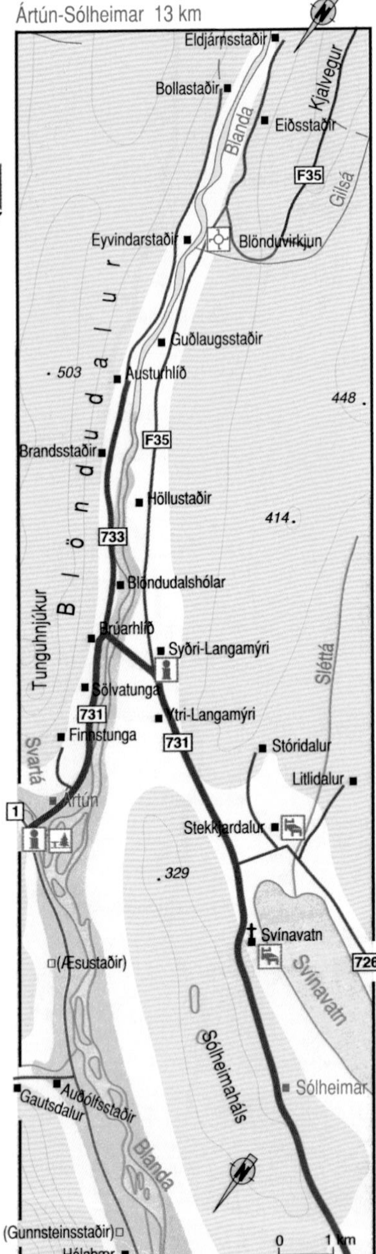

Sólheimar-Árún 13 km

733 Blöndudalsvegur, 10 km.

Eyvindarstaðir, formerly a substantial farm that owned all the land south to the glaciers.

Blöndustöð, a major hydro-electric power plant on the river Blanda, completed 1991. The dams created a huge lake, 30 km^2 on the moors. The plant itself is underground. Power 150 MW.

Gilsá, a river joining the Blanda south of Guðlaugsstaðir. Beginning of the track to Kjalvegur (F35) south across Auðkúluheiði moor. From Kjalvegur there is a jeep-track north of the mountain Sandkúlufell to Stórisandur sands, from where it is possible to descend to either the Vatnsdalur or Víðidalur valleys, or go west via Arnarvatnsheiði moor to the valleys of Borgarfjörður via Kalmanstunga.

Guðlaugsstaðir, a farm where there is a memorial to the professor and doctor, Guðmundur Hannesson (1866-1946), a pioneer in health care and organisation, who was born there. The farm has belonged to the same family since 1680.

Brandsstaðir, a farm, home of Björn Bjarnason, who wrote the *Brandsstaðir annals* covering the years 1783-1858.

Blöndudalshólar, a parsonage until 1880, and church till 1882. Not far from the bridge over the river Blanda.

731 Svínvetningabraut, 33 km.

Blanda, 125 km, one of the longest glacial rivers in Iceland. It comes mainly from the western part of the Hofsjökull glacier, the uppermost sources being below the mountain Blágnípa. Close to the farms it flows through big, wild gorges known as **Blöndugil**. There are only two bridges on the Blanda, one at Blönduós, the other in the lower part of the Blöndudalur valley.

Svínavatn, a farm and church beside a lake of the same name in the Svínadalur valley (see Road 727). There are fish in the lake, which is 11,78 km^2, but the winter ice is often unsafe and some pastors from Auðkúla have been drowned in it. The lake was thought to be haunted.

Interior of the church at Svínavatn.

1 Norðurlandsvegur, p. 69
726 Auðkúluvegur, p. 344
F35 Kjalvegur, p. 456

734 SVARTÁRDALSVEGUR

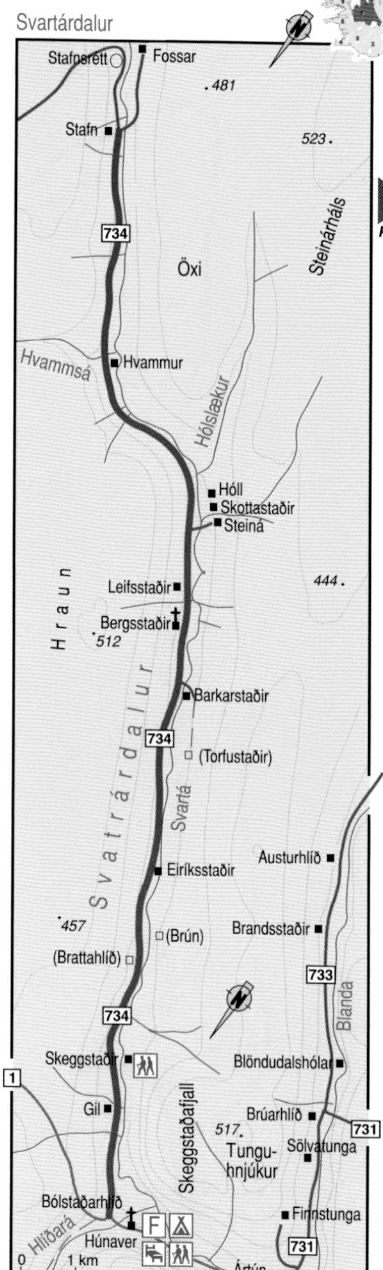

Fossar, ("Waterfalls") a farm in the Fossadalur valley, about 2 km south of Stafnsrétt, a sheep-gathering pen at 320 m above sea level. Long the home of moorland shepherds. From there it is possible to go by jeep to the lake Aðalmannsvatn and Álfgeirstungur, also by another track via Fossabrekka north of the glacier Hofsjökull. Near Fossar is the abandoned farm **Kóngsgarður**, birthplace of Sigurbjörn Sveinsson (1887-1950), popular author of children's books.

Stafn, at a height of 280 m this is one of furthest inland farms in the Svartárdalur valley. Nearby is **Stafnsrétt**, one of the biggest sheep-gathering pens in Iceland, always busy in autumn. A jeep-track leads from there over Kiðaskarð pass to Skagafjörður, and another via Eyvindarstaðaheiði moor south to the river Strangakvísl.

Bergsstaðir, a church and parsonage until the 20th century.

Eiríksstaðir, a farm.

Brattahlíð, an abandoned farm, was once called Eiríksstaðakot, but was changed to Brattahlíð when the house that still stands there was built in 1905.

Brún, an abandoned farm from which came the poet and horseman Sigurður Jónsson (1898-1970), who always added "from Brún" to his name.

Svartárdalur, the easternmost of the valleys in this county leading up to the highlands. Shallow, with little flat land but grassy slopes. **Svartá,** a good fishing river.

Húnaver, a community centre.

Bólstaðarhlíð, a church and substantial farm for centuries. For 300 years, 1528-1825, the home of successive generations of the same family, which produced numerous children, many of whom were famous or influential people in their time. Descendants are still known as the Bólstaðarhlíð family. The mouth of Svartárdalur, where Bólstaðarhlíð stands, is believed by some to be the Ævarsskarð mentioned in the Sagas.

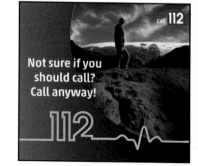

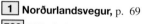

1 **Norðurlandsvegur,** p. 69 731 **Svínvetningabraut,** p. 346
733 **Blöndudalsvegur,** p. 346

4 P. 567

744 Þverárfjallsvegur, 39 km.

Norðurárdalur, a pretty side-valley northeast of the mouth of the Laxárdalur valley. There is a road through it, and over the mountain Þverárfjall to Laxárdalur in Skagafjörður.

Laxá, a good fishing-river, coming from Laxárdalur, a long valley extending to near Bólstaðarhlíð. There were once farms all along it, but now there are only four. This river was often dangerous in floods, and a number of people have drowned there.

Mánaskál, a farm where the settler Hólmgöngu-Máni ("Máni of the islet-duels") is said to have built his farm when he moved from Mánavík on Skagi. He is supposed to be buried in the Mánahaugur mound on Illviðrahnjúkur (969 m) in the Laxárdalur mountains. There are indeed signs of a rock-built mound, but it can supposedly bring bad luck to touch it.

742 Mýravegur, 6 km.

74 Skagastrandarvegur, p. 322

745 Skagavegur, p. 351

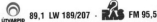

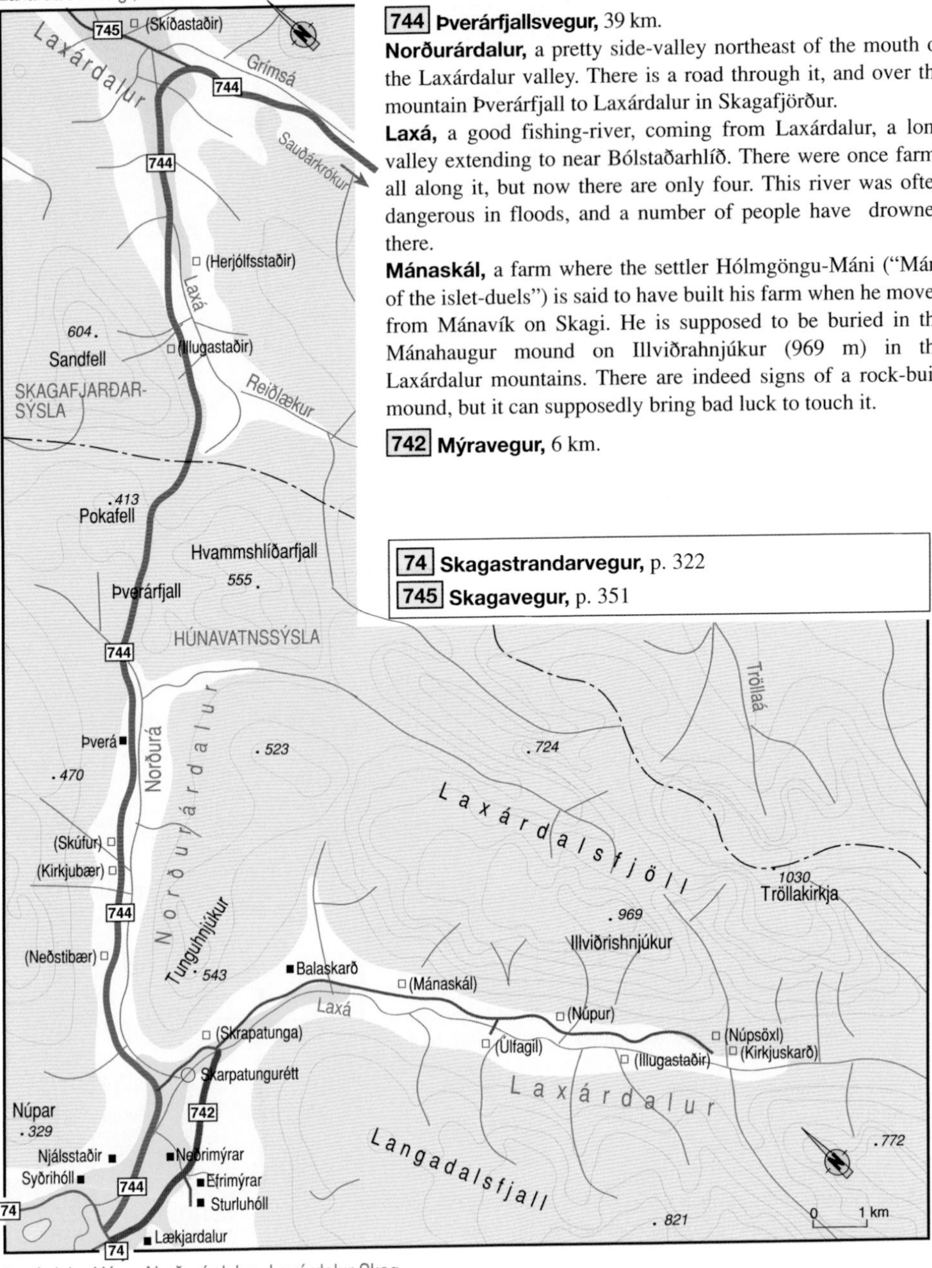

Laxárdalur Hún., Norðurárdalur, Laxárdalur Skag.

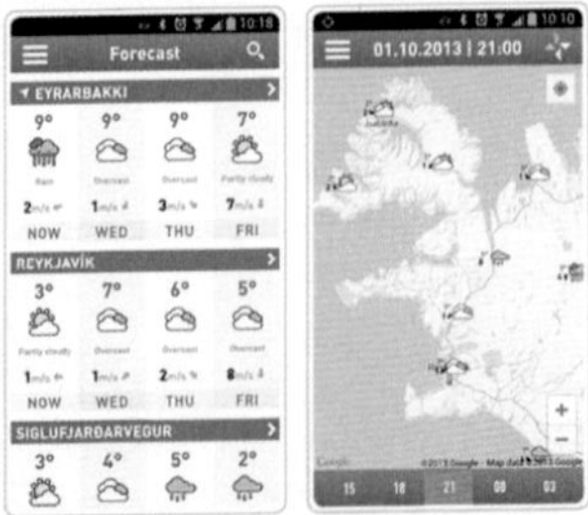

745 SKAGAVEGUR

Kyrpingsfjall, (98 m) gravel ridges rising to the north between the Laxá river and the valley Torfdalur. The southernmost and lowest ridge nearest Laxá is called Gullbrekka, below which is Gullkelda, a deep bog into which the farm Gullbrekka is said to have sunk with its occupants at the death of Þorgerður or Þorbjörg kólka of Kólkunes.

Laxá í Nesjum, a small river with some salmon.

The lighthouse in Kálfshamarsvík.

Kálfshamarsvík, a small bay, north of which is Kálfshamarsnes. Around 1900 there was a fishing station there, and a small settlement, but it was finally abandoned around the time of the depression, 1940. Interesting basalt columns. Signposts bearing the names of the buildings and inhabitants and much other information have been put up in various places in Kálfshamarvík. The signs rest on basalt columns.

Fossá, a waterfall falling from a 20 m high cliff, Króksbjarg, straight to the sea. It is best to see the waterfall from the sea. Just north of the waterfall is an unusual cliff, Bjargastapi.

Króksbjarg, 10 km of cliffs, 40-50 m high. At their southern base is a 16 m thick clay layer, on top of which are an 8 m layer of brown sandstone and a thick layer of basalt which has reversed magnetic polarisation.

Örlygsstaðir, a substantial farm on the Skagi peninsula, one of the so-called Brekkubæir. The home, in the 16th century, of Guðmundur Andrésson, one of the men who killed Clerk Kristján and his Danish followers in 1551 in revenge for the execution of the last Catholic Bishop in Iceland, Jón Arason, and his sons (see Road 45, Kirkjuból).

Hof, a farm and church, home of Jón Árnason (1819-88), librarian and important collector of folktales.

74 Skagastrandarvegur, p. 322

Tjörn-Skagaströnd 25 km

Skagaströnd-Tjörn 25 km

4 P. 567

MAP P. 323

Hóll-Tjörn 40 km

4 P. 567

Selvík, a bay providing shelter for boats, where there was once a fishing station, the remains of which are still visible. It was there that Kolbeinn ungi equipped his fleet for an attack on the Western fjords, resulting in the Flóabardagi battle in 1244.

Selnes, a farm. Jón Norðmann Jónasson (1898–1976) bought the farm and lived there till he died. He was considered peculiar man, wrote some books and had psychic experiences which he held lectures about the subject.

Ketubjörg, a rugged, sheer sea-cliff, the remains of an old volcano, the rock dating probably from the early Ice Age. Very impressive. Northeast of the cliffs is a pillar rock called Kerling ("Old woman").

Keta, a church. In the homefield is a rock, believed to be the home of "hidden people" who often came to the aid of people in distress.

Skagaheiði, wet and marshy moors.

Hraun, the northernmost farm on the west side of Skagafjarðarsýsla county. Nearby is Skagatá, the northern extremity of Skagi.

Ásbúðir, an abandoned farm, with rights to driftwood and eider duck colonies. To the east of the farm is the sea lagoon Ásbúðavatn.

Digrimúli, a basalt hill, with a good view of the Strandafjöll mountains.

Hafnir, a substantial farm into the 20th century, with rights to driftwood, eider duck colonies and seal hunting, from which as many as 20 rowing boats were operated for shark and other fish.

Torfadalsvatn, a good fishing lake.

Tjörn-Hóll 40 km

Sauðárkrókur, (pop. 2,564) a town at the head of Skagafjörður, see p. 326.

Veðramót, a farm. Home of Haraldur Björnsson (1891-1967), the first Icelander to become a professional actor, and Björn Sigurðsson MD (1913-1959), a scientist recognised world-wide for being the first to present theories about slow viral infections, c.f. his PhD thesis, "Immunological studies on paratuberculosis" (1955).

Heiði, a farm in the Gönguskörð valley, birthplace of botanist Stefán Stefánsson (1863-1921), the first headmaster of Menntaskólinn á Akureyri (Akureyri Junior College).

Gönguskörð, a shallow valley or pass at the southern end of the mountain Tindastóll, leading from above Sauðárkrókur to the head of Laxárdalur. On the mountain Tindastóll, near the abandoned farm Breiðsstaðir, about 15 km from Sauðárkrókur, lies a ski slope with a 1,250 m traction lift. Side valleys lead from it south and west into the mountains and on to Húnavatnssýsla. Excellente skiing area.

Hvammur, a church and parsonage.

Laxárdalur, a fairly long (14 km) grassy but rather narrow valley reaching from the Sævarlandsvík bay to Gönguskörð, the pass behind Tindastóll mountain. Through it flows Laxá, a fishing river.

Sævarland, the outermost farm in the Laxárdalur valley at the head of the delightful Sævarlandsvík bay. East of it the mountain Tindastóll ends in the wedge-shaped point Landsendi ("Land's end"). The Sævarlandsstapi crag off-shore near there. The islands Drangey and Málmey can be seen in the fjord in the distance.

Sauðárkrókur-Hóll 34 km

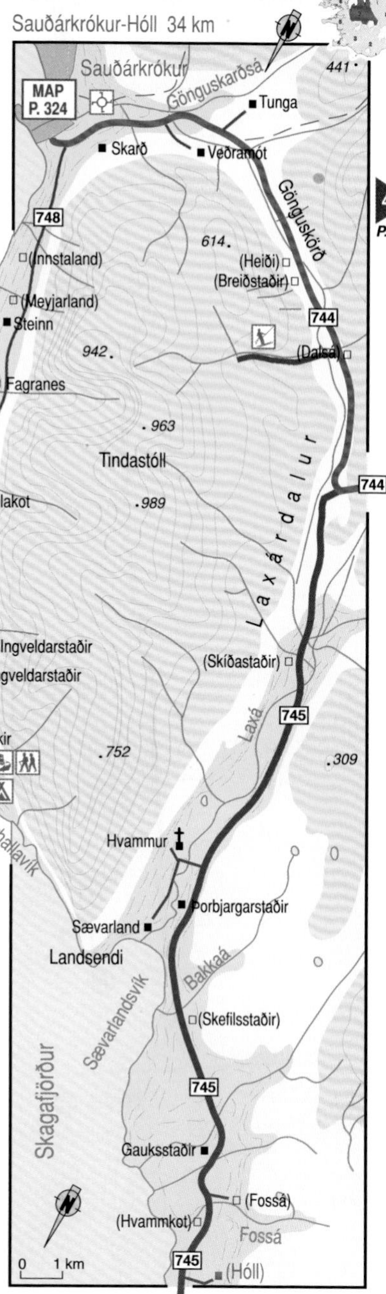

Hóll-Sauðárkrókur 34 km

744 **Þverárfjallsvegur,** p. 348 **748** **Reykjastrandarvegur,** p. 352

4 P. 567

Glerhallavík
Reykjadiskur
Grettislaug
Drangey
Reykir
529
(Sveinskot)
Ytri-Ingveldarstaðir
748
Syðri-Ingveldarstaðir
(Daðastaðir)
Mjólkurá
Hólkot
860
Tindastóll
Skagafjörður
Hólakot
748
Fagranes
942
Reykjaströnd
Steinn
(Meyjarland)
(Innstaland)
476
748
(Skarð)
744
Gönguskarðsá
Gönguskarðsárvirkjun
Sauðárkrókur
MAP P. 324
Sauðá
0 1 km
75
75

Sauðárkrókur-Reykir 17 km

Glerhallavík, a small bay below high cliffs. Famous for its beautiful stones washed out of the rock and polished by the surf. It is against the law to take stones from this protected area.

Grettislaug.

Reykir, a farm on the Reykjaströnd shore, the farm to which Grettir swam from Drangey to fetch fire. A semicircular point of land there is called Reykjadiskur, and on its southern side is the spring **Grettislaug,** where Grettir the strong bathed after swimming from Drangey. Jón Eiríksson of **Fagranes**, known as the Earl of Drangey, has had the area of the spring rebuilt. He has also rebuilt a small boat harbour and fishermen's dwelling as first steps in a programme to develop the area. Boat trips to **Drangey**.

Tindastóll, (989 m) one of the most imposing mountains of Skagafjörður, reaching from the Reykjaströnd coast to the Laxárdalur valley, ca. 20 km. Steep and rugged on the east, but more sloping and grassy on the west. Many folktales are connected with it. One is about the wishing-stone to be found in a well near Glerhallavík bay. It is said to float up every Midsummernight. The view from Tindastóll was the poet Matthías Jochumsson's inspiration in his poem about Skagafjörður. Nearby is the cove Baulubás and in it Bauluhellir ("Cow cave"), which got its name because cows walked through it from Atlastaðir. It used to be the home of sea-monsters. Tindastóll was the home of giants and trolls, their king living there and his daughter at Glerhallavík. One of the giants kidnapped a daughter of the Bishop of Hólar and kept her in his cave.

Reykjaströnd, the coastline north of Sauðárkrókur. A narrow strip of flat land, steep mountainside and rather barren country.

75 **Sauðárkróksbraut,** p. 323 744 **Þverárfjallsvegur,** p. 348

751 Efribyggðarvegur, 12 km.

752 Skagafjarðarvegur, 36,7 km.

Hafgrímsstaðir, there is the base camp for Arctic Rafting river rafting in Jökulsá East and West. They offer trips everyday on both rivers from May to September.

Mælifellshnjúkur, (1,138 m) one of the highest and most imposing mountains of Skagafjörður. It is said that 10 counties can be seen from there. A marked walking route.

Mælifell, a church and parsonage, a manor farm of old. The settlement land of Vékell hamrammi.

Bakkaflöt, a centre of river rafting for the rivers Austari-Jökulsá and Vestari Jökulsá, two rivers that are fed from the glacier Hofsjökull.

Skíðastaðir, birthplace of Pálmi Hannesson (1898-1956), a well-known naturalist, member of parliament and headmaster of Menntaskólinn í Reykjavík (Reykjavík College, formerly "The learned school").

Reykjafoss, a sizeable, pretty waterfall in the Svartá river, the biggest river of the district. There is a walking path following the fence at Vindheimamelar, passing Reykjafoss and a bridge to Svartá and on to Fosslaug, a natural pool.

Húseyjarkvísl, a deep and smooth-flowing river, formed from Svartá and other streams from the western mountains.

Hestavígshamar, ("Horse killing crag") a single crag on the west bank of Húseyjarkvísl. Former assembly site.

754 Héraðsdalsvegur, 7,6 km.

753 Vindheimavegur, 6,88 km.

Tungusveit, the district between the Héraðsvötn lakes to the east and the rivers Húseyjarkvísl and Svartá to the west. Some high rocky ridges, with marsh and moorland. About 200 m high in the north and 350 m in the south. Known as **Reykjatunga** in the north and **Eggjar** farther south.

Steinsstaðir, a farm in the Tungusveit district. Birthplace of Sveinn Pálsson, doctor and naturalist (1762-1840), who was the first person to make important discoveries about the movements of glaciers. Geothermal heat on the farm land at Steinsstaðalaug pool, where swimming was taught from 1822.

Reykir, church and old manor farm. Much geothermal heat. A swimming pool was built there in 1882. There is so much heat that the churchyard is actually "cozy", being probably the only warm graveyard in the world. The farmer, Kristján Jóhannesson, has built a house in the old style, of turf and stone, with a panelled interior, where he has set up his personal collection of old objects.

Kirkjuhóll, there was one of Icelands most know poet, Stephan G. Stephansson (1853–1927), born.

1 Norðurlandsvegur, p. 70 **75 Sauðárkróksbraut,** p. 323

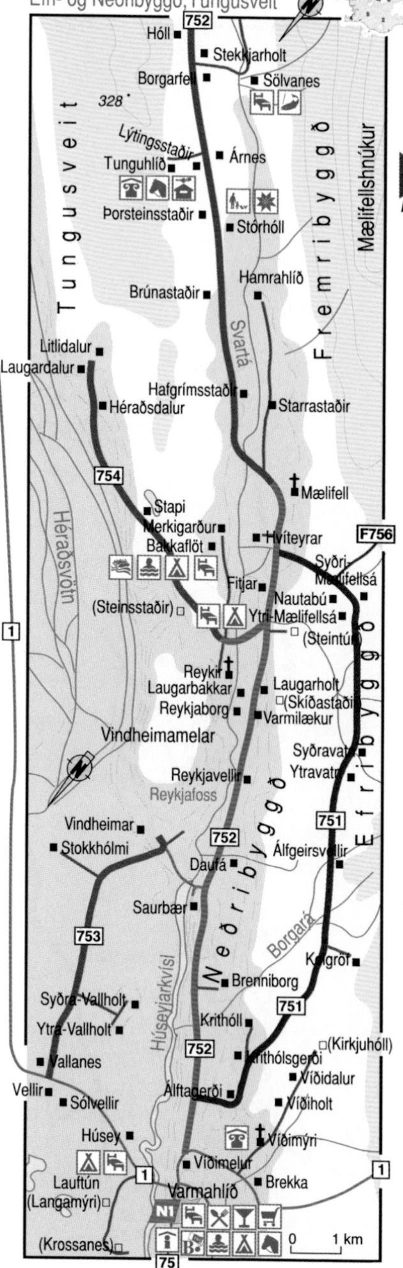

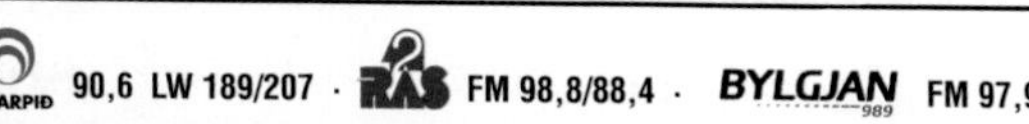

5 P. 568

Skagafjarðadalir-Kjálki

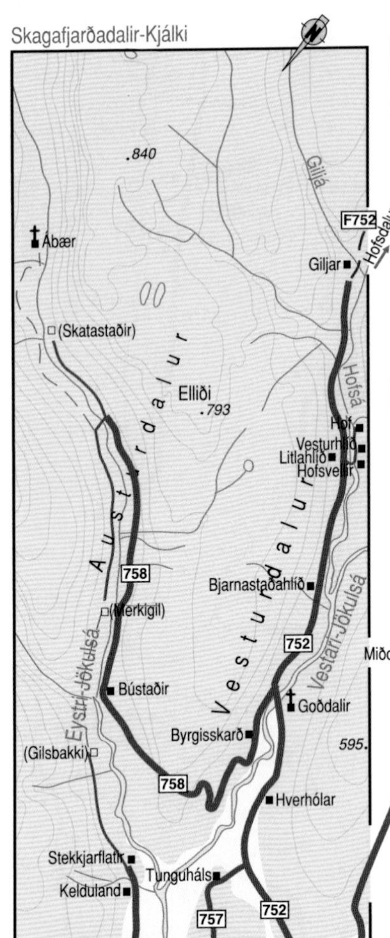

Kjálki-Skagafjarðardalir

752 **Skagafjarðarvegur,** 36,7 km.

Vesturdalur, a long, narrow valley, down which flows the mostly clear river Hofsá to join the Vestari-Jökulsá river. Several farms. From Þorljótsstaðir, abandoned since 1944, there is a jeep-track to Laugafell and the Hofsjökull glacier.

Hof, an old manor farm, the settlement land of Eiríkur Hróaldsson. The farm once owned land far into the highlands and gave its name to the glacier Hofsjökull.

Hofsdalur, a narrow valley, uninhabited above Goðdalir, through which flows the glacial river Vestari-Jökulsá.

Goðdalir, a church, and a parsonage until 1907, an old manor farm. The mountain above is called **Goðdalakista** ("Goðdalir's chest") (595 m). A jeep-track from there south to the mountains.

758 **Austurdalsvegur,** 19 km.

759 **Kjálkavegur,** 9,8 km.

Austurdalur, a 50 km long valley, narrow but fairly grassy, between high mountains. The river Eystri-Jökulsá flows down it, often in a deep gorge, difficult to cross. There is now a bridge between Merkigil and Ábær. The valley used to have a large number of inhabitants, now there is only one farm there.

Ábær, a church on farmland that has been abandoned since 1941. A famous ghost, Ábæjar-Skotta, who caused farmers in Skagafjörður all kinds of trouble, came from there. She was said to be seen in company with the ghost of a half-skinned bull calf, Þorgeirsboli, and when she was tired, she would sit on the skin he dragged behind him and let him pull her along.

Merkigil, ("Mark canyon") the only inhabited farm in Austurdalur east of the river Eystri-Jökulsá. Gets its name from the magnificent rocky gorge through which the river runs nearby.

Tunguháls, the outermost farm in Tungusveit. The Rev. Jónas Jónasson (1856-1918), scholar and author, usually associated with Hrafnagil in Eyjafjörður, was brought up there. Birthplace of the poet Elínborg Lárusdóttir (1891-1973).

755 **Svartárdalsvegur,** 6,7 km.

757 **Villinganesvegur,** 3,8 km

Kjálki, the area along the east of the river Héraðsvötn, from the river Norðurá to Merkigil in Austurdalur.

Flatatunga, a farm in the Kjálki area. Some very old wood carvings were preserved there, thought to be a detail from "The Last Judgement", which was carved in the 11th century in Byzantine style. Now in the National Museum.

Tyrfingsstaðir, an abandoned farm.

1 **Norðurlandsvegur,** p. 72 **F752** **Skagafjarðarleið,** p. 470-471

Hólar, Hjaltadalur

767 Hólavegur, 11 km að Hólum en 13,13 km að Hofi.

Hjaltadalur, a rather long, narrow valley, enclosed by high mountains (1,000-1,200 m) with passes and side-valleys. Shelterd and grassy.

Hof, a farm, the home of the settler Hjalti Þórðarson, for whom a magnificent funeral feast was held, according to "The Book of Settlements".

Hólar, (pop. 76) one of the Icelandic nation's principal historical, cultural, and ecclesiastical sites. People in the North still speak of travelling "home" to Hólar. Bishopric 1106-1798, and again from 1986. Cathedral college 1106-1802. Printing press 1530-1800. Seat of many famous bishops, e.g. Jón Ögmundarson, 1106-21, Jón Arason, 1524-50, the last Catholic Bishop in Iceland, and Guðbrandur Þorláksson, 1571-1627, whose printing of the first Icelandic Bible was crucial to the preservation of the language. The Cathedral, the oldest stone church in Iceland, built of red sandstone from the mountain Hólabyrða, consecrated in 1763 and reconsecrated 1988 after extensive renovation. Many ancient relics. A turf farmhouse **Nýibær** near the top of the field, built in 1860, has been in the care of the National Museum since 1956. Auðunarstofa, reconstruction of a house built in Hólar in early 14th century which lasted for 500 years. Traditional Norwegian log-stave house with turf roof. Bishop's office. Houses a collection of old books printed in Hólar and some of the Cathedral's treasures. Archeological research is being carried out at Hólar and in **Kolkuós**, the old harbour. Extensive program of concerts and church services throughout the summer, culminating in the Hólar festival mid August. An agricultural college was established at Hólar in 1882 which was the foundation of the present University College, specializing in equine science, rural tourism, aquatic science, archeology and cultural heritage.

Víðines, near Hólar. Site of the 1208 battle between the poet Kolbeinn Tumason and the forces of Bishop Guðmundur the good, in which Kolbeinn was slain.

Viðvík, a church and at one time a parsonage. In ancient times the home of Þorbjörn öngull, who killed Grettir the strong. Later the home of Jón Pétursson (1733-1801), a doctor famous for his cures and a book on medicine.

768 Hjaltadalsvegur, 12,14 km.

Reykir, the innermost farm in Hjaltadalur. It has two warm springs, Biskupslaug ("Bishop's pool"), a stone-built bathing pool of 42°-43°C where it is said the bishops bathed, and Hjúalaug ("Servants pool"). In 1928 they made a turf-built pool at Hjúalaug for teaching swimming.

769 Ásavegur, 7 km.

Neðri-Ás, ancient home of Þorvaldur Spak-Böðvarsson, the first Icelander to build a church at his farm, in 984. The site still bears the name Bænhús ("Chapel"). Excavations confirm site of an early church. Roadside memorial.

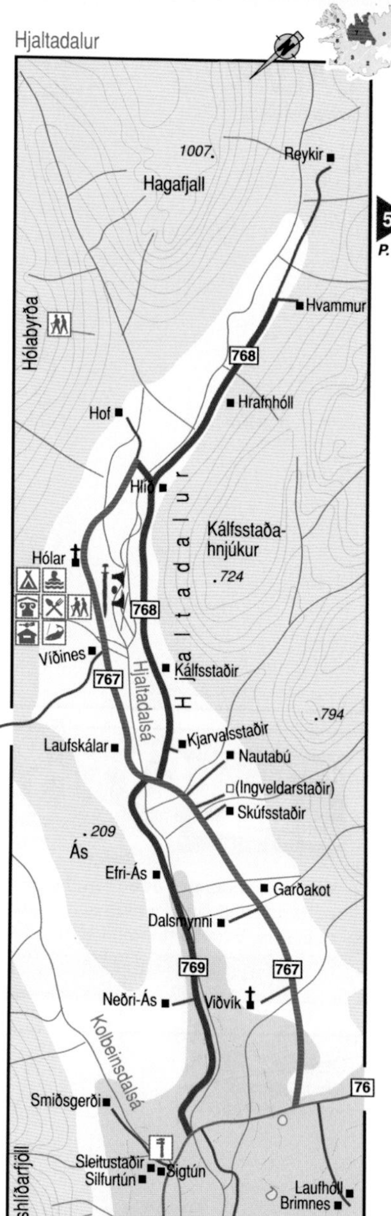

5 P. 568

76 Siglufjarðarvegur, p. 328

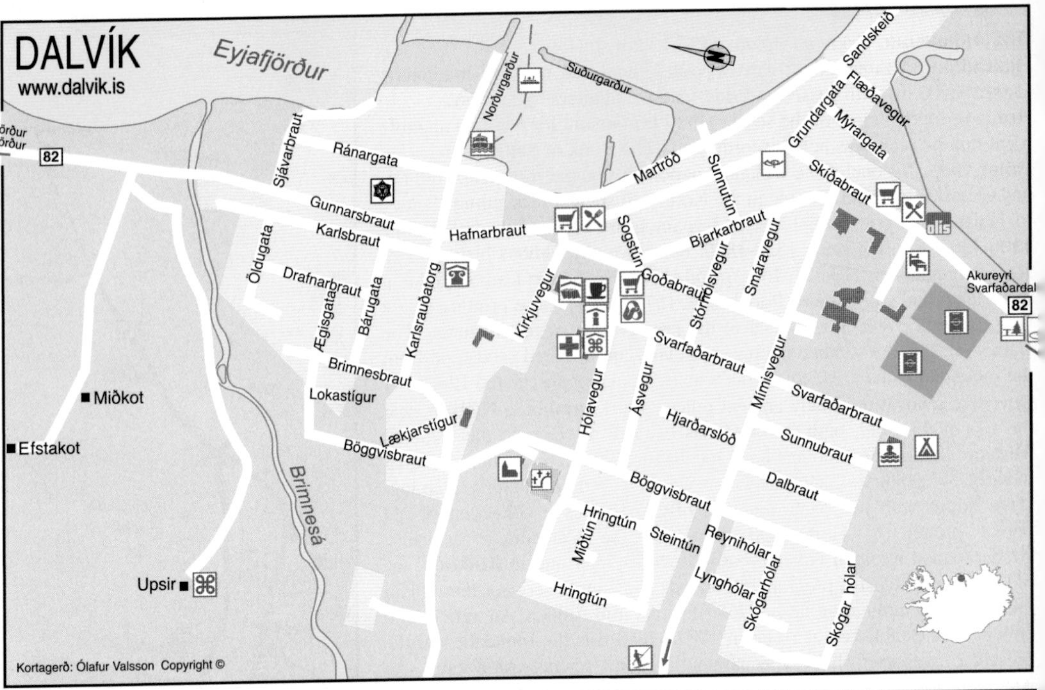

DALVÍK

www.dalvik.is

Eyjafjörður
Siglufjörður
Ólafsfjörður
82
Norðurgarður
Suðurgarður
Sandskeið
Grundargata
Flæðavegur
Mýrargata
Skíðabraut
Sjávarbraut
Ránargata
Martröð
Sunnutún
Gunnarsbraut
Karlsbraut
Hafnarbraut
Öldugata
Drafnarbraut
Ægisgata
Bárugata
Karlsrauðatorg
Kirkjuvegur
Sogstún
Goðabraut
Bjarkarbraut
Stórhólsvegur
Smáravegur
Akureyri
Svarfaðardal
82
Svarfaðarbraut
Mímisvegur
Brimnesbraut
Lokastígur
Lækjarstígur
Böggvisbraut
Hólavegur
Ásvegur
Hjarðarslóð
Sunnubraut
Dalbraut
Miðkot
Efstakot
Brimnesá
Böggvisbraut
Hringtún
Miðtún
Steintún
Reynihólar
Lynghólar
Skógarhólar
Skógar hólar
Hringtún
Upsir

Kortagerð: Ólafur Valsson Copyright ©

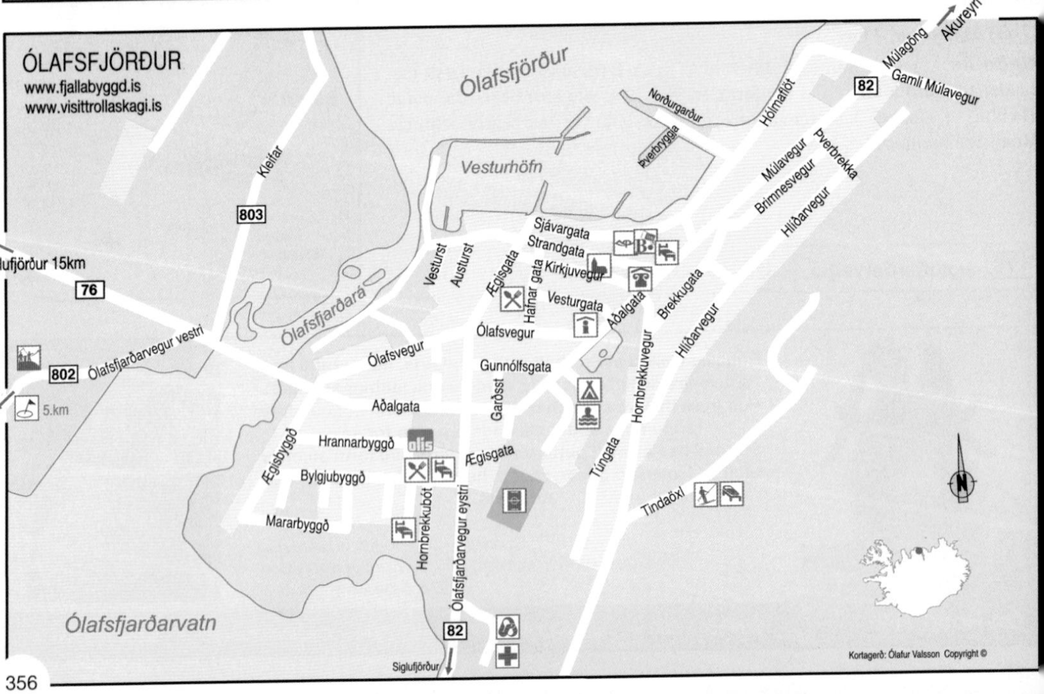

ÓLAFSFJÖRÐUR

www.fjallabyggd.is
www.visittrollaskagi.is

Ólafsfjörður
Múlagöng
Akureyri
82
Gamli Múlavegur
Norðurgarður
Hólmaflöt
Þverbryggja
Vesturhöfn
Kleifar
803
Múlavegur
Þverbrekka
Brimnesvegur
Hlíðarvegur
Sjávargata
Strandgata
Kirkjuvegur
Siglufjörður 15km
76
Vesturst
Austurst
Ægisgata
Hafnar gata
Vesturgata
Aðalgata
Brekkugata
Ólafsfjarðará
Ólafsvegur
Ólafsvegur
Hlíðarvegur
Ólafsfjarðarvegur vestri
802
5.km
Gunnólfsgata
Hornbrekkuvegur
Aðalgata
Garðsst
Hrannarbyggð
Ægisbyggð
Ægisgata
Bylgjubyggð
Túngata
Tindaöxl
Mararbyggð
Hornbrekkubót
Ólafsfjarðarvegur eystri
Ólafsfjarðarvatn
82
Siglufjörður

Kortagerð: Ólafur Valsson Copyright ©

Árskógsströnd, the coast from the abandoned farm Hillur north to Hámundarstaðaháls ridge. Broad, grassy lowland, many farms and fishing-villages. Árskógsströnd comprises the villages of **Hauganes** and **Árskógssandur**, each with a population of under 120. The ferry Sæfari plies between Árskógssandur and the island of Hrísey.

Fagriskógur, the outermost farm on the section of coast known as Gálmaströnd. The poet and playwright Davíð Stefánson (1895–1964) "from Fagriskógur", one of Iceland´s best-loved writers, was from there. Monument.

Kötlufjall, (964 m) the mountain above Fagriskógur, with many south-sloping terraces.

Arnarnes, a farm. The painter Kristín Jónsdóttir (1888-1959) came from there.

811 Hjalteyrarvegur, 3 km. **812 Bakkavegur,** 6 km.

Hjalteyri, a fishing-village and once a herring processing station.

Hvammsfjall, the northernmost of a fine row of peaks reminiscent of enormous house gables. Most of the peaks and the passes between them take their names from farms: Hofsskarð, Þríklakkar, Þrastarhólmshnjúkur, Hallgilsstaðahnjúkur, Staðarskarð above Möðruvellir, ending in Fálkahaus or Fornhagaöxl (703 m), an imposing rocky saddle.

Hof, one of outermost farms in the Hörgárdalur valley. Home of the botanist and folklorist Ólafur Davíðsson (1862-1903). He drowned in the river Hörgá.

813 Möðruvallavegur, 3,9 km.

Möðruvellir, a substantial farm of great historical importance for many centuries. Church and parsonage. A monastery was founded there in 1296, it was the seat of governors 1797–1874, and from 1888 to 1902 a high school, which was then moved to Akureyri and later became the Junior College of Akureyri. The poets Bjarni Thorarensen (1786–1841) and Davíð Stefánsson from Fagriskógur (1895-1964) are buried at Möðruvellir. Birthplace of Hannes Hafstein (1861–1922), poet and the first Icelandic Minister of State, Jón Sveinsson (Nonni) (1857-1944), author of many books in Icelandic and German, whose books have been translated to more than 40 languages, Hulda Á. Stefánsdóttir (1897–1989), writer and headmistress, and Steindór Steindórsson (1902–1997), writer, naturalist and headmaster. The church, built 1868, is one of the biggest country churches in Iceland. There have been more serious fires at Möðruvellir than anywhere else in Iceland.

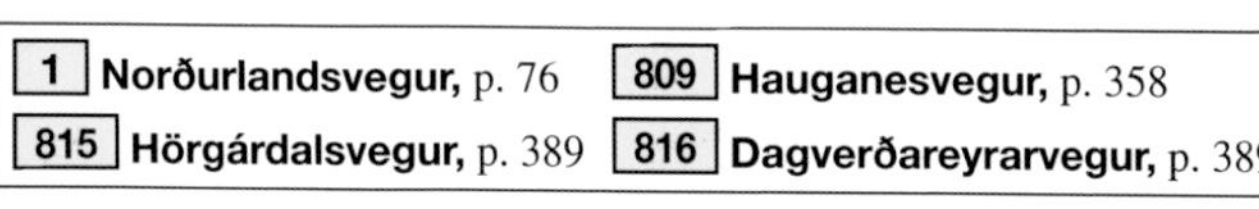

1 **Norðurlandsvegur,** p. 76
809 **Hauganesvegur,** p. 358
815 **Hörgárdalsvegur,** p. 389
816 **Dagverðareyrarvegur,** p. 389

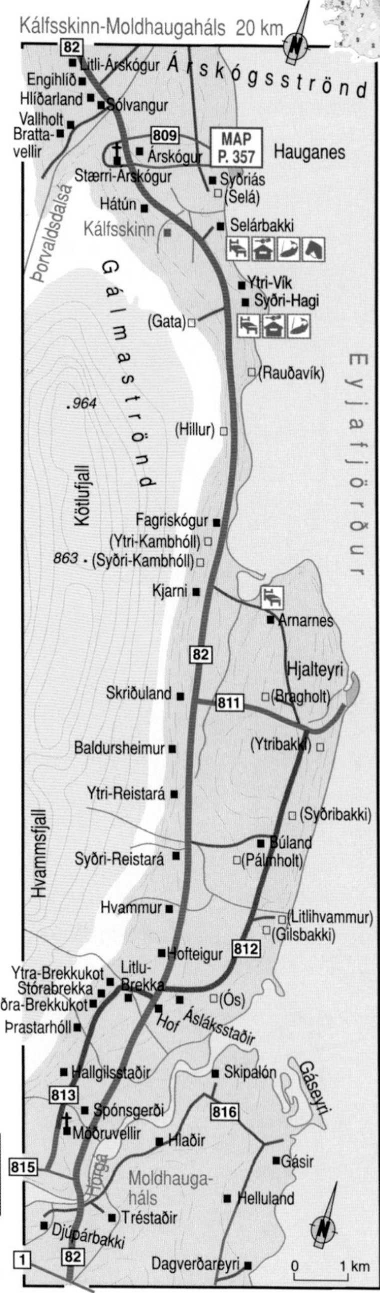

5 P. 568

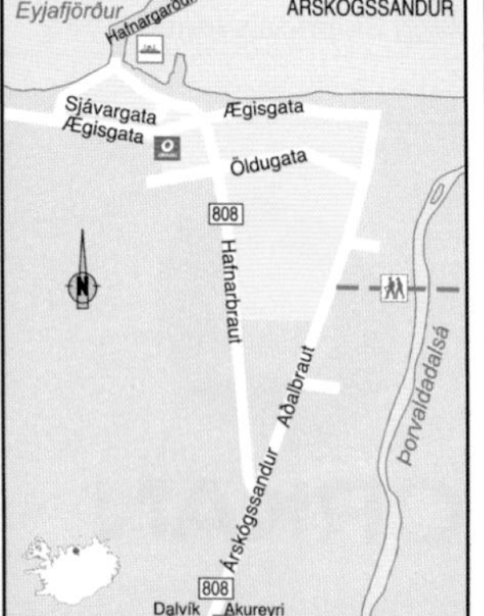

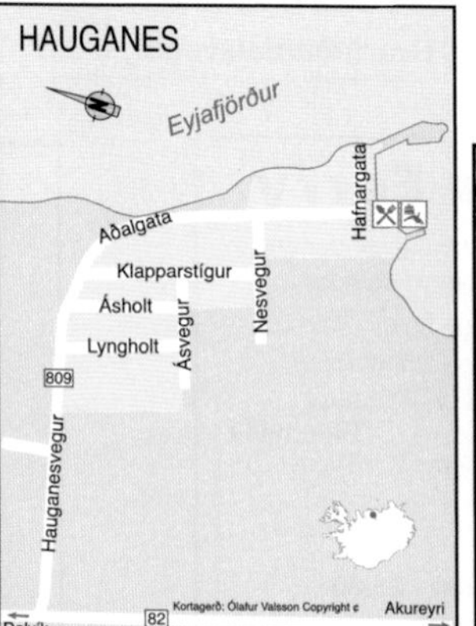

5 P. 568

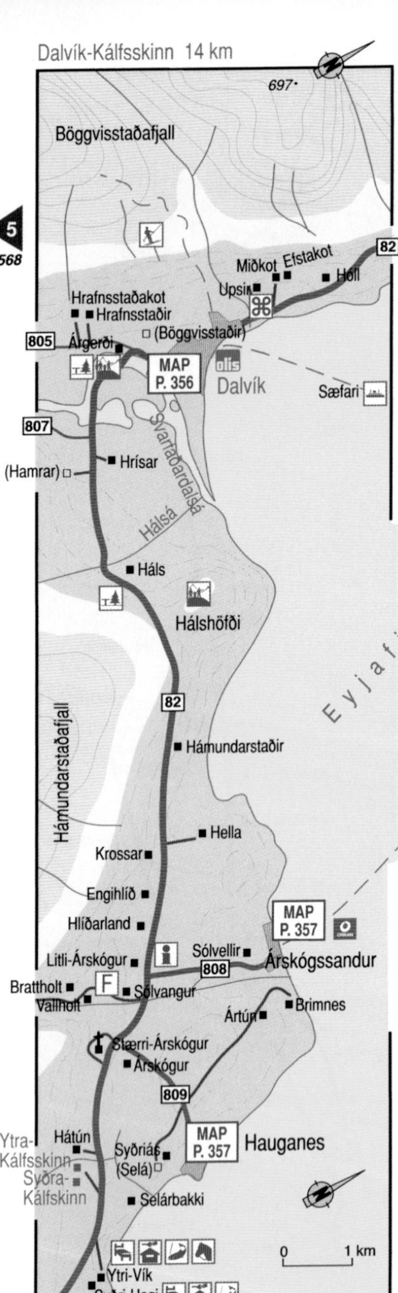

Hámundarstaðaháls, separates Árskógsströnd and Svarfaðardalur.

Hámundarstaðir, the outermost farm on Árskógsströnd, where the settlers Hámundur heljarskinn ("death's hide") and Helgi magri ("the lean") lived during their first winter in Eyjafjörður. South of the farm is a mountain, probably the Sólarfjall ("Sun mountain") mentioned in *Landnámabók*, ("The Book of Settlements") now called Hámundarstaðafjall. Wild primula (*Primula egaliksensis*), found nowhere else in Iceland, grows there.

Hrísey, (pop. 153) the second biggest island off Iceland, 8.0 km^2, ca. 2 km from Helluhöfði point on Árskógsströnd. Hrísey has a surface of approximately 11.5 square km. The island is approx. 7 km long and 2.5 km broad in the broadest place. North of the lighthouse is the highest point measuring 110 m. This highest point is named "Bratti" and from it there are rubble slopes towards the sea. Numerous man made embankments lie all over the island, the longest being almost 3 km long. These embankments are believed to be very old and some believe that they may have served as fences in the olden days. The" leylines" on the island are by many considered to be a spectacular source of energy and many visitors as well as inhabitants feel that this raw energy of the earth "charges their battery" in a unique way. Many birds nest on the island and because of the reservation of the wild fowl life the birds are unusually tame, especially the ptarmigan. Visitors must keep to marked walking paths. It is also possible to take trips on a hay cart towed by a tractor around the village and its surroundings. A village at the southern end is the only occupied part. Fishing and fish processing are the main industries. Geothermal heat. Quarantine centre imported pets. **www.hrisey.net**

808 Árskógssandsvegur, 2 km.

809 Hauganesvegur, 2,6 km.

Kálfsskinn, a farm where Hrærekur, king of the Upplendings in Norway, is said to be buried in the mound called **Hrærekshóll**. Two other kings lie buried in Iceland, the twin brothers Geirmundur and Hámundur heljarskinn (see road 590, Skarð). Monument.

805 Svarfaðardalsvegur, s. 387 | **807 Skíðadalsvegur,** s. 388

82 ÓLAFSFJARÐARVEGUR

Ólafsfjarðarmúli, the outermost mountain spur and cliffs between Eyjafjörður and Ólafsfjörður, ca. 400 m high, steep and with scree. Good view, the island Grímsey visible in clear weather. Landslides and avalanches can be expected. Tunnel opened 1991.
Hálfdanarhurð, a reddish patch on the slopes of Ólafsfjarðarmúli. Associated with the Rev. Hálfdan Narfason and his dealings with giants, trolls and the Devil (see Road 76, Fell and Málmey).
Mígindi, ("Pissing") a waterfall on Ólafsfjarðarmúli.
Sauðakot, an abandoned cottage farm. Monument to the last occupants.
Karlsá, an abandoned farm on the Upsaströnd coast. Monument to Eyvindur Jónsson (1678-1746), boatbuilder, said to have been the first Icelander to build a decked ocean-going ship.
Upsir, a farm above Dalvík, parsonage until 1851 and church until recently, when it was moved to Dalvík. Birthplace of Bjarni Pálsson (1719-79), Surgeon General (See Road 62, Svefneyjar.). The peak Upsi above the farm.
Upsaströnd, the coast line from Dalvík to Ólafsfjarðarmúli.
Dalvík, (pop. 1,334) a town with fishing, fish processing and trading. Good harbour. Community centre, museum, modern swimming pool with spectacular view. Some industry. In the summer of 1934 an earthquake destroyed or damaged most of the houses in the area. Hot spring domestic heating since 1969. The second weekend of August each year, local fishing and fish processing companies join forces to offer a great feast of seafood dishes and a programme of entertainment, all for free! The Great Fish Day is most certainly a day you do not want to miss. At Dalvík you may also find the Hvol museum. Quite a uniqe museum that is devided into three main parts including a room that is dedicated to Iceland's tallest man (2,34 m), a polar bear and birds as Dalvik's closest environment comprimises the Svarfaðardalur Nature Reserve is an area of about 8 square km. of wetland. Within the reserve are dry river-banks as well as marshes with sedge bogs, ditches and fertile ponds with reeds. This natural environment provides an excellent habitat for many species of breeding birds. (More information on www.dalvik.is or www.visittrollaskagi.is)
Háls, farm and birthplace of Pastor Friðrik Friðriksson (1868–1961) founder of the Icelandic YMCA in Reykjavík 1899. Memorial nearby.

803 **Kleifavegur,** p. 362 | 805 **Svarfaðardalsvegur,** p. 387
807 **Skíðadalsvegur,** p. 388

Ólafsfjörður-Dalvík 19 km

Hvannadalabjarg
Fossdalur
Arnfinnsfjall (Finnurinn)
Eyjafjörður
Ytriá
(Syðriá)
803
Ólafsfjörður
Ólafsfjarðarmúli
82
Ólafsfjörður
Brimnes
MAP P. 356
·981
Mígindisfoss
Hálfdanar-hurð
·1078
·1089
(Sauðakot)
82
·1012
Sauðanes-hnjúkar
(Sauðanes)
Drangar
·943
Karlsá
Upsaströnd
697·
(Karlsá)
Höll
Brimnesá
Miðkot
Efstakot
Upsir
Sæfari
Böggvisstaðafjall
MAP P. 356
Dalvík
Hrafnsstaðir
Hrafnsstaðakot
Árgerði
Svarfaðardalsá
805
Hrísar
Syðraholt
Ytraholt
Hamar
Háls
82
Helgafell
Skáldalækur
Ingvarir
Laugasteinn
Tjörn
807
0 1 km

Dalvík-Ólafsfjörður 19 km

5 P. 568

Grímsey

Grímsey, (pop. 67) a green island off Iceland's north coast, is the country's northernmost point. Grímsey, with its rich fishing grounds and rich bird life, is probably best known for its geographic position, right on the Arctic Circle. People travel from far and wide simply to step across that line. The island is 5.3 km in area, and its highest point is 105 m above sea level. It lies 41km off the Icelandic mainland. The islanders are cheerful and energetic. The local economy centres on the fisheries. Grímsey produces especially fine saltfish (salted cod), a delicacy in southern Europe and South America.

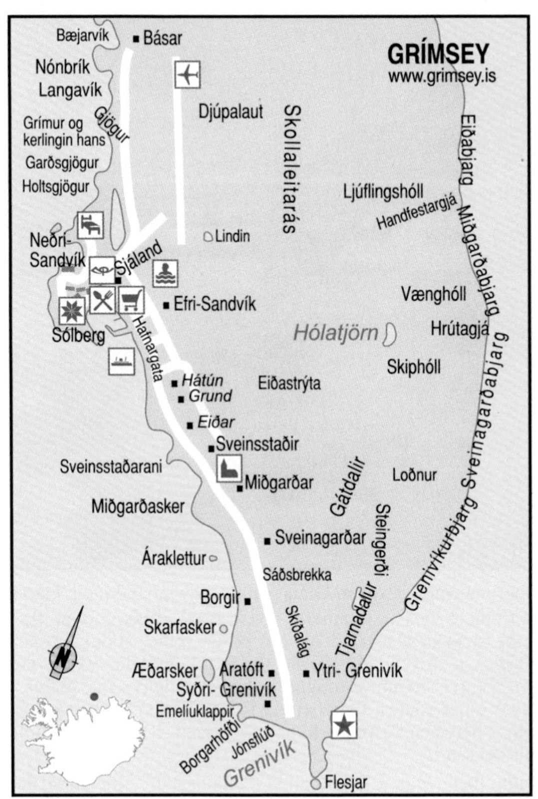

Múli, the community centre, houses a primary school, community hall, library, and health-care centre. Health-care services are provided by doctors from Akureyri on the mainland.

Miðgarðar Church was built in 1867, using driftwood (timber was always in short supply in Iceland). Recently renovated and painted in its original colours, the church is a fine building. The pastor of Dalvík now serves the parish.

An excellent swimming pool opened in 1989. Búðin general store serves the islanders' needs, with a wide range of goods. The island has two guesthouses, they are open all year round. In 1998 the crafts gallery Sól was opened by women on the island; it is open in summer on the days when the ferry calls at the island. The Krían restaurant, is open in summer.

The Sæfari ferry sails from Dalvík to Grímsey three days a week all year round. Regular flights are also operated three days a week in winter, and seven days a week in summer.

The islanders have their own "national" festival on November 11th each year, to mark the birthday of Dr. Daníel Willard Fiske, the island's American benefactor. Having seen Grímsey from the sea, Dr. Fiske was impressed that people lived on this remote island, and also by the fact that they were keen chess players! Around 1900, Dr. Fiske gave the Grímsey islanders the largest gift of money that Icelanders have ever received.

It is said that Grímsey (= Grímur's Island) got its name from a certain Grímur, the first settler on the island. Grímur's brother Kolbeinn is also commemorated by an island named after him, Kolbeinsey. Grímur is believed to have built a heathen temple at Kirkjuhóll, and according to folklore he wanted to be buried there, with a view of the sea and land. He is said to be buried with his wife on a cliff top at Sandvíkurgjögur.

Grímsey is said to be the home of many elves or "hidden people," whose church is supposed to be at Nónbrík.

At Prestaskvompa (Priest's Hollow) is a cave that passes under the whole island. Its name comes from the legend that a pastor rowed into the cave with four companions to explore: none of them was ever seen again.

Lágheiði-Ólafsfjörður 19 km

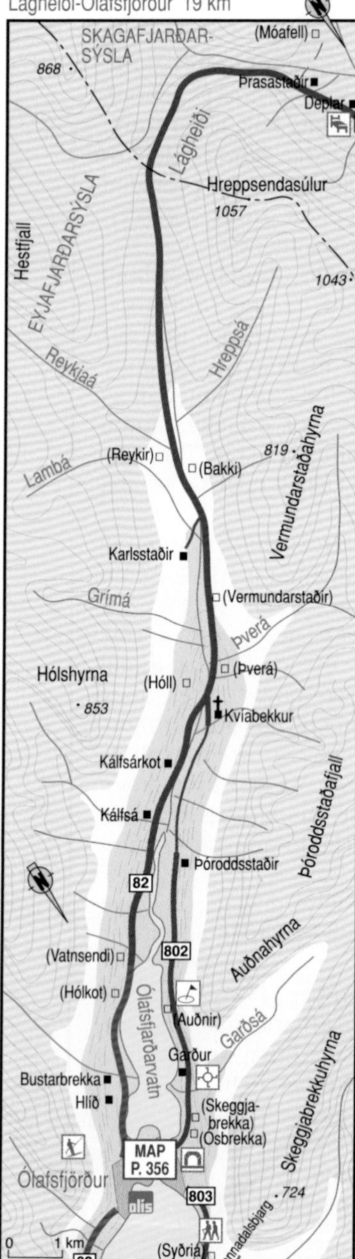

Ólafsfjörður-Lágheiði 19 km

Héðinsfjörður

© PGA

Reykir, the innermost farm in Ólafsfjörður, now abandoned. Geothermal heat. From there lies a mountain road, steep, 900m, over the heath Reykjaheiði to Svarfaðardalur. An old postal route, about 4 hours from farm to farm via Reykjaheiði. From the Svarfaðardalur valley the route goes from Böggvisstöðum throught the valley Böggvisstaðadalur. There are also two other routes. One between Ólafsfjörður and Svarfaðardalur and the other between Grímubrekkur and Drangi. It is also possible to go via Klaufabrekkur.

Hvanndalir, there was a field called "Ódáinsakur", meaning deathless meadow, where the eating of some of the vegetation gave eternal life. The farm there was abandoned when this "curse of eternal life" became too much to bear. Ruins of the farm still remain.

Kvíabekkur, a church and a parsonage until 1914. Around 1330 Lárentíus, Bishop of Hólar, founded a sort of old folks home there for retired priests. The home of governors, e.g. Þorkell Fjeldsted (1740-96), who was one of three men on a committee appointed by the Danish king in 1770 to investigate conditions in Iceland.

802 Garðsvegur, 2 km. From there lie the **Héðinsfjarðargöng**, 6,9 km long tunnel, connecting Siglufjörður and Ólafsjörður. Opened in 2010.

803 Kleifavegur, 2,7 km.

Gunnólfsá, a farm on the west of Ólafsfjörður, now a small village called Kleifar.

Ólafsfjörður, see p. 332.

76 Siglufjarðarvegur, p. 332

Midnight sun in Ólafsfjörður.

Stífla, ("Dam") the main valley of the Austur-Fljót district, taking its name from the Stífluhólar hills which block the valley. They were formed by landslides from the mountain Strengur on the east. A dam was built there when Skeiðsfoss was harnessed.

789 Sléttuvegur, 6,7 km.

Skeiðsfoss, a waterfall in the river Stífluá, harnessed for electricity for the town of Siglufjörður 1945. Most of the valley went under water.

Knappsstaðir, a church on land originally settled by Þórður knappur. The oldest wooden church in Iceland, consecrated 1840.

Lundur, a farm, birthplace of the novelist Guðrún frá Lundi (1887-1975), one of Iceland's most prolific and popular writers.

Hvarfdalur, a valley.

Hreppsendasúlur, (1,057 m) the mountain to the north of the Lágheiði moor.

Lágheiði, (409 m) a moor with a narrow road between the Fljót district and Ólafsfjörður. Grassy, but snowy in winter and often unpassable.

76 Siglufjarðarvegur, p. 330

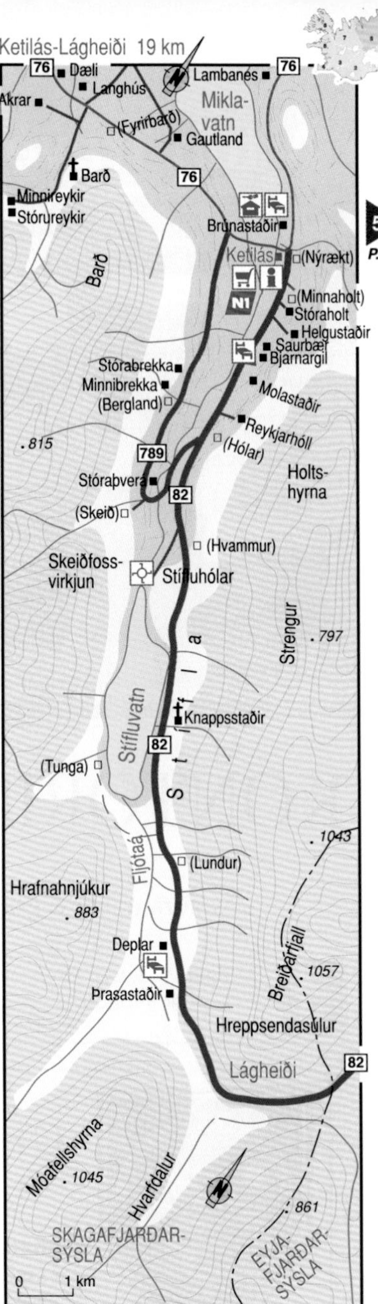

5
P. 568

Lágheiði-Ketilás 19 km

83 GRENIVÍKURVEGUR

Látraströnd, the coast of Eyjafjörður north of the village Grenivík, near Gjögurtá. Steep cliffs below the mountains. Formerly several farms and fishermen's homes but now all abandoned except one near Grenivík.

Kaldbakur, (1,167 m) the highest mountain on the Látrarströnd coast and the most impressive on the east of Eyjafjörður, a striking feature of the view north from Akureyri.

Grenivík, (pop. 274, 364 in the Grýtubakkahreppur district) a fishing village that began to form around 1900. Grenivík includes an elementary school, playschool, community centre, swimming pool, camping area, retirement home, health clinic, church and accommodations for travellers. There is a shop in the area, a savings bank, post office, hairdresser, dried fish factory, fish factory, garage, boat mechanic, and a pharmaceutical company. There are various activities in Grýtubakkahreppur, including the Magna Sports Club (est. 1915), Þráin Horseback Riding Club, a 9-hole golf course in Hvammur, Kaldbakur Tours (which takes skiers up Mount Kaldbakur in snow cats), Pólarhestar horse rental in Grýtubakki, swimming pool, fitness centre and a four-day hike along the Fjörður region and Látraströnd coast organized by Fjörðungar. The Grenivíkurgleði festival has become an annual event in Grenivík, held in August. This is a family festival featuring some of Iceland's great performers along with local acts, as well as grilling, singing, dancing, and a firework show.

831 Höfðavegur, 3,6 km.

Höfði, a parsonage until 1890, and church till 1880. A farm since the original settlement. Early this century the home of Þórður Gunnarsson (1865-1935) who along with his brothers operated fishing boats and was active in other spheres. These brothers were the most enterprising people on the east side of Eyjafjörður. There was a fishing centre at **Kljáströnd** and some farms, now abandoned.

Þengilhöfði, (261 m) a mountain south of Grenivík.

Höfðahverfi, a small farming district between the river Fnjóská and the village Grenivík, taking its name from **Þengilhöfði**.

Hléskógar, late in the 19th century a school for adolescents was set up and run there for several years through the agency of Einar Ásmundarsson from Nes. Now a guest house.

Ártún, a guesthouse and campsite.

Laufás, a parsonage and church, and an old farmhouse. Fertile farmland with many assets. The church was built in 1865 at the instigation of Rev. Björn Halldórsson, who also had the farmhouse built during his priesthood (1853-82). A very clear example of the northern type of farmhouses where the gables of all the front buildings face forwards. Behind the entrance building, a passage leads to rear buildings, which are arranged at right angles. Rev. Björn wrote many good hymns. His son was Bishop Þórhallur Bjarnarson (1846-1916). Birthplace of Tryggvi Gunnarsson (1835-1917), the master carpenter who built the church, later a member of parliament, bank director and important entrepreneur. Many other remarkable pastors have served at Laufás. Laufás has been a vicarage from the earliest Christian times. The last clergyman to live in the old farmhouse, Þorvaldur Þormar, moved into the new vicarage in 1936 where successive ministers of the Laufás parish lived until the year 2000.

1 **Norðurlandsvegur,** p. 86 | 835 **Fnjóskadalsv. eystri,** p. 397
F839 **Leirdalsheiðarvegur,** p. 478

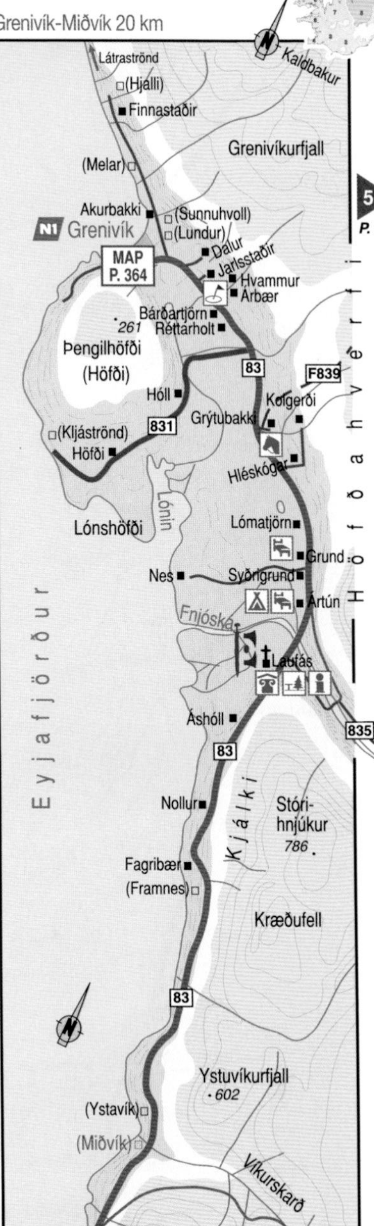

Tjörn-Kross 26 km

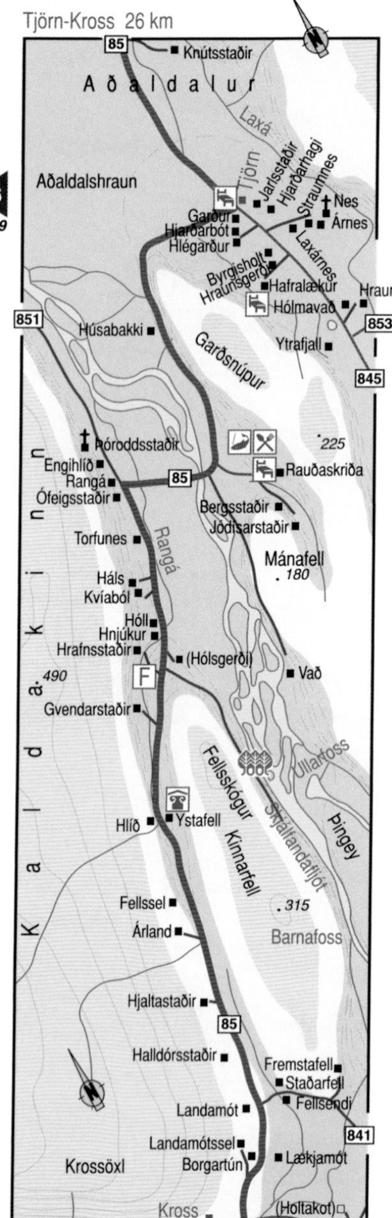

6
P. 569

Kross-Tjörn 26 km

Ljósavatnsskarð

Aðaldalur, ("Main valley") a broad lowland area at the head of Skjálfandaflói gulf, between the river Skjálfandafljót and Hvammsheiði moor, and then east of Fljótsheiði moor to the lake Vestmannsvatn. There is the Aðaldalshraun lava field, which comes from the Lake Mývatn area. Widespread birch bushes and strangely beautiful lava formations. Farms along the edge of the lava. Belts of sand along the coast.

Garðsnúpur, the steep northern end of Fljótsheiði ("River moor").

Rauðaskriða, ("Red landslide") a farm since the original settlement, often occupied by powerful Icelanders such as the district governors Hrafn Guðmundsson (d. 1432) and Hrafn Brandsson (15th century). The group of farms near Rauðaskriða is called **Skriðuhverfi**.

Skjálfandafljót, one of largest rivers of northern Iceland, with its source in Vonarskarð and the glaciers Tungnafellsjökull and Vatnajökull, with tributaries from the Ódáðahraun lava field. Flows through Bárðardalur valley. Many waterfalls, among them Aldeyjarfoss, Goðafoss and (near Kinnarfell) Barnafoss and Ullarfoss.

Ljósvetningabúð, community centre at the north end of the mountain Kinnarfell.

Ystafell, a farm, long the home of Sigurður Jónsson (1852-1926), the great cooperative leader and Minister of State. The birthplace in 1902 of the Federation of Icelandic Cooperatives, to which there is a memorial. Part of the protected **Fellsskógur** woods near Kinnarfell. An interesting transport exhibition, with vehicles of all ages and types open to the public.

Fellsskógur, one of the largest birch forests in Iceland. Part of a 22,000 ha nature reserve. National Forest.

Kaldakinn, the district north of Ljósavatnsskarð pass and west of the river Skjálfandafljót down to the sea. Above are the high Kinnarfjöll mountains (900-1,000 m) with their permanent snows.

1 **Norðurlandsvegur,** p. 88
845 **Aðaldalsvegur,** p. 400
853 **Hvammavegur,** p. 400
841 **Fremstafellsvegur,** p. 398
851 **Út-Kinnarvegur,** p. 402

Húsavík, (pop. 2,176) a fishing village and a perfect centre for individual tourists and groups travelling in the Northeast. Visitors can during their stay in Húsavík choose between hotels, guesthouses, cottages and camping. Húsavík is located on the Eastern Shore of Skjálfandi-bay facing the impressive Kinnarfjöll mountains across the bay. Húsavík offers an ample selection of easy hikes through varied landscape for example, along the shores of the bay, up the Húsavík mountain or around the lake **Botnsvatn** where trout fishing is free of charge. Even though fishing and fish processing is the important industry in Húsavík the town is now well known as the whale watching capital of Europe. Whale watching trips from Húsavík harbour on traditional wooden fishing boats, schooners and passenger boats are getting increasingly popular. The Husavik Whale Centre is the first and only information centre on whales in Iceland. The Church in Húsavík, built in 1907, is said to be the most beautiful wooden church in Iceland. In the Museum House are a folk museum for the area, a nature museum, art gallery, the library and district archives. A nice all year round heated swimming pool is open for visitors from early morning to late at night. Húsavík being located just south of the Arctic Circle enjoys 24 hours daylight in summer and the romantic midnight sun frequently paints the evening sky with colours beyond imagination. In the winter when the days are short and the nights are long the dark night sky is frequently decorated with millions of stars and flashing Northern Lights (Aurora Borealis). Winter excursions are constantly gaining popularity and options for winter tours and activities suitable to everyone increase yearly". The contrast of hot springs and geothermal areas against snow, ice and frozen waterfalls give explorers the experience of a lifetime.

Laxamýri, ("Salmon marsh") one of the biggest and wealthiest farms in Iceland, because of good farming land, salmon and eider ducks.

Laxá, a river that flows through an old lava-field with beautiful rock formations and some pseudo-craters; further up the river is the hydroelectric-power station Laxárvirkjun in a beautiful canyon.

Litlu-Núpar, there have some signs of an old settlement been found.

852 Sandsvegur, 6,49 km.

Sandur, a farm to north of Aðaldalshraun.

Knútsstaðir, a farm by the river Laxá, good fishing. In nearby lava there are strange hollow crater hills, some of which one can stand up in, the best known being **Knútsstaðaborg**.

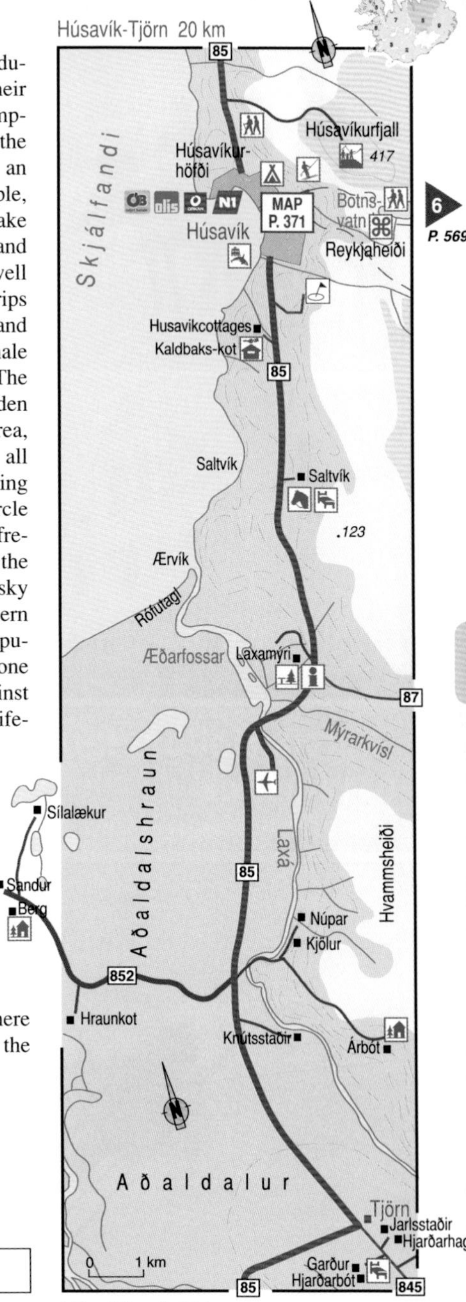

87 **Kísilvegur,** p. 386 845 **Aðaldalsvegur,** p. 400

Húsavík harbour

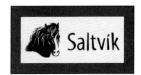

©OHS

Mánáreyjar, two small islands, Háey and Lágey ("High island and Low island"), 9 km off Tjörnes, belonging to the farm Máná.

Tjörnes, the peninsula between the Skjálfandaflói bay and Öxarfjörður. There is a mountain range along side it, and an old footpath and horse-trail across Tunguheiði moor between the farms Syðri-Tunga and Fjöll in the Kelduhverfi district. On the west and north there is a good deal of flat land with rivers running into the Skjálfandi bay, as well as some high sandstone ridges by the sea, 400-500 m thick, dating from the Tertiary period and the Ice Age. Towards the south there are alternate shell and lignite layers, showing big changes in sea level. In the southernmost and oldest of these are shells of creatures that now live only in warmer sea along west-European coasts. In younger layers there are cold-sea shells and at Breiðavík arctic shells. During World War I there was a lignite mine on Tjörnes in the land of the farms Hringver and Ytri-Tunga.

Máná, the northernmost farm in Tjörnes.

Mánárbakki, a farm and museum, and a weather station where research into the northern lights has been going on since 1984, financed by the Japanese government.

Breiðavík, a bay and a farm of the same name at the extreme northern point of the Tjörnes peninsula. Thick earth strata from the Ice Age. Excavations have been carried out near Breiðavík at what is thought to be the site of the settlement farm **Böðólfskytja**.

Hallbjarnarstaðir, a farm near which there are layers of shells of prehistoric origin in the cliffs. Long the home of Kári Sigurjónsson (1875-1949), who with scientists investigated the shells, though the pioneering work was done by Guðmundur G. Bárðarson (1880-1933), geologist.

Layers of shells in Hallbjarnarstaðakambur ridge.

Sólvangur, a community centre.

Ytritunga, a farm from which there is a road down to the sea, this being the best way to approach the prehistoric Tjörnes shell-layers in the cliffs both sides of the river Hallbjarnarstaðaá. There was a lignite mine on the farm land, and on the shore there is a boulder brought by ice from Greenland. Small pier, some fishing.

Kaldakvísl, the southernmost river on the Tjörnes peninsula.

Lundey, ("Puffin island") a 41 m high rocky island, belonging to the farm Héðinshöfði. Grassy on top, huge numbers of puffins breed there. Lighthouse.

Héðinshöfði, a farm, for 20 years the home of sheriff and parliamentarian Benedikt Sveinsson (1826-1899) who was prominent in the fight for independence, after the death of Jón Sigurðsson. His son, the poet Einar Benediktsson (1864-1940), who lies buried in the national cemetery at Þingvellir (see Road 36), was brought up there. Monument.

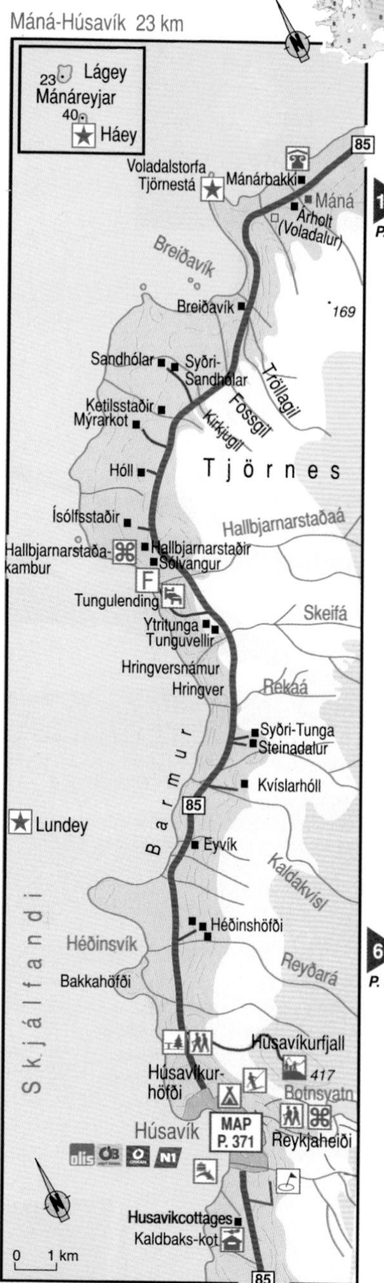

NORTH SAILING
SINCE 1995
ECO-FRIENDLY
WHALE WATCHING
+PUFFINS
#1
OF THINGS TO DO
IN HÚSAVÍK 2016
tripadvisor
BOOK ONLINE WWW.NORTHSAILING.IS
OR CALL +354 464 7272
HÚSAVÍK
the
WHALE CAPITAL
of
ICELAND
Gamli Baukur Restaurant
Adorning the Húsavík harbour front, Restaurant Gamli Baukur offers the atmosphere you're looking for. This driftwood-built house is the ideal place to sit down, enjoy the fresh local food or simply relax with a drink and observe the lively harbour area.
www.gamlibaukur.is
Tel. +354 464 2442
Order Here
Café Hvalbakur
The interior of this unique café has been beautifully crafted from the remains of an old oak fishing vessel keeping true to the spirit of North Sailing.
Café Hvalbakur offers a selection of food and drinks and is conveniently located directly under North Sailing's ticket office with a nice veranda offering great ocean view.
Tel. +354 464 7278

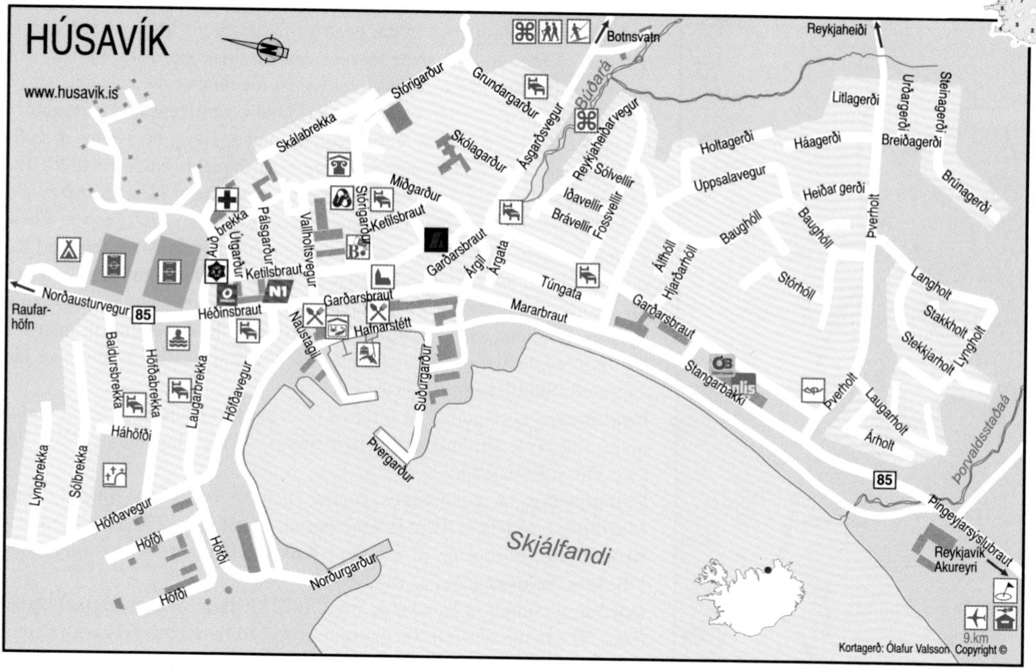

HÚSAVÍK

www.husavik.is

Skjálfandi

Kortagerð: Ólafur Valsson. Copyright ©

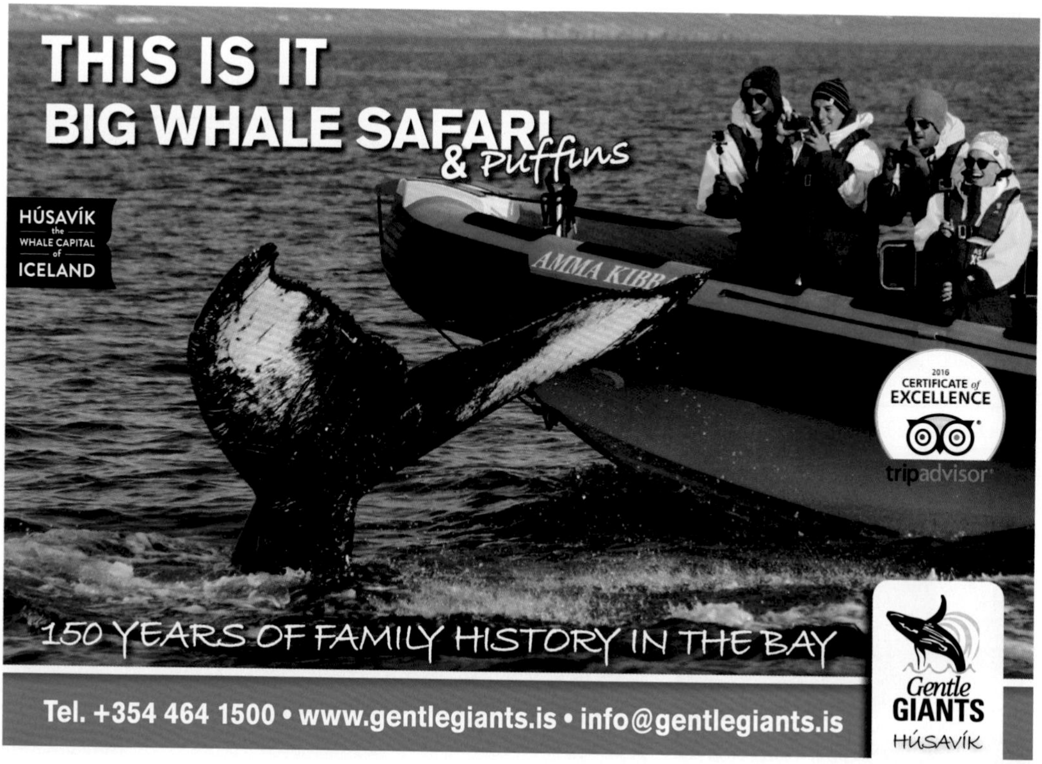

Kelduhverfi, the district at the head of Öxarfjörður between the mountains of Tjörnes and the river Jökulsá. Inland there are many fissures and chasms, difficult and dangerous to cross. At the time of the volcanic activity by Leirhnjúkur in 1975 (see Road 848) there were repeated earthquakes in the Kelduhverfi district, very frequent and some quite severe in early 1976. There was another series of severe earthquakes in early 1978. The land is thought to be spreading and indeed, many new fissures and cracks have appeared and some older ones have got wider and deeper. These changes can be seen as far north as the sea. At the same time the land has subsided by at least a meter. The greatest changes are in the area between the farms Lindarbrekka and Hlíðargerði, most obviously by the farms Lyngás, Framnes and Hlíðargerði. Warm water has come up in many of the fissures. Down on the flat land called Vestur-Sandur a new lake has appeared, **Skjálftavatn** ("Quake Lake").

Keldunes, a community of 6 farms near the Keldunes well, a big spring under the lava. Birthplace of High Sheriff Skúli Magnússon (1711-94) (see Viðey, Reykjavík).

Skúlagarður, a community centre, named for High Sheriff Skúli Magnússon, to whom there is a memorial, an eagle on a basalt column.

Krossdalur, birthplace of the poet Kristján Jónsson, called Fjallaskáld ("Poet of the mountains") (1842-69).

Garður, a church, a parsonage until 1872. A farm of the original settlement. The home of Þórir Skeggjason, who had fierce quarrels with Grettir the strong Ásmundarson.

Víkingavatn, a farm of the original settlement near a fishing-lake of same name.

Lón, ("Lagoon") named for the sizeable sea-lagoons emptying into the Lónsós estuary. Trout-fishing and nesting islets. Salmon farm.

Rifós, a salmon farm.

Auðbjargarstaðir, the westernmost farm in the Kelduhverfi district.

Imbuþúfa, view dial.

Hljóðaklettar

Ásbyrgi

866 Austursandsvegur, 10 km.

Sandá, a river.

Lundur, once a children's boarding school, built 1928, now there is a preschool and an elementary, summer hotel and a swimming pool.

865 Gilsbakkavegur, 4,5 km.

Skinnastaður, a church and parsonage, which according to folklore was the home of powerful priest-magicians, the Rev. Einar galdrameistari ("master magician") and Jón greipaglennir ("wide-hand"). At nearby Þangbrandslækur, the missionary Þangbrandur is said to have baptized the local people in a local stream.

Jökulsá á Fjöllum, one of greatest Icelandic rivers, the second longest at 206 km, and having the largest drainage basin, 8,000 km^2. It comes from Vatnajökull in two main streams, the eastern one being called Kreppa. Jökulsá divides into many forks before emptying into Öxarfjörður, the main one being Bakkahlaup, which flows through Kelduhverfi. Waterfalls: Selfoss, Dettifoss, Hafragilsfoss and Réttarfoss.

Jökulsárgljúfur, a National Park. In Ásbyrgi there is a Visitor Centre. The centre provides comprehensive information about the Park, its surroundings, hiking trails, natural attractions, history, services and recreational options. The Centre is open from May 1st to September 30th. Outside this period, the Centre opens by arrangement. Its purpose is to provide comprehensive information about the Park, its surroundings, hiking trails, natural attractions, history, services and recreational options. Ásbyrgi is a popular summer holiday destination and is within Vatnajökull National Park. The forest in Ásbyrgi is under the protection of the Forestry Service.

See information on Vatnajökull National Park on p. 122.

Ástjörn, a small but deep lake in a wooded dell just east of Ásbyrgi, peaceful and pretty.

Ás, an old manor farm, parsonage till 1816.

861 Ásbyrgisvegur, 3,52 km.

Ásbyrgi, a U-shaped depression about 3.5 km long, surrounded by cliffs up to 90 m high with a huge crag (2 km by 250 m) called Eyjan ("The island") in the open end of the U. Its origin is uncertain. It might have been formed by subsidence, or it could have been formed by floods in the river Jökulsá. There are also signs of sea-water having flowed into it. The legendary explanation is that it is a hoofprint made by Sleipnir, the eight-legged horse belonging to Óðinn, father of the gods, the crag Eyjan having been formed by the frog of his hoof. There is a small lake at the inner end. Vegetation ranges from moorland growth near the open end to thickly growing birch and rowan trees farther in. Ásbyrgi is a popular summer holiday destination and is within Vatnajökull National Park. The forest in Ásbyrgi is under the protection of the Forestry Service.

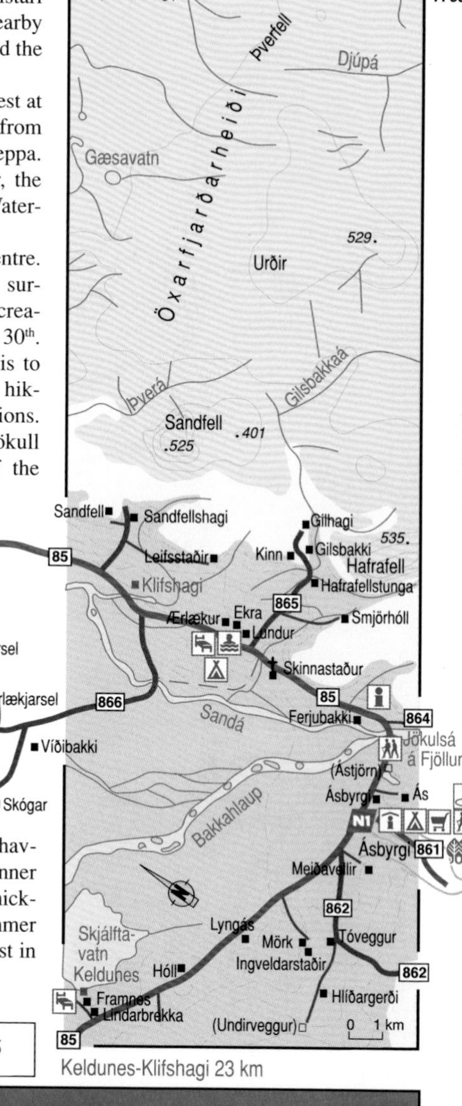

862 Dettifossvegur, p. 403 **864 Hólsfjallavegur,** p. 405

19
582

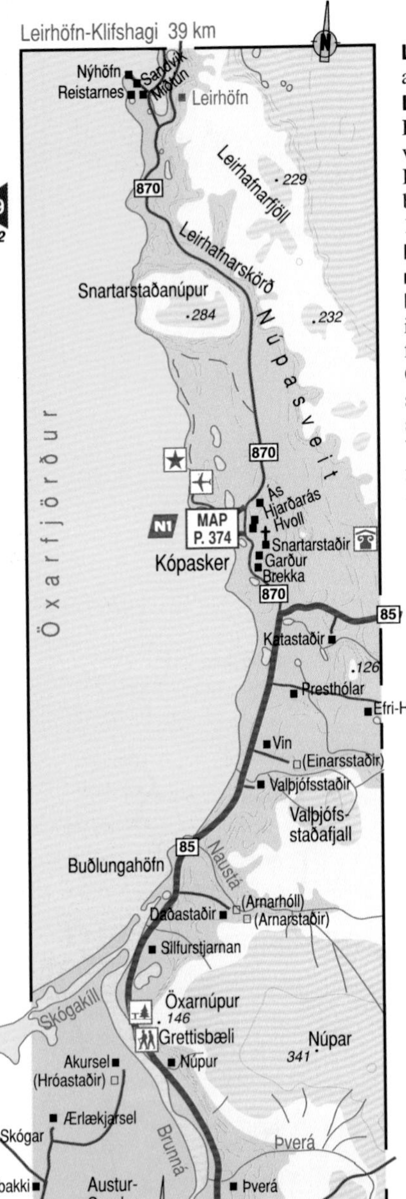

Leirhafnarskörð, a pass between the spur Snartarstaðanúpur (248 m) and the Leirhafnarfjöll mountains. Site of a small eruption in 1823.

Leirhöfn, a substantial farm, well-cultivated land. The farmer Helgi Kristjánsson (1894-1982) built a private library of about 10 thousand volumes which he gave to the county. It is now kept at Snartarstaðir at Kópasker. An excellent natural harbour, and harbour construction at near-by **Nýhöfn** for the many small boats that go fishing from there. Around 1950 farms were built there.

Hvallág, a beautiful rest stop by the see at the foot of **Snartarstaða-núpur** (284 m).

Núpasveit, the area between the spurs Öxarnúpur and Snartarstaðarnúpur, into the centre of which flowed lava from the Rauðhólar hills on Öxarfjarðarheiði moor.

Öxarfjörður, the area east of the river Jökulsá as far as the Öxarnúpur spur, with the delta Austursandur between the branches of Jökulsá. Gentle slopes with birch-trees merging into dwarf-willows. The river Sandá, a branch of Jökulsá, flows through it and joins Brunná, a mountain stream from the eastern moors. There is a good deal of geothermal energy there.

Snartarstaðir, a church since 1928. Site of official gatherings. A museum and county library in Núpasveitarskóli, an old school house built in 1928. The school operated there until 1983 when a new school was built at Kópasker. The Northern Þingeyjarsýsla Heritage Museum has a unique collection of local objects showing daily life in the 19th and 20th centuries. A wide arry of embroidery, woven goods, knitted clothing and many other unique and interesting handicrafts. Toys, a firefighting chart, guns, wood carvings and blacksmith objects can also be found there in addition to many other things. At the museum is also the library of Helgi Kristjánsson (1894-1982) from Leirhöfn. He was well known for bookbinding and woolen caps that he made.

Kópasker, (pop. 109) a village, a legalised port since 1879. Pier for oceangoing ships, airstrip. The main economy is based on services to the farms in the area as well as fisheries. There is a shop, gas station garage, health care centre, farmacy, bank, museum, campsite, hostel and guest-houses. On January 13th 1976 there was a very severe earthquake whose epicentre was out in the fjord, about 12 km northwest of the village. There was a great deal of damage, with severe cracks in many houses so that some could no longer be lived in. The water mains were in pieces and the harbour wall split along a fault, the two sides moving in opposite directions. Bridges in the area of Núpur were destroyed, the lava hills by Presthólar were damaged as if by an explosion and boulders fell from Öxarnúpur spur. At the village you will find a exhibition about this earth-quake at The Earthquake Center.

Silfurstjarnan, a fish farm with charr, halibut and turbot ideally situated in an area rich of geothermal water.

Öxarnúpur, (146 m) a sheer crag with scree at the foot, the easternmost spur of the mountain Núpar (341 m). On the crag is Grettisbæli ("Grettir's hide-out"), a rocky stronghold roofed by basalt columns, one of the places where Grettir the strong is said to have stayed for a while.

866 **Austursandsvegur,** p. 373 870 **Sléttuvegur,** p. 376

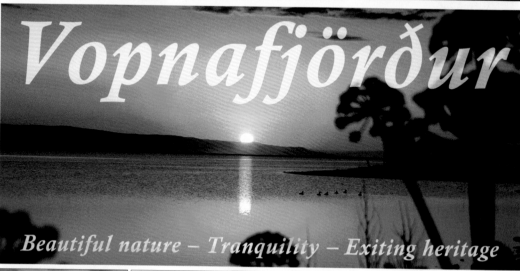

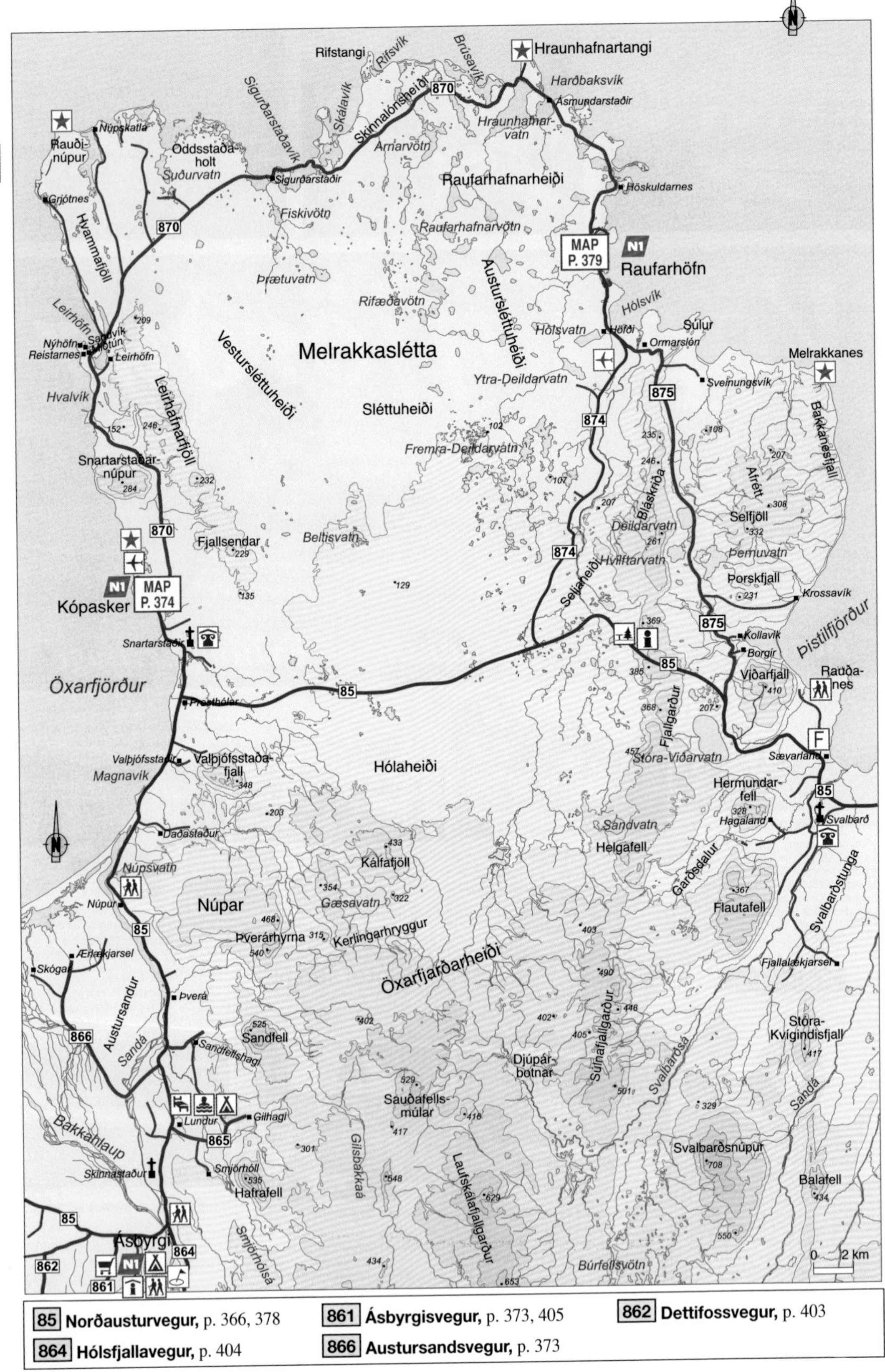

85 **Norðausturvegur,** p. 366, 378
861 **Ásbyrgisvegur,** p. 373, 405
862 **Dettifossvegur,** p. 403
864 **Hólsfjallavegur,** p. 404
866 **Austursandsvegur,** p. 373

© Björn Hróarsson

870 **Sléttuvegur,** 57,8 km.

Meyjarþúfa, ("Virgin's knoll") a small knoll with a staff on the top, between Harðbakur and the lake Hraunhafnarvatn, 200-300 m south of the road. According to legend the whole population of the Slétta area died of a plague, except for one woman in the eastern part and one man in the western part. They met up on Meyjarþúfa and laid the foundations for a new generation in the area.

Hraunhafnartangi, the northernmost point of Iceland, touches the Arctic Circle. Named for Hraunhöfn ("Lava harbour"), a small inlet nearby. An historical place, where *Fóstbræðra saga* tells us Þorgeir Hávarsson was slain and where his burial mound is said to be. Lighthouse.

Skinnalón, once a manor farm, now abandoned.

Rifstangi, long thought to be the northernmost point of Iceland. The farm **Rif** has been abandoned.

Blikalónsdalur, a grassy area of subsidence with cliffs along the edges in many places. It extends far south into the moors, dividing Vestursletta from Austurslétta, the western from the eastern part of the Melrakkaslétta plains. The farm Blikalón by the sea.

Oddsstaðir, once a manor farm, now abandoned.

Núpskatla, a farm beside the lake below the crater Rauðinúpur. Birthplace of the novelist Guðmundur Magnússon (1887-1918), whose pen-name was Jón Trausti.

Rauðinúpur, (73 m) a high crater at the northwestern tip of the Melrakkaslétta plains, erupted late in the Ice Age. Steep cliffs with many seabirds towards the sea but grassy at the inland end. At the northeastern corner is Karl, a big pinnacle rock, sometimes called Jón Trausti, for the novelist.

Gefla, a distinctive mountain in the northen end of Leirhafnarfjöll. An easy walk up the mountain and a great view of the Plain.

874 **Raufarhafnarvegur,** 20,1 km.

875 **Hálsavegur,** 20 km.

Melrakkaslétta, ("Arctic Foxes' plain") the peninsula between Öxarfjörður and Þistilfjörður between the spur Snartarstaðarnúður and the river Ormarsá. All flat and low except for the mountains Leirhafnarfjöll in the west. The northern and eastern coast is much-indented with coves, nesses and lagoons. Dry in the west but marshy in the east, with many lakes and tarns. Farms, many now abandoned, only along the coast. Much driftwood and trout-fishing, eider duck and seals are often spotted there. Foxes were widespread, hence the name, and polar bears occasionally drifted ashore on ice-floes. Melrakkaslétta boasts a large number of lakes inlets, where cayaking is possible. Information is available at Hotel Norðurljós in Raufarhöfn. Marked walking routes.

© Björn Hróarsson

Víðinesá-Raufarhöfn 29 km

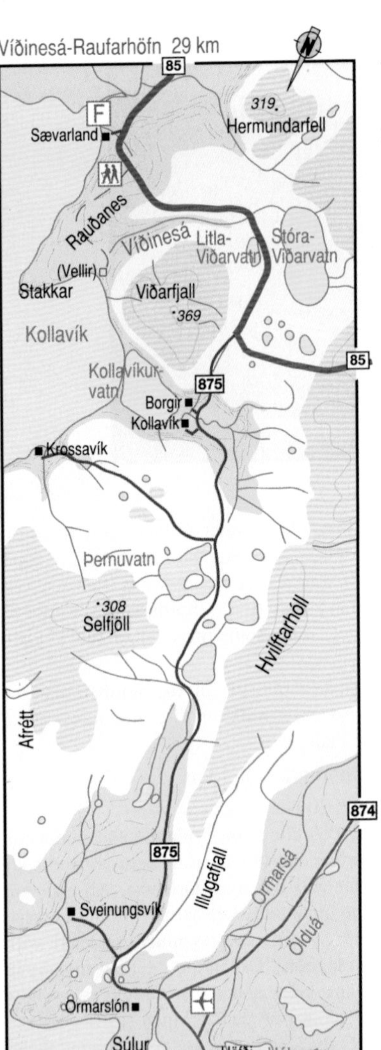

Raufarhöfn-Víðinesá 29 km

20
583

Viðarvatn, actually two lakes, **Stóra-Viðarvatn** and **Litla-Viðarvatn** ("Big and Little Viðarvatn"), good for fishing, southwest of Viðarfjall (410 m). From the larger lake the river Víðinesá flows out into Þistilfjörður.

Viðarfjall, (410 m) a mountain below which the shore, Borgarfjörur, is passable but dangerous.

Kollavík, a farm on a bay of the same name, a farm since the original settlement. The fishing-lake Kollavíkurvatn nearby.

Ormarslón, the easternmost farm on the Melrakkaslétta plain.

Ormarsá, a good fishing-river, the biggest on Melrakkaslétta.

Raufarhöfn, (pop. 173) a village which was once one of the biggest herring ports in Iceland. See town map, p. 379.

Heimskautsgerðið, (The Polar Enclosure) This is where the day is the longest in the summer and shortest in the winter. Around the summer solstice the sun does not set for several solar days. The light there is unique and owing to how low the surrounding landscape is nothing blocks the horizon for a total of 360°. The spectacular show put on by the interaction between light and shade there prompted men to contemplate how to capture all of this for exploitation by tourism. The first ideas were to somehow define the three hour periods of the solar day with some sort of solar watch and utilize the influence of the midnight sun to magnify the effect. But no matter what configuration was tried it was obvious that the conditions on the Melrakkaslétta plateau contained something even more powerful, something that was hidden there. Something was needed that could lift this idea to higher flights and intensify the sunset in a potent way. Bit by bit, things began to fall into place. In the end, a circle was formed with a diameter of 54 m, enclosed by a stacked rock wall. On the wall there are four gates with openings to the four cardinal points. The lower layer of the wall is about 2.5 m high. On top of it there are 68 gateways with a continuous rock layer upon them. The visual effect is that this upper layer floats on the rays of the midnight sun and at sunrise and sunset at other times of the year. In the middle of the circle there is an 8-10 m high pillar resting on four bollards. The spaces between the bollards point to the four gates so that the midnight sun will appear in the north gate. The spring equinox and fall equinox have also been kept in mind as well as the winter solstice when the sun barely peeks up over the horizon. Around the middle there are four columns, each one unique. Inside the wall there are 68 rocks, the dwarfs, which form a circle. The concept behind the dwarfs is taken from the Dwarf Tale in Völuspá. The dwarf concept is well-known throughout Europe where dwarfs and plants associated with the seasons have had the purpose of ensuring growth and prosperity in nature. With these concepts in mind the year circle of the dwarfs is formed inside the big wall circle. Each dwarf has his restricted role. The artist, Haukur Halldórsson, has drawn each individual dwarf according to his function. The author, Jónas Friðrik, has simultaneously written a poetic text about them. The cooperation of these two artists has awoken great expectations as they are actually working on designing merchandise for selling as souvenirs about the phenomenon discussed above – The Polar Enclosure.

Raufarhöfn

A village on the east of the Melrakkaslétta plain. In 1836 Raufarhöfn was officially designated a trading centre, having up to that time been simply a farm, named Reiðarhöfn in the 1703 census.

The rauf, or rift, that gives the village its name is a shallow channel between the Hólmi, which falls steeply to the sea but has a good deal of vegetation towards the top, and the Höfði, which is at the southern end of a fairly wide point of land, south of the so-called Klif. The Höfði, on which there is a lighthouse, has a rich birdlife. It is quite high and an excellent place from which to view the village and its harbour. Good trout-fishing in the area.

The harbour underwent extensive improvements in the beginning of the „herring years" around 1950, and piers were built making it possible to land great amounts of herring. Indeed, Raufarhöfn was for a while one of the main salting and processing centres in Iceland.

Raufarhöfn is the northernmost village in Iceland. There are the darkest winter nights but also the brightest summer nights and for a whole month in the summer the sun doesn't set. There is an airport near the village but no scheduled flights.

The church, designed by Guðjón Samúelsson, was built in 1927 and to a large extent rebuilt in 1979. The pulpit was once in the old church at Ásmundarstaðir, having been given to that church in 1851 by Danish merchants in Raufarhöfn. The altar piece is also from Ásmundarstaðir, painted in 1890 by Sveinungi Sveinungason (1840–1915).

Þistilfjörður

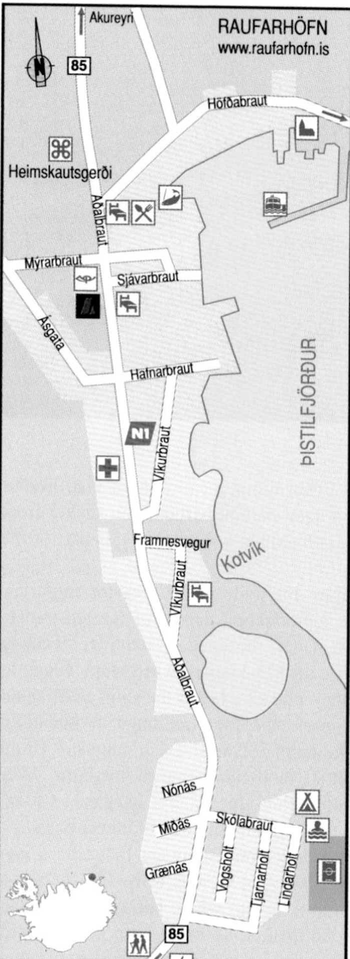

870 **Sléttuvegur,** p. 376

874 **Raufarhafnarvegur,** p. 376

875 **Hálsavegur,** p. 376

Heimskautsgerði

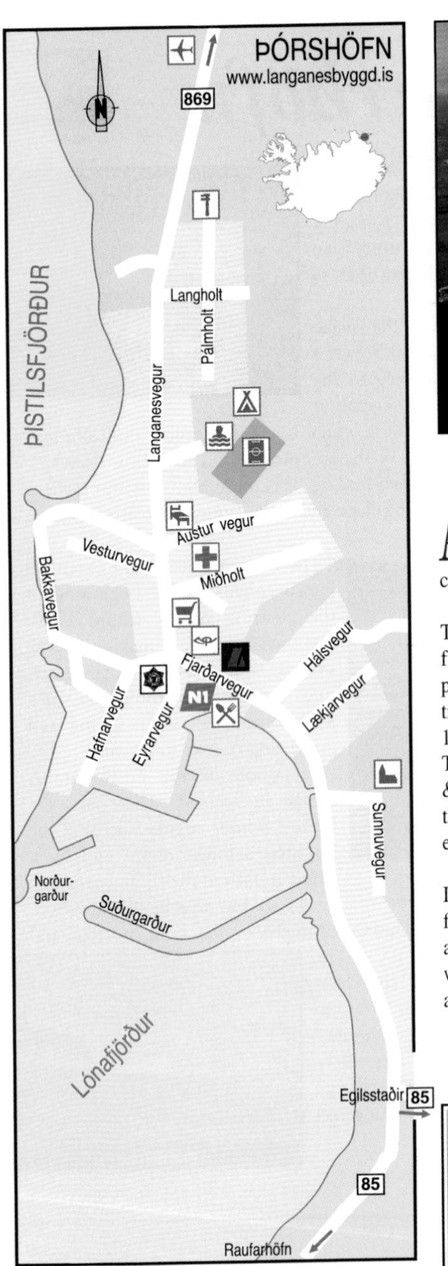

A village on the east side of Lónafjörður, a fjord out of Þistilfjörður to the southeast. There is a good natural harbour and shelter from the northeast wind, which is the main sea wind in this part of the country.

Þórshöfn has been the centre for trade in the area for centuries. Though it is mentioned in the authorization papers of foreign traders from the 16th century onwards, it only became an authorized trading post in 1846, when first private, then company-owned ships began to trade there regularly. Trading took place on board the ships until about 1880, when they built warehouses, the first buildings in Þórshöfn. To begin with, trade was in the hands of the Danish company Örum & Wulff, which built a substantial shop-cum-home in Þórshöfn. After that, trade was in the hands of various locals, the Langanes Co-op, established 1911, having run it the longest, but does no longer excist.

This prosperous community is based on fishing and fish-processing. In addition to the traditional processing of various white fish there is a factory producing capelin meal and a plant where herring and capelin are processed for the human food market. To make even better use of what the ocean has to offer, the most recent innovation is harvesting and processing mussels.

Þórshöfn Sport Centre

Þórshöfn, (pop. 346) a village with fishing, herring-salting, trading. There is the only place in Iceland that harvests ocean quahog (Arctica islandica), a species of an edible clam, native to the North Atlantic. At the restaurant Eyri one can try a special ocean quahog soup. In the village is an airport with daily flights, an elementary school, a church, a community centre, a health care centre, a bank, a swimming pool, a sport stadium, a campsite and a gas station. By the harbour is an art work by Kristín Alda Kjartansdóttir. The town festival „Kátir dagar" (Merry days) is an annual event. Just outside the village is Sauðaneshúsið, a museum open in summer. is an (www.lnb.is)

Hafralónsá, the biggest river in Þistilfjörður, coming from Hafralón far up on the moors but with tributaries whose sources are even farther away. Good fishing.

868 Laxárdalsvegur, 3,6 km.

Þistilfjörður, the bay between the Melrakkaslétta plain and the Langanes peninsula, with farms along its head, where there are low hills and valleys with many rivers, the main ones being Svalbarðsá, Sandá, Hölkná, Laxá, and Hafralónsá. All rise in the moors and most have trout and salmon. Formerly there were several farms on the extensive moors farther inland.

Rauðanes, fairly long peninsula with steep cliffs east of the mountain Viðarfjall. Many seabird nest there, and there are some picturesque pinnacle rocks, **Stakkar**, in the sea. The end of the peninsula has broken away and is called Stakkatorfa. There are caves under it, accessible by small boats in good weather. There are also caves in the cliffs. An area of natural beauty well worth seeing with marked walking paths.

Svalbarð, one of the biggest farms of the district, church, a parsonage till 1936, an ancient assembly site. On the walls of the church choir epitaphs have been written, believed to be the work of Bólu-Hjálmar (see Bóla, Skag). At Svalbarði you will find the Leader Sheep Centre. The number of Leader-sheep in the world is only around 1400 and they are all originally from Þingeyjarsýsla in the northern part of Iceland. They have exceptional sense of direction and danger and do in fact control the whole herd. There is also a café, souvenir shop, gallery and a view deck with interesting information about the Leader-sheep and the area.

Sævarland, a farm which was the birthplace of the painter Gunnlaugur Blöndal (1893-1962).

Öxarfjarðarheiði, the moor between Öxarfjörður and Þistilfjörður. A summer road, highest at Einarsskarð (380 m), 38 km long. Grassy moorland. Farms there now all abandoned.

Óttarshnjúkur, a mountain, marked walking routes.

Hrauntangi, a farm abandoned in 1943, the last farm on Öxarfjarðarheiði to be abandoned.

Rauðhólar, a row of craters from which lava has flowed down to the farms Presthólar in the Núpasveit district and Ormarslón on the Melrakkaslétta plain.

869 Langanesvegur, p. 408

Þórshöfn-Víðinesá 36 km

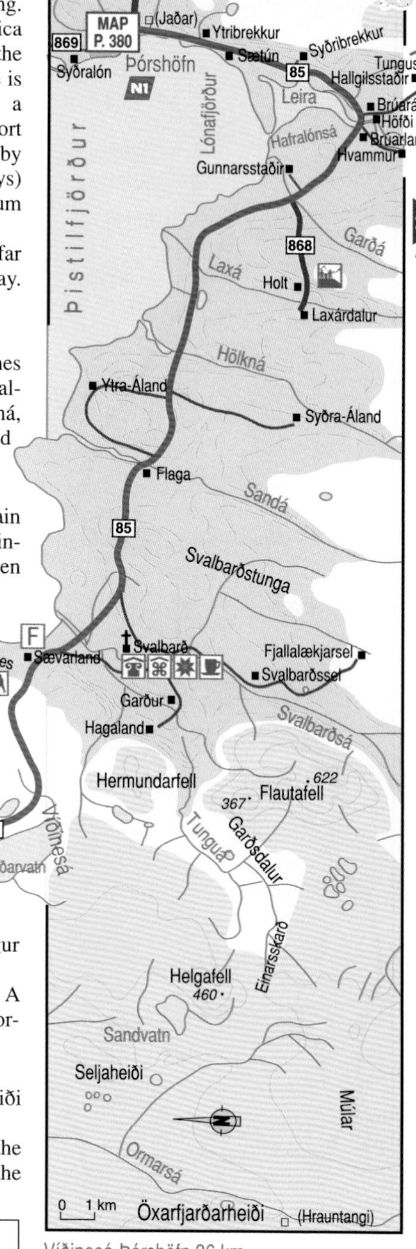

Víðinesá-Þórshöfn 36 km

Bakkafjörður-Þórshöfn 42 km

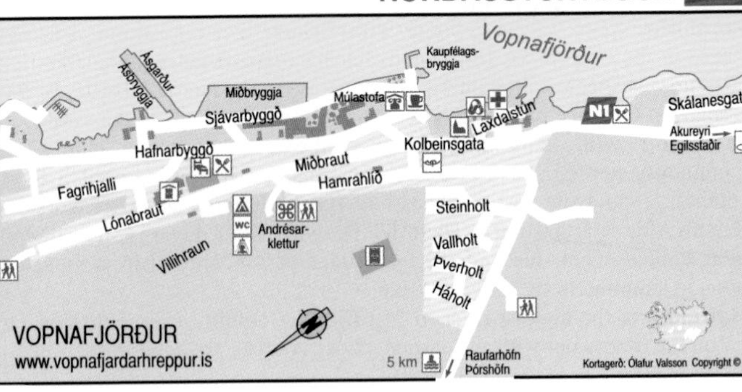

91 **Hafnarvegur í Bakkafirði,** 4,9 km.

Bakkafjörður, (pop. 77) a village in the land of Höfn which became an official trading place in 1883. Main occupations are fishing and service. At Bakkfjörður are elementary school, health care centre, community centre, campsite and a grocery store. Good walking routes in the area.

Skeggjastaðir, a church and parsonage. A little to the west is a strange rock, **Stapi**, rising straight out of the sea. The church was built in 1845, the pastor Rev. Hóseas Árnason paying out of his own pocket for all the work, since both the bishop and the local people refused to help. The Provost at Hof in Vopnafjörður, Rev. Guttormur Þorsteinsson, who owned Skoruvíkurfjörður on the Langanes peninsula, donated driftwood for the building.

Þorvaldsstaðir, a farm where the poet Magnús Stefánsson (1884-1942), whose pen-name was Örn Arnarson, grew up. He was born at Kverkártunga in the same district.

Djúpilækur, birthplace of the poet Kristján Einarsson (1916-94).

Miðfjarðará, the biggest river on the Langanesströnd coast, good salmon-fishing.

Gunnólfsvík, the northernmost farm on the Langanesströnd coast, now abandoned. Once a fishing-station. To north is **Gunnólfsvíkurfjall** (719 m). Good views. This marks the eastern end of the tuff area of northern Iceland, the west end of which is the valley Bárðardalur through which the river Skjálfandafljót runs (see Road 85).

Langanesströnd, the coast between the peninsulas Langanes and Digranes east of Bakkafjörður. There are three short fjords on the Bakkaflói bay: **Finnafjörður**, **Miðfjörður** and **Bakkafjörður** or Sandvík. Little real flat land, but big, low moors inland, from which run many streams. Similar scenery to that in Þistilfjörður. Farms now only along the coast, formerly also on the moors.

Brekknaheiði, the northern part of moors between Langanesströnd and Þistilfjörður, formerly called **Helkunduheiði**. Low hills alternate with marshes, small lakes and tarns, mostly below 200 m. There were formerly the boundaries between the 4 parts of Iceland, also between the bishoprics and still between Þingeyjarsýsla and Múlasýsla counties. The road reaches a height of 160 m.

Þórshöfn-Bakkafjörður 42 km

869 **Langanesvegur,** p. 408

85 NORÐAUSTURVEGUR

Vopnafjörður, a town situated on the southeastern shore of Kolbeinstangi spit. Population 511, whereas the population of the municipality as a whole is 645. Just offshore are two islets, Miðhólmi and Skiphólmi, which form the harbour. They are connected by a man-made breakwater that serves as protection from the ocean waves. A walking path leads along the breakwater. Vopnafjörður is an ancient trading post that thousands of people passed through during the Icelandic emigration to the West. The East Iceland Emigration Centre is an organization of volunteers interested in re-establishing contact with the descendants of the people who left after the eruption of Askja in 1875 and provide help to those descendants who come to visit their ancestral homeland. Its main industries are fishing, fish processing, and trade/services. Vopnafjörður has a primary school, a music school, a church, a hotel, a health centre, an information centre, a café and a swimming pool in Selárdalur, some 12 km away. There are beautiful walking routes in the area, information and a map can be found in the information centre. Múlastofa is located in Kaupvangur, cultural centre, and is dedicated to the memory of two brohters, Jón Múli and Jónas Árnason. Culture festival in relation to Múlistofa is held in the second week of August and a family festival, Vopnaskak, in the second week of July.

Rjúpnafell, a farm, now abandoned.

Ytri-Hlíð, a farm. A place of recreation.

Ljótsstaðir, a farm where Gunnar Gunnarsson (1889-1975), one of Iceland's greatest authors, was brought up. From 1907-39 he lived in Denmark and wrote in Danish, becoming one of the most popular novelists in Denmark at the time. The farm appears in the first part of his novel *Fjallkirkjan* (see Road 931, Skriðuklaustur).

Torfastaðir, a farm since the settlement, once a boarding school.

Vesturárdalur, the central valley of the Vopnafjörður area, off the Skógalón part of the Nýpslón lagoon, between low ridges, flat and grassy. The river Vesturá comes from Arnarvatn, salmon- and trout-river.

Nýpsfjörður, a short fjord off Vopnafjörður, with the long lagoon, Nýpslón off it. Nýpslón is divided into two by a low peninsula, the inner part being called Skógalón, with salmon, trout and sea fishing. Bridged in 1984.

Selárdalur, the northernmost of three valleys off Vopnafjörður, ca. 30 km long to the mountain Mælifell (822 m). Shallow with low moors and ridges on both sides. Selá is a good fishing river. 6-7 km from the road is the Selárfoss waterfall, and nearby some geothermal heat. The valley is now mostly uninhabited. The swimming pool in the valley, The Selárdalur swimming pool, is considered by many to be the most romantic pool in Iceland because it has no electricity and therefore relies on moonlight, aurora boreales and the stars for light as the day wanes. The dressing rooms are illuminated by candlelight. There is currently one inhabited farm in the valley.

913 Strandhafnarvegur, 12 km.

Ytri-Hágangur, (923 m) and **Syðri-Hágangur,** (952 m) two imposing mountains west of Sandvíkurheiði moor.

Sandvíkurheiði, (275 m) low moors between Bakkafjörður and Vopnafjörður, marshy with lakes and tarns. Many streams originate there.

91 Hafnarvegur, p. 382 | **914 Skógavegur,** p. 384

Vopnafjörður-Bakkafjörður 37 km

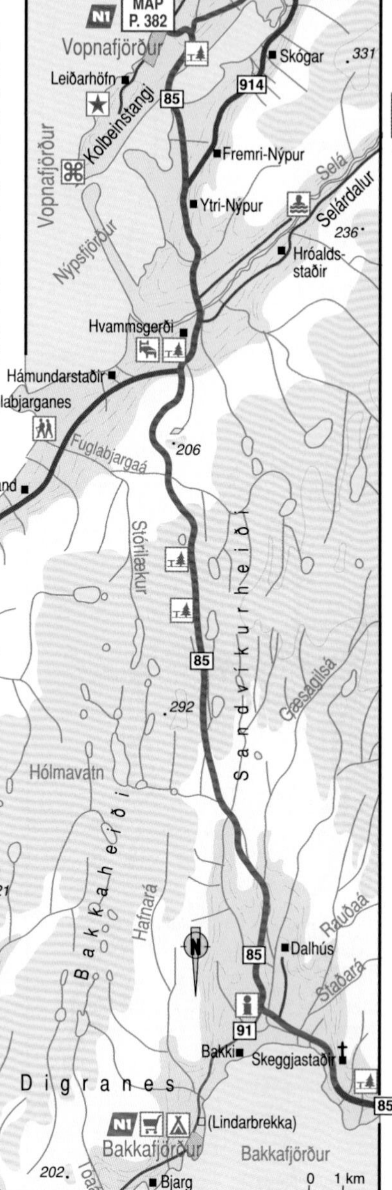

Bakkafjörður-Vopnafjörður 37 km

Kálffell-Vopnafjörður 39 km

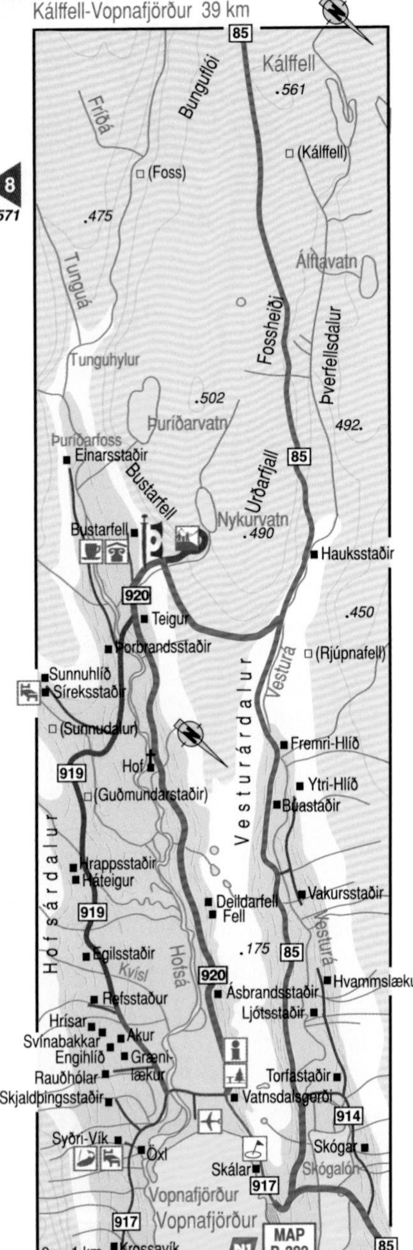

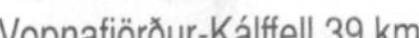
Vopnafjörður-Kálffell 39 km

920 **Hofsárdalsvegur,** 31,86 km

Bustarfell, a manor farm through the ages, with a long history. The farm has been in the same family since 1532. This turf house with red gables and grass-grown roof is one of the oldest and best preserved farms of its kind in Iceland. The house preserves much history about Iceland and its people. In 1770, sadly, the original farm burned down, but it was quickly rebuilt and was lived in until 1966. Then the family built a new house on Bustarfell which they still live in. Now there is a museum. The Museum, i.e. the relics, were given to Vopnafjörður by Elín Methúsalemsdóttir in the year 1982. The houses were sold to the Icelandic nation in 1943 by Methúsalem Methúsalemsson. They are now preserved by the Icelandic National Museum. A visit to the Museum at Bustarfell is a journey through the history of farming and changes in lifestyle from the beginning of the 18th century to the mid-20th century. The Museum shows clearly the lifestyle changes that occured from the time it was rebuilt until the family moved into the "new house". Guests can follow the difference in the standard for quality, for example when running water and a heating system were lead to the house. Beside Bustarfell Museum is Café Croft placed. It is little but very homelike and cosy where guests can sit down and enjoy coffee, tea or a chocolate along with a tasty traditional cakes and pies.

Bustarfell, sharp-topped mountain, with two lakes on top, Þuríðarvatn and Nykurvatn, good view. View-dial. Below the mountain is a farm of the same name.

914 **Skógavegur,** 7,7 km.

Hofsárdalur, the westernmost and biggest of the Vopnafjörður valleys, broad at the mouth but narrowing into Fossdalur. **Hofsá** is a good fishing river. To the east is a low ridge, to the west high mountains, **Smjörfjöll** ("Butter mountains") (1,251 m). Grassy, fertile farming area.

Teigur, a farm where the poetess Guðfinna Þorsteinsdóttir, pen-name Erla, (1891-1972) lived for many years. The geologist Dr. Sigurður Þórarinsson (1912-83), born at Hof, was brought up there.

Hof, a church, parsonage, historically important manor farm. Home of Brodd-Helgi and his son Bjarni Brodd-Helgason, mentioned in *Vopnfirðinga saga*. Among pastors who served there was Einar Jónsson (1853-1931) one of Iceland's best genealogists. There are a number of old ruins on the land of Hof.

919 **Sunnudalsvegur,** 16 km.

Fjallasíða, the row of farms below the mountains on the eastern side of Hofsárdalur.

Sunnudalur, a farm in a valley of the same name, now also called Hraunfellsdalur. Site of an ancient assembly, mentioned in the Sagas.

Hrappsstaðir, a farm. From there began the path over Smjörvatnsheiði moor to Fossavellir at Jökulsárhlíð. The route is about 38 km, steep in places and with heavy snow, highest point at 750 m. Once a route often travelled.

Refsstaður, a parsonage till 1786 and a church till 1812.

917 **Hlíðarvegur,** p. 423

Vegaskarð-Kálffell 34 km

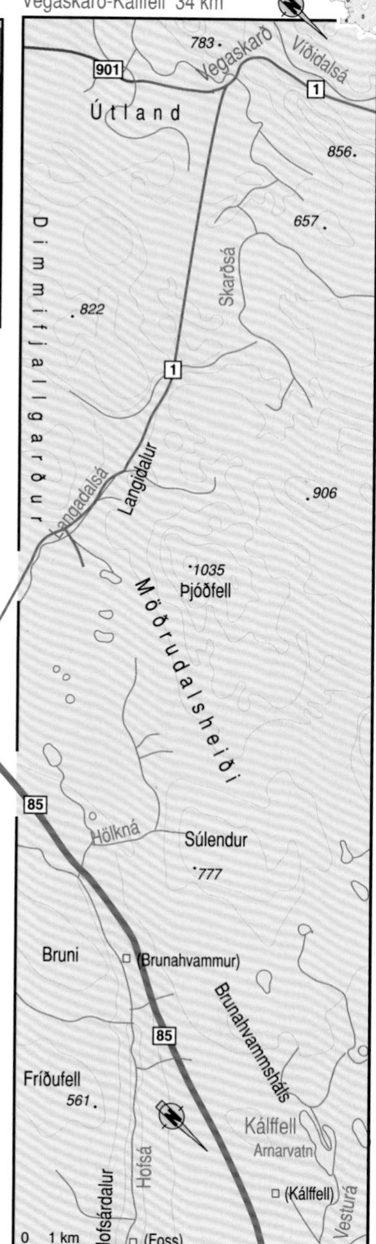

Kálffell-Vegaskarð 34 km

8 P. 571

© Björn Jonsson

In the Jökuldalur valley.

Dimmifjallgarður, ("Dark mountain range") going south from Haugsöræfi to Þjóðfell, most of its peaks being 600-900 m high. Formerly there was a route across there between the Hólsfjöll farms and Vopnafjörður, but it was difficult in winter and there were frequent accidents. In February 1874 two men were lost in a snow storm with their horse and cart. Their bodies were found 2 weeks later. The horse stood by them, alive but unable to move because its reins were frozen to the ground.

Haugsöræfi, a mountain range east of Hólsfjöll, up to 1,000 m high. There is a large lake there called Haugsvatn. An old route, about 70 km long, went across there between Vopnafjörður and Hólsfjöll, Vopnafjörður then being the trading post for the farmers. The mountain range gets its name from one of its peaks, Haugur (965 m).

Jökuldalsheiði, extensive moorland southwest of Vopnafjörður, about 60 km long. It lies in a depression bounded by the mountains Þjóðfell and Súlendur to the west, the ranges Þríhyrningsfjallgarður and Möðrudalsfjallgarður to the northwest and Jökuldalsfjöll to the east.

Langidalur, a narrow valley between the Möðrudalsfjallgarður range and the mountain Þjóðfell.

Þjóðfell, (1,035 m) a tuff mountain north of the eastern Möðrudalsfjallgarður range, Langidalur lying between them. The road to Vopnafjörður is southeast of Þjóðfell, called Biskupsáfangar at that point. The area northeast of Þjóðfell is called Þjóðfellsbungur, and the adjoining area Möðrudalsheiði.

Súlendur, (804 m) a mountain north of the road.

Brunahvammur, an abandoned farm in the valley Fossárdalur, named for Bruni, the mountain opposite. Birthplace of the poet Þorsteinn Valdimarsson (1918-77).

Foss, ("Waterfall") an abandoned farm in Hofsárdalur, the next farm beyond Burstarfell, named for a waterfall in the river Hofsá across from it. The Hofsá has salmon up as far as Foss.

1 **Austurlandsvegur,** p. 96 901 **Möðrudalsvegur,** p. 96

Laxamýri-Reykjahlíð 46 km

6 P. 569

Grísatungufjöll, (736 m) the southern end of the Tjörnes (see Road 85) mountains.

Reykjaheiði, high moorland between the districts Reykjahverfi and Kelduhverfi. Flattish, but with lava and isolated fells and spurs. Moorland vegetation. Big volcanic craters. Snowy and stormy, height 300-400 m. The Reykjaheiðarvegur route went across these moors, but was abandoned when the road was built round Tjörnes.

Þeistareykjabunga, (564 m) a shield volcano, always visible from the Reykjaheiðarvegur road and the Kelduhverfi district. South of it are the explosion craters Stóra-Víti ("Big Hell") and Litla-Víti ("Little Hell").

Þeistareykir, an abandoned farm towards the south of Reykjaheiði moor. Much geothermal heat and some sulphur mines, which were operated at one time. Good shepherd's hut. South of there is the mountain Bæjarfjall (570 m). Jeep-track from the Reykjaheiðarvegur road and Hólasandur.

Reykjahverfi, a farming area between the farms Laxamýri and Geitafell to the south. To the west is the Hvammsheiði moor, and to the east moors rising up towards the Lambafjöll mountains and Reykjaheiði. Heat has been piped from Reykjahverfi 18 km to Húsavík for domestic heating.

Skörð, a farm in Reykjahverfi. Home of a famous 19th century versifier, Skarða-Gísli, whose son was Arngrímur Gíslason málari (1829-87), a very artistic self-taught painter. See **Tjörn** in Svarfaðardalur.

Hveravellir, the main hot spring area in Reykjahverfi, with several farms. Hothouses, swimming pool and local community centre. The biggest springs are Syðstihver, Uxahver and Baðstofuhver (or Ystihver), one of biggest in Iceland. The river Mýrarkvísl, formed by several streams, flows from there and down near Laxamýri.

Lambafjöll, a large mountain range, the highest peak being Kista (843 m), to the north and east of which is the spur Höfuðreiðarmúli.

Geitafell, (432 m) a mountain and a farm of same name. View-dial on the mountain.

Hólasandur, a sand desert between the Laxárdalur valley and the Lake Mývatn district, formerly a much-travelled route. A major effort is under-way there to reclaim the land. The Kísilvegur road was built across Hólasandur in 1967. Extensive revegetation work done on behalf of local conservation group Húsgull and the Soil Conservation.

Sandvatn, a good fishing lake, only accessable by 4x4 cars.

1	**Norðurlandsvegur,** p. 92	85	**Norðausturvegur,** p. 367
845	**Aðaldalsvegur,** p. 400	848	**Mývatnsvegur,** p. 92
852	**Sandsvegur,** p. 367	853	**Hvammavegur,** p. 400
854	**Staðarbraut,** p. 400	855	**Fagranesvegur,** p. 400
856	**Laxárdalsvegur,** p. 400		

Reykjahlíð-Laxamýri 46 km

805 SVARFAÐARDALSVEGUR

Atlastaðir, the innermost farm in Svarfaðardalur, from where a route goes across Heljardalsheiði moor into the valley Kolbeinsdalur.

Klaufabrekkur, a farm, home of Klaufi, often mentioned in *Svarfdæla saga*. He earlier lived at Klaufanes, where some ruins of his dwellings have been excavated.

Urðir, a church and formerly the home of influential men.

Hreiðarsstaðir, a farm, once the home of Hreiðar heimski ("the foolish"), known as a great practical joker.

Steindyr, ("Stone doorway") on the Þverá river, which emerges from the Steindyragil gorge, where there are numerous plants and a pretty waterfall, **Steindyrafoss**.

Bakki, a farm. Three brothers, Gísli, Eiríkur and Helgi, the most notorious fools in Icelandic folklore, are supposed to have lived there.

Garðshorn ytra, monument to the first settler in the valley, Þorsteinn Svörfuður ("Trouble-maker"), source of the name Svarfaðardalur.

Grund, the land settled by Þorsteinn Svörfuður. Community centre, former assembly site. In the mountain above the farm is **Nykurtjörn**, a small lake in which a monster is supposed to have lurked.

Tjörn, a substantial farm and church and a parsonage till 1917, birthplace of Dr. Kristján Eldjárn (1916-82), 3rd President of Iceland. On the slope directly above the farm there was a cottage farm called Gullbringa. In 1884 the artist Arngrímur Gíslason from Skörð in the Reykjahverfi district moved in there and built a studio on to the cottage. This was probably the first artist's studio in the country. In the 80's the Central Bank of Iceland had the building, known as **Arngrímsstofa** ("Arngrímur's studio"), restored in memory of Kristján Eldjárn, who had written a book about Arngrímur in 1983. In the keeping of the National Museum since 1953 and is looked after by the family at Tjörn.

Húsabakki, there is the exhibition Birdland. The exhibition is focused on teaching children about birds and nature, but is also interesting to adults. There are marked walking paths leading from there through the Nature Reserve, Friðland Svarfdæla, the oldest wetland reserve in Iceland. Created in 1979 by local farmers.

Svarfaðardalur, a broad and fertile valley, with many farms and high beautiful mountains. At the bottom of Skíðadalur valley is the glacier **Gljúfurárjökull**. Svarfaðardalur has four beautiful churches, with old altar pieces. Birdland is an exhibition located at **Húsabakki**. The surrounding valley, Svarfaðardalur, is renowned for its diverse bird life, and marked trails will lead you from Húsabakki through the Svarfaðardalur Nature Reserve.

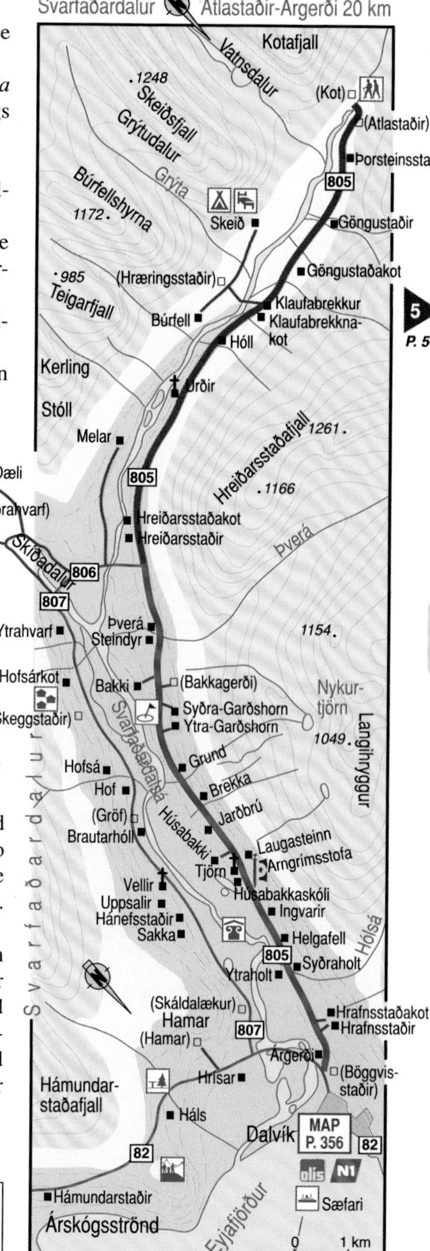

82 **Ólafsfjarðarvegur,** p. 358 — **806** **Tunguvegur,** p. 388

807 **Skíðadalsvegur,** p. 388

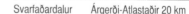

5
P. 568

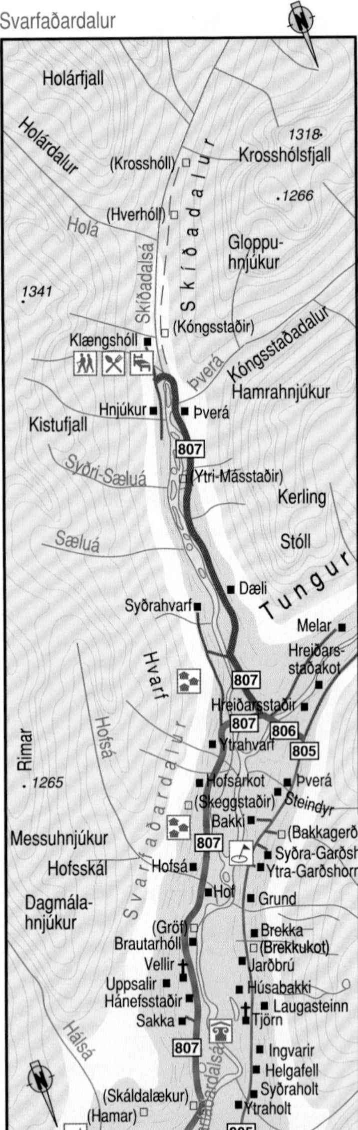

Svarfaðardalur

807 Skíðadalsvegur, 19,3 km.

Kóngsstaðir, an abandoned farm where trees have thrived since the land was put under protection. Good bilberry country.

Klængshóll, the innermost occupied farm in Skíðadalur.

Hofsá, a farm where there is a small wood, with a memorial to Soffonías Þorkelsson (1876-1964), a Canadian Icelander who made a handsome gift to promote forestry work there.

Hof, one of the larger farms in the valley. An old landslide from Hofsskál above the farm has formed clear ridges there. The peak **Messuhnjúkur**(1,100 m) above Hofsskál.

Vellir, a church, the home of Valla-Ljótur in Saga-times. The church was built in 1861 and has a 2-ton bell given by the Canadian Icelander Soffonías Þorkelsson (1876-1964), which was then the biggest bell in Iceland.

Hánefsstaðir, a farm where Eiríkur Hjartarson (1885-1981) started experimental forestry many years ago, but later gave all the land to the Eyjafjörður Forestry Club, which has since sold the farm but not the woodland. Monument to Eiríkur.

Brekkukot, an abandoned farm where Jóhann K. Pétursson, Jóhann Svarfdælingur (1913–1984), was brought up. He was for a time the tallest man in the world, 234 cm og 163 kg.

Sakka, a farm drawing its name from the marshy land around the farm.

Skáldalækur, a small river and a farm of the same name.

Háls, a farm. Rev. Friðrik Friðriksson (1868–1961), the founder of WMCY in Reykjavík 1899, was born there. A memorial to him and a history sign near the farm.

806 Tunguvegur, 1,4 km.

Stóll, ("Seat") a finely formed mountain between valleys, its highest peak, **Kerling** ("Old woman") (1,212 m), giving a fine view.

Tungur, the place where the valleys Svarfaðardalur and Skíðadalur join. Though there are now no trees, *Svarfdæla saga* says the area was so wooded as to provide the material to build an ocean-going ship.

Melar, a farm, where in 1625, at Melaeyrar, the first witch-burning in Iceland took place. Fossils of coniferous trees and cones have been found at a height of 300-350 m in the mountain above.

82 Ólafsfjarðarvegur, p. 358 **805 Svarfaðardalsvegur,** p. 387

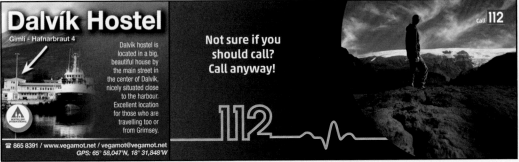

815 **816**

Hörgárdalur, a 50 km long valley on the west of Eyjafjörður, with many farms near its mouth, enclosed by high mountains with permanent snow-drifts. The Hörgá river, though it has the glacial colour, is a good fishing-river.

Þelamörk, the district on the east side of Hörgárdalur from the river Bægisá to the sea. Above are high peaks, the highest being **Strýta** (1,454 m) and **Kista** (1,447 m), near the **Vindheimajökull** glacier in Fossárdalur. Many farms.

815 **Hörgárdalsvegur,** 13,58 km.

816 **Dagverðareyrarvegur,** 10,4 km.

Fornhagi, a farm where Víga-Glúmur lies buried, according to the Sagas.
Auðbrekka, an old manor farm, birthplace of Þorleifur, father of Björn ríki ("the rich") (see Road 61, Vatnsfjörður).

Þríhyrningur, there grows a very rare mushroom, *Calvatia gigantea*, that can grow upto 1 m in diameter.

Möðruvellir, one of most historical places in northern Iceland. Church and parsonage (see Road 82). See road 82, p. 357.
Hlaðir, a farm, the home for many years of the author Ólöf Sigurðardóttir (1857–1933). Steindór Steindórsson frá Hlöðum ("from Hlaðir") (1902–1997), author of this book, was brought up there and uses the name of the farm.
Skipalón, the outermost farm on the east side of the Hörgárdalur valley. Made famous in the early 19th century by Þorsteinn Daníelsson (1786–1882), a builder who was also very enterprising in farming and fishing. The buildings he erected at Skipalón are still standing. Lónsstofa, a log built home dating from 1824, now plastered, in the keeping of the National Museum since 1986, and Smíðahús (Smithy), a tarred wooden building from 1843, in the keeping of the museum since 1985.
Gásir, a farm near the estuary of the river Hörgá, which was for many centuries the biggest port in northern Iceland. Silting in the river eventually made it unusable and trade was then moved to Akureyri. Grass-grown ruins of the old port.
Dagverðareyri, a farm where there was for a time herring processing and a herring factory. The same family has farmed there since the end of the 18th century.
Skjaldarvík, once two farms now combined and made into an old people's home, founded in 1943 by Stefán Jónsson, owner of the farms. In 1965 it was donated to the town of Akureyri, which now runs it. Nearby is a relay station of the State Broadcasting Service.

1 **Norðurlandsvegur,** p. 76
82 **Ólafsfjarðarvegur,** p. 357
813 **Möðruvallavegur,** p. 357

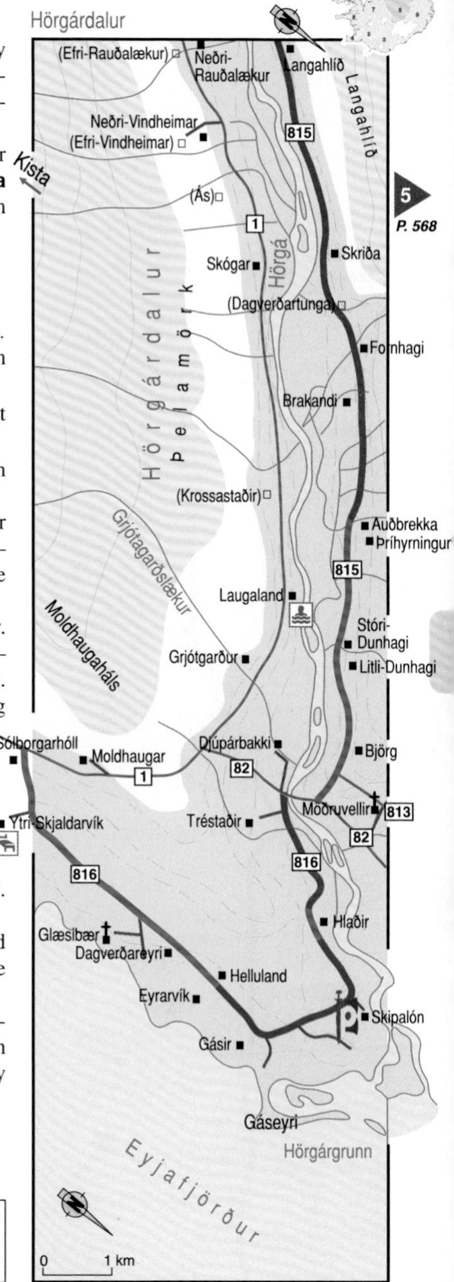

Hraundrangi
719
Staðarbakki
Flaga
Flöguháls
814
Myrká
Árhvammur
Auðnir
1068
Mýrkárbakki
Bakki
Búðarnes
Myrká
Steinsstaðir
(Efstalandskot)
Slembimúli
Hörgá
(Efstaland)
Baugasel
Gerði
Högg
(Miðland)
Staðartunguháls
Þúfnavellir
Barkárdalur
(Neðstaland)
Öxnadalsá
Bugur
Barká
1
814
Barká
Hörgárdalur
Staðartunga
Syðri-Bægisá
Öxnhóll
815
Ytri-Bægisá
Hallfríðarstaðir
855
Garðshorn
Neðri-Rauðalækur
Langahlíð
1
Lönguhlíðarfjall
(Efri-Vindheimar)
Neðri-Vindheimar
Selhnjúkur
815
Hörgá
Skógar
Skriða
(Dagverðartunga)
Ytri-Tunguá
Fornhagi
(Vaglir)
Brakandi
1
0 1 km

5 P. 568

Hjaltadalsheiði, (1,000 m) a moor which was formerly a much-travelled but dangerous route, with mountains (1,200-1,300 m) on both sides.

814 Staðarbakkavegur, 14,28 km.

Myrká, ("Dark river") a farm and a church until 1910 and parsonage till 1850. Connected with one of best known ghost stories of Icelandic folklore, *Djákninn á Myrká* ("The Deacon of Myrká"). It tells how the deacon at Myrká had invited the young woman Guðrún, from another farm, to the Christmas festivities at Myrká. Unfortunately, he drowned in the river Hörgá and was buried at Myrká the week before Christmas. Despite this, he came riding to her farm, where they had not heard of his death, put her behind him on the horse and set off for Myrká. As they rode the moon shone on the back of his head so Guðrún could see his white skull under his hat. She realised she was riding with a dead man, but gave no sign until they reached Myrká, where the deacon tried to drag her into his grave, which he had left open to go on this journey. She managed to get hold of the rope of the lych-gate bell and ring it, and he fell into the grave. The churchyard at Myrká is still well-maintained, and there is still a bell in the lych-gate, as in the folk-tale.

The church at Grund.

Þúfnavellir, a farm, behind it **Barkárdalur** valley, over 7 km². The river Barká comes from under it which is what gives the Hörgá river its glacial colour. In front of the glacier are the undulating Húðarhólar (475 m).

Barkárjökull, a glacier at the end of the valley.

815 Hörgárdalsvegur, 13,58 km.

Melar, community centre.

Skriða, ("Landslide") an ancient manor farm west of the Hörgá river, formerly called Langahlíð. The name was changed after it was buried by a landslide in 1397, in which 16 people lost their lives, including the farmer, Hrafn Bótólfsson, local governor. Early in the 19th century it was the home of Þorlákur Hallgrímsson (1754-1846) of Skriða. He was a pioneer in horticulture and forestry. Some of the trees he planted are still standing.

1 Norðurlandsvegur, p. 75

821 EYJAFJARÐARBRAUT VESTRI

824 Finnastaðavegur, 7 km.

Möðrufell, a farm, long the site of a leprosy hospital. The Möðrufell lavafield and the results of a landslide can be seen.

Klofasteinar, an old place of execution in the Möðrufellshraun lavafield.

Kerling, (1,538 m) the highest mountain in the settled parts of northern Iceland. A fine view from the top.

Grund, one of biggest and most historical manor farms in Eyjafjörður. The home of Sighvatur Sturluson and others of his family in the 13th century. Made famous by Grundar-Helga in 14th century, in connection with the Grundarbardagi ("Battle of Grund"). In the 16th century Þórunn, a daughter of the last Catholic bishop Jón Arason lived there, and the Grund Chairs, one of which is now in the National Muesum, date from her time. Grund was later the home of Magnús Sigurðsson (1846-1925), who made many improvements and built the present church, one of the finest in Iceland and now protected, in 1905. Historic forest from 1900, **Grundarreitur**. The early origins of forestation. Danish aspen and Swiss pine are common. National Forest.

Espihóll, a substantial farm, birthplace of historian Jón Espólín (1760–1836). Often mentioned in *Víga-Glúms saga*.

Botn, a summer camp for children with special needs.

Reykárhverfi, a small village with a school and a community centre. Some geothermal heat.

Jólagarðurinn, (the Christmas Garden), the first of its kind in Iceland.

Hrafnagil, a manor farm now and in the past, a church till 1862, parsonage till 1919. Þorgils skarði was slain there in 1258. Among famous clergymen who lived there were Bishop Jón Arason and the Rev. Jónas Jónasson (1856-1918), writer and scholar. A school and the Laugarborg community centre.

823 Miðbraut, 2,12 km

822 Kristnesvegur, 1,88 km.

Kristnes, (pop. 55) land settled by Helgi magri ("the lean"). In 1947 a tuberculosis sanatorium was opened there. It was the first large building in Iceland to be heated by water from hot springs. It is now a geriatric and rehabilitation hospital.

Kristnesskógur, diverse possibilities for outdoor recreation. Numerous tree species. National Forest.

Kjarni, formerly a substantial farm, now belonging to Akureyri. Forestry station since 1946. Kjarnaskógur ("The Kjarni woods"), Akureyri's outdoor recreation area, is on Kjarni land.

820 Flugvallarvegur, 0,19 km.

Samkomugerði-Akureyri 21 km

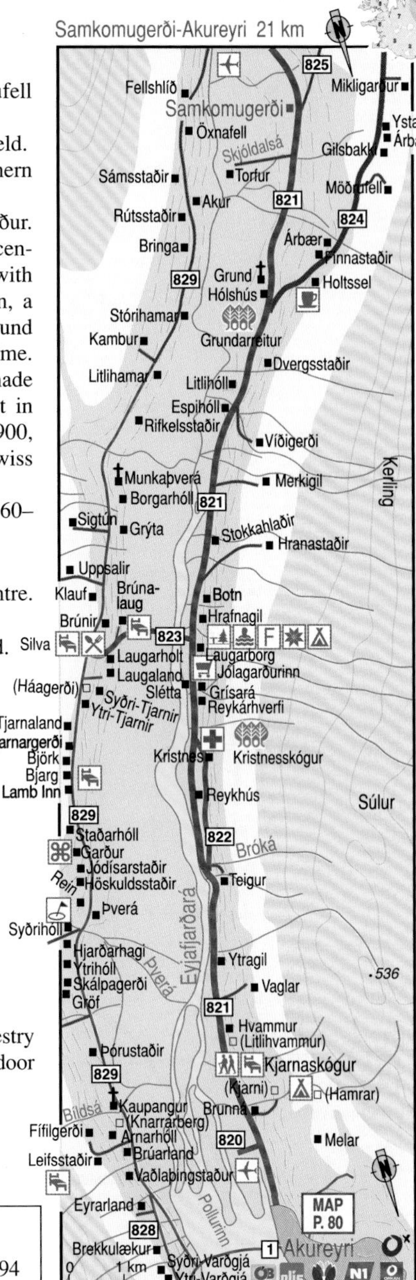

Akureyri-Samkomugerði 21 km

5 P. 568

1 **Norðurlandsvegur,** p. 85	825 **Dalsvegur,** p. 392
828 **Veigastaðavegur,** p. 394	829 **Eyjafjarðarbr. eystri,** p. 394

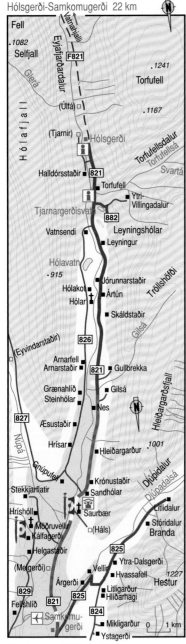

5 P. 568

Hólsgerði-Samkomugerði 22 km

Samkomugerði-Hólsgerði 22 km

Vatnahjalli, a terrace on the mountain south of the river Hafrá and Ullarvötn (or Urðarvötn) lakes. The traditional route from Eyjafjörður to southern Iceland, either via Kjölur or Stórisandur.

Eyjafjarðardalur, a valley. From there lies route F821 to Sprengisandur.

Úlfá, an abandoned farm. An avalanche fell there in 1925.

Tjarnir, now the innermost farm in Eyjafjörður.

Torfufellsdalur, a side-valley going off near Leyningshólar, the northern part being called Villingadalur from which the river **Torfufellsá** flows through a picturesque canyon.

882 Leyningshólavegur, 1,6 km.

Leyningshólar, a hilly area formed by landslide and glacial ridges. Nearby are some nice native woods, the only ones worthy of the name in Eyjafjörður and under the protection of the Eyjafjörður district Forestry Association since 1938-39. This is the only place where native birch has survived in the Eyjafjörður district. Some planting has also taken place.

Tjarnagerðisvatn, a lake by Leyningshólar.There is a "sibyl's grave" mound north of the lake.

Hleiðargarður, a farm for which one of the most notorious and destructive ghosts in the area, Hleiðargarðsskotta, was named.

Saurbær, a church, a parsonage till 1932. Turf church with timber-frame structure, built in 1858. Iceland's largest turf church. In the keeping of the National Museum since 1961. There was a monastery at Saurbær around 1200-1217. The building Sólgarður, by the farmstead, contains the fascinating trivia collection of Sverrir Hermannsson (1928-2008).

Melgerðismelar, site of an airfield built during World War II, for some years the main airfield in northern Iceland. Now only used for gliders. There is geological evidence that the Eyjafjörður fjord reached all the way to Melgerðismelar at the end of the Ice Age.

825 Dalsvegur, 7,4 km.

Djúpidalur, ("Deep valley") narrow and with such high mountains that for nearly half the year the sun can not be seen from the farm **Stóridalur,** formerly one of the manor farms of Eyjafjörður and site of one of three important pagan temples in the district.

Hvassafell, a farm famous at end of 15th century because of the "Hvassafell Case", where an accusation of incest let to a long struggle between secular and clerical powers. The Rev. Jónas Jónasson's novel *Randíður í Hvassafelli* is based on these events.

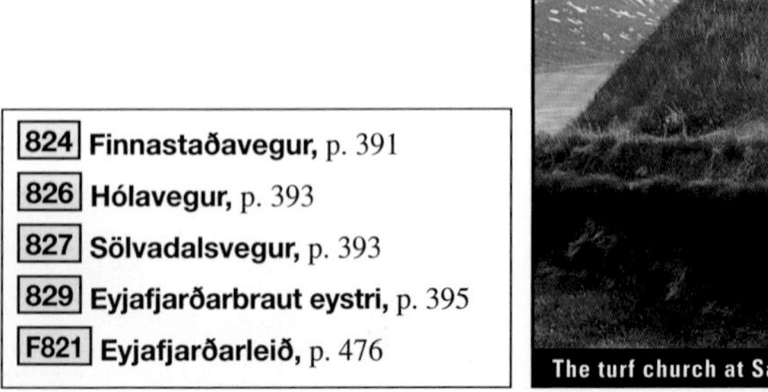

824 **Finnastaðavegur,** p. 391
826 **Hólavegur,** p. 393
827 **Sölvadalsvegur,** p. 393
829 **Eyjafjarðarbraut eystri,** p. 395
F821 **Eyjafjarðarleið,** p. 476

The turf church at Saurbær

827 **Sölvadalsvegur,** 11 km.

Laugafell, (892 m) and Laugafellshnjúkur (987 m) mountain peaks northeast of Hofsjökull. Both are visible from far and wide. Between them is the river Hnjúkskvísl, and to the north the river Laugakvísl. On a ridge leading northwest from Laugafell there are warm springs 40-50°C, from which flows a warm stream. Various kinds of grass flourish at nearby Valllendisbrekkur and around the springs although the altitude is over 700 m. In 1948 the Akureyri Tourist Association built a tourist hut there. Nearby is a rock with a small trough, probably man-made, containing lukewarm water. The story goes that Þórunn from Grund (see Road 821) brought her people to stay there in the 15th century during the Black Death, and made the pool.

Hólafjall, (1,002 m) the mountain above Hólar, a long spur between Eyjafjörður and the Sölvadalur valley. A fine view from the top.

Sölvadalur, a valley going southeast from Möðruvellir, ca. 25 km long. Formerly it had 9 farms but there are now only 3. The valley has often been hard hit by landslides and avalanches, most recently in June, 1995 when there was a landslide in Hólsfjall, 1 km long and half a km wide. It hurtled over the river Núpsá, filling its 50 m deep gorge and continuing onto the other bank. Its path lay from 50 to 150 m away from the farm buildings at Þormóðsstaðir. The climb onto Hólafjall starts at Þormóðsstaðir.

Gnúpufell, a farm across from Saurbær east of the Eyjafjarðará river. Mentioned in old tales. Site of one of the main pagan temples in Eyjafjörður. Bishop Guðbrandur Þorláksson had a printing-press there 1589-91.

826 **Hólavegur,** 12 km.

Hólar, a farm with remains of a 19th century turf farmhouse. In the care of the National Museum since 1990. A wooden church built in 1853 by the same carpenter as built the turf church at Saurbær. Just south of Hólar is **Hólavatn,** a fishing-lake and camp for Christian youth.

821 **Eyjafjarðarbraut vestri,** p. 392 **F821** **Eyjafjarðarleið,** p. 476
829 **Eyjafjarðarbraut eystri,** p. 394

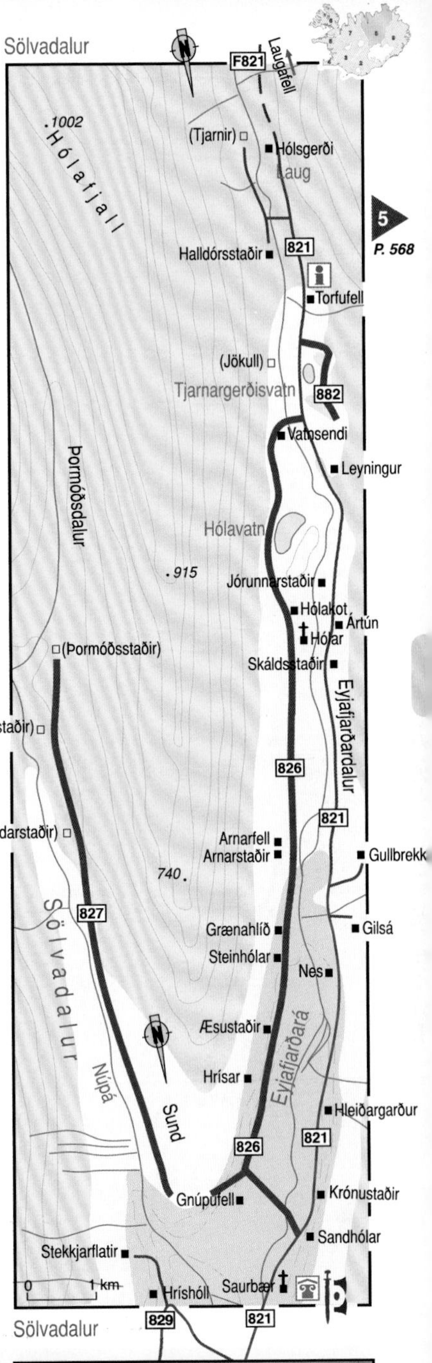

© Olgeir Andrésson www.olgeir.zenfolio.com

5 P. 568

Rifkelsstaðir-1 Norðurlandsvegur 16 km

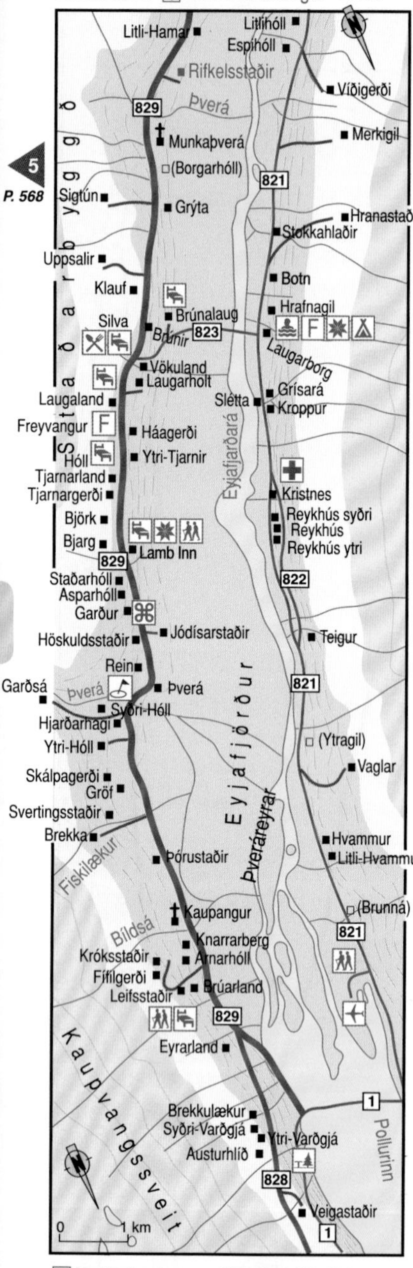

1 Norðurlandsvegur-Rifkelsstaðir 16 km

Munkaþverá, ("Þverá of the monks") has always been one of the most important substantial farms of the district. Church. The home, in Saga times, of Víga-Glúmur and a little later of Einar Eyjólfsson Þveræingur ("Of Þverá"), who probably built the first church there. According to *Ólafs saga helga* in *Heimskringla* Einar protested when his brother Guðmundur ríki ("the rich") of Möðruvellir suggested King Ólafur be given the island Grímsey, as he requested. Einar pointed out that the king could support a whole army on Grímsey from where he might then invade and conquer Iceland. His arguments were accepted and the idea was dropped. A monastery founded in 1155 remained there till the Reformation in 1550, after which Munkaþverá was long a residence of sheriffs and magistrates. The Vitaðsgjafi field there never lay fallow. In the churchyard is the Sturlungareitur ("Plot of the Sturlungas"), probably the grave of Sighvatur Sturluson and his sons, who fell in battle at Örlygsstaðir in Skagafjörður. Memorial to the last Catholic bishop Jón Arason, who studied in the monastery.

The church at Munkaþverár.

Grýta, a small farm near Munkaþverá, believed to be the birthplace of Jón Arason. Memorial garden to him.

Laugaland, a parsonage, school, the community centre Freyvangur. A girls' school from 1876 to the end of the 19th century, a school of domestic science 1937-75.

Þveráreyrar, sandspits north of the river Þverá. Where Eyjólfur ofsi and Hrafn Oddsson fought Þorgils skarða and Sturla Þórðarson in 1255, Eyjólfur was killed. **Staðarbyggð**, a settlement between the rivers.

Garðsárgil, rocky gorge in the Þverá river below the farm Garðsá. What was formerly a small wood has now grown into a pretty grove.

Kaupangssveit, the district between the farm Kaupangur and the Þverá river, off which goes Garðsárdalur.

Kaupangur, a church and substantial farm. Above it is the Bíldsárskarð pass over which there was a riding-trail into the Fnjóskadalur valley.

Bíldsá, small tributary just north of Kaupangur. *Landnámabók* ("The Book of Settlements") states that Helgi magri ("the lean") moored his ship by the river Bíldsá, the fjord having reached that far inland at the time.

828 Veigastaðavegur, 3,9 km.

Litla-Eyrarland, a farm near the site of the ancient Vaðlaþing assembly.

1 Norðurlandsvegur, p. 85	**821 Eyjafjarðarbraut vestri,** p. 391
822 Kristnesvegur, p. 391	**823 Miðbraut,** p. 391

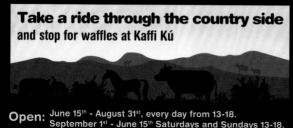

829 EYJAFJARÐARBRAUT EYSTRI

Eyjafjörður, the collective name for the whole district south of Akureyri, a 60 km long valley narrowing towards its head, where it is sometimes called Eyjafjörður Valley. Fertile and well cultivated, with many prosperous farms. High and imposing mountains, especially on the west. **Eyjafjarðará** is a smooth-flowing, rather deep river but does not have much fish.

Möðruvellir, a manor farm now and in the past. The home of Guðmundur ríki ("the rich") Eyjólfsson in Saga times. Early in the 15th century the home of Loftur ríki Guttormsson and later of his descendants. In the church there is a fine old altar-piece. In the churchyard there is the only remaining bell-gate of its kind, dating from around 1780. In the keeping of the National Museum since 1962.

Möðruvallafjall, the mountain above Möðruvellir, high and steep, but fairly grassy.

Kálfagerði, a farm, home of the 18th century Kálfagerði brothers, guilty of murder and other crimes.

Helgastaðir, a farm, the childhood home of the writer Páll J. Árdal (1857-1930), and birthplace of authoress Kristín Sigfúsdóttir (1876-1953).

Fellshlíð, a farm, birthplace of Hallgrímur Kristinsson (1876-1923), one of the leaders of the cooperative movement in Iceland.

Öxnafell, from there came Margrét J. Thorlacius (1908–1989), well-known in Iceland for clairvoyance and spiritual healing.

Rútsstaðir, a farm, birthplace of the Rev. Helgi Hálfdánarson (1826-1894), later the headmaster of the Theological college. He was a respected writer, historian and hymn-writer. His son was Bishop Jón Helgason (1866-1942) who was born at Garðar on Álftanes near Reykjavík.

Rifkelstaðir, a farm, site of one of the local pagan temples, Freyshof ("Temple of Freyr"), remains of which are said still to be visible.

821 **Eyjafjarðarbraut vestri,** p. 392
826 **Hólavegur,** p. 393
827 **Sölvadalsvegur,** p. 393

Möðruvellir-Rifkelsstaðir 13 km

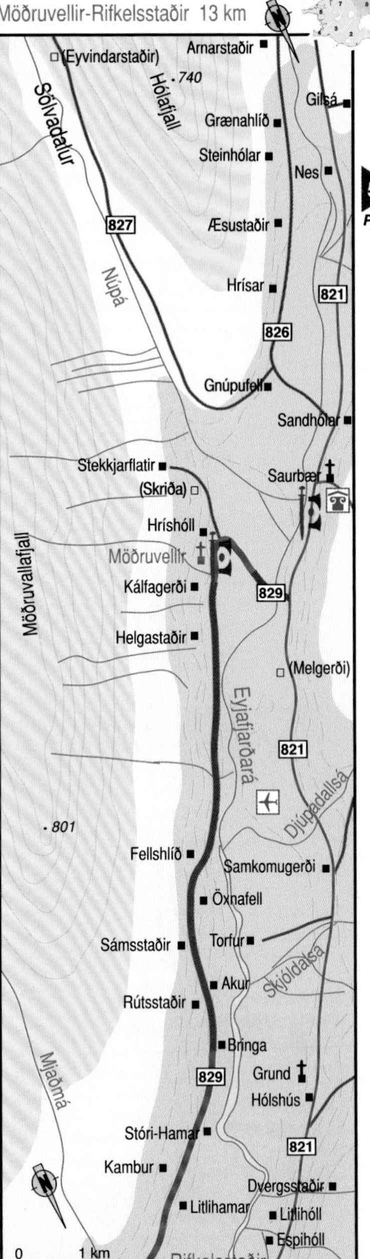

Rifkelsstaðir-Möðruvellir 13 km

The church and bell-gate at Mörðuvellir

The bell-gate

6
P. 569

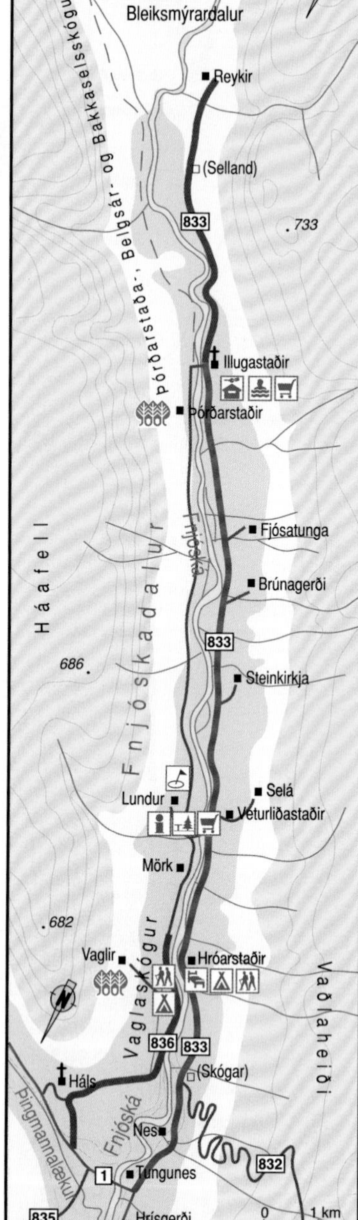

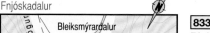

833 Illugastaðavegur, 20 km. **836 Vaglaskógarvegur,** 5,5 km.

Bleiksmýrardalur, a grassy, fertile valley through which flows the river Fnjóská. The last horse-fight in Iceland took place there at Vindhólanes in 1623.

Reykir, a farm in Fnjóskadalur. Geothermal heat and cultivation. Two very rare plants, Ólafur's eyebright and Wall speedwell grow there.

Selland, an abandoned farm where the printer Sigurður O. Björnsson (1901-75) started growing coniferous and birch trees in 1946.

Illugastaðir, an abandoned manor farm and a church in which is an old pulpit. The northern Iceland trade unions have built a number of summer houses there.

Þórðarstaðir, a farm, site of one of the finest birchwoods in Iceland. Home of 19th century scholar and book-collector Jónatan Þorláksson (1825-1906), who took great care of the trees. The woods there, at nearby Belgsá river and Bakkasel and the areas of Lundarskógur and Vaglaskógur form the largest woods in northern Iceland and one of greatest in the whole country. Near Þórðarstaðir is a bridge over the Fnjóská river.

Þórðarstaðaskógur, (incl. **Belgsáskógar** and **Bakkaselsskógar**) birch forest with large trees, also older plantings of Norwegian spruce and black pine. Belgsá and Bakkasel are within Þórðarstaðarskógur forest. A 4WD is required. National Forest.

Lundur, a farm since the settlement, east of the Fnjóská river. Protected woods, in the care of the Forestry Service. Home of versifier Björn Jónsson (1768-1845). A 9 hole golf course.

Vaglaskógur, second-largest forest in the country and one of the most beautiful. Popular for outdoor recreation, marked hiking paths. Large and straight birch trees, up to 13 m. Tree collection. National Forest.

Skógar, once a ferry point by Fnjóská, before the bridge was built, telephone and post office and a school from 1916-1972. Now it is a community centre for the people of Fnjóskadaldur and there is a café at Skógar during the summer months and a museum commemorating its former purpose.

832 Vaðlaheiðarvegur, 19 km, the old road over Vaðlaheiði, to Fnjóskadalur.

Vaðlaheiðargöng, a tunnel planned to open in the third quarter of 2018. It will have a length of 7,400 m and replace a 21 km section of route 1 including the Víkurskarð pass.

1 Norðurlandsvegur, p. 87 **835 Fnjóskadalsv. eystri,** p. 397

Fnjóskadalur

835 Fnjóskadalsvegur eystri, 22,4 km.

Dalsmynni, a deep pass, through which the Fnjóská has forced its way into Eyjafjörður. Steep, high mountains 800-1,000 m on both sides, very little flat land, danger of avalanches and landslides. Now no farms on the south side, but on the north are two prosperous farms, Skarð and Þverá. Some woods nearby.

In the Dalsmynni pass.

Flateyjardalsheiði, and Flateyjardalur, a continuation of Fnjóskadalur to the sea. The moors are above the valley, but there is good flat land near the sea, where it is grassy and there are fishing-rivers. Formerly there were several farms, the last one abandoned in 1954, but buildings still stand at Brettingsstaðir (once the site of a church) and Jökulsá. Fine scenery. The first part of the Saga of Finnbogi rammi took place in Flateyjardalur.

Garður, an abandoned farm. The first place in Iceland where wild gypsophilia was found.

Végeirsstaðir, an abandoned farm where the landowners planted various trees.

Hallgilsstaðir, a farm where Tryggvi Gunnarsson (1835-1917), later a member of parliament and bank director, started out as a farmer (see Road 83, Laufás).

834 Fnjóskadalsvegur vestri, 4,87 km.

Draflastaðir, a farm and a parsonage.

1 **Norðurlandsvegur,** p. 87
833 **Illugastaðavegur,** p. 396
836 **Vaglaskógarvegur,** p. 396
F899 **Flateyjardalsvegur,** p. 478

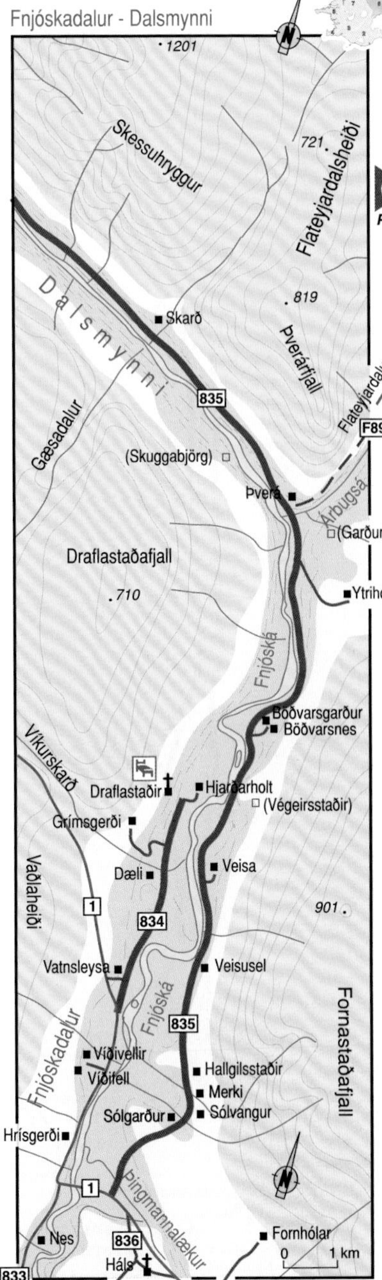

6
P. 569

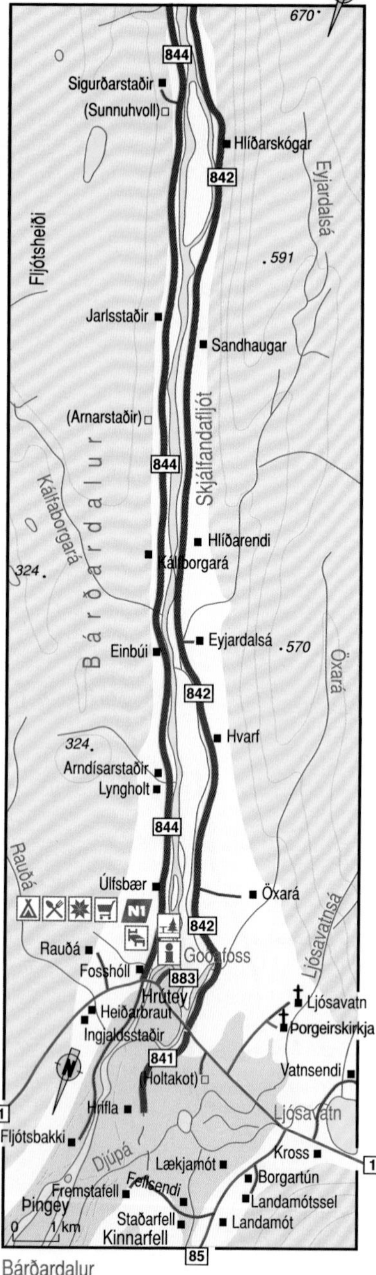

Bárðardalur

Ljósavatnsskarð

©Jónas Reynir Helgason

844 **Bárðardalsv. eystri,** 22,6 km. **883** **Goðafossvegur,** 0,34 km.

Bárðardalur, the valley opening between Ljósavatnsskarð pass and Goðafoss and reaching up onto the moors, one of the longest inhabited valleys in Iceland, but rather narrow and shallow. Basalt mountains up to 750 m on the west, Fljótsheiði moors, (528 m) on the east. The river Skjálfandafljót flows through the valley over the Bárðardalshraun lava field that probably came all the way from Trölladyngja in Ódáðahraun north of Vatnajökull more than 7,000 years ago. The valley is dry, mostly grassy, but with some soil erosion on the eastern side. Bushes on the western slopes. Few farms but good sheep pastures.

841 **Fremstafellsvegur,** 5,3 km. **842** **Bárðardalsv. vestri,** 37,66 km.

Sandhaugar, a farm mentioned in *Grettis saga*. Some woods now in the care of the Forestry Service.

Eyjadalsá, a church and parsonage till 1858. According to *Grettis saga* this is where the housewife at Sandhaugar was going when Grettir the strong carried her across the river Eyjadalsá.

Öxará, a farm since the settlement. The home of Þorkell hákur, with whom Skarphéðinn Njálsson argued at Alþingi and whom Guðmundur ríki slew, as told in the *Ljósvetninga saga*.

Goðafoss, ("Falls of the gods") among the finest in the country, not very high but cut into two horseshoe-shaped falls. Not far above the falls the river Skjálfandafljót divides in two, forming the island **Hrútey**. According to the Sagas Þorgeir of Ljósavatn threw his statues of the gods into the falls when Iceland converted to Christianity in the year 1000, hence the name. Just below Goðafoss is a hole through the lava known as Hansensgat ("Hansen's hole") into which a chemist from Akureyri named Hansen fell but survived unhurt. *Undirheimaförin* ("Journey to the Underworld") by the poet Kristján Jónsson, called Fjallaskáld, commemorates the event.

Hrifla, a farm on the banks of Skjálfandafljót. The birthplace of Jónas Jónsson (1875-1968), one of the most influential politicians of this century, and a great social innovator. He founded the Progressive Party.

Djúpá, ("Deep river") flowing from the lake Ljósavatn into the Skjálfandafljót river. The waterfall Barnafoss at the confluence.

1 **Norðurlandsvegur,** p. 88 **85** **Norðausturvegur,** p. 366

Ljósavatn

©Jónas Reynir Helgason

843 **Lundarbrekkuvegur,** 2,89 km.

Svartárkot, the innermost farm on the east side of the Bárðardalur valley, 400 m above sea level, near the moors and at the edge of the Ódáðahraun lava field. It is on the lake **Svartárvatn** to which farmer Einar Friðriksson brought trout spawn from Lake Mývatn late in the 19th century, a unique event in those days. Good fishing in the lake. The river Svartá, in which is the waterfall **Ullarfoss**, flows out of the lake, is joined by Suðurá, and flows into Skjálfandafljót a little north of the farm Víðiker. Jeep track from Svartárkot to the Dyngjufjöll mountains.

Víðiker, a farm at the edge of the moors east of the Bárðardalur valley. Birthplace of Hermann Jónasson (1858-1923), headmaster and member of parliament, known for his skill in interpreting dreams.

Lundarbrekka, church and farm east of the Skjálfandafljót river. Originally settled by Gnúpa-Bárður, the first settler in Bárðardalur, who later moved his whole household right across the central highlands to Fljótshverfi near Kirkjubæjarklaustur in the south. No doubt he was the first Icelander to take that route.

842 **Bárðardalsvegur vestri,** 37,6 km.

Mjóidalur, ("Narrow valley") a deserted valley off the Bárðardalur valley, where a farm of the same name was abandoned in 1894. That was the last home in Iceland of poet Stephan G. Stephansson, who emigrated to Canada (see Road 751).

Íshólsvatn, a trout lake in an uninhabited valley above the farm Mýri. Sprengisandsleið (Road F26) lies along its eastern shore.

Aldeyjarfoss, an impressive waterfall in the Skjálfandafljót river, in a unique setting of basalt columns and rock caves.

Aldeyjarfoss

Mýri, now the innermost farm in the west of the Bárðardalur valley. Beginning of Sprengisandsleið (Road F26).

Stóruvellir, a substantial farm of old, one of oldest stone houses in rural Iceland, built of Icelandic stone. A rare species of wild corn grows there. Suspension bridge over the river Skjálfandafljót. Nearby community centre, Kiðagil, and boarding school. Above the farm is the mountain Vallafjall (670 m). Kiðagil is located in the middle of Bárðardalur on the west side of Skjálfandafljót. It is named after Kiðagil at Sprengisandur which Grímur Thomsen wrote a poem about. Travellers used to rest there and graze their horses before or after crossing the Sprengisandur desert. In 1960 Kiðagil was donated by Páll H. Jónsson (1860-1955) so that a grammarschool could be built in the valley. Now there is a travel service all year. At Kiðagil is an exhibition, Outlaws at Ódáðahraun, myth or reality, that gives good insight to the life of icelandic outlaws. There is also an exhibition about the first journey on cars over Sprengisandur. Kiðagil is also a community centre.

844 **Bárðardalsvegur eystri,** p. 398 F26 **Sprengisandsleið,** p. 432

Bárðardalur

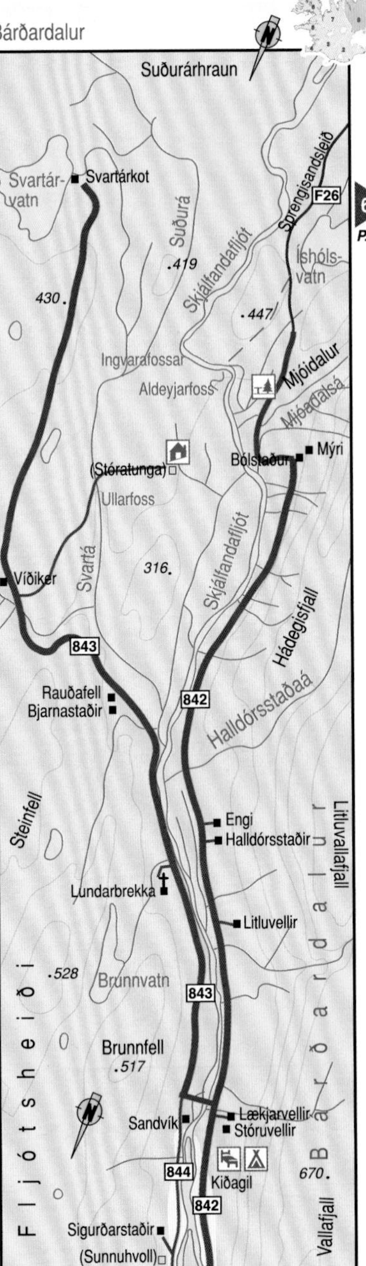

Bárðardalur

6
P. 569

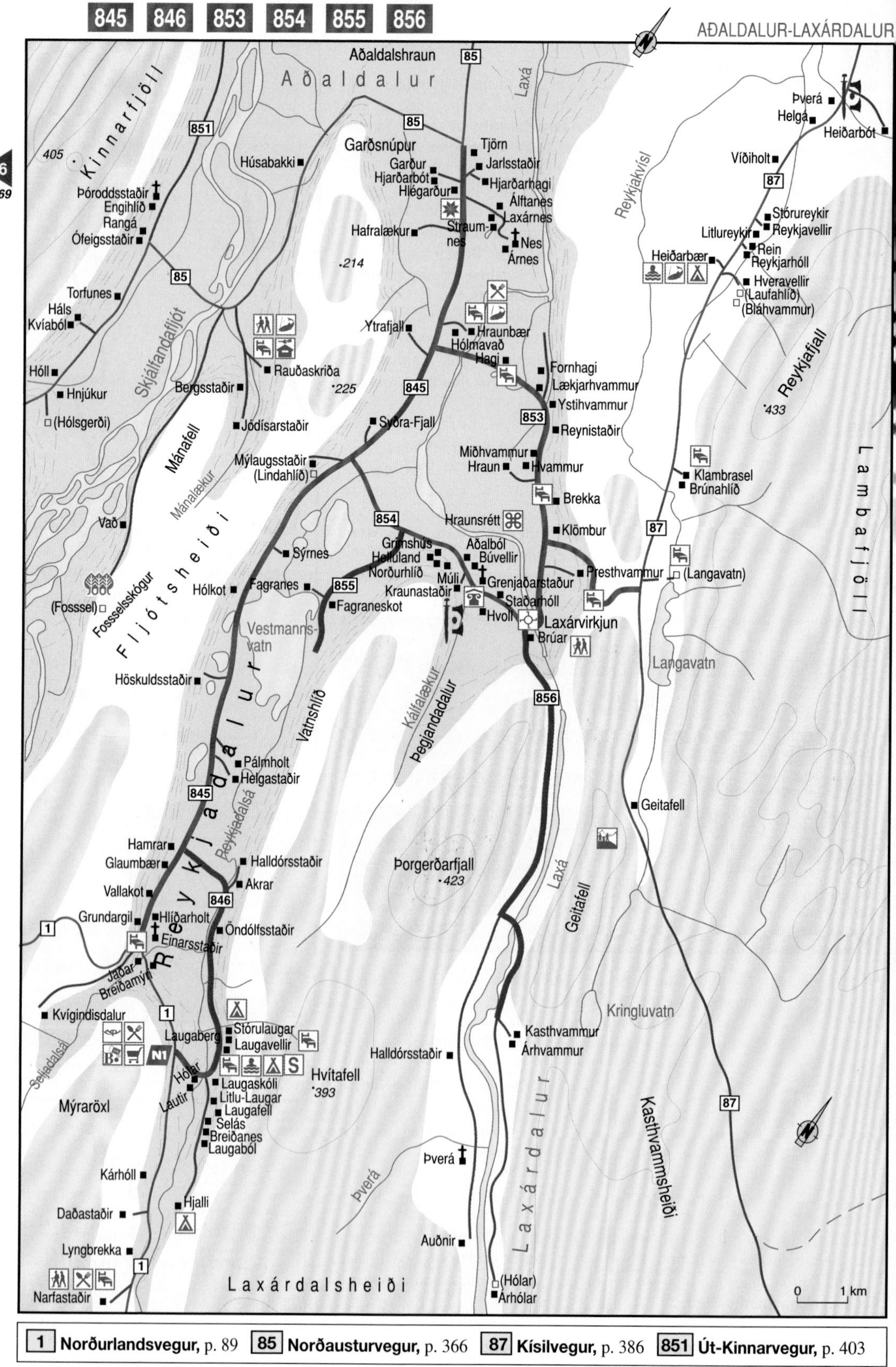
Aðaldalshraun
Aðaldalur
Kinnarfjöll
405
Laxá
Þverá
Helgá
Heiðarbót
Víðiholt
Reykjakvísl
Tjörn
Jarlsstaðir
Garðsnúpur
Garður
Hjarðarbót
Hlégarður
Hjarðarhagi
Álftanes
Laxárnes
Húsabakki
Þóroddsstaðir
Engihlíð
Rangá
Ófeigsstaðir
Hafralækur
Straum-nes
Nes
Árnes
Stórureykir
Litlureykir
Reykjavellir
Rein
Heiðarbær
Reykjarhóll
Hveravellir
(Laufahlíð)
(Bláhvammur)
214
Torfunes
Háls
Kvíaból
Skjálfandafljót
Ytrafjall
Hraunbær
Hólmavað
Hagi
Rauðaskriða
225
Fornhagi
Lækjarhvammur
Ystihvammur
Reykjafjall
433
Höll
Hnjúkur
(Hólsgerði)
Bergsstaðir
Jódísarstaðir
Syðra-Fjall
Reynistaðir
Mánafell
Mýlaugsstaðir
(Lindahlíð)
Miðhvammur
Hraun
Hvammur
Klambrasel
Brúnahlíð
Lambafjöll
Mánalækur
Vað
Brekka
Hraunsrétt
Klömbur
Fljótsheiði
Sýrnes
Grímshús
Helluland
Norðurhlíð
Aðalból
Búvellir
Presthvammur
(Langavatn)
Fossselsskógur
(Fosssel)
Hólkot
Fagranes
Fagraneskot
Kraunastaðir
Múli
Grenjaðarstaður
Staðarhóll
Hvoll
Laxárvirkjun
Brúar
Vestmannsvatn
Langavatn
Höskuldsstaðir
Kálfalækur
Þegjandadalur
Vatnshlíð
Reykjadalur
Pálmholt
Helgastaðir
Reykjadalsá
Geitafell
Hamrar
Glaumbær
Halldórsstaðir
Akrar
Þorgerðarfjall
423
Vallakot
Grundargil
Hlíðarholt
Einarsstaðir
Öndólfsstaðir
Jaðar
Breiðamýri
Kvígindisdalur
Kringluvatn
Stórulaugar
Laugaberg
Laugavellir
Kasthvammur
Árhvammur
Halldórsstaðir
Hólar
Hvítafell
393
Laugaskóli
Litlu-Laugar
Laugafell
Mýraröxl
Lautir
Selás
Breiðanes
Laugaból
Seljadalsá
Kasthvammsheiði
Laxárdalur
Þverá
Kárhóll
Hjalli
Daðastaðir
Auðnir
Lyngbrekka
Narfastaðir
Laxárdalsheiði
(Hólar)
Árhólar
0
1 km

1 Norðurlandsvegur, p. 89 85 Norðausturvegur, p. 366 87 Kísilvegur, p. 386 851 Út-Kinnarvegur, p. 403

845 **Aðaldalsvegur,** 17 km.

Nes, a farm and church, parsonage till 1860. Good fishing. Among those serving there was the poet Rev. Einar Sigurðsson of Nes (1538-1626), often associated with Heydalir (S-Múl) in the eastern fjords.

Hólmavað, a farm, birthplace of poet, writer and translator Jakobína Johnson (1883-1977), who for years lived and wrote in Seattle, USA.

Ytra-Fjall, a farm, long the home of writer and scholar Indriði Þorkelsson (1869-1943).

Syðra-Fjall, a farm. Þorkell Jóhannesson (1895-1960), professor, historian and rector of the University of Iceland came from there.

Vestmannsvatn, a fishing-lake, 2.38 km^2, fed by the river Reykjadalsá, emptied by Eyvindarlækur, with a much-indented shore and many grassy islets. To the east is the summer camp of the Church Youth Association the Hólar diocese.**Vatnshlíð,** wooded slope to the east of Vestmannsvatn lake.

Reykjadalur, a valley starting at Vestmannsvatn lake and reaching on to the moors. Shallow, with low moors on each side: Fljótsheiði to the west, Laxárdals- and Mývatnsheiði to the east. Grassy, several farms.

Helgastaðir, a farm of the original settlement, an ancient manor farm and church till 1872, parsonage till 1907.

Einarsstaðir, a substantial farm and a church.

846 **Austurhlíðarvegur,** 5,8 km.

Laugar, (pop. 128) a small school and commerce community in the eastern part of the Þingeyjar region. See p. 89.

Breiðamýri, a community centre and beside it a grove of trees planted some time before 1920.

853 **Hvammavegur,** 8 km.

Hagi II, from there came the artist Hringur Jóhannesson (1932–1996).

Hraunsrétt, a sheep fold, built in 1838.

Hvammar, several farms east of the river Laxá, north of power-station. Southernmost is Presthvammur, where the chieftain Áskell of *Reykdæla saga* is thought to have lived.

854 **Staðarbraut,** 6,9 km.

Múli, an old manor farm, church, and parsonage till 1880. Many well-known pastors have served there. In the 15th century there was Sveinbjörn Þórðarson, known as Barna-Sveinbjörn ("Sveinbjörn of the children") who fathered 50 children to whom he admitted, but it was thought there were more. Among his descendants were the bishops Jón Arason and Guðbrandur Þorláksson. Among other well-known incumbents were Þorleifur Skaftason (1663-1748), and Benedikt Kristjánsson (1824–1903). In the 12th century Oddur Helgason, Stjörnu-Oddi (Star-Oddi), a farmhand, lived at Múli. He was known for analysing the movement of the sun, moon and stars.

Grenjaðarstaður, an ancient manor farm, church and parsonage, considered one of best livings in Iceland. One of the large farm houses of the northern type, mostly built in the later half of the 19th century. Housed a post office in the later half of the 19th century, till around 1900. In the keeping of the National Museum since 1954. A folk museum since 1958.

Laxá, one of best known and most popular salmon rivers in the country. Comes from Lake Mývatn and has an average flow of 40 m^3/sec. Very beautiful with islets, pools and whirlpools. 340 islets with vegetation have been counted in the river, and there are twelve fords.

Laxárvirkjun, a hydro-electric station, near Brúar at the foot of Laxárgljúfur gorge, first built in 1939 but extended twice since. The gorge is deep and in places wild, with the waterfalls Brúarfossar (sometimes called Laxárfossar) at the lower end.

855 **Fagranesvegur,** 2,3 km.

856 **Laxárdalsvegur,** 13,76 km.

Laxárdalur, a shallow and fairly narrow valley, 26 km long from Brúar to Helluvað by Lake Mývatn. Laxá runs along it on a lava bed. Luxuriant vegetation.

Kringluvatn, a good fishing lake.

Þverá, a manor farm, mentioned in early history. A church of hewn stone, built 1878, with an altar-piece by Arngrímur Gíslason. The first cooperative in Iceland, Kaupfélag Þingeyinga, was founded at Þverá in 1882 in a turf farm house which is still standing, built in the latest half of the 19th century. In the keeping of the National Museum since 1968.

Auðnir, a farm, long the home of Benedikt Jónsson (1846-1939), prominent in social affairs of the district. His daughter, the writer Unnur Bjarklind, pen-name Hulda, (1881-1946), was born and brought up there.

Fosssel, an abandoned farm on Fljótsheiði, quite far to the north of the road. Extensive birchwoods, now protected by the Suður-Þingeyingar Forestry Association. The forest can be reached with a small car and has good hiking trails and rest stops. The view from there is good especially across to the island **Þingey**, used of old for official gatherings, in the Skjálfandafljót river on the west side. According to the Sagas the settler Bárður towed his ships up the Skjálfandafljót river to **Skipapollur** ("Boat pool") below Þingey.

Grenjaðarstaður

6 p. 569

Björg - Þóroddsstaður 13 km

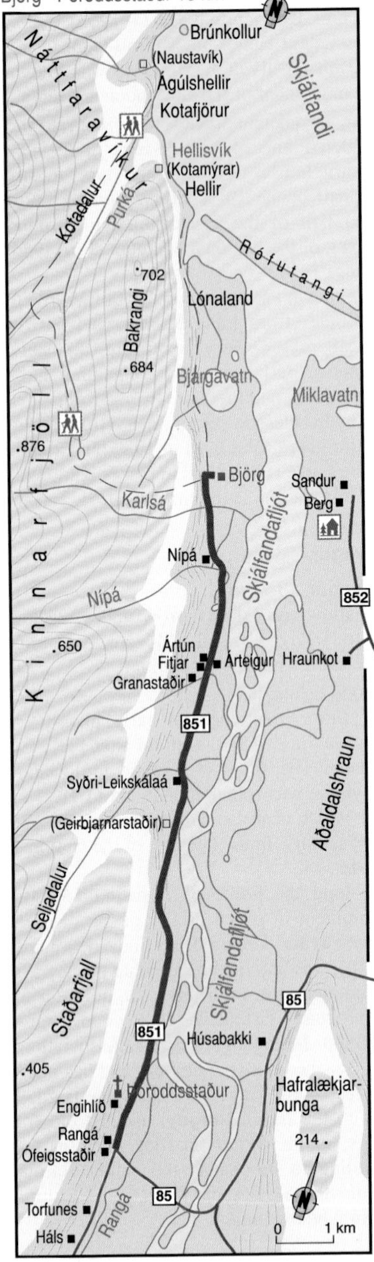

Þóroddsstaður- Björg 13 km

Náttfaravíkur, bays beneath the Víknafjöll mountains. The Book of Settlements relates how, when Garðar Svavarsson, one of the first Norsemen to visit Iceland, spent the winter in Húsavík, a boat broke free from his ship, and in it, a man called Náttfari, and a slave and a slave-woman, came ashore. Náttfari settled in Náttfaravíkur for a time, later moving to Reykjadalur, from where he was driven when other settlers arrived.

Bakrangi, (702 m) a mountain on the edge of Kaldakinn.

Björg, the northernmost farm in Kaldakinn, with rights to meadows and perquisites. Road 851 ends there, but there is a passable road extending another 5 km to the sea, to a point about an hour's walk from Naustavík. To walk north around Litlufjörubjarg and Hellisflös to Hellisvík it was necessary to wait for low tide and a calm sea. There, running south into the sheer cliff is a long cave known as Ágúlshellir or Þinghellir; according to a folktale it was the home of a giant named Ágúll, and in the 17th century a magician, Arnór Ólafsson of Sandur in Aðaldalur, is supposed to have had friendly dealings with him. It was not known exactly how long the cave was, as it was generally half full of gravel, but it was believed that a tunnel deep inside it led into another far bigger cave where Ágúll kept his hoard of gold. Various changes have taken place on the western shore of the Skjálfandaflói bay since 1970. Where it used to be possible to walk on the beach, the sea began eroding the cliffs and many old structural remains on the shore have been washed into the sea. The popular explanation is that there is a connection between this and the volcanic activity in the Þingeyjarsýslur counties during the same years. In 1973 the sea washed all the loose material out of the cave, revealing its floor at a depth of 50 m, but no tunnel to the hoard of gold came to light, and, worse still, the walking route north to Víkur is now completely impassable. A 10 m long tunnel was made leading out of the cave; this solved the problem to begin with, but after a few years the sea advanced so far into the shore from the west that the path is completely impassable. It is to be hoped that this impressive route will be opened up once again, but those intending to travel this way should seek guidance at Björg.

Þóroddsstaður, a farm, church site and vicarage until 1916.

85 **Norðausturvegur,** p. 367
852 **Sandsvegur,** p. 367
845 **Aðaldalsvegur,** p. 400

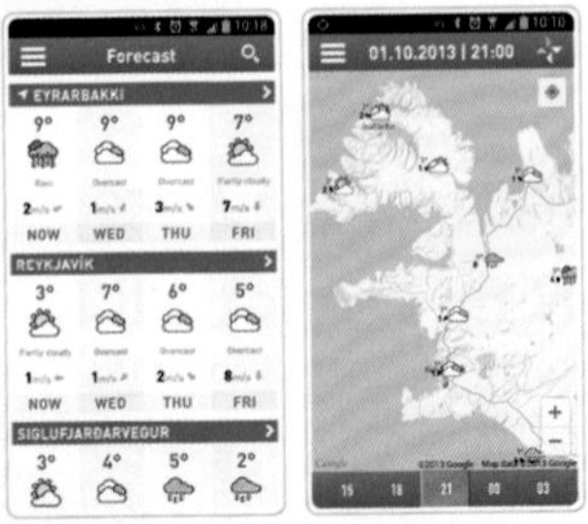

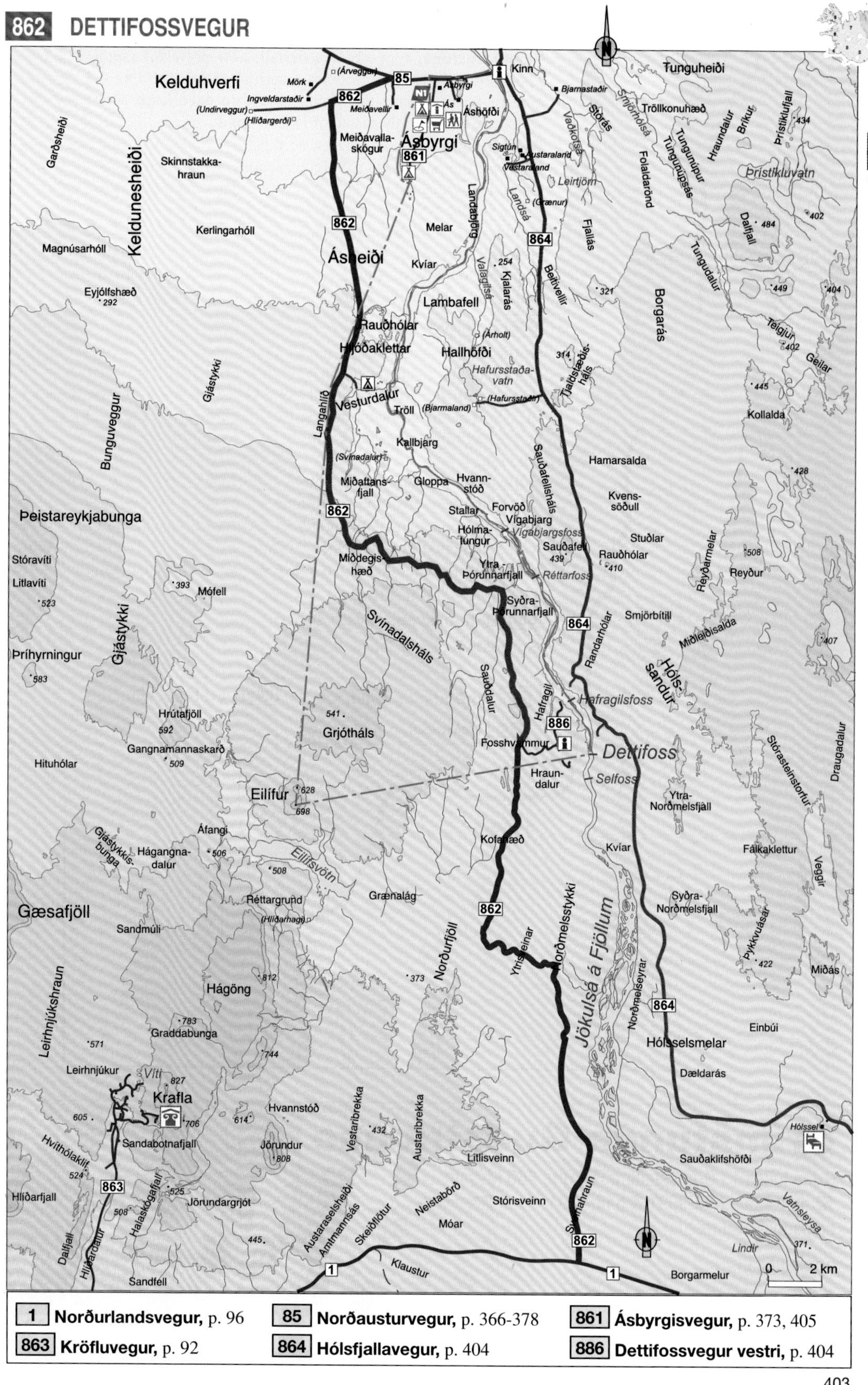
Kelduhverfi
Mörk
(Árvegur)
Ingveldarstaðir
(Undirveggur)
(Hlíðargerði)
Meiðavellir
Ásbyrgi
Ás
Áshöfði
Kinn
Bjarnastaðir
Tunguheiði
Tröllkonuhæð
Meiðavalla-
skógur
Sigtún
Austaraland
Vestaraland
Leirtjörn
(Grænur)
Skinnstakka-
hraun
Kelduneshéiði
Garðsheiði
Kerlingarhóll
Magnúsarhóll
Melar
Ásheiði
Kvíar
Landsá
Fjallás
Folaldaröind
Tungunúpur
Tungunúpsás
Hraundalur
Brikur
Pristikluffjall
Pristikluvatn
Dalfjall
Tungudalur
Borgarás
Eyjólfshæð
292
Lambafell
Kjalarás
Beitivellir
Rauðhólar
Hljóðaklettar
Hallhöfði
(Árholt)
Hafurssstaða-
vatn
(Hafursstaðir)
Teigjur
Geilar
Kollalda
Gjástykki
Bunguveggur
Vesturdalur
Tröll
(Bjarmaland)
Langahlíð
Kallbjarg
(Svínadalur)
Sauðafellsháls
Hamarsalda
Miðaftans-
fjall
Gloppa
Hvann-
stóð
Kvens-
söðull
Þeistareykjabunga
Stallar
Forvöð
Vígabjarg
Hólma-
tungur
Vígabjargsfoss
Stuðlar
Stóravíti
Litlavíti
523
Miðdegis-
hæð
Ytra-
Þórunnarfjall
Sauðafell
Rauðhólar
Réttarfoss
Reyðarmelar
Reyður
Mófell
Syðra-
Þórunnarfjall
Smjörbítill
Randarhólar
Miðleiðisalda
Svínadalsháls
Þríhyrningur
583
Sauðdalur
Hafragil
Hóls-
sandur
Hafragilsfoss
Hrútafjöll
Grjótháls
Fosshvammur
Dettifoss
Stórasteinstorfur
Draugadalur
Gangnamannaskarð
Hituhólar
Eilífur
Hraun-
dalur
Selfoss
Ytra-
Norðmelsfjall
Áfangi
Gjástykkis-
bunga
Hágangna-
dalur
Eilífsvötn
Kofahæð
Kvíar
Fálkaklettur
Veggir
Réttargrund
(Hlíðarhagi)
Grænalág
Syðra-
Norðmelsfjall
Gæsafjöll
Sandmúli
Norðurfjöll
Ytrisveinar
Norðmelsstykki
Jökulsá á Fjöllum
Pykkvuásar
Miðás
Hágöng
Norðmelseyrar
Leirhnjúkshraun
Graddabunga
Hólsselsmelar
Einbúi
Leirhnjúkur
Víti
Krafla
Dældarás
Hvannstóð
Hólssel
Hvíthólaklif
Sandabotnafjall
Vestaribrekka
Austaribrekka
Jörundur
Litlisveinn
Sauðaklifshöfði
Hlíðarfjall
Halaskógafjall
Jörundargrjót
Austaraselsheiði
Ammannsás
Skeiðflötur
Neistaborð
Stórisveinn
Svínahraun
Vatnsleysa
Dalfjall
Hlíðardalur
Móar
Klaustur
Lindir
Sandfell
Borgarmelur
0 2 km
19
P. 582
1 Norðurlandsvegur, p. 96
863 Kröfluvegur, p. 92
85 Norðausturvegur, p. 366-378
864 Hólsfjallavegur, p. 404
861 Ásbyrgisvegur, p. 373, 405
886 Dettifossvegur vestri, p. 404

Dettifoss-Grímsstaðir 28 km

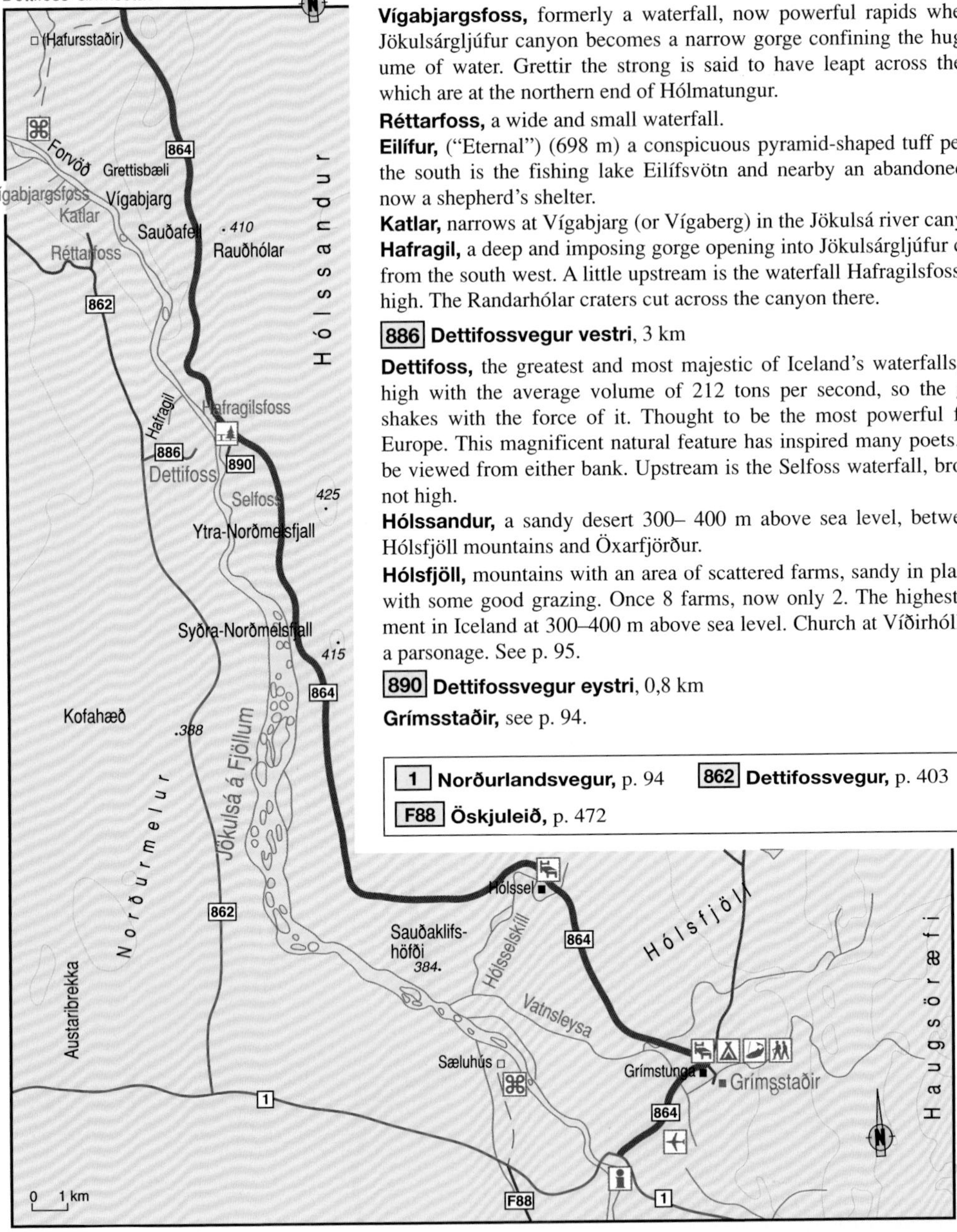

Vígabjargsfoss, formerly a waterfall, now powerful rapids where the Jökulsárgljúfur canyon becomes a narrow gorge confining the huge volume of water. Grettir the strong is said to have leapt across the falls, which are at the northern end of Hólmatungur.

Réttarfoss, a wide and small waterfall.

Eilífur, ("Eternal") (698 m) a conspicuous pyramid-shaped tuff peak. To the south is the fishing lake Eilífsvötn and nearby an abandoned farm now a shepherd's shelter.

Katlar, narrows at Vígabjarg (or Vígaberg) in the Jökulsá river canyon.

Hafragil, a deep and imposing gorge opening into Jökulsárgljúfur canyon from the south west. A little upstream is the waterfall Hafragilsfoss, 27 m high. The Randarhólar craters cut across the canyon there.

886 Dettifossvegur vestri, 3 km

Dettifoss, the greatest and most majestic of Iceland's waterfalls, 44 m high with the average volume of 212 tons per second, so the ground shakes with the force of it. Thought to be the most powerful falls in Europe. This magnificent natural feature has inspired many poets. It can be viewed from either bank. Upstream is the Selfoss waterfall, broad but not high.

Hólssandur, a sandy desert 300– 400 m above sea level, between the Hólsfjöll mountains and Öxarfjörður.

Hólsfjöll, mountains with an area of scattered farms, sandy in places but with some good grazing. Once 8 farms, now only 2. The highest settlement in Iceland at 300–400 m above sea level. Church at Víðirhóll. Once a parsonage. See p. 95.

890 Dettifossvegur eystri, 0,8 km

Grímsstaðir, see p. 94.

1 Norðurlandsvegur, p. 94
862 Dettifossvegur, p. 403
F88 Öskjuleið, p. 472

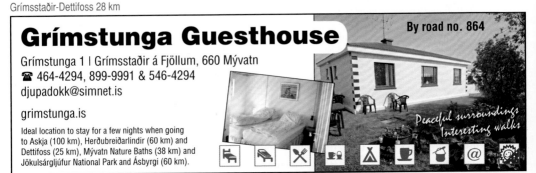

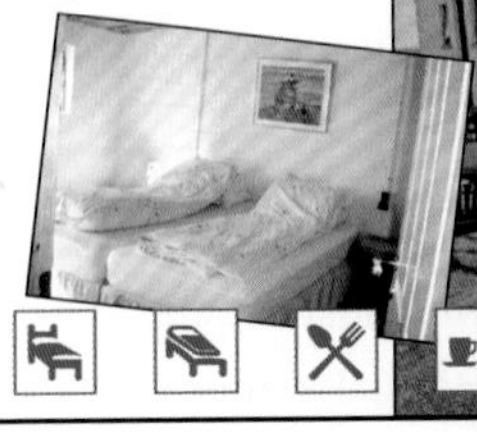

Grímsstaðir-Dettifoss 28 km

864 HÓLSFJALLAVEGUR

861 **Ásbyrgisvegur,** 3,5 km.

Ásheiði, a broad moor south and east of Ásbyrgi with a lot of low vegetation.

Jökulsárgljúfur, the largest river canyon in Iceland and most spectacular, about 25 km. The upper canyon, between the mountain Þórunnarfjall and Dettifoss, is up to 120 m deep. The land along the western bank up as far as Dettifoss is a National Park of over 120 km^2, established in 1973 and a part of Vatnajökull National Park since 2008. See p. 373.

Hljóðaklettar, ("Echo rocks") a group of rocks by the Jökulsá river that gets its name from strange echoes created by the numerous caves and uncommon rock formation.

Vesturdalur, a small valley south of Hljóðaklettar enclosed by cliffs. Wardens on site during the season.

Karl and **Kerling,** ("Old man" and "Old woman") two rocks in the Jökulsá river about 1 km south of Hljóðaklettar. Across the river is the cave Tröllahellir ("Giants' cave").

Hafursstaðir, an abandoned farm, once the uppermost in the Öxarfjörður district. There a difficult road leads to Forvöð and Skógarbjörg on the river across from Hólmatungur.

Svínadalur, an abandoned farm 250 m above sea level, interesting landscape, e.g. caves.

Hólmatungur, on the west side of the canyon. Many springs and tumbling brooks, woodland, rich in flowers, sheltered from most wind-directions, fine basalt columns. Unusual and beautiful scenery. Just to the south is Réttarfoss and the cliff Réttarbjarg.

Forvöð, opposite Hólmatungur in the Jökulsárgljúfur canyon. Pretty and unusual. A lone rock, Vígabjarg, with a path to **Grettisbæli** ("Grettir's hide-out"), another cave used by the outlaw Grettir the strong, at the top.

85 **Norðausturvegur,** p. 373 | **862** **Dettifossvegur,** p. 403

886 **Dettifossvegur vestri** p. 404 | **890** **Dettifossv. eystri** p. 404

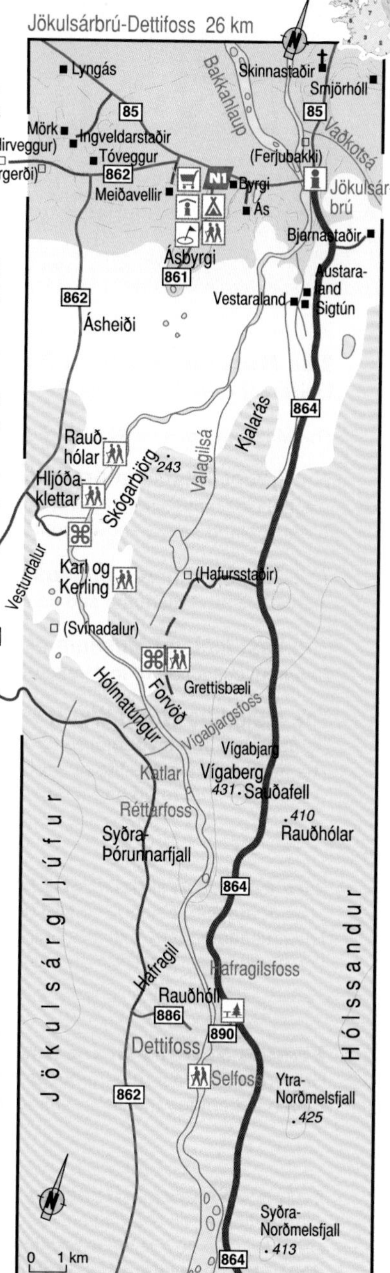

7 P. 570

For furher information:

The landscape around Svínadalur is unique and beautiful. One particular aspect worth mention is the cave Gloppuhellir by Jökulsá river. East of Svínadalur the same river falls through a narrow canyon. The vertical cliffs are called Kallbjörg (Calling cliffs). The distance between them is about 80 m, and people used to stand on each side and call out to each other across the river. The poet Jón Magnússon wrote a series of a verses about the last inhabitant of Svínadalur, Páll Jónsson (1870-1956), whose wife died on 15 December 1915, having six days previously given birth to triplets. A blizzard had been raging for days when this ocurred. When the storm allayed the new-born were brought from their birthplace by sled, in a tub used for bathing sheep, to be taken in by households where there was only one child.

Fjarðabyggð Museums

Open June - August from 13:00 till 17:00

or by arrangement.

☎ 470 9000 • sofn@fjardabyggd.is

The Museum House in Neskaupstaður

Egilsbraut 2, Neskaupstaður ☎ 470 9000 & 477 1446 • sofn@fjardabyggd.is

The Museum House at Norðfjörður hosts three museums under the same roof:

The Tryggvi Ólafsson Art Collection

Tryggvi Ólafsson, born in Norðfjörður 1940,
is one Iceland's best known contemporary artists.

The Jósafat Hinriksson Museum of Maritime and Handicraft Articles

An exhibition of maritime and handicraft artects, located in an old graceful warehouse.

The East Iceland Museum of Natural History

Beautiful collection of Icelandic birds, shellfish and stones.

The Icelandic World War II Museum

Heiðarvegur 37, Reyðarfjörður ☎ 470 9000 • sofn@fjardabyggd.is
The main theme is the life at wartime and the influences of the occupation for Icelanders.
Visitors are able to go into a replica of a barrack and cinema hall and see artefacts from the war.

The East Maritime Museum

Strandgata 39b, Eskifjörður ☎ 476 1605 & 470 9000 • sofn@fjardabyggd.is
The museum mostly exhibits objects and utensils relating to fishing and seafaring in general.
The museum is located in an old commercial building, „Gamla búð", built in 1816.

French Sailors in Iceland

Hafnargata 12 Fáskrúðsfjörður ☎ 470 9063 • sofn@fjardabyggd.is
A French heritage museum, telling the story of French sailors in Iceland though this exhibition.

Petra's Stone Collection

Stöðvarfjörður ☎ 475-8834
Open from 09:00 - 18:00 every day of the week from May till September.
One of the most interesting and unique collection of its kind, truly a magical world.

Information Centers for tourists in Fjarðabyggð:

The Museum House in Neskaupstaður, the swimming pool in Eskifjörður,
The Icelandic World War II Museum in Reyðjarfjörður, Gallerí Kolfreyja in Fáskrúðsfjörður,
Brekkan, shop and restaurant, in Stöðvarfjörður and at Sólbrekka in Mjóifjörður.

For further information go to www.visitfjardabyggd.is

FJARÐABYGGÐ fjardabyggd.is

Mjóifjörður Norðfjörður Eskifjörður Reyðarfjörður Fáskrúðsfjörður Stöðvarfjörður

Welcome to Fjarðabyggð

20
P. 583

Langanes

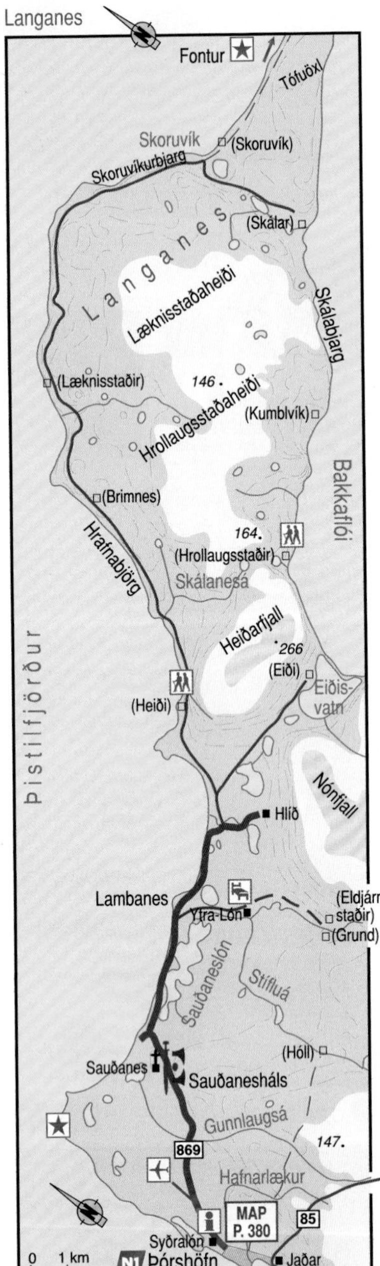

Langanes

Fontur or Langanesfontur, the outermost point of the Langanes peninsula, with high, sheer cliffs. Many ships had been wrecked nearby, the first lighthouse erected in 1910. Near the lighthouse is a rift in the cliffs, **Engelskagjá** ("The English gorge"), where shipwrecked English sailors are said to have managed to climb up. However, all but the captain died of exposure on way to the nearest farm. A cross marks the spot.

Skálar, a farm, abandoned since 1954. A fishing village grew up there early this century, having a population of 117 in 1924. Many Icelandic and Faroese fishermen went there in summer. Now deserted but remains visible. Churchyard. To the south is Skálabjarg (130 m), a bird-cliff.

Skoruvíkurbjarg, big bird-cliffs, one of the biggest Arctic tern breeding-grounds in Iceland. Easy access by jeep-track to the cliff edge, 33,23 km from Sauðanes. Recently a viewing deck was built there creating extraordinary experience for bird watchers. The deck stands 10 m out off the cliff and those who stand on it have in fact the ocean at their feet. At **Skoruvík**, east of the cliffs is much driftwood.

Heiðarfjall, (266 m) a mountain where there was an American radar starion in the second World War, 7,58 km from Sauðanes.

Eldjárnsstaðir, an abandoned farm, where a polar bear drifted ashore on an ice floe in 1918 and almost killed a man, but was itself killed.

Sauðanes, a church and parsonge. Rectory built of stone in 1879-81. This rectory, one of the few remaining stone houses in Iceland. The rocks used in its construction are from Brekknafjall and Prestlækjarbot. The doors and doorframes are made of solid redwood which had drifted ashore. In the keeping of the National Museum since 1989 and was formally opened after renovations in the summer of 2003. Fertile land, with an eider duck colony. In the summer time there is a information centre and café in the house.

Syðralón, a substantial farm on whose land is the village Þórshöfn.

Langanes, a large peninsula between Þistilfjörður and Bakkaflói, mountainous in the south but lower in the north but with high cliffs all around it. Breeding-place of gannet. Some flat land on the west, little on the east. Marshy in places. Has a raw, foggy climate. Little habitation, many farms having been abandoned in recent years.

Þórshöfn, (pop. 346 a village with fishing, herring-salting, trading. See road 85, p. 380.

85 **Norðausturvegur,** p. 381

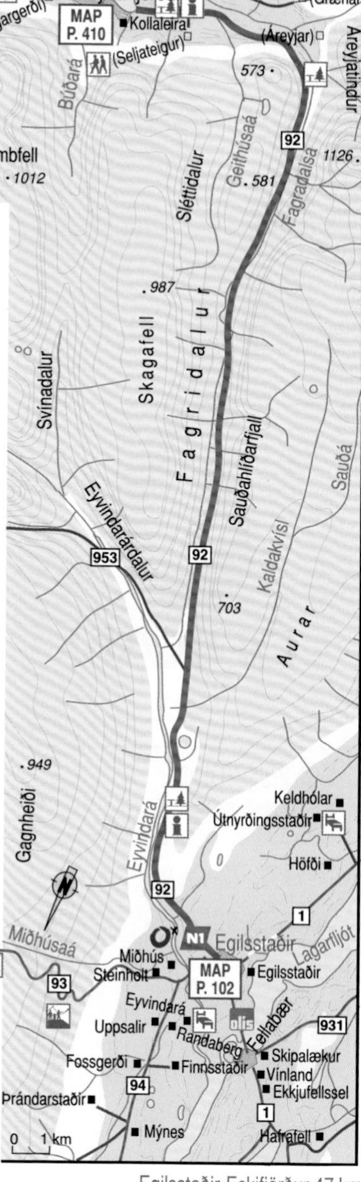

Eskifjörður, (pop. 997) a town since 1978, part of Fjarðabyggð, on the east side of a short fjord of the same name going north out of Reyðarfjörður. Fishing and fish processing. Community centre Valhöll, folk museum, maritime museum and a outdoor swimming pool. Trading started there ca. 1787.

Hólmatindur, (985 m) one of most majestic mountains off Reyðarfjörður, with the spur Hólmaháls ridge reaching onto the Hólmanes peninsula. Hólmanes and part of the ridge have been a nature reserve since 1973. On the mountain side of the road is the location of a cairn said to be the burial ground of a prophetess who stated that she would be the guardian of Reyðarfjörður as long as her bones remained unbroken.

Hólmar, a parsonage until 1930, church till 1909. A very wealthy farm in its time. Disputes in the Hólmar parish in 1880 led to the majority of the parishioners establishing the first Icelandic free-church congregation, which flourished for 50 years.

Sómastaðir, a house built of uncut stone in 1875, with mortar made of glacial clay, an unusual building technique in Iceland. The turf farmhouse, onto which it was built is now long gone. In the keeping of the National Museum since 1989. Now Alcoa Fjarðaál has built a state of the art aluminium smelter near to Sómastaðir.

Hraun, there stands the aluminum smelter of Alcoa Fjarðaál. It was opened in 2007 and produces 350 thousand tons of aluminum a year.

Reyðarfjörður, (pop. 1,189) a town founded at the turn of last century because of herring fishing, is now part of Fjarðarbyggð. After a road was built through the Fagridalur valley in 1909 the village grew larger. Trading, administration and industry. Community centre Félagslundur. A 9 hole golf course, recently made and a bit of a challange. A World War II Museum was opened in 1995 because there was an important military base located east of town. In January 1942 a platoon of British soldiers on winter exercises were caught in a very bad blizzard on the mountain above Eskifjörður. The family at Veturhús farm rescued and housed 48 of them but unfortunately another nine perished. Viw-dial.

1 **Austurlandsvegur,** p. 101
93 **Seyðisfjarðarvegur,** p. 414
94 **Borgarfjarðarvegur,** p. 415
96 **Suðurfjarðavegur,** p. 420
931 **Upphéraðsvegur,** p. 426
953 **Mjóafjarðarvegur,** p. 429
954 **Helgustaðavegur,** p. 412

Reyðarfjörður, 30 km long, the biggest of the Eastern fjords. Little flat land, but a short valley at the head.

Áreyjatindur, (971 m) an imposing mountain off Reyðarfjörður.

Fagridalur, a valley along which lies the main route from Egilsstaðir to Reyðarfjörður.

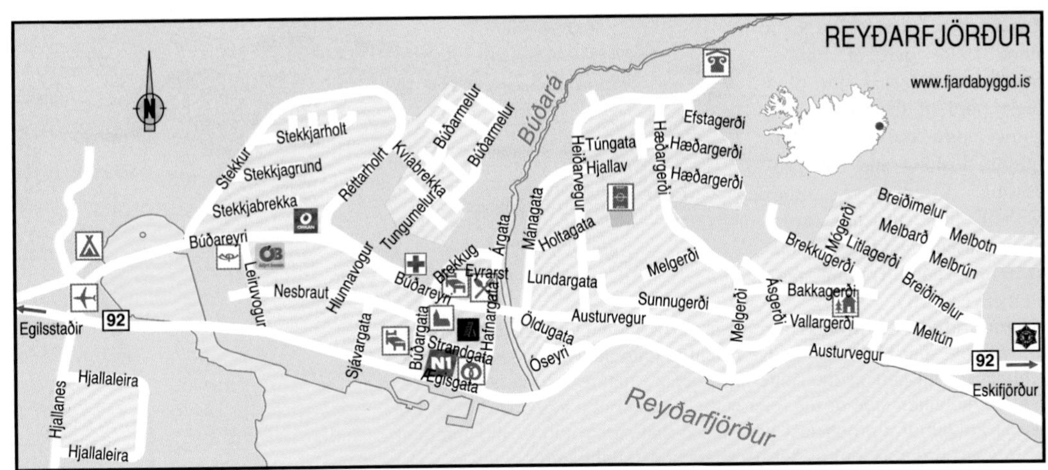
REYÐARFJÖRÐUR
www.fjardabyggd.is
Stekkjarholt
Stekkjagrund
Stekkur
Stekkjabrekka
Búðareyri
Leiruvegur
Nesbraut
Réttarholt
Kvíabrekka
Búðarmelur
Búðarmelur
Tungumelur
Hlunnavogur
Búðareyri
Brekkug
Eyrarst
Árgata
Búðará
Búðargata
Strandgata
Hafnargata
Sjávargata
Ægisgata
Mánagata
Holtagata
Heiðarvegur
Túngata
Hjallav
Hæðargerði
Efstagerði
Hæðargerði
Hæðargerði
Lundargata
Melgerði
Sunnugerði
Austurvegur
Öldugata
Óseyri
Melgerði
Ásgerði
Bakkagerði
Vallargerði
Brekkugerði
Mógerði
Litlagerði
Breiðimelur
Melbarð
Melbotn
Melbrún
Breiðimelur
Meltún
Austurvegur
Egilsstaðir
92
Hjallaleira
Hjallanes
Hjallaleira
Reyðarfjörður
92
Eskifjörður

ORKAN
Austfjarðaleið
Austfjarðaleið
Óseyri 1 – 730 Fjarðabyggð
Tel.: 477-1713 – www.austfjardaleid.is

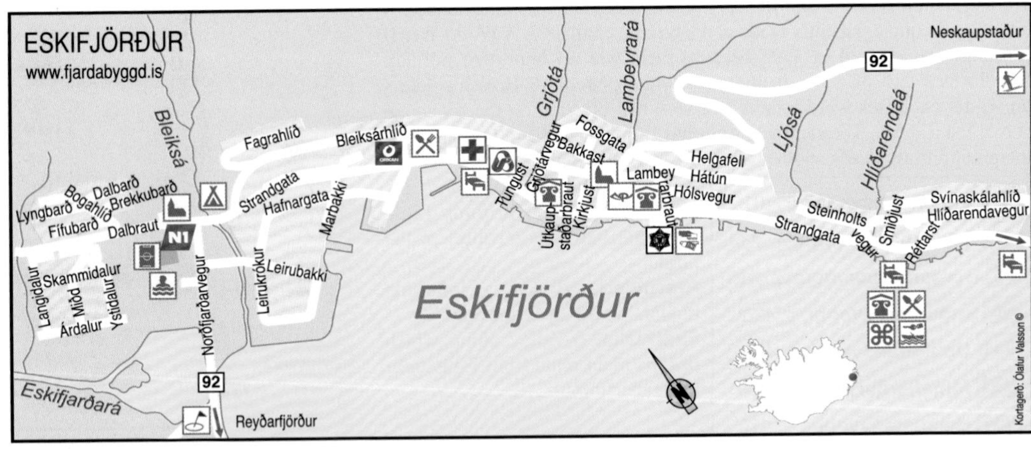
ESKIFJÖRÐUR
www.fjardabyggd.is
Bleiksá
Fagrahlíð
Bleiksárhlíð
Grjótá
Lambeyrará
Fossgata
Bakkast
Grjótárvegur
Tungust
Útkaupstaðarbraut
Kirkjust
Lambey
Helgafell
Hátún
Hólsvegur
Ljósá
Hlíðarendaá
Neskaupstaður
92
Lyngbarð
Bogahlíð
Dalbarð
Brekkubarð
Fífubarð
Dalbraut
Strandgata
Hafnargata
Marbakki
Leirukrókur
Leirubakki
Skammidalur
Langidalur
Miðd
Ystidalur
Árdalur
Norðfjarðarvegur
92
Eskifjarðará
Reyðarfjörður
Eskifjörður
Steinholts
vegur
Strandgata
Smiðjust
Réttarst
Svínaskálahlíð
Hlíðarendavegur
Kortagerð: Ólafur Valsson ©

Mjóeyri Travel Service
Strandgata 120
735 Eskifjörður
Tel.: 4771247
www.mjoeyri.is
mjoeyri@mjoeyri.is

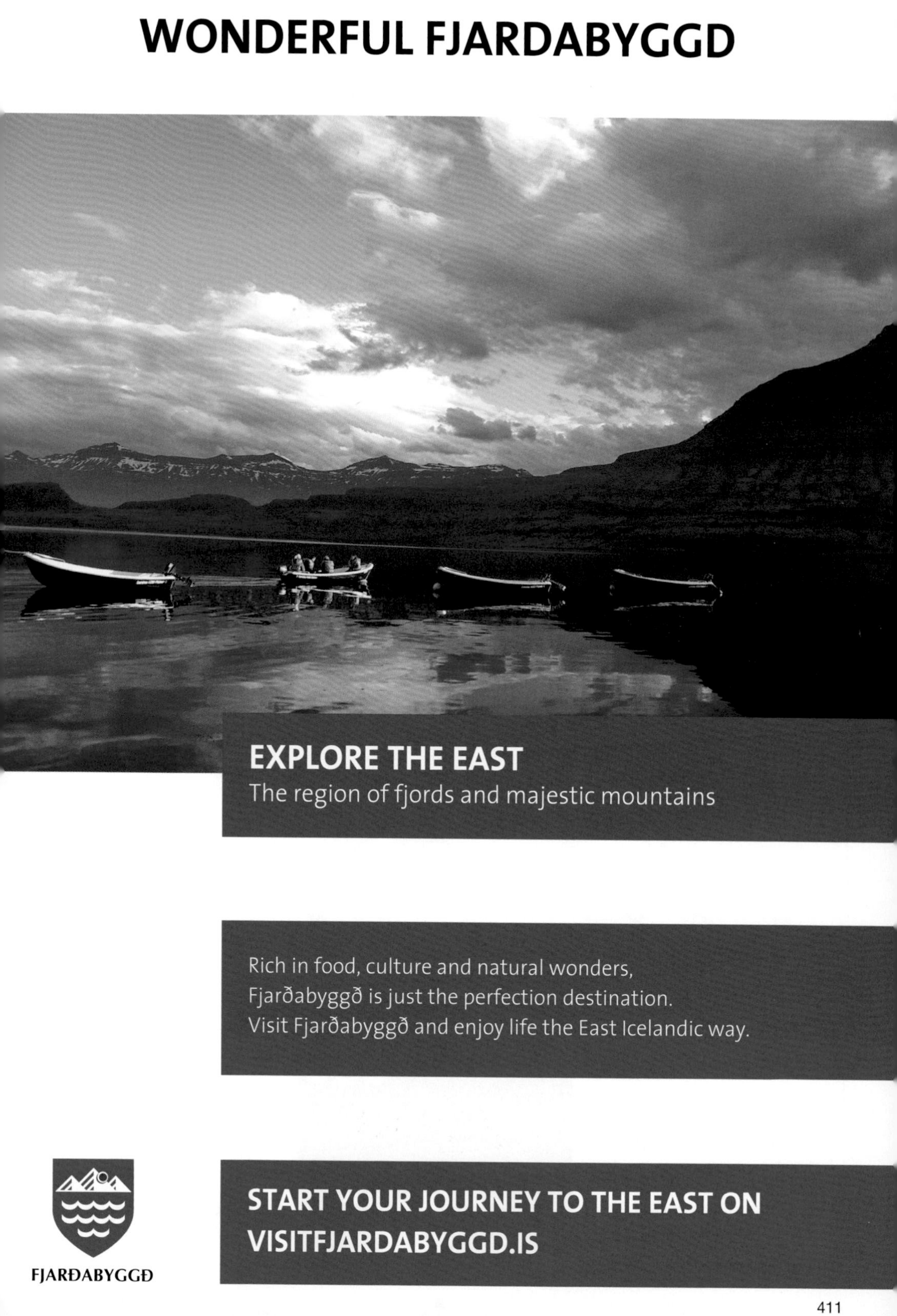

9
572

Neskaupstaður-Eskifjörður 25 km

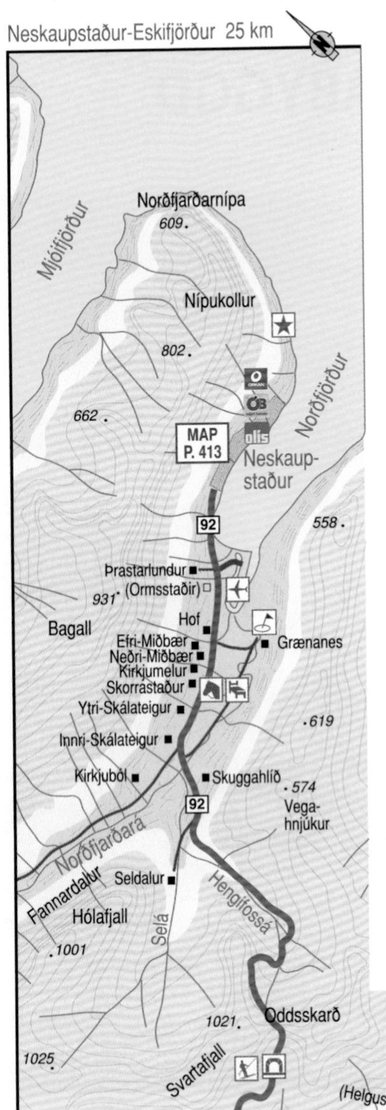

Eskifjörður-Neskaupstaður 25 km

Neskaupstaður, (pop. 1,470) the 2nd biggest town in eastern Iceland, built on the land of the farm Nes, originally settled by Egill rauði ("the red"). Fishing and allied industries, trading, and some farming. Authorized trading place since 1929, is now part of Fjarðabyggð. Hospital, Trades College, the community centre Egilsbúð and a nice newly renovated outdoor swimming pool. In a distinguished building from 1924, the Museum House, Safnahúsið, houses three separate art, folk and natural science museums, all under the same roof and beautifully situated in the town center next to the port area. Outside the town is a public park, a nature reserve. On December 20th, 1974, an avalanche fell on Neskaupstaður, killing 12. A number of protective barriers have been installed with the aim of avoiding further avalanches. A walk to the barriers is well worth the visit, they offer great view of the surrounding area. Yearly festivals in the town are Eistnaflug in July, the Seamen's Day, Barðneshlaup and Neistaflug held the first weekend of August, which daily is called the Tradesmen's Weekend.

Skorrastaður, a parsonage until 1894, church till 1896, when the church building was blown down. Now a farm with a ceramic gallery.

Norðfjörður, a short fjord, see p. 495.

Oddsskarð, (632 m) a pass over and through the mountain between Eskifjörður and Norðfjörður, with a 626 m long tunnel. There is a skiing and wintersport centre at Oddsskarð.

954 Helgustaðavegur, 11,4 km.

Stóra-Breiðuvík, the trading centre of Reyðarfjörður until the end of the Danish trade monopoly in 1787. Few remains. Possible to drive from there via Víkurheiði moor to Vöðlavík (Road 958).

Helgustaðir, an Iceland spar mine, one of the best in the world, in use from the 17th century until the 20th, remains still visible. The mine and its surroundings are a protected natural feature.

It is against the law to disturb or remove any of the stones.

Svínaskálastekkur, an abandoned farm. Birthplace of Dr. Richard Beck, professor, who emigrated to Canada and was a leader among Icelanders there. There was a whaling station there around 1900.

Mjóeyri, a place of the last execution in east Iceland, on September 30th 1786. The burial site can still be seen. Now Mjóeyri is a site of plenty for a tourist with guided tours, boat trips, see angling and accommodation. A beautiful shore line ideal for a pit stop.

958 Vöðlavíkurvegur, p. 494

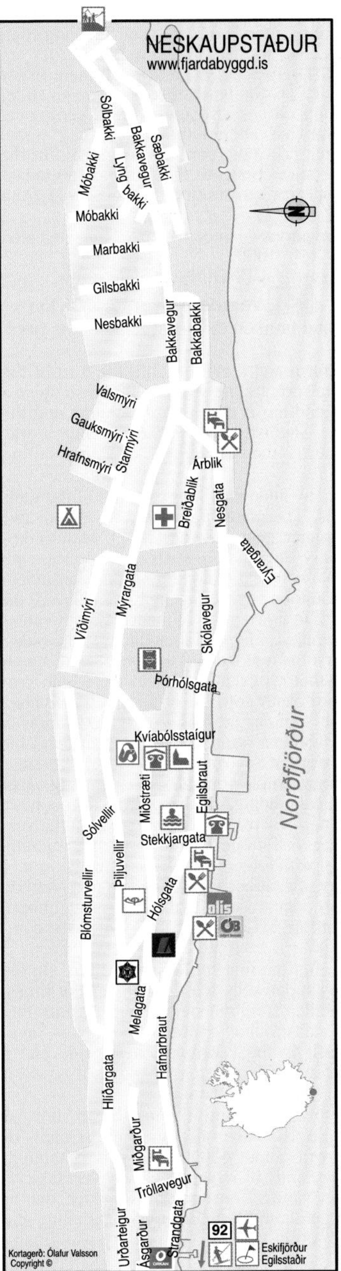

Neskaupstaður.

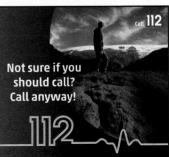

Seyðisfjörður-Egilsstaðir 26 km

9 P. 572

Egilsstaðir-Seyðisfjörður 26 km

Skálanes, a nature and heritage centre, on the south coast of Seyðisfjörður. In summer the centre provides services to tourists. Skálanesbjarg cliffs are home to thousands of sea birds. 47 different species go through there every year and 40 species nest there annually. At Skálanes there is a major eider duck nesting colony. The Skálanesbjarg cliff is also unique in a geological sense as it contains plutonic rock that has altered the surrounding stone, resulting in a veritable flora of zeolite. The most common mammals in the area are reindeer, fox, mink and field mice. Beneath the cliffs are abundant fishing grounds and different whale species can routinely be observed from the edge of the cliff.

Þórarinsstaðir, archaeological excavations in recent years have revealed remains of a stave church, dating from 940 -1000.

Hánefsstaðir, trading started there in around 1800. Now a dairy farm.

952 Hánefsstaðavegur, 7,51 km. **951 Vestdalseyrarvegur,** 8 km.

Brimnes, a historical fishing station and farm on the north shore of the fjord. Barely passable road. Lighthouse.

Dvergasteinn, ("Dwarfs' stone") a farm and a church until the turn of the century, parsonage till 1940. There is a rock by the shore which resembles a house and is called Dvergasteinn. Legend has it that both the church and the rock were once on the south side of Seyðisfjörður. Then the church was moved north to Dvergasteinn and shortly thereafter the rock came sailing across the fjord to the church.

Seyðisfjörður, (pop. 637) municipality by a long and narrow fiord of the same name, surrounded by rugged mountains. The municipality is divided into two parts, called Búðareyri and Alda. Commerce began there in 1843. Main industries now are fishing industry, iron industry and tourism. Posts of the police commissioner, pastor and doctor are there as well as a church, a hospital, an indoor swimming pool and steam bath, the community meeting hall, Herðubreið, the county library and a technology museum. In the vicinity of the technology museum one can visit the oldest mechanics smithy in Iceland in addition to the oldest telegraphy station in the country. The first town in Iceland to have electric streetlamps installed. Art exhibitions and numerous events are held the whole year round in Skaftafell, which is the visual art centre for East of Iceland. There are a number of festivals in town during the summer months. Art is flourishing in Seyðisfjörður. The international ferry, Norræna, sails between Iceland and the European continent the whole year and stops at Seyðisfjörður. As a result there is good tourist service in Seyðisfjörður. For exemple you can go sea angling, sight seeing, bird watching, kayaking, diving, paragliding, on a jeep safari or mountain biking. If you want to go hiking there are many marked hiking trails. In the year 1906, a sea telephone cable was laid to Seyðisfjörður from Europe, thus enabling Iceland to commence telecommunication with foreign countries. After the turn of the 19th century Seyðisfjörður was a very prosperous town, due to a good harbor. Otto Wathne (1834-1898), a Norwegian entrepreneur, lived there and a monument was later made in his honor and for Ingi T. Lárusson (1892-1946), the composer. www.seydisfjordur.is

Bjólfur, (1,085 m) a mountain named after the first settler in this fiord. On the highest peak of the mountain there was supposedly a temple in ancient times. Snow and mud avalanches have often fallen from the steep mountainsides that surround the town, sometimes with catastrophic consequences. Now, avalanche protection walls have been built in the Bjólfur mountainside and a snow avalanche inspector is posted in Seyðisfjörður all year round. It is possible to drive up there by a summer road, spectacular view.

Vestdalur, in the pass between Seyðisfjörður and Fljótsdalshérað, not far from Vestdalsvatn lake, where archaeologists have uncovered the remains of a woman from around 940, together with about 400 beads. This is thought to be one of Iceland's most remarkable finds of recent decades. Vestdalseyri and the valley of Vestdalur are on the Nature Conservation Register, due to their cultural features and diverse vegetation. **Vestdalseyri,** a trading and fishing post. The village that was built up in the late 19th century was finally abandoned in 1963.

Fjarðará, a river worth visiting. It has 25 waterfalls, Gufufoss being the most known. The river was harnessed in 1913 and again in 2007.

Fjarðarselsvirkjun is the country's oldest power plant (1913) still being used and the first alternating current power plant. Furthermore, the first high voltage line was laid to Seyðisfjörður from there. Next to the old power plant stands the first high voltage tower in Iceland. This old power plant has provided Seyðisfjörður with light and warmth for almost a century. www.fjardarsel.is

Stafir, the name given to two lines of cliffs, a lower and an upper line (Neðri-Stafur and Efri-Stafur), on the way up to Fjarðarheiði pass. A monument just on top of Neðri-Stafur to Þorbjörn Arnoddsson, a pioneer in winter transportation from Seyðisfjörður. Beside this monument, the river Fjarðará has carved pretty potholes in the basalt rock. The entrance to the skiing area shared by Seyðisfjörður and Fljótsdalshérað is just below Efri-Stafur.

Fjarðarheiði, (620 m) a moor crossed by a paved road, steep at both ends. Great views, view-dial on the northern edge. Possible to drive to Gagnheiði moor, site of a TV relay station and magnificent views.

Miðhúsaá, a river that runs from the Fjarðarheiði moor. In the river are some very beautifull waterfalls like Fardagafoss, behind it is a small cave with a guest book. It is said that a troll used to live there with a chest full of gold.

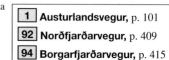

1 Austurlandsvegur, p. 101

92 Norðfjarðarvegur, p. 409

94 Borgarfjarðarvegur, p. 415

94 BORGARFJARÐARVEGUR

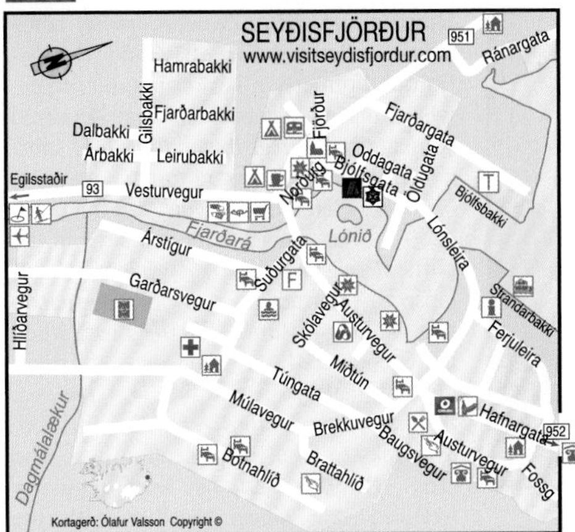

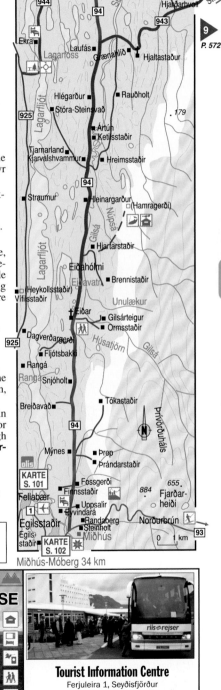

Móberg-Miðhús 34 km

Dyrfjöll, ("Doorway mountains") (1,136 m) the most impressive of the mountains in the Hérað district, split by the deep, rocky pass called Dyr ("Doorway").

Stórurð, west of Dyrfjöll, one of Icelands pearls of nature. Marked walking routes. See p. 418.

944 Lagarfossvegur, 10 km. **943 Hjaltastaðarvegur,** 10 km.

Lagarfoss, see p. 425.

Hjaltastaður, a church and a parsonage till 1919. Community centre, Hjaltalundur. It was there that the Hjaltastaður Devil, a well-known Icelandic ghost, was active in the late 17th century. He would speak to people insultingly for hours on end, challenge them to wrestling matches, bang doors, use bad language and shriek most dreadfully. The community centre Hjaltalundur is not far from Hjaltastaðir.

Eiðar, an historically important manor farm. Church, parsonage, swimming pool, sport statium, and facilities for large gatherings. Home of Helgi Ásbjarnarson of *Fljótsdæla saga*. A farmers' school was established there 1883, changed into a public school 1918. At present, however, no school of any kind is run at Eiðar. A hotel provides accommodation in summer. Radio relay station, sportsground, community centre. Some woods and walking routes by **Húsatjörn**. A biggish fishing lake, Eiðavatn, with the lovely wooded island **Eiðahólmi**.

Úthérað, the district from Eyvindará all the way to the sea, divided in two settlements, Eiðaþinghá on the south side and Hjaltastaðarþinghá or Útmannasveit on the north side. On the east side of the district are high picturesque tuff and basalt mountains. The highest ones are **Beinageitarfjall** 1107 m and Dyrfjöll 1136 m.

Miðhús, a farm with a good deal of woodland on the river Eyvindará across from Egilsstaðaskógur woods. In 1990 a store of silver was found there, the largest to have been found in Iceland. Objects from it are in the National Museum in Reykjavík.

1 Austurlandsvegur, p. 101 **93 Seyðisfjarðarvegur,** p. 414
925 Hróarstunguvegur, p. 425

Miðhús-Móberg 34 km

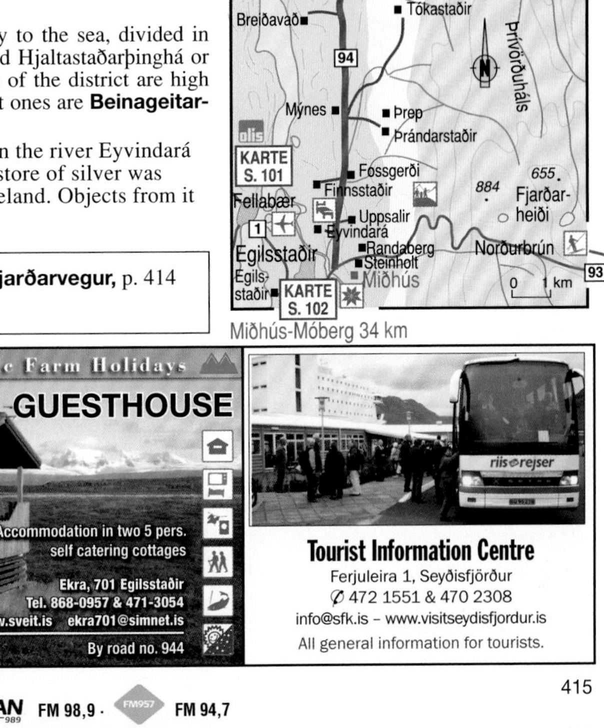

9 P. 572

Njarðvíkurskriður-Móberg 28 km

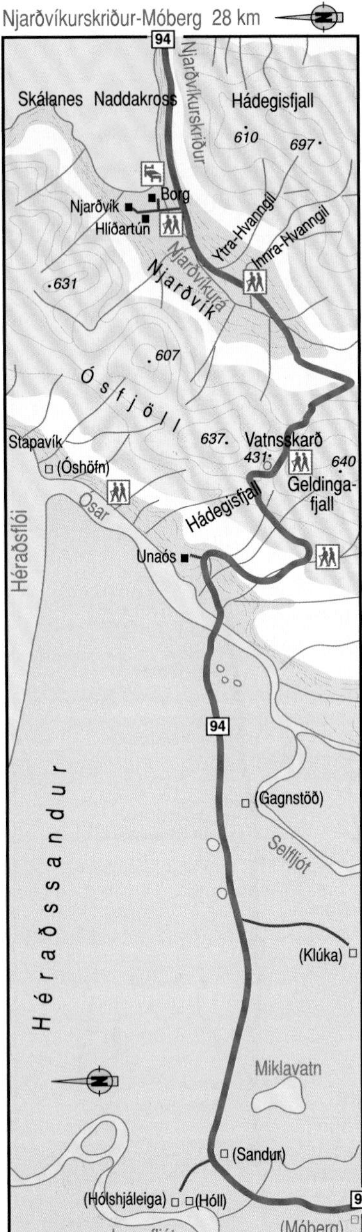

Móberg-Njarðvíkurskriður 28 km

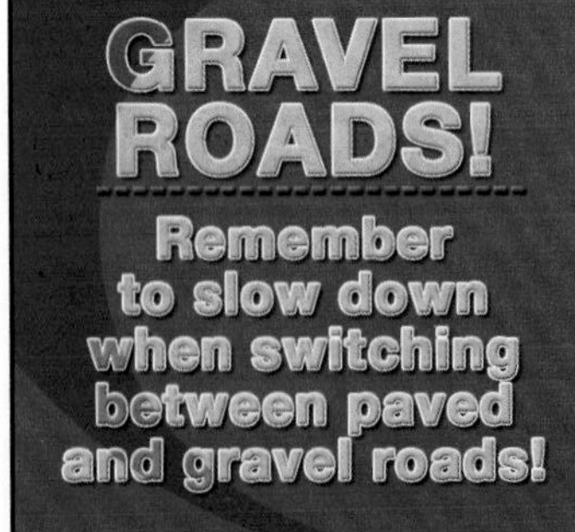

GRAVEL ROADS!
Remember to slow down when switching between paved and gravel roads!

Njarðvíkurskriður.

Njarðvíkurskriður, a very steep scree between the Njarðvík bay and Borgarfjörður. Formerly a very dangerous route, where the many accidents that occurred were at one time attributed to an evil spirit named Naddi. He is said to have dwelt in Naddagil ("Naddi's canyon"), at the north end of scree, where there is a cave in the cliffs at sea level, the cave has now collapsed. A farmer named Jón Bjarnason was walking by himself in this place when he encountered the monster and foght him, ultimately driving him into the sea. He then put up a cross in Skriður, in 1306, as thanks to God for protecting him. The cross, **Naddakross**, has been regularly renewed ever since, together with the inscription, *Effigiem Christi qui transis pronus honora*, which is to the effect that travellers should pray at the cross before continuing across the scree.

Njarðvík, the northernmost bay on the Eastern fjords, with a grassy, wooded valley at its head. A farm of the same name, frequently mentioned in local folklore, near which there is an ancient ruin, **Þorragarður**, said to date from Saga times, also some burial mounds. Þiðrandi Geitisson is said to have been slain at **Þiðrandaþúfa** ("Þiðrandi's hillock") at the farm Borg. Two skerries, called Gunnarssker, in the bay named for Gunnar Þiðrandabani ("Þiðrandi's bane"). There used to be a small turf-roofed church in Njarðvík; it was demolished in the middle of the 20th century.

Innra-Hvanngil, a rhyolite canyon with dark basaltic rocks just 200 m walk from the road.

Vatnsskarð, (431 m) a mountain pass, with road, named for a small lake at the north end.

Unaós, the outermost farm in Hjaltastaðarþinghá settlement, at the mouth of the Selfljót river, named for Uni Garðarsson the Dane. Uni was the son of Garðar Svavarsson, who discovered Iceland and called it Garðarshólmi ("Garðar's isle"). Harold Fairhair king of Norway sent Uni to Iceland to colonise it, for which he was to receive an earldom. From there he went south along the east of Iceland, staying with Úlfljótur in Skaftafell County. Úlfljótur slew Uni at his second attempt to escape after having got his host´s daughter with child. Therefore this first attempt of a Norwegian king to seize Iceland failed because Uni was slain by Icelanders.

Selfljót, a rather deep and quiet river. Formed from the Gilsá river, coming from the lake Vestdalsvatn, and many tributaries from the Úthérað mountains. A landing dock and a storehouse were constructed there in the middle of the 20th century for the benefit of local farmers. Good fishing. Where it flows into the sea it is called Óshöfn. This has sometimes been an anchorage. The sagas tells of a ship that was sailed into the inlet of Unaós and this is supported by the landmark names Ár (Oar), Skipaklettur (Ship Rock), Knörr (a type of ship) and Knarrará (Ship River) just beyond the bridge that stands there today.

Stórurð, west of Dyrfjöll, one of Icelands pearls of nature. Marked walking routes.

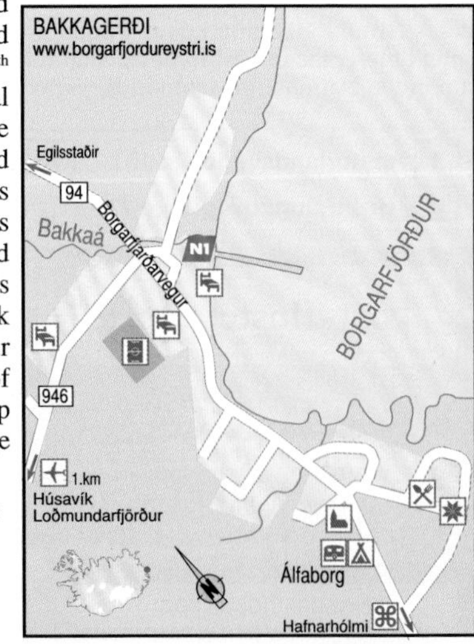

946 Hólalandsvegur, 7,6 km. **947 Desjarmýrarvegur,** 2,9 km.

Staðarfjall, a colourful rhyolite mountain with basalt arches above Desjarmýri. The story goes that the giantess Gellivör who lived there was turned to stone and can still be seen in the scree below the mountain.

Álfaborg, ("Elves' rock") a picturesque rock, from which the fjord gets its name. Said to be the home of elves. Public park. Viewdial.

Höfn, the outermost farm on the east side of Borgarfjörður with a harbour and a small island with a puffin colony. At the island Hafnarhólmi is an excellent view for bird watching. **www.puffins.is**

Bakki, a substantial farm, now abandoned. Mentioned in a story about Gunnar Þiðrandabani ("Þiðrandi's bane"). Some old relics have been found in ruins there. Around the turn of the century a great slab of stone was found during a dig. When it was raised they found a hollow beneath it. It was decided not to go on down into the hollow, the slab was replaced and a wall built on top of it. It is thought they had found the hiding place of Gunnar Þiðrandabani.

Bakkagerði, (pop. 86) a village in Borgarfjörður, and a trading post since 1894. Now fishing, fish processing, trade and farming. A church with a fine altar piece painted by Jóhannes S. Kjarval (1885-1972), who grew up in Borgarfjörður. It shows Christ giving the Sermon on the Mount, standing on Álfaborg with the Dyrfjöll mountains behind him. He is most definately one of the country's most beloved painter, and sketched the faces of most of his compatriots in the area in 1926. Kjarval revolutionized the country's art history. During his adult life, he spent many summers in the East to paint Mts Dyrfjöll and the colourful landscapes of Borgarfjordur east and its vicinity. He painted the altarpiece of the Bakkagerdi church in 1914. It was, and still is, the hamlet's most precious property. Most visitors of this area pay the church a visit to see it. Bræðslan is a very popular music festival held in Bakkagerði. The festival was first held in 2005 and has since then been an annual event on the last weekend of July. The festival venue takes place in a 40 years old fish factory that once a year is turned into a wonder world of music.

Borgarfjörður, a short, wide fjord and 10 km long, grassy, fertile valley of the same name. Magnificent, colourful mountains, especially Dyrfjöll and Staðarfjall, of rhyolite and basalt. Numerous rare and beautiful stones, minerals and plants are found there The stones can´t be collected unless with a permission from landowners. There is a good bird-watching hut on the beach by the pier. Most Icelandic birds with beach habitats can be observed from a hut. Beauiful walking routes. www.borgarfjordureystri.is

Geitavík, a farm on a small bay of the same name. Childhood home of artist Jóhannes S. Kjarval (1885-1972) who painted many pictures of Borgarfjörður, for instance, most of his famous "Heads" were painted there in the nineteen-forties. Monument to him.

Snotrunes, the outermost farm on the west side of Borgarfjörður. Named for an elf lady, who had a family in both this world and the hidden world of elves.

F946 Loðmundafjarðarleið, p. 492

Bakkagerði-Njarðvíkurskriður 8 km

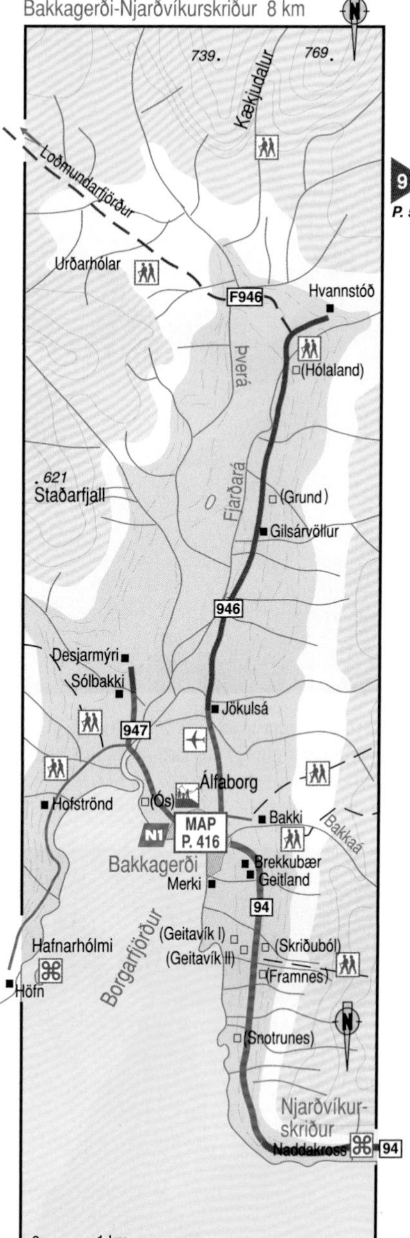

9
P. 572

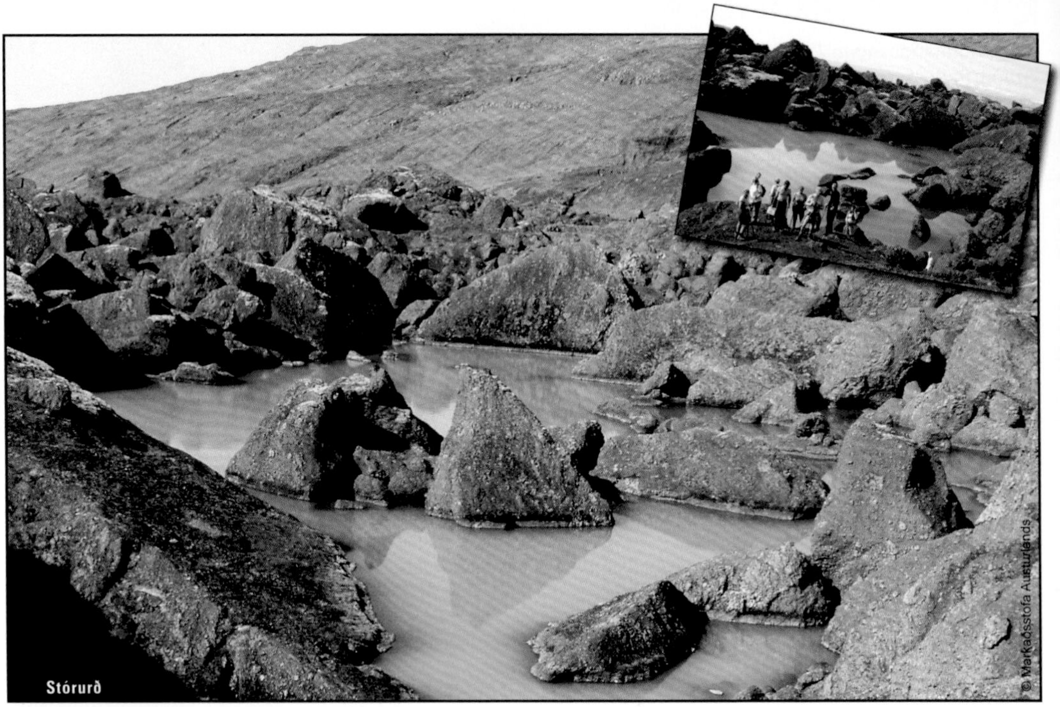

Stórurð

© Markaðsstofa Austurlands

Stórurð, massive rocks, one of East Iceland's most stupendous sights. They are thought to have fallen from the mountain above onto glacial ice, which then carried them farther down the valley before melting. See also p. 415.

Þerribjörg, below Kollumúli mountain (p. 423), consists of magnificent cliffs from a former central volcano. These were exposed in all their colourful beauty by the erosion of ocean breakers.

Þerribjörg

© Markaðsstofa Austurlands

www.olgeir.zenfolio.com

Hafnarnes-Reyðarfjörður 35 km

10 P. 573

Hafnarnes, an abandoned group of farms on the south side of Fáskrúðsfjörður. Formerly a busy fishing centre with 8 farms and a school. The French hospital was moved there from Fáskrúðsfjörður and served as flats and a school.

955 Vattarnesvegur, 49 km.

Víkurheiði, a hiking trail from the farm Vík over Víkurheiði to Stöðvarfjörður.

Fagraeyri, a German company built a whaling station here in 1903 and it was run until in1905. Remnants of the station can be seen here still. The station was purchased later by Chr. Salvesen and Co. And moved to the Falkland Islands when whaling commenced in the South Polar Sea. Fishing was carried out from Fagraeyri until 1950.

Sandfell, (743 m) a rhyolite mountain south of Fáskrúðsfjörður. It is a typical laccolith believed to be 600 m thick and one of the best examples of mountains from the tertier period in the northern hemisphere. It can be seen very clearly while travelling up the mountain how the basalt layers have been lifted and turned over on its south side while other layers lie untouched beneath it. This is a nice hiking trail, taking a total of 2-3 hours one way.

Stöðvarskarð, from the farm Merki is a hiking trail through Stöðvarskarð passage to the farm Stöð in Stöðvarfjörður. This trail follows an old electricity line road for the majority of the way.

Stuðlaheiði, lies between Fáskrúðsfjörður and Reyðarfjörður. Over this heathland is a hiking trail from Dalir in Fáskrúðsfjörður to the abondoned farm Stuðlar in Reyðarfjörður.

Reindalsheiði, from the farm Tunguholt in Tungudalur in Fáskrúðsafjörður there lies a marked hiking trail.

Gilsárfoss, a beautiful waterfall in the river Gilsá. There is a 15 minutes walk to the waterfall from the road.

Fáskrúðsfjarðargöng, a tunnel 5.9 km long through the mountainous land between Fáskrúðsfjörður and Reyðarfjörður.

Fáskrúðsfjörður, (Búðir) (pop. 705) a village on a rather long fjord of the same name which has a valley at the head with many wooded areas, the largest at Gestsstaðir, where wild aspen is found. Became part of Fjarðabyggð in 2006. Fishing and fish processing. Trading started ca. 1890. Formerly a base for French fishermen, who had their own hospital, chapel and cemetery. These beautiful old buildings opened in 2014 after careful restoration as an exclusive hotel and museum dedicated to the French heritage of Fáskrúðsfjörður. Until then you can learn aobut the local French history at the Frenchmen in Iceland Museum. The French used a big rock, which can still be seen in the village, as a bearing for landward sailing. They painted a black cross on it, and joined in prayer there before sailing out to sea. A memorial to Carl D. Tulinius, a merchant, Berg Hallgrímsson, a businessman and Dr. Charcot. Skrúður Community centre. A "French Days" festival is held in the last weekend in July each summer in Fáskrúðsfjörður. During this festival 1999, Foreign Minister Halldór Ásgrímsson unveiled a reproduction of Einar Jónsson´s bust of Dr. Charcot. The Icelandic government donated the bust to commemorate relations between Fáskrúðsfjörður and France. A swimming pool and camping grounds are located just outside the village.

Kolfreyjustaður, a church and parsonage. Among pastors there was Ólafur Indriðason (1796-1861), father of the poets Páll (1827-1905) and Jón (1850-1916) Ólafsson. Birthplace of Jón. Both brothers wrote many poems about the Kolfreyjustaður area. Just east of Kolfreyjustaður is a small peninsula called Hvalnes. There the French vessel Manon stranded in 1924. All the sailors were saved and the flotsam was auctioned away. A part of the old warehouse at Hafnargata 21 was built from Manon´s boards.

Reyðarfjörður-Hafnarnes 35 km

92 Norðfjarðarvegur, p. 409

936 Þórdalsheiðarvegur, p. 492

Andey, a island at the mouth of Fáskrúðsfjörður. Eider duck colony. In Andey you can also find puffins.

Skrúður, (161 m) a high grassy island with cliffs. Many seabirds, including gannet. Famous from a folktale about a giant said to have lived there in a cave, **Skrúðshellir**. He put a spell on the daughter of the pastor at Hólmur in Reyðarfjörður and lured her to Skrúður.

Skrúðshellir, a high, broad cave in the cliffs with a big scree at the back.

Vattarnes, a farm and fishing-station, close to shark-fishing grounds. Between Vattarnes and Kolfreyjustaður the road goes along the screes Vattarnesskriður and Staðarskriður. Farmers at Vattarnes have utilised the island Skrúður and grazed their sheep there all year round.

FÁSKRÚÐSFJÖRÐUR
www.austurbyggd.is

Heydalir, see p. 106.

97 Breiðdalsvíkurv., 1 km.

Breiðdalsvík, see p. 106.

Snæhvammur, the outermost farm on the northern side of the Breiðdalur valley. Late in the 18th century a polar bear was killed right at the front door after having chased a man who was walking there on his way from Stöðvarfjörður. Burial mounds have been found near Snæhvammur, with relics at least 1,000 years old, now kept in the National Museum. In 1940 a mine exploded on the beach nearby, causing damage. The farm was moved many years ago because of the danger of avalanches, but is now in danger from sand erosion.

Súlur, (664 m) interestingly shaped peak above Kambanes peninsula.

Kambanes, the end of the peninsula south of Stöðvarfjörður. Weatherstation and lighthouse. In 1942 a German plane attacked it and also the village of Breiðdalsvík.

Stöðvarfjörður, (pop. 184) a village on the north side of a small, pleasant fjord of the same name, with the short, grassy, wooded valleys Stöðvardalur and Jafnadalur at its head. Became part of Fjarðabyggð in 2006. Fishing, some farming, and trading since 1896. Petra's Stone Collection is truly unique, set in the home of the late Petra Sveinsdóttir (1922-2012). Accommodation and tourist services are offered in the old church building, no other church building in Iceland is known to accomodate such activities. Fishing, fish processing and commerce are the main industies there. The Snærós gallery is run by the the artists Ríkharður Valtingojer and Sigrún Friðriksdóttir. Various art items may be purchased at the gallery.

Saxa, an unusual bottleneck phenomenon just north of the buildings at Lönd, formed by shoreline cliffs which constrict bigger ocean swells until they spout high into the air at Saxa's landward end. Its name refers to slicing or cutting, and fits well with how Saxa chops up quantities of seaweed, hurling the bits onto the cliffs.

Jafnadalur, a north facing valley in Stöðvarfjörður fjord. A good walking path leads through the valley over Stöðvarskarð connecting it to Fáskrúðsfjörður fjord. At the end of the valley is Einbúi „The Hermit", a fairly unique and a solitary rock in otherwise flat surroundings. In Jafnadalur valley is also a beautiful 6 m stone arch, located on Álftafell mountain. Excellent hiking area.

1 **Austurlandsvegur,** p. 106
964 **Breiðdalsvegur,** p. 106
966 **Suðurbyggðarvegur,** p. 106

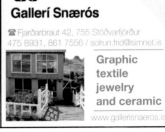

Ketilsstaðir-Jökulsárbrú 35 km

9 P. 572

Jökulsárbrú-Ketilsstaðir 35 km

Ketilsstaðir, the outermost farm in the Jökulsárhlíð district, with seal-hunting, driftwood and other natural advantages. From there the road crosses Hellisheiði moor to Vopnafjörður. A 3100 hectare area of land between Ketilasstaðir and Hjarðargrund in Jökuldalur has been fenced off and will be kept inaccessible to livestock from the beginning of spring until the first snow. The area will be divided into sections for forest planting and restoration of barren land, and grazing.

Kaldá, a deepish river in a deep canyon, rising in the Smjörfjöll mountains and flowing into Jökulsá.

921 Eyjavegur, 5,95 km. **922 Másselsvegur,** 6,74 km.

Sleðbrjótur, ("Sleigh breaker") a church and community centre, an ancient manor farm. Said to be named for an incident when some slaves broke their sled on their way from Vopnafjörður. They then met some slaves from the next farm and tried to buy their sled, but were refused. A fight broke out in which all the slaves were killed.

926 **Surtsstaðir,** a farm in the homefield of which is the rock Drykkjarsteinn ("Drinking stone"), about 10 m high, with a spring in it.

Fossvellir, the innermost farm in the Jökulsárhlíð district, beside the river Laxá which there descends in pretty falls. A former assembly site. There is an abattoir and freezing-plant at Fossvellir.

Smjörvatnsheiði, ("Butter lake moor") an old mountain route between Jökulsárhlíð and Vopnafjörður, with a refuge hut about mid-way. Now a jeep-track from Hofteigur in Jökuldalur. According to *Vopnfirðinga saga* the criminal Svartur was outlawed to these moors. He was particularly evil in that he stole and killed more sheep than he needed. Brodd-Helgi, a boy of 12 at the time, is said to have slain him in a hard battle, thus winning renown.

Jökulsárhlíð, the district along the east side of Fljótsdalshérað from Fossvellir. The mountains Smjörfjöll and Hlíðarfjöll beyond. Little flat land, what there is mostly along the Jökulsá river. High cliffs in the north along the coast. Fine views.

1 Austurlandsvegur, p. 100 **925 Hróarstunguvegur,** p. 425
926 Húseyjarvegur, p. 425

Krossvíkurfjöll, Vopnafjörður

Vindfell

Syðri-Vík, the first land to be settled in Vopnafjörður. The settler was Eyvindur Vopni of Strind in Norway, and he gave the fjord his name.

Krossavík, an ancient manor farm on the east of Vopnafjörður. Home of Geitir and his son Þorkell of *Vopnfirðinga saga*. The home around 1800 of sheriff Guðmundur Pétursson (1748-1811), a wealthy and enterprising man.

Vindfell, a farm where lignite is found.

Eyvindarstaðir, in Böðvarsdalur, scene of a battle between the Hofverjar ("Men of the farm Hof") and Þorkell Geitisson, 4 men on each side being slain, the battle scene is called **Hofsmannaflötur**.

Böðvarsdalur, a farm in a valley of the same name. Route from there, passable in summer, over Hellisheiði moor to Ketilsstaðir in the Jökulsárhlíð district.

Smjörfjöll, ("Butter mountains") between Vopnafjörður and Jökulsárhlíð, steep and rocky on the Vopnafjörður side. Mostly 1,200 m high, the highest 1,251 m. Little vegetation, rough and much scree, some rhyolite. Snowdrifts all summer in many places. Various streams become difficult to cross during thaws, though there is usually little water in them at other times.

Fagridalur, an abandoned farm and former weather station. Between Fagridalur and the spur Kollumúli is an uninhabited valley, Kattardalur. West of Fagridalur is the mountain **Búr** (516 m), with sheer cliffs descending into the sea and rocky coves below.

Kollumúli, (602 m) a spur with high cliffs at the outer end of the peninsula between Vopnafjörður and Héraðsflói. Bjarnarey island offshore.

Hellisheiði, (655 m) a mountain road across the moor between Vopnafjörður and Jökulsárhlíð, passable for all cars. Not kept open in the winter. Much used as a trade route to Vopnafjörður in former times, and as an emergency route when others were impassable.

85 **Norðausturvegur,** p. 384   919 **Sunnudalsvegur,** p. 384

Vatnsdalsgerði-Ketilsstaðir 31 km

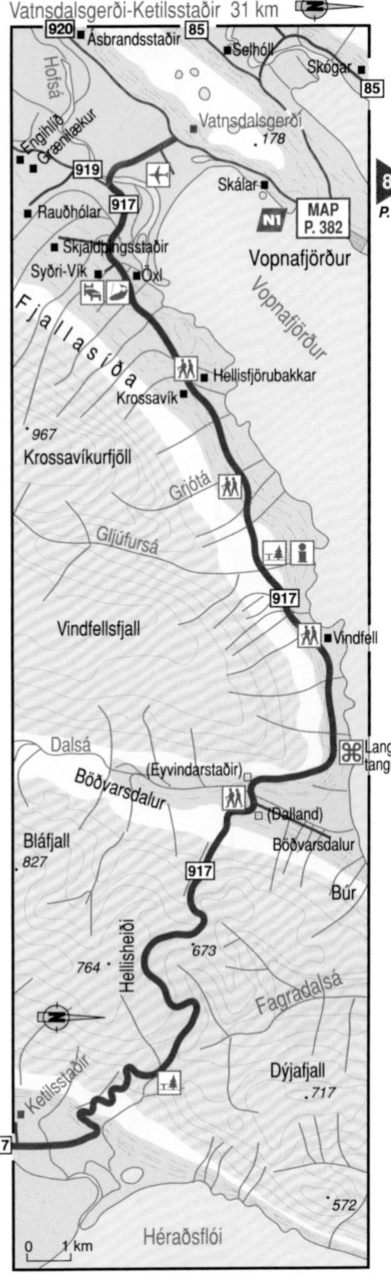

8 P. 571

Ketilsstaðir-Vatnsdalsgerði 31 km

Brú-Gilsá 31 km

923
Aðalból
Vaðbrekka
Hrafnkelsdalur
641
Hölkná
Brú
F910
907
Þverá
Jökulsá á Brú
923
Eiríksstaðir
Eiríksstaða-hneflar
947
922
Eyvindará
Búðará
Grund
(Stuðlafoss)
Kringilsá
923
Hákonarstaðir
Klaustursel
705
Þórfell
Jökulsá á Brú
Tregagilsá (Tregla)
Hnjúksvatn
Kiðufell
720
Merki
Arnórsstaða-hnjúkur
1
(Arnórsstaðir)
923
634
Valagilsá
Gilsá
792
Stóravatn
Skjöldólfsstaðir
1
0 1 km

Gilsá-Brú 31 km

8
P. 571

Snæfell, (1,833 m) the highest mountain in Iceland outside the main ice caps of Vatnajökull, conspicuous, with fine views from the top. An old volcano, the peak snow-covered. Local people say when it is clear over Snæfell in the evening, you can depend on good weather the next day. The local touring club has built a hut near the river Grjótá on the west of Snæfell. It is in this area that the majority of Iceland's wild reindeer are found (see Road F909).

Hrafnkelsdalur, a side-valley from the Jökuldalur valley, long and broad, often grassy with bushes. Geothermal heat in places. There are now only the 2 farms Vaðbrekka and Aðalból. Ruins of about 20 Saga age farms have been found there.

Aðalból, a farm about 80 km from the sea, once the home of Hrafnkell Freysgoði of *Hrafnkels saga*. Tracks for vehicles from there to the mountain Snæfell and other highland areas. The route up from the valley to Ytra-Kálfafell is rather steep and difficult, but then becomes relatively easy to the glacier Eyjabakkajökull.

Vaðbrekka, one of two inhabitaded farm in Hrafnkellsdalur. Almost midway between Vaðbrekka and Aðalból there is a pedestrian bridge across the river Hrafnkela on the land of Vaðbrekka. It was built to facilitate access to sheep sheds at Þórisstaðir.

907 Brúarvegur, frá Hringvegi á Austurleið F910, 21 km.

Brú, ("Bridge") the innermost farm in Jökuldalur, with land in to the glaciers and west to the river Kreppa. There was formerly a natural bridge over the Jökulsá river, which is where the name comes from. There is now a man-made bridge there. Four-wheel drive vehicles can be driven west across the moors south of the mountains Þríhyrningur and Mynnisfjallgarður and on track F905 south from Möðrudalur. It is also possible to drive (F910) east of Kreppa as far as the glacier Brúarjökull. Another track goes from Brú north across Jökuldalsheiði moor to join Highway 1 at the lake Sænautavatn.

Eiríksstaðir, a church, moved there from Brú. There is a magnificent view from Eiríksstaðahneflar (922 m and 947 m), two peaks above the farm.

Hákonarstaðir, a farm dating to the Settlement Era and situated beside the Jökulsá river, across from **Klaustursel**. The bridge over the Jökulsá to Klaustursel farmstead is the oldest in Iceland that is still in use. Specially manufactured in the USA, it was imported as parts, riveted together on site and erected in 1908. Klaustursel has a small zoo, with reindeer, fox, geese and other Icelandic animals, together with a gallery offering items made of reindeer leather.

1 Austurlandsvegur, p. 99
923 Jökuldalsvegur, p. 424
907 Brúarvegur, p. 99, 485
F910 Austurleið, p. 490

Snæfell

925 926 927

Hróarstunga, the area between the rivers Jökulsá á Brú and Lagarfljót from Ós to Rangá. The southernmost part is the Lágheiði moor, the northern end of Fljótsdalsheiði. Long and low hills with wet ground, fens and marshes in between, many lakes.

926 Húseyjarvegur, 21 km.

Húsey, the outermost farm in Hróarstunga in the middle of the flat land, near the confluence of the rivers Jökulsá and Lagarfljót. It once had the greatest amount of seal hunting in the Héraðsflói district.

925 Hróarstunguvegur, 42 km. 927 Brekkubæjarvegur, 7 km.

Litli-Bakki, close to Geirsstaðir. The ruins near Geirsstaðir date from about 980 and consist of a church, a house, an enclosing wall and some other remains. A replica of the church has been built there. It is also planned to rebuild the house and to use it and the church for living functions with people in Viking period costumes and farm animals on view to give an idea of life in the early days of Christianity in Iceland.

Hallfreðarstaðir, a farm, home for a time of poet Páll Ólafsson (1827-1905), who often mentioned the area in his verse. Memorial to him.

Skersl, some strange crags north of Kirkjubær, once the dwelling-place of the giant Þórir and his wife. Every year they put a spell on either the pastor or the shepherd in Kirkjubær that made them come to Skersl. A pastor named Eiríkur managed to change this, and they waited for him in their cave to no avail. In the end Þórir froze fast to the ice on Þórisvatn when fishing, and his wife turned into Skessusteinn ("Giantess rock").

Kirkjubær, a church and till recently a parsonage.

Lagarfoss, a waterfall in the river Lagarfljót opposite Kirkjubær, the only falls in this river. Lagarfoss is divided in the middle by a rock, where a salmon ladder was built in 1935. It has now been replaced. The west branch is rapids, the east branch plunges off a 6 m high ledge. Total drop: 11 m. The falls were harnessed for power in 1975, so their appearance has changed, and there is a bridge on the dam.

Galtastaðir fram, farm, dating from 1882, with living quarters above the cow-house, a storeroom, a kitchen with a stone stove, a pantry and a barn. It gives a good impression of how ordinary people in Iceland lived, using their cows as a source of heat. In the keeping of the National Museum since 1976.

Þinghöfði, an old assembly site by the river Krakalækur, mentioned in the Sagas. Ruins of booths still visible. Site during the 19th century of national meetings similar to the Kollubúðir meetings in the Western Fjords (see Road 608).

Urriðavatn, a fishing-lake with warm springs in it, water from which is piped to the towns Egilsstaðir and Fellabær. A farm of the same name beside the lake.

1 **Austurlandsvegur,** p. 101
917 **Hlíðarvegur,** p. 422
922 **Másselsvegur,** p. 422
929 **Hafrafellsvegur,** p. 101
944 **Lagarfossvegur,** p. 415

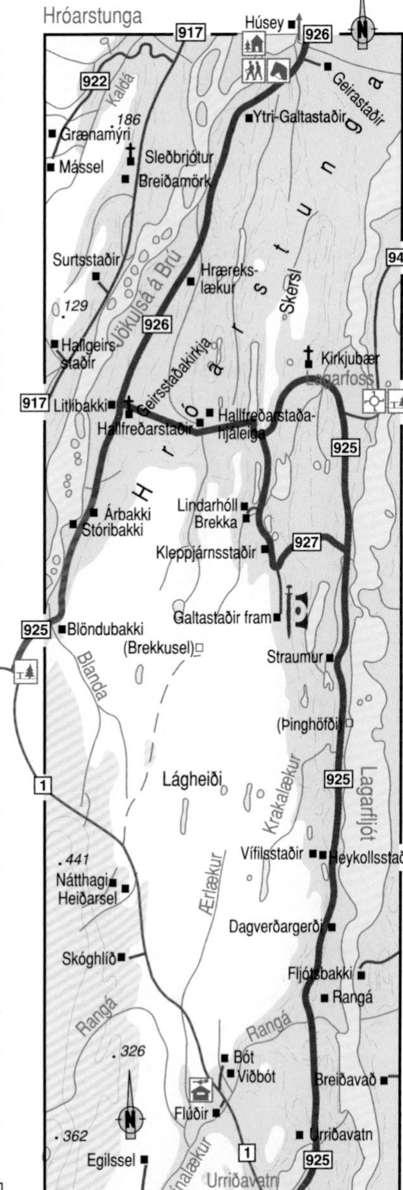

9
P. 572

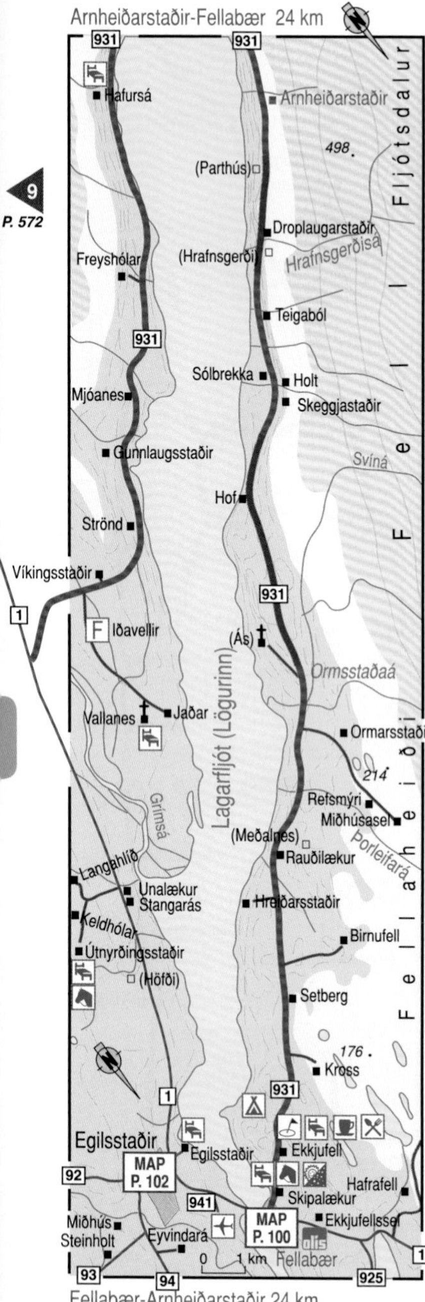

Fellabær-Arnheiðarstaðir 24 km

By Lagarfljót

Fljótsdalur, the valley district between the rivers Hrafnsgerðisá on the west and Gilsá on the east. The lower part of valley near the Lagarfljót river is broad with meadows, and about 10 km from Lagarfljót it divides into the narrow valleys Norðurdalur and Suðurdalur, between which is the mountain spur Múli (642 m).

Fellaheiði, (700 m) the moors above Fell west of the river Lagarfljót. Many lakes and tarns, with trout. Continuation to the south into Fljótsdalsheiði moor, where there are also numerous lakes, tarns, streams and brooks. Reindeer often come down there and even to the farms, especially if winter pastures are poor.

Ás, a church, a parsonage until 1880.

Meðalnes, an abandoned farm, once the home of the parents of the Icelandic-Canadian writer Jóhann Magnús Bjarnason (1866-1945).

Fell, the farming area along the western side of the river Lagarfljót. Rather barren, with many rocks, crags and marshes. Little meadow-land but good grazing. Several lakes and tarns.

Lagarfljót, a broad river, the inner part of which is a lake extending from Fljótsdalur to beyond Egilsstaðir. Deep, max. 112 m, average 50.7 m, at least 30 km long and 2.5 km at its broadest point, area 53 km^2. Natural gas in places. A little trout-fishing. There are many stories of a monster in the lake, known as Lagarfljótsormurinn ("The Lagarfljót serpent"). Near the bridge the lake becomes the river Lagarfljót, mostly quiet-flowing though deep, which marks the boundary between the counties of Norður-Múlasýsla and Suður-Múlasýsla. The summer of 1999 the passanger ship Lagafljótsormurinn began sailing on the river. The tours are very popular. The ship carries 130 passangers.

Fellabær, (pop. 404) a village across the bridge from Egilsstaðir. Main activities trading, service and industry.

941 Flugvallavegur, 0,55 km.

1 **Austurlandsvegur,** p. 101	92 **Norðfjarðarvegur,** p. 409
93 **Seyðisfjarðarvegur,** p. 414	94 **Borgarfjarðarvegur,** p. 415
925 **Hróarstunguvegur,** p. 425	

931 UPPHÉRAÐSVEGUR

Úlfsstaðir-Hrafnkelsstaðir 24 km

Vallanes, a church. Best known of pastors there was the poet Stefán Ólafsson (ca. 1619-88). After Hallgrímur Pétursson (see Saurbær, Borg) he was Iceland's greatest poet in the 17th century. He did many translations into and from Latin. He was also a song-writer and an astronomer. The community centre Iðavellir nearby. Vallanes today, is one of Iceland's largest farms growing entirely organic grains, fruits and vegetables.

Mjóanes, home of Helgi Ásbjarnarson, a Saga age chieftain of the Eastern fjords. Fenced to protect the woods from sheep.

Parthús, a sherpherds' hut, famous for the tale of the violent death there of one Parthúsa-Jón, at the hands of a ghost.

Hallormsstaður, a manor farm in its time. Church till 1895, parsonage till 1880. Domestic science school founded in 1930, still in use. Hallormsstaður is the main centre of the Forestry Service. Birthplace of Guðmundur Magnússon (1741-98), who lived most of his life abroad and published ancient literature, e.g. the first volume of the *Sæmundar-Edda*, 1787, in Latin translation, with notes and vocabulary. He also translated *Egils saga* into Latin, wrote an Icelandic-Latin dictionary, published a play by Terentius, 1780, and other works. Hotel, see add p. 103.

Hallormsstaðarskógur, ("Hallormsstaður woods") at the turn of the century considered to be the biggest woods in Iceland. Almost all of the woods protected from grazing animals between 1905 and 1927. Placed under nursery protection of the Forestry Service in 1907. The wood itself is now 740 km², and between 1965 and 1980 areas of land on both sides of the woods were brought inside fences along with the wood, the total fenced in area now being 1850 hectares (about 4,500 acres). The fence along the river Lagarfljót is 15 km long. In 1903 a nursery area, called Mörkin, was established to grow different kinds of native and foreign trees, and has flourished ever since. It is now possible to see 70 species of foreign trees there. In the Guttormslundur grove, named for Guttormur Pálsson, forester (1884-1964), is the tallest tree in Iceland, one of a number of Russian larches planted in 1938. The **Atlavík** bay on Lagarfljót is the best-known holiday area in Hallormsstaðarskógur, and there are 40 km of roads in the woods, many of which make excellent walking routes. National Forest.

Gilsá, a river forming the boundary between Norður-Múlasýsla and Suður-Múlasýsla counties.

Hrafnkelsstaðir, a farm in the lower Fljótsdalur valley, named for Hrafnkell Freysgoði of *Hrafnkels saga*. A lovely protected birchwood, **Ranaskógur**, nearby.

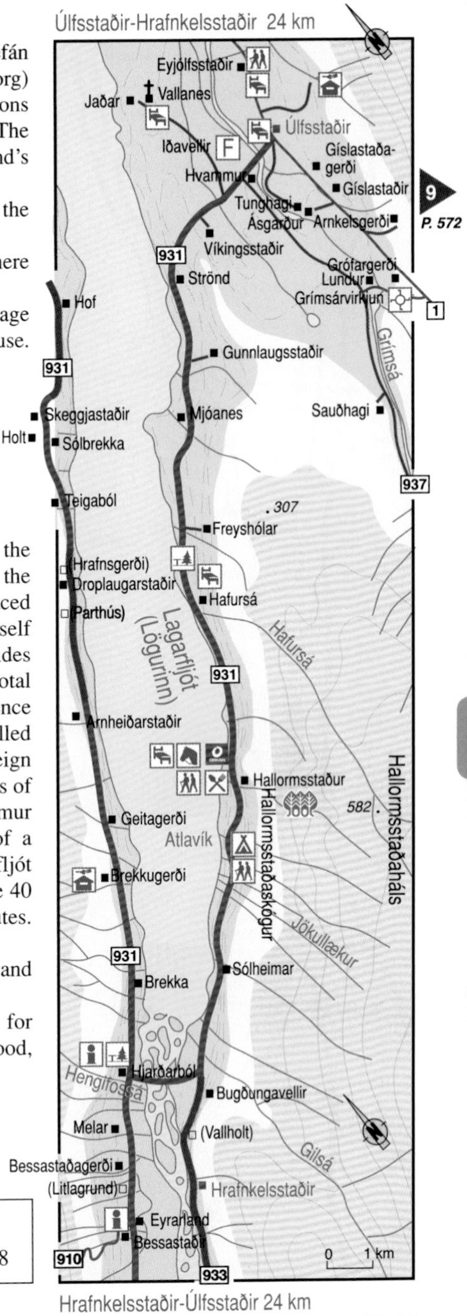

1 **Austurlandsvegur,** p. 101
937 **Skriðdalsvegur,** p. 105
910 **Austurleið,** p. 490
933 **Fljótsdalsvegur,** p. 428

Hrafnkelsstaðir-Úlfsstaðir 24 km

24 P. 587

9 P. 572

Arnaldsstaðaskógur, natural birch forest high on a steep mountain slope. Turn southwest from Highway 934 onto tracks north of Kelduá river. Steep hiking path. National Forest.

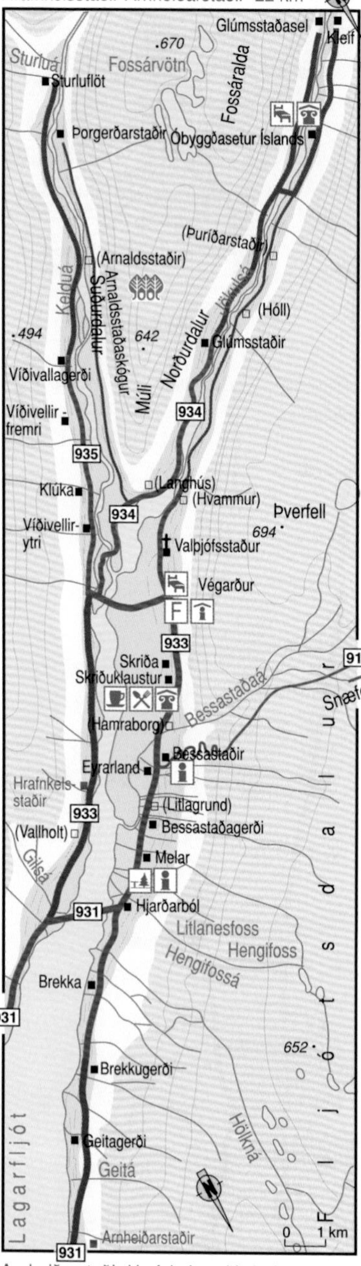

935 Suðurdalsvegur, 12,5 km. **933 Fljótsdalsvegur,** 17 km.

Sturluflöt, a rough track leads from there across the highlands from there south to Víðidalur í Lóni (see Stafafell, A-Skaft).

Kárahnjúkavirkjun, a power plant, with its generating station situated about 900 m inside Teigsbjarg mountain.

Valþjófsstaður, an ancient manor farm, church and parsonage. Community centre Végarður. The famous Valþjófsstaður church door, one of the finest items in the National Museum at Reykjavík, came from there. The door now on the church is an exact replica. Tröllkonustígur ("Giantess' path") above the farm. Once the home of the Þórarinsson brothers, Þorvarður, one of the most powerful men in Iceland in his day (d. 1297), and Oddur, a great warrior slain in 1255 at Geldingaholt.

Végarður, a community centre.

Skriðuklaustur, a substantial farm for centuries, site of a monastery from 1493 until the Reformation, then a church till 1792. Home of a number of prominent men, e.g. Sheriff Hans Wium (1715-88), who is buried there. In 1939 the author Gunnar Gunnarsson settled at Skriðuklaustur and built a large, unusual house, which he later presented to the Icelandic nation (see Road 85, Ljótsstaðir). For a time an experimental station for sheep-breeding and soil cultivation. Now a centre of culture and history, run by the Institute of Gunnar Gunnarsson, with various cultural activities and access to the ruins of the monastery. Klausturkaffi café offers launch and teatime buffet. In 2010 the Snæfell Visitor Centre for the east territory of Vatnajökull National Park was opened at Skriðuklaustur. The centre has an interesting exhibition on the area and the nature and a souvenir shop that focuses on locally produced products.

See information on Vatnajökull National Park on p. 122.

Hengifoss, ("Hanging falls") one of the highest waterfalls in Iceland, 128 m, in the river Hengifossá near the farm Brekka. In the gorge there, which is pretty and varied, are lignite and fossils. Another waterfall further downstream, Litlanesfoss, is set in basalt columns. A walking path leads to Hengifoss from the highway.

934 Múlavegur í Fljótsdal, 13 km. **910 Austurleið,** p. 490

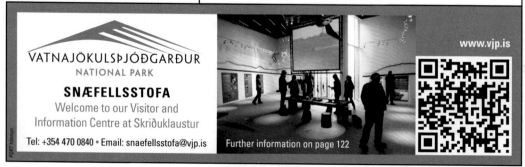

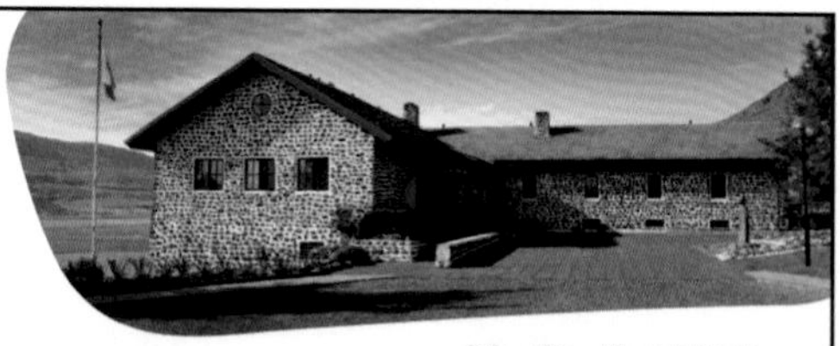

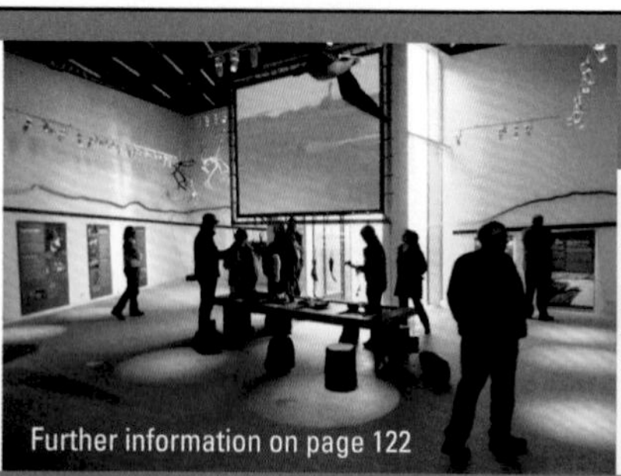

953 MJÓAFJARÐARVEGUR

Brekka-Fagridalur 32 km

Dalatangi, a weather station and lighthouse. One of the first lighthouses built in Iceland, 1895. In the keeping of the National Museum since 2003.

Mjóifjörður, a long, narrow fjord, surrounded by high mountains and steep cliffs. Today the fjord is largely uninhabited with few inhabitants, whereas in its heyday in 1902, there were 412. Became part of Fjarðabyggð in 2006. Some trout in the Fjarðará river. A lot of bilberries and other berries in August. Often good fishing in the fjord in late summer.

Brekkuþorp, an old fishing village. The first icehouse in Iceland was built there in 1895. Community centre Sólbrekka.

Asknes, site of a whaling-station built in 1901 by Norwegians. 14 whaling boats sailed from there in the early years of last century, and some 300-400 men worked at the station.

Fjörður, a farm of the original setlement, formerly the site of a church. It is at the sea end of **Fjarðardalur**, a pretty, wooded valley with many cliffs and waterfalls.

953 Mjóafjarðarvegur, 46,5 km, accessible to all cars. From Sólbrekka the road is hard to travel by car, but can easily be accessed by foot and is well worth the trip.

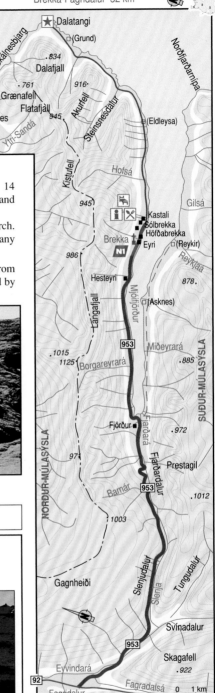

The Klifbrekkufossar waterfalls in Mjóifjörður.

92 Norðfjarðarvegur, p. 409

9 P. 572

Fagridalur-Brekka 32 km

22 P. 585

Nýidalur
Skrauti
Mjóháls
Vonarskarð
Ógöngur
Köldukvíslarjökull
Skerðingur
1127
Hofsjökull
Þórisjökull
Fjórðungakvísl
F26
Arnarfell hið litla
1140
Þórislón
Hreysiskvísl
Nyrðri-Háganga
1278
Hágöngur
Hágöngulón
Hamarskriki
1137
Arnarfell hið mikla
Kistualda
1284
Syðri-Háganga
Ólafsfell
926
Skrokkalda
Hágönguhraun
Tungnaárjökull
Söðulfell
765
Þjórsárver
Kvíslavatn
Vatnsleysuöldur
Þverfell
1032
Þúfuvötn
632
742
Hnöttóttaalda
Hnífá
Bláfjöll
Kerlingarfjöll
814
Stóra-Seta
Stóraverslón
Þveröldurvatn
Þveralda
Kaldakvísl
Ferðamannalda
Versalir
Jökulheimar
Fjórðungssandur
860
Eyvafen
Illugaver
Gjáfjöll
F26
Sauðafell
770
Tungnaá
Ljósufjöll
Lambafell
684
Kjalvötn
F229
Norðurleit
Þjórsá
Kjalöldur
Botnafjöll
740
728
Tungnaárfjöll
Langisjór
Rjúpnanefsvatn
Kaldakvísl
Útgönguhöfði
738
Austurbotnar
Þórisvatn
Klakkafell
Gljúfurleit
1090
Sveinstindur
Helguvatn
F26
Litlisjór
F228
Gljúfurleitarfoss
651
Veiðivötn
614
Vatnsfell
730
822
Þóristindur
Vatnaöldur
Lambafell
647
Grænifjallgarður
547
208
Hótel Háland
Krókslón
Hrauneyjalón
Sultartangalón
Búðarháls
Hrauneyjar
F235
Tungnaá
F26
Stóra-Melafell
F208
Eskihlíðarvatn
Löðmundur
1074
F208
0 2 km

14 P. 577

F26 **Sprengisandsleið (Ölduleið)** 107,9 km. A old route betweeen the South and the North. This old route across the interior between the north and south of Iceland is still in use today. Formerly the bishops of Skálholt used it on their way to the east of Iceland, as many place names indicate. Names like **Sveinar**, **Sprengir** og **Beinakerling** (see F752). Then it was more or less lost and out of use until the 18th and 19th centuries. The first trip by car was made in 1933. The oldest route was up from the Þjórsárdalur valley, on the west side of the Þjórsá river and across it at Sóleyjarhöfðavað ford, then north across the sands to the farm Mýri in the Bárðardalur valley, about 240 km (see Road 842). Less frequented was the route up from Galtalækur, along the east of the Þjórsá river to Sóleyjarhöfði, where the two routes came together. With the new power station on the Tungnaá river and bridges across it the **Sprengisandur** route has been moved further east away from Þjórsá, though there are several sideroads to the old route.

Versalir, a guesthouse and a restaurant since 1987. There is a junction just befor Versalir that divides Sprengisandsleið to two routes: **Kvíslaveituvegur** and **Ölduleið**.

Þúfuver, some wet grasslands along the Þjórsá river. Þúfuver and Eyvindarver belong to the broad, marshy grasslands called Þjórsárver. These grasslands are more extensive on the west side of the river and also more isolated and difficult to reach.

Fjórðungakvísl, a river formed by Hagakvísl and Nýjadalsá that come from Tungnafellsjökull. It later joins Bergvatnskvísl and more rivers to make Þjórsá, the longest river in Iceland.

Fjórðungsvatn, a shallow lake that sometimes almost disappears in dry periods. East of the lake is Fjórðungsalda, (969 m) a wide mountain ridge with a fine view from the top.

Eyvindarver, marshlands along the river Þjórsá, rich with bird-life mainly geese and swans. By Lindarbakki there are some ruins of a shelter built by the 18th century outlaw Fjalla-Evindur.

Innrahreysi, there are some ruins of a shelter of the outlaw Fjalla-Eyvindur. Eyvindur and his wife, Halla, were caught there in 1772.

Inn með Öldum, ("In along the ridges") a collective name for the road (or tracks) from the bridge on the Kaldakvísl river to the Nýidalur valley. This country is very barren and rocky. From south to north the four main ridges along the route are, **Þveralda** (728 m), **Hnöttóttaalda** (785 m), **Skrokkalda** (922 m) and **Kistualda** (786 m).

Vonarskarð, ("Hope pass") a mountain pass, really more of a wide valley between the two glaciers Vatnajökull and Tungnafellsjökull, 900 to 940 m above sea level, 15-20 km long and with about 13 km distance between the two glaciers. **Skjálfandafljót** and **Kaldakvísl** come from Vonarskarð.

Nýidalur, ("New valley") or **Jökuldalur,** ("Glacier valley") a valley on the southern side of Tungnafellsjökull. Its floor is about 800 m above sea level, yet surprisingly rich in vegetation. Probably the highest area of such vegetation in Iceland. This valley was off the beaten track and was found by three farmers from the north in 1845. Two tourist huts by the west entrance to the valley. The lodges in Nýidalur are just by the highland route over Sprengisandur. A warden is appointed during the summer. From the houses you can view the sout-west side of the glacier Tungnafellsjökull. The glacier can easily be accessed by foot about Mjóháls east of Vonarskarð.

26 **Landvegur,** p. 161 | **F208** **Fjallabaksleið nyrðri,** p. 436 | **F228** **Veiðivatnaleið,** p. 446
F229 **Jökulheimaleið,** p. 447 | **F235** **Langisjór,** p. 443

23 P. 586

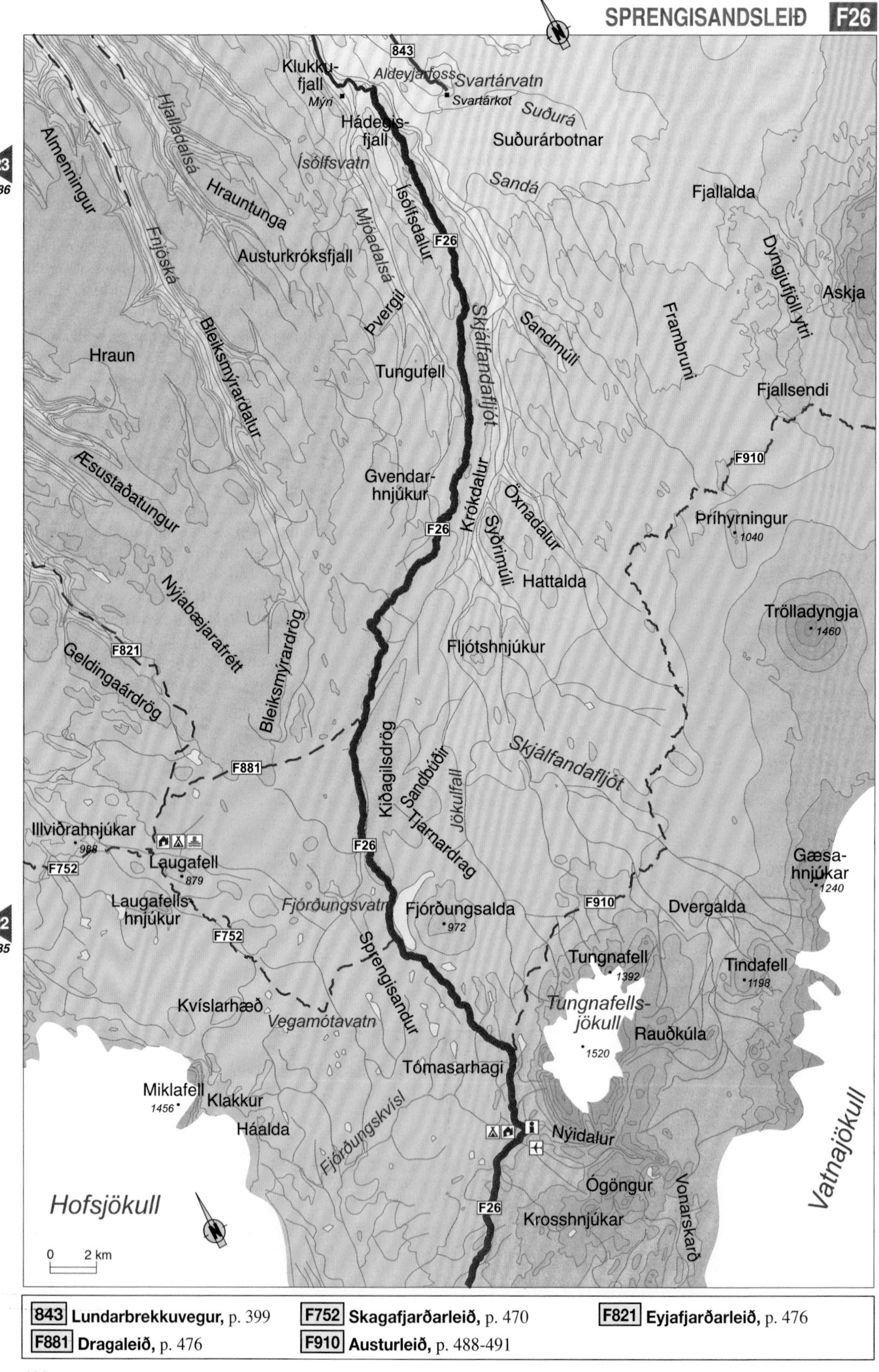

22 P. 585

843 **Lundarbrekkuvegur,** p. 399 **F752** **Skagafjarðarleið,** p. 470 **F821** **Eyjafjarðarleið,** p. 476
F881 **Dragaleið,** p. 476 **F910** **Austurleið,** p. 488-491

© Gunnar Guðjónsson

Hofsjökull

F26 **Sprengisandsleið (Bárðardalsleið)** 96 km. Passable for all jeeps, but with difficult rivers to cross.

Tómasarhagi, ("Tómas' pasture") a green area (mostly moss) west of the glacier Tungnafellsjökull, first found by Tómas Sæmundsson in 1835. There may possibly have been more vegetation there at that time.

Tungnafellsjökull, (1,540 m) a glacier mountain, 50 km^2, steep on the south and west sides. The German geologist Hans Reck was the first to do research work on Tungnafellsjökull in 1906. The route lies west of Fjórðungsvatn to Kiðagil.

Fjórðungsvatn, a shallow lake that sometimes almost disappears in dry periods. East of the lake is **Fjórðungsalda**, (972 m) a wide mountain ridge with a fine view from the top.

Sandbúðir, a weather station for some years in connection with plans to lay high-tension power lines across Sprengisandur. Now there is an automatic weather station.

Kiðagil, a narrow canyon about 6 km long going west from the river Skjálfandafljót. In times past this was the first stop to the north of the Sprengisandur desert. The canyon can not be seen from the road.

Kiðagilsdrög, a shallow valley up from Kiðagil.

Fremri-Mosar and **Ytri-Mosar,** some meager grasslands by the road with the stream Mosakvísl flowing north to Mjóadalsá.

Aldeyjarfoss, an impressive waterfall in the Skjálfandafljót river, in a unique setting of basalt columns and rock caves.

Svartárkot, a farm located innermost to the east in the valley of Bárðardalur. It stands on the heath at the edge of Ódáðarhraun, 400 m above sea level. A sizeable lake, named Svartárvatn, close by.

Mjóadalsá, a river by Mýri in the Bárðardalur valley. Formerly an obstacle to travel, bridge built in 1977.

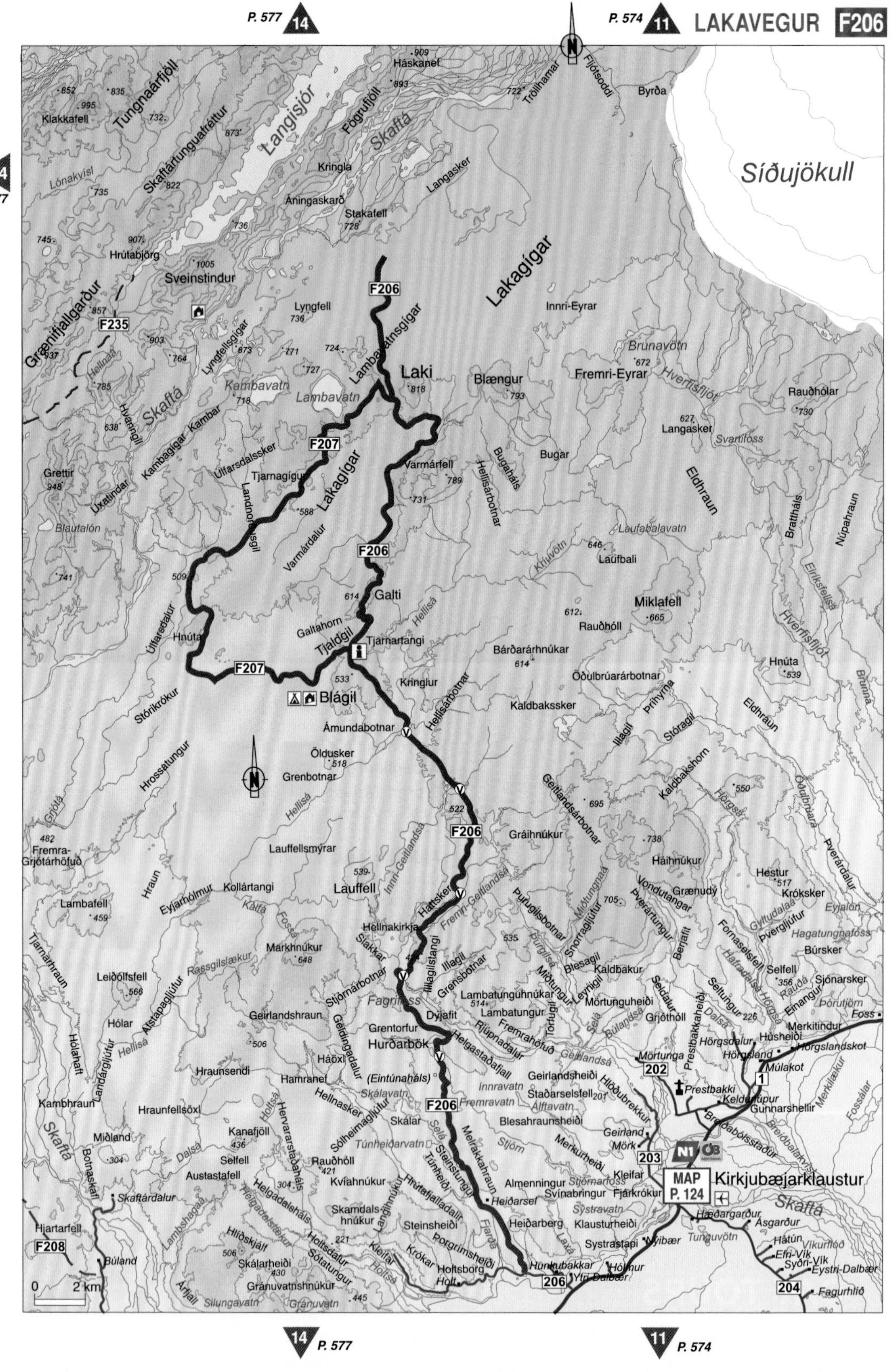
P. 577 14
P. 574 11
P. 577 14
Langisjór
Skaftá
Tungnaárfjöll
Skaftártunguafréttur
Fögrufjöll
Háskanef
Tröllhamar
Fljótsoddi
Byrða
Síðujökull
Klakkafell
Lónakvísl
Kringla
Langasker
Áningaskarð
Stakafell
Hrútabjörg
Sveinstindur
Lakagígar
Innri-Eyrar
F206
F235
Grænifjallgarður
Lyngfell
Lyngfellsgígar
Lambavatnsgígar
Laki
Blængur
Brunavötn
Fremri-Eyrar
Hverfisfljót
Rauðhólar
Kambavatn
Lambavatn
Langasker
Svartifoss
Hvarfingil
Kambar
Kambagígar
F207
Úlfarsdalssker
Tjarnagígur
Varmárfell
Bugar
Bugaháls
Hellisárbotnar
Eldhraun
Grettir
Uxatindar
Landnorðursgil
Blautalón
Varmárdalur
Laufabalavatn
Brattháls
Núpahraun
Laufbali
Galti
Miklafell
Rauðhóll
Galtahorn
Tjaldgil
Tjarnartangi
Hnúta
Úlfarsdalur
Bárðarárhnúkar
Blágil
Kringlur
Öðulbrúarárbotnar
Hnúta
Stórikrókur
Kaldbakssker
Ámundabotnar
Prihyrna
Illagil
Stóragil
Öldusker
Grenbotnar
Hrossatungur
Kaldbakshorn
Geirlandsárbotnar
Hörgsá
Hellisá
Grjótá
Fremra-Grjótárhöfuð
Lauffellsmýrar
Gráhnúkur
Háihnúkur
Lauffell
Hattsker
Hestur
Krókssker
Grænudý
Vondutangar
Hraun
Eyjarhólmur
Kollártangi
Lambafell
Hellnakirkja
Fremri-Geitlandsá
Þurugilsbotnar
Mörtunga
Kaldbakur
Markhnúkur
Illagil
Illagilstangi
Blesagil
Selfell
Sjónarsker
Leiðólfsfell
Stjórnárbotnar
Lambatunguhnúkar
Lambatungur
Mörtunguheiði
Hólar
Geirlandshraun
Dyjafit
Grjóthóll
Foss
Merkitindur
Grentorfur
Hurðarbök
Fremrahöfuð
Húsheiði
Hörgsdalur
Hörgsland
Hörgslandskot
Háöxl
Hraunsendi
Hamranef
(Eintúnaháls)
Helgastaðafjall
Geirlandsheiði
Mörtunga
202
Múlakot
Prestbakki
1
Kambhraun
Hellnasker
F206
Staðarselstell
Blesahraunsheiði
Keldunúpur
Gunnarshellir
Hraunfellsöxl
Skálar
Geirland
Mörk
203
Miðland
Kanafjöll
Selfell
Austastafell
Rauðhóll
Sólheimagljúfur
Steinstunga
Merkurheiði
Kleifar
Almenningur
Svínabringur
Fjarkrókur
MAP P. 124
Kirkjubæjarklaustur
Skaftárdalur
Kvíahnúkur
Hrútafjalladalur
Heiðarsel
Skaftá
Skamdalshnúkur
Steinsheiði
Heiðarberg
Klausturheiði
Hæðargarður
Ásgarður
Hjartarfell
F208
Búland
Hlíðskjál
Skálarheiði
Holtsdalur
Kleifar
Krókar
Holtsborg
Þorgrímsheiði
Systrastapi
Nýibær
Tunguvötn
Hátún
Efri-Vík
Syðri-Vík
Eystri-Dalbær
Hunkubakkar
Hólmur
206
Ytri-Dalbær
Holt
Gránuvatnshnúkur
Sótatungur
Arnjall
Silungavatn
Gránuvötn
Fagurhlíð
204
0 2 km
14 P. 577
11 P. 574

Fjaðrárgljúfur

F206 **Lakavegur** 48,8 km to the parking lot at Laki. Passable by all jeeps. On this route two rivers need to be crossed **Geirlandsá** and **Hellisá**.

Fjaðrárgljúfur, a canyon through tuff, 100 m deep, just below the farm Heiðarsel. There is a walking route along the eastern edge, and it is possible to walk up through the canyon, though then one must wade across the river.

Heiðarsel, a deserted farm on the east bank of the river Fjarðará. People lived on the farm until 1980s; it was the home of Þorbjörg Jónsdóttir (born in 1903), wife of the German folklorist Dr. Bruno Schweizer (1897 - 1958), documenting on paper and film some unique discription of the last stages of the Icelandic turf-roofed houses, work, transportation, and many other aspects of daily life in this static time that heralded the end of the ancient Icelandic rural community.

Selárgljúfur, a canyon just above the farm Heiðarsel.

Raflínuvegur ("Linesmen's road") a jeep-track at right angles to the road, leading east to the edge of the moor.

Eintúnaháls, ("One field ridge") an abandoned farm in a grassy, little valley, occupied from the early 19th century to 1934.

Fagrifoss, a waterfall just below the ford. Access is best from the east. The fords on the rivers Geirlandsá and Hellisá are problematic for smaller cars, and can become suddenly impassable when the rivers rise.

F207 **Hringleið** by Laki 23,9 km. Passable by all jeeps.

Laki, (818 m) a tuff mountain in the middle of the Lakagígar row of craters. Panoramic view in good weather.

Lakagígar, a 40 km long row of craters, from the river Skaftá up onto the Vatnajökull glacier. More than 100 craters, some as high as 100 m, now mostly moss-grown. An eruption started in the craters west of Laki in June 1783 and continued there in July, but moved to the eastern craters in the end of July and continued on till February 7th 1784. Source of the Skaftáreldar lava field. Lakagígar are a part of Vatnajökull National Park. The area contains some of the world's most remarkable geological formations while the plant and animal life is also of special interest. Because the area is very sensitive to encroachment, the aim of the conservation order is to preserve this unique and extremely sensitive area for future generations.

Galti, a steep mountain giving a good view over the moors.

Blágil, ("Blue canyons") a canyons west of the road near the Hellisá river. Mostly filled with lava from the Skaftáreldar eruptions. A park ranger station, cabin and a campground with limited services.

1 **Suðurlandsvegur,** p. 127	**202** **Prestbakkavegur,** p. 127	**203** **Geirlandsvegur,** p. 127
204 **Meðallandsvegur,** p. 162	**206** **Holtsvegur,** p. 128, 163	**F235** **Langisjór,** p. 443

14
P. 577

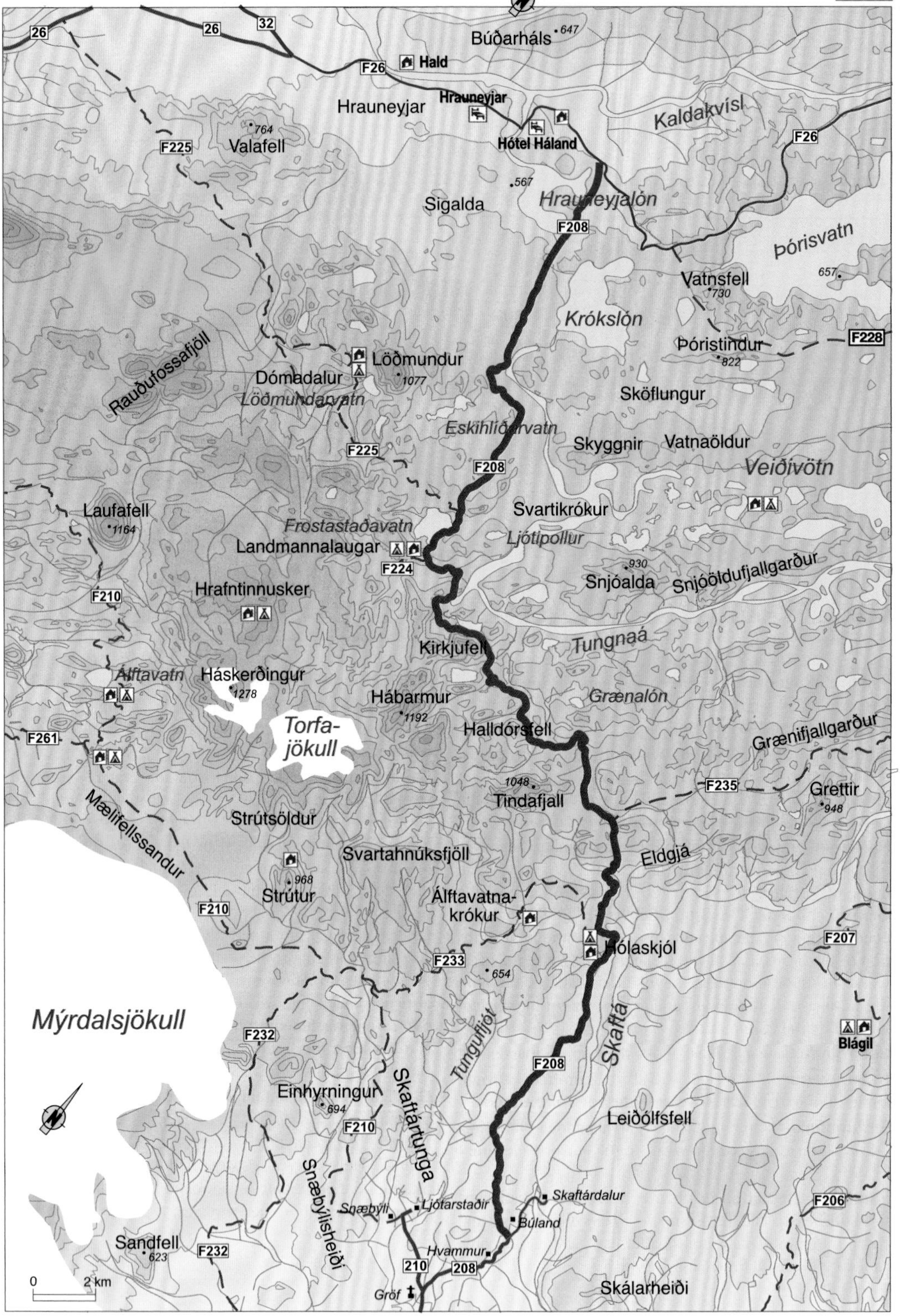

26
26
32
Búðarháls 647
Hald
F26
Hrauneyjar
Hrauneyjar
Hótel Háland
Kaldakvísl
F26
F225
Valafell
764
567
Sigalda
Hrauneyjalón
F208
Þórisvatn
657
Vatnsfell
730
Krókslón
Þóristindur
822
F228
Rauðufossafjöll
Löðmundur
1077
Dómadalur
Löðmundarvatn
Sköflungur
Eskihlíðarvatn
Skyggnir
Vatnaöldur
Veiðivötn
F225
F208
Svartikrókur
Laufafell
1164
Frostastaðavatn
Ljótipollur
Landmannalaugar
F224
930
Snjóalda
Snjóöldufjallgarður
F210
Hrafntinnusker
Tungnaá
Kirkjufell
Álftavatn
Háskerðingur
1278
Hábarmur
1192
Grænalón
Torfa-
jökull
Halldórsfell
F261
Grænifjallgarður
1048
Tindafjall
F235
Grettir
948
Mælifellssandur
Strútsöldur
Eldgjá
Svartahnúksfjöll
968
Strútur
F210
Álftavatna-
krókur
Hólaskjól
F207
F233
654
Mýrdalsjökull
Tungufljót
F232
Skaftá
Blágil
F208
Einhyrningur
694
Skaftártunga
F210
Leiðólfsfell
Snæbýlisheiði
Skaftárdalur
Snæbýli
Ljótarstaðir
Búland
F206
Sandfell
623
F232
Hvammur
210
208
0
2 km
Gröf
Skálarheiði

F208 Fjallabaksleið nyrðri (Sigölduleið) 85,4 km. Passable by all jeeps. Many small fords on the route.

Frostastaðavatn, a lake surrounded by lava, said to have once had a farm on its shore.

Ljótipollur, an explosion crater with colourful sides and greenish water.

Frostastaðaháls, connects the rhyolite mountains Norður-Námur and Suður-Námur.

Kýlingar, marshy grassland around two inlets from the Tungnaá river.

Kirkjufell, (964 m) an impressive table mountain of rhyolite.

Jökuldalir, valleys surrounded by impressive mountains, the highest being **Tindafjall** (1,048 m). The river Jökuldalakvísl is usually shallow but the riverbed may be soft and not safe to ford. Hut.

Hörðubreið,(812 m) a tuff mountain. The view in all directions from the Hörðubreiðarháls ridge just south of the mountain is the finest on these routes. Rain and fog are rather frequent.

Eldgjá, ("Fire canyon") a 40 km long volcanic rift reaching from the Mýrdalsjökull glacier to the mountain Gjátindur. Most impressive at the northern end where it is 600 m wide and 200 m deep. Extensive lava fields have come from Eldgjá and spread over the lowlands of Meðalland, Landbrot and Álftaver. Named by Þorvaldur Thoroddsen, the first geologist to study Eldgjá. He thought there had been only one eruption about 1,100 years ago but later research shows that there have been many eruptions, the lava of Álftaver being the oldest.

Eldgjá

Fremri-Tólfahringar and **Innri-Tólfahringar,** ("Ring of twelve") an area along the Skaftá river where it is said there were once 12 farms, with a church at Réttarfell, and hence the name. Ruins of two farms have been found there.

Svartinúpur, a low mountain and a farm of the same name, abandoned since the eruption of Katla in 1918.

Búland, the northernmost farm in the Skaftártunga district. Above Búland is a canyon, Granagil. There is an old burial cairn, **Granahaugar**, where Grani Gunnarsson was buried.

Skaftárdalur, the western most farm at Síða.

26 **Landvegur,** p. 160
210 **Ljótarstaðavegur,** p. 129
F207 **Lakagígavegur,** p. 437
F225 **Landmannaleið,** p. 444
F235 **Langisjór,** p. 443
32 **Þjórsárdalsvegur,** p. 175
F26 **Sprengisandsleið,** p. 430-433
F210 **Fjallabaksleið syðri,** p. 438-441
F232 **Öldufellsleið,** p. 448
F261 **Emstruleið,** p. 452
208 **Skaftártunguvegur,** p. 129
F206 **Lakavegur,** p. 434
F224 **Landmannalaugavegur,** p. 444
F233 **Álftavatnskrókur,** p. 449

14
P. 577

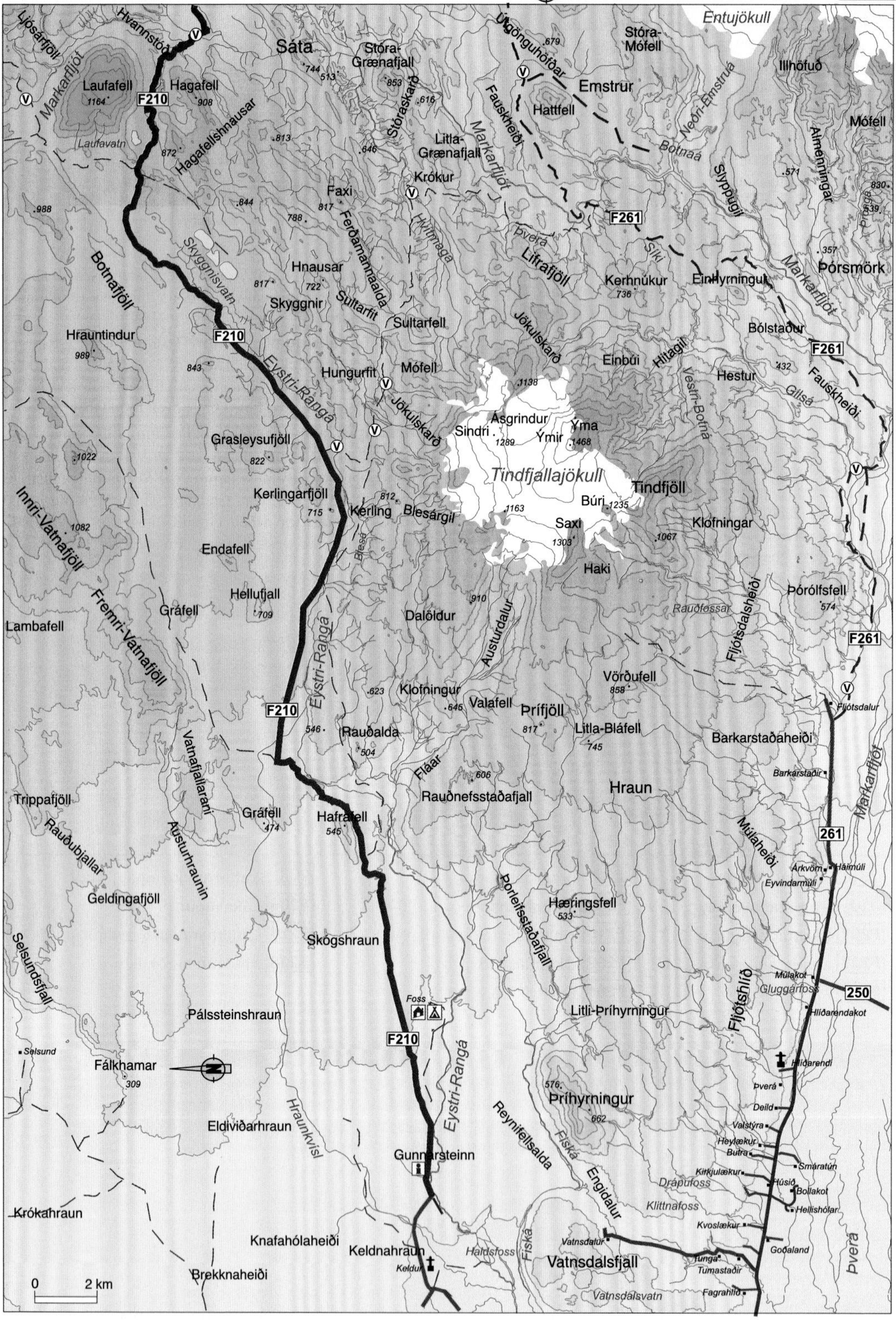

13
P. 576

Ljósárfjöll
Hvannstóð
Sáta
Stóra-Grænafjall
Laufafell
1164
Hagafell
908
Markarfljót
Laufavatn
Hagafellshnausar
872
813
853
616
744
513
Stóraskarð
646
Litla-Grænafjall
Krókur
Faxi
817
788
844
988
Ferðamannaalda
Hvítmaga
Skyggnisvatn
Botnafjöll
Hnausar
817
722
Skyggnir
Sultarfit
Sultarfell
Hrauntindur
989
843
F210
Eystri-Rangá
Hungurfit
Mófell
Jökulskarð
Grasleysufjöll
822
1022
Kerlingarfjöll
715
Kerling
812
Blesárgil
Innri-Vatnafjöll
1082
Endafell
Fremri-Vatnafjöll
Hellufjall
709
Gráfell
Lambafell
Dalöldur
910
Austurdalur
.623
Klofningur
.645
Valafell
546
Rauðalda
504
Fláar
606
Rauðnefsstaðafjall
Vatnafjallarani
Trippafjöll
Gráfell
474
Hafrafell
545
Rauðubjallar
Austurhraunin
Geldingafjöll
Skógshraun
Selsundsfjall
Foss
Pálssteinshraun
Selsund
Fálkhamar
309
Eldiviðarhraun
Hraunkvísl
Gunnarsteinn
Krókahraun
Knafahólaheiði
Keldnahraun
Keldur
Brekknaheiði
0 2 km
Útgönguhöfðar
679
Stóra-Mófell
Entujökull
Emstrur
Hattfell
Fauskheiði
Neðri-Emstruá
Illhöfuð
Mófell
Botnaá
Almenningar
Slyppugil
571
830
839
Þröngá
F261
Þverá
Lifrafjöll
Siki
357
Þórsmörk
Kerhnúkur
736
Einhyrningur
Markarfljót
Jökulskarð
Bólstaður
Einbúi
Hitagil
.432
Hestur
Vestri-Botna
Fauskheiði
Gilsá
.1138
Ásgrindur
Sindri
1289
Ýmir
Ýma
1468
Tindfjallajökull
Tindfjöll
Búri
1235
1163
Saxi
1303
Klofningar
1067
Haki
Rauðfossar
Fljótsdalsheiði
Þórólfsfell
574
Vörðufell
858
Þrífjöll
817
Litla-Bláfell
745
Fljótsdalur
Barkarstaðaheiði
Hraun
Barkarstaðir
Múlaheiði
261
Árkvörn
Hámúli
Eyvindarmúli
Þorleifsstaðafjall
Hæringsfell
533
Múlakot
Gluggafoss
250
Litli-Þríhyrningur
Fljótshlíð
Hlíðarendakot
Hlíðarendi
Þverá
576
Þríhyrningur
662
Deild
Valstýra
Reynifellsalda
Fiská
Heylækur
Butra
Smáratún
Engidalur
Kirkjulækur
Húsið
Dráþufoss
Bollakot
Klittnafoss
Hellishólar
Kvoslækur
Vatnsdalur
Goðaland
Haldsfoss
Vatnsdalsfjall
Tunga
Tumastaðir
Fagrahlíð
Vatnsdalsvatn
Þverá

Eystri-Rangá, a clear river with its source in Rangárbotnar, running into Þverá near Oddi in Rangárvallasýsla county. Average flow 44 m^3/sec.

Langvíuhraun, a lavafield that was very rough and difficult to cross until the 1947 eruption of Hekla filled it with pumice. Water from the river Eystri-Rangá has been diverted to the lava to promote vegetation and hinder erosion.

Hungurfit, grassland on the old Fjallabaksleið ("Behind the mountains") route. Jeep track from there to a bridge over Markarfljót, near Krókur. For mountain vehicles only.

Laufafell, (1,264 m) a majestic mountain, mostly rhyolite. A track, for mountain vehicles only, leads from this route west of Laufafell and Hrafntinnusker and on to Landmannaleið.

Ljósá, a river coming from the Reykjafjöll mountains and running into Markarfljót. South of Reykjadalir are **Ljósártungur**, mostly rhyolite. Lots of geothermal heat thereabout. To the east is **Launfitjarsandur**, probably an old lake-bed.

Torfahlaup, a narrow canyon on the Markarfljót river. Legend has it that a lad named Torfi, jumped over it carrying his sweetheart on his back, to escape from her family, who wanted him killed.

Álftavatn, a deep lake with good fishing. Two cabins built by the Touring Club of Iceland in 1979. The lodges are located in a beautiful spot on the north site of lake Álftavatn. A warden is appointed during the months of June, July and August. The camping site is located by the lake. Route to Torfahlaup along the lake past the mountain Torfatindur.

210 **Ljótarstaðavegur,** p. 129 | 250 **Dímonarvegur,** p. 138, 169 | 261 **Fljótshlíðarvegur,** p. 168, 169
F261 **Emstruleið,** p. 452

14
P. 577

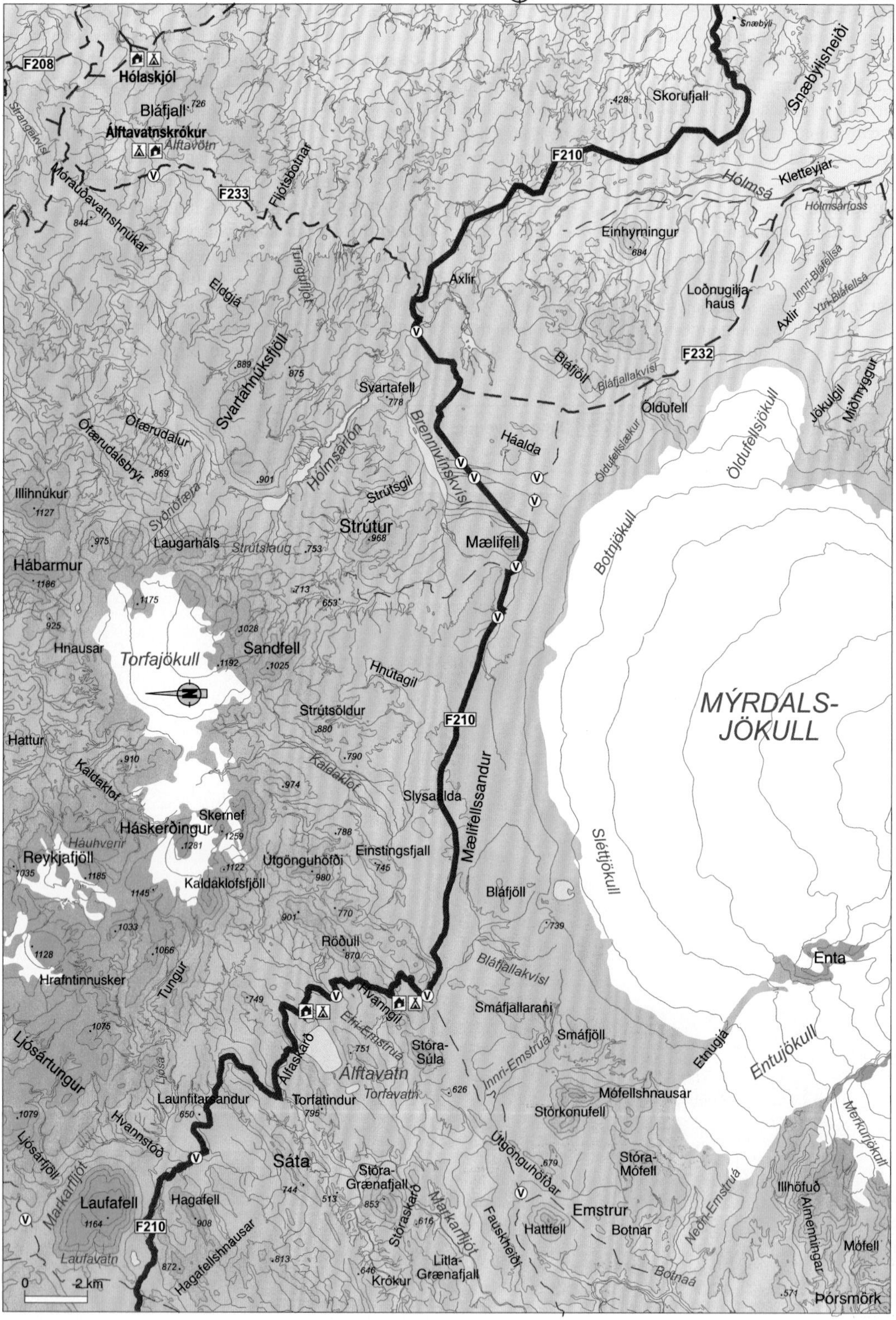

F208
Hólaskjól
Snæbýli
Snæbýlisheiði
Skorufjall
.428
Bláfjall .726
Álftavatnskrókur
Álftavötn
Strangakvísl
F210
Móraudavatnshnúkar
F233
Fljótsbotnar
Kletteyjar
Hólmsá
Hólmsárfoss
844
Einhyrningur
.684
Tungufljót
Eldgjá
Axlir
Loðnugilja-
haus
Innri-Bláfellsá
Ytri-Bláfellsá
Axlir
F232
Svartahnúksfjöll
.889
.875
Bláfjöll
Bláfjallakvísl
Svartafell
.778
Öldufell
Jökulgil
Miðhryggur
Brennivínskvísl
Ófærudalur
Hólmsárlón
Háalda
Ófærudalsbrýr
.869
.901
Strútsgil
Öldufellslækur
Öldufellsjökull
Illihnúkur
.1127
Syðri-Ófæra
Strútur
.968
.975
Laugarháls
Strútslaug
.753
Mælifell
Botnjökull
Hábarmur
.1186
.713
653
.1175
925
.1028
Hnausar
Torfajökull
Sandfell
.1192
.1025
Hnútagil
Strútsöldur
.880
F210
MÝRDALS-
JÖKULL
Hattur
.910
.790
Kaldaklof
Kaldaklof
.974
Mælifellssandur
Slysaalda
Skernef
Háskerðingur
.1259
.1281
Háuhverir
.788
Reykjafjöll
.1035
.1185
.1122
Útgönguhöfði
Einstingsfjall
.745
Sléttjökull
Kaldaklofsfjöll
980
1145
Bláfjöll
901
.770
.739
.1033
Röðull
.870
.1128
.1066
Enta
Tungur
Bláfjallakvísl
Hrafntinnusker
Hvanngil
.749
Smáfjallarani
.1075
Ljósártungur
Ljósá
Álftaskarð
Efri-Emstrurá
Stóra-
Súla
Smáfjöll
.751
Innri-Emstrurá
Etnugjá
Entujökull
Álftavatn
.626
Laufnitarsandur
Torfatindur
Torfavatn
Mófellshnausar
Stórkonufell
.1079
650
795
Hvannstóð
Markarfljótsjökull
Ljósárfjöll
Markarfljót
Sáta
Stóra-
Grænafjall
Útgönguhöfðar
.679
Stóra-
Mófell
Illhöfuð
Laufafell
Hagafell
744
513
853
Stóraskarð
.616
Markarfljót
Fauskheiði
Hattfell
Emstrur
Botnar
Syðri-Emstrurá
Almenningar
.1164
F210
908
Laufavatn
.813
.646
Litla-
Grænafjall
Krókur
Hagafellshnausar
872
Botnaá
Mófell
0 2 km
.571
Þórsmörk

F210 Fjallabaksleið syðri, Miðvegur (Ljótastaðavegur) 112,5 km, Ljótastaðavegur is 25 km. The route is passalbe for all jeeps, not small jeeps. Many rivers need to be crossed on this route. It is safer to have two jeeps. The main rivers that need to be crossed are: Markarfljót by Laufafell, Kaldaklofskvísl south of Hvanngil and Hólmsá south of Mælifellssandur.

Hvanngil, a small valley which has been a popular resting place for those travelling between Landmannalaugar and Þórsmörk. Sheperds' hut and accommodation. Good hiking area. A marked walking route (Laugavegur) to Hrafntinnusker and Landmannalaugar to the north and Emstrur and Þórsmörk to the south.

Mælifellssandur, sands between the glaciers Torfajökull and Mýrdalsjökull about 600 m above sea level. Once a much-used route, the western part named Gásasandur. A passable road but care must be taken because of quicksands.

Brytalækir, a short clear stream with its source in Mýrdalssandur, a tributaty of Hólmsá.

Slysaalda, ("Casualty ridge") a sand ridge in the western part of Mælifellssandur. In 1868 four people from Skaftafellssýsla county perished there, their remains not being discovered till ten years later. Memorial.

Mælifell, (791 m) a tuff mountain towards the east of Mælifellssandur. Good views.

Brennivínskvísl, ("The schnaps branch") a clear river, tributary of Hólmsá. The origins of its unusual name are unknown.

Hólmsárbotnar, southeast of the Torfajökull glacier.

Hólmsárlón, a lagoon of unusual beauty, and hot pools, among them **Strútslaug**.

Snæbýli, a farm in Skaftártunga. There Road 210 beginns.

F208 Fjallabaksleið nyrðri, p. 436 **F232 Öldufellsleið,** p. 448 **F233 Álftavatnskrókur,** p. 449

14
P. 577

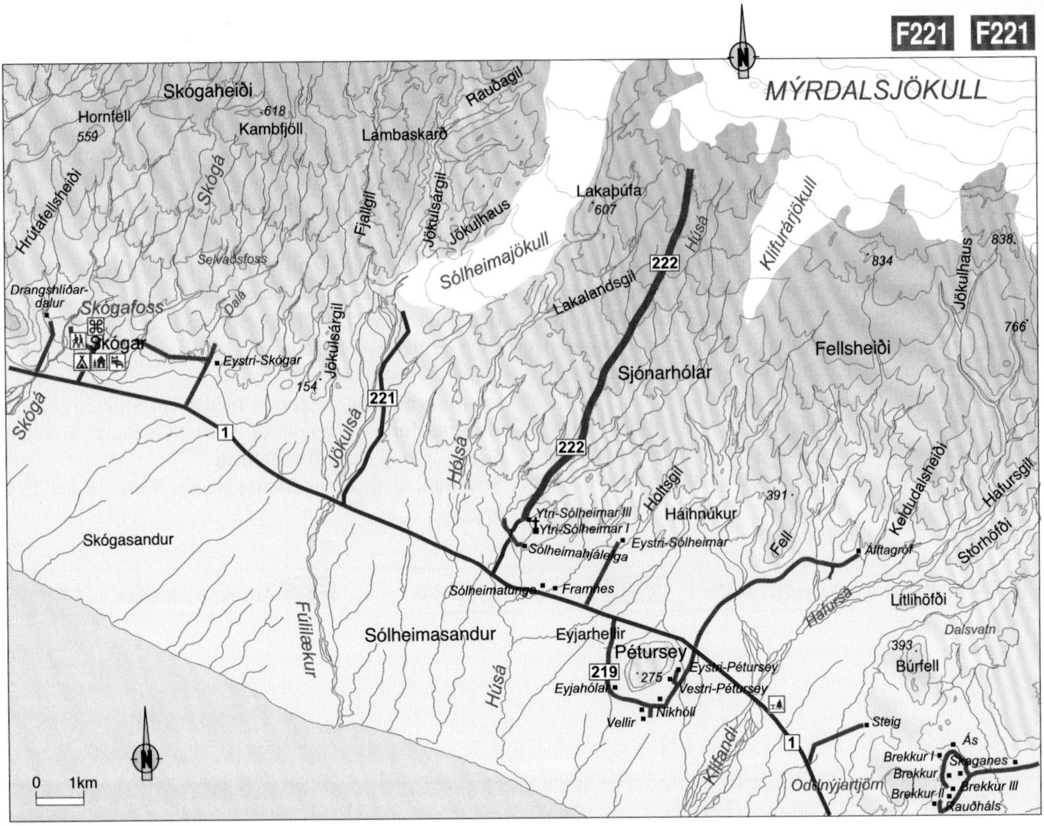

F221 **Sólheimajökulsvegur** 9,4 km. This route is passable for all jeeps. It is possible to take snowmobile tours on the glacier **Sólheimajökull**.

F222 **Mýrdalsjökulsvegur** 10 km.

1 **Suðurlandsvegur,** p. 133 **219** **Pétursseyjarsvegur,** p. 132

Skógarfoss, p. 133

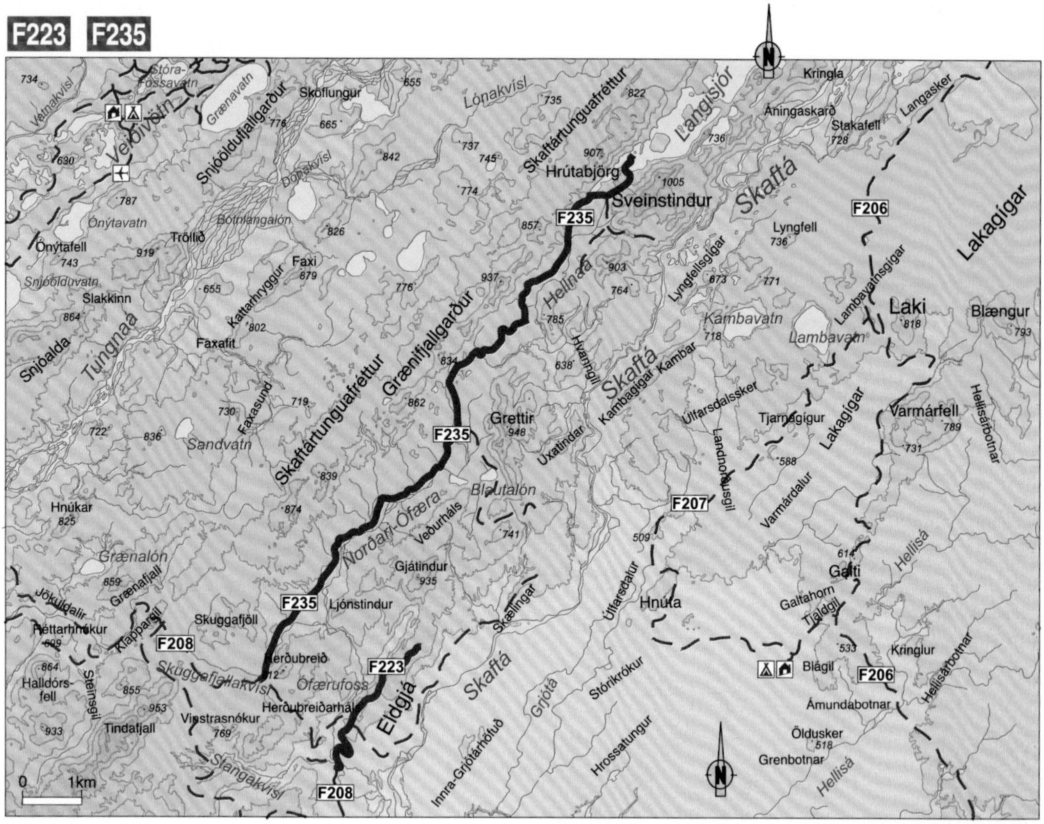

14 P. 577

F235 Langisjór, 25,4 km. Passable by all jeeps. A few rivers and creeks need to be crossed. There is a trail west of Hörðubreið leading to Langisjór, going over Skuggafjallakvísl and other rivers.

Langisjór, (Skaftárvatn) a lake 20 km long and 2 km wide.

Sveinstindur, (1089 m) mountain on the south side of Langisjór.

Breiðbakur, (1028 m) mountain. The highest mountain on the west of Langisjór, a jeep track leads to it. Beautiful view over Langisjór.

F223 Eldgjárvegur.

© Markaðsstofa Suðurlands

F206 Lakavegur, p. 434 **F207 Lakagígavegur,** p. 437 **F208 Fjallabaksleið nyrðri,** p. 436

14
P. 577

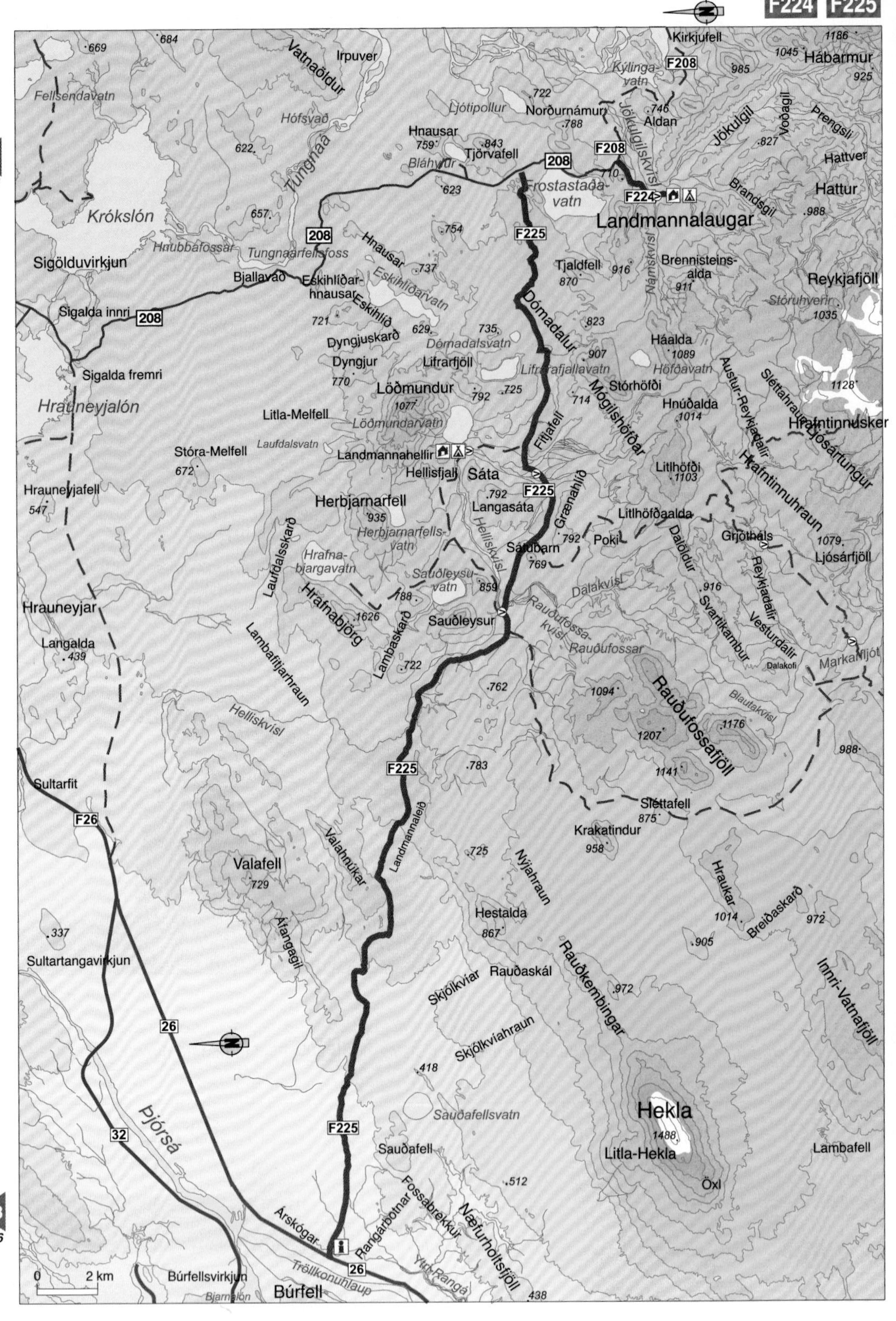

13
P. 576

Landmannalaugar

F224 **Landmannalaugavegur,** 2,5 km. Leads to F208 that goes to Landmannalaugar. Passable for small jeeps, crossing two small rivers, Námskvísl and Laugalæna. It is possible to leave small cars and walk to Landmannalaugar via walking bridges.

Landmannalaugar, one of Iceland's natural jewels and popular tourist attractions in Iceland. Streams of geothermal and spring water come from under a high wall of lava and mix to make streams and pools of just the right temperature for bathing. Though the altitude is over 600 m, the river banks are covered in grass and flowers. The very colourful rhyolite mountains surrounding it make this area quite unique. The Icelandic Touring Association has operated a mountain lodge in Landmannalaugar since 1951. The lodge is in the altitude of 600 m and is located by the edge of Laugahraun lava field. In walking distance from the lodge is a natural warm geothermal pool that is very popular for bathing. A warden is appointed during most of the year. There begins the popular 4 day trip from Landmannalaugar to Þórsmörk, Laugavegur route. The area around the lodge also offers numerous different hiking possibilities. Campsite. View dial at Bláhnúkur. The site is reasonably accessible in the summer and there are quite good summer roads leading to it.

Laugahraun, a dark rhyolite lava field with some obsidian from the Brennisteinsalda ridge, with steam and sulphur springs.

Jökulgil, a long, narrow valley between colourful rhyolite mountains.

Jökulgilskvísl, the river through the Jökulgil valley. It was a serious hindrance until bridged in 1966.

F225 **Landmannaleið (Dómadalsleið)** 40,9 km, from Landvegur. This route is passable for small jeeps, some small rivers need to be crossed. It is possible to drive to Landmannahellir, 8,5 km.

Sölvahraun, a lava field that was covered with moss, grass and dwarf shrubs until it the 1980 Hekla eruption.

Valagjá, an interesting crater east of Valahnúkur.

Rauðufossafjöll, ("Red falls mountains") (1,230 m) mountains named for the reddish explosion crater on their slopes, down which run the waterfalls Rauðufossar.

Kringla, a grassy plain the floor of which is at 590 m, encircled by mountains mostly around 1,000 m high.

Landmannahellir, a cave, a good place for a break on the old Dómadalur pass. The cave itself was once used as accommodation for those who had to travel through the highland pastures. Today at Landmannahellir there are fine cabins with decent facilitie designed to accommodate tourists and their travel horses.

Lóðmundur, (1,077 m) the highest mountain in this area, very impressive.

Dómadalur, a valley with a small lake named Dómadalsvatn.

26 **Landavegur,** p. 158-161 **32** **Þjórsárdalsvegur,** p. 175-176 **F26** **Sprengisandsleið,** p. 430-433
F208 **Fjallabaksleið nyrðri,** p. 436

14 P. 577

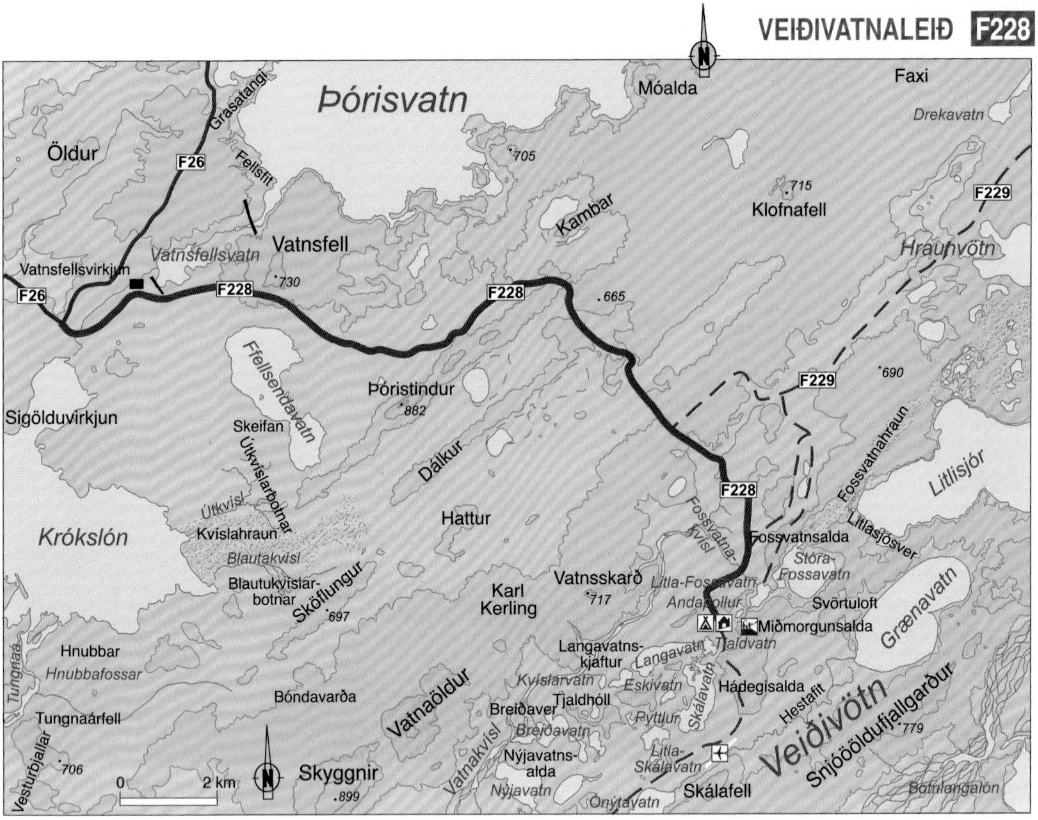

F228 Veiðivatnaleið, 21 km. This route is only passable by jeeps because of two deep fords that need to be crossed. There is a hut by Tjaldavatn. A view dial by Miðmorgunsalda.

F26 Sprengisandsleið, p. 430-433 **F229 Jökulheimaleið,** p. 447

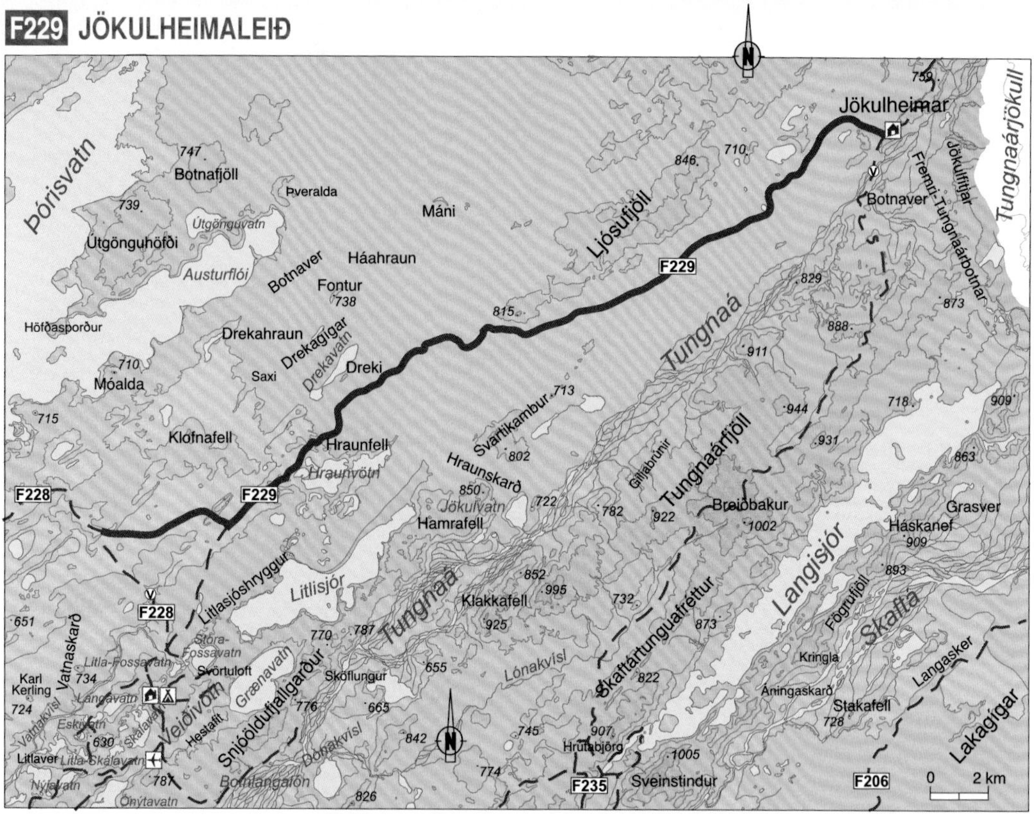

F229 JÖKULHEIMALEIÐ

14 P. 577

F229 Jökulheimaleið, 36,1 km. The route lies north of **Veiðivötn** to a cabin at the foot of Tungnaárjökull glacier. The route is passable for all jeeps. North of the cabin is an ill passable route to Vonarskarð called Bárðargata. It is also possible to go to Jökulheimar through a so called Jökulheimastyttingur which lies west of the main route and joins the main route on the south side of Drekavatn lake.

F206 Lakavegur, p. 434 **F228 Veiðivatnaleið,** p. 446 **F235 Langisjór,** p. 443

14
P. 577

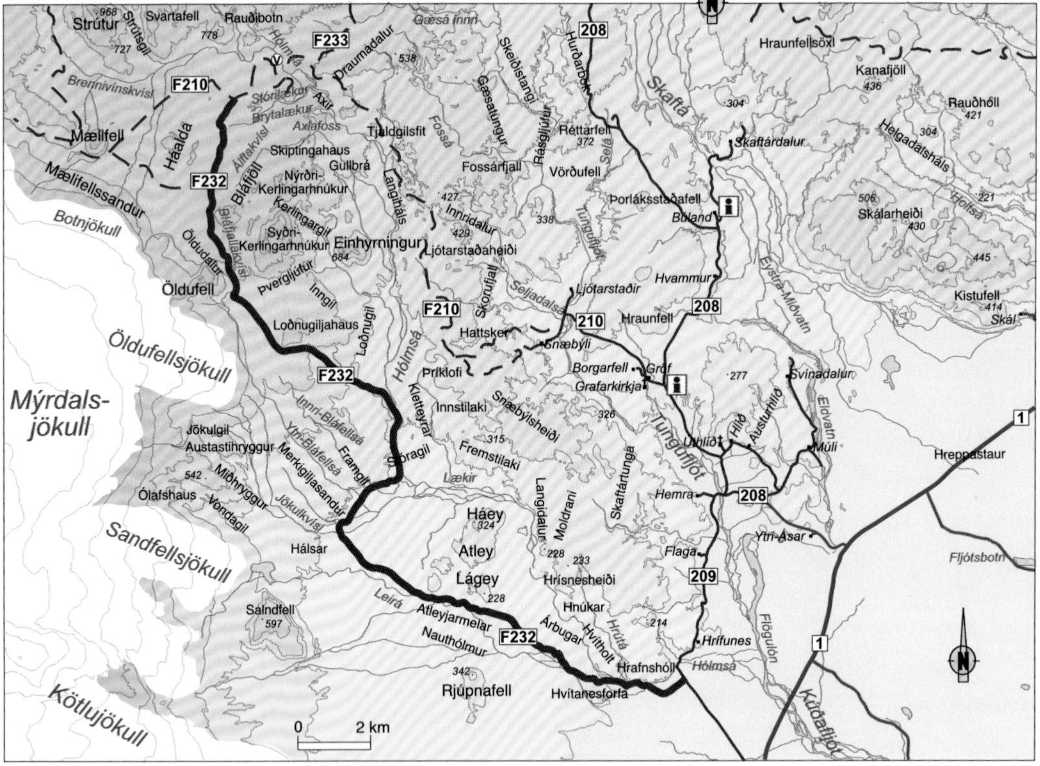

F232 Öldufellsleið 35,7 km. Passable by all jeeps. Considered one of the most beautiful routes of the country. The route lies close to Mýrdalsjökull. One ford needs to be crossed, Bláfjallakvísl.

Hólmsá, a river with its source under the glacier Torfajökull, running into Hólmsárbotnar, along the edge of Mýrdalssandur and into Kúðafljót. Tjaldagilsháls east of Hólmsá with a beautiful view.

1 **Suðurlandsvegur,** p. 129	208 **Skaftártunguvegur,** p. 129	209 **Hrífunesvegur,** p. 129
210 **Ljótarstaðavegur,** p. 129	F208 **Fjallabaksleið nyrðri,** p. 436	
F210 **Fjallabaksleið syðri,** p. 438-441	F233 **Álftavatnskrókur,** p. 449	

F233 ÁLFTAVATNSKRÓKUR

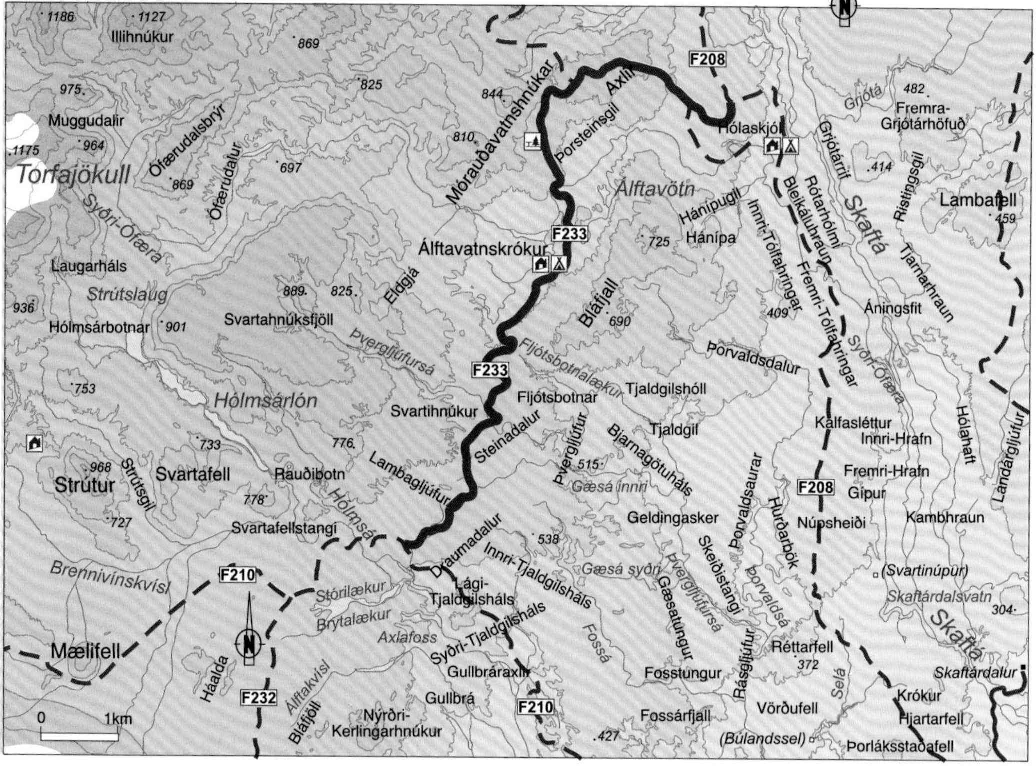

14 P. 577

F233 **Álftavatnskrókur,** 20,7 km going south west of route F208. Only passable by jeeps. A ford must be taken over the Syðri-Ófæra river which can be an obstacle for small jeeps.

Nyrðri-Ófæra and **Syðri-Ófæra,** ("Northern and southern impassable") two rivers that flow through the Eldgjá canyon and join the Skaftá river. The northern river enters the rift in two impressive waterfalls, Ófærufoss. A natural bridge across the lower falls collapsed in 1993. The southern river also plunges in a waterfall into the narrow canyon **Hánípugil**, just before it comes down to **Hánípufit**. a green spot on the west banks of the Skaftá river.

Ófærufoss.

F208 **Fjallabaksleið nyrðri,** p. 436 F210 **Fjallabaksleið syðri,** p. 438-441 F232 **Öldufellsleið,** p. 448

13 P. 576

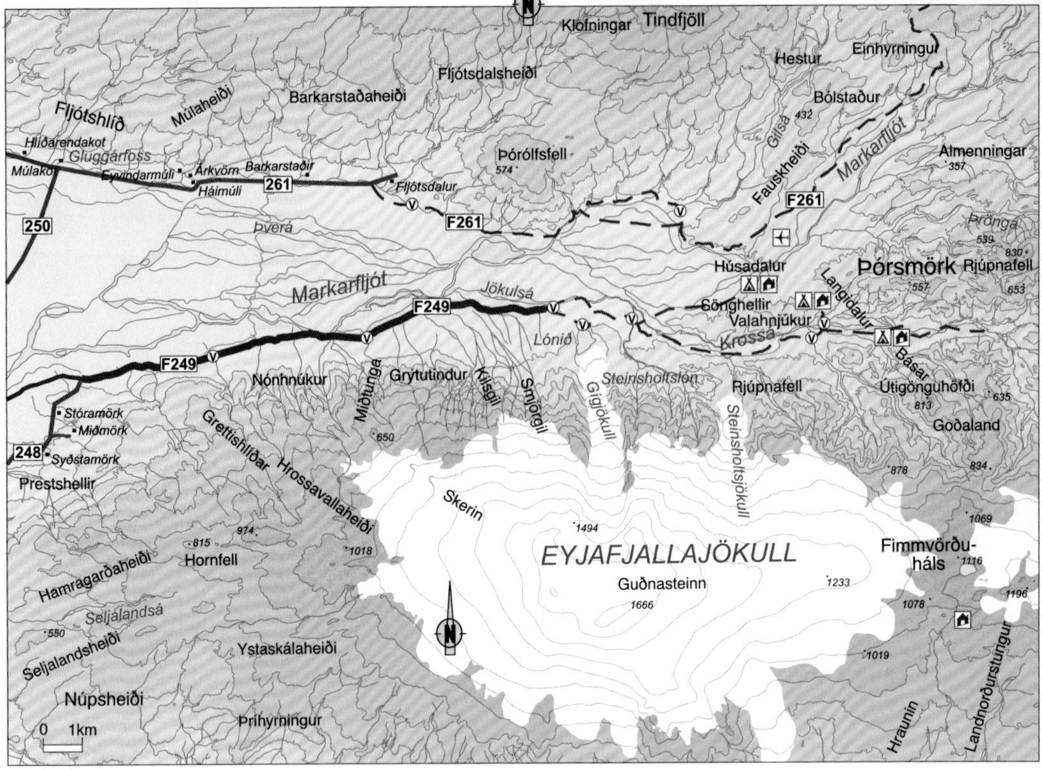

WARNING: Road F249 is not recommended for small cars, only for 4-wheel drive vehicles in convoy, because of dangerous rivers.

F249 Þórsmerkurvegur, 28,9 km. From the old bridge over Markarfljót to Gathillur. Some dangerous glacial rivers need to be crossed.

Nauthúsagil, a canyon by Stóra-Mörk.

Mörk, (Stóra-Mörk, Mið-Mörk and Syðsta-Mörk) the last farms on the way to Þórsmörk. Stóra-Mörk was often mentioned in *Njáls saga*.

Gígjökull, ("Crater glacier") a steep glacier-tongue coming down from the crater of the Eyjafjallajökull glacier, hence the name. The lake Jökullón in front of the glacier is more than 40 m deep and usually has icebergs floating on it. The glacier is getting smaller every year. The river Jökulsá runs from the lagoon to Markarfljót.

Steinholtsjökull, a glacier-tongue coming down from Eyjafjallajökull. In January 1967 a big part of the mountain Innstihaus broke off and fell down on the glacier causing a tremendous flood.

Stakkholtsgjá, a large canyon in the region of Stakkholt, with perpendicular walls up to 100 m high on both sides. The canyon divides in two, the left part ending in a narrow chasm with a lovely waterfall with very clear water. It takes about an hour to go through Stakkholtsgjá, and this must be done on foot.

Þórsmörk, the region west of the Mýrdalsjökull glacier between the rivers Krossá and Markarfljót. Famous for having a great variety of natural features and good weather, and therefore a very popular place for outings. Protected since 1921, in the care of the Forestry Service. National Forest. Cabins in the valleys Langidalur and Húsadalur. Campsites in Langidalur, the Össugil canyon in Húsadalur and the canyon Slyppugil. Skagfjörðsskáli is located by the roots of Langidalur in Þórsmörk not far from Krossá river. The lodge has two floors and it accommodates up to 75 people (in bunkers with mattresses). There are several beautiful hiking routes from Skagfjörðsskáli. Most people end their "Laugarvegur" hike in Langidalur. Landgræsla ríkisins, the Soil Conservation Service of Iceland has restored vegetation on barren land in Þórsmörk.

Goðaland, the region on the south side of Krossá, opposite Þórsmörk, great contrasts in nature with gullies, canyons and glaciers. Extensive birchwoods. Cabins of the touring club Útivist and a campsite at **Básar**.

248 Merkurvegur, p. 166 **250 Dímonarvegur,** p. 138, 169 **261 Fljótshlíðarvegur,** p. 168-169
F261 Emstruleið, p. 453, 453

www.laugarspa.com
LAUGARSPA
THE BEST HEALTH & BODY
EXPERIENCE ICELAND HAS TO OFFER

14
P. 577

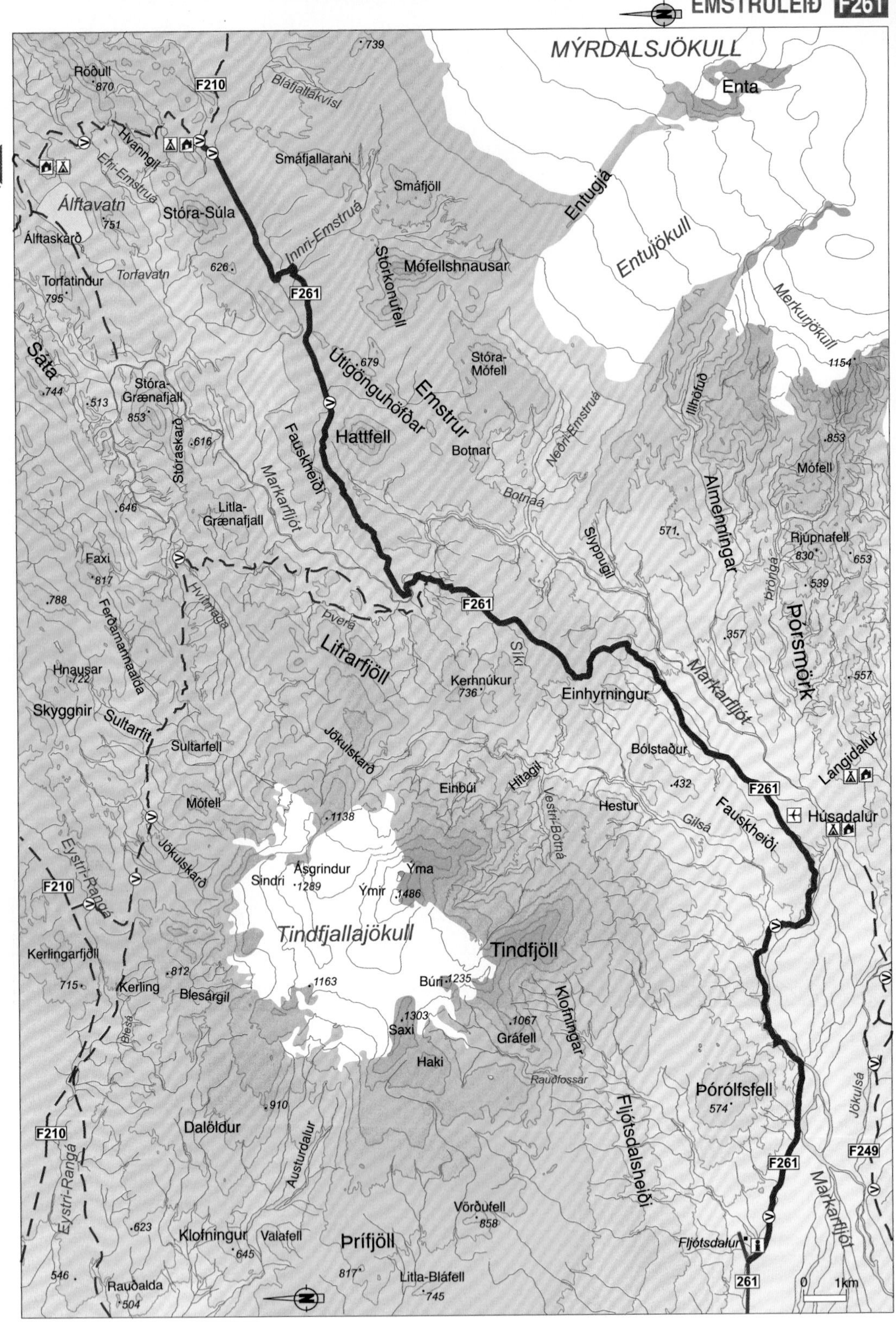

261 **Fljótshlíðarvegur,** p. 168-169	**F210** **Fjallabaksleið syðri,** p. 438-441	**F249** **Þórsmerkurvegur,** p. 450

F261 **Emstruleið** 37,3 km. Passable by all jeeps. The glacial river Gilsá needs to be crossed and also the river Bláfjallakvísl.

Gilsá, a river coming from the glacier Tindfjallajökull.

Markarfljótsgljúfur, a rugged canyon, 100 m deep, east of Einhyrningur.

Markarfljót, a 100 km long river, its drainage basin about 1,070 km^2, rising in the Reykjardalir valleys but mostly coming from the Mýrdalsjökull glacier. Bridge near Emstrur (1978), where the remains of an old ropeway can be seen.

Tröllagjá, a canyon through which the road goes, a river bed formed by Markarfljót in a massive débâcle 2,000-2,500 years ago.

Einhyrningur, ("Unicorn") (769 m) a mountain that from some angles resembles a horn. The settlement land of Sighvatur rauði is thought to be at its foot.

Hattfell (Hattafell), (909 m) a conspicuous mountain in the Emstrur area. To its southwest is the canyon Hattfellsgljúfur, an ancient riverbed.

Emstrur, the area north of the river Syðri-Emstruá, between Mýrdalsjökull and Markarfljót. Very little vegetation. Cabin built by the Touring Club of Iceland. The ITA lodges stand close by the river Sydri-Emstruá. A warden is appointed during the months of June, July and August. Close by the Emstrur lodges is the magnificent canyon Markarfljótsgljúfur that is well worth a short hike. A 4x4 path leads to the lodges.

Fremri-Emstruá, a river from under Entujökull, a tongue of the Mýrdalsjökull glacier. Bridged in 1978 by the Touring Club of Iceland then again in 1988 after the first footbridge was swept away in floods.

Innri-Emstruá, a river falling from the Mýrdalsjökull glacier into Markarfljót. Bridged in 1975.

Kaldaklofskvísl, a river that runs from the mountains Kaldaklofsfjöll into Markarfljót. There is a ford a little to the east of the Hvanngil canyon, but it can be dangerous in high water. Footbridge near the ford built by the Touring Club of Iceland in 1985.

At Húsadalur

At Húsadalur

21
P. 584

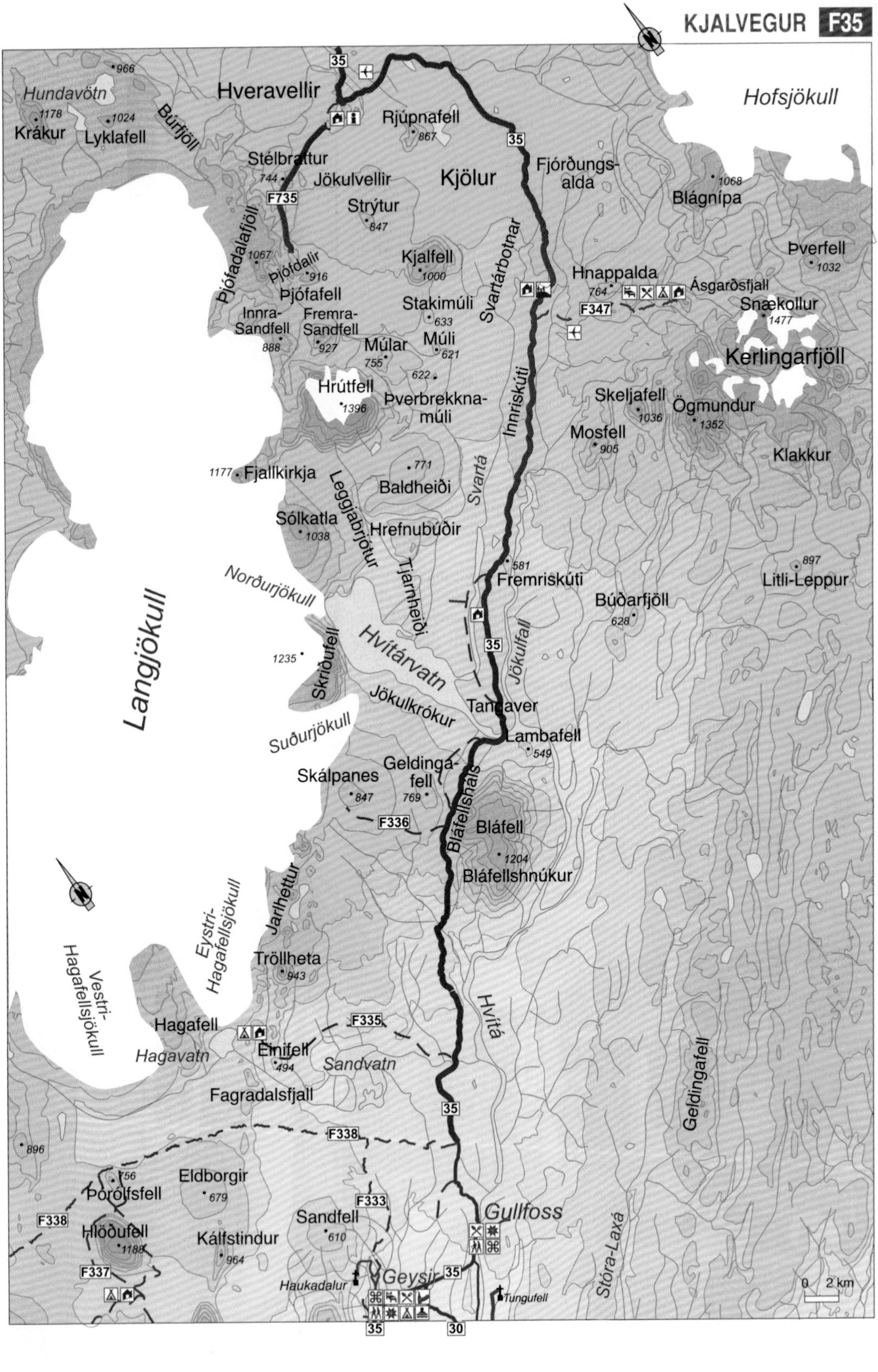

Hveravellir
Hundavötn
966
1178
Krákur
1024
Lyklafell
Búrfjöll
Rjúpnafell
867
Stélbrattur
744
Jökulvellir
Kjölur
F735
Strýtur
847
Fjórðungs-
alda
Hofsjökull
1068
Blágnípa
Þjófadalafjöll
1067
Þjófdalir
916
Þjófafell
Kjalfell
1000
Svartárbotnar
Hnappalda
764
Ásgarðsfjall
F347
Þverfell
1032
Snækollur
1477
Kerlingarfjöll
Innra-
Sandfell
888
Fremra-
Sandfell
927
Stakimúli
633
Múlar
755
Múli
621
622
Hrútfell
1396
Þverbrekkna-
múli
Innriskúti
Skeljafell
1036
Ögmundur
1352
Mosfell
905
Klakkur
1177
Fjallkirkja
771
Baldheiði
Svartá
Leggjabrjótur
Sólkatla
1038
Hrefnubúðir
Tjarnheiði
581
Fremriskúti
897
Litli-Leppur
Norðurjökull
Búðarfjöll
628
Langjökull
Hvítárvatn
1235
Skriðufell
Jökulfall
Jökulkrókur
Tangaver
Lambafell
549
Suðurjökull
Skálpanes
847
Geldinga-
fell
769
Bláfellsháls
F336
Bláfell
1204
Bláfellshnúkur
Jarlhettur
Eystri-
Hagafellsjökull
Vestri-
Hagafellsjökull
Tröllheta
943
Hvítá
Hagafell
F335
Hagavatn
Einifell
494
Sandvatn
Fagradalsfjall
Geldingafell
35
F338
896
756
Þórólfsfell
Eldborgir
679
F333
Gullfoss
F338
Hlöðufell
1188
Kálfstindur
964
Sandfell
610
Stóra-Laxá
F337
Geysir
Haukadalur
Tungufell
0 2 km
35
30

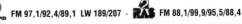

At Langjökull

F35 **Kjalvegur** ("Keel road") the south section, 88,2 km from the service centre by Gullfoss to the junction to Hveravellir. From there and north to road 731 are 79 km. This route is passible for all vehicles. Kjalvegur has always been a much-used mountain route between the north and south of Iceland, being easily accessible from Húnavatnssýsla, Skagafjörður and Eyjafjörður. The many grassy areas made this route easier than other inland tracks when people travelled on horseback. The oldest track was through the centre of Kjölur, on the east of Kjalfell, but after the incident at Beinahóll in 1780 people mostly used the western route through Þjófadalir.

F335 **Hagavatnsvegur** 16,7 km to the Icelandic Touring Association hut by Jarlhettur. Passable for allt small jeeps to the hut.

Hagavatn, a good-sized lake by the glacier edge. A tourist hut belonging to the Touring Club of Iceland. A warden is appointed during the months of July and August. **Farið** a river flowing from Hagavatn lake.

F336 **Skálpanesvegur** 7,9 km. The route is passable for all small jeeps to the hut.

Jarlhettur, a row of tuff peaks.

Skálpanes, an old shield volcano with lava flows towards Hvítárvatn and the roots of Bláfell.

Geldingafell, (763 m) a tuff mountain.

Bláfell, (1,204 m) the highest mountain in southwest Iceland.

Hvítá, a big glacial river coming from Hvítárvatn. There are plans to harness this river by the mountain Bláfell.

Hvítársandar, sands and barren land between Jökulfalla and Tjarnarheiði south to Hvítá.

Hvítárvatn, a lake 26.6 km^2, 419 m above sea level, 84 m deep. Glacier-coloured, it often has icebergs floating on it.

Karlsdráttur, a place where the glacier flows into Hvítárvatn lake. Patches with rich vegetation growing at approximately 420 - 440 meters above sea level

Hvítárnes, wide, wet and flat grasslands by Hvítárvatn. A tourist hut built 1930, rebuilt and improved since. a small creek on the north side of Hvítárvatn lake. A tourist hut built 1930, rebuilt and improved since. It was believed that a female ghost use to haunt the Hvítárnes area. On a rock south of the hut is a memorial to Tryggva Magnússon (1896-1943) a pioneer in highland travelling.

Tjarnheiði, an oasis east of Hvítárnes og Fúlakvísl.

Svartá, a river that runs from Kjalhraun lava field.

Hrefnubúðir, (648 m) a mountain on the north of Hvítárnes, with some birch bushes on the sides. This is about the highest that birch-bushes thrive in Iceland.

Baldheiði, a dolerite dome, 771 m.

Fúlakvísl, a river that runs from Langjökull to Hvítárvatn lake.

Fremriskúti, (572 m) and **Innriskúti,** (710 m) tuff mountains in southern Kjölur. Marked path from Innri-Skúti to a cabin belonging to the Touring Club of Iceland at Þverbrekkumúli.

Hrútfell, (1,410 m) a table mountain in the southwest area of Kjölur, with a 10 km^2 glacier top. One of the most majestic mountains in the area.

Gránunes, a field named after a mare.

F347 **Kerlingarfjallavegur** 10,5 km. Passable for jeeps. Some small rivers need to be crossed and ford over Blákvísl by Gýgjarfoss.

Árskarð, (also named Ásgarður) a pass or a canyon at the north side of Kerlingarfjöll.

Kerlingarfjöll, a cluster of majestic rhyolite peaks, some of them partially covered by glacier. Lots of geothermal heat in the valleys between the peaks. The highest peaks are **Snækollur** (1,477 m), **Loðmundur** (1,432 m) and **Mænir** (1,335 m). A visitors centre.

Kjalhraun, a lava field in the centre of Kjölur, 450 km^2. Some rocks and pinnacles around the crater **Strýtur** in the centre of the lavafield, otherwise rather flat and easy to cross, with a fair bit of vegetation.

Beinahóll or Beinabrekka ("Hill of bones") on a low lava ridge on the northeast of Kjalfell. In 1780 four men from Reynistaður in Skagafjörður perished there in bad weather together with a flock of sheep, hence the name.

Blágnípa, (1068 m) a table mountain on the west ridge of Hofsjökull.

Kjalfell, (1000 m) a small table mountain with dolerite on top.

Kjölur, the valley between the glaciers Hofsjökull and Langjökull, 25-30 km wide, 600 to 700 m above sea level. Mostly covered by lava and very barren.

Geirsalda, named after Geir G. Zoëga (1885-1959) road administrator. View dial.

Rjúpnafell, (867 m) tuff mountain.

30 **Skeiða- og Hrunamannavegur,** p. 173 | **35** **Biskupstungnabraut,** p. 183 | **F333** **Haukadalsvegur,** p. 461

F337 **Hlöðuvallavegur,** p. 458 | **F338** **Skjaldbreiðarvegur,** p. 460-461 | **F735** **Þjófadalavegur,** p. 456

21
P. 584

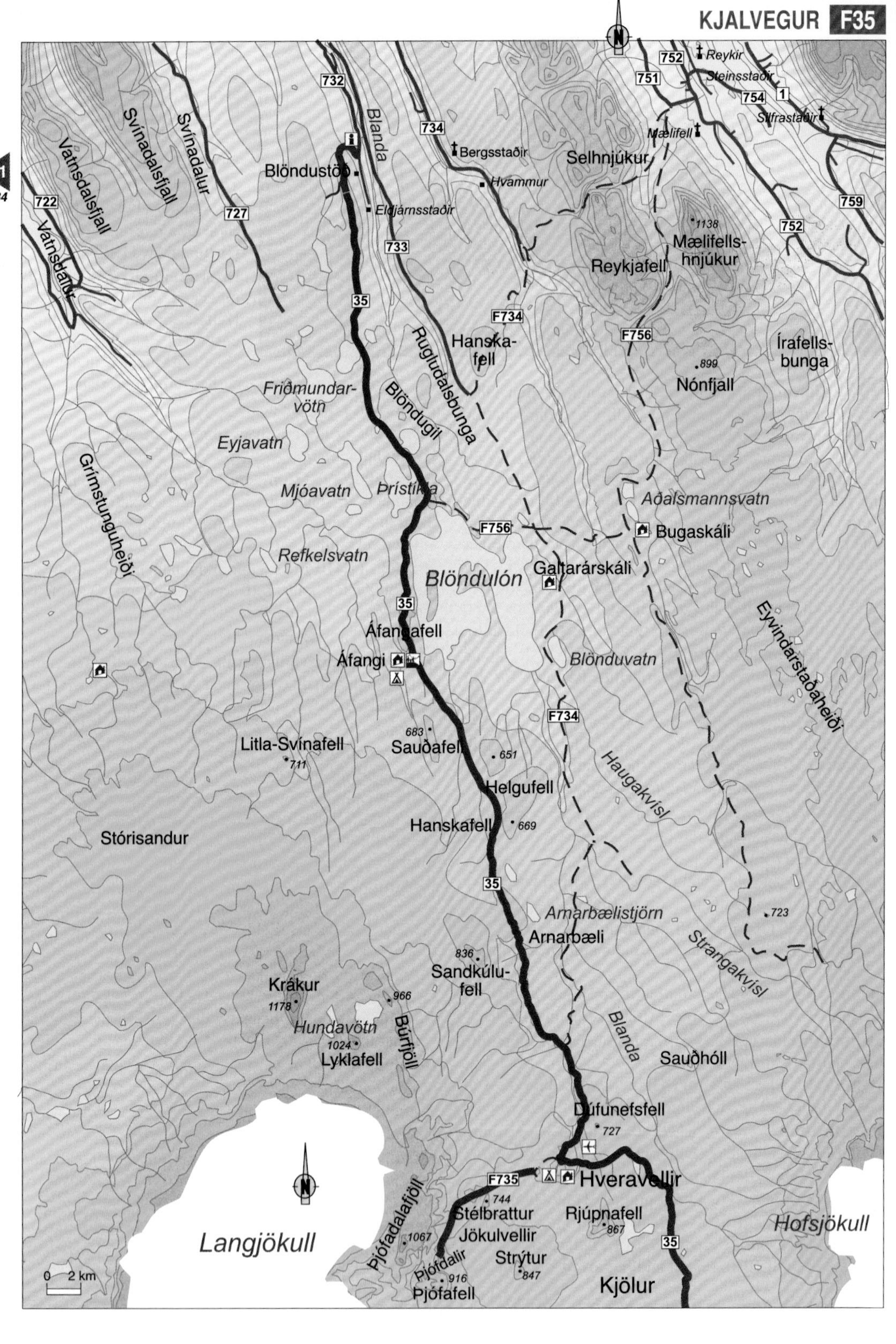
732
Blanda
734
Bergsstaðir
Selhnjúkur
752
Reykir
751
Steinsstaðir
754
1
Silfrastaðir
Mælifell
Blöndustöð
Hvammur
Eldjárnsstaðir
722
Vatnsdalsfjall
Svínadalsfjall
Svínadalur
727
Vatnsdalur
733
1138
Mælifells-
hnjúkur
Reykjafell
759
752
35
F734
Hanska-
fell
F756
Nónfjall
899
Írafells-
bunga
Rugludalsbunga
Friðmundar-
vötn
Blöndugil
Eyjavatn
Grímstunguheiði
Mjóavatn
Þrístikla
Aðalsmannsvatn
F756
Bugaskáli
Refkelsvatn
Blöndulón
Galtarárskáli
35
Áfangafell
Áfangi
Blönduvatn
Eyvindarstaðaheiði
F734
683
Sauðafell
651
Litla-Svínafell
711
Haugakvísl
Helgufell
Hanskafell
669
Stórisandur
35
Arnarbælistjörn
723
Arnarbæli
Strangakvísl
836
Sandkúlu-
fell
Krákur
1178
966
Hundavötn
1024
Lyklafell
Búrfjöll
Blanda
Sauðhóll
Dúfunefsfell
727
F735
Hveravellir
744
Stélbrattur
Rjúpnafell
867
Þjófadalafjöll
Langjökull
1067
Jökulvellir
Hofsjökull
35
Strýtur
847
Þjófadalir
916
Þjófafell
Kjölur
0 2 km

F35 **Kjalvegur norðurhluti,** 79 km from Hveravellir north to route 731. Passable for all cars.

F735 **Þjófadalsvegur** 12,7km. Passable for all cars to Hveravellir, only for jeeps from Hveravellir to Þröskuldar. From there is an 8-900m walk to a FÍ touring hut in Þjófadalur valley, built in 1939.

Þjófadalir, ("Thieves' valleys") some valleys east of the Langjökull glacier. The story, almost certainly apocryphal, is that 9 students from Hólar hid out there and lived off stolen sheep after having killed a serving woman at Hólar. The area can be reached by jeep-track from Hveravellir. A tourist hut built 1939. You can take several short but joyful hikes from the lodge, e.g. Hrufafell, Fagrahlíð and Jökulkrók by the edge of the glacier Langjökull.

Hveravellir, ("Hot spring plains") a geothermal area to the north of Kjalhraun, about 650 m above sea level, and one of the best known geothermal areas in Iceland. Many beautiful and peculiar hot springs, such as Bláhver, Öskurhólshver, Eyvindarhver, Bræðrahverir etc. Ruins of the shelter of the 18th century outlaw Fjalla-Eyvindur are to be found near the spring Eyvindarhver, where he is said to have boiled his meat. Memorial to the outlaw and his woman raised there in 1998. Tourist huts and other shelters, a bathing basin, and a weather report station. The Touring Club of Iceland built a house at Hveravellir in 1938. The house is heated with hot spring water, there is also a pool, suitable for bathing, just outsite the house. There is also a new and spacious mountain lodge at Hveravellir. **Hveravellir is a protected natural area that should not be spoiled in any way!** See more on Hveravellir, p. 459.

Dúfunefsfell, ("Dove nose mountain") (727 m) a high tuff mountain by the northern boundaries of Kjölur. Flat wasteland south of the mountain is believed to be **Dúfunefsskeið**, mentioned in *Landnámabók* ("The Book of Settlements") as the setting of the horse race between Þórir Dúfunef and the freed slave Örn.

F734 **Svartárdalsvegur (Vesturheiðarvegur-Kjalvegur hinn forni)** 56,9 km. A route from Kjalvegur route by Seyðisá. Goes down to Fossárdalur valley. Only a part of the route is passable for jeeps.

Seyðisá, a big clear river coming from the Búrfjöll mountains and taking in the rivers Þegjandi ("Keeping quiet") and Beljandi ("Roaring") on the way to the Blanda.

Blanda, 125 km, one of the longest glacial rivers in Iceland. It comes mainly from the western part of the Hofsjökull glacier, the uppermost sources being below the mountain Blágnípa.

Áfangi, a campsite and accommodation 40 km north of Hveravellir and 75 km from Blönduós.

Helgufell, (663 m) a prominent mountain in the middle of Auðkúluheiði moor.

Auðkúluheiði, a wide area or moorland with both scattered and continous grasslands between the river Blanda to the east, Grímstunguheiði moor to the west, and Hveravellir to the south. This area is mostly 400 to 500 m above sea level. A good deal of the northern part of the moor is under water since the Blanda was harnessed 1984-88, **Blönduvirkjun**. Among roads built there in connection with the building of the hydro-electric plant is one going over the mountain **Áfangafell**, from which there is a panoramic view. Shelter.

Þrístikla, a good-sized lake, as are the lakes Mjóavatn, Galtaból and Friðmundarvötn to the north of it.

F756 **Mælifellsdalur** 44,7 km. Passable for all jeep and small jeeps.

Mælifellshnjúkur, (1138 m), one of the highest and most imposing mountains of Skagafjörður. It is said that 10 counties can be seen from there. Marked walking route.

Blöndugil, an 18 km long canyon on the river Blanda, 50 to 100 m deep in many places. More info on **Blöndustöð** on p. 346.

Gilsá, a small river running into the Blanda where Kjalvegur comes down to the Blöndudalur valley.

1 **Norðurlandsvegur,** p. 72	**722** **Vatnsdalsvegur,** p. 343	**727** **Svínadalsvegur,** p. 344
733 **Blöndudalsvegur,** p. 346	**734** **Svartárdalsvegur,** p. 347	**751** **Efribyggðarvegur,** p. 353
752 **Skagafjarðarvegur,** p. 353-354	**754** **Héraðsdalsvegur,** p. 353	**759** **Kjálkavegur,** p. 354

© Gunnar Guðjónsson
Þjófadalir

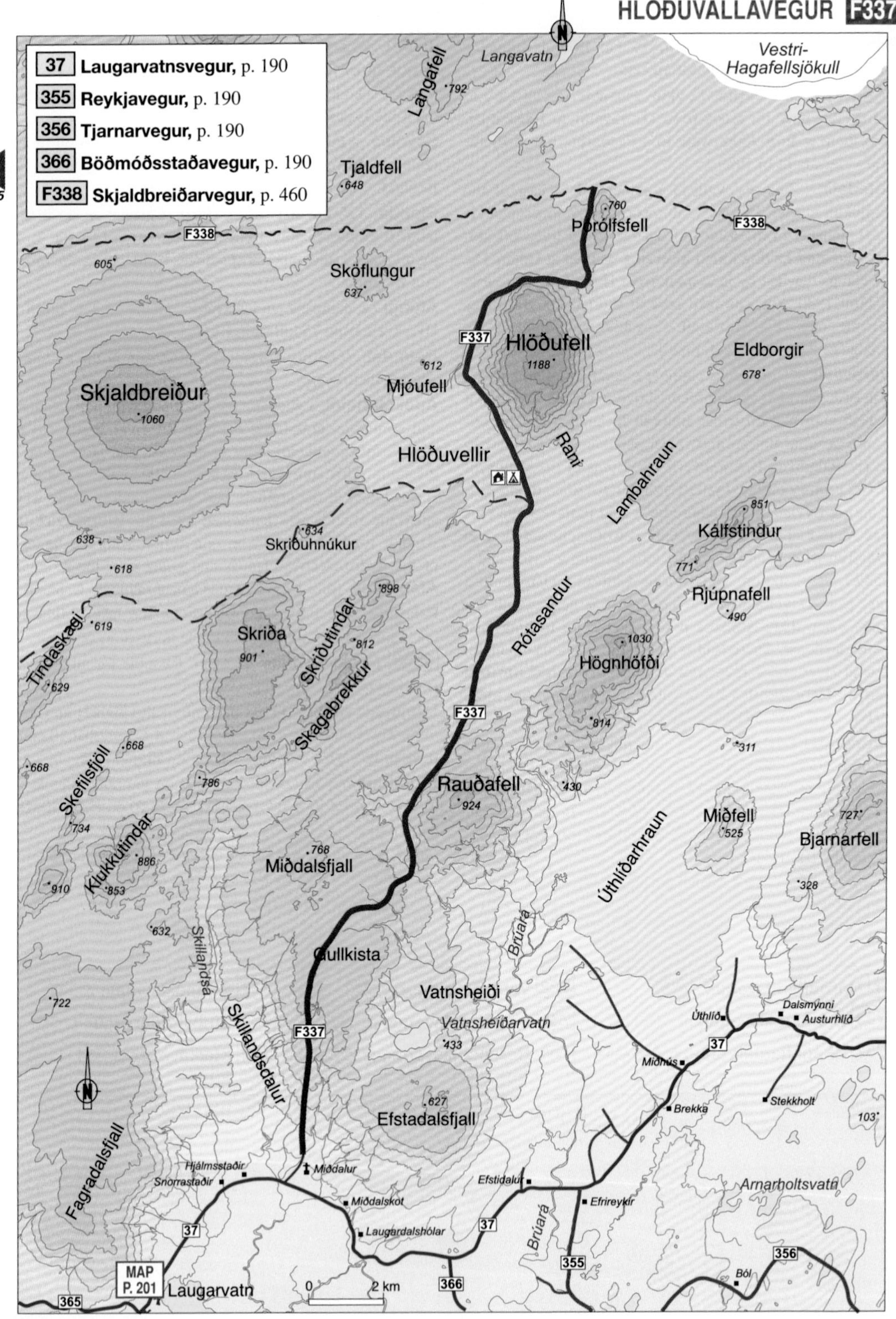

F337 Hlöðuvallavegur, 31,5 km. Route F337 if quite steep going up Miðdalsfjall mountain. This route goes to route F338 to Hlöðuvellir, it doesn´t matter on which side of the mountain the route is driven as it goes around the mountain. The route is fairly rough and can be a nuisance to small jeeps.

Gullkista, („Chest of Gold“) a box shaped peak on the mountain Miðdalsfjall (678 m).

WELCOME TO
HVERAVELLIR

Hveravellir is one of Iceland's natural wonders and popular with travellers in all seasons. The area is surrounded by spectacular landscape with glaciers and geysers such as Eyvindahver, Öskurhóll and Bláhver. Eyvindahver derives it names from the famous Icelandic saga about the couple Fjalla – Eyvindur (Mountain – Eyvindur) and Halla. They fled from the law into the highlands shortly after 1760 and spent some 20 years living in the wilderness. Remains from their stay can still be seen at Hveravellir.

To get to Hveravellir you drive Kjalvegur, which is one of the oldest roads in the highlands and lies through the centre of the country. Kjalvegur opens in the middle of June and closes depending on weather conditions in autumn.

Hveravellir has been a nature reserve since 1960. Accommodation is offered in two mountain huts which can accommodate up to 50 people. In Gamlaskála (The Old Hut) there are 30 beds in three dormitories as well as excellent kitchen and toilet facilities. Nýjaskála (The New Hut) has place for 20 guests in a dormitory and three smaller rooms. There is a good dining hall which seats 60 people, new toilet facilities and shower facilities for guests staying in the hut. In both huts, there is a choice between made-up beds and sleeping bag accommodation. Campers are welcome to pitch their tents or park their vans in this beautiful area between the glaciers.

The restaurant at Hveravellir is open all year. In summer, opening times are from morning til night, but to ensure service in winter, it is best to order beforehand. Pre-booking for groups in both summer and winter is essential.

Hveravellir has one of the best facilities for horses and riders in the highland with two stables and storage for saddles. Hay can be bought for the horses but has to be ordered in advance at the same time as the stables.

There are two bus companies offering daily bus tours from Reykjavík and Akureyri to Hveravellir, operation starts around mid June and is until around mid September. See further details at SBA **www.sba.is**

Usually you can get to Hveravellir by 4x4 but you better keep an eye on the weather before you take off and check if the roads are open in the wintertime, especially in the springtime when snow is melting. In the summertime the road is open for well equipped cars; note the road is gravel-surfaced.

HVERAVELLIR

Come to Hveravellir and enjoy!

HVERAVALLAFÉLAGIÐ EHF Tel: 452 4200 & 894 1293 www.hveravellir.is hveravellir@hveravellir.is

2
P. 565

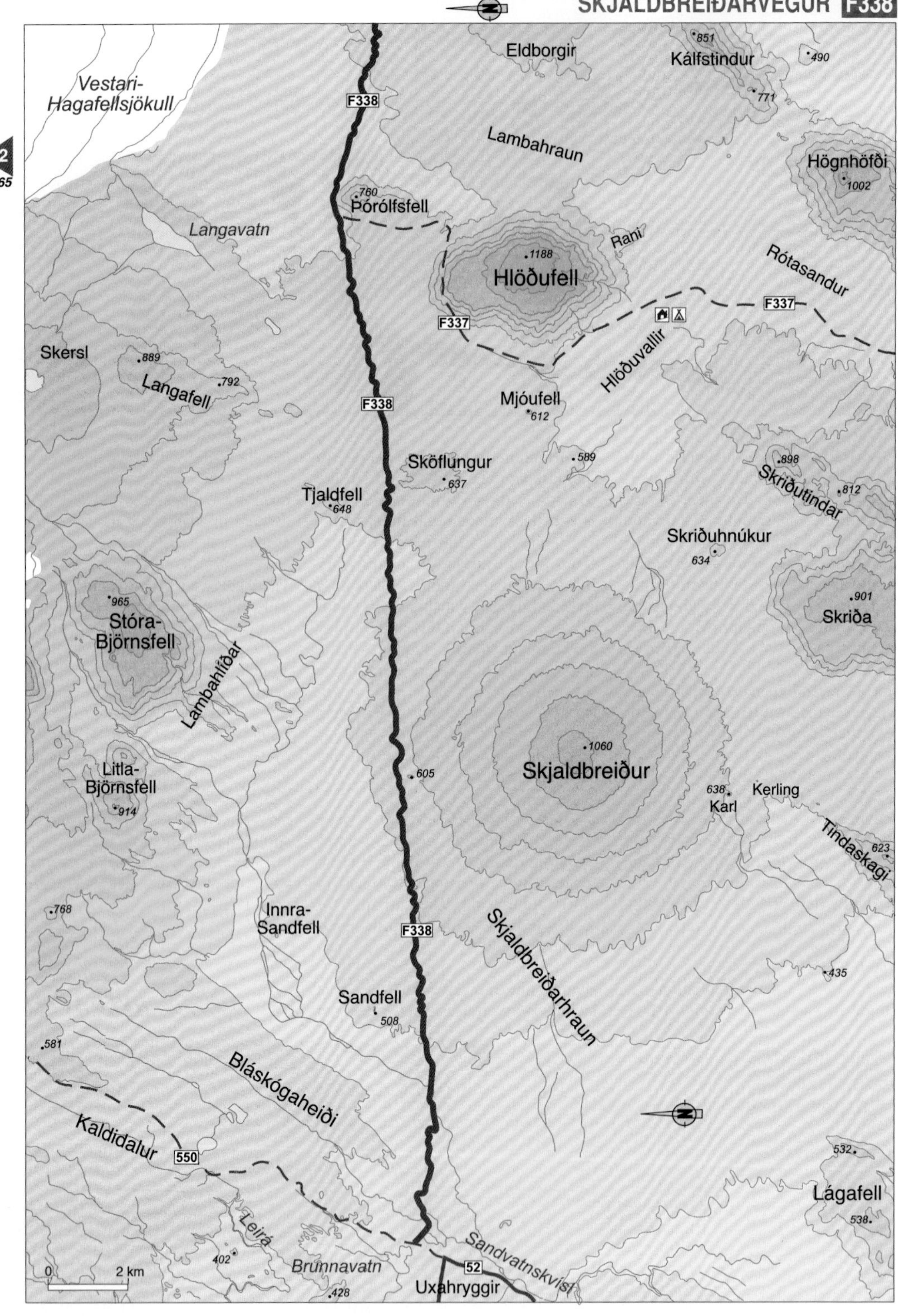

F338 Skjaldbreiðarvegur (Línuvegur), 48 km. Lies between F35 Kjalvegur and F550 Kaldadalsvegur. The route is passable by all jeeps but two fords need to be crossed. This route has a beautiful view to Langjökull.

F333 Haukadalsvegur.

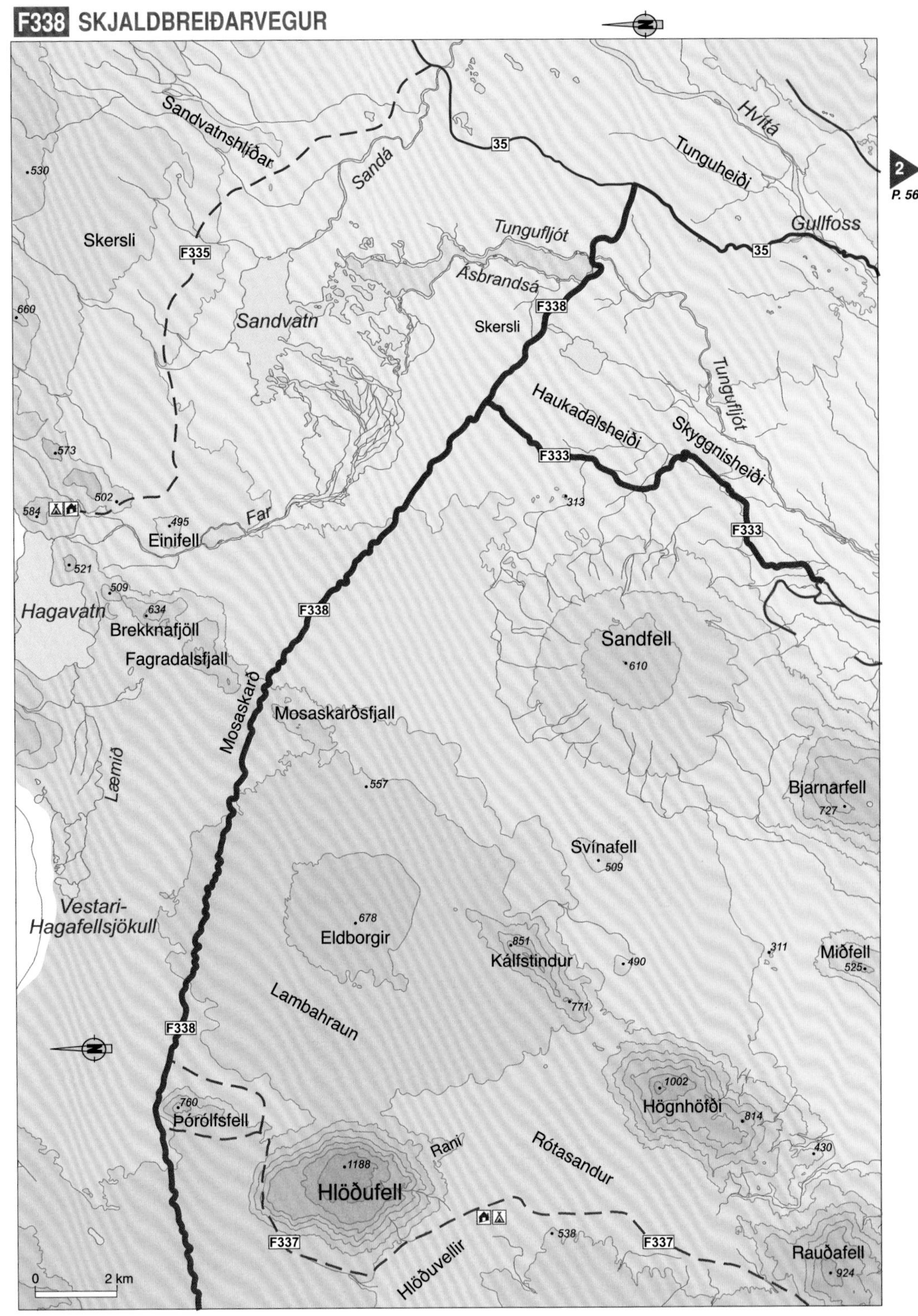

35 Biskupstungnabraut, p. 180-184	F335 Hagavatnsvegur, p. 455	F337 Hlöðuvallavegur, p. 458

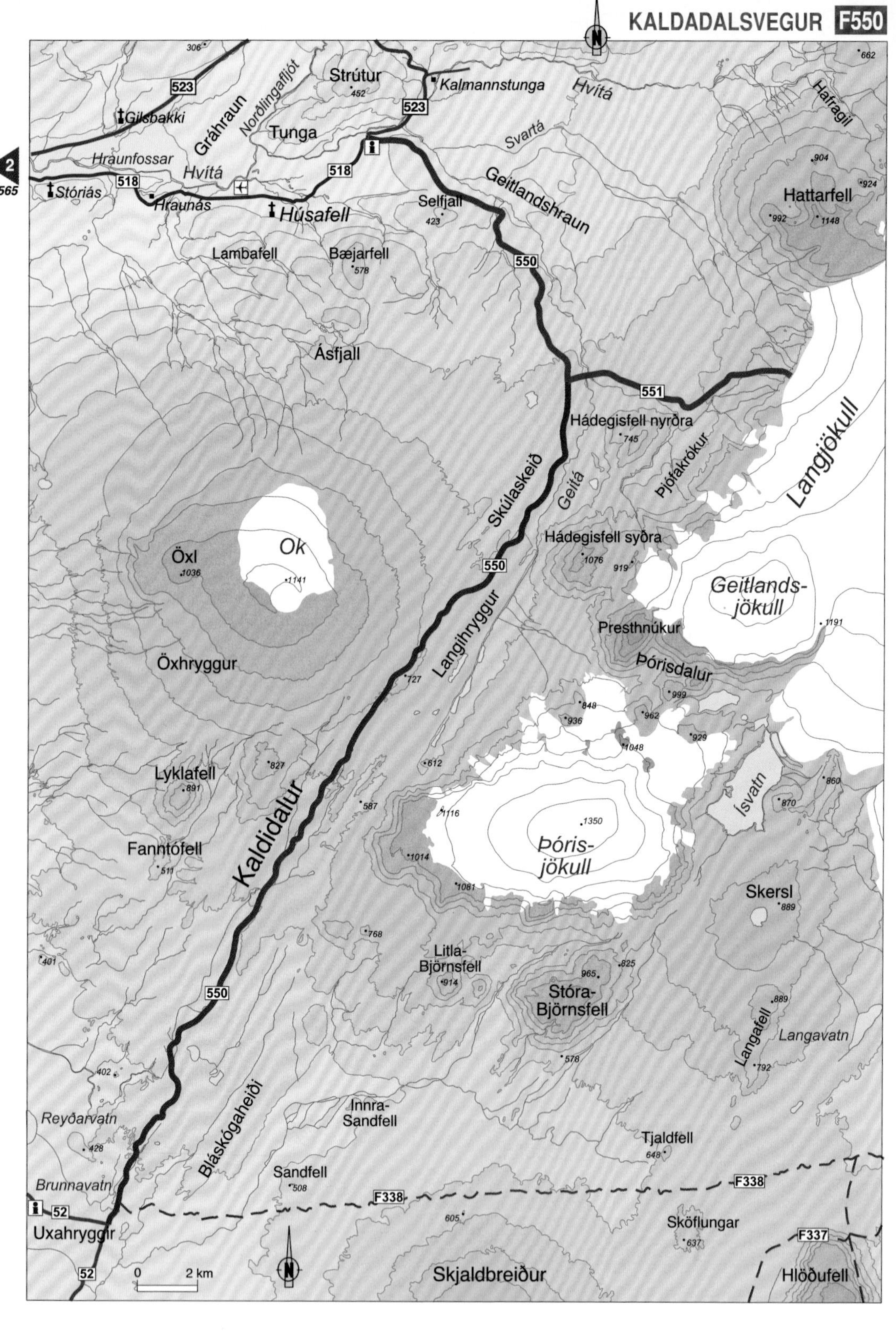
2
P. 565
Strútur
452
Kalmannstunga
Hvítá
Hafragil
662
523
Gilsbakki
Gráhraun
Norðlingafljót
Tunga
Svartá
904
924
Hraunfossar
Hvítá
518
Geitlandshraun
Hattarfell
992
1148
Stóriás
Hraunás
Húsafell
Selfjall
423
550
Lambafell
Bæjarfell
578
Ásfjall
551
Hádegisfell nyrðra
745
Þjófakrókur
Langjökull
Skúlaskeið
Geitá
Hádegisfell syðra
1076
919
Öxl
1036
Ok
1141
Geitlands-
jökull
1191
Presthnúkur
Langihryggur
Öxhryggur
Þórisdalur
727
999
848
936
962
929
1048
827
612
Lyklafell
891
860
Ísvatn
870
587
1116
1350
Fanntófell
511
Kaldidalur
1014
Þóris-
jökull
1081
Skersl
889
768
Litla-
Björnsfell
914
825
965
Stóra-
Björnsfell
401
889
Langafell
Langavatn
578
792
402
Bláskógaheiði
Innra-
Sandfell
Reyðarvatn
428
Tjaldfell
648
Brunnavatn
Sandfell
508
F338
52
605
Uxahryggir
Sköflungar
637
F337
0
2 km
Skjaldbreiður
Hlöðufell

550 **Kaldadalsvegur,** ("The cold valley route") 62,7 km between Þingvellir and Húsafell, **Kaldidalur** being the valley between Ok and Langjökull. This route is passable for all cars.

Björnsfell, **Stóra-Björnsfell** and **Litla-Björnsfell**, (914 m and 1,050 m) tuff mountains to the south of Þórisjökull.

Þórisjökull, (1350 m) a glacier covered tuff mountain, 33 km². Formerly a part of Langjökull but now separated from it by the valley Þórisdalur, well-known from *Grettis saga*.

Egilsáfangi, some grasslands by the road, an important resting place for travellers on horseback.

Beinakerling, ("Bone crone") a cairn by the road, one of the best known of this type of cairn. Travellers were supposed to compose some comment or greeting in verse, put it in a sheep's or cow's leg-bone and leave it in the Beinakerling for the next traveller who came along.

Hrúðurkarlar or **Hrúðurkatlar,** ("Barnacles") a cluster of tuff hills.

Fanntófell, a cone shaped tuff mountain to the south of Ok, the home of giants, according to folk tales.

551 **Langjökulsvegur** 7,7 km, from Kaldadalsvegur north of Hádegisfell to Langjökull. Passable for small jeeps. The route ends at the foot of Langjökull glacier.

Langjökull, Europe's second largest glacier. In June 2015 a man – made ice tunnels and caves will formally open in Langjökull. Inside the ice cave you will be able to view ice which has taken hundreds of years to develop. As you walk further along the tunnel, the ice gets older and the colour changes from white to deep-blue. The led lighted walls inside the tunnels are sheer-carved and you will find interior chambers containing exhibitions, a cafe and a small chapel.

Eiríksjökull, (1,675 m) a dome-shaped glacier dominating the view from the northern part of this route.

Hafrafell, (1,167 m) a mountain on the edge of Langjökull.

Geitlandshraun, an area of lava and sand below Geitlandsjökull to the west, between the rivers Geitá and Hvítá. The lava field, in which there are many caves, came from some craters by the glacier. The glacial river Svartá divides **Geitland** in two.

Geitá, a glacial river coming from the glaciers Geitlandsjökull and Þórisjökull. One of the rivers that join Hvítá in Borgarfjörður. Bridged to the west of Þjófakrókur.

52 **Uxahryggjavegur,** p. 236 **518** **Hálsasveitarvegur,** p. 263 **F337** **Hlöðuvallavegur,** p. 458
F338 **Skjaldbreiðarvegur,** p. 460

15
P. 578

BREIÐAFJÖRÐUR

Hellissandur
MAP P. 276
Rif
MAP P. 276
Keflavíkurbjarg
Björnssteinn
Bali
Keflavík
575
Ingjaldshóll
Gufuskálavör
(Gufuskálar)
Gufuskálar
Írskrabrunnur
Öndverðarnes
Skarðsvík
Fálki
574
579
(Írskubúðir)
Bekkjahraun
Gufuskálamóður
Neshraun
Prestahraun
Breiðidalur
Svöðufoss
Búrfell
232
Dýjadalsvatn
Hólmkelsá
(Foss)
Kerlingarfoss
Enni
419
Bæjarfoss
ÓLAFSVÍK
MAP P. 276
Gamlavík
(Haukabrekka)
Fróðárrif
Klettakotsvaðall
Sjávarfoss
Bugsvatn
Fróðá
54
Ennisdalur
Fossdalur
418
Rjúkandi
490
Hellisfjall
Svörtuloft
Saxhólsbjarg
Öndverðarneshólar
Stóri-Saxhóll
125
Saxhólahraun
Saxhóll
Sauðhóll
110
(Forni-Saxhóll)
(Saxhóll)
Fannhamrar
Klukkufoss
469
Hreggnasi
Skál
556
Hettudalir
570
Gerðubergsdalur
Tindfell
673
Fróðármúli
Kambsheiði
Miðfell
Bárðarkista
683
Geldingafell vestra
830
Táaghálsar
Rauðakúla
768
Geldingafell
633
824
Sandkúlur
844
Hamraendafjall
Lambhagatjarnir
(Garðar)
Svörtutindar
605
279
Blágilsjökull
SNÆFELLSJÖKULL
Jökulhálsjökull
Jökulháls
Beruvík
(Berutóftir)
Hnausahraun
Hnausahryggir
Gröf
Hamraendar
Beruvíkurlækur
Hyrningsjökull
Brennivínskúlur
657
Norðurþúfa
Miðþúfa
1446
Vesturþúfa
1442
Nátttmálahnúkur
574
Hnausar
(Litlalón)
Þverlækur
693
Hólatindajökull
Kvíahnúksjökull
Kálfatraðahraun
510
Botnsfjall
(Hólahólar)
Hólahólar
Kvíahnúkur
706
Kýrskarð
Klifhraun
Breiðavík
Beruvíkurhraun
Stagfell
Sönghellir
Stapafell
432
Sauðá
Stapagil
Eiríksbúð
Arnarstapi
Arnarfell
Djúpalónssandur
Dritvík
572
Merkjahryggur
Dagverðará
Tröllakirkja
(Einarslón)
Lónbjarg
Purkhólar
145
Laugarvatn
Bárðarlaug
574
Vatnshellir
Laugarbrekka
Brekkubær
Gíslabær
(Dagverðará)
Hellnar
Drangahraun
Svalþúfa
Hellnanes
(Malarrif)
Malarrif
Lóndrangar

FAXAFLÓI

0 1 km

Stapafell and Snæfellsjökull.

570 **Jökulhálsleið,** 18,5 km. From Stapafell north of Arnarstapi to Ólafsvík. This route is passable by all cars in the summer, but not untill July when all the snow has cleared.

Snæfellsjökull, (1,446 m), a national park, a central volcano and one of the most famous mountains in Iceland. Long thought to be the highest mountain in the country, probably because it stands alone and is the highest mountain rising straight up from the sea. Eggert Ólafsson and Bjarni Pálsson (see Road 62, Svefneyjar) are the first people known to have climbed it (in July 1753). The trip was considered highly dangerous at the time, though travel on the glacier is common today. At the top there is a large crater, 1 km in diameter with cliff-walls up to 200 m high by **Jökulþúfur**, three crags on the crater rim, but open to the west. There have been many eruptions under and around the glacier, though none since settlement times. Craters under the glacier have mostly produced acid (light-coloured) pumice and lava but on the lower land west and southwest of the glacier most eruptions have produced basalt. The most recent eruption was probably about 1,750 years ago, to the northwest of the glacier. Eruptions have often caused enormous flooding, e.g. along the course of the river Móðulækur. Around the turn of last century the glacier was twice the size it is today, then it grew rapidly smaller until about 1960, since when it has remained stable and even grown in places. There are still many moraines that show the former extent of the glacier. To the east and southeast of the ice there are thick layers of pumice, which was mined until 1935 and floated down along Kýrskarð pass in wooden troughs to the Klifhraun lava field, where water was used to pump it aboard freighters. Pumice has been mined there, but is now taken to Ólafsvík. New Age and mystic groups world-wide believe Snæfellsjökull to be a focus of power. It first became famous after the publication in 1864 of Jules Verne's *Journey to the Centre of the Earth.*

Kambsheiði, the moor between the Breiðavík and Fróðársveit districts. Many old routes crossed it, often dangerous and difficult to follow.

54 **Snæfellsnesvegur,** p. 238-250 **574** **Útnesvegur,** p. 270–275

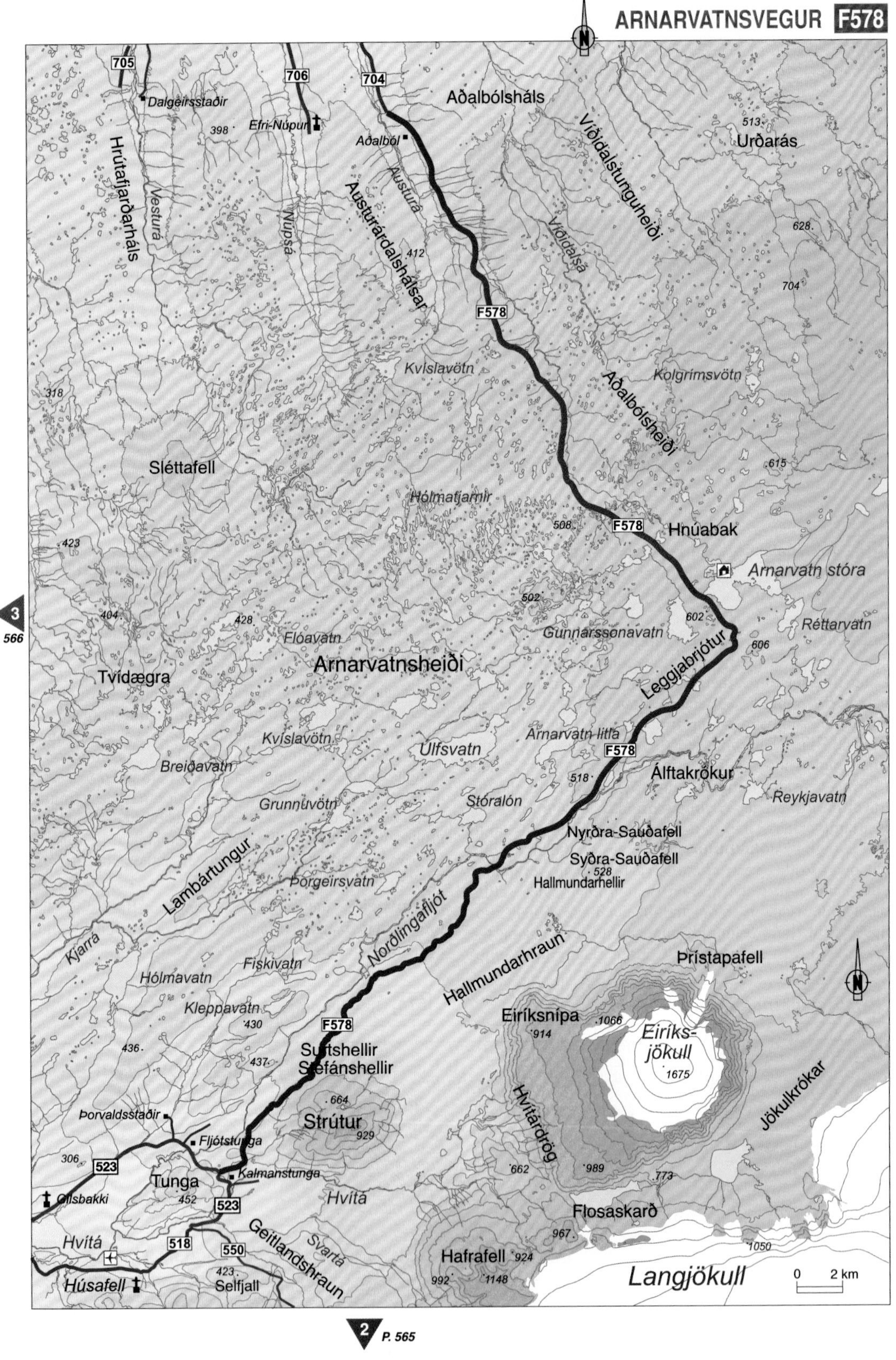
705
706
704
Dalgeirsstaðir
398
Efri-Núpur
Aðalból
Aðalbólsháls
Víðidalstunguheiði
513
Urðarás
Hrútafjarðarháls
Vesturá
Núpsá
Austurárdalsháls
Austurá
Austurárdalshálsar
412
Víðidalsá
628
704
F578
Kvíslavötn
Kolgrímsvötn
Aðalbólsheiði
318
Sléttafell
615
Hólmatjarnir
508
F578
Hnúabak
Arnarvatn stóra
423
502
602
404
428
Flóavatn
Gunnarssonavatn
Réttarvatn
606
Arnarvatnsheiði
Tvídægra
Leggjabrjótur
Kvíslavötn
Arnarvatn litla
Úlfsvatn
F578
Breiðavatn
518
Álftakrókur
Grunnuvötn
Stóralón
Reykjavatn
Nyrðra-Sauðafell
Syðra-Sauðafell
528
Lambártungur
Þorgeirsvatn
Hallmundarhellir
Norðlingafljót
Kjarrá
Fiskivatn
Hallmundarhraun
Þrístapafell
Hólmavatn
Kleppavatn
430
Eiríksnípa
914
1066
Eiríks-
jökull
1675
F578
436
437
Surtshellir
Stefánshellir
664
Strútur
929
Hvítárdrög
Jökulkrókar
Þorvaldsstaðir
Fljótstunga
306
523
Tunga
452
Kalmanstunga
662
989
773
Gilsbakki
523
Hvítá
Flosaskarð
Geitlandshraun
967
Hvítá
518
550
Svartá
1050
Hafrafell
924
Húsafell
423
Selfjall
992
1148
Langjökull
0
2 km

3
P. 566

2
P. 565

F578 Arnarvatnsvegur, 42 km from Kalmanstungu, by Lake Arnarvatn stóra to Núpsárbrú bridge in Austurárdal valley.

Stórisandur, west of Réttarvatn lake the Skagfirðingavegur route continues to the east to Grettishæð. From there it is possible to drive to Grímstunguheiði in Vatnsdalur valley. This route is very slow with larged rocks on the road. Not passable for small jeeps. By Grettishæð is a route to the south and the east through Krákshraun and east to route F35 Kjalvegur. This part of the route is also slow.

Víðgelmir, a cave down in the lava near the farm Fljótstunga, see p. 264.

Stefánshellir, a cave a little north of Surtshellir, see p. 264.

Hallmundarhraun, a lava field, thought to have been formed at the time of the settlement, coming from craters in Jökulkrókur between the glaciers Langjökull and Eiríksjökull and reaching down to the river Hvítá, where the Hraunfossar falls (see Road 518) come out from under it. The caves there are more numerous, larger and more famous than in any other lava field in Iceland. It is thought to be named for the giant Hallmundur of *Grettis saga*.

Kalmanshellir, a cave east of Eiríksjökull and north of Þrístapafell in Jökulkrókur, about 4 km long. Considered to be Icelands longest cave.

Hallmundarhellir, a cave south west of the mountain Syðra-Sauðafell.

Surtshellir, undoubtedly the most famous cave in Iceland. Right by the road just after it goes up onto the lava field. There are four openings, not all of a size for people to get through. The cave is 1970 m long, or 3500 m along with the cave Stefánshellir, which connects up to it, and with interesting side caves. Stone-built walls and bones have been found there. Outlawed thieves, called Hellismenn ("Cave men"), hid out in the caves in the 10th century, but were killed by farmers led by the chieftains of inland Borgarfjörður. According to *Hellismanna saga* the outlaws were sleeping in **Vopnalág** ("Weapon dell") at the southern end of the Þorvaldsháls ridge when the farmers attacked them.

Eiríksjökull, (1,675 m) the greatest mountain in this region, the highest west of the Vatnajökull glacier (apart from the highest point on the Hofsjökull ice cap) and the third-highest mountain in Iceland, outside the ice caps. Tuff with a basalt shield and an ice cap from which glaciers extend towards the north.

Arnarvatnsheiði, ("Eagle lake moor"), the moor north of the river Norðlingafljót, rocky, eroded hills but some vegetation by the many lakes, most of which are good fishing lakes.

Arnarvatnshæðir, hills southwest of the lake Arnarvatn stóra. Peat layers formed from angelica are found on the eastern slopes.

Réttarvatn, a lake to the east of Arnarvatnshæðir.

Tungukollur, (496 m) a small mountain on the road to Miðfjörður, offering a panoramic view of the moors.

Suðurmannasandfell, ("Southern men sand mountain") (718 m) a mountain providing the major landmark along the road to the Víðidalur valley.

Tvídægra, ("Two-day") flat, gently-sloping moors reaching north to Húnavatnssýsla county. A great deal of impassable boggy land with shallow lakes and tarns but with some low bare hills in between. Fishing in most of the lakes. Formerly people often travelled across the moor but it was difficult to find one's way and dangerous in winter and indeed many lost their lives there. To the west of the road to Miðfjörður were the Núpdælir paths south to Kalmanstunga. Even further to the west was another route going south to Borgarfjörður, and it was there that the Heiðarvíg ("Moor murders") took place when Víga-Barði of *Heiðarvíga saga* took revenge on the men of Borgarfjörður for having killed his brother.

Hveraborg, a geothermal area north of Tvídægra. A part of the hot water runs to Síká river, there it is possible to bath. A jeep track leads to Hverborg but the last part travellers need to walk for about an hour. There is a cabin at Hverborgir and it is possible to get a key at Staðarskáli in Hrútarfjörður.

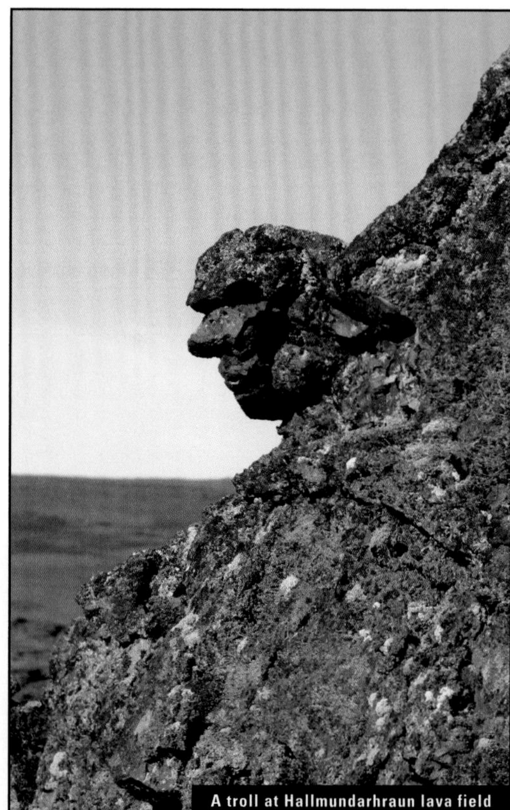

A troll at Hallmundarhraun lava field

518 Hálsasveitarvegur, p. 262
523 Hvítársíðuvegur, p. 263
550 Kaldadalsvegur, p. 263
704 Miðfjarðarvegur, p. 335
705 Vesturárdalsvegur, p. 335
706 Núpsdalsvegur, p. 336

2 P. 565

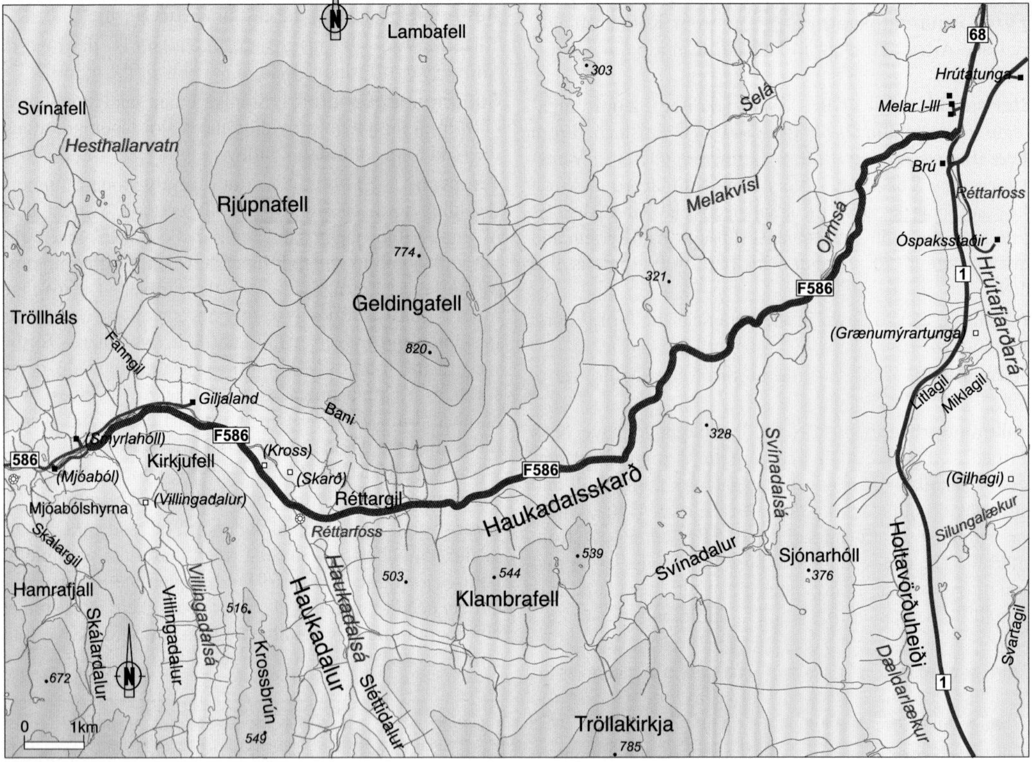

F586 Haukadalsskarðsvegur, 19,8 km. Between Haukadalur and Hrútafjörður, an ok jeep track through Haukadalsskarð. The route is passable for all jeeps, also small jeeps if the route is driven carefully. A small ford needs to be crossed by Haukadalsá.

Haukadalsskarð, a pass that was once an important route from the Haukadalur valley over to Hrútafjörður in the north. Little used now but passable for jeeps in the summer.

1 **Norðurlandsvegur,** p. 59 | 68 **Innstrandavegur,** p. 309-312 | 586 **Haukadalsskarðsvegur,** p. 277

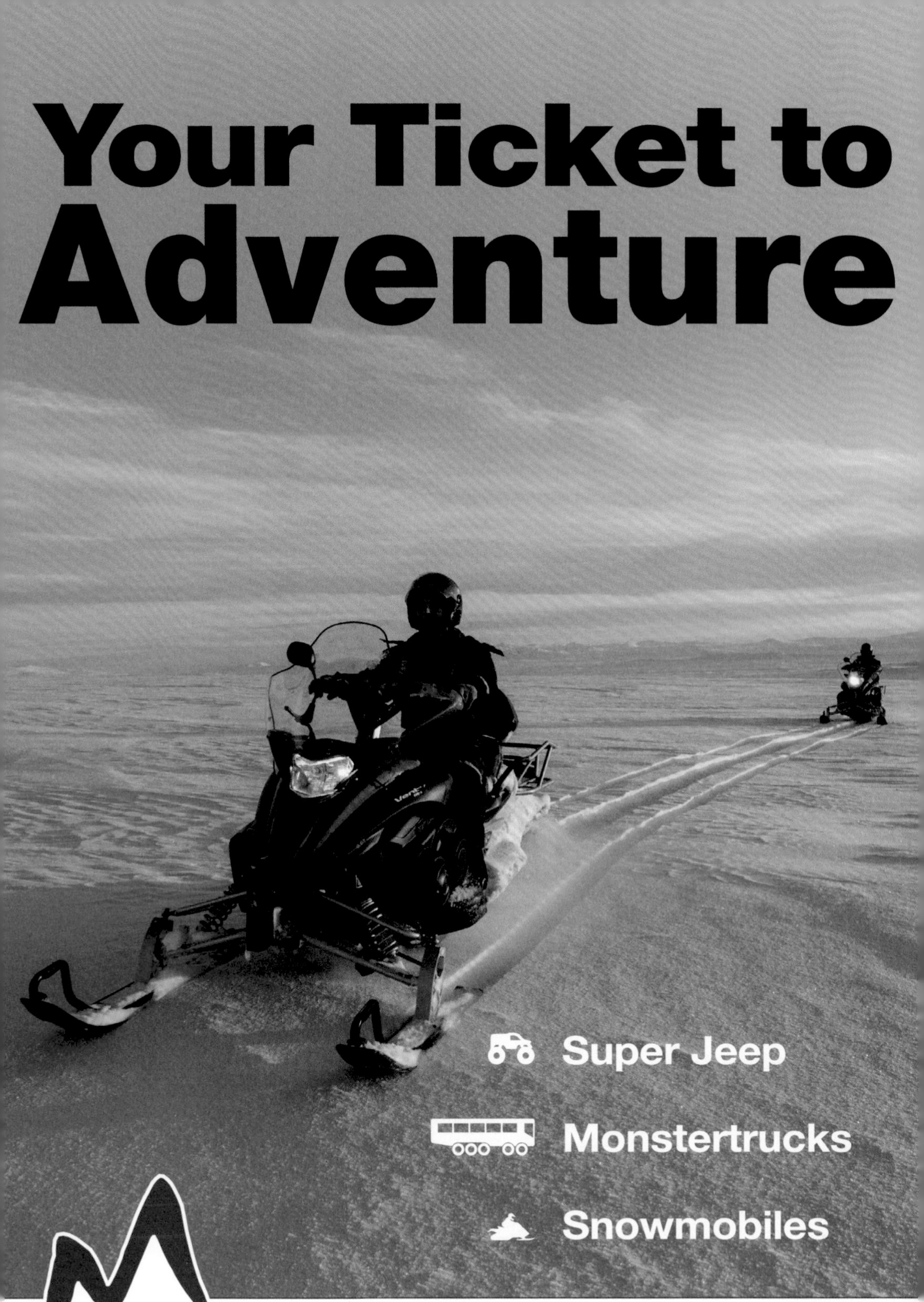

22
P. 585

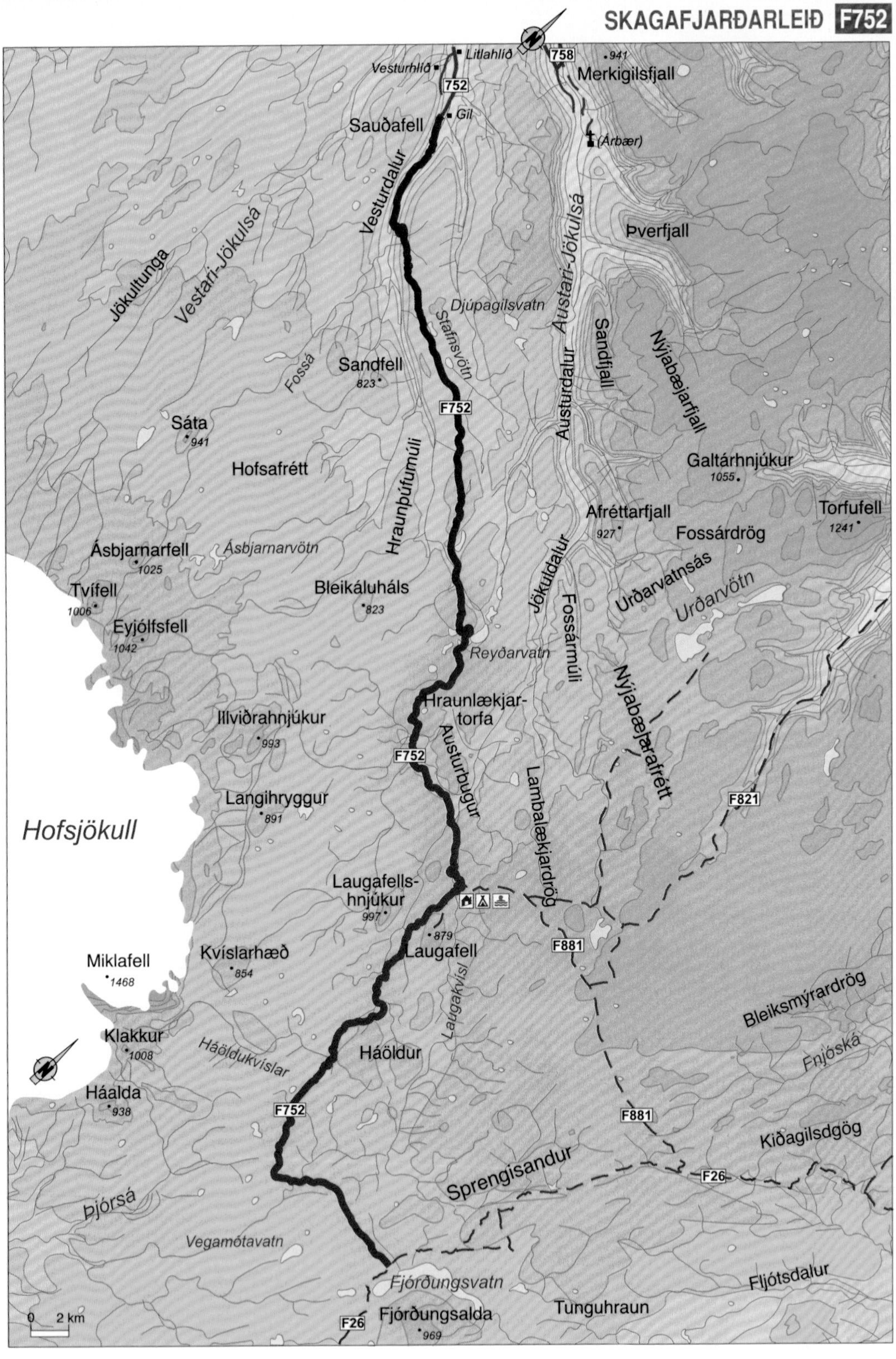

Litlahlíð
Vesturhlíð
752
758
•941
Merkigilsfjall
Sauðafell
Gil
(Árbær)
Vesturdalur
Vestari-Jökulsá
Jökultunga
Austari-Jökulsá
Þverfjall
Djúpagilsvatn
Stafnsvötn
Sandfjall
Nýjabæjarfjall
Fossá
Sandfell
823•
F752
Austurdalur
Sáta
•941
Hofsafrétt
Hraunþúfumúli
Galtárhnjúkur
1055•
Afréttarfjall
927•
Torfufell
1241•
Fossárdrög
Ásbjarnarfell
•1025
Ásbjarnarvötn
Jökuldalur
Urðarvatnsás
Urðarvötn
Tvífell
1006•
Bleikáluháls
•823
Fossármúli
Eyjólfsfell
1042•
Reyðarvatn
Hraunlækjar-
torfa
Nýjabæjarafrétt
Illviðrahnjúkur
•993
F752
Austurbugur
Lambalækjardrög
Langihryggur
•891
F821
Hofsjökull
Laugafells-
hnjúkur
997•
•879
Laugafell
F881
Miklafell
•1468
Kvíslarhæð
•854
Laugakvísl
Bleiksmýrardrög
Klakkur
•1008
Háöldukvíslar
Háöldur
Fnjóská
Háalda
•938
F752
F881
Kiðagilsdgög
Sprengisandur
F26
Þjórsá
Vegamótavatn
Fjórðungsvatn
Fljótsdalur
0 2 km
Fjórðungsalda
•969
F26
Tunguhraun

F752 **Skagafjarðarleið (Forsetavegur)** 30,2 km. he route is passable for all jeeps. There is one obstacle on the way, a ford on the Bergvatnskvísl river. It is easy in drought but the water can rise rapidly during rainy seasons and be dangerous for small jeeps. On the north side on this route is **Beinakerling** („ Bone crone") a cairn by the road, one of the best known of this type of cairn. Travellers were supposed to compose some comment or greeting in verse, put it in a sheep's or cow's leg-bone and leave it in the Beinakerling for the next traveller who came along.

Bergvatnskvísl, a clear river, the northernmost roots of the Þjórsá river, 230 km long, the longest river in Iceland.

Hofsjökull, 1800m) a glacier, 1000 km2. With some steep mountains like **Blágnípa** (1068 m), on the west side, **Arnarfell hið mikla** (1143 m), on the south side and **Miklafell** (1456 m), on the east side.

F752 **Skagafjarðarleið** 28,5 km from Laugafell to Gil in Vesturdalur, passable for all jeeps if there is not much water in the Hnjúkskvísl river.

Laugafell (892 m) and **Laugafellshnjúkur,** (997 m) two mountains which are prominent landmarks, rising as they do from rather flat country. To the northwest of Laugafell there are some geothermal springs 40-50°C, a bathing pool and a good tourist hut built 1948. The story goes that people lived there at one time, and there are some signs of ruins. A pool with changing rooms.

Austari-Jökulsá, a big glacial river collecting many streams and rivers from the Hofsjökull glacier and flowing down to the Austurdalur valley. This river used to be a big obstacle but now there is a bridge at Austurbugur.

Eyfirðingavegur, an old route from Þingvellir to North Iceland.

Strompleið, south of Orravatnsrústir ir a west bound route, passable for all jeeps.

Orravatnsrústir, grasslands around the lakes Reyðarvatn and Orravatn. Mostly wet ground with lots of cottongrass and sedge. This area is extremely marshy with hillocks tens of metres in diameter and up to three metres high, covered with dwarf shrubs. The river outlet for the area is Rústakvísl, later to join Hofsá. In the centre of the area is a small hill, Orrahaugur, where there is a good refuge hut.

Giljamúli, a mountain spur between the valleys Vesturdalur and Giljadalur, its highest point being Stafnsvatnahæð (716 m). There is a very poor road onto it from the abandoned farm Þorljótsstaðir and past the two lakes Stafnsvötn and Langavatn.

Reyðarfell, (802 m) a mountain north of the lake Reyðarvatn.

752 **Skagafjarðarvegur,** p. 353
758 **Austurdalsvegur,** p. 354
F26 **Sprengisandsleið,** p. 433
F821 **Eyjafjarðarleið,** p. 467
F881 **Dragaleið,** p. 476

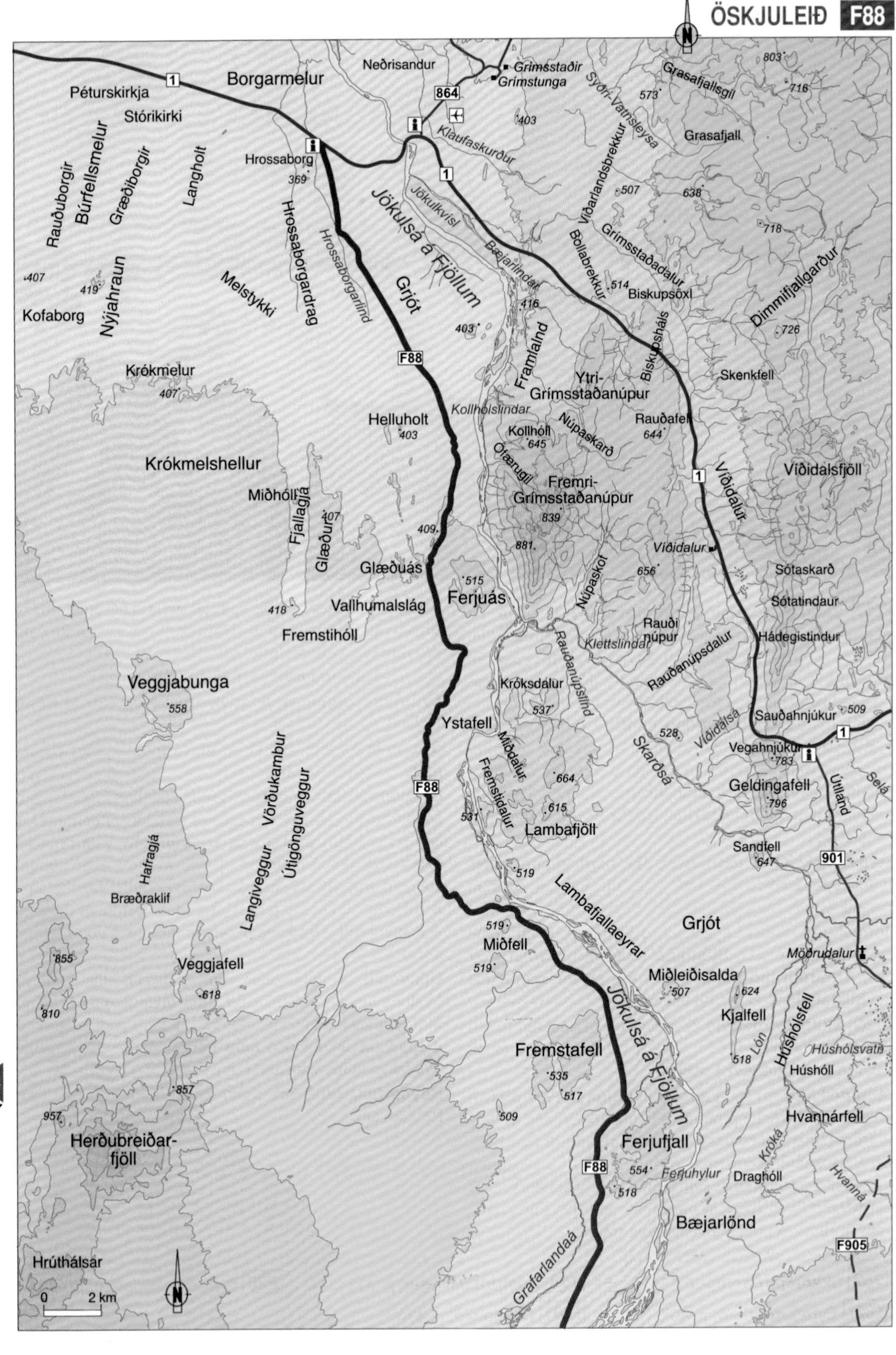

7 P. 570
24 P. 587

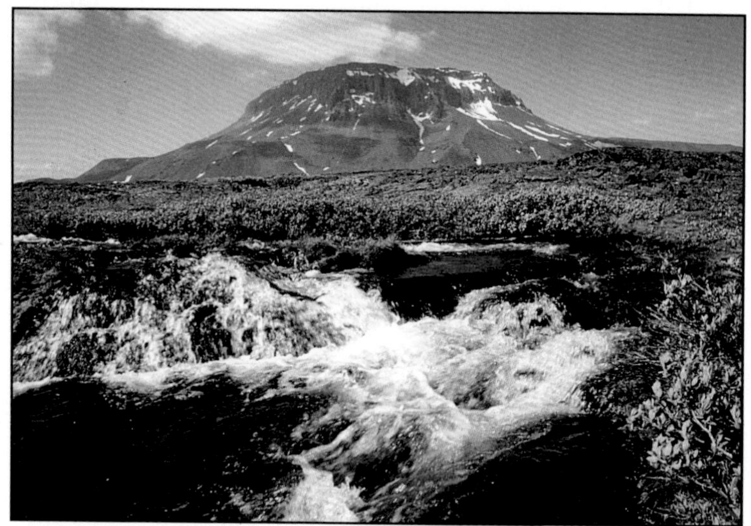

Herðubreið.

F88 **Öskjuleið,** 79,9 km, from the Ring Road by Hrossaborg. Passable by all jeeps, also small jeeps. A ford in Grafarlandaá and Lindá need to be passed.

Hrossaborg, an old crater, about 500 m long, rising about 40 m above the flat sands around it.

Herðubreiðarfjöll, (1,094 m) tuff mountains. Between them and the mountain **Hrúthálsar**, ridges (1,055 m), to the south is **Eggert** (1,332 m).

Grafarlönd, an area around the river Grafarlandaá with scattered vegetation. A nesting area for geese.

Kollóttadyngja, (1,177 m) a shield volcano with an 800 m wide crater at the top. In the floor of the crater, which is 30 m deep, there is a 70 m deep basin. One of the most regular shield volcanoes in Iceland. At Bræðrafell to the south of Kollóttadyngja there is a cabin belonging to the Touring Club of Akureyri, built in 1960.

Herðubreiðarlindir, an area of rich vegetation 5-6 km northeast of Herðubreið. Many springs appear from under the lava to make one stream or river, Lindaá. A wonderful oasis in the middle of black sands and lava. Ruins of a shelter, **Eyvindarkofi**, made by Fjalla-Eyvindur, the 18th century outlaw. A good tourist hut and a popular camping place. **Protected area**.

Herðubreið, (1,682 m) a table mountain with a crater at its top, rising 1,000 to 1,100 m above the surrounding highlands. One of the most majestic mountains in Iceland, with a nearly round base having a circumference of 8-9 km. The mountain is tuff with a basalt shield and steep screes all around. It was long held to be impossible to climb, the first ascent being in 1908 by Hans Reck and Sigurður Sumarliðason. The easiest route is directly from the west, but even this is difficult and there is always the very real danger of rockfalls.

1 **Austurlandsvegur,** p. 99 **864** **Hólsfjallavegur,** p. 404 **901** **Möðrudalsvegur,** p. 96
F905 **Arnardalsleið,** p. 484

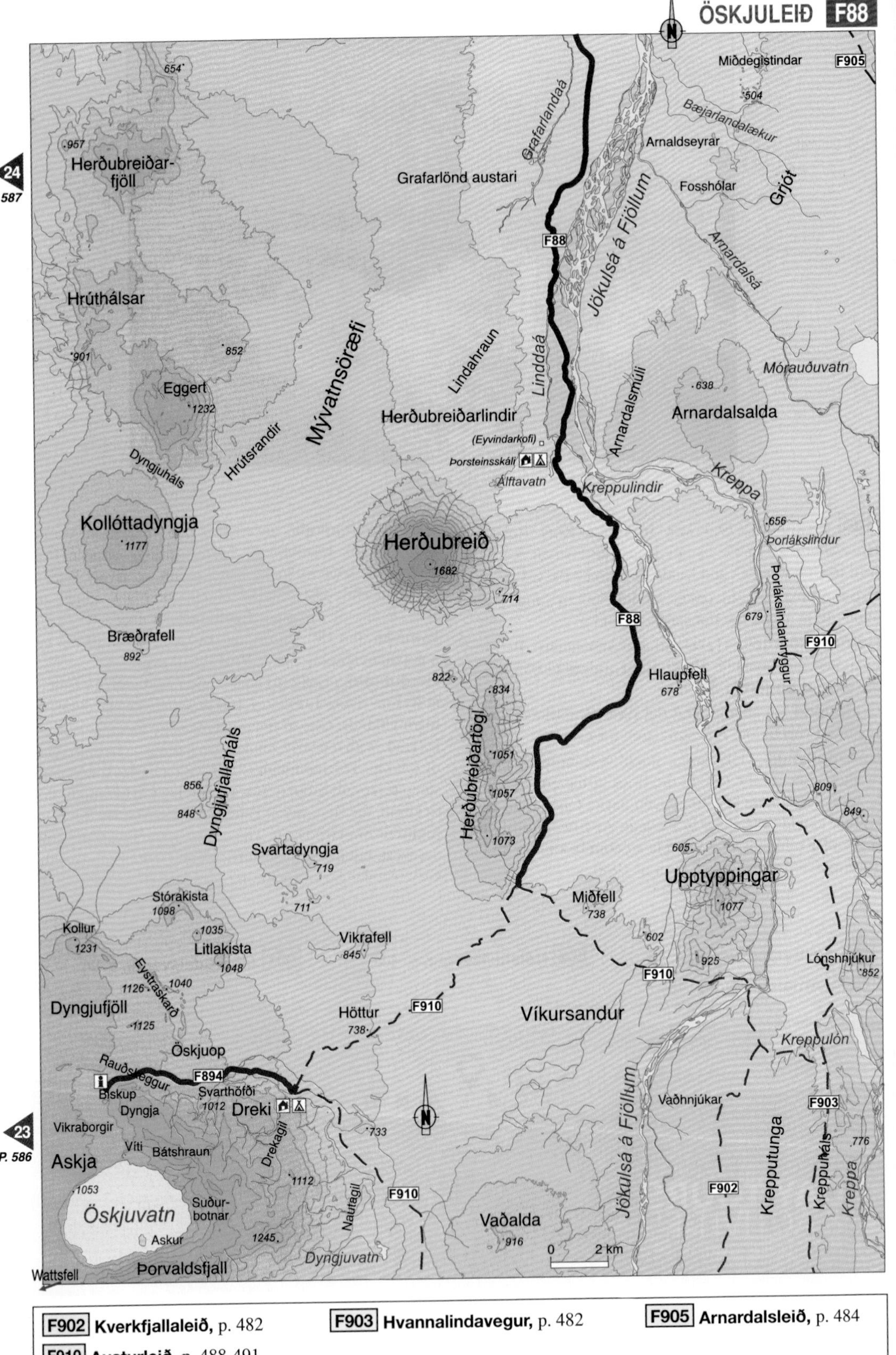

F902 **Kverkfjallaleið,** p. 482
F903 **Hvannalindavegur,** p. 482
F905 **Arnardalsleið,** p. 484
F910 **Austurleið,** p. 488-491

F894 **Öskjuvatnsvegur**, 7,8 km, of Austurleið route by Drekagil to Öskjuvatn. Passable for all cars to the parking lot by Öskuvatn.

Askja, a 50 km² caldera in the Dyngjufjöll mountains. The bottom, about 1,100 m above sea level, is mostly covered with rough lava. In the southeast corner, in a smaller caldera is the lake, Öskjuvatn, 217 m deep, and thus the second deepest lake in Iceland. The caldera and the lake were formed in the eruption of 1875, when there was a tremendous explosion in the small crater **Víti** ("Hell") on the northeastern shore of Öskjuvatn. This eruption produced more ash than any other eruption in Iceland, covering much of eastern Iceland, so that many farms had to be abandoned. This was a major cause of the emigrations to North America (see Road 77, Hofsós). There have been many other eruptions in Askja, the latest in 1961 when lava flowed from **Öskjuop**, the craters now named Vikraborgir. In 1907 two Germans, Walther von Knebel and Max Rudloff, were lost, presumed drowned, while doing research at Askja

Dyngjufjöll, a cluster of mountains around the Askja caldera, forming a square about 24 km a side, rising 600-700 m above the surrounding plateau and 100-200 m above the bottom of Askja. Evidence suggests that these mountains are the remnants of a huge volcanic zone from the ice age, that collapsed. There are many younger lava streams, almost no vegetation and geothermal heat in many places. The highest peak is Þorvaldstindur (1510 m) on the south rim, named for the 19th century geologist Þorvaldur Thoroddsen. The main passes into Askja are **Suðurskarð** on the south, **Jónsskarð** on the northwest and Öskjuop on the northeast, where the road-track is.

Dyngjufjöll ytri, (1,000 m) a 20 km long tuff ridge separating the Dyngjufjöll mountains from the Dyngjufjalladalur valley. Its higher end is named **Fjallsendi** ("Mountain's end").

Dyngjufjalladalur, a 15 km long valley through which lies the Gæsavatnaleið road going via Suðurárbotnar to Svartárkot in the Bárðardalur valley. Accessible ONLY to well equipped mountain vehicles. This route was first driven in July 1944.

Drekagil, ("Dragon canyon") in the eastern part of Dyngjufjöll. A cabin called Dreki built by the Touring Club of Akureyri. From here track F910 goes south by Dyngjufjöll, north of Trölladyngja and Tungnafellsjökull, joining Sprengisandsleið (F26) at Tómasarhagi. From Dreki to Tómasarhagi is about 100 km. **This route is only safe with two or more vehicles travelling in tandem.**

Kattbekingur, (1,055 m) a light brown, steep-sided tuff mountain with a sharp crest.

Vatnsfell, (1,308 m) a lone mountain in the Dyngjufjöll range. Originally named Wattsfell for W.L. Watts, an Englishman who, accompanied by the Icelandic guide "Glacier Páll", was the first to walk across Vatnajökull (1875). Excellent views.

5
P. 568

22
P. 585

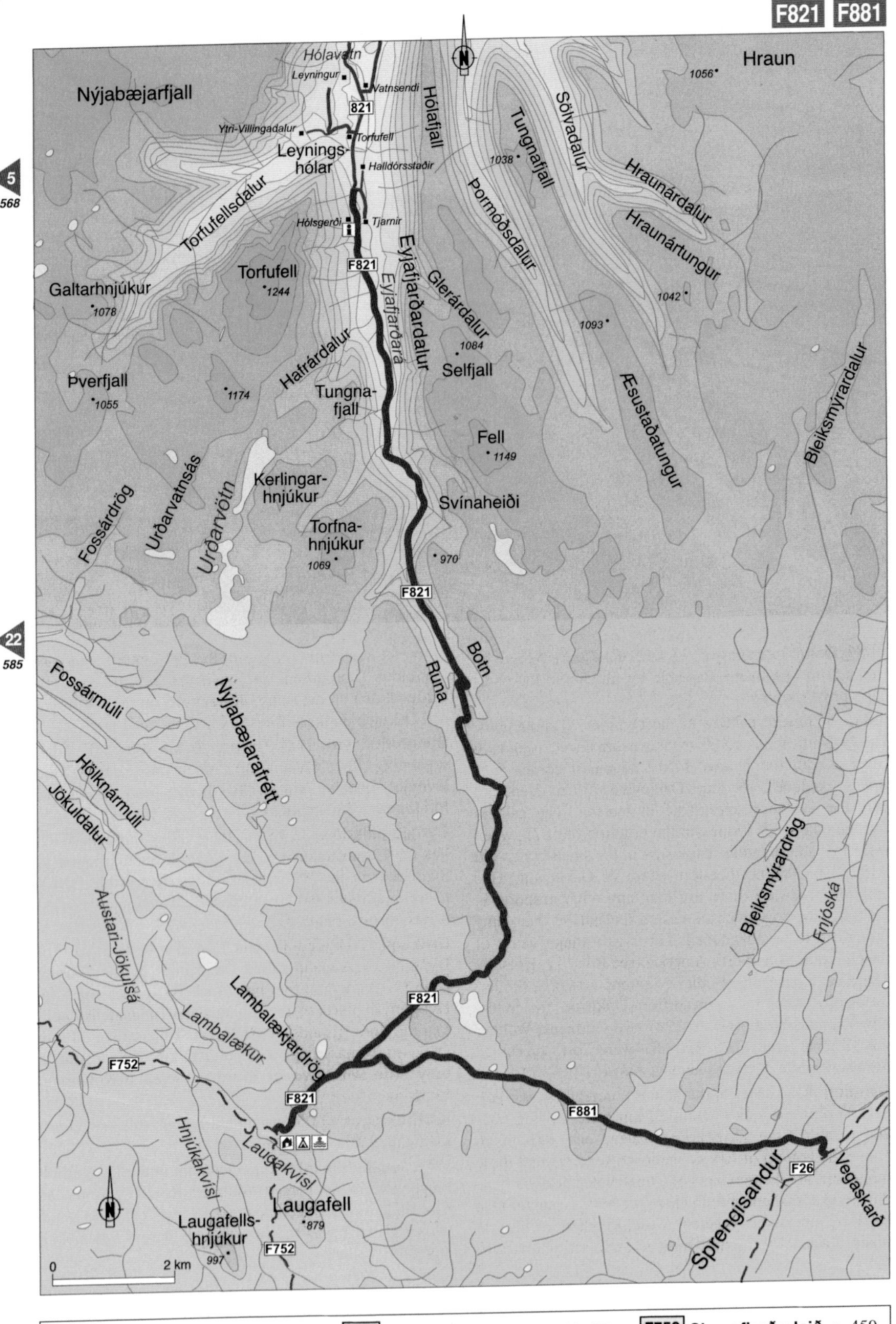

821	Eyjafjarðarbraut vestri, p. 392	F26	Sprengisandsleið, p. 430-433	F752	Skagafjarðarleið, p. 450

F881 **Dragaleið** 18,3 km, Westbound from route F26, Sprengisandsleið to Laugafell. The route is passable for all jeeps even small jeeps.

Sprengisandur, a wide and extensive desert in the centre of Iceland with indistinct boundaries, but usually understood to be between Eyvindarver/**Háumýrar**/**Þjórsárver** and Kiðagil and between the glaciers Hofsjökull and Tungnafellsjökull and the river Skjálfandafljót. Mostly about 700-800 m above sea level and about 30 by 70 km in area. In times past this route was not very much used, mostly because of the distance between grasslands. Since the road was made it has been used a good deal by motor vehicles in summertime.

F821 **Eyjafjarðarleið** 41,7 km. The route is passable for all jeeps. Many creeks cross the road and it is steep in places.

Nýibær, for some time a weather report station, now abandoned. The present road from Eyjafjörður is up through Runa and by Nýibær to Laugafell.

Hólafjall, a long, narrow mountain between Eyjafjörður and the valley Sölvadalur. A jeep-track, now abandoned, once ran along it, reaching an altitude of 1002 m. The view from Hólafjall is very good. From Þormóðsstaðir is a road on the northern end of Hólafjall, step but accessible for most cars.

Runa, the head of the Eyjafjörður valley.

6
P. 569

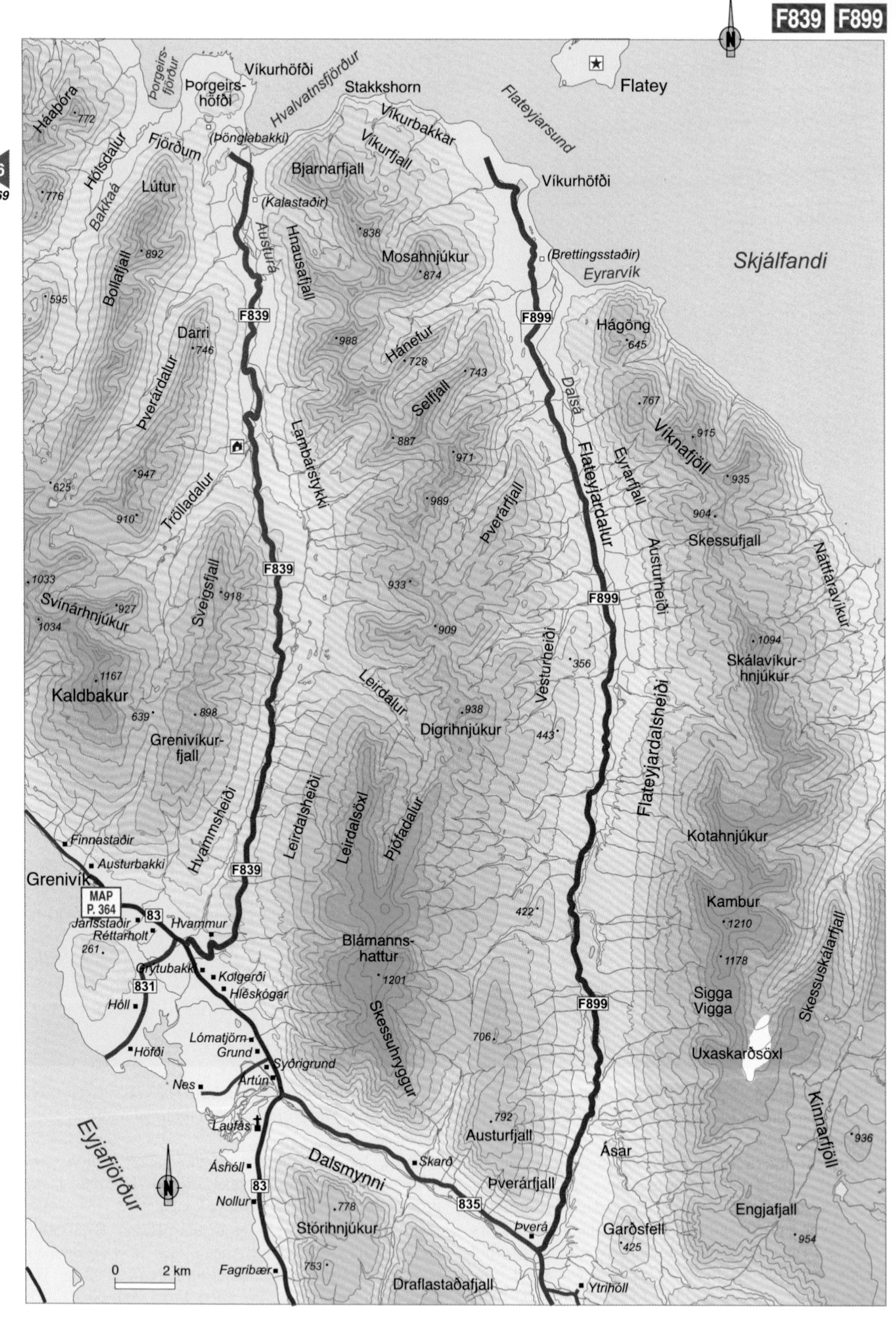
Víkurhöfði
Þorgeirs-
höfði
Þorgeirs-
fjörður
Hvalvatnsfjörður
Stakkshorn
Flatey
Flateyjarsund
Háaþóra
772
Fjörðum
(Þönglabakki)
Víkurbakkar
Víkurfjall
Bjarnarfjall
Víkurhöfði
Hólsdalur
Lútur
776
Bakkaá
(Kalastaðir)
838
Austurá
Hnausafjall
Mosahnjúkur
874
(Brettingsstaðir)
Eyrarvík
Skjálfandi
Bollafjall
892
595
F839
F899
Hágöng
645
Darri
746
988
Hánefur
728
743
Þverárdalur
Selfjall
Dalsá
767
Lambárstykki
887
971
Víknafjöll
915
935
947
625
Tröllladalur
910
989
Þverárfjall
Flateyjardalur
Eyrarfjall
904
Skessufjall
Austurheiði
Náttfaravíkur
Sveigsfjall
1033
918
933
927
Svínárhnjúkur
1034
909
1094
Skálavíkur-
hnjúkur
356
Vesturheiði
1167
Kaldbakur
Leirdalur
639
898
938
Digrihnjúkur
443
Flateyjardalsheiði
Grenivíkur-
fjall
Leirdalsheiði
Leirdalsöxl
Þjófadalur
Hvammsheiði
Kotahnjúkur
Finnastaðir
Austurbakki
Grenivík
MAP
P. 364
83
Jarlsstaðir
Hvammur
Kambur
Réttarholt
422
1210
261
Blámanns-
hattur
1178
Grýtubakki
Kolgerði
1201
Skessuskálarfjall
831
Hléskógar
Sigga
Vigga
Höll
Skessuhryggur
Lómatjörn
706
Höfði
Grund
Uxaskarðsöxl
Syðrigrund
Nes
Árún
Kinnarfjöll
Eyjafjörður
Laufás
792
Austurfjall
936
Ásar
Áshóll
Dalsmynni
Skarð
83
Þverárfjall
Nollur
835
778
Engjafjall
Stórihnjúkur
Þverá
Garðsfell
954
425
0
2 km
753
Fagribær
Draflastaðafjall
Ytrihóll

F839 **Leirdalsheiðarvegur** 34,4 km. The route is passable for all jeeps, also small jeeps. Some creeks and small fords need to be crossed. There is a hut at Flateyjardalsheiði heath.

Flateyjardalsheiði and **Flateyjardalur** stretch for 30 km from Fnjóskadalur valley to the sea. The valley is very fertile and colourful with fish in most rivers. In the Flateyjardalur valley where 5 farms, now all abandoned, the last one in 1953, Brettingsstaður. The valley is the scene of the story of Finnbogi rammi.

F899 **Flateyjardalsvegur** 27,5 km. Not passable for small jeeps.

Fjörður, two small fjords, **Hvalvatnsfjörður** and **Þorgeirsfjörður**, on the east of Eyjafjörður. Pleasant grassy valleys at their heads, with good trout streams. A jeep track from there over Leirdalsheiði moor to Grýtubakki in the Höfðahverfi district. A popular walking district.

Flatey (flat island), on Skjálfandi bay. Flatey befits its name by reaching a maximum altitude of only 22 m, in an area of 2.62 km². Although the island was inhabited from the 12th century till 1967, it was not until around 1943 that the population peaked at 120. Besides fishing and livestock farming, Flatey residents relied to some extent on driftwood, seals and birds. A cooperative store and primary school came into operation in the early 20th century, and several attractive houses are still maintained by descendents of former residents.

83 **Grenivíkurvegur,** p. 365 **831** **Höfðavegur,** p. 365 **835** **Fnjóskadalsvegur eystri,** p. 397

Call 112

Not sure if you should call? Call anyway!

112

© David Varga

23
P. 586

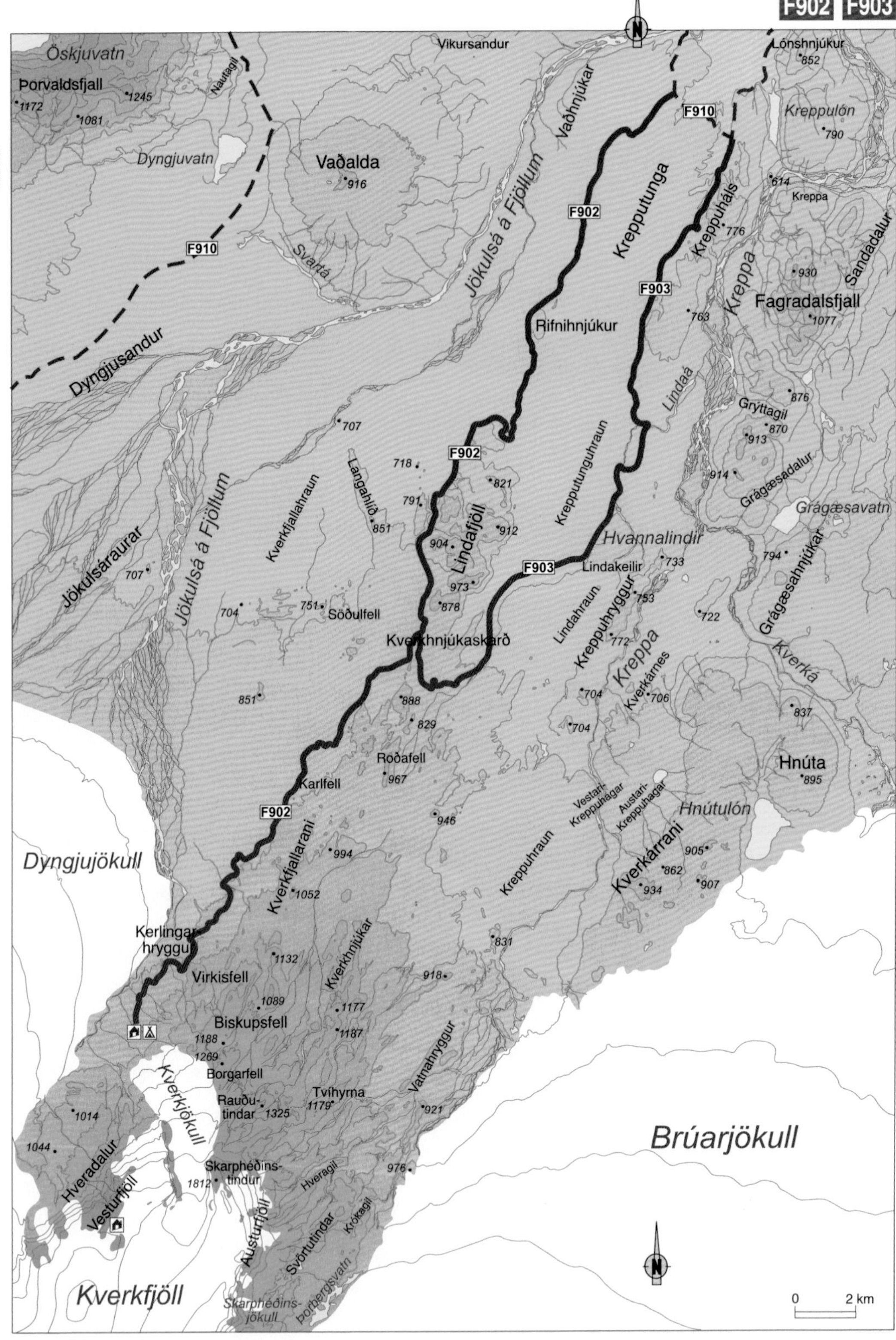

F910 **Austurleið**, p. 488-491

Öskjuvatn.

F902 **Kverkfjallavegur** 41,3 km. Accessible by jeeps.

Kverkfjallarani or **Kverkhnjúkarani**, a ridge.

Kverkfjöll, (1,920 m) a magnificent mountain range in northern Vatnajökull. One of the largest geothermal areas in the country on the west side of the mountains, creating many beautiful ice caves in the glacier. A good tourist hut north of Kverkfjöll and another one high in the mountains. Good walking routes.

F903 **Hvannalindavegur** 26,4 km. Accessible by jeeps.

Krepputunga, the district between the rivers Kreppa and Jökulsá á Fjöllum, 50-60 km long.

Hvannalindir, an area where several streams come up from under a lava field, surrounded by grasslands and other vegetation not usually seen at that height (650 m). Lindakeilir is a small cone shaped hill in the western part of the area. Many protected ruins in the lava edge, possibly made by the 18th century outlaw Fjalla-Eyvindur. A warden in the summer.

Fagradalsfjall, (1,022 m) the largest mountain in the Brúaröræfi wilderness.

24 P. 587

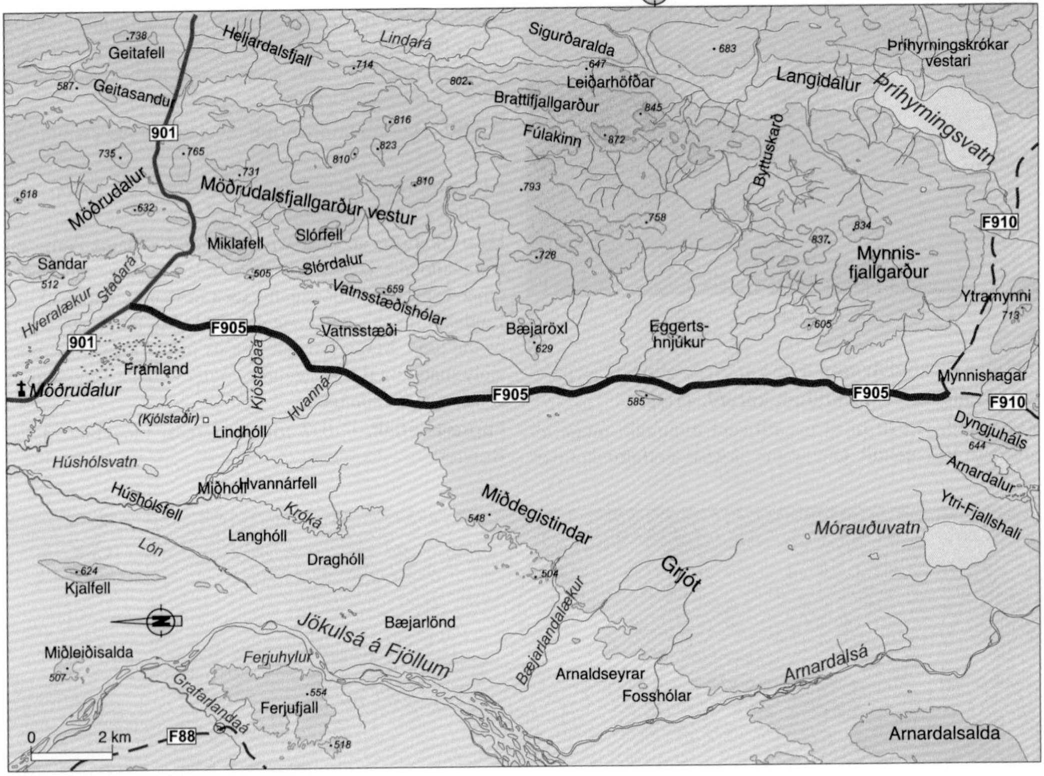

F905 **Arnardalsleið** 26,1 km. This route is passable by all jeeps, also small jeeps, though some fords need to be crossed.

Arnardalsfjöll, (679 and 671 m) two small but conspicuous mountains in the middle of Arnardalur.

Arnardalur, a lovely, broad valley west of the Fjallgarðar ranges, with good flat land, spring-fed rivers and areas of vegetation. North of the valley, there are two gravel ledges with a particularly well-formed glacial ridges on the northern one, west of the road. The crossroads at Ytra-Mynni are on the southern one. At the eastern end of the valley, accessible by jeep-track, are the ruins of the farm, **Dyngja**. Þorsteinn jökull was said to have fled to there at the time of the plague, around 1500. From the south of Arnardalur a jeep-track goes along Álftadalsdyngja to Brúarjökull and along Brúardalir east to Jökuldalur.

Grjót, a withered plain by Hvanná.

901 **Möðrudalsvegur,** p. 96 F88 **Öskjuleið,** p. 472 F910 **Austurleið,** p. 488-491

24 P. 587

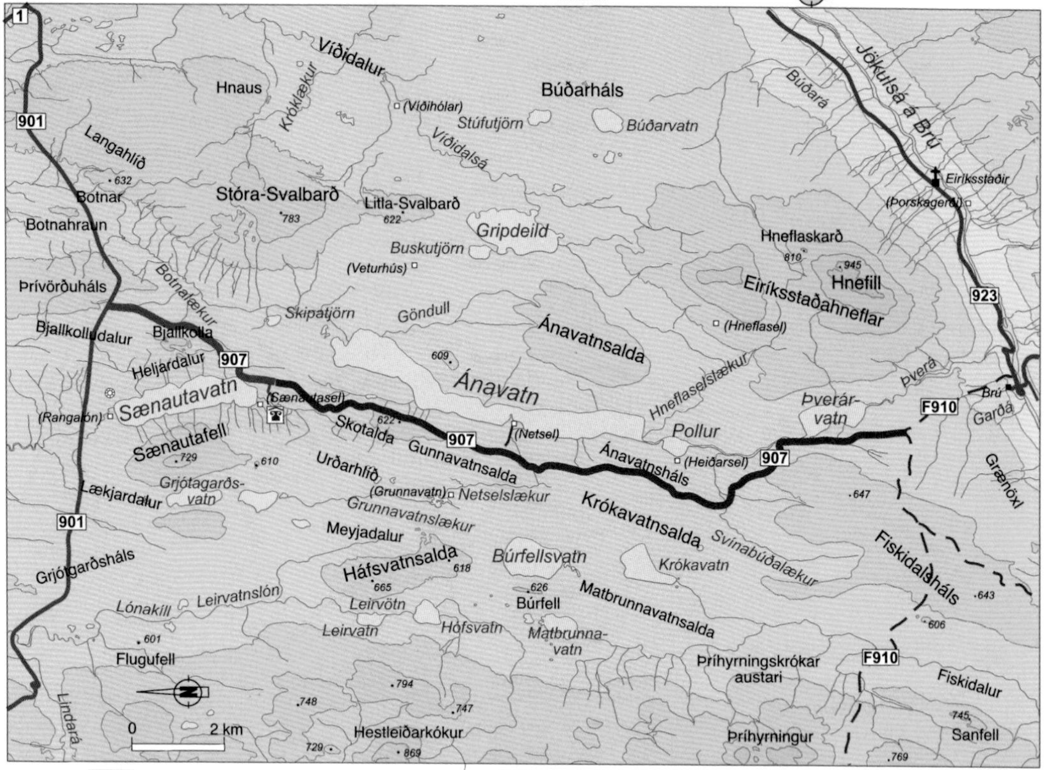

7 P. 570 24 P. 587

F907 Brúarvegur, 20,7 km. A route between route 1 and F910. Passable for all cars.

Sænautasel, an abandoned farm (occupied 1843–1943) at the southern end of the lake Sænautavatn ("Sea-monster lake"). It achieved notoriety through the Halldór Laxness' account A Midwinter Night on Jökuldalsheiði Moor. It was renovated in 1992-3 and is considered well worth a visit. Land reclamation and revegetation.

Jökuldalsheiði, the moor east of the Fjallgarðar ranges and west of the Jökuldalur valley. Hilly, with sparse vegetation and a number of good fishing lakes, among them Ánavatn which lies parallel to the road. A number of moorland farms were started there after 1840, some of them continuing into the 1940's. The farms that were inhabited the longest were Rangalón, on the north side of Sænautavatn lake by the main road, 1843-1924, **Ármótasel**, by the main road by Jökuldalur, 1853-1943, Veturhús, on the east side of Ánavatn lake, 1846-1941, **Heiðarsel,** on the west side of Ánavatn lake, 1857-1946, and Sænautasel, on the south side of Sænautavatn lake, 1843-1943.

Grunnavatn, an abandoned moor farm.

Netsel, an old abandoned moor farm where Þorsteinn Jökull from Brú lived for a year trying to avoid the plague.

1 **Norðurlandsvegur,** p. 96
901 **Möðrudalsvegur,** p. 96
923 **Jökuldalsvegur,** p. 424
F910 **Austurleið,** p. 488-491

24 P. 587

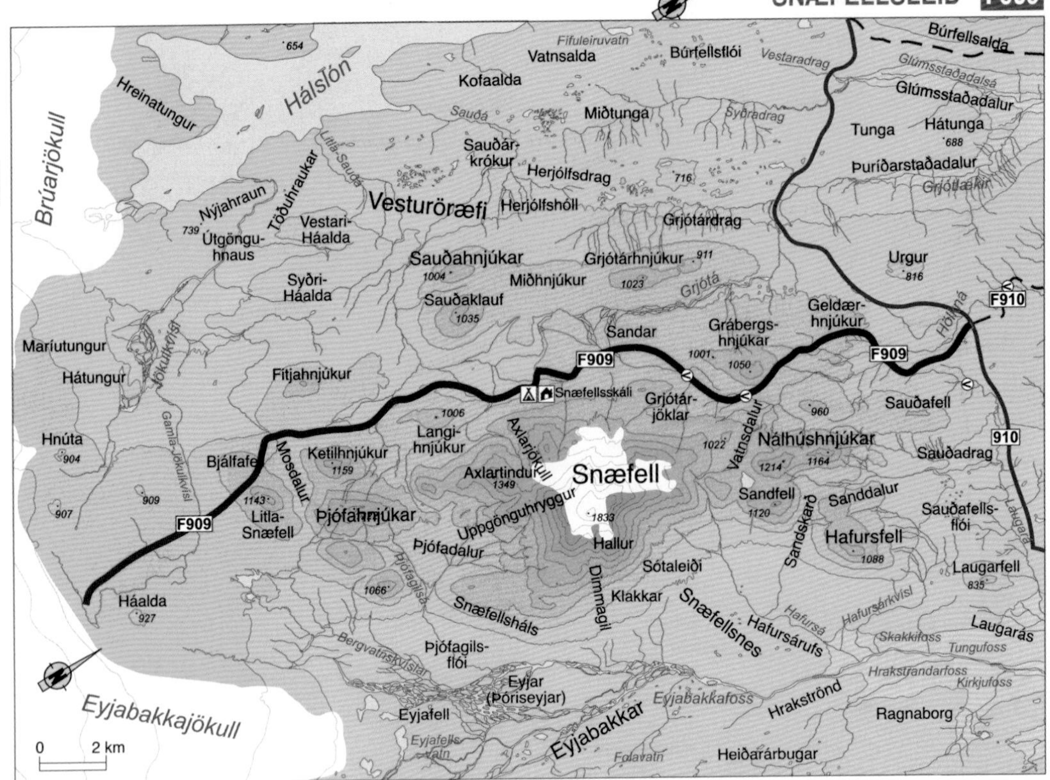

F909 **Snæfellsleið** 13,7 km. Passable for small jeep though some small creeks need to be passed on the way to the hut by the mountain Snæfell. The route continues for 18,2 km south of the hut towards Maríutungur on the east side of Brúarjökull.

Snæfell, (1,833 m) the highest mountain in Iceland outside the ice-caps. It is a conical central volcano, quite severely weathered by wind and glaciers. It is not clear when it last erupted, since neither lava nor ash-layers can clearly be identified with it. The first person known to attempt to climb the mountain was Sveinn Pálsson in 1794, but it was Guðmundur Snorrason from Bessastaðagerði in Fljótsdalur who first succeeded in conquering it in 1877. To the east of Snæfell the Eyjabakkajökull glacier stretches down onto Eyjabakkar, a marshy area of luxuriant vegetation at a height of 650-680 m soon to becoma a Ramsar-site. Important grazing and calving areas of the reindeer in the east are around Snæfell. Large herds can often be seen in Vesturöræfi, between Snæfell and Hálsalón. The animals are also spread around the highland west north and east of Snæfell and can sometimes be seen in the lowland in late winter. In the first half of the 20th century the reindeer mostly lived in the highland west of Snæfell, in Vesturöræfi and Kringilsárrani, but part of this area was covered by the surging glacier Brúarjökull in 1964. Reindeer have been imported to Iceland from Finnmark in Norway four times. In 1771 they were installed first in the Westman Islands and then in the Rangárvallasýsla county, but they became entirely extinct in the "Móðuharðindin" ("The hardship of the mist") of 1783-4. In 1777 they were imported to Hafnarfjörður near Reykjavík. These animals were the start of the Reykjanes stock which at one time was numbered in the hundreds but died out entirely before 1930. Reindeer that were released on Vaðlaheiði opposite Akureyri in 1784 became the stock of Þingeyjarsýsla county. It grew to more then thousand animals in the mid-19th century but the last of them disappeared in 1936. Finally, reindeer were put ashore in Vopnafjörður in 1787. They lived mostly on the moors from Möðrudalur south to Lón and probably numbered few thousand in the mid-19th century, but a period of hard weather towards the end of the century reduced their numbers there as elsewhere. By 1940 there were only a few hundred left, the only reindeer in Iceland. Since then their numbers have greatly increased, the population was estimated to be over 54.000 animals during the summer of 2012. They can now be found on moors and mountains from Jökulsá á Fjöllum south to Jökulsá á Breiðamerkursandi. Reindeer that stay close to farms and villages during late winter can cause damage to trees, fences and forestry projects. In later years hunting permits have been given for up to 1200 reindeer each year.

Brúarjökull, the biggest glacier coming from Vatnajökull.

F910 **Austurleið,** p. 488-491

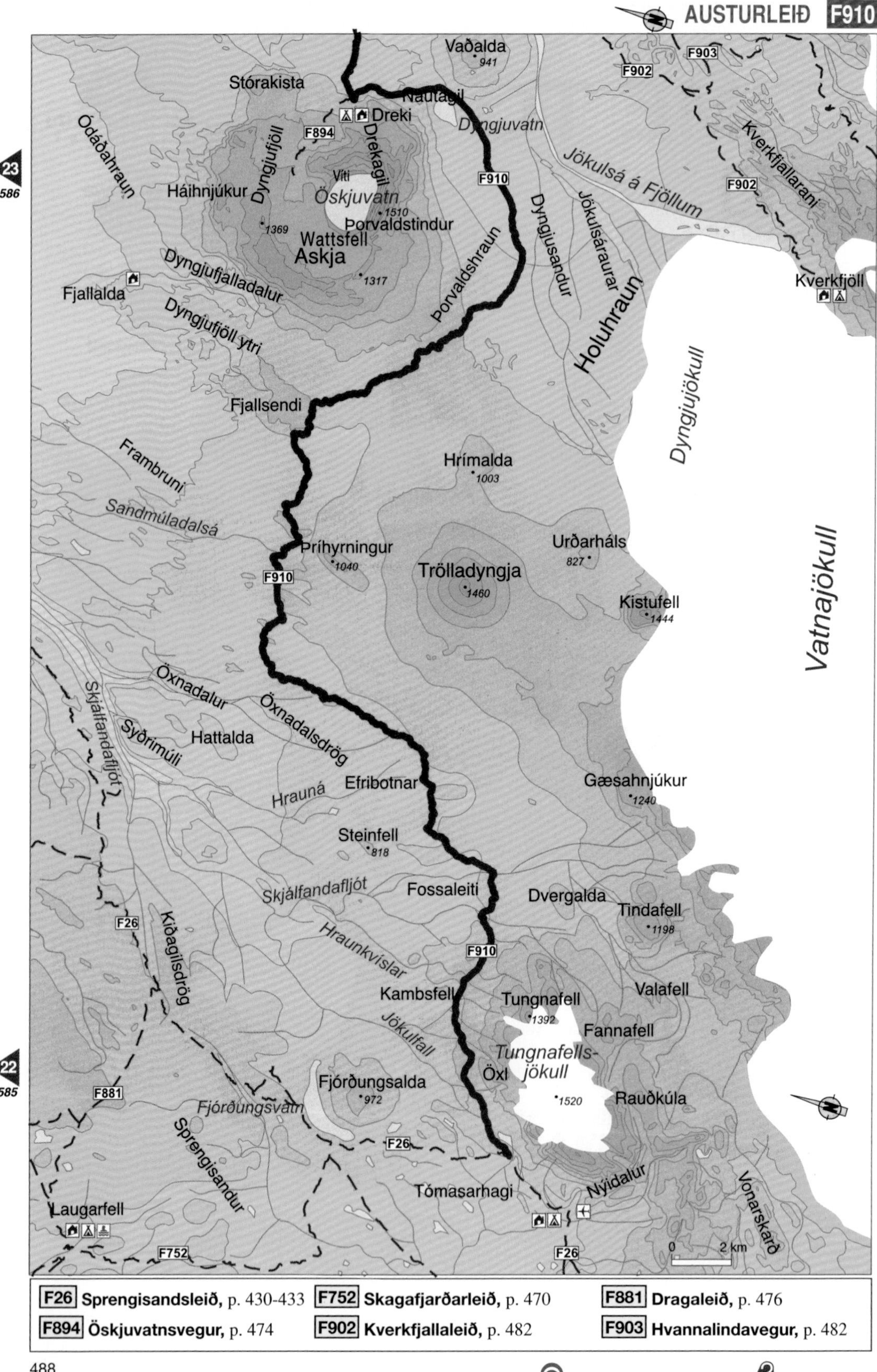

F26 Sprengisandsleið, p. 430-433	**F752 Skagafjarðarleið,** p. 470	**F881 Dragaleið,** p. 476
F894 Öskjuvatnsvegur, p. 474	**F902 Kverkfjallaleið,** p. 482	**F903 Hvannalindavegur,** p. 482

Hvannadalshnjúkur

F910 **Austurleið (Trölladyngjuleið)** 119,2 km. A difficult and a slow route. **Due to volcanic eruption which was in Holuhraun this road might be temporary closed.**

Tungnafell, (1,392 m) a mountain north of Tungnafellsjökull. The glacier is named for the mountain.

Jökulfall, one of the source tributaries of the river Skjálfandafljót, coming from Tungnafellsjökull.

Skjálfandafljót, one of largest rivers in the north, falling into the Skjálfandaflói bay. 178 km long and with a drainage area of 3,860 km^2. The bridge there was built in 1986.

Marteinsflæða, an area of vegetation named for Marteinn Þorgrímsson of Lake Mývatn who walked to there in the early 19th century, a considerable feat at that time.

Jökuldælaflæða, an area of vegetation found by men from the Jökuldalur valley in 1834.

Surtluflæða, ("Black ewe marshes") an area of rivers and vegetation discovered in 1880 and named for black shreds of wool found there.

Trölladyngja, (1,459 m) the greatest shield volcano in Iceland, about 10 km in diameter and rising 500-600 m above the surrounding area. The crater is 1,200-1,500 m long, 500 m wide and 100 m deep. Lavaflows are thought to have run down the Bárðardalur valley.

Þríhyrningur, (1,044 m) a prominent tuff crest north of the mountain Trölladyngja.

Ódáðahraun, ("Ill deeds lava field") the largest lava field in Iceland, bounded by Vatnajökull to the south, Skjálfandafljót to the west and Jökulsá á Fjöllum to the east. Its northern boundary is not so clear, but usually considered to be Highway 1 in the Lake Mývatn district. A desert with lava, sands, lot of mountains, cliffs, etc. Hardly any running water is found there, though there is some on the eastern and western edges. This area was unexplored and thus mysterious, giving rise to tales of extensive outlaw settlements. Organized travel and exploration was first begun in the early 19th century.

Holuhraun, ("Pitted lava") a large, sandy lava field north of Vatnajökull. Named in 1884 by Þorvaldur Thoroddsen the geologist. Towards the end of August 2014, an eruption occorred in Holuhraun and lasted for about six months.

Svartá, a 5 km long clear river running into Jökulsá á Fjöllum. In it is the waterfall Skínandi. It has a consistent flow of 20 m^3/sec. At the confluence it is, in winter, twice the size of the glacial river, though the latter is much the larger in the summer.

Vaðalda, (941 m) an old shield mountain on the west bank of the river Jökulsá, rising about 250 m above the surroundings.

Dyngjuvatn, a shallow lake. Can reach a length of 6 km during spring thaw but is much smaller later in the summer.

Gæsavatnaleið 59,1 km. A very difficult route and it is not advisable to go on one car.

Gæsavötn, ("Goose lakes") two shallow lakes 920-940 m above sea level. Named by two men who saw geese on the lake in 1880. Ruins of huts nearby but their origin unknown.

Kistufell, (1,446 m) a tuff mountain in northern Vatnajökull. In 1950 an Icelandic aircraft (Geysir) crash-landed on Bárðarbunga in Vatnajökull and the (successful) rescue operation had its headquarters near Kistufell. The crew was saved 6 days after the crash.

Dyngjuháls, (1,000-1,100 m) a volcanic ridge just north of Vatnajökull. Along the length of it run five parallel rows of craters from which both large and small lava flows have run to the north and west.

Vatnajökull, the largest glacier in Iceland and Europe, over 8000 km^2, its highest point being **Bárðarbunga** (2000 m). The highest point in Iceland is **Hvannadalshnjúkur** (2110 m) on the **Öræfajökull** glacier. The biggest glacier coming from Vatnajökull is Brúarjökull. Vatnajökull has been a National Park since 2008.

Urðarháls, (1,025 m) a glaciated, dolerite volcano, its crater about 1,100 m long, 800 m wide and 100 m at its deepest.

Dyngjujökull, one of Iceland's biggest outlet glaciers. Late on warm summer days melt water comes roaring off the glacier creating huge rivers that flow all over the sands east of the volcano Urðarháls. These are called **Síðdegisflæður** ("Evening morasses") and are very dangerous for all motor vehicles.

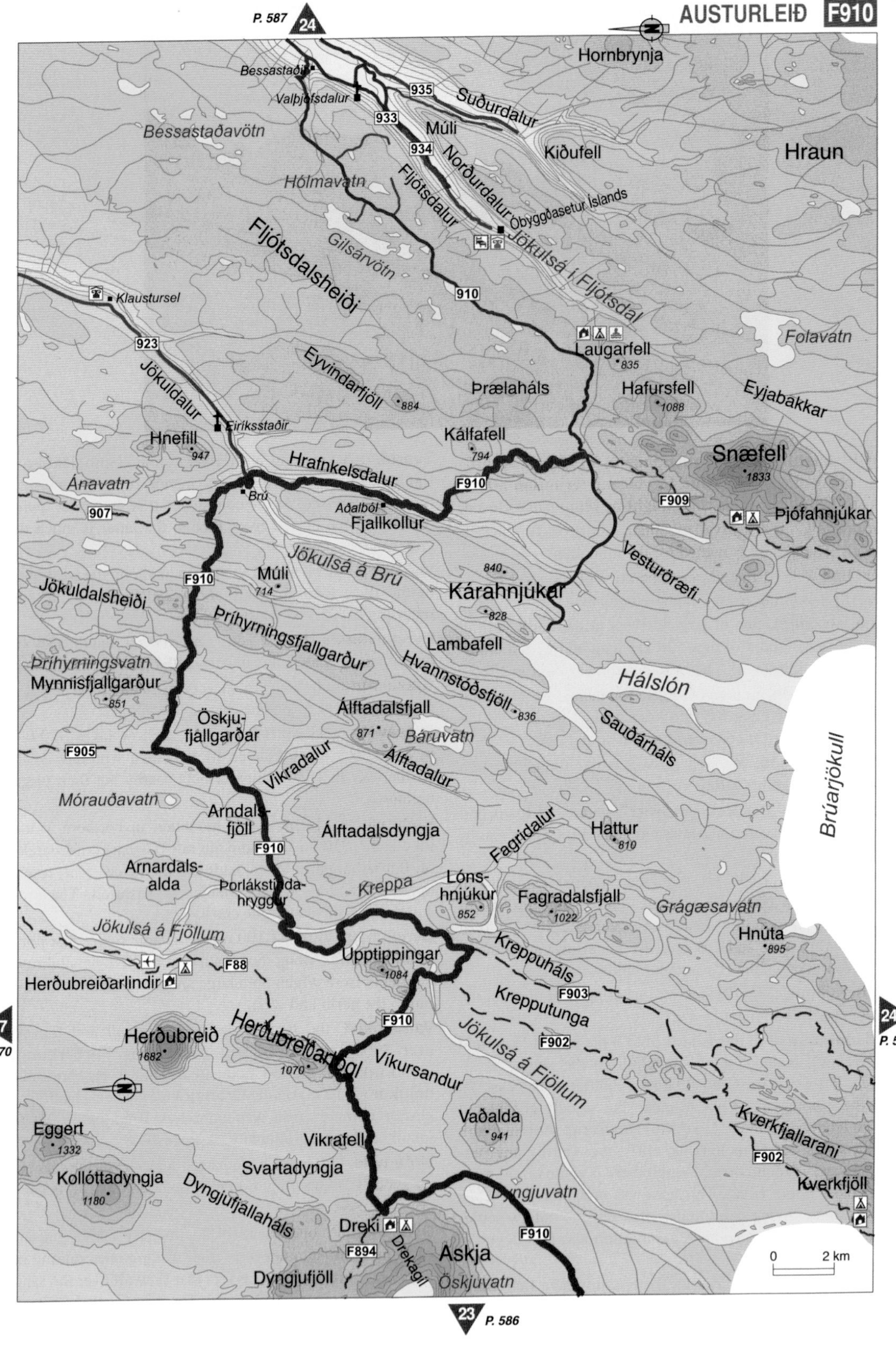
P. 587
24
Hornbrynja
Bessastaðir
Valþjófsdalur
935
Suðurdalur
933
Múli
934
Bessastaðavötn
Kiðufell
Hraun
Norðurdalur
Hólmavatn
Fljótsdalur
Óbyggðasetur Íslands
Fljótsdalsheiði
Gilsárvötn
Jökulsá í Fljótsdal
910
Klaustursel
Folavatn
Laugarfell
835
923
Eyvindarfjöll
884
Þrælahals
Hafursfell
1088
Eyjabakkar
Jökuldalur
Eiríksstaðir
Hnefill
947
Kálfafell
794
Snæfell
1833
Hrafnkelsdalur
Ánavatn
F910
Brú
Aðalból
Fjallkollur
F909
907
Þjófahnjúkar
Jökulsá á Brú
840
Vesturöræfi
F910
Múli
714
Kárahnjúkar
Jökuldalsheiði
828
Þríhyrningsfjallgarður
Lambafell
Þríhyrningsvatn
Hvannstóðsfjöll
Hálslón
Mynnisfjallgarður
851
836
Álftadalsfjall
Öskju-
fjallgarðar
871
Báruvatn
Sauðárháls
F905
Álftadalur
Vikradalur
Brúarjökull
Mórauðavatn
Arndals-
fjöll
Álftadalsdyngja
Fagridalur
Hattur
810
F910
Arnardals-
alda
Lóns-
hnjúkur
Kreppa
Þorlákstinda-
hryggur
852
Fagradalsfjall
1022
Grágæsavatn
Jökulsá á Fjöllum
Hnúta
895
Upptippingar
1084
Kreppuháls
F88
Herðubreiðarlindir
F903
Krepputunga
7
P. 570
F910
24
Herðubreið
1682
Herðubreiðartögl
1070
F902
Víkursandur
Jökulsá á Fjöllum
Vaðalda
941
Eggert
1332
Vikrafell
Kverkfjallarani
Svartadyngja
F902
Kollóttadyngja
1180
Dyngjufjallaháls
Kverkfjöll
Dyngjuvatn
Dreki
F910
F894
Drekagil
Askja
0
2 km
Dyngjufjöll
Öskjuvatn
23
P. 586

F910 **Austurleið** 148 km (the east section).

Jökulsá á Fjöllum, the largest river in the north, falling into Öxarfjörður, 206 km long with a drainage basin of 7,380 km² (1,700 of which is under the glacier). Its lower reaches often called Jökulsá í Öxarfirði. Bridge at Upptyppingar, built 1986.

Upptyppingar, (1,084 and 987 m) two pyramid shaped tuff mountains west of Jökulsá, prominent landmarks. There is a bridge on Jökulsá south of Upptyppingar, built in 1986.

Herðubreiðartögl, (1059 m) an 8 km long tuff ridge to the south of Herðubreið, rising to 450 m above the plateau.

Kreppa, is the name of deep and wide glacial river that has its source in the west part of the glacier Brúarjökull and joining Jökulsá by Herðubreiðarlindir. In August 1999 there was a flood in the rivers Kreppa and Jökulsá á Fjöllum. This flood, believed to be the greatest in the area for almost a hundred years, caused extensive damage to vegetation at Herðubreiðarlindir, cleared a path for a new branch out of Kreppa, and remodelled the landscape in other ways. The swollen rivers breached the road at Grímsstaðir á Fjöllum and Öxarfjörður, and swept the bridge across the river Sandá in Öxarfjörður out to sea.

Hvanná, a river that runs through the Byttuskarð pass between the two mountain ranges Brattifjallgarður and Mynnisfjallgarður.

Fjallgarðar, a series of mountain ranges reaching more or less all the way from the glacier to Melrakkaslétta (see Road 85). The different ranges have different names, such as Öskjufjallgarður, Mynnisfjallgarður, Dimmifjallgarður etc.

Þríhyrningsdalur, a broad dale in between the Fjallgarðar ranges with flat sands and sparse vegetation. The lake Þríhyrningsvatn at its northern end.

Brúaröræfi, (500-700 m) the wilderness from Brú at Jökuldalur, south from Arnardalur to Brúarjökull, between Jökulsá á Fjöllum and Dal.

Fagradalsfjall, (1022 m) the largest mountain in the Brúaröræfi wilderness.

Krepputunga, the district between Jökulsá á Fjöllum and Kreppa, 50-60 km long.

Hrafnkelsdalur, a rather long, broad valley leading off Jökuldalur, quite grassy with birch bushes and some geothermal activity. Ruins of 20 ancient farmsteads have been found there. The road up out of the valley is steep and generally not dependable. The river Hölkná, which has to be forded, is often very swollen.

Fljótsdalsheiði, a broad area of moorland, mostly covered with vegetation, between Jökuldalur and Fljótsdalur. In ages past the main route from Fljótsdalur to Aðalból in Hrafnkelsdalur lay across. A track, only accessable for altered jeeps leads from Kelduá to a mountain hut by Geldingafell.

Eyvindarfjöll, the glacier is named for Eyvindur Bjarnason, whom Hrafnkell Freysgoði killed there. Eyvindur was the brother of Sámur from Leikskálar.

907 **Brúarvegur,** p. 99
923 **Jökuldalsvegur,** p. 424
933 **Fljótsdalsvegur,** p. 428
934 **Múlavegur,** p. 428
935 **Suðurdalsvegur,** p. 428
F88 **Öskjuleið,** p. 472-475
F894 **Öskjuvatnsvegur,** p. 474
F902 **Kverkfjallaleið,** p. 482-483
F903 **Hvannalindavegur,** p. 482-483
F905 **Arnardalsleið,** p. 484
F909 **Snæfellsleið,** p. 486

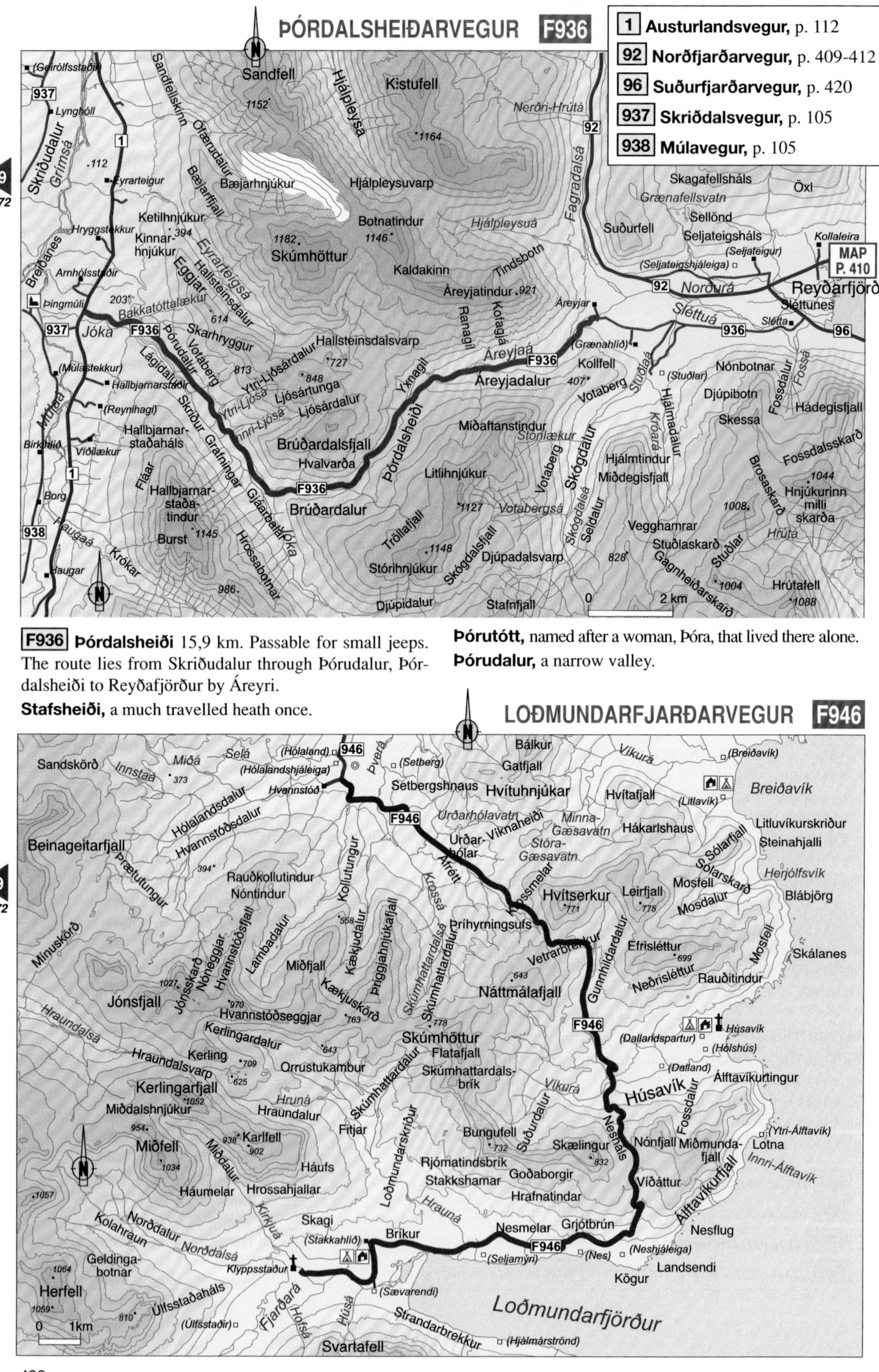

F936 Þórdalsheiði 15,9 km. Passable for small jeeps. The route lies from Skriðudalur through Þórudalur, Þórdalsheiði to Reyðafjörður by Áreyri.

Stafsheiði, a much travelled heath once.

Þórutótt, named after a woman, Þóra, that lived there alone.

Þórudalur, a narrow valley.

F946 **Loðmundafjörður,** 32,1 km. This route is only for experienced drivers on special jeeps.

Víknaslóðir is the name of the area from Héraðsflói to Seyðisfjörður. Amazing walking routes.

Hvítserkur, (774 m) a ignimbrite mountain northwest of Húsavík bay, with predominant white and pink colours, cut by dark basalt walls and streaks here and there. One of the most distinctive mountains in Iceland, often called Röndólfur ("The streaky one").

Breiðavík, a small and beautiful bay, reminiscent of Borgarfjörður. site of a lodge owned by the Touring Club of Fljótsdalur is located there.

Húsavíkurheiði, a pass over which it is possible to take the jeep-track to Húsavík in dry summer conditions, steep at the Húsavík end. Close to the cross roads to Loðmundarfjörður there is a clear profile of a face in the rock.

Húsavík, a little bay with a wide, short valley at its head. Formerly it had several farms, now all abandoned. The principal farm was Húsavík, a church. Part of the old churchyard has been broken off by the sea. A great variety of stones in the area. A mountain lodge owned by the travel agency of the district of Fljótsdalur is located there.

Álftavíkurtindur, (385 m) a peak well-known for its varied stones and for its spherulites. It is not readily accessible as only a narrow path leads there.

Nesháls, (435 m) a low ridge between Húsavík and Loðmundarfjörður, steep on both sides but with a jeep-track across it.

Skælingur, (832 m) a magnificent mountain with steep rock walls west from Nesháls. Visible from far out to sea. Seafarers call it "The Chinese Temple", the highest peak being reminiscent of a temple with a dome.

Loðmundarfjörður, a 7 km long fjord, rather deep. There is a wide, green valley, marshy in places, at its head, where there were once more than 10 farms, now all abandoned. The valley splits into two, Bárðarstaðadalur and Norðdalur, with the mountain **Herfell** (1,064 m) between them. The fjord is surrounded by a magnificent ring of mountains. An old riding path goes across Hjálmárdalsheiði moor to Seyðisfjörður. In Loðmundarfjörður there were once 10 farm, some of which were homes to two or three families. In 1860 the number of inhabitants was 143; by 1973 human habitation had ceased altogether. However, service is provided to tourists in Stakkahlíð in summer.

Nes, an abandoned farm on the north side of Loðmundarfjörður.

Karlfell, (926 m) an impressive rocky mountain, regular in shape and outstanding among the mountains of Loðmundarfjörður.

Stakkahlíð, formerly a manor farm, the largest in Loðmundarfjörður, abandoned in 1967. The farm buildings are well preserved. The view from there is very good. East of Stakkahlíð is **Stakkahlíðarhraun**, rhyolite screes from the mountain Flatafjall, rough in places. There were once plans to mine and export perlite from the screes. It is not quite clear how Stakkahlíðarhraun was formed and geologists do not agree on the subject. Jeep-tracks up to the screes. Close to the scree is Orrustukambur ("Battle crest") where petrified wood is to be found. The largest petrified trees to have been preserved in Iceland are kept by the Iceland Forestry Service at Hallormsstaður and on private land in Seyðisfjörður.

Sævarendi, an abandoned farm on the south side of Fjarðará. The farmer of Sævarendi was the last person to leave the district (1973).

Klyppsstaður, a farm and a church, formerly a parsonage, now deserted. Though the farm buildings have fallen, the church is still standing as are the crosses in the churchyard. Near the farm is the river **Kirkjuá** with a nice little waterfall. The river often flooded, causing serious damage to the farmlands. In 2009 a hut was built at Stakkahlíð.

946 **Hólalandsvegur,** p. 417

9
P. 572

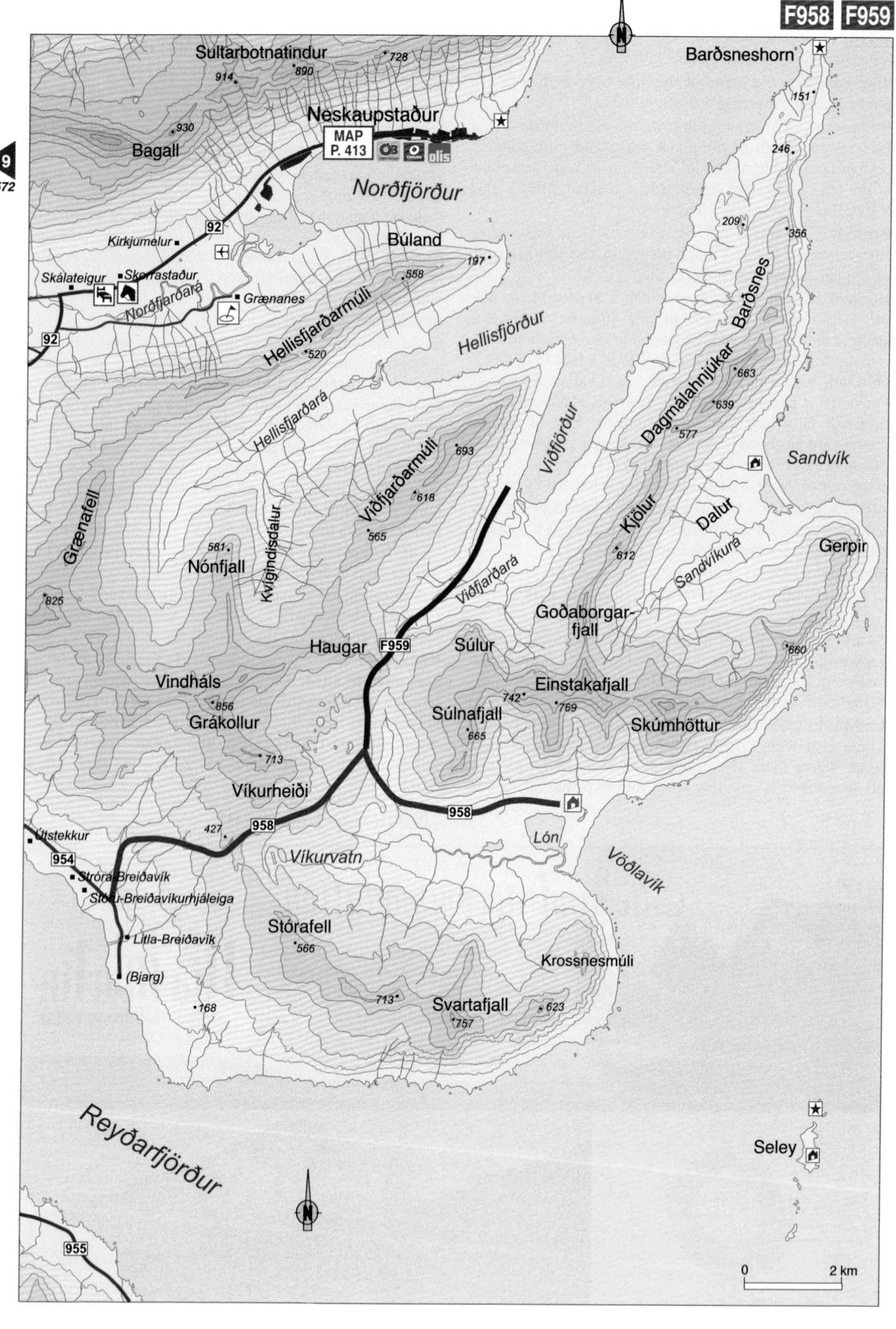
Sultarbotnatindur
728
890
914
Neskaupstaður
MAP
P. 413
olís
930
Bagall
Norðfjörður
Barðsneshorn
151
246
92
Kirkjumelur
Búland
197
209
356
Skálateigur
Skorrastaður
558
Norðfjarðará
Grænanes
Hellisfjarðarmúli
Hellisfjörður
Barðsnes
520
Dagmálahnjúkar
663
639
577
Hellisfjarðará
Viðfjörður
693
Viðfjarðarmúli
Sandvík
618
Grænafell
565
Kvígindisdalur
Kjölur
Dalur
581
Nónfjall
612
Sandvíkurá
Gerpir
Viðfjarðará
825
Goðaborgar-
fjall
Haugar
F959
Súlur
660
Vindháls
Einstakafjall
742
769
856
Grákollur
Súlnafjall
Skúmhöttur
665
713
Víkurheiði
958
Lón
427
Útstekkur
954
Víkurvatn
Vöðlavík
Stóra-Breiðavík
Stóru-Breiðavíkurhjáleiga
Stórafell
566
Litla-Breiðavík
Krossnesmúli
(Bjarg)
713
Svartafjall
623
168
757
Reyðarfjörður
Seley
955
0
2 km

Barðsneshorn, or Horn, is the outermost point of the highland peninsula Barðsnes. It falls very steeply to the sea, with many sheer cliffs. It and the mountain above it are of rhyolite and are steeply canted to the west. This appears to be the western side of a volcano which has mostly been worn away by the sea. On the west of the peninsula the rhyolite shows itself in **Rauðubjörg** ("Red cliffs"), which are multicoloured with a reddish gold cast and can be seen from Neskaupstaður. Down near sea level there are carbonated tree trunks 1-3 feet in diameter. These are considered to be the oldest vegetable remains in Iceland, probably about 15 million years old. There are many birds on Barðsnes and a spectacular view. The five farms that once were there have all been abandoned.

Norðfjarðarflói, devides into 3 fjords, **Norðfjörður**, Hellisfjörður and Viðfjörður.

Hellisfjörður, a fjord out of the Norðfjörður bay, with headlands Viðfjarðarmúli (689m) to the south and Hellisfjarðarmúli (558 m) to the north.

Viðfjörður, a fjord stretching south from the Norðfjörður bay where there was a farm of the same name, abandoned since 1955. The same family had lived there since 1750. The farm was said to have been haunted for centuries, the second quarter of the 20th century seeing particularly frequent and violent supernatural activity. Some blame these ghosts for the death by drowning of three brothers in 1936. The author Þórbergur Þórðarson (1889-1974) wrote about these ghosts in *Viðfjarðarundrin* ("The Viðfjörður wonders").

F959 **Viðarfjarðarvegur,** 8,6 km. Only for jeeps.

Sandvík, a bay to the north of the mountain **Gerpir**, the easternmost point of Iceland. Home of the ghost Sandvíkur-Glæsir ("The Sandvík dandy"), who wore a tie and tails and courteously took off his head in greeting.

F958 **Vaðlavíkurvegur,** 12,6 km from road 954. Passible by jeep.

Vöðlavík, a bay where there were two serious accidents. The boat *Bergvík* from the Westman Islands stranded in December 1993 and in January 1994 the salvage vessel *Goðinn* went down while attempting to tow the *Bergvík* away. One member of the crew of the *Goðinn* was lost, but the others were saved in a difficult and daring rescue operation performed by US helicopter crews from the Keflavík naval base.

92 **Norðfjarðarvegur,** p. 409-412 **954** **Helgustaðavegur,** p. 412 **955** **Vattarnesvegur,** p. 420

24 P. 587

10 P. 573

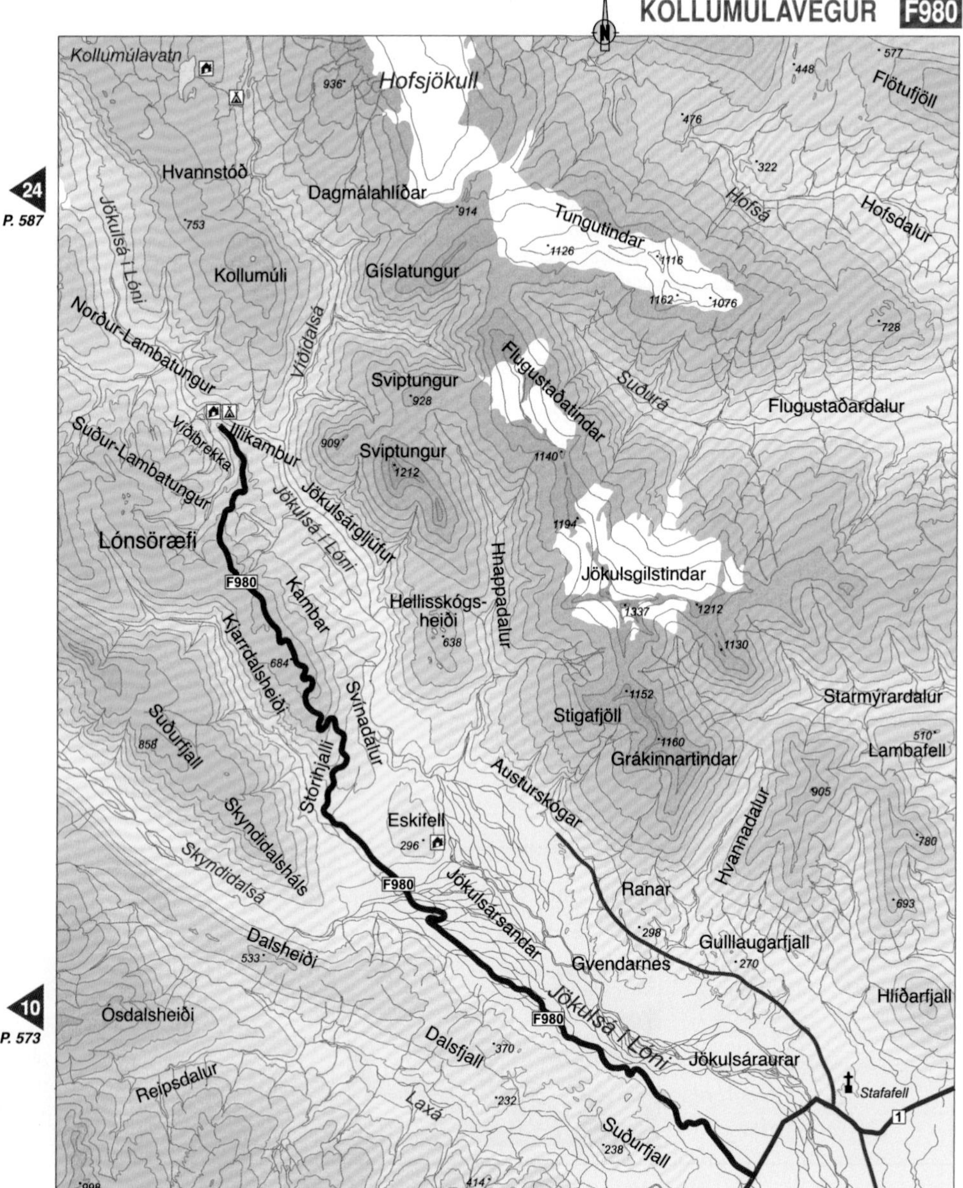

F980 Kollumúlavegur, 24,5 km off the main road by Þórisdalur in Lón to Illikambur. Only for large jeeps, traveling in tandem. **Skyndidalsá** a glacial river, a dangerous obstacle in rainy weather or when sun melts the glaciers. The river bed is soggy and treacherous. Dangerous to cross. Beyond the river is a jeep-track alongside Eskifell and up onto Illikambur by Kollumúli.

Jökulsá í Lóni, a sizeable glacial river having its source in the eastern part of Vatnajökull and flowing along Lón to the sea. Sometimes it flows along canyons, but towards the middle of the Lón district it spreads out along mud flats. A difficult river to ford.

Lónsöræfi, ("The Wilderness Lagoon") a broad unbuilt area east of Vatnajökull. In recent years it has become increasingly popular to walk in this area, huts have been put up and footbridges built on the most difficult rivers. Before the "mini-ice age" of 1600-1900 people travelling between different parts of Iceland often crossed Lónsöræfi, for instance from Þingeyjarsýsla county in the north to Hornafjörður in the southeast. This may explain why both the rivers Jökulsá í Lóni and Víðidalsá have fords called Norðlingavað ("Northerners' ford"). Lónsöræfi is rugged and dramatic countryside, very colourful. The central volcano piled its lava on top of that from the Álftafjarðar volcano by the Þvottá river. The mountains have numerous needles and pinnacles and are scored by canyons, so it is vital to follow designated walking routes carefully. To the north of Lónsöræfi is Hraun, a rocky moorland area of frequent fogs and snows, reaching north to Fljótsdalur. Apart from the glaciers, no place in Iceland has more precipitation. When it rains, rivers in the area can become unpassable torrents without warning.

1 **Austurlandsvegur,** p. 112

12 P. 575

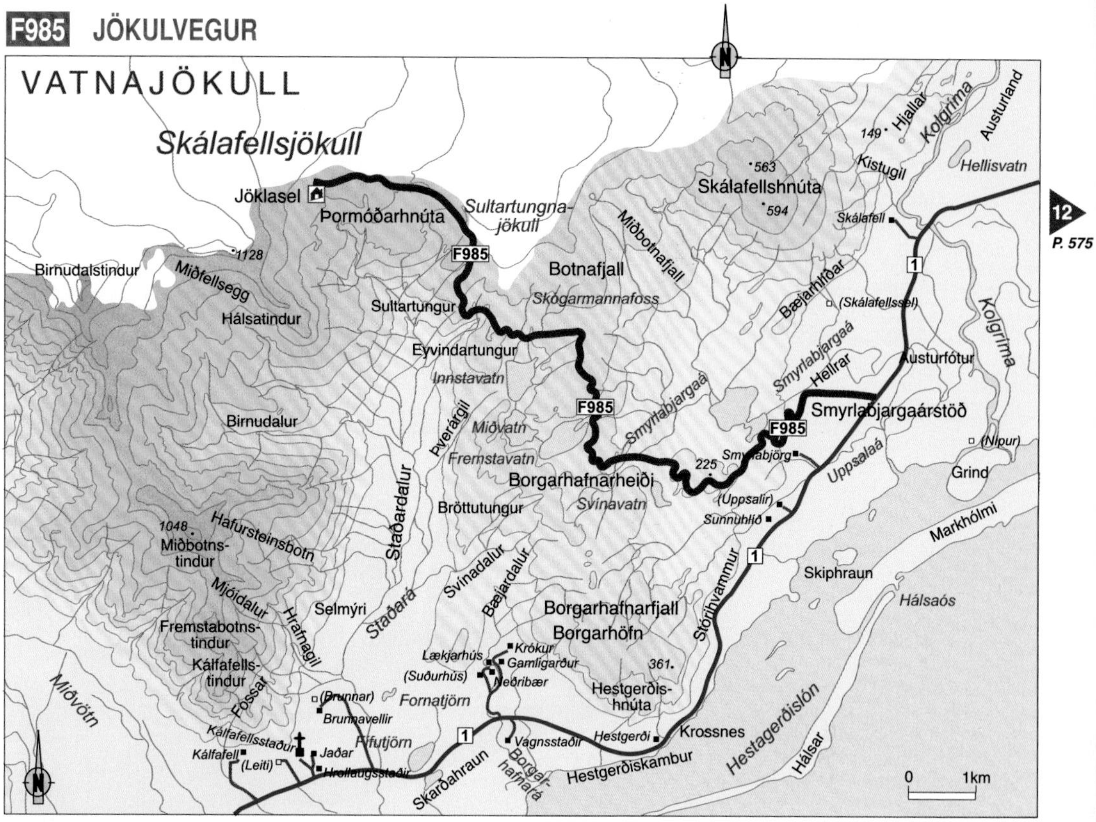

F985 Jökulvegur, 16,3 km, Passable by all jeeps, also small jeeps. Steep hills.

Birnudalstindur, (1,326 m) at the edge of the glacier, one of the highest mountains in the region.

Jöklasel, a centre of glacial activities and a restaurant. The view from Jöklasel is absolutely breathtaking.

1 Austurlandsvegur, p. 116

THE CAPITAL AREA
Reykjavík / Seltjarnarnes / Mosfellsbær
Kópavogur / Garðabær / Hafnarfjörður
© David Varga

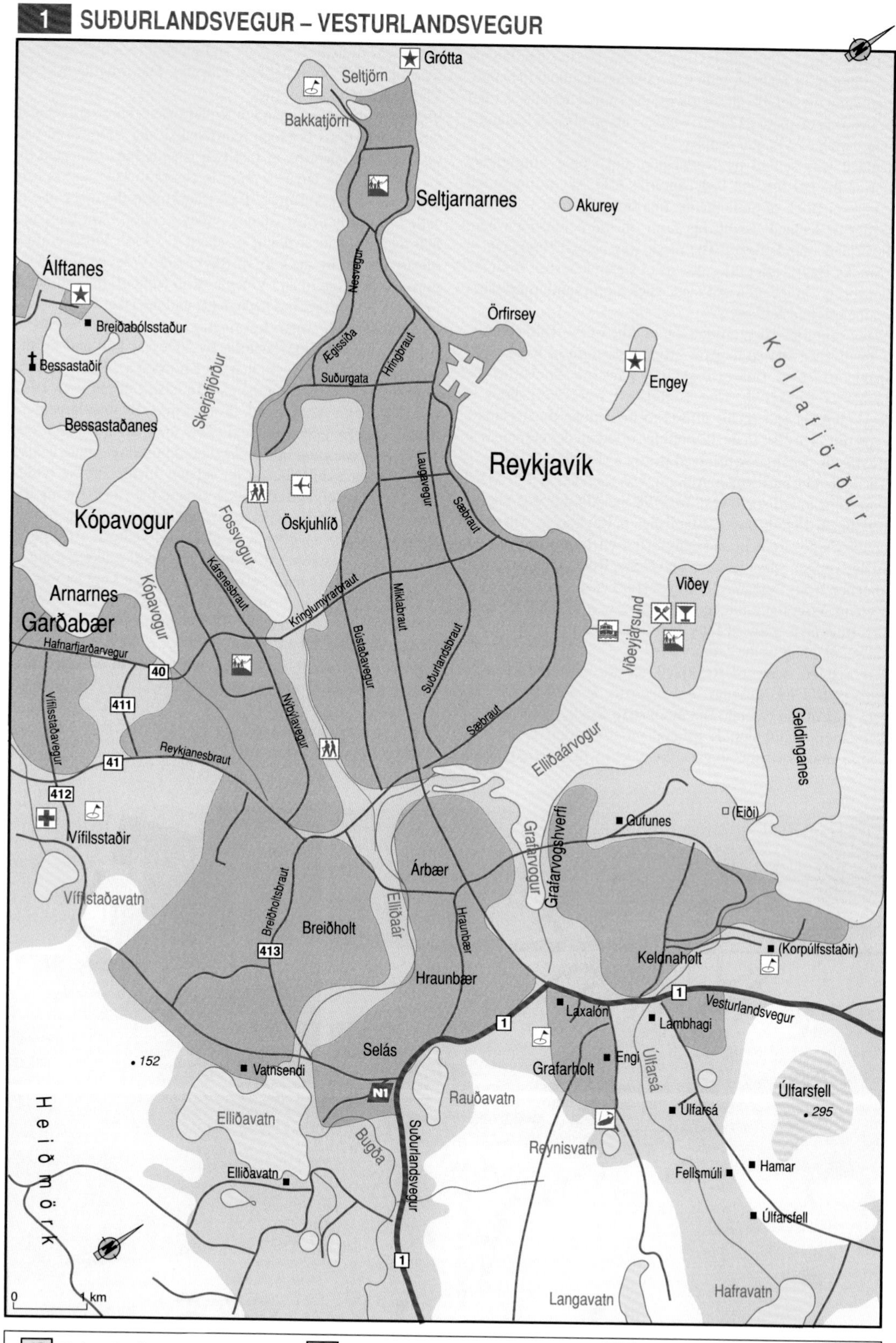

40 **Hafnarfjarðarvegur,** p. 202
41 **Reykjanesbraut,** p. 204-209
411 **Arnarnesvegur,** p. 204
412 **Vífilsstaðavegur,** p. 205
413 **Breiðholtsbraut,** p. 203

Reykjavík, is the nations capital and by far the largest community in Iceland, with a population of about 200,000. Including the neighbouring towns, the capital area has a total population of about 212,000, which is about 60% of Iceland's population of 338,000 people.

Iceland was settled by Norwegian and Celtic immigrants during the late 9th and 10th centuries A.D. According to the medieval Book of Settlements, Ingólfur Arnarson – the first settler of Iceland – built his farm on the peninsula where Reykjavík stands today. The place was named Reykjavík – "Smoky Bay" - after the columns of steam that rose from the hot springs in the area and made such a profound impression on the original settlers.

Many centuries later, around the middle of the 18th century, a small town started to grow around the farm of Reykjavík, thanks to Royal Treasurer Skúli Magnússon, known as the Father of Reykjavík, who established wool workshops at Reykjavík as part of his efforts to modernise the Icelandic economy. This led to the beginnings of urban development at Reykjavík. Reykjavík received its town charter in 1786.

The Icelandic parliament, Alþingi, was founded in 930 AD at Þingvellir in the southwest. In 1798 the Alþingi was abolished, but in 1845 it was re-established in Reykjavík, where the country's government and administration were now located. In due course, when Iceland won Home Rule and then independence from Danish rule, Reykjavík became the capital of Iceland. With the rapid economic progress of the 20th century, Reykjavík grew steadily, but developed especially fast in the second half of the century.

For a living view of Reykjavík's past, visit the open-air Reykjavík City Museum- Árbæjarsafn, located in the eastern part of the capital. The innovative Reykjavík 871 +/- 2 Settlement Exhibition is located on Aðalstræti in the city centre, allows visitors to view the recently discovered, oldest settlement ruins in Reykjavík and Iceland (possibly those of Ingólfur Arnarson or his descendents), featuring an original Viking age longhouse.

Viðey, is the largest island in Kollafjörður. There are regular ferry connections between Skarfabakki and Viðey. You can say that that island is in fact two islands but connected by an isthmus. The larger section is closer to land and is called Heimaey or Austurey (East island), but the other one is called Vesturey (West island). Viðey is only 3 km long and 800 m at its widest point, or about 1,5 km^2. Viðey is now mostly owned by the City of Reykjavík. Viðeyjarstofa, Viðeyjarkirkja (church) and Viðeyjarskóli (school) have all been restored. A new pier has been made and the island has electricity and running water. Information signs are by the end of the pier, behind Viðeyjarstofa, by Viðeyjarskóli and by the foundations of the houses that once formed a village. Viðeyjarskóli, the school, is on the eastern island. It ran from 1912 till 1941, with 40 students in its prime. Renovations were made between 1989-1993 and today there are good facilities for various occasion in the old school building. There is also a interesting exhibition on the islands history in the building. There are organized walkes around the island during the summer time. There are marked walking paths, a playground for children and a barbeque available for visitors. At Viðeyjarstofa is a restaurant. At Vesturey is a good walking route to the artwork of Richard Serra called Áfangi. On October 9th 2007 the light artwork of Yoko Ono, Imagine Peace Tower, was light for the first time. She dedicated the work to her husband's memory, John Lennon. Every year the Peace Tower is light on John Lennons birthday and turned of on December 8th, the anniversary of his death.

For further information and schedules go to:
www.elding.is or **www.videy.com**

Experience the history of Reykjavík in a lively and engaging way at the Reykjavík City Museum. Comprising five individual sites, the City Museum was founded to uphold and preserve Reykjavík's cultural heritage, which dates back to the arrival of the first settlers in the late 9th century.

Four of the museums are within walking distance of downtown Reykjavík, while the Árbær Open Air Museum is only a fifteen-minute-drive from the city center. The ferry to Viðey Island leaves from the Old Harbor in downtown Reykjavík.

Árbær Open Air Museum

This unique museum was founded in 1957 in order to give visitors a tangible sense of Reykjavík's past. It comprises a village-like collection of over twenty "homes," each of which is a separate exhibition. Visitors learn how Reykjavík developed from a few scattered farms into the capital of Iceland. During the summer months, staff wear period costumes, and domestic animals bite fresh grass around the site, but whatever time of the year you visit you will find plenty to whet your interest.

Opening hours:
June – August, daily 10:00 – 17:00
September – May, daily guided tours only at 13:00

Location:
Kistuhylur, 110 Reykjavík

Reykjavík Maritime Museum

Fishing has always played a major role in Iceland's history. However, before the superbly equipped modern trawlers appeared, ordinary farmer-fishermen regularly risked their lives in order to feed their families. See the craft and tools they used through the ages in this beautifully appointed maritime museum. Special attraction: the Coast Guard vessel Óðinn. Welcome aboard!

Opening hours:
Daily 10:00–17:00
Daily guided tours of the Vessel Óðinn at: 13, 14 and 15

Location:
Grandagarður 8, 101 Reykjavík

The Settlement Exhibition

Learn about Iceland's first settlers at The Settlement Exhibition, where multimedia technology takes you back to the Viking Age. The centerpiece of the exhibition is

an open excavation that houses the oldest remains of human habitation that have been found in Reykjavík, dating all the way back to the 9th century.

Settlement Sagas comprises some of the nation's most renowned documents, many of them written in the twelfth century but relating events that go back as far as 874 AD, when the first settlers are said to have come to Iceland. Recognised by the International World Heritage Programme as having outstanding cultural value, the documents on display include Landnámabók (the Book of the Settlement), Íslendingabók, Kjalnesingasaga, Jónsbók and the Bill of Purchase for Reykjavík (1615).

Opening hours for both exhibitions:
Daily 09:00 – 20:00

Location:
Aðalstræti 16 - 101 Reykjavík

Viðey Island

Viðey Island is situated just off the coast of Reykjavík. In addition to beautiful natural surroundings, ancient ruins and rich historical background, you can also see the "Imagine Peace Tower" by Yoko Ono and the Milestones project by Richard Serra. The island is also the nesting ground for over 30 species of birds.

Summer: Daily ferries from: Old harbor, Ægisgarður harbor and Skarfabakki harbor.
Winter: ferries only on Saturdays and Sunday from Skarfabakki.
See ferry schedule at www.videy.com

Reykjavík Museum of Photography

Visit exciting photographic exhibitions that focus on the capital's rich history and contemporary culture. The museum is a repository for nearly 5 million photographs taken by amateurs and professionals between 1870-2002. Around thirty thousand of these photographs are available on the museum's online gallery.

Opening hours:
Mondays – Thursdays 12:00 – 19:00
Friday 12:00 – 18:00, Weekends 13:00 – 17:00

Location:
Tryggvagata 15 (top floor), 101 Reykjavík

Free admission

1. **Ráðhúsið, Reykjavík City Hall,** is at the north-western corner of the lake Tjörnin on the corner of Tjarnargata and Vonarstræti. The building was designed by Margrét Harðardóttir and Steve Christer. Offices and meeting rooms are situated on the upper stories while the ground floor, which is open to the public from 8-17 on weekdays and 12-18 on weekends, is devoted to cultural activities of various kinds. In the main hall there is a huge three-dimensional map of Iceland.
2. **Aðalstræti,** ("Main Street") is Reykjavík's oldest street. Ingólfur Arnarson's farm is generally considered to have been situated at the southern end of the street, which must then have been the path he walked along down to the sea. While Reykjavík was small, Aðalstræti was the main street, lined with the homes of influential people, the meeting house and the town's main well, Ingólfsbrunnur ("Ingólfur's well"), outside the present No. 9. One of the oldest buildings in Reykjavík built around 1762, is No. 10, which is from the time of Skúli Magnússon. The Settlement exhibition Reykjavik 871±2 is based on archaeological finds in Reykjavík, well-preserved ruins of a Viking-Age long house from the 10th century and objects and remains of human habitation believed to date from the 9th-century settlement of Reykjavík. The exhibition gives a clear picture of the people and their way of life at this time, and the visitor can view the ruins and the objects connected to them in addition to information in the form of texts, pictures and multimedia designed to provide an extra focus on specific aspects of the history. The Settlement Exhibition is open every day from 10-17 and is located in Reykjavík old centre, on the corner of Aðalstræti and Suðurgata. Regular guided tours around the exhibition.
3. **Tourist Information Centre** – Reykjavík's official Tourist Information Centre, located at Aðalstræti 2, has all you need for a great holiday. Free booking service, tourist information for all parts of Iceland, money exchange, VAT cash refund, maps and brochures, internet and IP phone centre, Reykjavík Welcome Card and friendly staff.
4. **Grjótaþorp,** ("Grjóti village") is the area between Aðalstræti, Túngata, Garðastræti and Vesturgata. It takes its name from the farm Grjóti, a tenant farm of the original farm, Reykjavík. The majority of the houses are from the late 18th century and the streets have not been reorganized, so the "village" has a distinct flavour of times past.
5. **Austurstræti,** ("East Street") originally a path along the north side of Austurvöllur Green from Aðalstræti to Lækurinn ("The brook"). About 1820 the path was paved with stones and an open drain built alongside it. The path was then called Langastétt ("The long pavement"), or, in Danish, Lange Fortoug. In 1848 when a number of streets in Reykjavík were given names, Langastétt was named Austurstræti in view of the direction it took from Aðalstræti.
6. **Hafnarstræti,** ("Harbour Street") lies east from the northern end of Aðalstræti, north of and parallel to Austurstræti. Originally it was a path along the shoreline from Lækjartorg Square to Vesturgata, but received its present name in 1848. The curve on the street followed the curve of the shoreline. The land north of the street today is all land-fill.
7. **Reykjavík Art Museum,** located between Tryggvagata and Geirsgata. The exhibition halls are located on two floors. It also has a multi-purpose space and an outdoor area in an enclosed courtyard. Its many galleries house the diverse exhibitions of contemporary art and is a permanent residence for the works of Erró. The museum has a shop, a library and restaurant. The Museum is open daily from 10-17. Thursday 10-22. Free entrance.
8. **Alþingishúsið, Parliament House,** built in 1880-81 to the design of the Danish architect F. Meldahl. Its walls are of basalt which was quarried and cut on the Skólavörðuholt hill east of the Tjörnin Lake. Parliament was first convened in Alþingishúsið on July 1st in 1881. Since then, all its meetings have been held there apart from ceremonial meetings held at Þingvellir.
9. **Reykjavík Harbour,** right up to 1900 ships coming to Reykjavík had been forced to anchor out in the bay, people and goods being ferried to and from land in rowboats. Small piers had been built behind the shops on Hafnarstræti and elsewhere to receive them. Harbour construction started in 1913 and went well, so the first ship was able to dock in Reykjavík in 1915. The material for the harbour was mostly from the hills Skólavörðuholt and Öskjuhlíð. A railway was built between Öskjuhlíð and the harbour, along which a steam engine pulled cars loaded with stone. Various boat tours are available from Reykjavík Marina, including whale watching and sea angling tours. There are also a number of good restaurants located near the marina.
10. **Dómkirkjan, the Cathedral.** When the bishopric was moved from Skálholt to Reykjavík the old church on Aðalstræti was not considered grand enough, so it was decided to build a new one. Work started in 1788 and the cathedral was consecrated in 1796. It contains a number of noteworthy objects, among them a carved marble font by Bertel Thorvaldsen which he gave to the church in 1839. Since it was re-established in 1845, the opening of Parliament has always started with a service in Dómkirkjan.
11. **Arnarhóll,** is the grassy hill between Kalkofnsvegur, Hverfisgata, Ingólfsstræti and the Central Bank of Iceland. The name is thought to come from Landnámabók ("The Book of Settlements") where Ingólfur's high-seat posts are said to have been found "by Arnarhvál below the heath". The statue of Ingólfur Arnarson was unveiled on Arnarhóll on February 24th 1924.
12. **The Culture House,** is a listed building and its use today takes into consideration the building's protected status and historical value. It is a unique venue for promoting Icelandic history and cultural heritage. Exhibitions in the Culture House emphasize in particular the history and culture of Iceland, the country's independence and governance, as well as its ancient and modern literature. In the building there are facilities for exhibitions, meetings, gatherings, lectures, artistic events, public ceremonies and other occasions. The Culture House restaurant and souvenir shop are located on the ground floor.
13. **Þjóðleikhúsið, The National Theatre,** is on Hverfisgata, east of Safnahúsið. Construction started in 1928 to a design by State Architect Guðjón Samúelsson. Inside the theatre the walls are decorated with works by Guðmundur Einarsson from Miðdalur and Ríkarður Jónsson, and there are numerous busts and portraits of people who have influenced Icelandic art and culture over the years.
14. **Lækjartorg,** ("Brook square") is opposite the Government house north of Austurstræti. It has been of importance in the life of Reykjavík from earliest times. Farmers bringing wares to market ended their journey there, and commonly camped on Lækjartorg while they completed their business in town.
15. **Stjórnarráðshúsið, Government House,** on Lækjargata opposite Lækjartorg, was originally built as a prison. Construction began in 1761 and was completed in 1771. When Governor E.C.L. Moltke came to Iceland in 1819 he obtained permission to move into the building and had it extensively renovated. After that it was the home and workplace of the Governor while that post existed. From 1873-1904 it was the residence of the Governor-General, after which it housed the government when a Home Rule Minister was appointed in Reykjavík. It now houses the offices of the Prime Minister. It was on the steps of this building that Iceland was declared a sovereign state on December 1st 1918. On the lawn are two statues by Einar Jónsson: one, put up in 1931, of Hannes Hafstein, the first Icelander to be Home Rule Minister, and the other, from 1915, of King Christian IX of Denmark giving Icelanders their constitution.
16. **Bernhöftstorfa,** the area between Lækjargata, Bankastræti, Amtmannsstígur and Skólagata, is named for T.D. Bernhöft who ran a bakery at Bankastræti 2. The buildings on Bernhöftstorfa, along with Stjórnarráðshúsið and Menntaskólinn í Reykjavík and Íþaka, form the oldest row of houses in Reykjavík.
17. **Menntaskólinn í Reykjavík, The Reykjavík Secondary Grammar School.** When the Bessastaðir School was moved to Reykjavík a site "east of Lækurinn" was selected. The building was designed by Danish State Architect Jörgen Hansen Koch, the building materials imported ready-cut from Norway. Construction began in 1844 and teaching in the building in 1846. The full name of the school was then "The Learned School in Reykjavík". South of the main building is the school's library, built in 1866 with money donated by the Englishman Charles Kelsall. It was later named Íþaka in honour of Daniel Willard Fiske of Ithaca, N.Y, who donated a great many books and journals to the library.

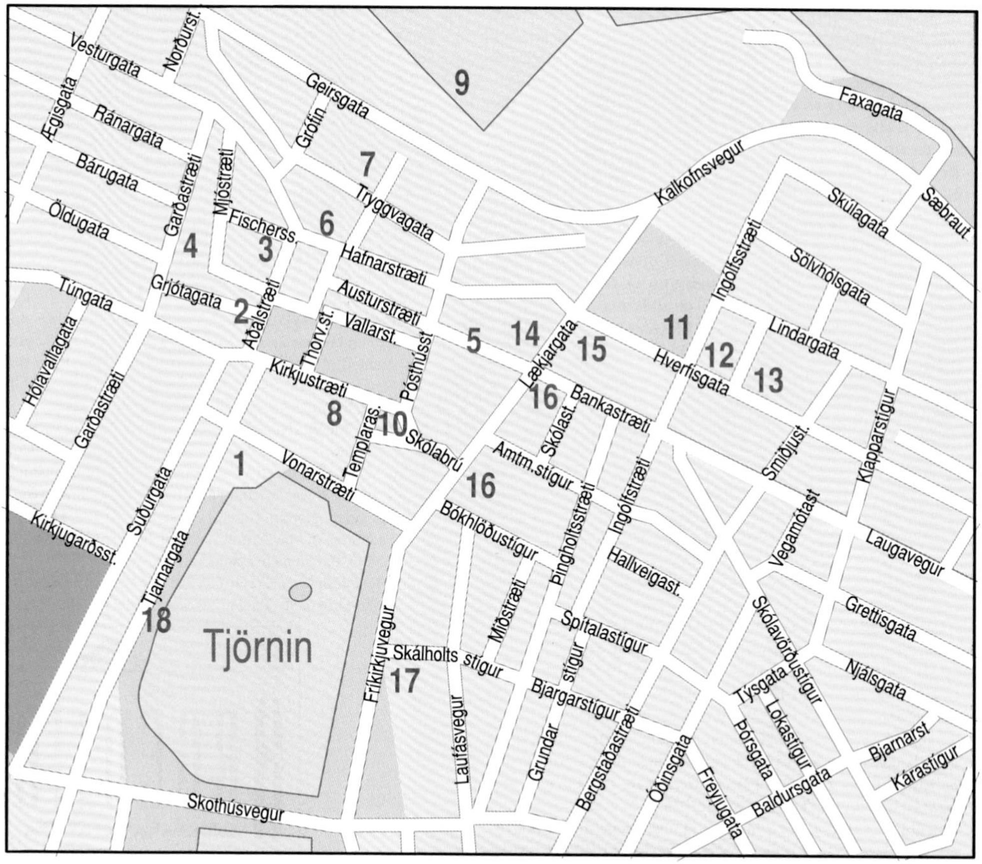

18. Tjarnargata, ("Pond Street") is the street along the western bank of the Tjörnin Lake. The northernmost end of it has a very long history indeed, since it is likely that it was a path from Ingólfur Arnarson's farm, Reykjavík, along the shore of Tjörnin to a well southwest of where the City Hall now stands. Most of the houses along the street, built of wood and clad with corrugated iron, are from just after the turn of the century. No. 32 is called Ráðherrabústaðurinn ("The Minister's Residence") and was originally built at Sólbakki in Önundarfjörður and belonged to a Norwegian, Hans Ellefsen. He is said to have either given it to Hannes Hafstein when he became Home Rule Minister in 1904 or sold it to him for 1 krona. It is now used by the Icelandic Government for official receptions.

19. **Suðurgata,** ("South Street") one of Reykjavík's oldest streets, runs from Túngata south to Skerjafjörður. There is a cemetery on Suðurgata. The cemetery for the church in Reykjavík appears to have originally been at the corner of Aðalstræti and Kirkjustræti, where there is now a little park, but by the early 19th century this was full. The area on Suðurgata was chosen as the new cemetery and the first burial there was in 1838. Many of the most influential Icelanders of the 19th and early 20th centuries are buried there.
20. **National and University Library of Iceland,** Arngrímsgata 3, combines the National Library (established 1918) and the University Library (established 1940) in one building which was opened on December 1st, 1994. In 1970 Parliament decided that a people´s library should be raised to commemorate the 1100th anniversary of the settlement of Iceland in 1974. Architect Manfreð Vilhjálmsson.
21. **Þjóðminjasafn Íslands, The National Museum.** On June 16th 1944 a meeting of both houses of Parliament agreed "to raise a building to house the National Museum and to start construction immediately." The building was completed and opened to the public in 1952, and has housed the museum ever since. The National Museum of Iceland is the country´s largest museum of cultural history and nurtures knowledge and innovation while maintaining a wide perspective and a sense of community. The museum's permanent exhibition, Making of a Nation – Heritage and History in Iceland is an exciting journey through time, presenting the nation's cultural history from settlement to present day. Special exhibitions feature highlights from the Museum's collections and archives, and are intended to shed light on particular subjects of cultural history as well as contemporary cultural issues.
22. **Háskóli Íslands, The University of Iceland.** Established in 1911 when three professional schools, the Theological School, the Law School and the Medical School, were combined. The main university building was built 1936-40 to the design of State Architect Guðjón Samúelsson. Sæmundur á selnum ("Sæmundur riding the seal"), a sculpture by Ásmundur Sveinsson, is on the lawn in front of the main building, and by the Geological Institute there is a memorial by Ríkarður Jónsson to the French scientist Dr. J.B. Charcot, who perished with the ship Pourqui pas? in 1936.
23. **Tjörnin,** ("The pond") is a lake in the centre of Reykjavík, originally formed by a lagoon inside the reef that used to be where Hafnarstræti now lies. There are two islets in Tjörnin. The one in the southern end is man-made and the one in the northern end, though natural, has been enlarged and turfed over to attract nesting birds. Bird-life is rich and varied on Tjörnin, especially in the spring. 40-50 kinds of birds spend some part of each year there, and 80 different kinds have been seen altogether.
24. **Listasafn Íslands, The National Art Gallery,** is at Fríkirkjuvegur 11. The building is from just before 1920, when it was an icehouse, called Herðubreið, which used ice taken from Tjörnin in the winter. In 1958 it was made into a night club, called Glaumbær. In 1971 there was a fire in Glaumbær which gutted it. After that the building was extended and renovated with an eye to its new role, and the National Art Gallery opened there in 1988.
25. **Sóleyjargata 1,** offices of the President of Iceland, Ólafur Ragnar Grímsson. Once home of the first president of Iceland, Sveinn Björnsson, and also, later, the home of Kristján Eldjárn, Iceland's third president.
26. **Hljómskálagarðurinn,** ("Bandstand Park") reaches from the southern end of the Tjörnin Lake to Hringbraut. In 1922 permission was granted to build the bandstand that still stands on the corner of Sóleyjargata and Skothúsvegur. It was to be, and still is, the headquarters of the Reykjavík City Band.
27. **Norræna húsið, Nordic House,** stands in Vatnsmýrin ("The water meadow"), east of the main University building. The Nordic Council decided in 1963 to build a Nordic cultural centre whose function was to strengthen the connection between Iceland and the other Nordic countries and to promote knowledge and understanding of the Nordic cultural heritage. The building was designed by the Finnish architect Alvar Aalto.
28. **Umferðarmiðstöðin,** ("Coach Terminal") at Vatnsmýrarvegur 10, houses the Bus Terminal (BSÍ). The Fly bus departs there to Keflavík International Airport.

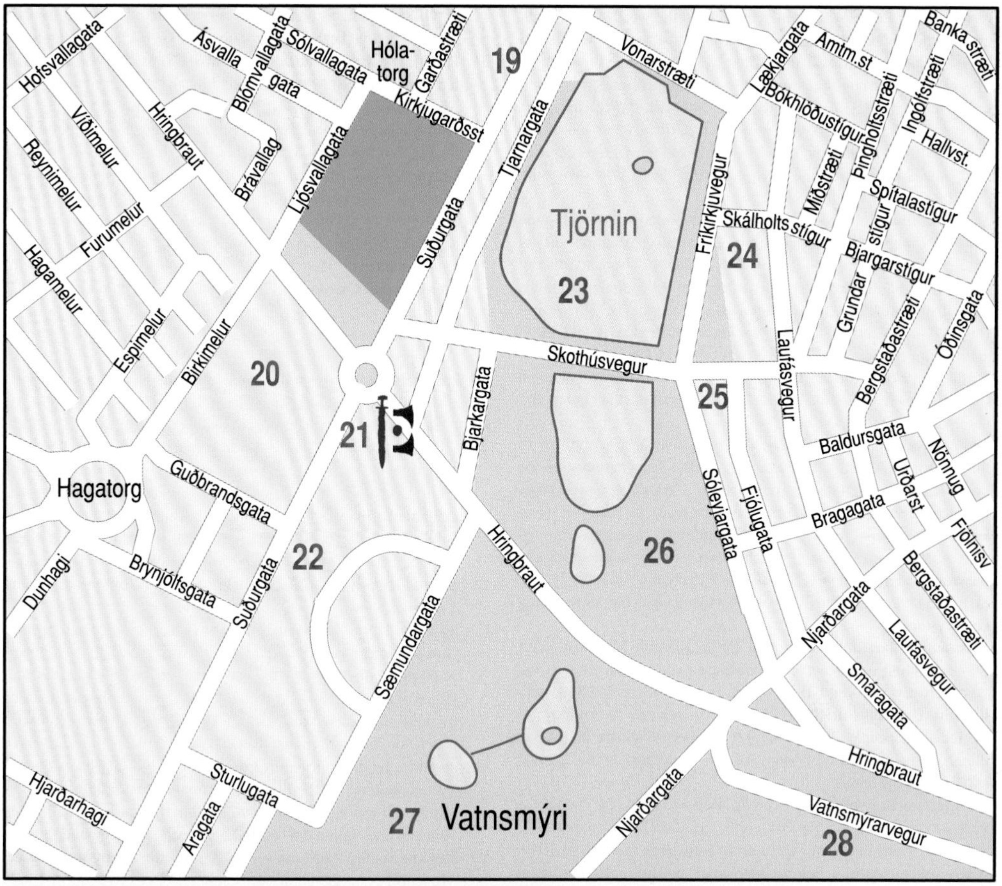

Hofsvallagata
Ásvallagata
Blómvallagata
Sólvallagata
Hólatorg
Garðastræti
19
Vonarstræti
Lækjargata
Amtm.st
Bankastræti
Kirkjugarðsst
Tjarnargata
Bókhlöðustígur
Þingholtsstræti
Ingólfsstræti
Hallvst.
Víðimelur
Hringbraut
Reynimelur
Brávallag
Ljósvallagata
Suðurgata
Tjörnin
Fríkirkjuvegur
Miðstræti
Spítalastígur
Skálholtsstígur
Bjargarstígur
Grundarstígur
24
Furumelur
Hagamelur
23
Espimelur
Birkimelur
20
Skothúsvegur
Laufásvegur
Bergstaðastræti
Óðinsgata
25
21
Bjarkargata
Baldursgata
Nönnug
Hagatorg
Guðbrandsgata
Urðarst.
Bragagata
Sóleyjargata
Fjólugata
Fjölnisv
22
26
Brynjólfsgata
Dunhagi
Suðurgata
Hringbraut
Bergstaðastræti
Njarðargata
Laufásvegur
Sæmundargata
Smáragata
Hringbraut
Hjarðarhagi
Sturlugata
Aragata
27 Vatnsmýri
Njarðargata
Vatnsmýrarvegur
28

29. **Örfirisey, or Effersey,** ("Ebb island") is to the west of the mouth of the older Reykjavík harbour. The island was once connected to the mainland by a narrow isthmus that went underwater at high tide. The isthmus has now been extended with landfill and is covered with buildings. Reykjavík bought the island in 1906 as part of the preparations for harbour construction. Örfirisey has long been associated with fishing and fish processing and one of the countries most advanced fish freezing and processing plants, now owned by Grandi hf., opened there in 1979.

30. **Skólavörðuholt,** ("School Cairn hill") is the basalt hill rising to the east of Lækjargata and Tjörnin. It was once called Arnarhólsholt. Its present name derives from the fact that when the school at Skálholt was moved to Reykjavík shortly before 1800 the students built a cairn there on the hill by the main road into Reykjavík. The School Cairn was a favourite place for the citizens of Reykjavík to walk to and admire the view until it was torn down in 1931 to make way for the statue of Leifur Eiríksson. There are a number of remarkable buildings at the top of the hill, such as Hallgrímskirkja church and the Einar Jónsson Museum.

31. **Hallgrímskirkja,** ("The church of Hallgrímur") is at the top of Skólavörðuholt. The idea of building a church in memory of the poet Hallgrímur Pétursson first arose in 1914. The first designs for such a church on Skólavörðuholt were made by State Architect Guðjón Samúelsson. The actual building process extended over many years and the church wasn't finally completed and consecrated until October 28th 1986. The church tower is 74.5 m high and offers a superb view of Reykjavík and the surrounding countryside.

32. **Listasafn Einars Jónssonar, The Einar Jónsson Museum,** is on Skólavörðuholt on the corner of Eiríksgata and Njarðargata. It was built between 1916 and 1923 by the sculptor Einar Jónsson, who lived in it until his death in 1954. He bequeathed the building to the Icelandic people along with all his works, which are on display there. There are casts of many of his sculptures in the garden surrounding the house.

33. **Reykjavíkurflugvöllur, Reykjavík Airport,** is in the Vatnsmýri meadow southwest of the Öskjuhlíð hill. The first commercially owned air plane in Iceland was sent to Reykjavík in a box in 1919. It was assembled in a field in Vatnsmýri and took off from there on September 3rd. For the next two decades this imperfect and primitive airstrip was the headquarters of whatever airlines operated there. When the British Army came to Iceland in 1940 they immediately started construction of a proper airport on the same site, and it is still there today. Now domestic flights and flights to Greenland and the Faroe Islands are operated from Reykjavík Airport.

34. **Öskjuhlíð/Perlan,** ("The Pearl"). Öskjuhlíð is a basalt hill (61m high) north of the Fossvogur inlet. At the end of the ice age, when the sea level was higher than it is today, Öskjuhlíð was an island. Some tide marks and marine eroded rocks are to be found at a height of about 45m. When the hot water heating system was constructed in the 30's storage tanks were built on top of Öskjuhlíð. They have now been replaced by larger ones, on top of which is the viewing platform and restaurant Perlan, which rotates. The Saga Museum located inside one of the tanks, transports you to the Viking Age and brings back to life renowned figures and major events in Icelandic history. Visitors to the museum are guided through the museum's many attractions as well as through a chronological history of the country. In this vibrant, multidimensional museum, both Icelandic and foreign visitors are given an opportunity to learn about Icelandic history in a way that is both educational and fun. The Museum is open every day from 10 -18 from April 1st - September 30th, from 12 -17 the rest of the year.

35. **Nauthólvík Geothermal Beach.** In Iceland the sea is normally far too cold to tempt swimmers, but at Nauthólsvík a thermal beach has been created, where natural hot water flows out into the sea, and you can frolic in the waves as if you were in the Mediterranean! A beach of golden sand has been made (Icelandic sand is usually black, which is less picturesque for a bathing beach), and by the beach a "pool" has been enclosed, where the water temperature is about 20ºC. Refreshments and various services are available at the beach. The geothermal beach is open daily 10-20 in the summer months .

36. **Reykjavík Art Museum - Kjarvalsstaðir** is located in the Miklatún Park, between Miklabraut and Flókagata. Built in honour of the painter Jóhannes Kjarval (d.1972), it was opened in 1973.

37. **Höfði,** a large timber house on Borgartún, built 1909 by the French for their consul. Now a hospitality house for the City of Reykjavík. Winston Churchill, the then British prime minister, visited at Höfði in 1941 during his visit to the British forces in Iceland. In 1986 summit talks between President Ronald Reagan and General Secretary Mikhaíl Gorbatsjov were held at Höfði.

38. **Laugardalur,** ("Hot spring valley") lies between the ridges Laugarás and Grensás, or more precisely between the streets Suðurlandsbraut and Laugarásvegur. The Laugardalsvöllur sports field was built there between 1950 and 1957 and was followed by one building after another. The Laugardalshöll sports stadium, the Laugardalslaug swimming pool, a Skating Rink and then more sports fields and office buildings. Laugardalur is now the main headquarters of all sports in Iceland that are associated with Íþróttasamband Íslands ("The Icelandic Sport Federation"). On August 18th 1961, Reykjavík's 175th birthday, Grasagarður Reykjavíkur ("The Reykjavík Botanical Gardens") was established. It contains examples of most Icelandic plants (about 300-350) as well as thousands of foreign plants. Þvottalaugarnar ("The washing springs") are hot springs where people, especially from Reykjavík, used to come to do their washing in memory of which Ásmundur Sveinsson's statue Þvottakonan ("The washerwoman") has been put up there. In 1928-30 drilling for hot water produced a considerable flow of water at 93°C. Hot water was piped to a number of buildings, first of all to the newly-built Austurbæjarskólinn junior school on Skólavörðuholt. This was the beginning of the massive operations to heat all of Reykjavík with natural hot water. In addition to the Reykjavík Botanical Gardens and the sporting facilities in Laugardalur, there is Húsdýragarðurinn, a Zoo containing all the domestic animals to be found on Icelandic farms, and Fjölskyldugarðurinn, a family fun park with all kinds of facilities and equipment for the amusement of young and old.

39. **Reykjavík Art Museum - The Ásmundur Sveinsson Sculpture Museum,** is on the corner of Sigtún and Reykjavegur. In 1942 the sculptor Ásmundur Sveinsson set about building this square house with its domed roof. He bequeathed his art gallery and collection to the city of Reykjavík and it was formally opened May 21st 1983.

40. **Árbæjarsafn, Árbær Museum.** Árbær is an old farm northeast of the Elliðaár Rivers and south of Vesturlandsvegur (Highway 1). In 1957 Reykjavík City Council decided to establish a folk museum to be housed at Árbær, whose old farm buildings formed the core of the museum. Old buildings of historical interest have been moved to Árbær from Reykjavík and elsewhere in the country. Árbær Museum tries to give a sense of the architecture and way of life in Reykjavík and during summer visitors can see domestic animals and lifestyles of the past. There are many exhibitions and events held at the Museum, including craft days, vintage car displays, Christmas exhibitions and much more. Árbær Museum is open every day from 10-17 in June, July and August. From September to May the Museum is open by arrangement and runs guided tours at 1pm Monday, Wednesday and Friday. A great fish restaurant, Gallerý fiskur is located within walking distance of the museum. The restaurant is family friendly, reasonably priced and of course there is fresh fish everyday.

41. **Elliðaárdalur,** ("The valley of the Elliðaár Rivers"). The Elliðaár Rivers are mentioned as early as in Landnámabók: "Ketilbjörn went to Iceland when there were a number of settlements on the coast. His ship was named Elliði. He came to the Elliðaár estuary below the heath." The hydro-electric plant near the river mouth began operating in 1921, and the rivers now belong to Reykjavík Electricity. Shortly before 1900, Englishmen started using the Elliðaár for angling since when other types of fishing have not been employed there. The rivers are now among the best salmon rivers in the country, and Reykjavík is probably the only capital city in the world to have such a river within its boundaries.

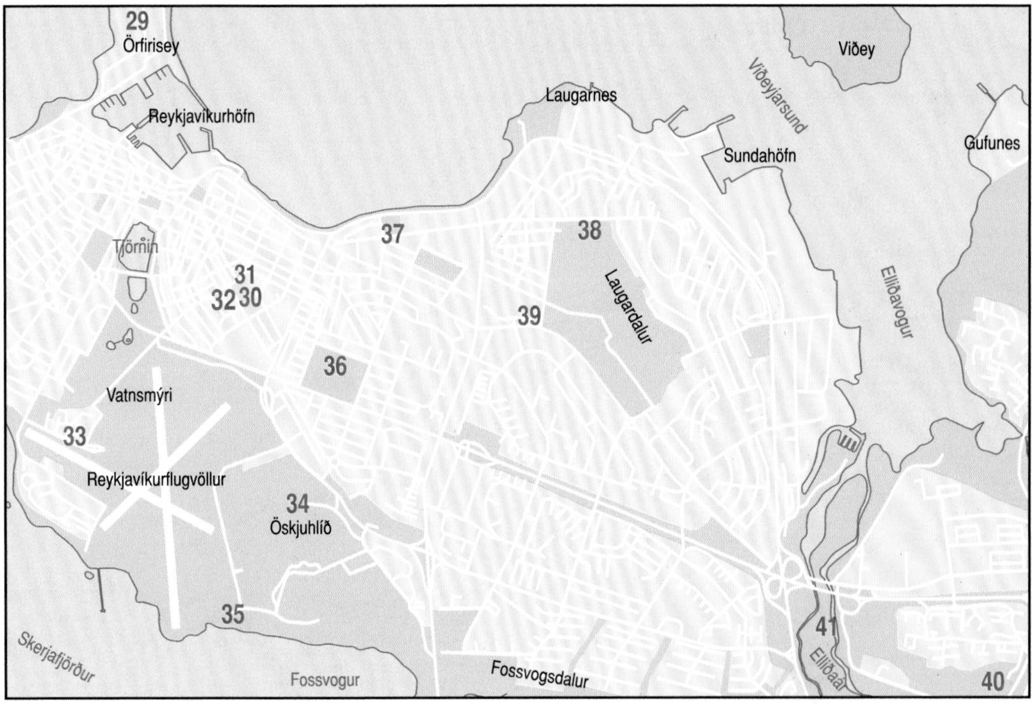
29
Örfirisey
Reykjavíkurhöfn
Laugarnes
Viðey
Viðeyjarsund
Sundahöfn
Gufunes
Tjörnin
37
38
31
32
30
Laugardalur
39
Elliðavogur
36
Vatnsmýri
33
Reykjavíkurflugvöllur
34
Öskjuhlíð
35
41
Skerjafjörður
Fossvogur
Fossvogsdalur
Elliðaár
40

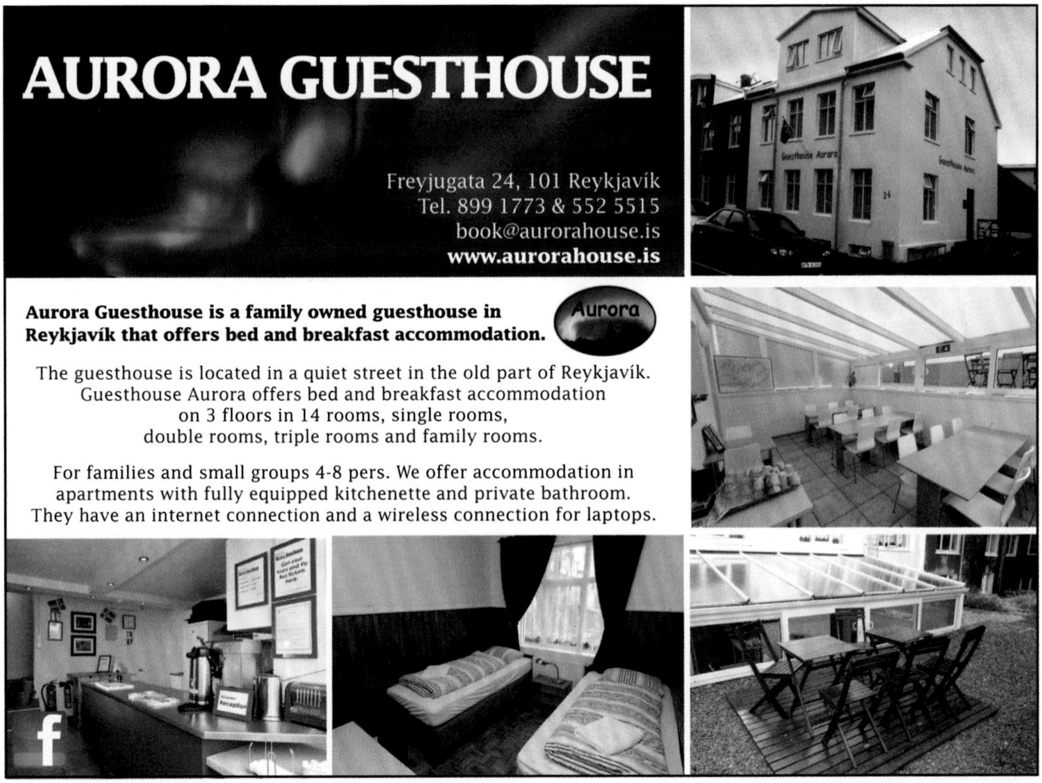
AURORA GUESTHOUSE
Freyjugata 24, 101 Reykjavík
Tel. 899 1773 & 552 5515
book@aurorahouse.is
www.aurorahouse.is
Aurora
Aurora Guesthouse is a family owned guesthouse in Reykjavík that offers bed and breakfast accommodation.
The guesthouse is located in a quiet street in the old part of Reykjavík. Guesthouse Aurora offers bed and breakfast accommodation on 3 floors in 14 rooms, single rooms, double rooms, triple rooms and family rooms.
For families and small groups 4-8 pers. We offer accommodation in apartments with fully equipped kitchenette and private bathroom. They have an internet connection and a wireless connection for laptops.

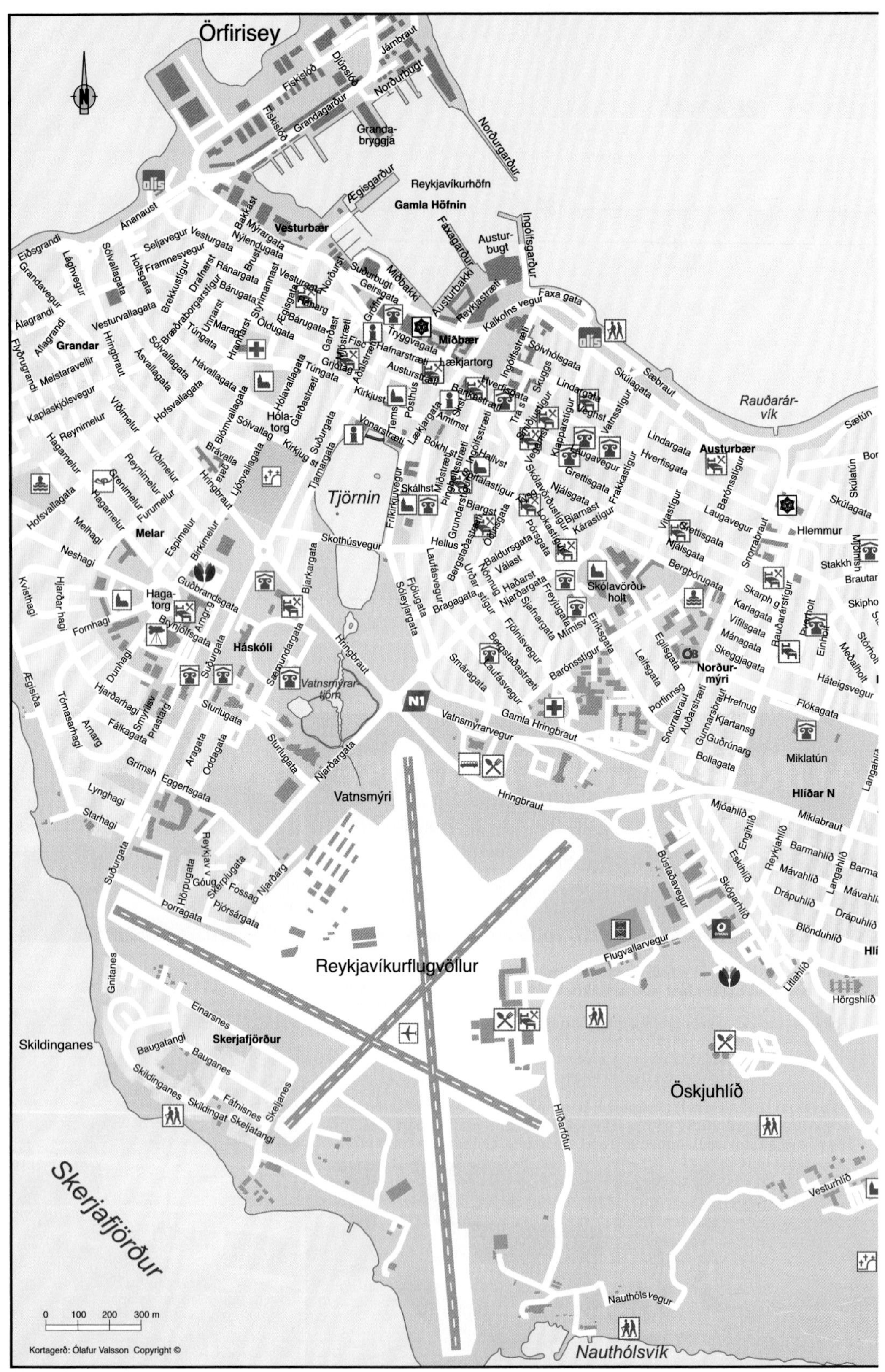
Örfirisey
Fiskislóð
Djúpslóð
Járnbraut
Norðurbugt
Grandagarður
Granda-
bryggja
Norðurgarður
Reykjavíkurhöfn
Ægisgarður
Gamla Höfnin
Ingólfsgarður
Faxagarður
Austur-
bugt
Ánanaust
Vesturbær
Eiðsgrandi
Grandavegur
Lágholtsvegur
Sólvallagata
Holtsgata
Seljavegur
Vesturgata
Framnesvegur
Mýrargata
Nýlendugata
Bakkast
Brekkustígur
Drafnarst
Ránargata
Bárugata
Bræðraborgarstígur
Stýrimannast
Ægisgata
Norðurst
Suðurbugt
Geirsgata
Miðbakki
Austurbakki
Reykjastræti
Kalkofns vegur
Faxa gata
Vesturvallagata
Álagrandi
Aflagrandi
Grandar
Flyðrugrandi
Hringbraut
Meistaravellir
Kaplaskjólsvegur
Túngata
Unnarst
Marargata
Öldugata
Garðast
Mjóstræti
Tryggvagata
Miðbær
Hafnarstræti
Lækjartorg
Austurstræti
Aðalstræti
Grjótag
Kirkjust
Pósthús
Templarasund
Hávallagata
Ásvallagata
Hofsvallagata
Blómvallagata
Sólvallag
Hóla-
torg
Garðastræti
Suðurgata
Vonarstræti
Tjarnargata
Kirkjug st
Tjörnin
Skálhst
Fríkirkjuvegur
Lækjargata
Amtmst
Bókhl st
Skólastræti
Bankastræti
Ingólfsstræti
Hverfisgata
Sölvhólsgata
Skuggas
Lindargata
Skúlagata
Sæbraut
Rauðarár-
vík
Klapparstígur
Vatnsstígur
Vegamótast
Laugavegur
Smiðjustígur
Grettisgata
Frakkastígur
Njálsgata
Skólavörðustígur
Bjarnarst
Kárastígur
Þórsgata
Lokastígur
Óðinsgata
Bjargarst
Spítalastígur
Hallvst
Þingholtsstræti
Grundarstígur
Bergstaðastræti
Hellus
Laufásvegur
Baldursgata
Válast
Nönnug
Urðarstígur
Haðarst
Njarðargata
Freyjugata
Fjölnisvegur
Sjafnargata
Mímisv
Eiríksgata
Skólavörðu-
holt
Lindargata
Hverfisgata
Austurbær
Barónsstígur
Vitastígur
Snorrabraut
Hlemmur
Skúlagata
Skúlatún
Sætún
Bergþórugata
Skarph g
Karlagata
Vífilsgata
Mánagata
Skeggjagata
Rauðarárstígur
Meðalholt
Einholt
Þverholt
Háteigsvegur
Stórholt
Skipholt
Brautarholt
Stakkholt
Mjölnish
Egilsgata
Leifsgata
Barónsstígur
Norður-
mýri
Þorfinnsg
Auðarstræti
Gunnarsbraut
Hrefnug
Kjartansg
Guðrúnarg
Bollagata
Flókagata
Miklatún
Hlíðar N
Miklabraut
Langahlíð
Gamla Hringbraut
Vatnsmýrarvegur
Hringbraut
Reynimelur
Víðimelur
Hagamelur
Grenimelur
Furumelur
Melhagi
Melar
Espimelur
Birkimelur
Neshagi
Kvisthagi
Hjarðar hagi
Fornhagi
Haga-
torg
Guðbrandsgata
Brynjólfsgata
Arngr
Háskóli
Suðurgata
Bjarkargata
Skothúsvegur
Sóleyjargata
Fjólugata
Bragagata
Smáragata
Bergstaðastræti
Laufásvegur
Sæmundargata
Hringbraut
Vatnsmýrar-
tjörn
Dunhagi
Hjarðarhagi
Smyrilsv
Þrastarg
Fálkagata
Arnarg
Tómasarhagi
Ægisíða
Sturlugata
Aragata
Oddagata
Sturlugata
Njarðargata
Grímsh
Eggertsgata
Vatnsmýri
Lynghagi
Starhagi
Suðurgata
Reykjav v
Hörpugata
Góug
Skerplugata
Fossag
Njarðarg
Þorragata
Þjórsárgata
Reykjavíkurflugvöllur
Mjóahlíð
Engihlíð
Eskihlíð
Reykjahlíð
Barmahlíð
Mávahlíð
Drápuhlíð
Blönduhlíð
Bústaðavegur
Skógarhlíð
Flugvallarvegur
Litlahlíð
Hörgshlíð
Gnitanes
Einarsnes
Skildinganes
Skerjafjörður
Baugatangi
Bauganes
Skildinganes
Skildingat
Fáfnisnes
Skeljanes
Skeljatangi
Hlíðarfótur
Öskjuhlíð
Vesturhlíð
Nauthólsvegur
Nauthólsvík
Skerjafjörður
0 100 200 300 m
Kortagerð: Ólafur Valsson Copyright ©

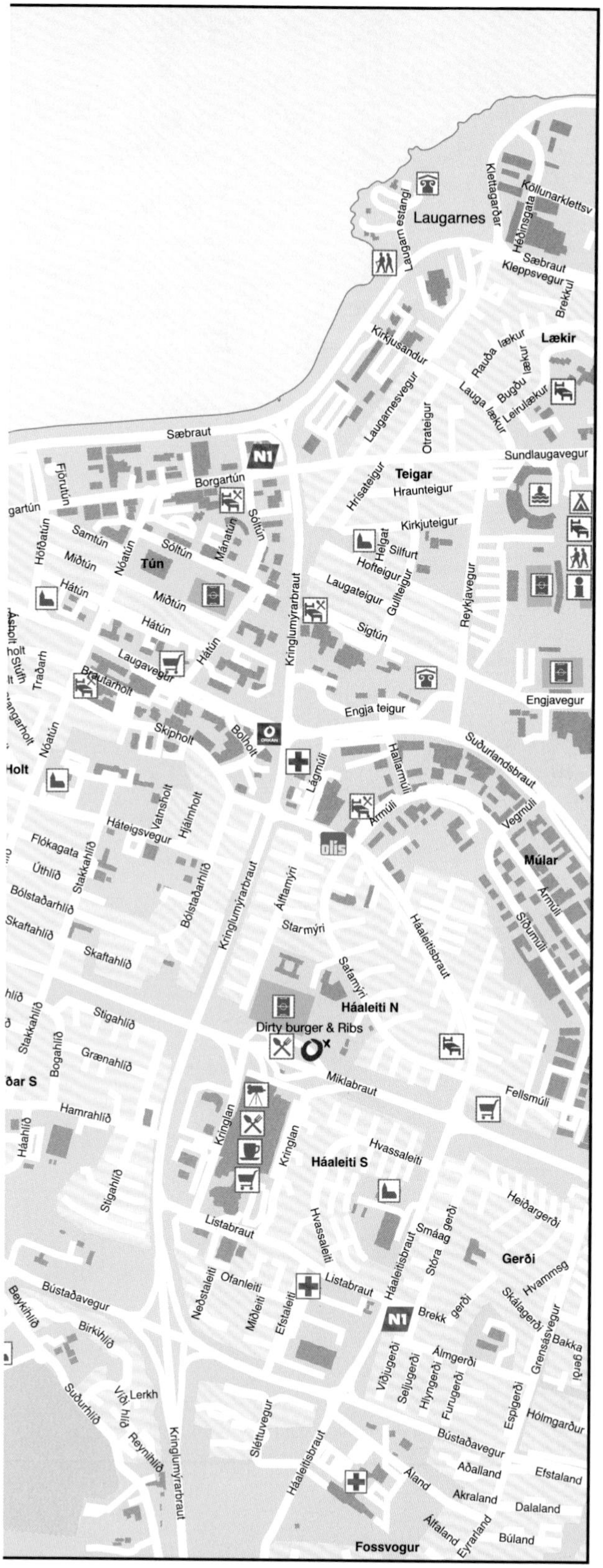

DIRTY BURGER & RIBS
Miklubraut 11 & Austurstræti 10
Tel. 546 2222 / www.dbr.is

ÍSLENSKI BARINN
ÍSLENSKI BARINN
THE ICELANDIC BAR · REYKJAVÍK
Unique bar/restaurant that serves all the Icelandic beer and spirits
Open every day from 11:30
Ingólfsstræti 1a, 101 Reykjavík
+354 517 6767 / postur@islenskibarinn.is
www.islenskibarinn.is

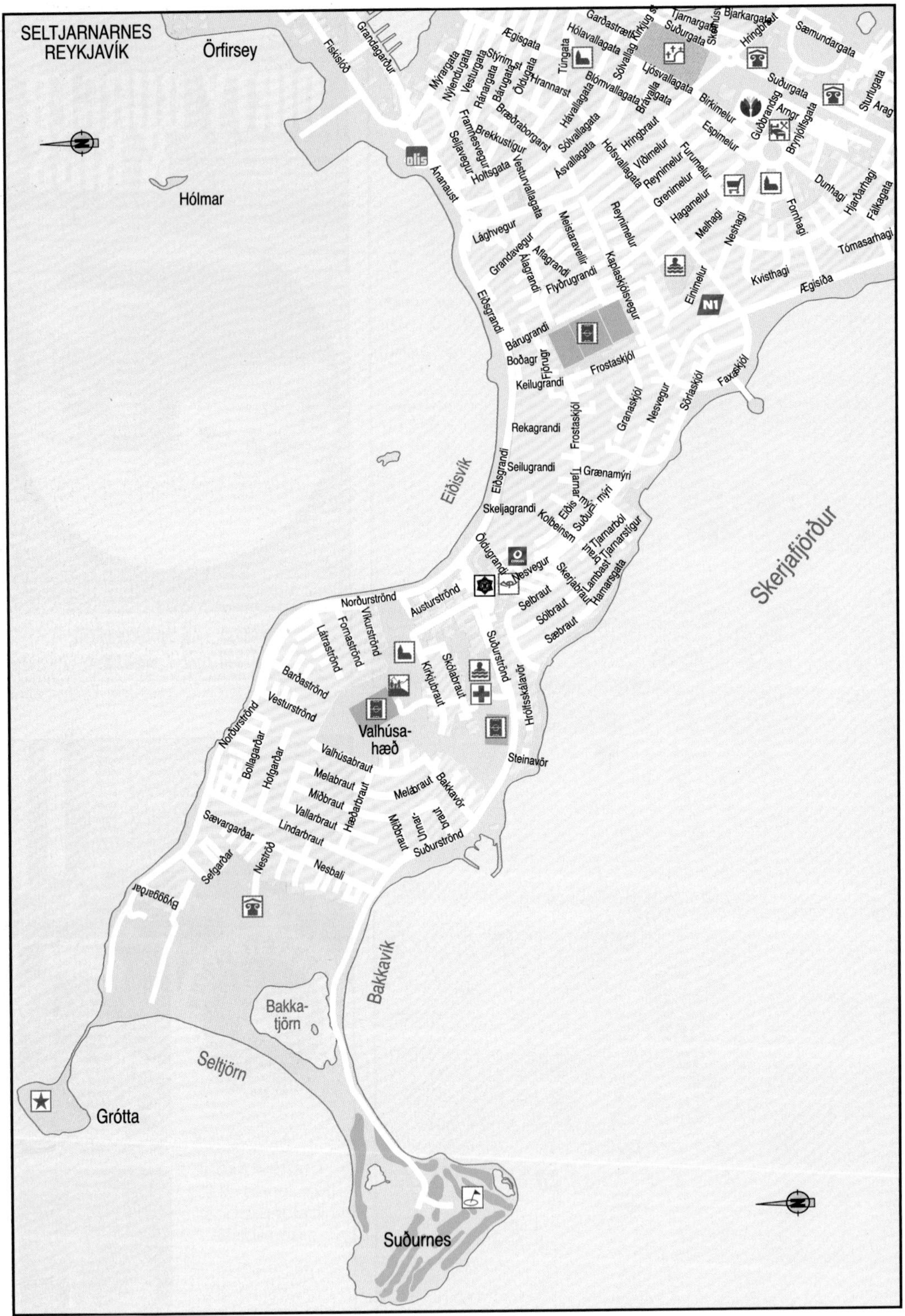
SELTJARNARNES
REYKJAVÍK
Örfirsey
Hólmar
Eiðisvík
Skerjafjörður
Valhúsa-
hæð
Bakkavík
Bakka-
tjörn
Seltjörn
Grótta
Suðurnes

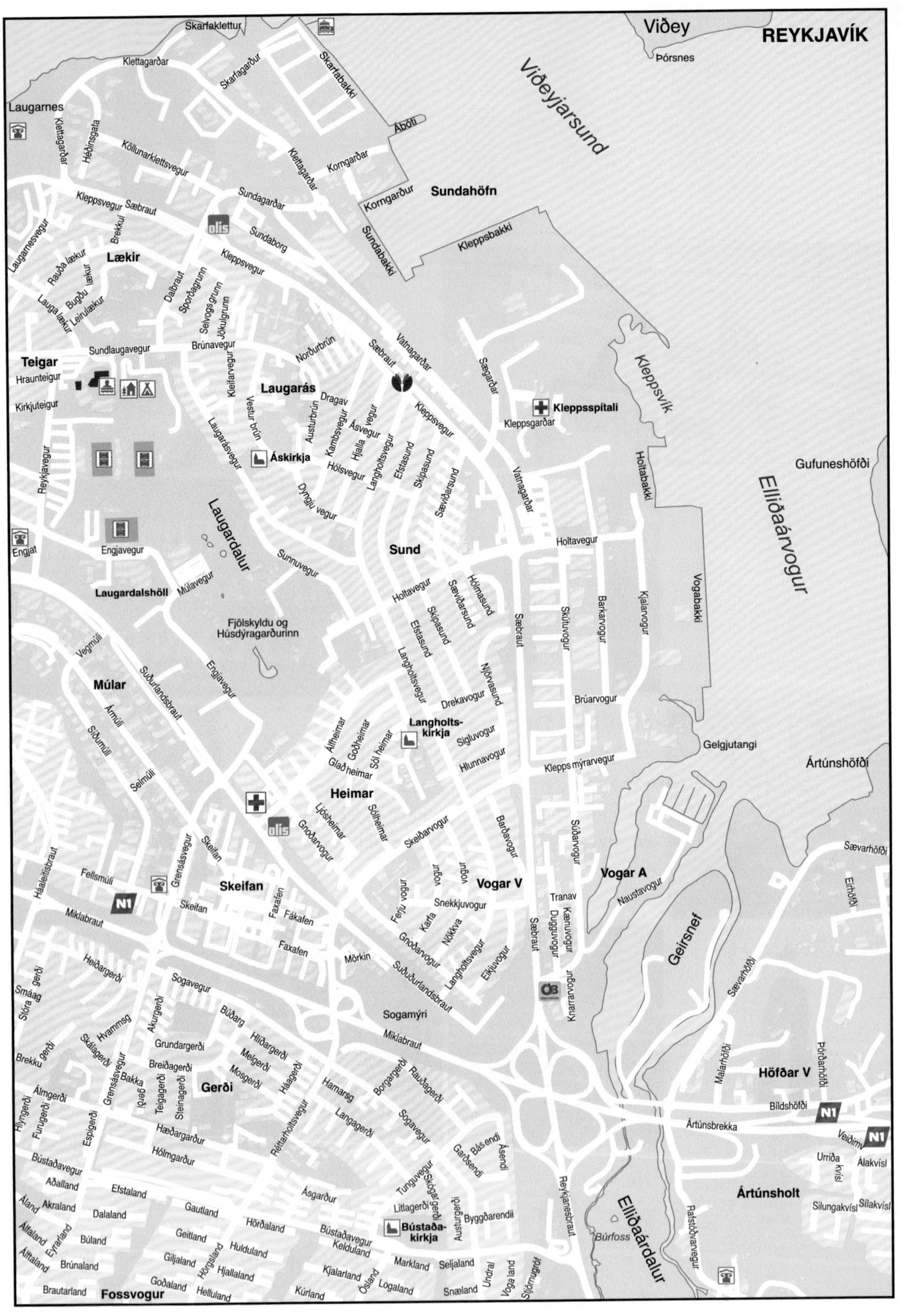
REYKJAVÍK
Viðey
Viðeyjarsund
Sundahöfn
Laugarnes
Lækir
Teigar
Laugarás
Áskirkja
Kleppsspítali
Kleppsvík
Gufuneshöfði
Elliðaárvogur
Sund
Laugardalur
Laugardalshöll
Fjölskyldu og Húsdýragarðurinn
Múlar
Langholts-kirkja
Heimar
Skeifan
Vogar V
Vogar A
Geirsnef
Gelgjutangi
Ártúnshöfði
Sogamýri
Gerði
Höfðar V
Ártúnsholt
Elliðaárdalur
Búrfoss
Bústaða-kirkja
Fossvogur

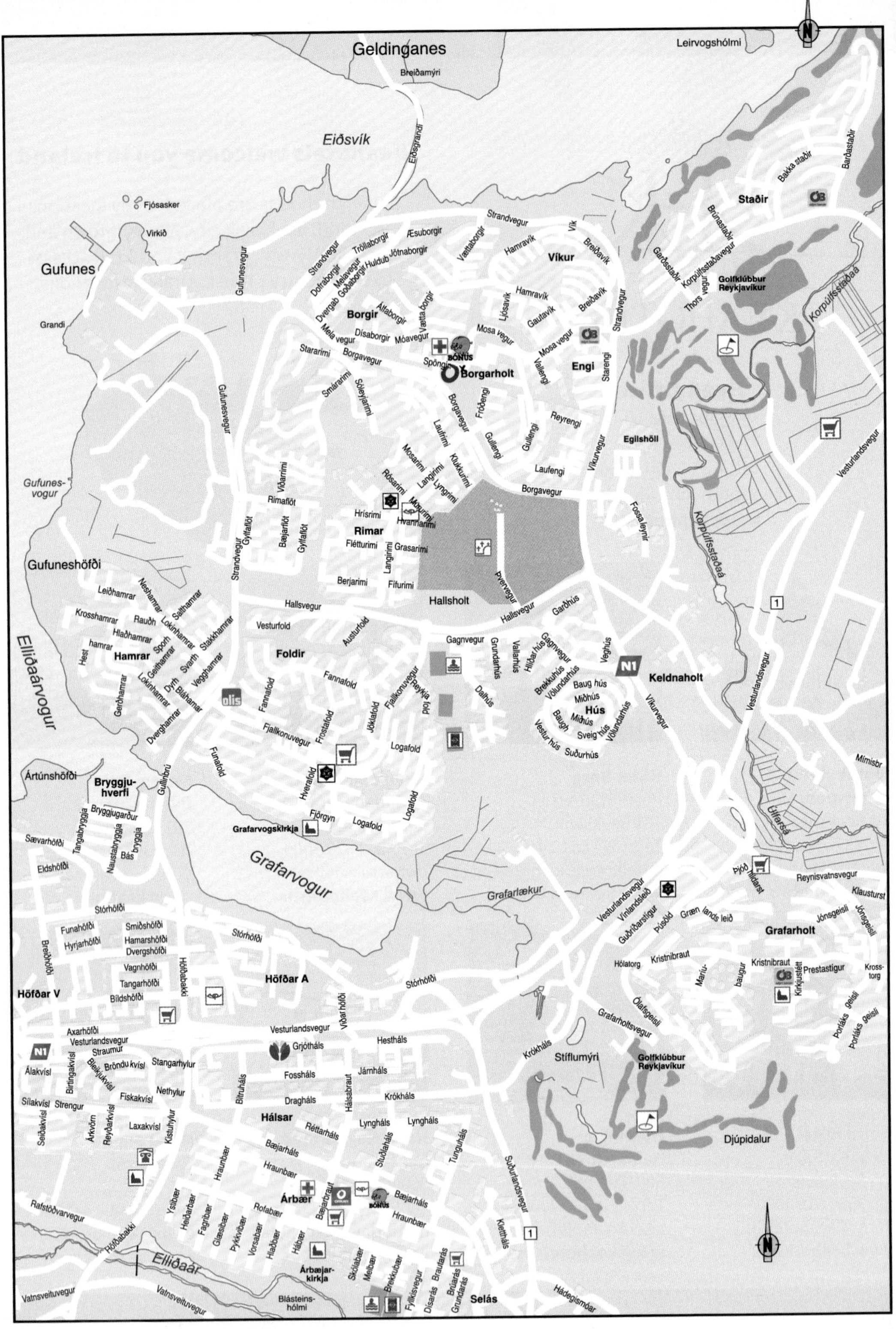
Geldinganes
Breiðamýri
Leirvogshólmi
Eiðsvík
Eiðsgrandi
Fjósasker
Virkið
Gufunes
Grandi
Gufunesvegur
Strandvegur
Tröllaborgir
Æsuborgir
Jötnaborgir
Vættaborgir
Dofraborgir
Dvergab
Borgir
Álfaborgir
Vætta borgir
Mela vegur
Dísaborgir
Móavegur
Stararimi
Borgavegur
Smárarimi
Sóleyjarimi
Spöngin
BÓNUS
Borgarholt
Hamravík
Víkur
Vík
Breiðavík
Ljósavík
Gautavík
Mosa vegur
Vallengi
Engi
Starengi
Strandvegur
Borgavegur
Fróðengi
Gullengi
Reyrengi
Laufengi
Laufrimi
Klukkurimi
Mosarimi
Langirimi
Lyngrimi
Rósarimi
Víðarrimi
Rimaflöt
Bæjarflöt
Gylfaflöt
Hrísrimi
Rimar
Flétturimi
Grasarimi
Hvannarimi
Berjarimi
Fífurimi
Hallsholt
Hallsvegur
Þorvegur
Garðhús
Vesturfold
Austurfold
Foldir
Gufunes-
vogur
Gufuneshöfði
Leiðhamrar
Neshamrar
Krosshamrar
Salthamrar
Hlaðhamrar
Stakkhamrar
Hamrar
Hest
Geirhamrar
Dverghamrar
Vegghamrar
Bláhamrar
Elliðaárvogur
Fannafold
Fjallkonuvegur
Frostafold
Jöklafold
Reykjafold
Logafold
Funafold
Hverafold
Fjörgyn
Grafarvogskirkja
Gagnvegur
Grundarhús
Vallarhús
Hlíðarhús
Veghús
Brekkuhús
Völundarhús
Baug hús
Miðhús
Hús
Dalhús
Vesturhús
Suðurhús
Keldnaholt
Víkurvegur
Vesturlandsvegur
Egilshöll
Fossaleynir
Korpúlfsstaðaá
Staðir
Bakkastaðir
Barðastaðir
Brúnastaðir
Garðsstaðir
Korpúlfsstaðavegur
Thors vegur
Golfklúbbur
Reykjavíkur
Mímisbr
Úlfarsá
Reynisvatnsvegur
Klausturst
Grafarholt
Kristnibraut
Prestastígur
Kirkjustétt
Kross-
torg
Óláfsgeisli
Þorláks geisli
Ártúnshöfði
Bryggju-
hverfi
Bryggjugarður
Gullinbrú
Sævarhöfði
Tangabryggja
Naustabryggja
Eldshöfði
Grafarvogur
Grafarlækur
Stórhöfði
Funahöfði
Hyrjarhöfði
Smiðshöfði
Hamarshöfði
Dvergshöfði
Vagnhöfði
Tangarhöfði
Bíldshöfði
Höfðabakki
Höfðar V
Höfðar A
Breiðhöfði
Vesturlandsvegur
Víkurvegur
Vínlandsleið
Guðríðarstígur
Þúsöld
Hólatorg
Grafarholtsvegur
Krókháls
Stíflumýri
Golfklúbbur
Reykjavíkur
Djúpidalur
Axarhöfði
Straumur
Álakvísl
Birtingakvísl
Stangarhylur
Nethylur
Fiskakvísl
Sílakvísl
Strengur
Laxakvísl
Kistuhylur
Seiðakvísl
Árkvörn
Reyðarkvísl
Grjótháls
Hestháls
Járnháls
Fossháls
Bitruháls
Hálsabraut
Draghals
Krókháls
Hálsar
Réttarháls
Lynghals
Stuðlaháls
Tunguháls
Bæjarháls
Hraunbær
Suðurlandsvegur
Árbær
Rafstöðvarvegur
Höfðabakki
Elliðaár
Ystibær
Heiðarbær
Fagribær
Glæsibær
Þykkvibær
Vorsabær
Hlaðbær
Hábær
Rofabær
Árbæjar-
kirkja
Skólabær
Melbær
Brekkubær
Fylkisvegur
Disarás
Brautarás
Brúarás
Grundarás
Selás
Hádegismóar
Kletthals
Vatnsveituvegur
Blásteins-
hólmi

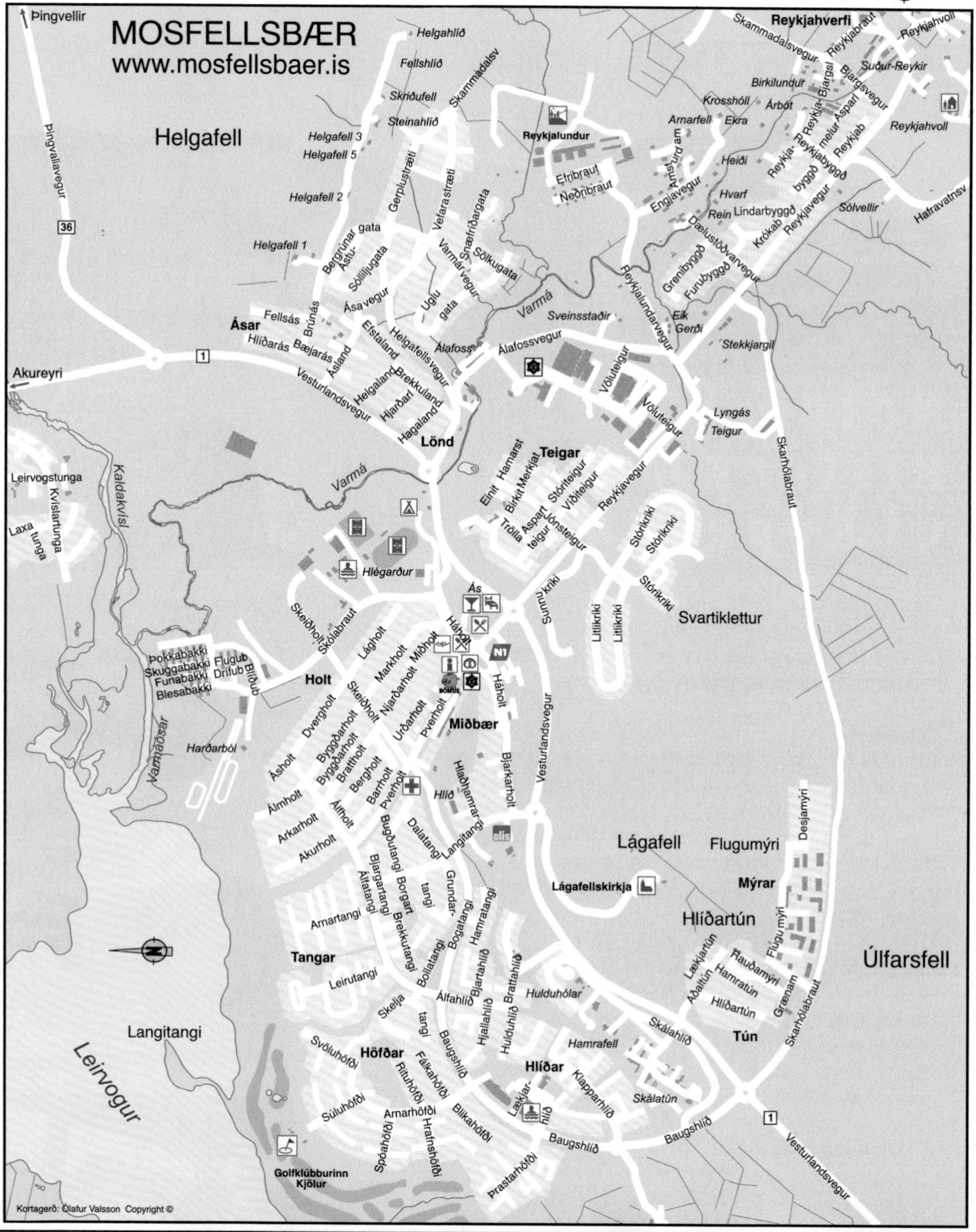

MOSFELLSBÆR
www.mosfellsbaer.is

Helgafell · Ásar · Lönd · Teigar · Holt · Miðbær · Tangar · Höfðar · Hlíðar · Tún · Reykjahverfi · Svartiklettur · Lágafell · Úlfarsfell · Langitangi · Leirvogur

Kortagerð: Ólafur Valsson Copyright ©

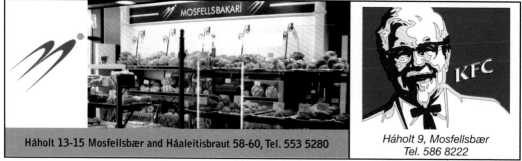

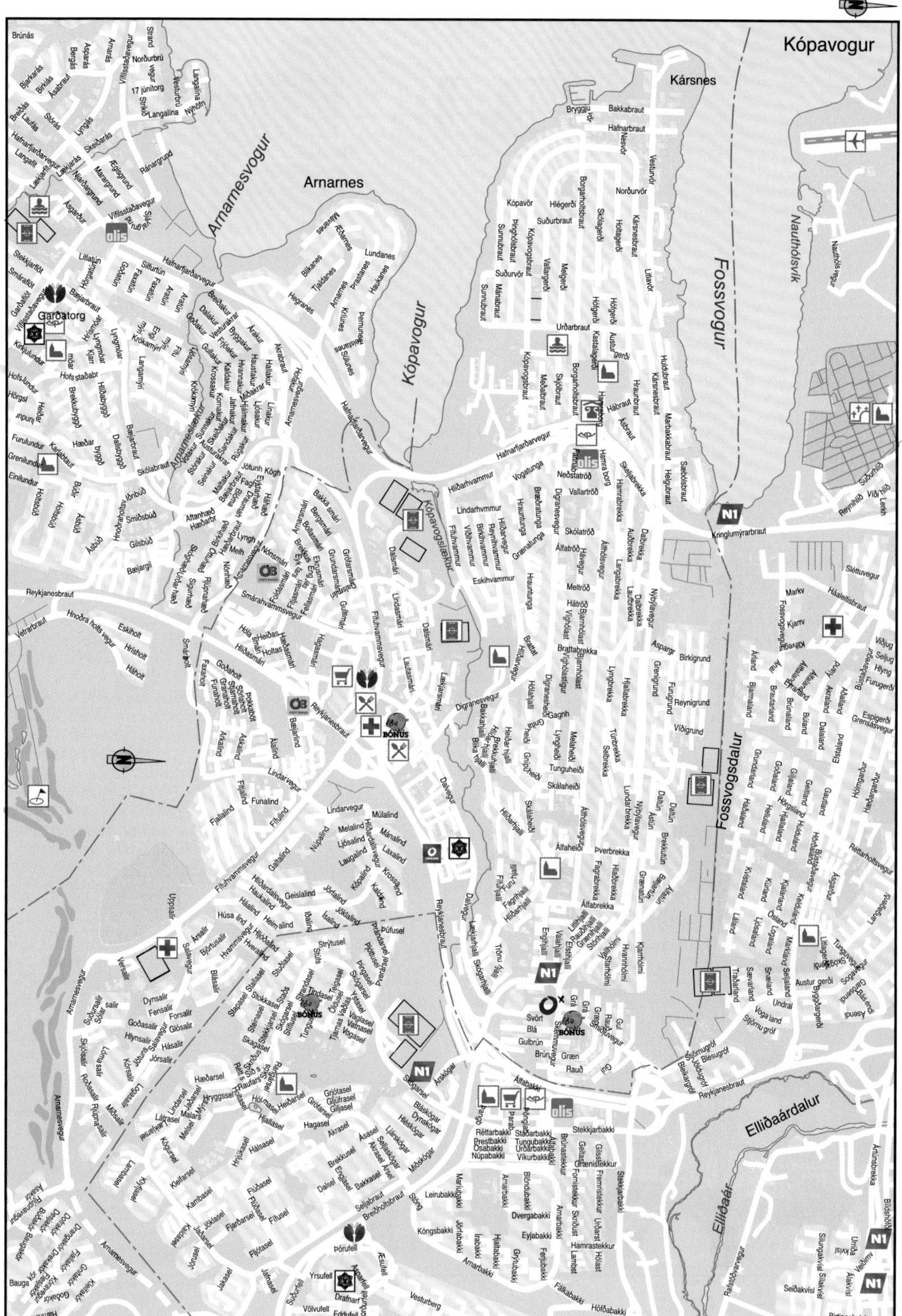

Kópavogur
Kársnes
Arnarnes
Arnarnesvogur
Kópavogur
Fossvogur
Nauthólsvík
Fossvogsdalur
Elliðaárdalur
Elliðaár
Garðatorg

Kópavogur Art Museum Gerðarsafn

Opening hours:

Every day except Mondays: 11:00 - 17:00.
Entrance: 500 ISK -

Hamraborg 4
200 Kópavogur
Tel: +354 570 0440
and +354 570 0442
Fax: +354 570 0441
www.gerdarsafn.is

LISTASAFN KÓPAVOGS
GERÐARSAFN

The Kópavogur, Library

Bókasafn Kópavogs

Opening hours:
Monday - Thursday: 10:00 - 19:00
Friday: 11:00 - 17:00.
Saturday: 13:00 - 17:00

Hamraborg 6a
200 Kópavogur
Tel: +354 570-0450
Fax: +354 570-0451
www.bokasafnkopavogs.is

Lindasafn, Library

Open 1st Sept. to 31st May
Mondays - Thursdays 14:00 - 19:00
Fridays 14:00 - 17:00
Saturdays from 1st Oct. 11:00-14:00

Lindaskóli, Núpalind 7
201 Kópavogur
Tel: +354 564-0621
lindasafn@kopavogur.is

Salurinn, Kópavogur Concert Hall

Information on concerts and ticket reservation: +354 5 700 400 and www.salurinn.is

Hamraborg 6
200 Kópavogur
Tel: +354 5 700 400
www.salurinn.is

Salurinn

Natural History Museum of Kópavogur

Opening hours:

Monday - Thursday: 10:00-19:00.
Friday: 11:00-17:00.
Saturday: 13:00-17:00.
Free entrance.

Hamraborg 6a
200 Kópavogur
Tel: +354 441-7200
www.natkop.is

Náttúrufræðistofa Kópavogs
Natural History Museum of Kópavogur

www.kopavogur.is

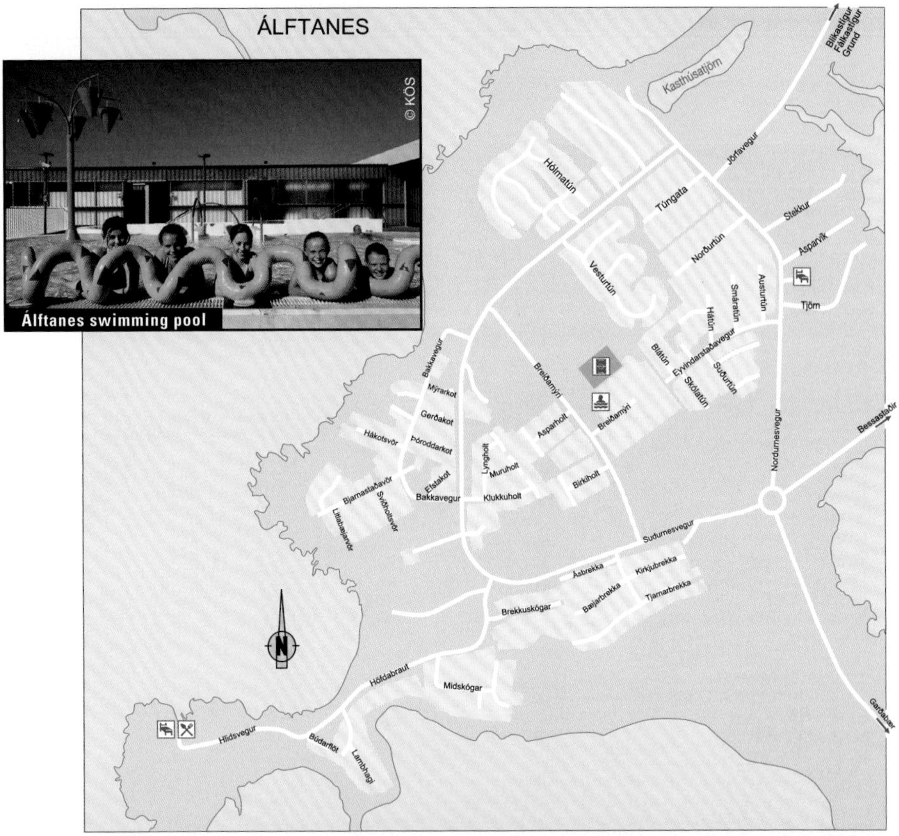

ÁLFTANES

© KÓS

Álftanes swimming pool

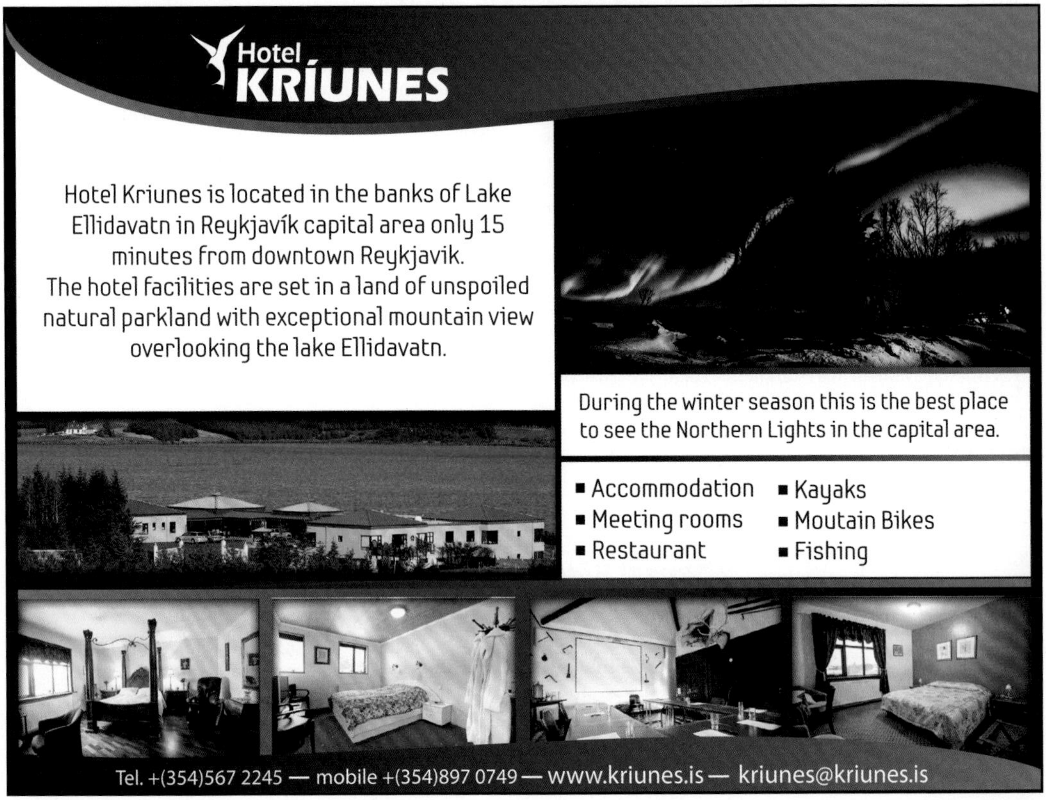

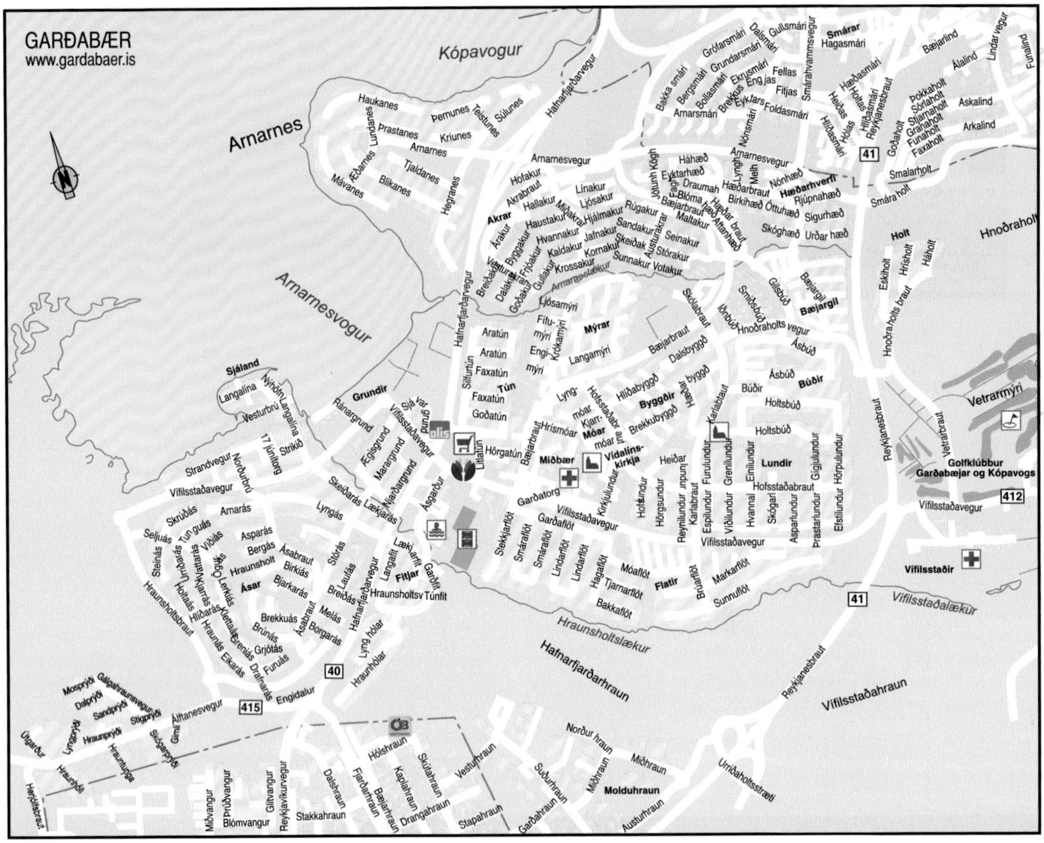

GARÐABÆR
www.gardabaer.is

Garðabær, (pop. 14,452) a municipality in the capital area is a community rich in unspoiled nature for the enjoyment of outdoor life by its residents. The peninsula Álftanes has a magnificent pastoral setting by the sea. It is home to the ancient farmstead of Bessastaðir, the official presidential residence. The lava landscape ("Búrfellshraun") is believed to be around 7200 years old and is one of the main natural features surrounding Garðabær. There is ample space for free outdoor activities and many hiking tracks, for example in the outdoor area "Heiðmörk". There are two lakes in the area of Garðabær, "Vífilsstaðavatn" and "Urriðavatn". Vífilsstaðavatn and its surroundings is a nature reserve and a fishing license can be purchased for Vífilsstaðavatn in the summers. There are two outdoor thermal pools in Garðabær, one at the sport center Ásgarður and „Álftaneslaug" featuring the one of the largest waterslide in the country and Iceland's only wave pool.
Places of cultural interest are: The Museum of Design and Applied Art, at the town's center in Garðatorg. Open from 12-17 (closed on Mondays). The old farm Krókur (built 1923) is open on Sunday afternoons during summertime. Hofsstaðir Archeaological site, the remains of the second largest farm from the age of settlement in Iceland (9th century) located at Kirkjulundur. Visitors can observe the archaeological remains and have a chance to learn more about the ruins through a multimedia, touch-screen exhibition. Free admission and open 24 hours a day.

Index and more information about Iceland

The Icelandic Horse

The Icelandic horse is rather small, its height usually being about 140 cm. It is sturdy and hardworking and has greater endurance than its foreign cousins. It has a characteristic varied colouring that breeders have attempted to preserve rather than eliminate. As a riding animal, the Icelandic horse is exceptional in that it has five gaits, called fet, skeið, tölt, brokk and stökk in Icelandic. It has become famous internationally for its various gaits and smooth movement. Icelandic horses are considered energetic and ready to run, and they are also admired for their even and friendly disposition. Icelandic farmers have traditionally been interested in the strength and endurance of horses.

Red skewbald

Black

Dark bay

Grey mare with a foal

Red-dun

Light black

Bay-roan

Bay skewbald

Pale dun, dun

Palamino

Buckskin

Blue dun

Silver dapple

Chestnut

Dapple grey

Black skewbald

Silver dapple, skewbald

Yellow dun

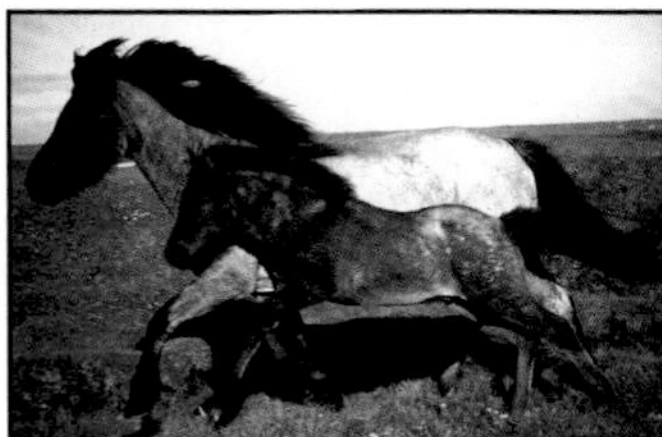
Dark roan stud mare
with a foal

Chestnut with white socks

Buckskin, light

The Icelandic Sheep

The Icelandic sheep is special in many ways. For example, leader sheep possessing the qualities of the Icelandic type do not exist anywhere else in the world. There are many stories of how they have rescued both men and other sheep from danger. Icelandic sheep are so-called short-tailed animals, a type which was formerly common in northwestern Europe, but which is now found in only few areas of the world. It is a strong, hardy species that has adapted well to Icelandic conditions. The majority of the national flock has horns, but polled sheep are also common.

White, polled ewe, with tan fibres and a black spot

White, horned ram, with a black cheek

Black, polled ewe

Dark-grey, polled ewe

White, polled ram

Grey, horned ewe

Homozygous grey, polled ewe

Brown, polled ewe lamb

Brown, horned ewe

Grey-brown, horned ram lamb

Black mouflon, horned ewe

Grey mouflon, horned ewe

Brown mouflon, polled ewe

Black badgerface, horned ram lamb, with a dark flank spot

Grey badgerface, horned ewe lamb

Brown badgerface, horned ewe

Black piebald, horned ewe, with dark eyerings only

Black piebald, polled ewe, with dark cheeks and a collar

Black piebald, horned ewe, with a hood

Black piebald, horned ewe, with dark outer socks

Black piebald, polled ewe, with patches

Grey piebald, polled ewe, with patches

Brown piebald, polled ewe lamb, with a hood

Brown piebald-mouflon, horned ram lamb, with an eagle head

Black mouflon-piebald, horned leader wether, with a blaze and socks

Black badgerface-piebald, horned ewe lamb

Black fourhorned ewe

Black piebald, fourhorned ram lamb, with patches

Black piebald, horned leader ram, with socks, head and nose spots

Brown piebald, horned leader ewe with black and brown piebald ewe lambs, all with white collars and stockings

Brown piebald polled ram, with a head spot and socks, the high crown showing the presence of the gene for fourhornednes

Black piebald, horned leader ewe, with a blaze, a collar and socks

The Icelandic Cattle

The Icelandic breed of cattle is smaller than cattle in neighbouring countries. It is a hardy and fertile type of cow and produces a great deal of milk. The number of dairy farmers is gradually declining as the productivity of individual farmers increases. There are currently about 1,100 milk farmers in the country. Most milk production and cattle breeding is conducted in the south, west and north-central areas of the country, near the major urban centres.

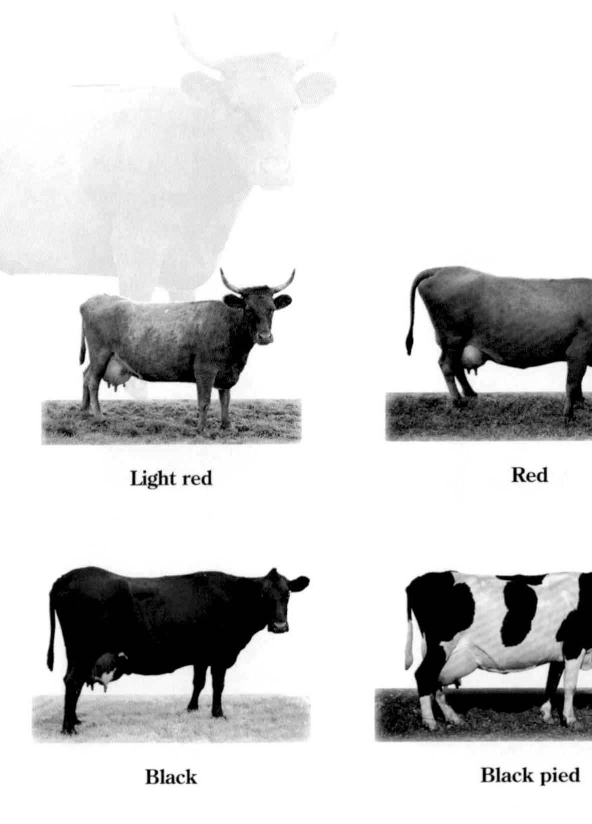

Light red

Red

Red pied, light

Black

Black pied

Red with white face

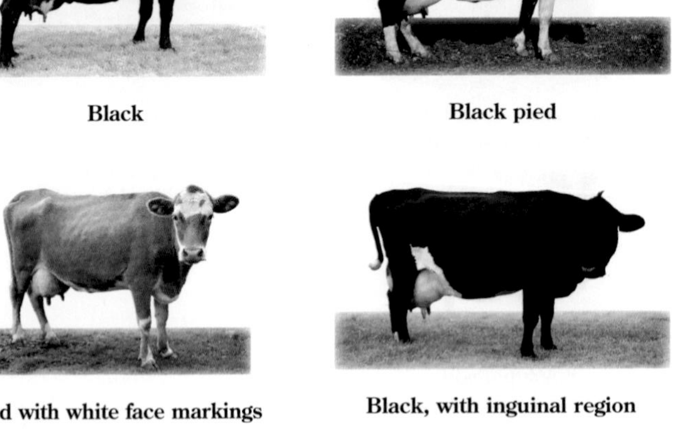

Red with white face markings

Black, with inguinal region

Black pied, extensive white

Brindle pied

Grey, blue roan

Brown, white face, socks

Grey

Red brindle

Brindle

White

White, red ears and muzzle

Dun, white dorsal line

Brown grey, white inguinal region

Brown, light

Brown, dark

Black sided, homozygous

Dun

Dun, white dorsal line

The Icelandic Dog

The Icelandic Sheepdog has assisted with guarding and hearding horses, cattle and sheep since it was brought here during the original settlement in Iceland. Research has shown that it is of Nordic origin like the Icelandic sheep and goats. Like the Icelandic goat the Icelandic Sheepdog was close to extinction in the mid 20th century. In the last decades some measures have been taken in reversing this process, both in Iceland and abroad. The main characteristics of the Icelandic Sheepdog are its pricked ears and curled tail and its many colours.

Light tan dog with a black mask and white collar

Reddish tan and light tan bitches, both with black masks

Black tricolour dog with a blaze

Tricolour and black masked puppies

Black tricolour dog

Reddish brown dog with a black mask

Black tricolour bitch puppy

Proud mother with her puppy, both light tan with black mask

Reddish tan dog with a white collar with a bitch of the same colour and another light tan bitch with a black mask

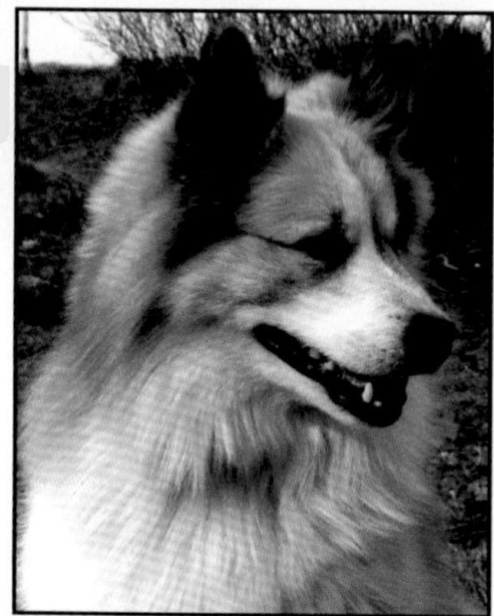

Reddish tan dog with
a white collar

Light tan three year old bitch

Reddish tan puppies, all with
black mask

Two bitches, one light tan,
the other reddish tan
with a white collar

Puppies, some with a blaze and
other with half a white face

Light tan two year old dog

A light reddish tan dog
on a winter's day

Reddish tan dog with a black
mask and a blaze

Light tan bitch
with a half a white face

Brown bitch

Light tan bitch with a white collar

Reddish tan dog
with a black mask

Reddish tan bitch with a white
collar and blaze

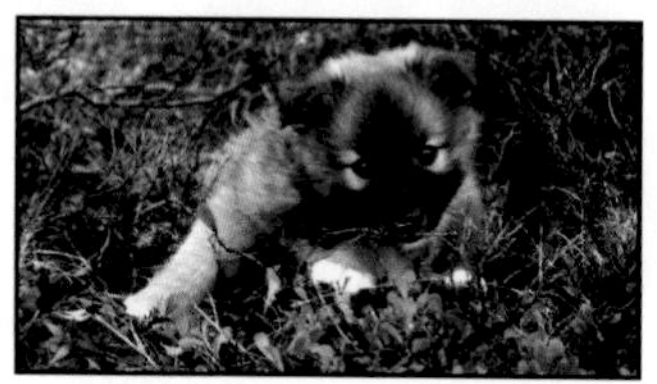

Reddish tan puppy with
a black mask, six weeks old

The Icelandic Goat

The Icelandic goat is now a unique breed, because it was brought here over 1100 years ago and no other goats have been introduced to this island since then. However, the stock currently consists of only about 520 animals, a number which undoubtedly puts it at great risk of dying out, compared to other goat breeds internationally.

Goats are thought to be the oldest species of livestock. Even though cow's milk has gained prominence in western farming, this is not usually the case in other parts of the world. Actually, goat milk is better suited to humans, as it is more easily digested and less likely to cause allergy. Above all, it is healthy for babies who are not fed on breast milk.

The largest herd of Icelandic goats now has its home at Háafell, where Jóhanna Þorvaldsdóttir and Þorbjörn Oddsson have raised goats for 25 years. In summer months the population of over a hundred adult animals increases by nearly a hundred kids.

As well as welcoming groups who want to get acquainted with this breed, the farm staff are gathering knowledge about it and utilising its hair, meat and milk, some of which is used for making cheese. The horns are also used for pretty crafted goods such as pocket snuff containers and buttons.

Those interested in learning more about any of these activities should contact Jóhanna, at **haafell@gmail.com**.

OPEN FARMS

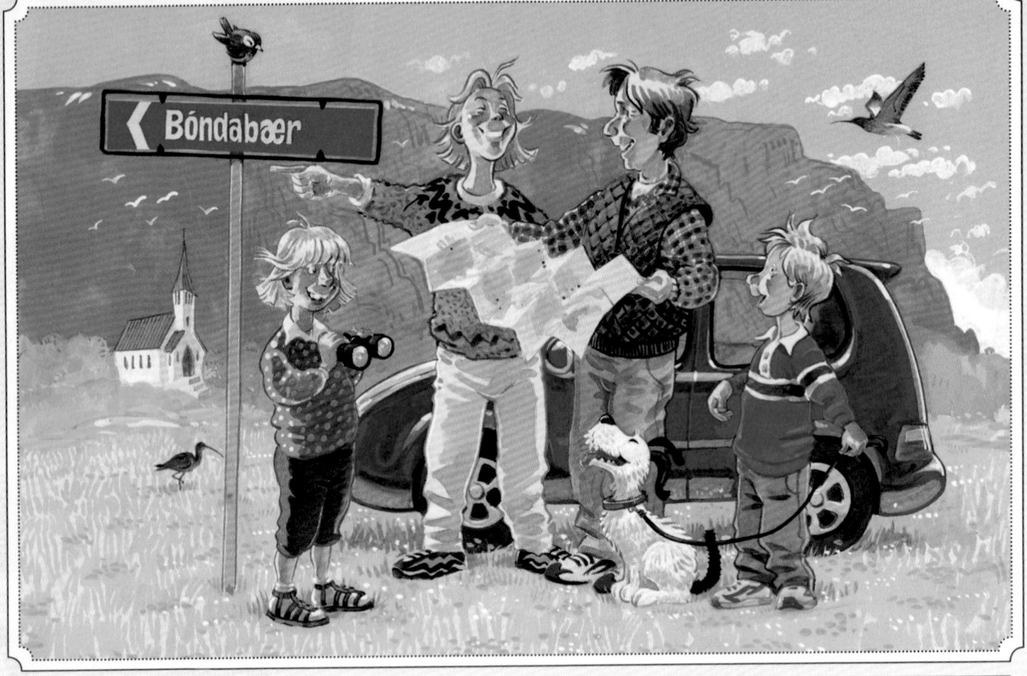

Bóndabær

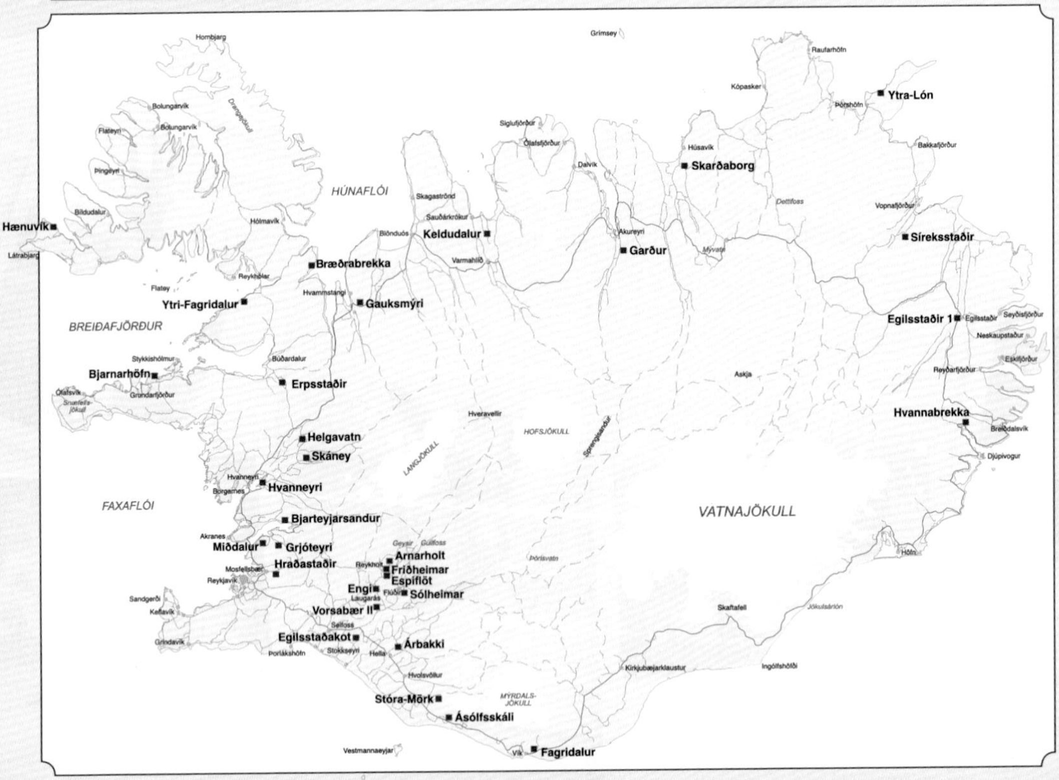

Hornbjarg
Grímsey
Raufarhöfn
Kópasker
Ytra-Lón
Þórshöfn
Bolungarvík
Flateyri
Þingeyri
Siglufjörður
Ólafsfjörður
Húsavík
Skarðaborg
Bakkafjörður
Dalvík
HÚNAFLÓI
Skagaströnd
Sauðárkrókur
Dettifoss
Vopnafjörður
Bíldudalur
Hænuvík
Hólmavík
Blönduós
Keldudalur
Akureyri
Garður
Mývatn
Síreksstaðir
Látrabjarg
Varmahlíð
Bræðrabrekka
Reykhólar
Flatey
Hvammstangi
Ytri-Fagridalur
Gauksmýri
BREIÐAFJÖRÐUR
Egilsstaðir 1
Egilsstaðir
Seyðisfjörður
Neskaupstaður
Stykkishólmur
Búðardalur
Eskifjörður
Bjarnarhöfn
Reyðarfjörður
Askja
Ólafsvík
Grundarfjörður
Erpsstaðir
Hveravellir
Hvannabrekka
HOFSJÖKULL
Breiðdalsvík
Helgavatn
Skáney
LANGJÖKULL
Djúpivogur
Hvanneyri
Borgarnes
FAXAFLÓI
VATNAJÖKULL
Bjarteyjarsandur
Akranes
Geysir
Gullfoss
Miðdalur
Grjóteyri
Arnarholt
Þórisvatn
Höfn
Hraðastaðir
Mosfellsbær
Reykholt
Friðheimar
Reykjavík
Espiflöt
Sandgerði
Engi
Laugarás
Flúðir
Sólheimar
Keflavík
Vorsabær II
Skaftafell
Jökulsárlón
Selfoss
Grindavík
Egilsstaðakot
Árbakki
Þorlákshöfn
Stokkseyri
Hella
Kirkjubæjarklaustur
Ingólfshöfði
Hvolsvöllur
Stóra-Mörk
MÝRDALSJÖKULL
Ásólfsskáli
Vestmannaeyjar
Vík
Fagridalur

Welcome to the countryside

– A Visit to an Open Farm

Open Farms is an opportunity to visit farms and get familiar with the work done in rural Iceland. Open Farms is a collaboration between the farms and The Farmers Association of Iceland. The farms represent a cross-section of Icelandic agriculture today.
Farmers take a fee for visits. Amounts are different based on the nature and scope of the services. In most cases the farmers only accept cash and visitors are politely asked to keep that in mind.

- More information on Open Farms can be found on **www.bondi.is**
- Have a nice trip, we hope you enjoy visiting the countryside!

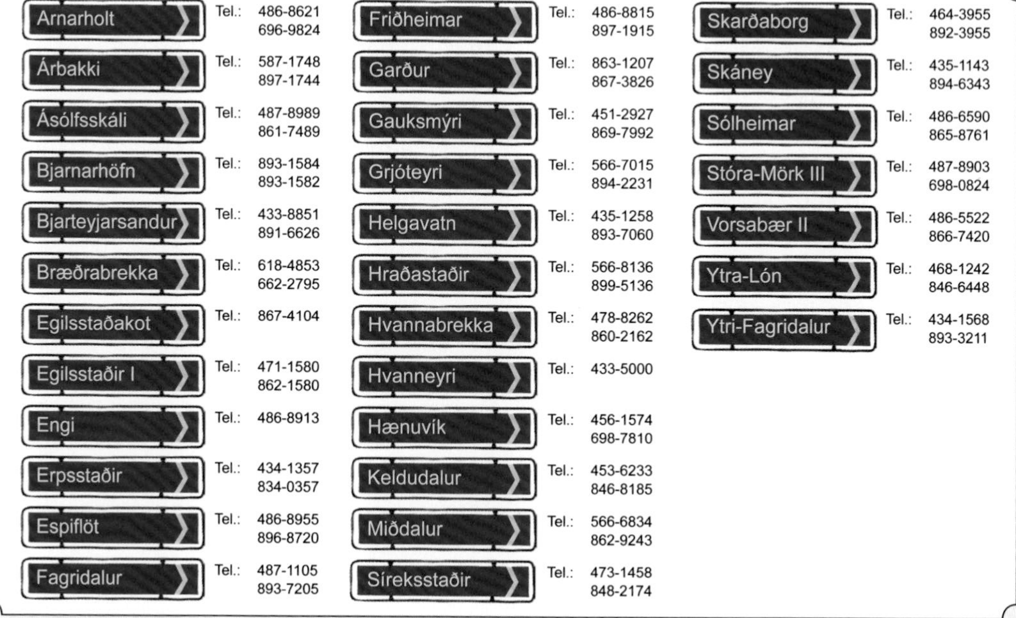

Farm	Tel.:
Arnarholt	486-8621 696-9824
Árbakki	587-1748 897-1744
Ásólfsskáli	487-8989 861-7489
Bjarnarhöfn	893-1584 893-1582
Bjarteyjarsandur	433-8851 891-6626
Bræðrabrekka	618-4853 662-2795
Egilsstaðakot	867-4104
Egilsstaðir I	471-1580 862-1580
Engi	486-8913
Erpsstaðir	434-1357 834-0357
Espiflöt	486-8955 896-8720
Fagridalur	487-1105 893-7205
Friðheimar	486-8815 897-1915
Garður	863-1207 867-3826
Gauksmýri	451-2927 869-7992
Grjóteyri	566-7015 894-2231
Helgavatn	435-1258 893-7060
Hraðastaðir	566-8136 899-5136
Hvannabrekka	478-8262 860-2162
Hvanneyri	433-5000
Hænuvík	456-1574 698-7810
Keldudalur	453-6233 846-8185
Miðdalur	566-6834 862-9243
Síreksstaðir	473-1458 848-2174
Skarðaborg	464-3955 892-3955
Skáney	435-1143 894-6343
Sólheimar	486-6590 865-8761
Stóra-Mörk III	487-8903 698-0824
Vorsabær II	486-5522 866-7420
Ytra-Lón	468-1242 846-6448
Ytri-Fagridalur	434-1568 893-3211

Farm Food Direct

Aided by the Farm Food Direct marketing programme, the production and sale of goods directly to consumers enables farmers to develop a wide range of products which have their origins in Icelandic nature.

More and more, Icelandic farmers are selling home-grown and homemade products, including handicrafts, straight from the farm. This trend is encouraged by increased tourism: consumers demand a greater selection of products that bring out local traits and traditions. Origin labelling attracts ever-increasing interest, together with good old-fashioned personal service.

Farm Food Direct is based on the following principles:

- Utilising historical traditions as well as innovative local techniques
- Preserving cultural heritage and introducing it to future generations
- Nurturing a mutual understanding between producers and consumers, bringing them closer together
- Returning to the original producer a larger part of the proceeds from the sale of goods and services

Another aim of Farm Food Direct is to support rural populations and employment. Finally, the goods sold under this programme are only made on a small scale, i.e. they are not mass-produced.

In early 2013, approximately 100 farms were involved, and their number is growing. These members are either already making or intend to start making Icelandic food products or handicrafts. While some are still developing their products, others have started to sell them. The opposite page lists the Farm Food Direct members when this book went to press.

The quality seal „First-hand"

In 2009, Farm Food Direct adopted a quality seal as a logo on product packaging. To use this seal, each farm must apply for permission, which is only granted if the farm fulfils both the quality requirements and an assessment by Farm Food Direct. The programme ensures that all necessary production licences have been obtained and that the farmstead and its vicinity are clean and tidy. However, programme members are not obligated to adopt this quality seal, although all of them must maintain the prescribed government licences, like any other production company.

An updated member list and information on product offerings and opening hours can be found at www.beintfrabyli.is and in the brochure The Ideal Holiday, available at most tourist facilities.

FARMS SELLING AT THE FARMSTEAD
DISTANCE SELLING ONLY
ALSO OFFER ACCOMMODATION

THE WEST AND WESTFJORDS

ÁLFTAVATN
BAKKI
BJARNARHÖFN
BJARTEYJARSANDUR
BRENNISTAÐIR
BRJÁNSLÆKUR
ERPSSTAÐIR
EYSTRI-LEIRÁRGARÐAR
GEMLUFALL
GLITSTAÐIR
GRÍMSSTAÐIR 2
HAGI 2
HÁAFELL
HÁLS
HUNDASTAPI
HÚSAVÍK
HVERINN-BJÖRK
LEIRULÆKUR
LITLA BREKKA – KVÍAHOLT
MIÐHÚS
NEÐRI-HÁLS
NEÐRI-HÓLL
NORÐTUNGA 3
NÚPUR II
SKÁLHOLT
STAÐUR
SUÐUR-BÁR GRUNDARFJÖRÐUR
YSTU-GARÐAR
YTRI-FAGRIDALUR
ÖRNÓLFSDALUR
ÞURRANES

THE NORTH

ÁSHÓLL
BÓLSTAÐARHLÍÐ 2
BREKKULÆKUR
DÆLI
FINNASTAÐIR
GARÐUR
GARÐUR 1
GIL
GRÆNAHLÍÐ
HAFNIR
HELLA - REYKKOFINN
HOLTSEL
HÖFÐI I
JÖRFI
MIÐHVAMMUR
LAUGARMÝRI
LITLA - HLÍÐ
STÓRI-DUNHAGI
LÓN II
SKARÐABORG
SKJALDARVÍK
STÓRHÓLL
SYÐRI-HAGI
VOGAFJÓS

THE EAST

AÐALBÓL
ÁSGARÐUR
BLÖNDUBAKKI
BORG, SKRIÐDAL
EGILSSTAÐIR I
HÓLABREKKA
KLAUSTURSEL
MIÐHÚS
MIÐSKER
MÖÐRUDALUR, Á EFRA-FJALLI
SELJAVELLIR
SÍREKSSTAÐIR
VALLANES

THE SOUTH

AKUR
ÁSGARÐUR
EFSTIDALUR II
EGILSSTAÐAKOT
ENGI
FAGRIDALUR
FOSSNES
GUNNARSHÓLMI
HEIÐMÖRK
HRÓLFSSTAÐAHELLIR
KALDBAKUR
LÁGAFELL
LANDNÁMSHÆNAN
LANGAMÝRI
LANGHOLTSKOT
NÝIBÆR
ORMSSTAÐIR
SKÁLMHOLT
SMÁRATÚN
SMYRLABJÖRG
SÓLHEIMAR
VEGATUNGA
VESTRA-FÍFLHOLT
ÞORVALDSEYRI

See map p. 538-539

Hornbjarg
Drangajökull
Bolungarvík
Flateyri
Ísafjörður
Núpur 2
Gemlufall
Þingeyri
Arnarfjörður
Bíldudalur
Patreksfjörður
Skálholt
Hagi 2
Látrabjarg
Brjánslækur
Staður
Reykhólar
Flatey
Hólmavík
Drangsnes
Bakki
Húsavík
Miðhús
HÚNAFLÓI
Hafnir
Siglufjörð
Hofsós
Skagaströnd
Sauðárkrókur
Blönduós
Gil
Varmahlíð
Laugarm
Bólstaðarhlíð
Jörfi
Dæli
Stórhóll
Hvammstangi
Laugarbakki
Brekkulækur
Litla-Hlíð
Ytri-Fagridalur
Þurranes
BREIÐAFJÖRÐUR
Stykkishólmur
Búðardalur
Vatn
Erpsstaðir
Suður-Bár
Bjarnarhöfn
Hellissandur
Ólafsvík
Grundarfjörður
Snæfells-
jökull
Neðri-Höll
Alftavatn
Arnarstapi
Ystu-Garðar
Glitstaðir
Örnólfsdalur
Norðtunga 3
Háafell
Grímsstaðir II
Hveravellir
LANGJÖKULL
Hundastapi
Ensku húsin
Kleppjárnsreykir
Brennistaðir
Leirulækur
Litla-Brekka
Borgarnes
FAXAFLÓI
Eystri-Leirárgarðar
Bjarteyjarsandur
Neðri-Háls
Háls
Akranes
Geysir
Gullfoss
Efsti-Dalur 2
Mosfellsbær
Vegatunga
Reykjavík
Gunnarshólmi
Ásgarður
Engi
Akur
Langholtskot
Laxárdalur
Heiðmörk
Keflavík
Sólheimar
Ormsstaðir
Fossnes
Skaftholt
Hveragerði
Langamýri
Skálmholt
Egilsstaðakot
Hrólfsstaðahellir
Kaldbakur
Grindavík
Landnámshænan
Hvolsvöllur
Smáratún
Vestra-Fíflholt
Búland
MÝRDALS
JÖKULL
Lágafell
Nýibær
Þorvaldseyri
Vestmannaeyjar

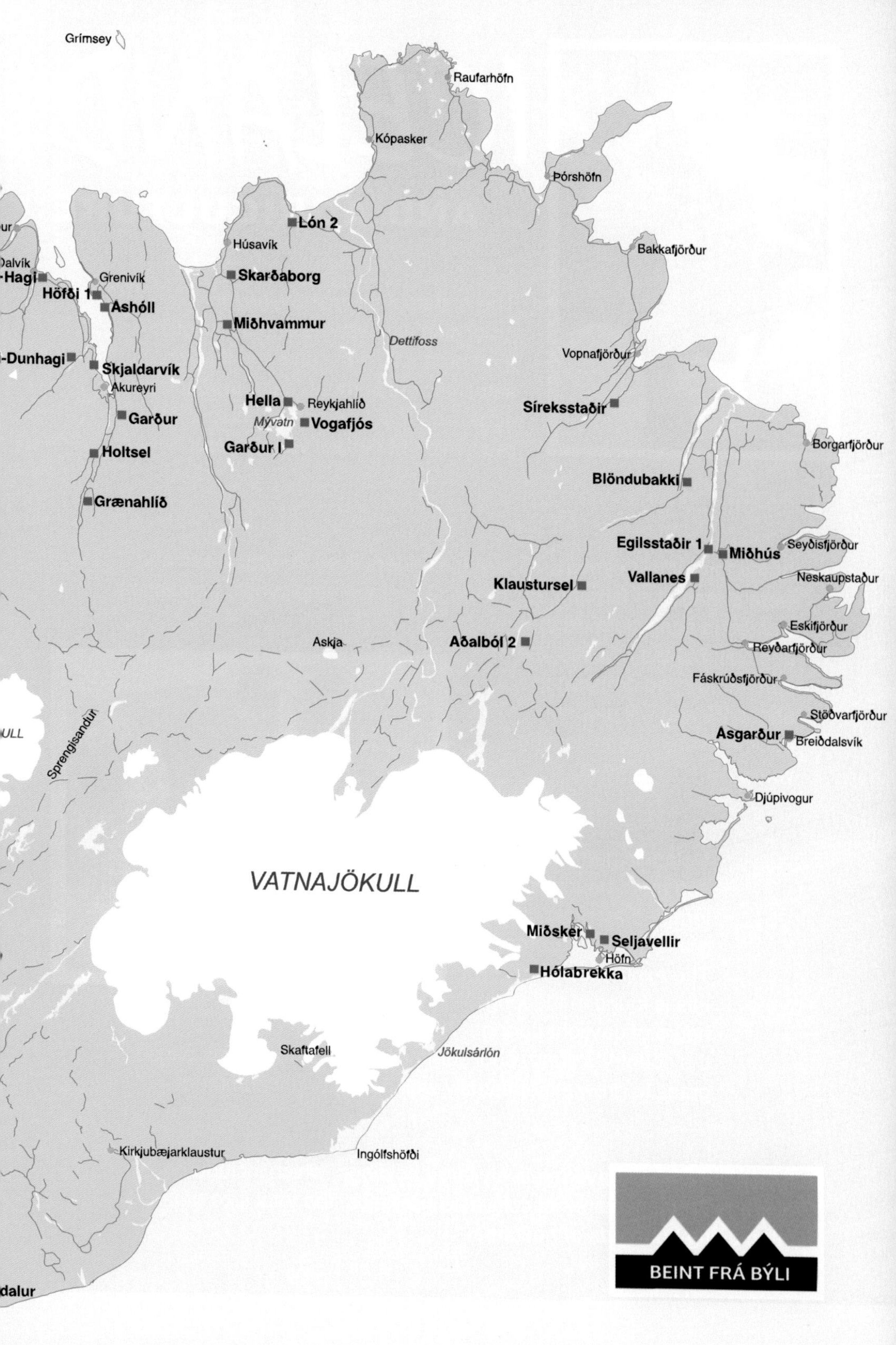
Grímsey
Raufarhöfn
Kópasker
Þórshöfn
Lón 2
Húsavík
Bakkafjörður
Grenivík
Höfði 1
Áshóll
Skarðaborg
Miðhvammur
Dettifoss
Vopnafjörður
Skjaldarvík
Akureyri
Hella
Reykjahlíð
Mývatn
Vogafjós
Garður
Garður I
Holtsel
Síreksstaðir
Borgarfjörður
Blöndubakki
Grænahlíð
Egilsstaðir 1
Miðhús
Seyðisfjörður
Vallanes
Neskaupstaður
Klaustursel
Eskifjörður
Askja
Aðalból 2
Reyðarfjörður
Fáskrúðsfjörður
Sprengisandur
Stöðvarfjörður
Ásgarður
Breiðdalsvík
Djúpivogur
VATNAJÖKULL
Miðsker
Seljavellir
Höfn
Hólabrekka
Skaftafell
Jökulsárlón
Kirkjubæjarklaustur
Ingólfshöfði
BEINT FRÁ BÝLI

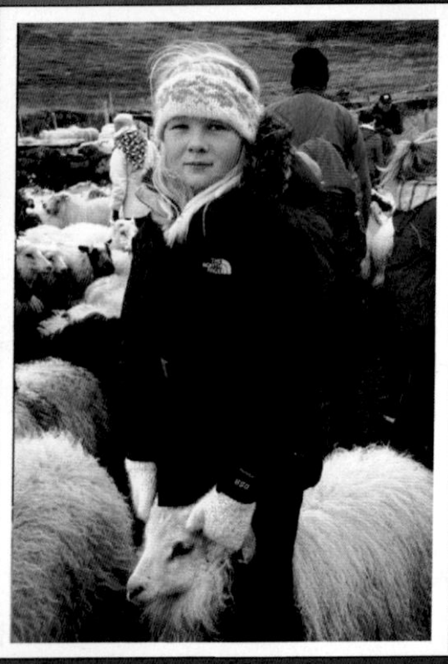

ICELAND
AND AGRICULTURE

There are unique conditions for producing wholesome and unpolluted food products in Iceland and the land is self-sufficient in meat, dairy products, eggs, and to a large extent also in the production of certain vegetables.

At the turn of last century, 73% of Icelanders lived in rural areas and were engaged in farming. By 1940, 32% of the employable population worked in agriculture. At the beginning of the nineties, the percentage had dropped to about 4% and will probably decline even more in coming years.

Icelandic grass is better and more nourishing forage than most other grass grown in Europe. The explanation for this is found in the long hours of daylight during the country´s short, cool summers. These conditions cause grass to grow exceptionally well during bright summers.

Icelandic farmers have relatively large holdings, which include on average 30-50 hectares of cultivated hayfields, the total size of farms often being hundreds of hectares.

One characteristic of Icelandic agriculture is the varied colouring of its native livestock. Horses, cattle and sheep exhibit many colour varieties, no particular variety having been favoured. However, emphasis has been placed on the wool of white sheep being pure white, as this variety is more valuable.

There are about 4000 full-time farmers in Iceland, and their numbers are decreasing, although the number of individuals deriving part of their income from farming is increasing. The majority of Icelandic farmers live on their own land, and holdings have often been in the same family for generations. Most do reasonably well, although very few can be said to belong to a high-income group.

Icelandic food production is based on purity, wholesomeness and sustainability. In Iceland there has been a ban on the use of antibiotics as feed additives and hormone implants as growth promoters, while the use of pesticides and herbicides is in general very restricted. The move towards organic agriculture in Iceland has not attracted quite the same attention as it has in some other European countries due to the fact that domestic products are already protected by strict regulations.

TRADITIONAL ICELANDIC FOOD

Hangikjöt – Smoked lamb

Smoked lamb, leg or shoulder, can be had on the bone, boned or cooked and sliced as luncheon meat. Raw hangikjöt should be boiled in unsalted water at a low heat for about 11/2 hours. In Iceland hangikjöt is traditionally served either hot or cold, with potatoes in a white (béchamel) sauce and green peas (variations according to taste). Popular as a luncheon meat, especially on Icelandic rye pancakes (flatbrauð). A favourite with Icelanders at any time, hangikjöt is traditional Christmas fare.

Svið – Singed sheep heads

Singed sheep heads should first be thoroughly rinsed and then boiled in well-salted water for 11/2 to 2 hours. Svið can be eaten hot or cold, with either plain boiled potatoes, mashed potatoes or swede turnips. A popular dish in Iceland, svið are an ideal item for a packed lunch. Also available ready-cooked, tinned or pressed and gelled (sviðasulta).

Saltkjöt – Salted lamb/mutton

Salted lamb/mutton needs to be boiled for 11/2 hours in unsalted water. It is served either hot or cold with potatoes or swede turnips and is frequently accompanied by split pea soup.

Lambakjöt – Lamb

Sheep breeding in Iceland goes back to the time of settlement, which explains the nations high consumption of lamb. In keeping with tradition, sheep are allowed to graze freely in mountain areas over the summer, feeding on the fresh grass and wild herbs that give Icelandic lamb its distinctive flavour.

Slátur – Blood and liver puddings

Slátur is a traditional Icelandic food, prepared every year in the months of September and October when the slaughtering season is at its peak. There are two types of slátur: blóðmör (blood pudding) and lifrarpylsa (liver pudding). Blóðmör consists of sheep´s blood, meal, suet and spices, mixed together and sewn up in sheep stomachs. Lifrarpylsa is quite similar, the difference being that instead of blood minced lamb liver is used. The puddings are boiled for 3 hours and generally served with creamed potatoes or mashed swede turnips. Precooked slátur which only needs to be heated and can also be fried is available at all stores.

Skyr – an Icelandic dairy product

Akin to yogurt and the German Quark, skyr is a dairy product with a very low fat content. Usually eaten with milk or cream, sometimes sprinkled with sugar and often berries when in season; it can of course be eaten plain. Varieties of skyr with added berries and fruits are also available.

Þorramatur – Traditional Icelandic foods

In addition to smoked and salted lamb, singed sheep heads, dried fish and rye pancakes (flatbrauð), traditional Icelandic food includes shark and various pickled foodstuffs, chiefly meat, that have been allowed to stand in whey for 3-4 months. Þorramatur is particularly associated with the period January-March.

Icelandic milk products

Icelandic milk is one of nature´s bounties, of which its countrymen are rightly proud. Through the centuries, this delicate product has been handled with respect and now, in recent years, with imaginative flair. The Icelandic dairy industry is subject to strict production control and all products must meet the high level of quality expected by the public.

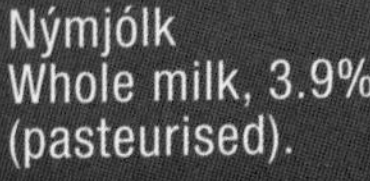

Nýmjólk
Whole milk, 3.9%
(pasteurised).

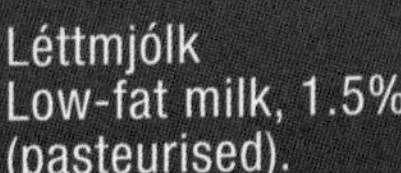

Léttmjólk
Low-fat milk, 1.5%
(pasteurised).

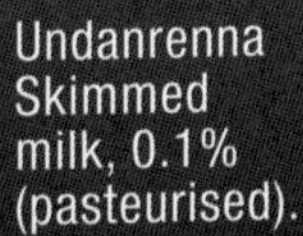

Undanrenna
Skimmed
milk, 0.1%
(pasteurised).

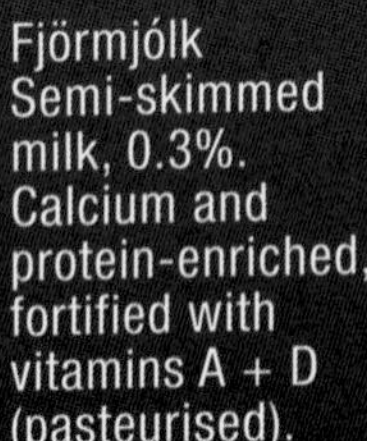

Fjörmjólk
Semi-skimmed
milk, 0.3%.
Calcium and
protein-enriched,
fortified with
vitamins A + D
(pasteurised).

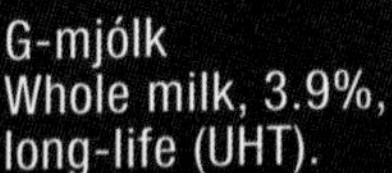

G-mjólk
Whole milk, 3.9%,
long-life (UHT).

Stoðmjólk
Follow-on milk for
babies aged 6-24
months.

Hleðsla
Protein drink with
chocolate flavor,low-fat,
0.5%, long-life (UHT).

Kókómjólk
Chocolate milk,
low-fat, 2.0%,
long-life (UHT).

Rjómi
Cream, 36%
(pasteurised).

Matreiðslurjómi
Light cream, 15%
(pasteurised).

Kaffirjómi
Coffee cream, 12%,
long-life (UHT).

Sýrður rjómi
Crème fraiche:
5%, 10% or 18%;
spiced/flavoured.

Súrmjólk
Cultured milk,
3.9%.

MS Léttmál - grísk jógúrt
Greek yoghurt with dates, almonds
and seeds. Protein 10g.

Skyr
Traditional Icelandic
non-fat dairy
product with creamy
texture. Plain or
flavoured with fruit.

Skyr.is
Flavoured skyr.
Incredibly healthy
dairy product with
creamy texture,
fat-free and high
in protein.

Skyr.is próteindrykkur
Protein skyr drink.
Low carb and fat-free.

Óskajógúrt
Yoghurt – plain,
with fruits or
flavoured, 3.4%,
low-fat 1.3%.

Létt drykkjarjógúrt
Flavoured, low-fat
drinking yoghurt,
1.3%.

Icelandic meat

Iceland offers a fine variety of meats: lamb, pork, and beef, as well as a limited amount of horse meat and reindeer. Meat display counters are always well stocked with quality fresh meat, handled by top class butchers. Iceland has strict regulations relating to the handling and storage of meat and the use of hormones is strictly forbidden.

ICELANDIC	ENGLISH
Kjöt	Meat
Lamb	Lamb
Naut	Beef
Svín	Pork
Folald	Horsemeat (Foal)
Hreindýr	Reindeer
Læri	Leg
Lærissneið	Slices of leg
Hryggur	Saddle/rack
Kótilettur/rifjur	Cutlets/chops
Frampartur	Shoulder
Frampartssneiðar	Shoulder slices
Hamborgarhryggur	Smoked saddle of pork
London lamb	Ligthly smoked lamb
Kjötfars	Sausage meat (f. Meatballs)
Kjöthakk	Minced meat
Lundir	Tenderloin
Hryggvöðvi (filé)	Fillet
Smásteik (gúllas)	Boneless stewing meat
Súpukjöt	Pot stew meat (with bones)
Afturhryggsneið (T-bein)	T-bone steak
Hamborgarar	Hamburgers
Rifjasteik	Rib steak
Skinka	Ham
Beikon (flesk)	Bacon
Saltkjöt	Salted meat
Reykt kjöt	Smoked meat
Kálfasneið (schnitzel)	Veal schnitzel
Hangikjöt	Smoked lamb

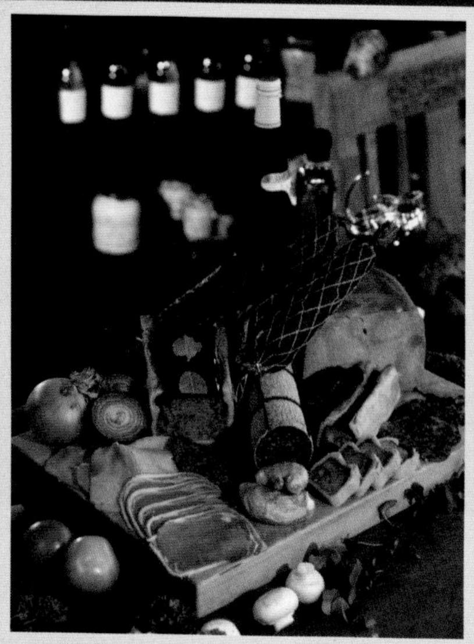

Þríbrot ehf

Spas and Natural Hot Pools

Hoffell

Extensive geothermal activity is one of Iceland‘s most distinctive features, with geothermal areas covering more of this country than any other. In fact, geothermal heat is known to be present at over 700 Icelandic sites. For geothermal warmth to reach the surface, water needs to bring it there from underneath.

Fontana

The island‘s geothermal activity clearly caught the attention of the early settlers, as they referred to geothermal phenomena in their place names. Thus a great number of the original names include terms such as varm (warm), reyk (smoke/steam) or laug (bathing pool). It is estimated that at least 55 place names, or around 2% of all saga place names, are linked to geothermal activity.

Snorralaug

Ever since the settlement, Icelanders have used geothermal water for washing and bathing. This is often mentioned in the sagas, with the most famous instance probably being that of Snorri Sturluson at Reykholt, in Borgarfjör›ur, West Iceland. Snorri, who was a productive saga writer, enjoyed relaxing in the hot water and discussing the topics of the day, just as people still do in hot tubs at modern swimming pools all around Iceland.

Jarðböðin

Laugarfell

At several places in Iceland, it so happens that geothermal water collects naturally at comfortable temperatures for bathing. In other places, people have come to nature's assistance to obtain the right temperatures and amount of water. Finally, in modern times many special swimming pools, hot tubs, etc. have been constructed. Therefore, it is often difficult to distinguish which pools are natural and which are not. For instance, there was no geothermal activity at the surface when construction started on the Blue Lagoon. Its water is pumped up out of drill holes and the surroundings are entirely designed by people. Thoses places are catagorized as spas.

NATURAL HOT POOLS:

P.	Name
203	Kvika / Seltjarnarnes
288	Hellulaug / Flókalundur
305	Pollurinn / Tálknafjörður
298	Heydalur / West fjords
298	Hörgslhíðarlaug / West fjords
318	Nauteyrarlaug / West fjords
352	Grettislaug / Skagafjörður
148	Klambragilslaug / Hveragerði
445	Landmannalaugar / Highland
455	Kerlingarfjöll / Highland
457	Hveravellir / Highland
471	Laugafell / Highland
475	Víti / Highland
490	Laugarfell / Highland

SPAS:

P.	Name
216	Bláa lónið / Blue Lagoon
500	Nauthólsvík / Reykjavík
92	Jarðböðin / Mývatn Nature Baths
117	Hoffell
173	Secret Lagoon / Flúðir
191	Fontana / Laugavatn

By scanning the QR-code you can access further information on those spas and natural hot pools throughout Iceland which are listed above.

Icelandic Lava Caves

In Iceland's lava fields, which cover about 11% of the country, there are about 600 known caves. Records tell of people having entered such caves before the year 1000. Surtshellir cave (note that hellir in any Icelandic name below means „cave") was in fact the first lava cave on earth to be mapped, as it was surveyed by the well-known Icelandic natural scientists Eggert Ólafsson and Bjarni Pálsson in 1756. As of 1970, however, fewer than 20 lava caves were known to exist in Iceland. This changed abruptly, because in 1979 the Icelandic speleologist Björn Hróarsson began to seek out, explore and study lava caves. In 1989, he founded the Icelandic Speleological Society and in 1990 published his book Hraunhellar á Íslandi (Lava Caves in Iceland), which described 150 lava caves. The work of the "cavemen" in the Icelandic Speleological Society has since been extremely successful and led to the discovery of a large number of lava caves, as evidenced by Björn Hróarsson's more recent book of 2006, Íslenskir hellar (Icelandic Caves), which lists about 520 lava caves. Thus, about 500 caves were discovered in the last quarter century, stretching to a total length of around 100 kilometres.

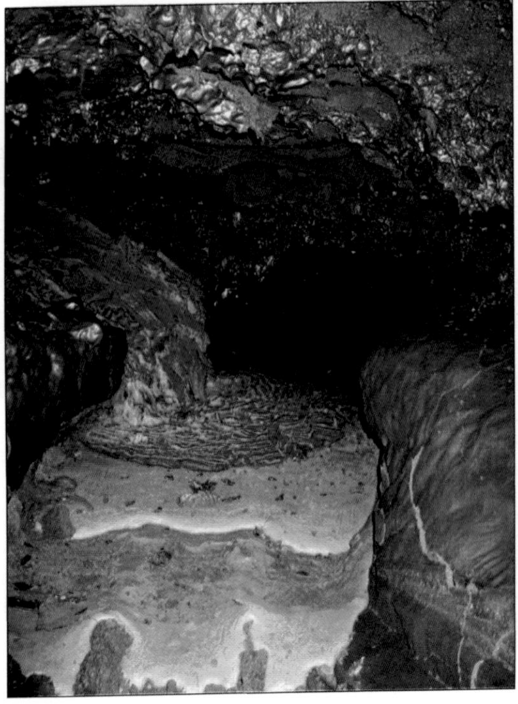

What is a lava cave?

There are many ways to define a lava cave, with no one definition being more correct than the others. A completely dark cavity in volcanic rock is one of the definitions used by lava cave experts in recent years. According to it, any hollow space in the lava not reached by any light would be called a lava cave. Others use a longer definition, requiring the hollow space both to be longer than 20 metres and passable to human beings in order to be called a lava cave. Lava caves are divided into a number of categories depending on how they were formed: lava tube caves, craters, blister caves, fissure caves, rootless vent caves, sea caves, erosional caves and, finally, man-made caves.

When we refer to the length of a cave, we mean the total cave length, that is, the length of the main passage together with the lengths of any side passages. The length of the main cavern alone is called the main passage length. Thus, in caves which have many long side passages there is a considerable difference between the total cave length and the main passage length. Where one cave begins and another ends is frequently a topic of debate! What makes a cave, where should the line be drawn between two caves in the same lava tube, and what constitutes a cave system? While it is difficult to give a definitive answer to these questions, certain points should be kept in mind. For instance, a cave is considered the same even if there are several openings where the roof has caved in. Also, a cave can be a single cave without being completely passable everywhere for a person remaining underground. Similarly, there do not need to be accessible connections between all parts of a single cave, so that the Icelandic caves named Hulduhellir, Stefánshellir and Surtshellir are in fact considered as one cave even though it is not possible to travel between them and Hulduhellir is entirely inaccessible. When referring to a cave's height, we mean the ceiling height, i.e. from floor to ceiling. The vertical depth of a cave, in contrast, refers to the difference between the altitudes of the cave floor at each end. Once the cave's depth and length are clear, it becomes possible to calculate its slope

The formation of lava caves

Magma from a volcanic eruption often flows into defined channels and tends to form tunnels through the spreading lava field. When the molten lava inside a tunnel runs out and leaves it empty at the end of an eruption, provided that the tunnel remains hollow while cooling and hardening, a lava tube forms. To describe these processes more exactly, we can say that when a lava stream follows the same course for some distance, it generally forms first a channel, open to the sky, and farther on a tunnel. Under the cover of lava that has already stiffened over the tunnel and may later become fairly smooth and passable for walkers, called pahoehoe lava, the molten stream underneath can flow long distances. Farther on, the molten lava is likely to start coming up here and there through openings to the surface, from where it flows in thin streams that pile together when stiffening and are then called ropy lava. When magma from the eruption stops feeding a tunnel, the tunnel empties to form a chamber. If the roof of this chamber is strong enough to hold itself up after cooling, this chamber will remain as a cave. However, in order for the chamber to become hollow in the first place, the slope of the tunnel must be steep enough for the lava left in it to run down the passage after fresh lava from behind stops pushing it. Flow in the tunnel stops when either the volcanic activity ends or the stream finds another passage. When new lava stops feeding into a tunnel with little slope and no longer pushes the previous lava forward, the lava present will solidify, filling the tunnel and leaving either no cave or one partly filled with lava, as many actually are. Moreover, the roof may be so weak that it collapses to some extent, leaving no cave but rather piles of fallen rubble in the lava channel. The viscosity of the lava, the quantity and speed of its flow and the landscape it crosses are also important in determining whether a lava cave forms.

Conservation

Lava caves are among Iceland's most vulnerable natural features. Damage to them cannot be taken back, but is permanent and irreparable. We need to bear in mind that man alone destroys caves; if no one ever visited them, they would generally remain unchanged and undamaged for thousands of years, or even hundreds of thousands, like many of Korea‘s largest caves.

Three approaches probably matter most for conserving lava caves. First of all, education; second, directing caving trips to caves which can tolerate the traffic; and third, closing off the most vulnerable caves to any traffic. Education and knowledge about the world of caves is extremely important for protecting them. The goal of visitors is and always must be to leave no traces behind. Nothing may be left except perhaps footprints, nothing may be taken away but photographs, and nothing may be broken. On the other hand, there

are numerous caves which can withstand traffic well, even the passage of whole groups, so long as the proper attitude, a good tour guide and adequate illumination are involved.

Caves are also threatened by the construction of power plants and roads. When lava fields are flooded, as by hydropower reservoirs, any caves there will be lost forever. An absolute demand must be that any caves in the lava fields be studied before being flooded, so as not to show disrespect of both nature and science. Seeing lava fields disappear under the reservoir of Hágöngumiðlun was painful, and the parties involved made no attempt to carry out speleological research. Not only must this neglect of research never be repeated, but other lava fields need protection from flooding. Lava fields and everything they contain are by nature too remarkable to destroy.

In a country where lava covers about 11% of the surface area, it is hardly possible to avoid routing any roads over lava fields, though it should be avoided insofar as possible. Wherever roads are built over lava, speleological research should be conducted on the intended route so that caves in the area can be left unharmed. Nowadays, environmental impact assessments are usually conducted before laying roads, but caves are generally not taken into consideration. This must change. For example, the cave Búri in Leitahraun was discovered on 7 May 2005, constituting one of the greatest cave discoveries in Iceland for centuries. Around the same time, a lava cave

was discovered on the island of Jeju, South Korea. That cave was named Yongchon and is about 2,450 metres long. Like Búri, it is one of the most important lava caves in its home country. As befits civilized societies, societies which take an interest in their natural treasures, Yongchon cave was sealed off within a week of being found. Two sturdy gates were erected at the entrance, with about five metres in between that were monitored by motion sensors directly connected to the nearest police station. All traffic in the cave would have to follow set rules. Within a few months of the discovery, books and pamphlets were published to introduce the cave to the public as well as the international scientific community. Here in Iceland, where nature conservation is unfortunately decades behind the standard in most other countries, nothing was done about the discovery of Búri.

Caring for caves

Most cave formations are very delicate, often unable to bear even the slightest touch without breaking. Usually, caves are completely untouched when discovered, even if five

or ten thousand years have passed since they were formed. A cave's climate stays stable, with similar temperature and humidity year-round, along with silence and an absence of light and life, so that there is almost no erosion. Caves have therefore generally remained unchanged for millennia, until the first humans arrive. As soon as the first rays of light cut through the hitherto permanent darkness, danger threatens.

There has been a disgraceful lack of good conduct in Icelandic lava caves. Throughout much of the twentieth century, most known caves were severely damaged, with lava formations being broken and removed and all sorts of rubbish left behind.

Raufarhólshellir was sheared of its beautiful formations in the first decades of the twentieth century. Stefánshellir was divested of its stalactites and lava straws soon after news of its location got out in the middle of the century. Víðgelmir was damaged and large amounts of trash left there in the 1940s and 1950s. The bones in Surtshellir, thousands of years old, disappeared. Similar stories can be told of most other caves that were known by around the middle of the twentieth century. Waste such as batteries, flares, plastic bags and bottles, clothing, string and the packaging from film, chocolate or drinks were often thrown aside on the spot.

Stalactites and other lava formations in the caves were broken off and removed, only to crumble and gather dust in people's homes, largely forgotten.

Spelunking equipment

Exploring caves rarely requires much special equipment. Illumination is the most important consideration. Two good lights are a must, as well as extra batteries. The light used must enable the spelunker to see well enough to avoid damaging the cave, and the energy source must be sufficient to provide full strength for the entire trip. While either good electric torches or diode lights will suffice, one has to have a backup light along in any case. Sufficient illumination is crucial for not damaging the cave. No open flame must ever be lit in caves, nor any flares or other light sources which cause pollution.

Helmets are very beneficial, for example bicycle helmets. The lack of erosion in caves means that nothing has blunted the edges of stones which have fallen from the ceiling. Bumping into them without a helmet can thus be very painful.

Fortunately, however, material very rarely collapses from a cave ceiling. Mostly, this happens during the first years after the cave is formed, while the lava is still cooling enough to crack and buckle, causing collapses which later become highly unlikely. The temperature in many Icelandic caves is about freezing or up to one to three degrees Celsius. In larger caves it is generally slightly warmer deep in the cave. As long as people keep moving, they tend not to feel the cold much since the air is completely still, but the chill sinks in when sweaty spelunkers sit down for a moment. Also, water is usually leaking from the cave ceiling. Even when the sun is shining brightly overhead and it has not rained for days or weeks, there will still be a steady drip inside the cave. For these reasons, spelunkers must protect themselves from wet as well as cold.

Since clothing often gets soiled and torn when exploring caves, it is wise not to wear expensive garments. It is also advisable to avoid wearing fabrics such as loose wool, which is likely to leave fibres behind in the cave. Gloves or mittens are necessary, but again woollen mittens are not a good choice. Leather or lined rubber gloves are well suited for spelunking.

Strong footwear is important because it is difficult to walk around on sharp, uneven stones. Fairly flexible hiking boots work best. If there is water in the cave, though, rubber boots may well be a better choice. Where ice covers the cave floor, it is often quite slippery, calling for some sort of spikes. In some cases it is necessary to use ropes or ladders to enter and explore the cave. Aluminium or cable ladders will manage in most cases, although some caves require a complete rappelling kit. In any case, a proper attitude towards nature is the most important factor in every cave trip. To leave the cave without a trace is the highest aim of any spelunker.

Dear Traveller

Iceland is unique, with incredible sights to please the eye and nourish the soul. On the other hand, not everyone sees and experiences this island in the same way. The psychic Erla Stefánsdóttir has for instance long been renowned among Icelanders for her visions, since she sees and feels wavelengths which reach far beyond what ordinary human eyes are capable of. We the editors of Iceland Road Atlas were thus curious to know how Erla views our landscape and wanted to give you, our Atlas readers, a chance to partake in this view, for your enlightenment and enjoyment.

Erla Stefánsdóttir

ERLA STEFÁNSDÓTTIR

Dear traveller,

On my journeys around Iceland, I have drawn this country's major energy lines onto maps. Most energy lines are either varying frequencies of yellow, or else violet or blue. The difference between such lines is that the blue ones, if they flow through a place we stay, affect how likely we are to perceive anyone moving between distinct worlds, whereas the violet ones flow between vegetation zones and the elf world, and the yellow ones provide unbelievable energy in many dimensions. If you should be planning to travel around the Ring Road by car, I advise you to drive slowly. Stop here and there, using not only your physical body but also your emotions, and look with your heart too. The earth's energy veil consists at once of the radiation and channels of the life force.

Such energy pathways exist in every dimension, as does indeed all of nature, which is full of life in countless forms, active at various frequencies. Iceland's energy is unique, matched in very few other places. Whether you are heading west or north, south or east, take care to notice especially the mountains, rivers, waterfalls, hay fields and forests. Try comparing two different mountains, or else different valleys or fjords, or lakes or rivers. You can also do special exercises for your senses of feeling, sight and hearing.

ICELAND'S ENERGY CENTRE

The biggest, most powerful energy lines in this country flow through Hofsjökull glacier, which is located in the middle of the island and is its primary energy centre. These lines connect the courses of energy and development for all conscious beings inhabiting Iceland. In addition, these energy lines are the divinity's means of connecting with creation - pathways which give us joy and strength while we explore the island. It is certainly better to return from your trip full of energy and happiness than exhausted. It is possible to read more about energy centres in my book Lífssýn mín ("My vision of life"), which was published in Icelandic in 2003. As emissions of and channels for the life force, energy paths form a grid over the entire earth, doing so in every world, from the physical up to the spiritual world, allowing us to say that the earth's energy system is reflected in God's embrace.

EARTH'S ENERGY LINES

The Chinese call these lines dragon paths and the Australian Aborigines song lines, while the English language also refers to them as ley or force lines. Energy lines are like currents of light flowing within every country as well as between countries. The greatest light currents may be over a hundred metres in height or breadth, whereas the smallest barely reach our ankles and resemble the blue trails left over the centuries by man's domestic animals.

While the largest and brightest energy flows are those between the world's energy centres, there are also very strong pathways between the energy centres inside each country. Thus, not only are there seven energy centres on the earth as a whole, but each country has its own particular seven energy centres.

EXPERIENCE FOR YOURSELF

You should definitely not try to rush through Iceland's largest and strongest life currents in one summer, since you must allow yourself enough time to experience their power. Take at least one month to make the most of each and every one, applying your mind as well as your feelings in many dimensions. Reflect upon your colours and the names of your centres in many worlds, because you will never appreciate their glory and sanctity by hurrying up that challenging slope in the physical realm alone. Instead, pause for a while; close your eyes. By daydreaming, you will bring your inner sight and hearing to play.

Akureyri's hidden worlds - the Angel City of Akureyri

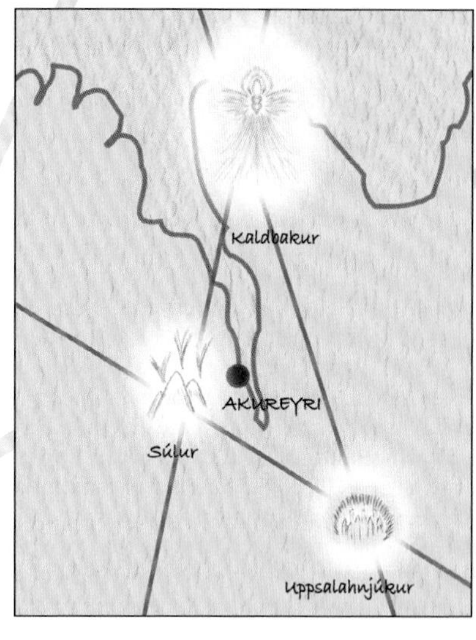

EARTH ENERGY

All types of life are imbued with a life force which has the flow and sound of a beautiful symphony and is the innate form of matter. Mother Earth is a living being, endowed with strength, awareness and life. The circulatory system or energy lines of earth are like a living light that flows between energy points. Whether such energy lines are called ley lines, dragon paths or song lines, they make up a densely woven grid extending throughout the world and linking together major and minor energy centres, vegetation zones and elf worlds. Moreover, these lines lend us, as the earth's inhabitants, power and joy. Iceland itself has seven energy centres, over which the island's brightest mountain gods tower majestically. Hofsjökull glacier is the primary centre, emitting energy currents which have 12 frequencies and range from blue water lines in the highest spheres of the material world and lowest spheres of the mental world, up to yellow lines in the highest spheres of the intuitive world. These currents of light connect the outposts of the island, guarded by those natural beings which are represented in the official Icelandic emblem. To the west is Snæfellsjökull, to the east Snæfell, to the north Kaldbakur, and to the south Mýrdalsjökull, not to mention the Queen of Icelandic Mountains, Herðubreið, and their prince, Hlöðufell.

ENERGY RELATED TO EYJAFJÖRÐUR

The energy line that flows directly north from Hofsjökull glacier fills Eyjafjörður with light and is directed towards Kaldbakur mountain, that is, towards the Goddess who grants us a promise of hope and sanctity. In general, Eyjafjörður's mountains and vegetation are inhabited by Iceland's gentlest supernatural beings: elves, hidden people, dwarves, gnomes, faeries and nymphs. The energy line to Kaldbakur is one of Iceland's strongest, so we should concentrate our inner consciousness on it and relish it. Eyjafjörður is a realm of supernatural beings, an area of true springtime and bliss even during the frosty northerlies of winter. The peaks of Súlur, Kaldbakur and Uppsalahnjúkur transmit soft violet rays one to another, forming a triangle of currents around Akureyri.

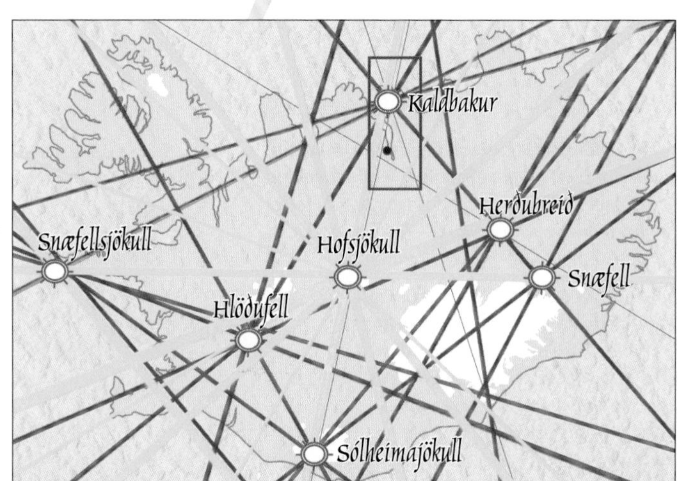

It is interesting to recall that Helgi the Lean, one of the original settlers of Iceland and a protector of this community, believed in the god Thor, whose "heaven" was Uppsalir (included in the name Uppsalahnjúkur). Many travellers make their way to Akureyri and could take advantage of a very interesting map of the "hidden worlds" of Akureyri, which is based on Erla's visions and philosophy and was published by Katrín Jónsdóttir. The Iceland Road Atlas has graciously received permission to publish three of the map's sixteen pages. If you are interested in seeing more of the map, please check in the tourist shops and the Eymundsson bookshop in Akureyri, or at the shops Betra Líf and Gjafir Jarðar in Reykjavík.

Three elf habitations on Vaðlaheiði heath

Sensing the past in the present

By fantasising, we can look forwards and backwards in time and have fun time-travelling around the fjord and valleys of Eyjafjörður, with its churches existing variously in the present or past. They are connected by bands of light which illuminate them like lighthouses, helping them impart their histories of varying length. Some churches date as far back as 1000 or even earlier, since many were built on the ruins of old pagan temples, as is often the case in Iceland. The churches need not be used much today for one to be able to enter and feel the presence of those previously occupying them in happiness or sorrow. The stillness communicates the proper tones, together with other indications of the nation's religious culture. Icelanders of earlier times had the talent of creating a path of light by knocking stones together into cairns, even though it was many kilometres between such cairns. Their horses were then capable of following such a path to the next farm, despite blizzards that blinded people.

ELF VILLAGES

Opposite Akureyri, three villages may be observed on the lower slopes of Vaðlaheiði. Elves live in one, hidden people in another, and a cluster of ten or twelve houses which I believe to represent previous human habitations appears above Festarklettur rock, which is east of and inland from the fjord. The ancient assembly site Vaðlaþing lies above Festarklettur, including a stone circle with sailcloth or skins stretched over it for a roof. Even today one can discern ships of different sizes there, indicating that the fjord once reached farther south, but has since filled with sediment through the ages. Thus it is hardly surprising that sharp-eyed Akureyri residents sometimes notice lights in windows across the fjord, in places without any houses in the physical world.

ORIGINAL EYJAFJÖRÐUR SETTLERS

Pioneers coming from Norway, like Helgi the Lean and his wife, Þórunn Hyrna, would clearly have entered this fjord from the north. The sagas report that they lived near Sólarfjall mountain and even on Hrísey island for their first year here, but later established the farm of Kristnes. Many of those moving here later stopped first at the medieval trading post of Gásir, which was a good place to moor ships and was close to fishing grounds. At Gásir I have seen visions which seem to be up to 1500 years old, involving people who are not Scandinavian, but have darker skin and stiff hair.

An elf residence on Vaðlaheiði

The colours of Akureyri's guardian angel are shades of blue-green, glistening with green and gold energy. These colours reveal the angel as harmonising with Iceland's fertility goddess.

Mount Kaldbakur, silvery blue-green, with thin violet-pink rays, is one of Iceland's greatest energy centres. In the green force emitted, elves and supernatural beings dance in the glow of this mountain goddess. You might meditate on and sound out green notes through the pendant on your necklace, so as to achieve divine harmony.

Our surrounding wealth

The hidden worlds are an inner revelation of nature. Nature, like all creation, is made up of countless spheres, since the creator of all controls everything around us. It is ours to enjoy this wealth, noting how it is truth itself and how you, I, every one of us and all of Iceland, nature and indeed the entire earth are united. Every backyard contains tree sprites, flower fairies, and grass elves, in addition to the inhabitants of possible cliffs, and little gnomes in small houses that look like stones. Walk slowly in the vicinity of your home - you and your family are not the only ones living there!

Tiny grass elves are a joy to see waking up in the spring as the grass turns green. After growing along with the grass, they fall asleep once again in autumn.

Jolly dwarves stay by the University of Akureyri, wearing cheerfully coloured clothes. They smile and wave when shown attention.

Of all the beings around us, the hidden people resemble us most. Usually they dress like 19TH - century Icelanders.

The fertility goddess of Iceland sends off her nymphs to places which are promising for vegetation. Here is one such nymph.

Gnomes are very small, perhaps up to 10 cm tall. Their houses are ornamented and they save their baby cradles and high chairs because upon reaching old age, they will start all over again.

INSTRUCTIONS FOR THE GENERAL PUBLIC REGARDING NATURAL DISASTER IN ICELAND

Text Color: Green = Precautions – Red = Preventive response

General Instructions

Preventive measures are an important part of dealing with danger

In homes and workplaces, individuals should talk about possible dangers, discuss safety measures, locate exits and know where safety equipment is kept. Knowledge of first aid is very practical and can save lives. The Icelandic Red Cross gives first aid courses for the general public.

You should know how to operate safety equipment.

In homes and in workplaces safety equipment should include:

- Fire extinguisher.
- Smoke detectors.
- Safety ladder or rope to evacuate high buildings.
- Tools such as a hammer, a saw, a screwdriver, an ax, a wrench and a crowbar.

Keep the following equipment in an emergency kit where everyone can find it:

- First-aid medical kit.
- Flashlight.
- Radio with batteries.
- First-aid instruction manual.
- List of important telephone numbers (relatives, service providers etc.).
- Your own emergency plan for the family/workplace.

Discuss and practice actions to be taken during an emergency situation (emergency plan). Let children participate so they will be prepared to respond appropriately.

General precautions if a dangerous situation develops:

Those who are in or near a town or village when a dangerous situation develops should report to the nearest emergency aid centre or contact the police. Emergency aid centres

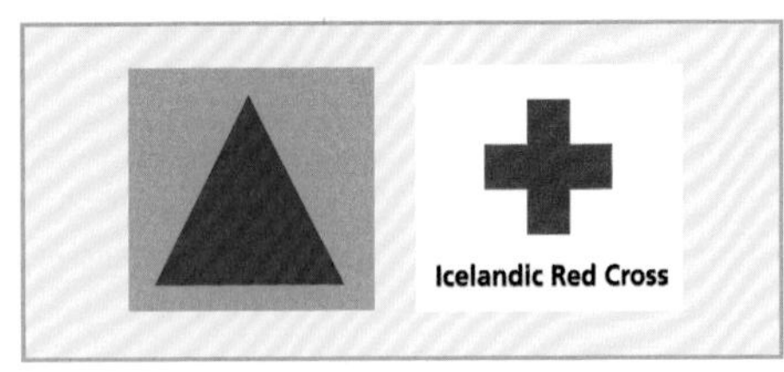

(Fjöldahjálparstöð) are identified by the logos (see picture) of the Red Cross (Rauði kross Íslands) and the Civil Protection (Almannavarnir).

- When an emergency is declared or a dangerous situation develops a SMS message will be sent to connected mobile phones in areas at risk with information and/or instructions of actions.
- If a dangerous situation develops, it is important that families gather together to coordinate their actions.
- If you evacuate your home, keep in mind that emergency aid centers are usually located in schools.
- If an emergency aid center is not nearby, contact the police (112) and notify them of your whereabouts.

Radio FM and LW

Announcements from the Civil Protection are sent to the State Radio (FM and LW) and TV as well as other media. Listen to the radio for announcements and news, and follow any instructions given.

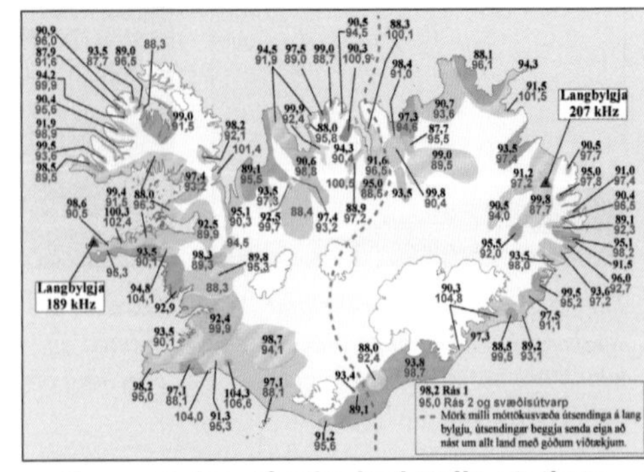

Frequencies of principal radio stations

- Report accidents and request assistance by calling **Emergency alert at 112.** • If you need assistance and the telephones do not work, and you have no other means of communication, put a cloth or a flag out of a window, or at some other noticeable location, outside the house. In case of emergency, flags or signals are a request for assistance.
- Do not use the telephone except for emergency purposes. Keep conversations to an absolute minimum or use text messages, twitter or facebook.
- Announcements from the Civil Protection are sent to the State Radio and TV as well as other media.

If in need for further information after a disaster, contact your Embassy, Consulate, Travel Agency or Tourist Information Centre. If those are not available, contact the Police at Emergency alert 112 or a helpful native.

Volcanic eruptions

Volcanic eruptions can begin without warning, but they are usually preceded by earthquakes that can be detected by seismograph. Eruptions can cause danger by lava flow and ash fall. The ash from a single eruption can fall throughout the country depending upon the weather. The falling ash can be unsafe and hazardous because of poisonous gases and materials. It especially poses a threat to animals. Clouds of ash can cause disturbances to air traffic. Always wear a helmet in the vicinity of eruptions.

- Avoid areas where ash is falling, because of the danger of lightning, and keep in mind that the falling ash may fall so densely as to block out sunlight. If hit by falling ash, take the shortest way out by moving perpendicular to the direction of the wind.
- Wear a dust mask or keep a wet cloth over your nostrils and mouth.
- Stay where the wind blows and do not go into low areas were gas can accumulate. The gas is a lethal poison, which in most cases has no smell and is difficult to detect.
- Shut windows in the path of the eruption and prevent fallen ash from entering the house through the chimney.

Lightning

Lightning is not common in Iceland and because of that people are often not prepared to protect themselves from the danger it poses. If a thunderstorm with lightning passes over, take the following precautions:

Outdoors:

- Avoid water, open and high areas. If you take refuge in a vehicle, keep the doors and window shut. Do not use radio-telephones or other telecommunications equipment.
- Avoid metallic objects which may conduct electricity such as power lines, fences, engines, machines etc.

Dangerous places include small huts, or shelters and areas close to trees. Seek shelter, if possible, in larger buildings or in vehicles

If you think lightning will strike near you, you should:

- Crouch with your feet together. Cover your ears with your hands to reduce the risk of hearing damage.
- Keep at least 5 meters away from the next person.

Indoors:

- Avoid water. Keep away from the buildings outside doors, windows and plumbing.
- Do not use telephones or headphones.
- Keep away from appliances, such as computers, power tools and television sets. Avoid metallic objects which may conduct electricity.
  Also keep away from antennas.

Electricity does not remain in persons hit by lightning, so necessary assistance can be rendered immediately. Apply first aid and call the Emergency Service 112.

www.almannavarnir.is

Civil Protection Natural Disaster

Instructions for the general public regarding natural disaster in Iceland

Avalanches

The Icelandic Meteorological Office and meteorological observers monitor the probability of avalanches near inhabited areas. If there is a danger of an avalanche, you should depart the affected area in accordance with instructions given.

If that is not possible, you should take the following measures:

- Spend as little time as possible outside and do not go near the avalanche area.
- Stay in that part of the house, which is farthest from the hillside. Close windows and doors tightly. Put shutters on windows facing the hillside.
- Do not stay in a basement unless it is completely underground and has a concrete roof.
- If you live in a remote area, you should establish contact by telephone, or radio, with someone outside the danger zone and communicate with him or her, regularly.

If the Chief of Police gives an evacuation order, you must comply. Local Civil Protection committees open emergency aid centre and maintain a register of people staying there until they are allowed to go back to their homes.

When traveling in mountainous areas where there is a danger of avalanches, for example on skis, snowboards, snowmobiles or motor vehicles, care should be taken not to start an avalanche by cutting the mountain side.

If you get caught in an avalanche you should:

- Keep your head up and use a swimming and rolling motion to stay near the surface
- Cover your face to prevent your mouth and nose from getting filled with snow if you are out of control.
- Move as much as you can to create space to breath when the avalanche is slowing down.
- Keep calm. Do not try to call for help, until you hear the rescuers.

ALWAYS BELIEVE THAT YOU WILL BE RESCUED. THAT WILL INCREASE THE POSSIBILITY OF BEING FOUND ALIVE!

Earthquake

There is seldom advance warning of an earthquake. Therefore, it is important to take security measures ahead of time and to learn how to respond.

Security measures:

- Secure cabinets, shelves and heavy objects to the floor or wall.
- Do not keep heavy objects on top of shelves or on walls.
- Secure heating equipment and radiators. Know where the water main and electric circuit breaker are.
- Secure picture frames and wall light fixtures with closed-loop hangers. Put security latches/child safety latches on cabinet doors.
- Prevent objects from falling on beds.
- Make sure that ceiling panels and raised floors are properly fastened. Cover windows to prevent flying glass in case they are broken. Locate beds and chairs away from windows if there is a danger of an earthquake.
- Announcements from the Civil Protection will be made on the State Radio in case of a natural disaster.

www.almannavarnir.is

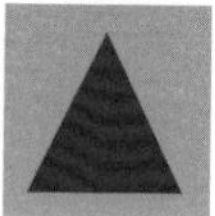

Preventive response:
It is good to remember the words DUCK, COVER, HOLD and how to react in the event of an earthquake. Those who are indoors when a large earthquake occurs should especially avoid:

- Furniture that may move.
- Objects that may fall from shelves and cabinets (especially in kitchens).
- Radiators that may move.
- Broken glass.
- Falling building parts.

Guard against falling objects by:

Ducking in an open doorway, covering the head (with one hand) and holding onto the doorway,

Ducking in the corner of a supporting wall, covering the head and holding on, if possible,

Ducking under a table, covering the head and holding onto a sturdy piece of a furniture

Do not run aimlessly inside or run outside in panic!

Those who are outside should:

- Find an open space and avoid buildings and electric poles. Keep a safe distance from man-made structures that are as tall as or taller than you.
- Duck and cover your head (at least with hands) if you cannot get to an open space.
- Avoid falling rocks and gravel slides in mountainous areas.
- Those who are driving should stop their automobiles in a safe place.

After an earthquake, one should:

- Wear shoes (if debris is on the floor).
- Obtain a first aid kit if needed.
- See if anyone is hurt, and if so, call the Emergency Service at 112. If it is not possible to get help by telephone, mark the place of the accident with a flag.
- Turn off the water and heat if a leak is unmanageable, and shut down the main electrical circuit if the building is damaged.
- See if there is a fire and do not use an open flame if there is danger of a fire starting.
- Leave calmly if you think the building is uninhabitable after an earthquake. Many accidents occur when people run out through debris after an earthquake.
- Dress appropriately for the weather conditions if you leave the building. Remember that the automobile is often the first heated shelter available
and it has a radio.
- Remember the emergency shelters in schools.
- Listen after announcements from
the Civil Protection that are sent to the Radio.
- Never touch damaged electric poles.

www.almannavarnir.is

When do mountain roads open?

On what factors does their opening depend?

How do I know which mountain roads are open?

ENVIRONMENT AGENCY OF ICELAND

ROAD AND COASTAL ADMINISTRATION 2017

Travel in the highlands of Iceland has increased considerably in recent years; this reflects an increase in leisure time, improvements in vehicles for rough-country travel, and awakening interest in year-round travel.

SENSITIVE ENVIRONMENT
Land which is more then 300 meters above sea level is classified as highland; the climate in the highlands is changeable, and these regions are generally blanketed with snow well into the summer months.

During the spring and early summer, when the snow melts and frozen earth thaws both roads and vegetation are in a vulnerable state and easily damaged. The greatest risk is due to the impact of premature traffic, especially when vehicles drive off-road to circumvent snowdrifts. Attempts to use snowmobiles in spring, when snowcover is decreasing, can also inflict damage.

The highland summer lasts only a month and a half, and this is the period of growth for highland vegetation, which is thus low-growing and sensitive to any disturbance. Even walkers can inflict permanent damage on vegetation. So all traveler in the highlands should treat the natural environment with care and respect.

OPENING OF MOUNTAIN ROADS
The state of snow cover is the most important factor on deciding when

mountain roads can be opened to traffic. Roads are often very wet following the spring melt, and this can also lead to roads remaining closed to traffic.

In cases where mountain roads pass through conservation areas, the roads may not be opened until the area as a whole is in a state to withstand the pressures of visitors, even if the road itself is clear of snow and could withstand traffic.

MOUNTARIN ROAD CONDITIONS
Since 1989, the Public Roads Administration and the Environmental and Food Agency have published maps showing the condition of mountain roads during the spring and early summer. The maps are issued for as long as any mountain road remains closed. http://www.road.is Up-to-date information on the state of the roads, including mountain roads, is available on telephone 1777.

ENVIRONMENTAL AGENCY OF ICELAND

ROAD AND COASTAL ADMINISTRATION

OPENING OF MOUNTAIN ROADS

Information on the approximate opening date of the principal mountain roads is given in the table; the map below shows the locations of mountain roads.

The first two columns of the table show the earliest and latest opening dates of the roads over the past 5 years. The third column shows the average date of opening during this period.

The road may not, in practice, be opened on the projected date, as the question whether a road has become passable is subject to weather conditions and the amount of snow in the highlands. More detailed information on the opening of highland roads can be found in maps issued by the Public Roads Administration and the Environmental and Food Agency during the spring and early summer, and published in the press. Further information on the state of the roads is also available on telephone 1777.

MOUNTAIN ROADS 2012 - 2016	Opening date earliest	Opening date laterst	Opening date median
Lakagígar, F206	05.06	09.07	23.06
Fjallabaksleið nyrðri, F208			
1. Sigalda - Landmannalaugar	31.05	26.06	15.06
2. Laugar - Eldgjá	07.06	17.07	27.06
3. Eldgjá - Skaftártunga	07.06	26.06	14.06
Fjallabaksleið syðri F210			
1. Keldur - Hvanngil	12.06	17.07	02.07
2. Hvanngil - Skaftártunga	12.06	23.07	01.07
Landmannaleið (Dómad.) F225	07.06	03.07	20.06
Emstruleið, F261	12.06	10.07	29.06
Kjalvegur, 35			
1. Gullfoss - Hveravellir	05.06	01.07	16.06
2. Hveravellir - Blönduvirkjun	05.06	25.06	14.06
Sprengisandur, F26			
1. Hrauneyjar - Nýidalur	15.06	10.07	26.06
2. Nýidalur - Bárðardalur	29.06	10.07	04.07
Skagafjarðarleið, F752	29.06	16.07	05.07
Eyjafjarðarleið, F821	01.07	24.07	10.07
Öskjuleið, F88			
1. Inn að Herðubreiðarlindum	14.06	26.06	22.06
2. Herðubreiðarlindir - Dreki	15.06	26.06	22.06
Öskjuvatnsvegur, F894	15.06	24.07	02.07
Vesturd. (Hljóðaklettar), F862	24.05	24.06	16.06
Kverkfjalaleið, F902	14.06	27.06	22.06
Uxahryggjavegur, 52	24.04	31.05	02.05
Kaldadalsvegur, 550	05.06	07.07	13.06

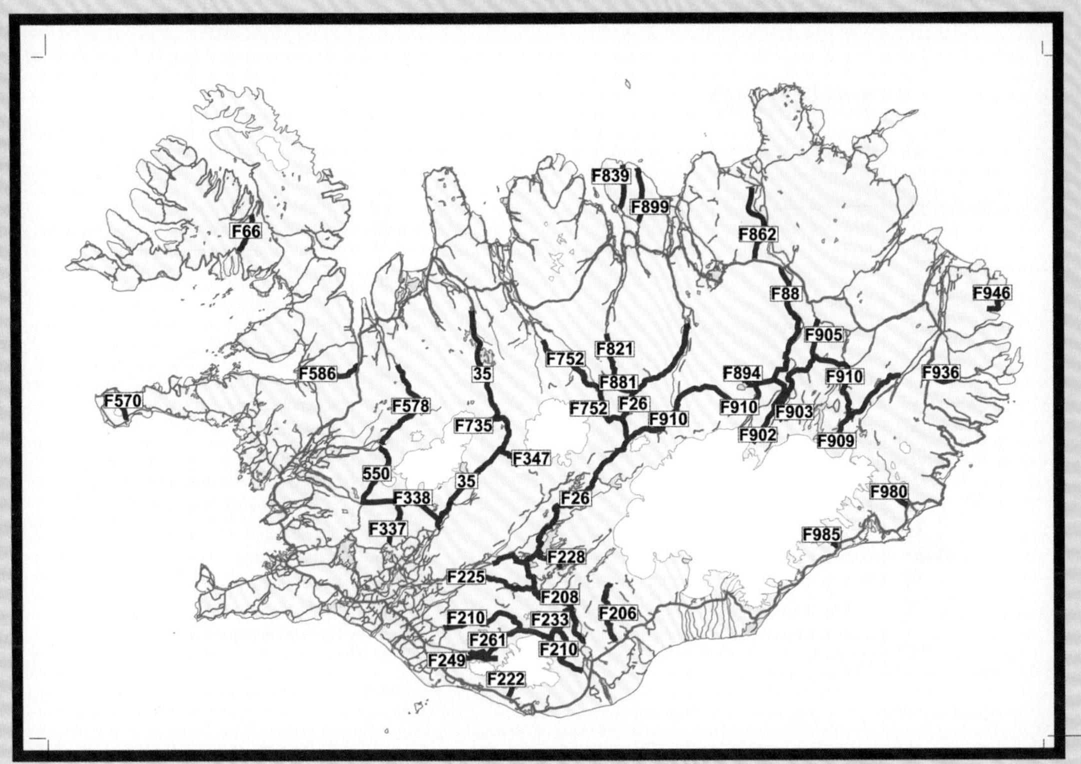

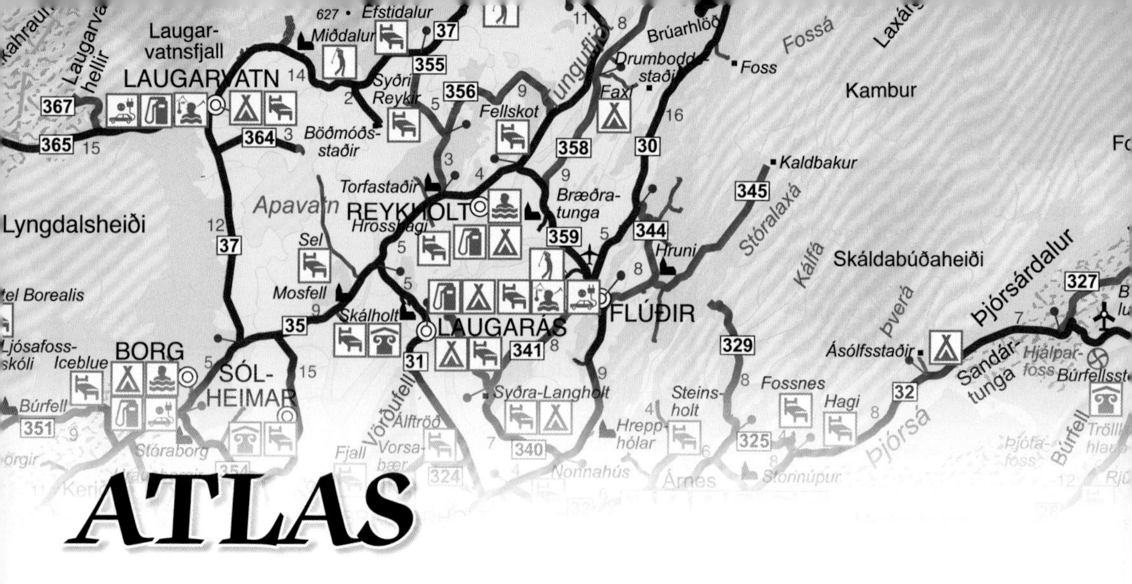

ATLAS

This edition includes a detailed 24-page Atlas on a scale of 1:500,000. The road system is according to the latest information from the Icelandic Road Administration. The Atlas includes symbols which indicate basic services available in the area.

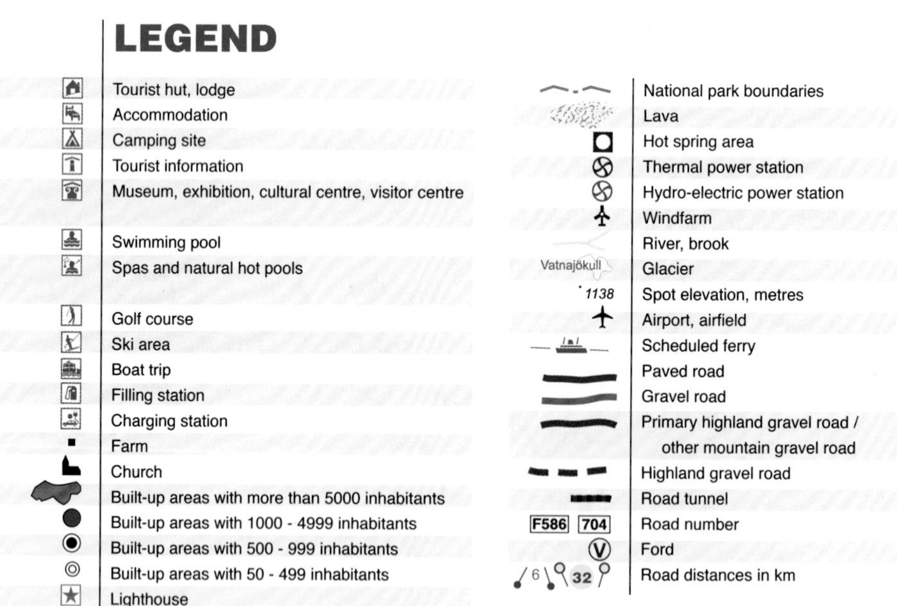

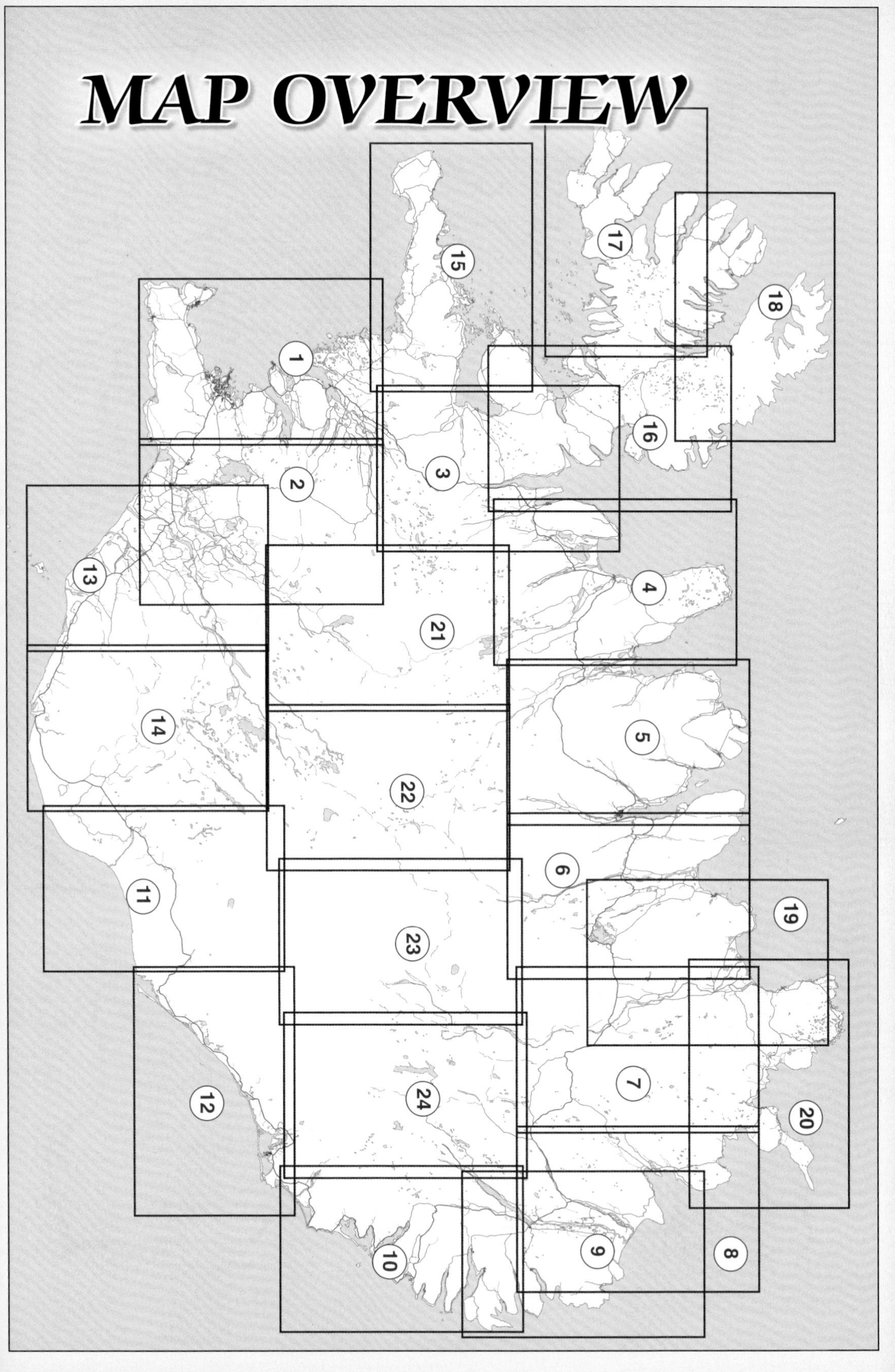
MAP OVERVIEW
1
2
3
4
5
6
7
8
9
10
11
12
13
14
15
16
17
18
19
20
21
22
23
24

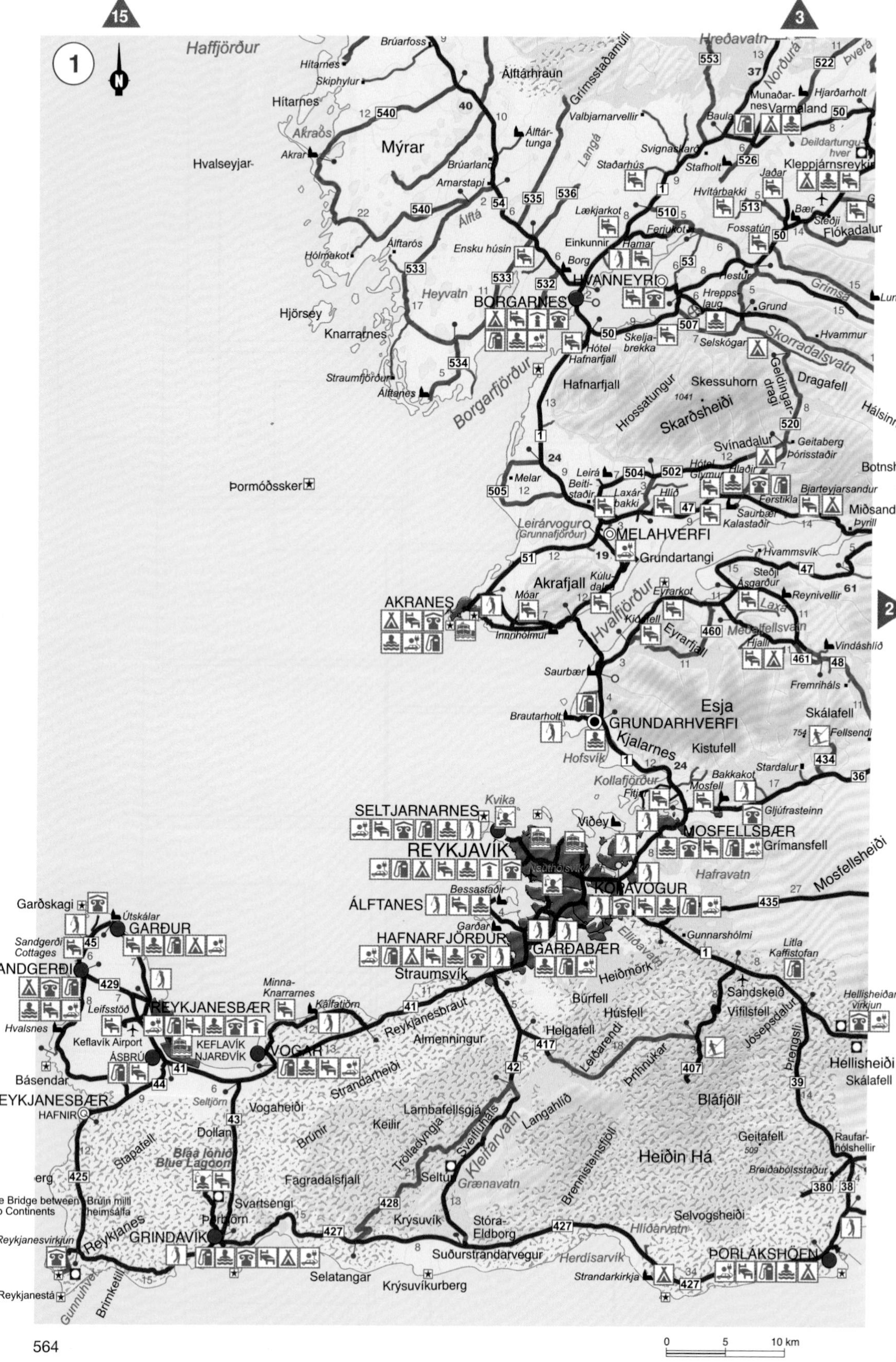
15
3
1
2
Haffjörður
Mýrar
Hvalseyjar-
Hítarnes
Akraós
Álftárhraun
Brúarfoss
Hreðavatn
Norðurá
Varmaland
Kleppjárnsreykir
Flókadalur
Deildartunguhver
Hjarðarholt
Stafholt
Svignaskarð
Valbjarnarvellir
Álftártunga
Arnarstapi
Brúarland
Álftá
Álftarós
Hólmakot
Ensku húsin
Heyvatn
BORGARNES
HVANNEYRI
Borg
Einkunnir
Hamar
Ferjukot
Lækjarkot
Staðarhús
Langá
Grímsstaðamúli
Hvítárbakki
Fossatún
Hestur
Hreppslaug
Grund
Grímsá
Skeljabrekka
Selskógar
Skorradalsvatn
Hvammur
Geldingardragi
Dragafell
Hálsinn
Hjörsey
Knarrarnes
Straumfjörður
Álftanes
Borgarfjörður
Hótel Hafnarfjall
Hafnarfjall
Skessuhorn
Hrossatungur
Skarðsheiði
Svínadalur
Geitaberg
Þórisstaðir
Hótel Glymur
Hlaðir
Bjarteyjarsandur
Ferstikla
Saurbær
Kalastaðir
Botnsh
Miðsandu
Þyrill
Þormóðssker
Melar
Leirá
Beitistaðir
Laxárbakki
Hlíð
Leirárvogur (Grunnafjörður)
MELAHVERFI
Grundartangi
Hvammsvík
Steðji
Ásgarður
Reynivellir
Akrafjall
Kúludalsá
Eyrarkot
Hvalfjörður
Laxá
Meðalfellsvatn
Kiðafell
Eyrarfjall
Hjalli
Vindáshlíð
AKRANES
Móar
Innnhólmur
Saurbær
Fremrihals
Esja
Skálafell
Brautarholt
GRUNDARHVERFI
Kjalarnes
Kistufell
Fellsendi
Hofsvík
Stardalur
Kollafjörður
Bakkakot
Mosfell
Fitjar
Gljúfrasteinn
SELTJARNARNES
Kvika
Viðey
MOSFELLSBÆR
Grímansfell
REYKJAVÍK
Nauthólsvík
Hafravatn
Mosfellsheiði
Bessastaðir
KÓPAVOGUR
ÁLFTANES
Garðar
Elliðavatn
Gunnarshólmi
HAFNARFJÖRÐUR
GARÐABÆR
Litla Kaffistofan
Straumsvík
Heiðmörk
Garðskagi
Útskálar
GARÐUR
Sandgerði Cottages
SANDGERÐI
Minna-Knarrarnes
Kálfatjörn
Reykjanesbraut
Búrfell
Húsfell
Sandskeið
Vífilsfell
Hellisheiðarvirkjun
Leifsstöð
REYKJANESBÆR
Hvalsnes
Keflavík Airport
KEFLAVÍK
NJARÐVÍK
ÁSBRÚ
VOGAR
Almenningur
Helgafell
Leiðarendi
Þríhnúkar
Jósepsdalur
Þrengsli
Hellisheiði
Skálafell
Básendar
Strandarheiði
Seltjörn
REYKJANESBÆR
HAFNIR
Vogaheiði
Lambafellsgjá
Sveifluháls
Langahlíð
Bláfjöll
Stapafell
Dollan
Bláa lónið
Blue Lagoon
Brúnir
Keilir
Trölladyngja
Kleifarvatn
Brennisteinsfjöll
Heiðin Há
Geitafell
Raufarhólshellir
Breiðabólsstaður
The Bridge between Two Continents
Brúin milli heimsálfa
Fagradalsfjall
Seltún
Grænavatn
Svartsengi
Reykjanesvirkjun
Reykjanes
Þorbjörn
GRINDAVÍK
Krýsuvík
Stóra-Eldborg
Selvogsheiði
Hlíðarvatn
Suðurstrandarvegur
Herdísarvík
ÞORLÁKSHÖFN
Strandarkirkja
Selatangar
Krýsuvíkurberg
Reykjanestá
Gunnuhver
Brimketill
0 5 10 km

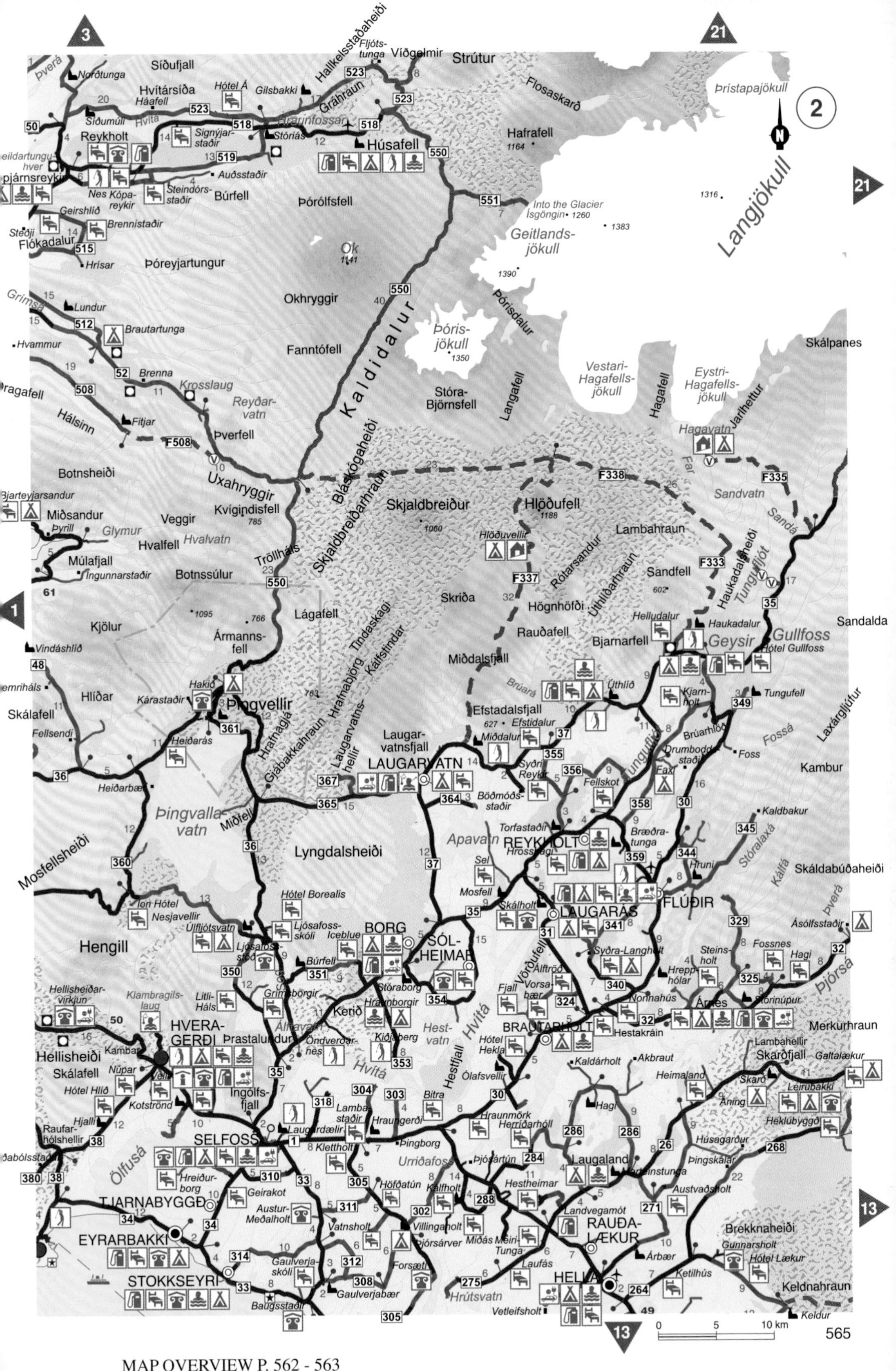

MAP OVERVIEW P. 562 - 563

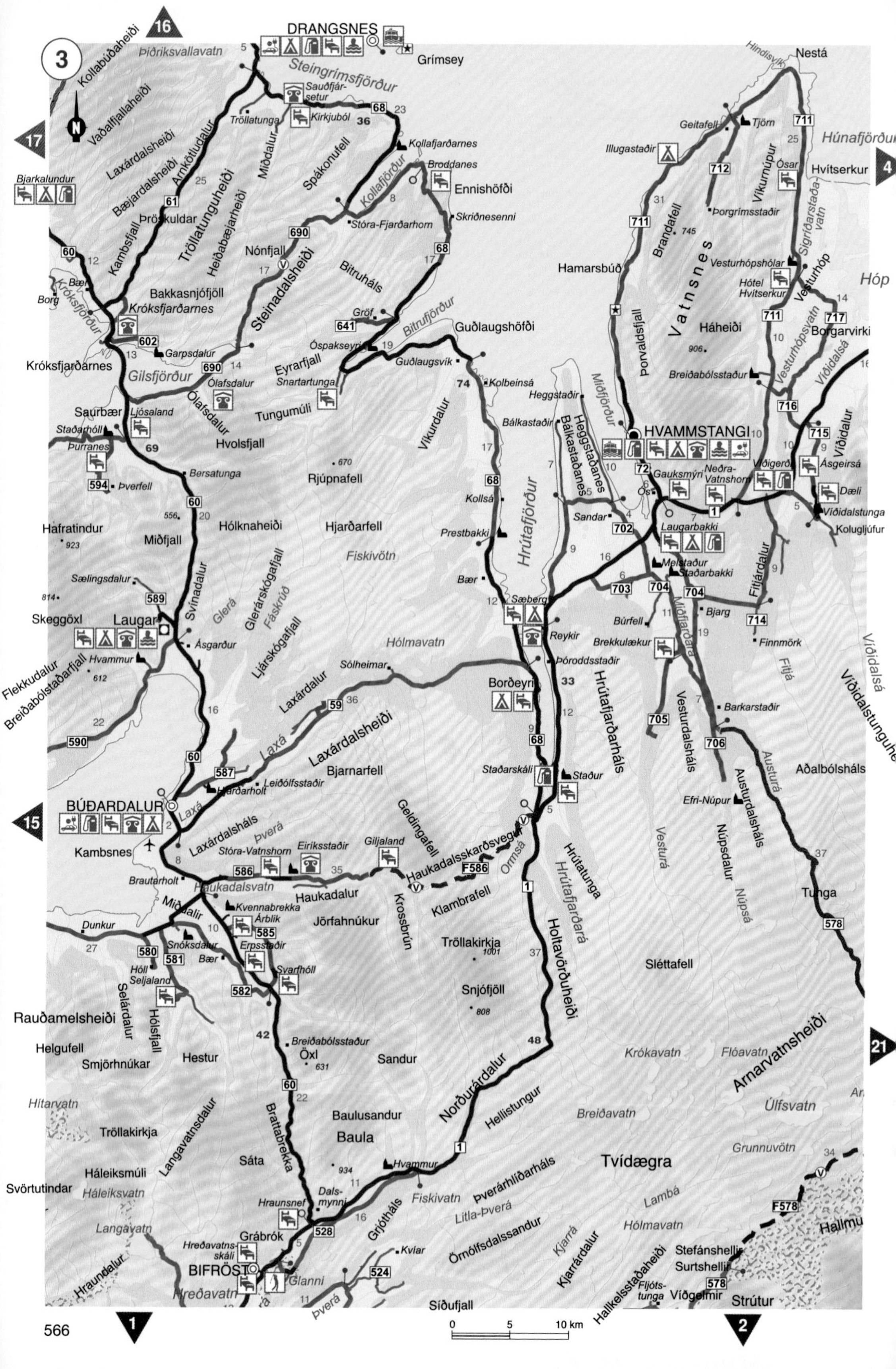
3
16
17
4
15
21
1
2
DRANGSNES
Grímsey
Steingrímsfjörður
Þiðriksvallavatn
Kollabúðaheiði
Vaðalfjallaheiði
Laxárdalsheiði
Bæjardalsheiði
Arnkötludalur
Tröllatunguheiði
Heiðabæjarheiði
Kambsfjall
Þröskuldar
Tröllatunga
Sauðfjársetur
Kirkjuból
Miðdalur
Spákonufell
Kollafjarðarnes
Broddanes
Ennishöfði
Skriðnesenni
Kollafjörður
Stóra-Fjarðarhorn
Nónfjall
Steinadalsheiði
Bitruháls
Bakkasnjófjöll
Krókfjarðarnes
Bær
Borg
Króksfjörður
Gróf
Bitrufjörður
Guðlaugshöfði
Óspakseyri
Guðlaugsvík
Garpsdalur
Gilsfjörður
Eyrarfjall
Snartartunga
Kolbeinsá
Ólafsdalur
Tungumúli
Víkurdalur
Saurbær
Ljósaland
Staðarhóll
Þurranes
Hvolsfjall
Bersatunga
Rjúpnafell
Þverfell
Hafratindur
Miðfjall
Hólknaheiði
Hjarðarfell
Fiskivötn
Kollsá
Prestbakki
Sælingsdalur
Skeggöxl
Laugar
Svínadalur
Glerá
Glerárskógafjall
Fáskrúð
Ljárskógafjall
Ásgarður
Hvammur
Flekkudalur
Breiðabólstaðarfjall
Hólmavatn
Sólheimar
Laxárdalur
Laxá
Laxárdalsheiði
Bjarnarfell
Hjarðarholt
Leiðólfsstaðir
BÚÐARDALUR
Laxárdalsháls
Þverá
Kambsnes
Stóra-Vatnshorn
Eiríksstaðir
Giljaland
Geldingafell
Haukadalsskarðsvegur
Brautarholt
Haukadalsvatn
Haukadalur
Miðdalir
Kvennabrekka
Árblik
Jörfahnúkur
Krossbrún
Klambrafell
Dunkur
Snóksdalur
Erpsstaðir
Tröllakirkja
Höll
Seljaland
Svarfhóll
Snjófjöll
Rauðamelsheiði
Selárdalur
Hólsfjall
Helgufell
Smjörhnúkar
Hestur
Breiðabólsstaður
Öxl
Sandur
Hítarvatn
Langavatnsdalur
Brattabrekka
Baulusandur
Baula
Norðurárdalur
Hellistungur
Sáta
Háleiksmúli
Svörtutindar
Háleiksvatn
Hvammur
Dalsmynni
Hraunsnef
Fiskivatn
Grjótháls
Langavatn
Grábrók
Hreðavatnsskáli
Hraundalur
BIFRÖST
Glanni
Hreðavatn
Kvíar
Þverá
Síðufjall
Sæberg
Reykir
Þóroddsstaðir
Borðeyri
Hrútafjörður
Bær
Staðarskáli
Staður
Hrútafjarðarháls
Hrútatunga
Hrútafjarðará
Holtavörðuheiði
Ormsá
Heggstaðir
Bálkastaðir
Heggstaðanes
Bálkastaðanes
Miðfjörður
Sandar
HVAMMSTANGI
Gauksmýri
Neðra-Vatnshorn
Víðigerði
Ásgeirsá
Dæli
Víðidalstunga
Kolugljúfur
Ós
Laugarbakki
Melstaður
Staðarbakki
Fitjárdalur
Bjarg
Búrfell
Brekkulækur
Miðfjarðará
Finnmörk
Fitjá
Vesturdalsháls
Barkarstaðir
Austurá
Austurdalsháls
Efri-Núpur
Núpsdalur
Núpsá
Vesturá
Tunga
Aðalbólsháls
Víðidalstunguheiði
Víðidalsá
Sléttafell
Krókavatn
Flóavatn
Arnarvatnsheiði
Úlfsvatn
Breiðavatn
Grunnuvötn
Tvídægra
Þverárhlíðarháls
Litla-Þverá
Lambá
Hólmavatn
Örnólfsdalssandur
Kjarrá
Kjarrárdalur
Hallkelsstaðaheiði
Fljótstunga
Víðgelmir
Stefánshellir
Surtshellir
Strútur
Hallmu
Nestá
Hindisvík
Geitafell
Tjörn
Illugastaðir
Húnafjörður
Víkurnúpur
Ósar
Hvítserkur
Sigríðarstaðavatn
Þorgrímsstaðir
Brandafell
Vatnsnes
Hamarsbúð
Vesturhópshólar
Hótel Hvítserkur
Vesturhóp
Hóp
Háheiði
Þorvaldsfjall
Borgarvirki
Vesturhópsvatn
Breiðabólsstaður
Víðidalsá
Víðidalur
0 5 10 km

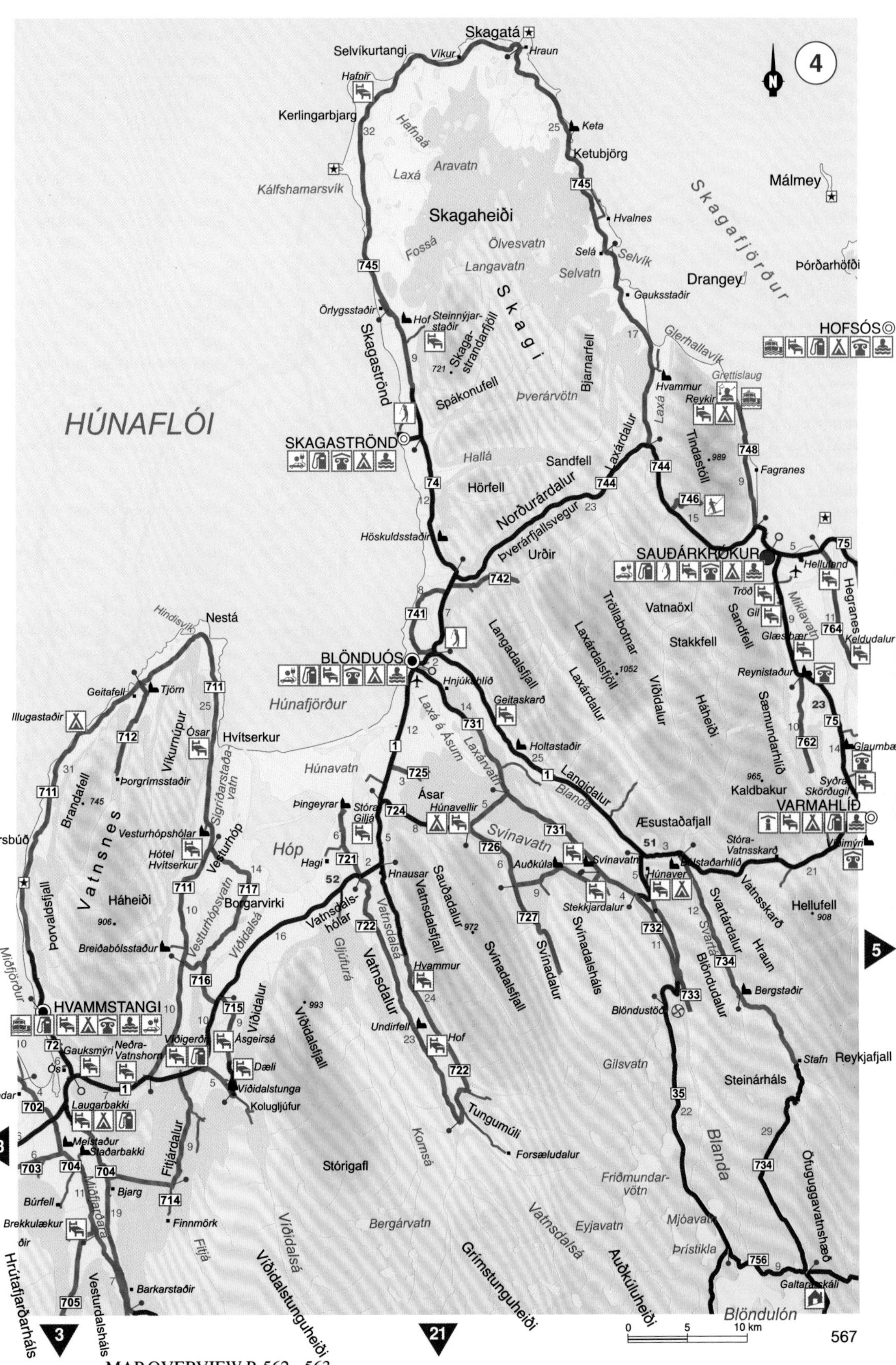

MAP OVERVIEW P. 562 - 563

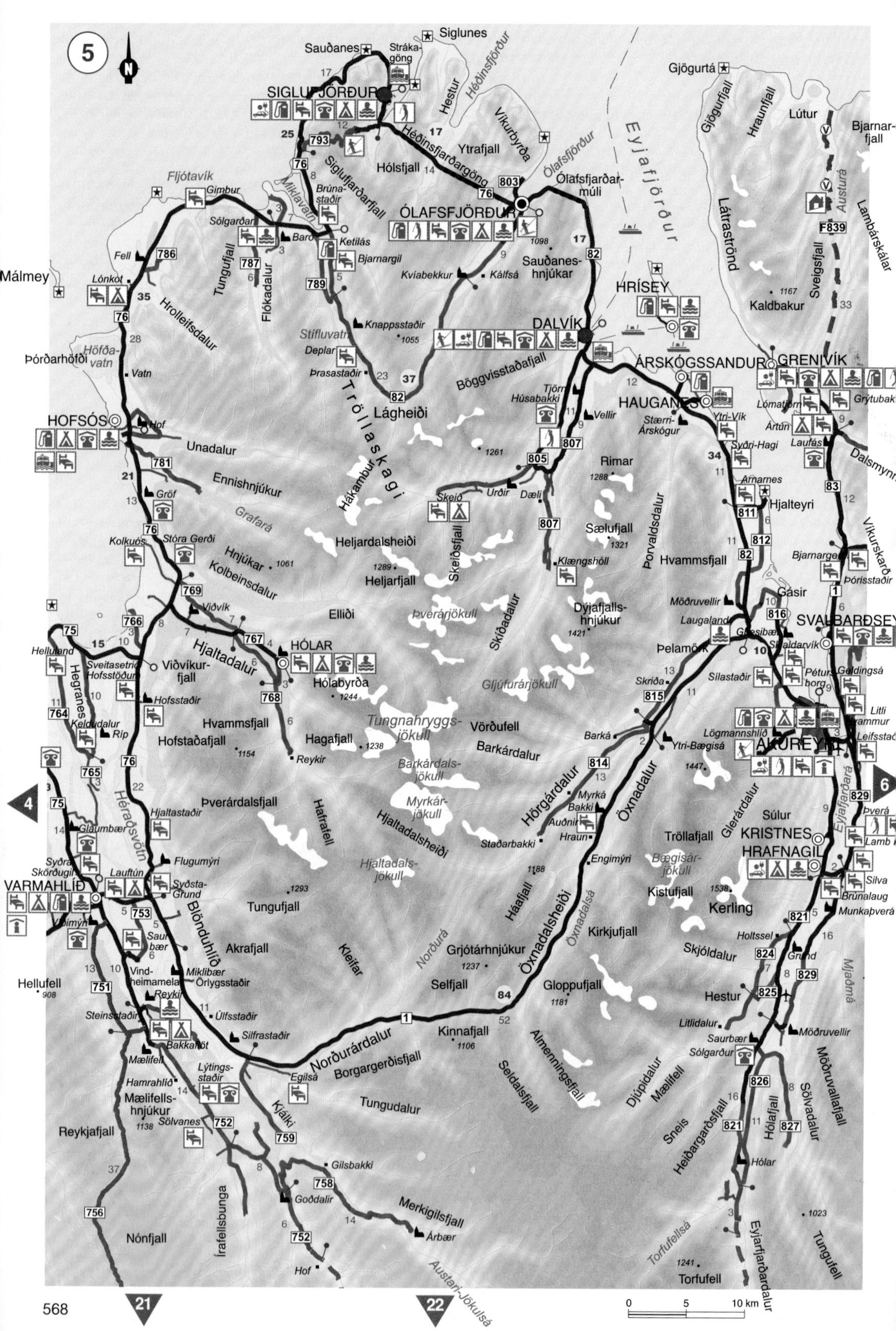
5
N
Siglunes
Sauðanes
Stráka-
göng
SIGLUFJÖRÐUR
Hestur
Héðinsfjörður
Vikurbyrða
Ytrafjall
Héðinsfjarðargöng
Siglufjarðarfjall
Hólsfjall
Ólafsfjörður
Ólafsfjarðar-
múli
ÓLAFSFJÖRÐUR
Eyjafjörður
Gjögurtá
Gjögurfjall
Hraunfjall
Lútur
Bjarnar-
fjall
Látraströnd
Austurá
Lambárskálar
F839
Sveigsfjall
Kaldbakur
Fljótavík
Gimbur
Miklavatn
Brúna-
staðir
Sólgarðar
Barð
Ketilás
Bjarnargil
Fell
Málmey
Lónkot
Tungufjall
Flókadalur
Hrolleifsdalur
Kvíabekkur
Kálfsá
Sauðanes-
hnjúkar
HRÍSEY
Knappsstaðir
Stífluvatn
Deplar
Þrasastaðir
Höfða-
vatn
Þórðarhöfði
Vatn
DALVÍK
Böggvisstaðafjall
ÁRSKÓGSSANDUR
GRENIVÍK
Tröllaskagi
Lágheiði
Tjörn
Húsabakki
Vellir
HAUGANES
Stærri-
Árskógur
Ytri-Vík
Lómatjörn
Grýtubakki
Ártún
Laufás
Dalsmynni
HOFSÓS
Hof
Unadalur
Ennishnjúkur
Gröf
Hákambur
Skeið
Urðir
Dæli
Rimar
Syðri-Hagi
Arnarnes
Hjalteyri
Grafará
Heljardalsheiði
Skeiðsfjall
Sælufjall
Þorvaldsdalur
Hvammsfjall
Víkurskarð
Kolkuós
Stóra Gerði
Hnjúkar
Kolbeinsdalur
Heljarfjall
Klængshóll
Bjarnargerði
Þórisstaðir
Viðvík
Elliði
Þverárjökull
Möðruvellir
Dýjafjalls-
hnjúkur
Gásir
SVALBARÐSEYRI
Laugaland
Hjaltadalur
HÓLAR
Skíðadalur
Glæsibær
Helluland
Sveitasetrið
Hofsstöðum
Viðvíkur-
fjall
Hólabyrða
Þelamörk
Skjaldarvík
Geldingsá
Hegranes
Gljúfurárjökull
Sílastaðir
Pétursborg
Hofsstaðir
Skriða
Keldudalur
Ríp
Tungnahryggs-
jökull
Vörðufell
Litli
Hvammur
Hvammsfjall
Hagafjall
Barká
Lögmannshlíð
Leifsstaðir
Hofstaðafjall
Barkárdalur
Ytri-Bægisá
AKUREYRI
Reykir
Barkárdals-
jökull
Hörgárdalur
Þverárdalsfjall
Hafrafell
Myrkár-
jökull
Myrká
Bakki
Öxnadalur
Glerárdalur
Héraðsvötn
Hjaltastaðir
Hjaltadalsheiði
Auðnir
Hraun
Súlur
Glaumbær
Staðarbakki
Tröllafjall
KRISTNES
Þverá
Syðra
Skörðugil
Flugumýri
Lauftún
Hjaltadals-
jökull
Engimýri
Bægisár-
jökull
HRAFNAGIL
Lamb
VARMAHLÍÐ
Syðsta-
Grund
Silva
Brúnalaug
Tungufjall
Háafjall
Kistufjall
Kerling
Munkaþverá
Víðimýri
Blönduhlíð
Öxnadalsheiði
Öxnadalsá
Saurbær
Akrafjall
Kleifar
Norðurá
Grjótárhnjúkur
Kirkjufjall
Holtssel
Skjóldalur
Grund
Mjaðmá
Vind-
heimamelar
Miklibær
Örlygsstaðir
Selfjall
Gloppufjall
Hellufell
Reykir
Hestur
Steinsstaðir
Úlfsstaðir
Kinnafjall
Litlidalur
Silfrastaðir
Norðurárdalur
Almenningsfjall
Möðruvellir
Saurbær
Sólgarður
Bakkaflöt
Mælifell
Lýtings-
staðir
Egilsá
Borgargerðisfjall
Seldalsfjall
Djúpidalur
Mælifell
Möðruvallafjall
Hamrahlíð
Mælifells-
hnjúkur
Sölvanes
Tungudalur
Kjálki
Sneis
Heiðargarðsfjall
Hólafjall
Sölvadalur
Reykjafjall
Gilsbakki
Hólar
Írafellsbunga
Goðdalir
Merkigilsfjall
Nónfjall
Árbær
Torfufellsá
Tungufell
Hof
Austari-Jökulsá
Torfufell
Eyjafjarðardalur
0
5
10 km
4
6
21
22

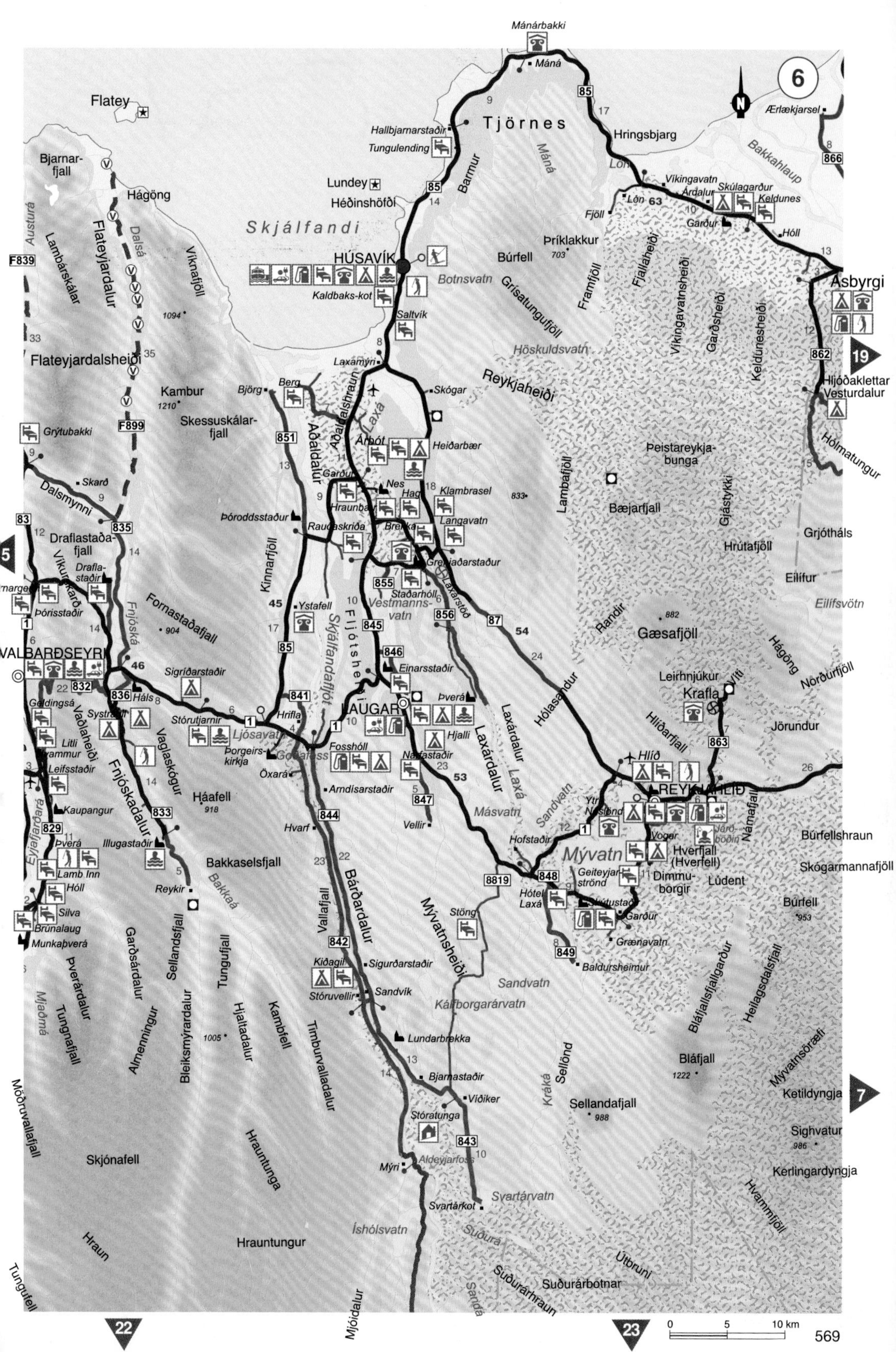

MAP OVERVIEW P. 562 - 563

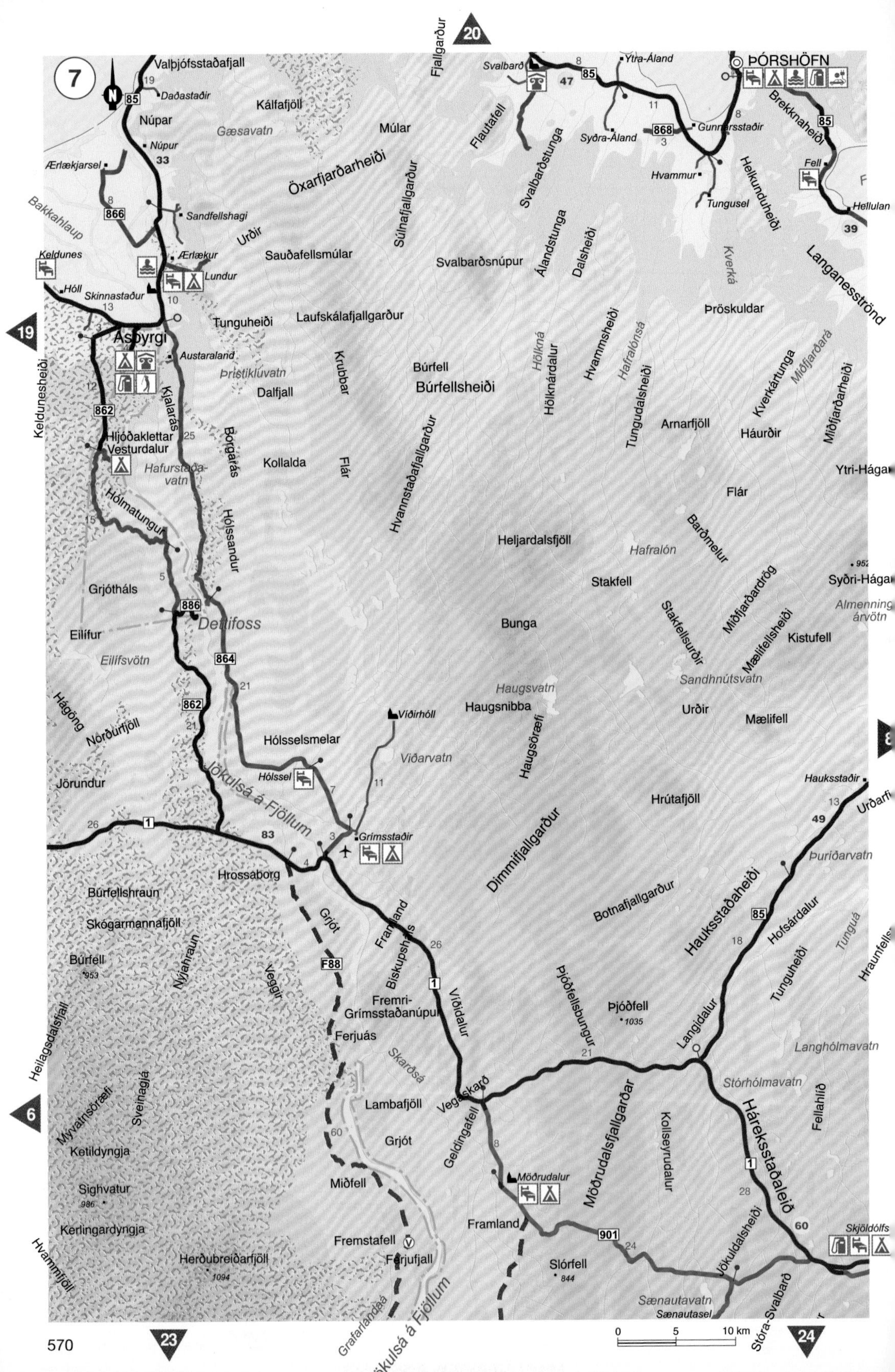
7
20
19
6
23
24
Valþjófsstaðafjall
Daðastaðir
Kálfafjöll
Núpar
Gæsavatn
Núpur
Múlar
Ærlækjarsel
Öxarfjarðarheiði
Bakkahlaup
Sandfellshagi
Súlnafjallgarður
Flautafell
Fjallgarður
Svalbarð
Ytra-Áland
ÞÓRSHÖFN
Brekknaheiði
Gunnarsstaðir
Syðra-Áland
Svalbarðstunga
Hvammur
Helkunduheiði
Fell
Tungusel
Hellulan
Langanesströnd
Kverká
Álandstunga
Dalsheiði
Svalbarðsnúpur
Urðir
Sauðafellsmúlar
Keldunes
Ærlækur
Lundur
Hóll
Skinnastaður
Tunguheiði
Laufskálafjallgarður
Þröskuldar
Ásbyrgi
Austaraland
Þristiklúvatn
Krubbar
Búrfell
Búrfellsheiði
Hölkná
Hölknárdalur
Hvammsheiði
Hafralónsá
Tungudalsheiði
Kverkártunga
Miðfjarðará
Miðfjarðarheiði
Keldunesheiði
Dalfjall
Kjalarás
Hljóðaklettar
Vesturdalur
Borgarás
Kollalda
Flár
Hvannstaðafjallgarður
Arnarfjöll
Háurðir
Ytri-Hága
Hafurstaðavatn
Hólmatungur
Hólssandur
Heljardalsfjöll
Hafralón
Barðmelur
Grjótháls
Stakfell
Miðfjarðardrög
Syðri-Hága
Almenningsárvötn
Eilífur
Dettifoss
Bunga
Stakfellsurðir
Mælifellsheiði
Kistufell
Eilífsvötn
Haugsvatn
Sandhnútsvatn
Hágöng
Norðurfjöll
Víðirhóll
Haugsnibba
Urðir
Mælifell
Hólsselsmelar
Víðarvatn
Haugsöræfi
Jörundur
Hólssel
Jökulsá á Fjöllum
Hauksstaðir
Hrútafjöll
Urðarfi
Grímsstaðir
Dimmifjallgarður
Þuríðarvatn
Hrossaborg
Búrfellshraun
Botnafjallgarður
Hauksstaðaheiði
Skógarmannafjöll
Grjót
Framland
Biskupsháls
Hofsárdalur
Tunguá
Búrfell
953
Nýjahraun
Veggir
Tunguheiði
Hraunfells
Víðidalur
Þjóðfellsbungur
Þjóðfell
1035
Fremri-Grímsstaðanúpur
Langidalur
Heilagsdalsfjall
Ferjuás
Langhólmavatn
Skarðsá
Vegaskarð
Stórhólmavatn
Mývatnsöræfi
Sveinagjá
Lambafjöll
Geldingafell
Möðrudalsfjallgarðar
Kollseyrudalur
Háreksstaðaleið
Fellahlíð
Ketildyngja
Grjót
Miðfell
Möðrudalur
Sighvatur
986
Kerlingardyngja
Framland
Jökuldalsheiði
Fremstafell
Ferjufjall
Herðubreiðarfjöll
1094
Slórfell
844
Skjöldólfs
Hvannfjöll
Sænautavatn
Sænautasel
Grafarlandaá
Stóra-Svalbarð
0
5
10 km

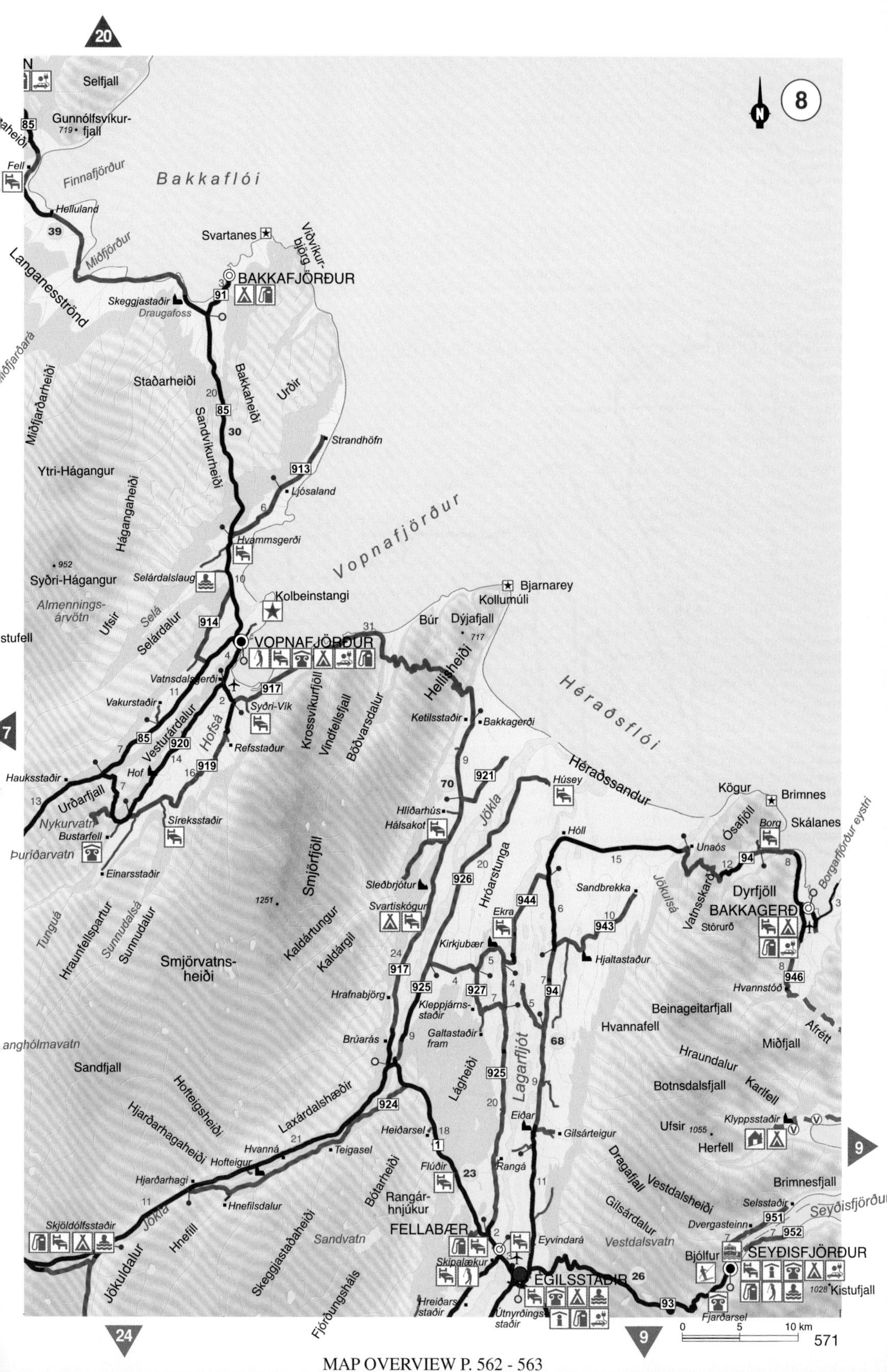

MAP OVERVIEW P. 562 - 563

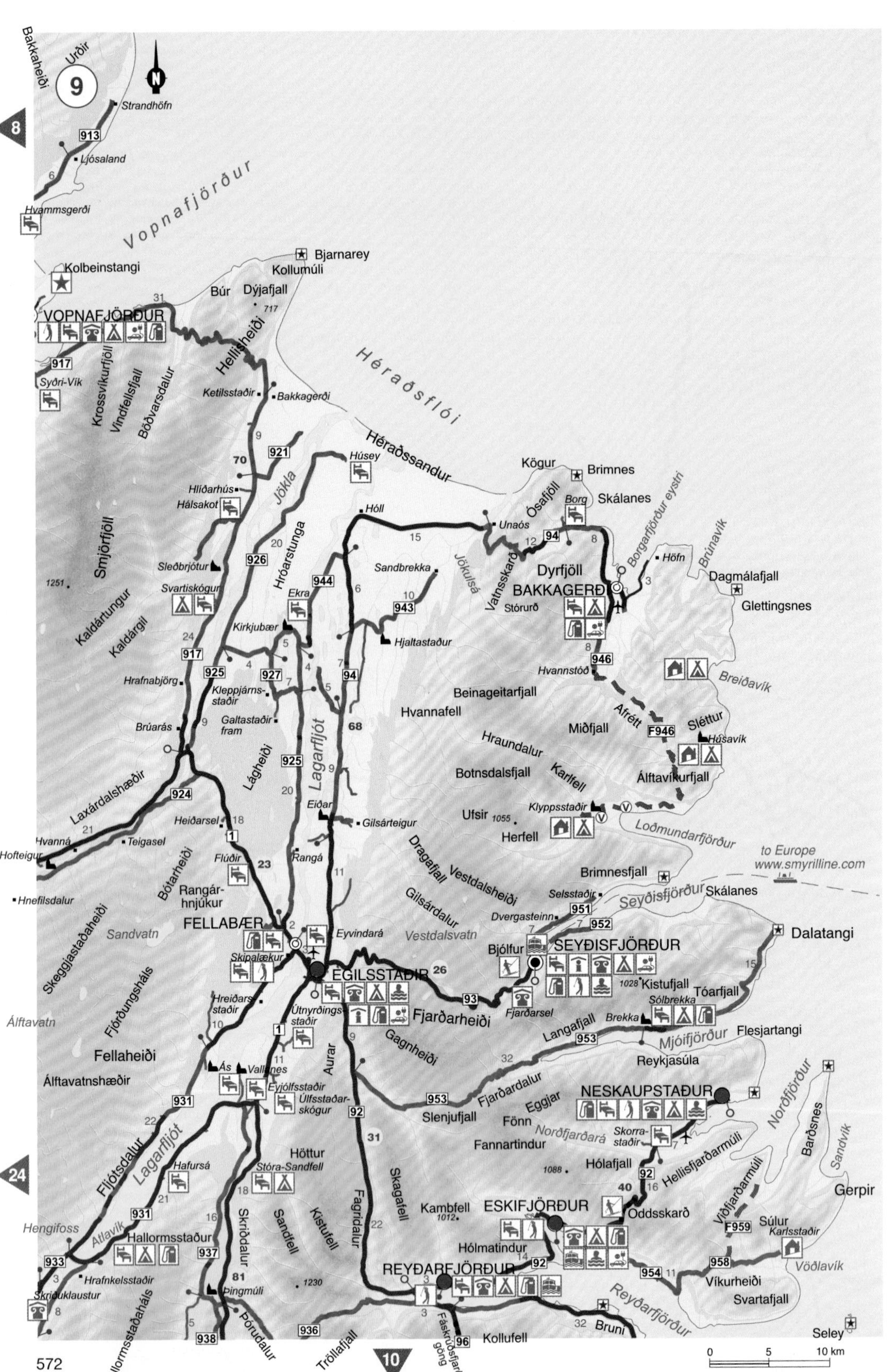

9
8
24
10
Vopnafjörður
Héraðsflói
Héraðssandur
VOPNAFJÖRÐUR
BAKKAGERÐI
SEYÐISFJÖRÐUR
EGILSSTAÐIR
FELLABÆR
NESKAUPSTAÐUR
ESKIFJÖRÐUR
REYÐARFJÖRÐUR
Bjarnarey
Kolbeinstangi
Strandhöfn
Ljósaland
Hvammsgerði
Syðri-Vík
Hellisheiði
Smjörfjöll
Dyrfjöll
Lagarfljót
Fjarðarheiði
Seyðisfjörður
Loðmundarfjörður
Mjóifjörður
Norðfjörður
Reyðarfjörður
Dalatangi
Gerpir
Hallormsstaður
to Europe
www.smyrilline.com
0
5
10 km

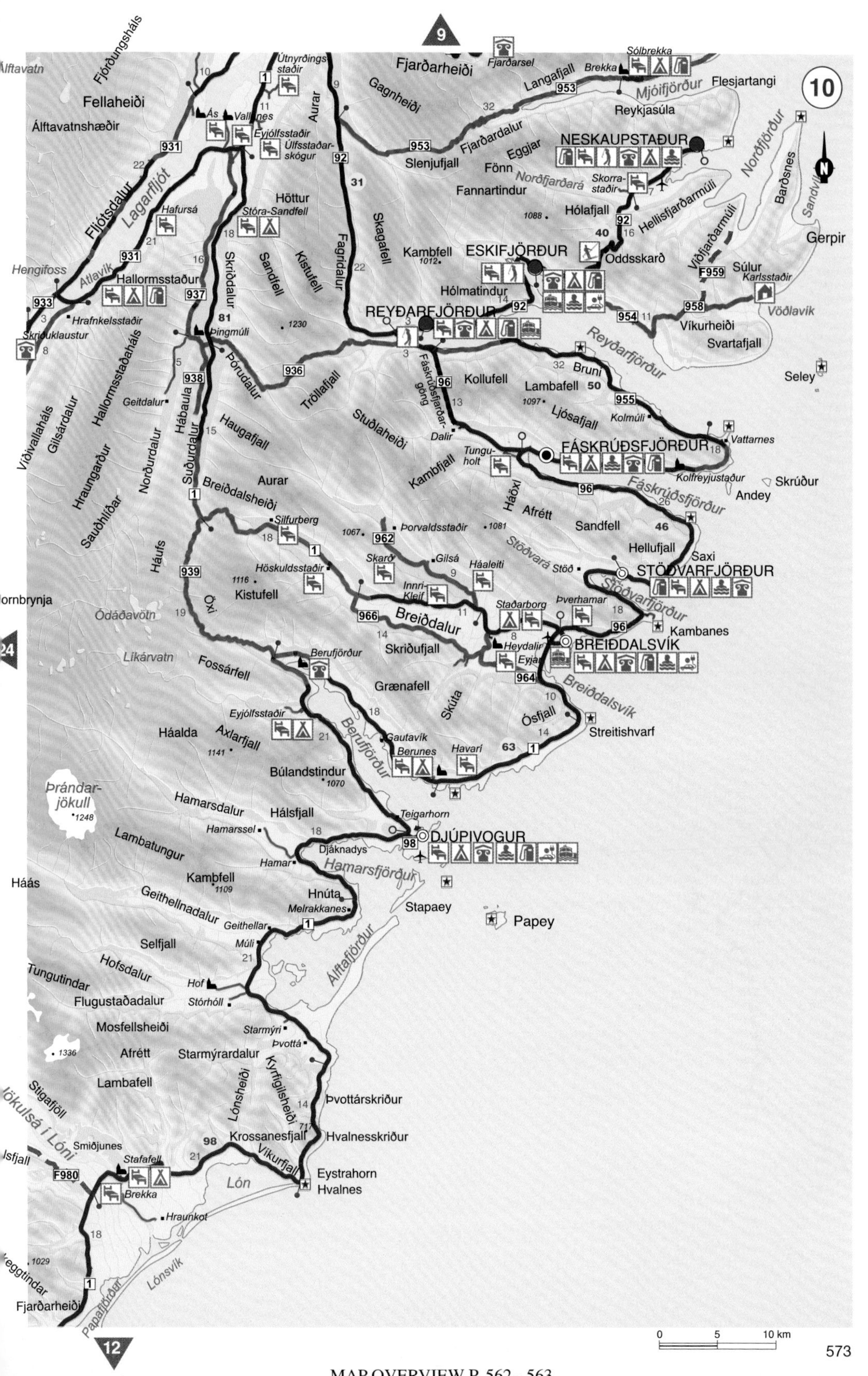

MAP OVERVIEW P. 562 - 563

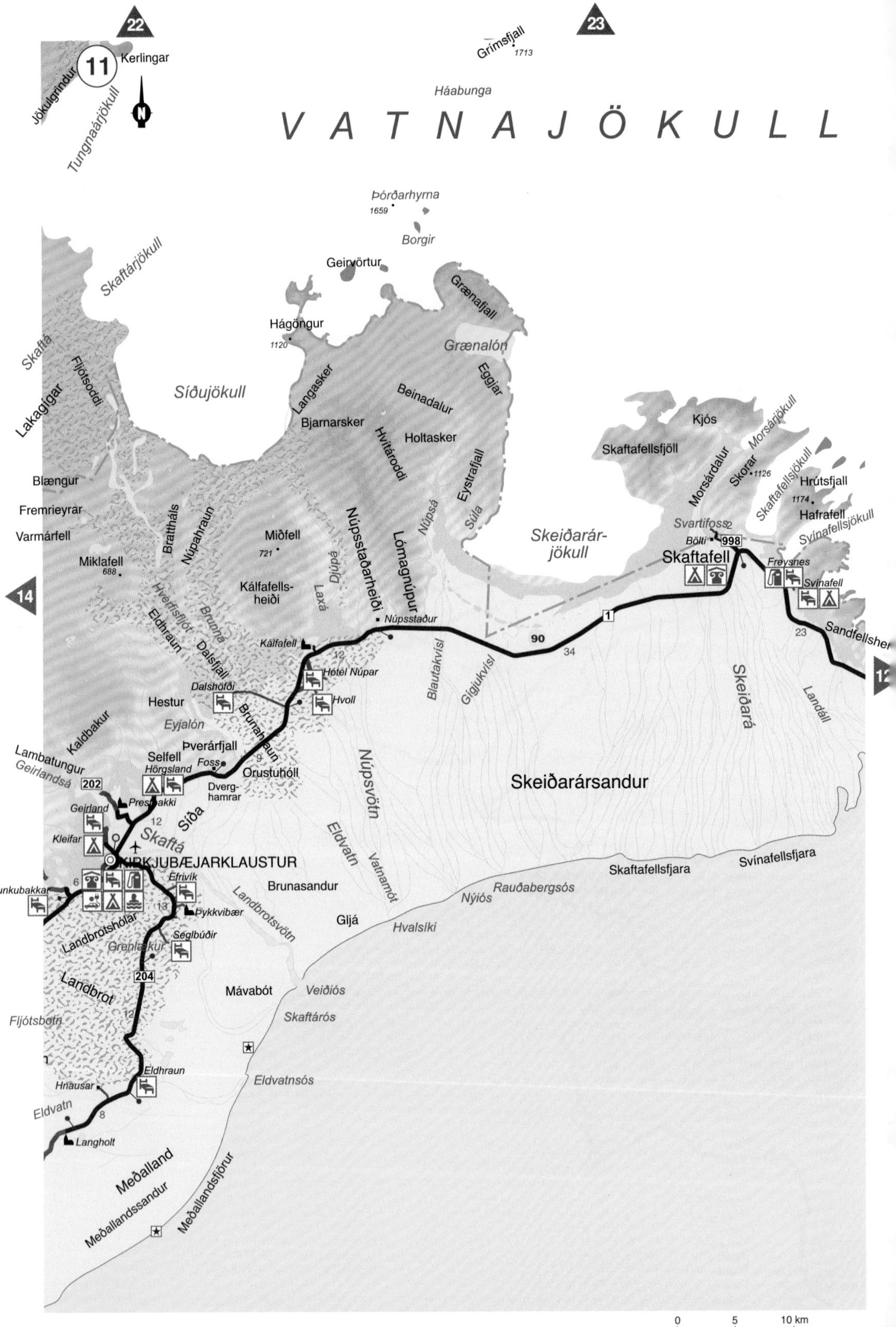

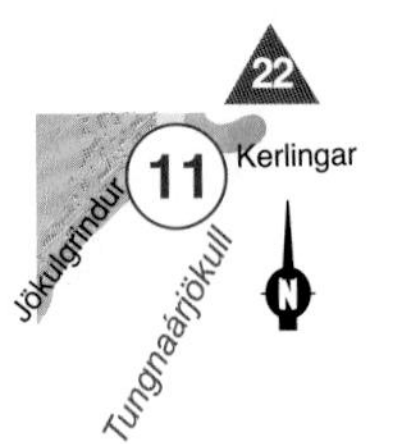

Háabunga

VATNAJÖKULL

Þórðarhyrna
1659
Borgir
Geirvörtur
Skaftárjökull
Grænafjall
Hágöngur
1120
Grænalón
Skaftá
Fljótsoddi
Síðujökull
Langasker
Eggjar
Beinadalur
Lakagígar
Bjarnarsker
Hvítároddi
Holtasker
Kjós
Morsárjökull
Skaftafellsfjöll
Blængur
Eystrafjall
Morsárdalur
Skorar
1126
Hrútsfjall
1174
Skaftafellsjökull
Hafrafell
Fremrieyrar
Bratthals
Núpahraun
Núpsstaðarheiði
Lómagnúpur
Núpsá
Súla
Skeiðarárjökull
Svartifoss 2
Svínafellsjökull
Varmárfell
Miðfell
721
Djúpá
Bölti
998
Skaftafell
Freysnes
Miklafell
688
Kálfafellsheiði
Laxá
Svínafell
14
Hverfisfljót
Brunná
Núpsstaður
1
Sandfellsheiði
Eldhraun
Dalsfjall
Kálfafell
12
90
34
23
Hótel Núpar
Blautakvísl
Gígjukvísl
Skeiðará
Dalshöfði
Hvoll
12
Landáll
Hestur
Brunahraun
Kaldbakur
Eyjalón
Lambatungur
Selfell
Þverárfjall
Núpsvötn
Geirlandsá
Hörgsland
Foss
8
Orustuhóll
202
Dverghamrar
Skeiðarársandur
Prestbakki
Geirland
12
Síða
Eldvatn
Kleifar
Skaftá
Vatnamót
KIRKJUBÆJARKLAUSTUR
Skaftafellsfjara
Svínafellsfjara
6
Efrivík
Brunasandur
Rauðabergsós
Hunkubakkar
13
Nýjós
Þykkvibær
Landbrotsvötn
Gljá
Hvalsíki
Landbrotshólar
Seglbúðir
Grenlækur
204
Landbrot
Mávabót
Veiðiós
Fljótsbotn
12
Skaftárós
Eldhraun
Hnausar
Eldvatnsós
Eldvatn
8
Langholt
Meðalland
Meðallandssandur
Meðallandsfjörur

0 5 10 km

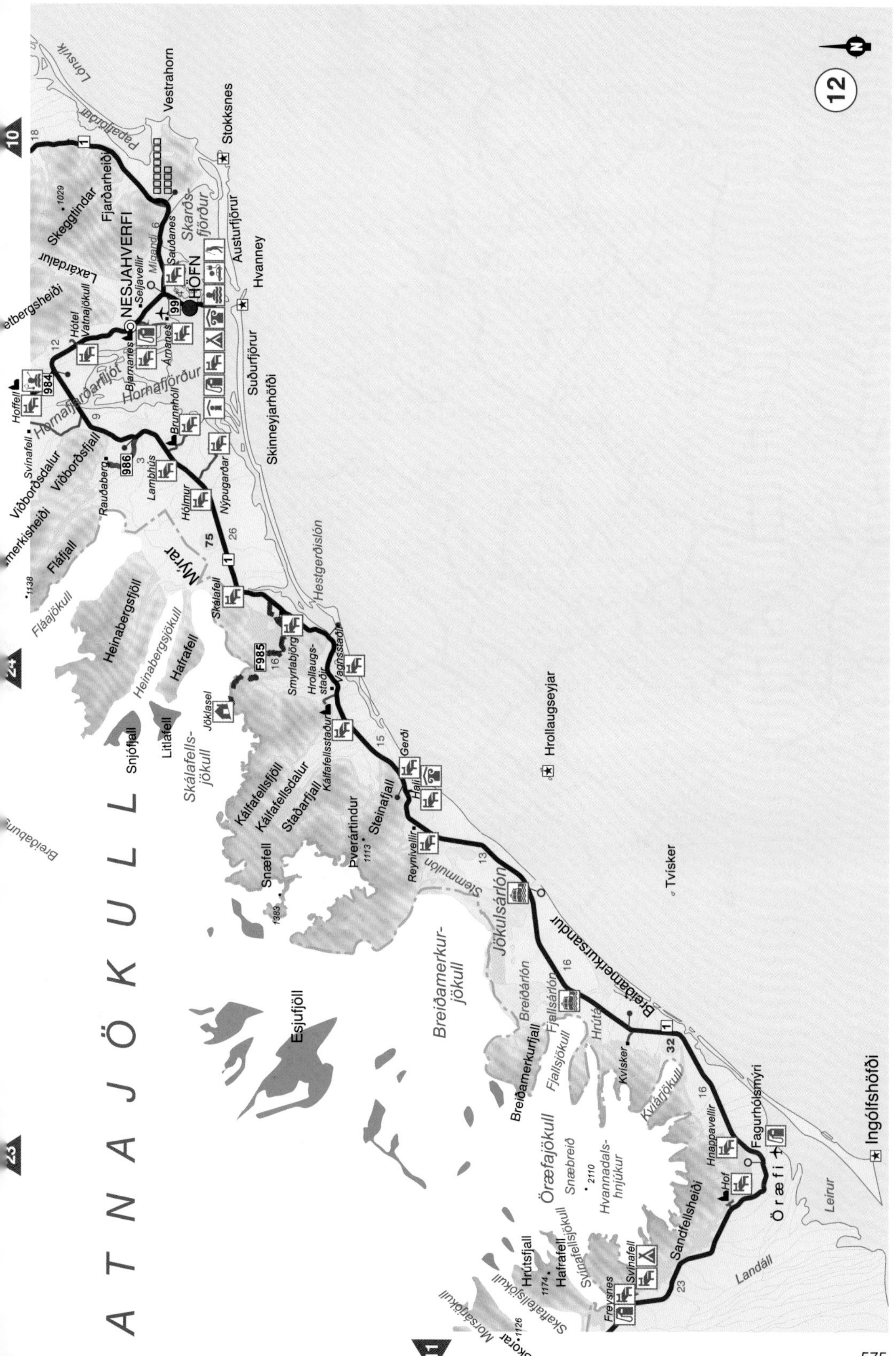

VATNAJÖKULL
12
0
5
10 km
Lónsvík
Vestrahorn
Papafjörður
Stokksnes
Fjarðarheiði
Skeggtindar
1029
Laxárdalur
NESJAHVERFI
Seljavellir
Miðgandi
Sauðanes
Skarðs-
fjörður
Austurfjörur
Hvanney
HÖFN
Hótel
Vatnajökull
Bjarnanes
Árnanes
Hornafjarðarfljót
Hornafjörður
Suðurfjörur
Skinneyjarhöfði
Hoffell
Svínafell
Viðborðsdalur
Viðborðsfjall
Brunnhóll
Lambhús
Rauðaberg
Hólmur
Nýpugarðar
Fláfjall
1138
Fláajökull
Mýrar
Heinabergsfjöll
Heinabergsjökull
Hafrafell
Skálafell
Hestgerðislón
Smyrlabjörg
Hrollaugs-
staðir
Vagnsstaðir
Jöklasel
Snjófjall
Litlafell
Skálafells-
jökull
Kálfafellsstaður
Kálfafellsfjöll
Kálfafellsdalur
Staðarfjall
Gerði
Hali
Steinafjall
Þverártindur
1113
Reynivellir
Hrollaugseyjar
Snæfell
1383
Steinmolin
Jökulsárlón
Tvísker
Breiðamerkursandur
Esjufjöll
Breiðamerkur-
jökull
Breiðárlón
Fjallsárlón
Breiðamerkurfjall
Fjallsjökull
Kvísker
Kvíárjökull
Fagurhólsmýri
Ingólfshöfði
Öræfajökull
Snæbreið
2110
Hvannadals-
hnjúkur
Hnappavellir
Hof
Ö r æ f i
Leirur
Sandfellsheiði
Svínafellsjökull
Hrútsfjall
Hafrafell
1174
Svínafell
Freysnes
Landáll
Skaftafellsjökull
Morsárjökull
Skorar
1126
Breiðabunga
1
75
26
F985
984
986
99
32
16
15
13
12
9
3
6
23
18
10
24
23
11

MAP OVERVIEW P. 562 - 563

MAP OVERVIEW P. 562 - 563

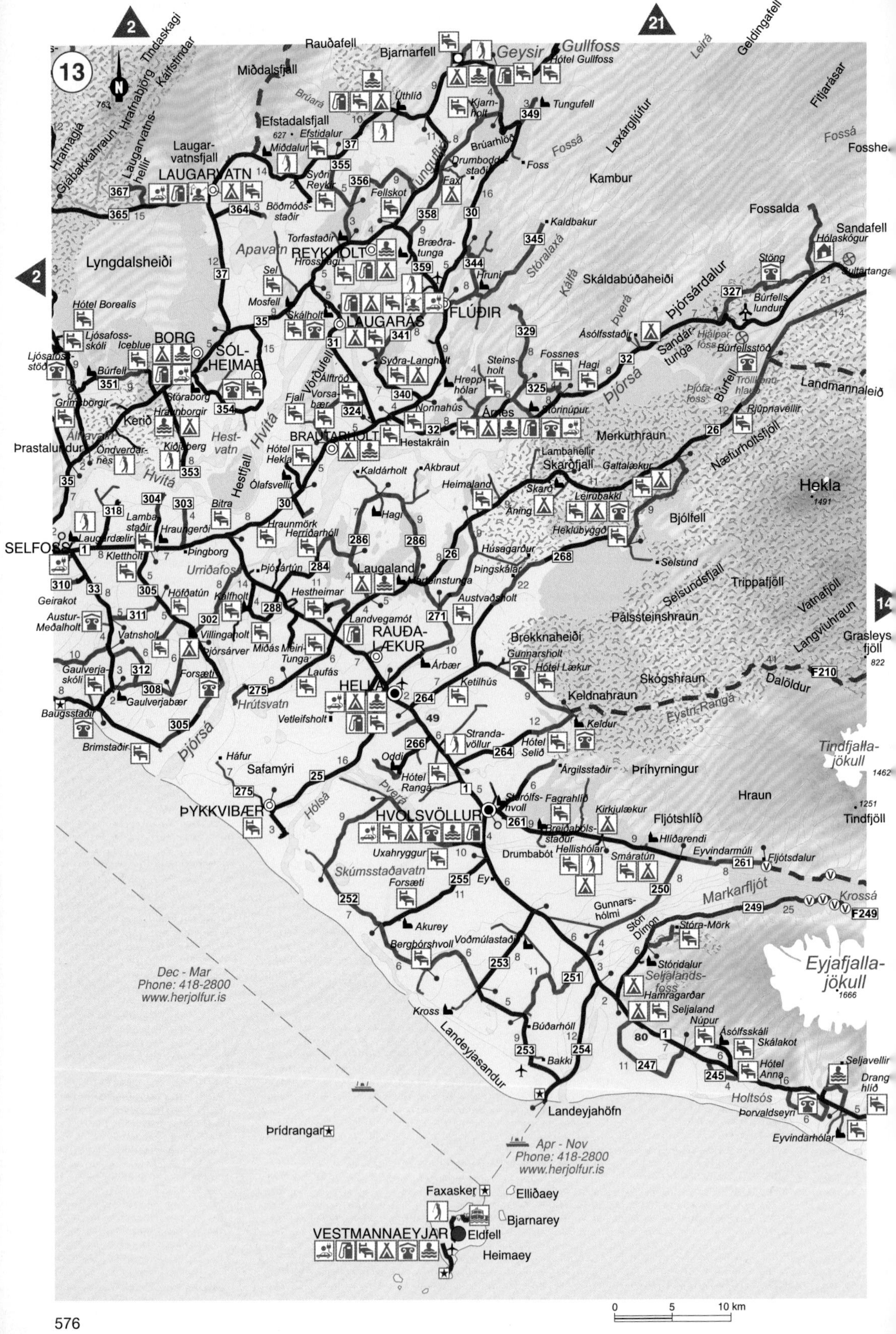

13
2
21
2
14
Rauðafell
Bjarnarfell
Geysir
Gullfoss
Hótel Gullfoss
Miðdalsfjall
Tindaskagi
Kálfstindar
Hrafnabjörg
Úthlíð
Kjarnholt
Tungufell
Efstadalsfjall
Efstidalur
Miðdalur
Laugarvatnsfjall
Laugarvatnshellir
Gjábakkahraun
Hrafnagjá
Brúarhlöð
Drumboddsstaðir
Foss
Fossá
Laxárgljúfur
Geldingafell
Fitjarásar
Fosshe
Leirá
Kambur
LAUGARVATN
Syðri Reykir
Fellskot
Faxi
Böðmóðsstaðir
Torfastaðir
Bræðratunga
Kaldbakur
Fossalda
Sandafell
Hólaskógur
Apavatn
REYKHOLT
Hrosshagi
Lyngdalsheiði
Sel
Mosfell
Hruni
Stóralaxá
Skáldabúðaheiði
Stöng
Sultartangi
Hótel Borealis
Skálholt
LAUGARÁS
FLÚÐIR
Kálfá
Þverá
Þjórsárdalur
Búrfellslundur
Ljósafossskóli
Iceblue
BORG
SÓLHEIMAR
Syðra-Langholt
Ásólfsstaðir
Sandártunga
Hjálparfoss
Búrfellsstöð
Ljósafossstöð
Búrfell
Stóraborg
Vörðufell
Álftröð
Hreppshólar
Steinsholt
Fossnes
Hagi
Tröllkonuhlaup
Landmannaleið
Grímsborgir
Fjall
Vorsabær
Þjórsá
Þjófafoss
Búrfell
Rjúpnavellir
Kerið
Hraunborgir
Hestvatn
Hvítá
Nónnahús
Árnes
Stórinúpur
Merkurhraun
Álftavatn
Þrastalundur
Öndverðarnes
Kiðjaberg
BRAUTARHOLT
Hótel Hekla
Hestakráin
Lambahellir
Skarðfjall
Galtalækur
Næfurholtsfjöll
Hestfjall
Kaldárholt
Akbraut
Heimaland
Skarð
Leirubakki
Hekla
1491
Ólafsvellir
Áning
Bjólfell
Lambastaðir
Bitra
Hraungerði
Hraunmörk
Hagi
Heklubyggð
SELFOSS
Laugardælir
Herríðarhóll
Húsagarður
Klettholt
Þingborg
Selsund
Urriðafoss
Þjórsártún
Laugaland
Marteinstunga
Þingskálar
Selsundsfjall
Trippafjöll
Vatnafjöll
Geirakot
Höfðatún
Kálfholt
Hestheimar
Austvaðsholt
Austur-Meðalholt
Landvegamót
Pálssteinshraun
Langviuhraun
Vatnsholt
Villingaholt
Miðás
Meiri-Tunga
RAUÐALÆKUR
Brekknaheiði
Þjórsárver
Árbær
Gunnarsholt
Grasleysfjöll
822
Gaulverjaskóli
Forsæti
Laufás
Hótel Lækur
Skógshraun
Dalöldur
F210
Ketilhús
Gaulverjabær
HELLA
Keldnahraun
Eystri-Rangá
Hrútsvatn
Vetleifsholt
Keldur
Baugsstaðir
Strandavöllur
Hótel Selið
Tindfjallajökull
1462
Brimstaðir
Háfur
Oddi
Árgilsstaðir
Þríhyrningur
Safamýri
Hótel Rangá
Stórólfshvoll
Fagrahlíð
Hraun
1251
ÞYKKVIBÆR
Hólsá
HVOLSVÖLLUR
Kirkjulækur
Fljótshlíð
Tindfjöll
Breiðabólsstaður
Hlíðarendi
Uxahryggur
Drumbabót
Hellishólar
Smáratún
Eyvindarmúli
Fljótsdalur
Skúmsstaðavatn
Forsæti
Ey
Markarfljót
Krossá
Gunnarshólmi
F249
Akurey
Stóri Dímon
Stóra-Mörk
Bergþórshvoll
Voðmúlastaðir
Stóridalur
Eyjafjallajökull
1666
Seljalandsfoss
Hamragarðar
Seljaland
Dec - Mar
Phone: 418-2800
www.herjolfur.is
Kross
Landeyjasandur
Búðarhóll
Núpur
Ásólfsskáli
Skálakot
Bakki
Hótel Anna
Seljavellir
Dranghlíð
Holtsós
Landeyjahöfn
Þorvaldseyri
Eyvindarhólar
Þrídrangar
Apr - Nov
Phone: 418-2800
www.herjolfur.is
Faxasker
Elliðaey
Bjarnarey
VESTMANNAEYJAR
Eldfell
Heimaey
0
5
10 km

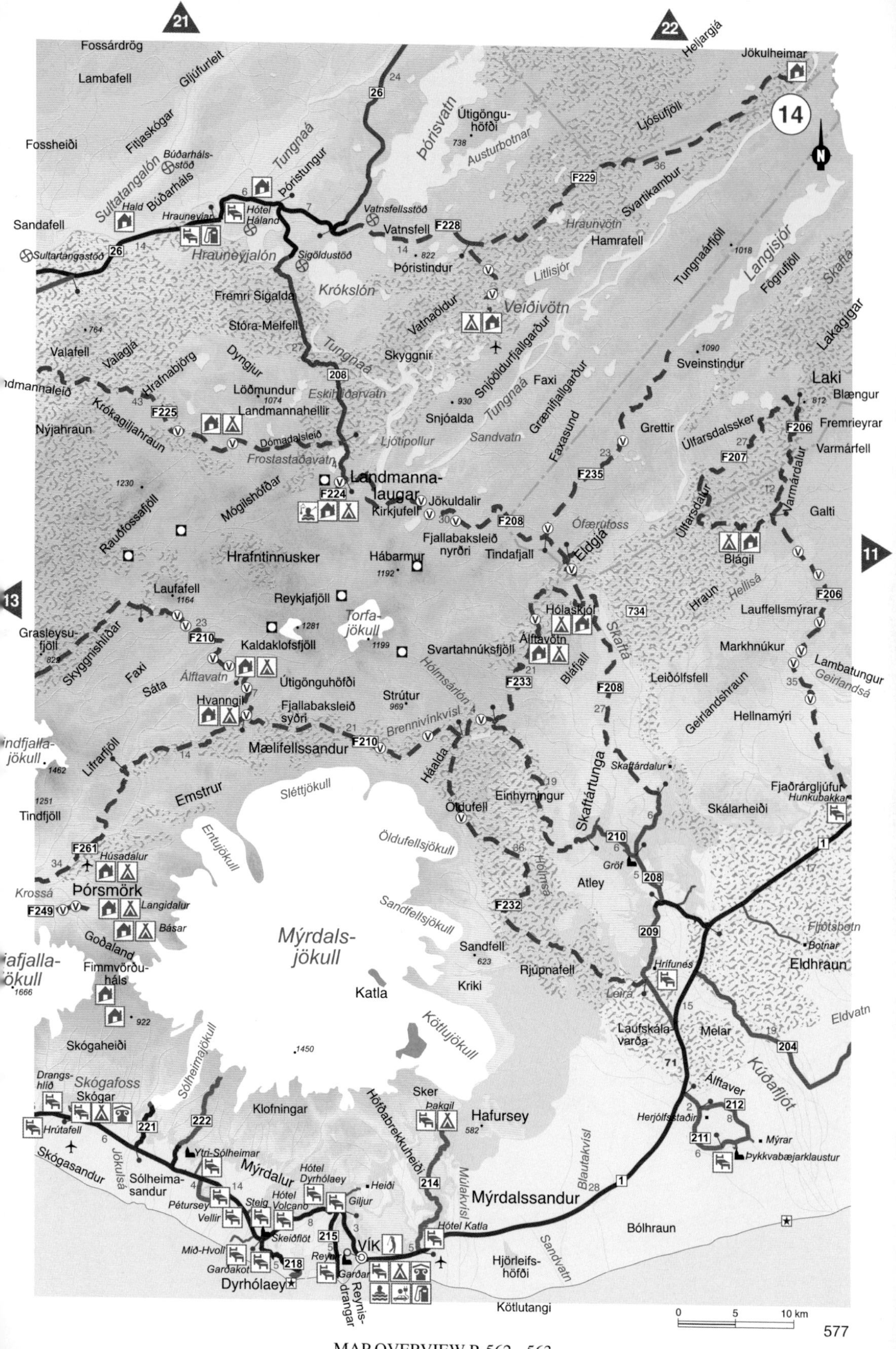

MAP OVERVIEW P. 562 - 563

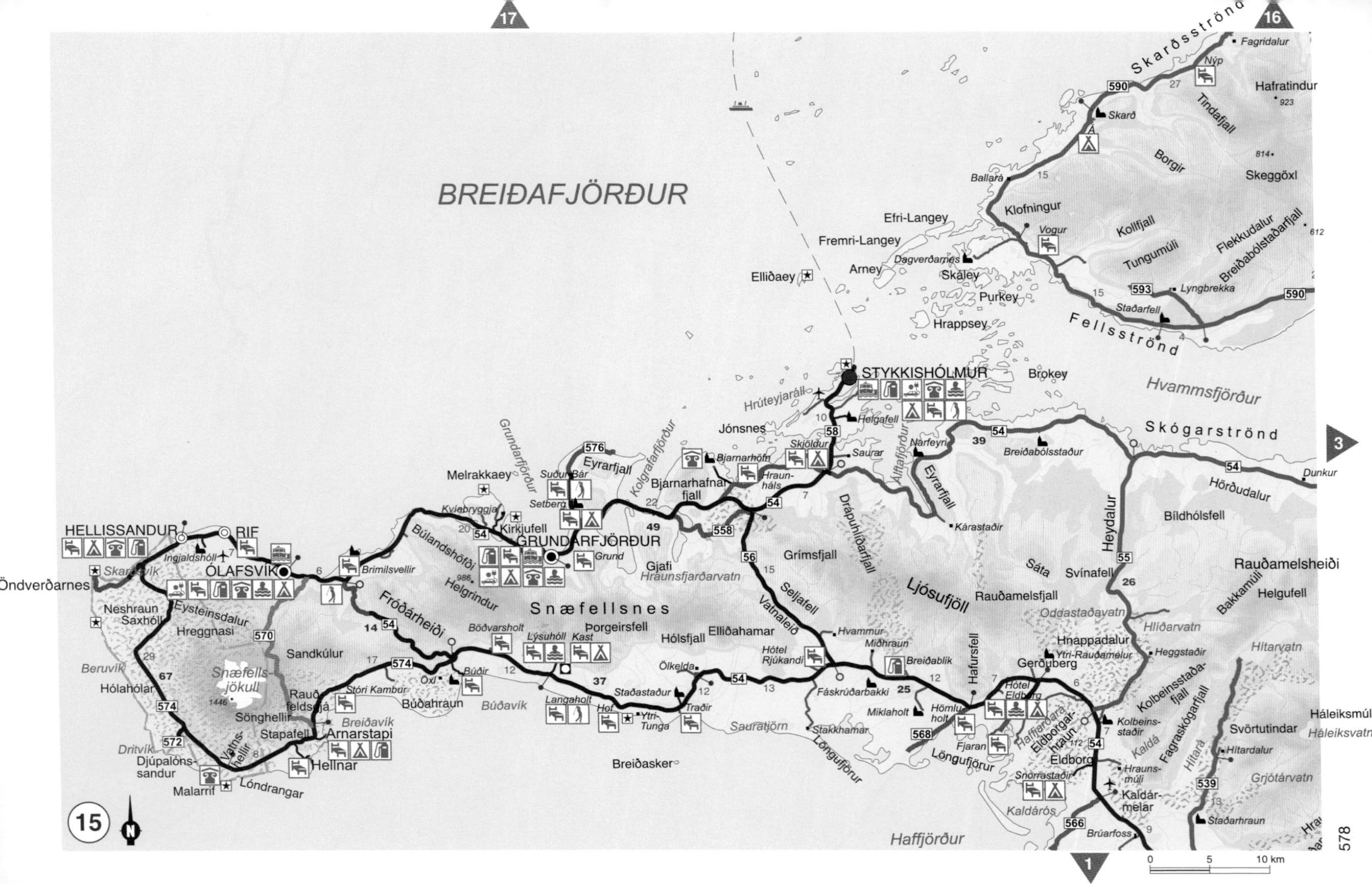
BREIÐAFJÖRÐUR
HELLISSANDUR
RIF
ÓLAFSVÍK
GRUNDARFJÖRÐUR
STYKKISHÓLMUR
Öndverðarnes
Skarðsvík
Ingjaldshóll
Neshraun
Saxhóll
Eysteinsdalur
Hreggnasi
Beruvík
Hólahólar
Snæfellsjökull
1446
Sönghellir
Vatnshellir
Dritvík
Djúpalónssandur
Malarrif
Lóndrangar
Stapafell
Rauðfeldsgjá
Arnarstapi
Hellnar
Breiðavík
Sandkúlur
Stóri Kambur
Búðahraun
Öxl
Búðir
Búðavík
Brimilsvellir
Fróðárheiði
Búlandshöfði
986
Helgrindur
Kvíabryggja
Melrakkaey
Kirkjufell
Grundarfjörður
Suður-Bár
Setberg
Eyrarfjall
Grund
Snæfellsnes
Böðvarsholt
Lýsuhóll
Kast
Þorgeirsfell
Langaholt
Hof
Ytri-Tunga
Staðastaður
Traðir
Ölkelda
Breiðasker
Sauratjörn
Kolgrafarfjörður
Bjarnarhafnarfjall
Bjarnarhöfn
Gjafi
Hraunsfjarðarvatn
Hólsfjall
Elliðahamar
Hótel Rjúkandi
Hraunháls
Skjöldur
Saurar
Jónsnes
Hrúteyjarál
Helgafell
Grímsfjall
Seljafell
Vatnaleið
Drápuhlíðarfjall
Hvammur
Miðhraun
Breiðablik
Fáskrúðarbakki
Stakkhamar
Löngufjörur
Miklaholt
Hömluholt
Hafursfell
Ljósufjöll
Álftafjörður
Narfeyri
Eyrarfjall
Kárastaðir
Breiðabólsstaður
Elliðaey
Fremri-Langey
Efri-Langey
Arney
Dagverðarnes
Skáley
Purkey
Hrappsey
Brokey
Hvammsfjörður
Skógarströnd
Dunkur
Hörðudalur
Bíldhólsfell
Heydalur
Sáta
Svínafell
Rauðamelsfjall
Rauðamelsheiði
Bakkamúli
Helgufell
Oddastaðavatn
Hlíðarvatn
Hnappadalur
Ytri-Rauðamelur
Gerðuberg
Heggstaðir
Hítarvatn
Hótel Eldborg
Haffjarðará
Eldborgarhraun
Eldborg
Fjaran
Snorrastaðir
Kaldárós
Kolbeinsstaðir
Kolbeinsstaðafjall
Kaldá
Hraunsmúli
Kaldármelar
Brúarfoss
Fagraskógarfjall
Hítará
Hítardalur
Svörtutindar
Háleiksmúli
Háleiksvatn
Grjótárvatn
Staðarhraun
Haffjörður
Fellsströnd
Staðarfell
Lyngbrekka
Klofningur
Vogur
Ballará
Kollfjall
Tungumúli
Flekkudalur
Breiðabólstaðarfjall
612
Borgir
Skeggöxl
814
Skarð
Tindafjall
Hafratindur
923
Nýp
Fagridalur
Skarðsströnd
0
5
10 km
15
17
16
3
1

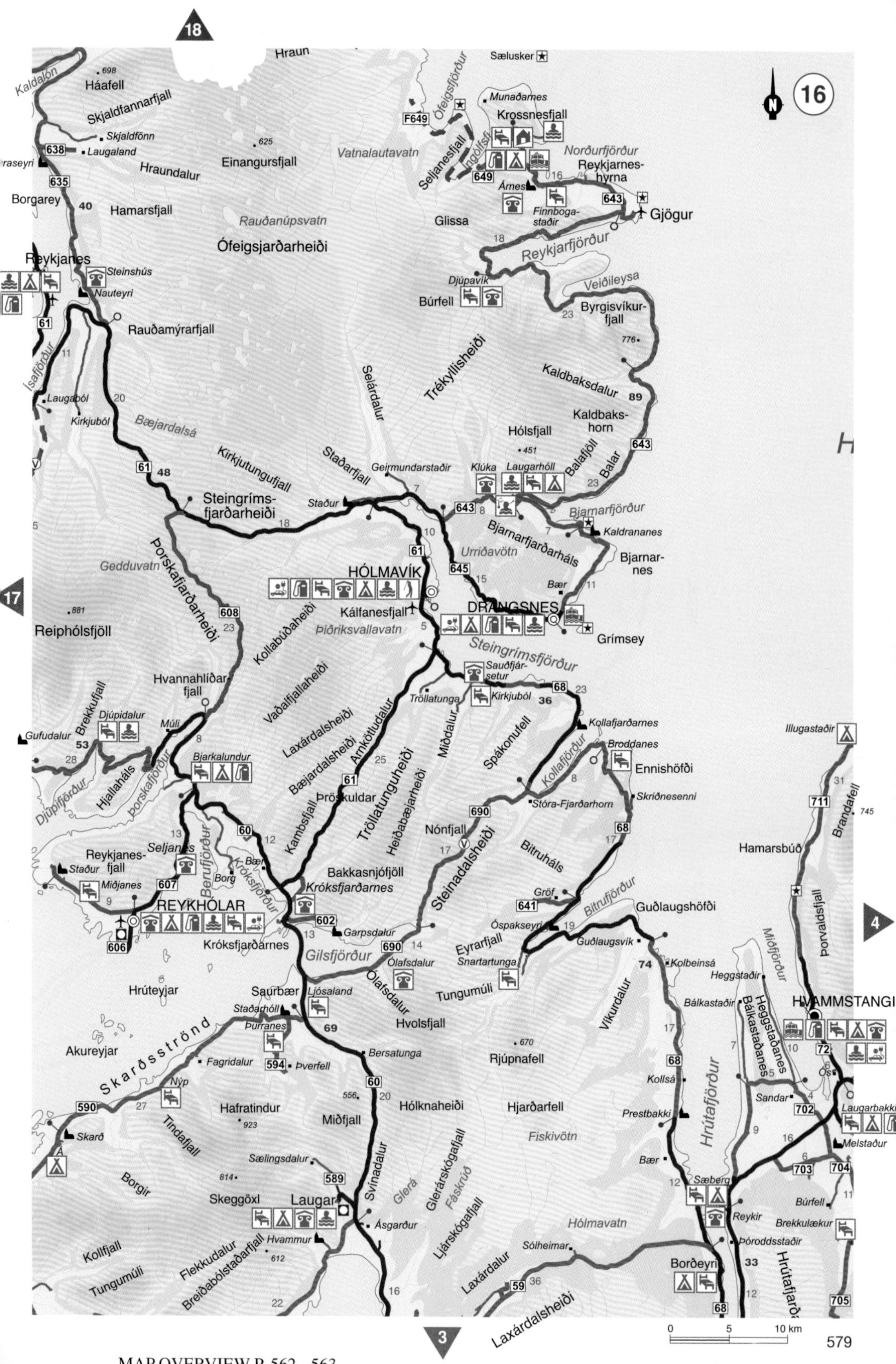

MAP OVERVIEW P. 562 - 563

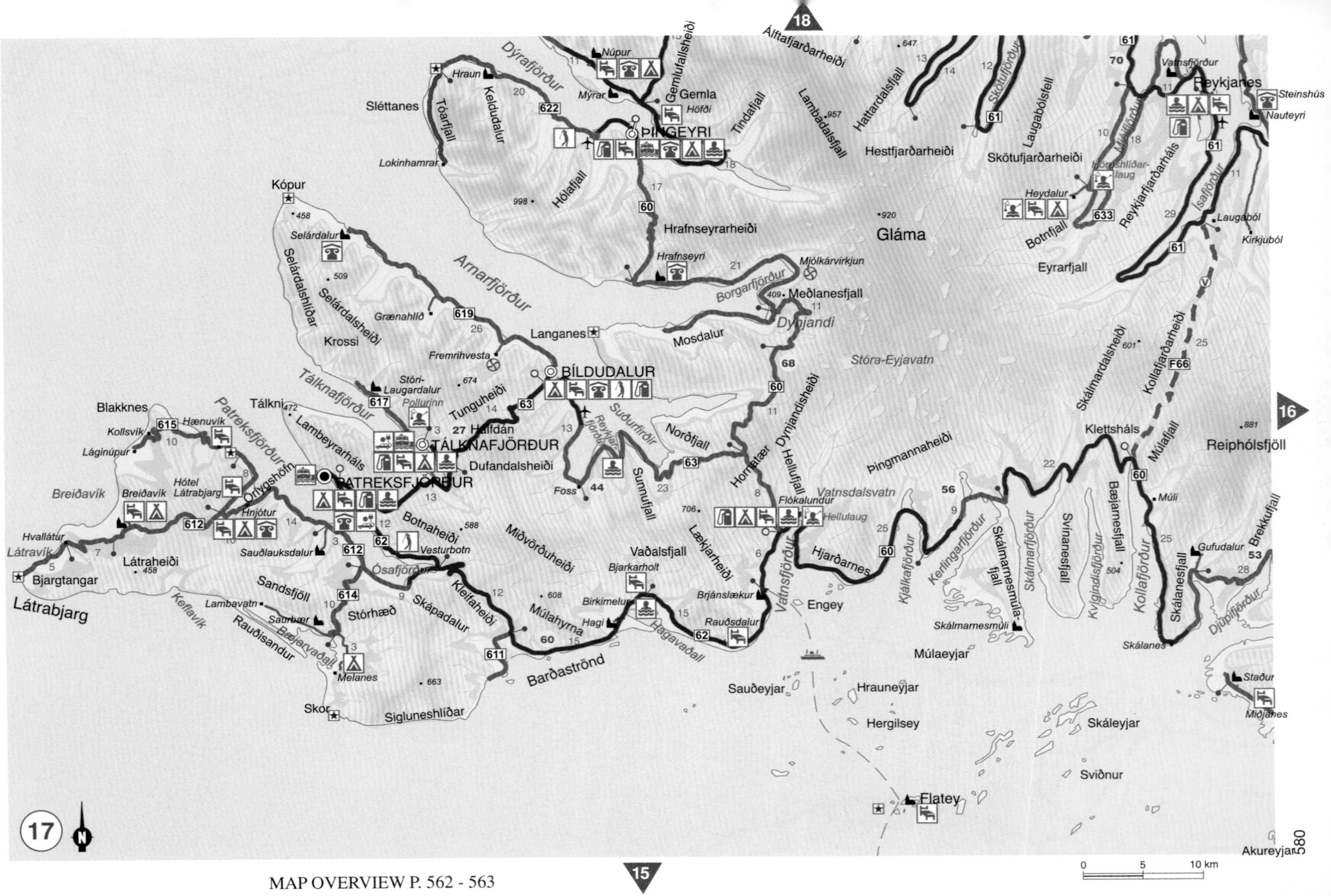

17

0 5 10 km

MAP OVERVIEW P. 562 - 563

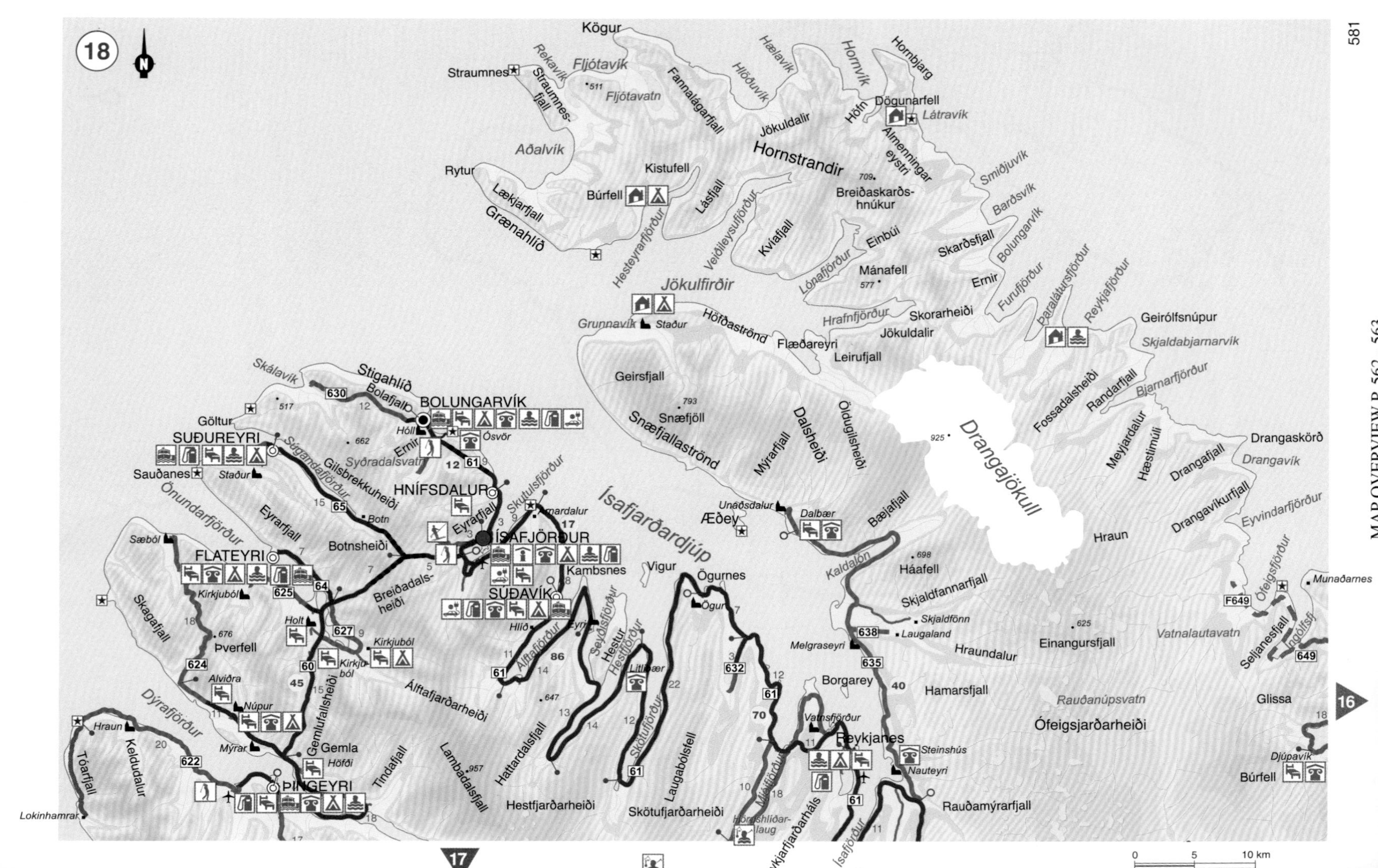

MAP OVERVIEW P. 562 - 563

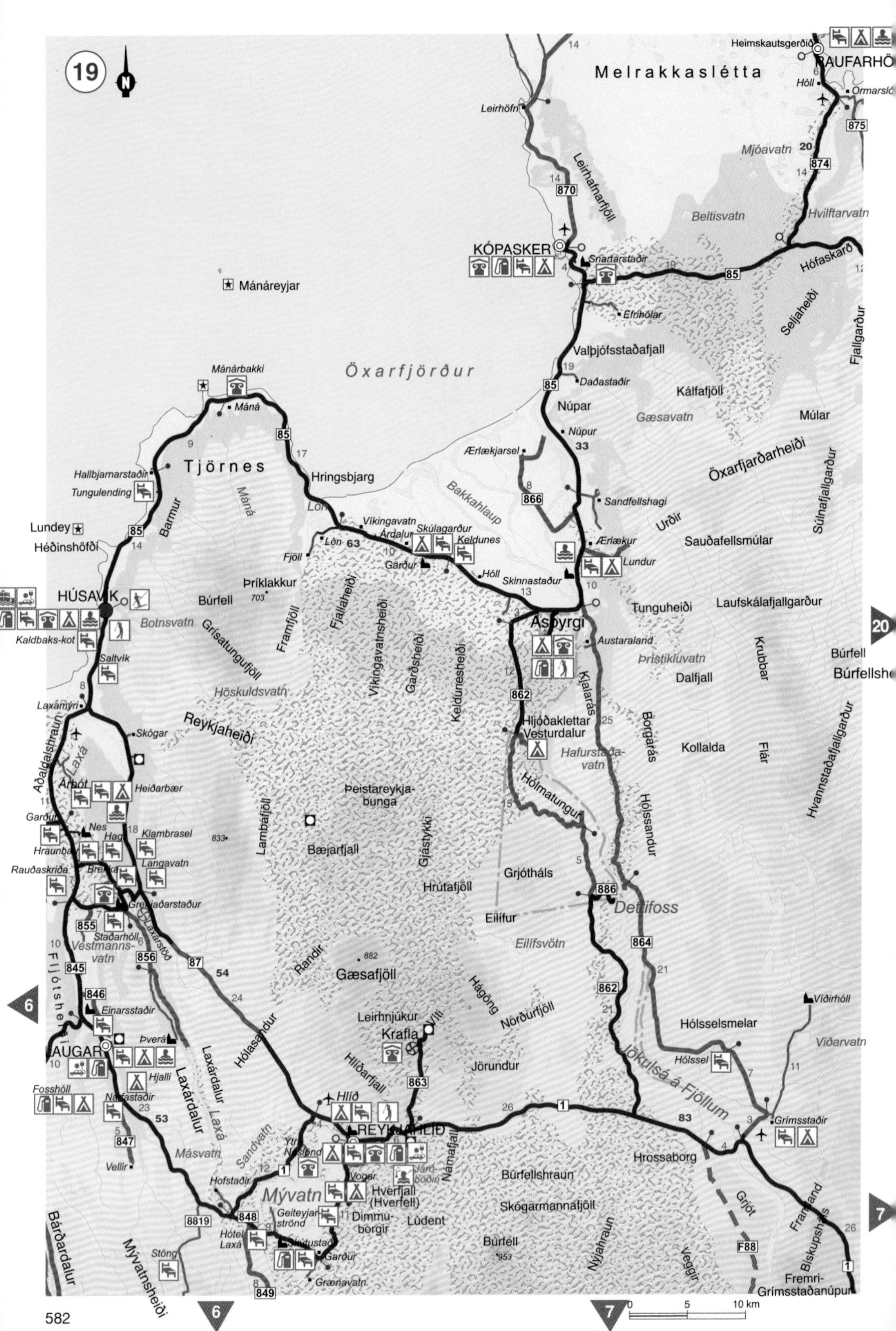
19
Melrakkaslétta
RAUFARHÖ
Heimskautsgerðið
Leirhöfn
KÓPASKER
Snartarstaðir
Mánáreyjar
Öxarfjörður
Mánárbakki
Máná
Tjörnes
Hallbjarnarstaðir
Tungulending
Lundey
Héðinshöfði
Hringsbjarg
HÚSAVÍK
Kaldbaks-kot
Saltvík
Botnsvatn
Grísatungufjöll
Höskuldsvatn
Reykjaheiði
Búrfell
Þríklakkur
Framfjöll
Fjallaheiði
Víkingavatnsheiði
Garðsheiði
Kelduneshreiði
Víkingavatn
Skúlagarður
Keldunes
Ásbyrgi
Skinnastaður
Lundur
Ærlækur
Sandfellshagi
Ærlækjarsel
Bakkahlaup
Núpar
Valþjófsstaðafjall
Daðastaðir
Kálfafjöll
Gæsavatn
Múlar
Öxarfjarðarheiði
Urðir
Sauðafellsmúlar
Tunguheiði
Laufskálafjallgarður
Krubbar
Búrfell
Dalfjall
Þristikluvatn
Austaraland
Hljóðaklettar
Vesturdalur
Hafurstaðavatn
Hólmatungur
Kollalda
Borgarás
Hólssandur
Þeistareykjabunga
Bæjarfjall
Lambafjöll
Gjástykki
Grjótháls
Hrútafjöll
Dettifoss
Eilífur
Eilífsvötn
Gæsafjöll
Randir
Hágöng
Norðurfjöll
Leirhnjúkur
Krafla
Víti
Jörundur
Hlíðarfjall
Hólasandur
Jökulsá á Fjöllum
Hólsselsmelar
Hólssel
Víðirhóll
Víðarvatn
Grímsstaðir
Hrossaborg
REYKJAHLÍÐ
Mývatn
Hverfjall (Hverfell)
Dimmuborgir
Lúdent
Búrfellshraun
Skógarmannafjöll
Búrfell
Námafjall
Laugar
Laxárdalur
Mývatnsheiði
Bárðardalur
Fljótsheiði
Vestmannsvatn
Grenjaðarstaður
Aðaldalshraun
Laxá
Heiðarbær
Skógar
Laxamýri
Hótel Laxá
Skútustaðir
Garður
Grænavatn
Sandvatn
Másvatn
Vellir
Fosshóll
Hjalli
Einarsstaðir
Þverá
Stöng
Hofstaðir
Fremri-Grímsstaðanúpur
Grjót
Veggir
Nýjahraun
0 5 10 km

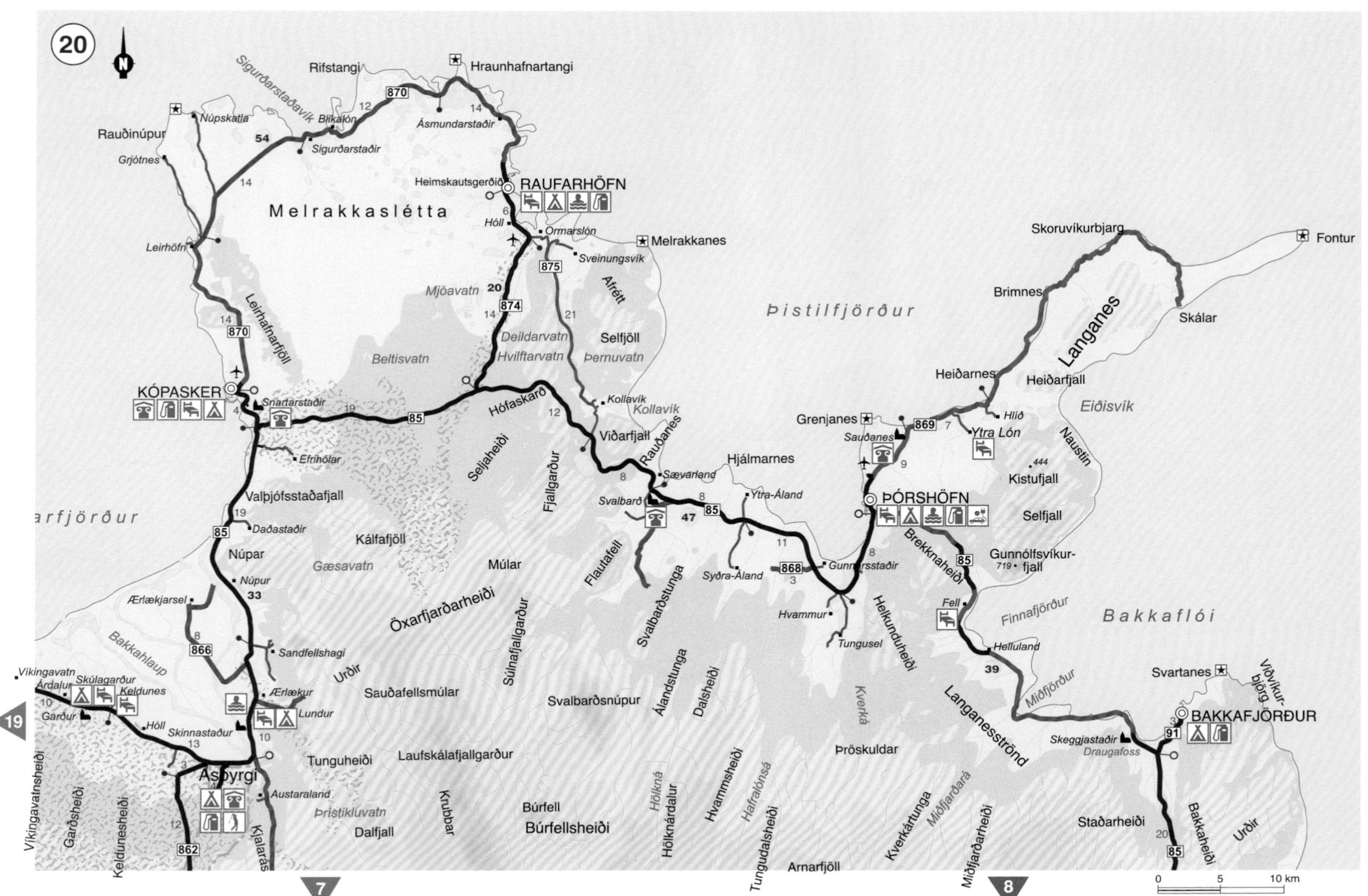

MAP OVERVIEW P. 562 - 563

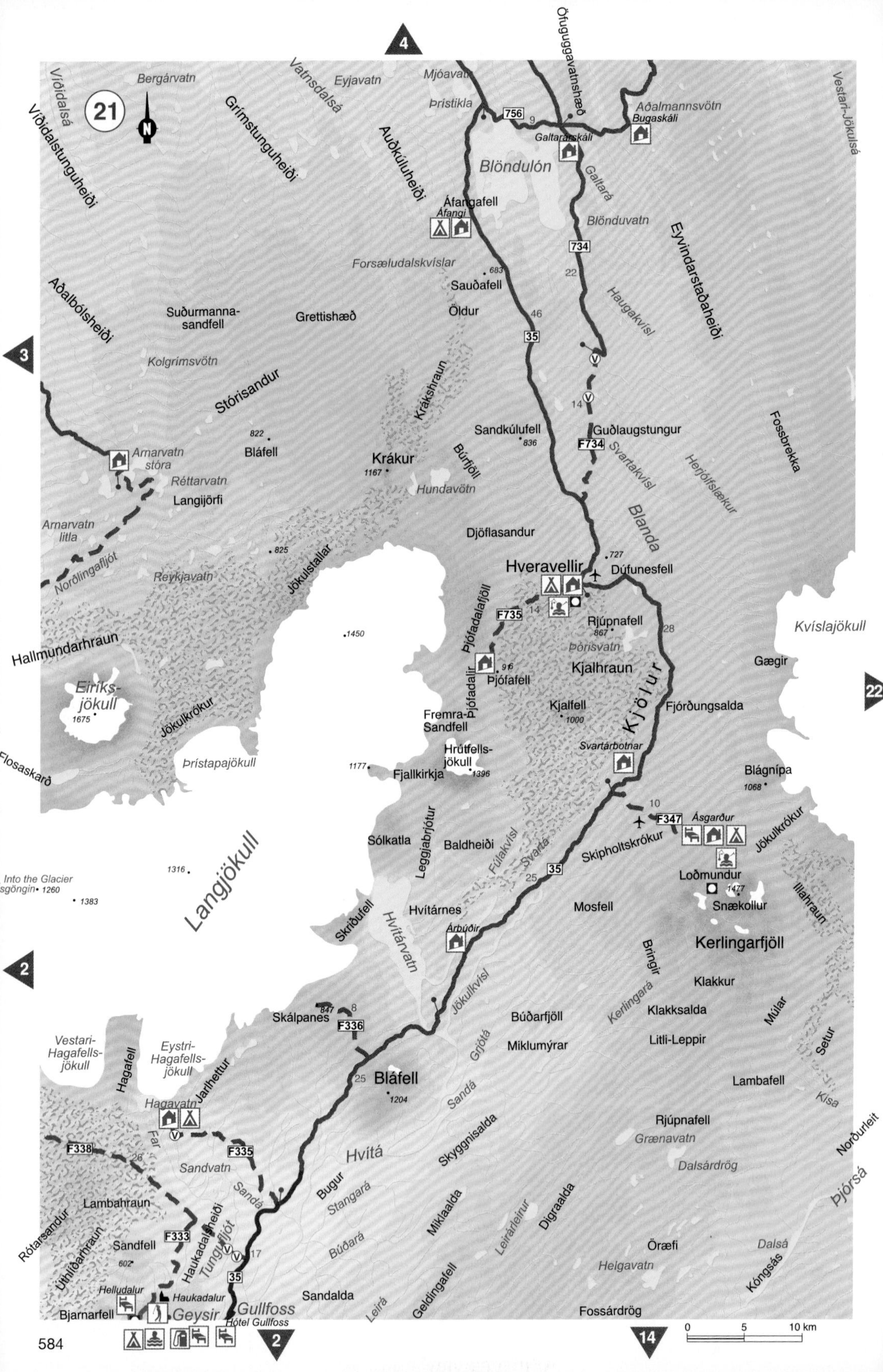
21
Langjökull
Hveravellir
Kjölur
Blöndulón
Kerlingarfjöll
Geysir
Gullfoss
Hótel Gullfoss
Bláfell
Hvítárvatn
Eiríksjökull
Þrístapajökull
Hrútfellsjökull
Kvíslajökull
Into the Glacier
Ísgöngin
Arnarvatn stóra
Áfangi
Bugaskáli
Galtaráarskáli
Svartárbotnar
Ásgarður
Árbúðir
Hagavatn
Helludalur
Haukadalur
Þjófadalir

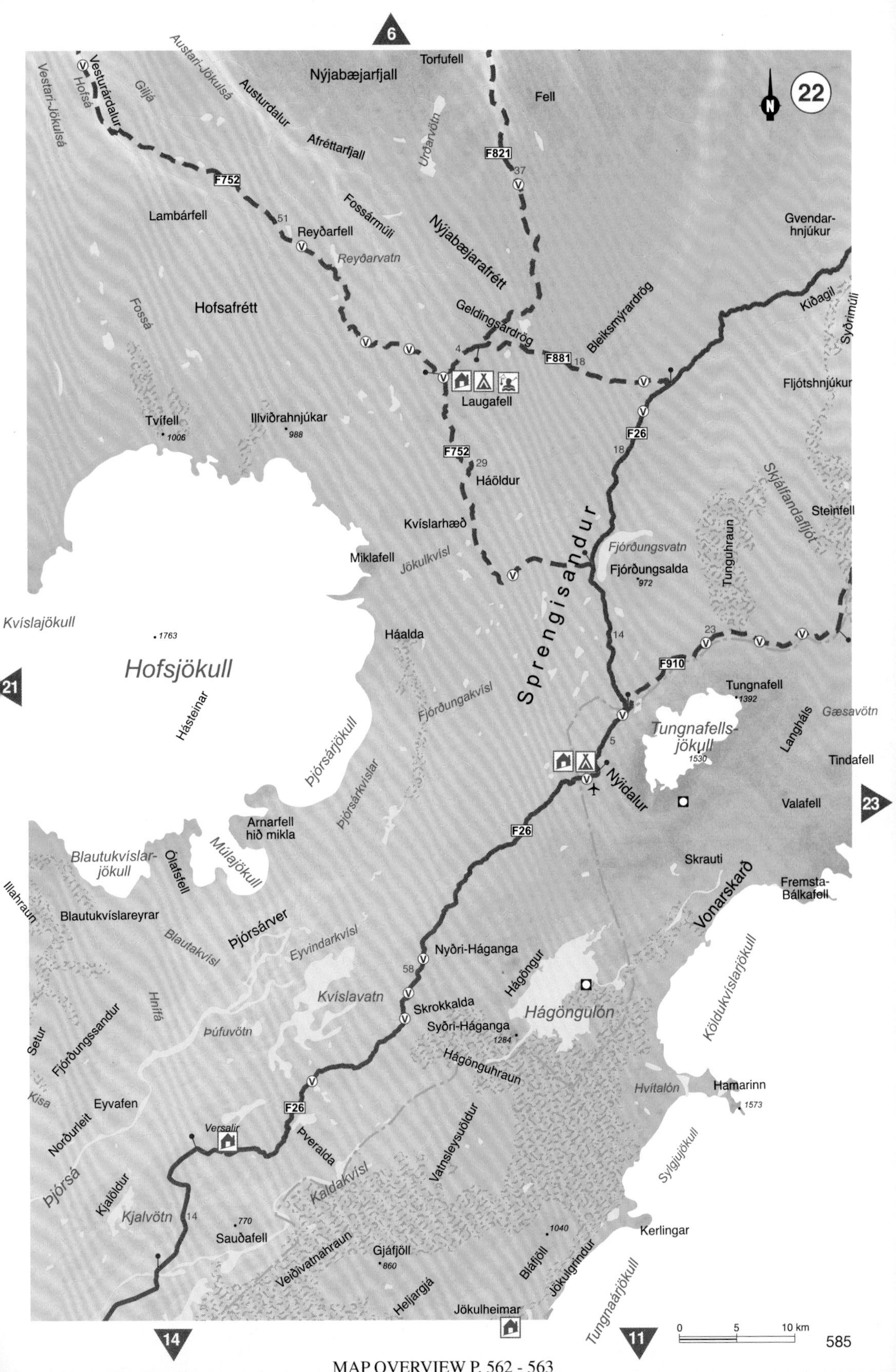

MAP OVERVIEW P. 562 - 563

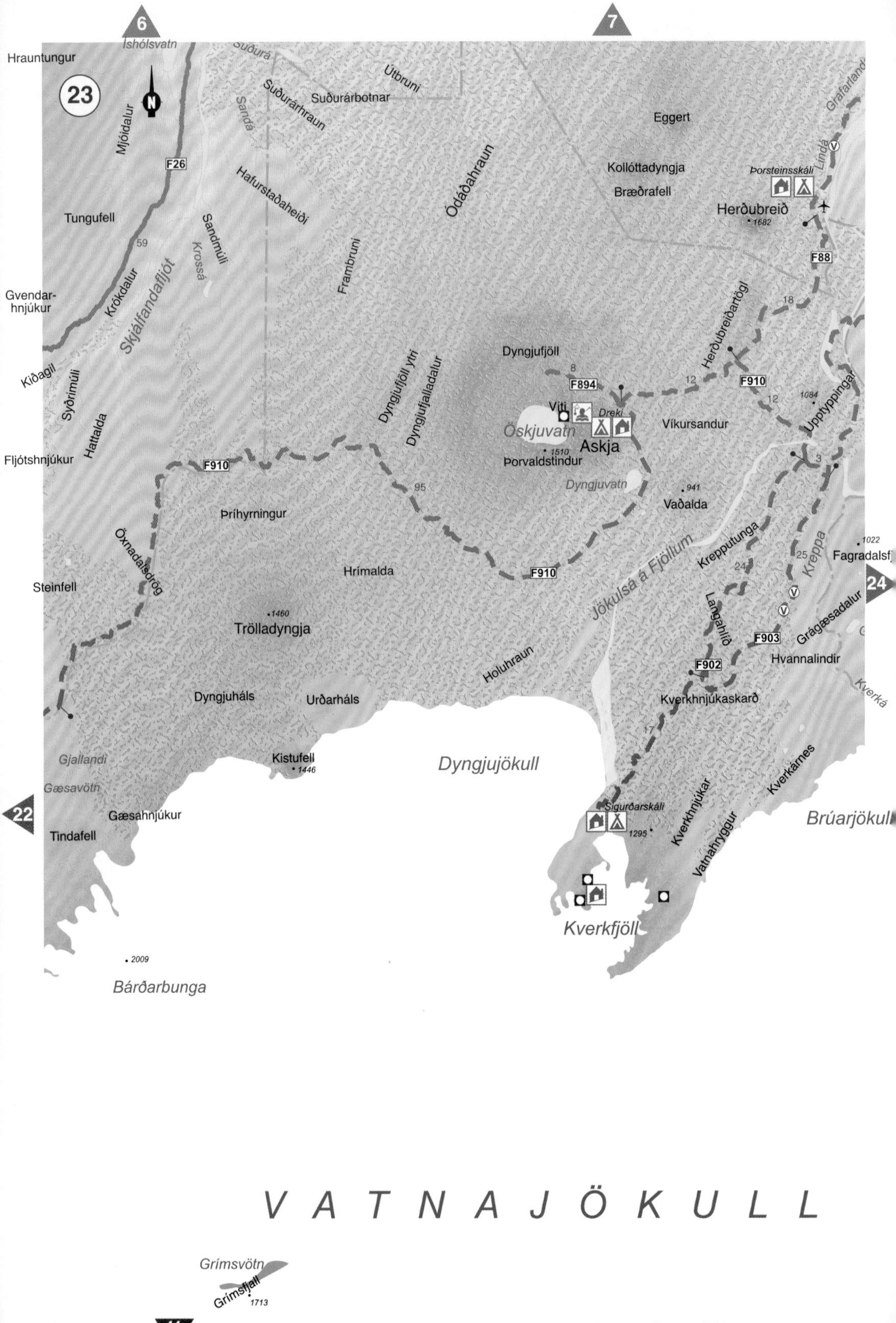

6
7
23
Hrauntungur
Íshólsvatn
Suðurá
Útbruni
Suðurárbotnar
Suðurárhraun
Sandá
Mjóidalur
F26
Eggert
Kollóttadyngja
Bræðrafell
Þorsteinsskáli
Grafarlönd
Lindá
Herðubreið
1682
F88
Hafurstaðaheiði
Ódáðahraun
Tungufell
Sandmúli
Krossá
59
Frambruni
Gvendar-
hnjúkur
Krókdalur
Skjálfandafljót
Herðubreiðartögl
18
Kiðagil
Syðrimúli
Hattalda
Fljótshnjúkur
Dyngjufjöll
8
F894
Dyngjufjöll ytri
Dyngjufjalladalur
Víti
Dreki
Öskjuvatn
Askja
1510
Þorvaldstindur
12
F910
1084
Upptyppingar
Víkursandur
F910
95
Dyngjuvatn
941
Vaðalda
3
Þríhyrningur
Öxnadalsdrög
Steinfell
Hrímalda
F910
Jökulsá á Fjöllum
Krepputunga
24
25
Kreppa
1022
Fagradalsfj
24
1460
Trölladyngja
Langahlíð
F903
Grágæsadalur
Hvannalindir
Holuhraun
F902
Kverkhnjúkaskarð
Kverká
Dyngjuháls
Urðarháls
17
Gjallandi
Kistufell
1446
Dyngjujökull
Kverkárnes
Gæsavötn
22
Gæsahnjúkur
Tindafell
Sigurðarskáli
1295
Kverkhnjúkar
Vatnahryggur
Brúarjökull
Kverkfjöll
2009
Bárðarbunga

V A T N A J Ö K U L L

11

0 5 10 km

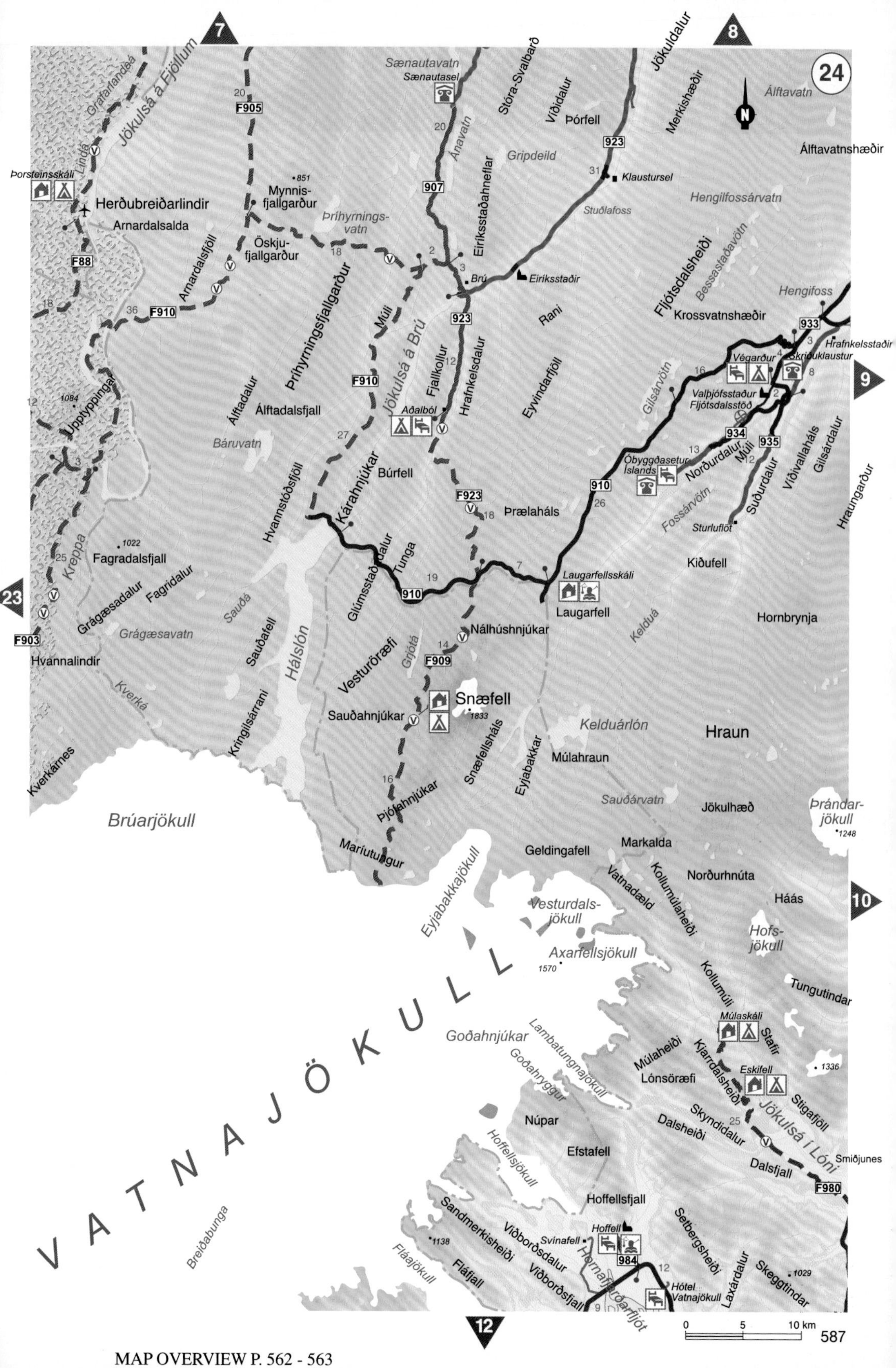

MAP OVERVIEW P. 562 - 563

INDEX

Safetravel
- For Your Safe Return

Driving in Iceland

Conditions in Iceland are in many ways unusual and often quite unlike what foreign drivers are accustomed to. It is therefore very important to find out how to drive in this country. We know that the landscapes are beautiful, which naturally draws the driver's attention away from the road. But in order to reach your destination safely, you must keep your full attention on driving.

- The speed limit is often 60 km/hr on thruways, but in residential areas it is usually only 30 km/hr.
- The main rule in rural areas is that gravel roads have a speed limit of 80 km/hr, and paved roads 90 km/hr.
- Watch out for single-lane bridges, they are many in Iceland. Slow down when getting close to them.
- Common place for accidents to occcur on rural roads is where a paved road suddenly changes to gravel. Reduce speed to avoid serious accidents.

Highland driving

Driving in the Icelandic highland is quite different from driving in the lowland. The conditions can change fast due to weather, rain and even sometimes snow. Therefore roads can be closed and rivers can be too big to cross.
Before you start your travel you should get information about the area as well as leave your travel plan with someone who can check up on you if needed. You can make your travel plan here.

- Start by checking if the area you are going to visit is open
- Get as much information about the area as you can
- Information centers, rangers and hut wardens can help you get the information needed
- Are you sure that you have the experience and knowledge needed to go the highland?
- If you are driving be on a 4x4 jeep, other cars will only get you into trouble
- If you are no sure how to cross a river skip it or wait for the next car to assist you ove

Get more information on www.safetravel.is

The emergency number in Iceland is 112

Safetravel

- For Your Safe Return

Outdoors

Good preparation is the key for a successful travel. Keep the below points in mind and remember that your first destination should always be **safetravel.is**

- Always leave your travel plan with someone who can react if needed
- Check the weather forecast. In Iceland the weather can change fast
- Remember to bring the right equiptment for the kind of travel you are planning
- Map, kompass and GPS should always be used when travel outside urban areas

Hiking

The first question that comes up for every hiker is where to go and what hiking trail to choose. Is it a well-known marked trail or off the beaten path? Regardless of what is decided, proper trail selection and route planning are essential components to a successful hike.

To ensure a better hike keep this in mind:

- When choosing a hiking trail, hikers should always use themselves as a frame of reference, i.e. their level of fitness and their experience and knowledge of hiking.
- Don't set out to do too much, plan reasonable distances each day.
- Keep in mind that even though a trail may have markers, visibility can be so poor that it is not possible to see from one mark to another.
- Compasses and GPS devices should be brought, alongside the knowledge of how to use them.
- A route plan is an important aid for every hiker. With a route plan you can plot day trips, distance to hike each day, write down accommodation details, a contingency plan if that might be needed, and other things that are important in making a good hike even better.
- The route plan should be left with a trustworthy person. He or she will then have exact information about the trip, in the event that a situation may arise in which it is needed.

Get more information on www.safetravel.is

The emergency number in Iceland is 112

Safetravel
- For Your Safe Return

Nature

The Icelandic nature is one of a kind and we are drawn to it again and again but at the same time travelling in the nature can be dangerous so we should keep the following in mind

- Get good information about the area you are travelling to
- Accidents are common when people get to close to the sea, cliff edges and hot springs.
- Sudden changes in weather are common especially in the highland
- When travelling the highland remember to check where you will find service. Often you have to drive a long way to get oil or food.

Off Road

Off road driving in Iceland is strictly prohibited and you can get very high fund braking those laws. Whilst travelling around the country, the highest respect for the Icelandic environment must be shown. It's good to remember to take nothing besides photographs and leave nothing behind except footprints.

- Check out the road map and see where the roads and trails are.
- Get information about the appropriate routes at visitor centres, and from rangers or staff.
- Find out in advance when mountain roads are likely to be open, along with other related information, at visitor centres.
- Get more information about driving in Iceland at www. safetravel.is
- The emergency number in Iceland is 112

Get more information on www.safetravel.is

The emergency number in Iceland is 112

ICELANDIC
FOLK LEGENDS